Gillette®

LEAGUE
Publications Ltd

RUGBY LEAGUE 2011-2012
Sweet sixteen

League Publications Ltd

First published in Great Britain in 2011 by
League Publications Ltd
Wellington House
Briggate
Brighouse
West Yorkshire HD6 1DN

Copyright © League Publications Ltd

A CIP catalogue record for this book is available from the British Library
ISBN 978-1-901347-24-1

Designed and Typeset by League Publications Limited
Printed by H Charlesworth & Co Ltd, Wakefield

Contributing Editor
Tim Butcher

Statistics, production and design
Daniel Spencer

Contributors

Malcolm Andrews
Neil Barraclough
Peter Bird
Jeff Bowron
Martin Butcher
Phil Caplan
Ian Cheveau
Tom Coates
Ben Collins
James Collins
Karl Connor
Sian Couch
Paul English
Simon Fitzjohn
Ian Golden
Shamoon Hafez
Malcolm Haigh
Roger Halstead
Phil Hodgson
Andrew Jackson
Chris Jackson

Conor Kelly
Steve Kilmartin
David Kuzio
Joanna Lester
Steve Mascord
Paddy McAteer
Keith McGhie
Joe Mills
David Parkinson
Arindam Rej
Ian Rigg
Mike Rylance
Martyn Sadler
David Saffer
Mike Sterriker
James Stott
Gareth Walker
Chris Westwood
Ricky Wilby
Gavin Willacy
Ian Wilson

Pictures

Rugby League Photos
RLA Images
SWPix
Action Photographics,
Australia
CameraSport
Varley Picture Agency
Glenn Ashley
Richard Beattie
Bob Brough
Gordon Clayton
Paul English
Steve Gaunt
Peter Green
Magi Haroun
Dave Howarth
Wayne Keegan
Richard Land
Ian Lovell
Allan McKenzie
Mike McKenzie
Marc Taylor
Mal Walker

Front cover photo
Magi Haroun

CONTENTS

ACKNOWLEDGEMENTS

Gillette Rugby League 2011-2012 is the 16th of League Publications Ltd's annual series of Rugby League Yearbooks, the ninth year of its production with the backing of world-leading brand Gillette.

As always, in compiling this historical record of the Rugby League year, we rely on the hard work and dedication of all the contributors to *Rugby Leaguer & Rugby League Express* and *Rugby League World* magazine. Without their efforts this yearbook would not be possible.

We are able to include some wonderful action photography provided by, in particular RLphotos.com, SWPix, Varley Picture Agency, Action Photographics in Sydney, Magi Haroun, CameraSport, Allan McKenzie and Peter Morley of RLA Images.

Thanks are due to the Rugby Football League for their help during the year, and in particular Oliver Barlow for his assistance in helping track down the dates of birth of players.

Acknowledgement also to the Rothmans Yearbook 1999, compiled by Ray Fletcher, the British Rugby Records Book from London Publications, and to the club officials, and some supporters, who helped us verify records.

The magnificent statistical review was put together meticulously, as always, by Daniel Spencer, who also designed the book.

Special mentions for Gareth Walker and Malcolm Andrews who wrote the Championship and NRL/State of Origin sections and to Paul English, Tom Coates and Lorraine Marsden for their assistance in proof reading. Thanks also to Opta Sportdata, who compiled the Opta Index Analysis in our mind-boggling statistical section.

TIM BUTCHER
Contributing Editor
Gillette Rugby League 2011-2012

INTRODUCTION

2011 was another year of ups and downs for the sport of Rugby League, and let's face it, we wouldn't have it any other way.

Naturally, there has been more ups for some, but putting patriotism and club affinity aside, our sport has served up rich entertainment once again.

It was a less than perfect finish for England as a feeling of déja vu descended on Elland Road during the second half of the Gillette Four Nations final. It was a disappointing end to what had been a thoroughly entertaining tournament in which England had shown genuine signs of being able to compete and beat the rest.

Alas, it was written in the stars that Australian captain Darren Lockyer, in the last competitive game of his 17-year career, would go out a winner and he even scored the last try of his side's 30-8 win. Although his very last touch was a badly-skewed conversion attempt, Lockyer bowed out with his reputation as an all-time great fully intact.

Though England fell at the final hurdle, there was enough in the previous three games to suggest a 2013 World Cup win might not be totally impossible.

Domestically, we had a season of one big major surprise, when Leeds Rhinos came up on the rails to win the Super League title from a fifth-placed finish. Unprecedented, unthinkable, but true. How good must it have felt for first-season coach Brian McDermott and his players, who were written off barely two months before the end of the regular season when the Rhinos languished in eighth spot. Such was their form that by the Gillette Four Nations kick-off, Leeds players made up one third of the England squad.

The Rhinos had to beat Hull FC at home and then Huddersfield Giants and Warrington on their own patch to win through to the Grand Final, so it was hard to argue they didn't deserve their place at Old Trafford, and then edged St Helens - for the fourth time in five years - to win the trophy. Was Wigan's title win in 2010 just a blip in Leeds' domination of English Rugby League? St Helens were the bridesmaid for the fifth year running, but their ability to at least get to the wedding was testament to their durability, with another season blighted by injury meaning they had to rely on an increasing number of home-grown talent to see them through.

In fact, one of the themes of 2011 was the emergence of some hot talent among English clubs. The RFL's 'club-trained' rules, which came into force from the start of the 2008 season as a means of encouraging Super League clubs to develop their own young players, was starting to bite. An investigative piece in *Rugby League World* magazine revealed that, after showing no sign of decrease from 2001 to 2008, the number of overseas players in Super League had dropped from 104 in 2007 to 69 in 2011.

Super League clubs were still allowed five non-Federation trained players and five quota players and still tried their best to get the most out of the system. Hull KR was the most prominent example this year as they tried to accommodate former Australian Test second-rower Willie Mason, who they had signed at the end of 2010. Mason, though counting as non-Fed trained, would only come off the quota if he had a Tongan passport. He didn't arrive in Hull until March, but without a Tongan passport in his possession, meaning Michael Dobson, conveniently injured, had to be taken off Rovers' books to make way. By the time Dobson was recovered, Mason, who hadn't been breaking many metaphorical pots on the field, still hadn't got his passport and was released, joining a French rugby union club. Red faces all round.

It was all change at Hull KR at the end of the season as coach Justin Morgan returned to Australia and was replaced by Newcastle Knights assistant coach Craig Sandercock. Hull FC, who flattered to deceive all year, experienced even greater flux, being taken over by former Hull soccer chairman Adam Pearson and then bringing in Shaun McRae as director of rugby, who then brought in Peter Gentle, assistant at Wests Tigers, as head coach for 2012.

Michael Maguire's success at Wigan in his first season, the former Melbourne assistant taking the Warriors to the 2010 Super League championship, had already set a trend. McRae's spell as head coach at Salford had ended in mid-season and he was replaced by Matt Parish, an assistant to Ricky Stuart, the New South Wales coach. Parish's tenure only lasted six games before he realised the size of the team-building task at the City Reds. Salford move into a new stadium at Barton for 2012 but without a coach going into the off-season, don't look in the best of positions to make the most of it. St Helens will also take up residency in a new home after a year's sojourn at Widnes.

Maguire has been enticed back to Australia by Russell Crowe and he will coach South Sydney in 2012. He couldn't finish off with a second Super League title, although a first win at Wembley since 1995 was compensation enough for the Warriors' fans. Former playing favourite Shaun Wane has moved up to head coach as planned. At the end of the year, Wigan tied up with Welsh Rugby League in a smart move after the demise of Crusaders.

The most traumatic week of the season came in July with the announcement of the second round of licences, with both Castleford and Wakefield vulnerable because of their inability to deliver a new stadium, a prerequisite set out three years before. By July, Wakefield, under new ownership since February after the club went into financial administration, were unbackable to be the club demoted, with Widnes Vikings having already elevated to Super League in March, and Halifax waiting in the wings having been told they met the criteria for a C-grade licence.

When the list of clubs for Super League was announced by RFL chairman Richard Lewis, Wakefield - to their surprise as well as everybody else's - were included in the list, but Crusaders were not, having withdrawn their application the night before. The Welsh Super League adventure was over after three years, with a string of top-quality players having recently signed contracts with the Wrexham-based club left with worthless pieces of paper. The RFL moved very quickly to declassify those mostly overseas players as non-Federation trained and take them off the quota to make it easier to get deals with other Super League clubs.

That didn't help Keith Senior, the Leeds centre who had his season ended by a knee injury, and had signed a two-year deal with the Welsh franchise. Senior made his feelings known on Twitter. So did many other players during the year as social networking took off big style. Hull KR's Ben Cockayne and Leeds' Ryan Bailey were two to get into hot water with injudicious posts.

Of the other clubs in Super League, we all expected Warrington to make the Super League Grand Final after edging Wigan to the League Leaders Shield, the Wolves earning a reputation for fast, open football but falling to a late penalty by Kevin Sinfield in their Qualifying semi-final. Castleford Tigers started off like a house on fire and topped the table for the early weeks of the season with Rangi Chase the outstanding player of the competition, earning the Albert Goldthorpe Medal and the Man of Steel, as well as a shock call-up for England. Bradford Bulls once again never got going, although one silver lining was a huge increase in their crowds. Huddersfield Giants, among the leaders for much of the year, were maddeningly erratic, their season tailing off, ending in a thrashing at Warrington in the play-offs, and then elimination at home to Leeds. Catalan Dragons

Introduction

also fell to heavy defeat and were eliminated at Wigan, but it was a season of real progress for them under new coach Trent Robinson, another former assistant coach in Australia, Robinson being named Super League coach of the year.

It was farewell to Crusaders and also to Harlequins, although in the latter case it was another name change at the end of the season, back to London Broncos. It had been a season of on-field struggle following the brightest of starts under young English coach Rob Powell. The counter balance was the continuing exponential growth of the community game in schools and clubs in the south of England. That development was happening too in Wales and there will be two Welsh clubs in Championship One in 2012, with a newly formed North Wales Crusaders joining South Wales Scorpions, who will be coached by former Barrow coach Dave Clark under the reciprocal relationship with Wigan, with the Warriors staff also strenghtening development work in the Principality.

In 2013, should they not be one of four teams to be promoted next season, the two Welsh clubs will be joined by four new clubs from outside the north of England in Championship One after the RFL announced its Championship review. One of the clubs desperate to win promotion in 2012 will be Barrow, who were ignominiously deducted all their league points for breaking operational rules and their chairman banned from the game for eight years. Barrow were champions in 2009 but in 2011 the champion team was Featherstone Rovers, who lost only one league game all year and beat Sheffield Eagles in the Grand Final to earn a tick on the next Super League application, as did Leigh Centurions, who scored a late winner to beat Halifax in the Northern Rail Cup Final. Swinton Lions will join them in the Championship in 2012 after winning automatic promotion as champions of Championship One, along with Keighley Cougars who won the play-off for the other spot.

And that's only a snapshot. There's a lot more to come in the following three hundred and odd pages. We are sure you will enjoy reliving the memories.

The Gillette Yearbook contains the full story of the domestic year, details of the international season and the Australian NRL season, and match facts for every Super League, Challenge Cup games involving professional teams, Championship and Championship One and Northern Rail Cup game. Every player who has played in Super League is also listed along with those players to have made their debuts this year. We have also selected five individuals who we judge to have made the biggest impact on Rugby League in 2011. For the second year we have published scoring and attendance records for every club. League Publications publishes the weekly newspaper *Rugby Leaguer & Rugby League Express*, as well as the monthly glossy magazine *Rugby League World* and the website *'totalrl.com'*. Many thanks once again to Gillette for their support for both this yearbook, and for the sport of Rugby League.

TIM BUTCHER
Contributing Editor
Gillette Rugby League 2011-2012

1
THE 2011 SEASON

DECEMBER 2010
Freeze a crowd

English Rugby League entered the last month of 2010 on the back of another third-placed finish in an international tournament, New Zealand beating Australia in the final of the Four Nations in Brisbane by 16-12, thanks to two late tries engineered by the brilliance of Rugby League World Golden Boot winner Benji Marshall.

As the UK was gripped by an early freeze and heavy snowfall at the end of November, the 2013 World Cup was launched at Media City in Salford. It was good timing after the Football Association's failure to secure the 2018 FIFA World Cup for England, and RFL Chairman Richard Lewis predicted that the 2013 World Cup would have a major economic impact. "The World Cup will generate an economic impact of £155 million in Yorkshire and the northwest, with over 200,000 fans expected to attend matches in these regions," said Lewis, speaking at the launch, which saw a firework display featuring England star Sam Tomkins and Wales' Lloyd White kicking goals over some giant posts. "The Rugby League World Cup will be the first major tournament after the London Olympics, and we have to maximise the opportunity of riding on the back of the Olympics. Our aim is to work hard over the next three years to deliver a tournament that England and Wales will be proud of."

If England as a team had disappointed in the Four Nations, several individuals impressed and were targeted by NRL clubs. Observers suggested an exodus of England's top stars would improve the chances of a home success in 2013, based on the development of Sam Burgess and Gareth Ellis since their moves down under. England captain James Graham was linked with a move to South Sydney, Sydney Roosters, Manly Sea Eagles, Wests Tigers, Penrith Panthers and the New Zealand Warriors, but denied rumours he was ready to leave St Helens a year before his contract was up.

His clubmate James Roby had also been tipped to move to the NRL at the end of 2011, but instead signed a new four-year deal at St Helens. Meanwhile the battle was hotting up for the services of another St Helens and England star, Kyle Eastmond, from the 2012 season. Saints were facing competition from NRL club Parramatta, as well as rugby union clubs.

The big off-field story of December was in Wales where the future of the Crusaders club was thrown in doubt when its parent company, Celtic Crusaders Ltd was served with a winding up order by HM Revenue and Customs at the end of Super League XV. Since moving the club to Wrexham from Bridgend less than a year before, the company had been hit by a succession of demands for money from a variety of claimants, with some players claiming the company had failed to make some pension payments that were due to them in accordance with the terms of their contracts. The club applied for protection from its creditors, and entered administration and was involved in talks with RFL officials throughout the autumn, who in early December gave clearance for directors Ian Roberts and Geoff Moss to resume their ownership of the Wrexham-based club. Crusaders came out of administration and the RFL explained that being in administration was no longer a bar to Super League membership. Crusaders would start the new season with a four-point deduction, not the maximum six, having agreed to carry over some of the debts of the old club. The RFL themselves were thought to be owed £700,000.

Despite being placed in administration in November, the Crusaders had made a number of signings or re-signings, and appointed Iestyn Harris as the club's new head coach for the 2011 season, succeeding Brian Noble, who stepped down from the position. Harris took up the role after leading the Welsh national side to victory in the Alitalia European Cup, with the Welsh now going forward to play in the next year's Four Nations tournament to be held in the northern hemisphere. Barry Eaton was rewarded for his work over the last five years as head coach of Keighley Cougars with a two-year contract as Harris's assistant.

Former Great Britain players Stuart Reardon and Paul Johnson, both ex-teammates of Harris at Bradford, joined, while Vince Mellars signed a three-year extension, with Peter Lupton and Frank Winterstein each extending their stays by two years. When the Crusaders came out of administration, Wakefield prop Richard Moore also signed.

Meanwhile South Wales Scorpions coach Anthony Seibold returned to Australia, giving a parting blast against the 2009 Crusaders management, who he accused of having deliberately misled their players and staff, causing them deep financial distress, before the club's move to Wrexham.

Crusaders may have survived but Championship One club Blackpool Panthers, which went into administration in early October, had its membership of the RFL cancelled after it failed to meet a deadline from the game's governing body.

By the end of December, one of the game's founding members, Wakefield Trinity, was hit by the news that their new stadium development near the M62, given the green light by local planners, was called in for a public inquiry by the Secretary of State for Communities, Eric Pickles. Wildcats Chairman Ted Richardson responded to critics who wrote off his club's chance of obtaining a second Super League licence the following July, after the Wildcats' prospects of being in their new stadium by the start of the 2012 season were effectively torpedoed.

Super League clubs had to submit their applications for new licences by April 2011, with the decision on which clubs were successful due to be made in July.

According to the RFL's licence criteria, "new stadiums or redevelopments of existing stadiums will only be taken into account if the RFL is satisfied that the stadium will be open or the redevelopment finished by the start of the 2012 season."

The Wildcats' historic Belle Vue stadium, the oldest still in the game, having been first used in 1879, had already been sold for development, with speculation linking Trinity with a temporary move to Barnsley.

With the RFL having pledged that a Championship club would be awarded a franchise, Super League licence applications were received from Barrow, Halifax and Widnes.

Whilst the Cumbrian club, with joint-record Great Britain cap-holder Garry Schofield their new head coach, went for the more conservative approach of emailing its bid to the RFL's Red Hall headquarters, Halifax and Widnes both delivered their bids with some style. Widnes, who had played in Super League as recently as 2005 and had appointed former Wigan and Great Britain forward Denis Betts as their head coach, had their bid delivered by 12-year-old season ticket holder Adam Blinston, accompanied by first-team player Anthony Thackeray. The pair travelled across the Pennines to Red Hall in a truck provided by the club's sponsor, Eddie Stobart Ltd. Halifax went one step further, and chartered a helicopter to take them to the bid presentation.

The UK government was again influencing the fortunes of Super League clubs via its Border Agency as it delayed several work visa applications. The highest profile was Hull Kingston Rovers marquee signing Willie Mason. To speed up the process, Mason had reportedly obtained a Tongan passport, but he had still not arrived by the end of the year. Even players who had previously been granted work visas were struggling. Tevita Leo-Latu, signed by Salford from Wakefield had his application turned down and the Reds hastily signed Wayne Godwin from Bradford to fill the hooking role vacated by the retired Malcolm Alker.

December 2010

No visa problems though for Canberra Test centre Joel Monaghan, who left his club in disgrace after a drunken Mad Monday prank with a dog was filmed by a friend and posted on the internet. Monaghan was linked with a host of clubs, Castleford and Catalans among them, but he finally signed for Warrington to link up with his elder brother Michael. The Wolves were able to sign Monaghan after prolific winger Chris Hicks decided to retire from the game and head back to Australia. Hicks, who became the first man to score a hat-trick in a Challenge Cup final at the new Wembley in the 30-6 win over Leeds Rhinos in 2010, signed a one-year contract extension in July, but subsequently had a change of heart. The timing of the arrangement, in the off-season, meant that any compensation paid by Warrington to 33-year-old Hicks would not count on the Wolves' salary cap for 2011. On his return to Australia Hicks was signed by Parramatta.

Huddersfield Giants were interested in making a bid for the Crusaders' forward Weller Hauraki, who played against England for the Maori in Auckland, but he opted to join Leeds Rhinos. Luke Robinson, one of the successes of England's campaign, pledged his long-term future to the Giants, penning a new five-year deal with the Giants, which superseded the contract he signed in June that had originally tied him to the club until 2012.

Catalans received a blow to their plans for the new season with former Australia Test forward Dane Carlaw leaving the club for personal reasons.

Castleford Tigers chief executive Richard Wright insisted his club had got the best possible deal in selling its 20-year-old back-row star Joe Westerman to Hull FC, with a six-figure transfer fee heading to the newly named Probiz Coliseum, Melbourne Storm centre Willie Isa signing for the Tigers.

Bradford Bulls insisted they would not agree to release halfback Matt Orford from the two final years of his three-year contract with the club. Orford returned to Australia after suffering a shoulder injury in Edinburgh in May on the Magic Weekend. He was wanted by Canberra Raiders as a replacement for their injured halfback Terry Campese, but the Raiders were reluctant to pay a fee. The Bulls moved quickly to secure a replacement with the signature of 23-year-old Canberra halfback Marc Herbert, who had spent much of the 2010 season on the sidelines with an ankle injury.

In one of the more surprising news stories of the off-season, Michael Worrincy left the Bulls to take up a one-year contract with NRL side Penrith Panthers, having agreed an early release from Bradford, although he didn't manage to break into first grade.

Harlequins appointed assistant Rob Powell as new head coach. The 30-year-old, whose route to the top was through the student and community game, had been in acting charge after Brian McDermott left for Leeds Rhinos in September.

Wakefield Trinity Wildcats appointed Glenn Morrison as captain and signed former Hull FC Challenge Cup winner Motu Tony, who had been playing rugby union.

Wigan's Australian fullback Cameron Phelps was looking for a new club, either in Super League or Australia, after being told he would not be offered a new contract by Wigan. And Hull FC's Australian star Shaun Berrigan headed back to Australia with a year still left on the four-year contract he signed when he joined Hull from Brisbane Broncos in 2008.

The RFL announced it would open the Engage Super League XVI season with a bang in Cardiff on the weekend of February 12th and 13th with seven round one games, most of them derbies. Fingers were crossed that the weather would be kind. The winter arrived early with heavy snow arriving across the UK at the end of November. The freeze had not relented by the Christmas period, with all the Boxing Day friendlies postponed.

Just about the only Rugby League action in December took place at Leigh Sports Village. On Christmas Monday, the Centurions beat Salford City Reds in a friendly. The underground heating also allowed both England Academy-Australian Schoolboys matches to be played earlier in the month, England winning both games, 38-30 and 34-22, under the leadership of Castleford hooker Adam Milner. One of England's stars, 18-year-old Bulls prop George Burgess, the younger brother of the Test star Sam, signed to play for the South Sydney Rabbitohs' Toyota Cup (under-20s) side.

JANUARY
New Year blues

Wigan winger Pat Richards added yet another award to his 2010 haul by being named by readers of League Express as the Super League player of the year. Richards - who broke the Wigan club record for points in a season with 462 - polled just under a half of all votes cast in the annual survey. Veteran broadcaster Ray French called the MBE awarded to him in the New Year's Honours List a reward for Rugby League. French, 71, was an international in League and union, and played for his home-town club St Helens and Widnes after switching codes in 1961. He usually featured in the second row, while also working as a school teacher at Cowley School in St Helens. He took over BBC TV commentaries from Eddie Waring in the 1981/2 season.

Former Workington Town and Whitehaven player Dave Smith, who established drugs and alcohol awareness charity The Ryan Smith Rising Sun Trust eleven-and-a-half years before, was awarded an MBE for services to people addicted to drugs. Smith, a former football director at Workington, launched the charity after the death of his son Ryan, who was then aged 18, from drugs problems.

The winter weather relented in the New Year, allowing several friendlies to go ahead. Leeds stand-off Danny McGuire watched from the sidelines as he recovered from knee ligament surgery as the Rhinos played out their traditional festive friendly against Wakefield a week after its postponement, with the Rhinos gaining a 40-22 victory.

The following day the Wolves warmed up, barely breaking sweat as they brushed aside Widnes at Stobart Stadium, by 48-18; Batley Bulldogs beat Dewsbury Rams 30-6 to lift the Roy Powell Trophy; and Featherstone Rovers bettered Hunslet 38-16 to win the Gareth Swift Memorial Trophy, launched in memory of the Rovers player who was killed in a motor accident the previous spring.

RFL Chief Executive Nigel Wood expressed his pride after all 89 Super League players from eleven different clubs involved in an intensive out-of-competition drugs testing programme by the UK Anti-Doping agency the previous November tested negative for banned substances. Rugby League was among the top three most-tested sports, alongside football and cycling.

Wigan signing Ryan Hoffman threw his support behind a proposed mid-season representative match between England and a team made up of Super League players from the southern hemisphere. The development came following England's 60-6 demolition of France in June 2010, a result which prompted the RFL to put in place a sterner test ahead of the 2011 Four Nations tournament.

Wakefield Trinity Wildcats supporters were told the future of the club was under threat, and called on to help generate £500,000 to safeguard its future. The government's decision to call the Wildcats' planning application in for a public inquiry put the club's future as a Super League outfit into severe doubt. The decision also meant that £350,000 promised by the developer of their proposed new stadium when planning permission was granted would be held back until after the public inquiry, placing tremendous financial strain on the club. Chairman Ted Richardson's entrance into an IVA (Individual Voluntary Arrangement) in 2010 meant he was no longer in a position to inject money and

January

League Express revealed that, in an attempt to maximise the club's profit, Belle Vue had been sold to a Richardson family company for £2.8 million, with a mortgage from the Bank of Ireland for £2 million. Wakefield supporters agreed to set up a Supporters' Trust in order to give supporters a stake in the running of the club in the long term.

Hull FC were on the lookout for a halfback after the departure of Shaun Berrigan and were linked with Crusaders' Jarrod Sammut, Warrington's Richie Myler and Batley's Gareth Moore, though coach Richard Agar reacted angrily to reports that Sean Long had been away from the club on compassionate leave. Hull did sign 19-year old halfback Chad McGlame from Scottish Rugby League Conference side Easterhouse Panthers from the east end of Glasgow on a 12-month contract.

Wolves coach Tony Smith denied Richie Myler was about to leave the club, whether on a permanent or temporary basis and the Crusaders dismissed speculation linking Sammut with a move away from the Racecourse Ground. The Crusaders won their first pre-season game of the year, when they travelled to Widnes and earned a 20-12 victory, with Sammut scoring a try for a side that fielded nine born and bred Welsh players.

Bradford finally secured an agreement to release Matt Orford to join NRL club Canberra Raiders. The Bulls still owed Orford some money under the terms of an image rights contract, but the club had been refusing to release his registration until Orford, or his new club, agreed to pay compensation to the Bulls for breaking his contract. The Bulls signed Kyle Briggs from Featherstone Rovers for an undisclosed fee on a two-year contract to strengthen their halfback options.

Huddersfield signed 24-year-old Jamie Simpson from South Sydney Rabbitohs to complete their overseas quota for the 2011 season. Simpson had won a battle against a rare form of cancer - Hodgkin's Lymphoma - that he was diagnosed with as a 15-year-old schoolboy in August 2002. England international Kevin Brown was made Giants captain.

Sean O'Loughlin, a member of a Wigan leadership team in 2010, was made sole captain by head coach Michael Maguire, who according to reports in Australia, had been sounded out by several Sydney clubs keen to know if he could obtain an early release from his contract with the Warriors. The Warriors were rocked by the news that marquee signing Brett Finch required surgery on a neck injury he picked up during training and could be out for up to three months.

Two Wigan players - winger Karl Pryce and young halfback Joe Mellor - went on season-long loan to Harlequins. On-trial Mark Calderwood made a try-scoring return to Rugby League on his Harlequins debut in a 70-6 romp over London Skolars at the Honourable Artillery Company in the City of London.

Emirates became the Official Airline of the RFL, the Super League and the England Rugby League team, leading to speculation on a Rugby League Nines competition in Dubai each year in January. An airline representative conceded that they would like to see Rugby League gain more recognition in the Middle East.

CARNEGIE CHALLENGE CUP - PRELIMINARY ROUND

Saturday 8th January 2011
Eccles 26 Castleford Panthers 6; Millom 6 Egremont Rangers 12;
Ovenden 26 Rochdale Mayfield 28; Shaw Cross Sharks 20 Stanley Rangers 21
Sunday 9th January 2011
St Albans Centurions 22 British Police 32
Saturday 15th January 2011
Bank Quay Bulls 26 Seaton Rangers 18; Oulton Raiders 23 Normanton Knights 22 (aet)
Sunday 16th January 2011
Loughborough University 38 Featherstone Lions 0;
Northampton Demons 46 Gloucestershire University 10

CARNEGIE CHALLENGE CUP - ROUND 1

Saturday 22nd January 2011
Drighlington 12 Hunslet Warriors 13 (aet); East Hull 24 Saddleworth Rangers 10;
East Leeds 36 Crosfields 6; Elland 16 Thatto Heath Crusaders 20;
Fryston 30 Stanningley 4; Leigh East 58 Heworth 6;
Leigh Miners Rangers 26 West Hull 10; Myton Warriors 34 Ince Rose Bridge 0;
Oldham St Annes 16 Hull Dockers 30; Rochdale Mayfield 38 Bank Quay Bulls 14;
Skirlaugh 16 Oulton Raiders 14; Nottingham Outlaws 30 Royal Air Force 22
Sunday 23rd January 2011
Loughborough University 18 Kippax Knights 10;
Northampton Demons 12 Leeds Met University 26; Royal Navy 28 British Police 14;
Stanley Rangers 18 Widnes St Maries 0 (conceded);
UCLan 12 Northumbria University 20; Valley Cougars 24 The Army 30;
Warrington Wizards 44 Carluke Tigers 18
Saturday 29th January 2011
Eccles 6 Wigan St Patricks 30; Wath Brow Hornets 18 Norland Sharks 0 (conceded);
Wigan St Judes 22 West Bowling 20
Sunday 30th January 2011
Castleford Lock Lane 38 Halton Simms Cross 4; Siddal 58 Eastmoor Dragons 18;
Waterhead 24 Egremont Rangers 28
Wednesday 2nd February 2011
Edge Hill University 6 Hull University 32
Saturday 5th February 2011
York Acorn 24 Milford Marlins 35
Saturday 12th February 2011
Kells 14 Bradford Dudley Hill 22

CARNEGIE CHALLENGE CUP - ROUND 2

Saturday 5th February 2011
Castleford Lock Lane 18 Stanley Rangers 16; East Hull 31 Myton Warriors 22;
East Leeds 4 Hull Dockers 64; Egremont Rangers 22 Wath Brow Hornets 10;
Hunslet Warriors 22 Wigan St Judes 16; Leeds Met University 44 Edge Hill University 14;
Leigh East 16 Thatto Heath Crusaders 18;
Loughborough University 18 Northumbria University 25;
The Army 27 Royal Air Force 16; Wigan St Patricks 16 Leigh Miners Rangers 18
Sunday 6th February 2011
Warrington Wizards 28 Royal Navy 20
Saturday 12th February 2011
Milford Marlins 24 Skirlaugh 16; Rochdale Mayfield 12 Siddal 25
Saturday 19th February 2011
Fryston 16 Bradford Dudley Hill 12

FEBRUARY
Starstruck in Wales

With the Super League season kick-off to be staged at the Millennium Stadium in Cardiff in the middle of February, there was a later start to the top-flight season in 2011, and no staggered start to accommodate the World Club Challenge. The champions, Wigan, were due to start their season with a testing derby against St Helens in Cardiff and play Australian Premiers St George Illawarra on the last Sunday of the month at the DW Stadium.

Warriors chairman Ian Lenagan proclaimed the decision by Sam and Joel Tomkins to sign new five-year contracts to the end of the 2015 season a boost to the game. Liam Farrell and Josh Charnley also signed new five-year contracts, while Darrell Goulding and Harrison Hansen committed to three-year contract extensions. Bookmakers William Hill installed Sam Tomkins and Hull KR's Michael Dobson as joint favourites to win the 2011 Albert Goldthorpe Medal.

Paul Wellens and James Graham were to be joint captains of St Helens, whose new signing, Australian international Josh Perry, would miss the season launch as he was recovering from a broken foot sustained the season before in the NRL.

Former Warriors hooker Jon Clarke revealed he had mixed emotions following Warrington's 24-18 defeat against Wigan in his Testimonial game at the Halliwell Jones Stadium on the first Tuesday of the month. Clarke scored the final try of the game in front of a crowd of 5,757 on a cold and windy February evening. Wolves' Welsh international winger Rhys Williams joined Crusaders on a month's loan.

His new clubmate Gareth Thomas revealed how a Rugby League World magazine article written by Jamie Jones-Buchanan led to Hollywood star Mickey Rourke deciding to make a film of the Welsh player's life. Rourke was expected to be in Cardiff for the Magic Weekend to hold talks with Thomas and gain an insight into the competitive nature of Rugby League.

Danny Orr was named Castleford Tigers captain for the second time in his career after his re-signing from Harlequins. Castleford were one of the clubs thought at the turn of the year to be most at risk of losing their Super League licence from 2012, having not made tangible progress on a new stadium to replace the newly renamed Probiz Coliseum. But the pressure on the Tigers was reduced by neighbours Wakefield Trinity's entry into administration on 1st February. Two individuals were in the running to buy the club, but when one of them, Steve Parkin, pulled out the way was cleared for Wakefield businessman Andrew Glover's 'Spirit of 1873' group to take over. The deal was not quite finalised as Super League XVI got underway in Cardiff.

February

Round 1

RFL Chief Executive Nigel Wood hailed Millennium Magic 2011 as the best ever start to a Super League season as Super League XVI began beneath the closed roof of the Millennium Stadium, allowing seven matches to be played at the same venue over the weekend of 12/13 February. The attendance for the opening day on Saturday, which featured four matches, was 30,891 whilst 29,323 people saw Sunday's three fixtures. The combined attendance of 60,214 was an increase on the crowds at the two Magic Weekends staged at Edinburgh's Murrayfield Stadium in 2009 (59,749) and 2010 (52,043).

Some were left questioning the decision to close the roof following an unusually high number of injuries, particularly on a bruising first day. The micro-climate caused the pitch to become slippery. Warrington, who were defeated 28-18 by Huddersfield Giants in the opener on the Saturday, finished the match with eleven men on the field, having used all of their substitutes and with Michael Monaghan in the sin bin.

Centre Matt King was the first to be carried off with knee ligament damage which sidelined him for the next eleven rounds, Chris Bridge suffered a hamstring injury, prop Mike Cooper was out until round eight with a dislocated shoulder, Simon Grix got a deadleg and Lee Briers was briefly knocked out and suffered concussion from a collision in the second half. And Ryan Hudson was helped from the field early in the Tigers' 40-20 derby victory against Wakefield later in the day after suffering neck injury.

Jamie Langley was forced to look on from the sidelines on the second day as the Bulls surrendered an 18-point lead in the second half, after the second-rower was withdrawn after dislocating his shoulder during the first half.

Danny Brough, Kevin Brown and youngster Keal Carlile played key roles in the Giants' 28-18 victory over Warrington. Brough scored two tries and four goals, Brown played a key captain's role, while coach Nathan Brown surprised the pundits by selecting hooker Carlile in his starting line-up. The game started well for Warrington when Joel Monaghan dived over just four minutes into his debut. But Carlile jumped on his own grubber kick after King made a mess of trying to clear the ball in his own in-goal area. Brough's missed conversion meant Warrington still held the lead, but the Giants' scrum-half made amends with a lung-bursting 90-metre dash for Huddersfield's second try. Briers' kick was palmed back by Joel Monaghan, but Brough reacted first and had just enough pace to keep out of Bridge's reach as he burst down the left flank. Minutes later, King was carried off and by half-time Cooper and Grix had also been confirmed as injury casualties who would not be returning. Darrell Griffin and Shaun Lunt both crossed from close range to take advantage of some increasingly weary Wolves defence. Warrington rallied, with Ben Westwood and Ryan Atkins going over late on, but their efforts sandwiched Brough's second touchdown – a superb 45-metre dash that left Paul Wood and Brett Hodgson chasing shadows – that sealed the win for Huddersfield.

Harlequins' rookie coach Rob Powell - appointed as Super League's youngest ever coach the previous November - said there was plenty more to come from Luke Gale after he scored all of the Londoners' points as they downed Catalan Dragons 11-4 on the Saturday, crossing for two tries, kicking a conversion and then adding a field goal for good measure.

Harlequins blasted into a ten-point lead in the first six minutes and then defended for their lives against a Catalans side lacking injured Thomas Bosc, and desperate to get back on track after 2010's disappointments. Catalans centre Setaimata Sa was knocked unconscious during a heavy tackle with Oliver Wilkes and play was stopped for over ten minutes while he received treatment. A 58th minute Gale one-pointer was to prove vital in the dying seconds of the match when the ball was sent wide to the right by the Catalans and new centre Ben Farrar sent in Damien Blanch to score on his debut. Scott Dureau failed with his conversion attempt from the touchline, leaving the Dragons trailing by seven points with 90 seconds left on the clock, not enough time for two scores.

Castleford coach Terry Matterson backed his young guns to light up Super League after the Tigers eased to an opening 40-20 victory over Wakefield in the third game. Teenagers Joe Arundel and Adam Milner both touched down in the eight-try romp which was inspired by a brilliant display from stand-off Rangi Chase. Kirk Dixon's break out of the Tigers' '20' with 13 minutes to go led to sub Daryl Millard's sin-binning for holding down and marked the end of a Wakefield comeback after tries to Dale Ferguson and Luke George had got them back to 28-20. A Paul Jackson try and Dean Widders' second touchdown finally settled the issue. Wakefield and the crowd were frustrated by the 37 penalties, 22 against them, awarded by referee James Child, most of them for offences at the play the ball and a record for a Super League game. RFL Match Officials Director Stuart Cummings denied he had introduced any radical changes to the refereeing of the tackle.

Saints - missing Leon Pryce with a groin strain - and Wigan drew the curtain of the first day with a 16-16 draw. Saints new head coach Royce Simmons had only returned to the UK the previous Thursday after he had flown back to Australia earlier in the month to be at the bedside of his dying father and the Warriors were coasting at 16-0 up with just 20 minutes to play before Saints ran in three late tries to snatch the unlikeliest of points. New Wigan signing Ryan Hoffman, who bagged the opening try, made a huge impression while late call-up Josh Charnley was outstanding. Even the early injury loss of Paul Deacon, principal kicker in the absence of Pat Richards, still not recovered from the Achilles injury he suffered in the 2010 Grand Final, had been negated, with the steepling kicks of Sam Tomkins wreaking havoc.

A Jon Wilkin try after 62 minutes began Saints' remarkable recovery, capitalising on the astonishing efforts of James Roby. Much of the talk surrounding Saints in 2011 had focussed on the absence of the retired Keiron Cunningham, now on the coaching staff, but Roby was imperious in keeping his side in contention.

The other factor that meant the contest literally went to the final kick - and an errant Kyle Eastmond field-goal attempt after the hooter had sounded, which would have given Saints an unlikely victory - was Wigan's last-quarter indiscipline. During the game Jon Wilkin made an official complaint against new Wigan prop Jeff Lima, alleging a dangerous tackle, resulting in Lima being suspended the following Tuesday by the RFL Disciplinary Committee for two matches.

Hollywood actor Mickey Rourke was a guest of Gareth Thomas on the Sunday and the American was impressed with what he saw as the Crusaders sailed to a 42-12 win over Salford City Reds. Crusaders ran in seven tries – including a hat-trick for Michael Witt and a Stuart Reardon brace – in an ultimately one-sided affair which marked a dream start for new head coach Iestyn Harris. Salford's afternoon was made even worse with Wayne Godwin's 80th minute sending off. The former Bradford hooker clobbered Clinton Schifcofske from behind as the Crusaders fullback squared up to Chris Nero. Godwin got a two-match ban.

Bradford Bulls, with new coach Mick Potter in charge for the first time, were left fuming after surrendering a 28-10 lead against Leeds as the Rhinos stormed back into the game in the last 17 minutes, scoring a late penalty try when Ben Jones-Bishop was tackled without the ball, to grab a 32-28 victory.

Bulls Chairman Peter Hood was angry, claiming that a series of marginal decisions had gone against his team as the game wore on. And, to make matters worse, the Bulls' coach broke down on the M4 as it was returning from Wales.

Matt Diskin, who joined the Bulls from Leeds during the close-season, was one of nine debutants for the Bulls. Diskin's former Leeds colleague Chev Walker, who returned after a year out with a broken leg whilst at Hull KR, was twice denied, on the first occasion by a despairing Ben Jones-Bishop tackle.

On the second occasion, video referee Richard Silverwood, who gave the deciding

19

score, denied him a try, ruling a knock-on, one of two Bulls' touchdowns that were chalked off on video evidence. With barely two minutes to go, and trailing by two points, Jones-Bishop, back from a season-long loan at Harlequins, broke clear from a Kallum Watkins pass, hacked on and was brought down by Bradford winger Gareth Raynor as he sped for glory.

Long-serving centre Keith Senior made his 400th appearance for the Rhinos. Senior was one of only three players, along with Sean Long and Paul Johnson, to have featured in every Super League campaign. New Bradford stand-off Kyle Briggs suffered knee ligament damage.

The Magic Weekend finished with a Hull derby. Hull FC, who the previous week had replaced sacked fullback Jordan Tansey by snapping up former Wigan fullback Cameron Phelps on a one-year deal, shot into a 14-0 lead in as many minutes thanks to Kirk Yeaman and Lee Radford tries and three Danny Tickle goals. But Rovers completed a weekend of comebacks. Inspired by Michael Dobson and his new playmaking partner Blake Green, Justin Morgan's side recovered from a sluggish start to score 28 unanswered points at one stage. Dobson and Green created or scored each of Rovers' tries, with back-rowers Clint Newton and Ben Galea causing havoc with their shrewd passing games.

The specifics of Tansey's latest misdemeanour, his third in twelve months, were the subject of speculation, after he was dropped for Hull FC's pre-season 22-20 friendly win at Castleford on the last Sunday of January, and was then absent from the club's media day.

The Robins that week revealed plans to replace the existing temporary seating behind the posts with a £6.5 million state-of-the-art structure.

Round 2

Wakefield Trinity were bought out of administration on the Thursday before round two by new owner Andrew Glover, who immediately signalled that the Wildcats, who were deducted four points by the RFL, would be in the market to sign new players.

Prior to coming out of administration, the Wildcats lost star players who had all played in round one, Sam Obst to Hull, Dale Ferguson to Huddersfield and Darryl Millard to the Catalans, and signed four young players, Greg Johnson and Josh Griffin from Huddersfield on permanent deals, while the club took prop forward Kyle Amor from Leeds and stand-off half Craig Harvey from Warrington on month-long loan deals. Young centre Aaron Murphy refused to leave the Wildcats, despite having been offered a deal by the Giants.

None of the new signings played on the Saturday in Perpignan as the Wildcats registered a stunning 38-14 victory against the Catalans, with Frankie Mariano, signed from Hull KR and former St Helens centre Chris Dean both scoring try-braces. Millard watched on from the stands as the Dragons slipped to their second defeat of the season at the hands of his former club.

Sam Obst made his debut for Hull FC on the Friday night. Obst was named on the bench for the match against Leeds at the KC Stadium, and was introduced after Sean Long failed to re-appear for the second half due to an Achilles injury.

Leeds strolled to a seventh successive Super League win over Hull FC, by 32-18, with a fine performance. The Rhinos were without five men before kick-off – Jamie Peacock, Danny McGuire, Ben Cross, Ryan Bailey and Ali Lauitiiti – and then lost three more during the course of an impressive triumph. Brent Webb was carried off after just eight minutes, Carl Ablett did not return after half-time and Brett Delaney lasted just seven minutes of the second half.

Hull had their own problems – most notably the loss of Long at half-time – but they were second best despite the sterling efforts of their captain Craig Fitzgibbon, who made 59 tackles, and Richard Whiting, who made several try-saving tackles in his unaccustomed position of fullback to keep the Airlie Birds in the game. For Leeds, Danny Buderus was the star, typified by the gamebreaking try he made for debutant Weller Hauraki.

Hull trailed 20-6 at the break, and fell further behind when Chris Clarkson went over early in the second half. Ben Jones-Bishop continued his good start to the season with an outstanding 70-metre dash. Hull had looked to be on the front foot when Long produced a grubber kick just before half-time, but Kevin Sinfield flicked the bouncing ball into Jones-Bishop's onrushing frame and the youngster surged upfield. By the time he'd gone past three Hull defenders, he was left with nobody else to beat and touched down with one second left of the first half, and Leeds were just about out of reach.

On the same night halfback Kyle Eastmond scored two tries as St Helens hammered Salford City Reds 56-22 at The Willows, although League Express revealed he had decided to accept an offer to join Bath rugby union club at the end of the season. Both sides were missing key players - the Reds still waiting for injured big-name signings Vinnie Anderson, Phil Bailey and Sean Gleeson to make their debuts - but it was the visitors who came roaring out of the blocks, with a seven-try blitz in the first 40 minutes, leaving the home fans baying for blood as coach Shaun McRae ran the gauntlet at half-time.

Saints, missing both their joint captains Paul Wellens (rib) and James Graham (shoulder), and with Leon Pryce still out with a groin strain, gave a runout at stand-off half to promising youngster Lee Gaskell, and they got the ball rolling as early as the third minute when a neat kick from Jamie Foster saw Chris Flannery nip in behind the defensive line to touch down. Eastmond's try on the half hour was already the final nail in the coffin for Salford.

Saints hooker James Roby and Castleford's Rangi Chase were the only two players to be named as the best players in both of their teams' matches and were locked at the top of the Albert Goldthorpe Medal table after two rounds

Chase played an instrumental role for the Tigers in their 18-12 victory over Huddersfield Giants on the Saturday. The Tigers, who fielded five players under the age of 21, were full value – despite the controversial nature of a try scored at a crucial stage - for a victory over a Giants side which was unchanged following their notable victory over Warrington in Cardiff. Hooker Adam Milner, who was drafted into the starting line-up when captain Ryan Hudson failed a fitness test on the Friday, and his own replacement Daryl Clark, who was on debut, were both highly impressive, and there were outstanding contributions from centre Joe Arundel, second-rower Oliver Holmes and prop Jon Walker.

The sin-binning of Shaun Lunt nine minutes from time ended the Giants' hopes of rescuing the situation as the Tigers led 18-6 thanks to two tries from Nick Youngquest, signed from Crusaders, and one more from Joe Arundel. The key moment was in the 56th minute when Youngquest claimed his touchdown. A Chase kick was well taken by Scott Grix, who was hauled over his tryline by a posse of tacklers. Chase appeared to have his hand on, or close to, the ball, which came loose. And, after video referral by referee Steve Ganson, Richard Silverwood awarded the touchdown, citing 'benefit of doubt'.

Warrington coach Tony Smith hailed the attitude of Lee Briers after he substituted the experienced stand-off in the first half of their dramatic 24-22 home win over Hull KR on the Sunday. Briers was hauled off after a disappointing opening quarter, with Smith confirming there was no injury. But the Welsh international returned to the action for the final 20 minutes, and had a hand in Brett Hodgson's late winner against the Robins. Rovers had battled back from 10-0 down to lead 22-14 heading into the final quarter, before Chris Riley's try set up a grandstand finale. The Wolves – with Briers back on the field – then laid siege to the Rovers line with wave after wave of attack. They created a host of clear-cut chances, but the Robins were still hanging on when winger Peter Fox cleared his line with a 40-metre break with four minutes remaining. Fox lost the ball in Joel Monaghan's cover tackle, and moments later Hodgson's six points were clinching it for Warrington. Clint Newton didn't deserve to finish on the losing side after titanic efforts in attack and defence.

On the Sunday, Wigan won 44-10 at Bradford, with Sam Tomkins in irrepressible form. Amos Roberts' second try, just before the hour, quashed the Bulls' brief fightback after Wigan went in at the break 26-0 ahead. The Bulls finally got onto the scoreboard four minutes after the restart when Elliott Whitehead atoned for earlier errors by chasing Matt Diskin's grubber in-goal to score for the fourth time this season. Ah Van converted and shortly after the Bulls' new Kiwi winger climbed, caught and grounded a Paul Sykes cross-field kick to the corner.

Some minds began to drift back to the Bulls' great comeback of 12 months before, when they had hauled themselves back from 20-0 down at the break to win. That was the last time Wigan lost on the road in Super League but Roberts' second try, following another flowing move on the hour, allayed any fears among the cherry and white. More wondrous Warriors' handling on their left flank led to George Carmont joining the try scorers and, to cap a magical personal performance, Sam Tomkins sliced through the Bulls defence to complete the Warriors joy, Paul Deacon finishing with an impressive haul of six out of eight conversions against the club he served for a decade.

Round 3

Warrington defeated St Helens for only the second time in a Super League game on the Friday night. The 25-18 success at Saints' temporary home at Stobart Stadium ended a run of 29 games without a win against their rivals. Lee Briers was the star turn with a virtuoso display that completely outshone Kyle Eastmond, just hours before the Saints scrum-half confirmed his cross-code switch. After a moderate performance, Eastmond pointedly left the field without acknowledging the Saints supporters, who responded by booing the halfback.

St Helens officials were thought to be debating a proposal to ask Bath Rugby Union club to amend their proposed contract with Eastmond so they could take the 21-year-old halfback immediately.

The Wolves established their dominance, and Briers – himself discarded by Saints as a youngster – was on hand to take advantage of the results. Saints, still without Josh Perry and Leon Pryce, struggled to offer any kind of threat for the first half hour. When they did eventually establish some pressure, they were met by a resolute Warrington defence that absorbed a punishing spell before the break.

Led by Garreth Carvell, Paul Wood and Adrian Morley – whose bone-rattling hit on Louie McCarthy-Scarsbrook set the tone in the first ten seconds – the Wolves always looked intent on wrecking Saints' first game at the Stobart Stadium. Briers' dummy to his left opened up enough space for him to wriggle past James Graham in the second minute, just seconds after Graham's indiscipline had allowed the Wolves to sweep up-field from an early penalty. Brett Hodgson added the conversion, and Warrington never looked back.

Michael Monaghan's impressive 40/20 kick - the first of the Super League season - gave the visitors a platform for their second score, when Hodgson's grubber bounced up perfectly for Richie Myler. Four minutes later Briers gathered his own grubber kick - albeit thanks to a lucky ricochet - and Saints were left wondering what had hit them. Louis Anderson put the game out of Saints' reach when he charged on to Myler's short pass early in the second half and skilfully held the ball off the ground to reach over for the try.

It was only at that point that the hosts produced anything of note in attack. Michael Shenton, signed from Castleford, reached over on the right side, then Eastmond and Lee Gaskell combined to work enough space for Chris Flannery to scythe through. There was enough time for Gaskell to add a third try for Saints, picking up the loose ball after Eastmond's kick deflected off Matty Blythe, but Briers' 71st-minute field goal had ensured that Warrington were guaranteed two points.

Salford coach Shaun McRae attempted to deflect credit onto his players after the Reds won their first game of the season at Wakefield on the Sunday. Salford's emphatic 32-6 win helped ease the pressure on McRae, after his side suffered heavy early defeats to Crusaders and St Helens. Former Red Jeremy Smith was finally able to make his Wakefield Trinity Wildcats debut after receiving clearance to play from the UK Border Agency.

The Wildcats were at home for the first time since Andrew Glover's takeover of the club and a near 7,000 crowd was present despite awful conditions. But rather than repeat the stirring performance that earned victory at Catalan Dragons seven days earlier, Wakefield were forced to look on as the Reds finally started to display the pre-season promise. In the front row, Ray Cashmere was outstanding, Stefan Ratchford and fullback Luke Patten were both constant dangers out wide and Mark Henry finished with two tries. Rob Parker's 57th minute try took the game firmly away from the Wildcats.

Hull Kingston Rovers scrum-half Michael Dobson missed the 31-18 home defeat to Catalans - their first win of the season - after being ruled out of action for around eight weeks because of an operation to cure an Achilles tendon and ankle problem, which he incurred in the Hull derby in Cardiff. It ended Dobson's run of 78 consecutive appearances, the longest current sequence in Super League. Dobson, 24, who won the Albert Goldthorpe Medal in 2009, had played in every Rovers game since his debut against Harlequins on May 25th, 2008.

The Robins were also missing Jake Webster, the Kiwi centre suspended for two matches after being found guilty of making dangerous contact with Warrington winger Chris Riley the week before. The RFL Disciplinary Committee ruled he had used his body to twist and apply pressure to Riley's leg. The hearing was told that Webster had received a formal caution over a similar offence in April 2010.

The Dragons came back from a 12-0 deficit after two tries from Blake Green, inspired by former Newcastle halfback Scott Dureau, with Damien Blanch getting two tries. Blanch's second, five minutes from time, put the visitors twelve points ahead and made the game safe.

Enigmatic former Hull favourite Danny Brough had a hand in all four Giants tries as Huddersfield beat Hull 20-10 at the Galpharm Stadium, his repeatedly punishing positional kicks giving the Black and Whites plenty of headaches. Hull got off to a bad start, going 10-0 behind in as many minutes but a Jordan Turner try and one from Will Sharp four minutes into the second half had Hull level. Eventually a determination to keep the ball alive from Eorl Crabtree, moved on by Brough, resulted in Michael Lawrence breaching the whitewash to edge the hosts ahead again. A few nervous moments in the home camp still followed, until a brilliantly weighted dab over the defence from Brough enabled Kevin Brown to collect and dance around Richard Whiting to put the result beyond doubt.

Bradford Bulls got their first win, by 30-26 in the Saturday TV game at Crusaders, whose coach Iestyn Harris was clearly frustrated after watching his side go 30-10 behind before mounting a three-try comeback in the last 11 minutes.

After the previous week's mauling by Wigan, Mick Potter made several changes. Ex-Wigan Warrior Shaun Ainscough was given his debut on the wing and made the most of it with a lively display, Patrick Ah Van moved into centre, while Danny Addy came in to replace Paul Sykes in the halves. In the pack, Chev Walker moved into the second row, although he lasted only 12 minutes before a chest injury forced him off. Brett Kearney bossed the game with his elusive running, slick passing and clever kicking game as Heath L'Estrange's try in the 63rd minute finally saw off the challenge of the valiant Welshmen.

Crusaders chief executive Rod Findlay maintained the future was bright for the Super League's only Welsh club, after they surpassed Ebbw Vale's total of 155 matches played between 1907 and 1912 to become Wales' most established Rugby League club.

With Castleford's game at Wigan postponed because of that weekend's World Club

February

Challenge, Harlequins moved clear at the top of the table after a stunning 36-26 Friday-night win at Leeds. Two late tries by the out-of-sorts Rhinos failed to lessen the impact of the pink-quartered Quins. Two-try Andy Ellis, his injury woes behind him, was a handful, while Chad Randall brought all his guile to the scrum-half role in a superb 80 minutes.

Twice in the second half he picked off interceptions to save tries. A key moment came when the score was 6-6. Quins won a goal-line drop-out, and Kevin Sinfield tried a short restart from under his sticks. Tony Clubb caught the ball and went over for the easiest try of the season.

Thirty-year-old Sinfield signed a new four-year contract the previous week to the end of the 2014 season. The former Waterhead amateur joined the Rhinos as a teenager and made his Super League debut aged just 16 in the home defeat to Sheffield Eagles on August 22nd, 1997.

SUPER LEAGUE TABLE - *Sunday 27th February*

	P	W	D	L	F	A	D	PTS
Harlequins	3	3	0	0	67	48	19	6
Castleford Tigers	2	2	0	0	58	32	26	4
Huddersfield Giants	3	2	0	1	60	46	14	4
Leeds Rhinos	3	2	0	1	90	82	8	4
Warrington Wolves	3	2	0	1	67	68	-1	4
Wigan Warriors	2	1	1	0	60	26	34	3
St Helens	3	1	1	1	90	63	27	3
Hull Kingston Rovers	3	1	0	2	74	77	-3	2
Catalan Dragons	3	1	0	2	49	67	-18	2
Bradford Bulls	3	1	0	2	68	102	-34	2
Salford City Reds	3	1	0	2	66	104	-38	2
Hull FC	3	0	0	3	50	86	-36	0
Crusaders *	3	1	0	2	86	62	24	-2
Wakefield T Wildcats *	3	1	0	2	64	86	-22	-2

* 4 points deducted for entering administration

* RFL Chairman Richard Lewis criticised the government for cutting out the Regional Development Agencies, one of which, for the northwest, had promised considerable financial support for the 2013 World Cup. He also suggested the BBC was in danger of losing the contract to broadcast the Challenge Cup from 2012.

World Club Challenge

St George Illawarra lifted the World Club Challenge for the first time in their history after a bruising and entertaining 21-15 win over Wigan at the DW Stadium on the Sunday night. The Dragons managed to shrug off a poor start - they trailed 8-0 after four minutes - to eventually hit back and outscore Super League champions Wigan four tries to two in front of 24,268 spectators.

Warriors coach Michael Maguire was dealt a major blow before the game with prop forward Stuart Fielden failing a late fitness test on a knee injury and he was replaced by Chris Tuson, meaning Andy Coley started in the front row. Centre Martin Gleeson did pass a late fitness test and took his place in the centres after limping off the previous weekend but he limped off again two minutes before the half-time break. It turned out to be his last Wigan appearance.

PROBIZ WORLD CLUB CHALLENGE

Sunday 27th February 2011

**WIGAN WARRIORS 15
ST GEORGE ILLAWARRA DRAGONS 21**

WARRIORS: 1 Sam Tomkins; 2 Darrell Goulding; 3 Martin Gleeson; 4 George Carmont; 19 Amos Roberts; 6 Paul Deacon; 7 Thomas Leuluai; 14 Paul Prescott; 9 Michael McIlorum; 10 Andy Coley; 11 Harrison Hansen; 16 Ryan Hoffman; 13 Sean O'Loughlin (C). Subs (all used): 12 Joel Tomkins; 23 Chris Tuson; 21 Lee Mossop; 22 Liam Farrell.
Tries: Carmont (2, 23); **Goals:** Deacon 3/4;
Field goal: S Tomkins (40).
DRAGONS: 1 Darius Boyd; 2 Brett Morris; 3 Mark Gasnier; 4 Matt Cooper; 5 Jason Nightingale; 6 Jamie Soward; 7 Ben Hornby (C); 8 Dan Hunt; 9 Nathan Fien; 10 Michael Weyman; 11 Beau Scott; 12 Ben Creagh; 13 Matt Prior. Subs (all used): 14 Michael Greenfield; 15 Trent Merrin; 16 Jon Green; 17 Cameron King.
Tries: Morris (10, 29), Cooper (16), King (55);
Goals: Soward 2/4; **Field goal:** Soward (70).
Rugby Leaguer & League Express Men of the Match:
Warriors: George Carmont; *Dragons:* Brett Morris.
Penalty count: 8-5; **Half-time:** 15-14;
Referee: Thierry Alibert;
Attendance: 24,268 *(at DW Stadium, Wigan).*

The Dragons, who were without head coach Wayne Bennett after he flew back to Australia to be with his gravely ill mother-in-law, named 13 of the 17 that won the NRL Grand Final with a 32-8 win over Sydney Roosters the previous October, with Neville Costigan, Jeremy Smith and Jarrod Saffy now not at the club. The other man to miss out was Australia Test hooker Dean Young because of a knee problem.

After just over a minute, George Carmont floated through the air to take a Paul

Thomas Leuluai finds his path blocked by Ben Hornby and Ben Creagh

Deacon kick that was aimed at exploiting Jamie Soward's vulnerability under a high ball. And, after Deacon added a penalty, Wigan looked to be coasting with an eight-point lead.

That impression was misleading, and the Dragons were able to exploit a weakness on the right side of Wigan's defence, with winger Brett Morris scoring two tries. George Carmont scored the try of the game when he broke from halfway in thrilling style but there were two incidents that did it for Wigan. An audacious try from dummy half by 19-year-old reserve hooker Cameron King gave St George a lead they would never lose after 55 minutes. And when Amos Roberts threw the ball into touch with three minutes to go, over the head of Darrell Goulding, it was Wigan's last shot.

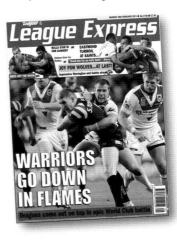

MARCH
The Big Willie show

Round 4

St Helens announced that England international Kyle Eastmond would be leaving the club at the end of the season to take up a lucrative three-year deal with rugby union side Bath. Eastmond insisted for the rest of this season his mind would be set on winning trophies for St Helens. Eastmond's decision led to calls for the competition's salary cap to be increased. On the first Saturday evening of March, in Perpignan, he played a key role in Saints' 22-16 victory against the Catalan Dragons, winning the maximum three Albert Goldthorpe Medal points. Saints had to overcome adversity, with Scott Moore taken off concussed and Leon Pryce lasting only four minutes of his 2011 debut after aggravating the groin strain that had ruled him out of the first three rounds. It meant Pryce would miss the first England Elite Squad training camp to be held at RAF Cranford in Lincolnshire.

Salford assistant coach Malcolm Alker was in charge of the City Reds team on the Friday night against Wigan at the Willows, after the club's announcement that head coach Shaun McRae would be stepping down for a month for health reasons. Alker prepared the team, and worked alongside Reds' Director of Rugby Steve Simms at the match, watching his side go down to a 32-16 defeat.

The Warriors ran in six tries in an entertaining clash, with scrum-half Thomas Leuluai grabbing a brace in a dazzling performance five days after Wigan's defeat to St George Illawarra in the World Club Challenge. In the post-match press conference, Wigan coach Michael Maguire fended off questions surrounding Martin Gleeson's future at the club. Gleeson had aggravated a hamstring injury in the World Club Challenge and was rumoured to be having off-field problems.

Hull Kingston Rovers' new signing Willie Mason finally arrived in the city, more than six months after the club announced it had signed him on a two-year contract, and he was due to be unveiled the following week. The Robins also signed a lower profile player when they snapped up David Scott, aged 17, from the Easterhouse Panthers club in Glasgow. Scott was the second player to come off the production line at the Panthers, after former teammate Chad McGlame joined Hull FC early in February.

Rovers were still struggling to find their form on the field and on the Sunday they lost 27-14 at Castleford as the Tigers maintained their 100 per cent start to the season. The Robins dominated much of the opening period and had forced two successive drop-outs to suggest that their 14-6 lead could be increased to a 12-point margin by the break. But a pass by stand-off Blake Green went to ground wide out and the Tigers grabbed a lifeline they badly needed in stunning style. Brett Ferres, playing in the centre, scooped up possession ten metres from his own line and, with an opportunity clearly available for his side, raced away, with Hull KR fullback Shaun Briscoe covering. Winger Nick Youngquest remained close to his touchline, receiving a well-timed pass from Ferres around halfway and speeding in for a touchdown which Kirk Dixon converted to reduce the deficit to 14-12 and transform the contest. Young gun teenage hooker Daryl Clark, who along with

26

Adam Milner, a year his senior, was keeping Ryan Hudson out of the side, went past three defenders six minutes into the second period to put the Tigers ahead for the first time.

The scheming of Michael Monaghan and Lee Briers, the spark of teenager Rhys Evans and the workrate of Ben Westwood saw Warrington Wolves emerge 40-24 winners at home to Leeds in the Saturday TV game, with the Rhinos scoring three times in the final 21 minutes after trailing 34-8 at one point. Evans, 18, was called into the side when Ryan Atkins withdrew with a knee strain. And he took his opportunity with both hands, scoring one first-half try and creating another for scrum-half Richie Myler. Bridgend-born Evans had moved north to further his Rugby League career along with twin brother Ben, a prop. He had been one of the stars of England Academy's autumn win over the Australian Schoolboys, scoring twice in the second Test win at Leigh.

Off the field, Wolves chief executive Andy Gatcliffe announced plans to increase the capacity of the Halliwell Jones to 15,000 by adding North East and South East corners of the stadium, the first part of a long-term plan to bring the capacity up to around the 20,000 mark within the next five years.

Wakefield skipper Glenn Morrison insisted the Wildcats could overcome their troubled start to Super League XVI and haul themselves off the foot of the table after his side went down 40-18 at Odsal in a game that saw former Bulls favourite Morrison make a key error, losing control as he stooped to touch down, having darted between the posts with his side just 12-6 in arrears.

Two quick-fire Bulls tries after Morrison's effort was ruled out, allied to a fine defensive effort after the break, swung the pendulum in Bradford's direction, prop Craig Kopczak scoring a hat-trick of tries.

Harlequins suffered their first defeat of the campaign but there wasn't much daylight between the sides as Huddersfield ran out 18-10 winners at the Stoop. The Giants gave debuts to 19-year-old former Wigan back-rower Jon Molloy as former Wakefield forward Dale Ferguson and Graeme Horne's try just after the interval gave Huddersfield breathing space at 16-4.

Hull FC cruised to their first win of the season, in a match that under-fire coach Richard Agar described as 'must-win', with a comprehensive eight-try, 42-18 victory over a disappointing Crusaders side. Former Crusaders coach Brian Noble - who had been linked with a possible move to Hull - was watching from the stands.

Sam Obst, signed from Wakefield after round one, was the gamestar, kicking well and linking superbly with the returning Richard Horne at halfback. Hull's two tries - from Obst and Will Sharp - in the opening five minutes of the second half put them 26-0 ahead and ended all thoughts of a Crusaders fightback.

* Chris Thorman broke Rugby League's all-time points-in-a-game record as York City Knights beat Northumbria University 132-0 in the third round of the Carnegie Challenge Cup on the first weekend of March, the highest score ever recorded in the Cup, beating the previous record of 120 points scored by Rochdale Hornets against Illingworth on 13th March, 2005. Thorman's 56-point haul for the Knights, made up of four tries and 20 goals, edged him ahead of Hull KR's George West, who racked up 53 points through 11 tries and ten goals against Cumbrian amateurs Brookland Rovers on March 4th, 1905.

Round 5

Willie Mason claimed his Hull KR debut "could not have gone any better" after he helped the Robins to a 40-22 win over the Crusaders at Craven Park on the Sunday. Mason played 54 minutes, having started in the second row for the first 24 minutes, before being reintroduced to the game with half an hour remaining. And he left a positive impression, laying on a try for Liam Watts and contributing some decent drives, despite being a touch off the pace in terms of match fitness. A healthy attendance of 8,602 watched Mason's debut. He said: "I haven't experienced a crowd like that before."

The Robins had terminated the contract of their star Australian halfback Michael Dobson, who had undergone ankle surgery, in order to fit Mason onto their overseas quota while the final details of his Tongan passport could be organised. "This is the biggest-name signing to come to Craven Park. He's certainly the biggest signing in the club's history," said Hull KR chief executive Mike Smith. "He is Rugby League's David Beckham, and we're pleased to be able to bring him here to this club, to Hull as a city and to Super League. We had to do our due diligence and we took our time before announcing him as a signing and we wanted to make sure everything was right."

The game saw Clint Newton injure medial ligaments in his knee, ending an impressive run of 67 consecutive appearances, a streak that started in round 1 of the 2009 Super League season.

Hull FC coach Richard Agar saw his side snatch defeat from the jaws of victory at Wigan on the Sunday. Hull's ill discipline was their downfall, as the champions came back from 12-4 down to win 14-12 in a bad-tempered affair that went down to the final hooter. Danny Tickle had the opportunity to claim a point right at the end, but his penalty attempt sailed wide of the uprights.

Agar was fuming about what he saw as Wigan's over-zealous tackling techniques, and he thought Sam Tomkins was fortunate not to join his brother Joel in being sent off. Joel Tomkins was dismissed after 69 minutes for elbowing Kirk Yeaman, but Agar was disappointed with the antics of Sam. "Sending off was 100 per cent the correct call. And if you look back at the brawl, Kirk and Joel Tomkins were in at each other when Sam comes in and gives three haymakers to the back of Kirk's head, so they were lucky just to have one bloke sent off. I'm quite happy that our blokes over the course of the 80 minutes responded in the way they did, because if they are not going to get the right protection during the game then they are quite right to do that."

The following Tuesday Sam Tomkins and Yeaman were both suspended for one match for fighting and Joel Tomkins copped two matches for leading with the elbow, an appeal being unsuccessful. Former Wigan player Cameron Phelps made his debut at fullback for Hull.

Warrington fielded just one overseas player in the side that beat Wakefield 22-4 at Belle Vue on the Friday - former Wildcats, Kiwi back-rower David Solomona the only non-Brit in the Wolves line-up. Ryan Atkins' walk-in try just after the break opened a 16-point gap which always looked too much for a Wakefield side struggling to prise any openings. Another former Wakefield player, Ben Westwood, was outstanding.

Castleford registered a 34-24 home win over Catalans in the Saturday TV game at the re-christened Probiz Coliseum. Catalans coach Trent Robinson was frustrated by a third successive defeat which had looked unlikely when his side, with scrum-half Scott Dureau (who finished with two tries and four goals and was involved in the Dragons' other two touchdowns) calling the shots, had dominated the early stages.

Robinson was particularly frustrated by the concession of a couple of long-range tries in the closing quarter that effectively put paid to his side's hopes. The Dragons were still very much in contention, at only 22-18 down, when Dureau fired a testing kick to the corner. Castleford winger Nick Youngquest, however, not only defused the threat – he turned defence into attack to stunning effect, blasting through a gap and rounding the covering Dureau before racing 90 metres for a rousing score that brought the crowd to its feet. With ten minutes left and Catalans again threatening, there was a similar touchdown, Tigers centre Joe Arundel scooping up possession after a Dragons move had broken down to sprint 80 metres for a try that settled the issue.

A stirring 46-12 home Rhinos victory over the Reds – who ran out of steam in the final quarter, conceding five tries – warmed up the crowd, on a cold night at Headingley. With a third of the Rhinos squad unavailable – Lee Smith, with a torn hamstring, joining the preponderance of props on the sidelines – the queue at the treatment room worsened when boom threequarter Ben Jones-Bishop dislocated his shoulder, scrambling to halt Jodie Broughton scoring in the corner after the visitors started brightly.

Leeds did not concede a point in the second half. Kallum Watkins led the way. The 19-year-old pulled off two try-saving tackles in seven minutes to get under Adam Sidlow and then race across to deny Stefan Ratchford, while his twinkling footwork and balanced strength brought him the game-turning try on the hour.

Huddersfield Giants swept to the top of the table as Kevin Brown inspired a surprisingly one-sided 50-16 victory over disappointing Bradford. The Bulls never recovered from a horror start that saw them concede three tries inside the first nine minutes, and they could have trailed by more than the 30-6 scoreline at half-time. Brown was a key figure throughout, with halfback partner Danny Brough chiming in with his virtuoso in-field kicking game. But the Giants were strong across the board, with Kiwi forwards David Fa'alogo and David Faiumu causing the visiting defence endless problems, along with two-try Graeme Horne. Rookie winger Jermaine McGillvary also finished with a try double.

Harlequins coach Rob Powell was refusing to look too far ahead after his team's outstanding start to the season, with four wins from their first five games, the latest a shock 27-16 victory against St Helens at the Stobart Stadium on the Friday night, with Kyle Eastmond bearing the brunt of the home crowd's dissatisfaction.

St Helens went into the contest wracked by injuries. Leon Pryce's groin had given out on him in Perpignan in the previous game; Kiwi centre Sia Soliola was missing with an ankle knock, Gary Wheeler's back ruled him out, Louie McCarthy-Scarsbrook failed a late fitness test and Jon Wilkin picked up a calf injury training with the England squad at RAF Cranwell during the week.

The Quins remained largely unchanged from the team that narrowly lost at Huddersfield last week. Aussie centre David Howell was missing through suspension, so on-loan Wigan Warrior Karl Pryce stepped into the centres, with devastating effect. Coach Rob Powell also handed a debut to veteran winger Mark Calderwood in the absence of Jamie O'Callaghan with a dead leg. Quins stand-off Luke Gale dominated the game with a fine display of tactical kicking and slick handling as Quins went 12-0 up in the opening six minutes.

One bit of good news for coach Royce Simmons was the belated debut of new prop Josh Perry. The former Manly front-rower looked a little rusty but put in a solid if unspectacular performance.

Round 6

Kyle Eastmond missed St Helens' 30-16 victory at Leeds in the Saturday TV game after he was suspended by the club for disciplinary reasons. Saints coach Royce Simmons was forced into a fourth different halfback pairing of the season in Lee Gaskell and Jonny Lomax. Lomax had been seen as a utility, but flourished at scrum-half and there was a great wing duel between 18-point Jamie Foster and Rhinos' try scoring teenage debutant Zak Hardaker, in for Ben Jones-Bishop. Jones-Bishop suffered a dislocated shoulder against Salford the previous week, and underwent an operation to repair the damage the day after. The Rhinos reacted quickly to the news by recalling Hardaker from his original club, Featherstone Rovers, where he was dual-registered. Two tries in four minutes just after the hour mark perfectly illustrated Saints' resilience and ability to ramp up the pressure, the game turner fittingly scored by the ubiquitous Paul Wellens.

Meanwhile the Rhinos were conducting an inquiry into an entry on their injured prop forward Ryan Bailey's Facebook page, on which Bailey was alleged to have made disparaging comments about Japanese people after the country was hit by a massive earthquake and tsunami, causing several thousand deaths. Bailey issued an apology and, on top of being fined by his club, volunteered to pay a donation to the Japanese tsunami relief fund.

Wigan coach Michael Maguire showed little surprise after teenage winger Josh Charnley, who had a successful short loan spell at Hull KR in 2010, played a starring role in the Warriors' hard fought 20-6 victory at Huddersfield on the Friday. Charnley, 19, making his fourth start of the season in Wigan colours, scored a try, made another and kicked four goals in addition to a making couple of spectacular try-saving tackles. The best try of the evening was Charnley's, when he dived outside Giants debutant Jamie Simpson to take a superb, precision kick from Sean O'Loughlin early in the second half. The final try that Charnley created for Ryan Hoffman, was a great one too, with the youngster dashing down the wing and delivering a great pass inside.

Nathan Brown made five changes in his 17-man squad from the one that had hammered Bradford 50-16 at the Galpharm Stadium five days before. One of the incomers was former Bulls junior Joe Wardle, who was making his debut in the centre after returning from a dual-registration stint with Barrow Raiders.

Wakefield defied the odds yet again with a monster effort against a Hull FC side that had run champions Wigan so close five days earlier. The 20-6 win at the KC Stadium wiped out the four-point deduction imposed for entering financial administration before the start of the season and the Wildcats climbed off the foot of the table for the first time.

Richard Horne made his 300th appearance for Hull FC, who welcomed back Sean Long after missing the last three games through injury. For Wakefield there was a first appearance of the season for stand-off Ben Jeffries. At the centre of the Wildcats' hardworking and enthusiastic effort was captain and man of the match Glenn Morrison. Tommy Lee's try and two goals from Josh Griffin at the start of the final quarter stretched the Wildcats' lead to 14-6 as desperate defence denied Hull a host of scoring chances.

Steve Menzies, still playing 80 minutes at the age of 37, played a major part in the Dragons' 32-22 Super League win over the Crusaders in Wrexham on the Friday night. The Welsh club were now bottom of the table. Scott Dureau was at the heart of every Dragons attack as their Welsh opponents had no answer to his pinpoint accurate bombs. The French side raced into a 12-0 lead and, despite a comeback in the second half that got them back to 22-all, the Crusaders were second best, Ben Farrar's second try eventually breaking their spirit.

Bradford's outstanding rearguard defensive effort at Odsal ended Castleford's undefeated start to the season. Inspired by lightning quick hooker Daryl Clark, the Tigers poured forward in the closing stages and threw everything they had at the home side. But in stark contrast to their woeful defensive display at the Galpharm Stadium, seven days earlier the Bulls held firm for an 18-14 win.

Bulls coach Mick Potter had plenty of heroes in his ranks, with Australian hooker Heath L'Estrange outstanding on his return to the side. Nick Scruton's big display up front was rewarded with a try double, while fullback Brett Kearney marshalled his side superbly amid the late Castleford onslaught. Castleford were still a chance to win the game up to the point when Paul Sykes took a huge Rangi Chase kick after the final siren.

Tigers prop Craig Huby signed a new three-year extension to his contract to keep him at the club until at least the end of the 2014 season. Huby, 24, was the club's longest serving Castleford player, having made his debut for his hometown club against Leeds Rhinos as a 16 year-old in 2003. His form in the opening weeks of the season had led several pundits to question why he hadn't been selected in Steve McNamara's England squad.

Hull Kingston Rovers badly missed Clint Newton on the Friday night as they went down 34-18 at The Willows, with Newton's countryman, Willie Mason, making his second appearance for the club, following his high-profile move from the NRL. "He was excellent last week, and did some decent things here," said Rovers' coach Justin Morgan. "But it's going to take him time to find his feet. He certainly put in the effort, but ask me about him in a month when I will have a better assessment." Centre Sean Gleeson made his first appearance in the Reds' colours after completing his recovery from an ankle problem.

Luke Patten was superb as the Reds ran in six tries.

And on the Sunday, Warrington surged to the top of the table with a club-record league win against the previously on-form Harlequins. The Wolves ran in 14 tries during a breathless 80 minutes, with Brett Hodgson booting 13 goals to claim the club's record tally for goals in a Super League match, while Chris Bridge scored a 19-minute hat-trick. The 82-6 reverse was Harlequins' heaviest ever Super League defeat.

Round 7

Warrington Wolves set down a marker after ending Wigan's unbeaten start to the league season on the last Friday of March. The Wolves dominated the champions in every department and the performance of the night came from Lee Briers, his dominating display completely overshadowing the debut of Warriors' halfback Brett Finch. Finch, who had finally recovered from neck surgery after a training injury on the off season, had not played in over six months before declaring himself fit for the top of the table clash at the DW Stadium.

The much-travelled halfback crowned his debut with a solo try after collecting his own grubber kick to score after it rebounded from the post, but he was clearly struggling for match fitness. Finch's try in the 26th minute levelled the scores after Matty Blythe - a back-rower filling in at centre for Matt King - had opened the scoring in the seventh minute. But Joel Monaghan's try seven minutes from the break and Brett Hodgson's second conversion had Warrington ahead 12-6 at half-time.

Warrington extended their lead further on 48 minutes when Briers targeted Josh Charnley with a high bomb, and Joel Monaghan out-jumped the youngster before grounding for his second score of the night. Hodgson's third conversion pushed the Wolves 18-6 ahead. The result was decided when a long ball from Wigan skipper Sean O'Loughlin intended for Stefan Marsh was intercepted by Richie Myler, who raced 55 metres unopposed to take the game away from the Champions. Hodgson's fourth goal made it 24-6 with 15 minutes remaining.

Sydney media reports suggested Hollywood star Russell Crowe's South Sydney Rabbitohs were targeting Wigan coach Michael Maguire for a return to Australia next year.

Wakefield Trinity Wildcats ran TV advertising on the main ITV network between popular soap operas Emmerdale and Coronation Street and were rewarded with a 9,000-strong crowd for their home game with Leeds. The Wildcats led 4-0 at half-time through a Greg Johnson try but the clinical finishing of Kallum Watkins - he scored four tries after the break - completed a 28-6 win for the Rhinos.

That week the Wildcats made a move to sign Sheffield Eagles prop forward Liam Higgins and took Warrington Wolves back-row forward Tyrone McCarthy on a month's loan.

Kyle Eastmond's suspension from the St Helens club was lifted after he was found guilty of making offensive gestures to supporters at the match against Harlequins on March 11 but the form of Jonny Lomax and Lee Gaskell saw him playing in the under-20s. On the Friday night, Jamie Foster and Paul Wellens scored two tries apiece as St Helens claimed their first 'home' win at the Stobart Stadium, by 28-16 over Bradford. Saints recovered from an early Shaun Ainscough try to make it third time lucky after losing to Warrington and Harlequins at Widnes's stadium, which they were sharing for a year until their new stadium was completed. Chris Flannery scored Saints' other try, with Lomax involved in all five as he impressed again in the halves alongside fellow youngster Gaskell.

Saints scored two tries while Paul Sykes was sin-binned late in the first half, and although the hosts had both Sia Soliola and Michael Shenton yellow-carded near the end, tries from Ainscough and Patrick Ah Van were too late for Bradford.

Salford City Reds cruised to a 22-10 victory in Perpignan. The scoreline should have been far greater as Catalans looked devoid of any imagination at halfback after the late withdrawal of the ill Scott Dureau. Salford started with Stefan Ratchford in the centres and that proved to be a masterstroke, with the halfback creating three of Salford's and four-try Jodie Broughton's tries.

The Reds learned that week that former Australian international Phil Bailey, signed ahead of 2011 following his release by Wigan, had announced his retirement from the sport after admitting defeat in his battle to overcome an Achilles tendon injury that had plagued him since the latter stages of last season. He failed to make a single appearance for the club.

Jordan Tansey, released by Hull FC, made his first appearance for the Crusaders in a ten-try 56-16 hammering at Castleford. The Tigers - with Rangi Chase continuing his magnificent form - were already 6-0 ahead, and showing signs of running rampant from a strong platform set by prop Nick Fozzard, when Vince Mellars, former Crusader Nick Youngquest and Michael Witt were shown yellow cards by whistler Ben Thaler in the 17th minute, after winger Kirk Dixon continuing his fine run of form by squeezing in at the corner after stand-off Chase and centre Joe Arundel had linked.

With numbers reduced, Castleford made use of the extra space, substitute hooker Daryl Clark making maximum use of territory gained by prop Paul Jackson by forcing his way past Clinton Schifcofske and substitute Gil Dudson. Schifcofske's exit was the prelude for tries shortly before half-time for Dixon – courtesy of Richie Mathers and Arundel – and benchman Dean Widders, Dixon's three goals from four attempts helping put the Tigers firmly in control at 22-0 ahead. Relieving news for the Crusaders was that Rhys Hanbury, Frank Winterstein and new signing from Melbourne Hep Cahill had their visa applications finally approved and were due to arrive that week.

Hull FC staged a grandstand finish to snatch a 40-30 victory - only their second league win of the season - from the jaws of defeat in a game that had the Stoop crowd on the edges of their seats from first whistle to last, bouncing back from a 14-point deficit with just 15 minutes to play. A Jordan Turner try finally edged Hull in front on 77 minutes and Kirk Yeaman sealed it in the final seconds with another.

The win put Hull FC level on points with Hull KR, who lost a protracted Saturday night TV game with Huddersfield at Craven Park by 38-16. With one floodlight failing towards the end of the first half and causing an extended half-time interval while repairs took place, there was plenty of incident. Danny Brough scored two tries, had a hand in two others and finished with an 18-point haul, Hull KR's key man Michael Dobson was still on the sidelines recovering from an ankle operation. Brough had plenty of support – winger Jermaine McGillvary was outstanding in attack and defence on the right, while Scott Grix barely put a foot wrong at fullback and Keith Mason led a big effort up front. Grix's 70th minute try finally took the contest away from dogged Rovers.

SUPER LEAGUE TABLE - *Sunday 27th March*

	P	W	D	L	F	A	D	PTS
Warrington Wolves	7	6	0	1	235	110	125	12
Castleford Tigers	6	5	0	1	189	104	85	10
Huddersfield Giants	7	5	0	2	172	108	64	10
St Helens	7	4	1	2	186	138	48	9
Wigan Warriors	6	4	1	1	132	84	48	9
Leeds Rhinos	7	4	0	3	204	170	34	8
Harlequins	7	4	0	3	140	204	-64	8
Bradford Bulls	7	3	0	4	158	212	-54	6
Salford City Reds	7	3	0	4	150	210	-60	6
Hull FC	7	2	0	5	150	168	-18	4
Hull Kingston Rovers	7	2	0	5	162	198	-36	4
Catalan Dragons	7	2	0	5	131	167	-36	4
Wakefield T Wildcats *	7	2	0	5	114	182	-68	0
Crusaders *	7	1	0	6	164	232	-68	-2

* 4 points deducted for entering administration

• *On 31st March Widnes Vikings learned that they had won a Super League licence for the 2012-2015 period. The other two Championship club applicants were Barrow, whose application fell short and Halifax, who fulfilled all the criteria but were not selected. RFL chief executive Nigel Wood confirmed that the RFL would again guarantee a licence for a Championship club from 2015.*

APRIL
Dragons fire up

Round 8

Leeds Rhinos looked back to their best for the first hour of their Friday night TV game at home to reigning champions Wigan as Kevin Sinfield slotted over his fifth goal to put the hosts 22-4 ahead - after Joel Tomkins gave Wigan a 4-0 lead in the 11th minute - and seemingly in total control. Jamie Jones-Buchanan, Danny Buderus and Brent Webb tries gave Leeds the ascendancy and the Rhinos also had three tries disallowed in the first half.

But the Warriors conjured an astonishing fight back, scoring three tries in 16 minutes - through Sam Tomkins, Darrell Goulding and Paul Prescott, two minutes from time - for a 22-all draw. And, pressing on the Rhinos line and in front of their own fans, they worked a position for a levelling penalty as the hooter sounded. With a minute to go, Brett Finch's long pass had put Sam Tomkins into space to link with brother Joel who found Liam Farrell on the inside. After hauling him down centimetres from the line, Buderus chose to hold down Farrell and concede a possible two-point kick rather than risking one last play and coming away with nothing as the Rhinos looked shot out wide on the left. Coolness personified, Sam Tomkins did the rest to end an epic.

The big talking point of the game was a tackle by Wigan prop Jeff Lima early in the second half when he came in as third man, appearing to attack the legs of Chris Clarkson. Lima had already received a two-match ban for a chicken-wing tackle earlier in the season and received another one-match suspension.

Hull FC promised to launch an official complaint to the RFL about referee James Child, who was at the centre of controversy following Hull's 20-18 home defeat to Castleford on the Friday night. Child dismissed Sean Long for leading with the elbow, after he had been sin-binned earlier in the game for fighting along with Castleford player Martin Aspinwall. Hull's Lee Radford was also shown a yellow card in the fifth minute for an alleged grapple tackle. Long, who was dismissed for the first time in a 17-year career, was suspended for two matches by the RFL Disciplinary Committee.

Kirk Dixon's fourth goal of the match after 69 minutes proved crucial, putting the Tigers eight points ahead. Richard Owen, who spent over a year on the sidelines after breaking his leg at Bradford in February 2010, scored a try on his return to action.

Hull Chairman Kath Hetherington questioned the competence of Child as a Super League match official, and asked the RFL to examine his performance. Coach Richard Agar, after his side's sixth defeat in the first eight rounds, blamed the reverse on the referee after more calls from fans for his sacking. Agar was called to an RFL Operational Rules Tribunal after being charged with breaching the Operational Rules and a breach of the RFL's Respect Policy and in May was fined £3,000, with a further £3,000 suspended until the end of the season.

Joe Wardle and fellow centre Michael Lawrence were singled out for praise by coach Nathan Brown after the Giants overcame a sketchy first-half showing at the Galpharm to beat Wakefield 34-10 on the Sunday. Just a Danny Brough penalty separated the sides after a disjointed first half but two tries in the final ten minutes were just enough to edge the Giants into second place above Castleford on points difference (although the Tigers still had a match in hand). Battling Wakefield gave debuts to prop Liam Higgins and Tyrone McCarthy.

Catalan Dragons defied the odds to come from behind for a thrilling 22-20 victory away to leaders Warrington. Not only did the Dragons come into the game with a record of two wins from seven, they also had six players out through injury. And when they suffered the early loss of fullback Clint Greenshields with a dislocated elbow, Warrington were expected to romp to another thumping victory after racking up 82 points in their previous home game against Harlequins. But a young French side dug deep to inflict Warrington's first defeat since the opening weekend in Cardiff. The game was decided on 71 minutes when Richie Myler tapped back a Lee Briers bomb on halfway. It didn't go near a teammate and Scott Dureau nipped in to gather and charge to the posts.

That week Wolves winger Joel Monaghan signed a three-year extension to his deal, keeping him at the club until the end of 2014. Paul Wood signed up until the end of 2013, while young Welsh centre Rhys Evans agreed an improved extended five-year contract.

Crusaders picked up an early-season double as they ended a six-match winless streak in a dour game against Salford on the Saturday. The Welsh side backed up their 42-12 win over the City Reds in Cardiff on the opening weekend of the season with a hard-fought win to finally move off minus points, having been deducted four points for entering administration before the start of the season.

The key to the Crusaders' win was Rhys Hanbury, who provided the organisational skills that Iestyn Harris' men had been lacking in recent weeks. Hanbury, whose return had been held up due to visa complications, started at scrum-half, with Jordan Tansey partnering him in the halves in the absence of the suspended Michael Witt. New signing Hep Cahill also made his debut after getting his visa along with Hanbury and Frank Winterstein.

Karl Pryce scored three tries for Harlequins and made another on his first return to Bradford, but it wasn't enough to prevent the Bulls recording their fourth win of the season, by 24-22, in a scrappy clash on the Sunday. Pryce terrorised the right side of the Bradford defence but the home side controlled the middle part of the game and looked well in control at 24-10 with less than ten minutes remaining. On-loan Wigan centre Pryce then created one try and scored another to set up a nervous final few seconds, as the Bulls held out. Craig Kopczak had an excellent game up front and 17-year-old Tom Burgess made a promising debut off the bench.

St Helens were close to their brilliant best as they ran in six tries at Widnes against a Hull KR side low on confidence and struggling with injuries. Coach Royce Simmons left out Kyle Eastmond again and stuck with the winning combination of Lee Gaskell and Jonny Lomax. Saints were still missing Leon Pryce, along with Francis Meli, Paul Clough and Jon Wilkin, who damaged nerves in his hand after a freak accident with a yard-brush earlier in the week. Gary Wheeler was moved off the bench into the centre berth, while Tommy Makinson was recalled. James Roby was brilliant once more as he dominated the ruck from start to finish.

The match kicked off with pageantry as a guard of honour of some former great Saints players welcomed James Graham onto the field to mark his 200th Saints appearance.

Round 9

Catalan Dragons coach Trent Robinson hailed the decision to stay in England after his club's win at Warrington as instrumental in gaining the scalp of Super League champions Wigan Warriors on the Friday night, with a 47-28 victory at the DW Stadium.

The talk before the game was all about the return of Pat Richards, who had shared the 2010 Albert Goldthorpe medal with teammate Sam Tomkins, but it was another

Australian, Scott Dureau, who ran the show as the Catalans destroyed the Warriors. Richards was making his first appearance of 2011 after recovering from the Achilles tendon injury he picked up in the Grand Final the previous October, but Dureau stole all the headlines and, backed up by the evergreen Steve Menzies and Ben Farrar, ran rings around Wigan. The former Newcastle Knights halfback bagged a brace, and kicked six goals and a field goal.

Huddersfield condemned Warrington to a second successive defeat with a 29-10 win at the Galpharm. Tries from the outstanding Scott Grix, Larne Patrick, Luke Robinson and boom rookie winger Jermaine McGillvary were supplemented by 13 points from the boot of Danny Brough. Lee Briers was missing with a deadleg picked up in the defeat to the Catalans. Giants coach Nathan Brown labelled close-season acquisition Luke O'Donnell as the "buy of the year".

Wakefield clinched their third victory of the campaign and went into positive league points with a 52-32 home win over Harlequins in a match played in sweltering conditions on the Sunday. Trinity had a firm grip on proceedings when halfbacks Ben Jeffries and Tommy Lee inspired an early 26-0 lead, before Quins gallantly fought back to 32-22 at one stage. But the sin-binning of Tony Clubb soon after proved decisive as the Wildcats regained control, and finished the afternoon with much to be positive about. Alongside Lee and Jeffries, young former Wigan reserve, loose forward Stuart Howarth had his best game in a Wakefield shirt, and Josh Griffin finished with an impressive 20-point haul. Up front, captain Glenn Morrison was outstanding, just edging a duel with opposite number Rob Purdham.

Castleford Tigers charged to the top of Super League with a ruthless 52-20 demolition of hapless Salford, whose off-field problems continued. Confusion reigned after reports on the Friday that assistant coach Malcolm Alker was sent home from a team training session by football director Steve Simms and told to stay away from the club until Monday. Simms refused to elaborate on the limited details of the alleged incident when questioned about Alker's absence from the match on the Sunday. Simms and Alker had overseen first-team matters at the Willows since February, when head coach Shaun McRae was granted leave from the club on medical grounds.

The Tigers ran in nine tries, including two each for Joe Arundel and Nick Youngquest, and Rangi Chase was once again the star of the show.

Castleford coach Terry Matterson had expressed his frustration at the decision made by the RFL to suspend Willie Isa for one match, after the disciplinary panel found him guilty of making dangerous contact during the previous week's victory over Hull FC. Isa was found to have forced Epalahame Lauaki's arm and shoulder in an abnormal direction and was also alleged to have used a grapple tackle on the same player six minutes later, but was cleared of that charge by the panel. Meanwhile the Tigers moved another step closer to moving into a new state-of-the-art stadium at Glasshoughton when they were given full planning permission for the project from Wakefield Council.

Hull KR got back to winning ways with a come-from-behind 38-28 triumph over Leeds in the Saturday TV game at Craven Park. Aside from when Crusaders were beaten in the euphoria of Willie Mason's debut, Justin Morgan's men had lost the five other games since Michael Dobson's ankle injury. Mason's impact on the field was limited and it was at the end of his first stint that the home revival started. Youngster Scott Taylor was the initial galvanising force, Liam Watts gave greater mobility and Matt Cook, on his seasonal debut, crossed for a try on the half hour to establish a two-score lead the hosts never lost. Sam Latus, on his first start in 2011 for out-of-form Peter Fox was a highlight and Ben Cockayne was typically enthusiastic at fullback in place of injured Shaun Briscoe. Ben Galea fully deserved the sealing score on 76 minutes.

Hull FC gave under-pressure coach Richard Agar some relief after back-to-back home defeats when they beat Bradford 34-24 at the KC Stadium on the Friday night. Hull slid to an early 12-0 deficit but after that initial spell, a tight affair was eventually settled by Tom

Briscoe's two late tries. It could have been so different. With the game poised at 24-24, and just 11 minutes left on the clock, Bradford's Marc Herbert had watched a field-goal attempt drift agonisingly wide. Then came the slice of luck that changed the game. Richard Horne, under pressure, produced a desperate, hurried kick that confused everybody and as the ball bounced around Craig Fitzgibbon gathered it and suddenly Hull had an overlap on the left. The loose forward promptly started the passing move that culminated in Briscoe's first. It was a pivotal moment of the match.

St Helens had the game with Crusaders won in the first half at the Racecourse Ground and went on to complete a 34-18 victory. The Welsh side were slow coming out of the traps again and were 12-0 down in the first seven minutes. Saints were outstanding in the first half hour. By that time they were already on 30 points and then managed to prevent a possible Crusaders comeback in the second half. James Roby ripped the Crusaders to shreds.

Royce Simmons asked supporters not to jeer union-bound scrum-half Kyle Eastmond, who was yet to force his way back into the first team since being suspended for making gestures to angry supporters after St Helens were defeated by Harlequins in round 5. Eastmond apologised for his actions, but had since been the subject of abuse from some sections of the club's support even though his suspension was lifted. Eastmond had been playing for Saints' Valvoline Cup side. "I probably shouldn't say this - but I just wish the crowd wouldn't boo. To me they are just booing the St Helens colours," said Simmons. Saints' first team had won four consecutive matches in Eastmond's absence.

Round 10

Huddersfield Giants went a point clear at the top of the table after a 38-6 thrashing of Leeds, just over 50 years since they last won a league game at Headingley. The Giants led 20-0 at half-time, and the score remained the same eight minutes into the second half when Ryan Bailey caught Kevin Brown late before appearing to drag him from the floor by his shirt and punch him again. That action provoked outrage from the Huddersfield ranks, with Brown's teammates rushing to his aid to attempt to settle the score during a 26-man battle. Referee Ben Thaler dismissed Bailey, before also showing the red card to Luke O'Donnell, complete with a ripped shirt, who further stoked the temperature by goading Leeds' fans as he left the field.

The incident provoked Giants coach Nathan Brown to produce an outburst against both Bailey and match officials after the game. Brown claimed that O'Donnell should have "knocked him (Bailey) out cold... and then given him some more." Brown looked as though he would escape censure until the RFL called him up following a news story in League Express three weeks later in which Leeds chief executive Gary Hetherington questioned why the Giants coach had not been reprimanded. At the end of June, Brown was fined £1,000 (£500 suspended for six months) after being found guilty of breaching the RFL's Operational Rules and the sport's Respect Policy.

Kirk Dixon salvaged a point in a thriller in the capital on the Friday night, as Castleford avoided defeat with a 26-all draw, but still slipped from first to third in the Super League table. Dixon's perfect goal-kicking proved decisive as the winger booted a last-gasp penalty from 45 metres, just as Quins looked to have snatched a famous victory. With 12 minutes to play the Tigers had been coasting at 24-10, only for a late trio of tries from Luke Dorn, Tony Clubb and Andy Ellis to turn things on their head. Harlequins' win ended a four-match losing streak, in front of their best crowd of the season - 4,128 - on the back of a promotion with the Evening Standard, the daily London newspaper.

Brett Hodgson produced a classic display of attacking fullback play as Warrington ended a two-match losing run with an emphatic 64-6 destruction of Crusaders at the Halliwell Jones Stadium. Hodgson finished with 28 points from two tries and ten goals from eleven attempts. The outstanding Ben Westwood also bagged a try-brace, as did centre Ryan Atkins, while hooker Michael Monaghan was at the hub of Warrington's best work. Winger Rhys Williams put in a top performance against the club he spent time on loan with earlier in the year.

St Helens moved into second spot with a nine-try 52-6 win at the Stobart Stadium - a fifth victory in succession - over Wakefield. In total, they had eight different scorers and eventually won comfortably against the gutsy Wildcats. Ade Gardner scored St Helens' fifth try after 53 minutes and, at 28-6, there was no way back for Wakefield.

Salford City Reds produced a fine display of attacking rugby to embarrass Bradford in glorious sunshine on the Saturday. With Manchester United and Manchester City meeting in the FA Cup at Wembley, a sparse crowd of 2,809 turned up at the Willows, but the loyal, vocal Reds fans in the Shed were treated to a masterclass, as Salford won 56-16. Daniel Holdsworth was in excellent form, and his link-up play with Luke Patten and Matty Smith was key as three tries in ten first-half minutes seemed to shock the Bulls, and they never got back into the game.

Rugby League's worst kept secret was finally unlocked following the Warriors' 28-16 away victory over Hull KR on the Friday night, when Wigan chairman Ian Lenagan confirmed Michael Maguire would leave his post at the end of the season to succeed John Lang as head coach of South Sydney Rabbitohs. The announcement brought to an end three weeks of increasing speculation surrounding the Wigan boss's future, which up until that win had coincided with a dip in form. Fullback Sam Tomkins proved a perfect link in attack and chipped in with some superb kicks, including a tremendous 40/20 as Wigan recorded their first win in four games.

Wigan centre Martin Gleeson, who had not played since the World Club Challenge at the end of February, joined Hull FC. Gleeson had been released from his contract by Wigan following revelations he had been the victim of an apparent blackmail, and after struggling to shake off a knee injury that had plagued him for the early part of the season. Gleeson wasn't in the side as Catalan Dragons beat Hull 28-10 - only their second Super League win at Stade Gilbert Brutus in thirteen months - to move up into sixth place in the table following their back-to-back wins against Warrington and Wigan. Over 8,000 fans packed into the stadium and stood as one to applaud Steve Menzies as he left the field in the dying moments of the game. Menzies belied his years and raced in from 80 metres to score the game-clinching score six minutes from time.

Round 11

Hull KR halfback and 2009 Albert Goldthorpe Medal winner Michael Dobson made his comeback in the Hull derby at the KC Stadium on Good Friday, although he couldn't stop the Black & Whites registering a 36-18 success.

His return left the future of Rovers' marquee signing, Willie Mason, clouded in doubt. Australian scrum-half Dobson - who underwent ankle surgery in early March - had been de-registered by the club, meaning he was classified as a free agent, to accommodate Mason while they waited for his Tongan passport, which would have allowed him to move off Rovers' import quota. When Rovers named their squad for the derby Mason was included. But, 24 hours later, Dobson was dramatically re-registered at Mason's expense. Mason - linked with a move to French rugby union club Toulon - watched from the sidelines at the KC Stadium. There was more controversy at Craven Park as it emerged Ben Cockayne faced investigations over an alleged racist comment on his Facebook page. The Good Friday defeat was the Robins' fourth from five games, and left them 12th in the Super League table.

With five minutes left on the clock, Rovers trailed by just four points thanks to some heroic, last-gasp defence. But the Airlie Birds ran in two late, converted tries from Kirk Yeaman - from a Willie Manu offload - and gamestar Tom Briscoe to seal the win, Martin

April

Gleeson making a try-scoring debut for his new club.

Australian fullback Brett Kearney suffered a broken hand during Bradford's Thursday night 30-22 home defeat by Leeds. The Rhinos, thrashed at home by high-flying Huddersfield the previous week, twice came from behind before a late Danny Buderus try sealed their first win in four games. Coach Brian McDermott praised his skipper Kevin Sinfield, who made vital contributions at crucial times, including a superb long pass that sent Ryan Hall over to put the Rhinos ahead for the first time midway through the second half. Hooker Paul McShane, who came off the bench and visibly gave the Rhinos extra impetus, poaching their opening try and having a hand in the second, was Leeds' best.

Both Wigan and Wakefield recorded stunning late derby wins by the same 28-24 score on Good Friday, with Liam Farrell's try sealing Wigan's win over St Helens and Frankie Mariano's effort doing the same for the Wildcats at Castleford.

The Wildcats were totally out of the contest a couple of minutes into the second period, when tries either side of the break had helped give the Tigers a 24-4 lead. But they posted four unanswered tries in the final thirty minutes of the game to clinch a stunning victory over their in-form neighbours. Wakefield scored what appeared to be little more than a consolation try when, shortly after Tigers winger Richard Owen had been unable to take a testing pass from stand-off Rangi Chase that could have put the game to bed, stand-off Kieran Hyde bustled his way over from short range. Winger Josh Griffin, who had been unable to convert centre Chris Dean's first-half try (scored from scrum-half Tommy Lee's high kick), added the extras and, crucially, Castleford winger Jordan Thompson was bundled into touch by centre Aaron Murphy and substitute Matthew Wildie when the Tigers launched a raid in response. Wakefield hauled themselves to within a manageable eight points as the game entered the final quarter, Griffin rising above Owen to collect Hyde's high kick and converting his own score from wide out.

With Wakefield suddenly confident after an indifferent opening period, Hyde made a telling break and found second row Paul Johnson on his shoulder. Johnson had enough power and pace to hold off the Tigers cover, crashing over under the posts, and Griffin's third goal left the visitors only two points behind and in rampant mood. Castleford, crucially, were penalised by referee James Child at a scrum awarded in their favour deep in the Wakefield half. The next set closed with Lee firing a kick across the posts which second row Mariano charged onto at pace for a try which led to Castleford players appealing vigorously for an offside ruling. Griffin extended the newly-found lead with his goal, and Wakefield dug deep into their resources to hold out in the closing stages.

The result was not enough to lift Wakefield out of the bottom two, but took them to within two points of 12th placed Hull KR, and within five of the play-offs.

Wigan showed true champion spirit by grasping victory from the jaws of defeat in an absolute thriller in the sunshine at the DW Stadium on Good Friday. The Warriors entered the clash without a home win over their rivals since 2007, and it needed a Liam Farrell try right on the hooter to end their hoodoo.

Saints, who played the whole of the second half with just 15 fit players following injuries to Paul Wellens and Gary Wheeler, did their fans proud after fighting back from 22-10 to lead 24-22 heading into the final minute. But the day belonged to Wigan, and Pat Richards in particular, with two tries and four goals.

Salford City Reds began the search for a new head coach after having received confirmation from current incumbent Shaun McRae that he would not be seeking re-appointment at the end of the 2011 season. McRae had been on sick leave for eight weeks, while Reds assistant coach Malcolm Alker remained suspended from the club after being ordered home from training a fortnight before by football director Steve Simms.

On Good Friday, six days after a morale-boosting 56-16 win over Bradford, they were brought crashing back down to earth by a rampant Warrington. The Wolves stunned a bumper Good Friday crowd in the Salford sunshine, running in ten tries to record their biggest winning margin over the City Reds in Super League, the 60-0 scoreline topping their 68-16 win in Edinburgh in 2010.

Lee Briers and Rhys Williams scored two tries apiece, with Brett Hodgson kicking all ten goals, although the game wasn't over at half-time when the Wolves led 18-0. But Luke Adamson was sin-binned in the 48th minute and Warrington scored two tries in his absence, and another two as the hosts were still trying to regroup. A total of seven second-half tries meant the visitors racked up their second successive 60-point haul.

Harlequins were left to reflect on another near miss against one of the competition's form sides when they were unable to hold on to the slender advantage they held late in the home game against Catalan Dragons on Good Friday. The 37-30 defeat at the Stoop came six days after Quins were also unable to hold on for the win against Castleford, and their winless run now spanned six matches.

Scott Dureau inspired the Catalan Dragons to their fourth successive win as they broke London hearts with a late flourish to seal the points. Dureau scored 19 points in total, grabbing two tries, and booting eleven points with five goals and a field goal. He was also sin-binned for dissent as the French side maintained its push up the Super League table.

Bottom club Crusaders stayed within two points of 13th-placed Wakefield after a remarkable 32-6 victory over level-top Huddersfield Giants at the Racecourse Ground. Jordan Tansey's 67th minute try sealed a historic win for the Welshmen that finally put them in the plus column in the league table. Evergreen fullback Clinton Schifcofske rolled back the years with a great all-round display.

* Engage Mutual Assurance that week announced that it would be ending its sponsorship at the end of the 2011 season after seven seasons as the major sponsor of Super League.

Round 12

Huddersfield returned to the top of the table as they finally shook off dogged Salford on Easter Tuesday. Danny Brough led the scoring, kicking seven goals out of eight attempts as the Giants bounced back from their shock Good Friday hammering at Crusaders with a 52-22 win. The Giants twice went behind in the opening quarter. Reds captain Daniel Holdsworth was the dominant figure early on as his pass sent Adam Sidlow charging over for the game's first try after eight minutes and he then produced perfect kicks to set up tries for himself and Mark Henry before half-time, all three of which he converted to keep the Reds in the game.

Luke O'Donnell and hooker Shaun Lunt both scored tries from close range before a superb long-range try created by a break by David Hodgson and finished off by Jamie Cording provided the home spark, then Dale Ferguson went over after Jermaine McGillvary had collected Brough's high kick. Henry's try had brought the visitors back to within six points at the break but it was virtually all Huddersfield in the second half, with skipper Kevin Brown at the centre of operations. Ferguson and Lunt both got second tries; the impressive Darrell Griffin proved unstoppable on the hour and Brown ended the forwards' try-scoring run when he jinked his way over on 66 minutes. Salford grabbed a consolation through Stefan Ratchford before Huddersfield had the final say when leading tryscorer McGillvary struck for his ninth touchdown of the season.

All eyes were on Danny McGuire as the Rhinos' key pivot returned after a seven-month absence because of a knee ligament injury, making an immediate impact when he came off the bench in the 26th minute of the 34-16 home win over Crusaders on Easter Monday. With the scores locked at nil-all, and Jarrod Sammut having just been hauled down centimetres short, McGuire immediately sparked the crowd and a three-try Rhinos blitz in the run up to half-time. Brett Delaney went 70 metres on a blindside break from a scrum; in the next set outstanding Rob Burrow's disguised flat pass sent in Carl Ablett and, with the hosts showing greater cohesion, McGuire cleverly shipped on Paul McShane's pass for Ablett to give Keith Senior the overlap and he stepped inside the cover.

A sensational Francis Meli try seven seconds from time and a conversion six metres in from touch by Jamie Foster earned St Helens a dramatic 22-20 home victory over Castleford. It was heartbreak for the Tigers, who led by eight points against a patched-up Saints side before late scores from Ade Gardner and then Meli gave the hosts the spoils.

Tom Armstrong, on dual registration with Leigh, made his first appearance of the year, scoring St Helens first try at the end of the first quarter, with his first touch of the ball. The Tigers levelled five minutes later when Stuart Jones rumbled over off a sweet Rangi Chase pass from close range. Kirk Dixon nudged the visitors 8-6 ahead with a 32nd-minute penalty after Chase was taken out after the kick. But just before the break Armstrong sneaked over in the corner, the Castleford defence half stopping when the ball was knocked from Sia Soliola's grasp in the build-up, Foster again goaling from the touchline.

Within two minutes of the restart Chase sold a huge dummy and strode through from 20 metres. Dixon again goaled to nudge the visitors ahead. A Chase pass led to a fine Cas handling movement which Jordan Thompson finished off. Dixon kicked the goal despite a split decision from the touch judges and the Tigers were eight to the good. St Helens weren't done as Jon Wilkin gathered his own kick and Michael Shenton fashioned the chance for Gardner to go in at the corner. Foster missed with the goal, but, just before the hooter, Meli crossed in the corner after a frantic series off offloads, and Foster made it a point-less Easter for the Tigers, who also lost form prop Craig Huby for the season with a fractured knee-cap.

Young fullback Louis Sheriff touched down on his debut as Hull KR bounced back from the Good Friday derby defeat. Justin Morgan also gave a debut to prop Richard Beaumont in the 37-24 win over Harlequins. For Quins it was seven games without a win, but they were only dead and buried when Michael Dobson kicked a field goal four minutes from time as twice they came back to level from 12-point deficits

Sam Tomkins was in mesmeric form as mis-firing Wigan eased to a 26-0 victory at battling Wakefield. Both sides looked flat after their last-gasp Good Friday derby successes but the champions had the class to take the two points, centres George Carmont and Joel Tomkins causing havoc in the second half. It looked ominous for over-stretched Wakefield when the Warriors scored the game's first try after two minutes, Pat Richards taking Sean O'Loughlin's monster pass to stroll into the left corner. A combination of stalwart defence, dropped ball and play-the-ball penalties kept the Wildcats in contention, although without Ben Jeffries they created very little in attack. Wigan added to their lead on the half-hour mark, Sam Tomkins supporting a break by Ryan Hoffman after he had been put through a gap by Brett Finch.

Sam Tomkins created a fabulous try just before the break when he re-gathered his chip over the defence and linked with older brother Joel to get winger Josh Charnley over in the right corner. Wigan missed a chance to increase their 14-0 lead early in the second half when Andy Coley broke through a series of attempted tackles but dropped the ball as he reached for the line. Wakefield dominated the third quarter and finally managed to threaten a try, hooker Matthew Wildie held up over the line and the indefatigable Glenn Morrison almost grounding Tommy Lee's grubber kick. But Joel Tomkins lifted the siege on the hour mark, dancing his way over on the right wing. And Wigan added a fifth try just before the final hooter when a great offload from Finch released Liam Farrell on halfway and he sent his skipper O'Loughlin over, with Richards kicking his third goal.

Hull completed a dream Easter weekend, recovering from 10-0 down for a 24-10 win at the Halliwell Jones Stadium that knocked Warrington off the top of the table. The Wolves were without Richard Myler, who fractured his cheekbone in the win at Salford three days earlier and also Chris Bridge but were able to welcome back Matt King for his first match since the season opener in Cardiff. Sean Long, who broke a finger against Hull KR was missing for Hull.

Warrington looked like they were in the mood after early tries from Joel Monaghan and Rhys Williams - his fourth try in three games since his return from a loan spell at the Crusaders. Brett Hodgson converted after hitting the post with his first effort. Richard Horne sparked Hull's recovery when he broke half the length of the field from a Cameron Phelps offload and Sam Obst kept the attack going with a probing kick. Hull eventually went over when Craig Fitzgibbon's short ball created a try for Danny Houghton. The Black and Whites went in front when Kirk Yeaman darted from dummy half and stepped his way to the line for a great score. Danny Tickle added his second goal and it was 12-10 to the visitors. The result was decided just after the hour when the Wolves mounted an attack to the left. Hodgson's pass for King was too high and King knocked the ball into the arms of Will Sharp, who raced 70 metres to the posts. Mickey Higham had a try ruled out for a forward pass before Yeaman grabbed his second try in the final minute after Adrian Morley's offload handed possession back to Hull.

A torrential downpour in the south of France ruined the TV spectacle in Perpignan as the Bulls managed to maintain their unbeaten league record at the Gilbert Brutus and the Dragons - missing Steve Menzies - remained unbeaten in April after an 8-8 draw.

In front of a capacity crowd, the Catalans opened the scoring in the 13th minute when Thomas Bosc found Scott Dureau and the in-form halfback put a pass behind two decoys to fullback Ben Farrar, who dummied and bounced off Patrick Ah Van to crash over. Dureau added the conversion to give the hosts a six-point lead. Bradford almost replied immediately when a Marc Herbert kick was knocked on over the line by Olivier Elima. Paul Sykes was sin-binned by Steve Ganson for repeatedly holding down and Sebastien Martins followed him for a high tackle. From the Martins sin-binning, Bradford gained field position and Heath L'Estrange managed to scramble over from acting half, the try given by the video referee. Ah Van added the extra two points to level the scores. Dureau put the hosts into the lead with a penalty eight minutes after the break but the Bulls levelled things eight minutes later when Ah Van converted a penalty for the visitors. There were chances for both teams to snatch victory in the final moments of the game. Dureau and Ah Van pushed kickable penalties wide and Dureau and Sykes failed with field-goal attempts in the soggy conditions.

SUPER LEAGUE TABLE - *Tuesday 26th April*

	P	W	D	L	F	A	D	PTS
Huddersfield Giants	12	9	0	3	331	188	143	18
St Helens	12	8	1	3	352	226	126	17
Warrington Wolves	12	8	0	4	399	191	208	16
Wigan Warriors	11	7	2	2	264	193	71	16
Castleford Tigers	11	7	1	3	331	218	113	15
Leeds Rhinos	12	6	1	5	324	306	18	13
Catalan Dragons	12	6	1	5	273	263	10	13
Hull FC	12	5	0	7	272	268	4	10
Harlequins	12	4	1	7	274	380	-106	9
Bradford Bulls	12	4	1	7	252	362	-110	9
Hull Kingston Rovers	12	4	0	8	287	348	-61	8
Salford City Reds	12	4	0	8	258	406	-148	8
Wakefield T Wildcats *	12	4	0	8	210	350	-140	4
Crusaders *	12	3	0	9	252	380	-128	2

* 4 points deducted for entering administration

* Crusaders star Gareth Thomas rubbed shoulders with celebrities and members of the Royal Family on the last Friday in April, the 29th, when he attended the wedding of Prince William and Kate Middleton as the country enjoyed a Friday Bank Holiday.

MAY
Wolves make hay

Round 13

Warrington ran riot as the sun shone at Odsal on the first Sunday of May to soar back to the top of the Super League table with a ruthless 11-try, 58-14 mauling of error-strewn Bradford. The Wolves, with Matt King impressive two games into his comeback from a round-one knee injury, scored at almost a point a minute for much of a first half, where every ricocheting ball seemed to pop into the hands of an Warrington attacker, and had 48 on the board before Bradford finally breached their line. The Bulls, lying in 11th spot, were thought to have made an offer to Hull Kingston Rovers to take Willie Mason on loan to the end of the season, but the former Australian international turned down a move.

The Giants had slipped up in Perpignan the night before as the Dragons maintained their unbeaten April with a 13-12 victory. A monster Scott Dureau field goal nine minutes from time decided the outcome, although the Giants might still have pinched it if not for stand-in fullback Cyril Stacul's tackle on Lee Gilmour as he strode through near the end. The Dragons ran with 13 French players and came up with the win despite missing the influential Clint Greenshields and Steve Menzies.

Gareth Thomas made it back from the Royal Wedding to Wrexham in time to score a try and create one for his winger Stuart Reardon against Wigan on the Sunday, although he couldn't prevent the Crusaders from falling to a 48-16 defeat.

The Warriors backed up wins over St Helens and Wakefield to extend their unbeaten run to four matches in a game they dominated from start to finish. Richard Moore was unavailable, having been banned for one match after being found guilty of punching Leeds fullback Brent Webb on Easter Monday. Sam Tomkins was unplayable, while the home side looked very tired following recent games against Leeds and Huddersfield. The Welsh side mounted a brief fightback in the second half but the champions were never in any danger.

Leeds' boom centre Kallum Watkins was ruled out long term with ligament damage to his wrist after the Rhinos' 48-6 win at Castleford in the Friday night TV game, the Tigers' third loss in a row. Jamie Peacock made his first outing since his knee injury at the same venue in 2010, coming off the bench in the 27th minute. The Tigers were still in the game midway through the second half and had what appeared good tries on the left ruled out for forward passes before the break. The try that sank them was classic Leeds as Peacock made a powerful bust on 63 minutes and fed Danny McGuire whose speed took him over.

Adam Clay had a Super League debut to remember as he bagged two tries to help Salford to a vital 34-16 televised win in the capital. The 20-year-old winger stepped in to fill in for the injured Mark Henry and made his presence count with a brace inside the opening 25 minutes, allowing the Reds, with Matty Smith on song, to cruise to a crucial two points that saw them leapfrog Harlequins in the table. The game hinged on a controversial call from the video referee on 61 minutes. Iafeta Palea'aesina looked to have been held short and made a second movement to ground the ball, only for the video referee to rule otherwise.

A dramatic 26-24 win over Hull KR at Belle Vue, known this year as Rapid Solictors Stadium, epitomised Wakefield's gutsy season to date, the Wildcats edging out the Robins courtesy of Kieran Hyde's controversial last-second penalty. The final hooter had already sounded by the time Hyde slotted the straight-forward kick from under the posts. It capped a remarkable late comeback for Wakefield, who had been the dominant team in establishing a 20-6 lead after the break before the visitors roared back into the contest.

Inspired by halves Michael Dobson and in particular Blake Green, Rovers scored three converted tries in 18 minutes to lead 24-20. But then the controversy started, as Bentham ruled that youngster Richard Beaumont knocked on in a heavy Glenn Morrison tackle when Rovers felt the ball had been ripped out. Seconds later Josh Griffin touched down in the corner to level the scores. Then, after Ben Galea had knocked on deep inside his own half, Bentham made his other decisive ruling. Bentham ruled a ball steal on Rinaldi, who was actually claiming a try under the posts.

Hull FC were within an inch of completing a dream extended holiday period - two Easter Bank Holidays were followed the next Friday by one more for the Royal Wedding and then Mayday - but St Helens showed tremendous resilience to fight back for a 24-all draw.

The Airlie Birds were full value for the 18-0 lead they held until five minutes before half-time and, after Saints had come back to lead 22-18, thought they had it won again when Kirk Yeaman gave them a two-point lead with just seven minutes to the final hooter. But a controversial call two minutes later allowed Jamie Foster to nonchalantly send over a 40-metre penalty to level the scores and set up a frantic finish as both sides failed with field-goal attempts - two of them from Saints in the last minute!

Despite the harsh penalty call that allowed Foster to level - Danny Washbrook judged by Steve Ganson to have fouled debutant Nathan Ashe when challenging for a bouncing Hull goal-line drop-out - a draw was a fair result. Yeaman's hat-trick took the headlines as he took his try-tally to 14 in 12 appearance.

Challenge Cup Round 4

There were no giant-killing acts in the Challenge Cup but Catalan Dragons scraped through, by 22-16, after a superb effort from the committed Centurions at Leigh Sports Village on the Friday. Leigh's halfback pairing of Jamie Ellis and Martyn Ridyard made the majority of play, before a starring role from the bench by Ian Henderson just helped tip the scales in the Dragons' favour. Leigh led 12-10 at half-time and after the Dragons second-half comeback, Stuart Donlan's try four minutes from time had the French side hanging on for dear life.

On the Sunday, Huddersfield won 28-18 at Batley, who held a four-point lead with only 15 minutes to go. But at that critical point the Bulldogs' enthusiastic second-rower Dane Manning was sent off for a high tackle. Within two minutes the Batley defence was split as centre Joe Wardle exploited an overlap by racing through for a try which levelled the scores. Then a Danny Kirmond run gave wingman David Hodgson plenty of space to score the try which took the Giants into the lead. Finally, Leroy Cudjoe collected a clearing kick and then meandered his way through an energy-drained Batley side to score between the sticks, giving Danny Brough an easy conversion.

Bradford didn't have it all their own way in the Sunday TV clash at the Shay, where they eventually won through 46-34. Former Fax favourite Shad Royston made a dream first return by opening the scoring and creating the Bulls' next two tries as the Super League outfit twice opened up a ten-point advantage in the early stages. Never-say-die Halifax bounced back every time the Bulls threatened to stretch their lead and, while never ahead, closed the gap to just two points after 33 minutes. It wasn't until successive tries and a penalty midway through the second half that the Bulls looked as if they had enough leeway to see them through to round five.

Danny McGuire limped out of the Rhinos' 30-20 Saturday TV victory over Crusaders. Ten points and two players down inside 14 minutes - Brent Webb suffering a dead leg when carving out the opening scoring chance, albeit from a forward pass, as well as McGuire tearing a quad muscle in the chase back to prevent Vince Mellars setting up Crusaders' second score - 2010's beaten finalists seemed to be taking an early exit. Showing tremendous fortitude, they hauled themselves back into contention with 24-unanswered points in a 19-minute blitz and, despite then losing back-rower Chris Clarkson with ankle damage, withstood a spirited Welsh fight back that had a scent of upset. Danny Buderus's try eight minutes from time, an unstoppable thrust from dummy half, turned a four-point gap into a match-clinching one.

Wigan coach Michael Maguire said he was satisfied with the club's 52-0 home win over Barrow on the Sunday. Pat Richards, the current Man of Steel and joint holder of the Albert Goldthorpe Medal, signed a new deal to keep him at the DW Stadium until the end of the 2013 season.

Lee Briers scored 32 points in Warrington's 80-0 home victory over Keighley on the Sunday, and was happy with the fifth-round draw that paired the holders with Swinton Lions. And Castleford coach Terry Matterson was delighted with the debut of young winger Greg Eden in his side's 72-10 win at Rochdale.

Round 14

Crusaders kept their hopes of not finishing bottom of the table alive with a 23-10 win over Wakefield Trinity Wildcats at a cold, wet Racecourse in Wrexham on the Friday, where they had to overcome a 10-0 half-time deficit to secure victory. Michael Witt passed, scored and kicked the Crusaders to victory but the win wasn't secure until Ryan O'Hara's try and Clinton Schifcofske's conversion gave Crusaders a seven-point gap with less than four minutes remaining. Now two points behind Wakefield on the ladder, the Crusaders went into a week off as the only Super League side not in action, following their Challenge Cup exit to Leeds.

Warrington were still top on points difference after their 62-0 televised defeat of Castleford Tigers on the Friday night at the Halliwell Jones Stadium. Nineteen-year-old stand-off Gareth O'Brien made his Super League debut after having made his first-team bow in the Challenge Cup the previous week against Keighley Cougars. On four minutes, O'Brien showed neat footwork and a clever dummy to squeeze over the line for the opening try and it was just about all Warrington after that. Lee Briers' kick-and-chase try on the stroke of half-time put the contest beyond all doubt, rounding off a miserable first half for the Tigers.

A Kris Welham hat-trick helped Hull Kingston Rovers to a comfortable 46-18 win over desperate Bradford at Craven Park on the Sunday. Ben Jeffries made a second debut for the Bulls after re-signing from Wakefield.

Wigan confirmed they had signed Gareth Hock on a five-year deal, with the former England back-rower close to completing a two-year suspension that was imposed when he tested positive for cocaine. On the Friday the reigning champions won 54-6 against Harlequins at the DW Stadium. The Warriors made sure there was no repeat of 2010's shock home defeat by Harlequins as they totally embarrassed the London side.

Catalans' unbeaten streak of seven matches came to an end at Headingley on the Friday night with a 30-6 defeat to Leeds, three tries in eight minutes in the run up to the final whistle - two from teenage winger Zak Hardaker - inflating the winning margin. Kevin Sinfield provided the glitter in a rain-soaked clash where defensive endeavour on both sides was admirable. Sinfield's 68th minute penalty to make it 14-6 was the catalyst for the Rhinos' impressive late onslaught.

Hull FC won 32-16 at Salford despite playing with just 15 men for over an hour after the loss of playmaker Sam Obst (hamstring) and the competition's leading tryscorer Kirk Yeaman with concussion. Three tries and 18 points in the opening ten minutes was a heartbreaker for the hosts, but Richard Horne's length-of-the-field interception, quickly followed by Will Sharp's try, was the killer blow. Hull coach Richard Agar praised ex-Wigan centre Martin Gleeson, whose arrival had coincided with an ongoing run of five unbeaten matches - four in the league.

When Stefan Ratchford conjured a try out of nothing on 47 minutes, mesmerising the Black and Whites' defence with a magnificent weaving run around three or four potential tacklers it was 24-16. For a few moments it was Hull under the cosh and making the mistakes but, as the Reds pressed for more points, Horne intercepted a loose pass and raced 70 metres upfield. Although eventually hauled down by a determined Matty Smith chase, the defence failed to regroup quickly enough to prevent Sharp scoring on the other wing to completely take the wind out of the Reds' sails. Gleeson then bundled his way over for his second try just after the hour and Salford never regained any momentum.

It looked as though injuries had finally got the better of St Helens after a 40-18 Saturday TV defeat at Huddersfield. Prop Josh Perry sustained a broken hand, with coach Royce Simmons already missing ten first-team players for the match, including four halfbacks. Giants halfbacks Kevin Brown and Danny Brough had hands in five of the Giants' eight tries, with Brough scoring a stunning individual effort himself in the first half.

Brough's superb try was not even the pick of the match, with Leroy Cudjoe producing a moment of sublime skill to lay on Michael Lawrence's brilliant team effort after the break. Brough's ball saw Lee Gilmour poke his head through the defensive line, palming off Michael Shenton before releasing Cudjoe. He sprinted clear down the left touchline and, as the cover came across, produced a superlative one-handed inside flick pass for the supporting Lawrence to finish with style.

Warrington, Huddersfield and Wigan were tied at the top of the table as Super League took another break for the Challenge Cup.

Challenge Cup Round 5

Lee Briers re-wrote the Warrington record books in the Wolves' stunning 112-0 home defeat of Swinton Lions on the Friday night. Briers became the highest points scorer in the history of the club, surpassing former Wilderspool favourite Steve Hesford. He then went on to set new Warrington records for points (44) and goals (16) in a match, to go alongside a well-taken hat-trick of tries. The scoreline was also a record win for the Warrington club. Swinton, on course for the third-tier, Championship One title, couldn't get hold of the ball for virtually the entire contest.

Bad news was that young Wolves stand-off Gareth O'Brien was stretchered from the field with knee ligament damage following a lengthy stoppage in the first half of the clash.

Sam Tomkins was led from the field after 30 minutes of Wigan's 26-22 win at Bradford, after he was knocked out in the act of scoring a try in an incident that saw Bradford Bulls winger Gareth Raynor sent from the field and subsequently suspended for two matches. Wigan breathed a sigh of relief as they made it through to the quarter-finals after being pushed all the way by the 12-man Bulls. They made sure of the victory with five minutes remaining when Liam Farrell steamed onto a short ball from Brett Finch to crash over. Pat Richards failed to add the extras but the Warriors now led 26-18. The Bulls did manage a last minute try from Patrick Ah Van as he grounded the ball in the corner and the winger was unable to add the extras as the hooter sounded with the Warriors hanging on.

Hull KR went to Salford on the Friday night after Willie Mason switched codes and joined French rugby union club Toulon and they comfortably accounted for the City Reds, 25-0. Salford Chairman John Wilkinson was on his way to Australia to find a new coach for the City Reds.

Leeds progressed with a 40-20 home win over Harlequins. Ali Lauitiiti, in his first match since a calf tear in March, crowned the try of the night in the 38th minute, involving six pairs of hands over 65 metres, which gave the hosts a two-score lead they never lost. But it was not until Chris Clarkson's late, superb solo effort from the base of a scrum on half way, that the Rhinos could breathe easily.

Keith Senior suffered a knee injury and scans later revealed that he had torn his anterior cruciate ligament and suffered cartilage damage. With his contract up at the end of the season, Senior looked like had played his last game, his 365th, for Leeds.

St Helens had an easier than expected 70-0 home win against Championship frontrunners Featherstone, with both sides in an injury crisis.

Keith Mason completed his return from injury five weeks ahead of schedule in the Giants' 30-16 victory over the Catalan Dragons on the Sunday in a tough tie made more unpredictable by the blustery gale. Danny Brough's creativity set up three of the Giants' first four tries, while Kevin Brown's imagination and evasiveness helped finish the job off. In between and especially in the second half, the efforts of the forwards, led by the irrepressible Darrell Griffin and epitomised by the strong-running of Lee Gilmour and Eorl Crabtree, kept the Giants just in the driving seat.

After a stuttering Championship campaign, Super League-bound Widnes came to life on the Saturday despite a 50-26 home defeat to on-form Hull FC. That Hull eventually won by 24 points was a harsh way to finish when, 12 minutes from time, Widnes only trailed by 12 points and were hammering at the visitors' line. But then England winger Tom Briscoe raced 90 metres after intercepting Chaz l'Anson's pass, and that was it.

The Saturday TV game produced the drama of the round, with Castleford winning at Wakefield by 20-18 after ten minutes of golden-point extra time.

Kirk Dixon had already kept the Tigers in the match with three successful kicks in normal time, but had a potentially decisive fourth chalked off after a 52nd minute try by scrum-half Danny Orr, despite it looking as though it was on target. Then in the 90th minute he was presented with a golden opportunity to settle the contest, when Dale Morton was penalised for a ball-steal 40 metres from the Wildcats' posts and inches from the left touchline. Dixon made sure with his pressure-cooker goal.

Round 15

Warrington completed a magnificent May, which had seen them score 354 points while conceding only 20, with a 42-6 win at the frustrated Rhinos. Michael Monaghan ran the show. His option-taking from dummy half was outstanding and his reverse pop-up pass for David Solomona's game-turning try was decisive. Richie Myler made his return after five weeks out with a fractured cheekbone. Having dug in to remain in contention by the break at 12-6 down - Danny Buderus muscling through Simon Grix, Brett Hodgson and Paul Wood as Warrington conceded their first points for over 210 minutes of rugby - the Rhinos conceded Solomona's try three minutes into the second half and the Wolves kicked on with four more tries.

Jonny Lomax returned from an ankle injury with a brilliant display against Crusaders on the Friday night, scoring a second-half try in St Helens' 28-12 home win. That try on 50 minutes made it 22-0 and was enough to see off a spirited rally from the Welsh side. Saints suffered a new injury blow to winger Ade Gardner when the former England international damaged his Achilles tendon, ruling him out for the rest of the season.

Huddersfield Giants coach Nathan Brown confirmed he was to stay with the club until the end of the 2012 season. The Giants celebrated with a 34-20 victory at Hull FC on Sunday as David Hodgson scored a hat-trick of tries. Hull could have won it, with Willie Manu's 70th-minute try cutting the gap to just two points, but the on-form Danny Brough came up with the crucial play by galloping 50 metres after Jordan Turner knocked on with open space at his mercy. Brough, who had represented Scotland at the 2008 World Cup, was expected to be called up for the England side for their mid-season international against a team made up of overseas players based in the UK, to be named the Exiles.

Catalan Dragons continued their march up the table with a comprehensive 42-22 win at Wakefield. Clint Greenshields returned after a two-month absence with a dislocated elbow to play a big part in the majority of the Dragons' tries. Damien Blanch's second touchdown, just four minutes after half-time, extended the score to 26-10, putting the match beyond Wakefield's reach.

Castleford and Harlequins fans were treated to a feast of points on the Sunday as the Tigers roared to a 10-try, 56-24 success in which mercurial stand-off Rangi Chase claimed four touchdowns, all registered in the second half, and was involved in three others. The first score of the game was one of the best solo efforts ever seen at the Wheldon Road ground, known in 2011 as the Probiz Coliseum. Harlequins fullback Jamie O'Callaghan, close to his own dead-ball line and faced with three challengers, collected a kick by Castleford hooker Adam Milner. O'Callaghan rounded the Tigers chase; eased past two or three others to clear the 20-metre zone and held off winger Richard Owen and Chase for a stunning length-of-the-field score.

On the same afternoon a hat-trick from Mark Henry at Odsal was not enough to stop revitalised Bradford ending a run of six league games without a win, with a 28-14 success over Salford that kept them in sight of the play-offs. Henry, out for the last month with a foot injury, crossed in the corner, once in the first half and twice in the second, each time hauling the City Reds back into the match. But Tom Burgess, still only 18, earned the Bulls three ultimately decisive tries with powerful initial surges just before the break.

The Bulls moved a point above Hull KR who went down 40-6 to Wigan at the DW Stadium on the Spring Bank Holiday Monday. Sam Tomkins was again the gamestar and was rewarded with a spectacular hat-trick - as was left winger Pat Richards, whose six goals gave him a points haul of 24 - in a game that was for the first hour much tighter than the scoreline suggested.

Rovers could have folded well before the first try of the second half, scored by Sam Tomkins 19 minutes after half-time. At that stage they trailed only by 16-6, having conceded a try as the half-time hooter sounded which could easily have been chalked off for Richards not having full control as he touched down Tomkins' kick to the left corner.

By then, Justin Morgan was operating with a 15-man squad, with right centre Jake Webster and prop Joel Clinton both having sustained shoulder injures midway through the first half. The injury ended Clinton's season. Tomkins' second try in the 59th minute was followed by three more converted scores to leave the game looking one-sided.

The win moved Wigan level at the top of the table with Warrington and Huddersfield, and with a game - the home tie with Castleford postponed to accommodate the World Club Challenge - in hand.

SUPER LEAGUE TABLE - *Monday 30th May*

	P	W	D	L	F	A	D	PTS
Warrington Wolves	15	11	0	4	561	211	350	22
Wigan Warriors	14	10	2	2	406	221	185	22
Huddersfield Giants	15	11	0	4	417	239	178	22
St Helens	15	9	2	4	422	302	120	20
Leeds Rhinos	15	8	1	6	408	360	48	17
Castleford Tigers	14	8	1	5	393	352	41	17
Catalan Dragons	15	8	1	6	334	327	7	17
Hull FC	15	6	1	8	348	342	6	13
Bradford Bulls	15	5	1	9	312	480	-168	11
Hull Kingston Rovers	15	5	0	10	363	432	-69	10
Salford City Reds	15	5	0	10	322	482	-160	10
Harlequins	15	4	1	10	320	524	-204	9
Wakefield T Wildcats *	15	5	0	10	268	439	-171	6
Crusaders *	15	4	0	11	303	466	-163	4

* 4 points deducted for entering administration

JUNE
England calling

Round 16

Wigan's eight-game winning streak came to an end when they suffered a 20-12 defeat to the Catalan Dragons in Montpellier on the Saturday, as the French team completed the double over the Champions.

Montpellier is officially the driest city in France, but was that weekend hit with a deluge. The game turned into an arm wrestle, with neither team ready to chance their arm, mainly down to some outstanding defence led by the likes of Paul Prescott, Harrison Hansen, Jeff Lima and Liam Farrell for Wigan and Jason Baitieri, Lopini Paea, David Ferriol and Steve Menzies - back from a hamstring injury sustained in round 11 - for Catalans.

It wasn't until ten minutes from time that the game was settled as Ian Henderson picked up from acting half and found Scott Dureau, who handed the ball on to Setaimata Sa. It was left to Clint Greenshields to send in Darryl Millard for his second of the night to give the Dragons a six-point-lead. Dureau added his fourth goal to extend the lead to two scores and eight points.

On the Friday night St Helens hooker James Roby suffered a broken cheekbone in the 42-16 televised win over Leeds Rhinos at the Saints' temporary home at the Stobart Stadium, Widnes. Although Roby played on until the end of the game, the injury was to rule him out of England reckoning for the game against the Exiles the following Friday.

Leeds conceded 42 points for the second week in a row even though they were still well in the contest at half-time, trailing only 6-4. But five tries in the space of 25 second-half minutes burned off the Rhinos. The tidal wave of red and white began when a neat chip by Jamie Foster was picked up, but then spilled on his own line by Brent Webb, forcing a goal-line drop-out. On the kick return, Louie McCarthy-Scarsbrook spun in the tackle and offloaded to the brilliant Jonny Lomax, who shrugged off three Rhinos defenders before somehow popping up the ball for Roby to dive over from close range. Ten minutes later a tired kick by Kevin Sinfield was plucked out of the air by Francis Meli, who scorched to the whitewash from 60 metres out. Minutes after, Paul Wellens chimed into the line to offload to Meli, who surged downfield and slipped the inside pass to Lomax, and he galloped home for the try to extend the lead to 24-4 with Foster's goal.

From the re-start, Sinfield's attempted short kick-off failed to reach the required ten metres, and from the resulting penalty Saints swept downfield and Scott Moore rounded off an excellent set play when Lee Gaskell put Sia Soliola through a large hole, and the big Kiwi was able to offload round the corner to the substitute hooker. In the 65th minute the shell-shocked Rhinos were huddled behind the posts again, when a penalty gifted Saints possession. Bearing down on the whitewash, a backhanded pass from Jon Wilkin somehow found Wellens, who breezed through the gap. Foster added the goal, and Saints moved out to a 36-4 lead.

The Rhinos went in for two consolation tries. On 68 minutes, Jamie Jones-Buchanan was able to latch onto a ball by Brett Delaney and force his way over from close range for the touchdown. Lee Smith added another four minutes later, when Leeds went on the blind side from a scrum and Webb found him with a well-timed pass. One minute from time Gaskell intercepted a wild pass by Sinfield to touch down under the posts.

As well as Roby, England coach Steve McNamara also lost the services of Danny Brough, who suffered ankle ligament damage while playing for the Giants against Castleford on the Sunday at Halifax.

The game, the first of three home Huddersfield home fixtures at the Shay because of pitch maintenance work at the Galpharm Stadium, was televised on the Sunday evening, but League bosses wished it hadn't been. A colour clash caused the match to be delayed for 25 minutes when both teams turned up with almost identical 'alternative' kits. Both clubs claimed that they had been told to wear their alternative strips by the RFL in an email earlier in the week. After much discussion, the Tigers were forced to abandon their shirts and change into an old Halifax strip that was in a cupboard under the main stand. The RFL confirmed that a full inquiry would be undertaken and a fortnight later Castleford were fined £500 for the mix-up. The Giants' seven-try, 40-18 win meant they kept the pressure on Warrington at the top of Engage Super League.

Another outstanding scrum-half, Sean Long, dislocated his shoulder in the Airlie Birds' 17-10 defeat at Hull KR on the Sunday. Long was making only his seventh appearance of the year for Hull, after suffering an injury-plagued start to the 2011 campaign, and was injured again in a collision with Robins back-rower Ben Galea. The 34-year-old was rushed straight to hospital amid fears his season could be over. It was, and he announced his retirement in August.

A stunning try by fullback Shaun Briscoe 15 minutes from time provided a spectacular climax to another nail-biting derby clash. With the scores locked at ten points all, but with Hull visibly reeling, Rovers produced the best score of a pulsating game. Blake Green broke through two tacklers and raced into the Hull '20' with an arcing run before sending the supporting Briscoe racing to the posts. Michael Dobson added the conversion and then sealed victory six minutes from the final hooter with a field goal to stay within a point of the play-off spots.

The Bulls followed up the previous week's win against Salford with a 30-16 victory at the Twickenham Stoop on the Saturday afternoon. Shad Royston capped another impressive performance with a stunning 90-metre solo try.

Warrington head coach Tony Smith paid tribute to his prop Paul Wood, who took to the field on the Friday night just hours after being at his wife's side when she gave birth to a baby daughter in the early hours of the morning. Wood was in fine form for the Wolves, scoring two of Warrington's ten tries in a 56-16 romp over Crusaders.

Stefan Ratchford, again playing at left centre, scored a sparkling hat-trick of tries in the Reds' 34-12 home win over Wakefield Trinity Wildcats on the Friday night. The 22-year-old had been linked with a host of clubs in recent weeks, including Wigan, Warrington and rugby union sides after turning down the offer of a new deal from the Reds.

In the week, Salford appointed 44-year-old former North Queensland Cowboys assistant Matt Parish, currently an assistant coach to Ricky Stuart with the New South Wales State of Origin team, as their new head coach.

Round 17

Wigan coach Michael Maguire refused to use the International Origin match as an excuse as his side blew a 22-4 lead at Castleford Tigers to draw 22-22 on the Sunday after England took on the Exiles at Headingley on the Friday night. The Warriors had seven players in the game, three for the Exiles and four for England, with centre George Carmont scoring the late winning try in a 16-12 win for the team made up of Super League's best Antipodean players. Sean O'Loughlin, Michael McIlorum, Thomas Leuluai, Pat Richards and Joel Tomkins all backed up, with only Sam Tomkins and Carmont not featuring against the Tigers.

On a terrible rainy day, the Super League champions were punished for not taking all their chances and could have easily tasted defeat as they were prevented from scoring a single point in the second half for the second week in a row. The Warriors led 22-4 at the break, with Wigan's representative quartet showing no signs of tiredness until the second half, when the champions looked out-of-sorts and the Tigers took full advantage, with Richard Mathers scoring in the corner to rescue a point with a minute to go.

Leeds bounced back from two consecutive defeats with a 44-14 watersplash win over Hull KR at Headingley on the Sunday. Brian McDermott's men came up with their most comprehensive performance of the campaign, running in eight tries, three of them to England winger Ryan Hall. Jamie Peacock's display – his 150th for the club - was the best since his return from injury. Hall's second try - topped by a fine touchline Kevin Sinfield goal - just before the hour mark, to make it 28-14, gave Leeds a lead that in the conditions was always likely to be decisive.

Salford were sniffing an upset at Halliwell Jones Stadium on the Sunday given that six of the Wolves players were backing up the Exiles game only 48 hours before. And so it proved as Daniel Holdsworth's top-class kicking game kept Warrington, who had head coach Tony Smith absent in the week on jury service, on the back foot throughout and engineered an 18-16 win. Mark Henry's 49th-minute try proved to be the difference. The Wolves did bite back three minutes from time when Richard Myler finished off a cross-field move. Brett Hodgson added a good kick to set up a grandstand finish, but Salford held out for a much-deserved victory.

Warrington and Wigan's slips gave the opportunity for Huddersfield to go clear at the top in what was expected to be a routine victory at struggling Wakefield, but the Wildcats made the most of the wet conditions to grind out a 13-10 win. With their Super League licence unlikely to be renewed the Wildcats had staged a supporters' meeting at the city's largest venue in midweek to announce plans for the refurbishment of their dilapidated Belle Vue home, as a stop-gap measure before their proposed move to a new stadium. Such was the response from their supporters two separate presentations had to be made to accommodate all the fans.

The team responded to the show of support as Gareth Moore, signed from Batley earlier in the season, kicked Wakefield to a hard-fought victory that ended a run of three straight defeats and eased them further away from the foot of the table, four points clear of Crusaders. Moore's four goals and field goal proved decisive. Huddersfield eventually outscored their hosts two tries to one but coach Nathan Brown was first to admit that: "it would have been an injustice had we scored again near the end and won the game." It was the Giants' first defeat since April 30.

Hull FC ground out a morale-boosting 38-6 victory over struggling Harlequins that put their play-off push back on track. Four of Hull's players - Willie Manu, Mark O'Meley, Craig Fitzgibbon and Tom Briscoe - had been involved in the Exiles match. But they were not given a testing workout and Manu, in particular, was outstanding.

With Sean Long out, Richard Horne and Sam Obst were re-united in the halfback positions but, once Horne went off injured, Joe Westerman played a great game at stand-off. Harlequins had been second best throughout the first half and it was clear that they would not be able to turn the tide once Briscoe established a 20-0 lead for Hull shortly before half-time.

Playing at the Gilbert Brutus for the first time in over six weeks, the Dragons led the Crusaders 24-6 with 12 minutes remaining, but the Welsh side showed a steely determination to drag themselves back into the contest. At 24-18, and with eight minutes remaining, the Crusaders were looking the more dominant of the two sides - until Scott Dureau settled Catalan nerves with a field goal to increase the gap to an insurmountable seven points with three minutes remaining. Then Damien Blanch showed a clean pair of heels to the Crusaders as he added his second of the night and tenth of the season to seal the win.

Bradford's revival continued as they almost beat St Helens at Odsal, Jamie Foster's 30-metre penalty goal after the final hooter securing a 14-14 draw. Referee James Child awarded the visitors the penalty six seconds from time when he ruled that Bradford prop Andy Lynch deliberately blocked Saints halfback Lee Gaskell as he chased his own kick through. The penalty was made infinitely more difficult by the torrential rain, but the young Saints winger held his nerve and shattered Bradford.

Hooker Heath L'Estrange suffered cruciate ligament damage during the first half, just days after signing a new contract extension with the Bulls, and was out for the season.

Round 18

Wigan won the third derby of the year at their old foes St Helens with something to spare. St Helens had no answer to Wigan's attacking flair in the first half, especially their high kicks. Brett Finch controlled everything in attack for the Warriors and capped off a fine performance with a try. Two tries in three minutes around the half-hour mark from Pat Richards and Joel Tomkins saw the Warriors lead 20-0 and gave St Helens too much to do in the second half. Finch's try six minutes after the turnaround finished off Saints, who scored twice before ending 32-10 in arrears.

The Warriors were still a point behind Warrington and Huddersfield, who both bounced back from their defeats the weekend before.

Matt King scored a hat-trick in his first game as a father as the Wolves recovered from their shock defeat to Salford with a 46-16 win at Hull KR. King had been absent the week before due to the birth of his first child. The Australian's two first-half tries, appropriately on Father's Day, came during a relentless ten-minute spell in which Warrington registered four tries. That put them 22-0 ahead and, from that point, there was no way back for lacklustre Rovers as their high-flying visitors finished with nine tries. Centre Ryan Atkins collected a pair of tries too as Rovers were out-classed.

Huddersfield coach Nathan Brown was delighted at the way his side bounced back from their shock 13-10 defeat in the rain to Wakefield and paid tribute to the contribution of David Hodgson after the winger's two tries secured a 28-20 home win over the Dragons in the Saturday TV game. Hodgson set the Giants on their way with a spectacular 90-metre opening score before all but sealing the victory and revenge for April's single point defeat in France with the final try of the game. In between, the hosts always held the upper hand but had to overcome stern Catalan resistance and a spirited, if short-lived, second-half fightback, when the visitors had been reduced to 12 men after Setaimata Sa was sin-binned for persistent team interference.

The signs of a Bulls revival after a three-match unbeaten run dissipated after an uninspiring home 28-14 defeat against Hull. Bradford included Nick Scruton on the bench after his recovery from a dislocated wrist, while Martin Gleeson remained absent for Hull, who later revealed that the former Great Britain centre had been granted sick leave due to a stress-related illness. Danny Tickle was the standout in a solid effort from the Hull pack.

Iestyn Harris described his side's home defeat as "extremely frustrating" as Crusaders were downed 12-7 by the Rhinos in dreadful weather conditions on the Friday night. The game produced 32 scrums thanks to the constant rain that made the ball greasy. "It was a good old-fashioned bash-each-other game of Rugby League, as that's all you could have in those conditions," was how Leeds coach Brian McDermott viewed it.

The Welsh side were 11 minutes away from securing an historic win, exactly a year to the weekend since they beat the Rhinos on their own patch, but Peter Lupton's early try and Michael Witt's penalty were cancelled out by a Danny McGuire score. Witt looked to have snatched it for the Welsh side with a field goal before Ali Lauitiiti secured a Leeds victory with five minutes remaining.

In a battle of basement sides, Harlequins - with Bradford loanee Kyle Briggs in at scrum-half - breathed some life into their season as they won for the first time in 13 games, a 40-22 success at the Stoop ensuring the visiting Wildcats did not leapfrog them in the table.

The game was all but finished as a contest by half-time, as the hosts scorched to a 24-4 lead, but the men from the capital ensured there was no collapse with a further three scores after the break. Wakefield were missing skipper Glenn Morrison with a dead leg picked up in the win over Huddersfield, and they struggled to find any rhythm.

Rangi Chase did not have hit the heights of some of his numerous dazzling displays in 2011, but he still stepped forward with the game's crucial plays to seal a gritty 15-8 win for Castleford at the rain-drenched Willows on the Friday night. With the sides locked at 8-8 after a tight, tense contest played in difficult conditions, Chase produced a 40/20 on the third tackle to lay the platform for a Danny Orr try. Minutes later the New Zealand halfback coolly slotted a field goal to deny the Reds a third straight Super League win for the first time since 2006. Orr's contribution to the Tigers' win was also huge. He combined well with Chase throughout, and secured a repeat set by swooping on a loose ball shortly after the Kiwi's 40/20 and just prior to his own try.

The Tigers were missing utility Martin Aspinwall, who was jailed for four months and banned from driving for two years after pleading guilty the previous Thursday to dangerous driving. Liverpool Crown Court heard how Aspinwall, 29, was involved in a high-speed police chase that resulted in him crashing his car in his home town of Wigan in January of 2011. The sentence came just four months after he was convicted of assault occasioning actual bodily harm in an incident involving former Wigan and Whitehaven player Rob Jackson. On that occasion Aspinwall escaped with a suspended sentence.

Tigers boss Terry Matterson had approached Leeds about a possible loan deal for Luke Burgess as a replacement for the incarcerated star, but Burgess turned down the approach. That week the Tigers made it clear that Aspinwall would remain within their first-team squad at the conclusion of his prison sentence. St Helens star Scott Moore was arrested that week on suspicion of drink-driving. The 23-year-old hooker had been dropped for the draw with Bradford, and was left out of the 19-man squad for the derby defeat to Wigan.

Round 19

Hull FC centre Kirk Yeaman scored a first-half try that took him to the top of the Super League tryscorers' chart against Wakefield at the Rapid Solicitors Stadium on the last Sunday of June. At half-time he suffered an epileptic fit in the Hull dressing-room. Yeaman had a history of epilepsy but this was his first seizure in ten years. At that stage Hull led by only 16-12 after being 12-0 down with ten minutes gone, but stand-off Richard Horne orchestrated his side to fine effect, building on a solid platform established by his pack to take his side to a 52-18 win.

Wakefield were on the wrong end of an extraordinary ten successive penalties, the first two of which were late in the first half, with the sequence not being halted until Hull were sanctioned by referee James Child in the 68th minute. Scrum-half Jeremy Smith also got himself sin-binned for dissent. It was all too much for a diminutive female spectator who dashed onto the pitch at the final hooter, berating Mr Child, who was protected by stewards.

Gareth Hock made his second debut for Wigan in their 46-12 win over Huddersfield at the DW Stadium, although it was the partnership of Brett Finch and Sam Tomkins that stole the headlines as Wigan coasted to victory on the Saturday evening.

Hock was making his return just two days after his two-year ban for taking cocaine ended and his presence lifted both the fans and the players, as the Warriors ran in eight tries against a team that, before this match, was above them on the league ladder. The 27-year-old, who had been handed the number 34 shirt, was named on the bench in place of the suspended Chris Tuson, who was sitting out one game after being cited for a dangerous tackle on Jon Wilkin in the previous week's win over St Helens. Sam Tomkins once again picked up three Albert Goldthorpe points as well as three more tries.

There was heavy rain on the Friday night, as the Bulls edged out Leeds 18-12, their first win over their derby rivals at Headingley since 2007. Matt Diskin, playing his first game at Headingley for Bradford, had an eventful evening, at one point being put on report for a challenge on his former team-mate Carl Ablett and then, at the end of the game, carrying the ball forward when a melee broke out between the two sets of players.

The steadfast Bulls supporters, who remained lashed to the core in the driving rain, cheered home Patrick Ah Van's four defining second-half penalties that won the game, at about the same time as Luke Burgess, whose younger brother Tom was rested by the Bulls, was touching down in Sydney after being released by the Rhinos, along with fellow prop Ben Cross.

Saints had not finished a season outside the top two since 2004, and a Friday 35-28 defeat at Warrington, a pulsating, rain-soaked 11-try thriller, left them five points behind the now clear leaders.

Warrington tore into an 18-0 lead inside 14 minutes but magnificent Saints staged an amazing comeback to lead 22-18 at the break. Three Wolves tries in ten minutes astride the hour mark gave them a 12-point lead again, although they needed a late field goal from Lee Briers to hold off another Saints comeback. Brett Hodgson was back to his best with an impeccable kicking performance and it was his 64th-minute try that finally tipped the balance the way of the home side. Wolves prop Adrian Morley was involved in a collision with St Helens player Chris Flannery and had to be helped from the field by the Wolves' physio.

Hull Kingston Rovers coach Justin Morgan insisted his immediate future was with the Robins, despite recent speculation he would not see out the season at Craven Park, having won just six of the first 18 matches. A Saturday 34-0 victory at Harlequins put the Robins in eleventh place in the Super League table with 14 points, five points behind eighth-placed Hull FC.

Prop Ray Cashmere played an influential role in Salford's 22-18 win over the Crusaders in Wrexham on the Friday night, but revealed the following day he had turned down the club's contract offer. It was déjà vu for the understrength Crusaders as they lost a home game in the last few minutes for the second week in a row after holding the lead for most of the night. Jordan James, with his first try of the season in just his eighth game, reached out brilliantly from Michael Witt's dangerous grubber just after the hour mark and Witt converted to give Crusaders the lead at 18-16. But the Reds regained the ball from a kick on the final tackle of a crucial set, and Adam Sidlow went through for the winner after Daniel Holdsworth's kick to the left.

The Dragons cemented fifth place in the table and drew level on points with St Helens as they bounced back from the narrow defeat to Huddersfield to run riot in the heat of the South of France with a 54-20 win over Castleford.

The only thing hotter than the weather in Perpignan were the plays produced by the Catalans, in particular a stunning ten-man, 90-metre try that was finished off by Damien Blanch and lifted the roof off the Stade Gilbert Brutus. For Castleford there were few positives in a game that saw them behind within five minutes and put to the sword by Scott Dureau, Darryl Millard, Steve Menzies and Ian Henderson. Three tries in the opening nine minutes of the second half ended any faint hopes the Tigers had of winning the game.

SUPER LEAGUE TABLE - *Sunday 26th June*

	P	W	D	L	F	A	D	PTS
Warrington Wolves	19	14	0	5	714	289	425	28
Wigan Warriors	18	12	3	3	518	285	233	27
Huddersfield Giants	19	13	0	6	507	336	171	26
St Helens	19	10	3	6	516	399	117	23
Catalan Dragons	19	11	1	7	459	405	54	23
Leeds Rhinos	19	10	1	8	492	441	51	21
Castleford Tigers	18	9	2	7	468	476	-8	20
Hull FC	19	9	1	9	476	397	79	19
Salford City Reds	19	8	0	11	404	543	-139	16
Bradford Bulls	19	7	2	10	388	550	-162	16
Hull Kingston Rovers	19	7	0	12	444	532	-88	14
Harlequins	19	5	1	13	382	648	-266	11
Wakefield T Wildcats *	19	6	0	13	333	575	-242	8
Crusaders *	19	4	0	15	362	587	-225	4

* 4 points deducted for entering administration

* The Rugby Football League reaffirmed its confidence in its strategy to increase participation despite news of reduced cash input from Sport England. Rugby League joined sports such as soccer and rugby union in having its funding cut. For the period 2011 to 2013, Sport England's investment in Rugby League was reduced by a total of £956,188 - a 3.35 per cent cut in the £29.4m funding for the four-year period from April 2009.

JULY
Warriors on top

Round 20

Leeds coach Brian McDermott refused to blame any of the match officials after his side went down to a narrow 26-24 defeat at the hands of Wigan Warriors on the Friday night despite a controversial call denying the Rhinos a late lead.

The Rhinos trailed by two points with four minutes remaining when Rhinos' stand-off Danny McGuire appeared to go over for the match-winning try. But referee Thierry Alibert referred the decision to video referee Steve Ganson, who decided that McGuire had dropped the ball under the attention of Sam Tomkins before kicking on to ground the ball. Ganson therefore overruled the try. Later that week RFL Match Officials Director Stuart Cummings admitted the try should have been awarded, as McGuire had drop-kicked the ball.

Two tries in the first five minutes of the second half, from Pat Richards and George Carmont, had swung the game. Richards then extended Wigan's lead by a further two points with his fifth goal of the night, after Jamie Peacock was penalised for offside, and the champions led 26-18 with 18 minutes remaining. But winger Zak Hardaker touched down McGuire's kick in the left corner and Kevin Sinfield added the conversion as the Rhinos trailed 26-24 with nine minutes left. Danny Buderus produced a wonder ball to send Ablett away, and from the play-the-ball it looked like McGuire had collected the match-winning try. The no-try decision won the game for Wigan, as they gratefully wound the clock down - declining two shots at goal with late penalties.

The win kept Wigan a point behind leaders Warrington with a game in hand. The Wolves beat Castleford away 48-18 on the Friday night. Matt King's hat-trick brightened up an uninspiring contest at the end of a week when the Aussie confirmed he would be returning home at the end of the season to join South Sydney. King's first game for the Rabbitohs next season was likely to be against his current club Warrington as the Wolves announced a pre-season friendly with the Souths in Australia. Warrington that week confirmed they had signed Penrith star Trent Waterhouse on a three-year deal.

Hull FC coach Richard Agar paid tribute to centre Kirk Yeaman after he returned to action just five days after having an epileptic fit during half-time of the away win at Wakefield. But he came straight back into the side at St Helens on the Friday night and produced a strong performance in his side's 28-14 defeat.

Two scoring bursts of 14 points in each half helped St Helens earn their first win in four games in a dogged contest at the Stobart Stadium. Royce Simmons' side scored three times without their opponents touching the ball midway through the first half, and after a Black and White revival, then added another 14 points during a period of second-half dominance to seal the two points. Tony Puletua's punishing runs were crucial for St Helens as Jonny Lomax's well-taken 68th-minute try ensured Saints would be ending their recent barren run

Crusaders' 40-12 defeat at Huddersfield on the Sunday made it mathematically impossible to match the previous season's feat and make the play-offs. A hat-trick of tries from in-form David Hodgson kept the Giants on the coat-tails of Warrington and Wigan at the summit of Super League as they ended their mid-season sojourn with a third Shay success on the bounce against a Crusaders team that conceded 20 penalties and had two men sin-binned.

Nevertheless, the Welsh club was seemingly building for the future by signing long-term deals with Michael Witt and halfback partner Rhys Hanbury, ruled out for the season after he underwent surgery on a shoulder injury suffered in the 56-16 home defeat to Warrington in June. They also announced the signing of South Sydney utility forward Shannan McPherson for the 2012 season.

Hull KR captain Mick Vella insisted to League Express that his club did not have an issue with player behaviour, and that the squad was united in support of their coach Justin Morgan, whose future remained unclear. Rovers recorded a breathtaking 70-14 home victory - their biggest Super League score - over Wakefield on the Sunday after a troubled week in which Ben Cockayne, 27, and Liam Watts, 20, were suspended by the club. It followed a police chase that ended in a car, alleged to have been driven by 2010 Albert Goldthorpe Rookie of the Year Watts, crashing into a wall. Cockayne had been in talks over a new two-year deal at Hull KR. The club's players were on a month-long alcohol ban, with chairman Neil Hudgell reportedly taking a more hands-on role in disciplinary matters.

The Robins were leading only 14-10 after half an hour, but piled on 56 points in the final 50 minutes. They ran in four tries in a blistering final nine minutes of the first half against a Wakefield side that had been competing before that. Peter Fox - the man brought in with Cockayne unavailable - was a hat-trick hero on his 100th Hull KR appearance. Kris Welham and Liam Colbon also ran in three tries apiece.

Catalan Dragons stepped up the pressure on the top four with a seven-try to four victory at Odsal, despite playing almost half the game with just 12 men. The dismissal of David Ferriol for a high tackle on James Donaldson six minutes after the break and a Tom Burgess try shortly afterwards gave Bradford an 18-12 lead and seemed to pave the way for the home side to step up their own push for the play-offs. But the French outfit responded to the handicap by stepping up a gear. The Dragons' three tries in 11 minutes either side of the hour switched the momentum decisively with 37-year-old Steve Menzies at the heart of the Dragons' great back-to-the-wall effort. Ferriol was banned for three matches.

Salford moved to within a point of the top eight play-off spots with a 26-18 home win over Harlequins on the Friday night. Quins had a host of injury problems, with key players such as Luke Dorn, Chris Melling and Chad Randall all missing, and they were unlucky to trail 8-6 at the break. The lowly Londoners managed to get themselves back in front during the second half and anticipated just a second Super League win in 15 as they led 18-14 heading into the closing stages. But Salford crossed twice in the last seven minutes, through Mark Henry and Ashley Gibson, to claim a fourth win in five and keep alive their hopes of snatching a play-off spot.

Round 3

Wigan won their match in hand, moved from round three to accommodate their participation in the World Club Challenge, beating Castleford 26-16 at the DW Stadium to go to the top of the table. But it was by no means plain sailing on a rainswept Wednesday night against a Castleford side in the midst of an injury crisis. The Tigers led 16-10 at half-time, and though the Warriors staged their traditional third-quarter rally, they were fortunate that video referee Phil Bentham chalked off a try by Brett Ferres on the hour, after numerous replays looked totally inconclusive.

Coach Terry Matterson's post-match assessment included some choice criticism of the Rugby Football League for its scheduling of the game. Matterson was proud of his players, but was clearly riled about the League's insistence on playing the match in midweek, rather than waiting for a possible blank weekend in August. Matterson had announced at the start of the week that he would return to Australia at the end of 2011.

Round 21

Warrington ended a three-match winless run against Huddersfield, edging a classic game of two halves in the driving rain by 28-16 on the Friday night. A four-try blitz in the opening 25 minutes left the Giants gasping for breath, as Brett Hodgson, Michael Monaghan and Richie Myler made a mockery of the awful conditions by conjuring up a feast of attacking rugby.

The Wolves were 12-0 up inside six minutes, with Hodgson waltzing over for an easy score before putting in the first of many teasing kicks for Joel Monaghan to pounce. The Giants never really recovered, as they were dominated in all areas, and it looked like Warrington were going to run up a huge score as they led 22-0 at the break. Although the Giants pulled it back to 22-16 at one stage, they never really looked like winning. Louis Anderson's try with two minutes remaining opened up a 12-point gap, ending any hope of a Huddersfield comeback.

Crusaders won a lot of respect from the fans who attended the 38-10 defeat to Hull KR at The Racecourse on the Saturday and from visiting coach Justin Morgan. With eight players suspended, and injuries on top of that, their supporters feared a hammering by the on-form Rovers. Crusaders had suspended seven players for indiscipline (drinking the night before the defeat at Huddersfield) - Lloyd White, Jordan Tansey, Jason Chan, Gil Dudson, Richard Moore, Peter Lupton and Jarrod Sammut - and Hep Cahill was serving a one-match ban for a late tackle on Kevin Brown in the defeat at The Shay.

Crusaders were the better side in the first half, despite going into the break with a two-point deficit. However Rovers came out all guns blazing in the second half and, as in the previous win at home to Wakefield, didn't give their opposition a look-in. Ben Galea's two quick second-half tries finally stamped Rovers' authority on the game.

Jordan Tansey apologised on behalf of the seven players suspended but more bad news was that Gareth Thomas broke an arm and was likely to be out for the season. Crusaders had confirmed the signing of Leeds' Keith Senior, currently sidelined with a knee injury, on a two-year deal.

St Helens moved within a point of third-placed Huddersfield with a 46-6 win at Wakefield on the Sunday. They went into the game against the Wildcats without fullback Paul Wellens, with a nagging Achilles tendon problem, to add to long-term injuries, with Leon Pryce, Josh Perry and Ade Gardner all unavailable. They then lost three more players during the match, including forward Paul Clough, who was making his comeback after being out for three months with a shoulder injury. Wakefield also lost threequarter Luke George for the season with an ankle injury.

In the end, the class of James Roby, power of Tony Puletua, and quick feet of Kyle Eastmond proved more than enough for Saints to maintain their top-four challenge. Prolific winger Jamie Foster helped himself to another 22 points

New Salford coach Matt Parish arrived in time to watch his new charges comprehensively beaten 52-16 at Hull on the Friday night. Salford's chance to leapfrog Hull into eighth place quickly dissolved after Danny Tickle's second converted try on 32 minutes made it 22-0. Tom Briscoe finished with a hat-trick, with Joe Westerman revelling when he was moved to stand-off.

Paul Deacon helped himself to a try double on the Saturday as Wigan stayed at the top – but only after a real tussle in the capital. Wigan rode their luck in the first half, emerging with a 14-6 interval lead but the Warriors - and especially Sam Tomkins - showed their class after the interval to eventually run out comfortable winners. Harlequins had 18-year-old Dan Sarginson from Hemel Hempstead making his home debut at stand-off.

On the Sunday, Castleford registered a sensational home 34-30 victory over Bradford. The Tigers twice recovered from near-oblivion at 12 points adrift to snatch an astonishing game. Castleford took the lead for the first time when second row Stuart Jones crashed over in the 66th minute and Kirk Dixon converted to end the scoring, if not the action. In a frantic last five minutes, Brett Ferres halted Bradford centre Elliott Whitehead, Jones was alert in dropping on a Ben Jeffries kick, and, in the closing seconds, Bulls prop Andy Lynch, a former Castleford favourite, lost the ball under pressure from Jones in driving to the line on the last tackle.

Leeds sank to eighth spot after a 38-18 defeat to the rampant Dragons in a hot and humid Perpignan. The Catalans' run of only four defeats in the last 18 games continued as they methodically took Leeds apart to climb level with St Helens in fourth and within a point of Huddersfield Giants in third place.

The home side were forced to deal with the late withdrawals of Jamal Fakir and Jean-Philippe Baile as well as the suspension of David Ferriol. They were replaced by the returning Vincent Duport, Cyrille Gossard and debutant Thibaut Ancely. Leeds were missing the suspended Rob Burrow, suspended for a dangerous tackle the previous week at Wigan.

A series of decisions in the Catalans' favour saw the hosts score 14 points without Leeds touching the ball in the run up to half-time as the three pivots for the Dragons - Ian Henderson, Scott Dureau, who suffered an ankle injury late on, and Steve Menzies - all turned in heroic efforts.

* RFL chief executive Nigel Wood hailed what he has described as the culmination of a golden decade for Rugby League, as the sport's latest annual report revealed the RFL and Super League (Europe) generated a record income of £22.8 million during 2010. Government funding rose from £4.4 million in 2009 to £7.5 million.

Round 22

Bradford gave their play-off hopes an invaluable life-line with an unexpected 36-0 trouncing of high-flying Huddersfield at a rainy Odsal on the Sunday. The Giants, who stood to go back up to third place had they emulated the other Super League front runners with victory, were instead nilled for the first time since their 48-0 thrashing at Catalan Dragons in May 2008. With mid-season signing from Wakefield Ben Jeffries the gamestar, the Bulls led 22-0 at half-time, with Paul Sykes scoring a try-double.

Giants halfback Danny Brough returned from injury and was relieved to come through the contest without aggravating the ankle injury that caused him to limp off the field during the Giants' 40-18 home win against Castleford on June 5. Brough had originally expected to be out for eight weeks, but returned to action after missing just five rounds of Super League.

Salford's new coach Matt Parish's first game in charge saw the Reds lead for much of a four-pointer at Hull Kingston Rovers on the Sunday, but a late collapse saw them finish on the wrong side of a 21-8 final scoreline. Matt Cook scored Rovers' second try - with the score at 8-8 and 11 minutes remaining - as they turned their fortunes around after half-time. Michael Dobson had eyed and missed a field goal moments earlier but, once he cashed in at the second attempt, it gave Rovers a late, seven-point lead that did irreparable damage to Salford's hopes of a play-off spot.

Rovers that week had parted company with utility player Ben Cockayne "by mutual consent" while prop forward Liam Watts returned to training after serving a three-week suspension imposed by the club.

Leeds ended a three-match losing run with a 20-0 home win in the rain over Hull FC. After a relatively even first 70 minutes, Hull skipper Craig Fitzgibbon leaving the fray with a calf strain 16 minutes in, Leeds cut loose. A Ben Jones-Bishop try on 73 minutes and

July

Kevin Sinfield's conversion made it 14-0 and Danny McGuire's converted try a minute from time sealed it. Jamie Peacock produced his most influential performance since returning from a knee reconstruction.

Wigan Warriors signed former Leeds Rhinos prop forward Ben Cross until the end of the season when the Australian prop would link up with Widnes for 2012. Cross made his debut off the bench in a 48-6 home win over struggling Wakefield. The threadbare Wildcats held their own for the opening 30 minutes, causing the Warriors a whole host of problems, but three tries in six minutes broke their spirit. The second half went the same way as the first, with the Wildcats showing plenty of fight but in the end Wigan's class shone through with three tries in the last 15 minutes. Gareth Hock turned in a stellar performance which saw him grab his first hat-trick for the club.

Chris Bridge was the star of the show for Warrington as they romped to an impressive 54-24 victory in the capital. Bridge grabbed four of the Wolves' nine tries as Tony Smith's men put Harlequins to the sword. A week from their Challenge Cup showdown with Wigan, Warrington looked ominous with the ball in hand as they strengthened their grip on second spot in Super League.

Crusaders welcomed back the "Wrexham Seven", suspended the previous week for breaching the club's code of conduct in a rumoured late-night drinking session, and managed to snatch a 26-20 defeat from the jaws of victory yet again at home, this time to Castleford.

Tigers' on-loan prop Rob Parker contentiously touched down in the dying minutes of the game for a try given the green light by the video referee, to the disgust of the home support who had already seen three home tries chalked off on video evidence. Lacking suspended linchpin Rangi Chase, the Tigers could count themselves fortunate to escape with the two points

Royce Simmons hailed James Roby after another outstanding performance on the Friday night, when he helped St Helens to a 40-18 home win against the Catalan Dragons. Young winger Jamie Foster grabbed the headlines with a personal haul of 28 points, but it was Roby, with outstanding distribution, tough defence and his usual attacking darts from dummy half, who was the true star. All of which meant the return of Leon Pryce went largely under the radar, despite all the pre-match focus falling on the ex-Bradford stand-off. Pryce was deemed fit enough to take a place on the bench, and was given a rousing reception when he was introduced on the hour to make only his second St Helens appearance of the season. His last, in Perpignan in round four, had lasted four minutes.

Challenge Cup Quarter Finals

Wigan's dream of a return to Wembley for the first time in 13 years remained alive after Josh Charnley's quick-fire double sealed a pulsating Challenge Cup quarter-final at Warrington.

Holders Warrington had somehow recovered from trailing 22-0 after less than half an hour to be within four points going into the final act of a contest that lived up to all expectations. But then Charnley – who had been frequently targeted by the Wolves throughout their thrilling comeback – scored twice in the space of four minutes to finally ease the Warriors to a 44-24 win. Charnley recovered from a difficult first half to score the game's two defining tries in the final quarter - the tie was very much in the balance at 24-28 with 18 minutes remaining - including a stunning 90-metre effort. Centre George Carmont was the stand-out in a superb match.

After the game Warriors coach Michael Maguire insisted there was nothing in an Andy Coley tackle that left Warrington forward David Solomona with a medial ligament injury. Solomona was helped off shortly after half-time, after twisting awkwardly in the tackle, which was made by Coley as Lee Mossop held the Kiwi forward up. The incident was looked at by the RFL match review panel the following Monday and no charge was made.

Home side Hull FC - who two days before had changed ownership - deservedly led 16-6 at half-time in their Sunday televised quarter-final but the Rhinos scored 18-unanswered points in the first 14 minutes after the break, with captain Kevin Sinfield breaking the club's all-time goal-kicking record in the process. Lewis Jones was the previous holder, with 1,244 goals in a career with Leeds between 1952 and 1964, and Sinfield needed three against Hull to pass that mark. Having successfully kicked his first two to level, Sinfield missed the next one. But he overtook the milestone on his next attempt. He finished with seven goals in the match to move his tally on to 1,249.

A spilled ball sparked a devastating period in which Hull hardly touched the ball as Leeds turned the game dramatically, with the likes of Rob Burrow and Ali Lauitiiti shining after emerging off the bench. Ben Jones-Bishop's deft touches made him stand out and he deserved two tries.

Leon Pryce moved a step closer to his best as he guided St Helens to their 11th successive Challenge Cup semi-final, as Saints ran in ten tries in a 54-6 win against a lacklustre Hull KR side. Pryce was in inspirational form in the first 40 minutes and the Robins could not lay a finger on him as he crossed for a try and had a hand in two others as Saints led 20-6 at the break.

The talking point of the half was a beer bottle thrown on to the field as Francis Meli was on the charge down the left side. The RFL was satisfied the ground safety personnel had adequately dealt with the incident after which two spectators were led away from the scene by stewards.

Castleford registered a 22-18 win over Huddersfield Giants, the 2009 finalists, at the Probiz Coliseum on the Sunday. Rangi Chase's position at the top of the Albert Goldthorpe Medal table helped to secure his availability. Chase had been banned by the RFL's disciplinary committee for two matches after being found guilty of punching in the Tigers' 34-30 victory over Bradford two weeks before. But the Tigers appealed against the decision, and in light of the player's previous good record and the position at the top of a competition for Super League's best and fairest player, his suspension was reduced to one match, ruling him out of the previous week's clash at the Crusaders, but freeing him for the crucial last-eight showdown with the Giants.

Castleford hung on to secure a place in the last four for the first time since 2002. Both sides scored four tries but the Tigers' Kirk Dixon landed three goals from four attempts, with Huddersfield's Danny Brough succeeding only once from the same number of shots, albeit all from wide out. The Giants had bounced back from 12-0 down midway through the first half to within a couple of points two minutes into the second period. But they were unable to build on winger Jermaine McGillvary's sensational length-of-the-field touchdown.

Bookmakers William Hill priced the Tigers as 12/1 outsiders to lift the Cup after they drew a semi-final derby against Leeds. Wigan were paired with St Helens and were 4/5 favourites.

However, the bookies had stopped taking bets on Super League licences. Wakefield Trinity Wildcats were unbackable favourites to lose their's the following Tuesday morning when RFL Chairman Richard Lewis was due to reveal the names of the 13 clubs to join Widnes Vikings in Super League for the next three seasons. A William Hill spokesman claimed in League Express that Wakefield's exclusion was a "foregone conclusion".

Round 23

The announcement of the second round of Super League licences on Tuesday 26th July proved to be more dramatic than expected.

Much to their own surprise, as well as everyone else's, Wakefield were still in Super League, thanks to the Crusaders' 11th-hour decision to withdraw their application to continue playing in the competition. The Wildcats' players and staff gathered at Belle Vue expecting a wake but it turned into a celebration party after watching the announcement from Old Trafford on TV.

Talks had been going on between Crusaders and the RFL for some weeks about their financial position and the club withdrew from the bidding process the day before the announcement. "The licensing system has proved its mettle with this announcement, because it is showing that it has made all clubs think very seriously about their business plans and their plans for the future," said RFL chairman Richard Lewis.

It was a shock to the Crusaders players, who had not been forewarned. Mark Bryant, tweeted that "the owners didn't even have the backbone to speak to players about their withdrawal," while Rhys Hanbury said that his recent three-year contract had been "written on toilet paper". It was a PR disaster for the game.

"It's not a great day for Rugby League in Wales," admitted the RFL's chief executive, Nigel Wood. "But it's not as catastrophic as some are suggesting. The game there is in far better shape than five or six years ago. Thousands more are playing and that will continue." Wood denied that the Wildcats were in Super League by default. Halifax, who had earlier in the year been told they met criteria weren't happy. "It seems a no-brainer as far as I'm concerned," said their chairman, Michael Steel. "If it's between Halifax and Wakefield, Halifax are in." Calls for an independent inquiry into what appeared a debacle were rebuffed by the RFL.

There was some doubt the Crusaders would fulfil their fixtures but the following Sunday, by an amazing quirk of fate, they played at Wakefield and put in their best performance of the season to beat the Wildcats 40-6. An RFL dispensation had given all the Crusaders players Federation-trained and non-quota status, making it easier for them to find other clubs for 2012. Jarrod Sammut was the first to sign for another club, agreeing to join Bradford at the end of the season. The Rugby League Players Association was besieged by domestic players currently out of contract and angry with the decision, believing it prejudiced their chances of finding new contracts. Wakefield had announced on the day before the game, the result of which moved Crusaders to within two points of Wakefield at the bottom, that coach John Kear's contract wasn't to be extended at the end of the season.

Three of the Crusaders try scorers were Welsh internationals, with two of those, Lloyd White and Elliot Kear, having seen their development flourish during the club's three-year Super League stay. White's two tries in the first nine minutes of the second half took the game firmly away from Wakefield.

Sam Tomkins was once again the star of the show as Wigan stayed on top with a 30-16 win at Hull FC, despite suffering a shoulder injury that saw him withdrawn for part of the game. On his return Tomkins' 72nd-minute long-range try sealed the win.

Warrington had their sights firmly set on knocking league leaders Wigan Warriors off their perch after they ran in 12 tries in a 64-6 victory against an outclassed Bradford at the Halliwell Jones Stadium on the Sunday. In a magnificent team performance former Bulls junior Ryan Atkins got four tries and Joel Monaghan also scored a hat-trick.

The Giants marked their return to the Galpharm with a Saturday TV, 46-26 win over Hull KR that belied their recent poor form. Danny Brough tormented rookie fullback Louis Sheriff with a string of uncatchable kicks, although when Jake Webster charged down the right wing and past fullback Scott Grix for a fantastic try on 52 minutes there were only four points in it. But seven minutes later Luke Robinson put Danny Kirmond over from short range to put eight points between the sides. Five minutes after, the Giants increased their lead further when a move started and finished by Grix saw Jermaine McGillvary break down the right touchline before kicking inside for the Giants fullback to pounce for his second.

The final nail in the coffin was hammered in by Eorl Crabtree, who broke through the goal-line defence to score. The Robins' frustration at how the game finished was summed up by Clint Newton, who spent the last ten minutes of the match in the dug-out after expressing his opinions to referee Thierry Alibert.

On the Sunday, St Helens were pulled back from an 18-point lead to be only 18-16 ahead as half-time approached, but recovered in style to finish comfortable 46-26 winners at Castleford. The Tigers, pressing hard, could have gone in front at the break when stand-off Rangi Chase's kick to the corner was palmed back by winger Kirk Dixon. Saints centre Kyle Eastmond, however, scooped up possession and raced away. Although Eastmond was hauled down by Adam Milner, and former Tigers favourite Michael Shenton was halted by Richard Owen in the next phase, St Helens were not to be denied, gamestar Paul Wellens crashing over despite the attentions of Ryan McGoldrick. Saints never looked back as winger Jamie Foster closed with seven goals from eight attempts.

Rob Purdham announced he would return to Cumbria at the end of the season and was in the Harlequins side that fell to a 48-22 defeat in Perpignan. The hosts ran into an unassailable 24-0 lead within 23 minutes that blew the Quins off the park. With both Steve Menzies and Scott Dureau missing, a new halfback partnership of Setaimata Sa and youngster Remy Marginet started for the home side. Damien Blanch's try just after half-time ended any hopes Harlequins had of coming back into the game.

Leeds won 30-22 at Salford on the Friday night and graced their final appearance at the Willows with a try that ranked among the best they had ever scored there. It came in the 17th minute after the hosts, with Matty Smith effective, had held sway in a penalty-ridden opening. Warrington-bound Stefan Ratchford put up a cross kick to the left, Jodie Broughton palmed it back but just behind the supporting Mark Henry. Local boy Kallum Watkins – restored to the Leeds line-up after wrist surgery that had kept him out since April – scooped up the rolling ball one-handed and majestically palmed off two would-be pursuers on an electrifying touchline break to half way. Danny Buderus made himself available up the middle in support and intelligently held the Reds cover at bay for long enough for Ryan Hall to loom on the left, the Leeds hooker firing out a pinpoint long pass for his winger to complete the exhilarating 100-metre breakout.

Kevin Sinfield's fifth goal, a touchline conversion of Lee Smith's late try, established a new Super League points total of 2,410.

SUPER LEAGUE TABLE - *Sunday 31st July*

	P	W	D	L	F	A	D	PTS
Wigan Warriors	23	17	3	3	686	353	333	37
Warrington Wolves	23	18	0	5	908	353	555	36
St Helens	23	14	3	6	676	463	213	31
Huddersfield Giants	23	15	0	8	609	438	171	30
Catalan Dragons	23	14	1	8	597	513	84	29
Leeds Rhinos	23	12	1	10	584	527	57	25
Castleford Tigers	23	11	2	10	588	646	-58	24
Hull FC	23	10	1	12	558	491	67	21
Hull Kingston Rovers	23	10	0	13	599	610	-11	20
Salford City Reds	23	9	0	14	476	664	-188	18
Bradford Bulls	23	8	2	13	488	682	-194	18
Harlequins	23	5	1	17	452	814	-362	11
Wakefield T Wildcats *	23	6	0	17	365	779	-414	8
Crusaders *	23	5	0	18	444	697	-253	6

* 4 points deducted for entering administration

AUGUST
Save the Cru

Challenge Cup Semi-finals

Wigan were the hot favourites to win the Carnegie Challenge Cup following their 18-12 semi-final victory against St Helens at Warrington on the Saturday, while Leeds Rhinos were the 11/4 underdog after they beat Castleford on the following day at Doncaster in golden-point extra time.

A top defensive performance and another sprinkling of Sam Tomkins magic sent Wigan back to Wembley for the first time in 13 years. Michael Maguire's charges built their victory on organisation without the ball, before making the most of it when they got their share of possession, most notably either side of half-time. When they did, Tomkins again produced moments of brilliance, scoring their crucial third try, having a hand in their second and having another disallowed. But he also played his full part in that defensive effort, coping superbly with a number of spiralling kicks that Leon Pryce sent his way, and pulling off a crucial tackle on Jonny Lomax alongside Thomas Leuluai early in the second half.

Josh Charnley followed up his quarter-final double over Warrington with another excellent try and a long-range break to set up George Carmont's opener.

It was by no means a one-sided affair, and although Saints failed to breach the Warriors' defensive line until the 65th minute, they played their full part in a gripping contest, not least when two quick Jamie Foster tries set up a grandstand finale.

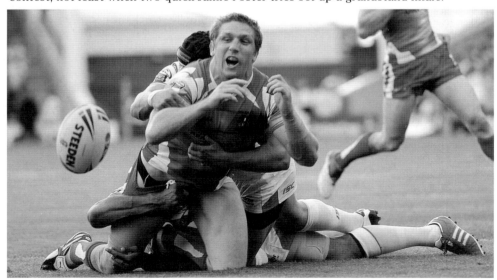

Wigan's Ryan Hoffman spills the ball under pressure from St Helens's Jonny Lomax

Leeds captain Kevin Sinfield hailed the 10-8 victory over Castleford as a classic after his goal won the game in golden-point extra time. Sinfield's clinching kick came after two minutes of extra time when Leeds won a penalty following Ryan McGoldrick's high shot on Danny McGuire.

At the start of the week, the story was that Castleford would be without Rangi Chase. The New Zealander reportedly had to return to Australia for a court case, relating to an assault that allegedly happened during his pre-Tigers days. Leeds were unconvinced at the start of the week and were proved right when Chase was on the teamsheet. Chase was on his way to Australia after the match, with the club succeeding in forcing a postponement to the court appearance.

Castleford had led 8-2 with 73 minutes on the clock after two Kirk Dixon penalty goals followed Chase's audacious try. The New Zealander, on his own 20-metre line, stepped inside cleverly, leaving Chris Clarkson trailing. He broke free down the left and then threw a dummy to catch out Brent Webb before eventually touching down.

Dramatically, Leeds were swiftly on level terms with six minutes left on the clock. Danny McGuire flung the ball out to

Leeds's Ryan Bailey halted by Castleford's Ben Davies and Brett Ferres

start a right-sided passing move that ended in Weller Hauraki delivering a timely pass out of the back of his hand to Kallum Watkins. The ball initially struck the centre's right boot but he collected and finished in the corner before Sinfield added the extras from wide out to make it 8-8.

Then came the heart-racing final moments. First, Sinfield attempted a field goal but Danny Orr charged it down and broke free before Watkins got back to drag him down. Next it was Chase's turn, with less than 15 seconds left on the clock, but his field-goal attempt drifted wide, leading to golden-point extra time.

After two minutes McGoldrick delivered the high shot on McGuire, who was stepping inside towards the tryline, and with a penalty awarded. Sinfield stepped up to win an epic Challenge Cup semi-final.

That weekend Hull KR were officially looking for a new coach, after months of speculation over Justin Morgan's future was ended with the news that the Australian would leave Craven Park at the end of the season. Hull FC coach Richard Agar rubbished media reports that he was to be the new coach at Wakefield Trinity Wildcats next season.

Round 24

Paul Wellens celebrated 400 St Helens appearances with a crucial try in a 19-6 home win over Huddersfield that just about guaranteed a top-three finish. Wellens left the field through a guard of honour formed by his team-mates.

Leon Pryce's try, when he took a ball from Lee Gaskell and stepped between Danny Kirmond and Larne Patrick, was all that separated the teams at half-time. And with the after-effects of the bruising Challenge Cup semi-final to contend with, plenty of people were tipping a Giants' victory. Wellens stepped up when his team needed him, coming from deep to charge on to Pryce's pass, and then forcing his way between Kevin Brown and Danny Brough for a try that eased St Helens' nerves, despite video-referee Ben Thaler looking closely to check whether Brown had been obstructed.

After a first half in which both sides had looked capable of conjuring errors, Saints' sudden 12-point advantage always looked like being enough, even with more than half an hour still to play. Louie McCarthy-Scarsbrook scored a brilliant try that sealed it. Receiving a pass from Jon Wilkin, he burst through one tackle and charged upfield on a 40-metre dash that saw him step round Scott Grix to score under the posts. More bad news for the Giants was that Luke O'Donnell had his campaign ended when he suffered knee ligament damage 12 minutes into the second half.

Hull FC spoiled Catalans' chance to go into fourth by hammering them 40-8 at the KC Stadium, also on the Friday night, boosting their own chances of finishing in the play-off places. Hull turned round only 16-4 ahead, but any Dragons hopes of a comeback disappeared in a stunning four-minute period at the start of the second half. There were less than 40 seconds on the clock when Tom Briscoe broke free down the left and passed inside to Richard Horne, who sent the supporting Cameron Phelps racing over near the corner. Danny Tickle added his fifth goal of the game, which took him past 1,000 points for the club.

Only two minutes later Hull stormed downfield again, and although Phelps was hauled down in the shadow of the Dragons' posts, Danny Houghton again sent out another scoring pass and Lee Radford dived over. Tickle added his sixth goal and Hull led 28-4. Joe Westerman added Hull's fifth try of the game when Horne regathered his own kick that rebounded off the Dragons' defence, and sent his halfback partner scampering over unopposed. And Kirk Yeaman produced arguably the most stunning score of the evening, sweeping through the cover and handing off a defender before sending Horne on a 30-metre run to the line.

Ben Cross broke his arm 35 minutes into the Warriors' home 52-18 win over Salford on Sunday. Sam Tomkins claimed four tries, including a first-half hat-trick and a spectacular closing effort, to take his tally up to 29 for the season. He had now scored in each of Wigan's last five games, and these latest scores saw him overhaul Hull KR's Kris Welham at the head of the Super League try-scoring charts.

Warrington had four key players helped off in the Sunday 66-12 home win over Wakefield. Brett Hodgson limped off in the second minute with a quad problem, and was quickly followed by Simon Grix, with a groin injury. Ben Westwood was also withdrawn before the half-hour mark with a knee complaint, and Rhys Evans followed him after the break with a suspected broken foot. Louis Anderson, Chris Bridge and Michael Monaghan all starred and Ryan Atkins finished with a smart hat-trick as the Wolves racked up a half century of points for the ninth time in Super League XVI.

Despite being on the end of another one-sided scoreline, Wakefield coach John Kear felt that his side improved from their heavy home defeat to Crusaders, and praised debutant Ryan Tongia, Ben Gledhill, Julien Rinaldi and Glenn Morrison.

The Rhinos confirmed themselves as one of the competition's form teams, having booked their place in the Challenge Cup Final and won their last three Super League matches. The Friday night 56-0 victory over Castleford took them to within three points of the top four. Jamie Jones-Buchanan gave a quality performance as the Rhinos ran riot. With Rangi Chase, the playmaker-in-chief, in Australia, the Tigers had also to do without Cup heroes Paul Jackson, Kirk Dixon, Ryan Hudson and Brett Ferres, while Greg Eden, earmarked as the eighteenth man, also pulled out at the last minute.

Tigers coach Terry Matterson joined the call for a reduction in the number of teams in Super League. "The guys have got to re-group, it's been a long year for us and I haven't seen an injury count like it," Matterson commented. "Our squad is not big enough to start with, but it's as big as it has ever been," he mused.

Crusaders climbed off bottom and above Wakefield on points difference with a 31-12 home win over Harlequins. Richard Moore's 67th-minute touchdown finally tipped the balance in favour of the home side.

A first win at Odsal for almost 20 years kept Hull KR's play-off ambitions well and truly alive, while all but mathematically extinguishing any lingering hopes Bradford had of making the top eight. Rovers moved to within a point of arch rivals and eighth placed Hull FC and just two behind Castleford with a 34-8 televised Sunday win. Three Rovers tries in an 11-minute spell either side of half-time knocked the wind out of the sails of Bradford, with Michael Dobson the guiding hand.

Elliott Whitehead was put on report for biting Hull KR back-rower Jordan Cox. At Tuesday's tribunal the Bulls produced evidence they claimed proved the player could not have been in control of his actions at the time of the offence as he had been knocked unconscious only four minutes before the incident. He was banned for five games.

Round 25

Eight days before Wigan's first Wembley Cup final since 1998, Sam Tomkins was in sensational form as he grabbed a brace of tries, one an amazing 95-metre solo effort, and had a hand in a few others as the Warriors hammered the Bulls 60-12 at the DW Stadium.

The Warriors looked like they were going to run away with it, with three tries in the opening 20 minutes as Sam Tomkins, George Carmont and Sean O'Loughlin ran the show. But after leading 14-0 they were outscored two tries to one in the final 20 minutes of the half. But after the break Wigan put the game to bed early with three tries in eight minutes, although Pat Richards' uncharacteristic kicking woes - he landed only six out of twelve attempts - kept the final score down. Australian halfback Marc Herbert had played his last game for the Bulls after breaking a hand.

It was different story for Wigan's Wembley opponents Leeds as Harlequins ended the Rhinos' five-match unbeaten run, running up a 26-0 lead just after half-time before a late Leeds response, with three tries in six minutes, gave the final 32-22 score line a flattering look.

It was not the sort of performance coach Brian McDermott was looking for in the run-up to his side's return to London and made Wigan hot favourites to lift the Cup. Harlequins were excellent in gaining their first double over the Rhinos since 1996, the first year of Super League. Luke Dorn's thrilling hat-trick took him above Scott Roskell as the leading career tryscorer for the London club, with 87. With Chris Bailey and, particularly, Jason Golden, who had been sidelined all season with a groin injury until round 22, at the heart of a solid pack performance, and Chad Randall, Luke Gale, Rob Purdham and Dorn polishing their best work, the hosts looked capable of ending the campaign as they began it, as a match for anyone.

McDermott faced an anxious wait, with centre pairing Kallum Watkins and Carl Ablett having left the Stoop injured. Watkins was helped off in the 67th minute with a twisted knee and looked a definite doubt for the following Saturday.

Warrington kept within a point of Wigan at the top of the table with a 25-12 win in Perpignan. The hosts were in good spirits, with the return of Steve Menzies and Jamal

Fakir, with Fakir was making his 100th appearance for the club but the Wolves had Lee Briers returning, and he controlled the game and added the gloss to a performance that saw Warrington just about deserve their win.

With eleven minutes remaining the Wolves took the lead for the first time. With the Catalans looking to break down the right hand side, Menzies had the ball stolen by Louis Anderson, who raced away before offloading to Ryan Atkins, who ran to the posts to score. Chris Bridge added the simple conversion to give the Wolves a six-point cushion heading into the final ten minutes. Briers extended that lead with a field goal from 35 metres out, and then scored a trademark interception try when a wide Catalan pass to the left saw him intercept and race 40 metres to touch down under the posts.

Ninth-placed Hull KR kept their quest for a play-off spot on track with a narrow 24-22 victory over St Helens at Craven Park on the Sunday. Earlier wins for Hull FC and Castleford that weekend meant that anything other than maximum points against Saints would have left Rovers needing other results to go their way. But the win meant they headed into their final two league games against Catalan Dragons and Castleford knowing that victory in both would guarantee them a play-off place, given that their nearest rivals played each other in Round 26.

It was Saints' fourth consecutive league defeat at Craven Park and they suffered injury blows to Chris Flannery, with a cartilage problem, and James Roby, who had his nose broken. The score was 18-16 to Rovers until midway through the second half. The home side finally wore down Saints, though, with back-to-back, goal-line drop-outs, before the on-form Craig Hall, coming back into a side after over two months out, scored a crucial try on 60 minutes.

Early-season front-runners Castleford battled back from 12-0 down to claim victory at the death in an exciting local derby at Wakefield. The lead changed hands no fewer than six times, with the Tigers having three claims for tries ruled out in the second half. Rangi Chase inspired the Tigers' first-half fightback and always looked likely to have the match-winning card up his sleeve. Dean Widders' 77th-minute try finally determined the outcome.

Hull FC looked to be coming into form at the right time with a 58-18 win in Wrexham on the Sunday. It was an emotionally charged occasion, as the Crusaders faced Super League opponents for the final time on home soil in their short three-year Super League history.

The Airlie Birds, the Crusaders' first ever Super League opponents in Bridgend in 2009, dominated proceedings at Wrexham as six tries before the interval demoralised Crusaders. Sam Obst scored a try-brace and was the highlight of many good performances in the Hull side.

A campaign to re-establish a Rugby League team in North Wales in time for the 2012 season had already attracted almost 3,000 messages of support. 'Save the Cru' - a group established by the current Crusaders club sponsors - had laid out plans to field a team within the Championship structure next season.

Huddersfield's chances of a top-two finish had gone and their top-four place was starting to look precarious after a 24-18 defeat at Salford on the Friday night. Former Leeds winger Danny Williams, who had made his Reds debut in mid-July after a spell in rugby union and a trial with Hull KR, scored a fine hat-trick as Salford responded to coach Matt Parish's criticism in the wake of the heavy defeat at Wigan. The Giants had not won away from home since May.

SUPER LEAGUE TABLE - *Sunday 21st August*

	P	W	D	L	F	A	D	PTS
Wigan Warriors	25	19	3	3	798	383	415	41
Warrington Wolves	25	20	0	5	999	377	622	40
St Helens	25	15	3	7	717	493	224	33
Huddersfield Giants	25	15	0	10	633	481	152	30
Catalan Dragons	25	14	1	10	617	578	39	29
Leeds Rhinos	25	13	1	11	662	559	103	27
Castleford Tigers	25	12	2	11	622	732	-110	26
Hull FC	25	12	1	12	656	517	139	25
Hull Kingston Rovers	25	12	0	13	657	640	17	24
Salford City Reds	25	10	0	15	518	734	-216	20
Bradford Bulls	25	8	2	15	508	776	-268	18
Harlequins	25	6	1	18	496	867	-371	13
Crusaders *	25	6	0	19	493	767	-274	8
Wakefield T Wildcats *	25	6	0	19	407	879	-472	8

* 4 points deducted for entering administration

CHALLENGE CUP FINAL
Wigan's Wembley Way

Hot favourites Wigan won their 18th Challenge Cup, Jeff Lima became the first prop forward to win the Lance Todd Trophy since Brian Lockwood in 1980, and the Rhinos lost at Wembley for the second year in a row, their captain Kevin Sinfield, along with Ryan Bailey and Rob Burrow, losing his fourth Challenge Cup final as Leeds skipper.

The bookies had Super League Champions Wigan as shoo-ins for their first Challenge Cup win since the 21-12 victory over St Helens at Murrayfield in 2002, and their first at Wembley since 1995. But that wasn't how it panned out in what was the most entertaining final since the return to Wembley in 2007. Leeds were still in the contest until Thomas Leuluai fought his way over from dummy-half with only four minutes left on the clock for the try that sealed the destiny of the Cup.

Video referee Steve Ganson took an age to decide whether Leuluai had grounded the ball properly, and the roar from the Wigan end was almost deafening as the try was given. Pat Richards hammered over his fourth conversion out of five attempts, and his kicking had proved crucial, with Kevin Sinfield only potting one out of four efforts, all of them from wide out, a measure itself of Wigan's rock-solid defence down the middle.

Lima collected the Lance Todd Trophy with a try in each half and a non-stop effort in attack and defence, amidst a solid team performance in which all the Wigan side played their part. Sam Tomkins was a handful throughout, and provided the space for brother Joel to score one of the great individual tries in the legend of Wembley finals. When Joel raced to the posts on the half-hour mark, Wigan led 16-0, and the bookies looked to have got their odds right. But the introduction of Burrow off the bench prior to that prompted the Rhinos to stage a magnificent comeback to set up a wonderful last quarter.

In the voting for the Lance Todd Trophy Lima was a narrow winner with eight votes, over the Rhinos' Rob Burrow, who picked up six. Other votes went to Joel Tomkins (5), Brett Finch (4), Sam Tomkins (3), Kevin Sinfield (1) and Danny McGuire (1). Other props to have won the award were George Nicholls (1978), Steve Pitchford (1977), Don Fox (1968), Frank Collier (1964), Alan Prescott (1956) and Frank Whitcombe (1948).

Wigan started the match confidently, looking as though they were going to run up a cricket score. Their first try came 90 seconds after Danny McGuire had kicked out on the full, under pressure from Harrison Hansen. Josh Charnley, one of the leading contenders

CARNEGIE CHALLENGE CUP FINAL

Saturday 27th August 2011

LEEDS RHINOS 18 WIGAN WARRIORS 28

RHINOS: 1 Brent Webb; 23 Ben Jones-Bishop; 19 Kallum Watkins; 12 Carl Ablett; 5 Ryan Hall; 13 Kevin Sinfield (C); 6 Danny McGuire; 8 Kylie Leuluai; 9 Danny Buderus; 10 Jamie Peacock; 11 Jamie Jones-Buchanan; 3 Brett Delaney; 20 Weller Hauraki. Subs (all used): 7 Rob Burrow; 16 Ryan Bailey; 17 Ian Kirke; 21 Chris Clarkson.
Tries: Hall (34, 71), Jones-Bishop (37), Ablett (59); **Goals:** Sinfield 1/4.
WARRIORS: 1 Sam Tomkins; 25 Josh Charnley; 12 Joel Tomkins; 4 George Carmont; 5 Pat Richards; 6 Paul Deacon; 17 Brett Finch; 15 Jeff Lima; 7 Thomas Leuluai; 10 Andy Coley; 11 Harrison Hansen; 16 Ryan Hoffman; 13 Sean O'Loughlin (C). Subs (all used): 22 Liam Farrell; 21 Lee Mossop; 9 Michael McIlorum; 14 Paul Prescott.
Tries: Charnley (9), Lima (24, 61), J Tomkins (29), Leuluai (78); **Goals:** Richards 4/5.
Rugby Leaguer & League Express Men of the Match:
Rhinos: Rob Burrow. *Warriors:* Jeff Lima.
Penalty count: 5-2; **Half-time:** 10-16; **Referee:** Phil Bentham; **Attendance:** 78,482 *(at Wembley Stadium).*

for this season's Rookie of the Year award, stepped nicely inside Danny McGuire, with Carl Ablett and Brent Webb unable to stop him from touching down, after a smart Wigan passing movement.

Shortly afterwards Webb was the recipient of a massive hit by Thomas Leuluai, and he seemed to be shaken up. It was Webb's dropping of a high bomb from Sam Tomkins that led directly to the second Wigan try, when Lima took a short pass from Paul Prescott near the Leeds line, with Kevin Sinfield tackling his legs, but unable to prevent the touchdown.

The third try came from a rushed kick by Watkins as he was heading under pressure towards the touchline. The ball bounced harmlessly to Sam Tomkins and he ran across the field and linked with his brother Joel. Joel galloped away down the right, and brushed off the covering McGuire before stepping inside Webb and burning off the valiant Jamie Peacock on his way to the posts.

But suddenly Leeds began to play. Rob Burrow had come onto the field shortly before Joel Tomkins' try, and his arrival had seemed to spark new life into the Rhinos, while Jamie Jones-Buchanan stepped up a gear.

Andy Coley's high tackle on Burrow gave Leeds the field position for Ryan Hall's first try, with Kevin Sinfield hitting the post with his attempted conversion. And after a great charge by Jones-Buchanan, the Rhinos scored on the right wing, this time with Ben Jones-Bishop touching down, and Sinfield adding the goal this time from the touchline.

After the interval Wigan, with Charnley playing with a broken finger and Lee Mossop having a dislocated shoulder popped back in, looked much more uncertain and after Ryan Hoffman's knock-on after 58 minutes, a Carl Ablett try put the Rhinos only two points behind. Sinfield couldn't add the goal, and the Rhinos couldn't quite get back on terms.

Paul Deacon collected a charged down Sinfield kick on halfway; Sam Tomkins made a half break; Liam Farrell drove in and on the next play Lima bumped off Ablett and Bailey and shot under Webb and Clarkson. Mossop's short pass to Lima was forward, but the Rhinos had ample opportunity to stop Lima if they could have. Richards' kick was a formality.

Farrell's high tackle on Burrow on his own 40-metre line gave Leeds the chance to get back again when McGuire's bullet pass squeezed Hall into the left corner. The video referee ratified it, but Sinfield missed again with the conversion.

The four-point deficit looked bridgeable, and from the restart Jones-Bishop skinned Richards and tore away down the right. Richards saved the day by tracking back and denying his opposite the pass inside to McGuire. Instead, Jones-Bishop kicked for the line, and neither Sam Tomkins nor McGuire could get to the ball before it ran dead.

Hall defused a Deacon bomb superbly, before Leeds launched another attack which ended with Chris Clarkson knocking on Sinfield's chip to the line.

It proved to be the Rhinos' last hurrah, as they kept Wigan inside their own '30' before Finch's long kick to touch was chased by Charnley. The winger's fly kick ahead seemed to bounce off Burrow, but Wigan, to the astonishment of the Leeds players, got the feed at the scrum.

It wasn't long before Leuluai shot in from dummy-half through Ian Kirke's and Clarkson's tackle.

Leeds' kick-off bounced into touch and the clock was run down with the game's only goal-line drop-out when Sam Tomkins ran the ball dead. As the hooter

Brent Webb arrives too late to stop Josh Charnley from scoring the first try of the Challenge Cup Final

sounded, McGuire was dumped by Thomas Leuluai, the second half ending just like the first as players rushed into a huddle.

It was a breathless finish to one of the best Challenge Cup finals in living memory.

After the game Sam Tomkins refused to comment about a V-sign he made to Leeds supporters when he was congratulating his team-mate Charnley on scoring Wigan's first try.

Tomkins was booed by a section of Leeds fans before the game and had been booed by a section of the crowd when he played for England against The Exiles at Headingley. The following Tuesday he was found guilty of minor misconduct by the RFL and given a £1,000 fine, suspended until the end of the 2012 season.

SEPTEMBER
Wolves at the door

Round 26

Warrington moved back to the top of Super League and into the driving seat for the League Leaders' Shield with a dominant 39-12 home win against Wigan in a fiery encounter on the first Sunday in September. The Wolves, with a superior points difference to Wigan, now only needed a point against Hull FC to finish top of the ladder. Wigan, who had prided themselves on their strong defence all season, could not live with the Wolves in the opening 25 minutes, as Matt King, Lee Briers and Michael Monaghan, twice, took advantage with well taken tries as they led 25-6 at the break. Wigan attempted to mount a comeback in the second half, but could only cross the Wolves' line once more as Warrington managed another 14 points.

The Wolves welcomed back skipper Adrian Morley after he had sat out the last seven matches with vision problems and dizziness. Morley was set to undergo eye surgery the following Monday after being on the sidelines for over two months following a head knock in the win against St Helens.

A bad-tempered affair saw two all-in brawls in the second half. The first incident saw Wigan fullback Sam Tomkins go in with his feet as Jon Clarke attempted to ground the ball. Lee Briers took offence, which sparked a 26-man brawl. Both Tomkins and Briers received a talking to from referee Richard Silverwood and the following week Sam Tomkins received a caution from the RFL.

The second incident, which was put on report, was for Gareth Hock punching Ben Harrison after a tackle and television replays showed Hock had gouged Harrison, which sparked the pushing and shoving. Hock was found guilty the following Tuesday and received four matches for the gouging and one for the punch, ending his season that had only begun in late June. Missing was David Solomona, who had been suspended for one game by the RFL Disciplinary Committee for making dangerous contact with Catalans player Jean-Philippe Baile in the round 15 game in Perpignan.

St Helens secured third spot as they ran in five tries against a spirited Salford side who ultimately pressed the self-destruct button, conceding 15 penalties in a 31-6 Saints win at the Stobart Stadium. Matty Ashurst's 55th-minute touchdown sealed the result and once again utility Jonny Lomax was the star of the show at scrum-half.

Leroy Cudjoe led a masterclass of Huddersfield threequarter play as the Giants booked fourth place and found some genuine form ahead of the play-offs with a 50-12 home hammering of Harlequins. The London side competed fully for long periods and made few mistakes. But they lacked the Giants' potency with the ball, with Cudjoe, Joe Wardle and boom rookie Jermaine McGillvary all helping themselves to try doubles.

Positions five to eight in the table were still in a state of flux going into the final round.

Leeds were still fourth, but only on points difference, as they banished Wembley blues with an 11-try, 64-20 rout of Wakefield. Ryan Hall claimed a hat-trick and Danny McGuire was back to his best. Ali Lauitiiti led the Rhinos out in his last regular season match at Headingley - after arriving in 2004 - before joining the Wildcats for 2012.

Leeds were now level on points with Catalans after the Dragons lost 30-28 to Hull KR in Perpignan, a result which threw the race for seventh and eighth spots wide open, with the Robins into the play-off positions for the first time since week three. Craig Hall's try in the 55th minute ended the Dragons spell of dominance and gave Rovers a key eight-point advantage. Meanwhile, Dragons Chairman Bernard Guasch labelled the signing of England International Leon Pryce as one of the biggest in the club's short history.

The Dragons' third straight defeat meant Rovers would face Castleford the following Sunday in a 'play-off' for the eighth and final play-off position. The same night Hull FC cemented their play-off spot with a 50-18 win at Castleford, who slipped into ninth. Richard Agar's men could still finish as high as fifth, depending on results in the final round of fixtures, but star forward Craig Fitzgibbon was a doubt for the last game against after suffering ankle ligament damage. Hull had racked up 148 points in three consecutive wins against Catalans, Crusaders and Castleford. Ryan McGoldrick's season came to a premature end when he received a two-match ban from the RFL Disciplinary Committee for a late, high tackle on Hull FC's Sam Obst.

That week former St Helens and Wigan coach Ian Millward, in his second spell at Leigh, was named as Terry Matterson's successor as head coach at Castleford, while former Hull scrum-half Sean Long was appointed assistant coach at Salford.

In a dead rubber, Bradford Bulls overcame a spirited display by the Crusaders – who were cheered on at Odsal by an enthusiastic band of supporters – to close their home campaign with a comfortable 48-24 victory. There was a return for Chev Walker who had featured in just eleven league matches - after missing four matches early in the campaign - with a torn pectoral muscle, before suffering a foot injury in the Challenge Cup tie against Halifax in May.

Round 27

Warrington secured the League Leaders' Shield and topped the table for the first time since 1973 when they won 34-12 at Hull FC on the Friday night. Ryan Atkins inspired a first-half performance that epitomised much of the Wolves' season in which they had amassed 1,072 points and ended Hull's run of three consecutive wins.

The Wolves had the game won by half-time, when they led 28-6, after Atkins broke the deadlock showing tremendous strength to wrestle the ball from Joe Westerman's grasp before sprinting 40 metres to touch down, beating the chasing Sam Obst, who tweaked a hamstring and was immediately withdrawn, with video referee Ian Smith ruling that the ball strip was legal.

Earlier that week Hull announced that coach Richard Agar would be leaving at the end of the season to make way for Shaun McRae as director of rugby, with responsibility to appoint a head coach. At the end of the following week Agar took up a three-year contract with Wakefield Trinity Wildcats.

Warrington's win set up a repeat of the previous year's play-off clash between the Wolves and Giants at the Halliwell Jones Stadium. Giants centre Leroy Cudjoe was certain to miss the game after picking up a knee injury in the 31-24 defeat to Leeds Rhinos at the Galpharm Stadium on the Sunday. Jamie Peacock, Kevin Sinfield and Danny McGuire all turned back the clock with inspired performances, with Ryan Hall grabbing two tries and Zak Hardaker showing up well in his new position at centre - Kallum Watkins still absent with a swollen knee.

The Rhinos headed into a home elimination play-off against Hull after securing a fifth-placed finish, with Catalan Dragons also getting home advantage in the first week eliminators by overpowering Salford on the Sunday at the last ever game at the Willows.

It was a moment in history as the Salford City Reds brought the curtain down on their 110 years at the Willows in front of a sell-out crowd - the first match at the famous old ground in 1901 saw Salford beat local rivals Swinton 2-0. As well as bidding farewell to their ground, the City Reds were saying goodbye to several players including Stefan Ratchford, Ray Cashmere, Mark Henry and Vinnie Anderson. Sadly for the Reds, the script went into the shredder, as with some considerable style the Dragons - with Thomas Bosc back after a series of injuries had almost wiped out his season - ran in seven tries in a 44-18 win.

Hull KR's Saturday-evening 26-24 win over Castleford made it three play-off series in a row for the Craven Park club - a trip to Perpignan their reward - while the Tigers dropped agonisingly out of the play-offs. The sides were on level terms, at 12-12, with only a couple of minutes remaining before the break, when Nick Fozzard was penalised, harshly, for a high tackle on Robins' young forward Scott Taylor. Rovers opted to go for goal, with Michael Dobson succeeding from 35 metres out. And with only seven seconds left on the first-half clock, Hull KR gained a scrum in the Tigers' '20'. Craig Hall drifted across from his left-wing position, coming into the line at exactly the right time to fire a pass to right winger Sam Latus, who crashed over the line, despite the robust and desperate challenge of Castleford substitute Daryl Clark.

The Tigers fought back to lead 24-22 after Jordan Thompson's 63rd minute try created by Rangi Chase's superb long pass but second rower Clint Newton - who had confirmed he would be heading back to the NRL with Penrith Panthers at the end of the season - and fullback Shaun Briscoe linked to send winger Latus over the line ten minutes from time.

St Helens coach Royce Simmons insisted his selection policy ahead of the club's 34-16 win at Harlequins was based entirely on necessity after he named an all-British squad, including 15 players who had come through the club's Academy. Winger Tom Armstrong proved the star of the show, grabbing a hat-trick that ensured the visitors came out on top, although that wasn't the case at the interval, as the London side led 12-4 and were dreaming of a first (and last) win at home against the Saints in the Harlequins guise, with the London club expected to revive the Broncos brand from 2012.

The Crusaders also played their last Super League game, which ended in a 42-10 defeat at Wigan on the Friday night. Before the game the Warriors celebrated their 'Heritage' with a host of former players welcomed onto the pitch with trophies from Wigan's past and present and a bumper crowd of over 19,000 turned out as the Warriors put the defeat at Warrington behind them with a seven-try display. An early Liam Farrell score in the second half put the game to bed and Wigan cantered to victory, although Jarrod Sammut will take away with him the accolade of scoring Crusaders' last try in Super League.

The defeat meant Crusaders finished with the wooden spoon as Wakefield gave coach John Kear a farewell party, battling out a 26-14 home win over Bradford.

The Wildcats went ahead through tries from Paul Johnson and Ryan Tongia, although the Bulls did gain brief hope, with Kyle Briggs and Shaun Ainscough touching down within two minutes of each other. But a further Trinity score, when Michael Korkidas crashed over a minute before the break, left the visitors, already with both hookers off injured, chasing a game they were struggling to get to grips with. Tommy Lee added a fourth try on

FINAL SUPER LEAGUE TABLE - *Sunday 11th September*

	P	W	D	L	F	A	D	PTS
Warrington Wolves	27	22	0	5	1072	401	671	44
Wigan Warriors	27	20	3	4	852	432	420	43
St Helens	27	17	3	7	782	515	267	37
Huddersfield Giants	27	16	0	11	707	524	183	32
Leeds Rhinos	27	15	1	11	757	603	154	31
Catalan Dragons	27	15	1	11	689	626	63	31
Hull Kingston Rovers	27	14	0	13	713	692	21	28
Hull FC	27	13	1	13	718	569	149	27
Castleford Tigers	27	12	2	13	664	808	-144	26
Bradford Bulls	27	9	2	16	570	826	-256	20
Salford City Reds	27	10	0	17	542	809	-267	20
Harlequins	27	6	1	20	524	951	-427	13
Wakefield T Wildcats *	27	7	0	20	453	957	-504	10
Crusaders *	27	6	0	21	527	857	-330	8

* 4 points deducted for entering administration

the hour to make it 22-8 and, after Shad Royston grabbed another back for Bradford, Julien Rinaldi got the fans in party mood by sealing the victory a minute from time.

SUPER LEAGUE PLAY-OFFS
Saints at the double

Week One

Qualifying Play-offs

WARRINGTON WOLVES 47 HUDDERSFIELD GIANTS 0

Warrington underlined their Grand Final favouritism with a 47-0 hammering of fourth-placed Huddersfield at the Halliwell Jones Stadium in the first play-off game on the Friday.

Wolves boss Tony Smith played his trump card an hour before kick off, confirming Adrian Morley's return to action after an eye operation by naming the England prop in his starting 13, while Huddersfield were still without knee injury victim Leroy Cudjoe.

Huddersfield had no answers - they conceded six penalties in the first eight minutes trying to slow down the onslaught - but when Chris Riley stepped past Graeme Horne after Chris Bridge's pass had skidded beneath Ryan Atkins, with Bridge nailing the touchline conversion, the hosts had a position of dominance they never looked like conceding. By half-time, the lead had been stretched to 25-0 through tries to Bridge and Joel Monaghan, Matt King, and a second from Riley plus a Lee Briers field goal two minutes from the break. Scott Grix's sin-binning three minutes after the turnaround compounded a miserable night for a Giants side that had been expected to be a serious challenge.

The result meant Warrington had a weekend off to recharge, while Huddersfield would face a sudden death match at home.

WIGAN WARRIORS 18 ST HELENS 26

On the Sunday, Jonny Lomax guided third-placed St Helens to victory over their fiercest rivals to put them 80 minutes away from a sixth successive Grand Final appearance.

Saints had all the early pressure and got the breakthrough when Lomax and Lee Gaskell combined to send Paul Wellens through Harrison Hansen and Paul Deacon to cross, Jamie Foster converting for a 6-0 lead. They were 12-0 to the good when Jon Wilkin sent Michael Shenton though a gap and he in turn sent an inside ball for Lomax to race in under the posts. A penalty for interference saw Foster slot over the extras for a 14-0 advantage.

Wigan eventually crossed over with seconds remaining to half-time when Sean O'Loughlin got the ball out to Pat Richards who went in and around the back of the posts, Wellens choosing to appeal to the referee instead of cutting Richards off. The winger converted as Wigan went in trailing 14-6 at the break.

After a penalty for a flop from Wilkin, Liam Farrell and Brett Finch combined to send O'Loughlin in under the posts. Richards' conversion made it 14-12 to St Helens but Wigan had their tails up. But a great break from Lomax sent Tommy Makinson surging through a gap and moments later Saints extended their lead when Wellens collected a neat inside ball from Lomax to grab his second. Foster's conversion put them 20-12 in front.

Just before the hour mark James Graham shipped a short ball for Louie McCarthy-Scarsbrook to burst over the line. Foster's conversion made the score 26-12. Joel Tomkins did give Wigan a fighting chance with 13 minutes remaining when he stormed onto a pass from Tommy Leuluai to ground the ball, and Richards' conversion made it 26-18. But St Helens' defence was magnificent.

Elimination Play-offs

CATALAN DRAGONS 56 HULL KINGSTON ROVERS 6

The sixth-placed Dragons announced themselves potential Grand Final candidates with a demolition job on Hull KR in baking hot Perpignan on the Saturday night. The home side raced into an early lead they would not relinquish and, as it turned out, Rovers could only muster a single try as they were completely outplayed from start to finish.

It could have all been different, as in the second minute Sam Latus broke down the Hull KR right, managed to step the covering Clint Greenshields and was just brought to ground by a despairing tackle by Ian Henderson. From the play-the-ball Rovers shipped the ball left with a try on the cards but Steve Menzies latched onto a Liam Watts pass and raced 80 metres down field before handing on to Damien Blanch to touch down in the corner for his first of the night. Scott Dureau failed with his attempt from close to the touchline but departing Rovers coach Justin Morgan acknowledged it was a game-changing incident.

When Dureau added a 35th minute penalty from twenty metres the Dragons had a 22-0 half-time lead after two tries from the brilliant Menzies and another from Blanch.

Darryl Millard's try in the first set of six after the half-time break wrecked any faint hopes the visitors had of a comeback.

LEEDS RHINOS 42 HULL FC 10

Leeds coach Brian McDermott described his side as 'dark horses' in the lead up to the play-offs and the comment didn't appear too far off the mark after a comprehensive Sunday-evening elimination of the black and whites in the last game of 2011 at Headingley.

In wet conditions, all four Rhinos props put in strong performances, Kevin Sinfield and Brent Webb at the back directed operations while centre pairing Brett Delaney in his initial role – covering for injured Kallum Watkins and Carl Ablett – and Zak Hardaker were outstanding.

The difference was exemplified in the closing minutes of the first half as Hull forced a drop out but misjudgement from Danny Tickle and Richard Whiting saw it go into touch. Danny McGuire sent on-form Ryan Bailey on the charge and he stood tall in the tackle to release Brent Webb with a one-handed pass for a crucial try two minutes before the break. Suddenly Hull were 18 points down.

"It was certainly no fairytale finish, it was as poorly as we have played for some time and we were beaten in every facet," coach Richard Agar said after seeing his tenure at the KC Stadium come to an end.

Week Two

Preliminary Semi-finals

HUDDERSFIELD GIANTS 28 LEEDS RHINOS 34

Leeds - after a season in which coach Brian McDermott had been ridiculed by supporters and the Rhinos had been largely written off as an ageing team whose best days had gone - were still on course to become the most unlikely Super League champions since the introduction of the play-offs in 1998.

Having survived one scare that saw their lead diminish from 16-0 to 16-12, Leeds then endured one of the most startling swings in momentum ever witnessed in the play-offs. They were cruising at 34-12 with only 12 minutes remaining, when three Huddersfield tries in five minutes put the Giants only six points adrift, and they still had five minutes left to find the score that would have led to golden-point extra time. But they fell agonisingly short, and their season came shuddering to a painful halt.

Stand-in centre, 19-year-old Zak Hardaker, scored a brilliant hat-trick, with injured duo Carl Ablett and Kallum Watkins still out. Ryan Bailey was a stand-out, only able to play after a one-match ban in midweek for running in with a knee raised in the win over Hull had been overturned on appeal.

Leeds were now facing a trip to the red-hot favourites Warrington Wolves, who selected the Rhinos as their opponents in the Clubcall.

WIGAN WARRIORS 44 CATALAN DRAGONS 0

Wigan proved they wouldn't relinquish their Super League crown without a fight after coming through a bruising encounter with the Dragons with flying colours. The game had to be played on Sunday evening because of a soccer fixture the day before and the opening 20 minutes were tight. If Thomas Bosc's ninth minute effort had been awarded when the score was 2-0 and Lopini Paea's try under the posts not disallowed for a forward pass with the score at 12-0 then there could easily have been a different outcome. But apart from those two lapses the Warriors defended well throughout the first half and managed to carve out three tries of their own, with Sam Tomkins showing signs of returning to his best as they led 18-0 at the break.

The start of the second half was a carbon copy of the first, with big hits flying about, but the champions' class told in the end as they ran in four tries in the last quarter to keep alive their hopes of a first league and cup double since 1995.

Stand-off Paul Deacon was a shock omission from the Wigan side as he was replaced in the halves by Thomas Leuluai, while Catalans prop David Ferriol had been suspended for one game after being found guilty of using his knees in the tackle against Hull KR. The win set up a revenge mission for Wigan against St Helens, this time away from home.

Week Three

Qualifying Semi-finals

WARRINGTON WOLVES 24 LEEDS RHINOS 26

Leeds Rhinos booked their sixth trip to Old Trafford in eight years as Kevin Sinfield's place in Headingley folklore was assured when, with 78 minutes and two seconds gone and the scores level, he stepped up and hit a penalty attempt straight through the uprights.

Sinfield had already had one attempt at goal, falling just short with a 50-metre penalty six minutes from time. But when Richie Myler shot out of the line in an attempt to block the Leeds skipper's 78th-minute field-goal attempt, touch-judge James Child and referee Steve Ganson made one of the biggest calls in recent memory. Sinfield kept his cool, Lee Briers and Matt King slumped to their knees, and the Rhinos' fans went delirious.

Carl Ablett, returning from injury, opened the scoring when he raced onto Danny McGuire's grubber. Sinfield's conversion gave Leeds a shock six-point lead. However, Chris Bridge sent Joel Monaghan over after King patted down Briers' cross-field kick. Warrington piled forward in search of a second, despite Brett Hodgson limping off after half an hour with an ankle ligament strain. Less than a minute later stand-in fullback Chris Riley was on hand to edge Warrington ahead from Michael Monaghan's pass as he stepped inside Ablett.

Leeds levelled within 50 seconds of the restart when Ryan Hall intercepted Simon Grix's pass to a two-man overlap just inside his own half, but when King took Myler's long pass and powered past four defenders to score from a quick tap penalty for offside eight minutes later, Warrington appeared back in control.

But Rob Burrow scampered clear on half way before finding McGuire on his shoulder. Ryan Atkins raced back to halt the Leeds halfback, but he lobbed out a perfect offload for Hall to claim his second try of the night. Then Burrow dashed over from 40 metres after supporting Webb's break before Riley's second, from Briers' inside pass levelled it up and set up an extraordinary finish. Leeds had become the first team outside the top four to make the Grand Final.

ST HELENS 26 WIGAN WARRIORS 18

St Helens ended Wigan's reign as Super League Champions, twice coming from behind to book their place in the Grand Final for the sixth consecutive season.

Wigan had the better of the opening 20 minutes. A penalty for not square saw them take the lead from the boot of Pat Richards. And it wasn't long before Wigan extended their advantage when Jamie Foster misjudged Thomas Leuluai's kick to allow Josh Charnley to swoop on the ball to score. Richards couldn't add the goal as Wigan led 6-0. But Saints levelled matters after a spell of pressure inside Wigan's half as Lee Gaskell, at the heart of all St Helens' attacks, took a ball from Jonny Lomax to ghost through and crash through Sam Tomkins over the line. Jamie Foster's conversion and a penalty saw Saints take a surprise 8-6 lead before Wigan hit back to lead at the break thanks to Eamon O'Carroll's first try of the season.

Richards thought he was on his way for the opening try of the second half as he raced down the touchline, but the touch-judge had adjudged that George Carmont had knocked the ball on in the tackle before the winger set off on his run. That let-off for Saints worked in their favour two minutes later, as Leuluai and Charnley failed to collect James Roby's kick, and Paul Wellens dived over to score his 200th career try. Foster converted and Saints now led 14-12.

Liam Farrell gave away a penalty deep inside his own half for not standing square, and Foster gave Saints a four-point lead with his fourth goal of the night. St Helens once again took full advantage, and a fantastic cut-out ball from Jon Wilkin saw Foster dive over in the corner. Although his conversion attempt was off target, Saints now led 20-12 with 21 minutes left and defended brilliantly before Roby scooted over from acting halfback. Foster's conversion made it 26-12 with five minutes to go.

Sam Tomkins capitalised on a kick from Sean O'Loughlin to touch down after the Warriors got the ball back from the kick-off and Richards converted. Wigan trailed 26-18 with three minutes remaining, and Saints held out.

For the first time in the Super League era, neither of the two top sides in the regular season - Warrington and Wigan - had reached the Grand Final.

SUPER LEAGUE GRAND FINAL
Leeds' famous five

Leeds' fifth Super League title win under the wet skies of Manchester went down as their greatest achievement. Not only did the Rhinos become the first team to win the Grand Final from outside the top three, ending the regular season in fifth position, but after round 21, when they lost to the Dragons in France, they were in eighth spot in the table, written off by some, including many of their own supporters.

The Rhinos proved themselves true champions as they stunned Saints with four tries in the last 16 minutes of the game. After an hour of a spectacular climax to the season St Helens, slight favourites before kick-off, had come back from an 8-2 half-time deficit to lead 16-8 on the back of 20 minutes of controlled football that had reaped two tries.

ENGAGE SUPER LEAGUE GRAND FINAL

Saturday 8th October 2011

LEEDS RHINOS 32 ST HELENS 16

RHINOS: 1 Brent Webb; 23 Ben Jones-Bishop; 27 Zak Hardaker; 12 Carl Ablett; 5 Ryan Hall; 13 Kevin Sinfield (C); 6 Danny McGuire; 8 Kylie Leuluai; 9 Danny Buderus; 10 Jamie Peacock; 11 Jamie Jones-Buchanan; 3 Brett Delaney; 21 Chris Clarkson. Subs (all used): 7 Rob Burrow; 16 Ryan Bailey; 17 Ian Kirke; 14 Ali Lauitiiti.
Tries: Burrow (34), Webb (65), Hall (70), Ablett (74), Hardaker (80); **Goals:** Sinfield 6/7.
SAINTS: 1 Paul Wellens (C); 28 Tom Makinson; 3 Michael Shenton; 5 Francis Meli; 22 Jamie Foster; 25 Lee Gaskell; 20 Jonny Lomax; 10 James Graham (C); 9 James Roby; 11 Tony Puletua; 12 Jon Wilkin; 4 Iosia Soliola; 16 Paul Clough. Subs (all used): 19 Andrew Dixon; 14 Scott Moore; 15 Louie McCarthy-Scarsbrook; 17 Gary Wheeler.
Tries: Makinson (50), Shenton (55); **Goals:** Foster 4/5.
Rugby Leaguer & League Express Men of the Match:
Rhinos: Rob Burrow; *Saints:* Lee Gaskell.
Penalty count: 5-7; **Half-time:** 8-2; **Referee:** Phil Bentham; **Attendance:** 69,107 *(at Old Trafford, Manchester).*

St Helens had lost both Paul Wellens and Michael Shenton to injury by the final quarter and three tries that took Leeds to their win were scored down Saints' right channel where Shenton had been impenetrable.

But nothing could take the glister off Leeds' fourth Super League title win of the last five years after a magnificent game.

Rob Burrow became the first player to win the Harry Sunderland Trophy twice in Super League Grand Finals. Coach Brian McDermott, the target of most of the criticism directed at Leeds during the season, persisted with using the former Great Britain scrum-half off the bench and his tactic was truly vindicated on the game's biggest stage. Burrow didn't come into the game until the 26th minute but eight minutes later he was in at the left of the posts for the first try of the game to complete one of the great individual scores of any final. And with just over ten minutes left on the clock it was Burrow who gave Leeds the lead again when he crabbed across to the left centre before shooting through and delivering the perfect pass for Ryan Hall to race into the corner.

Jamie Peacock recorded his seventh Grand Final win and was chiefly responsible for Leeds getting on the front foot in the opening stages. Kevin Sinfield captained and directed a Leeds Grand Final-winning side for the fifth time, kicking six goals from seven attempts, including a 45-metre shot on 67 minutes that levelled the scores. Back-rower

Carl Ablett's strength in the centre proved another of McDermott's masterstrokes. In the other centre was a winger, Zak Hardaker, a teenager who the previous year starred in the Championship, and who scored Leeds' last try just before the final hooter sounded.

The only change to the Rhinos side from the Qualifying semi-final win at Warrington was Ali Lauitiiti being named on the bench and playing his 200th game for Leeds, Weller Hauraki dropping out.

St Helens coach Royce Simmons had created the headline of the build-up by leaving Leon Pryce out of the 19-man squad, denying him the chance of a record tenth Grand Final appearance. Pryce's injury-hit season had allowed local product Lee Gaskell the chance to cement his place at stand-off. When he produced the only 40/20 of the game on 57 minutes, with Jamie Foster extending the lead to six points from a penalty straight after, the rangy Gaskell was on his way to being man of the match, that is before the Rhinos totally dominated the last quarter to inflict Saints' fifth successive Grand Final defeat.

The action was relentless from the first kick-off, but the first points didn't come until the 24th minute when Peacock was penalised for interference on Gaskell 15 metres from the posts. Foster stepped up to kick the first two points. Straight after, Sinfield levelled the scores with a 42-metre goal when Sia Soliola was penalised for knocking the ball out of Danny Buderus's hand after he was tackled.

There was nothing between the sides until the 34th minute when Burrow took the ball at first receiver 50 metres out with nothing obvious on. Burrow paused, stepped off his left foot, ducked under and through the tackles of Tony Puletua and Scott Moore and was away, stepping past Wellens and winning the race for the line. Sinfield's conversion made it 8-2.

Saints were relentless as more rain welcomed the sides back onto the pitch. Foster's restart bounced dead to signal the start of the onslaught. In the next five minutes Leeds had to drop out from under their own posts four times. Webb twice had to make Shenton grubbers safe, while Wellens trapped McGuire in-goal from Gaskell's grubber. Something had to give and in the 46th minute we thought it had when Andrew Dixon looked to have beaten Burrow and Jones-Buchanan to Lomax's grubber, but the video referee ruled Dixon has knocked on. It was a close call.

Leeds looked to have weathered the storm as Sinfield's raking kick forced Wellens back behind his line and James Graham knocked on 40 metres out. Sinfield hit a field-goal attempt to the right of the posts from 20 metres and at the other end of the field Peacock spilled the ball.

Tommy Makinson's grubber looked to have forced another GLDO but after referee Phil Bentham awarded the drop out, he was persuaded to go to the video ref, who ruled that

Rhinos crowned five-time Super League Champions

Makinson - by now filling in at fullback after Wellens had limped off - had reached out around Webb to touch down as the ball and the two players slid towards dead. Foster's conversion levelled the scores.

Within minutes, Saints were in front. Ben Jones-Bishop couldn't take a Lomax bomb and a complex set move from the scrum involving Roby, Lomax and Gaskell created the space for Shenton to go past Hall. Foster missed the conversion but after Gaskell's 40/20 - St Helens tried the same scrum move, this time with Roby running the ball in - Foster made it 14-8 with a penalty when Leeds were penalised for offside.

Sinfield put the kick-off straight into dead and Foster hammered over another two points from halfway.

The momentum was well and truly with Saints

Leeds captain Kevin Sinfield and Harry Sunderland winner Rob Burrow
show off the Super League trophy

but a high tackle by Moore on Jones-Bishop gave Leeds respite, and within seconds Shenton was lying prostrate after colliding with Soliola in a tackle on Chris Clarkson.

Leeds' speed of play went up a notch and though an attack petered out as McGuire's pass ended with Hall in touch, within three minutes Webb was over on the left through Soliola and Dixon's tackle. Sinfield kicked the touchline goal as coach Royce Simmons chose to take Graham, who was baffled by the move, off for a breather. Lauitiiti was on and a ball steal on him by Wilkin gave Sinfield the chance to level with a straight and true 45-metre kick.

Saints got the kick-off back but Jones-Bishop bundled Gaskell into touch before Burrow's second piece of magic was the gamebreaker. Moore once again couldn't collar Burrow as he ran to the left from dummy half. The speed of the break was breathtaking as Burrow dummied Francis Meli and, when James Roby tackled him from behind, delivered the perfect pass for Hall to score, despite Makinson's desperate tackle. Sinfield's kick was just wide.

A stunning ad-libbed attack at the end of the next set, when Sinfield feigned to kick on his own 40-metre line but instead sent Webb tearing through a gap, ended when Hardaker's kick was kicked dead by Meli. A minute later Buderus's pass sent Ablett into the left corner through Meli and Lomax's tackle. Sinfield nailed that kick and there was no way back for St Helens.

There was a minor melee four minutes from time when Ryan Bailey mediated in a tussle on the ground between Ablett and Wilkin and was immediately substituted. Lauitiiti looked to have ended his Leeds career with a try when he went under the posts after St Helens tried to keep the ball alive under their own posts but he was held up in a four-man tackle. But then Gaskell's chip was picked off by Hardaker who had the pace to make the line despite Foster's ankle tap. By the time Sinfield kicked his sixth goal the Rhinos' celebrations had already begun, with Bailey conducting the singing from behind Sinfield's back.

SUPER LEAGUE XVI AWARDS

MAN OF STEEL
Rangi Chase
(Castleford Tigers)

*(chosen by
players poll)*

SUPER LEAGUE DREAM TEAM
(previous appearances in italics)
1 Sam Tomkins (Wigan Warriors) *2009, 2010*
2 Tom Briscoe (Hull FC)
3 Kirk Yeaman (Hull FC) *2006*
4 George Carmont (Wigan Warriors) *2008*
5 Joel Monaghan (Warrington Wolves)
6 Rangi Chase (Castleford Tigers)
7 Scott Dureau (Catalan Dragons)
8 James Graham (St Helens) *2008, 2010*
9 James Roby (St Helens) *2007, 2010*
10 Garreth Carvell (Warrington Wolves)
11 Ben Westwood (Warrington Wolves) *2008, 2010*
12 Steve Menzies (Catalan Dragons)
13 Sean O'Loughlin (Wigan Warriors) *2010*

YOUNG PLAYER OF THE YEAR
Jonny Lomax (St Helens)

COACH OF THE YEAR
Trent Robinson (Catalan Dragons)

CLUB OF THE YEAR
Catalan Dragons

TOP TRY SCORER Sam Tomkins (Wigan Warriors)
for scoring 26 regular season tries

TOP METRE MAKER James Roby (St Helens)
for making 5,000 regular season metres

TOP TACKLER Danny Houghton (Hull FC)
for making 1,060 regular season tackles

MIKE GREGORY SPIRIT OF RUGBY LEAGUE AWARD
Harry Jepson

ALBERT GOLDTHORPE MEDAL
Rangi Chase (Castleford Tigers)

ROOKIE OF THE YEAR
Jermaine McGillvary
(Huddersfield Giants)

CLUB OF THE YEAR
Warrington Wolves

LIFETIME ACHIEVEMENT AWARD
Mike 'Stevo' Stephenson

CAREER ACHIEVEMENT AWARD
Robbie Hunter-Paul

2
CHAMPIONSHIPS 2011

CHAMPIONSHIP SEASON
Wild Rovers

FEATHERSTONE ROVERS eased some of the pain of 2010 by lifting the Championship title after a comprehensive Grand Final defeat of Sheffield.

Daryl Powell's superbly well-drilled and enterprising side again topped the table at the end of the regular season, but having lost the 2010 showpiece to Halifax in golden point extra-time, and then crashed out of the 2011 Northern Rail Cup in the same fashion, doubts surrounded their temperament in big games. But they blew that myth away as talisman Liam Finn inspired a complete demolition of the Eagles at Warrington, the superb scrum-half scoring 20 points in a 40-4 win.

It was rich reward for another admirable season under Powell, who retained his crown as Championship Coach of the Year after Rovers lost just one league game all season, at Leigh in March. Again their success was built on the two towers of strength up front, Stuart Dickens and Tony Tonks, with skipper Dickens joined in the Championship Dream Team by wingers Bryn Powell and Tommy Saxton plus stand-off Andy Kain.

Powell and Saxton were joint top try scorers, with Finn, Kain, Jonny Hepworth, Ian Hardman, Andrew Bostock, Sam Smeaton and impressive late-season arrival Ben Cockayne all also reaching double figures.

Unsung heroes included Tim Spears, Matty Dale and Ben Kaye, with the club continuing to push its excellent youth development programmes.

LEIGH CENTURIONS stood toe-to-toe with Featherstone for much of the season and also lifted the Northern Rail Cup after a memorable final, only for their season to peter out. The withdrawal of chairman Arthur Thomas's long-standing funding midway through the year led to financial worries that escalated after the campaign finished, and coach Ian Millward announced he would be departing to Castleford before the end of the season.

But Millward still oversaw a side that came within one match of the Grand Final, having already ticked the box for the next round of Super League applications with that stunning Blackpool win over Halifax. Tom Armstrong's last-gasp try sealed a thrilling 20-16 win, and gave the Centurions fans a day to remember.

The undoubted star of the season was scrum-half Jamie Ellis, who finished with 34 tries, the competition's Player and Young Player of the Year awards, and a move back into Super League with Hull FC.

His halfback partner Martyn Ridyard was another key figure, while back-rowers James Taylor, Stuart Littler and especially Tommy Goulden were among the stand-out players of the entire Championship. Centre Mick Nanyn continued his rise up Rugby League's all-time top points scorers list, and Chris Hill's magnificent form earned a move to Warrington Wolves.

And fortunately, after weeks of uncertainty, the club's future looked secured when the RFL agreed to advance central funding payments to help meet an unpaid tax bill and avoid a potential winding up order.

BATLEY BULLDOGS continued their rise up the Championship ladder, but their coach Karl Harrison still felt they should have achieved more than an early play-offs exit to Halifax.

Harrison's side mixed with the competition's best for much of the year, aside from a four-match losing streak in July.

Captain Paul Handforth was again the key man for much of the season, earning valuable support from returning scrum-half Paul Mennell. Winger Alex Brown finished as top try scorer with 12 despite a mid-season exit to rugby union, with hard-working second-rower Alex Bretherton finishing just one try behind.

Back row was certainly a strong point for the Bulldogs, with both Dane Manning making the Rugby League World Dream Team, while Byron Smith produced some of the best form of his career at prop.

Ian Preece, Wayne Reittie and Danny Maun were others to have their moments in what was general a positive campaign at Mount Pleasant.

There was disappointment when the popular Harrison announced he was leaving the club to join Halifax, and quickly took Handforth, Manning, Reittie, Adam Robinson and Sean Hesketh with him.

But that was quickly eased when the Bulldogs confirmed the appointment of John Kear as his successor, and a host of new signings brought fresh hope again at Batley, who were named Championship Club of the Year.

SHEFFIELD EAGLES were another club to continue in an upward trajectory as Mark Aston's team finished fourth and then made the Grand Final against the odds.

The Warrington showdown against Featherstone was undoubtedly one match too far for the gallant Eagles, but their loyal band of supporters will long cherish play-off wins over Widnes, Halifax and Leigh.

Samoans Misi Taulapapa and Quentin Laulu-Togagae alternated at fullback as Sheffield never lacked strike power from the back.

Papua New Guinean Menzie Yere, finished as top try scorer following a typically destructive campaign out wide, while experienced hooker Andrew Henderson was a model of consistency at number nine.

The club's own Player of the Year was loose forward Joe Hirst, and Dane McDonald and Alex Szostak are also deserving of mention.

But while those established figures – alongside long-serving props Mitchell Stringer and Jack Howieson – provided the backbone of the side, Aston's focus on youth development also paid rich dividends. Scholarship graduate Corey Hanson finished the season as a first team regular with 12 tries, while youngsters Sam Scott and Pat Smith also played big roles.

A fifth placed finish and first week play-offs exit was not the way that **WIDNES VIKINGS** would have chosen to march back into Super League.

An undefeated Northern Rail Cup group stages campaign – including winning at Featherstone – had hinted at a much brighter season, but a home loss to Hunslet followed by a thumping defeat to Leigh were a better indication of what was to come. Two wins in seven at that stage of the season saw the Vikings fall off the pace at the top, and thought a run of seven straight wins raised hopes of a play-off charge, the year ended with five consecutive defeats.

Having to announce which players would be leaving the club midway through the season can only have been a hindrance to coach Denis Betts, who will prefer to focus on the form of several emerging young players. One of those, Kiwi back-rower MacGraff Leuluai, was the Vikings' best in 2011, while prop Ben Kavanagh produced some encouraging display.

Elsewhere, Halifax-bound centre Steve Tyrer was top try and points scorer with 22 and 300 respectively, while winger Paddy Flynn – who will make the step up to the top flight - bagged 14 tries.

Reigning champions **HALIFAX** were playing catch-up for much of the season, before a late-season charge ultimately ran out of steam in the play-offs at Sheffield.

Championship Season

Before that, Grand Final-winning coach Matt Calland had steered Fax to the Northern Rail Cup final after another golden point win against Featherstone in the semi-final.

There, Fax were ahead against Leigh in the second half, before the scores were levelled and Tom Armstrong ultimately won it for the Centurions.

By that time, former Great Britain boss Brian Noble had been appointed as a coaching consultant at the club, and he stayed when Calland left not long after the NRC final. Damian Ball took charge on a caretaker basis, and after steering Fax into sixth spot, oversaw an excellent play-off win at Batley before they crashed out 50-12 at Sheffield the following week.

Hooker Sean Penkywicz was Fax's best for much of the year, while the back three of Miles Greenwood, and especially prolific wingers Paul White and Rob Worrincy, caused teams problems all season.

In the pack, Sam Barlow was always a handful and Makali Aizue became more prominent as the season unfolded, while Jacob Fairbank earned a Young Player of the Year nomination and Bob Beswick was rarely anything other than consistent.

It was all change at the club at the end of the season, with former playing favourite Karl Harrison taking up a three-year contract as coach.

HUNSLET HAWKS avoided relegation on merit under player-coach Paul March, whose side reflected his own tenacious approach for much of the season.

They got off to a flying start with a draw against York and victory at Widnes, and safety was eventually secured with a late-season win over Barrow and bonus point against Halifax.

In between the Hawks were often inconsistent but rarely lost their spirit, even though March himself was restricted to just 14 starts in all competitions. His twin brother David was again a hugely influential figure, while stand-off Danny Grimshaw was among the most potent attacking weapons in the competition.

Grimshaw just edged the equally impressive Danny Ratcliffe as top try scorer, with hard-working winger Waine Pryce not far behind. Tommy Haughey, James Houston and Adam Sullivan led the forward effort up front, while young prop Andrew Yates hinted at a bright future.

March made a surprise exit soon after the season had finished, and was replaced by respected former Keighley coach Barry Eaton.

YORK CITY KNIGHTS benefited from the RFL's end-of-year Championship restructuring to remain in the higher division despite initially finishing in a relegation place.

The Knights still had a chance of reaching the all-important eighth place going into the final game at Sheffield, before slipping to one of a number of heavy defeats.

But in between those they produced some excellent results under coach Dave Woods, not least completing the double over Dewsbury and comprehensively beating Halifax 22-8 in front of the television cameras in August.

It was not enough to save Woods his job – despite having led the Knights to promotion ahead of scheduled the previous year – and he was replaced by player-coach Chris Thorman during the close season.

Thorman was a key figure in several of the Knights' five league wins, while his halfback partner Jon Presley top scored with 14 tries in all competitions. Forward Matt Garside was the next highest with 11, hinting at a lack of strike power out wide.

York's strengths certainly seemed to come in the pack, where props Alex Benson and Nathan Freer were excellent, Duane Straugheir impressed in the second row, and Jack Lee never stopped prompting and probing from hooker.

DEWSBURY RAMS' Championship status was also preserved by the end-of-season reshuffle, and more specifically Barrow Raiders' demise.

Rams' coach Warren Jowitt felt that his side would have been clear of danger had they managed to win several close contest that ended in defeat, not least those two losses to rivals York.

A shocking mid-season run of form that saw Jowitt's side go 14 matches without a win in all competitions plunged them into relegation trouble, and although they rallied to win two from three, they still finished just one place above Toulouse.

But the Rams commendably stood by Jowitt following his achievements in the past season, and the former Hull and Bradford forward was confident of assembling a side capable of making the play-offs in 2012.

Scrum-half Dominic Brambani earned a return to Sheffield along with centre Scott Turner, but top try scorer Austin Buchanan and the ever-consistent Rob Spicer remained at the Rams.

Anthony England and James Lockwood were picked-up by Featherstone after their performances caught the eye, while other players worthy of mention include Michael Wainwright, James Craven and Luke Blake.

TOULOUSE OLYMPIQUE's final season in the Championship ended in disappointing fashion with just four league wins.

Their three-year adventure included several high points, but few of them came in 2011 as Gilles Dumas' squad struggled to compete.

Dumas certainly wasn't helped by arguably the most crippling injury list in the entire competition, which robbed him of key players for much of the season.

They still managed to beat Halifax at home early on, and staged a remarkable second-half comeback to beat York at the Huntington Stadium in July.

But sprinkled in between were a few heavy defeats, the worst of which was a 90-10 hammering at champions Featherstone in early July.

Young Australian halfback Darren Nicholls was arguably Toulouse's best player, and finished as top try scorer with 19 in total.

Utility back Gregory White also reached double figures, while the club's impressive development work saw the likes of Kevin Larroyer and Yoan Tisseyre play big roles.

Toulouse also made the knock-out stages of the Northern Rail Cup at their first attempt, and will maintain a link with the English game when they enter the competition again in 2012.

Few, if any, sets of supporters had to endure the kind of 2011 that **BARROW RAIDERS** fans did, as an already stuttering campaign was completely derailed by the club's major salary cap scandal.

Raiders had already been docked six points – effectively ending their play-off hopes – when they were eventually docked all 29 they had acquired for a series of breaches of operational rules.

That led to relegation and their controversial chairman Des Johnston being banned from being involved with the sport for eight years, and later debts of over £550,000 were revealed.

The club appointed a new board of directors and coach in local hero Darren Holt, and were looking to acquire a more stable footing for the long-term future.

Incredibly, Holt was the club's fourth coach of the year, after the prompt coming and going of first Garry Schofield and then his assistant Nigel Wright, before bringing Dave Clark back to Craven Park for a fourth stint in charge.

There were a handful of highlights for supporters to reflect on.

Among those was a stirring April win at Halifax and an August home win over in-form Sheffield, but less memorable was a thumping at Hunslet as their season faded away.

Fortunately for retiring legend Gary Broadbent it finished on a high with his late conversion in a 42-28 win in Toulouse, which also included a hat-trick for top try scorer Andy Ballard.

Centre Liam Harrison was outstanding and forwards Matt James and Michael Knowles rarely let their standards drop, but everyone connected with the club was hoping for significantly less drama in 2012.

CHAMPIONSHIP ONE SEASON
Pride in the Lions

SWINTON LIONS' blistering start to the Championship One season was enough to secure the competition's title and promotion to the higher level.

Coach of the Year Steve McCormack's side were always the division's pacesetters after going undefeated for their first 11 games, dropping a single point in a draw at Whitehaven.

They stuttered a little in July with two consecutive defeats, and finished with three losses from four, but by that time top spot was all but achieved after a supremely consistent first half of the campaign.

Key to that start were halfbacks Martin Ainscough and player-assistant coach Ian Watson, who provided the perfect balance of strike threat and organisation in the middle of the field.

That allowed the Lions' backs to thrive, not least fullback or winger Ian Mort, who set a new record for points in a season and was also top try scorer with 25 in all.

Mort was rewarded with the Championship One Player of the Year crown, and was joined in the Rugby League World Dream Team by Watson and veteran hooker Mark Smith.

Out wide, Rob Foxen and Gavin Dodd found themselves among the tries, though the Lions' success was ultimately built on the hard work of forwards such as Lee Wingfield, Dale Cunniffe, young prop Warren Thompson, impressive loose forward Phil Joseph and Darren Hawkyard.

With Karl Ashall, Mike Morrison and Neil Holland also contributing, the title was assured before a last day defeat to Rochdale in front of 1,063 at the Willows.

But just days later the season finished on a significant low point with the death of popular prop Dana Wilson in a car accident, casting a shadow on what was otherwise a memorable year for the club.

KEIGHLEY COUGARS were Swinton's biggest rivals for much of the season, and although their title challenge faltered amid mid-season inconsistency, they regrouped under player-coach Jason Demetriou to win the play-off final and promotion to the Championship.

Australian veteran Demetriou was Cougars' star man for the majority of the season, leading his side from the front from either stand-off or loose forward.

The arrival of London Skolars playmaker Jy-Mel Coleman eventually took some responsibilities off his shoulders, and it seemed to benefit the side in crucial wins over Rochdale in the play-offs and Workington in the final the week after.

Demetriou had several talented youngsters in his ranks, not least joint top try scorer Ben Sagar, back-rower Richard Jones and fullback James Haythornthwaite, plus dual registration signing Jake Normington. In the pack, Andy Shickell and Scott Law provided the platform for experienced hookers James Feather and Jamaine Wray to thrive, and Will Cartledge equalled Sagar's tally of 11 tries from the back row.

Olly Pursglove, Ryan Benjafield and Danny Lawton also played important roles, while Gavin Duffy's confirmed his status as one of the competition's best wingers.

With Michael Korkidas, Danny Jones and Paul March among Demetriou's new signings for 2012, there were high hopes at Cougar Park that the club could begin to recapture the golden era of the 1990s.

WORKINGTON TOWN fell one hurdle short of their ultimate goal of promotion, but that should not detract from another season of progress under joint coaches Martin Oglanby and Gary Charlton.

They were again nominated for the Coach of the Year award, while hooker Jack Pedley eased his disappointment at missing the play-off final with a broken ankle by taking the Young Player of the Year prize.

Pedley improved as the season unfolded – a pattern that was repeated by the squad as a whole, after a stuttering start and a run of one win from five games in April and May.

When they did find their feet, veteran halfback Darren Holt excelled, earning a nomination for the Player of the Year award.

His halfback partner Scott Kaighan ran in an impressive 25 tries in all, with threequarters Elliot Miller, John Patrick, Aaron Low and retiring veteran Neil Frazer also among the tries.

So too was outstanding Aussie back-rower Jarrad Stack, who led a big pack that also featured significant contributions from Kris Coward, Karl Olstrum, Mike Whitehead and mid-season signing Dave Armitstead.

Injuries hit the squad hard at times, but Brett Carter and Ruari McGoff remained consistent members of the team.

The aim now for Oglanby and Charlton will be to go one step further in 2012, as Town's sensible and gradual progression continues.

ROCHDALE HORNETS were another club who will look back on 2011 with pride despite falling, literally, minutes short of making the play-off final.

Young coach John Stankevitch's side were clinging onto a narrow lead in the final eliminator at Keighley before the Cougars stormed home in the closing minutes.

But for a team built on a strict budget, fourth place and a good play-off run represented a big effort for Hornets and Stankevitch, whose reputation continues to grow.

He had one of Championship One's stand-out players in back-rower Craig Ashall, who featured at hooker, second row and loose forward.

Stand-off Paul Crook and his outstanding kicking game came into its own in the closing stages of the season as Hornets recorded home play-off wins over Doncaster and Oldham, having won at champions Swinton the week before.

Dale Bloomfield narrowly edged out opposite winger Andy Saywell for the honour of leading try scorer, while hooker Steve McDermott came of age after skipper Phil Wood was ruled out for the vast majority of the season with a knee injury sustained in a friendly against Warrington.

Stankevitch also lost several other members of his squad to retirement or emigration towards the beginning of the year – but with John Cookson, Dayne Donoghue, Wayne English and Dave Newton providing consistency and commitment, they almost upset their more fancied rivals in the season run-in.

DONCASTER's league campaign was almost identical to Rochdale's, with points difference the only thing separating two clubs who run a strict pay-as-you-play policy.

That Hornets edged out Tony Miller's charges in the play-offs should not detract from an excellent campaign for the Dons, who will feel that they have much to build on for the 2012 season.

Championship One Season

Top try scorer Chris Spurr rolled back the years both at centre and second row, while Kyle Kesik earned a nomination for the Young Player of the Year award for his influential displays.

Fellow playmakers Scott Spaven, Craig Fawcett and Jack Ely were among others to impress, while Mick Butterfield was among Championship One's best fullbacks.

In the pack, Matt Carbutt, Craig Robinson and Adam Scott never wavered their efforts up front, and Grant Edwards made a big impact late in the campaign after returning from a nightmare injury.

The only real negative for the Dons was the mid-season story that broke in the national press, exposing their captain Shaun Leaf for betting against his own team.

Though the coverage was blown out of proportion in many people's eyes, Leaf was still banned 18 months by the RFL and will miss the entire 2012 season.

But there is still much for Miller and director Carl Hall to be positive about for the new season as they looked to continue their steady growth of the past two years.

WHITEHAVEN were always going to be up against it having incurred a nine-point deduction for entering administration, but would still have been in title contention were it not for a late-season stutter.

As it was, just three wins from their last seven league games ended any of those hopes, and they then exited the play-offs in the first week when they lost 34-16 at Doncaster.

But after the very existence of the club had come under threat at the beginning of the year, there was still much to admire in Haven's season.

David Seeds was nominated for the Coach of the Year as recognition for the role he played in first holding the club together and then assembling a fully competitive squad, before surprisingly stepping down at the end of the season.

He will be replaced by little-known Australian Don Gailer, who will have a hungry squad at his disposal, including 2011 Dream Team member Scott McAvoy, with Lee Doran becoming his assistant coach.

Among the other success stories of the season were young winger Loz Hamzat, established flyer Craig Calvert and hookers Carl Sice and Chris Smith, all of who were regularly among the tries.

Prop Paul Cullnean, young halfback Lewis Palfrey, fullback Craig Benson and loose forward Andrew Beattie were among other key Recreation Ground figures.

With more stability off the field this time around, Haven will hope to kick on further next season.

Having made four Grand Finals in a row prior to 2011, a seventh place finish and opening-week play-off exit could be seen as a failure for **OLDHAM**, but there was still much for the Roughyeds to be positive about.

Coach Tony Benson invested much of his faith in youth, which meant further development for the likes of Halifax-bound fullback Ben Heaton, threequarter Matthew Fogarty and winger Shaun Robinson.

Some of Oldham's older heads also had big campaigns, not least Dave Ellison, the vastly experienced Paul Noone and evergreen stand-off Neil Roden.

Hooker John Clough, winger Mark Brocklehurst and back-rower Valu Bentley were also mainstays of Benson's side.

But they were disappointed with the way their season ended with defeat in the play-offs at local rivals Rochdale, and will rue a sluggish start to the campaign.

A run of three straight league defeats in March and April, and another one in May and June, meant that they were always too far behind the division's pace setters to challenge for the title.

A comprehensive league double over Rochdale and stirring wins at Whitehaven and against Keighley showed what the Roughyeds were capable of on their day – and Benson was hoping for more of that on a consistent basis in 2012.

SOUTH WALES SCORPIONS failed to emulate their 2010 achievement of making the Championship One play-offs, but could still find plenty of cause for optimism about their future.

It was never going to be easy for the Scorpions in their second season in the competition, and they certainly weren't helped by the departure of respected and popular coach Anthony Seibold just prior to the start of the campaign.

The club chose not to directly replace him, instead using a combination of director of rugby Mark Rowley and captain Aled James.

And the makeshift team did manage to help Scorpions record a handful of notable results, not least a 40-20 May win over Oldham and a 32-24 victory against Keighley in June. But generally they lacked the consistency as a side to mount another successful play-off campaign.

Certain players certainly did not, however, with hooker Steve Parry a stand-out. Utility back Andrew Gay maintained his remarkable record of having played in every Scorpions game to date and top scored with 17 tries, while Christiaan Roets, Jamie Murphy, Curtis Cunningham and Ashley Bateman all played significant roles.

But perhaps the biggest plus was the form of youngsters Dalton Grant and Joe Burke, who ended up making their Super League debuts during a brief loan spell with Crusaders towards the end of the year.

LONDON SKOLARS' slow start to the season cost them a chance of making the top seven, but coach Joe Mbu saw enough promise to suggest they could make genuine progress up the table in 2012.

An excellent mid-campaign run that saw them win four times from six games raised hopes of a remarkable late charge, but they stuttered again towards the end.

Still, those home wins over Rochdale, Keighley, Oldham and South Wales Scorpions showed what Mbu's side were capable of on their day – the challenge now will be finding that form on a weekly basis.

One of the stars of the season was undoubtedly winger Ade Adebisi, who top scored with 17 tries. Another Skolars stalwart, Austen Aggrey, continued his remarkable transformation from winger to prop and caused problems for defences all season.

Other key performers included Dylan Skee and Oliver Purslow, while Mbu was cruelly robbed of two others, Neil Thorman and Matt Thomas, for much of the season through injury.

The club's outstanding community work in north London continued to bear fruit, with James Anthony and Aaron Small the latest two to make an impression at first team level.

GATESHEAD THUNDER finished bottom of the pile for a second consecutive season after a difficult campaign in the north east.

The year started with plenty of hope as respected coach Richard Pell recruited a host of new players. But the combinations never quite worked, and Pell moved on midway through the campaign, with director of rugby Chris Hood taking charge alongside former Thunder favourite Kevin Neighbour.

Neighbour was eventually appointed as the permanent successor following a series of encouraging performances towards the end of the season, which in general was one to forget. High points included a Challenge Cup win over amateurs Milford Marlins when many thought Thunder would slip up, and their only league points came courtesy of an April, 32-all draw at London Skolars.

There were also plenty of willing workers with the squad, including Player of the Year Will Bate, top points scorer Ryan Clarke, and hard-working regulars Jason Payne, Stephen Welton, and Michael Kelly.

Neighbour is confident he can inspire an upturn in fortunes in 2012, and with the club continuing to give its all in the local community, that would be welcomed by the sport.

NORTHERN RAIL CUP FINAL
Armstrong guns in

Jamie Ellis celebrates his second try of the game

Substitute Tom Armstrong's last-gasp try sealed a thrilling Northern Rail Cup win for Leigh in a classic final against Halifax.

Matt Calland's Fax dominated the first half and led 10-0 at the break, and Rob Worrincy's 67th minute try put them back in front going into the closing stages. But Leigh halfback Jamie Ellis then grabbed his second try to level the scores, and after Martyn Ridyard dummied a field-goal attempt, Armstrong crossed out wide to clinch matters with the last play of the game. It was heartbreaking for Fax, who led at half-time courtesy of Miles Greenwood and Stephen Bannister's tries.

With prop Chris Hill in outstanding form, Ian Millward's Centurions roared back after the restart, with Ellis and Hill crossing within nine second-half minutes of each other.

That was when Worrincy edged Halifax back in front, and they looked set to lift the trophy for the first time. But Ellis forced his way over again to set up the grandstand finale, and St Helens dual registration threequarter Armstrong then came up with his match-winning play.

Victory also meant that Leigh became the first club to tick the on-field playing box for the next round of Super League licence applications in 2014.

NORTHERN RAIL CUP FINAL

Sunday 17th July 2011

HALIFAX 16 LEIGH CENTURIONS 20

HALIFAX: 1 Miles Greenwood; 20 Paul White; 5 James Haley; 3 Jon Goddard; 23 Rob Worrincy; 6 Danny Jones; 7 Ben Black; 15 Jim Gannon; 13 Bob Beswick; 10 Neil Cherryholme; 16 Paul Smith; 24 Steve Bannister; 19 Jacob Fairbank. Subs (all used): 4 Dylan Nash; 8 Makali Aizue; 9 Sean Penkywicz; 12 Sam Barlow.
Tries: Greenwood (18), Bannister (28), Worrincy (67); **Goals:** Jones 2/4.
CENTURIONS: 1 Stuart Donlan; 2 Steve Maden; 3 Stuart Littler; 4 Mick Nanyn; 5 Dean McGilvray; 6 Martyn Ridyard; 25 Jamie Ellis; 8 Chris Hill; 9 John Duffy; 26 David Mills; 15 Andy Thornley; 12 Tommy Goulden; 11 James Taylor. Subs (all used): 7 Robbie Hunter-Paul; 13 Stephen Nash; 22 Tom Armstrong; 14 Adam Higson.
Tries: Ellis (47, 75), Hill (55), Armstrong (80); **Goals:** Nanyn 2/4.
Rugby Leaguer & League Express Men of the Match:
Halifax: Bob Beswick; *Centurions:* Chris Hill.
Penalty count: 9-7; **Half-time:** 10-0; **Referee:** Matthew Thomason; **Attendance:** 8,820 *(at Bloomfield Road, Blackpool).*

CHAMPIONSHIP PLAY-OFFS
In like Finn

Widnes Vikings' hopes of ending their stay in the Championship with a Grand Final appearance ended on the first weekend, as Sheffield Eagles began their own march to Warrington with a superb 36-20 win.

Fullback Quentin Laulu-Togagae started and finished the Sheffield scoring, crossing in the opening stages and then the 78th minute for Mark Aston's side. Widnes briefly threatened a comeback in the second half, but with Aussie Dane McDonald also crossing twice the Eagles eased into the next round.

They were joined there by Halifax, but produced an outstanding performance in front of the television cameras to beat Batley 32-22 at Mount Pleasant. Tries to Ian Preece and Daley Williams put the Bulldogs 12-0 up after 25 minutes, but they failed to take full advantage of the slope and were reeled into 12-6 at the break after James Haley's score. Further Fax tries to Stephen Bannister, Rob Worrincy, Sean Penkywicz and Bob Beswick sealed victory for the reigning champions, and ended a positive season for Batley on a disappointing note.

That meant that Halifax travelled to Sheffield on the second weekend, but it was a game too far for Damian Ball's side. The caretaker coach had to watch on as the Eagles brushed them aside 50-12 in a completely dominant performance. McDonald bagged another try double as did in-form hooker Andrew Henderson, helping Sheffield gain revenge for the 2010 play-offs exit at the Shay.

Sheffield's Misi Taulapapa tries to escape the clutches of Halifax's Sean Penkywicz

Championship Play-offs

Elsewhere that weekend, league leaders Featherstone Rovers booked their Grand Final place with an accomplished 35-20 win over Leigh.

Daryl Powell's charges got off to a flying start with Ben Cockayne and Ian Hardman tries within the first eight minutes. With winger Tom Saxton helping himself to a superb hat-trick of tries either side of half-time, Rovers eased to victory despite late tries to Martyn Ridyard and Mick Nanyn.

That meant a final eliminator between the Centurions and Eagles at the Leigh Sports Village, and it was Sheffield who prevailed 20-10. Aston's charges led 8-0 at the break courtesy of Sam Scott's sole first half try, and although Leigh hit back through Stuart Donlan, the visitors then took control. Two tries in three minutes from Vinny Finigan and Laulu-Togagae took the game away from the Centurions, and another late try from Nanyn came too late to make a difference.

Championship Grand Final

Featherstone Rovers capped three years of progress under coach Daryl Powell, as his on-field leader Liam Finn led his side to an emphatic Grand Final win.

Scrum-half Finn scored two first-half tries, made one for Ben Cockayne after the break, and kicked six goals from seven attempts.

Finn had plenty of support around him as Andy Kain terrorised the Sheffield defence early on and Jonny Hepworth caused endless problems from loose forward. Winger Tom Saxton followed up last year's man of the match performance

THE CO-OPERATIVE CHAMPIONSHIP GRAND FINAL

Sunday 2nd October 2011

FEATHERSTONE ROVERS 40 SHEFFIELD EAGLES 4

ROVERS: 1 Ian Hardman; 33 Ben Cockayne; 3 Sam Smeaton; 17 Greg Worthington; 5 Tom Saxton; 6 Andy Kain; 7 Liam Finn; 8 Tony Tonks; 9 Ben Kaye; 10 Stuart Dickens; 11 Jon Grayshon; 12 Tim Spears; 28 Jon Hepworth. Subs (all used): 18 Ross Divorty; 13 Matty Dale; 4 Andrew Bostock; 30 Kirk Netherton.
Tries: Spears (4), Finn (7, 39), Hardman (42), Cockayne (56), Hepworth (59), Saxton (79); **Goals:** Finn 6/7.
Sin bin: Netherton (54) - fighting.
EAGLES: 6 Quentin Laulu-Togagae; 5 Tim Bergin; 26 Corey Hanson; 1 Misi Taulapapa; 16 Vinny Finigan; 13 Dane McDonald; 7 Simon Brown; 8 Jack Howieson; 9 Andrew Henderson; 10 Mitchell Stringer; 11 Alex Szostak; 12 Peter Green; 19 Joe Hirst. Subs (all used): 22 Ryan Hepworth; 30 Sam Scott; 20 Pat Smith; 14 Jonny Woodcock.
Try: McDonald (12); **Goals:** Brown 0/1.
Sin bin: Hirst (54) - fighting.
Rugby Leaguer & League Express Men of the Match:
Rovers: Liam Finn; *Eagles:* Joe Hirst.
Penalty count: 7-11; **Half-time:** 18-4; **Referee:** Matthew Thomason; **Attendance:** 7,263 *(at Halliwell Jones Stadium, Warrington).*

with another stellar display, along with fellow back-three members Cockayne and Ian Hardman, and up front, the likes of Stuart Dickens, Tony Tonks and Tim Spears were physical and effective.

"It wasn't pretty at times, but these games are all about winning," Powell said, referring to the wet conditions. "It was so, so difficult to play expansive Rugby League out there, and that made it difficult for us because we're a footballing team – that's the way we've played all year.

"It's difficult to rein that in, but once we did that, that was the key really.

"I thought Sheffield gave us a real tough challenge after we got off to a good start, and put us under a lot of pressure."

Sheffield coach Mark Aston – Powell's long-time friend and former teammate – admitted it was one game too far for his brave side. Play-off wins over Widnes, Halifax and Leigh had taken their toll, and despite gutsy efforts from the likes of Joe Hirst and Andrew Henderson, they couldn't hold the rampant Featherstone attack.

"It was one too far for us, and we played against a very good Featherstone team," Aston said. "We've been outstanding for the last six weeks but today at times we looked like we had no idea out there.

"It's disappointing, but we have to look at the positives of what's happened this season. We got to a Grand Final, and we'll learn the lessons from that."

Sheffield were up against it from the fourth minute, when the first of several telling Kain contributions led to Tim Spears' opening try. Moments later Rovers were over again as Finn displayed his outstanding support play to make it 12-0.

Eagles rallied briefly and when Dane McDonald burrowed over from close range the gap was down to eight points. But crucially Powell's side scored again just before the

Tom Saxton and Andy Kain congratulate Jon Hepworth on his try

break through Finn, taking the contest away from their tiring opponents.

Four more tries followed in the second half as Rovers – cheered on by a huge support – celebrated in style.

Ian Hardman crossed within two minutes of the restart, before the prolific Cockayne grabbed his usual try. Loose forward Hepworth also got a deserved effort, before Saxton's late long-range effort put a seal on a stunning victory.

On the five-star performance of Finn, who polled 14 of the 19 votes for the Tom Bergin Trophy, Powell added: "Liam is an outstanding player and he's been outstanding for us for a couple of years now. He's a quality individual and a quality player, and I'm pleased he's here on a two-year contract."

CHAMPIONSHIP ONE PLAY-OFFS
Cougars return

Oldham's remarkable run of four consecutive Grand Finals came to an abrupt end at rivals Rochdale, who produced one of their best performances of the season to secure a 39-18 win. Stand-off Paul Crook was undoubtedly the key man, scoring two tries in a 21-point haul and seeing his kicking game cause the Roughyeds problems all afternoon. Three tries in the opening 16 minutes set Hornets on their way, and although Oldham responded through Neil Roden, Crook's second on 36 minutes game Hornets a commanding lead that they would never relinquish.

David Seeds' tenure as Whitehaven coach came to an end when he surprisingly resigned after their 34-16 defeat at Doncaster to spend more time with his family. Seeds had done a sterling job in helping to keep the club together after their financial woes, but his side were always struggling after falling 24-6 behind by half-time against an excellent Dons side.

Wingers Gareth Potts and Stuart Sanderson both bagged try doubles as Tony Miller's side booked a trip to Rochdale in the next round. There, they looked capable of advancing further as tries to Craig Robinson, Adam Scott and Chris Spurr put them 18-4 up at one point. But the home side roared back after the break, with winger Dale Bloomfield completing a hat-trick and Chris Hough scoring the match-winning try five minutes from the end of a 26-18 win.

Elsewhere that afternoon, Workington Town were booking their Grand Final place with a shock 19-10 win at Keighley. Town produced the perfect gameplan to beat the higher finishing Cougars, with Darren Holt's kicking game central to their win.

Veteran winger Neil Frazer scored twice and Elliot Miller once, leaving Keighley to face a sudden-death eliminator with Rochdale to reach the Grand Final. In that game seven days later, Jason Demetriou's side were still trailing by a point with ten minutes to go, with Rochdale hanging on amid a Cougar onslaught. Tries to Andy Saywell, Wayne English and Steve McDermott had kept John Stankevitch's side ahead on the scoreboard despite two Ben Sagar tries.

But the Cougars' dominance eventually told late on, with two tries to James Haythornthwaite and one to Jake Normington in the final stages completing a 38-23 win.

Championship One Grand Final

Jason Demetriou secured promotion for Keighley Cougars in his first season in charge as his influential performance was central to a comprehensive 32-12 win over Workington.

With Town having won at Cougar Park just two weeks earlier, a tight contest was expected between two well-matched sides. But instead Keighley got off to a flying start, and with Demetriou controlling matters from stand-off, they never relinquished their grip on the game.

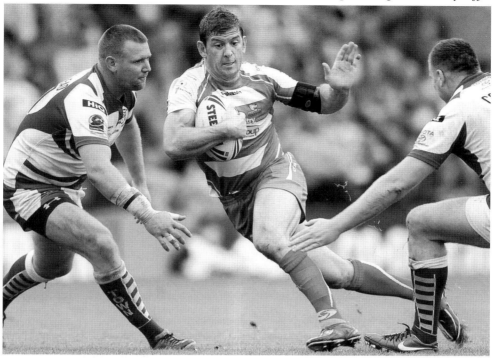

Keighley player-coach Jason Demetriou makes a break

Demetriou's squad had been among the favourites to win the Championship One title, only for a mid-season stutter to hit them hard. But they recovered well from that – and that play-off defeat to Workington – to secure their Championship place at the second time of asking.

The Cougars were 22-0 up after little more than half an hour, after tries to Danny Lawton, James Feather, Brendan Rawlins and Oliver Pursglove. They then stood firm as Town attempted a second-half comeback, which didn't get going until Scott Kaighan finally breached their defence in the 65th minute.

But the contest was over when powerful centre Jake Normington forced his way over soon after, making Neil Frazer's try – in his last appearance before retirement – scant consolation for Workington.

Normington's second in the final stages put a seal on victory, and allowed Demetriou to reflect on a job well done – not least in marshalling Darren Holt, who had been so influential in the meeting at Cougar Park.

"We needed to get to Holty," Demetriou said. "He kicked us to death the last two times we played. I nominated a couple of players and thought if we got him they didn't have a plan B. That's what happened – we took him out and they didn't have any answers.

"This is just as special as anything I did in Super League. I knew what it meant for everyone here at Keighley and I'm so proud of the players. They were awesome."

THE CO-OPERATIVE CHAMPIONSHIP ONE GRAND FINAL

Sunday 2nd October 2011

KEIGHLEY COUGARS 32 WORKINGTON TOWN 12

COUGARS: 18 James Haythornthwaite; 4 Danny Lawton; 22 Ben Sagar; 33 Jake Normington; 5 Gavin Duffy; 6 Jason Demetriou; 36 Jy-Mel Coleman; 17 Ryan Benjafield; 9 James Feather; 10 Scott Law; 11 Will Cartledge; 12 Oliver Pursglove; 21 Richard Jones. Subs (all used): 14 Jamaine Wray; 8 Andy Shickell; 16 Brendan Rawlins; 7 Ryan Smith.
Tries: Lawton (5), Feather (20), Rawlins (25), Pursglove (32), Normington (69, 77); **Goals:** Lawton 4/6.
TOWN: 1 Brett Carter; 2 Elliott Miller; 3 Jason Mossop; 4 Aaron Low; 5 Neil Frazer; 24 Darren Holt; 7 Scott Kaighan; 10 Kris Coward; 13 Karl Olstrum; 29 Dave Armitstead; 11 Mike Whitehead; 18 Joe McKenna; 12 Jarrad Stack. Subs (all used): 23 Marc Bainbridge; 15 Ruairi McGoff; 32 Chris Clough; 17 James Robinson.
Tries: Kaighan (65), Frazer (74); **Goals:** Holt 2/2.
Rugby Leaguer & League Express Men of the Match:
Cougars: Jason Demetriou; *Town:* Jarrad Stack.
Penalty count: 7-5; **Half-time:** 22-0; **Referee:** Tim Roby.
(at Halliwell Jones Stadium, Warrington).

THE CO-OPERATIVE CHAMPIONSHIP AWARDS

**DUAL CHAMPIONSHIP
AWARD WINNER:
Jamie Ellis
(Leigh Centurions)**

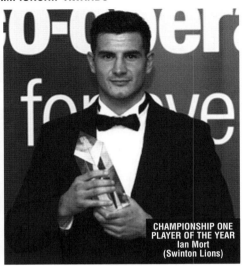

**CHAMPIONSHIP ONE
PLAYER OF THE YEAR
Ian Mort
(Swinton Lions)**

CHAMPIONSHIP

PLAYER OF THE YEAR
Jamie Ellis (Leigh Centurions)
Other nominees: Liam Finn (Featherstone Rovers),
Chris Hill (Leigh Centurions)

YOUNG PLAYER OF THE YEAR
Jamie Ellis (Leigh Centurions)
Other nominees: Jacob Fairbank (Halifax),
Dane Manning (Batley Bulldogs)

COACH OF THE YEAR
Daryl Powell (Featherstone Rovers)
Other nominees: Karl Harrison (Batley Bulldogs),
Ian Millward (Leigh Centurions)

RUGBY LEAGUE WORLD TEAM OF THE YEAR
1 Ian Hardman (Featherstone Rovers)
2 Tom Saxton (Featherstone Rovers)
3 Jon Hepworth (Featherstone Rovers)
4 Daley Williams (Batley Bulldogs)
5 Rob Worrincy (Halifax)
6 Paul Handforth (Batley Bulldogs)
7 Liam Finn (Featherstone Rovers)
8 Chris Hill (Leigh Centurions)
9 Andrew Henderson (Sheffield Eagles)
10 Stuart Dickens (Featherstone Rovers)
11 Tommy Goulden (Leigh Centurions)
12 Dane Manning (Batley Bulldogs)
13 Joe Hirst (Sheffield Eagles)

CLUB OF THE YEAR
Batley Bulldogs

COMMUNITY PROGRAMME OF THE YEAR
Gateshead Thunder

REFEREE OF THE YEAR
Matthew Thomason

CHAMPIONSHIP ONE

PLAYER OF THE YEAR
Ian Mort (Swinton Lions)
Other nominees: Craig Ashall (Rochdale Hornets),
Darren Holt (Workington Town),
Phil Joseph (Swinton Lions)

YOUNG PLAYER OF THE YEAR
Jack Pedley (Workington Town)
Other nominees: Karl Ashall (Swinton Lions),
Kyle Kesik (Doncaster)

COACH OF THE YEAR
Steve McCormack (Swinton Lions)
Other nominees:
Gary Charlton & Martin Oglanby (Workington Town),
David Seeds (Whitehaven)

RUGBY LEAGUE WORLD TEAM OF THE YEAR
1 Ian Mort (Swinton Lions)
2 Dale Bloomfield (Rochdale Hornets)
3 Scott McAvoy (Whitehaven)
4 Ben Sagar (Keighley Cougars)
5 Gavin Duffy (Keighley Cougars)
6 Jason Demetriou (Keighley Cougars)
7 Ian Watson (Swinton Lions)
8 Matt Carbutt (Doncaster)
9 Mark Smith (Swinton Lions)
10 Dave Armitstead (Workington Town)
11 Lee Doran (Whitehaven)
12 Jarrad Stack (Workington Town)
13 Craig Ashall (Rochdale Hornets)

RUGBY LEAGUE CONFERENCE

PLAYER OF THE YEAR
Alex Walmsley (Dewsbury Celtic)

YOUNG PLAYER OF THE YEAR
Martyn Smith (Hemel Stags)

COACH OF THE YEAR
Richard Knight (Huddersfield Underbank Rangers)

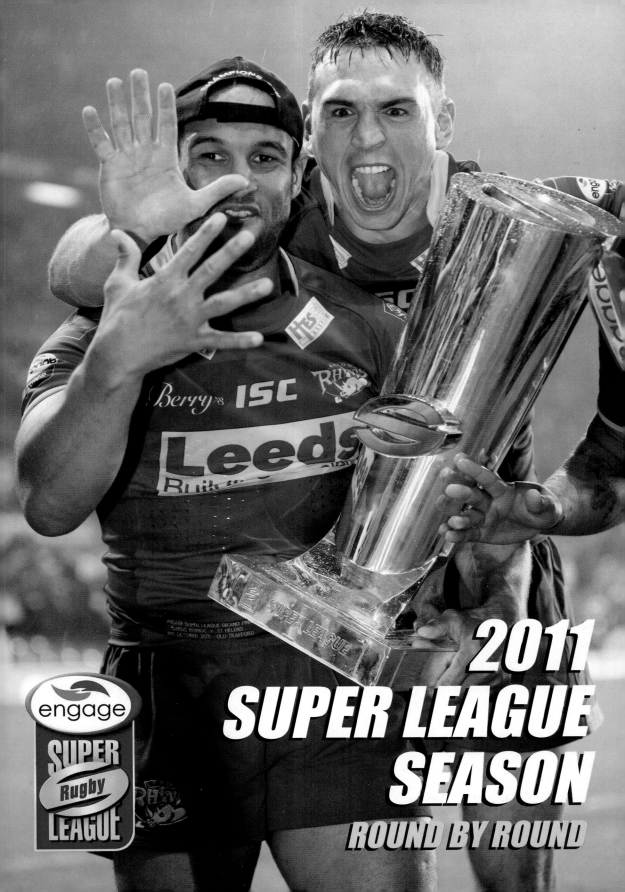

2011
SUPER LEAGUE
SEASON
ROUND BY ROUND

ABOVE: James Roby takes on Andy Coley and Jeff Lima as St Helens and Wigan fight out a thrilling draw

BELOW: Ben Galea bursts past Hull FC's Sean Long and Danny Houghton as Hull KR take the derby spoils

ROUND 1 - MILLENNIUM MAGIC

ABOVE: Brett Hodgson wrapped up by Michael Lawrence and Lee Gilmour as Huddersfield come out on top against Warrington

RIGHT: Leeds' Ben Jones-Bishop chases his kick through the Bradford defence on the way to being awarded a game-winning penalty try, after being tackled off the ball by Gareth Raynor

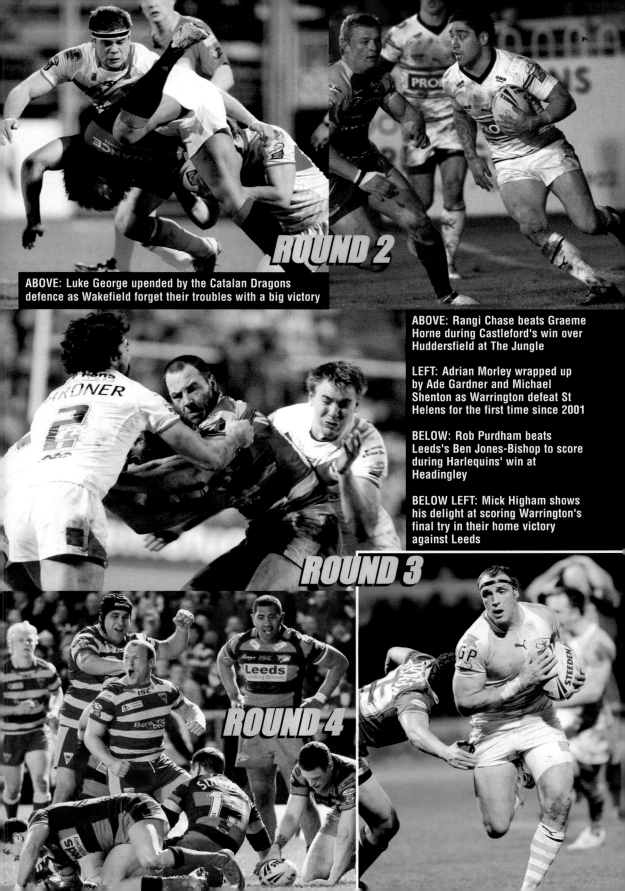

ROUND 2

ABOVE: Luke George upended by the Catalan Dragons defence as Wakefield forget their troubles with a big victory

ABOVE: Rangi Chase beats Graeme Horne during Castleford's win over Huddersfield at The Jungle

LEFT: Adrian Morley wrapped up by Ade Gardner and Michael Shenton as Warrington defeat St Helens for the first time since 2001

BELOW: Rob Purdham beats Leeds's Ben Jones-Bishop to score during Harlequins' win at Headingley

BELOW LEFT: Mick Higham shows his delight at scoring Warrington's final try in their home victory against Leeds

ROUND 3

ROUND 4

ABOVE: Luke Dorn, Nick Kouparitsas and Oliver Wilkes get to grips with James Graham as Harlequins stun St Helens

ROUND 5

BELOW: Olivier Elima brought down by Danny Orr as Bradford hand Castleford their first defeat of the season

ROUND 6

LEFT: Kirk Yeaman feels the force of Joel Tomkins, who was sent off for use of the elbow, as Wigan edge Hull FC

ROUND 8

ABOVE: Adrian Morley looks for a way past Sean O'Loughlin and Paul Prescott as Warrington defeat Wigan

LEFT: Frederic Vaccari races away from Chris Bridge on the way to scoring as Catalan Dragons upset Warrington

RIGHT: Brent Webb holds off Joel Tomkins to score during Leeds' thrilling draw with Wigan at Headingley

ROUND 9

ABOVE: Steve Menzies fends off George Carmont as Catalan Dragons power past Wigan

RIGHT: Vinnie Anderson tries to break free from Bryn Hargreaves and Matt Diskin as Salford demolish Bradford

ROUND 10

LEFT: Luke O'Donnell and Ryan Bailey, who were both dismissed for fighting, clash as Huddersfield win at Leeds for the first time since 1960

RIGHT: Jason Baitieri brought down by Luke Robinson, Lee Gilmour and Eorl Crabtree as Catalan Dragons edge past Huddersfield

LEFT: Tom Briscoe goes past Hull KR's Ben Cockayne as Hull FC emerge victorious in the Good Friday derby

RIGHT: Wigan's Liam Farrell swamped by jubilant teammates Sam Tomkins, Paul Deacon and Sean O'Loughlin following his last-gasp winning try against St Helens

ROUND 11

LEFT: Craig Fitzgibbon gets a pass away as Michael Monaghan closes in, during Hull FC's win at Warrington

LEFT: Stuart Reardon outjumps Danny Brough to claim a high ball as Crusaders defeat Huddersfield

ROUND 12

ROUND 13

ROUND 14

RIGHT: Scott Grix dives over for a try as Huddersfield see off St Helens

BELOW: Sam Tomkins gets the ball away under pressure from Clint Greenshields as Catalan Dragons complete the double over Wigan

RIGHT: Jermaine McGillvary crosses the line, as Rangi Chase looks on, during Huddersfield's victory over Castleford at The Shay. Due to a kit mix up, the Tigers were forced to turn out in Halifax colours!

ROUND 16

BELOW: Ryan Atkins looks for a way past Kevin Sinfield and Brett Delaney as Warrington take apart Leeds

ROUND 15

ROUND 18

ROUND 17

BELOW: A jubilant Mark Henry crashes past Brett Hodgson for a try as Salford stun Warrington

LEFT: Andy Lynch tackled by Iosia Soliola, James Roby and James Graham as Bradford and St Helens fight out a draw in the Odsal rain

BELOW: Glenn Morrison gets to grips with Huddersfield's Eorl Crabtree as Wakefield cut the Giants down to size

BELOW: Thomas Leuluai gets a kick away as Adam Milner challenges, during Castleford's draw with Wigan

BELOW: Chris Melling beats Dale Morton to score in the corner as Harlequins defeat Wakefield

RIGHT: Patrick Ah Van wrapped up by Leeds' Jamie Jones-Buchanan and Chris Clarkson during Bradford's derby victory at Headingley

ROUND 19

ROUND 20

BELOW: Ryan Hoffman moves in to tackle Jamie Peacock as Wigan hold off Leeds

ABOVE: Rangi Chase collared by Shad Royston as Castleford down Bradford in a thriller

BELOW: Paul Wellens reaches for the line under pressure from Willie Manu and Tom Briscoe as St Helens defeat Hull FC

ABOVE: Lopini Paea takes on Weller Hauraki as Catalan Dragons prove too strong for Leeds

BELOW: Gareth Raynor halted by Luke Robinson and Kevin Brown as Bradford sweep past Huddersfield

RIGHT: Richard Whiting brought down by Jamie Jones-Buchanan and Weller Hauraki as Leeds shut out Hull FC

ROUND 23

LEFT: Jason Chan looks for a way past Jeremy Smith and Chris Dean as Crusaders respond to their loss of a Super League licence with a big win at Wakefield

ROUND 24

RIGHT: Josh Hodgson beats Brett Kearney to score as Hull KR end Bradford's top eight hopes

ROUND 25

ABOVE: Michael Vella halted by Andrew Dixon, Louie McCarthy-Scarsbrook and James Roby as Hull KR hold off St Helens

RIGHT: Kevin Henderson wrestled to the ground by Ryan McGoldrick and Stuart Jones as Castleford edge out Wakefield

RIGHT: Lee Briers goes in under the posts during Warrington's victory over Wigan, a win that put the Wolves in the driving seat to win the League Leaders Shield

BELOW: Salford take to the field at The Willows for the final time, as they taste defeat against the Dragons

ROUND 27

RIGHT: Kris Welham tackled by Danny Orr and Dean Widders as Hull KR deny Castleford in the race for the play-offs

LEFT: Tom Makinson drags George Carmont into touch as St Helens defeat Wigan at the DW Stadium

ABOVE: Louis Anderson tackled by Graeme Horne and Larne Patrick as Warrington dismantle Huddersfield

QUALIFYING PLAY-OFFS

LEFT: Warrington captain Adrian Morley and coach Tony Smith show off the League Leaders Shield

ABOVE: Harrison Hansen dives over for a try as Wigan sweep past Catalan Dragons

RIGHT: Kevin Sinfield races away from Willie Manu on the way to scoring as Leeds eliminate Hull FC

ABOVE: Jamal Fakir takes on Michael Vella as Catalan Dragons end Hull KR's season

ELIMINATION PLAY-OFFS

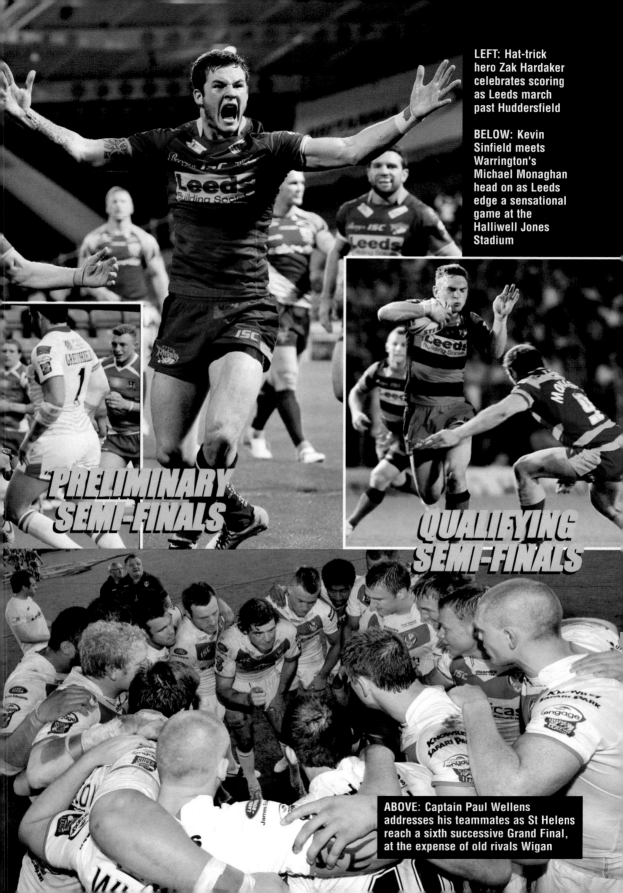

LEFT: Hat-trick hero Zak Hardaker celebrates scoring as Leeds march past Huddersfield

BELOW: Kevin Sinfield meets Warrington's Michael Monaghan head on as Leeds edge a sensational game at the Halliwell Jones Stadium

PRELIMINARY SEMI-FINALS

QUALIFYING SEMI-FINALS

ABOVE: Captain Paul Wellens addresses his teammates as St Helens reach a sixth successive Grand Final, at the expense of old rivals Wigan

LEFT: Rob Burrow leaves Tony Puletua and Scott Moore behind on the way to scoring an outstanding individual try

BELOW LEFT: James Roby tries to break free from the clutches of Ian Kirke and Carl Ablett

BELOW RIGHT: Kevin Sinfield lifts the Super League Trophy

GRAND FINAL

BELOW: Zak Hardaker slides past Jamie Foster to score the final try of the Super League season

3
PERSONALITIES OF 2011

Rangi Chase

Can a player have ever had a more eventful year than Castleford Tigers' mercurial stand-off Rangi Chase?

From start to finish, New Zealander Chase was making the headlines after he starred for the Tigers in their 40-20 opening day win at the Millennium Stadium against Wakefield, right through to his appearance in the Gillette Four Nations Final - for England. After Castleford's second round win over highly-fancied Huddersfield, he had collected the maximum six Albert Goldthorpe points and was on his way to winning the end-of-season medal awarded by *League Express* for Super League's best and fairest player. He was also crowned Man of Steel just after.

Not that it was all plain sailing. In round 21, Chase was found guilty of punching in a 34-30 home win over Bradford and banned for two matches. He appealed, using his position at the top of the Albert Goldthorpe Medal table to have the ban reduced to one game and secure his availability for Castleford's Challenge Cup quarter-final clash with Huddersfield. The Tigers won that game 22-18 to go into their first Challenge Cup semi-final since 2002.

The Tigers were desperately close to going one further, losing 10-8 to Leeds in the semi-final at Doncaster in golden-point extra-time. Castleford had led 8-2 with 73 minutes on the clock after two Kirk Dixon penalty goals followed an audacious try by Chase. On his own 20-metre line, he stepped inside leaving Chris Clarkson trailing, broke free down the left and then threw a dummy to fool Brent Webb before eventually touching down.

At the start of the week, the story was that Chase would miss the semi-final, having to return to Australia for a court case relating to an assault that happened during his pre-Tigers days. In fact, he was on his way to Australia after the match, with the club succeeding in forcing a postponement to the court appearance. Chase got a suspended sentence, missed a thrashing at Leeds the week after, but was back the following Sunday to pick up three more Goldthorpe points in a 34-30 win at Wakefield.

Before that, Chase had played for the Exiles in a 16-12 win over England in June and provided a spark at halfback that England lacked. At the end of the domestic season, Chase pledged his allegiance to England on the three-year residency rule. England coach Steve McNamara selected him for all four Gillette Four Nations games, which didn't please everybody, but the 30-8 final defeat to Australia capped off one heck of a year for Chase. Tigers fans breathed a sigh of relief when Chase signed a new contract that would keep him at the club until the end of the 2015 season.

Darren Lockyer

Darren Lockyer finally bowed out of Rugby League by lifting the 2011 Gillette Four Nations trophy, his reputation as the greatest player of his generation, if not of all time, guaranteed.

Lockyer was one of six candidates nominated before the final as contenders for the Golden Boot, awarded annually by *Rugby League World* magazine, and, following triumphs in 2003 and 2006, would have been a popular third-time winner.

Lockyer's career had been long and glorious. He made his Brisbane debut on 25 June 1995, coming off the bench as the Broncos hammered Parramatta 60-14 and soon, beginning with the 1997 Australian Super League tour, became a regular feature of Australian touring teams.

His first game on English soil was in the Wembley clash against Great Britain on 1st November 1997, when he was selected at fullback, which by then was his usual position. That was a game dominated by another Australian great, Laurie Daley, who scored three tries before half-time as the Aussies won 38-14. Lockyer had a solid, mistake-free game that didn't draw too many comments from the pundits.

A week later the Aussies went down to a 20-12 defeat at Old Trafford, with Lockyer kicking two goals, but with a young Adrian Morley being the star of the show for Great Britain. In the third Test the Aussies blitzed Great Britain 37-20 at Elland Road, with Lockyer playing a prominent role in several Australian tries and kicking a field goal.

From that point on he never missed a tour and played a major role in the Aussies' 2000 World Cup triumph. By 2003, Lockyer was the Australian captain in what turned out to be the last Ashes series, still playing at fullback and leading his team to three narrow Test victories in this country.

Anxious not to be the first Aussie Test captain to lose an Ashes series since 1970, his sheer will to win led his team to victory. And he was rewarded that year with the award of the Golden Boot for the first time.

2004 was the first year we held the Tri-Nations tournament in England, and by this time Lockyer was not only the Aussie captain, but he had moved to his original position of stand-off. In the final, Lockyer produced one of the greatest international performances as the Aussies led Great Britain 38-0 at half-time and went on to win 44-4.

Lockyer won the Golden Boot again in 2006, when he had a tremendous State of Origin series for Queensland, and scored the winning try in that year's Tri-Nations final against New Zealand. There'll be plenty of stand-offs vying for his green and gold number six shirt, but we are unlikely to see Darren Lockyer's like again.

Brian McDermott

Brian McDermott became the first coach to lead a side to the Super League title from outside the top three when Leeds beat St Helens 32-16 in 2011's thrilling Grand Final.

It was an amazing achievement by both the coach and his players in a season in which the Rhinos had been written off, even by many of their own supporters.

Four-times Super League champions Leeds had looked in danger of not reaching the play-offs for the first time since they were introduced in 1998 when they fell into eighth spot in the table following a 38-18 defeat against Catalan Dragons in early July.

But the Rhinos won ten of their next 12 fixtures, culminating in a stirring run through the play-offs with consecutive victories over Hull at home, and then away at Huddersfield and League Leaders Shield winners Warrington, and then came back from what looked a lost cause in the second half to beat St Helens in a wonderful match at Old Trafford.

Former Bradford prop McDermott, who had been a key member of the Bulls side in the glory years of the late 'nineties and early noughties and had spells as an assistant to Tony Smith at Huddersfield and Leeds, could hardly be described as a rookie. He served as head coach at Harlequins for four-and-a-half years before re-joining Leeds after SLXV as putative assistant to Brian McClennan but being promoted to head coach at Headingley barely three weeks into the off season.

Expectations at Headingley were certainly different to those in London and

Brian McDermott celebrates the Rhinos' Grand Final win with Harry Sunderland Trophy winner Rob Burrow

McDermott, missing both Danny McGuire and Jamie Peacock for almost all the first half of the season, quickly became a target of criticism as the Rhinos struggled for consistent form. Both coach and players handled the pressure with dignity and got on with the job in hand, with telling results.

'Gary Hetherington (chief executive) would have been questioned about 'who's this British coach you've got, he was at Harlequins last year, your team is too old, your halves don't do this and your props are too old',' McDermott said after the Grand Final. 'But the culture and philosophy we have at this club gets you through dark times.

'We finished fifth, and we'd like to be further up the table, but I don't think it's shock horror that Leeds Rhinos finished fifth. Not once has anyone whinged, moaned, blamed refs or looked for answers other than what's inside. That's why this is special. Coaching here is so special for the humility and integrity the players show."

Sam Tomkins

At the end of 2011, Sam Tomkins was rumoured to be the highest paid player in British Rugby League.

There was a certain symmetry to his year. In February, Sam, along with elder brother Joel, signed a new five-year contract with his club Wigan. And in November Sam signed another deal for the same length of time, on the day it was confirmed Joel had accepted an offer to play rugby union.

A compensation fee came to Wigan, but it was a fraction of the rumoured millions that were offered for a package for both siblings. Sam's new contract included a clause which meant the England fullback could not speak to either rugby union or NRL clubs for three years.

The deal was hailed as a boost for English Rugby League and it was certainly a fillip for England coach Steve McNamara. Sam's form for his club had been sensational all year as he was edged for the Albert Goldthorpe Medal by a single point and finished as Super League's joint top try-scorer alongside Leeds' Ryan Hall, with 28.

Sam Tomkins had emerged as the English club game's outstanding talent in the season he turned 22 years of age, but there were still question marks over whether he could take that onto a world stage. In June, when he played for England against the Exiles, many people were stunned as he was booed by sections of the Headingley crowd with his every touch - with suggestions that his competitive spirit on the pitch for Wigan at times edged into cheating. If Tomkins had taken the union shilling after that, not many people would have blamed him.

He didn't help himself in August when a moment of ill-judgement was captured on TV, clearly showing him flashing two fingers at the Leeds supporters as he congratulated Josh Charnley after Wigan's first try in their Carnegie Challenge Cup win over the Rhinos. The Rugby Football League handed him a suspended fine, as did his club Wigan, although he apologised for his actions.

There was no booing in the autumn when he starred in the Gillette Four Nations with three excellent performances in the pool games against Wales, Australia and New Zealand. He was not able to find his best form in England's 30-8 final defeat by Australia but that hardly damaged the reputation he had built since making his Wigan debut in a Challenge Cup tie with Whitehaven, scoring five tries in a 106-8 win, in May of 2008. Surprisingly he had to wait until the following February to make his Super League debut, against Harlequins in round three. Since then he has lit up the English game with his inimitable running style and speed off the mark, and Wigan fans in particular will be thankful their club has secured the services of Sam Tomkins for at least the next three years.

Daryl Powell

2011 was a particularly successful year for a man who has known plenty of achievements in his career.

By leading his Featherstone Rovers side to the Championship title, Daryl Powell completed a three-year journey to re-habilitate his coaching career after it had seemingly stalled at Leeds. After retiring from playing he spent two and a half years as head coach of the Rhinos, taking them to the Challenge Cup Final in 2003 before later that year being moved aside to make way for Tony Smith.

Leeds chief executive Gary Hetherington once said: 'It was his time as head coach which should be remembered. He agreed to take up the challenge during a bleak period in 2001 and immediately set about changing the culture and make up of the team. It was Daryl who introduced a rich crop of youngsters who have gone on to form the core of the present team. This was perhaps the single most important development in the club's recent history.'

Nevertheless Powell was moved up to director of rugby as new coach Smith transformed the Rhinos into a Championship-winning side. Powell drifted into the rugby union arm of the Leeds club as attacking coach, first team coach and subsequently assistant backs and skills coach. Surprisingly he didn't move on until the end of 2008 when he got his chance at first team coaching again with Featherstone.

In his first season Rovers finished in the last play-off position and came within one game of the Grand Final.

In 2010 they lost the showpiece to Halifax in golden point extra-time after winning the League Leaders Trophy with only two defeats all season. But in 2011,

after losing only one league game, at Leigh in March, Rovers were crowned champions after a comprehensive 40-4 defeat of Sheffield Eagles at Warrington.

That final pitted Powell against his friend and long-time playing partner at the Eagles, their coach and chief executive Mark Aston. The pair were the first two signings for the Sheffield club when they were formed by Hetherington in 1984. Powell's achievements from what were fairly humble beginnings were impressive, from two Divisional premierships and promotions with Sheffield to two Challenge Cup finals and one Grand Final with Leeds, those coming after a short spell with Keighley Cougars.

This year Powell retained his crown as Championship Coach of the Year, marking three years of steady progress at Post Office Road. It was no big surprise when England coach Steve McNamara named him as his assistant in March, Powell having won 33 caps for Great Britain during his playing career. He has fully earned his reputation as one of the brightest young English coaches in the game.

4
INTERNATIONAL YEAR

GILLETTE FOUR NATIONS
Australia on top again

Australia won the 2011 Gillette Four Nations, going through the tournament played in England and Wales unbeaten, and winning the final at Elland Road, Leeds against England by 30-8. England had won their place in the final with a 28-6 victory over New Zealand as they went one better than coach Steve McNamara's first tournament the year before when they came third. Wales were the fourth team in this year's tournament, having won the 2010 Alitalia European Cup, and though they didn't win a game, they gained much admiration for three tenacious displays.

England's preparation had included a game in June against the Exiles, a team made up of Antipodean players in Super League, who gave the Test side a sterner challenge than France had a year before, winning the game at Headingley 16-12. France themselves gave a much better showing in England's last warm-up the week before the tournament proper, losing 32-18 in front of a packed house in Avignon.

Castleford Tigers stand-off Rangi Chase, who in 2010 had played against England for the Maori and also represented the Exiles, made a shock decision to pledge allegiance to England and made his debut in Avignon, having qualified under a three-year residency rule. Also making debuts were Jack Reed, the Brisbane rookie centre, who was born in Keighley but moved to Australia as a youngster, and Wests Tigers loose forward Chris Heighington, who qualified through his English father.

2011 FOUR NATIONS SQUADS

AUSTRALIA: Darius Boyd (St George Illawarra Dragons); Daly Cherry-Evans (Manly Sea Eagles); Cooper Cronk (Melbourne Storm); Robbie Farah (Wests Tigers); Paul Gallen (Cronulla Sharks); Keith Galloway (Wests Tigers); Greg Inglis (South Sydney Rabbitohs); Chris Lawrence (Wests Tigers); Luke Lewis (Penrith Panthers); Darren Lockyer (Brisbane Broncos) (C); Josh Morris (Canterbury Bulldogs); Corey Parker (Brisbane Broncos); Beau Scott (St George Illawarra Dragons); Matt Scott (North Queensland Cowboys); David Shillington (Canberra Raiders); Billy Slater (Melbourne Storm); Cameron Smith (Melbourne Storm); Sam Thaiday (Brisbane Broncos); Johnathan Thurston (North Queensland Cowboys); Willie Tonga (North Queensland Cowboys); Akuila Uate (Newcastle Knights); Anthony Watmough (Manly Sea Eagles); Tony Williams (Manly Sea Eagles); Jharal Yow Yeh (Brisbane Broncos).

Manly's Glenn Stewart withdrew on compassionate grounds and was replaced by Beau Scott. His brother and teammate, fullback Brett Stewart, withdrew due to a knee injury. Willie Tonga was his replacement. South Sydney's Dave Taylor failed to recover in time from shoulder surgery but was not replaced.

ENGLAND: Carl Ablett (Leeds Rhinos); Ryan Bailey (Leeds Rhinos); Tom Briscoe (Hull FC); Garreth Carvell (Warrington Wolves); Rangi Chase (Castleford Tigers); Leroy Cudjoe (Huddersfield Giants); Gareth Ellis (Wests Tigers); James Graham (St Helens); Ryan Hall (Leeds Rhinos); Chris Heighington (Wests Tigers); Ben Jones-Bishop (Leeds Rhinos); Jamie Jones-Buchanan (Leeds Rhinos); Danny McGuire (Leeds Rhinos); Michael McIlorum (Wigan Warriors); Adrian Morley (Warrington Wolves); Jamie Peacock (Leeds Rhinos) (C); Jack Reed (Brisbane Broncos); James Roby (St Helens); Kevin Sinfield (Leeds Rhinos); Sam Tomkins (Wigan Warriors); Ben Westwood (Warrington Wolves); Gareth Widdop (Melbourne Storm); Jon Wilkin (St Helens); Kirk Yeaman (Hull FC).

St Helens' Jonny Lomax was ruled out with torn ankle ligaments and was replaced by Danny McGuire.

NEW ZEALAND: Gerard Beale (Brisbane Broncos); Adam Blair (Melbourne Storm); Lewis Brown (New Zealand Warriors); Kalifa Faifai Loa (North Queensland Cowboys); Nathan Fien (St George Illawarra Dragons); Kieran Foran (Manly Sea Eagles); Alex Glenn (Brisbane Broncos); Thomas Leuluai (Wigan Warriors); Kevin Locke (New Zealand Warriors); Issac Luke (South Sydney Rabbitohs); Simon Mannering (New Zealand Warriors); Sika Manu (Melbourne Storm); Benji Marshall (Wests Tigers) (C); Ben Matulino (New Zealand Warriors); Sam McKendry (Penrith Panthers); Fuifui Moimoi (Parramatta Eels); Jason Nightingale (St George Illawarra Dragons); Russell Packer (New Zealand Warriors); Kevin Proctor (Melbourne Storm); Jeremy Smith (Cronulla Sharks); Elijah Taylor (New Zealand Warriors); Bill Tupou (New Zealand Warriors); Jared Waerea-Hargreaves (Sydney Roosters).

Manu Vatuvei and Shaun Johnson (both New Zealand Warriors) and Steve Matai (Manly) withdrew from the original squad through injury, and were replaced by Kalifa Faifai Loa, Elijah Taylor and Krisnan Inu (New Zealand Warriors). Inu then pulled out for personal reasons and was replaced by Bill Tupou.

WALES: Chris Beasley (Central Comets); Andy Bracek (Crusaders); Lee Briers (Warrington Wolves) (C); Neil Budworth (Mackay Cutters); Geraint Davies (unattached); Ross Divorty (Featherstone Rovers); Gil Dudson (Crusaders); Ben Flower (Crusaders); Tyson Frizell (Cronulla Sharks); Andrew Gay (South Wales Scorpions); Aled James (South Wales Scorpions); Jordan James (Crusaders); Danny Jones (Halifax); Elliot Kear (Crusaders); Craig Kopczak (Bradford Bulls); Mark Lennon (Thirroul Butchers); Peter Lupton (Crusaders); Christiaan Roets (South Wales Scorpions); Matt Seamark (Wynnum Manly Seagulls); Ian Watson (Swinton Lions); Ian Webster (Central Comets); Lloyd White (Crusaders); Lee Williams (Crusaders); Rhys Williams (Warrington Wolves).

Crusaders' Gareth Thomas was named in the original squad, but retired from playing before the start of the tournament. He was replaced by Geraint Davies.

When Steve McNamara named his 24-man squad on the Monday after the Super League Grand Final there were a number of players unavailable through injury. Warrington's Chris Bridge needed knee surgery; St Helens centre Michael Shenton dislocated an elbow in the Grand Final, Huddersfield prop Eorl Crabtree and Wigan loose forward Sean O'Loughlin both needed shoulder surgery and South Sydney forward Sam Burgess had been sidelined since April with a damaged ankle. There was also no place in the squad for Wigan centre Joel

Tomkins, who asked not to be considered for 'personal reasons' five weeks before he signed for a rugby union club.

Rob Burrow, the star of the previous Saturday's Grand Final, was ruled out with a rib injury but Super League champions Leeds still had seven representatives in the squad. That number increased to eight when Jonny Lomax, the St Helens halfback, withdrew with torn ankle ligaments and Danny McGuire was called up as replacement.

Australian coach Tim Sheens also suffered from end-of-season unavailability, losing Petero Civoniceva, Jarryd Hayne, David Taylor and Justin Hodges to injury and Brett and Glenn Stewart due to personal reasons. Manly captain Jamie Lyons also made himself unavailable. Greg Inglis was passed fit to travel to the UK on the Monday before the tour after meeting with his surgeon, after undergoing minor surgery to clean out his right knee.

Kiwi coach Stephen Kearney had a number of unavailable players, Manu Vatuvei, knee, Shaun Johnson, back, and Steve Matai, neck, all ruled out for medical reasons. The trio were replaced by Warriors' Krisnan Inu and Elijah Taylor and North Queensland winger Kalifa Faifai Loa. Inu then withdrew for personal reasons and Warriors winger Bill Tupou was named as replacement.

Wales were rank outsiders as Iestyn Harris assembled a squad of mostly part-time players. Gareth Thomas was named in his squad but a few days before kick-off announced his retirement from playing.

Week two of the tournament was staged as a double header at Wembley Stadium, which attracted a crowd of 42,344, the biggest crowd for an international match in England since the World Cup final of 2000.

Australia got off to a winning start with a professional 26-12 win at Halliwell Jones Stadium on the last Friday in October. Stephen Kearney's side reeled in a 16-0 half-time deficit to trail by just four points going into the final quarter. But Australia stepped up their game again, as Johnathan Thurston's invention laid on the gamebreaking try for Darius Boyd and the other winger Akuila Uate - a star for Fiji in the 2008 World Cup - added another score in the dying minutes.

New Zealand had a bad start. Simon Mannering conceded a penalty on the last tackle of the opening set and hooker Cameron Smith sent prop Matt Scott bulldozing over by the posts. Just before the half-hour mark after giant Tongan Tony Williams took Thurston's pass, ran over the top of Benji Marshall and beat three other defenders to touch down. The pair combined again just before half-time. A superb ball from Thurston put Williams through a hole, and the halfback supported on the inside to take his pass to make it 16-0 at the break.

New Zealand found a way back into the contest soon after the restart when Kieran Foran's kick out wide caused problems and Jason Nightingale touched down. Seven minutes later the Kiwis were within four points after Gerard Beale sent Kalifa Faifai Loa over for Marshall to add a second conversion.

The Kangaroos struck the killer blow when Thurston attacked down the left and his delayed pass allowed Chris Lawrence to send Darius Boyd over in the corner. And Australia put a seal on their victory when Billy Slater's kick on the fly allowed Uate to touch down by the right corner flag.

GILLETTE FOUR NATIONS - GAME ONE

Friday 28th October 2011

AUSTRALIA 26 NEW ZEALAND 12

AUSTRALIA: 1 Billy Slater (Melbourne Storm); 2 Akuila Uate (Newcastle Knights); 3 Willie Tonga (North Queensland Cowboys); 4 Chris Lawrence (Wests Tigers); 5 Darius Boyd (St George Illawarra Dragons); 6 Darren Lockyer (Brisbane Broncos) (C); 7 Johnathan Thurston (North Queensland Cowboys); 8 Paul Gallen (Cronulla Sharks); 9 Cameron Smith (Melbourne Storm); 10 Matt Scott (North Queensland Cowboys); 11 Luke Lewis (Penrith Panthers); 12 Sam Thaiday (Brisbane Broncos); 13 Anthony Watmough (Manly Sea Eagles). Subs (all used): 14 Cooper Cronk (Melbourne Storm); 15 Keith Galloway (Wests Tigers); 16 David Shillington (Canberra Raiders); 17 Tony Williams (Manly Sea Eagles). **Tries:** M Scott (2), Williams (29), Thurston (37), Boyd (64), Uate (75); **Goals:** Thurston 3/5.
NEW ZEALAND: 1 Kevin Locke (New Zealand Warriors); 2 Kalifa Faifai Loa (North Queensland Cowboys); 3 Lewis Brown (New Zealand Warriors); 4 Gerard Beale (Brisbane Broncos); 5 Jason Nightingale (St George Illawarra Dragons); 6 Benji Marshall (Wests Tigers) (C); 7 Kieran Foran (Manly Sea Eagles); 8 Ben Matulino (New Zealand Warriors); 9 Issac Luke (South Sydney Rabbitohs); 10 Sam McKendry (Penrith Panthers); 11 Sika Manu (Melbourne Storm); 12 Simon Mannering (New Zealand Warriors); 13 Jeremy Smith (Cronulla Sharks). Subs (all used): 14 Thomas Leuluai (Wigan Warriors); 15 Fuifui Moimoi (Parramatta Eels); 16 Alex Glenn (Brisbane Broncos); 17 Jared Waerea-Hargreaves (Sydney Roosters).
Tries: Nightingale (48), Faifai Loa (55); **Goals:** Marshall 2/2.
Rugby Leaguer & League Express Men of the Match: *Australia:* Johnathan Thurston; *New Zealand:* Jason Nightingale.
Penalty count: 6-5; **Half-time:** 16-0; **Referee:** Phil Bentham (England); **Attendance:** 12,491 *(at Halliwell Jones Stadium, Warrington).*

The following day England accounted for Wales by 42-4, with Sam Tomkins scoring four tries. Wales coach Iestyn Harris was down to the bare bones as both Lloyd White and Peter Lupton failed fitness tests on hamstring strains they picked up in the 30-6 warm-up win over Ireland, though skipper Lee Briers made an expected return. After Jordan James was carried off, knocked out in the first tackle of the match and before the minute mark was reached, Tomkins had scythed through for his first in the left corner. It was 10-0 on 16 minutes as Tomkins grabbed his second, this time on the right after he tore onto a Sinfield pass. Within two minutes England were exploiting the centres again, as Chase went from dummy-half, sent Sinfield half through the left and he fed Kirk Yeaman.

GILLETTE FOUR NATIONS - GAME TWO

Saturday 29th October 2011

ENGLAND 42 WALES 4

ENGLAND: 1 Sam Tomkins (Wigan Warriors); 2 Ryan Hall (Leeds Rhinos); 3 Jack Reed (Brisbane Broncos); 4 Kirk Yeaman (Hull FC); 5 Tom Briscoe (Hull FC); 6 Kevin Sinfield (Leeds Rhinos); 7 Rangi Chase (Castleford Tigers); 8 Jamie Peacock (Leeds Rhinos) (C); 9 James Roby (St Helens); 10 James Graham (St Helens); 11 Gareth Ellis (Wests Tigers); 12 Ben Westwood (Warrington Wolves); 13 Chris Heighington (Wests Tigers). Subs (all used): 14 Gareth Widdop (Melbourne Storm); 15 Adrian Morley (Warrington Wolves); 16 Jamie Jones-Buchanan (Leeds Rhinos); 17 Jon Wilkin (St Helens).
Tries: Tomkins (1, 16, 50, 58), Reed (54), Heighington (76), Widdop (80); **Goals:** Sinfield 5/8.
WALES: 1 Danny Jones (Halifax); 2 Elliot Kear (Crusaders); 3 Ian Webster (Central Comets); 4 Christiaan Roets (South Wales Scorpions); 5 Rhys Williams (Warrington Wolves); 6 Lee Briers (Warrington Wolves) (C); 7 Matt Seamark (Wynnum Manly Seagulls); 8 Jordan James (Crusaders); 9 Neil Budworth (Mackay Cutters); 10 Gil Dudson (Crusaders); 11 Tyson Frizell (Cronulla Sharks); 12 Andy Bracek (Crusaders); 13 Ben Flower (Crusaders). Subs (all used): 14 Ian Watson (Swinton Lions); 15 Ross Divorty (Featherstone Rovers); 16 Aled James (South Wales Scorpions); 17 Craig Kopczak (Bradford Bulls).
Try: Kear (67); **Goals:** Briers 0/1.
Rugby Leaguer & League Express Men of the Match:
England: Kevin Sinfield; *Wales:* Danny Jones.
Penalty count: 4-7; **Half-time:** 14-0; **Referee:** Henry Perenara (New Zealand); **Attendance:** 10,377 *(at Leigh Sports Village).*

Tomkins got two more after the break and Jack Reed squeezed over on the right before the Welsh got their deserved try, as the ball was moved right at speed, with Briers, Danny Jones and Andy Bracek the link, allowing Elliot Kear to shoot into the right corner and plant the ball down with one hand while in mid-air. Two late tries from Gareth Widdop and Chris Heighington, gave the scoreboard a better look as a far as England were concerned.

The first game of a Bonfire Night double header saw New Zealand account for Wales 36-0. The Kiwis crossed three times in a totally dominant opening quarter through Jason Nightingale, Kevin Locke and Sika Manu, with Benji Marshall running riot on his first appearance on the Wembley stage. But the Dragons, led by their own talismanic stand-off in Lee Briers, and with their pack consistently standing up to their formidable opponents, competed fully for the rest of the game.

There was a towering performance from Craig Kopczak, who had an outstanding tournament and he gained ample support from the likes of Gil Dudson, Jordan James and Chris Beasley, leaving Harris to reflect on plenty of positives after the game. Kiwis coach Stephen Kearney was happy enough with the win, though he lost prop Sam McKendry for the rest of the tournament with a broken jaw sustained in a massive second-half shoulder charge by Kopczak, as well as Fuifui Moimoi with a shoulder injury.

Two Wales attacks at 16-0 almost yielded tries but instead they conceded twice again before the break through Manu and Gerard Beale tries to push the score out to 26-0. The third quarter was scoreless, the highlights coming from Kopczak, who replicated a stirring run against England with another impressive long-range charge, and then produced his huge hit on McKendry. The deadlock was eventually broken in the 62nd minute when Thomas Leuluai's smart ball left allowed Beale to bag his second. Leuluai was also involved in the final try five minutes from the end, when he split the Welsh defence up the middle and sent Nathan Fien away to the line.

Australia secured their place in the final in the second game of the Wembley double header with a 36-20 win over England. In a thrilling game, the turning point was the 48th minute denial of a try to England winger Tom Briscoe, referee Henry Perenara awarding a penalty for a double movement without referral to the video referee. Five minutes later Aussie sub Cooper Cronk sent Paul Gallen in to the right of the posts with a sweet short pass. Even with 25 minutes left on the clock, at 24-8, the result was decided.

Jack Reed got a try back when he out-leapt Darius Boyd to catch Kevin Sinfield's bomb 15 metres out, and was left with a clear run to the Aussie line. Boyd was playing fullback after Australia lost Billy Slater for the tournament in the 11th minute when he broke his collar bone trying to shoulder charge Ryan Hall into touch as he went over for England's first try. Boyd it was who scored the killer try with eight minutes remaining after a Thurston intercept of a Rangi Chase pass before Wests Tigers clubmates Chris Heighington and Chris Lawrence exchanged scores before the final whistle.

Leeds winger Hall scored England's second try, a beauty a minute from half-time when Sam Tomkins broke through off a Jon Wilkin pass just inside his own half and skipped out of the desperate tackle of Greg Inglis. Tomkins' audacious one-handed flick sent Reed racing away, and the centre delayed his pass to perfection to give Hall just enough time to score in the corner. Hall did magnificently to get the ball down in Boyd's attempted tackle.

In between the Kangaroos scored two converted tries, as first Luke Lewis went over in the left corner from Boyd's cut-out pass. Then, on the half-hour mark, Tony Williams bumped off Heighington ten metres out and steamrollered over. Inglis, in his first game of the tournament, scored in the fourth minute of the second half, the video referee ruling Thurston had not used a shepherd before releasing the try-making pass.

There was one more big talking point as Williams was put on report for a high shot on Westwood, just before the Briscoe incident. Williams received a one-match suspension later that week, meaning he would miss Australia's game in Wales.

GILLETTE FOUR NATIONS - GAME THREE

Saturday 5th November 2011

WALES 0 NEW ZEALAND 36

WALES: 1 Danny Jones (Halifax); 2 Elliot Kear (Crusaders); 3 Ian Webster (Central Comets); 4 Christiaan Roets (South Wales Scorpions); 5 Rhys Williams (Warrington Wolves); 6 Lee Briers (Warrington Wolves) (C); 7 Lloyd White (Crusaders); 8 Jordan James (Crusaders); 9 Neil Budworth (Mackay Cutters); 10 Gil Dudson (Crusaders); 11 Tyson Frizell (Cronulla Sharks); 12 Chris Beasley (Central Comets); 13 Ben Flower (Crusaders). Subs (all used): 14 Ian Watson (Swinton Lions); 15 Andy Bracek (Crusaders); 16 Ross Divorty (Featherstone Rovers); 17 Craig Kopczak (Bradford Bulls).
NEW ZEALAND: 1 Kevin Locke (New Zealand Warriors); 5 Jason Nightingale (St George Illawarra Dragons); 3 Lewis Brown (New Zealand Warriors); 4 Alex Glenn (Brisbane Broncos); 2 Gerard Beale (Brisbane Broncos); 6 Benji Marshall (Wests Tigers) (C); 7 Kieran Foran (Manly Sea Eagles); 8 Sam McKendry (Penrith Panthers); 9 Thomas Leuluai (Wigan Warriors); 10 Ben Matulino (New Zealand Warriors); 11 Sika Manu (Melbourne Storm); 12 Adam Blair (Melbourne Storm); 13 Jeremy Smith (Cronulla Sharks). Subs (all used): 14 Nathan Fien (St George Illawarra Dragons); 15 Jared Waerea-Hargreaves (Sydney Roosters); 16 Fuifui Moimoi (Parramatta Eels); 17 Elijah Taylor (New Zealand Warriors).
Tries: Nightingale (4), Locke (13), Manu (20, 31), Beale (39, 62), Fien (75); **Goals:** Marshall 4/7.
Rugby Leaguer & League Express Men of the Match:
Wales: Craig Kopczak; *New Zealand:* Benji Marshall.
Penalty count: 9-3; **Half-time:** 0-26; **Referee:** Matt Cecchin (Australia).

GILLETTE FOUR NATIONS - GAME FOUR

Saturday 5th November 2011

ENGLAND 20 AUSTRALIA 36

ENGLAND: 1 Sam Tomkins (Wigan Warriors); 2 Ryan Hall (Leeds Rhinos); 3 Jack Reed (Brisbane Broncos); 4 Kirk Yeaman (Hull FC); 5 Tom Briscoe (Hull FC); 6 Kevin Sinfield (Leeds Rhinos); 7 Rangi Chase (Castleford Tigers); 8 James Graham (St Helens); 9 James Roby (St Helens); 10 Jamie Peacock (Leeds Rhinos) (C); 11 Gareth Ellis (Wests Tigers); 12 Ben Westwood (Warrington Wolves); 13 Chris Heighington (Wests Tigers). Subs (all used): 14 Gareth Widdop (Melbourne Storm); 15 Adrian Morley (Warrington Wolves); 16 Jamie Jones-Buchanan (Leeds Rhinos); 17 Jon Wilkin (St Helens).
Tries: Hall (11, 39), Reed (60), Heighington (76); **Goals:** Sinfield 2/4.
AUSTRALIA: 1 Billy Slater (Melbourne Storm); 2 Akuila Uate (Newcastle Knights); 3 Chris Lawrence (Wests Tigers); 4 Greg Inglis (South Sydney Rabbitohs); 5 Darius Boyd (St George Illawarra Dragons); 6 Darren Lockyer (Brisbane Broncos) (C); 7 Johnathan Thurston (North Queensland Cowboys); 8 Paul Gallen (Cronulla Sharks); 9 Cameron Smith (Melbourne Storm); 10 Matt Scott (North Queensland Cowboys); 11 Luke Lewis (Penrith Panthers); 12 Sam Thaiday (Brisbane Broncos); 13 Anthony Watmough (Manly Sea Eagles). Subs (all used): 14 Cooper Cronk (Melbourne Storm); 15 Keith Galloway (Wests Tigers); 16 David Shillington (Canberra Raiders); 17 Tony Williams (Manly Sea Eagles).
Tries: Lewis (17), Williams (30), Inglis (44), Gallen (53), Boyd (72), Lawrence (79); **Goals:** Thurston 6/6.
On report: Williams (47) - alleged high tackle on Westwood.
Rugby Leaguer & League Express Men of the Match:
England: Ryan Hall; *Australia:* Johnathan Thurston.
Penalty count: 7-5; **Half-time:** 8-12;
Referee: Henry Perenara (New Zealand).

Attendance: 42,344 *(at Wembley Stadium).*

England kept alive their hopes with a 28-6 win against an aggressive Kiwi side in front of a packed house in Hull. Steve McNamara picked captain Jamie Peacock and James Graham who had both been injury doubts all week, though Gareth Ellis didn't recover. His place was taken by Jon Wilkin, with Garreth Carvell coming onto the bench for his first appearance in the tournament.

Rangi Chase provided a fine cameo in his match-up with Kiwi captain Benji Marshall, chasing him down and almost coming to blows on a couple of occasions. The Kiwis' over-physical approach led to their undoing, while a couple of incidents left two players on report. Jeremy Smith dropped on Sam Tomkins with an elbow to the face and was later suspended for one game. Issac Luke got two games for deliberately bending and twisting Chase's leg. By half-time the penalty count was 7-2 in the home side's favour, and Kiwi coach

Gillette Four Nations

Stephen Kearney admitted he had been relieved to only be 8-0 down at the break.

Although the game finished well for England, the start was almost disastrous when, in New Zealand's second set, Kevin Locke sent Kieran Foran over. Referee Mat Cecchin went to the video referee, and after several replays Ian Smith ruled two of the players in front of the kicker Marshall had encroached within ten metres of Tomkins when he dropped the ball.

It took England almost half an hour to break a scoring deadlock when Chase went left, and his link with Wilkin and Kirk Yeaman gave Tom Briscoe a clear run into the left corner. Kevin Sinfield's kicking was perfect all night and his penalty for the Luke offence completed the first-half scoring.

Another spectacular Ryan Hall try - this time a one-handed finish just before he hit the corner flag - eased any nerves. Sinfield goaled and 14-0 looked safe. Jason Nightingale's converted try just after the hour mark should have given New Zealand a bridgehead but Tom Briscoe ended the pressure when he stole the ball from Beale in a one-on-one as the Kiwis attacked on the right. The Hull flyer had a clear run to the line, but amazingly Simon Mannering raced back and caught him. Within a minute James Graham was over from Sinfield's pass after Westwood offloaded out of a tackle. Four minutes later Graham's delayed pass sent Jamie Jones-Buchanan through from 20 metres, and his smart inside pass sent Tomkins under the posts. Sinfield converted both tries.

Lee Briers did not have a fairytale ending to his international career as Wales eventually crashed to a 10-try, 56-14 hammering at the hands of Australia at Wrexham. But Iestyn Harris's side gave the Kangaroos a thorough test for 38 minutes, leading until two minutes before the break, when Cooper Cronk helped himself to a quick-fire brace of tries. That made the half-time score 18-8 in favour of the Aussies harsh on the Welsh. The Kangaroos took full advantage in the second half by running in seven more tries, including Cronk's hat-trick score.

Wales shocked everyone by taking a ninth minute lead when Briers put in a kick for Rhys Williams to touch down in the corner. Wales set their sights on a major upset with their second try in four minutes. A break from Briers put Wales in a strong position and he kept the ball alive to Danny Jones who in turn found Elliot Kear and the winger stepped inside to score in the right corner.

Two consecutive penalties eventually told as acting Aussie skipper Cameron Smith

GILLETTE FOUR NATIONS - GAME FIVE

Saturday 12th November 2011

ENGLAND 28 NEW ZEALAND 6

ENGLAND: 1 Sam Tomkins (Wigan Warriors); 2 Ryan Hall (Leeds Rhinos); 3 Jack Reed (Brisbane Broncos); 4 Kirk Yeaman (Hull FC); 5 Tom Briscoe (Hull FC); 6 Kevin Sinfield (Leeds Rhinos); 7 Rangi Chase (Castleford Tigers); 8 James Graham (St Helens); 9 James Roby (St Helens); 10 Jamie Peacock (Leeds Rhinos) (C); 11 Jon Wilkin (St Helens); 12 Ben Westwood (Warrington Wolves); 13 Chris Heighington (Wests Tigers). Subs (all used): 14 Gareth Widdop (Melbourne Storm); 15 Adrian Morley (Warrington Wolves); 16 Jamie Jones-Buchanan (Leeds Rhinos); 17 Garreth Carvell (Warrington Wolves).
Tries: Briscoe (28), Hall (44), Graham (72), Tomkins (77);
Goals: Sinfield 6/6.
NEW ZEALAND: 1 Kevin Locke (New Zealand Warriors); 5 Jason Nightingale (St George Illawarra Dragons); 4 Simon Mannering (New Zealand Warriors); 2 Gerard Beale (Brisbane Broncos); 6 Benji Marshall (Wests Tigers) (C); 7 Kieran Foran (Manly Sea Eagles); 8 Ben Matulino (New Zealand Warriors); 9 Thomas Leuluai (Wigan Warriors); 17 Russell Packer (New Zealand Warriors); 11 Sika Manu (Melbourne Storm); 10 Adam Blair (Melbourne Storm); 13 Jeremy Smith (Cronulla Sharks). Subs (all used): 12 Alex Glenn (Brisbane Broncos); 14 Issac Luke (South Sydney Rabbitohs); 16 Jared Waerea-Hargreaves (Sydney Roosters); 18 Elijah Taylor (New Zealand Warriors).
Try: Nightingale (61); **Goals:** Marshall 1/1.
On report: Smith (6) - alleged use of the forearm on Tomkins; Luke (40) - alleged dangerous tackle on Chase.
Rugby Leaguer & League Express Men of the Match:
England: James Graham; *New Zealand:* Simon Mannering.
Penalty count: 9-5; **Half-time:** 8-0; **Referee:** Matt Cecchin (Australia); **Attendance:** 23,447 *(at Kingston Communications Stadium, Hull).*

GILLETTE FOUR NATIONS - GAME SIX

Sunday 13th November 2011

WALES 14 AUSTRALIA 56

WALES: 1 Danny Jones (Halifax); 2 Elliot Kear (Crusaders); 3 Ian Webster (Central Comets); 4 Christiaan Roets (South Wales Scorpions); 5 Rhys Williams (Warrington Wolves); 6 Lee Briers (Warrington Wolves) (C); 7 Lloyd White (Crusaders); 8 Jordan James (Crusaders); 9 Neil Budworth (Mackay Cutters); 10 Craig Kopczak (Bradford Bulls); 11 Chris Beasley (Central Comets); 12 Andy Bracek (Crusaders); 13 Ben Flower (Crusaders). Subs (all used): 14 Mark Lennon (Thirroul Butchers); 15 Ross Divorty (Featherstone Rovers); 16 Aled James (South Wales Scorpions); 17 Gil Dudson (Crusaders).
Tries: R Williams (9), Kear (12), J James (49); **Goals:** Briers 1/3.
On report: Roets (69) - alleged dangerous tackle.
AUSTRALIA: 1 Darius Boyd (St George Illawarra Dragons); 5 Jharal Yow Yeh (Brisbane Broncos); 4 Chris Lawrence (Wests Tigers); 3 Greg Inglis (South Sydney Rabbitohs); 2 Josh Morris (Canterbury Bulldogs); 6 Cooper Cronk (Melbourne Storm); 7 Johnathan Thurston (North Queensland Cowboys); 8 Keith Galloway (Wests Tigers); 9 Cameron Smith (Melbourne Storm) (C); 10 David Shillington (Canberra Raiders); 15 Anthony Watmough (Manly Sea Eagles); 12 Beau Scott (St George Illawarra Dragons); 13 Corey Parker (Brisbane Broncos). Subs (all used): 14 Daly Cherry-Evans (Manly Sea Eagles); 18 Paul Gallen (Cronulla Sharks); 16 Matt Scott (North Queensland Cowboys); 17 Sam Thaiday (Brisbane Broncos).
Tries: Smith (25), Cronk (38, 40, 70), Cherry-Evans (42), Boyd (46), Thurston (60), Inglis (64), Yow Yeh (66), Morris (74);
Goals: Thurston 8/9, Smith 0/1.
Rugby Leaguer & League Express Men of the Match:
Wales: Lee Briers; *Australia:* Cooper Cronk.
Penalty count: 4-7; **Half-time:** 8-18; **Referee:** Phil Bentham (England); **Attendance:** 5,233 *(at The Racecourse Ground, Wrexham).*

snuck in from dummy half. The Kangaroos hit the front for the first time on 38 minutes when Smith threw a dummy and hit the gap before offloading for Cronk to score under the posts.

Things got even worse for Wales on the hooter as Thurston put Inglis through on the angle before handing on to the supporting Cronk for his second try. Thurston added all three conversions as the Kangaroos led 18-8 at half-time. And it was one-way traffic after the break, Jordan James' 49th minute try aside.

GILLETTE FOUR NATIONS - FINAL TABLE							
	P	W	D	L	F	A	D	Pts
Australia	3	3	0	0	118	46	72	6
England	3	2	0	1	90	46	44	4
New Zealand	3	1	0	2	54	54	0	2
Wales	3	0	0	3	18	134	-116	0

Darren Lockyer brought the curtain down on his glittering playing career in perfect style as he led another Australian side to another tournament win by 30-8, scoring the final try in the last minute at a sold-out Elland Road. England were well in the game until just before the hour mark, at least on the scoreboard, with the scores locked at 8-all. But a four-try blitz gave the final scoreline a one-sided look.

The third quarter was England's best, as they repeatedly made inroads in the Australia '20', but Kevin Sinfield's 53rd minute penalty from 20 metres out was England's only reward, and the green and gold response was uncontainable. Five minutes later right winger Jharal Yow Yeh started the scoring barrage when England were caught for numbers on their left.

For England, Chris Heighington missed out with a calf strain, which allowed Steve McNamara to have another prop, Garreth Carvell, on the bench, with Jon Wilkin starting for the second week in a row, alongside Gareth Ellis, who recovered from the back strain that kept him out the week before against the Kiwis.

England needed to produce their very best to have a chance of beating the Kangaroos, but they didn't. The halves, Rangi Chase and Kevin Sinfield, were tightly policed. Sam Tomkins was never allowed to cause havoc and never looked comfortable under the high kick.

Johnathan Thurston, who was in danger of missing the game with a reported groin strain, and with his left knee strapped, took the official man of the match award as he ran riot in the last quarter, scoring a try himself, making another for Greg Inglis, before Lockyer's party piece. Earlier Thurston had created Australia's first try in the third minute with a bomb to the right corner that Tom Briscoe couldn't take, allowing Sam Thaiday to open the scoring, as well as converting a perfect five from five.

Thurston was also involved in England's penalty try late in the first half when his high tackle on Ryan Hall was deemed by the video referee to have prevented the winger grounding cleanly.

Lockyer's destiny was always to finish a winner, and he rounded off what he described as "a tough win" with a try in the last minute as his stab to the post protector hit its target and bounced up perfectly for him to drop on the ball. His very last touch was the conversion attempt from almost in front of the sticks that skidded off the outside of his left boot towards the touchline.

GILLETTE FOUR NATIONS - FINAL

Saturday 19th November 2011

ENGLAND 8 AUSTRALIA 30

ENGLAND: 1 Sam Tomkins (Wigan Warriors); 2 Ryan Hall (Leeds Rhinos); 3 Jack Reed (Brisbane Broncos); 4 Kirk Yeaman (Hull FC); 5 Tom Briscoe (Hull FC); 6 Kevin Sinfield (Leeds Rhinos); 7 Rangi Chase (Castleford Tigers); 8 James Graham (St Helens); 9 James Roby (St Helens); 10 Jamie Peacock (Leeds Rhinos) (C); 11 Jon Wilkin (St Helens); 12 Gareth Ellis (Wests Tigers); 13 Ben Westwood (Warrington Wolves). Subs (all used): 14 Gareth Widdop (Melbourne Storm); 15 Adrian Morley (Warrington Wolves); 16 Jamie Jones-Buchanan (Leeds Rhinos); 17 Garreth Carvell (Warrington Wolves).
Try: Hall (36, pen); **Goals:** Sinfield 2/2.
AUSTRALIA: 1 Darius Boyd (St George Illawarra Dragons); 5 Jharal Yow Yeh (Brisbane Broncos); 4 Chris Lawrence (Wests Tigers); 3 Greg Inglis (South Sydney Rabbitohs); 2 Akuila Uate (Newcastle Knights); 6 Darren Lockyer (Brisbane Broncos) (C); 7 Johnathan Thurston (North Queensland Cowboys); 8 Paul Gallen (Cronulla Sharks); 9 Cameron Smith (Melbourne Storm); 10 Matt Scott (North Queensland Cowboys); 11 Luke Lewis (Penrith Panthers); 12 Sam Thaiday (Brisbane Broncos); 16 David Shillington (Canberra Raiders). Subs (all used): 13 Anthony Watmough (Manly Sea Eagles); 14 Cooper Cronk (Melbourne Storm); 15 Keith Galloway (Wests Tigers); 17 Tony Williams (Manly Sea Eagles).
Tries: Thaiday (4), Yow Yeh (57), Thurston (62), Inglis (69), Lockyer (79); **Goals:** Thurston 5/5, Lockyer 0/1.
Rugby Leaguer & League Express Men of the Match:
England: Ben Westwood; *Australia:* Cameron Smith.
Penalty count: 8-3; **Half-time:** 6-8; **Referee:** Matt Cecchin (Australia); **Attendance:** 34,174 *(at Elland Road, Leeds).*

WORLD CUP QUALIFIERS
The Italian Job

USA and Italy qualified for the 14-team World Cup to be staged in the UK in 2013.

The US Tomahawks, a representative side from the original AMNRL after several clubs broke away at the start of 2011 to form the USARL, were clear-cut winners of the Atlantic Zone, beating both South Africa and then Jamaica by the same scoreline, 40-4. All three games were staged at Campbell's Field in Camden, Philadelphia.

USA were to join Wales and the Cook Islands in Group D of the main tournament after winning a decider against Jamaica, who featured almost a full line-up of UK-based professionals.

Former Bradford coach Matthew Elliott was also able to call on Ryan McGoldrick for that crucial game - after his suspension from the end of the Super League season had been served the previous Sunday - and several players with NRL experience starred, including the Paulo brothers Joseph and Junior.

USA produced a terrific second-half performance to deny the rugby reggae boys, posting 36 unanswered points and spark wild celebrations. The game was scoreless for just over the opening quarter, Sheffield's Corey Hanson giving the Jamaicans the lead for the sole time in the 26th minute, Keighley's Jy-mel Coleman missing the conversion. The USA hit back four minutes before the break, substitute Stephen Howard crashing on to a fine short ball from stand-off David Miles, Joseph Paulo goaling to make it 6-4 at half-time. Scrum-half David Marando's try five minutes into the second period edged the hosts a converted score ahead, centre Mitchell Stevens extending the lead soon after. Although he missed both conversions, two penalties in as many minutes from Joseph Paulo around the hour mark made it 18-4 and sapped the Jamaican resistance.

USA finished strongly, Mark Cantoni crossing to effectively seal the win and they added three further touchdowns in the final seven minutes through Miles, Danny Howard and prop Mark Offerdahl with their seventh try.

Italy's qualification from the European Zone to go into the group with Scotland and Tonga, was less clear cut, as they snatched a last-gasp draw with Lebanon in Belgrade to qualify for their first ever appearance in the tournament on points difference.

The Azzurri and Cedars had been the standout sides in the qualifying games, unsurprisingly with their ability to call on players with experience in Australian competitions, including Sydney Roosters' former Golden Boot winner Anthony Minichiello, who captained Italy. Lebanon's failure to put more points past the Bears in Russia the previous weekend ultimately cost them.

Lebanon held a 19-18 lead with five minutes remaining but in an atmosphere of high tension, Italy scrum-half Ryan Ghietti slotted over the equalising field goal in the 78th minute, amid protests from Lebanon that the ball had not passed between the short uprights. The final whistle saw tears of despair from Lebanon's players who had also been involved in the 2008 World Cup qualifying campaign, when the Cedars again failed to qualify on points difference.

WORLD CUP QUALIFIERS - EUROPEAN ZONE

	P	W	D	L	F	A	D	Pts
Italy	3	2	1	0	163	31	132	5
Lebanon	3	2	1	0	147	23	124	5
Russia	3	1	0	2	42	152	-110	2
Serbia	3	0	0	3	38	184	-146	0

WORLD CUP QUALIFIERS - ATLANTIC ZONE

	P	W	D	L	F	A	D	Pts
USA	2	2	0	0	80	8	72	4
Jamaica	2	1	0	1	24	46	-22	2
South Africa	2	0	0	2	10	60	-50	0

WORLD CUP QUALIFIERS

EUROPEAN ZONE

Saturday 15th October 2011

ITALY 92 RUSSIA 6

ITALY: Anthony Minichiello (C); Christophe Calegari; Dom Nasso; Matt Parrata; Josh Mantellato; Ben Falcone; Ryan Ghietti; Alex Ranieri; Ray Nasso; Ryan Tramonte; Cameron Ciraldo; Joel Riethmuller; Rob Quitadamo. Subs (all used): Dean Vicelich; Cederic Prizzon; Matthew Sands; Rhys Lennarduzzi.
Tries: D Nasso (3, 12), Parrata (16, 49), Ciraldo (21), Quitadamo (24), Mantellato (39, 74), Riethmuller (47), Sands (53), Ghietti (56, 65), Vicelich (63), R Nasso (69), Lennarduzzi (77), Falcone (79); **Goals:** Mantellato 14/16.
RUSSIA: Maksim Suchkov; Petr Botnarash; Andrey Zdobnikov; Mikhail Burlutskiy; Rustam Bulanov; Aleksander Lysokon (C); Eduard Ososkov; Sergey Konstantinov; Vladimir Vlasyuk; Ilgiz Galimov; Alexey Nikolaev; Grigory Esin; Vadim Fedchuk. Subs (all used): Sergey Gaponov; Igor Chuprin; Vladimir Gotsulyak; Artem Grigoryan.
Try: Vlasyuk (36); **Goals:** Lysokon 1/1.
Half-time: 36-6; **Referee:** James Child (England).
(at Stadio di Plebiscito, Padova).

Sunday 16th October 2011

LEBANON 96 SERBIA 4

LEBANON: Adnan Saleh; Adnan El Zabedieh; Danny Barakat; Adham El Zabedieh; Clifton Nye; James Boustani; Nadim Couri; Khaled Deeb (C); Jamie Clark; Allen Soultan; Ahmed Ellaz; Steve Azzi; Ray Moujali. Subs (all used): Ali Kourouche; Nick Kassis; Ibrahim Ballout; Robin Hachache.
Tries: Adham El Zabedieh, Saleh 3, Barakat 3, Nye 2, Boustani 2, Deeb, Clark 3, Kassis, Adnan El Zabedieh; **Goals:** Couri 13/15, Ballout 1/1, Hachache 0/1.
SERBIA: Ivan Susnjara; Vladan Kikanovic; Milos Calic; Aleksandar Aleksic; Nebojsa Zivanovic; Adam Nedic; Dalibor Vukanovic (C); Ilija Radan; Niksa Unkovic; Lazar Zivkovic; Stefan Nedeljkovic; Soni Radovanovic; Austen Novakovic. Subs (all used): Dejan Lukenic; Danilo Delic; Zoran Pesic; Milan Susnjara.
Try: Nedic; **Goals:** Novakovic 0/1.
Half-time: 46-0; **Referee:** Ben Thaler (England).
(at Olympic Stadium, Tripoli).

Saturday 22nd October 2011

RUSSIA 0 LEBANON 32

RUSSIA: Maksim Suchkov; Mikhail Burlutskiy; Petr Botnarash; Vadim Fedchuk; Rustam Bulanov; Aleksander Lysokon (C); Eduard Ososkov; Sergey Konstantinov; Vladimir Vlasyuk; Ilgiz Galimov; Alexey Nikolaev; Grigory Esin; Sergey Gaponov. Subs (all used): Igor Chuprin; Anatoly Grigoriev; Vladimir Odnosumov; Artem Grigoryan.
LEBANON: Clifton Nye; Adnan El Zabedieh; Danny Barakat; Danny Chiha; Adham El Zabedieh; James Boustani; Nadim Couri; Charlie Farah; Jamie Clark; Khaled Deeb (C); Nick Kassis; Steve Azzi; Ray Moujali. Subs (all used): Walid Yassine; Ibrahim Ballout; Chris Saab; Robin Hachache.
Tries: Nye (6), Barakat (18, 39), Kassis (28), Adnan El Zabedieh (30), Azzi (64); **Goals:** Couri 3/5, Boustani 1/1.
Half-time: 0-26; **Referee:** Steve Ganson (England).
(at Vereya Stadium, Vereya).

Sunday 23rd October 2011

SERBIA 6 ITALY 52

SERBIA: Ivan Susnjara; Nebojsa Zivanovic; Milos Calic; Danilo Delic; Radovan Tajsic; Adam Nedic; Niksa Unkovic; Ilija Radan; Austen Novakovic; Dejan Lukenic; Lazar Zivkovic; Stefan Nedeljkovic; Soni Radovanovic (C). Subs (all used): Zoran Pesic; Vladan Kikanovic; Aleksandar Aleksic; Vuk Tvrdisic.
Try: Pesic (41); **Goals:** Nedic 1/1.
ITALY: Anthony Minichiello (C); Josh Mantellato; Dom Nasso; Matt Parrata; Fabrizio Ciaurra; Ben Stewart; Ryan Ghietti; Vic Mauro; Jonathan Marcinczak; Alex Ranieri; Cameron Ciraldo; Joel Riethmuller; Rhys Lennarduzzi. Subs (all used): Dean Vicelich; Matthew Sands; Ray Nasso; Ryan Tramonte.
Tries: Minichiello (5, 8, 50), Riethmuller (19), Parrata (28), Mantellato (31), D Nasso (45), Lennarduzzi (55, 65); **Goals:** Mantellato 8/9.
Half-time: 0-28; **Referee:** Ben Thaler (England).
(at Ministry of Interior Stadium, Belgrade).

Saturday 29th October 2011

SERBIA 28 RUSSIA 36

SERBIA: Ivan Susnjara; Aleksandar Aleksic; Milos Calic; Stevan Stevanovic; Radovan Tajsic; Adam Nedic; Dalibor Vukanovic (C); Ilija Radan; Austen Novakovic; Dejan Lukenic; Soni Radovanovic; Stefan Nedeljkovic; Vuk Tvrdisic. Subs (all used): Nebojsa Zivanovic; Zoran Pesic; Danilo Delic; Niksa Unkovic.
Tries: Pesic (35), Nedic (39), I Susnjara (62), Radan (68), Novakovic (71); **Goals:** Nedic 4/5.
RUSSIA: Maksim Suchkov; Rustam Bulanov; Petr Botnarash; Mikhail Burlutskiy; Alexey Volkov; Aleksander Lysokon (C); Eduard Ososkov; Sergey Konstantinov; Vladimir Vlasyuk; Vadim Fedchuk; Alexey Nikolaev; Ilgiz Galimov; Sergey Gaponov. Subs (all used): Artem Grigoryan; Anatoly Grigoriev; Grigory Esin; Igor Chuprin.
Tries: Volkov (5), Botnarash (24, 26, 79), Chuprin (46), Ososkov (55); **Goals:** Lysokon 6/7.
Half-time: 12-16; **Referee:** Mohammad Drizza (France).
(at Belgrade Police Academy, Belgrade).

ITALY 19 LEBANON 19

ITALY: Anthony Minichiello (C); Josh Mantellato; Dom Nasso; Matt Parrata; Christophe Calegari; Ryan Ghietti; Alex Ranieri; Ray Nasso; Vic Mauro; Cameron Ciraldo; Joel Riethmuller; Ben Falcone. Subs (all used): Dean Vicelich; Ryan Tramonte; Rob Quitadamo; Rhys Lennarduzzi.
Tries: Falcone (20), Stewart (31), Mantellato (35); **Goals:** Mantellato 3/3; **Field goal:** Ghietti (78).
LEBANON: Adnan Saleh; Adnan El Zabedieh; Danny Barakat; Adham El Zabedieh; Clifton Nye; James Boustani; Nadim Couri; Charlie Farah; Jamie Clark; Khaled Deeb (C); Ahmed Ellaz; Steve Azzi; Ray Moujali. Subs (all used): Chris Saab; Nick Kassis; Allen Soultan; Robin Hachache.
Tries: Adnan El Zabedieh (50), Moujali (54), Boustani (58); **Goals:** Couri 3/3; **Field goal:** Couri (75).
Half-time: 18-0; **Referee:** Thierry Alibert (France).
(at Belgrade Police Academy, Belgrade).

Italy's Josh Mantellato escapes the attentions of Lebanon's Clifton Nye

ATLANTIC ZONE

Saturday 15th October 2011

USA 40 SOUTH AFRICA 4

USA: Matt Petersen; Nate Smith; Mitchell Stevens; Michael Garvey; Sione Taufa; Joseph Paulo; David Marando; Junior Paulo; Apple Pope (C); Mark Offerdahl; Daniel Howard; Mark Cantoni; Sean Taylor. Subs (all used): Andrew Kneisly; Ian Elliott; Stephen Howard; Curtis Cunz.
Tries: Taylor 2, Cunz 2, Cantoni, Taufa, Howard, Stevens; **Goals:** Joseph Paulo 4/8.
SOUTH AFRICA: Christoff Swanepoel; Andre Olwagen; Henry du Toit; Hans du Plessis; Johan Fritz; Francois Greyvensteyn; Andre Loader (C); Christo Louw; Deon Kraemer; Christo Joubert; Rudi Prinsloo; Sivive Mpondo; Stevie Meyer. Subs (all used): Marcelle Slabbert; Gerrie Slabber; Jonothan Soares; JP Nel.
Try: Fritz; **Goals:** Loader 0/1.
Half-time: 24-0; **Referee:** Richard Silverwood (England).
(at Campbell's Field, Camden, New Jersey).

Wednesday 19th October 2011

JAMAICA 20 SOUTH AFRICA 6

JAMAICA: Paul White (C); Waine Pryce; Corey Hanson; Ryan Grant; Wayne Reittie; Karl Pryce; Jy-Mel Coleman; Romain Campbell; Jamaine Wray; Jode Sheriffe; Lamont Bryan; Danny Bravo; Joe Brown. Subs (all used): Roy Calvert; Richie Barnett; Tyronie Rowe; Ross Peltier.
Tries: White (5), Reittie (20, 72), Grant (62); **Goals:** Coleman 2/4.
SOUTH AFRICA: Hans du Plessis; Rudi Prinsloo; Henry du Toit; Riaan Englebrecht; Johan Fritz; Pieter Van der Nest; Andre Loader (C); Christo Louw; Gerrie Slabber; Christo Joubert; Jonothan Soares; Sivive Mpondo; Stevie Meyer. Subs (all used): Gerhardt de Wet; Marcelle Slabbert; Deon Kraemer; Francois Greyvensteyn.
Try: Prinsloo (40); **Goals:** Van der Nest 1/1.
Half-time: 10-6; **Referee:** Richard Silverwood (England).
(at Campbell's Field, Camden, New Jersey).

Sunday 23rd October 2011

USA 40 JAMAICA 0

USA: Matt Petersen; Sione Taufa; Mitchell Stevens; Ryan McGoldrick; Michael Garvey; David Myles; David Marando; Junior Paulo; Apple Pope (C); Mark Offerdahl; Daniel Howard; Mark Cantoni; Joseph Paulo. Subs (all used): Stephen Howard; Sean Taylor; Curtis Cunz; Andrew Kneisly.
Tries: S Howard (36), Marando (45), Stevens (51), Cantoni (68), Myles (73), D Howard (75), Offerdahl (77); **Goals:** Joseph Paulo 6/7.
JAMAICA: Paul White (C); Waine Pryce; Richie Barnett; Omari Caro; Wayne Reittie; Karl Pryce; Jy-Mel Coleman; Lamont Bryan; Jamaine Wray; Jode Sheriffe; Danny Bravo; Corey Hanson; Joe Brown. Subs (all used): Ryan Grant; Tyronie Rowe; Ashley Johnson; Ross Peltier.
Try: Hanson (26); **Goals:** Coleman 0/1.
Half-time: 6-4; **Referee:** Richard Silverwood (England).
(at Campbell's Field, Camden, New Jersey).

OTHER INTERNATIONALS
Too long in exile

International Origin Match

The Rugby Football League abandoned the mid-season Test against France, instead staging a match between England and a side selected from Antipodean players currently with Super League clubs, coached by Brian McClennan and known as 'Exiles'. The contest, staged on Friday 10th June at Headingley, certainly provided a bigger challenge for coach Steve McNamara's side as George Carmont's try 44 seconds from the end finally settled an intriguing clash by 16-12 in favour of the Exiles.

Wigan hooker Michael McIlorum was called up in place of St Helens' James Roby, who withdrew from the England squad after suffering a fractured eye socket in his side's victory over Leeds the previous Friday. McNamara opted not to draft in a replacement for scrum-half Danny Brough, who injured ankle ligaments in Huddersfield's victory over Castleford.

Victory for the combined nations side was just reward for an accomplished, gutsy performance while they possessed superior invention, not least from man of the match Rangi Chase. The in-form Castleford halfback combined thrillingly with fellow countryman Thomas Leuluai throughout the game, and the pair were arguably the difference between the two sides.

England lacked nothing in effort and endeavour, and had some mighty efforts among the forwards, especially James Graham and Ben Westwood. Sam Tomkins, despite being greeted by audible boos throughout from sections of the Headingley crowd, was lively in attack and produced two stunning try-saving tackles in defence, while Luke Robinson was especially dangerous from hooker in his first spell. But in attack they didn't have the creative nous of their opponents, and, Richie Myler's first-half try aside, they struggled to break down the resolute Exiles defence.

Exiles took the lead when Leuluai stepped past Jamie Peacock and sent Willie Manu roaring under the posts. England were level when Graham took a drive on halfway, stepped past Saints teammate Tony Puletua and handed off Danny Buderus before finding the supporting Myler.

England thought they had broken through again in the very next set of six, only for Adrian Morley's pass to Jon Wilkin to be ruled forward, with Myler again waiting on his shoulder. Instead, it was the Exiles who crossed next to take a half-time advantage when Chase and Leuluai's wide passes allowed Brett Hodgson to kick perfectly for Sia Soliola,

CARPLAN INTERNATIONAL ORIGIN MATCH

Friday 10th June 2011

ENGLAND 12 THE EXILES 16

ENGLAND: 1 Sam Tomkins (Wigan Warriors); 5 Tom Briscoe (Hull FC); 4 Chris Bridge (Warrington Wolves); 3 Michael Shenton (St Helens); 2 Ryan Hall (Leeds Rhinos); 6 Kevin Sinfield (Leeds Rhinos); 7 Richard Myler (Warrington Wolves); 8 James Graham (St Helens); 9 Luke Robinson (Huddersfield Giants); 10 Jamie Peacock (Leeds Rhinos) (C); 11 Jon Wilkin (St Helens); 12 Ben Westwood (Warrington Wolves); 13 Sean O'Loughlin (Wigan Warriors). Subs (all used): 14 Michael McIlorum (Wigan Warriors); 15 Adrian Morley (Warrington Wolves); 16 Garreth Carvell (Warrington Wolves); 17 Joel Tomkins (Wigan Warriors).
Tries: Myler (21), J Tomkins (69); **Goals:** Sinfield 2/2.
THE EXILES: 1 Brett Hodgson (Warrington Wolves); 2 Pat Richards (Wigan Warriors); 3 George Carmont (Wigan Warriors); 11 Iosia Soliola (St Helens); 5 Francis Meli (St Helens); 6 Rangi Chase (Castleford Tigers); 7 Thomas Leuluai (Wigan Warriors); 10 Mark O'Meley (Hull FC); 9 Danny Buderus (Leeds Rhinos) (C); 8 Tony Puletua (St Helens); 16 Louis Anderson (Warrington Wolves); 12 Willie Manu (Hull FC); 13 Craig Fitzgibbon (Hull FC). Subs (all used): 14 David Faiumu (Huddersfield Giants); 15 Kylie Leuluai (Leeds Rhinos); 18 Glenn Morrison (Wakefield Trinity Wildcats); 17 David Fa'alogo (Huddersfield Giants).
Tries: Manu (7), Meli (28), Carmont (80); **Goals:** Richards 2/3.
Rugby Leaguer & League Express Men of the Match:
England: Sam Tomkins; *The Exiles:* Rangi Chase.
Penalty count: 4-4; **Half-time:** 6-10; **Referee:** Richard Silverwood; **Attendance:** 14,174 *(at Headingley Carnegie, Leeds).*

who skilfully patted the ball inside for Francis Meli to touch down.

The second half developed into a tight battle before Joel Tomkins rushed off the line to intercept a Buderus pass from dummy-half, despite protests of offside from the Exiles. Tomkins then showed outstanding pace over the full length of the field to cross under the posts and, with Sinfield's conversion, give England a 12-10 lead.

With less than a minute remaining, the Exiles finally found a way through. Chase was the instigator, combining with Carmont to send Manu marauding through a gap. He was pulled down ten metres short. But on the next tackle Puletua again offloaded in the tackle, Carmont picked up the loose ball, and stepped inside four England defenders to plunge over for the winning try.

Gillette Four Nations - Warm-up matches

Almost seventeen thousand crammed into the Parc des Sports in Avignon the weekend before the Gillette Four Nations began, to see France give England a fitting warm-up for the tournament ahead. For the French, a late comeback and sizeable spells of dominance during the 80 minutes all but erased their modest showing against the England Knights six days before, despite a final scoreline of 32-18.

Ryan Hall scored in the right corner after only one minute and 29 seconds. Kevin Sinfield kicked a 40/20, and, one tackle after the scrum win, Sinfield and new boy Jack Reed sent in Hall on a huge overlap.

Debutants Reed, Rangi Chase and Chris Heighington all added to the England side. Reed scored a spectacular 80-metre try on 68 minutes when Gareth Widdop, who came on to replace Sam Tomkins at fullback with half an hour to go, ran at pace to release Reed down the right wing. The Keighley-born centre raced away, shrugged off the covering Thomas Bosc and rounded fullback Cyril Stacul to race to the posts.

After Hall's opening try France rallied before Olivier Elima beat Tomkins to the ball in-goal and the video referee decided he'd grounded cleanly. Thomas Bosc kicked the conversion and had the chance to extend the lead to 8-4 shortly after but

GILLETTE FOUR NATIONS - WARM-UP MATCHES

Friday 21st October 2011

FRANCE 18 ENGLAND 32

FRANCE: 1 Cyril Stacul (Catalan Dragons); 2 Vincent Duport (Catalan Dragons); 4 Mathias Pala (Catalan Dragons); 3 Jean-Philippe Baile (Catalan Dragons); 5 Frederic Vaccari (Catalan Dragons); 9 Dane Chisholm (Melbourne Storm); 7 Thomas Bosc (Catalan Dragons); 8 David Ferriol (Catalan Dragons); 6 Gregory Mounis (Catalan Dragons); 10 Remi Casty (Catalan Dragons); 11 Olivier Elima (Bradford Bulls) (C); 12 Cyrille Gossard (Catalan Dragons); 13 Jason Baitieri (Catalan Dragons). Subs (all used): 14 Eloi Pelissier (Catalan Dragons); 15 Jamal Fakir (Catalan Dragons); 16 Sebastien Raguin (Catalan Dragons); 17 Michael Simon (Catalan Dragons).
Tries: Elima (17), Pelissier (70), Duport (74); **Goals:** Bosc 3/4.
ENGLAND: 1 Sam Tomkins (Wigan Warriors); 2 Ryan Hall (Leeds Rhinos); 3 Jack Reed (Brisbane Broncos); 4 Kirk Yeaman (Hull FC); 5 Tom Briscoe (Hull FC); 6 Kevin Sinfield (Leeds Rhinos); 7 Rangi Chase (Castleford Tigers); 8 Jamie Peacock (Leeds Rhinos) (C); 9 James Roby (St Helens); 10 James Graham (St Helens); 11 Gareth Ellis (Wests Tigers); 12 Ben Westwood (Warrington Wolves); 13 Chris Heighington (Wests Tigers). Subs (all used): 14 Gareth Widdop (Melbourne Storm); 15 Adrian Morley (Warrington Wolves); 16 Jamie Jones-Buchanan (Leeds Rhinos); 17 Jon Wilkin (St Helens).
Tries: Hall (2), Yeaman (30), Briscoe (34, 50), Roby (38), Reed (68); **Goals:** Sinfield 4/6.
Rugby Leaguer & League Express Men of the Match:
France: Eloi Pelissier; *England:* James Roby.
Penalty count: 6-5; **Half-time:** 6-20; **Referee:** Matt Cecchin (Australia); **Attendance:** 16,866 *(at Parc des Sports, Avignon).*

Saturday 22nd October 2011

WALES 30 IRELAND 6

WALES: 1 Andrew Gay (South Wales Scorpions); 2 Elliot Kear (Crusaders); 3 Ian Webster (Central Comets); 4 Christiaan Roets (South Wales Scorpions); 5 Rhys Williams (Warrington Wolves); 6 Lloyd White (Crusaders); 7 Ian Watson (Swinton Lions); 8 Jordan James (Crusaders) (C); 9 Neil Budworth (Mackay Cutters); 17 Gil Dudson (Crusaders); 11 Tyson Frizell (Cronulla Sharks); 12 Andy Bracek (Crusaders). Subs (all used): 15 Peter Lupton (Crusaders); 16 Matt Seamark (Wynnum Manly Seagulls); 16 Ben Flower (Crusaders); 10 Craig Kopczak (Bradford Bulls); 19 Mark Lennon (Thirroul Butchers); 20 Geraint Davies (unattached); 21 Lee Williams (Crusaders); 22 Ross Divorty (Featherstone Rovers).
Tries: Gay (1), Roets (27), Frizell (30), Lennon (42), Kear (45), J James (70); **Goals:** White 0/1, Webster 3/5.
IRELAND: 1 Gregg McNally (Huddersfield Giants); 2 Tim Bergin (Sheffield Eagles); 3 Ian Cross (St Helens); 4 Elliott Cosgrove (Dewsbury Rams); 5 Joe Taylor (North Dublin Eagles); 6 Pat Smith (Sheffield Eagles); 7 Liam Finn (Featherstone Rovers) (C); 8 Luke Ambler (Harlequins); 9 Bob Beswick (Halifax); 10 Paddy Boyle (Oxford University); 11 Tyrone McCarthy (Warrington Wolves); 12 Ged Corcoran (Toulouse Olympique); 13 Callum Casey (Oldham). Subs (all used): 14 Sean Carmody (York City Knights); 15 Paddy Barcoe (Carlow Crusaders); 16 Tom McGarr (UWIC); 17 Aaron McCloskey (St Helens); 18 Joe Mulhern (Featherstone Rovers); 19 Andy McGrory (Coventry Bears).
Try: Bergin (77); **Goals:** Finn 1/1.
Rugby Leaguer & League Express Men of the Match:
Wales: Jordan James; *Ireland:* Tyrone McCarthy.
Penalty count: 5-5; **Half-time:** 14-0; **Referee:** Thierry Alibert (France); **Attendance:** 2,265 *(at The Gnoll, Neath).*

he missed from almost exactly the same spot when Jon Wilkin gave away his second penalty in as many minutes when he came off the bench.

Within four minutes Chase and Tomkins combined at speed with Kirk Yeaman, who went into the left corner, after James Roby's super-fast play-the-ball caught the French defence short of numbers.

Sinfield kicked the goal from the left touchline, and wasn't far wide a couple of minutes later, when Chase's looping pass to Yeaman allowed Tom Briscoe to skilfully squeeze into the same corner. The killer try came two minutes before the break, when Sinfield sent James Graham charging through the middle with an inside ball, and Graham sent clubmate, the unflagging Roby, under the sticks with a scissors pass.

Briscoe went in for his second on 50 minutes but it took another 18 minutes to breach a resolute French defence, with Widdop and Reed's wonder effort settling the outcome.

The last ten minutes belonged to France, and in particular substitute Eloi Pelissier. First, after a penalty for interference, the young Catalan hooker hoodwinked the left-side England defence with a dummy and go from a tap penalty. And minutes late Pelissier crabbed across field from a Baitieri offload and hit Duport with a perfect flat pass. The crowd went crazy as Duport, who only played three games for the Dragons in 2011 because of a ruptured anterior knee ligament injury, tore 60 metres downfield and around Widdop for a wonderful try.

Wales warmed up for the Gillette Four Nations with a 30-6 win over Ireland in Neath. Iestyn Harris gave 21 of his players a run, with Chris Beasley, Gareth Thomas, Lee Briers and Aled James sitting out the friendly. Beasley was still nursing an ankle injury picked up with Central Comets in Australia, James and Briers were recovering from an illness while Thomas was given leave for personal reasons. Later that week Thomas announced his retirement as a player. Jordan James stood out for his strength in attack and defence and scored a deserved try.

England Knights

At the start of the year England coach Steve McNamara announced a new England Knights programme featuring 25 players from 11 clubs to supplement the pool of players available to the national team.

In July, St Helens assistant Kieron Purtill was appointed head coach of the Knights side who were due to play two international fixtures in the autumn. The Knights played France at Leigh but the late

ENGLAND KNIGHTS TRAINING SQUAD
(announced in February)
Joe Arundel (Castleford Tigers); Ryan Atkins (Warrington Wolves); Jodie Broughton (Salford City Reds); Josh Charnley (Wigan Warriors); Paul Clough (St Helens); James Donaldson (Bradford Bulls); Liam Farrell (Wigan Warriors); Dale Ferguson (Huddersfield Giants); Luke Gale (Harlequins); Darrell Goulding (Wigan Warriors); Michael Lawrence (Huddersfield Giants); Jonny Lomax (St Helens); Shaun Lunt (Huddersfield Giants); Stefan Marsh (Wigan Warriors); Jermaine McGillvary (Huddersfield Giants); Scott Moore (St Helens); Lee Mossop (Wigan Warriors); Larne Patrick (Huddersfield Giants); Stefan Ratchford (Salford City Reds); Chris Riley (Warrington Wolves); Matty Smith (Salford City Reds); Jonathan Walker (Castleford Tigers); Kallum Watkins (Leeds Rhinos); Joe Westerman (Hull FC); Elliott Whitehead (Bradford Bulls).
In July, Hull FC's Danny Houghton and St Helens winger Jamie Foster were drafted into the squad with Hull KR's Liam Watts, who came down from the Elite Training Squad. St Helens halfback Jonny Lomax and Warrington centre Ryan Atkins were promoted to the England Elite Squad, whilst Castleford prop Jonathan Walker dropped out of the Knights programme after dislocating his knee in a club game.

cancellation of a tour by Samoa led to the second game being a hastily arranged fixture against Cumbria, who had also been due to meet the Samoans.

Aside from 30-year-old Ben Westwood, playing to get some game time ahead of England's Four Nations series after missing most of the domestic run-in with a knee injury, the Knights fielded a young side in a 38-18 win over France. The Knights dominated from start to finish with, in the first half especially, man of the match Richard Myler and Westwood influential in their left-hand side attack that tore the French defence apart time after time.

Myler opened the scoring and while France hogged possession after that they showed little creativity, and on the half-hour Danny Houghton crossed from dummy half. Greg Mounis claimed a similar try on 39 minutes before Myler shimmied his way through, handing on to the supporting Jodie Broughton, who left Vincent Duport trailing; Josh Charnley adding his third conversion for a 18-6 interval lead.

England extended their lead to 26-6 shortly after the restart: Matty Smith's kick to the corner was taken brilliantly by Charnley in the corner, and Charnley posted his second try soon after when fullback Dane Chisholm tried to keep the ball in play when a Matty Smith kick was heading for touch. Smith and Myler combined for Stefan Ratchford to post the Knights' sixth try, Westwood converting for a 32-6 lead. But France hit back, first through Eloi Pelissier and Cyril Stacul tries, Bosc converting both. England, however, had the last word, Luke Gale dummying his way under the posts and Charnley adding his fourth and final goal.

French coach Bobbie Goulding offered his resignation straight after the game, citing friction between the French Federation and Catalan Dragons, although 13 of his players were from the Dragons, but changed his mind before the weekend was out.

A week later the Knights got a sterner test against Cumbria at Whitehaven which they eventually won 26-12 with Myler again man of the match. The score stayed nil-nil for 26 minutes, when Zak Hardaker scorched down the right touchline and skipped past Brett Carter for a fine four-pointer created by Joe Westerman's surge and offload. Soon after the break, Myler ran to the right and sent Westerman through with a sharp inside ball, and there was Luke Gale on his shoulder to sprint to the line. But Cumbria stormed back with Jamie Butler, Liam Harrison, Carl Sice and Liam Campbell to the fore. Sice's pass ran along the ground, but Cumbria captain Kyle Amor toed it forward, raced on and touched down by the posts. But Sice went on a weaving run and tried a flat pass. Kris Welham juggled it, pouched it and raced 60 metres for the crucial six-pointer. Then Liam Watts crashed over off Matty Smith's short ball.

But Cumbria refused to fold and instead came storming back. Harrison, Mike Whitehead and Amor led the charge. Sice fed Campbell who released Brad Singleton for a well-deserved six points. Just before the end a Cumbrian error allowed Gale to dummy and accelerate away. He delivered a perfect long pass on the run for Charnley to dive in by the corner flag.

ANZAC matches

There were two ANZAC Tests in 2011, the ANZAC Day commemoration played in May at a packed Skilled Park on the Gold Coast and then another in Newcastle in October as a warm-up for the Gillette Four Nations.

In May, Billy Slater scored two tries for Australia as they overcame New Zealand to win 20-10. The Kiwis made too many handling errors throughout the match after Sam Rapira left the field, injuring his hand in the first carry of the game following a clash with Sam Thaiday, before Slater opened the scoring in the second minute. The second score came for the home side through Brisbane winger Jharal Yow Yeh as the Aussies went in at half-time with a 10-6 lead.

The Kiwis gave up possession five times in as many minutes in the second half, with Slater and then Jamal Idris making them pay with a try each. New Zealand responded

INTERNATIONAL FRIENDLIES

Saturday 15th October 2011

ENGLAND KNIGHTS 38 FRANCE 18

ENGLAND KNIGHTS: 1 Stefan Ratchford (Salford City Reds); 2 Josh Charnley (Wigan Warriors); 3 Joe Arundel (Castleford Tigers); 4 Kris Welham (Hull Kingston Rovers); 5 Jodie Broughton (Salford City Reds); 6 Richard Myler (Warrington Wolves); 7 Matty Smith (Salford City Reds); 8 Ben Harrison (Warrington Wolves); 9 Danny Houghton (Hull FC); 10 Lee Mossop (Wigan Warriors); 11 Joe Westerman (Hull FC) (C); 12 Ben Westwood (Warrington Wolves); 13 Liam Farrell (Wigan Warriors). Subs (all used): 14 Luke Gale (Harlequins); 15 Paul Clough (St Helens); 16 Michael Cooper (Warrington Wolves); 17 Liam Watts (Hull Kingston Rovers).
Tries: Myler (11), Houghton (31), Broughton (40), Charnley (46, 49), Ratchford (53), Gale (77); **Goals:** Charnley 4/6, Westwood 1/1.
FRANCE: 1 Dane Chisholm (Melbourne Storm); 2 Vincent Duport (Catalan Dragons); 3 Jean-Philippe Baile (Catalan Dragons); 4 Sebastien Raguin (Catalan Dragons); 5 Cyril Stacul (Catalan Dragons); 6 Thomas Bosc (Catalan Dragons); 7 Maxime Greseque (Pia); 8 David Ferriol (Catalan Dragons); 6 Gregory Mounis (Catalan Dragons); 10 Remi Casty (Catalan Dragons); 11 Olivier Elima (Bradford Bulls) (C); 12 Cyrille Gossard (Catalan Dragons); 13 Jason Baitieri (Catalan Dragons). Subs (all used): 14 Eloi Pelissier (Catalan Dragons); 15 Jamal Fakir (Catalan Dragons); 16 Michael Simon (Catalan Dragons); 17 Kane Bentley (Lezignan).
Tries: Mounis (39), Pelissier (61), Stacul (71); **Goals:** Bosc 3/3.
Rugby Leaguer & League Express Men of the Match:
England Knights: Richard Myler; *France:* Cyrille Gossard.
Penalty count: 10-8; **Half-time:** 22-8; **Referee:** Thierry Alibert (France);
Attendance: 2,071 *(at Leigh Sports Village).*

Saturday 22nd October 2011

CUMBRIA 12 ENGLAND KNIGHTS 26

CUMBRIA: 1 Brett Carter (Workington Town); 2 Chris Larkin (Barrow Raiders); 3 Jason Mossop (Workington Town); 18 Liam Harrison (Barrow Raiders); 5 Will Sharp (Hull FC); 6 Liam Campbell (Barrow Raiders); 7 Darren Holt (Workington Town); 19 Jamie Butler (Barrow Raiders); 9 Chris Smith (Whitehaven); 14 Kyle Amor (Wakefield Trinity Wildcats); 20 Mike Whitehead (Workington Town); 21 Oliver Wilkes (Harlequins) (C); 13 Brad Singleton (Leeds Rhinos). Subs (all used): 8 Carl Sice (Whitehaven); 12 Karl Olstrum (Workington Town); 17 Paul Culnean (Whitehaven); 10 Elliott Miller (Workington Town); 11 Aaron Low (Workington Town).
Tries: Amor (51), Singleton (74); **Goals:** Holt 1/1, Sharp 1/1.
ENGLAND KNIGHTS: 1 Chris Riley (Warrington Wolves); 2 Josh Charnley (Wigan Warriors); 3 Zak Hardaker (Leeds Rhinos); 4 Kris Welham (Hull Kingston Rovers); 5 Jodie Broughton (Salford City Reds); 6 Richard Myler (Warrington Wolves); 7 Luke Gale (Harlequins); 8 Lee Mossop (Wigan Warriors); 9 Scott Moore (St Helens); 10 Paul Clough (St Helens); 11 Joe Westerman (Hull FC) (C); 12 Chris Clarkson (Leeds Rhinos); 13 Liam Farrell (Wigan Warriors). Subs (all used): 14 Liam Watts (Hull Kingston Rovers); 15 Matty Smith (Salford City Reds); 16 James Donaldson (Bradford Bulls); 17 Joe Arundel (Castleford Tigers).
Tries: Hardaker (26), Gale (45), Welham (63), Watts (71), Charnley (79); **Goals:** Charnley 3/5.
Rugby Leaguer & League Express Men of the Match:
Cumbria: Liam Harrison; *England Knights:* Luke Gale.
Penalty count: 5-6; **Half-time:** 0-4; **Referee:** James Child (England);
Attendance: 1,163 *(at Recreation Ground, Whitehaven).*

with tries through Melbourne's Matt Duffie and St Helens-bound Lance Hohaia. Darren Lockyer equalled the record for Test appearances on the night by winning a 55th cap (not including his four for the Super League Tests in 1997).

There was a record attendance at Newcastle's Ausgrid Stadium in October as the Kangaroos were even more dominant in a 42-6 win. Lockyer played his last game on home soil and it couldn't have ended any sweeter, as he spearheaded a Kangaroos performance that had the Kiwis done for at half-time when they trailed 26-0.

The Kiwis were under the spell of Lockyer the magician right from the off, despite what looked a cynical effort when Warriors prop Russell Packer caught him late on the jaw as he made the first kick of the game. Packer went on report at the behest of the video referee and was subsequently banned for one game. By then Lockyer had created Australia's first try, Fijian Akuila Uate, tearing around to the right of the posts.

Autumn International Series

France won the three-nation series, with the European Cup suspended after its first year in 2010. Bobbie Goulding's side, made up predominantly of Catalan Dragons players, proved too strong for both Ireland and Scotland. In Perpignan, Melbourne's Dane Chisholm helped himself to three

ANZAC TEST

Friday 6th May 2011

AUSTRALIA 20 NEW ZEALAND 10

AUSTRALIA: 1 Billy Slater (Melbourne Storm); 5 Jharal Yow Yeh (Brisbane Broncos); 3 Greg Inglis (South Sydney Rabbitohs); 4 Justin Hodges (Brisbane Broncos); 2 Brett Morris (St George Illawarra Dragons); 6 Darren Lockyer (Brisbane Broncos) (C); 7 Johnathan Thurston (North Queensland Cowboys); 8 Petero Civoniceva (Penrith Panthers); 9 Cameron Smith (Melbourne Storm); 10 Matt Scott (North Queensland Cowboys); 11 Ben Creagh (St George Illawarra Dragons); 12 Sam Thaiday (Brisbane Broncos); 13 Paul Gallen (Cronulla Sharks). Subs (all used): 14 Cooper Cronk (Melbourne Storm); 15 Ben Hannant (Brisbane Broncos); 16 Jamal Idris (Bulldogs); 17 Kade Snowden (Cronulla Sharks).
Tries: Slater (3, 67), Yow Yeh (20), Idris (71); **Goals:** Thurston 2/4.
NEW ZEALAND: 1 Lance Hohaia (New Zealand Warriors); 5 Jason Nightingale (St George Illawarra Dragons); 3 Simon Mannering (New Zealand Warriors); 4 Shaun Kenny-Dowall (Sydney Roosters); 2 Matt Duffie (Melbourne Storm); 6 Benji Marshall (Wests Tigers); 8 Sam Rapira (New Zealand Warriors); 9 Nathan Fien (St George Illawarra Dragons); 10 Sam McKendry (Penrith Panthers); 11 Adam Blair (Melbourne Storm); 12 Bronson Harrison (Canberra Raiders); 13 Jeremy Smith (Cronulla Sharks). Subs (all used): 14 Issac Luke (South Sydney Rabbitohs); 15 Ben Matulino (New Zealand Warriors); 16 Fuifui Moimoi (Parramatta Eels); 18 Lewis Brown (New Zealand Warriors).
Tries: Duffie (36), Hohaia (75); **Goals:** Marshall 1/2.
Rugby Leaguer & League Express Men of the Match:
Australia: Paul Gallen; *New Zealand:* Kieran Foran.
Penalty count: 0-2; **Half-time:** 10-6; **Referee:** Richard Silverwood (England); **Attendance:** 26,301 *(at Skilled Park, Robina).*

TEST MATCH

Sunday 16th October 2011

AUSTRALIA 42 NEW ZEALAND 6

AUSTRALIA: 1 Billy Slater (Melbourne Storm); 2 Akuila Uate (Newcastle Knights); 3 Willie Tonga (North Queensland Cowboys); 4 Chris Lawrence (Wests Tigers); 5 Darius Boyd (St George Illawarra Dragons); 6 Darren Lockyer (Brisbane Broncos) (C); 7 Johnathan Thurston (North Queensland Cowboys); 8 Paul Gallen (Cronulla Sharks); 9 Cameron Smith (Melbourne Storm); 10 Matt Scott (North Queensland Cowboys); 11 Luke Lewis (Penrith Panthers); 12 Sam Thaiday (Brisbane Broncos); 13 Anthony Watmough (Manly Sea Eagles). Subs (all used): 14 Cooper Cronk (Melbourne Storm); 15 Keith Galloway (Wests Tigers); 16 David Shillington (Canberra Raiders); 17 Tony Williams (Manly Sea Eagles).
Tries: Uate (3, 6), Boyd (13, 70), Lawrence (21, 33), Galloway (63), Tonga (68); **Goals:** Thurston 4/7, Smith 1/1.
NEW ZEALAND: 1 Kevin Locke (New Zealand Warriors); 2 Kalifa Faifai Loa (North Queensland Cowboys); 3 Lewis Brown (New Zealand Warriors); 4 Gerard Beale (Brisbane Broncos); 5 Jason Nightingale (St George Illawarra Dragons); 6 Benji Marshall (Wests Tigers) (C); 7 Kieran Foran (Manly Sea Eagles); 8 Russell Packer (New Zealand Warriors); 9 Nathan Fien (St George Illawarra Dragons); 10 Sam McKendry (Penrith Panthers); 11 Alex Glenn (Brisbane Broncos); 12 Simon Mannering (New Zealand Warriors); 13 Jeremy Smith (Cronulla Sharks). Subs (all used): 14 Issac Luke (South Sydney Rabbitohs); 15 Fuifui Moimoi (Parramatta Eels); 16 Sika Manu (Melbourne Storm); 17 Jared Waerea-Hargreaves (Sydney Roosters).
Try: Locke (56); **Goals:** Luke 1/1.
On report: Packer (1) - alleged high tackle on Lockyer.
Rugby Leaguer & League Express Men of the Match:
Australia: Darren Lockyer; *New Zealand:* Kevin Locke.
Penalty count: 3-3; **Half-time:** 26-0; **Referee:** Phil Bentham (England); **Attendance:** 32,890 *(at Ausgrid Stadium, Newcastle).*

tries on his third appearance, while centre Jean-Philippe Baile, named man of the match for a non-stop performance, went over for two first-half tries in a 46-10 win. Halfback Thomas Bosc, showing his experience and authority in the middle of the field, claimed 18 points from a try and seven goals in front of a crowd of over ten thousand.

A week later, in the first ever game of Rugby League to be played at Thomond Park in Limerick, Mark Aston-coached Ireland led 12-10 before the French produced a superb final 15 minutes to win 34-16, Kane Bentley finishing with a hat-trick of tries. North Dublin Eagles winger Joe Taylor also scored a hat-trick.

Scotland had kicked off the series with a 26-6 win in Glasgow. Two tries on his debut by Glaswegian teenager David Scott of Hull KR proved crucial.

AUTUMN INTERNATIONAL SERIES

Sunday 16th October 2011

SCOTLAND 26 IRELAND 6

SCOTLAND: 1 Alex Hurst (Swinton Lions); 2 Crawford Matthews (Hull FC); 3 Josh Barlow (Halifax); 4 Dave Arnot (London Skolars); 5 David Scott (Hull Kingston Rovers); 6 Lee Paterson (Swinton Lions); 7 John Duffy (Leigh Centurions); 8 Jack Stearman (York City Knights); 9 Andrew Henderson (Sheffield Eagles) (C); 10 Neil Lowe (Hunslet Hawks); 11 Sam Barlow (Halifax); 12 Paddy Coupar (Edinburgh Eagles); 13 Alex Szostak (Sheffield Eagles). Subs (all used): 14 Jack Howieson (Sheffield Eagles); 15 Callum Cockburn (Edinburgh Eagles); 16 Michael Stewart (Gloucestershire University); 17 Giles Lomax (Edinburgh Eagles).
Tries: Hurst (4), J Barlow (25), Coupar (42), Scott (62, 79);
Goals: Hurst 1/2, Scott 2/3.
IRELAND: 1 Gregg McNally (Huddersfield Giants); 2 James Haley (Halifax); 3 Ian Cross (St Helens); 4 Elliott Cosgrove (Dewsbury Rams); 5 Joe Taylor (North Dublin Eagles); 6 Paul Handforth (Batley Bulldogs); 7 Liam Finn (Featherstone Rovers) (C); 8 Paddy Boyle (Oxford University); 9 Bob Beswick (Halifax); 10 Kyle Amor (Wakefield Trinity Wildcats); 11 Lemeki Vunipulu (Treaty City Titans); 12 Ged Corcoran (Toulouse Olympique); 13 Tyrone McCarthy (Warrington Wolves). Subs (all used): 14 Sean Carmody (York City Knights); 15 Paddy Barcoe (Carlow); 16 Callum Casey (Oldham); 17 Aaron McCloskey (St Helens).
Try: Finn (10); **Goals:** Finn 1/1.
Rugby Leaguer & League Express Men of the Match:
Scotland: David Scott; *Ireland:* Liam Finn.
Penalty count: 7-7; **Half-time:** 10-6; **Referee:** Steve Ganson (England);
Attendance: 802 *(at Scotstoun Stadium, Glasgow).*

Saturday 29th October 2011

FRANCE 46 SCOTLAND 10

FRANCE: 1 Cyril Stacul (Catalan Dragons); 2 Vincent Duport (Catalan Dragons); 3 Jean-Philippe Baile (Catalan Dragons); 4 Mathias Pala (Catalan Dragons); 5 Frederic Vaccari (Catalan Dragons); 6 Dane Chisholm (Melbourne Storm); 7 Thomas Bosc (Catalan Dragons); 8 Jamal Fakir (Catalan Dragons); 9 Kane Bentley (Lezignan); 10 Remi Casty (Catalan Dragons); 11 Olivier Elima (Bradford Bulls) (C); 12 Cyrille Gossard (Catalan Dragons); 13 Jason Baitieri (Catalan Dragons). Subs (all used): 14 Maxime Greseque (Pia); 15 Julian Bousquet (Catalan Dragons); 17 Michael Simon (Catalan Dragons); 19 Eloi Pelissier (Catalan Dragons).
Tries: Baile (8, 31), Chisholm (39, 61, 78), Duport (59), Bosc (73), Pala (75);
Goals: Bosc 7/8.
On report: Bentley (20) - alleged punching.
SCOTLAND: 1 Alex Hurst (Swinton Lions); 2 Crawford Matthews (Hull FC); 3 Ben Hellewell (Warrington Wolves); 4 Dave Arnot (London Skolars); 5 David Scott (Hull Kingston Rovers); 6 Lee Paterson (Swinton Lions); 7 John Duffy (Leigh Centurions); 8 Giles Lomax (Edinburgh Eagles); 9 Andrew Henderson (Sheffield Eagles); 10 Neil Lowe (Hunslet Hawks); 11 Sam Barlow (Halifax); 12 Paddy Coupar (Edinburgh Eagles); 13 Alex Szostak (Sheffield Eagles). Subs (all used): 14 Callum Cockburn (Edinburgh Eagles); 15 Michael Stewart (Gloucestershire University); 16 Jordan Rice (Gloucestershire University); 17 Nick Broere (Edinburgh Eagles).
Tries: Arnot (22), Hellewell (69); **Goals:** Hurst 0/1, Scott 1/1.
Rugby Leaguer & League Express Men of the Match:
France: Thomas Bosc; *Scotland:* Sam Barlow.
Penalty count: 10-8; **Half-time:** 16-4; **Referee:** Richard Silverwood (England);
Attendance: 10,313 *(at Stade Gilbert Brutus, Perpignan).*

Saturday 5th November 2011

IRELAND 16 FRANCE 34

IRELAND: 1 Gregg McNally (Huddersfield Giants); 2 Tim Bergin (Sheffield Eagles); 3 Ian Cross (St Helens); 4 Elliott Cosgrove (Dewsbury Rams); 5 Joe Taylor (North Dublin Eagles); 6 Paul Handforth (Batley Bulldogs); 7 Liam Finn (Featherstone Rovers) (C); 8 Kyle Amor (Wakefield Trinity Wildcats); 9 Bob Beswick (Halifax); 10 Luke Ambler (Harlequins); 11 Tyrone McCarthy (Warrington Wolves); 12 Ged Corcoran (Toulouse Olympique); 13 Callum Casey (Oldham). Subs (all used): 14 Pat Smith (Sheffield Eagles); 15 Paddy Barcoe (Carlow); 16 James Haley (Halifax); 17 Aaron McCloskey (St Helens).
Tries: Bergin (5), Taylor (15, 43, 74); **Goals:** Finn 0/4.
FRANCE: 1 Cyril Stacul (Catalan Dragons); 2 Vincent Duport (Catalan Dragons); 3 Mathias Pala (Catalan Dragons); 4 Jean-Philippe Baile (Catalan Dragons); 5 Frederic Vaccari (Catalan Dragons); 6 Dane Chisholm (Melbourne Storm); 7 Thomas Bosc (Catalan Dragons); 8 Jamal Fakir (Catalan Dragons); 9 Kane Bentley (Lezignan); 10 Remi Casty (Catalan Dragons); 11 Olivier Elima (Bradford Bulls) (C); 12 Cyrille Gossard (Catalan Dragons); 13 Jason Baitieri (Catalan Dragons). Subs (all used): 14 Eloi Pelissier (Catalan Dragons); 15 Michael Simon (Catalan Dragons); 16 Damien Cardace (Catalan Dragons); 17 Teddy Sadaoui (Carcassonne).
Tries: Bentley (9, 67, 75), Elima (60, 64), Bosc (72); **Goals:** Bosc 5/6.
Rugby Leaguer & League Express Men of the Match:
Ireland: Tyrone McCarthy; *France:* Kane Bentley.
Penalty count: 8-7; **Half-time:** 8-6; **Referee:** Richard Silverwood (England);
Attendance: 3,100 *(at Thomond Park, Limerick).*

AUTUMN INTERNATIONAL SERIES

	P	W	D	L	F	A	D	Pts
France	2	2	0	0	80	26	54	4
Scotland	2	1	0	1	36	52	-16	2
Ireland	2	0	0	2	22	60	-38	0

ACADEMY INTERNATIONALS

Saturday 4th December 2010

ENGLAND ACADEMY 38 AUSTRALIAN SCHOOLBOYS 30

ENGLAND ACADEMY: 1 Matthew Russell (Wigan Warriors); 2 Ryan King (Wigan Warriors); 3 Jordan Thompson (Castleford Tigers); 4 Rhys Evans (Warrington Wolves); 5 Reece Lyne (Hull FC); 6 Gareth O'Brien (Warrington Wolves); 7 Sam Powell (Wigan Warriors); 8 George Burgess (Bradford Bulls); 9 Adam Milner (Castleford Tigers) (C); 10 Ben Evans (Warrington Wolves); 11 Danny Bridge (Wigan Warriors); 12 Jack Hughes (Wigan Warriors); 13 James Laithwaite (Warrington Wolves). Subs (all used): 14 Adam O'Brien (Bradford Bulls); 15 Jared Stewart (Leeds Rhinos); 16 Greg Burke (Wigan Warriors); 17 Matthew Sarsfield (Wigan Warriors).
Tries: Bridge (2), King (33), Powell (55, 72), Sarsfield (65), Thompson (69);
Goals: G O'Brien 7/8.
AUSTRALIAN SCHOOLBOYS: 1 Henare Wells; 2 Jacob Gagan; 3 Tautau Moga; 4 Trent Jennings; 5 David Nofoaluma; 6 Jack Wighton; 7 Harry Seijka; 8 Chris Grevsmuhl; 9 Chad Redman; 10 Matthew Groat; 11 Lachlan Burr; 12 Vaipuna Tia Kilifi; 13 Paul Carter (C). Subs (all used): 14 Gerard McCallum; 15 Michael Chee-Kam; 16 Anthony Gadd; 17 David Klemmer.
Tries: Jennings (26), Tia Kilifi (36), Redman (42), Wighton (47), Carter (62);
Goals: Gadd 5/5.
Sin bin: Klemmer (37) - dissent.
Rugby Leaguer & League Express Men of the Match:
England: James Laithwaite; *Australia:* Harry Seijka.
Penalty count: 20-7; **Half-time:** 12-12; **Referee:** Steve Ganson (England);
Attendance: 732 *(at Leigh Sports Village).*

Friday 10th December 2010

ENGLAND ACADEMY 34 AUSTRALIAN SCHOOLBOYS 22

ENGLAND ACADEMY: 1 Matthew Russell (Wigan Warriors); 2 Ryan King (Wigan Warriors); 3 Jordan Thompson (Castleford Tigers); 4 Rhys Evans (Warrington Wolves); 5 Reece Lyne (Hull FC); 6 Gareth O'Brien (Warrington Wolves); 7 Sam Powell (Wigan Warriors); 8 George Burgess (Bradford Bulls); 9 Adam Milner (Castleford Tigers) (C); 10 Olsi Krasniqi (Harlequins); 11 Danny Bridge (Wigan Warriors); 12 Ben Evans (Warrington Wolves); 13 James Laithwaite (Warrington Wolves). Subs (all used): 14 Adam O'Brien (Bradford Bulls); 15 Jared Stewart (Leeds Rhinos); 16 Greg Burke (Wigan Warriors); 17 Matthew Sarsfield (Wigan Warriors).
Tries: Powell (15), Thompson (21, 46), B Evans (34), Russell (39), R Evans (65);
Goals: G O'Brien 5/7.
AUSTRALIAN SCHOOLBOYS: 1 Henare Wells; 2 Jacob Gagan; 3 Tautau Moga; 4 Trent Jennings; 5 Luke Pickerd; 6 Jack Wighton; 7 Harry Seijka; 8 Chris Grevsmuhl; 9 Chad Redman; 10 Matthew Groat; 11 Lachlan Burr; 12 Vaipuna Tia Kilifi; 13 Paul Carter (C). Subs (all used): 14 Cameron Cullen; 15 Ian Riccardi; 16 Anthony Gadd; 17 Matthew Eisenhuth.
Tries: Wells (5), Gagan (54), Carter (61), Jennings (72); **Goals:** Seijka 3/4.
Rugby Leaguer & League Express Men of the Match:
England: Ben Evans; *Australia:* Harry Seijka.
Penalty count: 6-2; **Half-time:** 22-4; **Referee:** Ben Thaler (England);
Attendance: 980 *(at Leigh Sports Village).*

Friday 3rd June 2011

FRANCE ACADEMY 19 ENGLAND ACADEMY 28

FRANCE ACADEMY: 1 Valentin Ferret (Lezignan); 2 Patrick Reynier (Pia); 3 Damien Cardace (Lezignan); 4 Charles Bouzinac (Lezignan); 5 Alexandre Doutres (St Esteve-XIII Catalan); 6 Karim Madani (St Esteve-XIII Catalan); 7 Yoan Didone (Albi); 8 Leo Baixas (Pia); 9 Joan Guasch (St Esteve-XIII Catalan); 10 Thibault Margalet (St Esteve-XIII Catalan); 11 Hakim Miloudi (St Esteve-XIII Catalan); 12 Mickael Rouch (Limoux); 13 Martial Romano (Carpentras). Subs (all used): 14 Maxime Scimone (St Esteve-XIII Catalan); 15 Yussuf Cal (Lyon); 16 Paul Ratier (Lezignan); 17 William Ousty (Tonneins).
Tries: Doutres (18), Miloudi (39), Cardace (66); **Goals:** Guasch 3/3.
Field goal: Guasch (70).
ENGLAND ACADEMY: 1 Jack Owens (Widnes Vikings); 2 Matthew Russell (Wigan Warriors); 3 Ryan Shaw (Warrington Wolves); 4 Ben Crooks (Hull FC); 5 Reece Lyne (Hull FC); 6 Dan Sarginson (Harlequins); 7 Daniel Yates (St Helens); 8 Brad Singleton (Leeds Rhinos) (C); 9 Liam Carberry (Wigan Warriors); 10 Greg Burke (Wigan Warriors); 11 Danny Bridge (Wigan Warriors); 12 Ben Currie (Warrington Wolves); 13 John Bateman (Bradford Bulls). Subs (all used): 14 Michael Bishay (Harlequins); 15 Jared Stewart (Leeds Rhinos); 16 Jordan Case (St Helens); 17 Daniel Smith (Leeds Rhinos).
Tries: Singleton (6), Lyne (30, 36, 60, 79), Shaw (42); **Goals:** Crooks 2/6.
Rugby Leaguer & League Express Men of the Match:
France: Joan Guasch; *England:* Reece Lyne.
Half-time: 12-14; **Referee:** Mohammed Drizza (France).
(at Stade Georges Guilhem, Palau).

EUROPEAN SHIELD: Norway 32 Germany 28; Germany 36 Malta 12; Malta 64 Norway 24
* Germany winners on points difference

EUROPEAN BOWL: Hungary 16 Czech Republic 38

MILAN KOSANOVIC CUP *(won by Russia):* Ukraine 4 Russia 26; Serbia 10 Ukraine 4; Serbia 28 Russia 36 *(World Cup double header)*

NORDIC CUP: Sweden 20 Norway 20; Denmark 28 Norway 8; Sweden 18 Denmark 52

AMATEUR FOUR NATIONS:
Ireland 22 Wales 54; England 30 Scotland 22; Wales 34 Scotland 22;
England 12 Ireland 26; Wales 30 England 24; Scotland 28 Ireland 18
Wales won all three games to claim the Grand Slam and an eighth title in 10 years

● Papua New Guinea and Fiji drew a two-match series in November. Fiji won the first game in Mount Hagen by 24-12, the Kumuls took the second in Port Moresby 26-0.
● The Australian Prime Minister's XIII beat Papua New Guinea by 36-22 in their annual clash amid chaotic scenes as an estimated ten thousand locals were locked out of the stadium in Lae.
● A proposed Test between New Zealand and the Cook Islands in Raratonga on October 7th was cancelled because of the involvement of the NZ Warriors in the NRL Grand Final.
● The proposed three-match tour of the UK and Eire by Samoa in October was cancelled at the eleventh hour when funding by the Samoan government was withdrawn.
● In March, Ireland beat USA Tomahawks 26-8 in the Donnybrook Cup international in Philadelphia
● Canada recorded a convincing 40-10 victory over Jamaica in Markham Ontario in the Caribbean Carnival Cup in late July.
● Canada secured a first-ever win over the USA in their Colonial Cup clash in Toronto, by 18-16.
● South Africa prepared for the World Cup Qualifiers in October with a 36-22 win against Canada in Toronto.

SEASON DOWN UNDER
Manly halt Kiwi charge

Manly Sea Eagles won their second Premiership in four seasons with an emphatic 24-10 victory over their surprise grand final opponents, the New Zealand Warriors in the 2011 decider.

Then, in a bizarre finish to the year, the Sea Eagles sacked their successful coach Des Hasler after he announced he would eventually join cross-city rivals Canterbury at the end of next season. With the Warriors' Ivan Cleary joining Penrith Panthers in 2012 fans face the unique situation of both grand final coaches being at the helm of opposition sides the year after their successes.

The Warriors had staged an astonishing finish to the season. After being thrashed 40-10 by the Brisbane Broncos in their qualifying final, they shocked Wests Tigers and Melbourne Storm in successive weekends. But their run came to an abrupt end when the chips were down in the one match that counted. At Homebush, in front of just under 82,000 fans, the Premiership proved too elusive.

The talent of Manly Sea Eagles, buoyed by the return from suspension of their loose forward Glenn Stewart, was enough to get the side from the northern beaches of Sydney over the line. Stewart, who won the Clive Churchill Medal as Man of the Match, had been banned for three matches for his role in a brawling encounter with the Storm at Brookvale Oval in late August. Kiwi hard man Adam Blair, his protagonist in a melee that broke out as the pair was heading for the sin bin after a previous fracas, was suspended for five games.

Stewart was not the only Sea Eagle who rose to the occasion in the grand final. As Hasler noted, he couldn't single out any player: "They were all great. There was a great attitude. It's a great club. I am so proud to be part of it all." It was an interesting comment considering the parting of the ways for Manly and Hasler a month later.

It was a torrid beginning with neither side willing to give an inch. The Warriors eventually broke the nil-all deadlock with a penalty goal by James Maloney after huge substitute forward George Rose was placed on report for using an elbow on the head of hooker Aaron Heremaia who had been tackled and was prone on the turf. The lead lasted just two minutes. Brett Stewart produced a brilliant solo run to score his 15th try in 20 appearances during 2011. And Lyon converted.

Just when it looked like there would be little separating the two sides at the interval, Manly pulled off a sensational play. The Sea Eagles took the ball almost the length of the pitch. Glenn Stewart put in a short kick. The movement broke down thanks to a great Sam Rapira tackle, but the Sea Eagles were rewarded when half Daly Cherry-Evans, the Dally M Rookie of the Year, dummied his way across the line to score next to the right upright.

It looked as if Manly had made sure of victory when Kris Inu fumbled the ball behind his own line and Manly's Kiwi international Keiran Foran pounced. Then Will Hopoate pulled off one of the great passes of the season, flicking the ball behind his back as he was being bundled into touch for Glenn Stewart to score.

Back-to-back tries within the space of six minutes to Vatuvei and back-rower Elijah Taylor – both set up by Johnson – had the Warriors back within striking distance with 10 minutes of the match remaining. But Lyon eventually sealed victory with his own late try.

Here's how the clubs fared in 2011.

MANLY SEA EAGLES (Premiers)

It was a case of sweet and sour for Manly. At the start of the season many critics believed they wouldn't even make the play-offs let alone be Premiership contenders. They had endured a couple of strife-torn seasons and were going to have to rely on some inexperienced young players. Yet those young players came up trumps and, with a consistency unmatched by other clubs, Manly finished second on the final Premiership table and then went one better on Grand Final Day. Coach Des Hasler was full of praise for the youngsters, including the youngest halves combination – 21-year-old Keiran Foran and Daly Cherry-Evans, one year his senior – to steer their side to success since the great Peter Sterling and Brett Kenny did the same for Parramatta in 1981.

No sooner had Hasler guided the Sea Eagles to Premiership success than he dropped a bombshell, announcing he would leave Brookvale at the end of the 2012 season to join the Canterbury Bulldogs.

It seemed unthinkable. Although he had started his senior career with Penrith and had a final year with Wests Magpies, Hasler was seen as a Sea Eagle through and through, with 13 seasons at Brookvale and 255 appearances in Manly colours. He had eight seasons as coach, winning Premierships in 2008 and 2011. Several of his coaching staff indicated they would follow him across the city to Canterbury. And there were rumours that a number of players may follow suit. Manly chiefs did not wait. They sacked Hasler and quickly turned to another Sea Eagle legend, Geoff Toovey, to succeed him in an attempt to stem the growing tide of defectors.

During 2011, many of the Manly players claimed individual honours. Co-captain (and former Man of Steel) Jamie Lyon was named Dally M Centre of the Year and, in a stellar season, would have undoubtedly played for Australia had he not asked not to be considered for selection. Cherry-Evans was Dally M Rookie of the Year and was chosen in Australia's squad for the Gillette Four Nations Tournament. Back-rowers Anthony Watmough and Tony Williams were also in the side that contested the tournament. Foran was in the Kiwis' line-up. Watmough, loose forward Glenn Stewart, prop Jason King and exciting young threequarter Will Hopoate all played State of Origin for New South Wales. At the end of the season Hopoate quit the game to spend two years as a Mormon missionary.

NEW ZEALAND WARRIORS (2nd)

The Warriors enjoyed what was arguably their best season since the original Auckland Warriors outfit joined the big league in 1995. They came from sixth place to reach the grand finals and in doing so overcome two of the more highly fancied sides, Wests Tigers and Melbourne Storm, in enthralling encounters. But, as with their grand final nemesis Manly, it was a bitter-sweet end to the season as their coach Ivan Cleary had already been poached by Penrith. Nevertheless they have found an able replacement in Brian McClennan, former Kiwi Test coach and mentor of both the Leeds Rhinos and the 2011 Exiles side that beat England.

Showing a great depth of talent, the Warriors also beat North Queensland 31-30 in extra time to win the Toyota Cup (under-20s) grand final. And their feeder club, the Auckland Vulcans went down 30-28 to Canterbury in the finale of the NSW Cup.

One of the keys to their success was the emergence of rookie scrum-half Shaun Johnson, who formed a deadly partnership with stand-off James Maloney. They were helped by a consistently solid display by the big forwards in the Warriors pack. Johnson was chosen in the Warriors squad for the Four Nations Tournament but had to withdraw through injury. However the Warriors were well-represented in the Test line-up – the club captain Simon Mannering, fullback Kevin Locke, winger Bill Tupou, utility Lewis Brown, props Ben Matulino and Russell Packer and second-rower Elijah Taylor. Prop Jacob Lillyman also played for Queensland's State of Origin side.

MELBOURNE STORM (3rd & Minor Premiers)

At the start of 2011 few of the experts expected Melbourne to be a legitimate challenger for Premiership honours. In the wake of the previous year's salary-cap scandal, their ranks had been decimated by the need to drastically cut the money being paid to their stars. Test centre Greg Inglis was the most notable departure, attracting a mammoth offer from South Sydney. But there were many lesser lights who also headed off – including the trio of Brett Finch, Ryan Hoffman and Jeff Lima, who all linked up with Wigan Warriors. However, the Storm had two things going for them – the genius of coach Craig Bellamy and the combination on the pitch of their three senior playmakers, hooker Cameron Smith, scrum-half Cooper Cronk and mercurial fullback Billy Slater.

The Storm players proved the critics wrong, taking out the Minor Premiership, before suffering a shock loss to the New Zealand Warriors in their preliminary final. During their run to the play-offs the Storm set a new club record of 12 straight victories. Slater won the Dally Medal as the NRL Player of the Year. Bellamy was Coach of the Year. Smith Captain of the Year and Representative Player of the Year (he also won the Wally Lewis Medal as the best player in the State of Origin series). And Cronk was Scrum Half of the Year. All three players were part of Australia's squad for the Gillette Four Nations Tournament, while big forwards Adam Blair, Sika Manu and Kevin Proctor were in the Kiwis line-up.

BRISBANE BRONCOS (4th)

When Ivan Henjak was sacked as Brisbane's coach during the pre-season preparations the omens did not look good for the Broncos. His assistant Anthony Griffin was thrust into the hot seat at short notice and rose to the occasion. He handled the task like a man who had been in the job for years. And with the inspirational Darren Lockyer directing his young troops on the pitch, the Broncos exceeded all expectations. Nevertheless a fairytale finish to Lockyer's club career did not eventuate. The Broncos were on a roll with eight consecutive victories after Lockyer's field goal in extra time gave them a 13-12 success over the Dragons in their semi-final. But the inspiring captain had suffered a depressed fracture of his left cheekbone and missed the preliminary final, where Manly pulled out all stops to finish the Queenslanders' season.

Lockyer was well supported by forwards Sam Thaiday and Corey Parker, who each had one of his best ever seasons. Thaiday was Dally M Second-rower of the Year and Parker made it back into the Queensland Origin side after an absence of six seasons and earned his first green and gold shirt. Both joined Lockyer in Australia's Four Nations squad together with fleet-footed winger Jharal Yow Yeh. Justin Hodges would have been there, too, but for injury. Utility back Gerard Beale and second-rower-cum-centre Alex Glenn made the Kiwis squad, while centre Jack Reed turned out for the country of his birth, England. Prop Ben Hannant also made Queensland's Origin squad.

Then there are the likes of young forwards Matt Gillett, Josh McGuire and Ben Te'o coming through the ranks.

WESTS TIGERS (5th)

After a mediocre first half to the season, when hampered by the absence through injury of several key players such as internationals Gareth Ellis, Chris Lawrence and Lote Tuqiri, the Tigers stormed home on the back of a club record nine consecutive victories. Then, after disposing of reigning Premiers St George Illawarra 21-12 in their qualifying final encounter, Wests blew their season's hopes in one awful 40 minutes. They had a commanding 18-6 half-time lead in their semi-final but allowed the New Zealand Warriors to regroup and score a try in the final minute of the match to win 22-20.

But there were many positives for Wests. Benji Marshall again showed why few players in the game can match his talents and it was a mid-season spray to his teammates that galvanised the Tigers. His inspirational displays almost won him the Dally M Medal (finishing just two points behind Billy Slater). He also topped the NRL pointscoring charts.

Once back in action Lawrence showed just how much his side had missed him with some sterling performances that won him a spot in Australia's Four Nations squad and the Test spot vacated by injured Justin Hodges. And prop Keith Galloway finally got due recognition for his efforts to join him in England. Back-rowers Ellis and Chris Heighington were chosen for the England squad. And Marshall, of course, was in Old Blighty, too, as captain of the Kiwis.

The 23-year-old centre Blake Ayshford came of age when he filled in for Lawrence and was one of the first chosen each week once the Test man returned to the fray. Tim Moltzen, later to be involved in a tug-o'-war with the Dragons, made the fullback spot his own. And 20-year-old prop Aaron Woods gave notice of future stardom.

ST GEORGE ILLAWARRA DRAGONS (6th)

Midway through the season the Dragons were sitting pretty at the top of the NRL Ladder, with a 10-match unbeaten streak. But they imploded post-Origin losing all but four of their final 14 games, including two in the play-offs (12-21 to the Tigers and 12-13 to the Broncos). Their reign as Premiers under supercoach Wayne Bennett was over two weeks before the grand final. They had saved their best for the last. When starved of the ball, they held an enthusiastic Brisbane outfit with some rugged defence, only to see the evergreen Darren Lockyer snap a field goal in 'golden point' extra time to break the deadlock.

But they did emerge with one title, the World Club Challenge after beating Wigan Warriors 21-15 at the DW Stadium.

Two Dragons made it into Australia's squad for the Gillette Four Nations Tournament – fullback Darius Boyd, who would be moving with Bennett to Newcastle the next year, and second-rower Beau Scott, who made his Test debut against Wales at Wrexham – while winger Jason Nightingale and hooker Nathan Fien turned out for the Kiwis. Winger Brett Morris and back-rower Ben Creagh played in the Anzac Test against New Zealand. And dual-international Mark Gasnier, stand-off Jamie Soward, utility forward Dean Young and prop Trent Merrin represented New South Wales at Origin level.

NORTH QUEENSLAND COWBOYS (7th)

It was a hot and cold season for the Cowboys. After being the worst-performing club in 2010 – only avoiding the wooden spoon because the Melbourne Storm were stripped of all points for cheating on the salary cap – the Townsville outfit emerged as a real Premiership threat. With five rounds of the competition proper remaining they were poised in third place. But they won only one match in the run home to finish in seventh spot and then crashed out in the first week of the play-offs, hammered 42-8 by eventual Premiers Manly.

They missed charismatic co-captain Johnathan Thurston through injury in a few vital clashes. Nonetheless there were some real stars in the ranks of the Cowboys. Off-season recruits Dallas Johnson and Glenn Hall from Super League, and Brent Tate from the New Zealand Warriors all proved great buys. Young forward Tariq Sims must have gone close to winning the Dally M award for Rookie of the Year. Winger Kalifa Faifai Loa so improved that by the end of the season he had achieved Test status. And similar dramatic progress saw hooker James Segeyaro and stand-off Ray Thompson chosen for the Papua New Guinea Kumuls in their annual clash with the Australian Prime Minister's XIII.

Once again Thurston reigned supreme. The Cowboys other co-captain Matt Scott was arguably the finest prop in the world and one of the first called up by Australia for the Four Nations. He and Thurston were joined in England by centre Willie Tonga (who was off to Parramatta in 2012). Fai fai Loa pulled on the Kiwi shirt. Veteran fullback Matt Bowen once again played for the Prime Minister's XIII.

NEWCASTLE KNIGHTS (8th)

It was a turbulent year for Newcastle. The Knights moved into private ownership, purchased by mining magnate Nathan Tinkler, who wiped out the club's debt and opened his cheque book to persuade the great coach Wayne Bennett to take over the reins from the popular Rick Stone.

The latter, to his credit, agreed to stay on under the man who had won seven Premierships with the Broncos and the Dragons. It was a measure of the man that Stone was responsible for lifting an injury-plagued Knights outfit into the play-offs against all odds. The fans responded with 30,729 packing Ausgrid Stadium to see Newcastle grab eighth spot with a do-or-die 40-24 effort against South Sydney.

The injury toll hit hard, with internationals Kurt Gidley, Adam 'Mad Dog' MacDougall and Wes Naiqama all lost for key games. But, when playing, Gidley was an inspirational captain. Had he not been injured he would have been on the plane to England for the Four Nations. But fellow-Knight Akuila Uate was. The exciting winger, who played for Fiji in the 2008 World Cup, scored 20 tries in his 23 NRL appearances. Both Gidley and Uate played for New South Wales in the Origin series.

CANTERBURY BULLDOGS (9th)

Once again Canterbury missed out on the play-offs. And it wasn't good enough for the back-room boys who showed 2009 Dally M Coach of the Year Kevin Moore the door before the season had ended. They replaced him with Jim Dymock as an interim coach before announcing Premiership-winning mentor Des Hasler would join the Bulldogs in 2012.

The speculation about Moore's future hardly helped the morale of the players. Neither did the news that club officials could find no room for captain Andrew Ryan in 2012, forcing him into retirement.

"It was certainly a disruption at a crucial stage of the season," said Canterbury's Origin hooker Michael Ennis. But the Bulldogs did come home under a wet sail, winning five of their last seven matches only to miss out on a spot in the finals' series on points-difference.

Fullback Ben Barba shared NRL try-scoring honours with Souths' Nathan Merritt, each snaring 23 four-pointers, and was rewarded with a spot on the bench of the Prime Minister's XIII for the clash with Papua New Guinea. Josh Morris was back in the green and gold for the Four Nations while fellow-centre Jamal Idris made Australia's side for the Anzac Test against the Kiwis but missed out when it came to the State of Origin series. Idris accepted a huge offer to switch to the Gold Coast in 2012.

SOUTH SYDNEY RABBITOHS (10th)

Once again South Sydney Rabbitohs unachieved. However they did have an excuse as they battled a growing list of injuries at vital stages of the season. Expectations were high after the signing of 2009 Golden Boot winner Greg Inglis. International forwards Roy Asotasi (New Zealand) and Sam Burgess (England) each played only a handful of games, while hard-working teammates in the pack also spent much of the season on the sidelines – Ben Lowe (playing just five games), Luke Stuart (five) and Scott Geddes (one).

The Rabbitohs, under the inspirational leadership of Michael Crocker, tried hard and a late-season run gave them an outside chance of sneaking into the play-offs. But a 40-24 capitulation to Newcastle in the final round dashed their hopes.

Several young players were blooded, including Burgess's brother Luke. The 24-year-old utility Chris McQueen, who missed the entire 2010 season after making just four appearances in his debut season, so shone that he got a run with the Prime Minister's XIII against the Kumuls. Also in that side was winger Nathan Merritt. He shared top billing on the NRL try-scoring lists with Newcastle's Akuila Uate, with 23 apiece. Merritt's tally took his career record to 115, making him only the fifth Rabbitoh to reach the century. The others are former Test stars Benny Wearing (144), Ian Moir (105), Harold Horder (102) and Bob McCarthy (100). Merritt also scored 19 while with Cronulla, Horder 50 for North Sydney and McCarthy 19 in Canterbury colours.

SYDNEY ROOSTERS (11th)

What a fall from grace it was for the Roosters. Last year they reached the grand final. In 2011 they were fighting to avoid the wooden spoon – an embarrassment only avoided when they won their final four games. Captain Braith Anasta expressed the players' disappointment: "We aren't proud of where we finished or of some of the games we played."

Much of the blame can be laid at the feet of enfant terrible Todd Carney, the talented but flawed playmaker, who once again embarrassed himself off the pitch. Roosters officials eventually lost patience and cut him from the club. Another former 'bad boy', hooker Jake Friend, turned his life around and had a great season. He received recognition with selection in the Prime Minister's XIII that beat Papua New Guinea at Lae. Also in that side was NSW Origin half Mitchell Pearce and loose forward Nate Myles, the latter also involved in a boozy off-field session with Carney.

Tough prop Jared Waerea-Hargreaves grabbed a spot with the Kiwis for the Four Nations, while winger Shaun Kenny-Dowall played for New Zealand in the Anzac Test. Fullback Anthony Minichiello made a return to the Origin arena before helping Italy qualify for the 2013 World Cup.

PENRITH PANTHERS (12th)

Off-pitch machinations dominated the Panthers' season. The season had hardly kicked off before the rumours began circulating that Matt Elliott's days as coach were numbered. The scuttlebuck hardly helped the morale of the players. Within less than two months the rumours had become reality. His contract would not be renewed at the end of the season. The former Bradford coach soldiered on until mid-June but by that time former Origin coach Phil 'Gus' Gould was firmly in control as director of football. Elliott departed, popular assistant coach Steve Georgallis was appointed caretaker coach before it was announced that Gould had signed his former protégé Ivan Cleary from the New Zealand Warriors.

A clean-out of players began, including the admired captain Petero Civoniceva, who was returning to his old club, Brisbane, and ex-Test man Trent Waterhouse, who headed for Warrington.

Throughout all the turmoil one player stood out like a beacon – utility star Luke Lewis and it was no coincidence that he was one of the first chosen for Australia's Four Nation line-up. Prop Sam McKendry made it into the Kiwis squad. And centre Michael Jennings and prop Tim Grant played for the Prime Minister's XIII in Papua New Guinea.

CRONULLA SHARKS (13th)

Cronulla Sharks, who have yet to win a Premiership since joining the big league in 1967, yet again struggled through lack of sufficient finance in 2011. Without cash reserves coach Shane Flanagan has had trouble attracting proven talent to the club – neither players nor coaching staff. And it showed.

As he pointed out, the four wingers who played in the senior side during the season scored a total of 14 tries between them. Akuila Uate (Newcastle) and Nathan Merritt (South Sydney) each scored 23 on his own. And the Sharks struggled to find a suitable scrum-half – although 'bad boy' Todd Carney will be in their ranks next season – basically because other clubs are not prepared to take the risk that he will get into trouble off the pitch yet again.

The Sharks finished 2011 with eight straight losses and you don't make the play-offs with a record like that.

On the positive side were the stirring displays by captain Paul Gallen, arguably the best loose forward in the world, but switched at Test and Origin levels to prop. During the NRL season, Gallen made 430 runs – almost 38 per cent more than any of his Cronulla teammates. In Origin II Gallen became only the second prop in history to play the full 80 minutes (the first was Glenn Lazarus). And in doing so he charged a total of 220 metres. He also made 30 tackles. He was also one of the first chosen for Australia to head for England and the Four Nations. His fellow-Shark Jeremy Smith was in the Kiwis squad. Prop Luke Douglas got a call up for the Prime Minister's XIII.

PARRAMATTA EELS (14th)

One can only sympathise with Parramatta's big-hearted captain Nathan Hindmarsh. In the words of the cliché, he gave a 110 per cent effort every weekend. He averaged 50 tackles and made around 100 metres in bone-jarring bursts per match. Indeed his 1200 tackles was an NRL record. If only some of his teammates had given half the effort. Only a last-round defeat of the Gold Coast Titans saved the Eels from the humiliation of picking up the wooden spoon. But no one blamed Hindmarsh. He won the Provan-Summons Medal, the People's Choice Dally M award decided by the fans, for a record-equalling fifth time and was handed the captaincy of the Prime Minister's XIII for the end-of-season clash with the Kumuls.

Admittedly, Parramatta suffered a heart-breaking string of narrow losses late in the season, including three under the grossly-unfair 'golden point' system, not used anywhere else in the Rugby League world – losing to the Panthers and Bulldogs in July and to the Roosters in the penultimate round of the season proper. But they did suffer some defeats that left them red-faced, not the least being a 56-6 thrashing at the hands of South Sydney, the Eels' worst performance since 1965. Fuifui Moimoi represented New Zealand and fellow prop Tim Mannah and winger Luke Burt the Prime Minister's XIII.

CANBERRA RAIDERS (15th)

For once the critics were predicting a promising season for Canberra Raiders in 2011 instead of tipping them to take out the wooden spoon. In recent years they had overachieved. This time it was the opposite. A spate of injuries and lack of consistency saw the Raiders struggling all year. The injuries included one to playmaker Terry Campese, who came back after a nine-month lay-off and lasted only 10 minutes before his season ended.

Exciting fullback Josh Dugan was another who struggled with injury, but still showed glimpses of form. Young half Josh McCrone also revealed the class that should make him one of the NRL's stars in the future. Prop David Shillington overcame injury worries to wear the green and gold and elusive winger Blake Ferguson was given his chance with the Prime Minister's XIII and scored a brace of tries against the Kumuls in Lae.

Evergreen Alan Tongue never gave up trying before bringing down the curtain on his 11-season, 220-match career in the final round against Canterbury.

GOLD COAST TITANS (16th)

Sixth in 2009 ... fourth in 2010 ... wooden spoon in 2011. What a comedown! For a senior side that had eight internationals in its ranks it was an unforgivable fall from grace. No wonder the Titans went on a wild spending spree for the next season.

It was hard to find any positives for the Gold Coast in a season in which coach John Cartwright admitted they underachieved. One was the form of 31-year-old veteran prop Luke Bailey, who won the club's Player of the Year award for the third straight season, a reward for his passion and pride. He averaged around 130 metres in bullocking runs and 35 tackles per match. Another bonus was the form of winger David Mead who scored a club record 16 tries before going on to give a good account of himself for Papua New Guinea in the clash with the Australian Prime Minister's XIII.

SEASON DOWN UNDER - ROUND-UP

NRL PREMIERSHIP FINALS SERIES

QUALIFYING FINALS

Friday 9th September 2011
Wests Tigers 21 ....St George Illawarra Dragons 12
Saturday 10th September 2011
Brisbane Broncos 40...New Zealand Warriors 10
Manly Sea Eagles 42.......................................North Queensland Cowboys 8
Sunday 11th September 2011
Melbourne Storm 18..Newcastle Knights 8

SEMI-FINALS

Friday 16th September 2011
Wests Tigers 20 ....New Zealand Warriors 22
Saturday 17th September 2011
Brisbane Broncos 13...............................St George Illawarra Dragons 12
(after golden point extra time)

PRELIMINARY FINALS

Friday 23rd September 2011
Manly Sea Eagles 26 ....Brisbane Broncos 14
Saturday 24th September 2011
Melbourne Storm 12.......................................New Zealand Warriors 20

GRAND FINAL

Sunday 2nd October 2011

MANLY SEA EAGLES 24 NEW ZEALAND WARRIORS 10

SEA EAGLES: 1 Brett Stewart; 2 Michael Robertson; 3 Jamie Lyon (C); 4 Steve Matai; 5 Will Hopoate; 6 Kieran Foran; 7 Daly Cherry-Evans; 8 Joe Galuvao; 9 Matt Ballin; 10 Brent Kite; 11 Anthony Watmough; 12 Tony Williams; 13 Glenn Stewart. Subs (all used): 14 Shane Rodney; 15 Jamie Buhrer; 16 Vic Mauro; 17 George Rose.
Tries: B Stewart (30), Cherry-Evans (40), G Stewart (56), Lyon (79);
Goals: Lyon 3/3, Robertson 1/1.
On report: Rose (27) - alleged use of the elbow on Heremaia.
WARRIORS: 1 Kevin Locke; 2 Bill Tupou; 3 Lewis Brown; 4 Kris Inu; 5 Manu Vatuvei; 6 James Maloney; 7 Shaun Johnson; 15 Russell Packer; 14 Lance Hohaia; 10 Jacob Lillyman; 12 Simon Mannering (C); 17 Elijah Taylor; 13 Micheal Luck. Subs (all used): 8 Sam Rapira; 9 Aaron Heremaia; 11 Feleti Mateo; 16 Ben Matulino.
Tries: Vatuvei (62), Taylor (68); **Goals:** Maloney 1/3.
On report: Heremaia (37) - alleged high tackle.
Rugby Leaguer & League Express Men of the Match:
Sea Eagles: Glenn Stewart; *Warriors:* Shaun Johnson.
Clive Churchill Medal (NRL Man of the Match):
Glenn Stewart (Manly Sea Eagles).
Half-time: 12-2; **Referees:** Tony Archer & Matt Cecchin;
Attendance: 81,988 *(at ANZ Stadium, Sydney).*

FINAL NRL PREMIERSHIP TABLE

	P	W	L	D	B	F	A	D	Pts
Melbourne Storm	24	19	5	0	2	521	308	213	42
Manly Sea Eagles	24	18	6	0	2	539	331	208	40
Brisbane Broncos	24	18	6	0	2	511	372	139	40
Wests Tigers	24	15	9	0	2	519	430	89	34
St George Illawarra Dragons	24	14	9	1	2	483	341	142	33
New Zealand Warriors	24	14	10	0	2	504	393	111	32
North Queensland Cowboys	24	14	10	0	2	532	480	52	32
Newcastle Knights	24	12	12	0	2	478	443	35	28
Canterbury Bulldogs	24	12	12	0	2	449	487	-40	28
South Sydney Rabbitohs	24	11	13	0	2	531	562	-31	26
Sydney Roosters	24	10	14	0	2	417	500	-83	24
Penrith Panthers	24	9	15	0	2	441	517	-87	22
Cronulla Sharks	24	7	17	0	2	428	557	-129	18
Parramatta Eels	24	6	17	1	2	385	538	-153	17
Canberra Raiders	24	6	18	0	2	423	623	-200	16
Gold Coast Titans	24	6	18	0	2	363	629	-266	16

TOP POINTSCORERS

		T	G	FG	Pts
Benji Marshall	Wests Tigers	13	78	3	211
James Maloney	New Zealand Warriors	9	79	2	206
Chris Sandow	South Sydney Rabbitohs	6	82	7	195
Luke Burt	Parramatta Eels	10	62	0	164
Cameron Smith	Melbourne Storm	2	78	0	164

TOP TRYSCORERS

Ben Barba	Canterbury Bulldogs	23
Nathan Merritt	South Sydney Rabbitohs	23
Akuila Uate	Newcastle Knights	20
David Mead	Gold Coast Titans	16
Brett Stewart	Manly Sea Eagles	15

TOYOTA CUP *(Under 20s)* GRAND FINAL
Sunday 2nd October 2011
New Zealand Warriors 31 ....North Queensland Cowboys 30
(after golden point extra time) (at ANZ Stadium, Sydney)

NEW SOUTH WALES CUP GRAND FINAL
Sunday 2nd October 2011
Canterbury Bulldogs 30 ....Auckland Vulcans 28
(at ANZ Stadium, Sydney)

QUEENSLAND CUP GRAND FINAL
Sunday 25th September 2011
Tweed Heads Seagulls 10 ....Wynnum Manly Seagulls 16
(at Suncorp Stadium, Brisbane)

DALLY M AWARDS
Dally M Medal (Player of the Year): Billy Slater (Melbourne Storm)
Provan-Summons Medal (People's Choice): Nathan Hindmarsh (Parramatta Eels)
Coach of the Year: Craig Bellamy (Melbourne Storm)
Captain of the Year: Cameron Smith (Melbourne Storm)
Representative Player of the Year: Cameron Smith (Melbourne Storm)
Rookie of the Year: Daly Cherry-Evans (Manly Sea Eagles)

ALL STARS GAME

Saturday 12th February 2011

NRL ALL STARS 28 NRL INDIGENOUS ALL STARS 12

NRL ALL STARS: 1 Josh Dugan (Canberra Raiders); 2 Akuila Uate (Newcastle Knights); 3 Michael Jennings (Penrith Panthers); 4 Jamie Lyon (Manly Sea Eagles); 5 Brett Morris (St George Illawarra Dragons); 6 Darren Lockyer (Brisbane Broncos) (C); 7 Benji Marshall (Wests Tigers); 8 Ben Hannant (Brisbane Broncos); 9 Cameron Smith (Melbourne Storm); 10 Matt Scott (North Queensland Cowboys); 11 Nathan Hindmarsh (Parramatta Eels); 12 Liam Fulton (Wests Tigers); 13 Paul Gallen (Cronulla Sharks). Subs (all used): 14 Dave Taylor (South Sydney Rabbitohs); 15 Ashley Harrison (Gold Coast Titans); 16 Feleti Mateo (New Zealand Warriors); 17 Shaun Kenny-Dowall (Sydney Roosters); 18 Michael Ennis (Bulldogs); 19 Petero Civoniceva (Penrith Panthers); 20 Kurt Gidley (Newcastle Knights).
Tries: Morris (3), Gallen (24), Kenny-Dowall (32), Uate (35), Dugan (71);
Goals: Smith 1/2, Marshall 2/2, Gidley 1/1.
On report: Fulton (49) - alleged dangerous tackle.
NRL INDIGENOUS ALL STARS: 20 Matt Bowen (North Queensland Cowboys); 2 Nathan Merritt (South Sydney Rabbitohs); 3 Willie Tonga (North Queensland Cowboys); 4 Beau Champion (Melbourne Storm); 5 Jharal Yow Yeh (Brisbane Broncos); 6 Scott Prince (Gold Coast Titans); 7 Johnathan Thurston (North Queensland Cowboys) (C); 8 Tom Learoyd-Lahrs (Canberra Raiders); 9 Travis Waddell (Canberra Raiders); 10 George Rose (Manly Sea Eagles); 11 Cory Paterson (Newcastle Knights); 12 Jamal Idris (Bulldogs); 13 Greg Bird (Gold Coast Titans). Subs (all used): 14 Ben Barba (Bulldogs); 15 Jamie Soward (St George Illawarra Dragons); 16 Carl Webb (Parramatta Eels); 17 Joel Moon (New Zealand Warriors); 18 Joel Thompson (Canberra Raiders); 19 Ryan James (Gold Coast Titans); 21 Anthony Mitchell (Parramatta Eels).
Tries: Barba (40), Merritt (59); **Goals:** Thurston 1/1, Prince 1/1.
Rugby Leaguer & League Express Men of the Match:
NRL All Stars: Josh Dugan; *NRL Indigenous All Stars:* Johnathan Thurston.
Preston Campbell Medal *(Man of the Match, judged by fans)*:
Josh Dugan (NRL All Stars).
Half-time: 22-6; **Referees:** Shayne Hayne, Henry Perenara, Gavin Badger & Ben Cummins; **Attendance:** 25,843 *(at Skilled Park, Robina).*

REPRESENTATIVE GAME

Sunday 25th September 2011

PAPUA NEW GUINEA 22 AUSTRALIAN PRIME MINISTER'S XIII 36

PAPUA NEW GUINEA: 1 David Mead (Gold Coast Titans); 2 Elijah Riyong (Port Moresby Vipers); 3 Richard Kambo (Hela Wigmen); 4 Chris Hogi (Goroka Lahanis); 5 Albert Patak (Rabaul Gurias); 6 Dion Aiye (Mt Hagen Eagles); 7 Ray Thompson (North Queensland Cowboys); 8 Gonzilla Urakusie (Goroka Lahanis); 9 James Segeyaro (North Queensland Cowboys); 10 Rodney Pora (Mt Hagen Eagles); 11 Glen Nami (Goroka Lahanis); 12 David Loko (Enga Mioks); 13 Paul Aiton (Cronulla Sharks) (C). Subs (all used): 14 Jessie Joe Parker (Hela Wigmen); 16 Larsen Marabe (Hela Wigmen); 17 Pidi Tongap (Rabaul Gurias); 18 Charlie Wabo (Mendi Muruks); 19 Joshua Abavu (Port Moresby Vipers); 20 Samuel Sok (Hela Wigmen).
Tries: Aiye, Parker, Thompson, Abavu; **Goals:** Nami 3/4.
AUSTRALIAN PRIME MINISTER'S XIII: 1 Matt Bowen (North Queensland Cowboys); 2 Blake Ferguson (Canberra Raiders); 3 Michael Jennings (Penrith Panthers); 4 Josh Morris (Canterbury Bulldogs); 5 Nathan Merritt (South Sydney Rabbitohs); 6 Greg Bird (Gold Coast Titans); 7 Mitchell Pearce (Sydney Roosters); 8 David Shillington (Canberra Raiders); 9 Jake Friend (Sydney Roosters); 10 Tim Mannah (Parramatta Eels); 11 Michael Crocker (South Sydney Rabbitohs); 12 Nathan Hindmarsh (Parramatta Eels) (C); 13 Nate Myles (Sydney Roosters). Subs (all used): 14 Tim Grant (Penrith Panthers); 15 Luke Douglas (Cronulla Sharks); 16 Chris McQueen (South Sydney Rabbitohs); 17 Luke Burt (Parramatta Eels); 18 Ben Barba (Canterbury Bulldogs).
Tries: Morris 2, Ferguson 2, Burt, Merritt;
Goals: Burt 3/3, Bowen 1/1, Crocker 1/1, Hindmarsh 1/1.
Half-time: 0-12; **Attendance:** 17,000 *(at Rugby League Oval, Lae).*

State Of Origin

Darren Lockyer, in his 17th and final season in the senior ranks, still played with the exuberance he showed when he made his State of Origin debut 13 years earlier. In July his Maroon teammates helped give him the finish he deserved when the curtain was rung down on his interstate career as Queensland stretched their record run in Origin series to six. To cap the fairytale it was Lockyer who set up the try that sealed victory over New South Wales 12 minutes before the final siren in the Origin decider at Suncorp Stadium.

Lockyer finished with a record 36 Origin appearances – two more than Allan Langer and four more than his successful coach Mal Meninga. The best of the New South Welshmen, Brad Fittler, played five games fewer than Lockyer. The NSW Blues had hoped to halt the Queensland juggernaut in 2011, with former Test mentor Ricky Stuart being handed the reins as full-time coach, taking a leaf out the Maroons' book. But while they stretched the Queenslanders, with captain Paul Gallen an inspirational leader in all three encounters, it proved to be a case of deja vu.

Lockyer showed in the first encounter just how desperate he was to win his final Origin series. So many times in the past he and Billy Slater have pulled games for Australia or Queensland out of the fire. So it was at the Lang Park complex in Brisbane in Origin I.

New South Wales had come back from a 10-point deficit to hit the lead with 11 minutes remaining on the clock. Then came a quick play-the-ball by Queensland prop Matt Scott and a magic pass from Lockyer put Slater into a gap and across the tryline for a Maroons victory.

The match was played at breakneck speed from the start. The genius of scrum-half Johnathan Thurston had the Queenslanders first on the scoreboard. Hooker Cameron Smith put a ball along the ground. Thurston missed it as he ran through but reached back behind his back to touch down.

STATE OF ORIGIN - GAME I

Wednesday 25th May 2011

QUEENSLAND 16 NEW SOUTH WALES 12

QUEENSLAND: 1 Billy Slater (Melbourne Storm); 2 Darius Boyd (St George Illawarra Dragons); 3 Dane Nielsen (Melbourne Storm); 4 Willie Tonga (North Queensland Cowboys); 5 Jharal Yow Yeh (Brisbane Broncos); 6 Darren Lockyer (Brisbane Broncos) (C); 7 Johnathan Thurston (North Queensland Cowboys); 8 Matt Scott (North Queensland Cowboys); 9 Cameron Smith (Melbourne Storm); 10 Petero Civoniceva (Penrith Panthers); 11 Nate Myles (Sydney Roosters); 12 Sam Thaiday (Brisbane Broncos); 13 Ashley Harrison (Gold Coast Titans). Subs (all used): 14 Cooper Cronk (Melbourne Storm); 15 Ben Hannant (Brisbane Broncos); 16 Jacob Lillyman (New Zealand Warriors); 17 Corey Parker (Brisbane Broncos).
Tries: Thurston (5), Yow Yeh (45), Slater (72); **Goals:** Thurston 2/4.
NEW SOUTH WALES: 1 Josh Dugan (Canberra Raiders); 2 Brett Morris (St George Illawarra Dragons); 3 Michael Jennings (Penrith Panthers); 4 Mark Gasnier (St George Illawarra Dragons); 5 Akuila Uate (Newcastle Knights); 6 Jamie Soward (St George Illawarra Dragons); 7 Mitchell Pearce (Sydney Roosters); 8 Jason King (Manly Sea Eagles); 17 Dean Young (St George Illawarra Dragons); 10 Kade Snowden (Cronulla Sharks); 11 Beau Scott (St George Illawarra Dragons); 12 Greg Bird (Gold Coast Titans); 13 Paul Gallen (Cronulla Sharks) (C). Subs (all used): 9 Michael Ennis (Bulldogs); 14 Ben Creagh (St George Illawarra Dragons); 15 Trent Merrin (St George Illawarra Dragons); 16 Tim Mannah (Parramatta Eels).
Tries: Pearce (64), Jennings (68); **Goals:** Soward 2/2.
Rugby Leaguer & League Express Men of the Match:
Queensland: Matt Scott; *New South Wales:* Paul Gallen.
Penalty count: 2-1; **Half-time:** 6-0; **Referees:** Tony Archer & Jared Maxwell; **Attendance:** 52,144 *(at Suncorp Stadium, Brisbane).*

Some 26 minutes into the action Queensland centre Willie Tonga dislocated his left shoulder in a collision with Blues fullback Josh Dugan. In any other match Tonga would have been replaced but this was an Origin encounter and he bravely soldiered on with winger Darius Boyd and Thurston providing extra defensive cover when the Blues tried to exploit the injury. At half-time Tonga was to reject further advice from Queensland team doctor Roy Saunders to quit.

Early into the second half young Jharal Yow Yeh scored off a kick along the ground by substitute Cooper Cronk. What a year it was for the 21-year-old Broncos winger. But the Blues eventually worked their way back into contention and, after good lead-up work by hooker Michael Ennis and Greg Bird, scrum-half Mitchell Pearce swerved his way through the defence to score. Four minutes later there was some more wonderful attack by the NSW players when Michael Jennings, who had not scored a try in any match all season, suddenly exploded. Substitute back-rower Ben Creagh had run as a decoy and Dugan served up the crispest of passes to the Penrith centre 10 metres inside the Queensland half. Jennings threw a dummy pass to Test winger Brett Morris before straightening up. He was across the stripe in the blink of an eyelid. Jamie Soward's successful conversion attempt put the New South

Welshmen ahead for the first time all night.

It was then that Lockyer danced like Fred Astaire and sent his waltzing partner Slater pirouetting across the tryline for the Maroons' victory.

What a difference 18 months made to Paul Gallen! At the start of the 2010 season he had a well-deserved reputation as one of the game's 'bad boys'. Then a few whispers in his ear from a couple of Rugby League legends whom he admired and a lot of self-discipline turned his life around. So much so that he ended up on the short list for that year's Golden Boot award.

But nothing prepared his critics for the Man of the Match performance in 2011's Origin II encounter as Gallen led his beloved New South Wales side to an upset victory over Queensland. Many members of the media believed coach Stuart had taken leave of his senses when he switched Gallen from loose forward into the front row and went into the do-or-die encounter with just two regular props. But the decision proved to be a stroke of genius.

STATE OF ORIGIN - GAME II

Wednesday 15th June 2011

NEW SOUTH WALES 18 QUEENSLAND 8

NEW SOUTH WALES: 1 Anthony Minichiello (Sydney Roosters); 2 Jarryd Hayne (Parramatta Eels); 3 Mark Gasnier (St George Illawarra Dragons); 4 Will Hopoate (Manly Sea Eagles); 5 Akuila Uate (Newcastle Knights); 6 Jamie Soward (St George Illawarra Dragons); 7 Mitchell Pearce (Sydney Roosters); 8 Tim Mannah (Parramatta Eels); 9 Michael Ennis (Bulldogs); 10 Paul Gallen (Cronulla Sharks) (C); 11 Beau Scott (St George Illawarra Dragons); 12 Ben Creagh (St George Illawarra Dragons); 13 Greg Bird (Gold Coast Titans). Subs (all used): 14 Trent Merrin (St George Illawarra Dragons); 15 Kurt Gidley (Newcastle Knights); 16 Anthony Watmough (Manly Sea Eagles); 17 Luke Lewis (Penrith Panthers).
Tries: Lewis (29), Hopoate (48), Minichiello (76); **Goals:** Soward 3/4.
QUEENSLAND: 1 Billy Slater (Melbourne Storm); 2 Darius Boyd (St George Illawarra Dragons); 3 Dane Nielsen (Melbourne Storm); 4 Greg Inglis (South Sydney Rabbitohs); 5 Jharal Yow Yeh (Brisbane Broncos); 6 Darren Lockyer (Brisbane Broncos) (C); 7 Johnathan Thurston (North Queensland Cowboys); 8 Matt Scott (North Queensland Cowboys); 9 Cameron Smith (Melbourne Storm); 10 Petero Civoniceva (Penrith Panthers); 11 Nate Myles (Sydney Roosters); 12 Sam Thaiday (Brisbane Broncos); 13 Ashley Harrison (Gold Coast Titans). Subs (all used): 14 Cooper Cronk (Melbourne Storm); 15 Corey Parker (Brisbane Broncos); 16 Dave Taylor (South Sydney Rabbitohs); 17 Ben Hannant (Brisbane Broncos).
Try: Smith (24); **Goals:** Thurston 2/2.
Rugby Leaguer & League Express Men of the Match:
New South Wales: Paul Gallen; *Queensland:* Ashley Harrison.
Penalty count: 5-4; **Half-time:** 6-8; **Referees:** Shayne Hayne & Ben Cummins; **Attendance:** 81,965 *(at ANZ Stadium, Sydney).*

In Origin I, lost narrowly by the Blues after a late sortie by the Queenslanders, the four NSW props made a total of 148 metres in the 80 minutes. In the second clash in Sydney, Gallen made 220 metres on his own – more than the total of the two starting Maroons front-rowers Petero Civoniceva and Matt Scott. Gallen also made 30 tackles.

Thanks to the 18-8 Gallen-inspired victory, the New South Welshmen were able to go to the decider in Brisbane three weeks later on level pegging.

The match was one of the most eagerly anticipated interstate clashes in years, with all tickets sold almost a week before the match. But on the night around 1,000 ticket-holders were worried about the torrential rain that hit the state in the days before the encounter and stayed at home. Nevertheless, 81,965 braved the inclement weather and all those fans dressed in blue reaped their reward.

Early in the action, the NSW players were under attack time and time again but produced some wonderful defence. Eventually the torrid assault took its toll and Cameron Smith darted across the line. Substitute prop Trent Merrin tried to hold him up, but the video referees ruled the ball had found the turf behind the stripe.

The Blues struck right back. Luke Lewis came off the bench and with his first touch made a break. A quick play-the-ball to 19-year-old debutant Will Hopoate set the scene for the perfect bomb that caught the Queenslanders floundering. Lewis leaped high, caught the ball and fell to the turf to score.

Right on half-time it was only desperate defence from Queensland that saved a try, with Aikula Uate cleaned up on the line by Slater. The Fijian winger's frantic pass went loose.

The second half opened with the Queenslanders on fire but the Blues were unfazed. Eight minutes into the half, scrum half Mitchell Pearce got some quick ball out wide to Hopoate who pushed through a diving tackle from Slater to plant the ball centimetres in from the left corner post. Jamie Soward's conversion put the home side ahead for the first time, 12-8.

As the clock wound down, twice Greg Inglis knocked on near the Queensland line giving the Blues a third set of six. Soward capitalised, dancing past a couple of would-be tacklers and unloading to the veteran Anthony Minichiello to seal the victory.

It was truly a fairy-tale finish to Darren Lockyer's years of playing State of Origin rugby.

Everyone among the 3.7 million who watched on Australian television and others around the world must have enjoyed the sensational display by 34 great players. There was another poignant moment after the full-time siren. Johnathon Thurston, injured in the 58th minute, appeared from the Queensland dressing room sitting in a wheel-chair, his left knee wrapped in an ice pack, to join in the celebrations. He was reluctant – but Meninga gave him a direct order to appear. And Thurston said later how glad he had done so, wheeled out by Sam Thaiday before being embraced by Lockyer and, later, by his fellow Maroons.

There was some incredibly early tough defence by both sides. It was a case of crunch, crunch, crunch from both teams.

Eventually, after concerted attack from the Queenslanders, with props Petero Civoniceva and Matt Scott leading the charge, Slater stood in a tackle and the ball continued to the left. Thurston pushed a kick into the corner and Greg Inglis scored. It was the latter's 11th try in 15 Origin appearances (and he was add to that number later in the evening).

The Queensland attack was unrelenting – especially from Slater who continually joined into the backline to challenge the besieged Blues.

Midway through the first half, Slater slipped a perfect short pass to a thundering Thaiday who was through the defence and over the tryline before the NSW players realised what was happening. Then, after some great lead-up work by Lockyer and Inglis, Smith pushed his way across the stripe from dummy half. Within two minutes the Maroons were in again. Lockyer kicked ahead, the ball bounced off Anthony Minichiello's shins and Jharal Yow Yeh dribbled ahead to score.

However, as the Maroons looked to have had the result wrapped up, the New South Welshmen grabbed two tries in the final minutes of the half. Five Queenslanders fumbled and allowed Minichiello to score, albeit off a suspicious pass. No sooner had play restarted than Fijian World Cup winger Akuila Uate was over wide out on the right to reduce the deficit to 14 points at the break.

Early in the second half the Maroons suffered a major blow with the injury to Thurston. But, if anything, it seemed to galvanise the Queenslanders.

It was then that the old firm of Lockyer and Slater, with help from Thaiday, crushed the Blues' vain hopes of a comeback with a sensational try.

Lockyer flung a pass wide to the right to Thaiday. The delighted Bronco accepted the ball and reversed it back inside. Who was waiting there to score? Take a bow Billy Slater!

The Queenslanders among the record Brisbane Origin crowd of 52,498 stood as one to hail the modern Emperor of Lang Park. The NSW supporters just shook their heads in amazement.

Just four minutes later victory was sealed when Inglis slipped past three or four would-be defenders to stretch the lead to 34-10. A length of the pitch try, scored by NSW second-rower, Greg Bird proved to be nothing more than a consolation.

STATE OF ORIGIN - GAME III

Wednesday 6th July 2011

QUEENSLAND 34 NEW SOUTH WALES 24

QUEENSLAND: 1 Billy Slater (Melbourne Storm); 2 Darius Boyd (St George Illawarra Dragons); 3 Justin Hodges (Brisbane Broncos); 4 Greg Inglis (South Sydney Rabbitohs); 5 Jharal Yow Yeh (Brisbane Broncos); 6 Darren Lockyer (Brisbane Broncos) (C); 7 Johnathan Thurston (North Queensland Cowboys); 8 Matt Scott (North Queensland Cowboys); 9 Cameron Smith (Melbourne Storm); 10 Petero Civoniceva (Penrith Panthers); 11 Sam Thaiday (Brisbane Broncos); 12 Ashley Harrison (Gold Coast Titans); 13 Nate Myles (Sydney Roosters). Subs (all used): 14 Cooper Cronk (Melbourne Storm); 15 Corey Parker (Brisbane Broncos); 16 Jacob Lillyman (New Zealand Warriors); 17 Ben Hannant (Brisbane Broncos).
Tries: Inglis (15, 68), Thaiday (24), Smith (30), Yow Yeh (32), Slater (64); **Goals:** Thurston 4/4, Smith 1/2.
On report: Smith (71) - alleged use of the knee.
NEW SOUTH WALES: 1 Anthony Minichiello (Sydney Roosters); 2 Brett Morris (St George Illawarra Dragons); 3 Mark Gasnier (St George Illawarra Dragons); 4 Jarryd Hayne (Parramatta Eels); 5 Akuila Uate (Newcastle Knights); 6 Jamie Soward (St George Illawarra Dragons); 7 Mitchell Pearce (Sydney Roosters); 8 Tim Mannah (Parramatta Eels); 9 Michael Ennis (Bulldogs); 10 Paul Gallen (Cronulla Sharks) (C); 11 Ben Creagh (St George Illawarra Dragons); 12 Glenn Stewart (Manly Sea Eagles); 13 Greg Bird (Gold Coast Titans); 18 Glenn Stewart (Manly Sea Eagles). Subs (all used): 14 Kurt Gidley (Newcastle Knights); 16 Anthony Watmough (Manly Sea Eagles); 17 Luke Lewis (Penrith Panthers); 20 Keith Galloway (Wests Tigers).
Tries: Minichiello (36), Uate (40), Hayne (71), Bird (78);
Goals: Soward 4/5.
Rugby Leaguer & League Express Men of the Match:
Queensland: Petero Civoniceva; *New South Wales:* Paul Gallen.
Penalty count: 3-4; **Half-time:** 24-10; **Referees:** Tony Archer & Shayne Hayne; **Attendance:** 52,498 *(at Suncorp Stadium, Brisbane).*

Wally Lewis Medal (Man of the Series): Cameron Smith (Queensland).

2011 REPRESENTATIVE SEASON

llette Four Nations ● Autumn International Series ● World Cup Qualifiers ● International Origin ● ANZAC Test ● State Of Origin

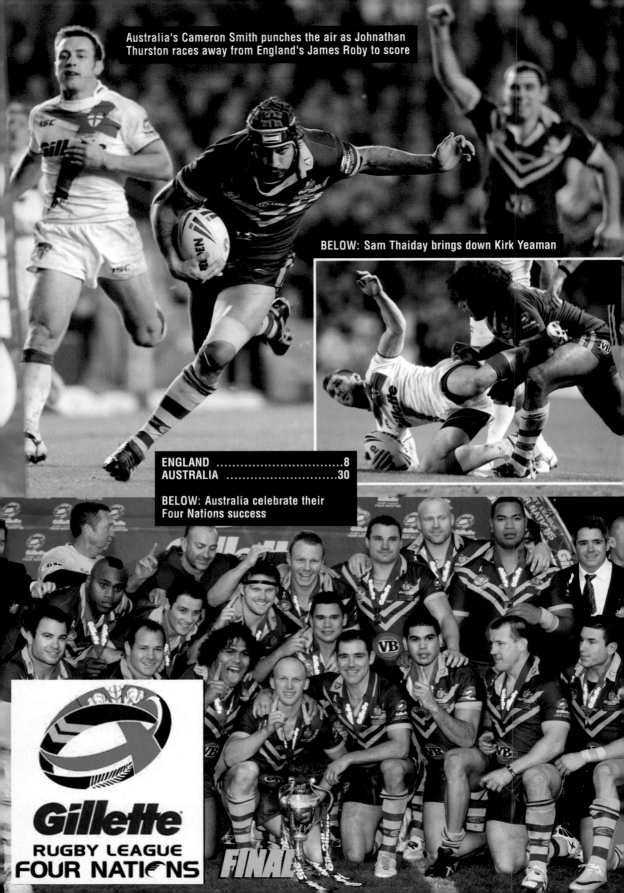

Australia's Cameron Smith punches the air as Johnathan Thurston races away from England's James Roby to score

BELOW: Sam Thaiday brings down Kirk Yeaman

ENGLAND 8
AUSTRALIA 30

BELOW: Australia celebrate their Four Nations success

Gillette

RUGBY LEAGUE
FOUR NATIONS

FINAL

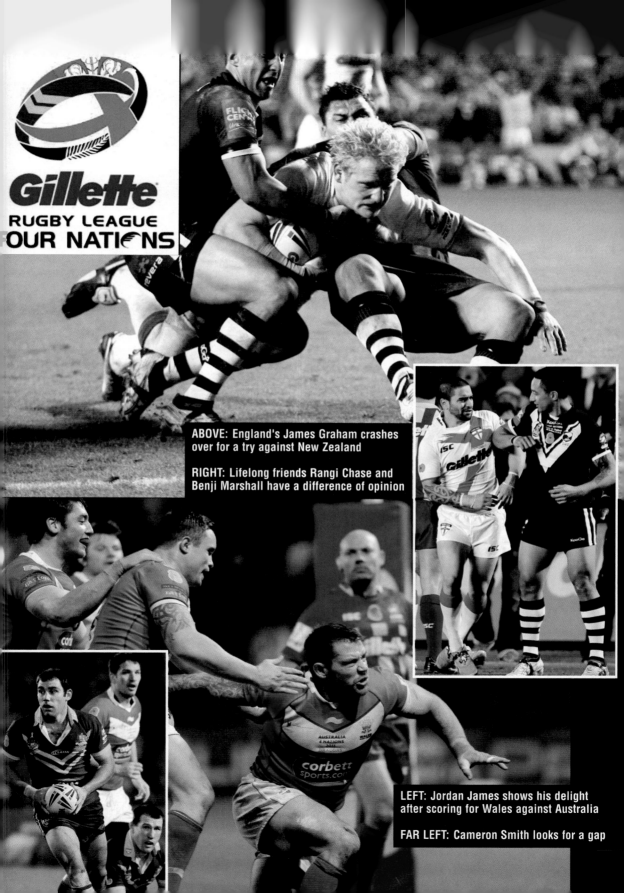

ABOVE: England's James Graham crashes over for a try against New Zealand

RIGHT: Lifelong friends Rangi Chase and Benji Marshall have a difference of opinion

LEFT: Jordan James shows his delight after scoring for Wales against Australia

FAR LEFT: Cameron Smith looks for a gap

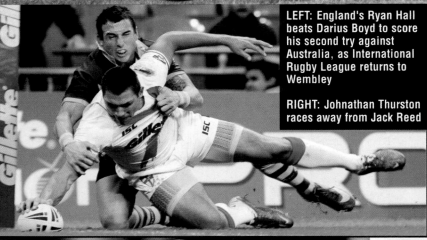

LEFT: England's Ryan Hall beats Darius Boyd to score his second try against Australia, as International Rugby League returns to Wembley

RIGHT: Johnathan Thurston races away from Jack Reed

LEFT: Matt Scott and Cameron Smith halt Adrian Morley

RIGHT: James Roby looks for support

LEFT: Wales' Elliot Kear claims a high ball against New Zealand

FAR LEFT: Sika Manu goes past Danny Jones to score

ABOVE: Australia's David Shillington tries to escape the clutches of New Zealand's Issac Luke

BELOW: England's Sam Tomkins goes over to score the last of his four tries against Wales

Gillette
RUGBY LEAGUE
FOUR NATIONS

LEFT: Scotland's Andrew Henderson on the charge against France

ABOVE: France's Olivier Elima and Thomas Bosc bring down Ireland's Tyrone McCarthy

AUTUMN INTERNATIONAL SERIES

ABOVE: The Ireland defence closes in on Scotland's Alex Szostak

ABOVE: Italy celebrate reaching the 2013 World Cup

LEFT: USA's Matt Petersen in action against Jamaica

WORLD CUP QUALIFIERS

LEFT: The Lebanon defence halts this Italy attack

RIGHT: No way through for Jamaica's Wayne Reittie against South Africa

ABOVE: England's Richard Myler contests a high ball with The Exiles's Brett Hodgson

LEFT: Exiles captain Danny Buderus celebrates George Carmont's last-gasp winning try

RIGHT: England Knights centre Kris Welham driven back against France

BELOW: England Knights duo Lee Mossop and James Donaldson ground Cumbria's Will Sharp

LEFT: England's Rangi Chase gets a pass away against France

BELOW: Wales's Andy Bracek and Peter Lupton close down Ireland's Callum Casey

INTERNATIONAL FRIENDLIES

FOUR NATIONS WARM-UPS

ANZAC TEST

ABOVE: New Zealand's Jason Nightingale upended by the challenge of Australia's Jamal Idris

BELOW: Australia's Willie Tonga dives over for a try against the Kiwis

TEST MATCH

RIGHT: Johnathan Thurston goes past Petero Civoniceva and Matt Scott during the NRL All Stars game

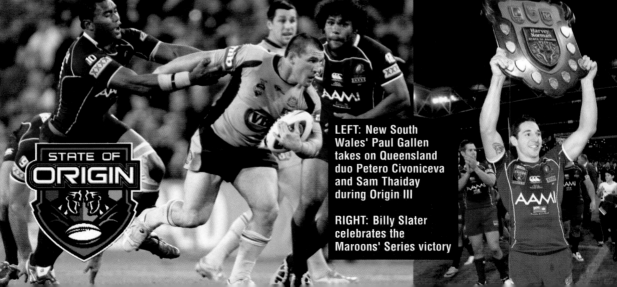

STATE OF ORIGIN

LEFT: New South Wales' Paul Gallen takes on Queensland duo Petero Civoniceva and Sam Thaiday during Origin III

RIGHT: Billy Slater celebrates the Maroons' Series victory

2011 DOMESTIC SEASON

Carnegie Challenge Cup ● NRL Grand Final ● World Club Challenge ● Championship Grand Finals ● Academy & Reserves

ROUND 4

Carnegie Challenge Cup

RIGHT: Bradford's Shad Royston crashes past Miles Greenwood to score against former club Halifax

RIGHT: Castleford's Kirk Dixon is mobbed by teammates after kicking the Tigers' golden point against Wakefield

ROUND 5

QUARTER FINALS

LEFT: Wigan's Pat Richards holds off Warrington's Joel Monaghan to score

ABOVE: St Helens's Leon Pryce and Wigan's Sam Tomkins contest a high ball

BELOW: Ali Lauitiiti shows his delight as Leeds captain Kevin Sinfield kicks the winning penalty in extra time against Castleford

SEMI-FINALS

RIGHT: Wigan's Joel Tomkins leaves Leeds' Jamie Peacock trailing on the way to scoring a sensational first-half try

BELOW: Brent Webb grounded by the challenge of Paul Deacon

BOTTOM: Wigan Warriors celebrate their Challenge Cup Final victory

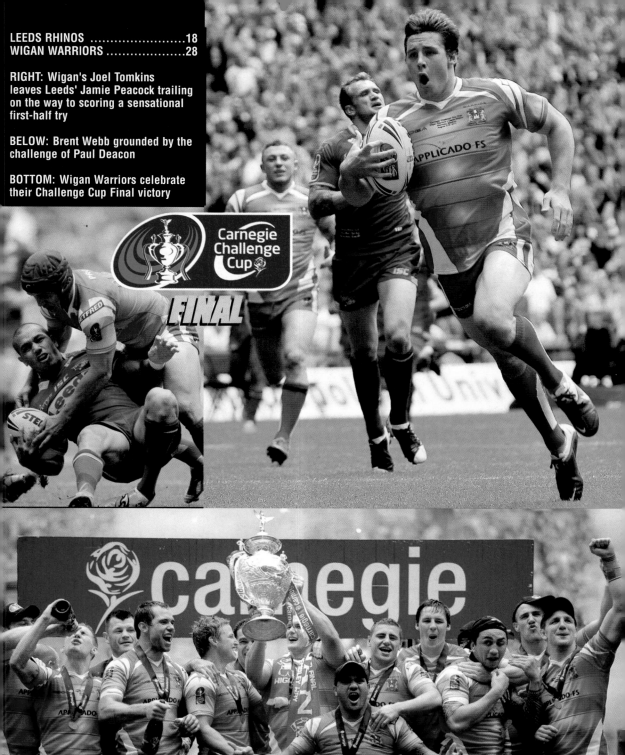

NRL

GRAND FINAL

ABOVE: Brett and Glenn Stewart celebrate with the Sea Eagles fans

LEFT: Sam Rapira driven back by Joe Galuvao

TOP LEFT: Jamie Lyon races through the Warriors defence

BELOW: New Zealand Warriors' Manu Vatuvei dives past Manly's Will Hopoate to score in the corner

PROBIZ
RUGBY LEAGUE
WORLD CLUB CHALLENGE

WIGAN WARRIORS **15**
ST GEORGE ILLAWARRA DRAGONS **21**

RIGHT: Wigan's Sam Tomkins tries to break free from St George Illawarra's Trent Merrin

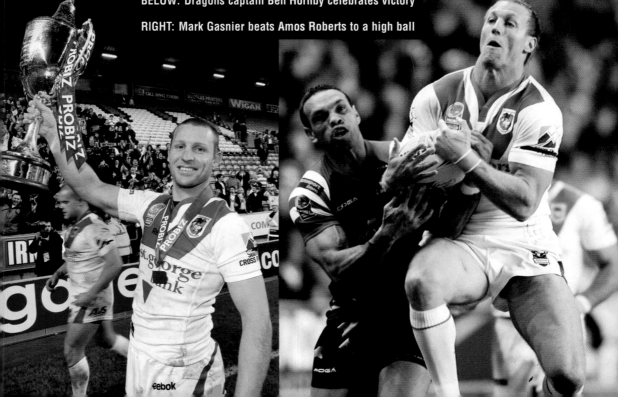

BELOW: Dragons captain Ben Hornby celebrates victory

RIGHT: Mark Gasnier beats Amos Roberts to a high ball

CHAMPIONS! Swinton Lions celebrate winning the Championship 1 title

The co-operative
CHAMPIONSHIP 1
GRAND FINAL

LEFT: Keighley's Jake Normington holds off Workington's Neil Frazer and Jason Mossop for a try as the Cougars clinch the second promotion place to the Championship

ABOVE: Skipper James Feather leads the Keighley celebrations

The co-operative
RUGBY LEAGUE CONFERENCE
GRAND FINAL

LEFT: Huddersfield Underbank's Nick Briggs scores against Kippax Knights as the Rangers make it third time lucky in the Conference Grand Final

FAR LEFT: Player-coach Richard Knight and captain Lee St Hilaire show their delight

FEATHERSTONE ROVERS 40
SHEFFIELD EAGLES 4

BELOW: Sheffield's Vinny Finigan can't prevent Featherstone's Jon Hepworth from scoring

The co-operative
CHAMPIONSHIP
GRAND FINAL

BELOW: Tony Tonks and Sam Scott clash as tempers flare

RIGHT: Rovers coach Daryl Powell and captain Stuart Dickens show off the Championship trophy

NORTHERN RAIL CUP
FINAL

HALIFAX 16
LEIGH CENTURIONS 20

LEFT: Coach Ian Millward leads the celebrations following Leigh's last-gasp Northern Rail Cup Final triumph over Halifax

ABOVE: Steve Maden wrapped up by Paul Smith and Sam Barlow

Valvoline CUP GRAND FINAL

RIGHT: Wigan's Joe Mellor makes a break through the Warrington defence

BELOW: The Warriors celebrate their Grand Final win

VALVOLINE CUP WINNERS 2011

RESERVES CHAMPIONSHIP - GRAND FINAL

RIGHT: The victorious Oldham side
BELOW: Oldham's Jamie Dallimore shows his delight at scoring against Widnes

NATIONAL CONFERENCE PREMIER DIVISION GRAND FINAL

Thatto Heath start the celebrations

LEFT: Shaun Quinn races away against Siddal

The co-operative WINN RUGBY LEAGUE CONFERENCE CHAMPIONS Parkside Hawks

5
STATISTICAL REVIEW

SUPER LEAGUE PLAYERS
1996-2011

Super League Players 1996-2011

PLAYER	CLUB	YEAR	APP	TRIES	GOALS	FG	PTS
Carl Ablett	Leeds	2004, 2006-11	84(32)	21	0	0	84
	London	2005	3(2)	0	0	0	0
Darren Abram	Oldham	1996-97	25(2)	11	0	0	44
Darren Adams	Paris	1996	9(1)	1	0	0	4
Guy Adams	Huddersfield	1998	1(2)	0	0	0	0
Luke Adamson	Salford	2006-07, 2009-11	61(32)	10	0	0	40
Matt Adamson	Leeds	2002-04	54(8)	9	0	0	36
Phil Adamson	St Helens	1999	(1)	0	0	0	0
Toby Adamson	Salford	2010	(1)	0	0	0	0
Danny Addy	Bradford	2010-11	9(16)	1	5	0	14
Ade Adebisi	London	2004	(1)	0	0	0	0
Patrick Ah Van	Bradford	2011	26	9	87	0	210
Jamie Ainscough	Wigan	2002-03	30(2)	18	0	0	72
Shaun Ainscough	Bradford	2011	11	7	0	0	28
	Wigan	2009-10	12	13	0	0	52
	Castleford	2010	7	4	0	0	16
Glen Air	London	1998-2001	57(13)	27	0	1	109
Makali Aizue	Hull KR	2007-09	18(32)	4	0	0	16
Darren Albert	St Helens	2002-05	105	77	0	0	308
Paul Alcock	Widnes	2003, 2005	1(7)	1	0	0	4
Neil Alexander	Salford	1998	(1)	0	0	0	0
Malcolm Alker	Salford	1997-2002, 2004-07, 2009-11	271(2)	40	0	1	161
Danny Allan	Leeds	2008-09	2(5)	0	0	0	0
Chris Allen	Castleford	1996	(1)	0	0	0	0
David Allen	Wigan	2003, 2005	6(15)	2	0	0	8
Gavin Allen	London	1996	10	0	0	0	0
John Allen	Workington	1996	20(1)	6	0	0	24
Ray Allen	London	1996	5(3)	3	0	0	12
Richard Allwood	Gateshead	1999	(4)	0	0	0	0
Sean Allwood	Gateshead	1999	3(17)	1	0	0	4
David Alstead	Warrington	2000-02	23(10)	3	0	0	12
Luke Ambler	Harlequins	2011	5(17)	1	0	0	4
	Leeds	2010	1(8)	1	0	0	4
Asa Amone	Halifax	1996-97	32(7)	10	0	0	40
Kyle Amor	Wakefield	2011	18(7)	5	0	0	20
	Leeds	2010	(3)	0	0	0	0
Thibaut Ancely	Catalans	2011	(2)	0	0	0	0
Grant Anderson	Castleford	1996-97	15(6)	3	0	0	12
Louis Anderson	Warrington	2008-11	92	18	0	0	72
Paul Anderson	St Helens	2005-06	48(5)	7	1	0	30
	Bradford	1997-2004	74(104)	30	0	0	120
	Halifax	1996	5(1)	1	0	0	4
Paul Anderson	Sheffield	1999	3(7)	1	0	0	4
	St Helens	1996-98	2(28)	4	1	0	18
Vinnie Anderson	Salford	2011	16(1)	6	0	0	24
	Warrington	2007-10	57(19)	22	0	0	88
	St Helens	2005-06	28(14)	17	0	0	68
Phil Anderton	St Helens	2004	1	0	0	0	0
Eric Anselme	Leeds	2008	2(2)	2	0	0	8
	Halifax	1997	(2)	0	0	0	0
Mark Applegarth	Wakefield	2004-07	20(5)	3	0	0	12
Graham Appo	Warrington	2002-05	60(13)	35	80	0	300
	Huddersfield	2001	7	4	0	0	16
Anthony Armour	London	2005	11(7)	1	0	0	4
Colin Armstrong	Workington	1996	11(2)	1	0	0	4
Tom Armstrong	St Helens	2009-11	10(5)	9	0	0	36
Richard Armswood	Workington	1996	5(1)	1	0	0	4
Danny Arnold	Salford	2001-02	26(13)	13	0	0	52
	Huddersfield	1998-2000	55(7)	26	0	0	104
	Castleford	2000	(4)	0	0	0	0
	St Helens	1996-97	40(1)	33	0	0	132
Joe Arundel	Castleford	2008, 2010-11	31(4)	13	2	0	56
Craig Ashall	St Helens	2006	1	1	0	0	4
Nathan Ashe	St Helens	2011	1(2)	0	0	0	0
Chris Ashton	Wigan	2005-07	44(2)	25	2	0	104
Matty Ashurst	St Helens	2009-11	12(39)	8	0	0	32
Martin Aspinwall	Castleford	2011	12(6)	2	0	0	8
	Huddersfield	2006-10	72(8)	22	0	0	88
	Wigan	2001-05	85(13)	27	0	0	108
Mark Aston	Sheffield	1996-99	67(6)	6	243	6	516
Paul Atcheson	Widnes	2002-04	16(35)	4	0	0	16
	St Helens	1998-2000	58(4)	18	0	0	72
	Oldham	1996-97	40	21	0	0	84
David Atkins	Huddersfield	2001	26(1)	4	0	0	16
Ryan Atkins	Warrington	2010-11	54	33	0	0	132
	Wakefield	2006-09	86(2)	45	0	0	180
Brad Attwood	Halifax	2003	(3)	0	0	0	0
Warren Ayres	Salford	1999	2(9)	1	2	0	8
Jerome Azema	Paris	1997	(1)	0	0	0	0
Marcus Bai	Bradford	2006	24	9	0	0	36
	Leeds	2004-05	57	42	0	0	168
David Baildon	Hull	1998-99	26(2)	4	0	0	16
Jean-Philippe Baile	Catalans	2008-11	54(7)	21	0	0	84
Andy Bailey	Hull	2004-05	2(8)	1	0	0	4
Chris Bailey	Harlequins	2011	24	3	0	0	12
Julian Bailey	Huddersfield	2003-04	47	13	0	0	52
Phil Bailey	Wigan	2007-10	84(4)	13	0	0	52
Ryan Bailey	Leeds	2002-11	138(81)	10	0	0	40
Jason Baitieri	Catalans	2011	8(19)	5	0	0	20
Simon Baldwin	Salford	2004-06	20(29)	3	0	0	12
	Sheffield	1999	7(15)	2	0	0	8
	Halifax	1996-98	41(15)	16	0	1	65
Rob Ball	Wigan	1998-2000	3(4)	0	0	0	0
Paul Ballard	Celtic	2009	2	0	0	0	0
	Widnes	2005	3(1)	2	0	0	8
Darren Bamford	Salford	2005	2(1)	0	0	0	0
Michael Banks	Bradford	1998	(1)	0	0	0	0
Steve Bannister	Harlequins	2007	(6)	0	0	0	0
	St Helens	2006-07	(3)	0	0	0	0
Frederic Banquet	Paris	1996	16(2)	7	4	0	36
Lee Bardauskas	Castleford	1996-97	(2)	0	0	0	0
Craig Barker	Workington	1996	(2)	0	0	0	0
Dwayne Barker	Harlequins	2008	5(5)	1	0	0	4
	London	2004	3	1	0	0	4
	Hull	2003	(1)	0	0	0	0
Mark Barlow	Wakefield	2002	(1)	0	0	0	0
Danny Barnes	Halifax	1999	2	0	0	0	0
Richie Barnett	Salford	2007	7	4	0	0	16
	Warrington	2006-07	26(10)	15	0	0	60
	Hull	2004-05	21(5)	21	0	0	84
	Widnes	2005	4	2	0	0	8
Richie Barnett	Hull	2003-04	31(1)	17	0	0	68
	London	2001-02	31(4)	13	0	0	52
David Barnhill	Leeds	2000	20(8)	5	0	0	20
Trent Barrett	Wigan	2007-08	53(1)	22	0	4	92
Paul Barrow	Warrington	1996-97	1(10)	1	0	0	4
Scott Barrow	St Helens	1997-2000	9(13)	1	0	0	4
Steve Barrow	London	2000	2	0	0	0	0
	Hull	1998-99	4(17)	1	0	0	4
	Wigan	1996	(8)	3	0	0	12
William Barthau	Catalans	2010	6(1)	0	3	0	6
Ben Barton	Huddersfield	1998	1(6)	1	0	0	4
Danny Barton	Salford	2001	1	0	0	0	0
Wayne Bartrim	Castleford	2002-03	41(2)	9	157	0	350
Greg Barwick	London	1996-97	30(4)	21	110	2	306
David Bastian	Halifax	1996	(2)	0	0	0	0
Ashley Bateman	Celtic	2009	1	0	0	0	0
John Bateman	Bradford	2011	2(1)	1	0	0	4
David Bates	Castleford	2001-02	(4)	0	0	0	0
	Warrington	2001	1(2)	0	0	0	0
Nathan Batty	Wakefield	2001	1(1)	0	0	0	0
Andreas Bauer	Hull KR	2007	10(2)	5	0	0	20
Russell Bawden	London	1996-97, 2002-04	50(49)	15	0	0	60
Neil Baxter	Salford	2001	1	0	0	0	0
Neil Baynes	Salford	1999-2002, 2004	84(19)	10	0	0	40
	Wigan	1996-98	(10)	1	0	0	4
Chris Beasley	Celtic	2009	15(5)	2	0	0	8
Chris Beattie	Catalans	2006	22(5)	3	0	0	12
Richard Beaumont	Hull KR	2011	(2)	0	0	0	0
Robbie Beazley	London	1997-99	48(15)	13	0	0	52
Robbie Beckett	Halifax	2002	27	15	0	0	60
Dean Bell	Leeds	1996	1	1	0	0	4
Ian Bell	Hull	2003	(1)	0	0	0	0
Mark Bell	Wigan	1998	22	12	0	0	48
Paul Bell	Leeds	2000	1	0	0	0	0
Steven Bell	Catalans	2009-10	43	14	0	0	56
Troy Bellamy	Paris	1997	5(10)	0	0	0	0
Adrian Belle	Huddersfield	1998	10(2)	0	0	0	0
	Oldham	1996	19	8	0	0	32
Jamie Benn	Castleford	1998, 2000	3(8)	1	15	0	34
Andy Bennett	Warrington	1996	6(5)	1	0	0	4
Mike Bennett	St Helens	2000-08	74(70)	15	0	0	60
Andrew Bentley	Catalans	2007-10	9(15)	1	0	0	4
John Bentley	Huddersfield	1999	13(4)	3	0	0	12
	Halifax	1996, 1998	22(3)	24	0	0	96
Kane Bentley	Catalans	2007-10	11(19)	5	0	0	20
Phil Bergman	Paris	1997	20(1)	14	0	0	56
Shaun Berrigan	Hull	2008-10	60(8)	12	0	0	48
Joe Berry	Huddersfield	1998-99	25(14)	3	0	0	12
David Berthezene	Salford	2007	9(1)	0	0	0	0
	Catalans	2006-07	5(14)	0	0	0	0
Colin Best	Hull	2003-04	57	34	0	0	136
Roger Best	London	1997-98	5	1	0	0	4
Bob Beswick	Wigan	2004-05	5(14)	2	0	0	8
Monty Betham	Wakefield	2006	26	2	0	0	8
Mike Bethwaite	Workington	1996	17(3)	1	0	0	4
Denis Betts	Wigan	1998-2001	82(24)	33	0	0	132
Cliff Beverley	Salford	2004-05	47(1)	14	0	0	56
Kyle Bibb	Wakefield	2008-10	1(24)	0	0	0	0
	Harlequins	2010	(2)	0	0	0	0
	Hull KR	2009	(2)	0	0	0	0
Adam Bibey	Widnes	2004	(2)	0	0	0	0
Ricky Bibey	Wakefield	2007-09	32(25)	1	0	0	4
	St Helens	2004	4(14)	0	0	0	0
	Wigan	2001-03	5(29)	1	0	0	4
Chris Birchall	Halifax	2002-03	24(22)	4	0	0	16
	Bradford	2000	(1)	0	0	0	0

PLAYER	CLUB	YEAR	APP	TRIES	GOALS	FG	PTS
Deon Bird	Castleford	2006	17(6)	5	0	0	20
	Widnes	2003-04	39(6)	9	0	0	36
	Wakefield	2002	10(1)	1	0	0	4
	Hull	2000-02	37(22)	20	0	0	80
	Gateshead	1999	19(3)	13	0	0	52
	Paris	1996-97	30	12	0	2	52
Greg Bird	Catalans	2009	20(2)	5	3	0	26
Nathan Blacklock	Hull	2005-06	44(3)	33	0	0	132
Richie Blackmore	Leeds	1997-2000	63	25	0	0	100
Anthony Blackwood							
	Crusaders	2010	1	0	0	0	0
	Celtic	2009	25	5	0	0	20
Luke Blake	Wakefield	2009	(2)	0	0	0	0
Matthew Blake	Wakefield	2003-04	1(5)	0	0	0	0
Steve Blakeley	Salford	1997-2002	103(5)	26	241	2	588
	Warrington	2000	4(3)	1	9	0	22
Richard Blakeway	Castleford	2002-04	1(14)	0	0	0	0
Damien Blanch	Catalans	2011	28	20	0	0	80
	Wakefield	2008-10	44(3)	31	0	0	124
	Castleford	2006	3(2)	0	0	0	0
Matt Blaymire	Wakefield	2007-11	96(3)	26	0	1	105
Ian Blease	Salford	1997	(1)	0	0	0	0
Jamie Bloem	Huddersfield	2003	18(4)	3	11	0	34
	Halifax	1998-2002	82(25)	25	100	2	302
Vea Bloomfield	Paris	1996	4(14)	3	0	0	12
Matty Blythe	Warrington	2007-11	18(20)	6	0	0	24
Ben Bolger	Harlequins	2010-11	4(15)	0	0	0	0
Pascal Bomati	Paris	1996	17(1)	10	0	0	40
Simon Booth	Hull	1998-99	15(9)	2	0	0	8
	St Helens	1996-97	10(4)	1	0	0	4
Steve Booth	Huddersfield	1998-99	16(4)	2	3	0	14
Alan Boothroyd	Halifax	1997	2(3)	0	0	0	0
Thomas Bosc	Catalans	2006-11	106(3)	31	291	3	709
John Boslem	Paris	1996	(5)	0	0	0	0
Liam Bostock	St Helens	2004	1	0	0	0	0
Liam Botham	Wigan	2005	5	0	0	0	0
	Leeds	2003-05	2(11)	4	0	0	16
	London	2004	6(2)	3	6	0	24
Frano Botica	Castleford	1996	21	5	84	2	190
Matthew Bottom	Leigh	2005	(1)	0	0	0	0
Hadj Boudebza	Paris	1996	(2)	0	0	0	0
David Boughton	Huddersfield	1999	26(1)	4	0	0	16
David Bouveng	Halifax	1997-99	66(2)	19	0	0	76
Tony Bowes	Huddersfield	1998	3(2)	0	0	0	0
Radney Bowker	London	2004	3	1	0	0	4
	St Helens	2001	(1)	0	0	0	0
David Boyle	Bradford	1999-2000	36(13)	15	0	1	61
Ryan Boyle	Salford	2010-11	42(4)	3	0	0	12
	Castleford	2006, 2008-09	(29)	2	0	0	8
Andy Bracek	Crusaders	2011	(2)	0	0	0	0
	Warrington	2005-08	7(49)	7	0	0	28
	St Helens	2004	(1)	0	0	0	0
David Bradbury	Hudds-Sheff	2000	21(2)	1	0	0	4
	Salford	1997-99	23(10)	6	0	0	24
	Oldham	1996-97	19(6)	9	0	0	36
John Braddish	St Helens	2001-02	1(1)	0	3	0	6
Graeme Bradley	Bradford	1996-98	62(1)	29	0	0	116
Nick Bradley-Qalilawa							
	Harlequins	2006	27	6	0	0	24
	London	2005	28	19	0	0	76
Darren Bradstreet	London	1999-2000	1(3)	0	0	0	0
Dominic Brambani							
	Castleford	2004	2(2)	0	0	0	0
Liam Bretherton	Wigan	1999	(5)	2	0	0	8
	Warrington	1997	(2)	0	0	0	0
Johnny Brewer	Halifax	1996	4(2)	2	0	0	8
Chris Bridge	Warrington	2005-11	115(12)	63	175	1	603
	Bradford	2003-04	2(14)	4	6	0	28
Lee Briers	Warrington	1997-2011	327(12)	122	808	65	2169
	St Helens	1997	3	0	11	0	22
Carl Briggs	Salford	1999	8(5)	3	0	1	13
	Halifax	1996	5(3)	1	0	0	4
Kyle Briggs	Bradford	2011	6	4	0	0	16
	Harlequins	2011	3	0	0	0	0
Mike Briggs	Widnes	2002	1(2)	1	0	0	4
Shaun Briscoe	Hull KR	2008-11	92	27	0	0	108
	Hull	2004-07	83(9)	50	0	0	200
	Wigan	2002-03	23(5)	11	0	0	44
Tom Briscoe	Hull	2008-11	76(3)	47	0	0	188
Darren Britt	St Helens	2002-03	41	3	0	0	12
Gary Broadbent	Salford	1997-2002	117(2)	22	0	0	88
Paul Broadbent	Wakefield	2002	16(5)	0	0	0	0
	Hull	2000-01	40(9)	3	0	0	12
	Halifax	1999	26(1)	2	0	0	8
	Sheffield	1996-98	63(1)	6	0	0	24
Andrew Brocklehurst							
	Salford	2004-07	34(23)	5	0	0	20
	London	2004	12(6)	2	0	0	8
	Halifax	2001-03	37(8)	2	0	0	8
Justin Brooker	Wakefield	2001	25	9	0	0	36
	Bradford	2000	17(4)	11	0	0	44
Danny Brough	Huddersfield	2010-11	42(3)	13	104	3	263
	Wakefield	2008-10	50(1)	14	174	4	408
	Castleford	2006	10	1	31	2	68
	Hull	2005-06	25(12)	3	85	1	183
Jodie Broughton	Salford	2010-11	50	26	0	0	104
	Hull	2008-09	9(3)	6	0	0	24
Alex Brown	Huddersfield	2009	1	0	0	0	0
Darren Brown	Salford	1999-2001	47(9)	11	6	0	56
Gavin Brown	Leeds	1996-97	5(2)	1	2	0	8
Kevin Brown	Huddersfield	2006-11	139	38	0	1	153
	Wigan	2003-06	46(18)	27	0	0	108
Lee Brown	Hull	1999	(1)	0	0	0	0
Michael Brown	Huddersfield	2008	(1)	0	0	0	0
Michael Brown	London	1996	(2)	0	0	0	0
Todd Brown	Paris	1996	8(1)	2	0	0	8
Adrian Brunker	Wakefield	1999	17	6	0	0	24
Lamont Bryan	Harlequins	2008-11	9(22)	2	0	0	8
Justin Bryant	Paris	1996	4(1)	0	0	0	0
	London	1996	7(8)	1	0	0	4
Mark Bryant	Crusaders	2010-11	42(8)	1	0	0	4
	Celtic	2009	23(3)	0	0	0	0
Austin Buchanan	Wakefield	2005-06	6	2	0	0	8
	London	2003	3(1)	2	0	0	8
Danny Buderus	Leeds	2009-11	57(14)	14	0	0	56
Neil Budworth	Celtic	2009	8(19)	0	0	0	0
	Harlequins	2006	2(19)	0	0	0	0
	London	2002-05	59(11)	4	1	0	18
James Bunyan	Huddersfield	1998-99	8(7)	2	0	0	8
Andy Burgess	Salford	1997	3(12)	0	0	0	0
Luke Burgess	Leeds	2008-11	10(63)	6	0	0	24
	Harlequins	2007	(2)	0	0	0	0
Sam Burgess	Bradford	2006-09	46(34)	14	5	0	66
Tom Burgess	Bradford	2011	1(17)	1	0	0	4
Joe Burke	Crusaders	2011	(1)	0	0	0	0
Mike Burnett	Harlequins	2011	16(4)	1	0	0	4
	Hull	2008-10	13(21)	3	0	0	12
Darren Burns	Warrington	2002-04	66(6)	19	0	0	76
Gary Burns	Oldham	1996	6	1	0	0	4
Paul Burns	Workington	1996	5(2)	1	0	0	4
Rob Burrow	Leeds	2001-11	211(79)	123	123	5	743
Dean Busby	Warrington	1999-2002	34(34)	7	0	0	28
	Hull	1998	8(6)	0	0	0	0
	St Helens	1996-98	1(7)	0	0	0	0
Tom Bush	Leeds	2010	3(1)	1	0	0	4
Ikram Butt	London	1996	5(1)	0	0	0	0
Shane Byrne	Huddersfield	1998-99	1(5)	0	0	0	0
Todd Byrne	Hull	2008-09	20	4	0	0	16
Didier Cabestany	Paris	1996-97	20(6)	2	0	0	8
Hep Cahill	Crusaders	2011	16	2	0	0	8
Joel Caine	Salford	2004	24	8	13	0	58
	London	2003	6	4	1	0	18
Mark Calderwood	Harlequins	2011	13	2	0	0	8
	Hull	2009-10	23	6	0	0	24
	Wigan	2006-08	64	23	0	0	92
	Leeds	2001-05	117(9)	88	0	0	352
Mike Callan	Warrington	2002	(4)	0	0	0	0
Matt Calland	Huddersfield	2003	2	0	0	0	0
	Hull	1999	1	0	0	0	0
	Bradford	1996-98	44(5)	24	0	0	96
Dean Callaway	London	1999-2000	26(24)	12	0	0	48
Laurent Cambres	Paris	1996	(1)	0	0	0	0
Chris Campbell	Warrington	2000	7(1)	2	0	0	8
Liam Campbell	Wakefield	2005	(1)	0	0	0	0
Logan Campbell	Hull	1998-99, 2001	70(13)	14	0	0	56
	Castleford	2000	14(2)	3	0	0	12
	Workington	1996	7(1)	1	0	0	4
Blake Cannova	Widnes	2002	(1)	0	0	0	0
Phil Cantillon	Widnes	2002-03	27(21)	18	0	0	72
	Leeds	1997	(1)	0	0	0	0
Daryl Cardiss	Warrington	2003-04	23(2)	3	4	0	20
	Halifax	1999-2003	91(8)	39	4	0	164
	Wigan	1996-98	12(6)	4	0	0	16
Dale Cardoza	Warrington	2002	5	1	0	0	4
	Halifax	2001	1	1	0	0	4
	Huddersfield	2000-01	20(9)	11	0	0	44
	Sheffield	1998-99	11(7)	3	0	0	12
Paul Carige	Salford	1999	24(1)	7	0	0	28
Dane Carlaw	Catalans	2008-09	58(15)	9	0	0	36
Keal Carlile	Huddersfield	2009, 2011	2(1)	1	0	0	4
	Bradford	2008	(1)	0	0	0	0
Jim Carlton	Huddersfield	1999	3(11)	2	0	0	8
George Carmont	Wigan	2008-11	112	51	0	0	204
Brian Carney	Warrington	2009	4	2	0	0	8
	Wigan	2001-05	91(10)	42	1	0	170
	Hull	2000	13(3)	7	0	0	28
	Gateshead	1999	3(2)	2	0	0	8
Martin Carney	Warrington	1997	(1)	0	0	0	0
Paul Carr	Sheffield	1996-98	45(5)	15	0	0	60
Bernard Carroll	London	1996	2(1)	1	0	0	4
Mark Carroll	London	1998	15(3)	1	0	0	4
Tonie Carroll	Leeds	2001-02	42(2)	30	0	0	120
Darren Carton	Workington	1996	10(3)	0	1	0	2
Steve Carter	Widnes	2002	14(7)	4	0	0	16
John Cartwright	Salford	1997	9	1	0	0	4
Garreth Carvell	Warrington	2009-11	62(8)	7	0	0	28
	Hull	2001-08	69(83)	22	0	0	88
	Leeds	1997-2000	(4)	0	0	0	0
	Gateshead	1999	4(4)	1	0	0	4

Super League Players 1996-2011

PLAYER	CLUB	YEAR	APP	TRIES	GOALS	FG	PTS
Garen Casey	Salford	1999	13(5)	3	23	0	58
Ray Cashmere	Salford	2009-11	63(3)	5	0	0	20
Mick Cassidy	Widnes	2005	24	0	0	0	0
	Wigan	1996-2004	184(36)	30	0	0	120
Remi Casty	Catalans	2006-11	33(83)	7	0	0	28
Ned Catic	Castleford	2008	7(7)	3	0	0	12
	Wakefield	2006-07	17(29)	4	0	0	16
Chris Causey	Warrington	1997-99	(18)	1	0	0	4
Jason Cayless	St Helens	2006-09	62(9)	7	0	0	28
Arnaud Cervello	Paris	1996	4	4	0	0	16
Marshall Chalk	Celtic	2009	13	4	0	0	16
Gary Chambers	Warrington	1996-2000	65(28)	2	0	0	8
Pierre Chamorin	Paris	1996-97	27(3)	8	3	0	38
Alex Chan	Catalans	2006-08	59(19)	11	0	0	44
Jason Chan	Crusaders	2010-11	48(1)	10	0	0	40
	Celtic	2009	17(6)	3	0	0	12
Joe Chandler	Leeds	2008	(1)	0	0	0	0
Chris Chapman	Leeds	1999	(1)	0	0	0	0
Damien Chapman	London	1998	6(2)	3	4	1	21
David Chapman	Castleford	1996-98	24(6)	8	0	0	32
Jaymes Chapman	Halifax	2002-03	5(8)	1	0	0	4
Richard Chapman	Sheffield	1996	1	1	2	0	8
Chris Charles	Salford	2004-06	59(16)	6	140	0	304
	Castleford	2001	1(4)	1	0	0	4
Olivier Charles	Catalans	2007	2	2	0	0	8
Josh Charnley	Wigan	2010-11	27(2)	24	5	0	106
	Hull KR	2010	5	5	0	0	20
Rangi Chase	Castleford	2009-11	73(5)	29	0	3	119
Andy Cheetham	Huddersfield	1998-99	30	11	0	0	44
Kris Chesney	London	1998	1(2)	0	0	0	0
Chris Chester	Hull KR	2007-08	28(6)	4	0	0	16
	Hull	2002-06	67(25)	13	0	0	52
	Wigan	1999-2001	21(22)	5	0	0	20
	Halifax	1996-99	47(14)	16	15	1	95
Lee Chilton	Workington	1996	10(3)	6	0	0	24
Gary Christie	Bradford	1996-97	4(7)	1	0	0	4
Daryl Clark	Castleford	2011	1(17)	7	0	0	28
Dean Clark	Leeds	1996	11(2)	3	0	0	12
Des Clark	St Helens	1999	4	0	0	0	0
	Halifax	1998-99	35(13)	6	0	0	24
Greg Clarke	Halifax	1997	1(1)	0	0	0	0
John Clarke	Oldham	1996-97	27(4)	5	0	0	20
Jon Clarke	Warrington	2001-11	217(25)	56	2	0	228
	London	2000-01	19(11)	2	0	0	8
	Wigan	1997-99	13(10)	3	0	0	12
Chris Clarkson	Leeds	2010-11	31(8)	7	0	0	28
Adam Clay	Salford	2011	2	3	0	0	12
Ryan Clayton	Castleford	2004, 2008-10	36(24)	5	0	0	20
	Salford	2006	3(8)	2	0	0	8
	Huddersfield	2005	4(6)	0	0	0	0
	Halifax	2000, 2002-03	28(12)	6	0	0	24
Gavin Clinch	Salford	2004	21(1)	1	0	1	5
	Halifax	1998-99, 2001-02	88(2)	26	45	5	199
	Hudds-Sheff	2000	18(2)	5	0	1	21
	Wigan	1999	10(2)	4	12	0	40
Joel Clinton	Hull KR	2010-11	30(7)	2	0	0	8
John Clough	Salford	2004-06	1(16)	0	0	0	0
Paul Clough	St Helens	2005-11	47(74)	14	0	0	56
Tony Clubb	Harlequins	2006-11	100(11)	29	0	0	116
Bradley Clyde	Leeds	2001	7(5)	1	0	0	4
Michael Coady	Leeds	2010	1	0	0	0	0
Evan Cochrane	London	1996	5(1)	1	0	0	4
Ben Cockayne	Hull KR	2007-11	76(26)	27	0	0	108
Liam Colbon	Hull KR	2009-11	51	20	0	0	80
	Wigan	2004-05, 2007-08	37(14)	15	0	0	60
Anthony Colella	Huddersfield	2003	5(1)	2	0	0	8
Liam Coleman	Leigh	2005	1(4)	0	0	0	0
Andy Coley	Wigan	2008-11	100(10)	8	0	0	32
	Salford	2001-02, 2004-07	112(34)	34	0	0	136
Richard Colley	Bradford	2004	1	0	0	0	0
Steve Collins	Hull	2000	28	17	0	0	68
	Gateshead	1999	20(4)	13	0	0	52
Wayne Collins	Leeds	1997	21	3	0	0	12
Aurelien Cologni	Catalans	2006	4(1)	3	0	0	12
Gary Connolly	Widnes	2005	20	4	1	0	18
	Wigan	1996-2002, 2004	168(10)	70	5	0	290
	Leeds	2003-04	27	6	0	0	24
Matt Cook	Hull KR	2010-11	9(16)	7	0	0	28
	Bradford	2005-09	11(52)	4	0	0	16
	Castleford	2008	2(1)	1	0	0	4
Mick Cook	Sheffield	1996	9(10)	2	0	0	8
Paul Cook	Huddersfield	1998-99	11(6)	2	13	0	34
	Bradford	1996-97	14(8)	7	38	1	105
Peter Cook	St Helens	2004	(1)	0	0	0	0
Paul Cooke	Wakefield	2010	16(1)	3	36	1	85
	Hull KR	2007-10	54(5)	8	76	2	186
	Hull	1999-2007	177(27)	32	333	4	798
Ben Cooper	Leigh	2005	25(1)	5	0	0	20
	Huddersfield	2000-01, 2003-04	28(12)	3	0	0	12
Michael Cooper	Warrington	2006-11	7(57)	5	0	0	20
	Castleford	2010	1(5)	2	0	0	8
Ged Corcoran	Halifax	2003	1(11)	0	0	0	0
Wayne Corcoran	Halifax	2003	4(2)	0	0	0	0
Jamie Cording	Huddersfield	2011	2(2)	1	0	0	4
Josh Cordoba	Hull	2009	8	1	0	0	4
Mark Corvo	Salford	2002	7(5)	0	0	0	0
Brandon Costin	Huddersfield	2001, 2003-04	69	42	93	3	357
	Bradford	2002	20(1)	8	0	0	32
Wes Cotton	London	1997-98	12	3	0	0	12
Phil Coussons	Salford	1997	7(2)	3	0	0	12
Alex Couttet	Paris	1997	1	0	0	0	0
Nick Couttet	Paris	1997	1	0	0	0	0
Jamie Coventry	Castleford	1996	1	0	0	0	0
Jimmy Cowan	Oldham	1996-97	2(8)	0	0	0	0
Will Cowell	Warrington	1998-2000	6(8)	1	0	0	4
Neil Cowie	Wigan	1996-2001	116(27)	10	0	1	41
Jordan Cox	Hull KR	2011	(6)	0	0	0	0
Mark Cox	London	2003	(3)	0	0	0	0
James Coyle	Wigan	2005	2(3)	1	0	0	4
Thomas Coyle	Wigan	2008	2(1)	0	0	0	0
Eorl Crabtree	Huddersfield	2001, 2003-11	92(127)	25	0	0	100
Andy Craig	Halifax	1999	13(7)	1	3	0	10
	Wigan	1996	5(5)	2	0	0	8
Owen Craigie	Widnes	2005	15	7	0	2	30
Scott Cram	London	1999-2002	65(7)	4	0	0	16
Steve Craven	Hull	1998-2003	53(42)	4	0	0	16
Nicky Crellin	Workington	1996	(2)	0	0	0	0
Jason Critchley	Wakefield	2000	1	4	0	0	16
	Castleford	1997-98	27(3)	11	0	0	44
Jason Croker	Catalans	2007-09	56(2)	11	0	1	45
Martin Crompton	Salford	1998-2000	30(6)	11	6	2	58
	Oldham	1996-97	36(1)	16	0	3	67
Paul Crook	Widnes	2005	2(2)	0	5	1	11
Paul Crook	Oldham	1996	4(9)	0	3	0	6
Jason Crookes	Bradford	2009-11	12(1)	0	0	0	0
Lee Crooks	Castleford	1996-97	27(2)	2	14	0	36
Alan Cross	St Helens	1997	(2)	0	0	0	0
Ben Cross	Wigan	2011	(4)	0	0	0	0
	Leeds	2011	1(9)	0	0	0	0
Steve Crossley	Bradford	2010-11	(9)	1	0	0	4
Garet Crossman	Hull KR	2008	8(18)	0	0	0	0
Steve Crouch	Castleford	2004	4(1)	2	0	0	8
Kevin Crouthers	Warrington	2001-03	12(1)	4	0	0	16
	London	2000	6(4)	1	0	0	4
	Wakefield	1999	4(4)	1	0	0	4
	Bradford	1997-98	3(9)	2	0	0	8
Matt Crowther	Hull	2001-03	48	20	166	0	412
	Hudds-Sheff	2000	10(4)	5	22	0	64
	Sheffield	1996-99	43(4)	22	10	0	108
Heath Cruckshank	Halifax	2003	19(1)	0	0	0	0
	St Helens	2001	1(12)	0	0	0	0
Leroy Cudjoe	Huddersfield	2008-11	92(1)	49	45	0	286
Paul Cullen	Warrington	1996	19	3	0	0	12
Francis Cummins	Leeds	1996-2005	217(13)	120	26	2	534
Keiron Cunningham	St Helens	1996-2010	357(24)	138	0	0	552
Liam Cunningham	Hull	2010	(1)	0	0	0	0
Andy Currier	Warrington	1996-97	(2)	1	0	0	4
Peter Cusack	Hull	2008-10	34(22)	3	0	0	12
Joe Dakuitoga	Sheffield	1996	6(3)	0	0	0	0
Matty Dale	Hull	2006, 2008	(7)	1	0	0	4
	Wakefield	2008	1(1)	0	0	0	0
Brett Dallas	Wigan	2000-06	156	89	0	0	356
Mark Dalle Cort	Celtic	2009	23	4	0	0	16
Paul Darbyshire	Warrington	1997	(6)	0	0	0	0
James Davey	Wakefield	2009-11	3(14)	1	0	0	4
Maea David	Hull	1998	1	0	0	0	0
Alex Davidson	Salford	2011	(1)	0	0	0	0
Paul Davidson	Halifax	2001-03	22(30)	10	0	0	40
	London	2000	6(10)	4	0	0	16
	St Helens	1998-99	27(16)	7	0	0	28
	Oldham	1996-97	17(18)	14	0	1	57
Ben Davies	Castleford	2011	3(2)	2	0	0	8
	Wigan	2010	(5)	0	0	0	0
Gareth Davies	Warrington	1996-97	1(6)	0	0	0	0
Geraint Davies	Celtic	2009	(7)	0	0	0	0
John Davies	Castleford	2010-11	(6)	1	0	0	4
Wes Davies	Wigan	1998-2001	22(22)	11	0	0	44
Brad Davis	Castleford	1997-2000, 2004, 2006	102(3)	31	43	10	220
	Wakefield	2001-03	51(12)	15	22	5	109
Matt Daylight	Hull	2000	17(1)	7	0	0	28
	Gateshead	1999	30	25	0	0	100
Michael De Vere	Huddersfield	2005-06	36	6	74	0	172
Paul Deacon	Wigan	2010-11	32(11)	4	14	0	44
	Bradford	1998-2009	258(43)	72	1029	23	2369
	Oldham	1997	(2)	0	0	0	0
Chris Dean	Wakefield	2011	20	8	0	0	32
	St Helens	2007-10	18(3)	9	0	0	36

PLAYER	CLUB	YEAR	APP	TRIES	GOALS	FG	PTS
Craig Dean	Halifax	1996-97	25(11)	12	1	1	51
Gareth Dean	London	2002	(4)	0	0	0	0
Yacine Dekkiche	Hudds-Sheff	2000	11(3)	3	0	0	12
Brett Delaney	Leeds	2010-11	46	11	0	0	44
Jason Demetriou	Wakefield	2004-10	174(3)	50	2	0	204
	Widnes	2002-03	47(1)	15	1	0	62
Martin Dermott	Warrington	1997	1	0	0	0	0
David Despin	Paris	1996	(1)	0	0	0	0
Fabien Devecchi	Paris	1996-97	17(10)	2	0	0	8
Paul Devlin	Widnes	2002-04	32	16	0	0	64
Stuart Dickens	Salford	2005	4(5)	0	4	0	8
Matt Diskin	Bradford	2011	17(6)	3	0	0	12
	Leeds	2001-10	195(37)	40	0	0	160
Andrew Dixon	St Helens	2009-11	17(25)	6	0	0	24
Kirk Dixon	Castleford	2008-11	86(1)	37	182	0	512
	Hull	2004-06	13(4)	7	4	0	36
Paul Dixon	Sheffield	1996-97	5(9)	1	0	0	4
Gareth Dobson	Castleford	1998-2000	(10)	0	0	0	0
Michael Dobson	Hull KR	2008-11	91	36	313	9	779
	Wigan	2006	14	5	61	0	142
	Catalans	2006	10	4	31	1	79
Michael Docherty	Hull	2000-01	(6)	0	0	0	0
Sid Domic	Hull	2006-07	39(4)	15	0	0	60
	Wakefield	2004-05	48	30	0	0	120
	Warrington	2002-03	41(4)	17	0	0	68
Scott Donald	Leeds	2006-10	131	77	0	0	308
James Donaldson							
	Bradford	2009-11	7(23)	2	0	0	8
Glen Donkin	Hull	2002-03	(10)	1	0	0	4
Stuart Donlan	Castleford	2008	20	8	0	0	32
	Huddersfield	2004-06	59(3)	15	0	0	60
	Halifax	2001-03	65(2)	22	0	0	88
Jason Donohue	Bradford	1996	(4)	0	0	0	0
Jeremy Donougher							
	Bradford	1996-99	40(21)	13	0	0	52
Justin Dooley	London	2000-01	37(18)	2	0	0	8
Dane Dorahy	Halifax	2003	20	7	45	0	118
	Wakefield	2000-01	16(2)	4	19	1	55
Luke Dorn	Harlequins	2006,					
		2009-11	83(1)	57	0	0	228
	Castleford	2008	25(1)	19	0	0	76
	Salford	2007	19(8)	11	0	0	44
	London	2005	28	23	0	0	92
Ewan Dowes	Hull	2003-11	169(51)	10	0	0	40
	Leeds	2001-03	1(9)	0	0	0	0
Adam Doyle	Warrington	1998	9(3)	4	0	0	16
Rod Doyle	Sheffield	1997-99	52(10)	10	0	0	40
Brad Drew	Huddersfield	2005-07,					
		2010	78(13)	18	13	1	99
	Wakefield	2008-09	27(9)	7	14	1	57
Damien Driscoll	Salford	2001	23(1)	1	0	0	4
Gil Dudson	Crusaders	2011	3(7)	0	0	0	0
	Celtic	2009	(1)	0	0	0	0
Jason Duffy	Leigh	2005	3(1)	0	0	0	0
John Duffy	Leigh	2005	21	6	0	0	24
	Salford	2000	3(11)	0	1	1	3
	Warrington	1997-99	12(12)	0	0	0	0
Tony Duggan	Celtic	2009	4	3	0	0	12
Andrew Duncan	London	1997	2(4)	2	0	0	8
	Warrington	1997	(1)	0	0	0	0
Andrew Dunemann							
	Salford	2006	25	1	0	2	6
	Leeds	2003-05	76(4)	11	0	2	46
	Halifax	1999-2002	68	19	0	1	77
Matt Dunford	London	1997-98	18(20)	3	0	1	13
Vincent Duport	Catalans	2007-09,					
		2011	30(14)	13	0	0	52
Jamie Durbin	Widnes	2005	1	0	0	0	0
	Warrington	2003	(1)	0	0	0	0
Scott Dureau	Catalans	2011	25	11	92	5	233
James Durkin	Paris	1997	(5)	0	0	0	0
Bernard Dwyer	Bradford	1996-2000	65(10)	14	0	0	56
Luke Dyer	Crusaders	2010	23(1)	5	0	0	20
	Celtic	2009	21	6	0	0	24
	Hull KR	2007	26	13	0	0	52
	Castleford	2006	17(2)	5	0	0	20
Adam Dykes	Hull	2008	12	1	0	2	6
Jim Dymock	London	2001-04	94(1)	15	0	1	61
Leo Dynevor	London	1996	8(11)	5	7	0	34
Jason Eade	Paris	1997	9	4	0	0	16
Michael Eagar	Hull	2004-05	12	4	0	0	16
	Castleford	1999-2003	130(2)	60	0	0	240
	Warrington	1998	21	6	0	0	24
Kyle Eastmond	St Helens	2007-11	46(20)	35	117	3	377
Greg Eastwood	Leeds	2010	5(12)	1	0	0	4
Barry Eaton	Widnes	2002	25	2	49	4	110
	Castleford	2000	1(4)	0	3	0	6
Greg Ebrill	Salford	2002	15(6)	1	0	0	4
Cliff Eccles	Salford	1997-98	30(5)	1	0	0	4
Chris Eckersley	Warrington	1996	1	0	0	0	0
Greg Eden	Castleford	2011	2	1	0	0	4
Steve Edmed	Sheffield	1997	15(1)	0	0	0	0
Mark Edmondson	Salford	2007	10(2)	0	0	0	0
	St Helens	1999-2005	27(75)	10	0	0	40

PLAYER	CLUB	YEAR	APP	TRIES	GOALS	FG	PTS
Diccon Edwards	Castleford	1996-97	10(5)	1	0	0	4
Grant Edwards	Castleford	2006	(2)	0	0	0	0
Max Edwards	Harlequins	2010	1	0	0	0	0
Peter Edwards	Salford	1997-98	35(2)	4	0	0	16
Shaun Edwards	London	1997-2000	32(8)	16	1	0	66
	Bradford	1998	8(2)	4	0	0	16
	Wigan	1996	17(3)	12	1	0	50
Danny Ekis	Halifax	2001	(1)	0	0	0	0
Abi Ekoku	Bradford	1997-98	21(4)	6	0	0	24
	Halifax	1996	15(1)	5	0	0	20
Shane Elford	Huddersfield	2007-08	26(1)	7	0	0	28
Olivier Elima	Bradford	2011	25	9	0	0	36
	Catalans	2008-10	56(10)	30	0	0	120
	Wakefield	2003-07	40(47)	13	0	0	52
	Castleford	2002	(1)	1	0	0	4
Abderazak Elkhalouki							
	Paris	1997	(1)	0	0	0	0
George Elliott	Leeds	2011	1	0	0	0	0
Andy Ellis	Harlequins	2010-11	26(11)	8	0	0	32
Gareth Ellis	Leeds	2005-08	109	24	1	0	98
	Wakefield	1999-2004	86(17)	21	2	0	88
James Ellis	St Helens	2009	1(2)	0	1	0	2
Danny Ellison	Castleford	1998-99	7(16)	6	0	0	24
	Wigan	1996-97	15(1)	13	0	0	52
Andrew Emelio	Widnes	2005	22(2)	8	0	0	32
Jake Emmitt	Castleford	2011	15(5)	0	0	0	0
	St Helens	2008-10	1(16)	1	0	0	4
Patrick Entat	Paris	1996	22	2	0	0	8
Jason Erba	Sheffield	1997	1(4)	0	0	0	0
Ryan Esders	Harlequins	2009-10	9(11)	3	0	0	12
	Hull KR	2009	(1)	0	0	0	0
James Evans	Castleford	2009-10	26(1)	13	0	0	52
	Bradford	2007-08	43(5)	20	0	0	80
	Wakefield	2006	6	3	0	0	12
	Huddersfield	2004-06	51	22	0	0	88
Paul Evans	Paris	1997	18	8	0	0	32
Rhys Evans	Warrington	2010-11	6(3)	2	0	0	8
Wayne Evans	London	2002	11(6)	2	0	0	8
Richie Eyres	Warrington	1997	2(5)	0	0	0	0
	Sheffield	1997	2(3)	0	0	0	0
Henry Fa'afili	Warrington	2004-07	90(1)	70	0	0	280
David Fa'alogo	Huddersfield	2010-11	29(7)	11	0	0	44
Sala Fa'alogo	Widnes	2004-05	8(15)	2	0	0	8
Richard Fa'aoso	Castleford	2006	10(15)	5	0	0	20
Maurie Fa'asavalu	St Helens	2004-10	5(137)	29	0	0	116
Bolouagi Fagborun							
	Huddersfield	2004-06	4(2)	1	0	0	4
Esene Faimalo	Salford	1997-99	23(25)	2	0	0	8
	Leeds	1996	3(3)	0	0	0	0
Joe Faimalo	Salford	1998-2000	23(47)	7	0	0	28
	Oldham	1996-97	37(5)	7	0	0	28
Jacob Fairbank	Huddersfield	2011	1	0	0	0	0
Karl Fairbank	Bradford	1996	17(2)	4	0	0	16
David Fairleigh	St Helens	2001	26(1)	8	0	0	32
David Faiumu	Huddersfield	2008-11	31(50)	9	0	0	36
Jamal Fakir	Catalans	2006-11	52(52)	10	0	0	40
Jim Fallon	Leeds	1996	10	5	0	0	20
Ben Farrar	Catalans	2011	13	3	0	0	12
Danny Farrar	Warrington	1998-2000	76	13	0	0	52
Andy Farrell	Wigan	1996-2004	230	77	1026	16	2376
Anthony Farrell	Widnes	2002-03	24(22)	4	1	0	18
	Leeds	1997-2001	99(23)	18	0	0	72
	Sheffield	1996	14(5)	5	0	0	20
Craig Farrell	Hull	2000-01	1(3)	0	0	0	0
Liam Farrell	Wigan	2010-11	16(27)	15	0	0	60
Abraham Fatnowna							
	London	1997-98	7(2)	2	0	0	8
	Workington	1996	5	2	0	0	8
Sione Faumuina	Castleford	2009	18	1	0	0	4
	Hull	2005	3	1	0	0	4
Vince Fawcett	Wakefield	1999	13(1)	2	0	0	8
	Warrington	1998	4(7)	1	0	0	4
	Oldham	1997	5	3	0	0	12
Danny Fearon	Huddersfield	2001	(1)	0	0	0	0
	Halifax	1999-2000	5(6)	0	0	0	0
Chris Feather	Castleford	2009	1(23)	0	0	0	0
	Bradford	2007-08	7(20)	1	0	0	4
	Leeds	2003-04,					
		2006	16(35)	6	0	0	24
	Wakefield	2001-02,					
		2004-05	29(32)	9	0	0	36
Dom Feaunati	Leigh	2005	4	1	0	0	4
	St Helens	2004	10(7)	7	0	0	28
Adel Fellous	Hull	2008	1(2)	0	0	0	0
	Catalans	2006-07	16(22)	4	0	0	16
Luke Felsch	Hull	2000-01	46(6)	7	0	0	28
	Gateshead	1999	28(1)	2	0	0	8
Leon Felton	Warrington	2002	4(2)	0	0	0	0
	St Helens	2001	1(1)	0	0	0	0
Dale Ferguson	Huddersfield	2011	11(6)	6	0	0	24
	Wakefield	2007-11	40(14)	12	0	0	48
Brett Ferres	Castleford	2009-11	63(3)	19	0	0	76
	Wakefield	2007-08	36(2)	6	5	0	34
	Bradford	2005-06	18(17)	11	2	0	48

Super League Players 1996-2011

PLAYER	CLUB	YEAR	APP	TRIES	GOALS	FG	PTS
David Ferriol	Catalans	2007-11	60(47)	8	0	0	32
Jason Ferris	Leigh	2005	4	1	0	0	4
Jamie Field	Wakefield	1999-2006	133(59)	19	0	0	76
	Huddersfield	1998	15(5)	0	0	0	0
	Leeds	1996-97	3(11)	0	0	0	0
Mark Field	Wakefield	2003-07	28(7)	3	0	0	12
Jamie Fielden	London	2003	(1)	0	0	0	0
	Huddersfield	1998-2000	4(8)	0	0	0	0
Stuart Fielden	Wigan	2006-11	104(24)	2	0	0	8
	Bradford	1998-2006	142(78)	41	0	0	164
Lafaele Filipo	Workington	1996	15(4)	3	0	0	12
Salesi Finau	Warrington	1996-97	16(15)	8	0	0	32
Brett Finch	Wigan	2011	21(3)	7	0	0	28
Vinny Finigan	Bradford	2010	4(1)	4	0	0	16
Liam Finn	Wakefield	2004	1(1)	0	1	0	2
	Halifax	2002-03	16(5)	2	30	1	69
Lee Finnerty	Halifax	2003	18(2)	5	2	0	24
Phil Finney	Warrington	1998	1	0	0	0	0
Simon Finnigan	Huddersfield	2009-10	22(5)	6	0	0	24
	Bradford	2008	14(13)	8	0	0	32
	Salford	2006-07	50	17	0	0	68
	Widnes	2003-05	51(19)	21	0	0	84
Matt Firth	Halifax	2000-01	12(2)	0	0	0	0
Andy Fisher	Wakefield	1999-2000	31(8)	4	0	0	16
Ben Fisher	Hull KR	2007-11	78(46)	18	0	0	72
Craig Fitzgibbon	Hull	2010-11	42(1)	9	8	0	52
Daniel Fitzhenry	Hull KR	2008-09	36(11)	14	0	0	56
Karl Fitzpatrick	Salford	2004-07, 2009-10	89(11)	33	2	0	136
Mark Flanagan	Wigan	2009	3(7)	1	0	0	4
Chris Flannery	St Helens	2007-11	89(7)	26	0	0	104
Darren Fleary	Leigh	2005	24	1	0	0	4
	Huddersfield	2003-04	43(8)	4	0	0	16
	Leeds	1997-2002	98(9)	3	0	0	12
Greg Fleming	London	1999-2001	64(1)	40	2	0	164
Adam Fletcher	Castleford	2006, 2008	16(7)	11	0	0	44
Bryan Fletcher	Wigan	2006-07	47(2)	14	0	0	56
Richard Fletcher	Castleford	2006	13(5)	3	4	0	20
	Hull	1999-2004	11(56)	5	0	0	20
Greg Florimo	Halifax	2000	26	6	4	0	32
	Wigan	1999	18(2)	7	1	0	30
Ben Flower	Crusaders	2010-11	10(23)	2	0	0	8
	Celtic	2009	2(15)	0	0	0	0
Jason Flowers	Salford	2004	6(1)	0	0	0	0
	Halifax	2002	24(4)	4	0	0	16
	Castleford	1996-2001	119(19)	33	0	1	133
Stuart Flowers	Castleford	1996	(3)	0	0	0	0
Adrian Flynn	Castleford	1996-97	19(2)	10	0	0	40
Wayne Flynn	Sheffield	1997	3(5)	0	0	0	0
Adam Fogerty	Warrington	1998	4	0	0	0	0
	St Helens	1996	13	1	0	0	4
Carl Forber	Leigh	2005	4	1	0	0	4
	St Helens	2004	1(1)	0	6	0	12
Paul Forber	Salford	1997-98	19(12)	4	0	0	16
Byron Ford	Hull KR	2007	13	6	0	0	24
James Ford	Castleford	2009	3(5)	1	0	0	4
Mike Ford	Castleford	1997-98	25(12)	5	3	3	23
	Warrington	1996	3	0	0	0	0
Jim Forshaw	Salford	1999	(1)	0	0	0	0
Mike Forshaw	Warrington	2004	20(1)	5	0	0	20
	Bradford	1997-2003	162(7)	32	0	0	128
	Leeds	1996	11(3)	5	0	0	20
Carl Forster	St Helens	2011	(1)	0	0	0	0
Mark Forster	Warrington	1996-2000	102(1)	40	0	0	160
David Foster	Halifax	2000-01	4(9)	0	0	0	0
Jamie Foster	St Helens	2010-11	39(3)	28	183	0	478
Peter Fox	Hull KR	2008-11	95	52	0	0	208
	Wakefield	2007	23	11	0	0	44
Nick Fozzard	Castleford	2011	7(10)	0	0	0	0
	St Helens	2004-08, 2010	100(25)	7	0	0	28
	Hull KR	2009	18(4)	1	0	0	4
	Warrington	2002-03	43(11)	2	0	0	8
	Huddersfield	1998-2000	24(8)	2	0	0	8
	Leeds	1996-97	6(16)	3	0	0	12
David Fraisse	Workington	1996	8	0	0	0	0
Daniel Frame	Widnes	2002-05	100(6)	24	0	0	96
Paul Franze	Castleford	2006	2(1)	0	0	0	0
Laurent Frayssinous	Catalans	2006	14(2)	3	32	0	76
Andrew Frew	Halifax	2003	17	5	0	0	20
	Wakefield	2002	21	8	0	0	32
	Huddersfield	2001	26	15	0	0	60
Dale Fritz	Castleford	1999-2003	120(4)	9	0	0	36
Gareth Frodsham	St Helens	2008-09	1(9)	0	0	0	0
Liam Fulton	Huddersfield	2009	12(3)	4	0	0	16
David Furner	Leeds	2003-04	45	8	23	0	78
	Wigan	2001-02	51(2)	21	13	0	110
David Furness	Castleford	1996	(1)	0	0	0	0
Matt Gafa	Harlequins	2006-09	81	26	16	0	136
Luke Gale	Harlequins	2009-11	56(12)	18	86	3	247
Ben Galea	Hull KR	2008-11	99(1)	27	0	0	108
Tommy Gallagher	Hull KR	2007	1(7)	0	0	0	0
	Widnes	2004	(6)	0	0	0	0
	London	2003	1(9)	1	0	0	4
Mark Gamson	Sheffield	1996	3	0	0	0	0
Jim Gannon	Hull KR	2007	7(16)	1	0	0	4
	Huddersfield	2003-06	79(14)	11	0	0	44
	Halifax	1999-2002	83(4)	14	0	0	56
Steve Garces	Salford	2001	(1)	0	0	0	0
Jean-Marc Garcia	Sheffield	1996-97	35(3)	22	0	0	88
Ade Gardner	St Helens	2002-11	218(12)	136	0	0	544
Matt Gardner	Harlequins	2009	6(3)	2	0	0	8
	Huddersfield	2006-07	22(3)	7	0	0	28
	Castleford	2004	1	1	0	0	4
Steve Gartland	Oldham	1996	1(1)	0	1	0	2
Daniel Gartner	Bradford	2001-03	74(1)	26	0	0	104
Dean Gaskell	Warrington	2002-05	58(1)	10	0	0	40
Lee Gaskell	St Helens	2010-11	22(6)	12	0	1	49
George Gatis	Huddersfield	2008	5(5)	1	0	0	4
Richard Gay	Castleford	1996-2002	94(16)	39	0	0	156
Andrew Gee	Warrington	2000-01	33(1)	4	0	0	16
Stanley Gene	Hull KR	2007-09	37(17)	9	0	0	36
	Bradford	2006	5(16)	8	0	0	32
	Huddersfield	2001, 2003-05	70(6)	27	0	0	108
	Hull	2000-01	5(23)	6	0	0	24
Steve Georgallis	Warrington	2001	5(1)	2	0	0	8
Luke George	Wakefield	2007-11	38(3)	24	0	0	96
Shaun Geritas	Warrington	1997	(5)	1	0	0	4
Anthony Gibbons	Leeds	1996	9(4)	2	0	1	9
David Gibbons	Leeds	1996	3(4)	2	0	0	8
Scott Gibbs	St Helens	1996	9	3	0	0	12
Ashley Gibson	Salford	2010-11	41(2)	18	0	0	72
	Leeds	2005-09	25(7)	13	9	0	70
Damian Gibson	Castleford	2003-04	40(3)	5	0	0	20
	Salford	2002	28	3	0	0	12
	Halifax	1998-2001	104(1)	39	0	0	156
	Leeds	1997	18	3	0	0	12
Matt Gidley	St Helens	2007-10	105	40	6	0	172
Tony Gigot	Catalans	2010-11	9(13)	0	3	0	6
Ian Gildart	Oldham	1996-97	31(7)	0	0	0	0
Chris Giles	Widnes	2003-04	35	12	0	0	48
	St Helens	2002	(1)	0	0	0	0
Peter Gill	London	1996-99	75(6)	20	0	0	80
Carl Gillespie	Halifax	1996-99	47(36)	13	0	0	52
Michael Gillett	London	2001-02	23(21)	12	2	0	52
Simon Gillies	Warrington	1999	28	6	0	0	24
Lee Gilmour	Huddersfield	2010-11	54	15	0	0	60
	St Helens	2004-09	149(3)	41	0	0	164
	Bradford	2001-03	44(31)	20	0	0	80
	Wigan	1997-2000	44(39)	22	0	0	88
Marc Glanville	Leeds	1998-99	43(3)	5	0	0	20
Eddie Glaze	Castleford	1996	1	0	0	0	0
Paul Gleadhill	Leeds	1996	4	0	0	0	0
Ben Gledhill	Wakefield	2010-11	(16)	0	0	0	0
Mark Gleeson	Warrington	2000-08	38(102)	12	0	0	48
Martin Gleeson	Hull	2011	6	4	0	0	16
	Wigan	2009-11	46(1)	19	0	0	76
	Warrington	2005-09	110(1)	44	0	0	176
	St Helens	2002-04	56(1)	25	0	0	100
	Huddersfield	1999-2001	47(9)	18	0	0	72
Sean Gleeson	Salford	2011	12	3	0	0	12
	Wakefield	2007-10	67(6)	20	0	0	80
	Wigan	2005-06	3(3)	0	0	0	0
Jon Goddard	Hull KR	2007	20	2	0	0	8
	Castleford	2000-01	(2)	0	0	0	0
Richard Goddard	Castleford	1996-97	11(3)	2	10	0	28
Brad Godden	Leeds	1998-99	47	15	0	0	60
Wayne Godwin	Salford	2011	18(5)	2	0	0	8
	Bradford	2008-10	16(44)	9	0	0	36
	Hull	2007	3(13)	1	0	0	4
	Wigan	2005-06	9(38)	6	0	0	24
	Castleford	2001-04	30(33)	18	56	0	184
Jason Golden	Harlequins	2009-11	34(12)	3	0	0	12
	Wakefield	2007-08	26(5)	1	0	0	4
Marvin Golden	Widnes	2003	4	1	0	0	4
	London	2001	17(2)	1	0	0	4
	Halifax	2000	20(2)	5	0	0	20
	Leeds	1996-99	43(11)	19	0	0	76
Brett Goldspink	Halifax	2000-02	64(5)	2	0	0	8
	Wigan	1999	6(16)	1	0	0	4
	St Helens	1998	19(4)	2	0	0	8
	Oldham	1997	13(2)	0	0	0	0
Lee Gomersall	Hull KR	2008	1	0	0	0	0
Luke Goodwin	London	1998	9(2)	3	1	1	15
	Oldham	1997	10	1	17	2	76
Aaron Gorrell	Catalans	2007-08	23	6	14	0	52
Andy Gorski	Salford	2001-02	(2)	0	0	0	0
Cyrille Gossard	Catalans	2006-11	53(27)	5	0	0	20
Bobbie Goulding	Salford	2001-02	31(1)	2	56	4	124
	Wakefield	2000	12	3	25	3	65
	Huddersfield	1998-99	27(1)	3	65	4	146
	St Helens	1996-98	42(2)	9	210	4	460
Darrell Goulding	Wigan	2005-11	67(22)	51	0	0	204
	Salford	2009	9	5	0	0	20
Mick Govin	Leigh	2005	5(6)	4	0	0	16
David Gower	Salford	2006-07	(16)	0	0	0	0
James Graham	St Helens	2003-11	132(63)	47	0	0	188

PLAYER	CLUB	YEAR	APP	TRIES	GOALS	FG	PTS
Nathan Graham	Bradford	1996-98	17(28)	4	0	1	17
Nick Graham	Wigan	2003	13(1)	2	0	0	8
Dalton Grant	Crusaders	2011	(1)	0	0	0	0
Jon Grayshon	Harlequins	2007-09	10(32)	4	0	0	16
	Huddersfield	2003-06	7(43)	5	0	0	20
Blake Green	Hull KR	2011	26	12	0	0	48
Brett Green	Gateshead	1999	10(2)	0	0	0	0
Toby Green	Huddersfield	2001	3(1)	1	0	0	4
Craig Greenhill	Castleford	2004	21(4)	1	0	0	4
	Hull	2002-03	56	3	2	0	16
Clint Greenshields							
	Catalans	2007-11	115	62	0	0	248
Brandon Greenwood							
	Halifax	1996	1	0	0	0	0
Gareth Greenwood							
	Huddersfield	2003	(1)	0	0	0	0
	Halifax	2002	1	0	0	0	0
Lee Greenwood	Huddersfield	2005	7	3	0	0	12
	London	2004-05	30(2)	19	0	0	76
	Halifax	2000-03	38(2)	17	0	0	68
	Sheffield	1999	1(1)	0	0	0	0
Maxime Greseque							
	Wakefield	2007	2(1)	0	0	0	0
Mathieu Griffi	Catalans	2006-08	1(25)	0	0	0	0
Darrell Griffin	Huddersfield	2007-11	65(60)	13	0	0	52
	Wakefield	2003-06	55(37)	9	3	0	42
Josh Griffin	Wakefield	2011	17	5	21	0	62
	Huddersfield	2009	2	0	0	0	0
Jonathan Griffiths							
	Paris	1996	(4)	1	0	0	4
Andrew Grima	Workington	1996	2(9)	2	0	0	8
Tony Grimaldi	Hull	2000-01	56(1)	14	0	0	56
	Gateshead	1999	27(2)	10	0	0	40
Danny Grimley	Sheffield	1996	4(1)	1	0	0	4
Scott Grix	Huddersfield	2010-11	33(11)	18	18	0	108
	Wakefield	2008-09	39(3)	18	0	0	72
Simon Grix	Warrington	2006-11	75(18)	25	0	0	100
	Halifax	2003	2(4)	0	0	0	0
Brett Grogan	Gateshead	1999	14(7)	3	0	0	12
Brent Grose	Warrington	2003-07	134(1)	55	0	0	220
David Guasch	Catalans	2010	1	0	0	0	0
Renaud Guigue	Catalans	2006	14(4)	3	0	0	12
Jerome Guisset	Catalans	2006-10	102(23)	9	0	0	36
	Wigan	2005	20(2)	3	0	0	12
	Warrington	2000-04	59(65)	21	0	0	84
Awen Guttenbeil	Castleford	2008	19	0	0	0	0
Reece Guy	Oldham	1996	3(4)	0	0	0	0
Tom Haberecht	Castleford	2008	2(2)	1	0	0	4
Gareth Haggerty	Harlequins	2008-09	8(28)	6	0	0	24
	Salford	2004-07	1(93)	15	0	0	60
	Widnes	2002	1(2)	1	0	0	4
Andy Haigh	St Helens	1996-98	20(16)	11	0	0	44
Scott Hale	St Helens	2011	(3)	1	0	0	4
Michael Haley	Leeds	2008	(1)	0	0	0	0
Carl Hall	Leeds	1996	7(2)	3	0	0	12
Craig Hall	Hull KR	2011	14	7	16	0	60
	Hull	2007-10	59(9)	39	11	0	178
Glenn Hall	Bradford	2010	7(18)	2	0	0	8
Martin Hall	Halifax	1998	2(10)	0	0	0	0
	Hull	1999	7	0	0	0	0
	Castleford	1998	4	0	0	0	0
	Wigan	1996-97	31(5)	7	6	0	40
Ryan Hall	Leeds	2007-11	106(2)	95	0	0	380
Steve Hall	Widnes	2004	1	0	0	0	0
	London	2002-03	35(3)	10	0	0	40
	St Helens	1999-2001	36(22)	19	0	0	76
Graeme Hallas	Huddersfield	2001	1	0	0	0	0
	Hull	1998-99	30(10)	6	39	1	103
	Halifax	1996	11(4)	5	0	0	20
Dave Halley	Bradford	2007-10	63(12)	20	0	0	80
	Wakefield	2009	5	4	0	0	16
Danny Halliwell	Salford	2007	2(3)	0	0	0	0
	Leigh	2005	5	3	0	0	12
	Halifax	2000-03	17(8)	4	0	0	16
	Warrington	2002	9(1)	8	0	0	32
	Wakefield	2002	3	0	0	0	0
Colum Halpenny	Wakefield	2003-06	103(1)	36	0	0	144
	Halifax	2002	22	12	0	0	48
Jon Hamer	Bradford	1996	(1)	0	0	0	0
Andrew Hamilton	London	1997, 2003	1(20)	3	0	0	12
John Hamilton	St Helens	1998	3	0	0	0	0
Karle Hammond	Halifax	2002	10(2)	2	14	0	36
	Salford	2001	2(3)	1	0	0	4
	London	1999-2000	47	23	2	3	99
	St Helens	1996-98	58(8)	28	0	4	116
Rhys Hanbury	Crusaders	2010-11	26(1)	14	0	0	56
Anthony Hancock	Paris	1997	8(6)	1	0	0	4
Michael Hancock	Salford	2001-02	12(24)	7	0	0	28
Gareth Handford	Castleford	2001	7(2)	0	0	0	0
	Bradford	2000	1(1)	0	0	0	0
Paul Handforth	Castleford	2006	2(15)	2	1	0	10
	Wakefield	2000-04	17(44)	10	13	0	66
Paddy Handley	Leeds	1996	1(1)	2	0	0	8
Dean Hanger	Warrington	1999	7(11)	3	0	0	12
	Huddersfield	1998	20(1)	5	0	0	20
Josh Hannay	Celtic	2009	17	2	24	0	56
Harrison Hansen	Wigan	2004-11	114(61)	34	0	0	136
Lee Hansen	Wigan	1997	10(5)	0	0	0	0
Shontayne Hape	Bradford	2003-08	123(2)	79	0	0	316
Lionel Harbin	Wakefield	2001	(1)	0	0	0	0
Zak Hardaker	Leeds	2011	14	11	0	0	44
Ian Hardman	Hull KR	2007	18	4	0	0	16
	St Helens	2003-07	32(11)	9	5	0	46
Jeff Hardy	Hudds-Sheff	2000	20(5)	6	0	1	25
	Sheffield	1999	22(4)	7	0	0	28
Spencer Hargrave	Castleford	1996-99	(6)	0	0	0	0
Bryn Hargreaves	Bradford	2011	19(5)	0	0	0	0
	St Helens	2007-10	53(44)	7	0	0	28
	Wigan	2004-06	16(12)	1	0	0	4
Lee Harland	Castleford	1996-2004	148(35)	20	0	0	80
Neil Harmon	Halifax	2003	13(3)	0	0	0	0
	Salford	2001	6(5)	0	0	0	0
	Bradford	1998-2000	15(13)	2	0	0	8
	Huddersfield	1998	12	1	0	0	4
	Leeds	1996	10	1	0	0	4
Ben Harris	Bradford	2005-07	70(4)	24	0	0	96
Iestyn Harris	Bradford	2004-08	109(11)	35	87	2	316
	Leeds	1997-2001	111(7)	57	490	6	1214
	Warrington	1996	16	4	63	2	144
Ben Harrison	Warrington	2007-11	65(40)	6	0	0	24
Karl Harrison	Hull	1999	26	2	0	0	8
	Halifax	1996-98	60(2)	2	0	0	8
Andrew Hart	London	2004	12(1)	2	0	0	8
Tim Hartley	Harlequins	2006	2	1	0	0	4
	Salford	2004-05	6(7)	5	0	0	20
Carlos Hassan	Bradford	1996	6(4)	2	0	0	8
Phil Hassan	Wakefield	2002	9(1)	0	0	0	0
	Halifax	2000-01	25(4)	3	0	0	12
	Salford	1998	15	2	0	0	8
	Leeds	1996-97	38(4)	12	0	0	48
Tom Haughey	Castleford	2006	1(3)	1	0	0	4
	London	2003-04	10(8)	1	0	0	4
	Wakefield	2001-02	5(12)	0	0	0	0
Simon Haughton	Wigan	1996-2002	63(46)	32	0	0	128
Solomon Haumono							
	Harlequins	2006	10(9)	6	0	0	24
	London	2005	24(5)	8	0	0	32
Weller Hauraki	Leeds	2011	14(10)	4	0	0	16
	Crusaders	2010	26(1)	11	0	0	44
Richie Hawkyard	Bradford	2007	1(2)	1	0	0	4
Andy Hay	Widnes	2003-04	50(2)	7	0	0	28
	Leeds	1997-2002	112(27)	43	0	0	172
	Sheffield	1996-97	17(3)	5	0	0	20
Adam Hayes	Hudds-Sheff	2000	2(1)	0	0	0	0
Joey Hayes	Salford	1999	9	2	0	0	8
	St Helens	1996-98	11(6)	7	0	0	28
James Haynes	Hull KR	2009	1	0	0	0	0
Mathew Head	Hull	2007	9(1)	1	0	1	5
Mitch Healey	Castleford	2001-03	68(1)	10	16	0	72
Daniel Heckenberg							
	Harlequins	2006-09	31(39)	4	0	0	16
Ricky Helliwell	Salford	1997-99	(2)	0	0	0	0
Tom Hemingway	Huddersfield	2005-09	7(7)	1	17	0	38
Bryan Henare	St Helens	2000-01	4(12)	1	0	0	4
Richard Henare	Warrington	1996-97	28(2)	24	0	0	96
Andrew Henderson							
	Castleford	2006, 2008	44(11)	4	0	0	16
Ian Henderson	Catalans	2011	27(2)	4	0	0	16
	Bradford	2005-07	33(37)	13	0	0	52
Kevin Henderson	Wakefield	2005-11	52(68)	9	0	0	36
	Leigh	2005	(1)	0	0	0	0
Mark Henry	Salford	2009-11	67	22	0	0	88
Brad Hepi	Castleford	1999, 2001	9(21)	3	0	0	12
	Salford	2000	3(5)	0	0	0	0
	Hull	1998	15(1)	3	0	0	12
Jon Hepworth	Castleford	2003-04	19(23)	7	8	0	44
	Leeds	2003	(1)	0	0	0	0
	London	2002	(2)	0	0	0	0
Marc Herbert	Bradford	2011	20	4	2	0	20
Ian Herron	Hull	2000	9	1	17	0	38
	Gateshead	1999	25	4	105	0	226
Jason Hetherington							
	London	2001-02	37	9	0	0	36
Gareth Hewitt	Salford	1999	2(1)	0	0	0	0
Andrew Hick	Hull	2000	9(9)	1	0	0	4
	Gateshead	1999	12(5)	2	0	0	8
Jarrad Hickey	Wakefield	2011	(8)	2	0	0	8
Chris Hicks	Warrington	2008-10	72	56	119	0	462
Paul Hicks	Wakefield	1999	(1)	0	0	0	0
Darren Higgins	London	1998	5(6)	2	0	0	8
Iain Higgins	London	1997-98	1(7)	2	0	0	8
Liam Higgins	Wakefield	2011	4(12)	0	0	0	0
	Castleford	2008-10	42(32)	2	0	0	8
	Hull	2003-06	1(34)	0	0	0	0
Mick Higham	Warrington	2009-11	13(46)	16	0	0	64
	Wigan	2006-08	61(28)	13	0	0	52
	St Helens	2001-05	43(56)	32	0	0	128
Chris Highton	Warrington	1997	1(1)	0	0	0	0

Super League Players 1996-2011

PLAYER	CLUB	YEAR	APP	TRIES	GOALS	FG	PTS
David Highton	London	2004-05	21(24)	2	0	0	8
	Salford	2002	4(5)	2	0	0	8
	Warrington	1998-2001	18(14)	2	0	0	8
Paul Highton	Salford	1998-2002, 2004-07	114(80)	14	0	0	56
	Halifax	1996-97	12(18)	2	0	0	8
Andy Hill	Huddersfield	1999	(4)	0	0	0	0
	Castleford	1999	4(4)	0	0	0	0
Chris Hill	Leigh	2005	(1)	0	0	0	0
Danny Hill	Wigan	2006-07	1(10)	0	0	0	0
	Hull KR	2007	2	0	0	0	0
	Hull	2004-06	4(6)	0	0	0	0
Howard Hill	Oldham	1996-97	22(12)	4	0	0	16
John Hill	St Helens	2003	(1)	0	0	0	0
	Halifax	2003	1(2)	0	0	0	0
	Warrington	2001-02	(4)	0	0	0	0
Scott Hill	Harlequins	2007-08	41(2)	13	0	0	52
Mark Hilton	Warrington	1996-2000, 2002-06	141(40)	7	0	0	28
Ian Hindmarsh	Catalans	2006	25	3	0	0	12
Brendan Hlad	Castleford	2008	(3)	0	0	0	0
Andy Hobson	Widnes	2004	5(13)	0	0	0	0
	Halifax	1998-2003	51(85)	8	0	0	32
Gareth Hock	Wigan	2003-09, 2011	100(43)	27	0	0	108
Tommy Hodgkinson	St Helens	2006	(1)	0	0	0	0
Andy Hodgson	Wakefield	1999	14(2)	2	1	0	10
	Bradford	1997-98	8(2)	4	0	0	16
Brett Hodgson	Warrington	2011	26	18	121	0	314
	Huddersfield	2009-10	45	13	166	0	384
David Hodgson	Huddersfield	2008-11	84	59	0	0	236
	Salford	2005-07	81	30	47	0	214
	Wigan	2000-04	90(19)	43	0	0	172
	Halifax	1999	10(3)	5	0	0	20
Elliot Hodgson	Huddersfield	2009	1	0	0	0	0
Josh Hodgson	Hull KR	2010-11	26(22)	2	0	0	8
	Hull	2009	(2)	0	0	0	0
Ryan Hoffman	Wigan	2011	28(1)	11	0	0	44
Darren Hogg	London	1996	(1)	0	0	0	0
Michael Hogue	Paris	1997	5(7)	0	0	0	0
Chris Holden	Warrington	1996-97	2(1)	0	0	0	0
Daniel Holdsworth	Salford	2010-11	45	12	114	1	277
Stephen Holgate	Halifax	2000	1(10)	0	0	0	0
	Hull	1999	1	0	0	0	0
	Wigan	1997-98	11(26)	2	0	0	8
	Workington	1996	19	3	0	0	12
Martyn Holland	Wakefield	2000-03	52(3)	6	0	0	24
Oliver Holmes	Castleford	2010-11	14(7)	1	0	0	4
Tim Holmes	Widnes	2004-05	15(4)	0	0	0	0
Graham Holroyd	Huddersfield	2003	3(5)	0	0	0	0
	Salford	2000-02	40(11)	8	75	5	187
	Halifax	1999	24(2)	3	74	5	165
	Leeds	1996-98	40(26)	22	101	8	298
Dallas Hood	Wakefield	2003-04	18(9)	1	0	0	4
Jason Hooper	St Helens	2003-07	89(6)	35	30	0	200
Lee Hopkins	Harlequins	2006-07	44(3)	11	0	0	44
	London	2005	29	6	0	0	24
Sean Hoppe	St Helens	1999-2002	69(16)	32	0	0	128
Graeme Horne	Huddersfield	2010-11	23(17)	11	0	0	44
	Hull	2003-09	49(74)	24	0	0	96
Richard Horne	Hull	1999-2011	286(11)	101	12	6	434
John Hough	Warrington	1996-97	9	2	0	0	8
Danny Houghton	Hull	2007-11	62(45)	12	0	0	48
Sylvain Houles	Wakefield	2003, 2005	8(1)	1	0	0	4
	London	2001-02	17(10)	11	0	0	44
	Hudds-Sheff	2000	5(2)	1	0	0	4
Harvey Howard	Wigan	2001-02	25(27)	1	0	0	4
	Bradford	1998	4(2)	1	0	0	4
	Leeds	1996	8	0	0	0	0
Kim Howard	London	1997	4(5)	0	0	0	0
Stuart Howarth	Wakefield	2011	17(2)	1	0	0	4
Stuart Howarth	Workington	1996	(2)	0	0	0	0
David Howell	Harlequins	2008-11	76	26	0	0	104
Phil Howlett	Bradford	1999	5(1)	2	0	0	8
Craig Huby	Castleford	2003-04, 2006, 2008-11	73(46)	19	37	0	150
Ryan Hudson	Castleford	2002-04, 2009-11	129(9)	30	0	0	120
	Huddersfield	1998-99, 2007-08	51(22)	10	0	0	40
	Wakefield	2000-01	42(9)	11	0	1	45
Adam Hughes	Widnes	2002-05	89(2)	45	51	0	282
	Halifax	2001	8(8)	8	0	0	32
	Wakefield	1999-2000	43(3)	21	34	0	152
	Leeds	1996-97	4(5)	4	0	0	16
Ian Hughes	Sheffield	1996	9(8)	4	0	0	16
Jack Hughes	Wigan	2011	(1)	0	0	0	0
Mark Hughes	Catalans	2006	23	9	0	0	36
Steffan Hughes	London	1999-2001	1(13)	1	0	0	4
David Hulme	Salford	1997-99	53(1)	5	0	0	20
	Leeds	1996	8(1)	2	0	0	8
Paul Hulme	Warrington	1996-97	23(1)	2	0	0	8
Gary Hulse	Widnes	2005	12(5)	2	0	0	8
	Warrington	2001-04	20(28)	8	0	1	33
Alan Hunte	Salford	2002	19(2)	9	0	0	36
	Warrington	1999-2001	83	49	0	0	196
	Hull	1998	21	7	0	0	28
	St Helens	1996-97	30(2)	28	0	0	112
Kieran Hyde	Wakefield	2010-11	11	4	4	0	24
Nick Hyde	Paris	1997	5(5)	1	0	0	4
Chaz I'Anson	Hull KR	2007-10	17(13)	3	0	0	12
Andy Ireland	Hull	1998-99	22(15)	0	0	0	0
	Bradford	1996	1	0	0	0	0
Kevin Iro	St Helens	1999-2001	76	39	0	0	156
	Leeds	1996	9	9	0	0	36
Willie Isa	Castleford	2011	7(2)	6	0	0	24
Andrew Isherwood	Wigan	1998-99	(5)	0	0	0	0
Olu Iwenofu	London	2000-01	2(1)	0	0	0	0
Chico Jackson	Hull	1999	(4)	0	0	0	0
Lee Jackson	Hull	2001-02	37(9)	12	1	0	50
	Leeds	1999-2000	28(24)	7	0	0	28
Michael Jackson	Sheffield	1998-99	17(17)	2	0	0	8
	Halifax	1996-97	27(6)	11	0	0	44
Paul Jackson	Castleford	2003-04, 2010-11	38(28)	2	0	0	8
	Huddersfield	1998, 2005-09	50(73)	4	0	0	16
	Wakefield	1999-2002	57(41)	2	0	0	8
Rob Jackson	Leigh	2005	20(3)	5	0	0	20
	London	2002-04	26(14)	9	0	0	36
Wayne Jackson	Halifax	1996-97	17(5)	2	0	0	8
Aled James	Crusaders	2011	1	0	0	0	0
	Celtic	2009	3(3)	0	0	0	0
	Widnes	2003	3	0	0	0	0
Andy James	Halifax	1996	(4)	0	0	0	0
Jordan James	Crusaders	2010-11	5(24)	3	0	0	12
	Celtic	2009	17(4)	1	0	0	4
	Wigan	2006	2(4)	3	0	0	12
Matt James	Harlequins	2010	2(2)	0	0	0	0
	Bradford	2006-09	1(23)	0	0	0	0
Pascal Jampy	Catalans	2006	4(7)	0	0	0	0
	Paris	1996-97	3(2)	0	0	0	0
Adam Janowski	Harlequins	2008	(1)	0	0	0	0
Ben Jeffries	Bradford	2008-09, 2011	57(3)	16	0	0	64
	Wakefield	2003-07, 2010-11	151(10)	70	27	6	340
Mick Jenkins	Hull	2000	24	2	0	0	8
	Gateshead	1999	16	3	0	0	12
Ed Jennings	London	1998-99	1(2)	0	0	0	0
Rod Jensen	Huddersfield	2007-08	26(3)	13	0	0	52
Anthony Jerram	Warrington	2007	(2)	0	0	0	0
Lee Jewitt	Salford	2007, 2009-11	11(52)	2	0	0	8
	Wigan	2005	(2)	0	0	0	0
Andrew Johns	Warrington	2005	3	1	12	1	29
Matthew Johns	Wigan	2001	24	3	0	1	13
Andy Johnson	Salford	2004-05	8(26)	7	0	0	28
	Castleford	2002-03	32(16)	11	0	0	44
	London	2000-01	24(21)	12	0	0	48
	Huddersfield	1999	5	1	0	0	4
	Wigan	1996-99	24(20)	19	0	0	76
Bruce Johnson	Widnes	2004-05	(4)	0	0	0	0
Dallas Johnson	Catalans	2010	26	1	0	0	4
Greg Johnson	Wakefield	2011	12	2	0	0	8
Jason Johnson	St Helens	1997-99	2	0	0	0	0
Mark Johnson	Salford	1999-2000	22(9)	16	0	0	64
	Hull	1998	10(1)	4	0	0	16
	Workington	1996	12	4	0	0	16
Nick Johnson	London	2003	(1)	0	0	0	0
Paul Johnson	Crusaders	2011	6(4)	0	0	0	0
	Wakefield	2010	12(3)	4	0	0	16
	Warrington	2007-09	37(9)	17	0	0	68
	Bradford	2004-06	46(8)	19	0	0	76
	Wigan	1996-2003	74(46)	54	0	0	216
Paul Johnson	Wakefield	2011	24(1)	5	0	0	20
	St Helens	2010	(2)	0	0	0	0
Richard Johnson	Bradford	2008	(2)	0	0	0	0
Ben Jones	Harlequins	2010	(2)	0	0	0	0
Chris Jones	Leigh	2005	1(1)	0	0	0	0
Danny Jones	Halifax	2003	1	0	0	0	0
David Jones	Oldham	1997	14(1)	5	0	0	20
Mark Jones	Warrington	1996	8(11)	2	0	0	8
Phil Jones	Leigh	2005	16	8	31	0	94
	Wigan	1999-2001	14(7)	6	25	0	74
Stacey Jones	Catalans	2006-07	39	11	43	3	133
Stephen Jones	Huddersfield	2005	(1)	0	0	0	0
Stuart Jones	Castleford	2009-11	54(17)	10	0	0	40
	Huddersfield	2004-08	96(22)	17	0	0	68
	St Helens	2003	(18)	2	0	0	8
	Wigan	2002	5(3)	1	0	0	4
Ben Jones-Bishop	Leeds	2008-09, 2011	18(2)	10	0	0	40
	Harlequins	2010	17	10	0	0	40

PLAYER	CLUB	YEAR	APP	TRIES	GOALS	FG	PTS
Jamie Jones-Buchanan							
	Leeds	1999-2011	176(58)	53	0	0	212
Tim Jonkers	Wigan	2006	3(1)	0	0	0	0
	Salford	2004-06	5(11)	0	0	0	0
	St Helens	1999-2004	41(64)	12	0	0	48
Darren Jordan	Wakefield	2003	(1)	0	0	0	0
Phil Joseph	Huddersfield	2004	7(6)	0	0	0	0
Warren Jowitt	Hull	2003	(2)	0	0	0	0
	Salford	2001-02	17(4)	2	0	0	8
	Wakefield	2000	19(3)	8	0	0	32
	Bradford	1996-99	13(25)	5	0	0	20
Chris Joynt	St Helens	1996-2004	201(14)	68	0	0	272
Gregory Kacala	Paris	1996	7	1	0	0	4
Andy Kain	Castleford	2004, 2006	9(7)	3	10	0	32
Mal Kaufusi	London	2004	1(3)	0	0	0	0
Ben Kaye	Harlequins	2009-10	2(13)	0	0	0	0
	Leeds	2008	2(2)	1	0	0	4
Elliot Kear	Crusaders	2010-11	16(1)	4	0	0	16
	Celtic	2009	3	0	0	0	0
Brett Kearney	Bradford	2010-11	44	18	0	0	72
Stephen Kearney	Hull	2005	22(2)	5	0	0	20
Damon Keating	Wakefield	2002	7(17)	1	0	0	4
Shaun Keating	London	1996	1(3)	0	0	0	0
Mark Keenan	Workington	1996	3(4)	1	0	0	4
Tony Kemp	Wakefield	1999-2000	15(5)	2	0	1	9
	Leeds	1996-98	23(2)	5	0	2	22
Damien Kennedy	London	2003	5(11)	1	0	0	4
Ian Kenny	St Helens	2004	(1)	0	0	0	0
Jason Kent	Leigh	2005	23	1	0	0	4
Shane Kenward	Wakefield	1999	28	6	0	0	24
	Salford	1998	1	0	0	0	0
Jason Keough	Paris	1997	2	1	0	0	4
Keiran Kerr	Widnes	2005	6	2	0	0	8
Martin Ketteridge	Halifax	1996	7(5)	0	0	0	0
Ronnie Kettlewell	Warrington	1996	(1)	0	0	0	0
Younes Khattabi	Catalans	2006-08	24(4)	10	0	0	40
David Kidwell	Warrington	2001-02	14(12)	9	0	0	36
Andrew King	London	2003	23(1)	15	0	0	60
Dave King	Huddersfield	1998-99	11(17)	2	0	0	8
James King	Leigh	2005	5(7)	0	0	0	0
Kevin King	Wakefield	2005	8(1)	2	0	0	8
	Castleford	2004	(1)	0	0	0	0
Matt King	Warrington	2008-11	91	58	0	0	232
Paul King	Wakefield	2010-11	10(19)	0	0	1	1
	Hull	1999-2009	136(93)	20	0	1	81
Andy Kirk	Wakefield	2005	6(3)	1	0	0	4
	Salford	2004	20	5	0	0	20
	Leeds	2001-02	4(4)	0	0	0	0
Ian Kirke	Leeds	2006-11	45(76)	8	0	0	32
John Kirkpatrick	London	2004-05	18(1)	5	0	0	20
	St Helens	2001-03	10(11)	10	0	0	40
	Halifax	2003	4	1	0	0	4
Danny Kirmond	Huddersfield	2008-11	18(31)	9	0	0	36
	Wakefield	2010	12(4)	1	0	0	4
Wayne Kitchin	Workington	1996	11(6)	3	17	1	47
Ian Knott	Leigh	2005	8(1)	2	0	0	8
	Wakefield	2002-03	34(5)	7	79	0	186
	Warrington	1996-2001	68(41)	24	18	0	132
Matt Knowles	Wigan	1996	(3)	0	0	0	0
Michael Knowles	Castleford	2006	(1)	0	0	0	0
Phil Knowles	Salford	1997	1	0	0	0	0
Simon Knox	Halifax	1999	(6)	0	0	0	0
	Salford	1998	1(1)	0	0	0	0
	Bradford	1996-98	9(19)	7	0	0	28
Toa Kohe-Love	Warrington	1996-2001, 2005-06	166(3)	90	0	0	360
	Bradford	2004	1(1)	0	0	0	0
	Hull	2002-03	42	19	0	0	76
Paul Koloi	Wigan	1997	1(2)	1	0	0	4
Craig Kopczak	Bradford	2006-11	20(80)	9	0	0	36
Michael Korkidas	Wakefield	2003-06, 2009-11	133(36)	15	0	0	60
	Huddersfield	2009	4(1)	1	0	0	4
	Castleford	2008	15(6)	1	0	0	4
	Salford	2007	26(1)	1	0	0	4
Nick Kouparitsas	Harlequins	2011	2(13)	1	0	0	4
Olsi Krasniqi	Harlequins	2010-11	3(20)	1	0	0	4
David Krause	London	1996-97	22(1)	7	0	0	28
Ben Kusto	Huddersfield	2001	21(4)	9	0	1	37
Adrian Lam	Wigan	2001-04	105(2)	40	1	9	171
Mark Lane	Paris	1996	(2)	0	0	0	0
Allan Langer	Warrington	2000-01	47	13	4	0	60
Kevin Langer	London	1996	12(4)	2	0	0	8
Junior Langi	Salford	2005-06	27(7)	7	0	0	28
Chris Langley	Huddersfield	2000-01	18(1)	3	0	0	12
Gareth Langley	St Helens	2006	1	1	3	0	10
Jamie Langley	Bradford	2002-11	149(48)	31	0	0	124
Andy Last	Hull	1999-2005	16(10)	4	0	0	16
Sam Latus	Hull KR	2010-11	18(3)	7	0	0	28
Epalahame Lauaki							
	Hull	2009-11	3(50)	4	0	0	16
Dale Laughton	Warrington	2002	15(1)	0	0	0	0
	Huddersfield	2000-01	36(2)	4	0	0	16
	Sheffield	1996-99	48(22)	5	0	0	20
Ali Lauitiiti	Leeds	2004-11	64(117)	58	0	0	232
Jason Laurence	Salford	1997	1	0	0	0	0
Graham Law	Wakefield	1999-2002	34(30)	6	40	0	104
Neil Law	Wakefield	1999-2002	83	39	0	0	156
	Sheffield	1998	1(1)	1	0	0	4
Dean Lawford	Widnes	2003-04	17(1)	5	2	4	28
	Halifax	2001	1(1)	0	0	0	0
	Leeds	1997-2000	15(8)	2	3	0	14
	Huddersfield	1999	6(1)	0	6	1	13
	Sheffield	1996	9(5)	2	1	1	11
Johnny Lawless	Halifax	2001-03	73(1)	10	0	0	40
	Hudds-Sheff	2000	19(6)	3	0	0	12
	Sheffield	1996-99	76(4)	11	0	0	44
Michael Lawrence							
	Huddersfield	2007-11	84(1)	26	0	0	104
Charlie Leaeno	Wakefield	2010	7(3)	2	0	0	8
Mark Leafa	Castleford	2008	5(9)	1	0	0	4
	Leigh	2005	28	2	0	0	8
Leroy Leapai	London	1996	2	0	0	0	0
Jim Leatham	Hull	1998-99	20(18)	4	0	0	16
	Leeds	1997	(1)	0	0	0	0
Andy Leathem	Warrington	1999	2(8)	0	0	0	0
	St Helens	1996-98	20(1)	1	0	0	4
Danny Lee	Gateshead	1999	16(2)	0	0	0	0
Jason Lee	Halifax	2001	10(1)	2	0	0	8
Mark Lee	Salford	1997-2000	25(11)	1	0	4	8
Robert Lee	Hull	1999	4(3)	0	0	0	0
Tommy Lee	Wakefield	2011	25	6	0	0	24
	Crusaders	2010	3(9)	0	0	0	0
	Hull	2005-09	44(27)	6	0	0	24
Matthew Leigh	Salford	2000	(6)	0	0	0	0
Chris Leikvoll	Warrington	2004-07	72(18)	4	0	0	16
Jim Lenihan	Huddersfield	1999	19(1)	10	0	0	40
Mark Lennon	Celtic	2009	10(3)	1	8	0	20
	Hull KR	2007	11(4)	5	7	0	34
	Castleford	2001-03	30(21)	10	21	0	82
Tevita Leo-Latu	Wakefield	2006-10	28(49)	10	0	0	40
Gary Lester	Hull	1998-99	46	17	0	0	68
Stuart Lester	Wigan	1997	1(3)	0	0	0	0
Heath L'Estrange	Bradford	2010-11	33(8)	6	0	0	24
Afi Leuila	Oldham	1996-97	17(3)	2	0	0	8
Kylie Leuluai	Leeds	2007-11	111(23)	13	0	0	52
Phil Leuluai	Salford	2007, 2009-11	7(47)	3	0	0	12
Thomas Leuluai	Wigan	2007-11	148	44	0	0	176
	Harlequins	2006	15(2)	6	0	0	24
	London	2005	20	13	0	0	52
Simon Lewis	Castleford	2001	4	3	0	0	12
Paul Leyland	St Helens	2006	1	0	0	0	0
Jon Liddell	Leeds	2001	1	0	0	0	0
Jason Lidden	Castleford	1997	15(1)	7	0	0	28
Danny Lima	Wakefield	2007	(3)	0	0	0	0
	Salford	2006	(7)	2	0	0	8
	Warrington	2004-06	15(47)	9	0	0	36
Jeff Lima	Wigan	2011	16(11)	1	0	0	4
Craig Littler	St Helens	2006	1	1	0	0	4
Stuart Littler	Salford	1998-2002, 2004-07, 2009-10	217(30)	65	0	0	260
Peter Livett	Workington	1996	3(1)	0	0	0	0
Scott Logan	Wigan	2006	10(11)	0	0	0	0
	Hull	2001-03	27(20)	5	0	0	20
Jamahl Lolesi	Huddersfield	2007-10	75(9)	27	0	0	108
Filimone Lolohea	Harlequins	2006	3(6)	0	0	0	0
	London	2005	8(15)	0	0	0	0
David Lomax	Huddersfield	2000-01	45(9)	4	0	0	16
	Paris	1997	19(2)	1	0	0	4
Jonny Lomax	St Helens	2009-11	47(2)	17	27	1	123
Dave Long	London	1999	(1)	0	0	0	0
Karl Long	London	2003	(1)	0	0	0	0
	Widnes	2002	1	0	0	0	4
Sean Long	Hull	2010-11	22	6	0	0	24
	St Helens	1997-2009	263(8)	126	826	20	2176
	Wigan	1996-97	1(5)	0	0	0	0
Davide Longo	Bradford	1996	1(3)	0	0	0	0
Gary Lord	Oldham	1996-97	28(12)	3	0	0	12
Paul Loughlin	Huddersfield	1998-99	34(2)	4	4	0	24
	Bradford	1996-97	36(4)	15	8	0	76
Rhys Lovegrove	Hull KR	2007-11	36(52)	10	0	0	40
Karl Lovell	Hudds-Sheff	2000	14	5	0	0	20
	Sheffield	1999	22(4)	8	0	0	32
James Lowes	Bradford	1996-2003	205	84	2	2	342
Laurent Lucchese	Paris	1996	13(5)	2	0	0	8
Zebastian Luisi	Harlequins	2006-07	23(2)	4	0	0	16
	London	2004-05	21(1)	7	0	0	28
Shaun Lunt	Huddersfield	2009-11	30(29)	30	0	0	120
Peter Lupton	Crusaders	2010-11	37(9)	10	0	0	40
	Celtic	2009	16(4)	4	0	0	16
	Castleford	2006, 2008	40	11	0	0	44
	Hull	2003-06	19(26)	10	3	0	46
	London	2000-02	10(15)	2	0	0	12
Andy Lynch	Bradford	2005-11	159(29)	46	0	0	184
	Castleford	1999-2004	78(48)	15	0	0	60
Reece Lyne	Hull	2010-11	11(1)	2	0	0	8
Jamie Lyon	St Helens	2005-06	54(1)	39	172	0	500

Super League Players 1996-2011

PLAYER	CLUB	YEAR	APP	TRIES	GOALS	FG	PTS
Duncan MacGillivray							
	Wakefield	2004-08	75(18)	6	0	0	24
Brad Mackay	Bradford	2000	24(2)	8	0	0	32
Graham Mackay	Hull	2002	27	18	24	0	120
	Bradford	2001	16(3)	12	1	0	50
	Leeds	2000	12(8)	10	2	0	44
Keiron Maddocks	Leigh	2005	1(3)	0	0	0	0
Steve Maden	Leigh	2005	23	9	0	0	36
	Warrington	2002	3	0	0	0	0
Mateaki Mafi	Warrington	1996-97	7(8)	7	0	0	28
Shaun Magennis	St Helens	2010-11	5(15)	3	0	0	12
Brendan Magnus	London	2000	3	1	0	0	4
Mark Maguire	London	1996-97	11(4)	7	13	0	54
Adam Maher	Hull	2000-03	88(4)	24	0	0	96
	Gateshead	1999	21(5)	3	0	0	12
Lee Maher	Leeds	1996	4(1)	0	0	0	0
Shaun Mahony	Paris	1997	5	0	0	0	0
Hutch Maiava	Hull	2007	(19)	1	0	0	4
David Maiden	Hull	2000-01	32(10)	11	0	0	44
	Gateshead	1999	5(16)	8	0	0	32
Craig Makin	Salford	1999-2001	24(20)	2	0	0	8
Tom Makinson	St Helens	2011	14(5)	7	6	0	40
Brady Malam	Wigan	2000	5(20)	1	0	0	4
Dominic Maloney	Hull	2009	(7)	0	0	0	0
Francis Maloney	Castleford	1998-99, 2003-04	71(7)	24	33	3	165
	Salford	2001-02	45(1)	26	5	0	114
	Wakefield	2000	11	1	1	0	6
	Oldham	1996-97	39(2)	12	91	2	232
George Mann	Warrington	1997	14(5)	1	0	0	4
	Leeds	1996	11(4)	2	0	0	8
Dane Manning	Leeds	2009	(1)	0	0	0	0
Misili Manu	Widnes	2005	1	0	0	0	0
Willie Manu	Hull	2007-11	105(17)	21	0	0	84
	Castleford	2006	19(4)	9	0	0	36
Darren Mapp	Celtic	2009	9(2)	1	0	0	4
David March	Wakefield	1999-2007	164(23)	34	126	0	388
Paul March	Wakefield	1999-2001, 2007	42(31)	17	23	0	114
	Huddersfield	2003-06	71(19)	17	36	1	141
Nick Mardon	London	1997-98	14	2	0	0	8
Remy Marginet	Catalans	2011	2	0	9	0	18
Frankie Mariano	Wakefield	2011	22(1)	6	0	0	24
	Hull KR	2010	(3)	0	0	0	0
Oliver Marns	Halifax	1996-2002	54(19)	23	0	0	92
Paul Marquet	Warrington	2002	23(2)	0	0	0	0
Callum Marriott	Salford	2011	(1)	0	0	0	0
Iain Marsh	Salford	1998-2001	1(4)	0	0	0	0
Lee Marsh	Salford	2001-02	3(4)	0	0	0	0
Stefan Marsh	Wigan	2010-11	12	3	0	0	12
Richard Marshall	Leigh	2005	4(16)	0	0	0	0
	London	2002-03	33(11)	1	0	0	4
	Huddersfield	2000-01	35(14)	1	0	0	4
	Halifax	1996-99	38(34)	2	0	0	8
Jason Martin	Paris	1997	15(2)	3	0	0	12
Scott Martin	Salford	1997-99	32(18)	8	0	0	32
Tony Martin	Crusaders	2010-11	40(1)	14	1	0	58
	Wakefield	2008-09	33	10	33	0	106
	London	1996-97, 2001-03	97(1)	36	170	1	485
Mick Martindale	Halifax	1996	(4)	0	0	0	0
Sebastien Martins	Catalans	2006, 2009-11	(21)	2	0	0	8
Tommy Martyn	St Helens	1996-2003	125(20)	87	63	12	486
Dean Marwood	Workington	1996	9(6)	0	22	0	44
Martin Masella	Warrington	2001	10(14)	5	0	0	20
	Wakefield	2000	14(8)	4	0	0	16
	Leeds	1997-1999	59(5)	1	0	0	4
Colin Maskill	Castleford	1996	8	1	1	0	6
Keith Mason	Huddersfield	2006-11	104(11)	3	0	0	12
	Castleford	2006	(2)	0	0	0	0
	St Helens	2003-05	33(23)	4	0	0	16
	Wakefield	2000-01	5(17)	0	0	0	0
Willie Mason	Hull KR	2011	6	1	0	0	4
Sammy Masselot	Wakefield	2011	(1)	0	0	0	0
Nathan Massey	Castleford	2008-11	6(13)	0	0	0	0
Vila Matautia	St Helens	1996-2001	31(68)	9	0	0	36
Feleti Mateo	London	2005	4(10)	1	0	0	4
Barrie-Jon Mather	Castleford	1998, 2000-02	50(12)	21	0	0	84
Richard Mathers	Castleford	2011	21(1)	7	0	0	28
	Warrington	2002, 2009-10	42(3)	11	0	0	44
	Wigan	2008-09	23(1)	2	0	0	8
	Leeds	2002-06	85(2)	26	0	0	104
Jamie Mathiou	Leeds	1997-2001	31(82)	3	0	0	12
Terry Matterson	London	1996-98	46	15	90	6	246
Luke May	Harlequins	2009-10	(3)	0	0	0	0
Casey Mayberry	Halifax	2000	1(1)	0	0	0	0
Chris Maye	Halifax	2003	3(4)	0	0	0	0
Joe Mbu	Harlequins	2006-09	33(20)	3	0	0	12
	London	2003-05	29(19)	4	0	0	16
Danny McAllister	Gateshead	1999	3(3)	1	0	0	4
	Sheffield	1996-97	33(7)	10	0	0	40
John McAtee	St Helens	1996	2(1)	0	0	0	0
Nathan McAvoy	Bradford	1998-2002, 2007	83(31)	46	0	0	184
	Wigan	2006	15(2)	5	0	0	20
	Salford	1997-98, 2004-05	57(4)	18	0	0	72
Tyrone McCarthy	Warrington	2009-11	1(9)	2	0	0	8
	Wakefield	2011	2(5)	1	0	0	4
Louie McCarthy-Scarsbrook							
	St Helens	2011	20(7)	8	0	0	32
	Harlequins	2006-10	41(50)	17	0	0	68
Dave McConnell	London	2003	(4)	0	0	0	0
	St Helens	2001-02	3(2)	4	0	0	16
Robbie McCormack	Wigan	1998	24	2	0	0	8
Steve McCurrie	Leigh	2005	7(3)	1	0	0	4
	Widnes	2002-04	55(22)	10	0	0	40
	Warrington	1998-2001	69(26)	31	0	0	124
Barrie McDermott	Leeds	1996-2005	163(69)	28	0	0	112
Brian McDermott	Bradford	1996-2002	138(32)	33	0	0	132
Ryan McDonald	Widnes	2002-03	6(4)	0	0	0	0
Wayne McDonald	Huddersfield	2005-06	11(23)	1	0	0	4
	Wigan	2005	(4)	0	0	0	0
	Leeds	2002-05	34(47)	14	0	0	56
	St Helens	2001	7(11)	4	0	0	16
	Hull	2000	5(8)	4	0	0	16
	Wakefield	1999	9(17)	8	0	0	32
Craig McDowell	Huddersfield	2003	(1)	0	0	0	0
	Warrington	2002	(1)	0	0	0	0
	Bradford	2000	(1)	0	0	0	0
Wes McGibbon	Halifax	1999	1	0	0	0	0
Jermaine McGillvary							
	Huddersfield	2010-11	33	23	0	0	92
Dean McGilvray	Salford	2009-10	14	4	0	0	16
	St Helens	2006-08	5(1)	1	0	0	4
Billy McGinty	Workington	1996	1	0	0	0	0
Ryan McGoldrick	Castleford	2006, 2008-11	116(1)	23	10	0	112
Kevin McGuinness							
	Salford	2004-07	63(3)	11	0	0	44
Casey McGuire	Catalans	2007-10	87(4)	27	0	0	108
Danny McGuire	Leeds	2001-11	201(37)	181	0	2	726
Gary McGuirk	Workington	1996	(4)	0	0	0	0
Michael McIlorum							
	Wigan	2007-11	38(50)	8	0	0	32
Richard McKell	Castleford	1997-98	22(7)	2	0	0	8
Chris McKenna	Bradford	2006-07	40(7)	7	0	0	28
	Leeds	2003-05	65(4)	18	0	0	72
Phil McKenzie	Workington	1996	4	0	0	0	0
Chris McKinney	Oldham	1996-97	4(9)	2	0	0	8
Mark McLinden	Harlequins	2006-08	46(1)	20	0	1	81
	London	2005	22(3)	8	0	0	32
Shayne McMenemy							
	Hull	2003-07	80(8)	12	0	0	48
	Halifax	2001-06	63	11	0	0	44
Andy McNally	London	2004	5(3)	0	0	0	0
	Castleford	2001, 2003	2(5)	1	0	0	4
Gregg McNally	Huddersfield	2011	1	0	6	0	12
Steve McNamara	Huddersfield	2001, 2003	41(9)	3	134	1	281
	Wakefield	2000	15(2)	2	32	0	72
	Bradford	1996-99	90(3)	14	348	7	759
Paul McNicholas	Hull	2004-05	28(12)	4	0	0	16
Neil McPherson	Salford	1997	(1)	0	0	0	0
Duncan McRae	London	1996	11(2)	3	0	1	13
Paul McShane	Leeds	2009-11	6(22)	5	0	0	20
	Hull	2010	(4)	0	0	0	0
Derek McVey	St Helens	1996-97	28(4)	6	1	0	26
Dallas Mead	Warrington	1997	2	0	0	0	0
Robbie Mears	Leigh	2005	8(6)	0	0	0	0
	Leeds	2001	23	6	0	0	24
Paul Medley	Bradford	1996-98	6(35)	9	0	0	36
Francis Meli	St Helens	2006-11	143(1)	89	0	0	356
Vince Mellars	Crusaders	2010-11	46	17	0	0	68
Chris Melling	Harlequins	2007-11	100(11)	33	6	0	144
	Wigan	2004-05	8(2)	1	3	0	10
Joe Mellor	Harlequins	2011	(1)	0	0	0	0
Paul Mellor	Castleford	2003-04	36(3)	18	0	0	72
Craig Menkins	Paris	1997	4(5)	0	0	0	0
Luke Menzies	Hull KR	2008	(1)	0	0	0	0
Steve Menzies	Catalans	2011	21(2)	14	0	0	56
	Bradford	2009-10	52(1)	24	1	0	98
Gary Mercer	Castleford	2002	(1)	0	0	0	0
	Leeds	1996-97, 2001	40(2)	9	0	0	36
	Warrington	2001	18	2	0	0	8
	Halifax	1998-2001	73(2)	16	0	0	64
Tony Mestrov	London	1996-97, 2001	59(8)	4	0	0	16
	Wigan	1998-2000	39(39)	4	0	0	12
Keiran Meyer	London	1996	4	1	0	0	4
Brad Meyers	Bradford	2005-06	40(11)	13	0	0	52

PLAYER	CLUB	YEAR	APP	TRIES	GOALS	FG	PTS
Gary Middlehurst	Widnes	2004	(2)	0	0	0	0
Simon Middleton	Castleford	1996-97	19(3)	8	0	0	32
Darryl Millard	Catalans	2011	22	8	0	0	32
	Wakefield	2010-11	21(1)	11	0	0	44
Shane Millard	Wigan	2007	19(6)	3	0	0	12
	Leeds	2006	6(21)	3	0	0	12
	Widnes	2003-05	69	23	0	0	92
	London	1998-2001	72(14)	11	1	0	46
David Mills	Harlequins	2006-07, 2010	25(32)	2	0	0	8
	Hull KR	2008-09	20(11)	1	0	0	4
	Widnes	2002-05	17(77)	8	0	0	32
Lewis Mills	Celtic	2009	(4)	0	0	0	0
Adam Milner	Castleford	2010-11	16(7)	5	0	0	20
Lee Milner	Halifax	1999	(1)	0	0	0	0
John Minto	London	1996	13	4	0	0	16
Lee Mitchell	Warrington	2007-11	8(27)	4	0	0	16
	Harlequins	2011	11(1)	1	0	0	4
Sam Moa	Hull	2009-11	18(41)	4	0	0	16
Martin Moana	Salford	2004	6(3)	1	0	0	4
	Halifax	1996-2001, 2003	126(22)	62	0	1	249
	Wakefield	2002	19(2)	10	0	0	40
	Huddersfield	2001	3(3)	2	0	0	8
Adam Mogg	Catalans	2007-10	74	19	0	1	77
Jon Molloy	Huddersfield	2011	1(1)	0	0	0	0
Steve Molloy	Huddersfield	2000-01	26(20)	3	0	0	12
	Sheffield	1998-99	32(17)	3	0	0	12
Chris Molyneux	Huddersfield	2000-01	1(18)	0	0	0	0
	Sheffield	1999	1(2)	0	0	0	0
Joel Monaghan	Warrington	2011	24	26	0	0	104
Michael Monaghan							
	Warrington	2008-11	104(1)	22	0	3	91
Adrian Moore	Huddersfield	1998-99	1(4)	0	0	0	0
Danny Moore	London	2000	7	0	0	0	0
	Wigan	1998-99	49(3)	18	0	0	72
Gareth Moore	Wakefield	2011	5	1	14	1	33
Jason Moore	Workington	1996	(5)	0	0	0	0
Richard Moore	Crusaders	2011	11(10)	1	0	0	4
	Wakefield	2007-10	50(44)	8	0	0	32
	Leigh	2005	2(5)	0	0	0	0
	Bradford	2002-04	1(26)	0	0	0	0
	London	2002, 2004	5(9)	2	0	0	8
Scott Moore	St Helens	2004-07, 2010-11	29(37)	9	0	0	36
	Huddersfield	2009	23(2)	9	0	0	36
	Castleford	2008	11(5)	1	0	0	4
Dennis Moran	Wigan	2005-06	39	17	1	1	71
	London	2001-04	107(2)	74	2	5	305
Willie Morganson	Sheffield	1997-98	18(12)	5	3	0	26
Paul Moriarty	Halifax	1996	3(2)	0	0	0	0
Adrian Morley	Warrington	2007-11	113(2)	7	0	0	28
	Bradford	2005	2(4)	0	0	0	0
	Leeds	1996-2000	95(14)	25	0	0	100
Chris Morley	Salford	1999	3(5)	0	0	0	0
	Warrington	1998	2(8)	0	0	0	0
	St Helens	1996-97	21(16)	4	0	0	16
Glenn Morrison	Wakefield	2010-11	43(1)	9	0	0	36
	Bradford	2007-09	48(2)	19	0	0	76
Iain Morrison	Hull KR	2007	5(6)	1	0	0	4
	Huddersfield	2003-05	11(23)	0	0	0	0
	London	2001	(1)	0	0	0	0
Dale Morton	Wakefield	2009-11	22(3)	8	5	0	42
Gareth Morton	Hull KR	2007	7(4)	3	23	0	58
	Leeds	2001-02	1(1)	0	0	0	0
Lee Mossop	Wigan	2008-11	15(37)	4	0	0	16
	Huddersfield	2009	1(4)	1	0	0	4
Aaron Moule	Salford	2006-07	45	17	0	0	68
	Widnes	2004-05	29	12	0	0	48
Wilfried Moulinec	Paris	1996	1	0	0	0	0
Gregory Mounis	Catalans	2006-11	113(39)	20	17	0	114
Mark Moxon	Huddersfield	1998-2001	20(5)	1	0	1	5
Brett Mullins	Leeds	2001	5(3)	1	0	0	4
Damian Munro	Widnes	2002	8(2)	1	0	0	4
	Halifax	1996-97	9(6)	8	0	0	32
Matt Munro	Oldham	1996-97	26(5)	8	0	0	32
Craig Murdock	Salford	2000	(2)	0	0	0	0
	Hull	1998-99	21(6)	8	0	2	34
	Wigan	1996-98	18(17)	14	0	0	56
Aaron Murphy	Wakefield	2008-11	57(2)	12	0	0	48
Jamie Murphy	Crusaders	2011	(2)	0	0	0	0
Justin Murphy	Catalans	2006-08	59	49	0	0	196
	Widnes	2004	5	1	0	0	4
Doc Murray	Warrington	1997	(2)	0	0	0	0
	Wigan	1997	6(2)	0	0	0	0
Scott Murrell	Hull KR	2007-11	102(15)	22	26	1	141
	Leeds	2005	(1)	0	0	0	0
	London	2004	3(3)	2	0	0	8
David Mycoe	Sheffield	1996-97	12(13)	1	0	0	4
Richard Myler	Warrington	2010-11	46(1)	31	1	0	126
	Salford	2009	18	11	0	0	44
Rob Myler	Oldham	1996-97	19(2)	6	0	0	24
Stephen Myler	Salford	2006	4(8)	1	15	0	34
	Widnes	2003-05	35(14)	8	74	0	180

PLAYER	CLUB	YEAR	APP	TRIES	GOALS	FG	PTS
Vinny Myler	Salford	2004	(4)	0	0	0	0
	Bradford	2003	(1)	0	0	0	0
Matt Nable	London	1997	2(2)	1	0	0	4
Brad Nairn	Workington	1996	14	4	0	0	16
Frank Napoli	London	2000	14(6)	2	0	0	8
Carlo Napolitano	Salford	2000	(3)	1	0	0	4
Stephen Nash	Salford	2007, 2009	2(18)	1	0	0	4
	Widnes	2005	4(1)	0	0	0	0
Jim Naylor	Halifax	2000	7(6)	2	0	0	8
Scott Naylor	Salford	1997-98, 2004	30(1)	9	0	0	36
	Bradford	1999-2003	127(1)	51	0	0	204
Adam Neal	Salford	2010-11	8(21)	0	0	0	0
Mike Neal	Salford	1998	(1)	0	0	0	0
	Oldham	1996-97	6(4)	3	0	0	12
Jonathan Neill	Huddersfield	1998-99	20(11)	0	0	0	0
	St Helens	1996	1	0	0	0	0
Chris Nero	Salford	2011	22	3	0	0	12
	Bradford	2008-10	65(5)	24	0	0	96
	Huddersfield	2004-07	97(8)	38	0	0	152
Jason Netherton	Hull KR	2007-11	46(53)	4	0	0	16
	London	2003-04	6	0	0	0	0
	Halifax	2002	2(3)	0	0	0	0
	Leeds	2001	(3)	0	0	0	0
Kirk Netherton	Castleford	2009-10	5(23)	3	0	0	12
	Hull KR	2007-08	9(15)	2	0	0	8
Paul Newlove	Castleford	2004	5	1	0	0	4
	St Helens	1996-2003	162	106	0	0	424
Richard Newlove	Wakefield	2003	17(5)	8	0	0	32
Clint Newton	Hull KR	2008-11	90(3)	37	0	0	148
Terry Newton	Wakefield	2010	(2)	0	0	0	0
	Bradford	2006-09	83(6)	26	0	0	104
	Wigan	2000-05	157(9)	62	0	0	248
	Leeds	1996-1999	55(14)	4	0	0	16
Gene Ngamu	Huddersfield	1999-2000	29(2)	9	67	0	170
Danny Nicklas	Hull	2010	(3)	0	0	0	0
Sonny Nickle	St Helens	1999-2002	86(18)	14	0	0	56
	Bradford	1996-98	25(16)	9	0	0	36
Jason Nicol	Salford	2000-02	52(7)	11	0	0	44
Tawera Nikau	Warrington	2000-01	51	7	0	0	28
Rob Nolan	Hull	1998-99	20(11)	6	0	0	24
Paul Noone	Harlequins	2006	5(2)	0	0	0	0
	Warrington	2000-06	60(59)	12	20	0	88
Chris Norman	Halifax	2003	13(3)	2	0	0	8
Paul Norman	Oldham	1996	(1)	0	0	0	0
Andy Northey	St Helens	1996-97	8(17)	2	0	0	8
Danny Nutley	Castleford	2006	28	3	0	0	12
	Warrington	1998-2001	94(1)	3	0	0	12
Tony Nuttall	Oldham	1996-97	1(7)	0	0	0	0
Adam O'Brien	Bradford	2011	(5)	0	0	0	0
Clinton O'Brien	Wakefield	2003	(2)	0	0	0	0
Gareth O'Brien	Warrington	2011	1	1	0	0	4
Sam Obst	Hull	2011	17(6)	6	0	0	24
	Wakefield	2005-11	100(28)	40	7	0	174
Jamie O'Callaghan							
	Harlequins	2008-11	54(3)	12	0	0	48
Eamon O'Carroll	Wigan	2006-11	2(59)	3	0	0	12
Matt O'Connor	Paris	1997	11(4)	1	26	2	58
Terry O'Connor	Widnes	2005	25	2	0	0	8
	Wigan	1996-2004	177(45)	9	0	0	36
Jarrod O'Doherty	Huddersfield	2003	26	3	0	0	12
David O'Donnell	Paris	1997	21	3	0	0	12
Luke O'Donnell	Huddersfield	2011	15	2	0	0	8
Martin Offiah	Salford	2000-01	41	20	0	2	82
	London	1996-99	29(3)	21	0	0	84
	Wigan	1996	8	7	0	0	28
Mark O'Halloran	London	2004-05	34(3)	10	0	0	40
Ryan O'Hara	Crusaders	2010-11	41(8)	3	0	0	12
	Celtic	2009	27	3	0	0	12
Hefin O'Hare	Huddersfield	2001, 2003-05	72(10)	27	0	0	108
Hitro Okesene	Hull	1998	21(1)	0	0	0	0
Anderson Okiwe	Sheffield	1997	1	0	0	0	0
Tom Olbison	Bradford	2009-11	9(13)	2	0	0	8
Jamie Olejnik	Paris	1997	11	8	0	0	32
Kevin O'Loughlin	Halifax	1997-98	2(4)	0	0	0	0
	St Helens	1997	(3)	0	0	0	0
Sean O'Loughlin	Wigan	2002-11	222(21)	49	3	2	204
Mark O'Meley	Hull	2010-11	46	9	0	0	36
Jules O'Neill	Widnes	2003-05	57(3)	14	158	7	379
	Wakefield	2005	10(2)	2	4	0	16
	Wigan	2002-03	29(1)	12	72	0	192
Julian O'Neill	Widnes	2002-05	57(39)	3	0	0	12
	Wakefield	2001	24(1)	2	0	0	8
	St Helens	1997-2000	95(8)	5	0	0	20
Mark O'Neill	Hull KR	2007	17	5	0	0	20
	Leeds	2006	1(8)	0	0	0	0
Steve O'Neill	Gateshead	1999	1(1)	0	0	0	0
Tom O'Reilly	Warrington	2001-02	8(6)	1	0	0	4
Matt Orford	Bradford	2010	12	3	31	2	76
Chris Orr	Huddersfield	1998	19(3)	2	0	0	8
Danny Orr	Castleford	1997-2003, 2011	176(20)	70	292	3	867
	Harlequins	2007-10	90(4)	13	96	0	244
	Wigan	2004-06	66(2)	18	12	0	96

Super League Players 1996-2011

PLAYER	CLUB	YEAR	APP	TRIES	GOALS	FG	PTS
Gareth Owen	Salford	2010	(3)	0	0	0	0
Nick Owen	Leigh	2005	8(1)	1	11	0	26
Richard Owen	Castleford	2008-11	67(3)	34	0	0	136
Lopini Paea	Catalans	2011	14(6)	3	0	0	12
Mathias Pala	Catalans	2011	2	0	0	0	0
Iafeta Palea'aesina							
	Salford	2011	2(20)	1	0	0	4
	Wigan	2006-10	55(77)	16	0	0	64
Jason Palmada	Workington	1996	12	2	0	0	8
Junior Paramore	Castleford	1996	5(5)	3	0	0	12
Paul Parker	Hull	1999-2002	23(18)	9	0	0	36
Rob Parker	Castleford	2011	4(2)	2	0	0	8
	Salford	2009-11	23(14)	4	0	0	16
	Warrington	2006-08	10(56)	6	0	0	24
	Bradford	2000,					
		2002-05	19(76)	14	0	0	56
	London	2001	9	1	0	0	4
Wayne Parker	Halifax	1996-97	12(1)	0	0	0	0
Ian Parry	Warrington	2001	(1)	0	0	0	0
Jules Parry	Paris	1996	10(2)	0	0	0	0
Regis Pastre-Courtine							
	Paris	1996	4(3)	4	0	0	16
Andrew Patmore	Oldham	1996	8(5)	3	0	0	12
Larne Patrick	Huddersfield	2009-11	5(51)	11	0	0	44
Luke Patten	Salford	2011	27	5	0	0	20
Henry Paul	Harlequins	2006-08	60(1)	8	94	2	222
	Bradford	1999-2001	81(5)	29	350	6	822
	Wigan	1996-98	60	37	23	0	194
Junior Paul	London	1996	3	1	0	0	4
Robbie Paul	Salford	2009	2(24)	2	0	0	8
	Huddersfield	2006-07	44(8)	7	0	0	28
	Bradford	1996-2005	198(31)	121	0	3	490
Jason Payne	Castleford	2006	1(1)	0	0	0	0
Danny Peacock	Bradford	1997-99	32(2)	15	0	0	60
Jamie Peacock	Leeds	2006-11	136(9)	17	0	0	68
	Bradford	1999-2005	163(25)	38	0	0	152
Martin Pearson	Wakefield	2001	21(1)	3	60	3	135
	Halifax	1997-98,					
		2000	55(6)	24	181	0	458
	Sheffield	1999	17(6)	9	36	2	110
Jacques Pech	Paris	1996	16	0	0	0	0
Mike Pechey	Warrington	1998	6(3)	2	0	0	8
Bill Peden	London	2003	21(3)	7	0	0	28
Adam Peek	Crusaders	2010-11	5(22)	1	0	0	4
	Celtic	2009	5(12)	3	0	0	12
Eloi Pelissier	Catalans	2011	1(22)	2	0	0	8
Dimitri Pelo	Catalans	2007-10	79	37	0	0	148
Sean Penkywicz	Huddersfield	2004-05	21(11)	7	0	0	28
	Halifax	2000-03	29(27)	8	0	0	32
Julian Penni	Salford	1998-99	4	0	0	0	0
Kevin Penny	Wakefield	2011	5	1	0	0	4
	Harlequins	2010	5	3	0	0	12
	Warrington	2006-09	39(1)	26	0	0	104
Lee Penny	Warrington	1996-2003	140(5)	54	0	0	216
Paul Penrice	Workington	1996	11(2)	2	0	0	8
Chris Percival	Widnes	2002-03	26	6	0	0	24
Apollo Perelini	St Helens	1996-2000	103(16)	27	0	0	108
Mark Perrett	Halifax	1996-97	15(4)	4	0	0	16
Josh Perry	St Helens	2011	7(4)	0	0	0	0
Shane Perry	Catalans	2009	8(8)	1	0	0	4
Adam Peters	Paris	1997	16(3)	0	0	0	0
Dominic Peters	London	1998-2003	58(11)	12	0	0	48
Mike Peters	Warrington	2000	2(12)	1	0	0	4
	Halifax	2000	1	0	0	0	0
Willie Peters	Widnes	2004	9	3	0	2	14
	Wigan	2000	29	15	5	6	76
	Gateshead	1999	27	11	1	6	52
Matt Petersen	Wakefield	2008-09	14	3	0	0	12
Adrian Petrie	Workington	1996	(1)	0	0	0	0
Cameron Phelps	Hull	2011	19	2	0	0	8
	Wigan	2008-10	43(1)	14	4	0	64
Rowland Phillips	Workington	1996	22	1	0	0	4
Nathan Picchi	Leeds	1996	(1)	0	0	0	0
Ian Pickavance	Hull	1999	4(2)	2	0	0	8
	Huddersfield	1999	3(14)	0	0	0	0
	St Helens	1996-98	12(44)	6	0	0	24
James Pickering	Castleford	1999	1(19)	0	0	0	0
Steve Pickersgill	Warrington	2005-09	1(36)	0	0	0	0
Nick Pinkney	Salford	2000-02	64	29	0	0	116
	Halifax	1999	26(2)	13	0	0	52
	Sheffield	1997-98	33	10	0	0	40
Mikhail Piskunov	Paris	1996	1(1)	1	0	0	4
Darryl Pitt	London	1996	2(16)	4	0	1	17
Jay Pitts	Leeds	2009-11	8(14)	2	0	0	8
	Wakefield	2008-09	9(8)	2	0	0	8
Andy Platt	Salford	1997-98	20(3)	1	0	0	4
Michael Platt	Bradford	2007-11	93(5)	29	0	0	116
	Castleford	2006	26	7	0	0	28
	Salford	2001-02	3	1	0	0	4
Willie Poching	Leeds	2002-06	58(73)	44	0	0	176
	Wakefield	1999-2001	65(4)	20	0	0	80
Quentin Pongia	Wigan	2003-04	15(10)	0	0	0	0
Dan Potter	Widnes	2002-03	34(2)	6	0	0	24
	London	2001	1(3)	1	0	0	4
Craig Poucher	Hull	1999-2002	31(5)	5	0	0	20
Bryn Powell	Salford	2004	1(1)	0	0	0	0
Daio Powell	Sheffield	1999	11(3)	2	0	0	8
	Halifax	1997-98	30(3)	17	0	0	68
Daryl Powell	Leeds	1998-2000	49(30)	12	0	2	50
Karl Pratt	Bradford	2003-05	35(19)	18	0	0	72
	Leeds	1999-2002	62(12)	33	0	0	132
Paul Prescott	Wigan	2004-11	42(73)	3	0	0	12
Steve Prescott	Hull	1998-99,					
		2001-03	99	46	191	3	569
	Wakefield	2000	22(1)	3	13	0	38
	St Helens	1996-97	32	15	17	0	94
Lee Prest	Workington	1996	(1)	0	0	0	0
Gareth Price	Salford	2002	(2)	0	0	0	0
	London	2002	2(2)	3	0	0	12
	St Helens	1999	(11)	2	0	0	8
Gary Price	Wakefield	1999-2001	55(13)	11	0	0	44
Richard Price	Sheffield	1996	1(2)	0	0	0	0
Tony Priddle	Paris	1997	11(7)	3	0	0	12
Karl Pryce	Harlequins	2011	11(7)	12	0	0	48
	Wigan	2009-10	11(2)	12	0	0	48
	Bradford	2003-06	28(19)	33	1	0	134
Leon Pryce	St Helens	2006-11	133(3)	64	0	0	256
	Bradford	1998-2005	159(29)	86	0	0	344
Waine Pryce	Wakefield	2007	10(2)	4	0	0	16
	Castleford	2000-06	97(12)	49	0	0	196
Tony Puletua	St Helens	2009-11	66(12)	33	0	0	132
Andrew Purcell	Castleford	2000	15(5)	3	0	0	12
	Hull	1999	27	4	0	0	16
Rob Purdham	Harlequins	2006-11	112(3)	18	131	1	335
	London	2002-05	53(15)	16	2	1	69
Luke Quigley	Catalans	2007	16(1)	1	0	0	4
Damien Quinn	Celtic	2009	20(1)	4	12	0	40
Scott Quinnell	Wigan	1996	6(3)	1	0	0	4
Florian Quintilla	Catalans	2008-09	1(4)	0	0	0	0
Lee Radford	Hull	1998,					
		2006-11	136(28)	22	1	0	90
	Bradford	1999-2005	79(65)	18	12	0	96
Kris Radlinski	Wigan	1996-2006	236(1)	134	1	0	538
Sebastien Raguin	Catalans	2007-11	90(13)	26	0	0	104
Adrian Rainey	Castleford	2002	4(7)	1	0	0	4
Andy Raleigh	Huddersfield	2006-11	74(46)	13	0	0	52
Jean-Luc Ramondou							
	Paris	1996	1(1)	1	0	0	4
Chad Randall	Harlequins	2006-11	141(2)	37	0	1	149
Craig Randall	Halifax	1999	8(11)	4	0	0	16
	Salford	1997-98	12(18)	4	0	0	16
Scott Ranson	Oldham	1996-97	19(2)	7	0	0	28
Aaron Raper	Castleford	1999-2001	48(4)	4	2	1	21
Stefan Ratchford	Salford	2007,					
		2009-11	65(5)	23	20	0	132
Mike Ratu	Hull KR	2010	5	1	0	0	4
	Leeds	2007, 2009	1(5)	1	0	0	4
Paul Rauhihi	Warrington	2006-09	67(20)	10	0	0	40
Ben Rauter	Wakefield	2001	15(6)	4	0	0	16
Gareth Raynor	Bradford	2011	18	4	0	0	16
	Crusaders	2010	7	4	0	0	16
	Hull	2001-09	186	102	0	0	408
	Leeds	2000	(3)	0	0	0	0
Tony Rea	London	1996	22	4	0	0	16
Stuart Reardon	Crusaders	2011	25	11	0	0	44
	Bradford	2003-05,					
		2010	78(11)	37	0	0	148
	Warrington	2006-08	48	12	0	0	48
	Salford	2002	7(1)	3	0	0	12
Mark Reber	Wigan	1999-2000	9(9)	5	0	0	20
Alan Reddicliffe	Warrington	2001	1	0	0	0	0
Tahi Reihana	Bradford	1997-98	17(21)	0	0	0	0
Paul Reilly	Wakefield	2008	5(2)	1	0	0	4
	Huddersfield	1999-2001,					
		2003-07	150(8)	35	1	0	142
Robert Relf	Widnes	2002-04	68(2)	5	0	0	20
Steve Renouf	Wigan	2000-01	55	40	0	0	160
Steele Retchless	London	1998-2004	177(6)	13	0	0	52
Scott Rhodes	Hull	2000	2	0	0	0	0
Phillipe Ricard	Paris	1996-97	2	0	0	0	0
Andy Rice	Huddersfield	2000-01	2(13)	1	0	0	4
Basil Richards	Huddersfield	1998-99	28(17)	1	0	0	4
Craig Richards	Oldham	1996	1	0	0	0	0
Pat Richards	Wigan	2006-11	160	116	595	3	1657
Andy Richardson	Hudds-Sheff	2000	(2)	0	0	0	0
Sean Richardson	Widnes	2002	2(18)	1	0	0	4
	Wakefield	1999	5(1)	0	0	0	0
	Castleford	1996-97	3(8)	1	0	0	4
Mark Riddell	Wigan	2009-10	45(11)	5	2	0	24
Neil Rigby	St Helens	2006	(1)	0	0	0	0
Shane Rigon	Bradford	2001	14(11)	12	0	0	48
Craig Rika	Halifax	1996	2	0	0	0	0
Chris Riley	Warrington	2005-11	87(10)	61	0	0	244
	Harlequins	2011	3	2	0	0	8
Peter Riley	Workington	1996	7(5)	0	0	0	0
Julien Rinaldi	Wakefield	2002,					
		2010-11	27(9)	6	0	0	24
	Bradford	2009	(7)	1	0	0	4
	Harlequins	2007-08	4(43)	9	0	0	36
	Catalans	2006	16(6)	3	1	0	14

PLAYER	CLUB	YEAR	APP	TRIES	GOALS	FG	PTS
Dean Ripley	Castleford	2004	3(4)	1	0	0	4
Leroy Rivett	Warrington	2002	9	1	0	0	4
	Hudds-Sheff	2000	5(1)	1	0	0	4
	Leeds	1996-2000	39(15)	21	0	0	84
Jason Roach	Warrington	1998-99	29(7)	15	0	0	60
	Castleford	1997	7	4	0	0	16
Ben Roarty	Castleford	2006	11(6)	2	0	0	8
	Huddersfield	2003-05	52	5	0	0	20
Amos Roberts	Wigan	2009-11	47(2)	27	5	0	118
Mark Roberts	Wigan	2003	(3)	0	0	0	0
Robert Roberts	Huddersfield	2001	(1)	0	0	0	0
	Halifax	2000	(3)	0	0	0	0
	Hull	1999	24(2)	4	13	4	46
Chad Robinson	Harlequins	2009	13(1)	2	0	0	8
Craig Robinson	Wakefield	2005	(1)	0	0	0	0
Jason Robinson	Wigan	1996-2000	126(1)	87	0	1	349
Jeremy Robinson	Paris	1997	10(3)	1	21	0	46
John Robinson	Widnes	2003-04	7	1	0	0	4
Luke Robinson	Huddersfield	2008-11	97(6)	26	4	0	112
	Salford	2005-07	79	28	10	2	134
	Wigan	2002-04	17(25)	9	6	1	49
Will Robinson	Castleford	2004	9	4	3	0	22
	Hull	2000	22	4	0	0	16
	Gateshead	1999	28	9	0	0	36
James Roby	St Helens	2004-11	94(114)	57	0	0	228
Mike Roby	St Helens	2004	(1)	0	0	0	0
Carl Roden	Warrington	1997	1	0	0	0	0
Matt Rodwell	Warrington	2002	10	3	0	0	12
Darren Rogers	Castleford	1999-2004	162(1)	81	0	0	324
	Salford	1997-98	42	16	0	0	64
Jamie Rooney	Wakefield	2003-09	113(7)	60	314	21	889
	Castleford	2001	2(1)	0	6	0	12
Jonathan Roper	Castleford	2001	13	7	12	0	52
	Salford	2000	1(4)	1	3	0	10
	London	2000	4	0	0	0	0
	Warrington	1996-2000	75(8)	33	71	0	274
Scott Roskell	London	1996-97	30(2)	16	0	0	64
Steve Rosolen	London	1996-98	25(9)	10	0	0	40
Adam Ross	London	1996	(1)	0	0	0	0
Paul Round	Castleford	1996	(3)	0	0	0	0
Steve Rowlands	Widnes	2004-05	18(3)	2	15	0	38
	St Helens	2003	(1)	0	0	0	0
Paul Rowley	Leigh	2005	15(7)	3	0	0	12
	Huddersfield	2001	24	3	0	0	12
	Halifax	1996-2000	107(3)	27	1	3	113
Nigel Roy	London	2001-04	100	39	0	0	156
Nicky Royle	Widnes	2004	13	7	0	0	28
Shad Royston	Bradford	2011	17(1)	10	0	0	40
Chris Rudd	Warrington	1996-98	31(17)	10	16	0	72
Sean Rudder	Catalans	2006	22(1)	6	0	0	24
	Castleford	2004	9(3)	2	0	0	8
James Rushforth	Halifax	1997	(4)	0	0	0	0
Danny Russell	Huddersfield	1998-2000	50(13)	8	0	0	32
Ian Russell	Oldham	1997	1(3)	1	0	0	4
	Paris	1996	3	0	0	0	0
Richard Russell	Castleford	1996-98	37(4)	2	0	0	8
Robert Russell	Salford	1998-99	2(1)	0	1	0	2
Sean Rutgerson	Salford	2004-06	60(9)	4	0	0	16
Chris Ryan	London	1998-99	44(3)	17	10	0	88
Sean Ryan	Castleford	2004	11(5)	2	0	0	8
	Hull	2002-03	53	8	0	0	32
Justin Ryder	Wakefield	2004	19(3)	11	0	0	44
Jason Ryles	Catalans	2009	19(2)	2	0	0	8
Setaimata Sa	Catalans	2010-11	41(4)	12	0	0	48
Teddy Sadaoui	Catalans	2006	7	0	0	0	0
Matt Salter	London	1997-99	14(34)	0	0	0	0
Ben Sammut	Hull	2000	20	4	67	0	150
	Gateshead	1999	26(2)	6	17	0	58
Jarrod Sammut	Crusaders	2010-11	17(16)	17	0	0	68
Dean Sampson	Castleford	1996-2003	124(28)	24	0	0	96
Paul Sampson	London	2004	1(2)	1	0	0	4
	Wakefield	2000	17	8	0	0	32
Lee Sanderson	London	2004	1(5)	1	7	0	18
Jason Sands	Paris	1996-97	28	0	0	0	0
Mitchell Sargent	Castleford	2008-10	37(21)	6	0	0	24
Dan Sarginson	Harlequins	2011	8	5	0	0	20
Lokeni Savelio	Halifax	2000	2(11)	0	0	0	0
	Salford	1997-98	18(20)	0	0	0	0
Tom Saxton	Salford	2007	5	0	0	0	0
	Wakefield	2006	9(6)	2	0	0	8
	Hull	2005	19(8)	3	0	0	12
	Castleford	2002-04	37(12)	11	0	0	44
Jonathan Scales	Halifax	2000	1	0	0	0	0
	Bradford	1996-98	46(4)	24	0	0	96
Andrew Schick	Castleford	1996-98	45(13)	10	0	0	40
Clinton Schifcofske							
	Crusaders	2010-11	44	5	115	0	250
Garry Schofield	Huddersfield	1998	(2)	0	0	0	0
Gary Schubert	Workington	1996	(1)	0	0	0	0
Matt Schultz	Hull	1998-99	23(9)	2	0	0	8
	Leeds	1996	2(4)	0	0	0	0
John Schuster	Halifax	1996-97	31	9	127	3	293
Nick Scruton	Bradford	2009-11	43(19)	4	0	0	16
	Leeds	2002, 2004-08	11(53)	3	0	0	12
	Hull	2004	2(16)	3	0	0	12

PLAYER	CLUB	YEAR	APP	TRIES	GOALS	FG	PTS
Danny Sculthorpe	Huddersfield	2009	5(8)	0	0	0	0
	Wakefield	2007-09	14(28)	1	0	0	4
	Castleford	2006	18(1)	4	0	1	17
	Wigan	2002-05	13(49)	7	0	0	28
Paul Sculthorpe	St Helens	1998-2008	223(4)	94	356	7	1095
	Warrington	1996-97	40	6	0	0	24
Mick Seaby	London	1997	3(2)	1	0	0	4
Danny Seal	Halifax	1996-99	8(17)	3	0	0	12
Matt Seers	Wakefield	2003	11(1)	2	0	0	8
Anthony Seibold	London	1999-2000	33(19)	5	0	0	20
Keith Senior	Leeds	1999-2011	319(2)	159	0	0	636
	Sheffield	1996-99	90(2)	40	0	0	160
Fili Seru	Hull	1998-99	37(1)	13	0	0	52
Anthony Seuseu	Halifax	2003	1(11)	1	0	0	4
Jerry Seuseu	Wigan	2005-06	29(9)	1	0	0	4
Will Sharp	Hull	2011	12(8)	7	0	0	28
	Harlequins	2008-10	65(1)	19	0	0	76
Darren Shaw	Salford	2002	5(9)	1	0	0	4
	London	1996, 2002	22(8)	3	0	0	12
	Castleford	2000-01	50(6)	1	0	0	4
	Sheffield	1998-99	51(1)	3	0	1	13
Mick Shaw	Halifax	1999	5	1	0	0	4
	Leeds	1996	12(2)	7	0	0	28
Phil Shead	Paris	1996	3(2)	0	0	0	0
Richard Sheil	St Helens	1997	(1)	0	0	0	0
Kelly Shelford	Warrington	1996-97	25(3)	4	0	2	18
Michael Shenton	St Helens	2011	28	9	0	0	36
	Castleford	2004, 2006, 2008-10	97(2)	46	0	0	184
Ryan Sheridan	Castleford	2004	2	0	0	0	0
	Widnes	2003	14(3)	2	0	0	8
	Leeds	1997-2002	123(7)	46	0	1	185
	Sheffield	1996	9(3)	5	0	1	21
Louis Sheriff	Hull KR	2011	2	1	0	0	4
Rikki Sheriffe	Bradford	2009-10	51	14	0	0	56
	Harlequins	2006-08	35(1)	16	0	0	64
	Halifax	2003	6(1)	3	0	0	12
Ian Sherratt	Oldham	1996	5(3)	1	0	0	4
Brent Sherwin	Catalans	2010	12	1	0	1	5
	Castleford	2008-10	48(1)	4	0	3	19
Peter Shiels	St Helens	2001-02	44(3)	11	0	0	44
Gary Shillabeer	Huddersfield	1999	(2)	0	0	0	0
Mark Shipway	Salford	2004-05	30(12)	3	0	0	12
Ian Sibbit	Bradford	2011	9(5)	0	0	0	0
	Salford	2005-07, 2009-10	64(17)	11	0	0	44
	Warrington	1999-2001, 2003-04	63(18)	24	0	0	96
Mark Sibson	Huddersfield	1999	2	2	0	0	8
Adam Sidlow	Salford	2009-11	23(38)	11	0	0	44
Jon Simms	St Helens	2002	(1)	0	0	0	0
Craig Simon	Hull	2000	23(2)	8	0	0	32
	Gateshead	1999	25(4)	6	0	0	24
Michael Simon	Catalans	2010-11	1(27)	1	0	0	4
Darren Simpson	Huddersfield	1998-99	17(1)	5	0	0	20
Jamie Simpson	Huddersfield	2011	8(1)	0	0	0	0
Robbie Simpson	London	1999	6(7)	0	0	0	0
Kevin Sinfield	Leeds	1997-2011	325(25)	53	1138	21	2509
Matt Sing	Hull	2007-08	41	14	0	0	56
Wayne Sing	Paris	1997	18(1)	2	0	0	8
Brad Singleton	Leeds	2011	(1)	0	0	0	0
Fata Sini	Salford	1997	22	7	0	0	28
John Skandalis	Huddersfield	2007-08	37(5)	4	0	0	16
Dylan Skee	Harlequins	2008-09	(3)	0	0	0	0
Ben Skerrett	Castleford	2003	(1)	0	0	0	0
Kelvin Skerrett	Halifax	1997-99	31(6)	2	0	0	8
	Wigan	1996	1(8)	0	0	0	0
Troy Slattery	Wakefield	2002-03	33(5)	4	0	0	16
	Huddersfield	1999	3	1	0	0	4
Mick Slicker	Huddersfield	2001, 2003-05	17(48)	2	0	0	8
	Sheffield	1999	(3)	1	0	0	4
	Halifax	1997	2(5)	0	0	0	0
Ian Smales	Castleford	1996-97	10(8)	5	0	0	20
Aaron Smith	Castleford	2006	(2)	0	0	0	0
	Bradford	2003-04	12(1)	3	0	0	12
Andy Smith	Harlequins	2007	6(3)	3	0	0	12
	Bradford	2004-06	9(9)	4	0	0	16
	Salford	2005	4	1	0	0	4
Byron Smith	Castleford	2004	(9)	0	0	0	0
	Halifax	2003	6(1)	0	0	0	0
Chris Smith	Hull	2001-02	12	3	0	0	12
	St Helens	1998-2000	62(9)	26	0	0	104
	Castleford	1996-97	36(1)	12	0	0	48
Craig Smith	Wigan	2002-04	77(3)	10	0	0	40
Damien Smith	St Helens	1998	21(1)	8	0	0	32
Danny Smith	Paris	1996	10(2)	1	15	0	34
	London	1996	2(1)	1	0	0	4
Darren Smith	St Helens	2003	25(1)	14	0	0	56
Gary Smith	Castleford	2001	(1)	0	0	0	0
Hudson Smith	Bradford	2000	8(22)	2	0	0	8
	Salford	1999	23(2)	5	0	0	20
James Smith	Salford	2000	23(3)	6	0	0	24

175

Super League Players 1996-2011

PLAYER	CLUB	YEAR	APP	TRIES	GOALS	FG	PTS
Jamie Smith	Hull	1998-99	24(6)	6	12	0	48
	Workington	1996	5(3)	0	1	0	2
Jason Smith	Hull	2001-04	61(3)	17	0	1	69
Jeremy Smith	Wakefield	2011	9(1)	1	0	0	4
	Salford	2009-10	27(17)	2	0	0	8
Kris Smith	London	2001	(1)	0	0	0	0
	Halifax	2001	(1)	0	0	0	0
Lee Smith	Leeds	2005-11	117(7)	60	34	1	309
Leigh Smith	Workington	1996	9	4	0	0	16
Mark Smith	Widnes	2005	12(15)	4	0	0	16
	Wigan	1999-2004	35(77)	8	0	0	32
Martyn Smith	Harlequins	2010	(2)	0	0	0	0
Matty Smith	Salford	2010-11	48(4)	10	4	1	49
	St Helens	2006-08,					
		2010	17(2)	3	10	1	33
	Celtic	2009	15(1)	3	2	1	17
Michael Smith	Hull KR	2007	(3)	1	0	0	4
	Castleford	1998,					
		2001-04	86(33)	32	0	0	128
	Hull	1999	12(6)	3	0	0	12
Paul Smith	Huddersfield	2004-06	52(17)	13	0	0	52
Paul Smith	Warrington	2001	(1)	0	0	0	0
	Castleford	1997-2000	6(37)	3	0	0	12
Paul Smith	London	1997	7(1)	2	0	0	8
Peter Smith	Oldham	1996	2	0	0	0	0
Richard Smith	Wakefield	2001	8(1)	1	0	0	4
	Salford	1997	(1)	1	0	0	4
Tim Smith	Wigan	2008-09	13(8)	2	0	0	8
Tony Smith	Hull	2001-03	43(5)	26	0	0	104
	Wigan	1997-2000	66(5)	46	0	0	184
	Castleford	1996-97	18(2)	10	0	0	40
Tony Smith	Workington	1996	9	1	0	0	4
Tyrone Smith	Harlequins	2006-07	49(3)	13	0	0	52
	London	2005	20(4)	11	0	0	44
Rob Smyth	Leigh	2005	15(1)	4	0	0	16
	Warrington	2000-03	65	35	20	0	180
	London	1998-2000	32(2)	9	15	0	66
	Wigan	1996	11(5)	16	0	0	64
Marc Sneyd	Salford	2010-11	5(12)	1	1	0	6
Steve Snitch	Castleford	2010-11	27(10)	8	0	0	32
	Wakefield	2002-05,					
		2009	33(55)	9	0	0	36
	Huddersfield	2006-08	24(35)	12	0	0	48
Bright Sodje	Wakefield	2000	15	4	0	0	16
	Sheffield	1996-99	54	34	0	0	136
Iosia Soliola	St Helens	2010-11	30(1)	2	0	0	8
David Solomona	Warrington	2010-11	8(44)	13	0	0	52
	Bradford	2007-09	44(9)	19	0	0	76
	Wakefield	2004-06	73(3)	26	0	0	104
Alfred Songoro	Wakefield	1999	8(5)	4	0	0	16
Romain Sort	Paris	1997	(1)	0	0	0	0
Paul Southern	Salford	1997-2002	79(33)	6	13	0	50
	St Helens	2002	1(1)	0	0	0	0
Cain Southernwood							
	Bradford	2010	2	0	0	0	0
Roy Southernwood							
	Wakefield	1999	1	0	0	0	0
	Halifax	1996	2	0	0	0	0
Jason Southwell	Huddersfield	2004	(1)	0	0	0	0
Waisale Sovatabua							
	Wakefield	2001-03	44(3)	19	0	0	76
	Hudds-Sheff	2000	23(1)	8	0	0	32
	Sheffield	1996-99	56(17)	19	0	1	77
Yusef Sozi	London	2000-01	(5)	0	0	0	0
Scott Spaven	Hull KR	2010	(2)	0	0	0	0
Andy Speak	Castleford	2001	4(4)	0	0	0	0
	Wakefield	2000	6(5)	2	0	0	8
	Leeds	1999	4	1	0	0	4
Tim Spears	Castleford	2003	(3)	0	0	0	0
Ady Spencer	London	1996-99	8(36)	5	0	0	20
Jack Spencer	Salford	2009-11	(7)	0	0	0	0
Rob Spicer	Wakefield	2002-05	28(18)	4	0	0	16
Russ Spiers	Wakefield	2011	(2)	0	0	0	0
Stuart Spruce	Widnes	2002-03	45(4)	19	0	0	76
	Bradford	1996-2001	107(2)	57	0	0	228
Lee St Hilaire	Castleford	1997	4(2)	0	0	0	0
Marcus St Hilaire	Bradford	2006-07	34(1)	12	0	0	48
	Huddersfield	2003-05	72(2)	30	0	0	120
	Leeds	1996-2002	59(33)	31	0	0	124
Cyril Stacul	Catalans	2007-11	55(1)	17	0	0	68
Dylan Stainton	Workington	1996	2(3)	0	0	0	0
Mark Stamper	Workington	1996	(1)	0	0	0	0
John Stankevitch	Widnes	2005	17(5)	0	0	0	0
	St Helens	2000-04	74(40)	25	0	0	100
Gareth Stanley	Bradford	2000	1	1	0	0	4
Craig Stapleton	Salford	2009	24	2	0	0	8
	Leigh	2005	27(1)	4	0	0	16
Graham Steadman							
	Castleford	1996-97	11(17)	5	0	0	20
Jon Steel	Hull KR	2007-08	18	6	0	0	24
Jamie Stenhouse	Warrington	2000-01	9(3)	3	0	0	12
Gareth Stephens	Sheffield	1997-99	23(6)	2	0	0	8
David Stephenson							
	Hull	1998	11(7)	3	0	0	12
	Oldham	1997	10(8)	2	0	0	8

PLAYER	CLUB	YEAR	APP	TRIES	GOALS	FG	PTS
Francis Stephenson							
	London	2002-05	42(34)	5	0	0	20
	Wigan	2001	2(9)	0	0	0	0
	Wakefield	1999-2000	50(1)	6	0	0	24
Paul Sterling	Leeds	1997-2000	79(12)	50	0	0	200
Paul Stevens	Oldham	1996	2(1)	0	0	0	0
	London	1996	(1)	0	0	0	0
Warren Stevens	Leigh	2005	4(14)	1	0	0	4
	Warrington	1996-99,					
		2002-05	17(66)	1	0	0	4
	Salford	2001	(8)	0	0	0	0
Anthony Stewart	Harlequins	2006	4	0	0	0	0
	Salford	2004-06	51(2)	15	0	0	60
	St Helens	1997-2003	93(23)	44	0	0	176
Troy Stone	Widnes	2002	18(6)	1	0	0	4
	Huddersfield	2001	12(1)	1	0	0	4
James Stosic	Wakefield	2009	8(10)	1	0	0	4
Lynton Stott	Wakefield	1999	21	4	6	1	29
	Sheffield	1996-98	40(4)	15	0	0	60
Mitchell Stringer	Salford	2005-06	12(4)	0	0	0	0
	London	2004-05	10(19)	0	0	0	0
Graham Strutton	London	1996	9(1)	2	0	0	8
Matt Sturm	Leigh	2005	8(19)	3	0	0	12
	Warrington	2002-04	1(18)	0	0	0	0
	Huddersfield	1998-99	46	8	0	0	32
Anthony Sullivan	St Helens	1996-2001	137(2)	105	0	0	420
Michael Sullivan	Warrington	2006-07	21(16)	8	1	0	34
Phil Sumner	Warrington	1996	(5)	0	0	0	0
Simon Svabic	Salford	1998-2000	13(5)	3	19	0	50
Luke Swain	Salford	2009-10	54	3	0	0	12
Richard Swain	Hull	2004-07	89	5	0	0	20
Anthony Swann	Warrington	2001	3	1	0	0	4
Logan Swann	Warrington	2005-06	49(1)	17	0	0	68
	Bradford	2004	25	6	0	0	24
Willie Swann	Warrington	1996-97	25(2)	6	0	0	24
Nathan Sykes	Castleford	1996-2004	158(52)	3	0	0	12
Paul Sykes	Bradford	1999-2002,					
		2008-11	97(4)	35	62	2	266
	Harlequins	2006-07	31(2)	15	47	1	155
	London	2001-05	95(1)	26	220	3	547
Wayne Sykes	London	1999	(2)	0	0	0	0
Semi Tadulala	Wakefield	2004-07,					
		2011	92	37	0	0	148
	Bradford	2008-09	49	30	0	0	120
Whetu Taewa	Sheffield	1997-98	33(7)	8	0	0	32
Alan Tait	Leeds	1996	3(3)	1	0	0	4
Willie Talau	Salford	2009-10	22	4	0	0	16
	St Helens	2003-08	130(1)	50	0	0	200
Ian Talbot	Wakefield	1999	9(5)	2	31	0	70
	Wigan	1997	3	1	0	0	4
Albert Talipeau	Wakefield	2004	2(3)	0	0	0	0
Gael Tallec	Halifax	2000	5(19)	3	0	0	12
	Castleford	1998-99	19(21)	3	0	0	12
	Wigan	1996-97	8(12)	3	0	0	12
Joe Tamani	Bradford	1996	11(3)	4	0	0	16
Ryan Tandy	Hull KR	2007	8(4)	2	0	0	8
Andrew Tangata-Toa							
	Huddersfield	1999	15	2	0	0	8
David Tangata-Toa							
	Celtic	2009	1(18)	4	0	0	16
	Hull KR	2007	(17)	3	0	0	12
Jordan Tansey	Crusaders	2011	14(4)	5	0	0	20
	Hull	2009-10	30	9	0	0	36
	Leeds	2006-08	18(32)	19	3	0	82
Kris Tassell	Wakefield	2002	24	10	0	0	40
	Salford	2000-01	35(10)	12	0	0	48
Shem Tatupu	Wigan	1996	(3)	0	0	0	0
Tony Tatupu	Wakefield	2000-01	20	2	0	0	8
	Warrington	1997	21(1)	6	0	0	24
James Taylor	Leigh	2005	(4)	0	0	0	0
Joe Taylor	Paris	1997	9(5)	2	0	0	8
Lawrence Taylor	Sheffield	1996	(1)	0	0	0	0
Scott Taylor	Hull KR	2009-11	7(18)	2	0	0	8
Frederic Teixido	Sheffield	1999	(4)	0	0	0	0
	Paris	1996-97	2(3)	1	0	0	4
Lionel Teixido	Catalans	2006-07	11(13)	3	0	0	12
Karl Temata	Harlequins	2006-11	94(22)	7	0	0	28
	London	2005	1(2)	1	0	0	4
Jason Temu	Hull	1998	13(2)	1	0	0	4
	Oldham	1996-97	25(3)	1	0	0	4
Paul Terry	London	1997	(1)	0	0	0	0
Anthony Thackeray							
	Castleford	2008	3(6)	0	0	0	0
	Hull	2007	2	0	0	0	0
Jamie Thackray	Crusaders	2010	1(16)	2	0	0	8
	Hull	2005-06,					
		2008-09	37(45)	6	0	0	24
	Leeds	2006-07	5(27)	7	0	0	28
	Castleford	2003-04	7(11)	3	0	0	12
	Halifax	2000-02	10(38)	3	0	0	12
Adam Thaler	Castleford	2002	(2)	0	0	0	0
Gareth Thomas	Crusaders	2010-11	27(1)	6	0	0	24
Giles Thomas	London	1997-99	1(2)	0	0	0	0
Rob Thomas	Harlequins	2011	(2)	0	0	0	0

176

PLAYER	CLUB	YEAR	APP	TRIES	GOALS	FG	PTS
Steve Thomas	London	2004	4(2)	0	0	0	0
	Warrington	2001	2	0	0	0	0
Alex Thompson	Warrington	2009	(1)	1	0	0	4
Alex Thompson	Sheffield	1997	4(11)	0	0	0	0
Bobby Thompson	Salford	1999	28	5	2	0	24
Jordan Thompson							
	Castleford	2009-11	19(11)	10	0	0	40
Sam Thompson	Harlequins	2009	(2)	0	0	0	0
	St Helens	2008	(5)	0	0	0	0
Chris Thorman	Hull	2009	19(2)	1	0	0	4
	Huddersfield	2000-01, 2005-08	126(20)	51	320	3	847
	London	2003	26(1)	7	81	1	191
	Sheffield	1999	5(13)	2	8	1	25
Tony Thorniley	Warrington	1997	(5)	0	0	0	0
Andy Thornley	Salford	2009	(1)	1	0	0	4
Danny Tickle	Hull	2007-11	128	33	402	1	937
	Wigan	2002-06	94(36)	34	200	2	538
	Halifax	2000-02	25(17)	10	91	2	224
Kris Tickle	Warrington	2001	(1)	0	0	0	0
John Timu	London	1998-2000	57(3)	11	0	0	44
Kerrod Toby	London	1997	2(2)	0	0	0	0
Tulsen Tollett	London	1996-2001	105(5)	38	49	1	251
Joel Tomkins	Wigan	2005-11	94(39)	46	0	0	184
Sam Tomkins	Wigan	2009-11	77(5)	55	7	1	235
Glen Tomlinson	Wakefield	1999-2000	41(5)	8	0	0	32
	Hull	1998	5	1	0	0	4
	Bradford	1996-97	27(13)	12	0	0	48
Ryan Tongia	Wakefield	2011	4	2	0	0	8
Ian Tonks	Castleford	1996-2001	32(50)	11	13	0	70
Motu Tony	Wakefield	2011	6(3)	1	0	0	4
	Hull	2005-09	76(20)	25	0	0	100
	Castleford	2004	8(1)	1	0	0	4
Mark Tookey	Harlequins	2006	12(14)	1	0	0	4
	London	2005	13(14)	5	0	0	20
	Castleford	2004	2(8)	1	0	0	4
Clinton Toopi	Leeds	2006-08	40(3)	9	0	0	36
David Tootill	Harlequins	2008	(4)	0	0	0	0
Paul Topping	Oldham	1996-97	23(10)	1	19	0	42
Patrick Torreilles	Paris	1996	9(1)	1	25	0	54
Albert Torrens	Huddersfield	2006	7	5	0	0	20
Mat Toshack	London	1998-2004	120(21)	24	0	0	96
Julien Touxagas	Catalans	2006-11	14(45)	4	0	0	16
Darren Treacy	Salford	2002	24(1)	6	1	0	26
Dean Treister	Hull	2003	16(1)	3	0	0	12
Rocky Trimarchi	Crusaders	2010	16(8)	0	0	0	0
Steve Trindall	London	2003-05	40(20)	3	0	0	12
Shane Tronc	Wakefield	2010	8(3)	2	0	0	8
George Truelove	Wakefield	2002	2	1	0	0	4
	London	2000	5	1	0	0	4
Va'aiga Tuigamala							
	Wigan	1996	21	10	3	0	46
Fereti Tuilagi	St Helens	1999-2000	43(15)	21	0	0	84
	Halifax	1996-98	55(3)	27	0	0	108
Sateki Tuipulotu	Leeds	1996	6(3)	1	2	0	8
Tame Tupou	Bradford	2007-08	10(7)	8	0	0	32
Neil Turley	Leigh	2005	6(3)	2	20	1	49
Darren Turner	Huddersfield	2000-01, 2003-04	42(13)	13	0	0	52
	Sheffield	1996-99	41(29)	15	0	0	60
Ian Turner	Paris	1996	1(1)	1	0	0	4
Jordan Turner	Hull	2010-11	41(2)	19	0	0	76
	Salford	2006-07, 2009	22(10)	4	1	0	18
Chris Tuson	Wigan	2008, 2010-11	5(27)	2	0	0	8
	Castleford	2010	3(5)	0	0	0	0
Gregory Tutard	Paris	1996	1(1)	0	0	0	0
Brendon Tuuta	Warrington	1998	18(2)	4	0	0	16
	Castleford	1996-97	41(1)	3	0	0	12
Steve Tyrer	Salford	2010	20	6	9	0	42
	Celtic	2009	8	2	5	0	18
	St Helens	2006-08	17(3)	12	42	0	132
Mike Umaga	Halifax	1996-97	38(1)	16	5	0	74
Kava Utoikamanu	Paris	1996	6(3)	0	0	0	0
Frederic Vaccari	Catalans	2010-11	31	17	0	0	68
David Vaealiki	Wigan	2005-07	67(1)	17	0	0	68
Joe Vagana	Bradford	2001-08	176(44)	17	0	0	68
Nigel Vagana	Warrington	1997	20	17	0	0	68
Tevita Vaikona	Bradford	1998-2004	145(2)	89	0	0	356
Lesley Vainikolo	Bradford	2002-07	132(4)	136	1	0	546
Eric Van Brussell	Paris	1996	2	0	0	0	0
Jace Van Dijk	Celtic	2009	19	1	1	0	6
Richard Varkulis	Warrington	2004	4(1)	3	0	0	12
Marcus Vassilakopoulos							
	Sheffield	1997-99	15(11)	3	10	2	34
	Leeds	1996-97	1(3)	0	0	0	0
Josh Veivers	Wakefield	2011	10(2)	2	22	0	52
Phil Veivers	Huddersfield	1998	7(6)	1	0	0	4
	St Helens	1996	(1)	1	0	0	4
Michael Vella	Hull KR	2007-11	111(5)	13	0	0	52
Bruno Verges	Catalans	2006	25	6	0	0	24
Eric Vergniol	Paris	1996	14(1)	6	0	0	24
Gray Viane	Salford	2007	9	2	0	0	8
	Castleford	2006	20(7)	14	0	0	56
	Widnes	2005	20	13	0	0	52
	St Helens	2004	4	1	0	0	4
Adrian Vowles	Castleford	1997-2001, 2003	125(1)	29	1	1	119
	Wakefield	2002-03	24(3)	6	1	0	26
	Leeds	2002	14(3)	2	0	0	8
Michael Wainwright							
	Castleford	2008-10	70	22	0	0	88
	Wakefield	2004-05	21(10)	8	0	0	32
Mike Wainwright	Salford	2000-02, 2007	75(3)	9	0	0	36
	Warrington	1996-99, 2003-07	168(14)	23	0	0	92
Adam Walker	Huddersfield	2010-11	(2)	0	0	0	0
Ben Walker	Leeds	2002	23(1)	8	100	0	232
Chev Walker	Bradford	2011	9(2)	1	0	0	4
	Hull KR	2008-09	24(7)	5	0	0	20
	Leeds	1999-2006	142(19)	77	0	0	308
Chris Walker	Catalans	2010	11	6	2	0	28
Jonathan Walker	Castleford	2010-11	(12)	0	0	0	0
Jonny Walker	Wigan	2010	(1)	0	0	0	0
Matt Walker	Huddersfield	2001	3(6)	0	0	0	0
Anthony Wall	Paris	1997	9	3	3	0	18
Mark Wallace	Workington	1996	14(1)	3	0	0	12
Joe Walsh	Huddersfield	2009	1(1)	1	0	0	4
	Harlequins	2007-08	1(4)	0	0	0	0
Lucas Walshaw	Wakefield	2011	(1)	0	0	0	0
Kerrod Walters	Gateshead	1999	10(12)	2	1	0	10
Kevin Walters	Warrington	2001	1	0	0	0	0
Jason Walton	Salford	2009	(5)	0	0	0	0
Barry Ward	St Helens	2002-03	20(30)	4	0	0	16
Danny Ward	Harlequins	2008-11	89(7)	4	0	0	16
	Hull KR	2007	11(9)	0	0	0	0
	Castleford	2006	18(7)	2	0	0	8
	Leeds	1999-2005	70(48)	9	0	1	37
Joe Wardle	Huddersfield	2011	13	4	0	0	16
	Bradford	2010	1(1)	0	0	0	0
Phil Waring	Salford	1997-99	6(8)	2	0	0	8
Brett Warton	London	1999-2001	49(7)	14	133	0	322
Kyle Warren	Castleford	2002	13(14)	3	0	0	12
Danny Washbrook							
	Hull	2005-11	92(30)	11	0	0	44
Adam Watene	Wakefield	2006-08	45(8)	5	0	0	20
	Bradford	2006	(4)	0	0	0	0
Frank Watene	Wakefield	1999-2001	24(37)	6	0	0	24
Kallum Watkins	Leeds	2008-11	29(7)	17	0	0	68
Dave Watson	Sheffield	1998-99	41(4)	4	0	0	16
Ian Watson	Salford	1997, 2002	24(17)	8	3	5	43
	Workington	1996	4(1)	1	15	0	34
Kris Watson	Warrington	1996	11(2)	2	0	0	8
Brad Watts	Widnes	2005	6	3	0	0	12
Liam Watts	Hull KR	2008, 2010-11	24(24)	5	0	0	20
Michael Watts	Warrington	2002	3	0	0	0	0
Brent Webb	Leeds	2007-11	122(1)	71	0	0	284
Jason Webber	Salford	2000	25(1)	10	0	0	40
Ian Webster	St Helens	2006	1	0	0	0	0
Jake Webster	Hull KR	2008-11	82(1)	31	7	0	138
James Webster	Hull	2008	1	0	0	0	0
	Hull KR	2007-08	36	2	0	2	10
Pat Weisner	Hull KR	2007	(2)	0	0	0	0
	Harlequins	2006	10(6)	3	0	0	12
Taylor Welch	Warrington	2008	1	0	0	0	0
Kris Welham	Hull KR	2007-11	90(2)	57	1	0	230
Paul Wellens	St Helens	1998-2011	333(23)	162	34	1	717
Jon Wells	Harlequins	2006-09	66	10	0	0	40
	London	2004-05	42(2)	19	0	0	76
	Wakefield	2003	22(1)	1	0	0	4
	Castleford	1996-2002	114(14)	49	0	0	196
Dwayne West	St Helens	2000-02	8(16)	6	0	0	24
	Wigan	1999	(7)	0	0	0	0
Joe Westerman	Hull	2011	19(7)	8	20	0	72
	Castleford	2008-10	68(7)	29	151	0	418
Craig Weston	Widnes	2002, 2004	23(9)	2	1	2	12
	Huddersfield	1998-99	46(1)	15	15	0	90
Ben Westwood	Warrington	2002-11	222(8)	77	55	0	418
	Wakefield	1999-2002	31(7)	8	1	0	34
Andrew Whalley	Workington	1996	(2)	0	0	0	0
Paul Whatuira	Huddersfield	2010	59	23	0	0	92
Scott Wheeldon	Hull KR	2009-11	28(36)	4	0	0	16
	Hull	2006-08	2(60)	4	0	0	16
Gary Wheeler	St Helens	2008-11	23(8)	9	3	0	42
Matt Whitaker	Castleford	2006	8(2)	0	0	0	0
	Widnes	2004-05	10(20)	9	0	0	36
	Huddersfield	2003-04	3(14)	0	0	0	0
David White	Wakefield	2000	(1)	0	0	0	0
Josh White	Salford	1998	18(3)	5	5	1	31
	London	1997	14(2)	8	0	1	33
Lloyd White	Crusaders	2010-11	13(11)	8	0	0	32
	Celtic	2009	6	1	0	0	4
Paul White	Salford	2009	1	1	0	0	4
	Wakefield	2006-07	24(12)	12	0	0	48
	Huddersfield	2003-05	11(32)	17	16	0	100

177

Super League Players 1996-2011

PLAYER	CLUB	YEAR	APP	TRIES	GOALS	FG	PTS
Elliott Whitehead	Bradford	2009-11	48(9)	15	0	0	60
Richard Whiting	Hull	2004-11	123(33)	48	8	2	210
Danny Whittle	Warrington	1998	(2)	0	0	0	0
David Whittle	St Helens	2002	1(2)	0	0	0	0
	Warrington	2001	1(2)	0	0	0	0
Jon Whittle	Wakefield	2006	8(2)	3	0	0	12
	Widnes	2005	13	2	0	0	8
	Wigan	2003	1	0	0	0	0
Dean Widders	Castleford	2009-11	25(32)	23	0	0	92
Stephen Wild	Salford	2011	21	1	0	0	4
	Huddersfield	2006-10	116(2)	33	0	0	132
	Wigan	2001-05	67(20)	24	0	0	96
Matthew Wildie	Wakefield	2010-11	5(13)	2	0	0	8
Oliver Wilkes	Harlequins	2010-11	39(13)	4	0	0	16
	Wakefield	2008-09	41(13)	6	0	0	24
	Wigan	2006	1(5)	0	0	0	0
	Leigh	2005	13(1)	1	0	0	4
	Huddersfield	2000-01	1(6)	0	0	0	0
	Sheffield	1998	(1)	0	0	0	0
Jon Wilkin	St Helens	2003-11	172(27)	58	0	1	233
Alex Wilkinson	Hull	2003-04	11(4)	1	0	0	4
	Huddersfield	2003	8	4	0	0	16
	London	2002	5(1)	0	0	0	0
	Bradford	2000-01	3(3)	1	0	0	4
Bart Williams	London	1998	5(3)	1	0	0	4
Daley Williams	Salford	2006-07	9(2)	4	0	0	16
Danny Williams	Harlequins	2006	9(13)	4	0	0	16
	London	2005	1(16)	0	0	0	0
Danny Williams	Salford	2011	6	8	0	0	32
	Leeds	2006, 2008	13(2)	7	0	0	28
	Hull	2008	3	0	0	0	0
Dave Williams	Harlequins	2008-11	1(17)	0	0	0	0
Desi Williams	Wigan	2004	2	0	0	0	0
Jonny Williams	London	2004	(4)	0	0	0	0
Lee Williams	Crusaders	2011	1(7)	0	0	0	0
Rhys Williams	Warrington	2010-11	10(1)	7	0	0	28
	Crusaders	2011	6	3	0	0	12
Luke Williamson	Harlequins	2009-10	39	6	0	0	24
John Wilshere	Salford	2006-07, 2009	72(2)	32	142	0	412
	Leigh	2005	26	8	6	0	44
	Warrington	2004	5	2	0	0	8
Craig Wilson	Hull	2000	2(16)	1	0	1	5
	Gateshead	1999	17(11)	5	0	1	21
George Wilson	Paris	1996	7(2)	3	0	0	12
John Wilson	Catalans	2006-08	69	23	0	0	92
Richard Wilson	Hull	1998-99	(13)	0	0	0	0
Scott Wilson	Warrington	1998-99	23(2)	6	0	0	24
Johan Windley	Hull	1999	2(2)	1	0	0	4
Paul Wingfield	Warrington	1997	5(3)	6	1	0	26
Frank Winterstein	Crusaders	2010-11	26(19)	4	0	0	16
	Wakefield	2009	(5)	0	0	0	0
Lincoln Withers	Crusaders	2010-11	47	4	0	0	16
	Celtic	2009	21	6	0	0	24
Michael Withers	Wigan	2007	6(1)	1	0	0	4
	Bradford	1999-2006	156(6)	94	15	4	410
Michael Witt	Crusaders	2010-11	39	13	47	4	150
Jeff Wittenberg	Huddersfield	1998	18(1)	1	0	0	4
	Bradford	1997	8(9)	4	0	0	16
Kyle Wood	Huddersfield	2011	1(5)	0	0	0	0
	Castleford	2010	1(4)	0	0	0	0
Martin Wood	Sheffield	1997-98	24(11)	4	18	2	54
Nathan Wood	Warrington	2002-05	90	38	0	3	155
	Wakefield	2002	11	2	0	0	8
Paul Wood	Warrington	2000-11	105(141)	38	0	0	152
Phil Wood	Widnes	2004	2(1)	0	0	0	0
Darren Woods	Widnes	2005	(1)	0	0	0	0
David Woods	Halifax	2002	18(2)	8	0	0	32
Simon Worrall	Leeds	2008-09	5(16)	1	0	0	4
Michael Worrincy	Bradford	2009-10	12(34)	12	0	0	48
	Harlequins	2006-08	20(12)	10	0	0	40
Rob Worrincy	Castleford	2004	1	0	0	0	0
Troy Wozniak	Widnes	2004	13(7)	1	0	0	4
Matthew Wray	Wakefield	2002-03	13(3)	2	0	0	8
David Wrench	Wakefield	2002-06	28(52)	6	0	0	24
	Leeds	1999-2001	7(17)	0	0	0	0
Craig Wright	Castleford	2000	1(9)	0	0	0	0
Nigel Wright	Huddersfield	1999	4(6)	1	0	0	4
	Wigan	1996-97	5(5)	2	0	1	9
Ricky Wright	Sheffield	1997-99	2(13)	0	0	0	0
Vincent Wulf	Paris	1996	13(4)	4	0	0	16
Andrew Wynyard	London	1999-2000	34(6)	4	0	0	16
Bagdad Yaha	Paris	1996	4(4)	2	4	0	16
Malakai Yasa	Sheffield	1996	1(3)	0	0	0	0
Kirk Yeaman	Hull	2001-11	117(17)	124	0	0	496
Grant Young	London	1998-99	22(2)	2	0	0	8
Nick Youngquest	Castleford	2011	14	12	0	0	48
	Crusaders	2010	26(1)	9	0	0	36
Ronel Zenon	Paris	1996	(4)	0	0	0	0
Nick Zisti	Bradford	1999	6(1)	0	0	0	0
Freddie Zitter	Catalans	2006	1	0	0	0	0

NEW FACES - Players making their Super League debuts in 2011

PLAYER	CLUB	DEBUT vs	ROUND	DATE
Patrick Ah Van	Bradford	Leeds (MM)	1	13/2/11
Thibaut Ancely	Catalans	Leeds (MM)	21	10/7/11
Nathan Ashe	St Helens	Hull (a)	13	2/5/11
Chris Bailey	Harlequins	Catalans (MM)	1	12/2/11
Jason Baitieri	Catalans	Hull KR (a)	3	27/2/11
John Bateman	Bradford	Catalans (a)	12	25/4/11
Richard Beaumont	Hull KR	Harlequins (h)	12	25/4/11
Kyle Briggs	Bradford	Leeds (MM)	1	13/2/11
Tom Burgess	Bradford	Harlequins (h)	8	3/4/11
Joe Burke	Crusaders	Hull KR (h)	21	9/7/11
Hep Cahill	Crusaders	Salford (a)	8	2/4/11
Daryl Clark	Castleford	Huddersfield (h)	2	19/2/11
Adam Clay	Salford	Harlequins (a)	13	30/4/11
Jamie Cording	Huddersfield	Bradford (h)	5	13/3/11
Jordan Cox	Hull KR	Huddersfield (a)	23	30/7/11
		(first team debut: York (a), CCR4, 8/5/11)		
Ben Cross	Leeds	Bradford (MM)	1	13/2/11
Alex Davidson	Salford	Hull KR (h)	6	18/3/11
Scott Dureau	Catalans	Harlequins (MM)	1	12/2/11
Greg Eden	Castleford	Warrington (h)	20	1/7/11
		(first team debut: Rochdale (a), CCR4, 8/5/11)		
George Elliott	Leeds	Crusaders (h)	12	25/4/11
Jacob Fairbank	Huddersfield	Hull KR (h)	23	30/7/11
		(first team debut: Batley (a), CCR4, 8/5/11)		
Ben Farrar	Catalans	Harlequins (MM)	1	12/2/11
Brett Finch	Wigan	Warrington (h)	7	25/3/11
Carl Forster	St Helens	Harlequins (a)	27	10/9/11
Dalton Grant	Crusaders	Hull KR (h)	21	9/7/11
Blake Green	Hull KR	Hull (MM)	1	13/2/11
Scott Hale	St Helens	Huddersfield (h)	14	14/5/11
Zak Hardaker	Leeds	St Helens (h)	6	19/3/11
Marc Herbert	Bradford	Wakefield (h)	4	6/3/11
Jarrad Hickey	Wakefield	Salford (a)	16	3/6/11
Ryan Hoffman	Wigan	St Helens (MM)	1	12/2/11
Stuart Howarth	Wakefield	Catalans (a)	2	19/2/11
Jack Hughes	Wigan	Harlequins (h)	14	13/5/11
		(first team debut: Barrow (h), CCR4, 8/5/11)		
Willie Isa	Castleford	Bradford (MM)	6	20/3/11
Greg Johnson	Wakefield	Warrington (h)	5	11/3/11
Nick Kouparitsas	Harlequins	Catalans (MM)	1	12/2/11
Jeff Lima	Wigan	St Helens (MM)	1	12/2/11
Tom Makinson	St Helens	Salford (a)	2	18/2/11
Remy Marginet	Catalans	St Helens (a)	22	15/7/11
Callum Marriott	Salford	Hull KR (h)	6	18/3/11
Willie Mason	Hull KR	Crusaders (h)	5	13/3/11
Sammy Masselot	Wakefield	Hull KR (a)	20	3/7/11
Gregg McNally	Huddersfield	Crusaders (h)	20	3/7/11
Joe Mellor	Harlequins	St Helens (a)	5	11/3/11
Jon Molloy	Huddersfield	Harlequins (a)	4	4/3/11
Joel Monaghan	Warrington	Huddersfield (MM)	1	12/2/11
Gareth Moore	Wakefield	Salford (a)	16	3/6/11
Jamie Murphy	Crusaders	Hull KR (a)	5	13/3/11
Adam O'Brien	Bradford	Huddersfield (a)	5	13/3/11
Gareth O'Brien	Warrington	Castleford (h)	14	13/5/11
		(first team debut: Keighley (h), CCR4, 8/5/11)		
Luke O'Donnell	Huddersfield	Warrington (MM)	1	12/2/11
Lopini Paea	Catalans	Harlequins (MM)	1	12/2/11
Mathias Pala	Catalans	Bradford (h)	12	25/4/11
Luke Patten	Salford	Crusaders (MM)	1	13/2/11
Eloi Pelissier	Catalans	Wakefield (h)	2	19/2/11
Josh Perry	St Helens	Harlequins (h)	5	11/3/11
Shad Royston	Bradford	Leeds (MM)	1	13/2/11
Dan Sarginson	Harlequins	Salford (a)	20	3/7/11
		(first team debut: Gateshead (a), CCR4, 6/5/11)		
Louis Sheriff	Hull KR	Harlequins (h)	12	25/4/11
Jamie Simpson	Huddersfield	Bradford (h)	5	13/3/11
Brad Singleton	Leeds	Salford (h)	5	11/3/11
Russ Spiers	Wakefield	Castleford (MM)	1	12/2/11
Rob Thomas	Harlequins	Bradford (a)	8	3/4/11
Ryan Tongia	Wakefield	Warrington (a)	24	14/8/11
Josh Veivers	Wakefield	Castleford (MM)	1	12/2/11
Lucas Walshaw	Wakefield	Leeds (a)	26	2/9/11
Lee Williams	Crusaders	Salford (h)	19	24/6/11
		(first team debut: Eastmoor Dragons (h), CCR3, 10/3/07)		

OLD FACES - Players making their debuts for new clubs in 2011

PLAYER	CLUB	DEBUT vs	ROUND	DATE
Shaun Ainscough	Bradford	Crusaders (a)	3	26/2/11
Luke Ambler	Harlequins	Catalans (MM)	1	12/2/11
Kyle Amor	Wakefield	Salford (h)	3	27/2/11
Vinnie Anderson	Salford	Crusaders (h)	8	2/4/11
Martin Aspinwall	Castleford	Huddersfield (h)	2	19/2/11
Damien Blanch	Catalans	Harlequins (MM)	1	12/2/11
Andy Bracek	Crusaders	Bradford (a)	26	4/9/11
Kyle Briggs	Harlequins	Wakefield (h)	18	18/6/11
Mike Burnett	Harlequins	Catalans (MM)	1	12/2/11
Mark Calderwood	Harlequins	St Helens (a)	5	11/3/11
Ben Cross	Wigan	Wakefield (h)	22	15/7/11
Ben Davies	Castleford	Crusaders (a)	22	16/7/11
Chris Dean	Wakefield	Castleford (MM)	1	12/2/11
Matt Diskin	Bradford	Leeds (MM)	1	13/2/11
Olivier Elima	Bradford	Leeds (MM)	1	13/2/11
Jake Emmitt	Castleford	Wakefield (MM)	1	12/2/11
Dale Ferguson	Huddersfield	Harlequins (a)	4	4/3/11
Nick Fozzard	Castleford	Catalans (h)	5	12/3/11
Martin Gleeson	Hull	Hull KR (h)	11	22/4/11
Sean Gleeson	Salford	Hull KR (h)	6	18/3/11
Wayne Godwin	Salford	Crusaders (MM)	1	13/2/11
Josh Griffin	Wakefield	Bradford (a)	4	6/3/11
Craig Hall	Hull KR	Catalans (a)	3	27/2/11
Bryn Hargreaves	Bradford	Leeds (MM)	1	13/2/11
Weller Hauraki	Leeds	Hull (a)	2	18/2/11
Ian Henderson	Catalans	Harlequins (MM)	1	12/2/11
Liam Higgins	Wakefield	Huddersfield (a)	8	3/4/11
Brett Hodgson	Warrington	Huddersfield (MM)	1	12/2/11
Ben Jeffries	Bradford	Hull KR (a) (D2)	14	15/5/11
Paul Johnson	Crusaders	Salford (MM)	1	13/2/11
Paul Johnson	Wakefield	Castleford (MM)	1	12/2/11
Ben Jones-Bishop	Leeds	Bradford (MM) (D2)	1	13/2/11
Tommy Lee	Wakefield	Castleford (MM)	1	12/2/11
Frankie Mariano	Wakefield	Catalans (a)	2	19/2/11
Richard Mathers	Castleford	Wakefield (MM)	1	12/2/11
Tyrone McCarthy	Wakefield	Huddersfield (a)	8	3/4/11
Louie McCarthy-Scarsbrook	St Helens	Wigan (MM)	1	12/2/11
Steve Menzies	Catalans	Harlequins (MM)	1	12/2/11
Darryl Millard	Catalans	Hull KR (a)	3	27/2/11
Lee Mitchell	Harlequins	Hull KR (a)	12	25/4/11
Richard Moore	Crusaders	Salford (MM)	1	13/2/11
Chris Nero	Salford	Crusaders (MM)	1	13/2/11
Sam Obst	Hull	Leeds (h)	2	18/2/11
Danny Orr	Castleford	Wakefield (MM) (D2)	1	12/2/11
Iafeta Palea'aesina	Salford	Crusaders (MM)	1	13/2/11
Rob Parker	Castleford	Wigan (a)	3	6/7/11
Kevin Penny	Wakefield	Catalans (a)	2	19/2/11
Cameron Phelps	Hull	Wigan (a)	5	13/3/11
Karl Pryce	Harlequins	Leeds (a)	3	25/2/11
Gareth Raynor	Bradford	Leeds (MM)	1	13/2/11
Stuart Reardon	Crusaders	Salford (MM)	1	13/2/11
Chris Riley	Harlequins	Castleford (a)	15	29/5/11
Will Sharp	Hull	Hull KR (MM)	1	13/2/11
Michael Shenton	St Helens	Wigan (MM)	1	12/2/11
Ian Sibbit	Bradford	Leeds (MM)	1	13/2/11
Jeremy Smith	Wakefield	Salford (h)	3	27/2/11
Semi Tadulala	Wakefield	Hull KR (a) (D2)	20	3/7/11
Jordan Tansey	Crusaders	Castleford (a)	7	27/3/11
Motu Tony	Wakefield	Huddersfield (h)	17	12/6/11
Chev Walker	Bradford	Leeds (MM)	1	13/2/11
Joe Wardle	Huddersfield	Wigan (h)	6	18/3/11
Joe Westerman	Hull	Hull KR (MM)	1	13/2/11
Stephen Wild	Salford	Crusaders (MM)	1	13/2/11
Danny Williams	Salford	Hull KR (a)	22	17/7/11
Rhys Williams	Crusaders	Salford (MM)	1	13/2/11
Kyle Wood	Huddersfield	Hull (h)	3	27/2/11
Nick Youngquest	Castleford	Wakefield (MM)	1	12/2/11

SUPER LEAGUE XVI
Club by Club

11 November 2010 - Danny Sculthorpe leaves the club by mutual consent.

12 November 2010 - Michael Worrincy joins NRL club Penrith Panthers for 2011.

22 December 2010 - Wayne Godwin signs for Salford.

28 December 2010 - George Burgess leaves to join brother Sam at South Sydney Rabbitohs.

6 January 2011 - Glenn Hall granted early release after one year of three-year contract.

12 January 2011 - stand-off Kyle Briggs signs from Featherstone on two-year deal.

17 January 2011 - Matt Orford released from remaining two years of three-year contract.

30 January 2011 - 40-16 home victory over Wakefield in final pre-season game.

13 February 2011 - last-minute 32-28 round-one defeat by Leeds Rhinos at Millennium Stadium, Cardiff.

20 February 2011 - 44-10 home defeat by Wigan in round 2.

26 February 2011 - Heath L'Estrange suffers ankle ligament damage in 30-26 round three win at Crusaders.

6 March 2011 - Marc Herbert makes debut and Craig Kopczak scores hat-trick in 40-18 home win over Wakefield.

25 March 2011 - Nick Scruton dislocates wrist in 28-16 defeat by St Helens at Stobart Stadium, Widnes.

28 March 2011 - Nick Scruton signs three-year contract to end of 2014.

3 April 2011 - Danny Addy fractures thumb in 24-22 home victory over Harlequins.

11 April 2011 - Tom Olbison signs four-year contract to end of 2014.

14 April 2011 - Michael Platt signs new two-year contract.

21 April 2011 - Brett Kearney breaks hand in 30-22 home defeat to Leeds Rhinos.

25 April 2011 - 8-8 Easter Monday draw with Catalan Dragons in Perpignan.

1 May 2011 - Shaun Ainscough suffers ankle injury in 58-14 home defeat by Warrington.

7 May 2011 - Ben Jeffries re-signs from Wakefield on 18-month deal.

8 May 2011 - Chev Walker breaks ankle in 46-34 Cup victory at Halifax.

15 May 2011 - 46-18 defeat at Hull KR leaves Bulls in 12th spot.

KEY DATES - BRADFORD BULLS

22 May 2011 - Gareth Raynor gets two-match ban, sent off in 26-22 home Cup defeat by Wigan.

29 May 2011 - 28-14 home victory against Salford.

4 June 2011 - 30-16 victory at Harlequins.

6 June 2011 - Heath L'Estrange signs new three-year contract to end of 2014.

12 June 2011 - Heath L'Estrange's season ends when he ruptures knee ligaments in 14-14 home draw with St Helens.

15 June 2011 - Kyle Briggs joins Harlequins on month's loan.

17 June 2011 - St George Illawarra centre Keith Lulia signs two-year contract from 2012.

19 June 2011 - Nick Scruton returns in 28-14 home defeat by Hull FC.

21 June 2011 - Shaun Ainscough undergoes ankle surgery.

27 June 2011 - Brett Kearney signs new two-year contract with additional 12-month option.

30 June 2011 - Dave Halley released and joins Keighley.

16 July 2011 - Gareth Raynor signs new one-year contract to end of 2012 season.

22 July 2011 - Harlequins scrum-half Luke Gale joins on two-year contract from 2012.

28 July 2011 - Crusaders halfback Jarrod Sammut signs one-year contract for 2012.

1 August 2011 - Patrick Ah Van to leave at end of season to join Widnes.

3 August 2011 - Penrith Panthers back Adrian Purtell signs on three-year deal from 2012.

5 August 2011 - Matt Diskin out for season after surgery on shoulder injury.

11 August 2011 - Shaun Ainscough agrees one-year contract extension for 2012.

11 August 2011 - Shad Royston turns down contract offer to join French side Pia.

16 August 2011 - Elliott Whitehead gets five-match ban for biting Hull KR's Jordan Cox in previous Sunday's 34-8 home defeat to Hull KR.

19 August 2011 - Marc Herbert breaks hand in 60-12 defeat at Wigan.

23 August 2011 - Nick Scruton's season over after undergoing surgery to repair ligament damage to wrist.

11 September 2011 - Chev Walker signs new one-year contract for 2012.

12 September 2011 - 17-year-old stand-off Marcus Elliott joins from Rhinos Academy on two-year contract.

13 September 2011 - chairman Peter Hood apologises to fans for disappointing season after round 27 defeat at Wakefield means 10th placed finish.

22 September 2011 - Andy Lynch released from last year of contract to join Hull FC; Gareth Raynor's contract ended with immediate effect following breach of club discipline.

7 October 2011 - Welsh international Elliot Kear signs on three-year contract.

15 October 2011 - Parramatta prop Manase Manuokafoa signs one-year deal.

CLUB RECORDS
Highest score: 98-6 v Toulouse, 19/4/2008 **Highest score against:** 18-75 v Leeds, 14/9/31 **Record attendance:** 69,429 v Huddersfield (CC), 14/3/53
MATCH RECORDS
Tries: 6 Eric Batten v Leeds, 15/9/45 Trevor Foster v Wakefield, 10/4/48 Steve McGowan v Barrow, 8/11/92 Lesley Vainikolo v Hull, 2/9/2005 **Goals:** 15 Iestyn Harris v Toulouse, 15/4/2008 **Points:** 36 John Woods v Swinton, 13/10/85
SEASON RECORDS
Tries: 63 Jack McLean 1951-52 **Goals:** 213 *(inc 5fg)* Henry Paul 2001 **Points:** 457 Henry Paul 2001
CAREER RECORDS
Tries: 261 Jack McLean 1950-56 **Goals:** 1,165 *(inc 25fg)* Paul Deacon 1998-2009 **Points:** 2,605 Paul Deacon 1998-2009 **Appearances:** 588 Keith Mumby 1973-90; 1992-93

BRADFORD BULLS

DATE	FIXTURE	RESULT	SCORERS	LGE	ATT
13/2/11	Leeds (MM) ●	L28-32	t:Whitehead(3),Ah Van,Diskin g:Ah Van(4)	8th	N/A
20/2/11	Wigan (h)	L10-44	t:Whitehead,Ah Van g:Ah Van	11th	15,348
26/2/11	Crusaders (a)	W26-30	t:Lynch,Royston,Ainscough,Diskin,L'Estrange g:Ah Van(5)	10th	2,615
6/3/11	Wakefield (h)	W40-18	t:Olbison,Royston(2),Kopczak(3),Ainscough g:Ah Van(6)	8th	12,835
13/3/11	Huddersfield (a)	L50-16	t:Ainscough,Herbert,Raynor g:Ah Van(2)	9th	9,466
20/3/11	Castleford (h)	W18-14	t:Elima,Scruton(2) g:Ah Van(3)	8th	14,348
25/3/11	St Helens (a)	L28-16	t:Ainscough(2),Ah Van g:Ah Van(2)	8th	7,676
3/4/11	Harlequins (h)	W24-22	t:Elima,Diskin,Kearney,Sykes g:Ah Van(4)	7th	12,354
8/4/11	Hull FC (a)	L34-24	t:Sykes,Royston(2),Walker g:Ah Van(4)	8th	11,346
16/4/11	Salford (a)	L56-16	t:Lynch,Herbert(2) g:Herbert(2)	10th	2,809
21/4/11	Leeds (h)	L22-30	t:Ah Van,Lynch,Elima(2) g:Ah Van(3)	10th	19,275
25/4/11	Catalan Dragons (a)	D8-8	t:L'Estrange g:Ah Van(2)	10th	9,496
1/5/11	Warrington (h)	L14-58	t:Kopczak,Lynch,Whitehead g:Ah Van	11th	14,134
8/5/11	Halifax (a) (CCR4)	W34-46	t:Royston,Raynor(2),Platt,Whitehead,Ah Van,Burgess,Sibbit g:Ah Van(7)	N/A	5,045
15/5/11	Hull KR (a)	L46-18	t:Briggs,Raynor,Lynch g:Ah Van(3)	12th	7,923
22/5/11	Wigan (h) (CCR5)	L22-26	t:Whitehead,Ah Van(2),Royston g:Ah Van(3)	N/A	5,828
29/5/11	Salford (h)	W28-14	t:Briggs(2),Sykes,L'Estrange,Jeffries g:Ah Van(4)	9th	12,487
4/6/11	Harlequins (a)	W16-30	t:Ah Van(2),Royston,Whitehead,Lynch g:Ah Van(5)	9th	4,253
12/6/11	St Helens (h)	D14-14	t:Kearney,Lynch g:Ah Van(3)	10th	13,224
19/6/11	Hull FC (h)	L14-28	t:Royston(2),Lynch g:Ah Van	10th	14,414
24/6/11	Leeds (a)	W12-18	t:Elima(2) g:Ah Van(5)	10th	18,095
2/7/11	Catalan Dragons (h)	L28-34	t:Elima,Burgess,Jeffries,Raynor g:Ah Van(6)	11th	12,670
10/7/11	Castleford (a)	L34-30	t:Kearney(2),Raynor,Royston,Sykes g:Ah Van(5)	11th	7,004
17/7/11	Huddersfield (h)	W36-0	t:Jeffries,Sykes(2),Platt,Ah Van,Kearney g:Ah Van(4),Sykes(2)	10th	14,047
31/7/11	Warrington (a)	L64-6	t:Ah Van g:Ah Van	11th	10,641
14/8/11	Hull KR (h)	L8-34	t:Herbert g:Ah Van(2)	10th	13,441
19/8/11	Wigan (a)	L60-12	t:Kopczak,Bateman g:Ah Van(2)	11th	13,940
4/9/11	Crusaders (h)	W48-24	t:Elima(2),Kearney(2),Kopczak,Ainscough,Ah Van,Lynch g:Ah Van(8)	11th	12,998
9/9/11	Wakefield (a)	L26-14	t:Briggs,Ainscough,Royston g:Ah Van	10th	6,502

● Played at Millennium Stadium, Cardiff

	D.O.B.	APP ALL	APP SL	TRIES ALL	TRIES SL	GOALS ALL	GOALS SL	FG ALL	FG SL	PTS ALL	PTS SL
Danny Addy	15/1/91	5(9)	5(9)	0	0	0	0	0	0	0	0
Patrick Ah Van	17/3/88	28	26	12	9	97	87	0	0	242	210
Shaun Ainscough	27/11/89	11	11	7	7	0	0	0	0	28	28
John Bateman	30/9/93	2(2)	2(1)	1	1	0	0	0	0	4	4
Kyle Briggs	7/12/87	8	6	4	4	0	0	0	0	16	16
Tom Burgess	21/4/92	1(19)	1(17)	2	1	0	0	0	0	8	4
Jason Crookes	21/4/90	6	6	0	0	0	0	0	0	0	0
Steve Crossley	28/11/89	(2)	(2)	0	0	0	0	0	0	0	0
Matt Diskin	27/1/82	17(7)	17(6)	3	3	0	0	0	0	12	12
James Donaldson	14/9/91	5(7)	4(7)	0	0	0	0	0	0	0	0
Olivier Elima	19/5/83	26	25	9	9	0	0	0	0	36	36
Bryn Hargreaves	14/11/85	20(6)	19(5)	0	0	0	0	0	0	0	0
Marc Herbert	7/1/87	21	20	4	4	2	2	0	0	20	20
Ben Jeffries	4/9/80	15	14	3	3	0	0	0	0	12	12
Brett Kearney	29/9/83	21	21	7	7	0	0	0	0	28	28
Craig Kopczak	20/12/86	12(16)	11(15)	6	6	0	0	0	0	24	24
Jamie Langley	21/12/83	14(1)	13(1)	0	0	0	0	0	0	0	0
Heath L'Estrange	21/5/85	8(8)	6(8)	3	3	0	0	0	0	12	12
Andy Lynch	20/10/79	29	27	9	9	0	0	0	0	36	36
Adam O'Brien	11/7/93	(6)	(5)	0	0	0	0	0	0	0	0
Tom Olbison	20/3/91	9(7)	9(6)	1	1	0	0	0	0	4	4
Michael Platt	23/3/84	19(2)	17(2)	2	1	0	0	0	0	8	4
Gareth Raynor	24/2/78	20	18	6	4	0	0	0	0	24	16
Shad Royston	29/11/82	19(1)	17(1)	12	10	0	0	0	0	48	40
Nick Scruton	24/12/84	1(13)	1(13)	2	2	0	0	0	0	8	8
Ian Sibbit	15/10/80	11(5)	9(5)	1	0	0	0	0	0	4	0
Paul Sykes	11/8/81	16	16	6	6	2	2	0	0	28	28
Chev Walker	9/10/82	10(2)	9(2)	1	1	0	0	0	0	4	4
Elliott Whitehead	4/9/89	23(3)	21(3)	8	6	0	0	0	0	32	24

Andy Lynch

LEAGUE RECORD
P27-W9-D2-L16
(10th, SL)
F570, A826, Diff-256
20 points.

CHALLENGE CUP
Round Five

ATTENDANCES
Best - v Leeds (SL - 19,275)
Worst - v Wigan (CC - 5,828)
Total (SL only) - 181,575
Average (SL only) - 13,967
(Up by 5,531 on 2010)

11 November 2010 - prop Jonathan Walker signs two-year contract extension; Huddersfield release Martin Aspinwall to join on one-year deal.

15 December 2010 - Melbourne Storm centre Willie Isa joins on one-year deal from 2011.

17 December 2010 - The Jungle renamed the Probiz Coliseum on back of new sponsorship deal.

31 January 2011 - 22-20 home defeat by Hull FC in final warm-up game.

12 February 2011 - 40-20 round-one victory over Wakefield Wildcats at Millennium Stadium.

19 February 2011 - 17-year-old Daryl Clark makes debut in 18-12 home victory over Huddersfield.

25 February 2011 - Jordan Thompson joins York on month's loan.

12 March 2011 - 34-24 home victory over Catalan Dragons makes it four from four.

17 March 2011 - Craig Huby signs three-year contract extension to end of 2014.

20 March 2011 - 18-14 defeat by Bradford at Odsal ends winning start.

7 April 2011 - planning consent given for new stadium at Glasshoughton.

10 April 2011 - leading tryscorer Nick Youngquest suffers knee injury in 52-20 home victory over Salford.

15 April 2011 - last-minute Kirk Dixon penalty goal secures 26-26 draw at Harlequins.

22 April 2011 - shock 28-24 Good Friday home defeat by Wakefield.

25 April 2011 - Craig Huby fractures knee cap in 22-20 Easter Monday defeat at St Helens as Francis Meli scores seven seconds from time.

8 May 2011 - 72-10 win at Rochdale in Challenge Cup fourth round.

13 May 2011 - 62-0 defeat at Warrington.

21 May 2011 - long-range Kirk Dixon penalty ten minutes into golden-point time secures 20-18 Challenge Cup fifth round win at Wakefield.

29 May 2011 - Rangi Chase scores four second-half tries in 56-24 home victory over Harlequins.

5 June 2011 - Jonathan Walker dislocates knee in 40-18 defeat against Huddersfield at the Shay. Tigers play in Halifax shirts after kit mix up.

16 June 2011 - Martin Aspinwall jailed for four months for dangerous driving offence.

17 June 2011 - Castleford fined £500 for kit mix-up two weeks before.

25 June 2011 - 54-20 hammering by Catalan Dragons in Perpignan.

KEY DATES - CASTLEFORD TIGERS

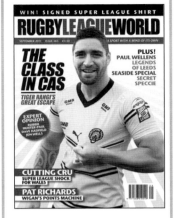

1 July 2011 - Rob Parker joins on month's loan from Salford.

4 July 2011 - Terry Matterson to leave at end of season after six years as head coach.

4 July 2011 - Kirk Dixon signs three-year contract extension to end of 2014 season.

5 July 2011 - Danny Orr signs new deal for 2012.

7 July 2011 - Jordan Thompson signs new deal taking him to end of 2013.

8 July 2011 - Wigan prop Ben Davies joins on month's loan.

13 July 2011 - Rangi Chase has two-game ban, for punching during 34-30 home win over Bradford the previous Sunday, halved on appeal.

24 July 2011 - 22-18 home win over Huddersfield in Challenge Cup quarter-final.

26 July 2011 - Tigers awarded grade C licence for 2012 to 2015.

31 July 2011 - John Davies banned for one game for dangerous contact in 46-26 home defeat by St Helens.

7 August 2011 - 10-8 Cup semi-final exit to Leeds after Kevin Sinfield golden-point penalty.

11 August 2011 - Stuart Jones signs new one-year contract.

18 August 2011 - Nathan Massey signs two-year contract; Paul Jackson one year.

31 August 2011 - Ian Millward appointed head coach from 2012 on three-year deal.

2 September 2011 - Willie Isa to leave at end of season to join Widnes.

3 September 2011 - Ryan McGoldrick gets two-match ban for high tackle in 50-18 home defeat by Hull FC.

5 September 2011 - young winger Greg Eden turns down new two-year contract to join Huddersfield.

10 September 2011 - 26-24, round 27 defeat at Hull KR, knocks Tigers out of play-off spots.

13 September 2011 - Rangi Chase awarded Albert Goldthorpe Medal.

14 September 2011 - assistant coach Andy Hay departs club.

20 September 2011 - Terry Matterson to join North Queensland Cowboys as assistant.

27 September 2011 - Rangi Chase signs two-year contract extension to end of 2015.

30 September 2011 - Wakefield outside back Josh Griffin joins on one-year deal; Richard Owen signs new four-year contract.

3 October 2011 - Rangi Chase wins Man of Steel and commits international future to England.

5 October 2011 - Leigh prop Steve Nash joins on two-year deal.

6 October 2011 - Adam Milner signs new contract to end of 2014.

7 October 2011 - academy products James Clare, Ben Johnson and Charlie Martin sign full-time contracts.

20 October 2011 – Daryl Clark signs new five-year deal to end of 2016.

3 November 2011 - Stuart Donlan appointed new assistant coach.

CLUB RECORDS

Highest score:
106-0 v Rochdale, 9/9/2007
Highest score against:
12-76 v Leeds, 14/8/2009
Record attendance:
25,449 v Hunslet (CC), 9/3/35

MATCH RECORDS

Tries:
5 Derek Foster v Hunslet, 10/11/72
John Joyner v Millom, 16/9/73
Steve Fenton v Dewsbury, 27/1/78
Ian French v Hunslet, 9/2/86
St John Ellis v Whitehaven, 10/12/89
Goals: 17 Sammy Lloyd v Millom, 16/9/73
Points: 43 Sammy Lloyd v Millom, 16/9/73

SEASON RECORDS

Tries: 40 St John Ellis 1993-94
Goals: 158 Sammy Lloyd 1976-77
Points: 334 Bob Beardmore 1983-84

CAREER RECORDS

Tries: 206 Alan Hardisty 1958-71
Goals: 875 Albert Lunn 1951-63
Points: 1,870 Albert Lunn 1951-63
Appearances: 613 John Joyner 1973-92

CASTLEFORD TIGERS

DATE	FIXTURE	RESULT	SCORERS	LGE	ATT
12/2/11	Wakefield (MM) ●	W40-20	t:Arundel,Ferres,Youngquest,Widders(2),Chase,Milner,Jackson g:Dixon(4)	1st	N/A
19/2/11	Huddersfield (h)	W18-12	t:Youngquest(2),Arundel g:Dixon(3)	1st	5,992
6/3/11	Hull KR (h)	W27-14	t:Holmes,Youngquest,Clark,Dixon g:Dixon(5) fg:Chase	1st	8,537
12/3/11	Catalan Dragons (h)	W34-24	t:Huby,Jones,Dixon,Chase,Youngquest,Arundel g:Dixon(5)	2nd	4,889
20/3/11	Bradford (a)	L18-14	t:Chase,Clark g:Dixon(3)	3rd	14,348
27/3/11	Crusaders (h)	W56-16	t:Dixon(2),Clark(2),Widders,Ferres,Isa,Mathers,Youngquest,Arundel g:Dixon(8)	2nd	6,030
1/4/11	Hull FC (a)	W18-20	t:Owen,Isa(2) g:Dixon(4)	3rd	11,856
10/4/11	Salford (h)	W52-20	t:Youngquest(2),Dixon,Mathers,Arundel(2),Widders,Clark,Owen g:Dixon(8)	1st	6,741
15/4/11	Harlequins (a)	D26-26	t:Owen(2),Chase,Clark g:Dixon(5)	3rd	4,128
22/4/11	Wakefield (h)	L24-28	t:Mathers,Aspinwall,Thompson,Orr g:Dixon(4)	4th	9,020
25/4/11	St Helens (a)	L22-20	t:Jones,Chase,Thompson g:Dixon(4)	5th	8,010
29/4/11	Leeds (h)	L6-48	t:Arundel g:Dixon	5th	9,860
8/5/11	Rochdale (a) (CCR4)	W10-72	t:Dixon(2),Arundel(2),Chase,Snitch(2),Clark(2),Massey(2),Milner,Owen g:Dixon(9),Orr	N/A	1,675
13/5/11	Warrington (a)	L62-0		6th	10,715
21/5/11	Wakefield (a) (CCR5)	W18-20 (aet)	t:Ferres,Chase,Orr g:Dixon(4)	N/A	6,604
29/5/11	Harlequins (h)	W56-24	t:Dixon,Mathers,Thompson,Owen,Chase(4),Clark,Milner g:Dixon(8)	6th	7,072
5/6/11	Huddersfield (a) ●●	L40-18	t:Owen(2),Orr g:Dixon(3)	7th	5,237
12/6/11	Wigan (h)	D22-22	t:Widders,Arundel(2),Aspinwall,Mathers g:Dixon	7th	7,263
17/6/11	Salford (a)	W8-15	t:Thompson,Orr g:Dixon(3) fg:Chase	7th	3,587
25/6/11	Catalan Dragons (a)	L54-20	t:Owen(2),Widders,Mathers g:Dixon(2)	7th	8,695
1/7/11	Warrington (h)	L18-48	t:Ferres,Chase,Hudson,Eden g:Orr	7th	5,947
6/7/11	Wigan (a)	L26-16	t:Jones,Owen,J Davies g:Arundel(2)	7th	13,096
10/7/11	Bradford (h)	W34-30	t:Milner,Arundel(2),Chase,Parker,Jones g:Dixon(5)	6th	7,004
16/7/11	Crusaders (a)	W20-26	t:Thompson,Youngquest,B Davies,Parker g:Dixon(5)	6th	3,055
24/7/11	Huddersfield (h) (CCQF)	W22-18	t:Dixon,Thompson,Orr,Hudson g:Dixon(3)	N/A	6,336
31/7/11	St Helens (h)	L26-46	t:Chase,Dixon,Youngquest,Owen,Widders g:Dixon(3)	7th	6,802
7/8/11	Leeds (CCSF) ●●●	L8-10 (aet)	t:Chase g:Dixon(2)	N/A	13,158
12/8/11	Leeds (a)	L56-0		7th	15,156
20/8/11	Wakefield (a)	W30-34	t:Mathers,Isa(2),B Davies,Youngquest,Widders g:Orr(5)	7th	6,784
3/9/11	Hull FC (h)	L18-50	t:Orr,Youngquest,Isa g:Orr(3)	9th	7,866
10/9/11	Hull KR (a)	L26-24	t:Orr,Owen,Snitch,Thompson g:Orr(4)	9th	8,936

● Played at Millennium Stadium, Cardiff   ●● Played at The Shay, Halifax   ●●● Played at Keepmoat Stadium, Doncaster

		APP		TRIES		GOALS		FG		PTS	
	D.O.B.	ALL	SL	ALL	SL	ALL	SL	ALL	SL	ALL	SL
Joe Arundel	22/8/91	30	26	13	11	2	2	0	0	56	48
Martin Aspinwall	21/10/81	13(6)	12(6)	2	2	0	0	0	0	8	8
Rangi Chase	11/4/86	28(1)	24(1)	15	12	0	0	2	2	62	50
Daryl Clark	10/2/93	1(20)	1(17)	9	7	0	0	0	0	36	28
Ben Davies	2/11/89	3(4)	3(2)	2	2	0	0	0	0	8	8
John Davies	8/1/91	(5)	(5)	1	1	0	0	0	0	4	4
Kirk Dixon	19/7/84	25	21	10	7	102	84	0	0	244	196
Greg Eden	14/11/90	3	2	1	1	0	0	0	0	4	4
Jake Emmitt	4/10/88	17(5)	15(5)	0	0	0	0	0	0	0	0
Brett Ferres	17/4/86	25(1)	22(1)	4	3	0	0	0	0	16	12
Nick Fozzard	22/7/77	9(10)	7(10)	0	0	0	0	0	0	0	0
Oliver Holmes	7/8/92	16(3)	14(3)	1	1	0	0	0	0	4	4
Craig Huby	21/5/86	9(2)	9(2)	1	1	0	0	0	0	4	4
Ryan Hudson	20/11/79	18(3)	15(2)	2	1	0	0	0	0	8	4
Willie Isa	1/1/89	8(3)	7(2)	6	6	0	0	0	0	24	24
Paul Jackson	29/9/78	16(5)	14(5)	1	1	0	0	0	0	4	4
Stuart Jones	7/12/81	23	21	4	4	0	0	0	0	16	16
Nathan Massey	11/7/89	5(10)	5(7)	2	0	0	0	0	0	8	0
Richard Mathers	24/10/83	22(1)	21(1)	7	7	0	0	0	0	28	28
Ryan McGoldrick	12/1/81	15(1)	12(1)	0	0	0	0	0	0	0	0
Adam Milner	19/12/91	19(3)	16(3)	4	3	0	0	0	0	16	12
Danny Orr	17/5/78	28(1)	25	7	5	14	13	0	0	56	46
Richard Owen	25/4/90	24	20	13	12	0	0	0	0	52	48
Rob Parker	5/9/81	6(2)	4(2)	2	2	0	0	0	0	8	8
Steve Snitch	22/2/83	8(6)	7(5)	3	1	0	0	0	0	12	4
Jordan Thompson	4/9/91	10(8)	9(5)	7	6	0	0	0	0	28	24
Jonathan Walker	20/2/91	(5)	(5)	0	0	0	0	0	0	0	0
Dean Widders	25/10/79	6(19)	5(18)	8	8	0	0	0	0	32	32
Nick Youngquest	28/7/83	16	14	12	12	0	0	0	0	48	48

Rangi Chase

LEAGUE RECORD
P27-W12-D2-L13
(9th, SL)
F664, A808, Diff-144
26 points.

CHALLENGE CUP
Semi-Finalists

ATTENDANCES
Best - v Leeds (SL - 9,860)
Worst - v Catalan Dragons
(SL - 4,889)
Total (SL only) - 93,023
Average (SL only) - 7,156
(Up by 540 on 2010)

22 November 2010 - Dane Carlaw released from remaining 12 months of contract.

22 January 2011 - 34-22 home defeat to Crusaders in pre-season clash.

2 February 2011 - young hooker Eloi Pelissier signs new two-year deal.

9 February 2011 - France prop Remi Casty signs new four-year contract until end 2014.

12 February 2011 - 11-4 round-one defeat by Harlequins in Cardiff.

16 February 2011 - Darryl Millard signs from Wakefield Wildcats.

19 February 2011 - shock 38-14 home defeat by Wakefield Wildcats.

27 February 2011 - 31-18 round 3 victory over Hull KR at Craven Park is first of season.

5 March 2011 - 22-16 home defeat to St Helens.

12 March 2011 - Lopini Paea damages ankle ligaments in 34-24 defeat at Castleford.

18 March 2011 - Scott Dureau stars in 32-22 victory over Crusaders in Wrexham.

26 March 2011 - Scott Dureau misses 22-10 home defeat by Salford with sickness bug.

3 April 2011 - Clint Greenshields suffers rib dislocation in shock 22-20 victory at Warrington.

8 April 2011 - Scott Dureau stars in stunning 47-28 victory at Wigan.

16 April 2011 - 28-10 home victory over Hull FC is first of season at Gilbert Brutus.

22 April 2011 - Steve Menzies damages hamstring in 37-30 round 11 Good Friday victory at Harlequins.

25 April 2011 - Thomas Bosc makes comeback in 8-8 home draw with Bradford after eight months out with knee problem.

30 April 2011 - monster Scott Dureau field goal seals 13-12 home victory over Huddersfield.

6 May 2011 - Ben Farrar and Remi Casty suffer knee injuries as Dragons scrape 22-16 Cup win at Championship leaders Leigh.

13 May 2011 - 30-6 defeat at Leeds.

22 May 2011 - Lopini Paea back but Cyril Stacul breaks ankle in round five 30-16 Challenge Cup defeat at Huddersfield.

23 May 2011 - William Barthau joins Dewsbury on dual registration.

KEY DATES - CATALAN DRAGONS

29 May 2011 - Clint Greenshields makes comeback in 42-22 victory at Wakefield.

4 June 2011 - Steve Menzies back for 20-12 round-16 victory over Wigan in Montpellier.

11 June 2011 - 31-18 home victory over Crusaders consolidates fifth spot.

18 June 2011 - Sebastien Raguin suspended for one game for dangerous tackle in 28-20 defeat at Huddersfield.

25 June 2011 - Remi Casty makes comeback in 54-20 home thrashing of Castleford. Setaimata Sa suffers hamstring injury.

27 June 2011 - League Express reveals Louis Anderson has signed from Warrington for 2012 on a three-year contract.

1 July 2011 - Darryl Millard signs contract for 2012.

5 July 2011 - David Ferriol gets three-match ban after being sent off in previous Saturday's 34-28 win at Bradford for high tackle on James Donaldson.

6 July 2011 - Clint Greenshields signs new 12-month contract.

7 July 2011 - Steve Menzies ends speculation by signing new 12-month contract.

14 July 2011 - Setaimata Sa signs new 12-month contract.

26 July 2011 - Dragons awarded B licence for 2012 to 2015.

2 August 2011 - Jean-Philippe Baile and Cyrille Gossard sign new two-year contracts; William Barthau one year.

3 August 2011 - Thomas Bosc and Greg Mounis sign new two-year contracts.

23 August 2011 - Saints' Leon Pryce signs three-year deal from 2012.

8 September 2011 - Ben Farrar, out since May with knee injury, declines second year option and is released.

17 September 2011 - 56-6 home Elimination Play-off win over Hull KR.

20 September 2011- David Ferriol banned for one game for running with knees in win over Hull KR.

25 September 2011 - 44-0 defeat at Wigan in Preliminary Semi-final ends Dragons' season.

CLUB RECORDS

Highest score:
74-12 v Batley, 29/5/2010
Highest score against:
12-60 v Leeds, 15/9/2006
Record attendance: 18,150 v Warrington
(in Barcelona), 20/6/2009

MATCH RECORDS

Tries:
4 Justin Murphy v Warrington, 13/9/2008
Goals:
11 Thomas Bosc v Featherstone, 31/3/2007
11 Thomas Bosc v Batley, 29/5/2010
Points:
26 Thomas Bosc v Featherstone, 31/3/2007

SEASON RECORDS

Tries: 27 Justin Murphy 2006
Goals: 123 Thomas Bosc 2008
Points: 275 Thomas Bosc 2008

CAREER RECORDS

Tries: 67 Clint Greenshields 2007-2011
Goals:
351 *(inc 5fg)* Thomas Bosc 2006-2011
Points: 839 Thomas Bosc 2006-2011
Appearances:
164 Gregory Mounis 2006-2011

CATALAN DRAGONS

DATE	FIXTURE	RESULT	SCORERS	LGE	ATT
12/2/11	Harlequins (MM) ●	L4-11	t:Blanch	9th	N/A
19/2/11	Wakefield (h)	L14-38	t:Raguin,Stacul g:Dureau(3)	10th	7,113
27/2/11	Hull KR (a)	W18-31	t:Mounis,Sa,Blanch(2),Raguin,Menzies g:Dureau(3) fg:Dureau	9th	8,092
5/3/11	St Helens (h)	L16-22	t:Sa,Menzies,Dureau g:Dureau(2)	11th	7,095
12/3/11	Castleford (a)	L34-24	t:Dureau(2),Blanch,Stacul g:Dureau(4)	11th	4,889
18/3/11	Crusaders (a)	W22-32	t:Greenshields(3),Farrar(2) g:Dureau(6)	10th	3,517
26/3/11	Salford (h)	L10-22	t:Stacul,Raguin g:Gigot	12th	7,156
3/4/11	Warrington (a)	W20-22	t:Millard,Vaccari,Ferriol,Dureau g:Dureau(3)	9th	10,956
8/4/11	Wigan (a)	W28-47	t:Vaccari(2),Menzies(2),Casty,Dureau(2),Blanch g:Dureau(7) fg:Dureau	7th	13,134
16/4/11	Hull FC (h)	W28-10	t:Baile,Blanch,Vaccari,Menzies,Henderson g:Dureau(4)	6th	8,025
22/4/11	Harlequins (a)	W30-37	t:Dureau(2),Pelissier,Baitieri,Stacul(2) g:Dureau(5),Mounis fg:Dureau	6th	2,069
25/4/11	Bradford (h)	D8-8	t:Farrar g:Dureau(2)	7th	9,496
30/4/11	Huddersfield (h)	W13-12	t:Ferriol,Baitieri g:Dureau(2) fg:Dureau	7th	8,025
6/5/11	Leigh (a) (CCR4)	W16-22	t:Blanch,Baile,Stacul,Henderson g:Dureau,Bosc(2)	N/A	2,237
13/5/11	Leeds (a)	L30-6	t:Henderson g:Bosc	7th	13,273
22/5/11	Huddersfield (a) (CCR5)	L30-16	t:Henderson,Baile,Stacul g:Dureau(2)	N/A	3,198
29/5/11	Wakefield (a)	W22-42	t:Vaccari(2),Baile,Blanch(2),Greenshields,Sa,Mounis g:Dureau(5)	7th	4,561
4/6/11	Wigan (h) ●●	W20-12	t:Baile,Millard(2) g:Dureau(4)	5th	9,372
11/6/11	Crusaders (a)	W31-18	t:Millard,Baile,Sa,Blanch(2) g:Dureau(5) fg:Dureau	5th	7,125
18/6/11	Huddersfield (h) ●●●	L28-20	t:Dureau,Blanch,Baitieri,Baile g:Dureau(2)	6th	5,132
25/6/11	Castleford (h)	W54-20	t:Menzies,Paea(2),Blanch,Dureau,Greenshields,Baitieri,Vaccari(2),Baile g:Dureau(7)	5th	8,695
2/7/11	Bradford (a)	W28-34	t:Greenshields(2),Blanch(2),Raguin,Henderson,Dureau g:Dureau(3)	5th	12,670
10/7/11	Leeds (h)	W38-18	t:Raguin,Vaccari(2),Blanch,Menzies,Greenshields,Duport g:Dureau(5)	5th	10,688
15/7/11	St Helens (a)	L40-18	t:Menzies(2),Vaccari,Greenshields g:Marginet	5th	7,026
30/7/11	Harlequins (h)	W48-22	t:Greenshields(2),Baile,Mounis(2),Baitieri,Blanch,Simon g:Marginet(8)	5th	8,471
12/8/11	Hull FC (a)	L40-8	t:Millard,Duport	5th	10,739
20/8/11	Warrington (a)	L12-25	t:Blanch,Menzies g:Dureau(2)	5th	9,495
3/9/11	Hull KR (h)	L28-30	t:Sa,Baile,Millard(2),Raguin g:Dureau(4)	6th	8,252
11/9/11	Salford (a)	W18-44	t:Sa(2),Menzies(2),Paea,Bosc,Henderson g:Dureau(6),Bosc(2)	6th	10,146
17/9/11	Hull KR (h) (EPO)	W56-6	t:Blanch(3),Menzies(2),Millard,Pelissier,Raguin,Stacul,Greenshields g:Dureau(8)	N/A	8,413
25/9/11	Wigan (a) (PSF)	L44-0		N/A	6,790

● Played at Millennium Stadium, Cardiff
●● Played at Stade Yve du Manoir, Montpellier
●●● Played at The Shay, Halifax

	D.O.B.	APP ALL	APP SL	TRIES ALL	TRIES SL	GOALS ALL	GOALS SL	FG ALL	FG SL	PTS ALL	PTS SL
Thibaut Ancely	18/5/88	(2)	(2)	0	0	0	0	0	0	0	0
Jean-Philippe Baile	7/6/87	22(2)	20(2)	10	8	0	0	0	0	40	32
Jason Baitieri	2/7/89	8(21)	8(19)	5	5	0	0	0	0	20	20
Damien Blanch	24/5/83	30	28	21	20	0	0	0	0	84	80
Thomas Bosc	5/8/83	8	6	1	1	5	3	0	0	14	10
Remi Casty	5/2/85	20(5)	19(5)	1	1	0	0	0	0	4	4
Vincent Duport	15/12/87	3	3	2	2	0	0	0	0	8	8
Scott Dureau	29/7/86	27	25	11	11	95	92	5	5	239	233
Jamal Fakir	30/8/82	10(14)	9(13)	0	0	0	0	0	0	0	0
Ben Farrar	2/12/86	14	13	3	3	0	0	0	0	12	12
David Ferriol	24/4/79	23(2)	21(2)	2	2	0	0	0	0	8	8
Tony Gigot	27/12/90	5(3)	5(2)	0	0	1	1	0	0	2	2
Cyrille Gossard	7/2/82	1(6)	1(6)	0	0	0	0	0	0	0	0
Clint Greenshields	11/1/82	20	20	12	12	0	0	0	0	48	48
Ian Henderson	23/4/83	28(3)	27(2)	6	4	0	0	0	0	24	16
Remy Marginet	27/5/89	2	2	0	0	9	9	0	0	18	18
Sebastien Martins	18/11/84	(8)	(8)	0	0	0	0	0	0	0	0
Steve Menzies	4/12/73	21(2)	21(2)	14	14	0	0	0	0	56	56
Darryl Millard	20/2/85	23	22	8	8	0	0	0	0	32	32
Gregory Mounis	18/1/85	29(2)	28(1)	4	4	1	1	0	0	18	18
Lopini Paea	19/4/84	15(6)	14(6)	3	3	0	0	0	0	12	12
Mathias Pala	14/6/89	2	2	0	0	0	0	0	0	0	0
Eloi Pelissier	18/6/91	2(22)	1(22)	2	2	0	0	0	0	8	8
Sebastien Raguin	14/2/79	27(3)	25(3)	7	7	0	0	0	0	28	28
Setaimata Sa	14/9/87	24	23	7	7	0	0	0	0	28	28
Michael Simon	2/4/87	2(19)	1(18)	1	1	0	0	0	0	4	4
Cyril Stacul	12/10/84	18	16	8	6	0	0	0	0	32	24
Julien Touxagas	12/2/84	(3)	(2)	0	0	0	0	0	0	0	0
Frederic Vaccari	7/11/87	19	17	11	11	0	0	0	0	44	44

Scott Dureau

LEAGUE RECORD
P27-W15-D1-L11
(6th, SL/Preliminary Semi-Final)
F689, A626, Diff+63
31 points.

CHALLENGE CUP
Round Five

ATTENDANCES
Best - v Leeds (SL - 10,688)
Worst - v St Helens (SL - 7,095)
Total (SL, inc play-offs) - 117,421
Average (SL, inc play-offs) - 8,387
(Up by 1,573 on 2010)

11 November 2010 - former Wigan, Bradford and Wakefield utility Paul Johnson joins on one-year deal.

12 November 2010 - released Jamie Thackray signs for Barrow Raiders.

19 November 2010 - Weller Hauraki joins Leeds Rhinos as Crusaders line up Melbourne back-rower Hep Cahill.

22 November 2010 - first-team coach Jon Sharp released.

8 December 2010 - Rod Findlay appointed chief executive.

9 December 2010 - Barry Eaton appointed new assistant coach.

10 December 2010 - Crusaders readmitted to Super League but deducted four league points for 2011 for breaching insolvency rules.

24 December 2010 - officially out of administration after the sale of the club to Geoff Moss and Ian Roberts completed.

27 December 2010 - Richard Moore joins from Wakefield on three-year contract

8 February 2011 - Wales winger Rhys Williams joins on one-month loan from Warrington.

13 February 2011 - Hollywood actor Mickey Rourke watches impressive 42-12 victory over Salford City Reds at Millennium Stadium.

20 February 2011 - 20-18 defeat by Harlequins at the Stoop.

18 March 2011 - 32-22 home defeat by Catalans sends Crusaders to bottom of table.

21 March 2011 - Jordan Tansey, sacked by Hull, joins on 18-month contract.

23 March 2011 - Andy Bracek, carrying a knee injury, signs 18-month deal.

27 March 2011 - Lincoln Withers suffers hamstring strain in 56-16 thrashing at Castleford. Michael Witt banned for one game for punching.

27 March 2011 - Rhys Hanbury arrives after visa hold-up.

30 March 2011 - Frank Winterstein and new signing Hep Cahill finally arrive after visa hold-ups.

2 April 2011 - Rhys Hanbury stars as 16-10 round-eight victory at Salford cancels out points deduction.

22 April 2011 - stunning 32-6 Good Friday victory over Huddersfield at the Racecourse.

25 April 2011 - Richard Moore suspended for one match for punching in 34-16 Easter Monday defeat at Leeds.

4 May 2011 - Gil Dudson (to end of 2014) and Paul Johnson (one-year extension to end of 2012) sign new deals.

7 May 2011 - 30-20 round four Challenge Cup defeat at Leeds.

11 May 2011 - Ben Flower signs three-year contract extension to end of 2014.

24 May 2011 - Rhys Hanbury signs new three-year contract extension to end of 2014 season.

KEY DATES - CRUSADERS

2 June 2011 - Gil Dudson joins Championship side Halifax on dual-registration.

15 June 2011 - Gareth Thomas signs new one-year contract to end of 2012 season.

29 June 2011 - utility forward Shannan McPherson signs from South Sydney on a two-year contract from 2012.

30 June 2011 - Michael Witt signs new three-year contract to end of 2014.

7 July 2011 - Keith Senior signs two-year contract from 2012.

7 July 2011 - Jason Chan, Gil Dudson, Richard Moore, Peter Lupton, Jordan Tansey, Jarrod Sammut and Lloyd White suspended by club for breaches of club discipline before 40-12 defeat away at Huddersfield.

9 July 2011 - Gareth Thomas breaks left arm during 38-10 home defeat by Hull KR.

12 July 2011 - Hep Cahill signs for Super League-bound Widnes.

14 July 2011 - suspension lifted on seven players.

25 July 2011 - Crusaders withdraw from Super League from 2012 on eve of licence announcement.

28 July 2011 - Jarrod Sammut signs for Bradford for 2012.

28 July 2011 - RFL special dispensation classes Crusaders players as non-quota and Federation Trained.

29 July 2011 - Crusaders confirm they will fulfil remaining five fixtures.

31 July 2011 - 40-6 win at Wakefield ends run of eight defeats.

4 August 2011 - Jason Chan signs three-year deal with Huddersfield.

5 August 2011 - Michael Witt and Mark Bryant sign with Harlequins from 2012.

8 August 2011 - Vince Mellars signs three-year contract with Wakefield.

12 August 2011 - Richard Moore signs for Leeds Rhinos on three-year deal.

12 August 2011 - Gil Dudson gets two matches for fighting in 31-12 home win over Harlequins which takes Crusaders off bottom of table..

13 August 2011 - Ryan O'Hara joins Hull KR for 2012.

21 August 2011 - 58-18 defeat to Hull FC in last home Super League game.

2 September 2011 - Crusaders apply to join Championship.

7 September 2011 - Rhys Hanbury signs two-year deal with Widnes.

8 September 2011 - Jordan James signs for Salford from 2012.

9 September 2011 - 42-10 defeat in round 27 at Wigan, coupled with Wakefield's 26-14 win over Bradford means wooden spoon.

14 September 2011 - Rod Findlay steps down as chief executive.

23 September 2011 - application for Championship membership turned down by RFL.

27 September 2011 - Lincoln Withers signs for Hull KR.

7 October 2011 - Tony Martin signs for Hull FC; Elliot Kear signs for Bradford.

10 October 2011 - Crusaders accepted for Championship One in 2012.

11 October 2011 - head coach Iestyn Harris joins Wigan as assistant to new coach Shaun Wane.

25 October 2011 - Gareth Thomas retires with immediate effect.

CLUB RECORDS
Highest score: 84-10 v Hunslet, 11/8/2007 **Highest score against:** 0-68 v Leeds, 2/8/2009 **Record attendance:** 10,334 v Leeds, 29/1/2010
MATCH RECORDS
Tries: 4 Tony Duggan v Lokomotiv Moscow, 12/3/2006 Carl de Chenu v London Skolars, 14/4/2006 Craig Richards v Blackpool, 9/4/2007 Damien Quinn v Swinton, 28/4/2007 Paul Ballard v London Skolars, 7/7/2007 **Goals:** 12 Damien Quinn v St Albans, 26/2/2006 **Points:** 32 Damien Quinn v St Albans, 26/2/2006
SEASON RECORDS
Tries: 40 Tony Duggan 2007 **Goals:** 96 Mark Lennon 2008 **Points:** 252 Damien Quinn 2007
CAREER RECORDS
Tries: 101 Tony Duggan 2006-2009 **Goals:** 190 Damien Quinn 2006-2009 **Points:** 612 Damien Quinn 2006-2009 **Appearances:** 112 Damien Quinn 2006-2009

CRUSADERS

DATE	FIXTURE	RESULT	SCORERS	LGE	ATT
13/2/11	Salford (MM) ●	W42-12	t:R Williams,Witt(3),Reardon(2),Chan g:Schifcofske(7)	14th	N/A
20/2/11	Harlequins (a)	L20-18	t:Sammut(2),Flower g:Schifcofske(3)	13th	1,776
26/2/11	Bradford (h)	L26-30	t:Witt,Thomas,Sammut,Schifcofske,Martin g:Schifcofske(3)	13th	2,615
4/3/11	Hull FC (a)	L42-18	t:R Williams(2),Sammut g:Schifcofske(3)	13th	10,422
13/3/11	Hull KR (a)	L40-22	t:Reardon(2),Sammut,Lupton g:Schifcofske(3)	13th	8,602
18/3/11	Catalan Dragons (h)	L22-32	t:Sammut,Martin,Mellars(2) g:Schifcofske,Witt(2)	14th	3,517
27/3/11	Castleford (a)	L56-16	t:Reardon,Martin,Mellars g:Schifcofske(2)	14th	6,030
2/4/11	Salford (a)	W10-16	t:Tansey,Sammut,Thomas g:Schifcofske(2)	13th	3,416
8/4/11	St Helens (h)	L18-34	t:Thomas,Martin,White g:Schifcofske,Witt(2)	14th	4,002
15/4/11	Warrington (a)	L64-6	t:Hanbury g:Schifcofske	14th	10,002
22/4/11	Huddersfield (h)	W32-6	t:Chan,Hanbury,Schifcofske,Cahill,Tansey,Reardon g:Schifcofske(4)	14th	3,008
25/4/11	Leeds (a)	L34-16	t:Tansey,Witt,Hanbury g:Schifcofske(2)	14th	14,165
1/5/11	Wigan (h)	L16-48	t:Thomas,Witt,Reardon g:Schifcofske(2)	14th	5,037
7/5/11	Leeds (a) (CCR4)	L30-20	t:Cahill,Hanbury,Kear,Lupton g:Schifcofske(2)	N/A	10,954
13/5/11	Wakefield (h)	W23-10	t:Witt,Mellars,O'Hara,Hanbury g:Schifcofske(3) fg:Witt	14th	3,241
27/5/11	St Helens (a)	L28-12	t:Sammut,White g:Schifcofske(2)	14th	6,752
3/6/11	Warrington (h)	L16-56	t:Kear,Cahill,Sammut g:Schifcofske(2)	14th	4,907
11/6/11	Catalan Dragons (a)	L31-18	t:White,Tansey,Sammut g:Schifcofske(3)	14th	7,125
17/6/11	Leeds (h)	L7-12	t:Lupton g:Witt fg:Witt	14th	3,035
24/6/11	Salford (h)	L18-22	t:Martin,Flower,J James g:Witt(3)	14th	2,576
3/7/11	Huddersfield (a) ●●	L40-12	t:Martin(2) g:Witt(2)	14th	4,892
9/7/11	Hull KR (h)	L10-38	t:Kear,Winterstein g:Schifcofske	14th	2,820
16/7/11	Castleford (h)	L20-26	t:Chan,White,Tansey,Sammut g:Schifcofske(2)	14th	3,055
31/7/11	Wakefield (a)	W6-40	t:Withers,White(2),Reardon,Mellars,J James,Kear g:Schifcofske(3),Witt(2),Martin	14th	6,428
12/8/11	Harlequins (h)	W31-12	t:Chan,Reardon,White,Moore,Kear g:Schifcofske(5) fg:Witt	13th	2,259
21/8/11	Hull FC (h)	L18-58	t:Mellars,Martin,Lupton g:Schifcofske(3)	13th	3,827
4/9/11	Bradford (a)	L48-24	t:White,Reardon(2),Lupton,Martin g:Schifcofske(2)	13th	12,998
9/9/11	Wigan (a)	L42-10	t:Lupton,Sammut g:Schifcofske	14th	19,104

● Played at Millennium Stadium, Cardiff
●● Played at The Shay, Halifax

		APP		TRIES		GOALS		FG		PTS	
	D.O.B.	ALL	SL	ALL	SL	ALL	SL	ALL	SL	ALL	SL
Andy Bracek	21/3/84	(2)	(2)	0	0	0	0	0	0	0	0
Mark Bryant	10/4/81	16(7)	16(6)	0	0	0	0	0	0	0	0
Joe Burke	18/5/90	(1)	(1)	0	0	0	0	0	0	0	0
Hep Cahill	15/10/86	17	16	3	2	0	0	0	0	12	8
Jason Chan	26/1/84	22(1)	22(1)	4	4	0	0	0	0	16	16
Gil Dudson	16/6/90	3(8)	3(7)	0	0	0	0	0	0	0	0
Ben Flower	19/10/87	9(14)	9(13)	2	2	0	0	0	0	8	8
Dalton Grant	21/4/90	(1)	(1)	0	0	0	0	0	0	0	0
Rhys Hanbury	27/8/85	10	9	5	4	0	0	0	0	20	16
Aled James	17/2/82	1	1	0	0	0	0	0	0	0	0
Jordan James	24/5/80	5(10)	5(10)	2	2	0	0	0	0	8	8
Paul Johnson	25/11/78	6(4)	6(4)	0	0	0	0	0	0	0	0
Elliot Kear	29/11/88	12(1)	11(1)	5	4	0	0	0	0	20	16
Peter Lupton	7/3/82	16(3)	15(3)	6	5	0	0	0	0	24	20
Tony Martin	7/10/78	24	24	9	9	1	1	0	0	38	38
Vince Mellars	27/1/84	24	23	6	6	0	0	0	0	24	24
Richard Moore	2/2/81	12(10)	11(10)	1	1	0	0	0	0	4	4
Jamie Murphy	29/12/89	(2)	(2)	0	0	0	0	0	0	0	0
Ryan O'Hara	18/8/80	18(7)	17(7)	1	1	0	0	0	0	4	4
Adam Peek	5/2/77	(3)	(3)	0	0	0	0	0	0	0	0
Stuart Reardon	13/10/81	26	25	11	11	0	0	0	0	44	44
Jarrod Sammut	15/2/87	7(15)	7(14)	12	12	0	0	0	0	48	48
Clinton Schifcofske	10/11/75	25	24	2	2	63	61	0	0	134	130
Jordan Tansey	9/9/86	14(4)	14(4)	5	5	0	0	0	0	20	20
Gareth Thomas	25/7/74	18	17	4	4	0	0	0	0	16	16
Lloyd White	9/10/88	13(6)	12(6)	8	8	0	0	0	0	32	32
Lee Williams	19/2/88	1(7)	1(7)	0	0	0	0	0	0	0	0
Rhys Williams	8/12/89	6	6	3	3	0	0	0	0	12	12
Frank Winterstein	17/12/86	14(5)	13(5)	1	1	0	0	0	0	4	4
Lincoln Withers	7/5/81	20	20	1	1	0	0	0	0	4	4
Michael Witt	1/1/84	25	24	7	7	12	12	3	3	55	55

Jarrod Sammut

LEAGUE RECORD
P27-W6-D0-L21
(14th, SL)
F527, A857, Diff-330
8 points. *(4 points deducted for
entering administration)*

CHALLENGE CUP
Round Four

ATTENDANCES
Best - v Wigan (SL - 5,037)
Worst - v Harlequins (SL - 2,259)
Total (SL only) - 43,899
Average (SL only) - 3,377
(Down by 1,244 on 2010)

19 November 2010 - assistant Rob Powell appointed head coach on two-year contract.

25 November 2010 - former Hull KR winger Jack Latus joins on trial.

21 December 2010 - Hull FC forward Mike Burnett signs on season-long loan.

14 January 2011 - Gus Mackay replaces Paul Blanchard as chief executive.

18 January 2011 - Mark Calderwood handed trial until end of February.

22 January 2011 - 70-6 defeat of London Skolars to win Capital Challenge in Rob Powell's first game in charge.

25 January 2011 - Wigan duo Karl Pryce and Joe Mellor join on one-month loan deals.

30 January 2011 - 34-26 victory at Leigh Centurions.

12 February 2011 - 11-4 victory over Catalan Dragons in round 1 at Millennium Stadium.

20 February 2011 - Karl Temata returns from 2010 knee injury in 20-18 home victory over Crusaders in round 2.

23 February 2011 - Featherstone sign prop Dave Williams on month's loan.

25 February 2011 - shock 36-26 victory over Leeds Rhinos in round 3 at Headingley.

4 March 2011 - 18-10 home defeat by Huddersfield in round 4.

11 March 2011 - 27-16 victory over St Helens in round 5 at Halton Stadium.

20 March 2011 - 82-6 defeat by Warrington Wolves in round 6 at Halliwell Jones Stadium.

27 March 2011 - 40-30 home defeat by Hull FC in round 7.

3 April 2011 - Karl Pryce scores hat-trick in 24-22 defeat by Bradford Bulls in round 8 at Odsal.

10 April 2011 - 52-32 defeat at Wakefield in round 9.

15 April 2011 - Rob Purdham suffers shoulder injury in round 10, 26-26 home draw with Castleford.

20 April 2011 - Lee Mitchell joins from Warrington on month's loan.

22 April 2011 - 37-30 home defeat by Catalan Dragons in round 11.

25 April 2011 - 37-24 defeat at Hull KR.

30 April 2011 - Luke Dorn suffers hamstring injury in 34-16 home defeat by Salford in round 13.

13 May 2011 - 54-6 defeat by Wigan in round 14 at DW Stadium.

KEY DATES - HARLEQUINS

20 May 2011 - Luke Dorn returns but suffers recurrence of hamstring injury in 40-20 Challenge Cup fifth round exit at Leeds.

24 May 2011 - fullback Chris Riley becomes sixth loan recruit.

29 May 2011 - 56-24 defeat at Castleford in round 15.

4 June 2011 - 30-16 home defeat by Bradford Bulls in round 16.

12 June 2011 - 38-6 defeat by Hull FC in round 17 at KC Stadium.

15 June 2011 - Bradford stand-off Kyle Briggs becomes Harlequins seventh loanee of the season.

18 June 2011 - 40-22 home victory over Wakefield Wildcats ends 13-game winless run in league.

1 July 2011 - Kyle Briggs breaks wrist in 26-18 round 20 defeat at Salford and returns to Bradford.

13 July 2011 - Chad Randall signs new two-year contract to end of 2013.

16 July 2011 - Jason Golden makes first appearance of season in round 22, 54-24 home defeat by Warrington.

22 July 2011 - skipper Rob Purdham announces he will leave at end of season after ten-year spell in London.

22 July 2011 - Luke Gale signs for Bradford for 2012.

30 July 2011 - David Howell banned for six matches for biting in 48-22 defeat at Catalans.

3 August 2011 - Andy Ellis joins Wakefield Trinity Wildcats.

5 August 2011 - Crusaders Michael Witt signs three-year contract from 2012 and Mark Bryant for two years.

9 August 2011 - Craig Gower, currently playing rugby union at Bayonne, signs two-year deal from 2012.

11 August 2011 - Dan Sarginson extends contract by a year to end of 2013.

12 August 2011 - local youngster Kieran Dixon signs two-year contract.

18 August 2011 - Shane Rodney joins from Manly and Antonio Kaufusi from Newcastle on three-year contracts.

20 August 2011 - 32-22 home win over Leeds ends chances of wooden spoon.

26 August 2011 - Julien Rinaldi returns on two-year contract from 2012.

7 September 2011 - Manly winger Michael Robertson joins on 12-month deal, with an option for a second year.

7 September 2011 - Hull KR duo Liam Colbon and Matt Cook join on two-year deals.

22 September 2011 - Australian prop Jarrad Hickey signs from Wakefield on 12-month contract.

1 November 2011 - Harlequins change name to London Broncos.

190

HARLEQUINS
RUGBY LEAGUE

HARLEQUINS

DATE	FIXTURE	RESULT	SCORERS	LGE	ATT
12/2/11	Catalan Dragons (MM) ●	W4-11	t:Gale(2) g:Gale fg:Gale	4th	N/A
20/2/11	Crusaders (h)	W20-18	t:Gale,Dorn(2) g:Gale(4)	3rd	1,776
25/2/11	Leeds (a)	W26-36	t:Gale,Clubb,Ellis(2),Purdham,Bailey g:Gale(6)	1st	14,350
4/3/11	Huddersfield (h)	L10-18	t:Pryce,Melling g:Purdham	4th	2,624
11/3/11	St Helens (a)	W16-27	t:Dorn,Pryce,Clubb,Kouparitsas g:Gale(5) fg:Gale	4th	6,050
20/3/11	Warrington (a)	L82-6	t:Dorn g:Gale	5th	11,506
27/3/11	Hull FC (h)	L30-40	t:Melling,Clubb,Dorn,Gale,Randall g:Gale(5)	7th	3,052
3/4/11	Bradford (a)	L24-22	t:Pryce(3),Clubb g:Gale(3)	8th	12,354
10/4/11	Wakefield (a)	L52-32	t:Bailey,O'Callaghan,Purdham,Melling,Pryce,Dorn g:Gale(4)	9th	5,412
15/4/11	Castleford (h)	D26-26	t:Bryan,Clubb(2),Dorn,Ellis g:Gale(3)	8th	4,128
22/4/11	Catalan Dragons (h)	L30-37	t:O'Callaghan,Gale,Ellis,Pryce,Randall g:Gale(5)	8th	2,069
25/4/11	Hull KR (a)	L37-24	t:Wilkes,Temata,Dorn,Mitchell g:Gale(4)	9th	7,139
30/4/11	Salford (h)	L16-34	t:Burnett,Ambler,Melling g:Gale(2)	10th	1,957
6/5/11	Gateshead (a) (CCR4)	W0-70	t:Wilkes,Gale,Bolger(2),O'Callaghan,Howell,Clubb(3),Sarginson, Melling,Kouparitsas,Randall g:Gale(7),Melling(2)	N/A	402
13/5/11	Wigan (a)	L54-6	t:Calderwood g:Gale	11th	12,813
20/5/11	Leeds (a) (CCR5)	L40-20	t:Melling,Dorn,Calderwood,Bolger g:Gale(2)	N/A	7,147
29/5/11	Castleford (a)	L56-24	t:O'Callaghan,Riley(2),Wilkes(2) g:Gale(2)	12th	7,072
4/6/11	Bradford (h)	L16-30	t:Pryce(2),Temata g:Gale(2)	12th	4,253
12/6/11	Hull FC (a)	L38-6	t:Melling g:Gale	12th	11,139
18/6/11	Wakefield (h)	W40-22	t:Gale,Bailey,Dorn,Clubb,Melling,Randall,O'Callaghan g:Gale(6)	12th	2,875
25/6/11	Hull KR (h)	L0-34		12th	2,927
1/7/11	Salford (a)	L26-18	t:Sarginson(2),Clubb g:Gale(3)	12th	3,065
9/7/11	Wigan (h)	L6-38	t:Pryce g:Gale	12th	4,423
16/7/11	Warrington (h)	L24-54	t:Gale,Dorn,Sarginson,Ellis g:Gale(4)	12th	3,842
30/7/11	Catalan Dragons (a)	L48-22	t:Wilkes,Pryce,Randall,Clubb g:Purdham,Melling(2)	12th	8,471
12/8/11	Crusaders (a)	L31-12	t:Sarginson(2) g:Gale(2)	12th	2,259
20/8/11	Leeds (h)	W32-22	t:Dorn(3),O'Callaghan,Calderwood g:Gale(6)	12th	3,241
4/9/11	Huddersfield (a)	L50-12	t:Melling,Clubb g:Gale(2)	12th	5,220
10/9/11	St Helens (h)	L16-34	t:Temata,Pryce,O'Callaghan g:Gale(2)	12th	3,546

● Played at Millennium Stadium, Cardiff

		APP		TRIES		GOALS		FG		PTS	
	D.O.B.	ALL	SL	ALL	SL	ALL	SL	ALL	SL	ALL	SL
Luke Ambler	18/12/89	6(18)	5(17)	1	1	0	0	0	0	4	4
Chris Bailey	5/7/82	25	24	3	3	0	0	0	0	12	12
Ben Bolger	13/9/89	(6)	(4)	3	0	0	0	0	0	12	0
Kyle Briggs	7/12/87	3	3	0	0	0	0	0	0	0	0
Lamont Bryan	12/4/88	(8)	(8)	1	1	0	0	0	0	4	4
Mike Burnett	6/10/88	17(4)	16(4)	1	1	0	0	0	0	4	4
Mark Calderwood	25/10/81	15	13	3	2	0	0	0	0	12	8
Tony Clubb	12/6/87	29	27	13	10	0	0	0	0	52	40
Luke Dorn	2/7/82	23	22	14	13	0	0	0	0	56	52
Andy Ellis	15/12/84	17(9)	16(8)	5	5	0	0	0	0	20	20
Luke Gale	22/6/88	28	26	9	8	84	75	2	2	206	184
Jason Golden	6/11/85	2(3)	2(3)	0	0	0	0	0	0	0	0
David Howell	18/11/83	14	12	1	0	0	0	0	0	4	0
Nick Kouparitsas	26/2/84	3(13)	2(13)	2	1	0	0	0	0	8	4
Olsi Krasniqi	26/6/92	2(13)	1(12)	0	0	0	0	0	0	0	0
Chris Melling	21/9/84	27	25	9	7	4	2	0	0	44	32
Joe Mellor	28/11/90	(1)	(1)	0	0	0	0	0	0	0	0
Lee Mitchell	8/9/88	11(1)	11(1)	1	1	0	0	0	0	4	4
Jamie O'Callaghan	21/9/90	26(1)	25(1)	7	6	0	0	0	0	28	24
Karl Pryce	27/7/86	11(7)	11(7)	12	12	0	0	0	0	48	48
Rob Purdham	14/4/80	17(2)	17(2)	2	2	2	2	0	0	12	12
Chad Randall	30/12/80	27	25	5	4	0	0	0	0	20	16
Chris Riley	22/2/88	3	3	2	2	0	0	0	0	8	8
Dan Sarginson	26/5/93	8(1)	8	6	5	0	0	0	0	24	20
Karl Temata	12/7/78	16(9)	14(9)	3	3	0	0	0	0	12	12
Rob Thomas	9/10/90	(2)	(2)	0	0	0	0	0	0	0	0
Danny Ward	15/6/80	26	24	0	0	0	0	0	0	0	0
Oliver Wilkes	2/5/80	21(6)	19(6)	5	4	0	0	0	0	20	16
Dave Williams	29/1/87	(12)	(10)	0	0	0	0	0	0	0	0

Tony Clubb

LEAGUE RECORD
P27-W6-D1-L20
(12th, SL)
F524, A951, Diff-427
13 points.

CHALLENGE CUP
Round Five

ATTENDANCES
Best - v Wigan (SL - 4,423)
Worst - v Crusaders (SL - 1,776)
Total (SL only) - 40,713
Average (SL only) - 3,132
(Down by 248 on 2010)

12 November 2010 - Luke Robinson to miss start of 2011 season after undergoing surgery on left elbow.

14 December 2010 - Jamahl Lolesi not allocated squad number following major back surgery.

21 December 2010 - Jermaine McGillvary signs new three-year contract.

3 January 2011 - Matthew Sarsfield joins from Wigan on three-year deal.

14 January 2011 - South Sydney release centre Jamie Simpson to sign three-year deal with Huddersfield.

12 February 2011 - 28-18 victory over Warrington in round 1 at Millennium Stadium.

15 February 2011 - Dale Ferguson signs two-and-a-half-year deal after Wakefield go in to administration.

19 February 2011 - Keal Carlile is withdrawn with extreme fatigue in 18-12 defeat at Castleford Tigers.

24 February 2011 - Hooker David Faiumu signs new contract until end of 2013.

13 March 2011 - 50-16 home victory over Bradford Bulls moves Giants top after round 5.

18 March 2011 - Luke Robinson makes injury comeback in 20-6 home defeat by Wigan.

3 April 2011 - Keith Mason damages knee ligaments in 34-10 home victory over Wakefield Wildcats.

8 April 2011 - Andy Raleigh injures eye in 29-10 home victory over Warrington Wolves in round 9.

15 April 2011 - Luke O'Donnell sent off in 38-6 victory at Leeds, the first win at Headingley in over 50 years.

22 April 2011 - shock 32-6 Good Friday defeat by Crusaders in round 11 at Wrexham.

26 April 2011 - Danny Brough scores 2,000th career point in 52-22 Easter Monday home victory over Salford in round 12.

30 April 2011 - Graeme Horne suspended for one match for dangerous contact after 13-12 defeat at Catalan Dragons.

6 May 2011 - Nathan Brown charged with breaching RFL's Respect Policy after outburst following win at Leeds in April.

12 May 2011 - Shaun Lunt signs contract extension until end of 2015.

14 May 2011 - Luke O'Donnell injures hamstring warming up for 40-18 home victory over St Helens in round 14.

17 May 2011 - Keith Mason signs contract to end of 2015 season.

KEY DATES - HUDDERSFIELD GIANTS

20 May 2011 - Scott Grix signs new contract until end of 2014 season.

22 May 2011 - Keith Mason returns in 30-16 Challenge Cup round four home win over Catalans.

25 May 2011 - Nathan Brown, linked with coaching vacancies in the NRL, signs 12-month contract extension to end 2012.

26 May 2011 - Keal Carlile undergoes surgery on congenital heart problem.

29 May 2011 - David Hodgson scores hat-trick in 34-20 victory at Hull FC.

5 June 2011 - Danny Brough injures ankle in 40-18 victory over Castleford Tigers in round 16 at Shay Stadium.

12 June 2011 - shock 13-10 defeat at Wakefield.

23 June 2011 - Lee Gilmour signs two-year contract extension to end 2013

25 June 2011 - 46-12 defeat at Wigan puts Giants in third spot.

26 June 2011 - Nathan Brown fined £1,000 for criticising match officials, half of it suspended for six months, after comments in the wake of 38-6 win over Leeds at Headingley on April 15.

4 July 2011 - Joe Wardle signs new contract to end of 2014.

5 July 2011 - Shaun Lunt out for season after surgery on long-standing groin injury.

18 July 2011 - David Hodgson to leave for Hull KR at end of season.

24 July 2011 - 22-18 defeat at Castleford in Challenge Cup quarter-final.

4 August 2011 - Crusaders' Jason Chan signs three-year deal from 2012.

11 August 2011 - Michael Lawrence signs new five-year deal to end 2016.

12 August 2011 - Luke O'Donnell's season ends with knee injury during 19-6 defeat at St Helens.

13 August 2011 - Graeme Horne signs for Hull KR from 2012.

16 August 2011 - Jermaine McGillvary signs new five-year contract to end of 2016.

1 September 2011 - Leroy Cudjoe signs new five-year contract to end of 2016.

2 September 2011 - 17-year-old prop Josh Johnson signs three-year full-time contract .

6 September 2011 - Gregg McNally and Keal Carlile not offered contracts for 2012.

7 September 2011 - Castleford threequarter Greg Eden joins on two-year deal.

8 September 2011 - Luke George re-signs from Wakefield on two-year contract.

16 September 2011 - 47-0 Qualifying Play-off defeat at Warrington.

23 September 2011 - 34-28 elimination at home to Leeds in Preliminary Semi-final.

3 October 2011 - Featherstone prop Tony Tonks joins on 12-month deal.

7 October 2011 - Wakefield centre Aaron Murphy joins on four-year contract; Andy Raleigh and Danny Kirmond move in opposite direction.

19 October 2011 - Tommy Lee, released by Wakefield, signs one-year contract.

CLUB RECORDS

Highest score:
142-4 v Blackpool G, 26/11/94
Highest score against:
12-94 v Castleford, 18/9/88
Record attendance:
32,912 v Wigan, 4/3/50
15,629 v Leeds, 10/2/2008 *(new ground)*

MATCH RECORDS

Tries:
10 Lionel Cooper v Keighley, 17/11/51
Goals:
18 Major Holland v Swinton Park, 28/2/14
Points:
39 Major Holland v Swinton Park, 28/2/14

SEASON RECORDS

Tries: 80 Albert Rosenfeld 1913-14
Goals: 147 Ben Gronow 1919-20
Points: 332 Pat Devery 1952-53

CAREER RECORDS

Tries: 420 Lionel Cooper 1947-55
Goals: 958 Frank Dyson 1949-63
Points: 2,072 Frank Dyson 1949-63
Appearances: 485 Douglas Clark 1909-29

HUDDERSFIELD GIANTS

DATE	FIXTURE	RESULT	SCORERS	LGE	ATT
12/2/11	Warrington (MM) ●	W28-18	t:Carlile,Brough(2),Griffin,Lunt g:Brough(4)	3rd	N/A
19/2/11	Castleford (a)	L18-12	t:McGillvary(2) g:Brough(2)	7th	5,992
27/2/11	Hull FC (h)	W20-10	t:Hodgson(2),Lawrence,Brown g:Brough(2)	3rd	8,822
4/3/11	Harlequins (a)	W10-18	t:O'Donnell,McGillvary,Horne g:Brough(3)	2nd	2,624
13/3/11	Bradford (h)	W50-16	t:McGillvary(2),Cudjoe,Fa'alogo,Grix,Patrick,Horne(2),Ferguson g:Brough(7)	1st	9,466
18/3/11	Wigan (h)	L6-20	t:Robinson g:Brough	4th	8,151
26/3/11	Hull KR (a)	W16-38	t:McGillvary,Brough(2),Lawrence,Grix,Robinson,Hodgson g:Brough(5)	3rd	7,502
3/4/11	Wakefield (h)	W34-10	t:Robinson,Horne(2),Lawrence(2),Lunt g:Brough(5)	2nd	7,267
8/4/11	Warrington (h)	W29-10	t:Grix,Patrick,Robinson,McGillvary g:Brough(6) fg:Brough	2nd	7,224
15/4/11	Leeds (a)	W6-38	t:Ferguson(2),McGillvary,Lunt(2),Robinson g:Brough(7)	1st	14,768
22/4/11	Crusaders (a)	L32-6	t:Brough g:Brough	2nd	3,008
26/4/11	Salford (h)	W52-22	t:O'Donnell,Lunt(2),Cording,Ferguson(2),Griffin,Brown,McGillvary g:Brough(7),Cudjoe(2)	1st	6,042
30/4/11	Catalan Dragons (a)	L13-12	t:Gilmour,Grix g:Brough(2)	2nd	8,025
8/5/11	Batley (a) (CCR4)	W18-28	t:Brown,Gilmour,Brough,Wardle,Hodgson,Cudjoe g:Brough(2)	N/A	2,676
14/5/11	St Helens (h)	W40-18	t:Crabtree(2),Brough,Brown,Lawrence,Wardle,Grix g:Brough(6)	2nd	7,843
22/5/11	Catalan Dragons (h) (CCR5)	W30-16	t:McGillvary,Cudjoe,Hodgson,Brown(2),Griffin g:Brough(3)	N/A	3,198
29/5/11	Hull FC (a)	W20-34	t:Lawrence,Hodgson(3),Brough,Gilmour g:Brough(5)	3rd	11,274
5/6/11	Castleford (h) ●●	W40-18	t:Cudjoe(2),Crabtree,Hodgson,Gilmour,McGillvary,Fa'alogo g:Brough(4),Cudjoe(2)	2nd	5,237
12/6/11	Wakefield (a)	L13-10	t:Lunt,Wardle g:Cudjoe	2nd	5,436
18/6/11	Catalan Dragons (h) ●●	W28-20	t:Hodgson(2),Faiumu,Griffin,Brown g:Grix(4)	2nd	5,132
25/6/11	Wigan (a)	L46-12	t:Hodgson,Kirmond g:Grix(2)	3rd	19,169
3/7/11	Crusaders (h) ●●	W40-12	t:Fa'alogo,Wardle,Brown,Hodgson(3),Lawrence g:McNally(6)	3rd	4,892
8/7/11	Warrington (a)	L28-16	t:McGillvary,Fa'alogo,Brown g:Grix(2)	3rd	10,283
17/7/11	Bradford (a)	L36-0		4th	14,047
24/7/11	Castleford (a) (CCQF)	L22-18	t:Grix,McGillvary,Cudjoe,Lawrence g:Brough	N/A	6,336
30/7/11	Hull KR (h)	W46-26	t:Cudjoe,Faiumu,Grix(2),Horne(2),Kirmond,Crabtree g:Grix(5),Cudjoe(2)	4th	6,464
12/8/11	St Helens (a)	L19-6	t:Fa'alogo g:Grix	4th	6,421
19/8/11	Salford (a)	L24-18	t:McGillvary,Gilmour,Fa'alogo g:Grix(3)	4th	3,458
4/9/11	Harlequins (h)	W50-12	t:Cudjoe(2),Wardle,Horne,McGillvary(3),Brough,Grix g:Brough(7)	4th	5,220
11/9/11	Leeds (h)	L24-31	t:Lawrence,Robinson,Patrick,McGillvary g:Brough(4)	4th	10,428
16/9/11	Warrington (a) (QPO)	L47-0		N/A	10,006
23/9/11	Leeds (h) (PSF)	L28-34	t:Grix(2),Ferguson,Fa'alogo(2) g:Brough(4)	N/A	7,872

● Played at Millennium Stadium, Cardiff ●● Played at The Shay, Halifax

		APP		TRIES		GOALS		FG		PTS	
	D.O.B.	ALL	SL	ALL	SL	ALL	SL	ALL	SL	ALL	SL
Danny Brough	15/1/83	26	23	9	8	88	82	1	1	213	197
Kevin Brown	2/10/84	28	26	9	6	0	0	0	0	36	24
Keal Carlile	20/3/90	2	2	1	1	0	0	0	0	4	4
Jamie Cording	30/12/89	3(2)	2(2)	1	1	0	0	0	0	4	4
Eorl Crabtree	2/10/82	22(8)	20(7)	4	4	0	0	0	0	16	16
Leroy Cudjoe	7/4/88	30	27	9	6	5	5	0	0	46	34
David Fa'alogo	4/9/80	17(2)	17(2)	8	8	0	0	0	0	32	32
Jacob Fairbank	4/3/90	2	1	0	0	0	0	0	0	0	0
David Faiumu	30/4/83	11(16)	11(14)	2	2	0	0	0	0	8	8
Dale Ferguson	13/4/88	13(6)	11(6)	6	6	0	0	0	0	24	24
Lee Gilmour	12/3/78	28	25	5	4	0	0	0	0	20	16
Darrell Griffin	19/6/81	20(7)	18(6)	4	3	0	0	0	0	16	12
Scott Grix	1/5/84	29(1)	27(1)	11	10	18	18	0	0	80	76
David Hodgson	8/8/81	21	18	15	13	0	0	0	0	60	52
Graeme Horne	22/3/85	11(9)	11(9)	8	8	0	0	0	0	32	32
Danny Kirmond	11/11/85	8(10)	6(9)	2	2	0	0	0	0	8	8
Michael Lawrence	12/4/90	27	24	9	8	0	0	0	0	36	32
Shaun Lunt	15/4/86	7(11)	6(10)	7	7	0	0	0	0	28	28
Keith Mason	20/1/82	12(7)	11(6)	0	0	0	0	0	0	0	0
Jermaine McGillvary	16/5/88	30	28	18	16	0	0	0	0	72	64
Gregg McNally	2/1/91	1	1	0	0	6	6	0	0	12	12
Jon Molloy	23/3/91	1(2)	1(1)	0	0	0	0	0	0	0	0
Luke O'Donnell	22/10/80	16	15	2	2	0	0	0	0	8	8
Larne Patrick	3/11/88	3(25)	1(24)	3	3	0	0	0	0	12	12
Andy Raleigh	17/3/81	5(7)	5(7)	0	0	0	0	0	0	0	0
Luke Robinson	25/7/84	20(5)	18(5)	6	6	0	0	0	0	24	24
Jamie Simpson	6/9/86	8(1)	8(1)	0	0	0	0	0	0	0	0
Adam Walker	20/2/91	(1)	(1)	0	0	0	0	0	0	0	0
Joe Wardle	22/9/91	15	13	5	4	0	0	0	0	20	16
Kyle Wood	18/6/89	1(7)	1(5)	0	0	0	0	0	0	0	0

Jermaine McGillvary

LEAGUE RECORD
P27-W16-D0-L11
(4th, SL/Preliminary Semi-Final)
F707, A524, Diff+183
32 points.

CHALLENGE CUP
Quarter Finalists

ATTENDANCES
Best - v Leeds (SL - 10,428)
Worst - v Catalan Dragons
(CC - 3,198)
Total (SL, inc play-offs) - 100,060
Average (SL, inc play-offs) - 7,147
(Down by 86 on 2010)

22 December 2010 - Mike Burnett joins Harlequins on season-long loan deal.

26 December 2010 - Shaun Berrigan leaves after release from final year of contract.

26 January 2011 - Craig Fitzgibbon handed captaincy for 2011 season.

28 January 2011 - young Scottish centre Chad McGlame signs one-year deal; teenage halfback Danny Nicklas ruled out for season with torn ACL.

8 February 2011 - Jordan Tansey contract terminated for disciplinary reasons.

9 February 2011 - Cameron Phelps signs until end of 2011 season.

13 February 2011 - 34-22 defeat by Hull KR in round 1 at Millennium Stadium.

18 February 2011 - new signing from Wakefield Sam Obst makes debut in 32-18 home defeat by Leeds in round 2.

4 March 2011 - Sam Obst stars in 42-18 home victory over Crusaders in round 4.

13 March 2011 - Kirk Yeaman gets one-match ban for fighting after 14-12 defeat at Wigan.

18 March 2011 - 20-6 home defeat by Wakefield leaves Hull third from bottom after round 6.

1 April 2011 - coach Richard Agar criticises referee after 20-18 home defeat by Castleford in which Sean Long is sent off.

5 April 2011 - Sean Long suspended for two games for striking.

7 April 2011 - RFL charge Richard Agar with breaching RFL's Respect Policy.

15 April 2011 - Martin Gleeson, released by Wigan, signs 18-month contract to end of 2012 season.

22 April 2011 - Sean Long fractures thumb in 36-18 Good Friday home victory over Hull KR in round 11.

25 April 2011 - 24-10 Easter Monday victory at league leaders Warrington puts Hull in top-eight.

2 May 2011 - 24-24 Bank Holiday Monday home draw with St Helens in round 13 after leading 18-0.

4 May 2011 - Richard Agar fined £6,000, half suspended until end of season, following criticism of referee James Child after defeat to Castleford at KC Stadium on 1 April.

7 May 2011 - 82-0 home win over Oldham in Challenge Cup.

21 May 2011 - 50-26 win at Widnes in fifth round of Challenge Cup

30 May 2011 - fullback Wade McKinnon signs from Wests Tigers on three-year deal from 2012.

KEY DATES - HULL F.C.

1 June 2011 - Jamie Ellis signs from Leigh on two-year contract from 2012.

2 June 2011 - Aaron Heremaia signs two-year contract from NZ Warriors for 2012.

5 June 2011 - Sean Long dislocates shoulder in 17-10 defeat by Hull KR in round 16 at Craven Park.

10 June 2011 - Martin Gleeson given sick leave because of stress-related illness.

12 June 2011 - 38-6 home victory over Harlequins in round 17.

30 June 2011 - Australian halfback Brett Seymour signs from NZ Warriors on three-year contract.

15 July 2011 - Richard Horne signs new two-year contract to end of 2013 season.

22 July 2011 - Sam Moa signs new contract for 2012.

22 July 2011 - club taken over by former Hull City chairman Adam Pearson.

24 July 2011 - 38-22 home defeat to Leeds in Challenge Cup quarter-final.

10 August 2011 - Sean Long confirms retirement after 21 appearances in two injury-hit seasons.

12 August 2011 - Kirk Yeaman gets one match ban for punching in 40-8 home win over Catalans.

6 September 2011 - Wigan prop forward Eamon O'Carroll signs on three-year deal.

6 September 2011 - Shaun McRae to become Director of Rugby from 1 October and will appoint new first team coach.

7 September 2011 - Danny Houghton signs two-year contract extension to end of 2014.

7 September 2011 - captain Craig Fitzgibbon confirms retirement after severe ankle injury sustained in 50-18, round 26 win at Castleford which guarantees play-off finish.

9 September 2011 - Richard Agar announced as new coach of Wakefield.

12 September 2011 - Wests Tigers assistant Peter Gentle announced as new head coach on three-year contract.

18 September 2011 - 42-10 elimination at Leeds.

19 September 2011 - Ewan Dowes, Cameron Phelps, Danny Washbrook and Epalahame Lauaki all released.

19 September 2011 - Wakefield sign Danny Washbrook.

22 September 2011 - Martin Gleeson and Mike Burnett released.

23 September 2011 - rising star Luke Briscoe signs for Leeds.

6 October 2011 - Lee Radford announces retirement and takes up assistant coach role.

7 October 2011 - centre Tony Martin signs 12-month contract; Andy Hay joins on three-year deal as assistant coach.

11 October 2011 - James Rule resigns from chief executive role.

HULL F.C.

HULL F.C.

DATE	FIXTURE	RESULT	SCORERS	LGE	ATT
13/2/11	Hull KR (MM) ●	L22-34	t:Yeaman(2),Radford,Sharp g:Tickle(3)	11th	N/A
18/2/11	Leeds (h)	L18-32	t:O'Meley(2),Sharp g:Tickle(3)	9th	12,515
27/2/11	Huddersfield (a)	L20-10	t:Turner,Sharp g:Westerman	12th	8,822
4/3/11	Crusaders (h)	W42-18	t:Tickle(2),Whiting,Obst,Sharp,Horne,Yeaman,Briscoe		
			g:Tickle(4),Westerman	9th	10,422
13/3/11	Wigan (a)	L14-12	t:Westerman,Briscoe g:Tickle,Westerman	10th	15,346
18/3/11	Wakefield (h)	L6-20	t:Tickle g:Tickle	12th	11,032
27/3/11	Harlequins (a)	W30-40	t:Tickle,Yeaman(2),Briscoe,Lauaki,Obst,Turner g:Tickle(6)	10th	3,052
1/4/11	Castleford (h)	L18-20	t:Yeaman,Tickle,Fitzgibbon g:Westerman,Tickle(2)	11th	11,856
8/4/11	Bradford (h)	W34-24	t:Yeaman,Tickle,Radford,Turner,Briscoe(2) g:Tickle(5)	10th	11,346
16/4/11	Catalan Dragons (a)	L28-10	t:Briscoe,Obst g:Fitzgibbon	11th	8,025
22/4/11	Hull KR (h)	W36-18	t:Yeaman(2),Long,Gleeson,Whiting,Briscoe g:Tickle(6)	9th	19,795
25/4/11	Warrington (a)	W10-24	t:Houghton,Yeaman(2),Sharp g:Tickle(4)	8th	12,036
2/5/11	St Helens (h)	D24-24	t:Yeaman(3),Briscoe g:Tickle(4)	8th	11,933
7/5/11	Oldham (h) (CCR4)	W82-0	t:Obst(2),Turner(3),Houghton,Sharp,Whiting(2),Gleeson,Lyne(2),		
			Horne,Moa,Radford g:Whiting(11)	N/A	6,235
13/5/11	Salford (a)	W16-32	t:Yeaman,Gleeson(2),Briscoe,Radford,Sharp g:Tickle(4)	8th	3,983
21/5/11	Widnes (a) (CCR5)	W26-50	t:Whiting,Sharp,Horne(2),Westerman,Lauaki,Briscoe(2),Phelps		
			g:Tickle(4),Westerman(3)	N/A	3,387
29/5/11	Huddersfield (h)	L20-34	t:Dowes,O'Meley,Manu g:Tickle(4)	8th	11,274
5/6/11	Hull KR (a)	L17-10	t:Yeaman,Gleeson g:Tickle	8th	10,250
12/6/11	Harlequins (h)	W38-6	t:Turner,Manu,Obst,Briscoe,Horne,Moa,Whiting g:Tickle(4),Westerman	8th	11,139
19/6/11	Bradford (a)	W14-28	t:Horne,Moa,Westerman,Yeaman,Fitzgibbon g:Tickle(4)	8th	14,414
26/6/11	Wakefield (a)	W18-52	t:Westerman,Yeaman,Horne,Tickle,Whiting(2),Turner,O'Meley,		
			Briscoe,Radford g:Tickle(6)	8th	7,965
1/7/11	St Helens (a)	L28-14	t:Briscoe(2),Turner g:Westerman	8th	7,053
8/7/11	Salford (h)	W52-16	t:Tickle(2),Briscoe(3),Turner(2),Westerman,Washbrook g:Tickle(8)	7th	11,699
15/7/11	Leeds (a)	L20-0		8th	14,809
24/7/11	Leeds (h) (CCQF)	L22-38	t:Obst,Turner(2),Westerman g:Tickle(3)	N/A	9,496
29/7/11	Wigan (h)	L16-30	t:Yeaman,Turner,Manu g:Tickle(2)	8th	11,729
12/8/11	Catalan Dragons (h)	W40-8	t:Moa,Manu,Phelps,Radford,Westerman,Horne g:Tickle(8)	8th	10,739
21/8/11	Crusaders (a)	W18-58	t:Fitzgibbon(2),O'Meley,Whiting,Radford,Houghton,Phelps,		
			Westerman,Turner,Obst(2) g:Westerman(5),Tickle(2)	8th	3,827
3/9/11	Castleford (a)	W18-50	t:Yeaman,Turner(2),Briscoe(2),Manu(2),Houghton,Sharp		
			g:Westerman(7)	7th	7,866
9/9/11	Warrington (h)	L12-34	t:Westerman(2) g:Westerman(2)	8th	16,121
18/9/11	Leeds (a) (EPO)	L42-10	t:Whiting,Briscoe g:Tickle	N/A	9,075

● Played at Millennium Stadium, Cardiff

		APP		TRIES		GOALS		FG		PTS	
	D.O.B.	ALL	SL	ALL	SL	ALL	SL	ALL	SL	ALL	SL
Jack Aldous	3/4/91	(1)	0	0	0	0	0	0	0	0	0
Tom Briscoe	19/3/90	31	28	21	19	0	0	0	0	84	76
Ewan Dowes	4/3/81	3(20)	2(18)	1	1	0	0	0	0	4	4
Craig Fitzgibbon	16/6/77	21(1)	21(1)	4	4	1	1	0	0	18	18
Martin Gleeson	28/5/80	7	6	5	4	0	0	0	0	20	16
Richard Horne	16/7/82	29	26	8	5	0	0	0	0	32	20
Danny Houghton	25/9/88	31	28	4	3	0	0	0	0	16	12
Liam Kent	9/4/91	(1)	0	0	0	0	0	0	0	0	0
Epalahame Lauaki	27/1/84	1(29)	(27)	2	1	0	0	0	0	8	4
Sean Long	24/9/76	2	2	1	1	0	0	0	0	4	4
Reece Lyne	2/12/92	5(2)	5(1)	2	0	0	0	0	0	8	0
Willie Manu	20/3/80	24(6)	21(6)	5	5	0	0	0	0	20	20
Sam Moa	14/6/86	21(8)	18(8)	4	3	0	0	0	0	16	12
Sam Obst	26/11/80	19(6)	17(6)	9	6	0	0	0	0	36	24
Mark O'Meley	22/5/81	27	25	5	5	0	0	0	0	20	20
Cameron Phelps	11/2/85	21	19	3	2	0	0	0	0	12	8
Lee Radford	26/3/79	10(16)	10(13)	7	6	0	0	0	0	28	24
Will Sharp	12/5/86	14(9)	12(8)	9	7	0	0	0	0	36	28
Danny Tickle	10/3/83	28	26	9	9	90	83	0	0	216	202
Jordan Turner	9/1/89	22(2)	19(2)	17	12	0	0	0	0	68	48
Danny Washbrook	18/9/85	5(14)	4(13)	1	1	0	0	0	0	4	4
Joe Westerman	15/11/89	21(7)	19(7)	10	8	23	20	0	0	86	72
Richard Whiting	20/12/84	28(2)	25(2)	10	7	11	0	0	0	62	28
Kirk Yeaman	15/9/83	28	26	21	21	0	0	0	0	84	84

Kirk Yeaman

LEAGUE RECORD
P27-W13-D1-L13
(8th, SL/Elimination Play-Off)
F718, A569, Diff+149
27 points.

CHALLENGE CUP
Quarter Finalists

ATTENDANCES
Best - v Hull KR (SL - 19,795)
Worst - v Oldham (CC - 6,235)
Total (SL only) - 161,600
Average (SL only) - 12,431
(Down by 1,583 on 2010)

12 October 2010 - Canterbury Bulldogs stand-off Blake Green signs on two-year deal.

13 February 2011 - 34-22 victory over Hull FC in round 1 at Millennium Stadium.

20 February 2011 - Jake Webster gets two-match ban for dangerous contact after 24-22 defeat at Warrington in round 2.

27 February 2011 - Michael Dobson has surgery on Achilles and ankle injuries and after run of 78 consecutive games misses 31-18 home defeat by Catalan Dragons.

8 March 2011 - Willie Mason unveiled after six-month wait to take up two-year contract because of passport and visa issues. Injured Michael Dobson is de-registered.

13 March 2011 - Willie Mason makes debut in 40-22 home victory over Crusaders.

1 April 2011 - Shaun Briscoe injures knee in 34-16 defeat by St Helens in round 8 at Stobart Stadium.

14 April 2011 - hooker Josh Hodgson signs two-year contract extension to end of 2013.

21 April 2011 - Michael Dobson re-registered with the RFL; Willie Mason de-registered 'whilst the passport process is finalised'.

22 April 2011 - 36-18 Good Friday defeat at Hull FC in round 11.

25 April 2011 - 37-24 home victory over Harlequins in round 12.

15 May 2011 - Kris Welham scores hat-trick in 46-18 home victory over Bradford in round 14.

22 May 2011 - Willie Mason signs for French rugby union club Toulon.

3 June 2011 - Jason Netherton signs new two-year contract until end of 2013.

5 June 2011 - 17-10 home victory over Hull FC in round 16.

6 June 2011 - Scott Taylor signs new two-year contract to end of 2013.

8 June 2011 - former Leeds Rhinos winger Danny Williams is taken on trial.

17 June 2011 - Liam Salter signs first professional 12-month contract for 2012.

22 June 2011 - coach Justin Morgan insists he intends to see out remaining 18 months on his contract in wake of 46-16 home defeat by Warrington.

29 June 2011 - Ben Cockayne suspended for an alleged breach of club discipline, six weeks after final warning following an offensive post by him on Facebook. Liam Watts also suspended.

KEY DATES - HULL KINGSTON ROVERS

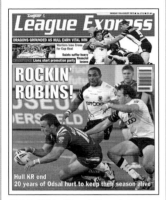

12 July 2011 - Shaun Briscoe to be released at end of season while Ben Galea signs for another 12 months to end 2012.

15 July 2011 - Shaun Briscoe signs for Widnes.

15 July 2011 - Ben Cockayne leaves by mutual consent.

18 July 2011 - Huddersfield winger David Hodgson signs three-year contract from 2012.

20 July 2011 - Liam Watts back in training after being suspended by Rovers on June 29.

24 July 2011 - 54-6 defeat at St Helens in Challenge Cup quarter-final.

3 August 2011 - Michael Dobson and Blake Green sign until end of 2014 after extending contracts from end 2012.

4 August 2011 - Justin Morgan to leave at end of season, six years after joining from Toulouse in 2005.

11 August 2011 - Joel Clinton out for season after surgery on shoulder injury suffered in loss to Wigan in May.

13 August 2011 - Ryan O'Hara, off quota after Crusaders withdraw licence application, and Huddersfield's Graeme Horne sign two-year contracts from 2012.

24 August 2011 - Blake Green loses appeal against one-match ban imposed for dangerous throw on St Helens winger Jamie Foster during 24-22 home win.

25 August 2011 - Sam Latus and Richard Beaumont sign two-year contracts.

29 August 2011 - Samoa international Misi Taulapapa signs from Sheffield Eagles on 12-month deal.

1 September 2011 - captain Mick Vella to retire at end of season.

3 September 2011 - 30-28 win at Catalans sets up last-round sudden-death decider with Castleford at Craven Park.

5 September 2011 - Clint Newton released from last year of contract to return to the NRL with Penrith. Ben Fisher to leave the club at end of season after not being offered new contract.

10 September 2011 - 26-24 round 27 home win over Castleford ensures seventh-placed finish.

17 September 2011 - 56-6 Elimination Play-off defeat at Catalans Dragons.

20 September 2011 - Scott Murrell banned for one game for high tackle in Catalans defeat.

26 September 2011 - Newcastle Knights assistant Craig Sandercock is new head coach on two-year contract, with the option of a third season.

27 September 2011 - former Crusaders hooker Lincoln Withers signs two-year deal.

6 October 2011 - prop Micky Paea joins from Canterbury Bulldogs on two-year deal.

10 October 2011 - Huddersfield hooker Keal Carlile joins on two-year deal.

11 October 2011 - Stanley Gene appointed under-18s coach.

27 October 2011 - Newcastle back row forward Constantine Mika joins on two-year contract.

5 November 2011 - Newcastle fullback Shannon McDonnell joins on 12-month contract.

CLUB RECORDS

Highest score:
100-6 v Nottingham City, 19/8/90
Highest score against:
8-76 v Halifax, 20/10/91
Record attendance:
27,670 v Hull FC, 3/4/53 *(Boothferry Park)*
10,250 v Hull FC, 5/6/2011 *(Craven Park)*

MATCH RECORDS

Tries: 11 George West
v Brooklands Rovers, 4/3/1905
Goals:
14 Alf Carmichael v Merthyr, 8/10/1910
Mike Fletcher v Whitehaven, 18/3/90
Colin Armstrong v Nottingham City, 19/8/90
Damien Couturier v Halifax, 23/4/2006
Points: 53 George West
v Brooklands Rovers, 4/3/1905

SEASON RECORDS

Tries: 45 Gary Prohm 1984-85
Goals: 199 Mike Fletcher 1989-90
Points: 450 Mike Fletcher 1989-90

CAREER RECORDS

Tries: 207 Roger Millward 1966-80
Goals: 1,268 Mike Fletcher 1987-98
Points: 2,760 Mike Fletcher 1987-98
Appearances: 489 Mike Smith 1975-91

HULL KINGSTON ROVERS

DATE	FIXTURE	RESULT	SCORERS	LGE	ATT
13/2/11	Hull FC (MM) ●	W22-34	t:Green,Newton,Galea(2),Welham(2) g:Dobson(4),Welham	2nd	N/A
20/2/11	Warrington (a)	L24-22	t:Newton(2),Green,Briscoe g:Dobson(3)	6th	10,899
27/2/11	Catalan Dragons (h)	L18-31	t:Green(2),Briscoe g:Hall(3)	8th	8,092
6/3/11	Castleford (a)	L27-14	t:Newton,Hall,Galea g:Hall	10th	8,537
13/3/11	Crusaders (h)	W40-22	t:Galea,Murrell,Watts,Welham(2),Webster,Green g:Hall(6)	8th	8,602
18/3/11	Salford (a)	L34-18	t:Hall(2),Murrell g:Hall(3)	9th	4,408
26/3/11	Huddersfield (h)	L16-38	t:Welham(2),Fisher g:Hall,Murrell	11th	7,502
1/4/11	St Helens (a)	L34-16	t:Welham(2),Webster g:Hall(2)	12th	7,740
9/4/11	Leeds (h)	W38-28	t:Vella,Welham,Cook,Murrell,Colbon,Latus,Galea g:Murrell(5)	11th	8,653
15/4/11	Wigan (h)	L16-28	t:Cook,Mason,Cockayne g:Murrell(2)	12th	8,703
22/4/11	Hull FC (a)	L36-18	t:Cook,Welham,Cockayne g:Dobson(3)	12th	19,795
25/4/11	Harlequins (h)	W37-24	t:Webster,Sheriff,Dobson,Galea,Murrell,Fisher g:Dobson(5),Murrell fg:Dobson	11th	7,139
1/5/11	Wakefield (a)	L26-24	t:Cockayne(2),Welham,Green g:Dobson(4)	12th	7,283
8/5/11	York (a) (CCR4)	W22-64	t:Fox(2),Green,Galea,Sheriff,Dobson,Cook,Cox(2),Welham,Webster g:Dobson(10)	N/A	2,463
15/5/11	Bradford (h)	W46-18	t:Welham(3),Green,Webster,Dobson,Watts,Fox g:Dobson(7)	9th	7,923
20/5/11	Salford (a) (CCR5)	W0-25	t:Green,Cockayne,Welham,Webster g:Dobson(4) fg:Dobson	N/A	2,087
30/5/11	Wigan (a)	L40-6	t:Welham g:Dobson	10th	14,779
5/6/11	Hull FC (h)	W17-10	t:Welham,Briscoe(2) g:Dobson(2) fg:Dobson	10th	10,250
12/6/11	Leeds (a)	L44-14	t:Cockayne,Welham,Hall g:Dobson	11th	13,669
19/6/11	Warrington (h)	L16-46	t:Green,Colbon,Taylor g:Dobson(2)	11th	8,143
25/6/11	Harlequins (a)	W0-34	t:Webster(2),Colbon,Green,Newton,Dobson g:Dobson(5)	11th	2,927
3/7/11	Wakefield (h)	W70-14	t:Colbon(3),Fox(3),Welham(3),Webster(2),Dobson,Newton(2) g:Dobson(7)	10th	8,025
9/7/11	Crusaders (a)	W10-38	t:Latus,Galea(3),Briscoe,Newton,Dobson g:Dobson(5)	9th	2,820
17/7/11	Salford (h)	W21-8	t:Galea,Cook,Welham g:Dobson(4) fg:Dobson	9th	7,834
24/7/11	St Helens (a) (CCQF)	L54-6	t:Galea g:Dobson	N/A	6,449
30/7/11	Huddersfield (a)	L46-26	t:Taylor,Hodgson,Fisher,Webster g:Dobson(5)	9th	6,464
14/8/11	Bradford (a)	W8-34	t:Galea,Murrell,Fox,Hodgson,Welham,Green g:Dobson(5)	9th	13,441
21/8/11	St Helens (h)	W24-22	t:Green(2),Latus,Hall g:Dobson(4)	9th	8,356
3/9/11	Catalan Dragons (a)	W28-30	t:Lovegrove,Welham(2),Latus,Hall g:Dobson(5)	8th	8,252
10/9/11	Castleford (h)	W26-24	t:Dobson,Vella,Latus(2),Webster g:Dobson(3)	7th	8,936
17/9/11	Catalan Dragons (a) (EPO)	L56-6	t:Hall g:Dobson	N/A	8,413

● Played at Millennium Stadium, Cardiff

	D.O.B.	APP		TRIES		GOALS		FG		PTS	
		ALL	SL	ALL	SL	ALL	SL	ALL	SL	ALL	SL
Richard Beaumont	2/2/88	(2)	(2)	0	0	0	0	0	0	0	0
Shaun Briscoe	23/2/83	24	22	5	5	0	0	0	0	20	20
Joel Clinton	8/12/81	9(5)	8(4)	0	0	0	0	0	0	0	0
Ben Cockayne	20/7/83	13(6)	11(6)	6	5	0	0	0	0	24	20
Liam Colbon	30/9/84	13	13	6	6	0	0	0	0	24	24
Matt Cook	14/11/86	5(5)	4(4)	5	4	0	0	0	0	20	16
Jordan Cox	27/5/92	(7)	(6)	2	0	0	0	0	0	8	0
Michael Dobson	29/5/86	23	20	7	6	91	76	4	3	214	179
Ben Fisher	4/2/81	8(20)	8(17)	3	3	0	0	0	0	12	12
Peter Fox	5/11/83	20	17	7	5	0	0	0	0	28	20
Ben Galea	16/8/78	31	28	13	11	0	0	0	0	52	44
Blake Green	19/9/86	29	26	14	12	0	0	0	0	56	48
Craig Hall	21/2/88	14	14	7	7	16	16	0	0	60	60
Josh Hodgson	31/10/89	23(8)	20(8)	2	2	0	0	0	0	8	8
Sam Latus	21/10/89	11(3)	11(3)	6	6	0	0	0	0	24	24
Rhys Lovegrove	11/3/87	8(15)	7(13)	1	1	0	0	0	0	4	4
Willie Mason	15/4/80	6	6	1	1	0	0	0	0	4	4
Scott Murrell	5/9/85	22(7)	20(7)	5	5	9	9	0	0	38	38
Jason Netherton	5/10/82	14(8)	12(7)	0	0	0	0	0	0	0	0
Clint Newton	18/6/81	17(2)	16(2)	8	8	0	0	0	0	32	32
Louis Sheriff	6/9/92	3	2	2	1	0	0	0	0	8	4
Scott Taylor	27/2/91	7(15)	7(14)	2	2	0	0	0	0	8	8
Michael Vella	19/2/78	26	24	2	2	0	0	0	0	8	8
Liam Watts	8/7/90	11(9)	11(8)	2	2	0	0	0	0	8	8
Jake Webster	29/10/83	25	22	12	10	0	0	0	0	48	40
Kris Welham	12/5/87	31	28	26	24	1	1	0	0	106	98
Scott Wheeldon	23/2/86	9(12)	7(11)	0	0	0	0	0	0	0	0

Kris Welham

LEAGUE RECORD
P27-W14-D0-L13
(7th, SL/Elimination Play-Off)
F713, A692, Diff+21
28 points.

CHALLENGE CUP
Quarter Finalists

ATTENDANCES
Best - v Hull FC (SL - 10,250)
Worst - v Harlequins (SL - 7,139)
Total (SL only) - 108,158
Average (SL only) - 8,320
(Up by 86 on 2010)

KEY DATES - LEEDS RHINOS

22 March 2011 - Zak Hardaker ruled out for 6-8 weeks after he breaks finger in domestic accident.

22 March 2011 - Ryan Bailey fined and warned by the club as to his future conduct after posting insensitive comments after the Japanese tsunami.

23 March 2011 - prop Kyle Amor extends loan spell at Wildcats.

1 April 2011 - 22-22 home draw with Wigan Warriors in round 8.

9 April 2011 - 38-28 defeat by Hull KR in round 9 at Craven Park. Carl Ablett receives one-match ban for dangerous contact.

15 April 2011 - 38-6 home defeat by Huddersfield in round 10. Ryan Bailey gets one-match ban after being sent off for throwing punches during brawl.

25 April 2011 - Danny McGuire returns from long-term knee injury in 34-16 home victory over Crusaders in round 12.

29 April 2011 - Jamie Peacock makes comeback from long-term knee injury in round 13, 48-6 victory at Castleford.

24 May 2011 - Keith Senior ruled out for season with knee injury sustained in 40-20 Carnegie Challenge Cup home win over Harlequins.

16 June 2011 - front-row forwards Luke Burgess and Ben Cross released with immediate effect.

24 June 2011 - Weller Hauraki banned for one game for dangerous contact in 18-12 home defeat to Bradford.

29 June 2011 - Brent Webb agrees new contract for 2012.

30 June 2011 - Kylie Leuluai to retire at end of 2012 season after agreeing new 12-month contract .

1 July 2011 - Rob Burrow banned for one game for dangerous contact in 26-24 defeat at Wigan.

4 July 2011 - Ian Kirke signs new two-year contract.

5 July 2011 - Keith Senior to leave Rhinos at end of season.

6 July 2011 - Jamie Peacock signs new 12-month contract.

7 July 2011 - Keith Senior to join Crusaders on two-year contract.

24 July 2011 - 38-22 win at Hull FC in Challenge Cup quarter-final.

7 August 2011 - Kevin Sinfield golden-point penalty wins Challenge Cup semi-final with Castleford by 10-8.

9 August 2011 - Ali Lauitiiti to leave at end of season after seven-and-a-half seasons at Headingley.

19 October 2010 - Matt Diskin signs for Bradford.

4 November 2010 - Tom Bush joins York City Knights.

8 November 2010 - Luke Ambler signs season-long loan deal at Harlequins.

19 November 2010 - Crusaders forward Weller Hauraki signs three-year contract.

20 November 2010 - former Leeds and Bradford hooker James Lowes joins as assistant coach.

15 December 2010 - Academy scrum-half Rory Kettlewell signs from Wigan in two-year deal.

17 December 2010 - Chris Clarkson ruled out for six weeks following operation on fractured thumb.

1 January 2011 - 40-6 home win over Wakefield to win Festive Charity Trophy.

28 January 2011 - 32-0 win over Crusaders at Wrexham in final pre-season game.

13 February 2011 - late Ben Jones-Bishop penalty try secures 32-28 victory over Bradford in round 1 at Millennium Stadium.

16 February 2011 - Ryan Hall, Ben Jones-Bishop, Chris Clarkson and Kallum Watkins sign deals keeping them at Leeds until end of 2014 season.

24 February 2011 - skipper Kevin Sinfield signs new four-year deal to end of 2014 season.

25 February 2011 - Kylie Leuluai suffers pectoral tear in 36-26 home defeat by Harlequins in round 3.

5 March 2011 - 40-24 defeat by Warrington Wolves in round 4 at Halliwell Jones Stadium; Ben Cross issued one-match ban for late and high tackle on Richard Myler.

11 March 2011 - Ben Jones-Bishop dislocates shoulder in 46-12 home victory over Salford in round 5.

19 March 2011 - Zak Hardaker makes debut in 30-16 home defeat by St Helens in round 6.

12 August 2011 – Crusaders prop Richard Moore signs thee-year contract for 2012.

27 August 2011 - 28-18 defeat by Wigan at Wembley.

18 September 2011 - 42-10 win at Headingley eliminates Hull FC.

23 September 2011 - rising Hull FC star Luke Briscoe signs three-year contract.

23 September 2011 - 34-28 win at Galpharm eliminates Huddersfield in Preliminary Semi-final.

30 September 2011 - late Kevin Sinfield penalty secures 26-24 Qualifying semi-final win at Warrington.

3 October 2011 - Kyle Amor signs three-year contract with Wakefield, but Leeds retain option to re-sign after one year.

8 October 2011 - Rob Burrow wins Harry Sunderland award in 32-16 win over St Helens; the fifth Grand Final win in eight years, this time from fifth-place.

13 October 2011 - Darrell Griffin signs from Huddersfield on three-year contract.

CLUB RECORDS

Highest score:
106-10 v Swinton, 11/2/2001
Highest score against:
6-74 v Wigan, 20/5/92
Record attendance:
40,175 v Bradford, 21/5/47

MATCH RECORDS

Tries:
8 Fred Webster v Coventry, 12/4/13
Eric Harris v Bradford, 14/9/31
Goals:
17 Iestyn Harris v Swinton, 11/2/2001
Points:
42 Iestyn Harris v Huddersfield, 16/7/99

SEASON RECORDS

Tries: 63 Eric Harris 1935-36
Goals: 168 *(inc 2fg)* Iestyn Harris 1999
Points: 431 Lewis Jones 1956-57

CAREER RECORDS

Tries: 391 Eric Harris 1930-39
Goals:
1,306 *(inc 27fg)* Kevin Sinfield 1997-2011
Points: 2,920 Lewis Jones 1952-64
Appearances: 625 John Holmes 1968-89

LEEDS RHINOS

DATE	FIXTURE	RESULT	SCORERS	LGE	ATT
13/2/11	Bradford (MM) ●	W28-32	t:Jones-Bishop(3),Hall,Leuluai,Burrow g:Sinfield(4)	5th	N/A
18/2/11	Hull FC (a)	W18-32	t:Webb,Hall,Burrow,Jones-Bishop,Clarkson,Hauraki g:Sinfield(3) fg:Burrow,Sinfield	2nd	12,515
25/2/11	Harlequins (h)	L26-36	t:Clarkson,Sinfield,Hall,Smith,Jones-Buchanan g:Sinfield(3)	4th	14,350
5/3/11	Warrington (a)	L40-24	t:Watkins,Webb,Hall(2) g:Sinfield(4)	7th	11,438
11/3/11	Salford (h)	W46-12	t:Senior,Jones-Buchanan,Hauraki,Watkins,Webb,Ablett(2),Lauitiiti g:Sinfield(7)	6th	13,068
19/3/11	St Helens (h)	L16-30	t:Hall,Hardaker,McShane g:Sinfield(2)	6th	16,035
27/3/11	Wakefield (a)	W6-28	t:Watkins(4),Buderus g:Sinfield(4)	6th	8,763
1/4/11	Wigan (h)	D22-22	t:Jones-Buchanan,Buderus,Webb g:Sinfield(5)	6th	16,118
9/4/11	Hull KR (a)	L38-28	t:Smith,Watkins(2),Hall,McShane g:Sinfield(4)	6th	8,653
15/4/11	Huddersfield (h)	L6-38	t:Burrow g:Sinfield	7th	14,768
21/4/11	Bradford (a)	W22-30	t:McShane,Jones-Buchanan,Senior,Hall,Buderus g:Sinfield(5)	7th	19,275
25/4/11	Crusaders (h)	W34-16	t:Delaney,Ablett,Senior(2),Burrow,Leuluai g:Sinfield(5)	6th	14,165
29/4/11	Castleford (a)	W6-48	t:Watkins,Jones-Buchanan,Hall(2),McGuire,Burrow,McShane,Kirke g:Sinfield(8)	6th	9,860
7/5/11	Crusaders (h) (CCR4)	W30-20	t:McShane,Pitts,Burrow,Hall,Buderus g:Sinfield(5)	N/A	10,954
13/5/11	Catalan Dragons (h)	W30-6	t:Hall,Leuluai,Hardaker(2),Burrow g:Sinfield(5)	5th	13,273
20/5/11	Harlequins (h) (CCR5)	W40-20	t:Hardaker,Jones-Buchanan,Delaney,Lauitiiti,Leuluai,Hall,Clarkson g:Sinfield(6)	N/A	7,147
27/5/11	Warrington (h)	L6-42	t:Buderus g:Sinfield	5th	17,276
3/6/11	St Helens (a)	L42-16	t:Jones-Buchanan,Smith g:Sinfield(4)	6th	9,062
12/6/11	Hull KR (h)	W44-14	t:Smith,Hall(3),Hauraki,McGuire,Hardaker,Delaney g:Sinfield(6)	6th	13,669
17/6/11	Crusaders (a)	W7-12	t:McGuire,Lauitiiti g:Sinfield(2)	5th	3,035
24/6/11	Bradford (h)	L12-18	t:Hall,Jones-Buchanan g:Sinfield(2)	6th	18,095
1/7/11	Wigan (a)	L26-24	t:Jones-Bishop,Webb,Hardaker(2) g:Sinfield(4)	6th	16,426
10/7/11	Catalan Dragons (a)	L38-18	t:Hall,Jones-Buchanan,Buderus g:Sinfield(3)	8th	10,688
15/7/11	Hull FC (h)	W20-0	t:Hall,Jones-Bishop,McGuire g:Sinfield(4)	7th	14,809
24/7/11	Hull FC (a) (CCQF)	W22-38	t:Jones-Bishop(2),Lauitiiti,Delaney,Ablett(2) g:Sinfield(7)	N/A	9,496
29/7/11	Salford (a)	W22-30	t:Hall,Bailey,McGuire,Webb,Smith g:Sinfield(5)	6th	4,024
7/8/11	Castleford (CCSF) ●●	W8-10 (aet)	t:Watkins g:Sinfield(3)	N/A	13,158
12/8/11	Castleford (h)	W56-0	t:Jones-Buchanan,Hall,Watkins,Webb(2),Jones-Bishop,Lauitiiti,Burrow(2),McGuire g:Sinfield(6),Burrow(2)	6th	15,156
20/8/11	Harlequins (a)	L32-22	t:Hall,McGuire,Burrow,Pitts g:Sinfield(3)	6th	3,241
27/8/11	Wigan (CCF) ●●●	L18-28	t:Hall(2),Jones-Bishop,Ablett g:Sinfield	N/A	78,482
2/9/11	Wakefield (h)	W64-20	t:Hall(3),Jones-Bishop,Ablett,McGuire(2),Lauitiiti,Buderus,Peacock,Smith g:Sinfield(10)	5th	15,511
11/9/11	Huddersfield (a)	W24-31	t:Hardaker,Webb,Hall(2),Jones-Buchanan g:Sinfield(5) fg:Sinfield	5th	10,428
18/9/11	Hull FC (h) (EPO)	W42-10	t:Jones-Buchanan,Jones-Bishop,Webb,Hauraki,Sinfield,McGuire,Bailey g:Sinfield(7)	N/A	9,075
23/9/11	Huddersfield (a) (PSF)	W28-34	t:Jones-Bishop,Hardaker(3),Webb(2) g:Sinfield(5)	N/A	7,872
30/9/11	Warrington (a) (QSF)	W24-26	t:Ablett,Hall(2),Burrow g:Sinfield(5)	N/A	12,074
8/10/11	St Helens (GF) ●●●●	W32-16	t:Burrow,Webb,Hall,Ablett,Hardaker g:Sinfield(6)	N/A	69,107

● Played at Millennium Stadium, Cardiff ●● Played at Keepmoat Stadium, Doncaster
●●● Played at Wembley Stadium ●●●● Played at Old Trafford, Manchester

		APP		TRIES		GOALS		FG		PTS	
	D.O.B.	ALL	SL	ALL	SL	ALL	SL	ALL	SL	ALL	SL
Carl Ablett	19/12/85	31	26	9	6	0	0	0	0	36	24
Ryan Bailey	11/11/83	9(16)	8(13)	2	2	0	0	0	0	8	8
Danny Buderus	6/2/78	33(2)	28(2)	7	6	0	0	0	0	28	24
Luke Burgess	20/2/87	5(7)	5(6)	0	0	0	0	0	0	0	0
Rob Burrow	26/9/82	22(12)	19(10)	12	11	2	2	1	1	53	49
Chris Clarkson	7/4/90	23(6)	19(5)	3	2	0	0	0	0	12	8
Ben Cross	6/12/78	1(9)	1(9)	0	0	0	0	0	0	0	0
Brett Delaney	26/10/85	27	22	4	2	0	0	0	0	16	8
George Elliott	21/9/91	1	1	0	0	0	0	0	0	0	0
Ryan Hall	27/11/87	35	30	32	28	0	0	0	0	128	112
Zak Hardaker	17/10/91	15	14	12	11	0	0	0	0	48	44
Weller Hauraki	18/2/85	16(11)	14(10)	4	4	0	0	0	0	16	16
Ben Jones-Bishop	24/8/88	18(1)	15(1)	13	10	0	0	0	0	52	40
Jamie Jones-Buchanan	1/8/81	34	30	12	11	0	0	0	0	48	44
Ian Kirke	26/12/80	5(28)	5(23)	1	1	0	0	0	0	4	4
Ali Lauitiiti	13/7/79	6(15)	6(13)	6	4	0	0	0	0	24	16
Kylie Leuluai	29/3/78	28(3)	24(2)	4	3	0	0	0	0	16	12
Danny McGuire	6/12/82	17(5)	15(3)	10	10	0	0	0	0	40	40
Paul McShane	19/11/89	3(15)	3(13)	5	4	0	0	0	0	20	16
Jamie Peacock	14/12/77	22(1)	17(1)	1	1	0	0	0	0	4	4
Jay Pitts	9/12/89	4(9)	3(9)	2	1	0	0	0	0	8	4
Keith Senior	24/4/76	16	14	4	4	0	0	0	0	16	16
Kevin Sinfield	12/9/80	36	31	2	2	160	138	2	2	330	286
Brad Singleton	29/10/92	(1)	(1)	0	0	0	0	0	0	0	0
Lee Smith	8/8/86	15(2)	13(2)	6	6	0	0	0	0	24	24
Kallum Watkins	12/3/91	16(1)	14(1)	11	10	0	0	0	0	44	40
Brent Webb	8/11/80	30	26	13	13	0	0	0	0	52	52

Kevin Sinfield

LEAGUE RECORD
P27-W15-D1-L11
(5th, SL/Grand Final Winners,
Champions)
F757, A603, Diff+154
31 points.

CHALLENGE CUP
Runners-Up

ATTENDANCES
Best - v Bradford (SL - 18,095)
Worst - v Harlequins (CC - 7,147)
Total (SL, inc play-offs) - 205,368
Average (SL, inc play-offs) - 14,669
(Down by 568 on 2010)

11 September 2010 - Ian Sibbit leaves for Bradford Bulls.

22 September 2010 - Jeremy Smith joins Wakefield.

16 November 2010 - Phil Veivers appointed new assistant coach for 2011 season.

22 December 2010 - Bradford hooker Wayne Godwin signs on three-year deal.

27 December 2010 - 13-12 defeat at Leigh in first warm-up game.

13 January 2011 - Daniel Holdsworth named captain for 2011 season.

16 January 2011 - 30-24 loss to Wigan in friendly at the Willows; Wayne Godwin handed one-match suspension for dangerous throw.

30 January 2011 - 40-6 defeat at Hull KR in final pre-season game; Ray Cashmere, one match for dissent, and Ryan Boyle, two matches for dangerous tackle, both banned.

13 February 2011 - Wayne Godwin suspended for two matches for running in and punching Clinton Schifcofske after the final whistle of round 1, 42-12 defeat by Crusaders at Millennium Stadium.

18 February 2011 - 56-22 home defeat by St Helens in round 2.

27 February 2011 - 32-6 victory at Wakefield Wildcats in round 3.

2 March 2011 - coach Shaun McRae takes month's leave on medical advice. Phil Veivers in Australia following bereavement, assistant Malcolm Alker takes charge.

4 March 2011 - 32-16 home defeat by Wigan Warriors in round 4.

11 March 2011 - 46-12 defeat at Leeds Rhinos in round 5.

17 March 2011 - Ray Cashmere is banned for one match for punching Brent Webb.

18 March 2011 - 34-18 home victory over Hull KR in round 6.

22 March 2011 - Phil Bailey announces retirement due to Achilles injury without making an appearance for the Reds.

26 March 2011 - Jodie Broughton scores four tries in 22-10 victory over Catalan Dragons in round 7 at Stade Gilbert Brutus.

2 April 2011 - 16-10 home defeat by Crusaders in round 8.

7 April 2011 - Marc Sneyd signs new two-year contract.

8 April 2011 - assistant coach Malcolm Alker sent home from training by football manager Steve Simms and suspended by club.

KEY DATES - SALFORD CITY REDS

10 April 2011 - 52-20 defeat by Castleford Tigers in round 9 at The Jungle.

16 April 2011 - 56-16 home victory over Bradford Bulls in round 10.

21 April 2011 - Shaun McRae confirms he will not be seeking re-appointment at end of season.

22 April 2011 - 60-0 home defeat by Warrington in round 11.

26 April 2011 - 52-22 defeat at Huddersfield Giants in round 12.

29 April 2011 - Shaun McRae leaves with immediate effect.

30 April 2011 - 34-16 victory at Harlequins in round 13.

13 May 2011 - 32-16 home defeat by Hull FC in round 14.

29 May 2011 - 28-14 defeat at Bradford Bulls in round 15.

2 June 2011 - Australian Matt Parish appointed new head coach.

3 June 2011 - 34-12 home victory over Wakefield Wildcats in round 16.

12 June 2011 - 18-16 victory at Warrington in round 17.

17 June 2011 - 15-8 home defeat by Castleford Tigers in round 18.

1 July 2011 - Rob Parker joins Castleford on month's loan.

1 July 2011 - 26-18 home win over Harlequins puts Salford clear in ninth spot.

8 July 2011 - 16-year-old halfback Theo Fages joins from French club Pia on two-and-a-half-year deal.

8 July 2011 - 52-16 defeat at Hull FC.

17 July 2011 - 21-8 defeat at Hull KR in Matt Parish's first game in charge sees Reds go 11th.

26 July 2011 - Stefan Ratchford turns down new deal and set for move to Warrington at the end of season.

19 August 2011 - Sean Long appointed assistant coach after retiring from playing.

22 August 2011 - South Sydney prop or second-rower Shannan McPherson signs three-year contract from 2012.

31 August 2011 - Wakefield prop Ben Gledhill signs three-year deal.

8 September 2011 - NZ Warriors utility back Joel Moon and Crusaders prop forward Jordan James sign two-year deals.

11 September 2011 - 44-18 defeat to Catalans ends 100 years at the Willows and means 11th placed-finish.

10 October 2011 - Matt Ashurst signs from St Helens on three-year deal.

17 November 2011 - Matt Parish quits as coach.

CLUB RECORDS

Highest score:
100-12 v Gateshead, 23/3/2003
Highest score against:
16-96 v Bradford, 25/6/2000
Record attendance:
26,470 v Warrington, 13/2/37

MATCH RECORDS

Tries:
6 Frank Miles v Lees, 5/3/1898
Ernest Bone v Goole, 29/3/1902
Jack Hilton v Leigh, 7/10/39
Goals:
14 Steve Blakeley v Gateshead, 23/3/2003
Points:
39 Jim Lomas v Liverpool City, 2/2/1907

SEASON RECORDS

Tries: 46 Keith Fielding 1973-74
Goals: 221 David Watkins 1972-73
Points: 493 David Watkins 1972-73

CAREER RECORDS

Tries: 297 Maurice Richards 1969-83
Goals: 1,241 David Watkins 1967-79
Points: 2,907 David Watkins 1967-79
Appearances:
498 Maurice Richards 1969-83

SALFORD CITY REDS

DATE	FIXTURE	RESULT	SCORERS	LGE	ATT
13/2/11	Crusaders (MM) ●	L42-12	t:Holdsworth,Patten g:Holdsworth(2)	13th	N/A
18/2/11	St Helens (h)	L22-56	t:Patten,Gibson,Ratchford,Broughton g:Holdsworth(3)	12th	5,929
27/2/11	Wakefield (a)	W6-32	t:Ratchford,Wild,Henry(2),Parker,Sidlow g:Holdsworth(4)	11th	6,823
4/3/11	Wigan (h)	L16-32	t:Gibson,Parker,Nero g:Ratchford,Sneyd	12th	6,266
11/3/11	Leeds (a)	L46-12	t:Ratchford,Sidlow g:Holdsworth(2)	12th	13,068
18/3/11	Hull KR (h)	W34-18	t:Boyle,Broughton,Ratchford,Smith,Gleeson,Sneyd g:Holdsworth(4),Ratchford	11th	4,408
26/3/11	Catalan Dragons (a)	W10-22	t:Broughton(4) g:Holdsworth(3)	9th	7,156
2/4/11	Crusaders (h)	L10-16	t:Cashmere,Broughton g:Holdsworth	10th	3,416
10/4/11	Castleford (a)	L52-20	t:Broughton,Anderson,Holdsworth,Sidlow g:Holdsworth(2)	12th	6,741
16/4/11	Bradford (h)	W56-16	t:Holdsworth,Henry(2),Gibson(3),Broughton,Smith,Ratchford,Adamson g:Holdsworth(8)	9th	2,809
22/4/11	Warrington (h)	L0-60		11th	7,496
26/4/11	Huddersfield (a)	L52-22	t:Sidlow,Holdsworth,Henry,Ratchford g:Holdsworth(3)	12th	6,042
30/4/11	Harlequins (a)	W16-34	t:Clay(2),Godwin,Patten,Nero,Palea'aesina,Anderson g:Holdsworth(3)	9th	1,957
8/5/11	Hunslet (a) (CCR4)	W2-68	t:Adamson(2),Palea'aesina(2),Neal,Jewitt,Broughton(2),Ratchford, Nero,Clay(2) g:Holdsworth(6),Ratchford(3),Smith	N/A	649
13/5/11	Hull FC (h)	L16-32	t:Clay,Gibson,Ratchford g:Holdsworth(2)	10th	3,983
20/5/11	Hull KR (h) (CCR5)	L0-25		N/A	2,087
29/5/11	Bradford (a)	L28-14	t:Henry(3) g:Holdsworth	11th	12,487
3/6/11	Wakefield (h)	W34-12	t:Holdsworth,Ratchford(3),Broughton,Jewitt,Adamson g:Holdsworth(3)	11th	3,213
12/6/11	Warrington (a)	W16-18	t:Gleeson,Patten,Henry g:Holdsworth(3)	9th	10,339
17/6/11	Castleford (h)	L8-15	t:Broughton,Holdsworth	9th	3,587
24/6/11	Crusaders (a)	W18-22	t:Godwin,Adamson,Ratchford,Sidlow g:Holdsworth(3)	9th	2,576
1/7/11	Harlequins (h)	W26-18	t:Gibson(2),Anderson,Broughton,Henry g:Holdsworth(3)	9th	3,065
8/7/11	Hull FC (a)	L52-16	t:Broughton,Anderson,Nero g:Holdsworth(2)	10th	11,699
17/7/11	Hull KR (a)	L21-8	t:Anderson g:Holdsworth(2)	11th	7,834
29/7/11	Leeds (h)	L22-30	t:Patten,Broughton,Anderson,Jewitt g:Holdsworth(3)	10th	4,024
14/8/11	Wigan (a)	L52-18	t:Williams(2),Gleeson g:Holdsworth(3)	11th	13,607
19/8/11	Huddersfield (h)	W24-18	t:Holdsworth,Williams(3) g:Holdsworth(4)	10th	3,458
2/9/11	St Helens (a)	L31-6	t:Williams g:Holdsworth	10th	7,377
11/9/11	Catalan Dragons (h)	L18-44	t:Williams(2),Adamson g:Holdsworth(3)	11th	10,146

● Played at Millennium Stadium, Cardiff

		APP		TRIES		GOALS		FG		PTS	
	D.O.B.	ALL	SL	ALL	SL	ALL	SL	ALL	SL	ALL	SL
Luke Adamson	17/11/87	20(7)	18(7)	6	4	0	0	0	0	24	16
Vinnie Anderson	14/2/79	16(2)	16(1)	6	6	0	0	0	0	24	24
Ryan Boyle	17/10/87	24(2)	22(2)	1	1	0	0	0	0	4	4
Jodie Broughton	9/1/88	29	27	16	14	0	0	0	0	64	56
Ray Cashmere	12/1/80	25(2)	24(1)	1	1	0	0	0	0	4	4
Adam Clay	7/10/90	4	2	5	3	0	0	0	0	20	12
Alex Davidson	1/11/92	(1)	(1)	0	0	0	0	0	0	0	0
Ashley Gibson	25/9/86	17	16	8	8	0	0	0	0	32	32
Sean Gleeson	29/11/87	13	12	3	3	0	0	0	0	12	12
Wayne Godwin	13/3/82	19(5)	18(5)	2	2	0	0	0	0	8	8
Mark Henry	19/4/81	25	25	10	10	0	0	0	0	40	40
Daniel Holdsworth	27/4/84	28	26	7	7	74	68	0	0	176	164
Lee Jewitt	14/2/87	2(22)	2(20)	3	2	0	0	0	0	12	8
Callum Marriott	30/5/93	(1)	(1)	0	0	0	0	0	0	0	0
Adam Neal	21/5/90	4(21)	4(19)	1	0	0	0	0	0	4	0
Chris Nero	14/2/81	24	22	4	3	0	0	0	0	16	12
Iafeta Palea'aesina	10/2/82	3(21)	2(20)	3	1	0	0	0	0	12	4
Rob Parker	5/9/81	1(3)	1(3)	2	2	0	0	0	0	8	8
Luke Patten	9/1/80	29	27	5	5	0	0	0	0	20	20
Stefan Ratchford	19/7/88	27(1)	25(1)	12	11	5	2	0	0	58	48
Adam Sidlow	25/10/87	9(12)	8(12)	5	5	0	0	0	0	20	20
Matty Smith	23/7/87	28(1)	26(1)	2	2	1	0	0	0	10	8
Marc Sneyd	9/2/91	2(11)	1(10)	1	1	1	1	0	0	6	6
Jack Spencer	21/12/90	(4)	(4)	0	0	0	0	0	0	0	0
Stephen Wild	26/4/81	22	21	1	1	0	0	0	0	4	4
Danny Williams	26/9/86	6	6	8	8	0	0	0	0	32	32

Jodie Broughton

LEAGUE RECORD
P27-W10-D0-L17
(11th, SL)
F542, A809, Diff-267
20 points.

CHALLENGE CUP
Round Five

ATTENDANCES
Best - v Catalan Dragons
(SL - 10,146)
Worst - v Hull KR (CC - 2,087)
Total (SL only) - 61,800
Average (SL only) - 4,754
(Up by 588 on 2010)

17 November 2010 - Kyle Eastmond undergoes more ankle surgery after surgeons discover problems in his other ankle.

25 November 2010 - reserve halfback Jamie Ellis joins Leigh.

29 November 2010 - James Roby signs new four-year deal to end of 2014.

30 November 2010 - Gareth Frodsham joins Widnes Vikings on year-long loan.

23 January 2011 - 52-20 Karalius Cup win over Widnes Vikings at the Stobart Stadium.

1 February 2011 - Paul Wellens and James Graham handed joint captaincy for 2011 season.

12 February 2011 - comeback 16-16 draw with Wigan Warriors in round 1 at Millennium Stadium.

22 February 2011 - young halfback Adam Swift signs two-year contract.

25 February 2011 - Kyle Eastmond booed after 25-18 home defeat by Warrington Wolves in round 3.

1 March 2011 - Kyle Eastmond rejects new contract and will join Bath rugby union at end of season.

5 March 2011 - Leon Pryce comeback in 22-16 victory at Catalan Dragons lasts four minutes before groin strain recurs.

8 March 2011 - Jon Wilkin damages calf whilst training with England.

11 March 2011 - Josh Perry makes debut in 27-16 home defeat by Harlequins in round 5.

16 March 2011 - Kyle Eastmond suspended by club for making gestures at crowd after Harlequins game.

19 March 2011 - Paul Clough suffers injury to neck nerve in 30-16 victory at Leeds in round 6.

22 March 2011 - Lee Gaskell signs three-year contract to end of 2013 season.

22 March 2011 - Scott Moore gets one-match ban for dangerous tackle on Kevin Sinfield.

KEY DATES - ST HELENS

25 March 2011 - Kyle Eastmond suspension lifted but he is dropped for 28-16 victory over Bradford - the first 'home' win of the season.

29 March 2011 - Jon Wilkin suffers nerve damage in hand after accident at home.

5 April 2011 - coach Royce Simmons calls for fans to stop booing Kyle Eastmond in under-20s games.

12 April 2011 - Kiwi World Cup winner Lance Hohaia signs from NZ Warriors on four-year deal from 2012.

15 April 2011 - Lee Gaskell fractures ankle in 52-6 home victory over Wakefield Wildcats in round 10.

22 April 2011 - 28-24 defeat by Wigan in round 11 at DW Stadium.

27 April 2011 - James Graham signs three-year deal with Canterbury Bulldogs from next season.

2 May 2011 - Kyle Eastmond makes return in 24-24 draw with Hull FC in round 13 at KC Stadium.

4 May 2011 - Gold Coast forward Anthony Laffranchi signs two-year contract from 2012.

10 May 2011 - Tony Puletua signs new two-year contract.

27 May 2011 - Ade Gardner tears Achilles tendon in 28-12 home victory over Crusaders in round 15.

1 June 2011 - Josh Perry serves one-match ban after fighting with Crusaders' Ben Flower.

3 June 2011 - James Roby fractures eye socket in 42-16 home victory over Leeds Rhinos in round 16 and misses England game with Exiles following Friday.

12 June 2011 - James Roby plays and Jamie Foster kicks penalty after final hooter to secure 14-14 draw at Bradford.

17 June 2011 - Michael Shenton injures ankle in 32-10 home defeat by Wigan Warriors in round 18.

24 June 2011 - Louie McCarthy-Scarsbrook gets one-match ban for high tackle on Adrian Morley in 35-28 defeat at Warrington.

1 July 2011 - Josh Perry to miss rest of season after hamstring injury in 28-14 home win over Hull FC.

12 July 2011 - Chris Flannery commits for sixth season after signing new deal for 2012.

15 July 2011 - Leon Pryce makes second comeback in 40-18 home win over Catalans.

19 July 2011 - Mark Flanagan signs from Wests Tigers on two-year deal from 2012.

6 August 2011 - 18-12 Challenge Cup semi-final defeat to Wigan.

18 August 2011 - Tommy Makinson, two years and Scott Hale, one year, sign new contracts.

23 August 2011 - Leon Pryce signs for Catalan Dragons.

13 September 2011 - Ade Gardner signs new two-year contract.

18 September 2011 - 26-18 win at Wigan in Qualifying Play-off.

1 October 2011 - 26-18 home win over Wigan secures sixth successive Grand Final spot.

8 October 2011 - 32-16 Old Trafford defeat to Leeds means fifth runners-up spot in last five years.

10 October 2011 - Scott Moore signs for Widnes; Matt Ashurst signs for Salford.

28 October 2011 - chief executive Tony Colquitt to stand down at end of year.

31 October 2011 - the death of club legend Len Killeen is announced.

CLUB RECORDS
Highest score: 112-0 v Carlisle, 14/9/86
Highest score against: 6-78 v Warrington, 12 April 1909
Record attendance: 35,695 v Wigan, 26/12/49

MATCH RECORDS
Tries: 6 Alf Ellaby v Barrow, 5/3/32 Steve Llewellyn v Castleford, 3/3/56 Steve Llewellyn v Liverpool, 20/8/56 Tom van Vollenhoven v Wakefield, 21/12/57 Tom van Vollenhoven v Blackpool, 23/4/62 Frank Myler v Maryport, 1/9/69 Shane Cooper v Hull, 17/2/88
Goals: 16 Paul Loughlin v Carlisle, 14/9/86
Points: 40 Paul Loughlin v Carlisle, 14/9/86

SEASON RECORDS
Tries 62 Tom van Vollenhoven 1958-59
Goals: 214 Kel Coslett 1971-72
Points: 452 Kel Coslett 1971-72

CAREER RECORDS
Tries: 392 Tom van Vollenhoven 1957-68
Goals: 1,639 Kel Coslett 1962-76
Points: 3,413 Kel Coslett 1962-76
Appearances: 531 Kel Coslett 1962-76

ST HELENS

DATE	FIXTURE	RESULT	SCORERS	LGE	ATT
12/2/11	Wigan (MM) ●	D16-16	t:Wilkin,Puletua,Meli g:Foster(2)	6th	N/A
18/2/11	Salford (a)	W22-56	t:Flannery,Eastmond(2),Roby,Meli,Lomax,Gardner,Gaskell,Clough,Shenton g:Foster(8)	4th	5,929
25/2/11	Warrington (h)	L18-25	t:Shenton,Flannery,Gaskell g:Lomax,Foster(2)	7th	10,514
5/3/11	Catalan Dragons (a)	W16-22	t:Flannery,Gardner,Graham,Shenton g:Eastmond(3)	6th	7,095
11/3/11	Harlequins (h)	L16-27	t:Meli,Graham,Roby g:Eastmond,Foster	7th	6,050
19/3/11	Leeds (a)	W16-30	t:Foster(2),Shenton,Meli,Wellens g:Foster(5)	6th	16,035
25/3/11	Bradford (h)	W28-16	t:Foster(2),Wellens(2),Flannery g:Foster(4)	4th	7,676
1/4/11	Hull KR (h)	W34-16	t:Soliola,McCarthy-Scarsbrook(2),Wellens,Foster,Graham g:Foster(5)	4th	7,740
8/4/11	Crusaders (a)	W18-34	t:Lomax,Gaskell,Wellens,Gardner(2),Roby g:Foster(5)	3rd	4,002
15/4/11	Wakefield (h)	W52-6	t:Foster(2),Lomax,Shenton,Gardner,Wheeler,Wellens,Puletua,Makinson g:Foster(8)	2nd	7,003
22/4/11	Wigan (a)	L28-24	t:Shenton,Foster(2),Makinson g:Foster(4)	3rd	24,057
25/4/11	Castleford (h)	W22-20	t:Armstrong(2),Gardner,Meli g:Foster(3)	2nd	8,010
2/5/11	Hull FC (a)	D24-24	t:Foster,Roby,Gardner,Puletua g:Foster(4)	3rd	11,933
7/5/11	Sheffield (h) (CCR4)	W52-26	t:Foster(2),Soliola,Meli(2),Shenton,Wilkin,Eastmond,Flannery g:Foster(8)	N/A	3,563
14/5/11	Huddersfield (a)	L40-18	t:McCarthy-Scarsbrook,Ashurst,Gardner g:Foster(3)	4th	7,843
22/5/11	Featherstone (h) (CCR5)	W70-0	t:Meli,Thompson,Wellens,Graham,Ashe,Shenton(2),Ashurst,Makinson(2),Soliola,Armstrong g:Foster(11)	N/A	2,905
27/5/11	Crusaders (h)	W28-12	t:Foster(2),Wilkin,Lomax,Gaskell g:Foster(4)	4th	6,752
3/6/11	Leeds (h)	W42-16	t:Graham,Roby,Meli,Lomax,Moore,Wellens,Gaskell g:Foster(7)	4th	9,062
12/6/11	Bradford (a)	D14-14	t:McCarthy-Scarsbrook,Makinson g:Foster(3)	4th	13,224
17/6/11	Wigan (h)	L10-32	t:Puletua,Makinson g:Makinson	4th	11,540
24/6/11	Warrington (a)	L35-28	t:Graham,Gaskell,Foster,Puletua(2) g:Foster(4)	4th	13,024
1/7/11	Hull FC (h)	W28-14	t:Flannery,Meli(2),Makinson,Lomax g:Foster(4)	4th	7,053
10/7/11	Wakefield (a)	W6-46	t:Eastmond(2),Foster(2),Wilkin,Lomax,Meli,Flannery g:Foster(7)	4th	5,985
15/7/11	Catalan Dragons (h)	W40-18	t:Foster(3),Meli(2),Shenton g:Foster(8)	3rd	7,026
24/7/11	Hull KR (h) (CCQF)	W54-6	t:Pryce,Soliola,Wilkin(2),Makinson(2),Moore,Lomax,Roby,Shenton g:Foster(7)	N/A	6,449
31/7/11	Castleford (a)	W26-46	t:Graham,Shenton,McCarthy-Scarsbrook,Wellens(2),Puletua,Gaskell,Eastmond g:Foster(7)	3rd	6,802
6/8/11	Wigan (CCSF) ●●	L12-18	t:Foster(2) g:Foster(2)	N/A	12,713
12/8/11	Huddersfield (h)	W19-6	t:Pryce,Wellens,McCarthy-Scarsbrook g:Foster(3) fg:Gaskell	3rd	6,421
21/8/11	Hull KR (a)	L24-22	t:Foster(2),Ashurst,Gaskell g:Foster(3)	3rd	8,356
2/9/11	Salford (a)	W31-6	t:Soliola,Makinson,Meli,Ashurst,Gaskell g:Foster(5) fg:Lomax	3rd	7,377
10/9/11	Harlequins (a)	W16-34	t:Armstrong(3),Gaskell,Hale,McCarthy-Scarsbrook g:Makinson(5)	3rd	3,546
18/9/11	Wigan (a) (QPO)	W18-26	t:Wellens(2),Lomax,McCarthy-Scarsbrook g:Foster(5)	N/A	12,893
1/10/11	Wigan (h) (QSF)	W26-18	t:Gaskell,Wellens,Foster,Roby g:Foster(5)	N/A	9,421
8/10/11	Leeds (GF) ●●●	L32-16	t:Makinson,Shenton g:Foster(4)	N/A	69,107

● Played at Millennium Stadium, Cardiff
●● Played at Halliwell Jones Stadium, Warrington
●●● Played at Old Trafford, Manchester

		APP		TRIES		GOALS		FG		PTS	
	D.O.B.	ALL	SL	ALL	SL	ALL	SL	ALL	SL	ALL	SL
Tom Armstrong	12/9/89	4(6)	4(4)	6	5	0	0	0	0	24	20
Nathan Ashe	15/10/91	3(2)	1(2)	1	0	0	0	0	0	4	0
Matty Ashurst	1/11/89	5(11)	4(10)	4	3	0	0	0	0	16	12
Paul Clough	27/9/87	6(9)	6(8)	1	1	0	0	0	0	4	4
Andrew Dixon	28/2/90	3(15)	3(14)	0	0	0	0	0	0	0	0
Kyle Eastmond	17/7/89	11(6)	10(5)	6	5	4	4	0	0	32	28
Chris Flannery	5/6/80	16(4)	13(4)	7	6	0	0	0	0	28	24
Carl Forster	4/6/92	(1)	(1)	0	0	0	0	0	0	0	0
Jamie Foster	27/7/90	29(3)	25(3)	25	21	151	123	0	0	402	330
Ade Gardner	24/6/83	17	15	8	8	0	0	0	0	32	32
Lee Gaskell	28/10/90	21(5)	21(4)	11	11	0	0	1	1	45	45
James Graham	10/9/85	32	28	7	6	0	0	0	0	28	24
Scott Hale	14/12/91	(4)	(3)	1	0	0	0	0	0	4	4
Jonny Lomax	4/9/90	29	27	9	8	1	1	1	1	39	35
Shaun Magennis	2/12/89	4(15)	2(14)	0	0	0	0	0	0	0	0
Tom Makinson	10/10/91	16(6)	14(5)	11	7	6	6	0	0	56	40
Louie McCarthy-Scarsbrook	14/1/86	21(10)	20(7)	8	8	0	0	0	0	32	32
Francis Meli	20/8/80	28	24	15	12	0	0	0	0	60	48
Scott Moore	23/1/88	4(21)	4(19)	2	1	0	0	0	0	8	4
Josh Perry	4/2/81	8(4)	7(4)	0	0	0	0	0	0	0	0
Leon Pryce	9/10/81	7(1)	5(1)	2	1	0	0	0	0	8	4
Tony Puletua	25/6/79	23(3)	21(3)	7	7	0	0	0	0	28	28
James Roby	22/11/85	33	29	7	6	0	0	0	0	28	24
Michael Shenton	22/7/86	32	28	13	9	0	0	0	0	52	36
Iosia Soliola	4/8/86	29	25	5	2	0	0	0	0	20	8
Warren Thompson	24/2/90	(1)	0	1	0	0	0	0	0	4	0
Paul Wellens	27/2/80	28	25	14	13	0	0	0	0	56	52
Gary Wheeler	30/9/89	6(3)	6(3)	1	1	0	0	0	0	4	4
Jon Wilkin	11/1/83	27(2)	23(2)	6	3	0	0	0	0	24	12

Jamie Foster

LEAGUE RECORD
P27-W17-D3-L7
(3rd, SL/Grand Final Runners-Up)
F782, A515, Diff+267
37 points.

CHALLENGE CUP
Semi-Finalists

ATTENDANCES
Best - v Wigan (SL - 11,540)
Worst - v Featherstone (CC - 2,905)
Total (SL, inc play-offs) - 111,645
Average (SL, inc play-offs) - 7,975
(Down by 3,594 on 2010)

26 November 2010 - new partnership with West Yorkshire Windows announced.

9 December 2010 - Glenn Morrison awarded captaincy for 2011 season; Richard Moore and Jessie Joe Parker released.

6 January 2011 - meeting with shareholders sees appeal for funds.

21 January 2011 - James Davey to be dual registered with Featherstone for 2011 season.

30 January 2011 - 40-16 loss to Bradford in pre-season game at the Grattan Stadium.

1 February 2011 - Wakefield go into administration.

12 February 2011 - 40-20 defeat by Castleford Tigers in round 1 at Millennium Stadium.

14 February 2011 - administrator accepts bid from Hull FC for Sam Obst.

15 February 2011 - administrator accepts bid from Huddersfield Giants for Dale Ferguson.

16 February 2011 - administrator accepts bid for Darryl Millard from Catalan Dragons.

17 February 2011 - club is taken over by local businessman Andrew Glover of West Yorkshire Windows.

18 February 2011 - Wakefield docked four points for going into administration.

19 February 2011 - shock 38-14 victory over Catalan Dragons in round 2 at Stade Gilbert Brutus.

18 March 2011 - 20-6 victory over Hull FC in round 6 at KC Stadium.

23 March 2011 - Leeds prop Kyle Amor extends loan spell.

28 March 2011 - Warrington forward Tyrone McCarthy joins on month's loan.

31 March 2011 - Sheffield forward Liam Higgins signs until end of 2012 season.

10 April 2011 - 52-32 home victory over Harlequins in round 9.

14 April 2011 - prop Jarrad Hickey signs two-year contract.

20 April 2011 - Batley scrum-half Gareth Moore signs two-year contract.

22 April 2011 - 28-24 Good Friday victory at Castleford Tigers in round 11.

25 April 2011 - 26-0 Easter Monday home defeat by Wigan Warriors in round 12.

1 May 2011 - 26-24 home victory over Hull KR in round 13.

7 May 2011 - Ben Jeffries leaves for Bradford Bulls.

13 May 2011 - 23-10 defeat at Crusaders in round 14.

20 May 2011 - Frankie Mariano signs new two-year contract to end of 2013.

KEY DATES - WAKEFIELD T WILDCATS

21 May 2011 - penalty in 10th minute of golden point extra time leads to 20-18 Challenge Cup defeat at home to Castleford.

26 May 2011 - Matthew Wildie signs two-year contract extension to end of 2013.

8 June 2011 - public meeting at Cedar Court attracts over a thousand supporters.

12 June 2011 - 13-10 home victory over Huddersfield Giants in round 17.

26 June 2011 - Glenn Morrison breaks hand in 52-18 home defeat by Hull FC.

1 July 2011 - Semi Tadulala signs contract to end of season.

13 July 2011 - 20-year-old loose forward Chris Annakin signs new two-year contract to end of 2013.

26 July 2011 - Wildcats awarded C grade licence for 2012 to 2015.

30 July 2011 - John Kear to leave at end of season.

1 August 2011 - 19-year-old halfback Liam Kay signs new two-year contract to end of 2013.

3 August 2011 - Harlequins hooker Andy Ellis signs three-year contract from 2012.

4 August 2011 - Villeneuve forward Samy Masselot signs full-time 12-month contract following trials.

5 August 2011 - Papua New Guinea international Ryan Tongia signs to end of season.

5 August 2011 - Oliver Wilkes returns from Harlequins on two-year contract.

8 August 2011 - Vince Mellars joins from Crusaders on three-year contract.

9 August 2011 - Newcastle forward Steve Southern joins on a three-year contract.

10 August 2011 - Peter Fox re-signs from Hull KR on three-year deal and Ali Lauitiiti on two-year contract.

12 August 2011 - Paul King joins Whitehaven with immediate effect.

26 August 2011 - Julien Rinaldi to join Harlequins at end of season.

31 August 2011 - Ben Gledhill joins Salford.

7 September 2011 - Matt Blaymire announces his retirement through knee injury.

8 September 2011 - Luke George to join Huddersfield at end of year.

9 September 2011 - Richard Agar announced as new coach on three-year contract.

16 September 2011 - Cronulla centre Dean Collis, Richard Agar's first signing, joins on three-year contract.

19 September 2011 - Hull FC's Danny Washbrook joins on three-year deal.

28 September 2011 - James Webster leaves Hull and appointed assistant on three-year deal.

3 October 2011 - Kyle Amor signs three-year contract, but Leeds retain option to re-sign after one year.

7 October 2011 - Andy Raleigh joins on two-year contract; Danny Kirmond on three-year deal. Aaron Murphy goes in opposite direction to Huddersfield.

10 October 2011 - Ben Cockayne joins on 12-month contract.

18 October 2011 - Tommy Lee released; former Academy scrum-half Kyle Wood re-signs from Huddersfield on two-year deal.

22 October 2011 - Glenn Morrison signs new 12-month player/coaching contract.

24 October 2011 - Michael Korkidas joins Keighley.

29 October 2011 - halfback Isaac John joins from NZ Warriors on three-year contract.

2 November 2011 - Tim Smith, released by Cronulla, signs 12-month deal, subject to visa application.

4 November 2011 - Josh Veivers and Stuart Howarth released.

11 November 2011 - Glenn Morrison forced to retire after injuring shoulder in pre-season training.

CLUB RECORDS

Highest score:
90-12 v Highfield, 27/10/92
Highest score against:
0-86 v Castleford, 17/4/95
Record attendance:
30,676 v Huddersfield, 26/2/21

MATCH RECORDS

Tries:
7 Fred Smith v Keighley, 25/4/59
Keith Slater v Hunslet, 6/2/71
Goals:
13 Mark Conway v Highfield, 27/10/92
Points:
36 Jamie Rooney v Chorley, 27/2/2004

SEASON RECORDS

Tries: 38 Fred Smith 1959-60
David Smith 1973-74
Goals: 163 Neil Fox 1961-62
Points: 407 Neil Fox 1961-62

CAREER RECORDS

Tries: 272 by Neil Fox 1956-69; 1970-74
Goals: 1,836 by Neil Fox 1956-69; 1970-74
Points: 4,488 by Neil Fox 1956-69; 1970-74
Appearances:
605 Harry Wilkinson 1930-49

WAKEFIELD T WILDCATS

DATE	FIXTURE	RESULT	SCORERS	LGE	ATT
12/2/11	Castleford (MM) ●	L40-20	t:Rinaldi,Ferguson(2),George g:Veivers(2)	12th	N/A
19/2/11	Catalan Dragons (a)	W14-38	t:Mariano(2),Penny,Dean(2),Hyde,George g:Veivers(5)	14th	7,113
27/2/11	Salford (h)	L6-32	t:Lee g:Veivers	14th	6,823
6/3/11	Bradford (a)	L40-18	t:Mariano,George,Hyde g:Veivers(3)	14th	12,835
11/3/11	Warrington (h)	L6-22	t:Griffin g:Griffin	14th	5,073
18/3/11	Hull FC (a)	W6-20	t:Mariano,Lee,Amor g:Griffin(4)	13th	11,032
27/3/11	Leeds (h)	L6-28	t:G Johnson g:Griffin	13th	8,763
3/4/11	Huddersfield (a)	L34-10	t:Dean,Jeffries g:Veivers	14th	7,267
10/4/11	Harlequins (h)	W52-32	t:Lee,Morrison,Howarth,Griffin,George,Jeffries(2),Dean,P Johnson g:Griffin(8)	13th	5,412
15/4/11	St Helens (a)	L52-6	t:Dean g:Griffin	13th	7,003
22/4/11	Castleford (a)	W24-28	t:Dean,Hyde,Griffin,P Johnson,Mariano g:Griffin(4)	13th	9,020
25/4/11	Wigan (h)	L0-26		13th	8,163
1/5/11	Hull KR (h)	W26-24	t:Amor,Dean,Davey,Murphy,Griffin g:Hyde(3)	13th	7,283
8/5/11	Doncaster (a) (CCR4)	W10-50	t:Amor,Griffin(2),Murphy,Henderson,Morton,Dean,Veivers,Hyde g:Veivers(7)	N/A	1,823
13/5/11	Crusaders (a)	L23-10	t:Morton(2) g:Griffin	13th	3,241
21/5/11	Castleford (h) (CCR5)	L18-20 (aet)	t:Morrison,Lee g:Veivers(5)	N/A	6,604
29/5/11	Catalan Dragons (h)	L22-42	t:G Johnson,Wildie,Mariano,McCarthy g:Veivers(3)	13th	4,561
3/6/11	Salford (a)	L34-12	t:Lee,Hickey g:Moore(2)	13th	3,213
12/6/11	Huddersfield (h)	W13-10	t:George g:Moore(4) fg:Moore	13th	5,436
18/6/11	Harlequins (a)	L40-22	t:Morton,Rinaldi,Hickey,P Johnson g:Moore(3)	13th	2,875
26/6/11	Hull FC (h)	L18-52	t:Moore,Amor,George g:Moore(3)	13th	7,965
3/7/11	Hull KR (a)	L70-14	t:Henderson,Lee,George g:Griffin	13th	8,025
10/7/11	St Helens (h)	L6-46	t:Murphy g:Hyde	13th	5,985
15/7/11	Wigan (a)	L48-6	t:Griffin g:Veivers	13th	13,095
31/7/11	Crusaders (h)	L6-40	t:Veivers g:Veivers	13th	6,428
14/8/11	Warrington (a)	L66-12	t:Amor,Smith g:Veivers(2)	14th	10,296
20/8/11	Castleford (h)	L30-34	t:Morrison,P Johnson,Wildie,Tadulala,Dean g:Morton(5)	14th	6,784
2/9/11	Leeds (a)	L64-20	t:Tongia,Veivers,Tony,Amor g:Moore(2)	14th	15,511
9/9/11	Bradford (h)	W26-14	t:P Johnson,Tongia,Korkidas,Lee,Rinaldi g:Veivers(3)	13th	6,502

● Played at Millennium Stadium, Cardiff

		APP		TRIES		GOALS		FG		PTS	
	D.O.B.	ALL	SL	ALL	SL	ALL	SL	ALL	SL	ALL	SL
Kyle Amor	26/5/87	19(8)	18(7)	6	5	0	0	0	0	24	20
Matt Blaymire	10/6/82	11	11	0	0	0	0	0	0	0	0
James Davey	21/8/89	3(8)	3(7)	1	1	0	0	0	0	4	4
Chris Dean	17/1/88	20(1)	20	9	8	0	0	0	0	36	32
Dale Ferguson	13/4/88	1	1	2	2	0	0	0	0	8	8
Luke George	30/10/87	17	16	7	7	0	0	0	0	28	28
Ben Gledhill	18/9/89	(9)	(9)	0	0	0	0	0	0	0	0
Josh Griffin	9/5/90	19	17	7	5	21	21	0	0	70	62
Kevin Henderson	1/10/81	8(16)	7(15)	2	1	0	0	0	0	8	4
Jarrad Hickey	7/5/85	(8)	(8)	2	2	0	0	0	0	8	8
Liam Higgins	19/7/83	4(12)	4(12)	0	0	0	0	0	0	0	0
Stuart Howarth	25/1/90	19(2)	17(2)	1	1	0	0	0	0	4	4
Kieran Hyde	10/10/89	12	10	4	3	4	4	0	0	24	20
Ben Jeffries	4/9/80	5	5	3	3	0	0	0	0	12	12
Greg Johnson	20/2/90	13	12	2	2	0	0	0	0	8	8
Paul Johnson	13/3/88	25(1)	24(1)	5	5	0	0	0	0	20	20
Paul King	28/6/79	2(11)	1(10)	0	0	0	0	0	0	0	0
Michael Korkidas	12/1/81	16(5)	15(4)	1	1	0	0	0	0	4	4
Tommy Lee	1/2/88	27	25	7	6	0	0	0	0	28	24
Frankie Mariano	10/5/87	23(2)	22(1)	6	6	0	0	0	0	24	24
Sammy Masselot	1/9/89	(1)	(1)	0	0	0	0	0	0	0	0
Tyrone McCarthy	21/4/88	2(5)	2(5)	1	1	0	0	0	0	4	4
Darryl Millard	20/2/85	(1)	(1)	0	0	0	0	0	0	0	0
Gareth Moore	3/6/89	5	5	1	1	14	14	1	1	33	33
Glenn Morrison	28/5/76	23	21	3	2	0	0	0	0	12	8
Dale Morton	31/10/90	11	9	4	3	5	5	0	0	26	22
Aaron Murphy	26/11/88	22	20	3	2	0	0	0	0	12	8
Sam Obst	26/11/80	1	1	0	0	0	0	0	0	0	0
Kevin Penny	3/10/87	5	5	1	1	0	0	0	0	4	4
Julien Rinaldi	27/4/79	22(2)	21(2)	3	3	0	0	0	0	12	12
Jeremy Smith	18/7/81	9(1)	9(1)	1	1	0	0	0	0	4	4
Russ Spiers	28/4/91	(2)	(2)	0	0	0	0	0	0	0	0
Semi Tadulala	3/3/78	7	7	1	1	0	0	0	0	4	4
Ryan Tongia	31/5/90	4	4	2	2	0	0	0	0	8	8
Motu Tony	29/5/81	6(3)	6(3)	1	1	0	0	0	0	4	4
Josh Veivers	9/12/89	12(2)	10(2)	3	2	34	22	0	0	80	52
Lucas Walshaw	4/8/92	(1)	(1)	0	0	0	0	0	0	0	0
Matthew Wildie	25/10/90	5(14)	4(13)	2	2	0	0	0	0	8	8

Glenn Morrison

LEAGUE RECORD
P27-W7-D0-L20
(13th, SL)
F453, A957, Diff-504
10 points. *(4 points deducted for entering administration)*

CHALLENGE CUP
Round Five

ATTENDANCES
Best - v Leeds (SL - 8,763)
Worst - v Catalan Dragons (SL - 4,561)
Total (SL only) - 85,178
Average (SL only) - 6,552
(Up by 568 on 2010)

Classy Wolves put Rhinos to the sword

19 November 2010 - assistant coach James Lowes leaves club.

22 November 2010 - Willie Poching confirmed as new assistant coach.

3 December 2010 - Joel Monaghan signs on 12-month contract.

14 December 2010 - released winger Chris Hicks joins Parramatta.

23 January 2011 - Joel Monaghan makes try-scoring debut in 58-10 win over Leigh at Leigh Sports Village.

2 February 2011 - Jon Clarke Testimonial postponed because of snow.

3 February 2011 - Louis Anderson injures knee in 24-18 loss to Wigan in Jon Clarke Testimonial game at the Halliwell Jones Stadium.

7 February 2011 - Rhys Williams joins Crusaders on loan.

12 February 2011 - Matt King injures knee in 28-18 defeat by Huddersfield Giants in round 1 at Millennium Stadium.

20 February 2011 - 24-22 home victory over Hull KR in round 2.

25 February 2011 - Louis Anderson suffers knee cartilage damage in 25-18 victory at St Helens.

5 March 2011 - Rhys Evans makes home debut in 40-24 victory over Leeds in round 4.

7 March 2011 - reserve halfback Craig Harvey decides to quit the game.

11 March 2011 - 22-6 victory at Wakefield Wildcats in round 5.

15 March 2011 - Lee Briers signs 12-month contract extension to end of 2012 season.

20 March 2011 - 82-6 home victory over Harlequins in round 6.

25 March 2011 - 24-6 victory at Wigan in round 7 ends Warriors' unbeaten start.

28 March 2011 - Tyrone McCarthy joins Wakefield on month's loan.

30 March 2011 - Joel Monaghan agrees three-year contract extension.

3 April 2011 - shock 22-20 home defeat by Catalan Dragons in round 8.

KEY DATES - WARRINGTON WOLVES

8 April 2011 - 29-10 defeat by Huddersfield Giants in round 9 at Galpharm Stadium.

15 April 2011 - 64-6 home victory over Crusaders in round 10.

20 April 2011 - Lee Mitchell joins Harlequins on month's loan; Rhys Evans agrees dual registration with Leigh.

22 April 2011 - Richie Myler fractures cheekbone in 60-0 victory at Salford.

25 April 2011 - 24-10 home defeat by Hull FC in round 12.

8 May 2011 - Ben Harrison damages ankle in 80-0 Challenge Cup win over Keighley.

13 May 2011 - 62-0 home victory over Castleford Tigers in round 14.

20 May 2011 - Lee Briers becomes club's all-time top points scorer, and sets new marks for points (44) and goals (16) in a match in 112-0 home Challenge Cup win over Swinton.

24 May 2011 - Chris Riley joins Harlequins on loan.

27 May 2011 - Richie Myler makes comeback in 42-6 victory at Leeds in round 15.

9 June 2011 - Garreth Carvell signs contract until end of 2013; Chris Bridge agrees three-year deal until November 2015 and David Solomona 12-month deal.

11 June 2011 - club mourns Paul Darbyshire, who dies at the age of 41 from motor neurone disease.

12 June 2011 - 18-16 home defeat by Salford City Reds in round 17

19 June 2011 - 46-16 victory over Hull KR in round 18 at Craven Park.

24 June 2011 - Adrian Morley suffers eye injury in 35-28 home win over St Helens.

29 June 2011 - Test forward Trent Waterhouse signs three-year deal from 2012.

6 July 2011 - Wolves reserve side wins RL Nines final at Headingley.

8 July 2011 - Leigh prop Chris Hill signs two-year contract from 2012.

12 July 2011 - Louis Anderson to join Catalans, and Matt King South Sydney, at end of season.

23 July 2011 - 44-24 Challenge Cup quarter-final defeat by Wigan.

26 July 2011 - Academy international Danny Bridge joins from Wigan.

27 July 2011 - Salford's Stefan Ratchford signs three-year deal from 2012.

31 July 2011 - Mickey Higham banned for two games for dangerous contact in 64-6 home win over Bradford.

14 August 2011 - Ben Westwood tears medial ligament in 66-12 home win over Wakefield.

4 September 2011 - 39-12 home win over Wigan puts Wolves on top of table.

THE EDGE OF GLORY!

6 September 2011 - Jon Clarke to join Super League-bound Widnes at end of season.

9 September 2011 - 34-12 win at Hull FC seals League Leaders Trophy.

13 September 2011 - Wolves win Albert Goldthorpe Team of the Year.

16 September 2011 - 47-0 hammering of Huddersfield in home Qualifying Play-off.

25 September 2011 - Wolves choose Leeds Rhinos in Clubcall.

30 September 2011 - 26-24 Qualifying semi-final defeat after late Kevin Sinfield penalty.

13 October 2011 - Richie Myler and Ryan Atkins extend contracts by two years to end of 2015.

13 October 2011 - Simon Grix agrees three-year extension to end of 2015.

13 October 2011 - Matty Blythe signs three-year extension to end of 2014; Rhys Williams signs one-year extension for 2012.

CLUB RECORDS

Highest score:
112-0 v Swinton, 20/5/2011
Highest score against:
12-84 v Bradford, 9/9/2001
Record attendance:
34,404 v Wigan, 22/1/49 *(Wilderspool)*
14,206 v Wakefield, 21/2/2004
(Halliwell Jones Stadium)

MATCH RECORDS

Tries:
7 Brian Bevan v Leigh, 29/3/48
Brian Bevan v Bramley, 22/4/53
Goals:
16 Lee Briers v Swinton, 20/5/2011
Points:
44 Lee Briers v Swinton, 20/5/2011

SEASON RECORDS

Tries: 66 Brian Bevan 1952-53
Goals: 170 Steve Hesford 1978-79
Points: 363 Harry Bath 1952-53

CAREER RECORDS

Tries: 740 Brian Bevan 1945-62
Goals: 1,159 Steve Hesford 1975-85
Points: 2,466 Lee Briers 1997-2011
Appearances: 620 Brian Bevan 1945-62

WARRINGTON WOLVES

DATE	FIXTURE	RESULT	SCORERS	LGE	ATT
12/2/11	Huddersfield (MM) ●	L28-18	t:J Monaghan,Westwood,Atkins g:Hodgson(3)	10th	N/A
20/2/11	Hull KR (h)	W24-22	t:J Monaghan,Myler,Atkins,Riley,Hodgson g:Hodgson(2)	8th	10,899
25/2/11	St Helens (a)	W18-25	t:Briers(2),Myler,Anderson g:Hodgson(4) fg:Briers	5th	10,514
5/3/11	Leeds (h)	W40-24	t:Evans,Briers,Myler,Riley,Grix,J Monaghan,Higham g:Hodgson(6)	3rd	11,438
11/3/11	Wakefield (a)	W6-22	t:Riley,Bridge,Atkins,Myler g:Westwood(3)	3rd	5,073
20/3/11	Harlequins (h)	W82-6	t:Bridge(3),Briers,Solomona(2),Myler,Evans,Westwood(2),Morley,Blythe, Mitchell,Hodgson g:Hodgson(13)	1st	11,506
25/3/11	Wigan (a)	W6-24	t:Blythe,J Monaghan(2),Myler g:Hodgson(4)	1st	21,056
3/4/11	Catalan Dragons (h)	L20-22	t:J Monaghan(2),Riley,Myler g:Hodgson(2)	1st	10,956
8/4/11	Huddersfield (a)	L29-10	t:Hodgson(2) g:Hodgson	4th	7,224
15/4/11	Crusaders (h)	W64-6	t:Hodgson(2),Westwood(2),Williams,Anderson,Atkins(2),Bridge, J Monaghan,Myler g:Hodgson(10)	4th	10,002
22/4/11	Salford (a)	W0-60	t:Atkins,Myler,Briers(2),Bridge,Carvell,J Monaghan,Williams(2),Wood g:Hodgson(10)	1st	7,496
25/4/11	Hull FC (h)	L10-24	t:J Monaghan,Williams g:Hodgson	3rd	12,036
1/5/11	Bradford (a)	W14-58	t:Anderson(2),Atkins(2),M Monaghan,King,J Monaghan,Hodgson,Higham, Bridge,Briers g:Hodgson(7)	1st	14,134
8/5/11	Keighley (h) (CCR4)	W80-0	t:Atkins(3),Grix,Wood,Cooper,Briers(2),O'Brien,Williams(2),King, M Monaghan,Evans g:Briers(12)	N/A	6,583
13/5/11	Castleford (h)	W62-0	t:O'Brien,Briers(2),King(2),Hodgson,Grix(2),Higham,Solomona,J Monaghan g:Hodgson(7),Briers(2)	1st	10,715
20/5/11	Swinton (h) (CCR5)	W112-0	t:J Monaghan(4),Briers(3),Atkins,Carvell(3),Grix,M Monaghan,Riley(3), Westwood,Williams,Bridge g:Briers(16)	N/A	4,440
27/5/11	Leeds (a)	W6-42	t:Briers(2),J Monaghan,Solomona,Bridge,M Monaghan,King g:Hodgson(7)	1st	17,276
3/6/11	Crusaders (a)	W16-56	t:King,Morley,Westwood,Atkins,Wood(2),Hodgson(3),Myler g:Hodgson(8)	1st	4,907
12/6/11	Salford (h)	L16-18	t:Bridge,Briers,Myler g:Hodgson(2)	1st	10,339
19/6/11	Hull KR (a)	W16-46	t:Grix,King(3),Atkins(2),Briers,Williams,Myler g:Hodgson(5)	1st	8,143
24/6/11	St Helens (h)	W35-28	t:M Monaghan,Williams,King,Westwood,Wood,Hodgson g:Hodgson(5) fg:Briers	1st	13,024
1/7/11	Castleford (a)	W18-48	t:Hodgson(2),Myler,Blythe,King(3),J Monaghan,Atkins g:Hodgson(6)	1st	5,947
8/7/11	Huddersfield (h)	W28-16	t:Hodgson,J Monaghan(2),Myler,Anderson g:Hodgson(4)	2nd	10,283
16/7/11	Harlequins (a)	W24-54	t:Carvell,Bridge(4),J Monaghan,Briers,Myler,Wood g:Hodgson(8),Briers	2nd	3,842
23/7/11	Wigan (h) (CCQF)	L24-44	t:King(2),Myler(2),Solomona g:Hodgson(2)	N/A	13,105
31/7/11	Bradford (h)	W64-6	t:Atkins(4),King(2),J Monaghan(3),Hodgson(2),M Monaghan g:Hodgson(5),Bridge(3)	2nd	10,641
14/8/11	Wakefield (h)	W66-12	t:Bridge,Atkins(3),Myler,J Monaghan,King(2),Anderson(2),Cooper g:Hodgson,Bridge(10)	2nd	10,296
20/8/11	Catalan Dragons (a)	W12-25	t:Bridge(2),Atkins,Briers g:Bridge(4) fg:Briers	2nd	9,495
4/9/11	Wigan (h)	W39-12	t:King,Briers,M Monaghan(2),Clarke,J Monaghan g:Bridge(7) fg:M Monaghan	1st	13,024
9/9/11	Hull FC (a)	W12-34	t:Atkins,Riley(2),M Monaghan,Bridge,J Monaghan g:Bridge(4),Briers	1st	16,121
16/9/11	Huddersfield (h) (QPO)	W47-0	t:Riley(2),Bridge,J Monaghan(2),King,Hodgson,Myler,Atkins g:Bridge(2),Briers(3) fg:Briers	N/A	10,006
30/9/11	Leeds (h) (QSF)	L24-26	t:J Monaghan,Riley(2),King g:Bridge(4)	N/A	12,074

● Played at Millennium Stadium, Cardiff

		APP		TRIES		GOALS		FG		PTS	
	D.O.B.	ALL	SL	ALL	SL	ALL	SL	ALL	SL	ALL	SL
Louis Anderson	27/6/85	20	19	7	7	0	0	0	0	28	28
Ryan Atkins	7/10/85	28	25	26	22	0	0	0	0	104	88
Matty Blythe	20/11/88	14(8)	12(7)	3	3	0	0	0	0	12	12
Chris Bridge	5/7/84	27	25	19	18	34	34	0	0	144	140
Lee Briers	14/6/78	25	23	21	16	35	7	4	4	158	82
Garrett Carvell	21/4/80	28(3)	25(3)	5	2	0	0	0	0	20	8
Jon Clarke	4/4/79	2(16)	2(14)	1	1	0	0	0	0	4	4
Michael Cooper	15/9/88	6(17)	5(15)	2	1	0	0	0	0	8	4
Rhys Evans	30/10/92	6(3)	6(2)	3	2	0	0	0	0	12	8
Simon Grix	28/9/85	25(2)	22(2)	6	4	0	0	0	0	24	16
Ben Harrison	24/2/88	14(9)	13(9)	0	0	0	0	0	0	0	0
Mick Higham	18/9/80	2(20)	1(19)	3	3	0	0	0	0	12	12
Brett Hodgson	12/2/78	27	26	18	18	123	121	0	0	318	314
Matt King	22/8/80	21	18	22	19	0	0	0	0	88	76
Tyrone McCarthy	21/4/88	(3)	(3)	0	0	0	0	0	0	0	0
Lee Mitchell	8/9/88	(5)	(5)	1	1	0	0	0	0	4	4
Joel Monaghan	22/4/82	26	24	30	26	0	0	0	0	120	104
Michael Monaghan	13/5/80	30(1)	28	9	7	0	0	1	1	37	29
Adrian Morley	10/5/77	21(2)	20(1)	2	2	0	0	0	0	8	8
Richard Myler	21/5/90	27	26	19	17	0	0	0	0	76	68
Gareth O'Brien	31/10/91	3	1	2	1	0	0	0	0	8	4
Chris Riley	22/2/88	12	10	13	10	0	0	0	0	52	40
David Solomona	26/1/78	5(23)	4(21)	5	4	0	0	0	0	20	16
Ben Westwood	25/7/81	24(2)	22(2)	9	7	3	3	0	0	42	34
Rhys Williams	8/12/89	11	9	9	6	0	0	0	0	36	24
Paul Wood	10/10/81	12(14)	11(13)	6	5	0	0	0	0	24	20

Joel Monaghan

LEAGUE RECORD
P27-W22-D0-L5
(1st, SL/Qualifying Semi-Final)
F1072, A401, Diff+671
44 points.

CHALLENGE CUP
Quarter Finalists

ATTENDANCES
Best - v Wigan (CC - 13,105)
Worst - v Swinton (CC - 4,440)
Total (SL, inc play-offs) - 167,239
Average (SL, inc play-offs) - 11,149
(Up by 411 on 2010)

19 November 2010 - Paul Deacon signs new one-year playing contract.

23 November 2010 - Karl Pryce signs new one-year deal; departure of Cameron Phelps confirmed.

3 December 2010 - Chris Tuson signs for next two years, with an option for 2013.

14 December 2010 - released Mark Riddell joins Sydney Roosters for 2011.

13 January 2011 - Brett Finch undergoes neck surgery after training injury.

25 January 2011 - Karl Pryce and Joe Mellor join Harlequins on loan.

28 January 2011 - Sean O'Loughlin named captain for 2011 season.

2 February 2011 - 24-18 win over Warrington in Jon Clarke Testimonial at the Halliwell Jones Stadium.

4 February 2011 - Sam and Joel Tomkins and Liam Farrell and Josh Charnley sign new five-year contracts to end of 2015; Darrell Goulding and Harrison Hansen pen three-year deals.

7 February 2011 - coach Michael Maguire dismisses speculation linking him with a return to the NRL.

12 February 2011 - 16-16 draw with St Helens in round 1 at Millennium Stadium - prop Jeff Lima handed two-match suspension for two dangerous tackles.

27 February 2011 - 21-15 defeat to St George Illawarra in World Club Challenge.

8 March 2011 - Stuart Fielden out of action for at least three months after knee surgery.

13 March 2011 - Joel and Sam Tomkins receive two-match ban and one-match ban respectively after 14-12 home victory over Hull FC.

25 March 2011 - Brett Finch makes debut in 24-6 home defeat by Warrington in round 6.

30 March 2011 - Ben Davies joins Barrow on month's loan, Jack Hughes signs dual-registration.

1 April 2011 - Jeff Lima gets one-match ban for dangerous contact in round 7, 22-22 draw at Leeds.

5 April 2011 - Martin Gleeson released from contract.

6 April 2011 - Gareth Hock returns to training, almost three months before drug ban expires.

8 April 2011 - Pat Richards makes seasonal debut in 47-28 home defeat by Catalan Dragons in round 8.

16 April 2011 - coach Michael Maguire to leave at end of season to take over at South Sydney.

22 April 2011 - last-minute Liam Farrell try secures 28-24 home victory over St Helens in round 10.

KEY DATES - WIGAN WARRIORS

6 May 2011 - Pat Richards signs contract extension for 2012 and 2013.

8 May 2011 - 52-0 home win over Barrow in fourth round of Challenge Cup.

11 May 2011 - Gareth Hock signs five-year contract to end of 2015.

22 May 2011 - 26-22 Carnegie Challenge Cup fifth round win at Bradford.

6 June 2011 - Thomas Leuluai dismisses talk he will follow coach Michael Maguire to South Sydney at end of season.

17 June 2011 - Chris Tuson receives one-match ban for dangerous contact in 32-10 victory over St Helens in round 17 at Stobart Stadium.

25 June 2011 - Gareth Hock returns from two-year drugs ban in 46-12 home win over Huddersfield.

1 July 2011 - Andy Coley banned for one match for running in and punching in 26-24 home win over Leeds..

8 July 2011 - Ben Davies joins Castleford on loan.

12 July 2011 - released Leeds prop Ben Cross signs to end of season.

12 July 2011 - George Carmont postpones retirement plans to play on in 2012.

14 July 2011 - Ryan Hoffman confirms he will return to Melbourne at end of season.

23 July 2011 - 44-24 Challenge Cup quarter-final win at holders Warrington.

27 July 2011 - Stuart Fielden ruled out for rest of season after tearing pectoral muscle in training, after four months out with knee injury.

27 July 2011 - Young forward Danny Bridge leaves to join brother Chris at Warrington.

6 August 2011 - 18-12 Cup semi-final win over St Helens.

14 August 2011 - Ben Cross breaks arm in 52-18 home win over Salford.

22 August 2011 - Andy Coley confirms he is to retire at end of season.

27 August 2011 - 28-18 Wembley win over Leeds secures first Challenge Cup since 2002.

30 August 2011 - Sam Tomkins fined £1,000, suspended until the end of 2012 season for minor misconduct following obscene gesture towards a section of Leeds Rhinos supporters at Wembley.

4 September 2011 - 39-12 defeat at Warrington puts Wolves on top of table.

6 September 2011 - Eamon O'Carroll signs for Hull FC.

6 September 2011 - Gareth Hock handed five-match ban for gouging and punching in Warrington defeat.

18 September 2011 - 26-18 home defeat to St Helens in Qualifying Play-off.

25 September 2011 - 44-0 home defeat of Catalans in Preliminary Semi-final.

1 October 2011 - 26-18 away defeat to St Helens in Qualifying Semi-final ends season.

11 October 2011 - Shaun Wane appointed new head coach on two-year contract with option for third season; Iestyn Harris joins as assistant.

11 October 2011 - Paul Deacon retires and joins backroom staff.

2 November 2011 - Epalahame Lauaki joins from Hull FC on three-year contract.

7 November 2011 - Sam Tomkins signs new, improved five-year contract. Brother Joel joins Saracens rugby union club.

CLUB RECORDS

Highest score:
116-0 v Flimby & Fothergill, 14/2/25
Highest score against:
0-75 v St Helens, 26/6/2005
Record attendance:
47,747 v St Helens, 27/3/59 *(Central Park)*
25,004 v St Helens, 25/3/2005
(JJB Stadium)

MATCH RECORDS

Tries: 10 Martin Offiah v Leeds, 10/5/92
Shaun Edwards v Swinton, 29/9/92
Goals: 22 Jim Sullivan
v Flimby & Fothergill, 14/2/25
Points: 44 Jim Sullivan
v Flimby & Fothergill, 14/2/25

SEASON RECORDS

Tries: 62 Johnny Ring 1925-26
Goals: 186 Frano Botica 1994-95
Points: 462 Pat Richards 2010

CAREER RECORDS

Tries: 478 Billy Boston 1953-68
Goals: 2,317 Jim Sullivan 1921-46
Points: 4,883 Jim Sullivan 1921-46
Appearances: 774 Jim Sullivan 1921-46

WIGAN WARRIORS

DATE	FIXTURE	RESULT	SCORERS	LGE	ATT
12/2/11	St Helens (MM) ●	D16-16	t:Hoffman,Hansen,Carmont g:Deacon,S Tomkins	6th	N/A
20/2/11	Bradford (a)	W10-44	t:Roberts(2),Hansen,Leuluai,Farrell,Goulding,Carmont,S Tomkins g:Deacon(6)	5th	15,348
27/2/11	St George Illawarra (WCC) ●●	L15-21	t:Carmont(2) g:Deacon(3) fg:S Tomkins	N/A	24,268
4/3/11	Salford (a)	W16-32	t:Hansen,Leuluai(2),Mossop,Charnley,Goulding g:Deacon(4)	5th	6,266
13/3/11	Hull FC (h)	W14-12	t:Hoffman,Charnley(2) g:S Tomkins	5th	15,346
18/3/11	Huddersfield (a)	W6-20	t:O'Loughlin,Charnley,Hoffman g:Charnley(4)	4th	8,151
25/3/11	Warrington (h)	L6-24	t:Finch g:Charnley	5th	21,056
1/4/11	Leeds (a)	D22-22	t:J Tomkins,S Tomkins,Goulding,Prescott g:S Tomkins(3)	5th	16,118
8/4/11	Catalan Dragons (h)	L28-47	t:S Tomkins,McIlorum,Carmont,O'Loughlin,Marsh g:Richards(4)	5th	13,134
15/4/11	Hull KR (a)	W16-28	t:J Tomkins,Hoffman,Charnley,Leuluai,Carmont g:Richards(4)	5th	8,703
22/4/11	St Helens (h)	W28-24	t:Charnley(2),Richards(2),Farrell g:Richards(4)	5th	24,057
25/4/11	Wakefield (a)	W0-26	t:Richards,S Tomkins,Charnley,J Tomkins,O'Loughlin g:Richards(3)	4th	8,163
1/5/11	Crusaders (a)	W16-48	t:Richards,Charnley(2),S Tomkins(2),Leuluai,Finch,McIlorum g:Richards(7),O'Loughlin	4th	5,037
8/5/11	Barrow (h) (CCR4)	W52-0	t:Leuluai(2),Coley,Carmont,Deacon,S Tomkins(2),O'Loughlin,Richards g:Richards(8)	N/A	8,026
13/5/11	Harlequins (h)	W54-6	t:Richards(2),Hoffman,Carmont,S Tomkins(2),Leuluai(2),O'Loughlin g:Richards(9)	3rd	12,813
22/5/11	Bradford (a) (CCR5)	W22-26	t:Richards(2),S Tomkins,Finch,Farrell g:Richards(3)	N/A	5,828
30/5/11	Hull KR (h)	W40-6	t:S Tomkins(3),Richards(3),Carmont g:Richards(6)	2nd	14,779
4/6/11	Catalan Dragons (a) ●●●	L20-12	t:S Tomkins(2) g:Richards(2)	3rd	9,372
12/6/11	Castleford (a)	D22-22	t:Finch,Charnley,Prescott,J Tomkins g:Richards(3)	3rd	7,263
17/6/11	St Helens (a)	W10-32	t:Mossop,Richards,J Tomkins,Finch,Lima g:Richards(6)	3rd	11,540
25/6/11	Huddersfield (h)	W46-12	t:S Tomkins(3),Leuluai,Carmont,Richards,Charnley,Mossop g:Richards(7)	2nd	19,169
1/7/11	Leeds (h)	W26-24	t:Charnley,Hoffman,Richards,Carmont g:Richards(5)	2nd	16,426
6/7/11	Castleford (h)	W26-16	t:Charnley(2),Farrell,Carmont,Hoffman g:Deacon(3)	1st	13,096
9/7/11	Harlequins (a)	W6-38	t:Richards,Hoffman,Hansen,Deacon(2),Marsh,Finch g:Richards(5)	1st	4,423
15/7/11	Wakefield (h)	W48-6	t:Hock(3),Carmont,Richards,S Tomkins(2),Charnley g:Richards(8)	1st	13,095
23/7/11	Warrington (a) (CCQF)	W24-44	t:Hansen,S Tomkins,Coley,Richards(2),Charnley(2),O'Loughlin g:Richards(6)	N/A	13,105
29/7/11	Hull FC (a)	W16-30	t:S Tomkins(2),Richards(2),Carmont g:Richards(5)	1st	11,729
6/8/11	St Helens (CCSF) ●●●●	W12-18	t:Carmont,Charnley,S Tomkins g:Richards(3)	N/A	12,713
14/8/11	Salford (h)	W52-18	t:S Tomkins(4),Coley,Charnley,McIlorum,Farrell,J Tomkins g:Richards(8)	1st	13,607
19/8/11	Bradford (h)	W60-12	t:Carmont(2),Hoffman,Richards(3),S Tomkins(2),Charnley(2),O'Loughlin,Hansen g:Richards(6)	1st	13,940
27/8/11	Leeds (CCF) ●●●●●	W18-28	t:Charnley,Lima(2),J Tomkins,Leuluai g:Richards(4)	N/A	78,482
4/9/11	Warrington (a)	L39-12	t:Deacon,O'Loughlin g:Richards(2)	2nd	13,024
9/9/11	Crusaders (h)	W42-10	t:Finch,Charnley(2),Hoffman,Farrell,Richards,J Tomkins g:Richards(7)	2nd	19,104
18/9/11	St Helens (h) (QPO)	L18-26	t:Richards,O'Loughlin,J Tomkins g:Richards(3)	N/A	12,893
25/9/11	Catalan Dragons (h) (PSF)	W44-0	t:Charnley,Hoffman,Farrell,Carmont,Finch,S Tomkins,Hansen g:Richards(8)	N/A	6,790
1/10/11	St Helens (a) (QSF)	L26-18	t:Charnley,O'Carroll,S Tomkins g:Richards(3)	N/A	9,421

● Played at Millennium Stadium, Cardiff ●● Played at DW Stadium ●●● Played at Stade Yve du Manoir, Montpellier
●●●● Played at Halliwell Jones Stadium, Warrington ●●●●● Played at Wembley Stadium

		APP		TRIES		GOALS		FG		PTS	
	D.O.B.	ALL	SL	ALL	SL	ALL	SL	ALL	SL	ALL	SL
George Carmont	30/6/78	33	28	18	14	0	0	0	0	72	56
Josh Charnley	26/6/91	32(1)	27(1)	27	23	5	5	0	0	118	102
Andy Coley	7/7/78	27(5)	21(5)	3	1	0	0	0	0	12	4
Ben Cross	6/12/78	(5)	(4)	0	0	0	0	0	0	0	0
Paul Deacon	13/2/79	23(6)	19(4)	4	3	17	14	0	0	50	40
Liam Farrell	2/7/90	9(19)	7(16)	7	6	0	0	0	0	28	24
Stuart Fielden	14/9/79	1	1	0	0	0	0	0	0	0	0
Brett Finch	20/8/81	26(3)	21(3)	8	7	0	0	0	0	32	28
Martin Gleeson	28/5/80	3	2	0	0	0	0	0	0	0	0
Darrell Goulding	3/3/88	13(2)	11(2)	3	3	0	0	0	0	12	12
Harrison Hansen	26/10/85	29(2)	25(2)	7	6	0	0	0	0	28	24
Gareth Hock	5/9/83	2(7)	2(6)	3	3	0	0	0	0	12	12
Ryan Hoffman	26/1/84	34(1)	28(1)	11	11	0	0	0	0	44	44
Jack Hughes	4/1/92	(2)	(1)	0	0	0	0	0	0	0	0
Thomas Leuluai	22/6/85	35	29	11	8	0	0	0	0	44	32
Jeff Lima	4/7/82	20(12)	16(11)	3	1	0	0	0	0	12	4
Stefan Marsh	3/9/90	7	7	2	2	0	0	0	0	8	8
Michael McIlorum	10/1/88	21(15)	18(12)	3	3	0	0	0	0	12	12
Lee Mossop	17/1/89	14(15)	13(11)	3	3	0	0	0	0	12	12
Eamon O'Carroll	13/6/87	(4)	(4)	1	1	0	0	0	0	4	4
Sean O'Loughlin	24/11/82	34(1)	28(1)	9	7	1	1	0	0	38	30
Paul Prescott	1/1/86	9(20)	8(16)	2	2	0	0	0	0	8	8
Pat Richards	27/2/82	27	22	26	21	139	115	0	0	382	314
Amos Roberts	2/11/80	5(1)	4(1)	2	2	0	0	0	0	8	8
Joel Tomkins	21/3/87	28(4)	23(3)	9	8	0	0	0	0	36	32
Sam Tomkins	23/3/89	34	28	33	28	5	5	1	0	143	122
Chris Tuson	25/2/90	2(18)	2(15)	0	0	0	0	0	0	0	0

Sam Tomkins

LEAGUE RECORD
P27-W20-D3-L4
(2nd, SL/Qualifying Semi-Final)
F852, A432, Diff+420. 43 points.

CHALLENGE CUP: Winners

ATTENDANCES
Best - v St George Illawarra
(WCC - 24,268)
Worst - v Catalan Dragons
(PSF - 6,790)
Total (SL, inc play-offs) - 229,305
Average (SL, inc play-offs) - 15,287
(Up by 110 on 2010)

SUPER LEAGUE XVI
Round by Round

ROUND 1 - MILLENNIUM MAGIC

Saturday 12th February 2011

HUDDERSFIELD GIANTS 28 WARRINGTON WOLVES 18

GIANTS: 1 Scott Grix; 20 Jermaine McGillvary; 3 Leroy Cudjoe; 2 Michael Lawrence; 5 David Hodgson; 6 Kevin Brown (C); 7 Danny Brough; 8 Eorl Crabtree; 22 Keal Carlile; 15 Keith Mason; 4 Lee Gilmour; 12 David Fa'alogo; 11 Luke O'Donnell (D). Subs (all used): 14 Shaun Lunt; 19 Graeme Horne; 13 David Faiumu; 10 Darrell Griffin.
Tries: Carlile (10), Brough (30, 71), Griffin (46), Lunt (65); **Goals:** Brough 4/6.
Sin bin: Griffin (76) - fighting.
WOLVES: 1 Brett Hodgson (D); 5 Joel Monaghan (D); 4 Chris Bridge; 23 Ryan Atkins; 3 Matt King; 6 Lee Briers; 7 Richard Myler; 8 Adrian Morley (C); 9 Michael Monaghan; 13 Ben Harrison; 11 Louis Anderson; 12 Ben Westwood; 17 Simon Grix. Subs (all used): 26 David Solomona; 16 Paul Wood; 14 Mick Higham; 18 Michael Cooper.
Tries: J Monaghan (4), Westwood (69), Atkins (78); **Goals:** Hodgson 3/3.
Sin bin: M Monaghan (76) - fighting.
Rugby Leaguer & League Express Men of the Match: *Giants:* Danny Brough; *Wolves:* David Solomona.
Penalty count: 12-13; **Half-time:** 10-6;
Referee: Ben Thaler.

CATALAN DRAGONS 4 HARLEQUINS 11

DRAGONS: 1 Clint Greenshields; 2 Damien Blanch (D); 3 Ben Farrar (D); 4 Setaimata Sa; 5 Cyril Stacul; 14 Tony Gigot; 7 Scott Dureau (D); 8 David Ferriol; 15 Jean-Philippe Baile; 23 Lopini Paea (D); 17 Cyrille Gossard; 12 Sebastien Raguin; 13 Gregory Mounis (C). Subs (all used): 9 Ian Henderson (D); 10 Remi Casty; 11 Steve Menzies (D); 22 Jamal Fakir.
Try: Blanch (78); **Goals:** Dureau 0/1.
HARLEQUINS: 1 Luke Dorn; 2 Jamie O'Callaghan; 3 Tony Clubb; 4 David Howell; 5 Chris Melling; 6 Luke Gale; 7 Chad Randall; 17 Danny Ward; 9 Andy Ellis; 10 Oliver Wilkes; 13 Rob Purdham (C); 16 Mike Burnett (D); 12 Chris Bailey (D). Subs (all used): 15 Luke Ambler (D); 11 Nick Kouparitsas (D); 19 Lamont Bryan; 21 Olsi Krasniqi.
Tries: Gale (3, 6); **Goals:** Gale 1/2; **Field goal:** Gale (62).
Rugby Leaguer & League Express Men of the Match: *Dragons:* Steve Menzies; *Harlequins:* Luke Gale.
Penalty count: 9-11; **Half-time:** 0-10;
Referee: Robert Hicks.

CASTLEFORD TIGERS 40
WAKEFIELD TRINITY WILDCATS 20

TIGERS: 1 Richard Mathers (D); 2 Kirk Dixon; 13 Brett Ferres; 4 Joe Arundel; 3 Nick Youngquest (D); 6 Rangi Chase; 7 Danny Orr (C) (D2); 10 Craig Huby; 9 Ryan Hudson; 11 Jake Emmitt (D); 14 Stuart Jones; 24 Oliver Holmes; 12 Steve Snitch. Subs (all used): 16 Adam Milner; 25 Dean Widders; 8 Paul Jackson; 15 Jonathan Walker.
Tries: Arundel (5), Ferres (31), Youngquest (34), Widders (39, 78), Chase (41), Milner (50), Jackson (72); **Goals:** Dixon 4/8.
Sin bin: Arundel (23) - persistent offending.
On report: Snitch (18) - alleged dangerous contact.
WILDCATS: 1 Matt Blaymire; 23 Josh Veivers (D); 3 Aaron Murphy; 18 Chris Dean (D); 5 Luke George; 27 Kieran Hyde; 7 Sam Obst; 8 Michael Korkidas; 9 Julien Rinaldi; 17 Paul Johnson (D); 12 Dale Ferguson; 13 Glenn Morrison (C); 14 Tommy Lee (D). Subs (all used): 4 Darryl Millard; 10 Paul King; 28 Russ Spiers (D); 11 Kevin Henderson.
Tries: Rinaldi (19), Ferguson (26, 57), George (64); **Goals:** Veivers 2/4.
Sin bin: Obst (38) - persistent offending; Millard (67) - persistent offending.
Rugby Leaguer & League Express Men of the Match: *Tigers:* Rangi Chase; *Wildcats:* Julien Rinaldi.
Penalty count: 22-15; **Half-time:** 18-10;
Referee: James Child.

ST HELENS 16 WIGAN WARRIORS 16

SAINTS: 1 Paul Wellens (C); 2 Ade Gardner; 3 Michael Shenton (D); 20 Jonny Lomax; 5 Francis Meli; 17 Gary Wheeler; 7 Kyle Eastmond; 10 James Graham (C); 9 James Roby; 15 Louie McCarthy-Scarsbrook (D); 4 Iosia Soliola; 12 Jon Wilkin; 14 Scott Moore. Subs (all used): 11 Tony Puletua; 16 Paul Clough; 19 Andrew Dixon; 22 Jamie Foster.
Tries: Wilkin (62), Puletua (68), Meli (75); **Goals:** Foster 2/3.
WARRIORS: 1 Sam Tomkins; 2 Darrell Goulding; 3 Martin Gleeson; 4 George Carmont; 25 Josh Charnley; 6 Paul Deacon; 7 Thomas Leuluai; 10 Andy Coley; 9 Michael McIlorum; 15 Jeff Lima (D); 16 Ryan Hoffman (D); 12 Joel Tomkins; 13 Sean O'Loughlin (C). Subs (all used): 14 Paul Prescott; 11 Harrison Hansen; 21 Lee Mossop; 22 Liam Farrell.
Tries: Hoffman (9), Hansen (28), Carmont (49); **Goals:** Deacon 1/1, S Tomkins 1/2.
On report:
Lima (52) - alleged dangerous contact on Wilkin.
Rugby Leaguer & League Express Men of the Match: *Saints:* James Roby; *Warriors:* Ryan Hoffman.
Penalty count: 10-3; **Half-time:** 0-12;
Referee: Richard Silverwood.

Attendance: 30,891 *(at Millennium Stadium, Cardiff).*

Sunday 13th February 2011

CRUSADERS 42 SALFORD CITY REDS 12

CRUSADERS: 1 Clinton Schifcofske (C); 5 Stuart Reardon (D); 2 Gareth Thomas; 4 Vince Mellars; 26 Rhys Williams (D); 3 Tony Martin; 6 Michael Witt; 20 Gil Dudson; 9 Lincoln Withers; 10 Mark Bryant; 21 Paul Johnson (D); 12 Jason Chan; 16 Ben Flower. Subs (all used): 14 Adam Peek; 22 Richard Moore (D); 8 Ryan O'Hara; 7 Jarrod Sammut.
Tries: R Williams (3), Witt (16, 60, 64), Reardon (20, 68), Chan (54); **Goals:** Schifcofske 7/9.
CITY REDS: 1 Luke Patten (D); 5 Ashley Gibson; 4 Chris Nero (D); 3 Mark Henry; 2 Jodie Broughton; 14 Matty Smith; 7 Daniel Holdsworth (C); 10 Lee Jewitt; 9 Wayne Godwin (D); 22 Adam Neal; 15 Luke Adamson; 18 Adam Sidlow; 13 Stephen Wild (D). Subs (all used): 16 Rob Parker; 17 Iafeta Palea'aesina (D); 6 Stefan Ratchford; 25 Jack Spencer.
Tries: Holdsworth (12), Patten (25);
Goals: Holdsworth 2/2.
Dismissal: Godwin (80) - punch on Schifcofske.
Rugby Leaguer & League Express Men of the Match: *Crusaders:* Michael Witt; *City Reds:* Chris Nero.
Penalty count: 6-6; **Half-time:** 18-12;
Referee: Thierry Alibert.

BRADFORD BULLS 28 LEEDS RHINOS 32

BULLS: 25 Shad Royston (D); 5 Patrick Ah Van (D); 1 Michael Platt; 4 Chev Walker (D); 19 Gareth Raynor (D); 32 Kyle Briggs (D); 6 Brett Kearney; 10 Andy Lynch (C); 9 Heath L'Estrange; 15 Bryn Hargreaves (D); 11 Olivier Elima (D); 12 Elliott Whitehead; 13 Jamie Langley. Subs (all used): 14 Matt Diskin (D); 8 Nick Scruton; 16 Craig Kopczak; 17 Ian Sibbit (D).
Tries: Whitehead (12, 19, 53), Ah Van (24), Diskin (43); **Goals:** Ah Van 4/5.
RHINOS: 1 Brent Webb; 23 Ben Jones-Bishop (D2); 3 Brett Delaney; 4 Keith Senior; 5 Ryan Hall; 13 Kevin Sinfield (C); 7 Rob Burrow; 8 Kylie Leuluai; 9 Danny Buderus; 15 Ben Cross (D); 11 Jamie Jones-Buchanan; 14 Ali Lauitiiti; 12 Carl Ablett. Subs (all used): 18 Luke Burgess; 17 Ian Kirke; 22 Jay Pitts; 19 Kallum Watkins.
Tries: Jones-Bishop (5, 62, 78 - pen), Hall (32), Leuluai (65), Burrow (69); **Goals:** Sinfield 4/7.
Sin bin: Delaney (9) - professional foul.
Rugby Leaguer & League Express Men of the Match: *Bulls:* Elliott Whitehead; *Rhinos:* Ben Jones-Bishop.
Penalty count: 12-15; **Half-time:** 16-10;
Referee: Steve Ganson.

HULL FC 22 HULL KINGSTON ROVERS 34

HULL: 3 Richard Whiting; 2 Will Sharp (D); 5 Tom Briscoe; 4 Kirk Yeaman; 21 Reece Lyne; 19 Jordan Turner; 7 Sean Long; 8 Mark O'Meley; 9 Danny Houghton; 10 Lee Radford; 16 Willie Manu; 12 Danny Tickle; 13 Craig Fitzgibbon (C). Subs (all used): 17 Ewan Dowes; 23 Sam Moa; 15 Epalahame Lauaki; 11 Joe Westerman (D).
Tries: Yeaman (4, 79), Radford (9), Sharp (70); **Goals:** Tickle 3/5.
ROVERS: 1 Shaun Briscoe; 2 Peter Fox; 3 Kris Welham; 4 Jake Webster; 5 Liam Colbon; 6 Blake Green (D); 7 Michael Dobson; 20 Michael Vella (C); 9 Ben Fisher; 10 Joel Clinton; 11 Clint Newton; 12 Ben Galea; 13 Scott Murrell. Subs (all used): 18 Josh Hodgson; 15 Scott Wheeldon; 14 Liam Watts; 28 Ben Cockayne.
Tries: Green (21), Newton (29), Galea (32, 46), Welham (56, 76); **Goals:** Dobson 4/5, Welham 1/1.
Rugby Leaguer & League Express Men of the Match: *Hull:* Danny Houghton; *Rovers:* Michael Dobson.
Penalty count: 9-8; **Half-time:** 14-18;
Referee: Phil Bentham.

Attendance: 29,323 *(at Millennium Stadium, Cardiff).*

ROUND 2

Friday 18th February 2011

HULL FC 18 LEEDS RHINOS 32

HULL: 3 Richard Whiting; 2 Will Sharp; 16 Willie Manu; 4 Kirk Yeaman; 5 Tom Briscoe; 19 Jordan Turner; 7 Sean Long; 8 Mark O'Meley; 9 Danny Houghton; 10 Lee Radford; 11 Joe Westerman; 12 Danny Tickle; 13 Craig Fitzgibbon (C). Subs (all used): 30 Sam Obst (D); 23 Sam Moa; 14 Danny Washbrook; 15 Epalahame Lauaki.
Tries: O'Meley (15, 51), Sharp (70); **Goals:** Tickle 3/3.
RHINOS: 1 Brent Webb; 23 Ben Jones-Bishop; 19 Kallum Watkins; 4 Keith Senior; 5 Ryan Hall; 13 Kevin Sinfield (C); 7 Rob Burrow; 8 Kylie Leuluai; 9 Danny Buderus; 18 Luke Burgess; 11 Jamie Jones-Buchanan; 3 Brett Delaney; 12 Carl Ablett. Subs (all used): 17 Ian Kirke; 21 Chris Clarkson; 20 Weller Hauraki (D); 2 Lee Smith.
Tries: Webb (2), Hall (27), Burrow (35), Jones-Bishop (40), Clarkson (48), Hauraki (61); **Goals:** Sinfield 3/6;
Field goals: Burrow (77), Sinfield (79).
Rugby Leaguer & League Express Men of the Match: *Hull:* Mark O'Meley; *Rhinos:* Danny Buderus.
Penalty count: 8-5; **Half-time:** 6-20;
Referee: Richard Silverwood; **Attendance:** 12,515.

SALFORD CITY REDS 22 ST HELENS 56

CITY REDS: 1 Luke Patten; 2 Jodie Broughton; 3 Mark Henry; 4 Chris Nero; 5 Ashley Gibson; 6 Stefan Ratchford; 7 Daniel Holdsworth (C); 8 Ray Cashmere; 14 Matty Smith; 16 Rob Parker; 15 Luke Adamson; 18 Adam Sidlow; 13 Stephen Wild. Subs (all used): 10 Lee Jewitt; 17 Iafeta Palea'aesina; 22 Adam Neal; 25 Jack Spencer.
Tries: Patten (13), Gibson (41), Ratchford (74), Broughton (80); **Goals:** Holdsworth 3/4.
SAINTS: 20 Jonny Lomax; 2 Ade Gardner; 3 Michael Shenton; 5 Francis Meli; 22 Jamie Foster; 25 Lee Gaskell; 7 Kyle Eastmond; 15 Louie McCarthy-Scarsbrook; 9 James Roby (C); 11 Tony Puletua; 13 Chris Flannery; 4 Iosia Soliola; 12 Jon Wilkin. Subs (all used): 14 Scott Moore; 16 Paul Clough; 21 Shaun Magennis; 28 Tom Makinson (D).
Tries: Flannery (3), Eastmond (9, 31), Roby (21), Meli (27), Lomax (35), Gardner (37), Gaskell (42), Clough (46), Shenton (60); **Goals:** Foster 8/10.
On report: Moore (41) - alleged high tackle; McCarthy-Scarsbrook (65) - alleged grapple tackle.
Rugby Leaguer & League Express Men of the Match: *City Reds:* Daniel Holdsworth; *Saints:* James Roby.
Penalty count: 7-8; **Half-time:** 6-38;
Referee: Robert Hicks; **Attendance:** 5,929.

Saturday 19th February 2011

CATALAN DRAGONS 14
WAKEFIELD TRINITY WILDCATS 38

DRAGONS: 3 Ben Farrar; 2 Damien Blanch; 15 Jean-Philippe Baile; 4 Setaimata Sa; 5 Cyril Stacul; 14 Tony Gigot; 7 Scott Dureau; 8 David Ferriol; 9 Ian Henderson; 10 Remi Casty; 11 Steve Menzies; 12 Sebastien Raguin; 13 Gregory Mounis (C). Subs (all used): 17 Cyrille Gossard; 22 Jamal Fakir; 23 Lopini Paea; 26 Eloi Pelissier (D).
Tries: Raguin (38), Stacul (64); **Goals:** Dureau 3/3.
WILDCATS: 23 Josh Veivers; 2 Kevin Penny (D); 3 Aaron Murphy; 18 Chris Dean; 5 Luke George; 27 Kieran Hyde; 14 Tommy Lee; 8 Michael Korkidas; 9 Julien Rinaldi; 17 Paul Johnson; 13 Glenn Morrison (C); 21 Frankie Mariano (D); 22 Stuart Howarth (D). Subs (all used): 10 Paul King; 11 Kevin Henderson; 24 James Davey; 28 Russ Spiers.
Tries: Mariano (8, 53), Penny (18), Dean (48, 60), Hyde (72), George (79); **Goals:** Veivers 5/8.
Rugby Leaguer & League Express Men of the Match: *Dragons:* Lopini Paea; *Wildcats:* Chris Dean.
Penalty count: 6-7; **Half-time:** 8-14;
Referee: Ben Thaler; **Attendance:** 7,113.

CASTLEFORD TIGERS 18 HUDDERSFIELD GIANTS 12

TIGERS: 1 Richard Mathers; 2 Kirk Dixon; 4 Joe Arundel; 13 Brett Ferres; 3 Nick Youngquest; 6 Rangi Chase; 7 Danny Orr (C); 8 Paul Jackson; 16 Adam Milner; 10 Craig Huby; 11 Jake Emmitt; 24 Oliver Holmes; 14 Stuart Jones. Subs (all used): 27 Daryl Clark (D); 20 Martin Aspinwall (D); 25 Dean Widders; 15 Jonathan Walker.
Tries: Youngquest (14, 56), Arundel (61);
Goals: Dixon 3/6.
GIANTS: 1 Scott Grix; 20 Jermaine McGillvary; 3 Leroy Cudjoe; 2 Michael Lawrence; 5 David Hodgson; 6 Kevin Brown (C); 7 Danny Brough; 8 Eorl Crabtree; 22 Keal Carlile; 15 Keith Mason; 4 Lee Gilmour; 12 David Fa'alogo; 11 Luke O'Donnell. Subs (all used): 14 Shaun Lunt; 19 Graeme Horne; 13 David Faiumu; 10 Darrell Griffin.
Tries: McGillvary (42, 80); **Goals:** Brough 2/2.
Sin bin: Lunt (71) - late challenge on Chase.
Rugby Leaguer & League Express Men of the Match: *Tigers:* Rangi Chase; *Giants:* Scott Grix.
Penalty count: 9-2; **Half-time:** 8-0;
Referee: Steve Ganson; **Attendance:** 5,992.

Sunday 20th February 2011

HARLEQUINS 20 CRUSADERS 18

HARLEQUINS: 1 Luke Dorn; 2 Jamie O'Callaghan; 3 Tony Clubb; 4 David Howell; 5 Chris Melling; 7 Chad Randall; 6 Luke Gale; 10 Oliver Wilkes; 9 Andy Ellis; 17 Danny Ward; 13 Rob Purdham (C); 16 Mike Burnett; 12 Chris Bailey. Subs (all used): 8 Karl Temata; 15 Luke Ambler; 19 Lamont Bryan; 11 Nick Kouparitsas.
Tries: Gale (21), Dorn (26, 41); **Goals:** Gale 4/4.
CRUSADERS: 1 Clinton Schifcofske (C); 5 Stuart Reardon; 3 Tony Martin; 2 Gareth Thomas; 26 Rhys Williams; 6 Michael Witt; 7 Jarrod Sammut; 8 Ryan O'Hara; 9 Lincoln Withers; 10 Mark Bryant; 21 Paul Johnson; 12 Jason Chan; 16 Ben Flower. Subs (all used): 20 Gil Dudson; 22 Richard Moore; 15 Jordan James; 23 Peter Lupton.
Tries: Sammut (12, 35), Flower (61);
Goals: Schifcofske 3/3.
Rugby Leaguer & League Express Men of the Match: *Harlequins:* Luke Dorn; *Crusaders:* Jarrod Sammut.
Penalty count: 13-6; **Half-time:** 14-12;
Referee: James Child; **Attendance:** 1,776.

BRADFORD BULLS 10 WIGAN WARRIORS 44

BULLS: 25 Shad Royston; 5 Patrick Ah Van; 1 Michael Platt; 4 Chev Walker; 19 Gareth Raynor; 3 Paul Sykes; 6 Brett Kearney; 8 Nick Scruton; 9 Heath L'Estrange; 10 Andy Lynch (C); 11 Olivier Elima; 12 Elliott Whitehead; 15 Bryn Hargreaves. Subs (all used): 14 Matt Diskin; 16 Craig Kopczak; 17 Ian Sibbit; 23 Tom Olbison.
Tries: Whitehead (44), Ah Van (56); **Goals:** Ah Van 1/2.
On report: Sibbit (39) - alleged dangerous contact.
WARRIORS: 1 Sam Tomkins; 2 Darrell Goulding; 3 Martin Gleeson; 4 George Carmont; 19 Amos Roberts; 6 Paul Deacon; 7 Thomas Leuluai; 14 Paul Prescott; 9 Michael McIlorum; 8 Stuart Fielden; 16 Ryan Hoffman; 11 Harrison Hansen; 13 Sean O'Loughlin (C). Subs (all used): 10 Andy Coley; 12 Joel Tomkins; 21 Lee Mossop; 22 Liam Farrell.
Tries: Roberts (11, 59), Hansen (15), Leuluai (31), Farrell (36), Goulding (40), Carmont (75), S Tomkins (78); **Goals:** Deacon 6/8.

Rugby Leaguer & League Express Men of the Match: *Bulls:* Brett Kearney; *Warriors:* Sam Tomkins.
Penalty count: 9-8; **Half-time:** 0-26;
Referee: Phil Bentham; **Attendance:** 15,348.

WARRINGTON WOLVES 24
HULL KINGSTON ROVERS 22

WOLVES: 1 Brett Hodgson; 2 Chris Riley; 20 Matty Blythe; 23 Ryan Atkins; 5 Joel Monaghan; 6 Lee Briers; 7 Richard Myler; 8 Adrian Morley (C); 9 Michael Monaghan; 10 Garreth Carvell; 12 Ben Westwood; 11 Louis Anderson; 26 David Solomona. Subs (all used): 13 Ben Harrison; 16 Paul Wood; 14 Mick Higham; 19 Lee Mitchell.
Tries: J Monaghan (3), Myler (9), Atkins (40), Riley (60), Hodgson (78); **Goals:** Hodgson 2/5.
ROVERS: 1 Shaun Briscoe; 2 Peter Fox; 4 Jake Webster; 3 Kris Welham; 5 Liam Colbon; 6 Blake Green; 7 Michael Dobson; 20 Michael Vella (C); 18 Josh Hodgson; 10 Joel Clinton; 11 Clint Newton; 12 Ben Galea; 13 Scott Murrell. Subs (all used): 14 Liam Watts; 15 Scott Wheeldon; 16 Jason Netherton; 28 Ben Cockayne.
Tries: Newton (16, 31), Green (20), Briscoe (46);
Goals: Dobson 3/4.
Rugby Leaguer & League Express Men of the Match: *Wolves:* Ben Westwood; *Rovers:* Clint Newton.
Penalty count: 7-5; **Half-time:** 14-16;
Referee: Thierry Alibert; **Attendance:** 10,899.

ROUND 3

Friday 25th February 2011

LEEDS RHINOS 26 HARLEQUINS 36

RHINOS: 23 Ben Jones-Bishop; 2 Lee Smith; 19 Kallum Watkins; 4 Keith Senior; 5 Ryan Hall; 13 Kevin Sinfield (C); 7 Rob Burrow; 8 Kylie Leuluai; 9 Danny Buderus; 18 Luke Burgess; 21 Chris Clarkson; 14 Ali Lauitiiti; 11 Jamie Jones-Buchanan. Subs (all used): 15 Ben Cross; 17 Ian Kirke; 20 Weller Hauraki; 22 Jay Pitts.
Tries: Clarkson (6), Sinfield (38), Hall (50), Smith (78), Jones-Buchanan (79); **Goals:** Sinfield 3/5.
HARLEQUINS: 1 Luke Dorn; 2 Jamie O'Callaghan; 3 Tony Clubb; 4 David Howell; 5 Chris Melling; 6 Luke Gale; 7 Chad Randall; 17 Danny Ward; 9 Andy Ellis; 10 Oliver Wilkes; 13 Rob Purdham (C); 16 Mike Burnett; 12 Chris Bailey. Subs (all used): 8 Karl Temata; 15 Luke Ambler; 11 Nick Kouparitsas; 31 Karl Pryce (D).
Tries: Gale (16), Clubb (24), Ellis (32, 75), Purdham (60), Bailey (66); **Goals:** Gale 6/6.
Rugby Leaguer & League Express Men of the Match: *Rhinos:* Kylie Leuluai; *Harlequins:* Chris Bailey.
Penalty count: 4-1; **Half-time:** 12-18;
Referee: Ben Thaler; **Attendance:** 14,350.

ST HELENS 18 WARRINGTON WOLVES 25

SAINTS: 1 Paul Wellens (C); 2 Ade Gardner; 3 Michael Shenton; 20 Jonny Lomax; 5 Francis Meli; 25 Lee Gaskell; 7 Kyle Eastmond; 10 James Graham (C); 9 James Roby; 15 Louie McCarthy-Scarsbrook; 13 Chris Flannery; 4 Iosia Soliola; 12 Jon Wilkin. Subs (all used): 11 Tony Puletua; 14 Scott Moore; 16 Paul Clough; 22 Jamie Foster.
Tries: Shenton (66), Flannery (76), Gaskell (79);
Goals: Lomax 1/1, Foster 2/2.
WOLVES: 1 Brett Hodgson; 2 Chris Riley; 20 Matty Blythe; 23 Ryan Atkins; 5 Joel Monaghan; 6 Lee Briers; 7 Richard Myler; 8 Adrian Morley (C); 9 Michael Monaghan; 10 Garreth Carvell; 11 Louis Anderson; 12 Ben Westwood; 26 David Solomona. Subs (all used): 13 Ben Harrison; 14 Mick Higham; 16 Paul Wood; 24 Rhys Evans.
Tries: Briers (2, 20), Myler (16), Anderson (53);
Goals: Hodgson 4/4; **Field goal:** Briers (71).
Rugby Leaguer & League Express Men of the Match: *Saints:* James Roby; *Wolves:* Lee Briers.
Penalty count: 7-5; **Half-time:** 0-18;
Referee: Phil Bentham; **Attendance:** 10,514.

Saturday 26th February 2011

CRUSADERS 26 BRADFORD BULLS 30

CRUSADERS: 1 Clinton Schifcofske (C); 5 Stuart Reardon; 3 Tony Martin; 2 Gareth Thomas; 26 Rhys Williams; 6 Michael Witt; 7 Jarrod Sammut; 8 Ryan O'Hara; 9 Lincoln Withers; 10 Mark Bryant; 23 Peter Lupton; 12 Jason Chan; 16 Ben Flower. Subs (all used): 14 Adam Peek; 15 Jordan James; 20 Gil Dudson; 22 Richard Moore.
Tries: Witt (21), Thomas (47), Sammut (69), Schifcofske (78), Martin (80); **Goals:** Schifcofske 3/5.
BULLS: 25 Shad Royston; 18 Shaun Ainscough (D); 1 Michael Platt; 5 Patrick Ah Van; 19 Gareth Raynor; 6 Brett Kearney; 21 Danny Addy; 15 Bryn Hargreaves; 9 Heath L'Estrange; 10 Andy Lynch (C); 4 Chev Walker; 12 Elliott Whitehead; 11 Olivier Elima. Subs (all used): 8 Nick Scruton; 14 Matt Diskin; 16 Craig Kopczak; 23 Tom Olbison.
Tries: Lynch (9), Royston (29), Ainscough (34), Diskin (43), L'Estrange (63); **Goals:** Ah Van 5/5.
Rugby Leaguer & League Express Men of the Match: *Crusaders:* Clinton Schifcofske; *Bulls:* Brett Kearney.
Penalty count: 9-7; **Half-time:** 6-18;
Referee: Richard Silverwood; **Attendance:** 2,615.

Sunday 27th February 2011

HUDDERSFIELD GIANTS 20 HULL FC 10

GIANTS: 1 Scott Grix; 20 Jermaine McGillvary; 3 Leroy Cudjoe; 2 Michael Lawrence; 5 David Hodgson; 6 Kevin Brown (C); 7 Danny Brough; 8 Eorl Crabtree; 14 Shaun Lunt; 10 Darrell Griffin; 4 Lee Gilmour; 12 David Fa'alogo; 11 Luke O'Donnell. Subs (all used): 18 Larne Patrick; 19 Graeme Horne; 13 David Faiumu; 23 Kyle Wood (D).
Tries: Hodgson (3, 9), Lawrence (62), Brown (74);
Goals: Brough 2/4.
HULL: 3 Richard Whiting; 2 Will Sharp; 19 Jordan Turner; 4 Kirk Yeaman; 5 Tom Briscoe; 6 Richard Horne; 30 Sam Obst; 8 Mark O'Meley; 9 Danny Houghton; 10 Lee Radford; 11 Joe Westerman; 12 Danny Tickle; 13 Craig Fitzgibbon (C). Subs (all used): 23 Sam Moa; 14 Danny Washbrook; 15 Epalahame Lauaki; 16 Willie Manu.
Tries: Turner (28), Sharp (44);
Goals: Tickle 0/1, Westerman 1/1.
Rugby Leaguer & League Express Men of the Match: *Giants:* Danny Brough; *Hull:* Craig Fitzgibbon.
Penalty count: 7-8; **Half-time:** 10-4;
Referee: Robert Hicks; **Attendance:** 8,822.

HULL KINGSTON ROVERS 18 CATALAN DRAGONS 31

ROVERS: 1 Shaun Briscoe; 2 Peter Fox; 3 Kris Welham; 19 Craig Hall (D); 5 Liam Colbon; 6 Blake Green; 13 Scott Murrell; 20 Michael Vella (C); 18 Josh Hodgson; 10 Joel Clinton; 11 Clint Newton; 12 Ben Galea; 16 Jason Netherton. Subs (all used): 15 Scott Wheeldon; 22 Scott Taylor; 28 Ben Cockayne; 14 Liam Watts.
Tries: Green (6, 12), Briscoe (47); **Goals:** Hall 3/3.
DRAGONS: 3 Ben Farrar; 2 Damien Blanch; 4 Setaimata Sa; 18 Darryl Millard (D); 5 Cyril Stacul; 14 Tony Gigot; 7 Scott Dureau; 8 David Ferriol; 9 Ian Henderson; 10 Remi Casty; 11 Steve Menzies; 12 Sebastien Raguin; 13 Gregory Mounis (C). Subs: 22 Jamal Fakir; 23 Lopini Paea; 24 Jason Baitieri (D); 26 Eloi Pelissier (not used).
Tries: Mounis (16), Sa (39), Blanch (43, 75), Raguin (60), Menzies (68); **Goals:** Dureau 3/6;
Field goal: Dureau (78).
Rugby Leaguer & League Express Men of the Match: *Rovers:* Blake Green; *Dragons:* Scott Dureau.
Penalty count: 6-7; **Half-time:** 12-12;
Referee: James Child; **Attendance:** 8,092.

WAKEFIELD TRINITY WILDCATS 6
SALFORD CITY REDS 32

WILDCATS: 23 Josh Veivers; 2 Kevin Penny; 3 Aaron Murphy; 18 Chris Dean; 5 Luke George; 16 Jeremy Smith (D); 14 Tommy Lee; 8 Michael Korkidas; 9 Julien Rinaldi; 17 Paul Johnson; 21 Frankie Mariano; 13 Glenn Morrison (C); 22 Stuart Howarth. Subs (all used): 20 Ben Gledhill; 24 James Davey; 31 Kyle Amor (D); 11 Kevin Henderson.
Try: Lee (23); **Goals:** Veivers 1/1.
CITY REDS: 1 Luke Patten; 2 Jodie Broughton; 3 Mark Henry; 4 Chris Nero; 5 Ashley Gibson; 6 Stefan Ratchford; 7 Daniel Holdsworth (C); 8 Ray Cashmere; 14 Matty Smith; 19 Ryan Boyle; 15 Luke Adamson; 18 Adam Sidlow; 13 Stephen Wild. Subs (all used): 16 Rob Parker; 17 Iafeta Palea'aesina; 23 Marc Sneyd; 10 Lee Jewitt.
Tries: Ratchford (1), Wild (5), Henry (16, 74), Parker (57), Sidlow (71); **Goals:** Holdsworth 4/6.
Sin bin: Boyle (60) - late challenge on Smith.
Rugby Leaguer & League Express Men of the Match: *Wildcats:* Glenn Morrison; *City Reds:* Ray Cashmere.
Penalty count: 9-2; **Half-time:** 6-16;
Referee: Steve Ganson; **Attendance:** 6,823.

ROUND 4

Friday 4th March 2011

HARLEQUINS 10 HUDDERSFIELD GIANTS 18

HARLEQUINS: 1 Luke Dorn; 2 Jamie O'Callaghan; 3 Tony Clubb; 4 David Howell; 5 Chris Melling; 6 Luke Gale; 7 Chad Randall; 10 Oliver Wilkes; 9 Andy Ellis; 17 Danny Ward; 13 Rob Purdham (C); 16 Mike Burnett; 12 Chris Bailey. Subs (all used): 15 Luke Ambler; 8 Karl Temata; 31 Karl Pryce; 11 Nick Kouparitsas.
Tries: Pryce (15), Melling (74);
Goals: Gale 0/1, Purdham 1/1.
GIANTS: 1 Scott Grix; 20 Jermaine McGillvary; 3 Leroy Cudjoe; 4 Lee Gilmour; 5 David Hodgson; 6 Kevin Brown (C); 7 Danny Brough; 8 Eorl Crabtree; 13 David Faiumu; 10 Darrell Griffin; 32 Jon Molloy (D); 12 David Fa'alogo; 11 Luke O'Donnell. Subs (all used): 14 Shaun Lunt; 18 Larne Patrick; 19 Graeme Horne; 37 Dale Ferguson (D).
Tries: O'Donnell (25), McGillvary (32), Horne (47);
Goals: Brough 3/3.
Rugby Leaguer & League Express Men of the Match: *Harlequins:* Chris Bailey; *Giants:* Scott Grix.
Penalty count: 7-3; **Half-time:** 4-12;
Referee: Phil Bentham; **Attendance:** 2,624.

HULL FC 42 CRUSADERS 18

HULL: 3 Richard Whiting; 2 Will Sharp; 19 Jordan Turner; 4 Kirk Yeaman; 5 Tom Briscoe; 6 Richard Horne; 30 Sam Obst; 8 Mark O'Meley; 9 Danny Houghton; 10 Lee Radford; 11 Joe Westerman; 12 Danny Tickle; 13 Craig Fitzgibbon (C). Subs (all used): 14 Danny Washbrook; 15 Epalahame Lauaki; 16 Willie Manu; 23 Sam Moa.
Tries: Tickle (6, 25), Whiting (19), Obst (41), Sharp (44), Horne (51), Yeaman (62), Briscoe (77);
Goals: Tickle 4/6, Westerman 1/2.
CRUSADERS: 1 Clinton Schifcofske (C); 5 Stuart Reardon; 2 Gareth Thomas; 4 Vince Mellars; 26 Rhys Williams; 3 Tony Martin; 6 Michael Witt; 8 Ryan O'Hara; 9 Lincoln Withers; 10 Mark Bryant; 23 Peter Lupton; 12 Jason Chan; 16 Ben Flower. Subs (all used): 20 Gil Dudson; 7 Jarrod Sammut; 22 Richard Moore; 14 Adam Peek.
Tries: R Williams (60, 74), Sammut (66);
Goals: Schifcofske 3/3.
Rugby Leaguer & League Express Men of the Match: *Hull:* Sam Obst; *Crusaders:* Rhys Williams.
Penalty count: 9-2; **Half-time:** 16-0;
Referee: Ben Thaler; **Attendance:** 10,422.

SALFORD CITY REDS 16 WIGAN WARRIORS 32

CITY REDS: 1 Luke Patten; 2 Jodie Broughton; 4 Chris Nero; 5 Ashley Gibson; 3 Mark Henry; 6 Stefan Ratchford (C); 14 Matty Smith; 8 Ray Cashmere; 9 Wayne Godwin; 10 Lee Jewitt; 18 Adam Sidlow; 15 Luke Adamson; 13 Stephen Wild. Subs (all used): 16 Rob Parker; 17 Iafeta Palea'aesina; 22 Adam Neal; 23 Marc Sneyd.
Tries: Gibson (17), Parker (38), Nero (68);
Goals: Ratchford 1/1, Smith 0/1, Sneyd 1/1.
WARRIORS: 1 Sam Tomkins; 2 Darrell Goulding; 24 Stefan Marsh; 4 George Carmont; 25 Josh Charnley; 6 Paul Deacon; 7 Thomas Leuluai; 10 Andy Coley; 9 Michael McIlorum; 14 Paul Prescott; 11 Harrison Hansen; 16 Ryan Hoffman; 13 Sean O'Loughlin (C). Subs (all used): 12 Joel Tomkins; 15 Jeff Lima; 21 Lee Mossop; 22 Liam Farrell.
Tries: Hansen (2), Leuluai (11, 42), Mossop (25), Charnley (56), Goulding (78); **Goals:** Deacon 4/6.
Rugby Leaguer & League Express Men of the Match: *City Reds:* Luke Patten; *Warriors:* Thomas Leuluai.
Penalty count: 7-3; **Half-time:** 10-16;
Referee: James Child; **Attendance:** 6,266.

Saturday 5th March 2011

CATALAN DRAGONS 16 ST HELENS 22

DRAGONS: 3 Ben Farrar; 2 Damien Blanch; 12 Sebastien Raguin; 18 Darryl Millard; 5 Cyril Stacul; 14 Tony Gigot; 7 Scott Dureau; 8 David Ferriol; 9 Ian Henderson; 10 Remi Casty; 11 Steve Menzies; 4 Setaimata Sa; 13 Gregory Mounis (C). Subs (all used): 22 Jamal Fakir; 23 Lopini Paea; 24 Jason Baitieri; 26 Eloi Pelissier.
Tries: Sa (25), Menzies (61), Dureau (78);
Goals: Dureau 2/3.
SAINTS: 1 Paul Wellens (C); 2 Ade Gardner; 3 Michael Shenton; 20 Jonny Lomax; 5 Francis Meli; 6 Leon Pryce; 7 Kyle Eastmond; 10 James Graham (C); 9 James Roby; 15 Louie McCarthy-Scarsbrook; 13 Chris Flannery; 12 Jon Wilkin; 14 Scott Moore. Subs (all used): 11 Tony Puletua; 16 Paul Clough; 19 Andrew Dixon; 25 Lee Gaskell.
Tries: Flannery (17), Gardner (22), Graham (37), Shenton (47); **Goals:** Eastmond 3/5.
Rugby Leaguer & League Express Men of the Match: *Dragons:* Setaimata Sa; *Saints:* Kyle Eastmond.
Penalty count: 7-5; **Half-time:** 4-16;
Referee: Thierry Alibert; **Attendance:** 7,095.

WARRINGTON WOLVES 40 LEEDS RHINOS 24

WOLVES: 1 Brett Hodgson; 2 Chris Riley; 20 Matty Blythe; 24 Rhys Evans; 5 Joel Monaghan; 6 Lee Briers; 7 Richard Myler; 8 Adrian Morley (C); 9 Michael Monaghan; 10 Garreth Carvell; 12 Ben Westwood; 26 David Solomona; 13 Ben Harrison. Subs (all used): 16 Paul Wood; 15 Jon Clarke; 17 Simon Grix; 14 Mick Higham.
Tries: Evans (21), Briers (26), Myler (28), Riley (40), Grix (42), J Monaghan (55), Higham (69);
Goals: Hodgson 6/7.
RHINOS: 1 Brent Webb; 2 Lee Smith; 19 Kallum Watkins; 4 Keith Senior; 5 Ryan Hall; 13 Kevin Sinfield (C); 7 Rob Burrow; 18 Luke Burgess; 9 Danny Buderus; 11 Jamie Jones-Buchanan; 14 Ali Lauitiiti; 20 Weller Hauraki; 12 Carl Ablett. Subs (all used): 23 Ben Jones-Bishop; 15 Ben Cross; 21 Chris Clarkson; 17 Ian Kirke.
Tries: Watkins (11), Webb (59), Hall (66, 78);
Goals: Sinfield 4/5.
Rugby Leaguer & League Express Men of the Match: *Wolves:* Ben Westwood; *Rhinos:* Kevin Sinfield.
Penalty count: 6-8; **Half-time:** 22-8;
Referee: Steve Ganson; **Attendance:** 11,438.

Sunday 6th March 2011

BRADFORD BULLS 40
WAKEFIELD TRINITY WILDCATS 18

BULLS: 25 Shad Royston; 19 Gareth Raynor; 5 Patrick Ah Van; 1 Michael Platt; 18 Shaun Ainscough; 6 Brett Kearney; 7 Marc Herbert (D); 10 Andy Lynch (C); 14 Matt Diskin; 15 Bryn Hargreaves; 23 Tom Olbison; 12 Elliott Whitehead; 11 Olivier Elima. Subs (all used): 8 Nick Scruton; 17 Ian Sibbit; 16 Craig Kopczak; 21 Danny Addy.
Tries: Olbison (10), Royston (23, 60), Kopczak (33, 35, 72), Ainscough (68); **Goals:** Ah Van 6/7.
WILDCATS: 23 Josh Veivers; 2 Kevin Penny; 3 Aaron Murphy; 29 Josh Griffin (D); 5 Luke George; 27 Keiran Hyde; 14 Tommy Lee; 8 Michael Korkidas; 9 Julien Rinaldi; 17 Paul Johnson; 21 Frankie Mariano; 13 Glenn Morrison (C); 22 Stuart Howarth. Subs (all used): 20 Ben Gledhill; 24 James Davey; 31 Kyle Amor; 11 Kevin Henderson.
Tries: Mariano (4), George (65), Hyde (80);
Goals: Veivers 3/3.
Rugby Leaguer & League Express Men of the Match: *Bulls:* Craig Kopczak; *Wildcats:* Glenn Morrison.
Penalty count: 11-9; **Half-time:** 24-6;
Referee: Robert Hicks; **Attendance:** 12,835.

CASTLEFORD TIGERS 27 HULL KINGSTON ROVERS 14

TIGERS: 1 Richard Mathers; 2 Kirk Dixon; 13 Brett Ferres; 4 Joe Arundel; 3 Nick Youngquest; 6 Rangi Chase; 7 Danny Orr (C); 8 Paul Jackson; 16 Adam Milner; 10 Craig Huby; 24 Oliver Holmes; 14 Stuart Jones; 11 Jake Emmitt. Subs (all used): 27 Daryl Clark; 20 Martin Aspinwall; 25 Dean Widders; 15 Jonathan Walker.
Tries: Holmes (6), Youngquest (34), Clark (46), Dixon (69); **Goals:** Dixon 5/6; **Field goal:** Chase (79).

ROVERS: 1 Shaun Briscoe; 2 Peter Fox; 19 Craig Hall; 3 Kris Welham; 5 Liam Colbon; 6 Blake Green; 13 Scott Murrell; 20 Michael Vella (C); 18 Josh Hodgson; 14 Liam Watts; 11 Clint Newton; 12 Ben Galea; 16 Jason Netherton. Subs (all used): 15 Scott Wheeldon; 28 Ben Cockayne; 22 Scott Taylor; 9 Ben Fisher.
Tries: Newton (10), Hall (16), Galea (29); **Goals:** Hall 1/3.
Rugby Leaguer & League Express Men of the Match: *Tigers:* Paul Jackson; *Rovers:* Scott Murrell.
Penalty count: 9-8; **Half-time:** 12-14;
Referee: Richard Silverwood; **Attendance:** 8,537.

ROUND 5

Friday 11th March 2011

LEEDS RHINOS 46 SALFORD CITY REDS 12

RHINOS: 1 Brent Webb; 23 Ben Jones-Bishop; 19 Kallum Watkins; 4 Keith Senior; 5 Ryan Hall; 13 Kevin Sinfield (C); 7 Rob Burrow; 11 Jamie Jones-Buchanan; 9 Danny Buderus; 17 Ian Kirke; 20 Weller Hauraki; 14 Ali Lauitiiti; 12 Carl Ablett. Subs (all used): 21 Chris Clarkson; 22 Jay Pitts; 24 Paul McShane; 28 Brad Singleton (D).
Tries: Senior (18), Jones-Buchanan (28), Hauraki (30), Watkins (60), Webb (64), Ablett (70, 74), Lauitiiti (79); **Goals:** Sinfield 7/9.
CITY REDS: 1 Luke Patten; 2 Jodie Broughton; 4 Chris Nero; 5 Ashley Gibson; 3 Mark Henry; 6 Stefan Ratchford; 7 Daniel Holdsworth (C); 8 Ray Cashmere; 9 Wayne Godwin; 19 Ryan Boyle; 22 Adam Neal; 15 Luke Adamson; 13 Stephen Wild. Subs (all used): 25 Jack Spencer; 18 Adam Sidlow; 17 Iafeta Palea'aesina; 14 Matty Smith.
Tries: Ratchford (5), Sidlow (38); **Goals:** Holdsworth 2/2.
Rugby Leaguer & League Express Men of the Match: *Rhinos:* Brent Webb; *City Reds:* Stefan Ratchford.
Penalty count: 6-7; **Half-time:** 18-12;
Referee: Thierry Alibert; **Attendance:** 13,068.

ST HELENS 16 HARLEQUINS 27

SAINTS: 1 Paul Wellens (C); 2 Ade Gardner; 3 Michael Shenton; 20 Jonny Lomax; 5 Francis Meli; 25 Lee Gaskell; 7 Kyle Eastmond; 10 James Graham (C); 9 James Roby; 8 Josh Perry (D); 16 Paul Clough; 13 Chris Flannery; 11 Tony Puletua. Subs (all used): 14 Scott Moore; 19 Andrew Dixon; 21 Shaun Magennis; 22 Jamie Foster.
Tries: Meli (47), Graham (54), Roby (80);
Goals: Eastmond 1/2, Foster 1/1.
HARLEQUINS: 1 Luke Dorn; 23 Mark Calderwood (D); 3 Tony Clubb; 31 Karl Pryce; 5 Chris Melling; 6 Luke Gale; 7 Chad Randall; 17 Danny Ward; 9 Andy Ellis; 10 Oliver Wilkes; 16 Mike Burnett; 13 Rob Purdham (C); 12 Chris Bailey. Subs (all used): 8 Karl Temata; 11 Nick Kouparitsas; 15 Luke Ambler; 32 Joe Mellor (D).
Tries: Dorn (2), Pryce (6), Clubb (22), Kouparitsas (56); **Goals:** Gale 5/5; **Field goal:** Gale (75).
Rugby Leaguer & League Express Men of the Match: *Saints:* Paul Wellens; *Harlequins:* Luke Gale.
Penalty count: 5-5; **Half-time:** 0-20;
Referee: Gareth Hewer; **Attendance:** 6,050.

WAKEFIELD TRINITY WILDCATS 6 WARRINGTON WOLVES 22

WILDCATS: 3 Aaron Murphy; 30 Greg Johnson (D); 29 Josh Griffin; 18 Chris Dean; 5 Luke George; 27 Kieran Hyde; 14 Tommy Lee; 8 Michael Korkidas; 9 Julien Rinaldi; 17 Paul Johnson; 21 Frankie Mariano; 13 Glenn Morrison (C); 22 Stuart Howarth. Subs (all used): 20 Ben Gledhill; 26 Matthew Wildie; 31 Kyle Amor; 11 Kevin Henderson.
Try: Griffin (65); **Goals:** Griffin 1/1.
WOLVES: 4 Chris Bridge; 2 Chris Riley; 20 Matty Blythe; 23 Ryan Atkins; 24 Rhys Evans; 6 Lee Briers (C); 7 Richard Myler; 10 Garreth Carvell; 14 Mick Higham; 16 Paul Wood; 12 Ben Westwood; 17 Simon Grix; 13 Ben Harrison. Subs (all used): 26 David Solomona; 19 Lee Mitchell; 21 Tyrone McCarthy; 15 Jon Clarke.
Tries: Riley (6), Bridge (13), Atkins (46), Myler (58); **Goals:** Westwood 3/4.
Rugby Leaguer & League Express Men of the Match: *Wildcats:* Tommy Lee; *Wolves:* Ben Westwood.
Penalty count: 15-9; **Half-time:** 0-10;
Referee: Richard Silverwood; **Attendance:** 5,073.

Saturday 12th March 2011

CASTLEFORD TIGERS 34 CATALAN DRAGONS 24

TIGERS: 1 Richard Mathers; 2 Kirk Dixon; 4 Joe Arundel; 13 Brett Ferres; 3 Nick Youngquest; 6 Rangi Chase; 7 Danny Orr (C); 8 Paul Jackson; 16 Adam Milner; 10 Craig Huby; 24 Oliver Holmes; 11 Jake Emmitt; 14 Stuart Jones. Subs (all used): 19 Nick Fozzard (D); 20 Martin Aspinwall; 25 Dean Widders; 27 Daryl Clark.
Tries: Huby (16), Jones (25), Dixon (50), Chase (57), Youngquest (59), Arundel (70); **Goals:** Dixon 5/6.
DRAGONS: 1 Clint Greenshields; 2 Damien Blanch; 3 Ben Farrar; 18 Darryl Millard; 5 Cyril Stacul; 4 Setaimata Sa; 7 Scott Dureau; 22 Jamal Fakir; 9 Ian Henderson; 23 Lopini Paea; 11 Steve Menzies; 12 Sebastien Raguin; 24 Jason Baitieri. Subs (all used): 8 David Ferriol; 10 Remi Casty; 13 Gregory Mounis (C); 14 Tony Gigot.
Tries: Dureau (4, 38), Blanch (9), Stacul (75);
Goals: Dureau 4/5.
Rugby Leaguer & League Express Men of the Match: *Tigers:* Rangi Chase; *Dragons:* Scott Dureau.
Penalty count: 9-12; **Half-time:** 12-18;
Referee: Phil Bentham; **Attendance:** 4,889.

Sunday 13th March 2011

HUDDERSFIELD GIANTS 50 BRADFORD BULLS 16

GIANTS: 1 Scott Grix; 20 Jermaine McGillvary; 3 Leroy Cudjoe; 2 Michael Lawrence; 36 Jamie Simpson (D); 6 Kevin Brown (C); 7 Danny Brough; 8 Eorl Crabtree; 13 David Faiumu; 15 Keith Mason; 12 David Fa'alogo; 19 Graeme Horne; 11 Luke O'Donnell. Subs (all used): 18 Larne Patrick; 14 Shaun Lunt; 26 Jamie Cording (D); 37 Dale Ferguson.
Tries: McGillvary (2, 45), Cudjoe (6), Fa'alogo (9), Grix (16), Patrick (27), Horne (30, 68), Ferguson (63); **Goals:** Brough 7/10.
Sin bin: O'Donnell (48) - professional foul.
BULLS: 3 Paul Sykes; 18 Shaun Ainscough; 1 Michael Platt; 5 Patrick Ah Van; 19 Gareth Raynor; 6 Brett Kearney; 7 Marc Herbert; 10 Andy Lynch (C); 14 Matt Diskin; 15 Bryn Hargreaves; 23 Tom Olbison; 12 Elliott Whitehead; 11 Olivier Elima. Subs (all used): 8 Nick Scruton; 17 Ian Sibbit; 16 Craig Kopczak; 27 Adam O'Brien (D).
Tries: Ainscough (21), Herbert (73), Raynor (78);
Goals: Ah Van 2/3.
Rugby Leaguer & League Express Men of the Match: *Giants:* Kevin Brown; *Bulls:* Elliott Whitehead.
Penalty count: 11-9; **Half-time:** 30-6;
Referee: James Child; **Attendance:** 9,466.

HULL KINGSTON ROVERS 40 CRUSADERS 22

ROVERS: 1 Shaun Briscoe; 2 Peter Fox; 4 Jake Webster; 3 Kris Welham; 19 Craig Hall; 6 Blake Green; 13 Scott Murrell; 14 Liam Watts; 9 Ben Fisher; 16 Jason Netherton; 11 Clint Newton (C); 23 Willie Mason (D); 12 Ben Galea. Subs (all used): 15 Scott Wheeldon; 28 Ben Cockayne; 18 Josh Hodgson; 8 Rhys Lovegrove.
Tries: Galea (6), Murrell (8), Watts (17), Welham (38, 77), Webster (54), Green (57); **Goals:** Hall 6/7.
CRUSADERS: 1 Clinton Schifcofske (C); 5 Stuart Reardon; 3 Tony Martin; 4 Vince Mellars; 26 Rhys Williams; 6 Michael Witt; 7 Jarrod Sammut; 8 Ryan O'Hara; 9 Lincoln Withers; 10 Mark Bryant; 23 Peter Lupton; 12 Jason Chan; 16 Ben Flower. Subs (all used): 22 Richard Moore; 20 Gil Dudson; 19 Lloyd White; 25 Jamie Murphy (D).
Tries: Reardon (26, 71), Sammut (65), Lupton (68);
Goals: Schifcofske 3/4.
Rugby Leaguer & League Express Men of the Match: *Rovers:* Blake Green; *Crusaders:* Richard Moore.
Penalty count: 9-8; **Half-time:** 24-6;
Referee: Robert Hicks; **Attendance:** 8,602.

WIGAN WARRIORS 14 HULL FC 12

WARRIORS: 1 Sam Tomkins; 2 Darrell Goulding; 24 Stefan Marsh; 4 George Carmont; 25 Josh Charnley; 6 Paul Deacon; 7 Thomas Leuluai; 10 Andy Coley; 9 Michael McIlorum; 14 Paul Prescott; 11 Harrison Hansen; 16 Ryan Hoffman; 13 Sean O'Loughlin (C). Subs (all used): 12 Joel Tomkins; 15 Jeff Lima; 21 Lee Mossop; 22 Liam Farrell.
Tries: Hoffman (3), Charnley (55, 74);
Goals: S Tomkins 1/3, Deacon 0/1.
Dismissal: J Tomkins (69) - use of the elbow on Yeaman.
HULL: 20 Cameron Phelps (D); 2 Will Sharp; 3 Richard Whiting; 4 Kirk Yeaman; 5 Tom Briscoe; 6 Richard Horne; 30 Sam Obst; 8 Mark O'Meley; 9 Danny Houghton; 10 Lee Radford; 11 Joe Westerman; 12 Danny Tickle; 13 Craig Fitzgibbon (C). Subs (all used): 14 Danny Washbrook; 15 Epalahame Lauaki; 16 Willie Manu; 17 Ewan Dowes.
Tries: Westerman (8), Briscoe (16);
Goals: Tickle 1/3, Westerman 1/1.
Rugby Leaguer & League Express Men of the Match: *Warriors:* Sam Tomkins; *Hull:* Craig Fitzgibbon.
Penalty count: 13-8; **Half-time:** 4-10;
Referee: Steve Ganson; **Attendance:** 15,346.

ROUND 6

Friday 18th March 2011

CRUSADERS 22 CATALAN DRAGONS 32

CRUSADERS: 1 Clinton Schifcofske (C); 5 Stuart Reardon; 2 Gareth Thomas; 4 Vince Mellars; 26 Rhys Williams; 6 Michael Witt; 7 Jarrod Sammut; 20 Gil Dudson; 9 Lincoln Withers; 10 Mark Bryant; 23 Peter Lupton; 12 Jason Chan; 3 Tony Martin. Subs (all used): 22 Richard Moore; 19 Lloyd White; 16 Ben Flower; 8 Ryan O'Hara.
Tries: Sammut (35), Martin (42), Mellars (57, 61);
Goals: Schifcofske 1/2, Witt 2/2.
DRAGONS: 1 Clint Greenshields; 2 Damien Blanch; 3 Ben Farrar; 18 Darryl Millard; 5 Cyril Stacul; 4 Setaimata Sa; 7 Scott Dureau; 22 Jamal Fakir; 9 Ian Henderson; 10 Remi Casty; 11 Steve Menzies; 12 Sebastien Raguin; 13 Gregory Mounis (C). Subs (all used): 15 Jean-Philippe Baile; 17 Cyrille Gossard; 24 Jason Baitieri; 20 Michael Simon.
Tries: Greenshields (9, 39, 50), Farrar (13, 66);
Goals: Dureau 6/7.
Rugby Leaguer & League Express Men of the Match: *Crusaders:* Richard Moore; *Dragons:* Scott Dureau.
Penalty count: 3-8; **Half-time:** 6-16;
Referee: James Child; **Attendance:** 3,517.

HUDDERSFIELD GIANTS 6 WIGAN WARRIORS 20

GIANTS: 1 Scott Grix; 36 Jamie Simpson; 3 Leroy Cudjoe; 29 Joe Wardle (D); 5 David Hodgson; 6 Kevin Brown (C); 7 Danny Brough; 15 Keith Mason; 14 Shaun Lunt; 10 Darrell Griffin; 4 Lee Gilmour; 12 David Fa'alogo; 11 Luke O'Donnell. Subs (all used): 9 Luke Robinson; 13 David Faiumu; 8 Eorl Crabtree; 19 Graeme Horne.
Try: Robinson (23); **Goals:** Brough 1/1.
WARRIORS: 19 Amos Roberts; 2 Darrell Goulding; 24 Stefan Marsh; 4 George Carmont; 25 Josh Charnley; 13 Sean O'Loughlin (C); 7 Thomas Leuluai; 14 Paul Prescott; 9 Michael McIlorum; 10 Andy Coley; 11 Harrison Hansen; 16 Ryan Hoffman; 22 Liam Farrell. Subs: 15 Jeff Lima; 21 Lee Mossop; 23 Chris Tuson; 31 Joe Mellor (not used).
Tries: O'Loughlin (3), Charnley (43), Hoffman (78);
Goals: Charnley 4/4.
Rugby Leaguer & League Express Men of the Match: *Giants:* Scott Grix; *Warriors:* Josh Charnley.
Penalty count: 8-7; **Half-time:** 6-8;
Referee: Ben Thaler; **Attendance:** 8,151.

HULL FC 6 WAKEFIELD TRINITY WILDCATS 20

HULL: 20 Cameron Phelps; 2 Will Sharp; 3 Richard Whiting; 5 Tom Briscoe; 21 Reece Lyne; 6 Richard Horne; 7 Sean Long; 17 Ewan Dowes; 9 Danny Houghton; 10 Lee Radford; 11 Joe Westerman; 12 Danny Tickle; 13 Craig Fitzgibbon (C). Subs (all used): 14 Danny Washbrook; 15 Epalahame Lauaki; 16 Willie Manu; 30 Sam Obst.
Try: Tickle (43); **Goals:** Tickle 1/1.
WILDCATS: 3 Aaron Murphy; 30 Greg Johnson; 18 Chris Dean; 29 Josh Griffin; 5 Luke George; 6 Ben Jeffries; 14 Tommy Lee; 8 Michael Korkidas; 9 Julien Rinaldi; 17 Paul Johnson; 13 Glenn Morrison (C); 21 Frankie Mariano; 22 Stuart Howarth. Subs (all used): 10 Paul King; 11 Kevin Henderson; 26 Matthew Wildie; 31 Kyle Amor.
Tries: Mariano (18), Lee (64), Amor (80);
Goals: Griffin 4/4.
Rugby Leaguer & League Express Men of the Match: *Hull:* Sam Obst; *Wildcats:* Glenn Morrison.
Penalty count: 10-11; **Half-time:** 0-6;
Referee: Thierry Alibert; **Attendance:** 11,032.

SALFORD CITY REDS 34 HULL KINGSTON ROVERS 18

CITY REDS: 1 Luke Patten; 2 Jodie Broughton; 6 Stefan Ratchford; 20 Sean Gleeson (D); 3 Mark Henry; 14 Matty Smith; 7 Daniel Holdsworth (C); 19 Ryan Boyle; 9 Wayne Godwin; 18 Adam Sidlow; 15 Luke Adamson; 4 Chris Nero; 13 Stephen Wild. Subs (all used): 22 Adam Neal; 23 Marc Sneyd; 28 Callum Marriott (D); 29 Alex Davidson (D).
Tries: Boyle (11), Broughton (18), Ratchford (52), Smith (57), Gleeson (61), Sneyd (78);
Goals: Holdsworth 4/5, Ratchford 1/1.
ROVERS: 1 Shaun Briscoe; 4 Jake Webster; 19 Craig Hall; 3 Kris Welham; 5 Liam Colbon; 6 Blake Green (C); 13 Scott Murrell; 15 Scott Wheeldon; 9 Ben Fisher; 14 Liam Watts; 23 Willie Mason; 12 Ben Galea; 16 Jason Netherton. Subs (all used): 8 Rhys Lovegrove; 10 Joel Clinton; 18 Josh Hodgson; 28 Ben Cockayne.
Tries: Hall (38, 43), Murrell (46); **Goals:** Hall 3/3.
Rugby Leaguer & League Express Men of the Match: *City Reds:* Luke Patten; *Rovers:* Craig Hall.
Penalty count: 5-8; **Half-time:** 10-6;
Referee: Gareth Hewer; **Attendance:** 4,408.

Saturday 19th March 2011

LEEDS RHINOS 16 ST HELENS 30

RHINOS: 1 Brent Webb; 27 Zak Hardaker (D); 19 Kallum Watkins; 4 Keith Senior; 5 Ryan Hall; 13 Kevin Sinfield (C); 7 Rob Burrow; 11 Jamie Jones-Buchanan; 9 Danny Buderus; 17 Ian Kirke; 20 Weller Hauraki; 14 Ali Lauitiiti; 12 Carl Ablett. Subs (all used): 21 Chris Clarkson; 18 Luke Burgess; 15 Ben Cross; 24 Paul McShane.
Tries: Hall (35), Hardaker (45), McShane (56);
Goals: Sinfield 2/3.
SAINTS: 1 Paul Wellens (C); 2 Ade Gardner; 3 Michael Shenton; 5 Francis Meli; 22 Jamie Foster; 25 Lee Gaskell; 20 Jonny Lomax; 8 Josh Perry; 9 James Roby; 10 James Graham (C); 16 Paul Clough; 13 Chris Flannery; 11 Tony Puletua. Subs (all used): 14 Scott Moore; 21 Shaun Magennis; 18 Matty Ashurst; 17 Gary Wheeler.
Tries: Foster (21, 78), Shenton (50), Meli (63), Wellens (67); **Goals:** Foster 5/5.
Rugby Leaguer & League Express Men of the Match: *Rhinos:* Jamie Jones-Buchanan; *Saints:* Jonny Lomax.
Penalty count: 6-5; **Half-time:** 6-6;
Referee: Richard Silverwood; **Attendance:** 16,035.

Sunday 20th March 2011

BRADFORD BULLS 18 CASTLEFORD TIGERS 14

BULLS: 3 Paul Sykes; 18 Shaun Ainscough; 1 Michael Platt; 25 Shad Royston; 5 Patrick Ah Van; 6 Brett Kearney; 7 Marc Herbert; 10 Andy Lynch (C); 14 Matt Diskin; 15 Bryn Hargreaves; 11 Olivier Elima; 12 Elliott Whitehead; 13 Jamie Langley. Subs (all used): 8 Nick Scruton; 9 Heath L'Estrange; 16 Craig Kopczak; 23 Tom Olbison.
Tries: Elima (11), Scruton (40, 45); **Goals:** Ah Van 3/3.
TIGERS: 1 Richard Mathers; 2 Kirk Dixon; 4 Joe Arundel; 13 Brett Ferres; 3 Nick Youngquest; 6 Rangi Chase; 7 Danny Orr (C); 8 Paul Jackson; 16 Adam Milner; 10 Craig Huby; 24 Oliver Holmes; 11 Jake Emmitt; 14 Stuart Jones. Subs (all used): 19 Nick Fozzard; 20 Martin Aspinwall; 17 Willie Isa (D); 27 Daryl Clark.
Tries: Chase (4), Clark (55); **Goals:** Dixon 3/3.
Rugby Leaguer & League Express Men of the Match: *Bulls:* Heath L'Estrange; *Tigers:* Daryl Clark.
Penalty count: 7-9; **Half-time:** 12-8;
Referee: Robert Hicks; **Attendance:** 14,348.

WARRINGTON WOLVES 82 HARLEQUINS 6

WOLVES: 1 Brett Hodgson; 5 Joel Monaghan; 20 Matty Blythe; 4 Chris Bridge; 24 Rhys Evans; 6 Lee Briers; 7 Richard Myler; 10 Garreth Carvell; 9 Michael Monaghan; 16 Paul Wood; 17 Simon Grix; 12 Ben Westwood; 13 Ben Harrison. Subs (all used): 8 Adrian Morley (C); 26 David Solomona; 19 Lee Mitchell; 15 Jon Clarke.
Tries: Bridge (6, 14, 25), Briers (20), Solomona (35, 49), Myler (38), Evans (44), Westwood (54, 74), Morley (57), Blythe (61), Mitchell (65), Hodgson (79); **Goals:** Hodgson 13/14.
HARLEQUINS: 1 Luke Dorn; 5 Chris Melling; 4 David Howell; 31 Karl Pryce; 2 Jamie O'Callaghan; 6 Luke Gale; 7 Chad Randall; 17 Danny Ward; 9 Andy Ellis; 10 Oliver Wilkes; 3 Tony Clubb; 13 Rob Purdham (C); 12 Chris Bailey. Subs (all used): 8 Karl Temata; 15 Luke Ambler; 19 Lamont Bryan; 11 Nick Kouparitsas.
Try: Dorn (32); **Goals:** Gale 1/1.
Sin bin: Ward (56) - professional foul.
Rugby Leaguer & League Express Men of the Match: *Wolves:* Chris Bridge; *Harlequins:* Lamont Bryan.
Penalty count: 14-4; **Half-time:** 36-6;
Referee: Steve Ganson; **Attendance:** 11,506.

ROUND 7

Friday 25th March 2011

ST HELENS 28 BRADFORD BULLS 16

SAINTS: 1 Paul Wellens (C); 2 Ade Gardner; 3 Michael Shenton; 5 Francis Meli; 22 Jamie Foster; 25 Lee Gaskell; 20 Jonny Lomax; 10 James Graham (C); 9 James Roby; 8 Josh Perry; 13 Chris Flannery; 4 Iosia Soliola; 11 Tony Puletua. Subs (all used): 15 Louie McCarthy-Scarsbrook; 17 Gary Wheeler; 18 Matty Ashurst; 21 Shaun Magennis.
Tries: Foster (15, 43), Wellens (21, 37), Flannery (47);
Goals: Foster 4/6.
Sin bin: Soliola (67) - grapple tackle;
Shenton (74) - dangerous contact.
BULLS: 3 Paul Sykes; 18 Shaun Ainscough; 1 Michael Platt; 25 Shad Royston; 5 Patrick Ah Van; 6 Brett Kearney; 7 Marc Herbert; 10 Andy Lynch (C); 14 Matt Diskin; 15 Bryn Hargreaves; 11 Olivier Elima; 12 Elliott Whitehead; 13 Jamie Langley. Subs (all used): 8 Nick Scruton; 9 Heath L'Estrange; 16 Craig Kopczak; 23 Tom Olbison.
Tries: Ainscough (4, 77), Ah Van (63); **Goals:** Ah Van 2/3.
Sin bin: Sykes (36) - holding down.
Rugby Leaguer & League Express Men of the Match: *Saints:* Jonny Lomax; *Bulls:* Marc Herbert.
Penalty count: 8-4; **Half-time:** 16-6;
Referee: Richard Silverwood; **Attendance:** 7,676.

WIGAN WARRIORS 6 WARRINGTON WOLVES 24

WARRIORS: 1 Sam Tomkins; 2 Darrell Goulding; 24 Stefan Marsh; 4 George Carmont; 25 Josh Charnley; 17 Brett Finch (D); 7 Thomas Leuluai; 10 Andy Coley; 9 Michael McIlorum; 14 Paul Prescott; 11 Harrison Hansen; 16 Ryan Hoffman; 13 Sean O'Loughlin (C). Subs (all used): 15 Jeff Lima; 21 Lee Mossop; 23 Chris Tuson; 19 Amos Roberts.
Try: Finch (21); **Goals:** Charnley 1/1.
WOLVES: 1 Brett Hodgson; 5 Joel Monaghan; 20 Matty Blythe; 4 Chris Bridge; 24 Rhys Evans; 6 Lee Briers; 7 Richard Myler; 10 Garreth Carvell; 9 Michael Monaghan; 8 Adrian Morley (C); 17 Simon Grix; 12 Ben Westwood; 13 Ben Harrison. Subs (all used): 14 Mick Higham; 26 David Solomona; 16 Paul Wood; 15 Jon Clarke.
Tries: Blythe (7), J Monaghan (33, 48), Myler (64);
Goals: Hodgson 4/4.
Rugby Leaguer & League Express Men of the Match: *Warriors:* Andy Coley; *Wolves:* Lee Briers.
Penalty count: 10-5; **Half-time:** 6-12;
Referee: Thierry Alibert; **Attendance:** 21,056.

Saturday 26th March 2011

CATALAN DRAGONS 10 SALFORD CITY REDS 22

DRAGONS: 1 Clint Greenshields; 2 Damien Blanch; 3 Ben Farrar; 18 Darryl Millard; 5 Cyril Stacul; 4 Setaimata Sa; 14 Tony Gigot; 22 Jamal Fakir; 9 Ian Henderson; 10 Remi Casty; 11 Steve Menzies; 12 Sebastien Raguin; 13 Gregory Mounis (C). Subs (all used): 15 Jean-Philippe Baile; 20 Michael Simon; 24 Jason Baitieri; 8 David Ferriol.
Tries: Stacul (27), Raguin (61); **Goals:** Gigot 1/2.
CITY REDS: 1 Luke Patten; 2 Jodie Broughton; 20 Sean Gleeson; 6 Stefan Ratchford; 3 Mark Henry; 14 Matty Smith; 7 Daniel Holdsworth (C); 18 Adam Sidlow; 9 Wayne Godwin; 19 Ryan Boyle; 4 Chris Nero; 15 Luke Adamson; 13 Stephen Wild. Subs (all used): 23 Marc Sneyd; 8 Ray Cashmere; 10 Lee Jewitt; 22 Adam Neal.
Tries: Broughton (10, 13, 43, 70); **Goals:** Holdsworth 3/4.
Rugby Leaguer & League Express Men of the Match: *Dragons:* Setaimata Sa; *City Reds:* Jodie Broughton.
Penalty count: 8-3; **Half-time:** 4-10;
Referee: Robert Hicks; **Attendance:** 7,156.

HULL KINGSTON ROVERS 16 HUDDERSFIELD GIANTS 38

ROVERS: 1 Shaun Briscoe; 2 Peter Fox; 3 Kris Welham; 19 Craig Hall; 4 Jake Webster; 6 Blake Green; 13 Scott Murrell; 14 Liam Watts; 18 Josh Hodgson; 10 Joel Clinton; 23 Willie Mason; 12 Ben Galea (C); 16 Jason Netherton. Subs (all used): 8 Rhys Lovegrove; 22 Scott Taylor; 21 Sam Latus; 9 Ben Fisher.
Tries: Welham (2, 67), Fisher (48);
Goals: Hall 1/2, Murrell 1/1.
GIANTS: 1 Scott Grix; 20 Jermaine McGillvary; 3 Leroy Cudjoe; 2 Michael Lawrence; 5 David Hodgson; 6 Kevin Brown (C); 7 Danny Brough; 8 Eorl Crabtree; 13 David Faiumu; 15 Keith Mason; 4 Lee Gilmour; 17 Danny Kirmond; 11 Luke O'Donnell. Subs (all used): 9 Luke Robinson; 37 Dale Ferguson; 18 Larne Patrick; 16 Andy Raleigh.
Tries: McGillvary (7), Brough (14, 58), Lawrence (42), Grix (70), Robinson (77), Hodgson (80);
Goals: Brough 5/7.
Rugby Leaguer & League Express Men of the Match: *Rovers:* Kris Welham; *Giants:* Danny Brough.
Penalty count: 9-4; **Half-time:** 6-12;
Referee: Steve Ganson; **Attendance:** 7,502.

Sunday 27th March 2011

HARLEQUINS 30 HULL FC 40

HARLEQUINS: 1 Luke Dorn; 5 Chris Melling; 3 Tony Clubb; 4 David Howell; 2 Jamie O'Callaghan; 6 Luke Gale; 7 Chad Randall; 17 Danny Ward; 9 Andy Ellis; 10 Oliver Wilkes; 13 Rob Purdham (C); 16 Mike Burnett; 12 Chris Bailey. Subs (all used): 8 Karl Temata; 31 Karl Pryce; 11 Nick Kouparitsas; 19 Lamont Bryan.
Tries: Melling (14), Clubb (19), Dorn (51), Gale (53), Randall (58); **Goals:** Gale 5/5.
HULL: 6 Richard Horne; 2 Will Sharp; 3 Richard Whiting; 4 Kirk Yeaman; 5 Tom Briscoe; 30 Sam Obst; 7 Sean Long; 17 Ewan Dowes; 9 Danny Houghton; 10 Lee Radford; 11 Joe Westerman; 12 Danny Tickle; 13 Craig Fitzgibbon (C). Subs (all used): 16 Willie Manu; 19 Jordan Turner; 15 Epalahame Lauaki; 23 Sam Moa.
Tries: Tickle (7), Yeaman (29, 80), Briscoe (42), Lauaki (65), Obst (71), Turner (77);
Goals: Tickle 6/6, Westerman 0/1.
Rugby Leaguer & League Express Men of the Match: *Harlequins:* Andy Ellis; *Hull:* Sam Obst.
Penalty count: 3-4; **Half-time:** 12-12;
Referee: Phil Bentham; **Attendance:** 3,052.

CASTLEFORD TIGERS 56 CRUSADERS 16

TIGERS: 1 Richard Mathers; 2 Kirk Dixon; 4 Joe Arundel; 17 Willie Isa; 3 Nick Youngquest; 6 Rangi Chase; 7 Danny Orr (C); 19 Nick Fozzard; 16 Adam Milner; 10 Craig Huby; 14 Stuart Jones; 20 Martin Aspinwall; 13 Brett Ferres. Subs (all used): 8 Paul Jackson; 11 Jake Emmitt; 25 Dean Widders; 27 Daryl Clark.
Tries: Dixon (5, 35), Clark (29, 48), Widders (39), Ferres (51), Isa (55), Mathers (61), Youngquest (73), Arundel (79); **Goals:** Dixon 8/10.
Sin bin: Youngquest (17) - fighting.
CRUSADERS: 1 Clinton Schifcofske (C); 5 Stuart Reardon; 3 Tony Martin; 4 Vince Mellars; 27 Jordan Tansey (D); 6 Michael Witt; 7 Jarrod Sammut; 8 Ryan O'Hara; 9 Lincoln Withers; 10 Mark Bryant; 2 Gareth Thomas; 12 Jason Chan; 22 Richard Moore. Subs (all used): 20 Gil Dudson; 19 Lloyd White; 16 Ben Flower; 25 Jamie Murphy.
Tries: Reardon (66), Martin (69), Mellars (73);
Goals: Schifcofske 2/3.
Sin bin: Witt (17) - fighting; Mellars (17) - fighting; Schifcofske (30) - delaying restart.
Rugby Leaguer & League Express Men of the Match: *Tigers:* Rangi Chase; *Crusaders:* Tony Martin.
Penalty count: 15-3; **Half-time:** 22-0;
Referee: Ben Thaler; **Attendance:** 6,030.

WAKEFIELD TRINITY WILDCATS 6 LEEDS RHINOS 28

WILDCATS: 3 Aaron Murphy; 30 Greg Johnson; 29 Josh Griffin; 18 Chris Dean; 5 Luke George; 6 Ben Jeffries; 14 Tommy Lee; 8 Michael Korkidas; 9 Julien Rinaldi; 17 Paul Johnson; 21 Frankie Mariano; 13 Glenn Morrison (C); 22 Stuart Howarth. Subs (all used): 23 Josh Veivers; 26 Matthew Wildie; 31 Kyle Amor; 11 Kevin Henderson.
Try: G Johnson (24); **Goals:** Griffin 1/2.
RHINOS: 1 Brent Webb; 19 Kallum Watkins; 12 Carl Ablett; 4 Keith Senior; 5 Ryan Hall; 13 Kevin Sinfield (C); 7 Rob Burrow; 8 Kylie Leuluai; 9 Danny Buderus; 16 Ryan Bailey; 21 Chris Clarkson; 20 Weller Hauraki; 11 Jamie Jones-Buchanan. Subs (all used): 22 Jay Pitts; 24 Paul McShane; 18 Luke Burgess; 15 Ben Cross.
Tries: Watkins (44, 56, 60, 76), Buderus (73);
Goals: Sinfield 4/6.
Sin bin: Burgess (27) - interference.
Rugby Leaguer & League Express Men of the Match: *Wildcats:* Chris Dean; *Rhinos:* Kallum Watkins.
Penalty count: 11-12; **Half-time:** 4-0;
Referee: James Child; **Attendance:** 8,763.

ROUND 8

Friday 1st April 2011

HULL FC 18 CASTLEFORD TIGERS 20

HULL: 20 Cameron Phelps; 2 Will Sharp; 3 Richard Whiting; 4 Kirk Yeaman; 5 Tom Briscoe; 6 Richard Horne; 7 Sean Long; 23 Sam Moa; 9 Danny Houghton; 10 Lee Radford; 11 Joe Westerman; 12 Danny Tickle; 13 Craig Fitzgibbon (C). Subs (all used): 30 Sam Obst; 16 Willie Manu; 15 Epalahame Lauaki; 17 Ewan Dowes.
Tries: Yeaman (18), Tickle (50), Fitzgibbon (72);
Goals: Westerman 1/1, Tickle 2/3.
Dismissal: Long (75) - use of the elbow.
Sin bin: Radford (5) - grapple tackle;
Long (65) - fighting.
TIGERS: 1 Richard Mathers; 2 Kirk Dixon; 4 Joe Arundel; 17 Willie Isa; 5 Richard Owen; 6 Rangi Chase; 7 Danny Orr (C); 8 Paul Jackson; 9 Ryan Hudson; 11 Jake Emmitt; 14 Stuart Jones; 20 Martin Aspinwall; 13 Brett Ferres. Subs (all used): 10 Craig Huby; 19 Nick Fozzard; 25 Dean Widders; 27 Daryl Clark.
Tries: Owen (13), Isa (36, 58); **Goals:** Dixon 4/6.
Sin bin: Aspinwall (65) - fighting.
Rugby Leaguer & League Express Men of the Match: *Hull:* Craig Fitzgibbon; *Tigers:* Danny Orr.
Penalty count: 13-14; **Half-time:** 6-10;
Referee: James Child; **Attendance:** 11,856.

LEEDS RHINOS 22 WIGAN WARRIORS 22

RHINOS: 1 Brent Webb; 19 Kallum Watkins; 12 Carl Ablett; 4 Keith Senior; 5 Ryan Hall; 13 Kevin Sinfield (C); 7 Rob Burrow; 16 Ryan Bailey; 9 Danny Buderus; 8 Kylie Leuluai; 20 Weller Hauraki; 22 Jay Pitts; 11 Jamie Jones-Buchanan. Subs (all used): 17 Ian Kirke; 21 Chris Clarkson; 24 Paul McShane; 15 Ben Cross.
Tries: Jones-Buchanan (18), Buderus (20), Webb (60);
Goals: Sinfield 5/5.
WARRIORS: 1 Sam Tomkins; 2 Darrell Goulding; 12 Joel Tomkins; 4 George Carmont; 19 Amos Roberts; 13 Sean O'Loughlin (C); 7 Thomas Leuluai; 10 Andy Coley; 9 Michael McIlorum; 14 Paul Prescott; 11 Harrison Hansen; 16 Ryan Hoffman; 22 Liam Farrell. Subs (all used): 15 Jeff Lima; 17 Brett Finch; 21 Lee Mossop; 23 Chris Tuson.
Tries: J Tomkins (11), S Tomkins (64), Goulding (72), Prescott (78); **Goals:** S Tomkins 3/5.
Sin bin: Lima (46) - dangerous contact on Clarkson.
Rugby Leaguer & League Express Men of the Match: *Rhinos:* Danny Buderus; *Warriors:* Thomas Leuluai.
Penalty count: 9-11; **Half-time:** 12-4;
Referee: Richard Silverwood; **Attendance:** 16,118.

ST HELENS 34 HULL KINGSTON ROVERS 16

SAINTS: 1 Paul Wellens (C); 2 Ade Gardner; 3 Michael Shenton; 17 Gary Wheeler; 22 Jamie Foster; 25 Lee Gaskell; 20 Jonny Lomax; 8 Josh Perry; 9 James Roby; 10 James Graham (C); 13 Chris Flannery; 4 Iosia Soliola; 11 Tony Puletua. Subs (all used): 14 Scott Moore; 15 Louie McCarthy-Scarsbrook; 18 Matty Ashurst; 28 Tom Makinson.
Tries: Soliola (15), McCarthy-Scarsbrook (20, 25), Wellens (37), Foster (58), Graham (63);
Goals: Foster 5/6.
ROVERS: 1 Shaun Briscoe; 2 Peter Fox; 19 Craig Hall; 3 Kris Welham; 4 Jake Webster; 6 Blake Green; 13 Scott Murrell; 10 Joel Clinton; 18 Josh Hodgson; 14 Liam Watts; 23 Willie Mason; 12 Ben Galea (C); 16 Jason Netherton. Subs (all used): 8 Rhys Lovegrove; 9 Ben Fisher; 21 Sam Latus; 22 Scott Taylor.
Tries: Welham (12, 78), Webster (68); **Goals:** Hall 2/3.
Rugby Leaguer & League Express Men of the Match: *Saints:* James Roby; *Rovers:* Jake Webster.
Penalty count: 10-4; **Half-time:** 24-6;
Referee: Ben Thaler; **Attendance:** 7,740.

Saturday 2nd April 2011

SALFORD CITY REDS 10 CRUSADERS 16

CITY REDS: 1 Luke Patten; 2 Jodie Broughton; 20 Sean Gleeson; 6 Stefan Ratchford; 3 Mark Henry; 14 Matty Smith; 7 Daniel Holdsworth (C); 8 Ray Cashmere; 9 Wayne Godwin; 19 Ryan Boyle; 4 Chris Nero; 15 Luke Adamson; 13 Stephen Wild. Subs (all used): 11 Vinnie Anderson (D); 18 Adam Sidlow; 10 Lee Jewitt; 22 Adam Neal.
Tries: Cashmere (50), Broughton (54);
Goals: Holdsworth 1/2.
CRUSADERS: 1 Clinton Schifcofske (C); 5 Stuart Reardon; 3 Tony Martin; 2 Gareth Thomas; 4 Vince Mellars; 27 Jordan Tansey; 17 Rhys Hanbury; 22 Richard Moore; 19 Lloyd White; 10 Mark Bryant; 11 Hep Cahill (D); 12 Jason Chan; 21 Paul Johnson. Subs (all used): 16 Ben Flower; 8 Ryan O'Hara; 23 Peter Lupton; 7 Jarrod Sammut.
Tries: Tansey (40), Sammut (46), Thomas (71);
Goals: Schifcofske 2/3.
Sin bin: Mellars (11) - persistent offending.
Rugby Leaguer & League Express Men of the Match: *City Reds:* Daniel Holdsworth; *Crusaders:* Rhys Hanbury.
Penalty count: 13-11; **Half-time:** 0-6;
Referee: Steve Ganson; **Attendance:** 3,416.

Sunday 3rd April 2011

BRADFORD BULLS 24 HARLEQUINS 22

BULLS: 3 Paul Sykes; 18 Shaun Ainscough; 4 Chev Walker; 25 Shad Royston; 5 Patrick Ah Van; 6 Brett Kearney; 7 Marc Herbert; 10 Andy Lynch (C); 14 Matt Diskin; 15 Bryn Hargreaves; 11 Olivier Elima; 23 Tom Olbison; 20 James Donaldson. Subs (all used): 21 Danny Addy; 12 Elliott Whitehead; 16 Craig Kopczak; 29 Tom Burgess (D).
Tries: Elima (37), Diskin (40), Kearney (52), Sykes (63);
Goals: Ah Van 4/5.
HARLEQUINS: 1 Luke Dorn; 5 Chris Melling; 3 Tony Clubb; 31 Karl Pryce; 23 Mark Calderwood; 6 Luke Gale; 7 Chad Randall; 17 Danny Ward; 9 Andy Ellis; 8 Karl Temata; 13 Rob Purdham (C); 11 Nick Kouparitsas; 12 Chris Bailey. Subs (all used): 10 Oliver Wilkes; 26 Rob Thomas (D); 19 Lamont Bryan; 2 Jamie O'Callaghan.
Tries: Pryce (15, 43, 79), Clubb (71); **Goals:** Gale 3/4.
Rugby Leaguer & League Express Men of the Match: *Bulls:* Brett Kearney; *Harlequins:* Karl Pryce.
Penalty count: 13-7; **Half-time:** 10-4;
Referee: Thierry Alibert; **Attendance:** 12,354.

HUDDERSFIELD GIANTS 34 WAKEFIELD TRINITY WILDCATS 10

GIANTS: 3 Leroy Cudjoe; 20 Jermaine McGillvary; 29 Joe Wardle; 2 Michael Lawrence; 36 Jamie Simpson; 9

Luke Robinson (C); 7 Danny Brough; 15 Keith Mason; 14 Shaun Lunt; 16 Andy Raleigh; 37 Dale Ferguson; 19 Graeme Horne; 13 David Faiumu. Subs (all used): 1 Scott Grix; 18 Larne Patrick; 10 Darrell Griffin; 17 Danny Kirmond.
Tries: Robinson (7), Horne (42, 63), Lawrence (57, 70), Lunt (75); **Goals:** Brough 5/7.
WILDCATS: 3 Aaron Murphy; 30 Greg Johnson; 18 Chris Dean; 29 Josh Griffin; 5 Luke George; 6 Ben Jeffries; 14 Tommy Lee; 8 Michael Korkidas; 9 Julien Rinaldi; 17 Paul Johnson; 13 Glenn Morrison (C); 21 Frankie Mariano; 22 Stuart Howarth. Subs (all used): 23 Josh Veivers; 25 Liam Higgins (D); 33 Tyrone McCarthy (D); 31 Kyle Amor.
Tries: Dean (12), Jeffries (51);
Goals: Griffin 0/2, Veivers 1/1.
Rugby Leaguer & League Express Men of the Match:
Giants: David Faiumu; *Wildcats:* Ben Jeffries.
Penalty count: 13-12; **Half-time:** 6-4;
Referee: Robert Hicks; **Attendance:** 7,267.

WARRINGTON WOLVES 20 CATALAN DRAGONS 22

WOLVES: 1 Brett Hodgson; 5 Joel Monaghan; 4 Chris Bridge; 24 Rhys Evans; 2 Chris Riley; 6 Lee Briers; 7 Richard Myler; 8 Adrian Morley (C); 9 Michael Monaghan; 10 Garreth Carvell; 17 Simon Grix; 20 Matty Blythe; 15 Jon Clarke. Subs (all used): 16 Paul Wood; 14 Mick Higham; 26 David Solomona; 18 Michael Cooper.
Tries: J Monaghan (8, 25), Riley (46), Myler (66);
Goals: Hodgson 2/4.
DRAGONS: 1 Clint Greenshields; 19 Frederic Vaccari; 15 Jean-Philippe Baile; 18 Darryl Millard; 5 Cyril Stacul; 3 Ben Farrar; 7 Scott Dureau; 8 David Ferriol; 9 Ian Henderson; 10 Remi Casty; 11 Steve Menzies; 12 Sebastien Raguin; 13 Gregory Mounis (C). Subs (all used): 20 Michael Simon; 21 Sebastien Martins; 24 Jason Baitieri; 26 Eloi Pelissier.
Tries: Millard (15), Vaccari (34), Ferriol (55), Dureau (71); **Goals:** Dureau 3/4.
Sin bin: Henderson (79) - delaying restart.
Rugby Leaguer & League Express Men of the Match:
Wolves: David Solomona; *Dragons:* Scott Dureau.
Penalty count: 16-8; **Half-time:** 10-10;
Referee: Phil Bentham; **Attendance:** 10,956.

ROUND 9

Friday 8th April 2011

CRUSADERS 18 ST HELENS 34

CRUSADERS: 1 Clinton Schifcofske (C); 5 Stuart Reardon; 3 Tony Martin; 2 Gareth Thomas; 4 Vince Mellars; 6 Michael Witt; 17 Rhys Hanbury; 22 Richard Moore; 19 Lloyd White; 10 Mark Bryant; 11 Hep Cahill; 12 Jason Chan; 21 Paul Johnson. Subs (all used): 13 Frank Winterstein; 27 Jordan Tansey; 8 Ryan O'Hara; 16 Ben Flower.
Tries: Thomas (22), Martin (42), White (65);
Goals: Schifcofske 1/1, Witt 2/2.
SAINTS: 1 Paul Wellens (C); 2 Ade Gardner; 3 Michael Shenton; 17 Gary Wheeler; 22 Jamie Foster; 25 Lee Gaskell; 20 Jonny Lomax; 10 James Graham (C); 9 James Roby; 8 Josh Perry; 13 Chris Flannery; 4 Iosia Soliola; 11 Tony Puletua. Subs: 12 Jon Wilkin; 15 Louie McCarthy-Scarsbrook; 21 Shaun Magennis; 28 Tom Makinson (not used).
Tries: Lomax (4), Gaskell (7), Wellens (18), Gardner (28, 79), Roby (30); **Goals:** Foster 5/6.
Rugby Leaguer & League Express Men of the Match:
Crusaders: Hep Cahill; *Saints:* James Roby.
Penalty count: 10-9; **Half-time:** 6-30;
Referee: Robert Hicks; **Attendance:** 4,002.

HUDDERSFIELD GIANTS 29 WARRINGTON WOLVES 10

GIANTS: 1 Scott Grix; 20 Jermaine McGillvary; 3 Leroy Cudjoe; 2 Michael Lawrence; 36 Jamie Simpson; 6 Kevin Brown (C); 7 Danny Brough; 8 Eorl Crabtree; 9 Luke Robinson; 16 Andy Raleigh; 4 Lee Gilmour; 37 Dale Ferguson; 11 Luke O'Donnell. Subs (all used): 14 Shaun Lunt; 13 David Faiumu; 18 Larne Patrick; 17 Danny Kirmond.
Tries: Grix (4), Patrick (22), Robinson (34), McGillvary (79); **Goals:** Brough 6/6; **Field goal:** Brough (63).
WOLVES: 1 Brett Hodgson; 5 Joel Monaghan; 20 Matty Blythe; 23 Ryan Atkins; 24 Rhys Evans; 4 Chris Bridge; 7 Richard Myler; 8 Adrian Morley (C); 9 Michael Monaghan; 10 Garreth Carvell; 11 Louis Anderson; 12 Ben Westwood; 13 Ben Harrison. Subs (all used): 15 Jon Clarke; 16 Paul Wood; 18 Michael Cooper; 26 David Solomona.
Tries: Hodgson (8, 40); **Goals:** Hodgson 1/2.
Rugby Leaguer & League Express Men of the Match:
Giants: Scott Grix; *Wolves:* Brett Hodgson.
Penalty count: 10-5; **Half-time:** 18-10;
Referee: Richard Silverwood; **Attendance:** 7,224.

HULL FC 34 BRADFORD BULLS 24

HULL: 20 Cameron Phelps; 2 Will Sharp; 19 Jordan Turner; 4 Kirk Yeaman; 5 Tom Briscoe; 6 Richard Horne; 30 Sam Obst; 8 Mark O'Meley; 9 Danny Houghton; 23 Sam Moa; 16 Willie Manu; 12 Danny Tickle; 13 Craig Fitzgibbon (C). Subs (all used): 15 Epalahame Lauaki; 11 Joe Westerman; 3 Richard Whiting; 10 Lee Radford.
Tries: Yeaman (24), Tickle (31), Radford (39), Turner (43), Briscoe (71, 78); **Goals:** Tickle 5/6.
BULLS: 6 Brett Kearney; 18 Shaun Ainscough; 4 Chev Walker; 25 Shad Royston; 5 Patrick Ah Van; 3 Paul Sykes; 7 Marc Herbert; 10 Andy Lynch (C); 14 Matt Diskin; 15 Bryn Hargreaves; 12 Elliott Whitehead; 23 Tom Olbison; 20 James Donaldson. Subs (all used): 9 Heath L'Estrange; 29 Tom Burgess; 16 Craig Kopczak; 17 Ian Sibbit.
Tries: Sykes (4), Royston (10, 50), Walker (36);
Goals: Ah Van 4/4.
Sin bin: Sibbit (48) - grapple tackle.
Rugby Leaguer & League Express Men of the Match:
Hull: Danny Tickle; *Bulls:* Marc Herbert.
Penalty count: 10-8; **Half-time:** 18-18;
Referee: Ben Thaler; **Attendance:** 11,346.

WIGAN WARRIORS 28 CATALAN DRAGONS 47

WARRIORS: 1 Sam Tomkins; 2 Darrell Goulding; 24 Stefan Marsh; 4 George Carmont; 5 Pat Richards; 17 Brett Finch; 7 Thomas Leuluai; 10 Andy Coley; 9 Michael McIlorum; 14 Paul Prescott; 12 Joel Tomkins; 16 Ryan Hoffman; 13 Sean O'Loughlin (C). Subs (all used): 11 Harrison Hansen; 21 Lee Mossop; 23 Chris Tuson; 25 Josh Charnley.
Tries: S Tomkins (2), McIlorum (40), Carmont (69), O'Loughlin (75), Marsh (79); **Goals:** Richards 4/5.
DRAGONS: 5 Cyril Stacul; 2 Damien Blanch; 18 Darryl Millard; 4 Setaimata Sa; 19 Frederic Vaccari; 3 Ben Farrar; 7 Scott Dureau; 8 David Ferriol; 9 Ian Henderson; 10 Remi Casty; 11 Steve Menzies; 12 Sebastien Raguin; 13 Gregory Mounis (C). Subs (all used): 20 Michael Simon; 21 Sebastien Martins; 24 Jason Baitieri; 26 Eloi Pelissier.
Tries: Vaccari (7, 42), Menzies (10, 37), Casty (17), Dureau (22, 57), Blanch (61); **Goals:** Dureau 7/9;
Field goal: Dureau (78).
Rugby Leaguer & League Express Men of the Match:
Warriors: Sam Tomkins; *Dragons:* Scott Dureau.
Penalty count: 11-7; **Half-time:** 10-30;
Referee: James Child; **Attendance:** 13,134.

Saturday 9th April 2011

HULL KINGSTON ROVERS 38 LEEDS RHINOS 28

ROVERS: 28 Ben Cockayne; 21 Sam Latus; 3 Kris Welham; 4 Jake Webster; 5 Liam Colbon; 6 Blake Green; 13 Scott Murrell; 20 Michael Vella (C); 18 Josh Hodgson; 10 Joel Clinton; 23 Willie Mason; 8 Rhys Lovegrove; 12 Ben Galea. Subs (all used): 22 Scott Taylor; 14 Liam Watts; 17 Matt Cook; 9 Ben Fisher.
Tries: Vella (19), Welham (22), Cook (31), Murrell (36), Colbon (42), Latus (61), Galea (76); **Goals:** Murrell 5/7.
RHINOS: 1 Brent Webb; 19 Kallum Watkins; 2 Lee Smith; 4 Keith Senior; 5 Ryan Hall; 13 Kevin Sinfield (C); 7 Rob Burrow; 17 Ian Kirke; 9 Danny Buderus; 16 Ryan Bailey; 11 Jamie Jones-Buchanan; 21 Chris Clarkson; 12 Carl Ablett. Subs (all used): 15 Ben Cross; 20 Weller Hauraki; 22 Jay Pitts; 24 Paul McShane.
Tries: Smith (4), Watkins (14, 78), Hall (50), McShane (66); **Goals:** Sinfield 4/5.
Rugby Leaguer & League Express Men of the Match:
Rovers: Ben Galea; *Rhinos:* Kallum Watkins.
Penalty count: 11-3; **Half-time:** 24-10;
Referee: Thierry Alibert; **Attendance:** 8,653.

Sunday 10th April 2011

CASTLEFORD TIGERS 52 SALFORD CITY REDS 20

TIGERS: 1 Richard Mathers; 5 Richard Owen; 4 Joe Arundel; 2 Kirk Dixon; 3 Nick Youngquest; 6 Rangi Chase; 7 Danny Orr (C); 11 Jake Emmitt; 9 Ryan Hudson; 10 Craig Huby; 20 Martin Aspinwall; 24 Oliver Holmes; 13 Brett Ferres. Subs (all used): 8 Paul Jackson; 19 Nick Fozzard; 25 Dean Widders; 27 Daryl Clark.
Tries: Youngquest (5, 40), Dixon (28), Mathers (35), Arundel (38, 77), Widders (48), Clark (56), Owen (68);
Goals: Dixon 8/9.
CITY REDS: 1 Luke Patten; 2 Jodie Broughton; 4 Chris Nero; 6 Stefan Ratchford; 3 Mark Henry; 14 Matty Smith; 7 Daniel Holdsworth (C); 8 Ray Cashmere; 9 Wayne Godwin; 19 Ryan Boyle; 15 Luke Adamson; 11 Vinnie Anderson; 13 Stephen Wild. Subs (all used): 23 Marc Sneyd; 17 Iafeta Palea'aesina; 22 Adam Neal; 18 Adam Sidlow.
Tries: Broughton (15), Anderson (17), Holdsworth (43), Sidlow (80); **Goals:** Holdsworth 2/4.
Sin bin: Wild (53) - late challenge.
Rugby Leaguer & League Express Men of the Match:
Tigers: Rangi Chase; *City Reds:* Jodie Broughton.
Penalty count: 6-7; **Half-time:** 30-10;
Referee: Phil Bentham; **Attendance:** 6,741.

WAKEFIELD TRINITY WILDCATS 52 HARLEQUINS 32

WILDCATS: 1 Matt Blaymire; 2 Kevin Penny; 18 Chris Dean; 5 Luke George; 29 Josh Griffin; 6 Ben Jeffries; 14 Tommy Lee; 31 Kyle Amor; 9 Julien Rinaldi; 17 Paul Johnson; 21 Frankie Mariano; 13 Glenn Morrison (C); 22 Stuart Howarth. Subs (all used): 33 Tyrone McCarthy; 26 Matthew Wildie; 25 Liam Higgins; 20 Ben Gledhill.
Tries: Lee (5), Morrison (16), Howarth (21), Griffin (26), George (28), Jeffries (41, 67), Dean (59), P Johnson (78); **Goals:** Griffin 8/10.
HARLEQUINS: 1 Luke Dorn; 5 Chris Melling; 4 David Howell; 31 Karl Pryce; 2 Jamie O'Callaghan; 6 Luke Gale; 7 Chad Randall; 10 Oliver Wilkes; 9 Andy Ellis; 8 Karl Temata; 13 Rob Purdham (C); 3 Tony Clubb; 12 Chris Bailey. Subs (all used): 18 Dave Williams; 15 Luke Ambler; 11 Nick Kouparitsas; 20 Ben Bolger.
Tries: Bailey (32), O'Callaghan (43), Purdham (51), Melling (53), Pryce (72), Dorn (74); **Goals:** Gale 4/6.
Sin bin: Clubb (58) - persistent offending.
Rugby Leaguer & League Express Men of the Match:
Wildcats: Glenn Morrison; *Harlequins:* Rob Purdham.
Penalty count: 9-9; **Half-time:** 26-6;
Referee: Tim Roby; **Attendance:** 5,412.

ROUND 10

Friday 15th April 2011

HARLEQUINS 26 CASTLEFORD TIGERS 26

HARLEQUINS: 1 Luke Dorn; 2 Jamie O'Callaghan; 3 Tony Clubb; 4 David Howell; 5 Chris Melling; 6 Luke Gale; 7 Chad Randall; 15 Luke Ambler; 9 Andy Ellis; 8 Karl Temata; 12 Chris Bailey; 13 Rob Purdham (C); 10 Oliver Wilkes. Subs (all used): 18 Dave Williams; 19 Lamont Bryan; 20 Ben Bolger; 31 Karl Pryce.
Tries: Bryan (16), Clubb (29, 72), Dorn (68), Ellis (78);
Goals: Gale 3/5.
TIGERS: 1 Richard Mathers; 2 Kirk Dixon; 13 Brett Ferres; 4 Joe Arundel; 5 Richard Owen; 6 Rangi Chase; 7 Danny Orr (C); 8 Paul Jackson; 9 Ryan Hudson; 10 Craig Huby; 20 Martin Aspinwall; 25 Dean Widders; 24 Oliver Holmes. Subs (all used): 11 Jake Emmitt; 12 Steve Snitch; 19 Nick Fozzard; 27 Daryl Clark.
Tries: Owen (21, 45), Chase (26), Clark (48);
Goals: Dixon 5/5.
Rugby Leaguer & League Express Men of the Match:
Harlequins: Luke Dorn; *Tigers:* Rangi Chase.
Penalty count: 8-6; **Half-time:** 10-12;
Referee: Matthew Thomasson; **Attendance:** 4,128.

HULL KINGSTON ROVERS 16 WIGAN WARRIORS 28

ROVERS: 28 Ben Cockayne; 5 Liam Colbon; 4 Jake Webster; 3 Kris Welham; 21 Sam Latus; 6 Blake Green; 13 Scott Murrell; 10 Joel Clinton; 18 Josh Hodgson; 20 Michael Vella (C); 23 Willie Mason; 8 Rhys Lovegrove; 12 Ben Galea. Subs (all used): 22 Scott Taylor; 9 Ben Fisher; 14 Liam Watts; 17 Matt Cook.
Tries: Cook (28), Mason (44), Cockayne (65);
Goals: Murrell 2/3.
WARRIORS: 1 Sam Tomkins; 25 Josh Charnley; 12 Joel Tomkins; 4 George Carmont; 5 Pat Richards; 6 Paul Deacon; 7 Thomas Leuluai; 10 Andy Coley; 9 Michael McIlorum; 15 Jeff Lima; 11 Harrison Hansen; 16 Ryan Hoffman; 13 Sean O'Loughlin (C). Subs (all used): 14 Paul Prescott; 17 Brett Finch; 21 Lee Mossop; 22 Liam Farrell.
Tries: J Tomkins (15), Hoffman (20), Charnley (30), Leuluai (48), Carmont (77); **Goals:** Richards 4/6.
On report: Lima (80) - alleged dangerous contact.
Rugby Leaguer & League Express Men of the Match:
Rovers: Michael Vella; *Warriors:* Sam Tomkins.
Penalty count: 6-7; **Half-time:** 6-16;
Referee: Thierry Alibert; **Attendance:** 8,703.

LEEDS RHINOS 6 HUDDERSFIELD GIANTS 38

RHINOS: 1 Brent Webb; 19 Kallum Watkins; 3 Brett Delaney; 4 Keith Senior; 5 Ryan Hall; 13 Kevin Sinfield (C); 7 Rob Burrow; 16 Ryan Bailey; 9 Danny Buderus; 8 Kylie Leuluai; 11 Jamie Jones-Buchanan; 21 Chris Clarkson; 17 Ian Kirke. Subs (all used): 15 Ben Cross; 18 Luke Burgess; 20 Weller Hauraki; 24 Paul McShane.
Try: Burrow (53); **Goals:** Sinfield 1/1.
Dismissal: Bailey (48) - fighting.
Sin bin: Webb (75) - professional foul.
GIANTS: 1 Scott Grix; 20 Jermaine McGillvary; 3 Leroy Cudjoe; 2 Michael Lawrence; 36 Jamie Simpson; 6 Kevin Brown (C); 7 Danny Brough; 8 Eorl Crabtree; 9 Luke Robinson; 10 Darrell Griffin; 4 Lee Gilmour; 37 Dale Ferguson; 11 Luke O'Donnell. Subs (all used): 19 Graeme Horne; 18 Larne Patrick; 13 David Faiumu; 14 Shaun Lunt.
Tries: Ferguson (17, 31), McGillvary (20), Lunt (56, 79), Robinson (76); **Goals:** Brough 7/7.
Dismissal: O'Donnell (48) - fighting.
Sin bin: Grix (64) - professional foul.
Rugby Leaguer & League Express Men of the Match:
Rhinos: Kylie Leuluai; *Giants:* Dale Ferguson.
Penalty count: 10-12; **Half-time:** 0-20;
Referee: Ben Thaler; **Attendance:** 14,768.

ST HELENS 52 WAKEFIELD TRINITY WILDCATS 6

SAINTS: 1 Paul Wellens (C); 2 Ade Gardner; 3 Michael Shenton; 17 Gary Wheeler; 22 Jamie Foster; 25 Lee Gaskell; 20 Jonny Lomax; 10 James Graham (C); 9 James Roby; 15 Louie McCarthy-Scarsbrook; 13 Chris Flannery; 4 Iosia Soliola; 11 Tony Puletua. Subs (all used): 12 Jon Wilkin; 14 Scott Moore; 21 Shaun Magennis; 28 Tom Makinson.
Tries: Foster (17, 32), Lomax (25), Shenton (37), Gardner (53), Wheeler (57), Wellens (67), Puletua (72), Makinson (79); **Goals:** Foster 8/9.
WILDCATS: 1 Matt Blaymire; 2 Kevin Penny; 18 Chris Dean; 5 Luke George; 29 Josh Griffin; 6 Ben Jeffries; 14 Tommy Lee; 31 Kyle Amor; 9 Julien Rinaldi (C); 17 Paul Johnson; 33 Tyrone McCarthy; 21 Frankie Mariano; 22 Stuart Howarth. Subs (all used): 10 Paul King; 11 Kevin Henderson; 25 Liam Higgins; 26 Matthew Wildie.
Try: Dean (45); **Goals:** Griffin 1/1.
Rugby Leaguer & League Express Men of the Match:
Saints: Jonny Lomax; *Wildcats:* Julien Rinaldi.
Penalty count: 5-2; **Half-time:** 24-6;
Referee: Steve Ganson; **Attendance:** 7,003.

WARRINGTON WOLVES 64 CRUSADERS 6

WOLVES: 1 Brett Hodgson; 22 Rhys Williams; 17 Simon Grix; 23 Ryan Atkins; 5 Joel Monaghan; 4 Chris Bridge; 7 Richard Myler; 8 Adrian Morley (C); 9 Michael Monaghan; 10 Garreth Carvell; 11 Louis Anderson; 12 Ben Westwood; 13 Ben Harrison. Subs (all used): 26 David Solomona; 18 Michael Cooper; 16 Paul Wood; 14 Mick Higham.
Tries: Hodgson (20, 70), Westwood (25, 47), Williams (31), Anderson (35), Atkins (41, 58), Bridge (50), J Monaghan (73), Myler (75); **Goals:** Hodgson 10/11.
Sin bin: Bridge (69) - fighting.

CRUSADERS: 1 Clinton Schifcofske (C); 27 Jordan Tansey; 3 Tony Martin; 2 Gareth Thomas; 4 Vince Mellars; 6 Michael Witt; 17 Rhys Hanbury; 22 Richard Moore; 9 Lincoln Withers; 8 Ryan O'Hara; 11 Hep Cahill; 21 Paul Johnson; 23 Peter Lupton. Subs (all used): 10 Mark Bryant; 15 Jordan James; 13 Frank Winterstein; 7 Jarrod Sammut.
Try: Hanbury (3); **Goals:** Schifcofske 1/1.
Sin bin: Mellars (69) - fighting.
Rugby Leaguer & League Express Men of the Match: *Wolves:* Brett Hodgson; *Crusaders:* Gareth Thomas.
Penalty count: 9-3; **Half-time:** 24-6;
Referee: Tim Roby; **Attendance:** 10,002.

Saturday 16th April 2011

SALFORD CITY REDS 56 BRADFORD BULLS 16

CITY REDS: 1 Luke Patten; 2 Jodie Broughton; 5 Ashley Gibson; 6 Stefan Ratchford; 3 Mark Henry; 14 Matty Smith; 7 Daniel Holdsworth (C); 8 Ray Cashmere; 9 Wayne Godwin; 19 Ryan Boyle; 4 Chris Nero; 11 Vinnie Anderson; 13 Stephen Wild. Subs (all used): 23 Marc Sneyd; 17 Iafeta Palea'aesina; 15 Luke Adamson; 18 Adam Sidlow.
Tries: Holdsworth (15), Henry (17, 70), Gibson (25, 60, 64), Broughton (36), Smith (50), Ratchford (68), Adamson (80); **Goals:** Holdsworth 8/10.
BULLS: 6 Brett Kearney; 19 Gareth Raynor; 3 Paul Sykes; 4 Chev Walker; 18 Shaun Ainscough; 32 Kyle Briggs; 7 Marc Herbert; 10 Andy Lynch (C); 9 Heath L'Estrange; 16 Craig Kopczak; 11 Olivier Elima; 12 Elliott Whitehead; 23 Tom Olbison. Subs (all used): 20 James Donaldson; 14 Matt Diskin; 29 Tom Burgess; 15 Bryn Hargreaves.
Tries: Lynch (2), Herbert (42, 77); **Goals:** Herbert 2/3.
Rugby Leaguer & League Express Men of the Match: *City Reds:* Daniel Holdsworth; *Bulls:* Marc Herbert.
Penalty count: 13-7; **Half-time:** 24-6;
Referee: James Child; **Attendance:** 2,809.

CATALAN DRAGONS 28 HULL FC 10

DRAGONS: 5 Cyril Stacul; 2 Damien Blanch; 15 Jean-Philippe Baile; 4 Setaimata Sa; 19 Frederic Vaccari; 3 Ben Farrar; 7 Scott Dureau; 8 David Ferriol; 9 Ian Henderson; 10 Remi Casty; 11 Steve Menzies; 12 Sebastien Raguin; 13 Gregory Mounis (C). Subs (all used): 20 Michael Simon; 21 Sebastien Martins; 24 Jason Baitieri; 26 Eloi Pelissier.
Tries: Baile (25), Blanch (28), Vaccari (46), Menzies (74), Henderson (76); **Goals:** Dureau 4/5.
HULL: 20 Cameron Phelps; 21 Reece Lyne; 19 Jordan Turner; 4 Kirk Yeaman; 5 Tom Briscoe; 6 Richard Horne; 30 Sam Obst; 8 Mark O'Meley; 9 Danny Houghton; 23 Sam Moa; 11 Joe Westerman; 12 Danny Tickle; 13 Craig Fitzgibbon (C). Subs (all used): 3 Richard Whiting; 10 Lee Radford; 15 Epalahame Lauaki; 17 Ewan Dowes.
Tries: Briscoe (12), Obst (35);
Goals: Tickle 0/1, Fitzgibbon 1/1.
Rugby Leaguer & League Express Men of the Match: *Dragons:* Steve Menzies; *Hull:* Craig Fitzgibbon.
Penalty count: 6-7; **Half-time:** 12-10;
Referee: Richard Silverwood; **Attendance:** 8,025.

ROUND 11

Thursday 21st April 2011

BRADFORD BULLS 22 LEEDS RHINOS 30

BULLS: 25 Shad Royston; 19 Gareth Raynor; 1 Michael Platt; 4 Chev Walker; 5 Patrick Ah Van; 6 Brett Kearney; 7 Marc Herbert; 10 Andy Lynch (C); 9 Heath L'Estrange; 16 Craig Kopczak; 11 Olivier Elima; 12 Elliott Whitehead; 20 James Donaldson. Subs (all used): 14 Matt Diskin; 15 Bryn Hargreaves; 23 Tom Olbison; 29 Tom Burgess.
Tries: Ah Van (7), Lynch (10), Elima (47, 62);
Goals: Ah Van 3/5.
RHINOS: 1 Brett Webb; 19 Kallum Watkins; 3 Brett Delaney; 4 Keith Senior; 5 Ryan Hall; 13 Kevin Sinfield (C); 7 Rob Burrow; 18 Luke Burgess; 9 Danny Buderus; 8 Kylie Leuluai; 11 Jamie Jones-Buchanan; 21 Chris Clarkson; 12 Carl Ablett. Subs (all used): 15 Ben Cross; 17 Ian Kirke; 20 Weller Hauraki; 24 Paul McShane.
Tries: McShane (25), Jones-Buchanan (35), Senior (53), Hall (55), Buderus (78); **Goals:** Sinfield 5/6.
Rugby Leaguer & League Express Men of the Match: *Bulls:* Olivier Elima; *Rhinos:* Paul McShane.
Penalty count: 10-7; **Half-time:** 12-10;
Referee: Thierry Alibert; **Attendance:** 19,275.

Friday 22nd April 2011

HULL FC 36 HULL KINGSTON ROVERS 18

HULL: 20 Cameron Phelps; 3 Richard Whiting; 33 Martin Gleeson (D); 4 Kirk Yeaman; 5 Tom Briscoe; 6 Richard Horne; 7 Sean Long; 8 Mark O'Meley; 9 Danny Houghton; 23 Sam Moa; 16 Willie Manu; 12 Danny Tickle; 13 Craig Fitzgibbon (C). Subs (all used): 30 Sam Obst; 11 Joe Westerman; 17 Ewan Dowes; 15 Epalahame Lauaki.
Tries: Yeaman (2, 78), Long (21), Gleeson (32), Whiting (65), Briscoe (80); **Goals:** Tickle 6/7.
ROVERS: 28 Ben Cockayne; 21 Sam Latus; 3 Kris Welham; 4 Jake Webster; 2 Peter Fox; 6 Blake Green; 7 Michael Dobson; 20 Michael Vella (C); 18 Josh Hodgson; 10 Joel Clinton; 17 Matt Cook; 12 Ben Galea; 13 Scott Murrell. Subs (all used): 8 Rhys Lovegrove; 22 Scott Taylor; 16 Jason Netherton; 9 Ben Fisher.
Tries: Cook (8), Welham (27), Cockayne (72);
Goals: Dobson 3/3.
Rugby Leaguer & League Express Men of the Match: *Hull:* Tom Briscoe; *Rovers:* Blake Green.
Penalty count: 6-3; **Half-time:** 16-12;
Referee: Phil Bentham; **Attendance:** 19,795.

CRUSADERS 32 HUDDERSFIELD GIANTS 6

CRUSADERS: 1 Clinton Schifcofske (C); 5 Stuart Reardon; 3 Tony Martin; 4 Vince Mellars; 27 Jordan Tansey; 6 Michael Witt; 17 Rhys Hanbury; 8 Ryan O'Hara; 19 Lloyd White; 22 Richard Moore; 11 Hep Cahill; 12 Jason Chan; 23 Peter Lupton. Subs (all used): 7 Jarrod Sammut; 10 Mark Bryant; 13 Frank Winterstein; 15 Jordan James.
Tries: Chan (3), Hanbury (16), Schifcofske (31), Cahill (38), Tansey (67), Reardon (70); **Goals:** Schifcofske 4/6.
Sin bin: Witt (13) - dissent; Moore (77) - grapple tackle.
GIANTS: 1 Scott Grix; 20 Jermaine McGillvary; 3 Leroy Cudjoe; 2 Michael Lawrence; 36 Jamie Simpson; 6 Kevin Brown (C); 7 Danny Brough; 8 Eorl Crabtree; 9 Luke Robinson; 10 Darrell Griffin; 4 Lee Gilmour; 12 David Fa'alogo; 19 Graeme Horne. Subs (all used): 13 David Faiumu; 14 Shaun Lunt; 18 Larne Patrick; 17 Danny Kirmond.
Try: Brough (42); **Goals:** Brough 1/1.
Rugby Leaguer & League Express Men of the Match: *Crusaders:* Clinton Schifcofske; *Giants:* Shaun Lunt.
Penalty count: 8-6; **Half-time:** 20-0;
Referee: Steve Ganson; **Attendance:** 3,008.

HARLEQUINS 30 CATALAN DRAGONS 37

HARLEQUINS: 1 Luke Dorn; 5 Chris Melling; 4 David Howell; 3 Tony Clubb; 2 Jamie O'Callaghan; 6 Luke Gale; 7 Chad Randall (C); 15 Luke Ambler; 9 Andy Ellis; 17 Danny Ward; 16 Mike Burnett; 12 Chris Bailey; 10 Oliver Wilkes. Subs (all used): 11 Nick Kouparitsas; 19 Lamont Bryan; 18 Dave Williams; 31 Karl Pryce.
Tries: O'Callaghan (21), Gale (44), Ellis (58), Pryce (62), Randall (68); **Goals:** Gale 5/5.
DRAGONS: 5 Cyril Stacul; 2 Damien Blanch; 15 Jean-Philippe Baile; 4 Setaimata Sa; 19 Frederic Vaccari; 3 Ben Farrar; 7 Scott Dureau; 8 David Ferriol; 9 Ian Henderson; 10 Remi Casty; 12 Sebastien Raguin; 11 Steve Menzies; 13 Gregory Mounis (C). Subs (all used): 21 Sebastien Martins; 20 Michael Simon; 24 Jason Baitieri; 26 Eloi Pelissier.
Tries: Dureau (13, 25), Pelissier (28), Baitieri (37), Stacul (54, 79); **Goals:** Dureau 5/6, Mounis 1/1;
Field goal: Dureau (74).
Sin bin: Dureau (63) - dissent.
Rugby Leaguer & League Express Men of the Match: *Harlequins:* Andy Ellis; *Dragons:* Steve Menzies.
Penalty count: 14-2; **Half-time:** 6-22;
Referee: Ben Thaler; **Attendance:** 2,069.

WIGAN WARRIORS 28 ST HELENS 24

WARRIORS: 1 Sam Tomkins; 25 Josh Charnley; 12 Joel Tomkins; 4 George Carmont; 5 Pat Richards; 6 Paul Deacon; 7 Thomas Leuluai; 10 Andy Coley; 9 Michael McIlorum; 15 Jeff Lima; 11 Harrison Hansen; 16 Ryan Hoffman; 13 Sean O'Loughlin (C). Subs (all used): 14 Paul Prescott; 17 Brett Finch; 21 Lee Mossop; 22 Liam Farrell.
Tries: Charnley (37, 49), Richards (45, 56), Farrell (80);
Goals: Richards 4/5.
SAINTS: 1 Paul Wellens (C); 2 Ade Gardner; 3 Michael Shenton; 5 Francis Meli; 22 Jamie Foster; 20 Jonny Lomax; 17 Gary Wheeler; 10 James Graham (C); 9 James Roby; 15 Louie McCarthy-Scarsbrook; 12 Jon Wilkin; 4 Iosia Soliola; 11 Tony Puletua. Subs (all used): 18 Matty Ashurst; 14 Scott Moore; 21 Shaun Magennis; 28 Tom Makinson.
Tries: Shenton (13), Foster (27, 74), Makinson (69);
Goals: Foster 4/5.
Rugby Leaguer & League Express Men of the Match: *Warriors:* Pat Richards; *Saints:* James Roby.
Penalty count: 1-5; **Half-time:** 4-10;
Referee: Richard Silverwood; **Attendance:** 24,057.

SALFORD CITY REDS 0 WARRINGTON WOLVES 60

CITY REDS: 1 Luke Patten; 2 Jodie Broughton; 5 Ashley Gibson; 6 Stefan Ratchford; 3 Mark Henry; 14 Matty Smith; 7 Daniel Holdsworth (C); 8 Ray Cashmere; 9 Wayne Godwin; 19 Ryan Boyle; 11 Vinnie Anderson; 4 Chris Nero; 13 Stephen Wild. Subs (all used): 15 Luke Adamson; 22 Adam Neal; 23 Marc Sneyd; 18 Adam Sidlow.
Sin bin: Adamson (48) - punching.
WOLVES: 1 Brett Hodgson; 5 Joel Monaghan; 4 Chris Bridge; 23 Ryan Atkins; 22 Rhys Williams; 6 Lee Briers; 7 Richard Myler; 8 Adrian Morley (C); 9 Michael Monaghan; 16 Paul Wood; 11 Louis Anderson; 12 Ben Westwood; 13 Ben Harrison. Subs (all used): 14 Mick Higham; 17 Simon Grix; 10 Garreth Carvell; 18 Michael Cooper.
Tries: Atkins (17), Myler (28), Briers (33, 56), Bridge (43), Carvell (50), J Monaghan (59), Williams (61, 68), Wood (74); **Goals:** Hodgson 10/10.
Rugby Leaguer & League Express Men of the Match: *City Reds:* Jodie Broughton; *Wolves:* Lee Briers.
Penalty count: 5-7; **Half-time:** 0-18;
Referee: Robert Hicks; **Attendance:** 7,496.

CASTLEFORD TIGERS 24
WAKEFIELD TRINITY WILDCATS 28

TIGERS: 1 Richard Mathers; 2 Kirk Dixon; 22 Jordan Thompson; 4 Joe Arundel; 5 Richard Owen; 6 Rangi Chase; 7 Danny Orr (C); 19 Nick Fozzard; 9 Ryan Hudson; 11 Jake Emmitt; 14 Stuart Jones; 13 Brett Ferres; 20 Martin Aspinwall. Subs (all used): 8 Paul Jackson; 10 Craig Huby; 25 Dean Widders; 27 Daryl Clark.
Tries: Mathers (5), Aspinwall (8), Thompson (40), Orr (42); **Goals:** Dixon 4/4.
WILDCATS: 1 Matt Blaymire; 30 Greg Johnson; 18 Chris Dean; 3 Aaron Murphy; 29 Josh Griffin; 27 Kieran Hyde; 14 Tommy Lee; 31 Kyle Amor; 9 Julien Rinaldi; 17 Paul Johnson; 13 Glenn Morrison (C); 21 Frankie Mariano; 22 Stuart Howarth. Subs (all used): 10 Paul King; 11 Kevin Henderson; 25 Liam Higgins; 26 Matthew Wildie.
Tries: Dean (15), Hyde (52), Griffin (63), P Johnson (64), Mariano (69); **Goals:** Griffin 4/5.
Rugby Leaguer & League Express Men of the Match: *Tigers:* Danny Orr; *Wildcats:* Glenn Morrison.
Penalty count: 2-8; **Half-time:** 18-4;
Referee: James Child; **Attendance:** 9,020.

ROUND 12

Monday 25th April 2011

WAKEFIELD TRINITY WILDCATS 0
WIGAN WARRIORS 26

WILDCATS: 1 Matt Blaymire; 30 Greg Johnson; 18 Chris Dean; 3 Aaron Murphy; 19 Dale Morton; 27 Kieran Hyde; 14 Tommy Lee; 31 Kyle Amor; 26 Matthew Wildie; 10 Paul King; 13 Glenn Morrison (C); 11 Kevin Henderson; 22 Stuart Howarth. Subs (all used): 17 Paul Johnson; 8 Michael Korkidas; 24 James Davey; 33 Tyrone McCarthy.
WARRIORS: 1 Sam Tomkins; 25 Josh Charnley; 12 Joel Tomkins; 4 George Carmont; 5 Pat Richards; 17 Brett Finch; 7 Thomas Leuluai; 10 Andy Coley; 9 Michael McIlorum; 21 Lee Mossop; 11 Harrison Hansen; 16 Ryan Hoffman; 13 Sean O'Loughlin (C). Subs (all used): 14 Paul Prescott; 6 Paul Deacon; 15 Jeff Lima; 22 Liam Farrell.
Tries: Richards (2), S Tomkins (30), Charnley (36), J Tomkins (60), O'Loughlin (77); **Goals:** Richards 3/5.
Rugby Leaguer & League Express Men of the Match: *Wildcats:* Glenn Morrison; *Warriors:* Sam Tomkins.
Penalty count: 6-7; **Half-time:** 0-14;
Referee: Robert Hicks; **Attendance:** 8,163.

HULL KINGSTON ROVERS 37 HARLEQUINS 24

ROVERS: 26 Louis Sheriff (D); 2 Peter Fox; 3 Kris Welham; 4 Jake Webster; 28 Ben Cockayne; 6 Blake Green; 7 Michael Dobson; 20 Michael Vella (C); 9 Ben Fisher; 14 Liam Watts; 17 Matt Cook; 12 Ben Galea; 13 Scott Murrell. Subs (all used): 24 Richard Beaumont (D); 10 Joel Clinton; 8 Rhys Lovegrove; 18 Josh Hodgson.
Tries: Webster (12), Sheriff (14), Dobson (33), Galea (38), Murrell (66), Fisher (79);
Goals: Dobson 5/5, Murrell 1/1; **Field goal:** Dobson (76).
HARLEQUINS: 1 Luke Dorn; 5 Chris Melling; 3 Tony Clubb; 4 David Howell; 2 Jamie O'Callaghan; 6 Luke Gale; 7 Chad Randall (C); 10 Oliver Wilkes; 9 Andy Ellis; 17 Danny Ward; 16 Mike Burnett; 33 Lee Mitchell (D); 15 Luke Ambler. Subs (all used): 11 Nick Kouparitsas; 8 Karl Temata; 18 Dave Williams; 31 Karl Pryce.
Tries: Wilkes (21), Temata (26), Dorn (48), Mitchell (59);
Goals: Gale 4/4.
Rugby Leaguer & League Express Men of the Match: *Rovers:* Ben Galea; *Harlequins:* Luke Dorn.
Penalty count: 8-5; **Half-time:** 24-12;
Referee: Richard Silverwood; **Attendance:** 7,139.

LEEDS RHINOS 34 CRUSADERS 16

RHINOS: 1 Brent Webb; 32 George Elliott (D); 3 Brett Delaney; 4 Keith Senior; 5 Ryan Hall; 13 Kevin Sinfield (C); 7 Rob Burrow; 8 Kylie Leuluai; 9 Danny Buderus; 16 Ryan Bailey; 11 Jamie Jones-Buchanan; 21 Chris Clarkson; 12 Carl Ablett. Subs (all used): 18 Luke Burgess; 24 Paul McShane; 17 Ian Kirke; 6 Danny McGuire.
Tries: Delaney (29), Ablett (32), Senior (39, 77), Burrow (45), Leuluai (79); **Goals:** Sinfield 5/6.
CRUSADERS: 1 Clinton Schifcofske (C); 5 Stuart Reardon; 3 Tony Martin; 2 Gareth Thomas; 27 Jordan Tansey; 6 Michael Witt; 17 Rhys Hanbury; 8 Ryan O'Hara; 19 Lloyd White; 22 Richard Moore; 11 Hep Cahill; 21 Paul Johnson; 23 Peter Lupton. Subs (all used): 7 Jarrod Sammut; 15 Jordan James; 12 Jason Chan; 13 Frank Winterstein.
Tries: Tansey (52), Witt (68), Hanbury (74);
Goals: Schifcofske 2/3.
Rugby Leaguer & League Express Men of the Match: *Rhinos:* Rob Burrow; *Crusaders:* Michael Witt.
Penalty count: 11-6; **Half-time:** 18-0;
Referee: James Child; **Attendance:** 14,165.

ST HELENS 22 CASTLEFORD TIGERS 20

SAINTS: 28 Tom Makinson; 2 Ade Gardner; 3 Michael Shenton; 5 Francis Meli; 22 Jamie Foster; 12 Jon Wilkin; 20 Jonny Lomax; 10 James Graham (C); 9 James Roby; 15 Louie McCarthy-Scarsbrook; 18 Matty Ashurst; 4 Iosia Soliola; 11 Tony Puletua. Subs (all used): 14 Scott Moore; 21 Shaun Magennis; 19 Andrew Dixon; 24 Tom Armstrong.
Tries: Armstrong (19, 35), Gardner (73), Meli (80);
Goals: Foster 3/4.
TIGERS: 1 Richard Mathers; 2 Kirk Dixon; 22 Jordan Thompson; 4 Joe Arundel; 5 Richard Owen; 6 Rangi Chase; 7 Danny Orr (C); 8 Paul Jackson; 16 Adam Milner; 10 Craig Huby; 14 Stuart Jones; 24 Oliver Holmes; 20 Martin Aspinwall. Subs (all used): 9 Ryan Hudson; 11 Jake Emmitt; 13 Brett Ferres; 12 Steve Snitch.
Tries: Jones (24), Chase (42), Thompson (64);
Goals: Dixon 4/4.
Rugby Leaguer & League Express Men of the Match: *Saints:* James Roby; *Tigers:* Rangi Chase.
Penalty count: 3-3; **Half-time:** 12-8;
Referee: Phil Bentham; **Attendance:** 8,010.

Wakefield captain Glenn Morrison leads the celebrations after a thrilling derby win against Castleford

WARRINGTON WOLVES 10 HULL FC 24

WOLVES: 1 Brett Hodgson; 5 Joel Monaghan; 3 Matt King; 23 Ryan Atkins; 22 Rhys Williams; 6 Lee Briers; 15 Jon Clarke; 8 Adrian Morley (C); 9 Michael Monaghan; 16 Paul Wood; 11 Louis Anderson; 12 Ben Westwood; 13 Ben Harrison. Subs (all used): 14 Mick Higham; 20 Matty Blythe; 10 Garreth Carvell; 26 David Solomona.
Tries: J Monaghan (7), Williams (15);
Goals: Hodgson 1/2.
HULL: 20 Cameron Phelps; 3 Richard Whiting; 33 Martin Gleeson; 4 Kirk Yeaman; 5 Tom Briscoe; 6 Richard Horne; 30 Sam Obst; 8 Mark O'Meley; 9 Danny Houghton; 23 Sam Moa; 16 Willie Manu; 12 Danny Tickle; 13 Craig Fitzgibbon (C). Subs (all used): 14 Danny Washbrook; 2 Will Sharp; 17 Ewan Dowes; 15 Epalahame Lauaki.
Tries: Houghton (22), Yeaman (31, 75), Sharp (63);
Goals: Tickle 4/4.
Rugby Leaguer & League Express Men of the Match: *Wolves:* Ben Westwood; *Hull:* Kirk Yeaman.
Penalty count: 7-3; **Half-time:** 10-12;
Referee: Ben Thaler; **Attendance:** 12,036.

CATALAN DRAGONS 8 BRADFORD BULLS 8

DRAGONS: 3 Ben Farrar; 2 Damien Blanch; 15 Jean-Philippe Baile; 27 Mathias Pala (D); 5 Cyril Stacul; 6 Thomas Bosc (C); 7 Scott Dureau; 20 Michael Simon; 9 Ian Henderson; 10 Remi Casty; 4 Setaimata Sa; 12 Sebastien Raguin; 13 Gregory Mounis. Subs (all used): 22 Jamal Fakir; 21 Sebastien Martins; 24 Jason Baitieri; 26 Eloi Pelissier.
Try: Farrar (13); **Goals:** Dureau 2/3.
Sin bin: Martins (35) - high tackle;
Mounis (56) - holding down.
BULLS: 25 Shad Royston; 19 Gareth Raynor; 1 Michael Platt; 4 Chev Walker; 5 Patrick Ah Van; 3 Paul Sykes; 7 Marc Herbert; 10 Andy Lynch (C); 14 Matt Diskin; 16 Craig Kopczak; 11 Olivier Elima; 17 Ian Sibbit; 31 John Bateman (D). Subs (all used): 9 Heath L'Estrange; 12 Elliott Whitehead; 15 Bryn Hargreaves; 22 Steve Crossley.
Try: L'Estrange (32); **Goals:** Ah Van 2/3.
Sin bin: Sykes (26) - holding down.
Rugby Leaguer & League Express Men of the Match: *Dragons:* Ian Henderson; *Bulls:* Andy Lynch.
Penalty count: 12-11; **Half-time:** 6-6;
Referee: Steve Ganson; **Attendance:** 9,496.

Tuesday 26th April 2011

HUDDERSFIELD GIANTS 52 SALFORD CITY REDS 22

GIANTS: 1 Scott Grix; 20 Jermaine McGillvary; 29 Joe Wardle; 2 Michael Lawrence; 5 David Hodgson; 6 Kevin Brown (C); 7 Danny Brough; 16 Andy Raleigh; 14 Shaun Lunt; 10 Darrell Griffin; 37 Dale Ferguson; 26 Jamie Cording; 11 Luke O'Donnell. Subs (all used): 13 David Faiumu; 8 Eorl Crabtree; 23 Kyle Wood; 32 Jon Molloy.
Tries: O'Donnell (14), Lunt (25, 55), Cording (28), Ferguson (34, 46), Griffin (59), Brown (64), McGillvary (76); **Goals:** Brough 7/8, Grix 1/1.
CITY REDS: 1 Luke Patten; 2 Jodie Broughton; 5 Ashley Gibson; 6 Stefan Ratchford; 3 Mark Henry; 14 Matty Smith; 7 Daniel Holdsworth (C); 8 Ray Cashmere; 9 Wayne Godwin; 19 Ryan Boyle; 15 Luke Adamson; 18 Adam Sidlow; 13 Stephen Wild. Subs (all used): 10 Lee Jewitt; 23 Marc Sneyd; 17 Iafeta Palea'aesina; 25 Jack Spencer.
Tries: Sidlow (8), Holdsworth (19), Henry (38), Ratchford (71); **Goals:** Holdsworth 3/4.
Rugby Leaguer & League Express Men of the Match: *Giants:* Darrell Griffin; *City Reds:* Daniel Holdsworth.
Penalty count: 10-6; **Half-time:** 24-18;
Referee: Thierry Alibert; **Attendance:** 6,042.

ROUND 13

Friday 29th April 2011

CASTLEFORD TIGERS 6 LEEDS RHINOS 48

TIGERS: 1 Richard Mathers; 2 Kirk Dixon; 22 Jordan Thompson; 4 Joe Arundel; 5 Richard Owen; 6 Rangi Chase; 7 Danny Orr (C); 8 Paul Jackson; 16 Adam Milner; 12 Steve Snitch; 14 Stuart Jones; 24 Oliver Holmes; 13 Brett Ferres. Subs (all used): 11 Jake Emmitt; 20 Martin Aspinwall; 23 Ryan McGoldrick; 27 Daryl Clark.
Try: Arundel (71); **Goals:** Dixon 1/1.
RHINOS: 1 Brent Webb; 19 Kallum Watkins; 3 Brett Delaney; 4 Keith Senior; 5 Ryan Hall; 13 Kevin Sinfield (C); 7 Rob Burrow; 8 Kylie Leuluai; 24 Paul McShane; 18 Luke Burgess; 11 Jamie Jones-Buchanan; 21 Chris Clarkson; 12 Carl Ablett. Subs (all used): 6 Danny McGuire; 10 Jamie Peacock; 15 Ben Cross; 17 Ian Kirke.
Tries: Watkins (2), Jones-Buchanan (20), Hall (53, 80), McGuire (63), Burrow (69), McShane (73), Kirke (77);
Goals: Sinfield 8/9.
Rugby Leaguer & League Express Men of the Match: *Tigers:* Rangi Chase; *Rhinos:* Jamie Jones-Buchanan.
Penalty count: 9-7; **Half-time:** 0-12;
Referee: Richard Silverwood; **Attendance:** 9,860.

Saturday 30th April 2011

CATALAN DRAGONS 13 HUDDERSFIELD GIANTS 12

DRAGONS: 5 Cyril Stacul; 2 Damien Blanch; 15 Jean-Philippe Baile; 3 Ben Farrar; 19 Frederic Vaccari; 6 Thomas Bosc (C); 7 Scott Dureau; 8 David Ferriol; 9 Ian Henderson; 22 Jamal Fakir; 10 Remi Casty; 12 Sebastien Raguin; 13 Gregory Mounis. Subs (all used): 20 Michael Simon; 28 Julien Touxagas; 24 Jason Baitieri; 26 Eloi Pelissier.

Tries: Ferriol (2), Baitieri (59); **Goals:** Dureau 2/2;
Field goal: Dureau (71).
GIANTS: 1 Scott Grix; 20 Jermaine McGillvary; 3 Leroy Cudjoe; 2 Michael Lawrence; 36 Jamie Simpson; 6 Kevin Brown (C); 7 Danny Brough; 16 Andy Raleigh; 13 David Faiumu; 19 Graeme Horne; 4 Lee Gilmour; 37 Dale Ferguson; 11 Luke O'Donnell. Subs (all used): 8 Eorl Crabtree; 9 Luke Robinson; 10 Darrell Griffin; 18 Larne Patrick.
Tries: Gilmour (5), Grix (21); **Goals:** Brough 2/2.
Rugby Leaguer & League Express Men of the Match: *Dragons:* Cyril Stacul; *Giants:* Luke O'Donnell.
Penalty count: 4-3; **Half-time:** 6-12;
Referee: Ben Thaler; **Attendance:** 8,025.

HARLEQUINS 16 SALFORD CITY REDS 34

HARLEQUINS: 1 Luke Dorn; 5 Chris Melling; 4 David Howell; 3 Tony Clubb; 2 Jamie O'Callaghan; 6 Luke Gale; 7 Chad Randall (C); 15 Luke Ambler; 9 Andy Ellis; 17 Oliver Wilkes. Subs (all used): 11 Nick Kouparitsas; 8 Karl Temata; 18 Dave Williams; 31 Karl Pryce.
Tries: Burnett (2), Ambler (45), Melling (77);
Goals: Gale 2/3.
CITY REDS: 1 Luke Patten; 2 Jodie Broughton; 6 Stefan Ratchford; 5 Ashley Gibson; 27 Adam Clay (D); 14 Matty Smith; 7 Daniel Holdsworth (C); 8 Ray Cashmere; 9 Wayne Godwin; 17 Iafeta Palea'aesina; 11 Vinnie Anderson; 4 Chris Nero; 13 Stephen Wild. Subs (all used): 22 Adam Neal; 15 Luke Adamson; 19 Ryan Boyle; 10 Lee Jewitt.
Tries: Clay (9, 22), Godwin (28), Patten (33), Nero (37), Palea'aesina (61), Anderson (72); **Goals:** Holdsworth 3/8.
Rugby Leaguer & League Express Men of the Match: *Harlequins:* Luke Ambler; *City Reds:* Matty Smith.
Penalty count: 7-5; **Half-time:** 4-22;
Referee: Robert Hicks; **Attendance:** 1,957.

Sunday 1st May 2011

BRADFORD BULLS 14 WARRINGTON WOLVES 58

BULLS: 25 Shad Royston; 18 Shaun Ainscough; 1 Michael Platt; 4 Chev Walker; 5 Patrick Ah Van; 3 Paul Sykes; 7 Marc Herbert; 10 Andy Lynch (C); 14 Matt Diskin; 16 Craig Kopczak; 11 Olivier Elima; 17 Ian Sibbit; 23 Tom Olbison. Subs (all used): 12 Elliott Whitehead; 9 Heath L'Estrange; 15 Bryn Hargreaves; 22 Tom Burgess.
Tries: Kopczak (67), Lynch (71), Whitehead (78);
Goals: Ah Van 1/3.
WOLVES: 1 Brett Hodgson; 5 Joel Monaghan; 4 Chris Bridge; 23 Ryan Atkins; 3 Matt King; 6 Lee Briers; 17 Simon Grix; 8 Adrian Morley (C); 9 Michael Monaghan; 16 Paul Wood; 11 Louis Anderson; 12 Ben Westwood; 13 Ben Harrison. Subs (all used): 14 Mick Higham; 18 Michael Cooper; 10 Garreth Carvell; 26 David Solomona.

217

Tries: Anderson (4, 15), Atkins (9, 54), M Monaghan (25), King (28), J Monaghan (32), Hodgson (45), Higham (56), Bridge (76), Briers (79); **Goals:** Hodgson 7/11.
Rugby Leaguer & League Express Men of the Match: *Bulls:* Andy Lynch; *Wolves:* Matt King.
Penalty count: 8-5; **Half-time:** 0-32;
Referee: Thierry Alibert; **Attendance:** 14,134.

CRUSADERS 16 WIGAN WARRIORS 48

CRUSADERS: 1 Clinton Schifcofske (C); 5 Stuart Reardon; 3 Tony Martin; 2 Gareth Thomas; 27 Jordan Tansey; 6 Michael Witt; 17 Rhys Hanbury; 10 Mark Bryant; 19 Lloyd White; 16 Ben Flower; 11 Hep Cahill; 12 Jason Chan; 13 Frank Winterstein. Subs (all used): 7 Jarrod Sammut; 8 Ryan O'Hara; 21 Paul Johnson; 20 Gil Dudson.
Tries: Thomas (55), Witt (64), Reardon (66); **Goals:** Schifcofske 2/3.
WARRIORS: 1 Sam Tomkins; 25 Josh Charnley; 2 Darrell Goulding; 4 George Carmont; 5 Pat Richards; 17 Brett Finch; 7 Thomas Leuluai; 10 Andy Coley; 9 Michael McIlorum; 21 Lee Mossop; 16 Ryan Hoffman; 22 Liam Farrell; 13 Sean O'Loughlin (C). Subs (all used): 14 Paul Prescott; 6 Paul Deacon; 15 Jeff Lima; 23 Chris Tuson.
Tries: Richards (3), Charnley (20, 43), S Tomkins (25, 78), Leuluai (28), Finch (40), McIlorum (61); **Goals:** Richards 7/7, O'Loughlin 1/1.
Rugby Leaguer & League Express Men of the Match: *Crusaders:* Gareth Thomas; *Warriors:* Sam Tomkins.
Penalty count: 8-6; **Half-time:** 0-30;
Referee: James Child; **Attendance:** 5,037.

WAKEFIELD TRINITY WILDCATS 26 HULL KINGSTON ROVERS 24

WILDCATS: 1 Matt Blaymire; 5 Luke George; 18 Chris Dean; 3 Aaron Murphy; 29 Josh Griffin; 27 Kieran Hyde; 14 Tommy Lee; 31 Kyle Amor; 9 Julien Rinaldi; 17 Paul Johnson; 13 Glenn Morrison (C); 21 Frankie Mariano; 22 Stuart Howarth. Subs (all used): 33 Tyrone McCarthy; 10 Paul King; 24 James Davey; 25 Liam Higgins.
Tries: Amor (7), Dean (19), Davey (44), Murphy (51), Griffin (76); **Goals:** Griffin 0/1, Hyde 3/4.
ROVERS: 28 Ben Cockayne; 2 Peter Fox; 19 Craig Hall; 3 Kris Welham; 21 Sam Latus; 6 Blake Green; 7 Michael Dobson; 20 Michael Vella (C); 9 Ben Fisher; 15 Scott Wheeldon; 12 Ben Galea; 17 Matt Cook; 13 Scott Murrell. Subs (all used): 16 Jason Netherton; 24 Richard Beaumont; 18 Josh Hodgson; 22 Scott Taylor.
Tries: Cockayne (15, 60), Welham (54), Green (72); **Goals:** Dobson 4/4.
Rugby Leaguer & League Express Men of the Match: *Wildcats:* Julien Rinaldi; *Rovers:* Blake Green.
Penalty count: 6-3; **Half-time:** 8-6;
Referee: Phil Bentham; **Attendance:** 7,283.

Monday 2nd May 2011

HULL FC 24 ST HELENS 24

HULL: 3 Richard Whiting; 2 Will Sharp; 33 Martin Gleeson; 4 Kirk Yeaman; 5 Tom Briscoe; 6 Richard Horne; 30 Sam Obst; 8 Mark O'Meley; 9 Danny Houghton; 23 Sam Moa; 16 Willie Manu; 12 Danny Tickle; 13 Craig Fitzgibbon (C). Subs (all used): 14 Danny Washbrook; 11 Joe Westerman; 17 Ewan Dowes; 15 Epalahame Lauaki.
Tries: Yeaman (10, 30, 73), Briscoe (14); **Goals:** Tickle 4/4.
SAINTS: 24 Tom Armstrong; 2 Ade Gardner; 3 Michael Shenton; 5 Francis Meli; 22 Jamie Foster; 12 Jon Wilkin; 7 Kyle Eastmond; 10 James Graham (C); 9 James Roby; 15 Louie McCarthy-Scarsbrook; 18 Matty Ashurst; 4 Iosia Soliola; 11 Tony Puletua. Subs (all used): 8 Josh Perry; 21 Shaun Magennis; 19 Andrew Dixon; 27 Nathan Ashe (D).
Tries: Foster (35), Roby (51), Gardner (56), Puletua (59); **Goals:** Foster 4/5.
Rugby Leaguer & League Express Men of the Match: *Hull:* Tom Briscoe; *Saints:* Jon Wilkin.
Penalty count: 4-6; **Half-time:** 18-4;
Referee: Steve Ganson; **Attendance:** 11,933.

ROUND 14

Friday 13th May 2011

CRUSADERS 23 WAKEFIELD TRINITY WILDCATS 10

CRUSADERS: 1 Clinton Schifcofske (C); 5 Stuart Reardon; 2 Gareth Thomas; 4 Vince Mellars; 18 Elliot Kear; 6 Michael Witt; 17 Rhys Hanbury; 10 Mark Bryant; 19 Lloyd White; 22 Richard Moore; 11 Hep Cahill; 13 Frank Winterstein; 23 Peter Lupton. Subs (all used): 27 Jordan Tansey; 8 Ryan O'Hara; 16 Ben Flower; 7 Jarrod Sammut.
Tries: Witt (43), Mellars (49), O'Hara (76), Hanbury (79); **Goals:** Schifcofske 3/4; **Field goal:** Witt (67).
WILDCATS: 1 Matt Blaymire; 29 Josh Griffin; 18 Chris Dean; 3 Aaron Murphy; 19 Dale Morton; 27 Kieran Hyde; 14 Tommy Lee; 17 Paul Johnson; 9 Julien Rinaldi; 31 Kyle Amor; 13 Glenn Morrison (C); 21 Frankie Mariano; 22 Stuart Howarth. Subs (all used): 10 Paul King; 11 Kevin Henderson; 25 Liam Higgins; 16 Jeremy Smith.
Tries: Morton (8, 12); **Goals:** Griffin 1/2.
Rugby Leaguer & League Express Men of the Match: *Crusaders:* Michael Witt; *Wildcats:* Dale Morton.
Penalty count: 6-4; **Half-time:** 0-10;
Referee: Phil Bentham; **Attendance:** 3,241.

LEEDS RHINOS 30 CATALAN DRAGONS 6

RHINOS: 2 Lee Smith; 27 Zak Hardaker; 3 Brett Delaney; 4 Keith Senior; 5 Ryan Hall; 13 Kevin Sinfield (C); 7 Rob Burrow; 8 Kylie Leuluai; 9 Danny Buderus; 10 Jamie Peacock; 11 Jamie Jones-Buchanan; 22 Jay Pitts; 12 Carl Ablett. Subs (all used): 17 Ian Kirke; 18 Luke Burgess; 20 Weller Hauraki; 24 Paul McShane.
Tries: Hall (21), Leuluai (51), Hardaker (71, 74), Burrow (79); **Goals:** Sinfield 5/6.
DRAGONS: 5 Cyril Stacul; 2 Damien Blanch; 15 Jean-Philippe Baile; 27 Mathias Pala; 19 Frederic Vaccari; 4 Setaimata Sa; 6 Thomas Bosc; 8 David Ferriol; 9 Ian Henderson; 22 Jamal Fakir; 12 Sebastien Raguin; 13 Gregory Mounis (C); 24 Jason Baitieri. Subs (all used): 21 Sebastien Martins; 20 Michael Simon; 28 Julien Touxagas; 14 Tony Gigot.
Try: Henderson (61); **Goals:** Bosc 1/1.
Rugby Leaguer & League Express Men of the Match: *Rhinos:* Brett Delaney; *Dragons:* Jean-Philippe Baile.
Penalty count: 8-8; **Half-time:** 6-0;
Referee: Robert Hicks; **Attendance:** 13,273.

SALFORD CITY REDS 16 HULL FC 32

CITY REDS: 1 Luke Patten; 2 Jodie Broughton; 6 Stefan Ratchford; 5 Ashley Gibson; 27 Adam Clay; 14 Matty Smith; 7 Daniel Holdsworth (C); 8 Ray Cashmere; 9 Wayne Godwin; 17 Iafeta Palea'aesina; 11 Vinnie Anderson; 4 Chris Nero; 13 Stephen Wild. Subs (all used): 10 Lee Jewitt; 22 Adam Neal; 15 Luke Adamson; 19 Ryan Boyle.
Tries: Clay (17), Gibson (39), Ratchford (47); **Goals:** Holdsworth 2/3.
HULL: 20 Cameron Phelps; 3 Richard Whiting; 33 Martin Gleeson; 4 Kirk Yeaman; 5 Tom Briscoe; 6 Richard Horne; 30 Sam Obst; 8 Mark O'Meley; 9 Danny Houghton; 23 Sam Moa; 16 Willie Manu; 12 Danny Tickle; 13 Craig Fitzgibbon (C). Subs (all used): 17 Ewan Dowes; 10 Lee Radford; 2 Will Sharp; 11 Joe Westerman.
Tries: Yeaman (2), Gleeson (4, 62), Briscoe (10), Radford (30), Sharp (55); **Goals:** Tickle 4/6.
Rugby Leaguer & League Express Men of the Match: *City Reds:* Matty Smith; *Hull:* Craig Fitzgibbon.
Penalty count: 3-5; **Half-time:** 10-24;
Referee: Ben Thaler; **Attendance:** 3,983.

WARRINGTON WOLVES 62 CASTLEFORD TIGERS 0

WOLVES: 1 Brett Hodgson; 5 Joel Monaghan; 4 Chris Bridge; 23 Ryan Atkins; 3 Matt King; 6 Lee Briers; 27 Gareth O'Brien; 8 Adrian Morley (C); 9 Michael Monaghan; 10 Garreth Carvell; 11 Louis Anderson; 12 Ben Westwood; 17 Simon Grix. Subs (all used): 14 Mick Higham; 16 Paul Wood; 18 Michael Cooper; 26 David Solomona.
Tries: O'Brien (4), Briers (7, 37), King (16, 59), Hodgson (24), Grix (47, 51), Higham (55), Solomona (71), J Monaghan (77); **Goals:** Hodgson 7/9, Briers 2/2.
TIGERS: 1 Richard Mathers; 2 Kirk Dixon; 23 Ryan McGoldrick; 4 Joe Arundel; 5 Richard Owen; 6 Rangi Chase; 7 Danny Orr (C); 21 Nathan Massey; 9 Ryan Hudson; 19 Nick Fozzard; 13 Brett Ferres; 14 Stuart Jones; 20 Martin Aspinwall. Subs (all used): 11 Jake Emmitt; 16 Adam Milner; 24 Oliver Holmes; 25 Dean Widders.
Rugby Leaguer & League Express Men of the Match: *Wolves:* Gareth O'Brien; *Tigers:* Richard Mathers.
Penalty count: 2-2; **Half-time:** 28-0;
Referee: Steve Ganson; **Attendance:** 10,715.

WIGAN WARRIORS 54 HARLEQUINS 6

WARRIORS: 1 Sam Tomkins; 25 Josh Charnley; 12 Joel Tomkins; 4 George Carmont; 5 Pat Richards; 17 Brett Finch; 7 Thomas Leuluai; 10 Andy Coley; 9 Michael McIlorum; 21 Lee Mossop; 22 Liam Farrell; 16 Ryan Hoffman; 13 Sean O'Loughlin (C). Subs (all used): 15 Jeff Lima; 6 Paul Deacon; 33 Jack Hughes; 23 Chris Tuson.
Tries: Richards (3, 80), Hoffman (7), Carmont (11), S Tomkins (12, 53), Leuluai (20, 24), O'Loughlin (27); **Goals:** Richards 9/9.
HARLEQUINS: 2 Jamie O'Callaghan; 5 Chris Melling; 31 Karl Pryce; 3 Tony Clubb; 23 Mark Calderwood; 6 Luke Gale; 7 Chad Randall (C); 17 Danny Ward; 9 Andy Ellis; 15 Luke Ambler; 12 Chris Bailey; 11 Nick Kouparitsas; 10 Oliver Wilkes. Subs (all used): 8 Karl Temata; 33 Lee Mitchell; 21 Olsi Krasniqi; 16 Mike Burnett.
Try: Calderwood (78); **Goals:** Gale 1/1.
Rugby Leaguer & League Express Men of the Match: *Warriors:* Thomas Leuluai; *Harlequins:* Luke Gale.
Penalty count: 2-6; **Half-time:** 42-0;
Referee: James Child; **Attendance:** 12,813.

Saturday 14th May 2011

HUDDERSFIELD GIANTS 40 ST HELENS 18

GIANTS: 1 Scott Grix; 20 Jermaine McGillvary; 29 Joe Wardle; 3 Leroy Cudjoe; 2 Michael Lawrence; 6 Kevin Brown (C); 7 Danny Brough; 8 Eorl Crabtree; 9 Luke Robinson; 10 Darrell Griffin; 4 Lee Gilmour; 37 Dale Ferguson; 17 Danny Kirmond. Subs (all used): 14 Shaun Lunt; 13 David Faiumu; 26 Jamie Cording; 18 Larne Patrick.
Tries: Crabtree (8, 58), Brough (33), Brown (51), Lawrence (54), Wardle (61), Grix (75); **Goals:** Brough 6/7.
SAINTS: 1 Paul Wellens (C); 2 Ade Gardner; 3 Michael Shenton; 5 Francis Meli; 22 Jamie Foster; 27 Nathan Ashe; 12 Jon Wilkin; 10 James Graham (C); 9 James Roby; 8 Josh Perry; 4 Iosia Soliola; 18 Matty Ashurst; 21 Shaun Magennis. Subs (all used): 15 Louie McCarthy-Scarsbrook; 28 Tom Makinson; 24 Tom Armstrong; 29 Scott Hale (D).
Tries: McCarthy-Scarsbrook (44), Ashurst (66), Gardner (70); **Goals:** Foster 3/3.
Rugby Leaguer & League Express Men of the Match: *Giants:* Kevin Brown; *Saints:* James Roby.
Penalty count: 4-4; **Half-time:** 12-0;
Referee: Thierry Alibert; **Attendance:** 7,843.

Sunday 15th May 2011

HULL KINGSTON ROVERS 46 BRADFORD BULLS 18

ROVERS: 1 Shaun Briscoe; 2 Peter Fox; 3 Kris Welham; 4 Jake Webster; 28 Ben Cockayne; 6 Blake Green; 7 Michael Dobson; 20 Michael Vella (C); 18 Josh Hodgson; 15 Scott Wheeldon; 8 Rhys Lovegrove; 12 Ben Galea; 16 Jason Netherton. Subs (all used): 10 Joel Clinton; 14 Liam Watts; 9 Ben Fisher; 17 Matt Cook.
Tries: Welham (9, 12, 58), Green (25), Webster (31), Dobson (33), Watts (42), Fox (76); **Goals:** Dobson 7/8.
BULLS: 25 Shad Royston; 19 Gareth Raynor; 1 Michael Platt; 12 Elliott Whitehead; 5 Patrick Ah Van; 33 Ben Jeffries (D2); 32 Kyle Briggs; 10 Andy Lynch (C); 9 Heath L'Estrange; 15 Bryn Hargreaves; 17 Ian Sibbit; 23 Tom Olbison; 20 James Donaldson. Subs (all used): 16 Craig Kopczak; 29 Tom Burgess; 14 Matt Diskin; 13 Jamie Langley.
Tries: Briggs (4), Raynor (27), Lynch (50); **Goals:** Ah Van 3/3.
Rugby Leaguer & League Express Men of the Match: *Rovers:* Kris Welham; *Bulls:* Ben Jeffries.
Penalty count: 6-10; **Half-time:** 28-12;
Referee: Richard Silverwood; **Attendance:** 7,923.

ROUND 15

Friday 27th May 2011

LEEDS RHINOS 6 WARRINGTON WOLVES 42

RHINOS: 2 Lee Smith; 27 Zak Hardaker; 3 Brett Delaney; 12 Carl Ablett; 5 Ryan Hall; 13 Kevin Sinfield (C); 6 Danny McGuire; 8 Kylie Leuluai; 9 Danny Buderus; 10 Jamie Peacock; 11 Jamie Jones-Buchanan; 14 Ali Lauitiiti; 20 Weller Hauraki. Subs (all used): 17 Ian Kirke; 16 Ryan Bailey; 22 Jay Pitts; 7 Rob Burrow.
Try: Buderus (34); **Goals:** Sinfield 1/1.
WOLVES: 1 Brett Hodgson; 22 Rhys Williams; 4 Chris Bridge; 23 Ryan Atkins; 5 Joel Monaghan; 6 Lee Briers; 7 Richard Myler; 8 Adrian Morley (C); 9 Michael Monaghan; 10 Garreth Carvell; 3 Matt King; 12 Ben Westwood; 17 Simon Grix. Subs (all used): 16 Paul Wood; 26 David Solomona; 18 Michael Cooper; 14 Mick Higham.
Tries: Briers (9, 79), J Monaghan (19), Solomona (43), Bridge (63), M Monaghan (65), King (76); **Goals:** Hodgson 7/8.
Rugby Leaguer & League Express Men of the Match: *Rhinos:* Lee Smith; *Wolves:* Michael Monaghan.
Penalty count: 6-9; **Half-time:** 6-12;
Referee: James Child; **Attendance:** 17,276.

ST HELENS 28 CRUSADERS 12

SAINTS: 1 Paul Wellens (C); 2 Ade Gardner; 3 Michael Shenton; 5 Francis Meli; 22 Jamie Foster; 25 Lee Gaskell; 20 Jonny Lomax; 10 James Graham (C); 9 James Roby; 15 Louie McCarthy-Scarsbrook; 4 Iosia Soliola; 12 Jon Wilkin; 21 Shaun Magennis. Subs (all used): 7 Kyle Eastmond; 8 Josh Perry; 18 Matty Ashurst; 19 Andrew Dixon.
Tries: Foster (1, 38), Wilkin (44), Lomax (50), Gaskell (72); **Goals:** Foster 4/5.
CRUSADERS: 1 Clinton Schifcofske (C); 5 Stuart Reardon; 12 Jason Chan; 4 Vince Mellars; 18 Elliot Kear; 6 Michael Witt; 17 Rhys Hanbury; 8 Ryan O'Hara; 19 Lloyd White; 22 Richard Moore; 11 Hep Cahill; 13 Frank Winterstein; 23 Peter Lupton. Subs (all used): 7 Jarrod Sammut; 10 Mark Bryant; 16 Ben Flower; 27 Jordan Tansey.
Tries: Sammut (57), White (78); **Goals:** Schifcofske 2/2.
Rugby Leaguer & League Express Men of the Match: *Saints:* Jonny Lomax; *Crusaders:* Rhys Hanbury.
Penalty count: 9-4; **Half-time:** 10-0;
Referee: Ben Thaler; **Attendance:** 6,752.

Sunday 29th May 2011

HULL FC 20 HUDDERSFIELD GIANTS 34

HULL: 20 Cameron Phelps; 2 Will Sharp; 33 Martin Gleeson; 4 Kirk Yeaman; 5 Tom Briscoe; 6 Richard Horne; 30 Sam Obst; 8 Mark O'Meley; 9 Danny Houghton; 23 Sam Moa; 16 Willie Manu; 12 Danny Tickle; 13 Craig Fitzgibbon (C). Subs (all used): 11 Joe Westerman; 17 Ewan Dowes; 19 Jordan Turner; 15 Epalahame Lauaki.
Tries: Dowes (15), O'Meley (65), Manu (70); **Goals:** Tickle 4/4.
GIANTS: 1 Scott Grix; 20 Jermaine McGillvary; 3 Leroy Cudjoe; 2 Michael Lawrence; 5 David Hodgson; 6 Kevin Brown (C); 7 Danny Brough; 15 Keith Mason; 9 Luke Robinson; 10 Darrell Griffin; 17 Danny Kirmond; 4 Lee Gilmour; 13 David Faiumu. Subs (all used): 12 David Fa'alogo; 14 Shaun Lunt; 18 Larne Patrick; 16 Andy Raleigh.
Tries: Lawrence (6), Hodgson (26, 45, 68), Brough (71), Gilmour (76); **Goals:** Brough 5/7.
Rugby Leaguer & League Express Men of the Match: *Hull:* Danny Houghton; *Giants:* David Hodgson.
Penalty count: 11-6; **Half-time:** 8-10;
Referee: Thierry Alibert; **Attendance:** 11,274.

BRADFORD BULLS 28 SALFORD CITY REDS 14

BULLS: 25 Shad Royston; 24 Jason Crookes; 5 Patrick Ah Van; 12 Elliott Whitehead; 3 Paul Sykes; 33 Ben Jeffries; 32 Kyle Briggs; 10 Andy Lynch (C); 14 Matt

Diskin; 15 Bryn Hargreaves; 11 Olivier Elima; 23 Tom Olbison; 13 Jamie Langley. Subs (all used): 9 Heath L'Estrange; 16 Craig Kopczak; 20 James Donaldson; 29 Tom Burgess.
Tries: Briggs (6, 73), Sykes (30), L'Estrange (36), Jeffries (39); **Goals:** Ah Van 4/5.
CITY REDS: 1 Luke Patten; 2 Jodie Broughton; 6 Stefan Ratchford; 20 Sean Gleeson; 3 Mark Henry; 14 Matty Smith; 7 Daniel Holdsworth (C); 8 Ray Cashmere; 23 Marc Sneyd; 19 Ryan Boyle; 4 Chris Nero; 11 Vinnie Anderson; 13 Stephen Wild. Subs (all used): 10 Lee Jewitt; 22 Adam Neal; 17 Iafeta Palea'aesina; 18 Adam Sidlow.
Tries: Henry (18, 57, 63); **Goals:** Holdsworth 1/3.
Rugby Leaguer & League Express Men of the Match: *Bulls:* Tom Burgess; *City Reds:* Mark Henry.
Penalty count: 9-4; **Half-time:** 22-4;
Referee: Richard Silverwood; **Attendance:** 12,487.

CASTLEFORD TIGERS 56 HARLEQUINS 24

TIGERS: 1 Richard Mathers; 2 Kirk Dixon; 17 Willie Isa; 4 Joe Arundel; 5 Richard Owen; 6 Rangi Chase; 7 Danny Orr (C); 19 Nick Fozzard; 16 Adam Milner; 11 Jake Emmitt; 14 Stuart Jones; 13 Brett Ferres; 12 Steve Snitch. Subs (all used): 15 Jonathan Walker; 22 Jordan Thompson; 25 Dean Widders; 27 Daryl Clark.
Tries: Dixon (6), Mathers (25), Thompson (27), Owen (40), Chase (44, 64, 73, 77), Clark (49), Milner (67); **Goals:** Dixon 8/11.
HARLEQUINS: 2 Jamie O'Callaghan; 5 Chris Melling; 31 Karl Pryce; 3 Tony Clubb; 34 Chris Riley (D); 12 Chris Bailey; 6 Luke Gale; 8 Karl Temata; 7 Chad Randall (C); 17 Danny Ward; 16 Mike Burnett; 33 Lee Mitchell; 10 Oliver Wilkes. Subs (all used): 15 Luke Ambler; 21 Olsi Krasniqi; 9 Andy Ellis; 11 Nick Kouparitsas.
Tries: O'Callaghan (3), Riley (12, 38), Wilkes (19, 57); **Goals:** Gale 2/5.
Rugby Leaguer & League Express Men of the Match: *Tigers:* Rangi Chase; *Harlequins:* Chris Riley.
Penalty count: 7-6; **Half-time:** 22-18;
Referee: Robert Hicks; **Attendance:** 7,072.

WAKEFIELD TRINITY WILDCATS 22 CATALAN DRAGONS 42

WILDCATS: 23 Josh Veivers; 19 Dale Morton; 18 Chris Dean; 3 Aaron Murphy; 30 Greg Johnson; 26 Matthew Wildie; 14 Tommy Lee; 8 Michael Korkidas; 24 James Davey; 17 Paul Johnson; 13 Glenn Morrison (C); 11 Kevin Henderson; 22 Stuart Howarth. Subs (all used): 21 Frankie Mariano; 31 Kyle Amor; 25 Liam Higgins; 33 Tyrone McCarthy.
Tries: G Johnson (2), Wildie (38), Mariano (47), McCarthy (75); **Goals:** Veivers 3/4.
DRAGONS: 1 Clint Greenshields; 2 Damien Blanch; 15 Jean-Philippe Baile; 18 Darryl Millard; 19 Frederic Vaccari; 4 Setaimata Sa; 7 Scott Dureau; 8 David Ferriol; 9 Ian Henderson; 22 Jamal Fakir; 23 Lopini Paea; 12 Sebastien Raguin; 13 Gregory Mounis (C). Subs (all used): 20 Michael Simon; 21 Sebastien Martins; 24 Jason Baitieri; 26 Eloi Pelissier.
Tries: Vaccari (12, 29), Baile (16), Blanch (24, 44), Greenshields (64), Sa (71), Mounis (78);
Goals: Dureau 5/8.
Rugby Leaguer & League Express Men of the Match: *Wildcats:* Glenn Morrison; *Dragons:* Clint Greenshields.
Penalty count: 12-9; **Half-time:** 10-20;
Referee: Tim Roby; **Attendance:** 4,561.

Monday 30th May 2011

WIGAN WARRIORS 40 HULL KINGSTON ROVERS 6

WARRIORS: 1 Sam Tomkins; 25 Josh Charnley; 12 Joel Tomkins; 4 George Carmont; 5 Pat Richards; 17 Brett Finch; 6 Paul Deacon; 10 Andy Coley; 7 Thomas Leuluai; 21 Lee Mossop; 11 Harrison Hansen; 16 Ryan Hoffman; 13 Sean O'Loughlin (C). Subs (all used): 14 Paul Prescott; 9 Michael McIlorum; 15 Jeff Lima; 23 Chris Tuson.
Tries: S Tomkins (2, 59, 68), Richards (10, 40, 72), Carmont (77); **Goals:** Richards 6/7.
ROVERS: 1 Shaun Briscoe; 2 Peter Fox; 4 Jake Webster; 3 Kris Welham; 28 Ben Cockayne; 6 Blake Green; 7 Michael Dobson; 20 Michael Vella (C); 18 Josh Hodgson; 15 Scott Wheeldon; 8 Rhys Lovegrove; 12 Ben Galea; 13 Scott Murrell. Subs (all used): 17 Matt Cook; 10 Joel Clinton; 16 Jason Netherton; 9 Ben Fisher.
Try: Welham (36); **Goals:** Dobson 1/1.
Rugby Leaguer & League Express Men of the Match: *Warriors:* Sam Tomkins; *Rovers:* Rhys Lovegrove.
Penalty count: 2-4; **Half-time:** 16-6;
Referee: Phil Bentham; **Attendance:** 14,779.

ROUND 16

Friday 3rd June 2011

CRUSADERS 16 WARRINGTON WOLVES 56

CRUSADERS: 1 Clinton Schifcofske (C); 18 Elliot Kear; 4 Vince Mellars; 2 Gareth Thomas; 27 Jordan Tansey; 6 Michael Witt; 17 Rhys Hanbury; 8 Ryan O'Hara; 9 Lincoln Withers; 22 Richard Moore; 11 Hep Cahill; 13 Frank Winterstein; 12 Jason Chan. Subs (all used): 7 Jarrod Sammut; 16 Ben Flower; 10 Mark Bryant; 23 Peter Lupton.
Tries: Kear (17), Cahill (28), Sammut (33);
Goals: Schifcofske 2/3.
WOLVES: 1 Brett Hodgson; 3 Matt King; 4 Chris Bridge; 23 Ryan Atkins; 22 Rhys Williams; 6 Lee Briers; 7 Richard Myler; 8 Adrian Morley (C); 9 Michael Monaghan; 10 Garreth Carvell; 11 Louis Anderson; 12 Ben Westwood; 17 Simon Grix. Subs (all used): 16 Paul Wood; 26 David Solomona; 18 Michael Cooper; 14 Mick Higham.
Tries: King (7), Morley (10), Westwood (37), Atkins (38), Wood (40, 47), Hodgson (43, 63, 66), Myler (51); **Goals:** Hodgson 8/10.
Rugby Leaguer & League Express Men of the Match: *Crusaders:* Hep Cahill; *Wolves:* Brett Hodgson.
Penalty count: 5-8; **Half-time:** 16-28;
Referee: Robert Hicks; **Attendance:** 4,907.

SALFORD CITY REDS 34 WAKEFIELD TRINITY WILDCATS 12

CITY REDS: 1 Luke Patten; 2 Jodie Broughton; 6 Stefan Ratchford; 20 Sean Gleeson; 3 Mark Henry; 14 Matty Smith; 7 Daniel Holdsworth (C); 8 Ray Cashmere; 9 Wayne Godwin; 19 Ryan Boyle; 15 Luke Adamson; 4 Chris Nero; 11 Vinnie Anderson. Subs (all used): 17 Iafeta Palea'aesina; 10 Lee Jewitt; 22 Adam Neal; 18 Adam Sidlow.
Tries: Holdsworth (5), Ratchford (15, 21, 59), Broughton (26), Jewitt (47), Adamson (72);
Goals: Holdsworth 3/6, Ratchford 0/1.
WILDCATS: 1 Matt Blaymire; 30 Greg Johnson; 3 Aaron Murphy; 18 Chris Dean; 29 Josh Griffin; 35 Gareth Moore (D); 14 Tommy Lee; 8 Michael Korkidas; 9 Julien Rinaldi; 31 Kyle Amor; 21 Frankie Mariano; 13 Glenn Morrison (C); 33 Tyrone McCarthy. Subs (all used): 11 Kevin Henderson; 24 James Davey; 25 Liam Higgins; 36 Jarrad Hickey (D).
Tries: Lee (2), Hickey (65); **Goals:** Moore 2/2.
Rugby Leaguer & League Express Men of the Match: *City Reds:* Stefan Ratchford; *Wildcats:* Josh Griffin.
Penalty count: 7-3; **Half-time:** 16-6;
Referee: James Child; **Attendance:** 3,213.

ST HELENS 42 LEEDS RHINOS 16

SAINTS: 1 Paul Wellens (C); 28 Tom Makinson; 3 Michael Shenton; 5 Francis Meli; 22 Jamie Foster; 25 Lee Gaskell; 20 Jonny Lomax; 10 James Graham (C); 9 James Roby; 15 Louie McCarthy-Scarsbrook; 4 Iosia Soliola; 12 Jon Wilkin; 11 Tony Puletua. Subs (all used): 7 Kyle Eastmond; 14 Scott Moore; 19 Andrew Dixon; 21 Shaun Magennis.
Tries: Graham (29), Roby (42), Meli (52), Lomax (56), Moore (58), Wellens (65), Gaskell (79); **Goals:** Foster 7/7.
RHINOS: 1 Brent Webb; 27 Zak Hardaker; 2 Lee Smith; 3 Brett Delaney; 5 Ryan Hall; 6 Danny McGuire; 7 Rob Burrow; 8 Kylie Leuluai; 9 Danny Buderus; 10 Jamie Peacock; 11 Jamie Jones-Buchanan; 12 Carl Ablett; 13 Kevin Sinfield (C). Subs (all used): 14 Ali Lauitiiti; 16 Ryan Bailey; 20 Weller Hauraki; 24 Paul McShane.
Tries: Jones-Buchanan (67), Smith (71);
Goals: Sinfield 4/4.
Rugby Leaguer & League Express Men of the Match: *Saints:* Francis Meli; *Rhinos:* Jamie Jones-Buchanan.
Penalty count: 7-7; **Half-time:** 6-4;
Referee: Phil Bentham; **Attendance:** 9,062.

Saturday 4th June 2011

HARLEQUINS 16 BRADFORD BULLS 30

HARLEQUINS: 34 Chris Riley; 2 Jamie O'Callaghan; 3 Tony Clubb; 31 Karl Pryce; 5 Chris Melling; 12 Chris Bailey; 6 Luke Gale; 17 Danny Ward; 7 Chad Randall (C); 8 Karl Temata; 16 Mike Burnett; 33 Lee Mitchell; 10 Oliver Wilkes. Subs (all used): 21 Olsi Krasniqi; 15 Luke Ambler; 9 Andy Ellis; 11 Nick Kouparitsas.
Tries: Pryce (6, 69), Temata (59); **Goals:** Gale 2/3.
BULLS: 25 Shad Royston; 24 Jason Crookes; 5 Patrick Ah Van; 12 Elliott Whitehead; 1 Michael Platt; 33 Ben Jeffries; 7 Marc Herbert; 10 Andy Lynch (C); 14 Matt Diskin; 16 Craig Kopczak; 11 Olivier Elima; 23 Tom Olbison; 13 Jamie Langley. Subs (all used): 9 Heath L'Estrange; 21 Danny Addy; 20 James Donaldson; 29 Tom Burgess.
Tries: Ah Van (23, 42), Royston (38), Whitehead (66), Lynch (80); **Goals:** Ah Van 5/6.
Rugby Leaguer & League Express Men of the Match: *Harlequins:* Karl Pryce; *Bulls:* Shad Royston.
Penalty count: 9-6; **Half-time:** 4-12;
Referee: Thierry Alibert; **Attendance:** 4,253.

CATALAN DRAGONS 20 WIGAN WARRIORS 12

DRAGONS: 1 Clint Greenshields; 2 Damien Blanch; 15 Jean-Philippe Baile; 18 Darryl Millard; 19 Frederic Vaccari; 4 Setaimata Sa; 7 Scott Dureau; 8 David Ferriol; 9 Ian Henderson; 24 Jason Baitieri; 23 Lopini Paea; 12 Sebastien Raguin; 13 Gregory Mounis (C). Subs (all used): 11 Steve Menzies; 20 Michael Simon; 22 Jamal Fakir; 26 Eloi Pelissier.
Tries: Baile (7), Millard (28, 70); **Goals:** Dureau 4/4.
WARRIORS: 1 Sam Tomkins; 25 Josh Charnley; 12 Joel Tomkins; 4 George Carmont; 5 Pat Richards; 17 Brett Finch; 6 Paul Deacon; 14 Paul Prescott; 7 Thomas Leuluai; 21 Lee Mossop; 11 Harrison Hansen; 16 Ryan Hoffman; 13 Sean O'Loughlin (C). Subs (all used): 9 Michael McIlorum; 15 Jeff Lima; 22 Liam Farrell; 23 Chris Tuson.
Tries: S Tomkins (21, 34); **Goals:** Richards 2/2.
Rugby Leaguer & League Express Men of the Match: *Dragons:* Jason Baitieri; *Warriors:* Sam Tomkins.
Penalty count: 9-8; **Half-time:** 14-12;
Referee: Richard Silverwood; **Attendance:** 9,372 *(at Stade Yve du Manoir, Montpellier).*

Sunday 5th June 2011

HULL KINGSTON ROVERS 17 HULL FC 10

ROVERS: 1 Shaun Briscoe; 28 Ben Cockayne; 19 Craig Hall; 3 Kris Welham; 5 Liam Colbon; 6 Blake Green; 7 Michael Dobson; 20 Michael Vella (C); 18 Josh Hodgson; 15 Scott Wheeldon; 12 Ben Galea; 8 Rhys Lovegrove; 13 Scott Murrell. Subs (all used): 16 Jason Netherton; 9 Ben Fisher; 22 Scott Taylor; 11 Clint Newton.
Tries: Welham (38), Briscoe (56, 65);
Goals: Dobson 2/3; **Field goal:** Dobson (74).
HULL: 19 Jordan Turner; 3 Richard Whiting; 33 Martin Gleeson; 4 Kirk Yeaman; 5 Tom Briscoe; 6 Richard Horne; 7 Sean Long; 8 Mark O'Meley; 9 Danny Houghton; 23 Sam Moa; 16 Willie Manu; 12 Danny Tickle; 13 Craig Fitzgibbon (C). Subs (all used): 30 Sam Obst; 15 Epalahame Lauaki; 17 Ewan Dowes; 11 Joe Westerman.
Tries: Yeaman (14), Gleeson (50); **Goals:** Tickle 1/2.
Rugby Leaguer & League Express Men of the Match: *Rovers:* Kris Welham; *Hull:* Richard Horne.
Penalty count: 5-3; **Half-time:** 4-4;
Referee: Steve Ganson; **Attendance:** 10,250.

HUDDERSFIELD GIANTS 40 CASTLEFORD TIGERS 18

GIANTS: 1 Scott Grix; 20 Jermaine McGillvary; 29 Joe Wardle; 2 Michael Lawrence; 5 David Hodgson; 3 Leroy Cudjoe; 7 Danny Brough; 8 Eorl Crabtree; 9 Luke Robinson (C); 10 Darrell Griffin; 4 Lee Gilmour; 19 Graeme Horne; 12 David Fa'alogo. Subs (all used): 15 Keith Mason; 18 Larne Patrick; 17 Danny Kirmond; 13 David Faiumu.
Tries: Cudjoe (4, 32), Crabtree (25), Hodgson (44), Gilmour (52), McGillvary (68), Fa'alogo (74);
Goals: Brough 4/5, Cudjoe 2/2.
Sin bin: McGillvary (54) - dissent.
TIGERS: 1 Richard Mathers; 2 Kirk Dixon; 22 Jordan Thompson; 4 Joe Arundel; 5 Richard Owen; 6 Rangi Chase; 7 Danny Orr (C); 8 Paul Jackson; 16 Adam Milner; 11 Jake Emmitt; 14 Stuart Jones; 13 Brett Ferres; 20 Martin Aspinwall. Subs (all used): 15 Jonathan Walker; 19 Nick Fozzard; 25 Dean Widders; 27 Daryl Clark.
Tries: Owen (13, 76), Orr (61); **Goals:** Dixon 3/3.
Rugby Leaguer & League Express Men of the Match: *Giants:* Luke Robinson; *Tigers:* Richard Owen.
Penalty count: 10-6; **Half-time:** 18-6; **Referee:** Ben Thaler; **Attendance:** 5,237 *(at The Shay, Halifax).*

ROUND 17

Saturday 11th June 2011

CATALAN DRAGONS 31 CRUSADERS 18

DRAGONS: 1 Clint Greenshields; 2 Damien Blanch; 15 Jean-Philippe Baile; 18 Darryl Millard; 19 Frederic Vaccari; 4 Setaimata Sa; 7 Scott Dureau; 8 David Ferriol; 26 Eloi Pelissier; 24 Jason Baitieri; 11 Steve Menzies; 12 Sebastien Raguin; 13 Gregory Mounis (C). Subs (all used): 9 Ian Henderson; 20 Michael Simon; 22 Jamal Fakir; 23 Lopini Paea.
Tries: Millard (27), Baile (35), Sa (55), Blanch (58, 80);
Goals: Dureau 5/5; **Field goal:** Dureau (77).
CRUSADERS: 1 Clinton Schifcofske (C); 5 Stuart Reardon; 3 Tony Martin; 4 Vince Mellars; 18 Elliot Kear; 6 Michael Witt; 27 Jordan Tansey; 10 Mark Bryant; 9 Lincoln Withers; 16 Ben Flower; 11 Hep Cahill; 13 Frank Winterstein; 12 Jason Chan. Subs (all used): 7 Jarrod Sammut; 8 Ryan O'Hara; 15 Jordan James; 19 Lloyd White.
Tries: White (52), Tansey (69), Sammut (72);
Goals: Schifcofske 3/4.
Rugby Leaguer & League Express Men of the Match: *Dragons:* Scott Dureau; *Crusaders:* Jarrod Sammut.
Penalty count: 9-8; **Half-time:** 12-2;
Referee: Steve Ganson; **Attendance:** 7,125.

Sunday 12th June 2011

HULL FC 38 HARLEQUINS 6

HULL: 3 Richard Whiting; 21 Reece Lyne; 19 Jordan Turner; 4 Kirk Yeaman; 5 Tom Briscoe; 6 Richard Horne; 30 Sam Obst; 8 Mark O'Meley; 9 Danny Houghton; 10 Lee Radford; 12 Danny Tickle; 16 Willie Manu; 11 Joe Westerman. Subs (all used): 17 Ewan Dowes; 15 Epalahame Lauaki; 23 Sam Moa; 13 Craig Fitzgibbon (C).
Tries: Turner (5), Manu (9), Obst (32), Briscoe (40), Horne (47), Moa (50), Whiting (69);
Goals: Tickle 4/5, Westerman 1/2.
HARLEQUINS: 34 Chris Riley; 23 Mark Calderwood; 3 Tony Clubb; 2 Jamie O'Callaghan; 5 Chris Melling; 12 Chris Bailey; 6 Luke Gale; 8 Karl Temata; 7 Chad Randall (C); 17 Danny Ward; 16 Mike Burnett; 10 Oliver Wilkes; 21 Olsi Krasniqi. Subs (all used): 18 Dave Williams; 15 Luke Ambler; 19 Lamont Bryan; 9 Andy Ellis.
Try: Melling (57); **Goals:** Gale 1/1.
Rugby Leaguer & League Express Men of the Match: *Hull:* Joe Westerman; *Harlequins:* Luke Gale.
Penalty count: 6-5; **Half-time:** 20-0;
Referee: Richard Silverwood; **Attendance:** 11,139.

WARRINGTON WOLVES 16 SALFORD CITY REDS 18

WOLVES: 1 Brett Hodgson; 4 Chris Bridge; 20 Matty Blythe; 23 Ryan Atkins; 22 Rhys Williams; 6 Lee Briers; 7 Richard Myler; 8 Adrian Morley (C); 9 Michael Monaghan; 10 Garreth Carvell; 26 David Solomona; 12 Ben Westwood; 17 Simon Grix. Subs (all used): 14 Mick Higham; 16 Paul Wood; 18 Michael Cooper; 21 Tyrone McCarthy.
Tries: Bridge (11), Briers (27), Myler (77);
Goals: Hodgson 2/3.
CITY REDS: 1 Luke Patten; 3 Mark Henry; 20 Sean Gleeson; 6 Stefan Ratchford; 2 Jodie Broughton; 14 Matty Smith; 7 Daniel Holdsworth (C); 8 Ray Cashmere; 9 Wayne Godwin; 19 Ryan Boyle; 15 Luke Adamson; 4 Chris Nero; 11 Vinnie Anderson. Subs (all used): 10 Lee Jewitt; 17 Iafeta Palea'aesina; 18 Adam Sidlow; 22 Adam Neal.

Tries: Gleeson (19), Patten (45), Henry (49);
Goals: Holdsworth 3/3.
Rugby Leaguer & League Express Men of the Match:
Wolves: Garreth Carvell; *City Reds:* Daniel Holdsworth.
Penalty count: 12-5; **Half-time:** 10-6;
Referee: Ben Thaler; **Attendance:** 10,339.

CASTLEFORD TIGERS 22 WIGAN WARRIORS 22

TIGERS: 1 Richard Mathers; 2 Kirk Dixon; 22 Jordan Thompson; 4 Joe Arundel; 5 Richard Owen; 23 Ryan McGoldrick; 7 Danny Orr (C); 8 Paul Jackson; 16 Adam Milner; 11 Jake Emmitt; 13 Brett Ferres; 20 Martin Aspinwall; 9 Ryan Hudson. Subs (all used): 6 Rangi Chase; 19 Nick Fozzard; 25 Dean Widders; 21 Nathan Massey.
Tries: Widders (38), Arundel (59, 72), Aspinwall (65), Mathers (79); **Goals:** Dixon 1/5.
WARRIORS: 19 Amos Roberts; 25 Josh Charnley; 12 Joel Tomkins; 2 Darrell Goulding; 5 Pat Richards; 17 Brett Finch; 6 Paul Deacon; 21 Lee Mossop; 7 Thomas Leuluai; 15 Jeff Lima; 11 Harrison Hansen; 16 Ryan Hoffman; 23 Chris Tuson. Subs (all used): 9 Michael McIlorum; 13 Sean O'Loughlin (C); 22 Liam Farrell; 14 Paul Prescott.
Tries: Finch (10), Charnley (27), Prescott (35), J Tomkins (40); **Goals:** Richards 3/4.
Rugby Leaguer & League Express Men of the Match:
Tigers: Rangi Chase; *Warriors:* Jeff Lima.
Penalty count: 7-9; **Half-time:** 4-22;
Referee: Phil Bentham; **Attendance:** 7,263.

WAKEFIELD TRINITY WILDCATS 13 HUDDERSFIELD GIANTS 10

WILDCATS: 15 Motu Tony (D); 19 Dale Morton; 5 Luke George; 3 Aaron Murphy; 29 Josh Griffin; 35 Gareth Moore; 16 Jeremy Smith; 8 Michael Korkidas; 24 James Davey; 31 Kyle Amor; 21 Frankie Mariano; 17 Paul Johnson; 13 Glenn Morrison (C). Subs (all used): 36 Jarrad Hickey; 26 Matthew Wildie; 25 Liam Higgins; 11 Kevin Henderson.
Try: George (4); **Goals:** Moore 4/4;
Field goal: Moore (63).
GIANTS: 3 Leroy Cudjoe; 20 Jermaine McGillvary; 29 Joe Wardle; 2 Michael Lawrence; 5 David Hodgson; 6 Kevin Brown (C); 23 Kyle Wood; 8 Eorl Crabtree; 14 Shaun Lunt; 16 Andy Raleigh; 4 Lee Gilmour; 17 Danny Kirmond; 26 Jamie Cording. Subs (all used): 9 Luke Robinson; 15 Keith Mason; 19 Graeme Horne; 18 Larne Patrick.
Tries: Lunt (56), Wardle (75); **Goals:** Cudjoe 1/2.
Rugby Leaguer & League Express Men of the Match:
Wildcats: Gareth Moore; *Giants:* Keith Mason.
Penalty count: 8-5; **Half-time:** 10-0;
Referee: Thierry Alibert; **Attendance:** 5,436.

BRADFORD BULLS 14 ST HELENS 14

BULLS: 6 Brett Kearney; 24 Jason Crookes; 5 Patrick Ah Van; 12 Elliott Whitehead; 19 Gareth Raynor; 33 Ben Jeffries; 7 Marc Herbert; 10 Andy Lynch (C); 14 Matt Diskin; 16 Craig Kopczak; 11 Olivier Elima; 17 Ian Sibbit; 13 Jamie Langley. Subs (all used): 9 Heath L'Estrange; 23 Tom Olbison; 20 James Donaldson; 29 Tom Burgess.
Tries: Kearney (11), Lynch (27); **Goals:** Ah Van 3/4.
SAINTS: 1 Paul Wellens (C); 28 Tom Makinson; 3 Michael Shenton; 7 Kyle Eastmond; 22 Jamie Foster; 25 Lee Gaskell; 20 Jonny Lomax; 10 James Graham (C); 9 James Roby; 15 Louie McCarthy-Scarsbrook; 4 Iosia Soliola; 12 Jon Wilkin; 11 Tony Puletua. Subs (all used): 8 Josh Perry; 13 Chris Flannery; 19 Andrew Dixon; 24 Tom Armstrong.
Tries: McCarthy-Scarsbrook (6), Makinson (36);
Goals: Foster 3/4.
Rugby Leaguer & League Express Men of the Match:
Bulls: Brett Kearney; *Saints:* Tony Puletua.
Penalty count: 6-4; **Half-time:** 12-12;
Referee: James Child; **Attendance:** 13,224.

LEEDS RHINOS 44 HULL KINGSTON ROVERS 14

RHINOS: 1 Brent Webb; 27 Zak Hardaker; 2 Lee Smith; 3 Brett Delaney; 5 Ryan Hall; 6 Danny McGuire; 7 Rob Burrow; 16 Ryan Bailey; 24 Paul McShane; 10 Jamie Peacock; 11 Jamie Jones-Buchanan; 12 Carl Ablett; 13 Kevin Sinfield (C). Subs (all used): 8 Kylie Leuluai; 20 Weller Hauraki; 17 Ian Kirke; 9 Danny Buderus.
Tries: Smith (5), Hall (21, 56, 68), Hauraki (33), McGuire (41), Hardaker (60), Delaney (73);
Goals: Sinfield 6/8.
ROVERS: 1 Shaun Briscoe; 28 Ben Cockayne; 3 Kris Welham; 19 Craig Hall; 5 Liam Colbon; 6 Blake Green; 7 Michael Dobson; 20 Michael Vella (C); 18 Josh Hodgson; 15 Scott Wheeldon; 12 Ben Galea; 8 Rhys Lovegrove; 13 Scott Murrell. Subs (all used): 16 Jason Netherton; 11 Clint Newton; 9 Ben Fisher; 22 Scott Taylor.
Tries: Cockayne (15), Welham (39), Hall (45);
Goals: Dobson 1/3.
Rugby Leaguer & League Express Men of the Match:
Rhinos: Brent Webb; *Rovers:* Shaun Briscoe.
Penalty count: 3-4; **Half-time:** 16-10;
Referee: Robert Hicks; **Attendance:** 13,669.

ROUND 18

Friday 17th June 2011

CRUSADERS 7 LEEDS RHINOS 12

CRUSADERS: 27 Jordan Tansey; 5 Stuart Reardon; 3 Tony Martin; 2 Gareth Thomas; 4 Vince Mellars; 6 Michael Witt (C); 19 Lloyd White; 10 Mark Bryant; 9 Lincoln Withers; 8 Ryan O'Hara; 12 Jason Chan; 13 Frank Winterstein; 23 Peter Lupton. Subs (all used): 21 Paul Johnson; 15 Jordan James; 16 Ben Flower; 7 Jarrod Sammut.
Try: Lupton (9); **Goals:** Witt 1/2; **Field goal:** Witt (73).
RHINOS: 1 Brent Webb; 27 Zak Hardaker; 3 Brett Delaney; 2 Lee Smith; 5 Ryan Hall; 6 Danny McGuire; 7 Rob Burrow; 8 Kylie Leuluai; 24 Paul McShane; 10 Jamie Peacock; 11 Jamie Jones-Buchanan; 20 Weller Hauraki; 13 Kevin Sinfield (C). Subs (all used): 14 Ali Lauitiiti; 9 Danny Buderus; 16 Ryan Bailey; 17 Ian Kirke.
Tries: McGuire (69), Lauitiiti (75); **Goals:** Sinfield 2/2.
Rugby Leaguer & League Express Men of the Match:
Crusaders: Jordan Tansey; *Rhinos:* Kevin Sinfield.
Penalty count: 8-12; **Half-time:** 4-0;
Referee: Ben Thaler; **Attendance:** 3,035.

SALFORD CITY REDS 8 CASTLEFORD TIGERS 15

CITY REDS: 1 Luke Patten; 2 Jodie Broughton; 6 Stefan Ratchford; 20 Sean Gleeson; 3 Mark Henry; 14 Matty Smith; 7 Daniel Holdsworth (C); 8 Ray Cashmere; 9 Wayne Godwin; 19 Ryan Boyle; 15 Luke Adamson; 4 Chris Nero; 11 Vinnie Anderson. Subs (all used): 10 Lee Jewitt; 22 Adam Neal; 17 Iafeta Palea'aesina; 18 Adam Sidlow.
Tries: Broughton (32), Holdsworth (61);
Goals: Holdsworth 0/2.
TIGERS: 1 Richard Mathers; 2 Kirk Dixon; 22 Jordan Thompson; 4 Joe Arundel; 3 Nick Youngquest; 6 Rangi Chase; 7 Danny Orr (C); 8 Paul Jackson; 9 Ryan Hudson; 11 Jake Emmitt; 12 Steve Snitch; 13 Brett Ferres; 23 Ryan McGoldrick. Subs (all used): 19 Nick Fozzard; 21 Nathan Massey; 25 Dean Widders; 27 Daryl Clark.
Tries: Thompson (42), Orr (73); **Goals:** Dixon 3/3;
Field goal: Chase (76).
Rugby Leaguer & League Express Men of the Match:
City Reds: Lee Jewitt; *Tigers:* Rangi Chase.
Penalty count: 5-4; **Half-time:** 4-2;
Referee: Phil Bentham; **Attendance:** 3,587.

ST HELENS 10 WIGAN WARRIORS 32

SAINTS: 1 Paul Wellens (C); 28 Tom Makinson; 3 Michael Shenton; 5 Francis Meli; 22 Jamie Foster; 25 Lee Gaskell; 20 Jonny Lomax; 10 James Graham (C); 9 James Roby; 15 Louie McCarthy-Scarsbrook; 4 Iosia Soliola; 12 Jon Wilkin; 11 Tony Puletua. Subs (all used): 7 Kyle Eastmond; 13 Chris Flannery; 18 Matty Ashurst; 21 Shaun Magennis.
Tries: Puletua (59), Makinson (63);
Goals: Makinson 1/1, Foster 0/1.
WARRIORS: 1 Sam Tomkins; 25 Josh Charnley; 12 Joel Tomkins; 4 George Carmont; 5 Pat Richards; 17 Brett Finch; 6 Paul Deacon; 21 Lee Mossop; 7 Thomas Leuluai; 15 Jeff Lima; 11 Harrison Hansen; 16 Ryan Hoffman; 13 Sean O'Loughlin (C). Subs (all used): 9 Michael McIlorum; 10 Andy Coley; 14 Paul Prescott; 23 Chris Tuson.
Tries: Mossop (14), Richards (28), J Tomkins (31), Finch (46), Lima (76); **Goals:** Richards 6/6.
Rugby Leaguer & League Express Men of the Match:
Saints: Jonny Lomax; *Warriors:* Brett Finch.
Penalty count: 6-2; **Half-time:** 0-20;
Referee: Thierry Alibert; **Attendance:** 11,540.

Saturday 18th June 2011

HARLEQUINS 40 WAKEFIELD TRINITY WILDCATS 22

HARLEQUINS: 1 Luke Dorn; 5 Chris Melling; 3 Tony Clubb; 2 Jamie O'Callaghan; 23 Mark Calderwood; 6 Luke Gale; 35 Kyle Briggs (D); 17 Danny Ward; 7 Chad Randall (C); 10 Oliver Wilkes; 16 Mike Burnett; 33 Lee Mitchell; 12 Chris Bailey. Subs (all used): 21 Olsi Krasniqi; 15 Luke Ambler; 9 Andy Ellis; 26 Rob Thomas.
Tries: Gale (4), Bailey (17), Dorn (24), Clubb (31), Melling (51), Randall (63), O'Callaghan (65);
Goals: Gale 6/7.
WILDCATS: 15 Motu Tony; 19 Dale Morton; 3 Aaron Murphy; 5 Luke George; 29 Josh Griffin; 35 Gareth Moore; 16 Jeremy Smith; 8 Michael Korkidas; 24 James Davey; 31 Kyle Amor; 21 Frankie Mariano; 18 Chris Dean; 17 Paul Johnson. Subs (all used): 11 Kevin Henderson; 9 Julien Rinaldi (C); 25 Liam Higgins; 36 Jarrad Hickey.
Tries: Morton (40), Rinaldi (60), Hickey (69), P Johnson (80); **Goals:** Moore 3/4.
Sin bin: Smith (57) - dissent.
Rugby Leaguer & League Express Men of the Match:
Harlequins: Luke Gale; *Wildcats:* Julien Rinaldi.
Penalty count: 10-9; **Half-time:** 24-4;
Referee: Robert Hicks; **Attendance:** 2,875.

HUDDERSFIELD GIANTS 28 CATALAN DRAGONS 20

GIANTS: 1 Scott Grix; 20 Jermaine McGillvary; 29 Joe Wardle; 3 Leroy Cudjoe; 5 David Hodgson; 6 Kevin Brown (C); 9 Luke Robinson; 8 Eorl Crabtree; 14 Shaun Lunt; 15 Keith Mason; 4 Lee Gilmour; 37 Dale Ferguson; 12 David Fa'alogo. Subs (all used): 13 David Faiumu; 10 Darrell Griffin; 17 Danny Kirmond; 18 Larne Patrick.
Tries: Hodgson (28, 69), Faiumu (33), Griffin (43), Brown (60); **Goals:** Grix 4/6.
DRAGONS: 1 Clint Greenshields; 2 Damien Blanch; 15 Jean-Philippe Baile; 18 Darryl Millard; 19 Frederic Vaccari; 4 Setaimata Sa; 7 Scott Dureau; 8 David Ferriol; 9 Ian Henderson; 23 Lopini Paea; 11 Steve Menzies; 12 Sebastien Raguin; 13 Gregory Mounis (C). Subs (all used): 20 Michael Simon; 22 Jamal Fakir; 24 Jason Baitieri; 26 Eloi Pelissier.
Tries: Dureau (37), Blanch (50), Baitieri (62), Baile (64);
Goals: Dureau 2/4.
Sin bin: Sa (59) - holding down.
Rugby Leaguer & League Express Men of the Match:
Giants: David Hodgson; *Dragons:* Clint Greenshields.
Penalty count: 12-6; **Half-time:** 8-4; **Referee:** Richard Silverwood; **Attendance:** 5,132 *(at The Shay, Halifax)*.

Sunday 19th June 2011

BRADFORD BULLS 14 HULL FC 28

BULLS: 6 Brett Kearney; 24 Jason Crookes; 25 Shad Royston; 12 Elliott Whitehead; 5 Patrick Ah Van; 33 Ben Jeffries; 7 Marc Herbert; 10 Andy Lynch (C); 14 Matt Diskin; 16 Craig Kopczak; 11 Olivier Elima; 17 Ian Sibbit; 13 Jamie Langley. Subs (all used): 1 Michael Platt; 8 Nick Scruton; 21 Danny Addy; 29 Tom Burgess.
Tries: Royston (37, 39), Lynch (52); **Goals:** Ah Van 1/3.
HULL: 3 Richard Whiting; 21 Reece Lyne; 19 Jordan Turner; 4 Kirk Yeaman; 5 Tom Briscoe; 6 Richard Horne; 30 Sam Obst; 8 Mark O'Meley; 9 Danny Houghton; 13 Craig Fitzgibbon (C); 16 Willie Manu; 12 Danny Tickle; 11 Joe Westerman. Subs (all used): 17 Ewan Dowes; 15 Epalahame Lauaki; 23 Sam Moa; 10 Lee Radford.
Tries: Horne (15), Moa (18), Westerman (23), Yeaman (46), Fitzgibbon (78); **Goals:** Tickle 4/5.
Rugby Leaguer & League Express Men of the Match:
Bulls: Shad Royston; *Hull:* Danny Tickle.
Penalty count: 7-12; **Half-time:** 8-16;
Referee: Phil Bentham; **Attendance:** 14,414.

HULL KINGSTON ROVERS 16 WARRINGTON WOLVES 46

ROVERS: 1 Shaun Briscoe; 28 Ben Cockayne; 3 Kris Welham; 19 Craig Hall; 5 Liam Colbon; 6 Blake Green; 7 Michael Dobson; 16 Jason Netherton; 18 Josh Hodgson; 20 Michael Vella (C); 11 Clint Newton; 12 Ben Galea; 22 Scott Taylor. Subs (all used): 15 Scott Wheeldon; 13 Scott Murrell; 8 Rhys Lovegrove; 14 Liam Watts.
Tries: Green (50), Colbon (62), Taylor (65);
Goals: Dobson 2/3.
WOLVES: 1 Brett Hodgson; 3 Matt King; 4 Chris Bridge; 23 Ryan Atkins; 22 Rhys Williams; 6 Lee Briers; 7 Richard Myler; 8 Adrian Morley (C); 9 Michael Monaghan; 10 Garreth Carvell; 17 Simon Grix; 12 Ben Westwood; 13 Ben Harrison. Subs (all used): 14 Mick Higham; 18 Michael Cooper; 20 Matty Blythe; 26 David Solomona.
Tries: Grix (20), King (22, 25, 67), Atkins (29, 52), Briers (42), Williams (47), Myler (75);
Goals: Hodgson 5/9.
Rugby Leaguer & League Express Men of the Match:
Rovers: Ben Galea; *Wolves:* Chris Bridge.
Penalty count: 9-11; **Half-time:** 0-22;
Referee: Steve Ganson; **Attendance:** 8,143.

ROUND 19

Friday 24th June 2011

CRUSADERS 18 SALFORD CITY REDS 22

CRUSADERS: 27 Jordan Tansey; 5 Stuart Reardon; 2 Gareth Thomas; 4 Vince Mellars; 18 Elliot Kear; 3 Tony Martin; 6 Michael Witt (C); 8 Ryan O'Hara; 9 Lincoln Withers; 15 Jordan James; 12 Jason Chan; 13 Frank Winterstein; 11 Hep Cahill. Subs: 16 Ben Flower; 7 Jarrod Sammut; 20 Gil Dudson (not used); 24 Lee Williams.
Tries: Martin (2), Flower (24), J James (61);
Goals: Witt 3/3.
CITY REDS: 1 Luke Patten; 2 Jodie Broughton; 6 Stefan Ratchford; 5 Ashley Gibson; 3 Mark Henry; 14 Matty Smith; 7 Daniel Holdsworth (C); 8 Ray Cashmere; 9 Wayne Godwin; 19 Ryan Boyle; 4 Chris Nero; 15 Luke Adamson; 11 Vinnie Anderson. Subs (all used): 17 Iafeta Palea'aesina; 18 Adam Sidlow; 10 Lee Jewitt; 22 Adam Neal.
Tries: Godwin (15), Adamson (30), Ratchford (46), Sidlow (77); **Goals:** Holdsworth 3/4.
Rugby Leaguer & League Express Men of the Match:
Crusaders: Michael Witt; *City Reds:* Daniel Holdsworth.
Penalty count: 6-7; **Half-time:** 12-10;
Referee: Robert Hicks; **Attendance:** 2,576.

LEEDS RHINOS 12 BRADFORD BULLS 18

RHINOS: 1 Brent Webb; 2 Lee Smith; 3 Brett Delaney; 12 Carl Ablett; 5 Ryan Hall; 13 Kevin Sinfield (C); 7 Rob Burrow; 8 Kylie Leuluai; 9 Danny Buderus; 10 Jamie Peacock; 20 Weller Hauraki; 11 Jamie Jones-Buchanan; 21 Chris Clarkson. Subs (all used): 16 Ryan Bailey; 17 Ian Kirke; 14 Ali Lauitiiti; 24 Paul McShane.
Tries: Hall (20), Jones-Buchanan (29); **Goals:** Sinfield 2/2.
BULLS: 6 Brett Kearney; 24 Jason Crookes; 5 Patrick Ah Van; 12 Elliott Whitehead; 19 Gareth Raynor; 33 Ben Jeffries; 7 Marc Herbert; 10 Andy Lynch (C); 14 Matt Diskin; 16 Craig Kopczak; 13 Jamie Langley; 17 Ian Sibbit; 11 Olivier Elima. Subs (all used): 15 Bryn Hargreaves; 8 Nick Scruton; 21 Danny Addy; 1 Michael Platt.
Tries: Elima (23, 33); **Goals:** Ah Van 5/7.
On report: Diskin (50) - alleged high tackle on Ablett.
Rugby Leaguer & League Express Men of the Match:
Rhinos: Carl Ablett; *Bulls:* Ian Sibbit.
Penalty count: 10-12; **Half-time:** 12-10;
Referee: Steve Ganson; **Attendance:** 18,095.

WARRINGTON WOLVES 35 ST HELENS 28

WOLVES: 1 Brett Hodgson; 3 Matt King; 4 Chris Bridge; 23 Ryan Atkins; 22 Rhys Williams; 6 Lee Briers; 7 Richard Myler; 8 Adrian Morley (C); 9 Michael Monaghan; 10 Garreth Carvell; 17 Simon Grix; 12 Ben Westwood; 13 Ben Harrison. Subs (all used): 14 Mick Higham; 16 Paul Wood; 20 Matty Blythe; 26 David Solomona.
Tries: M Monaghan (1), Williams (7), King (14), Westwood (55), Wood (62), Hodgson (64);
Goals: Hodgson 5/6; **Field goal:** Briers (75).
SAINTS: 1 Paul Wellens (C); 28 Tom Makinson; 4 Iosia Soliola; 5 Francis Meli; 22 Jamie Foster; 25 Lee Gaskell; 20 Jonny Lomax; 10 James Graham (C); 9 James Roby;

15 Louie McCarthy-Scarsbrook; 12 Jon Wilkin; 13 Chris Flannery; 11 Tony Puletua. Subs (all used): 7 Kyle Eastmond; 8 Josh Perry; 14 Scott Moore; 19 Andrew Dixon.
Tries: Graham (18), Gaskell (21), Foster (24), Puletua (34, 73); **Goals:** Foster 4/5.
Rugby Leaguer & League Express Men of the Match:
Wolves: Brett Hodgson; *Saints:* Tony Puletua.
Penalty count: 12-10; **Half-time:** 18-22;
Referee: Richard Silverwood; **Attendance:** 13,024.

Saturday 25th June 2011

HARLEQUINS 0 HULL KINGSTON ROVERS 34

HARLEQUINS: 1 Luke Dorn; 5 Chris Melling; 3 Tony Clubb; 2 Jamie O'Callaghan; 23 Mark Calderwood; 35 Kyle Briggs; 6 Luke Gale; 8 Karl Temata; 7 Chad Randall; 10 Oliver Wilkes; 16 Mike Burnett; 33 Lee Mitchell; 12 Chris Bailey. Subs (all used): 13 Rob Purdham (C); 15 Luke Ambler; 9 Andy Ellis; 21 Olsi Krasniqi.
ROVERS: 1 Shaun Briscoe; 28 Ben Cockayne; 3 Kris Welham; 4 Jake Webster; 5 Liam Colbon; 6 Blake Green; 7 Michael Dobson; 20 Michael Vella (C); 9 Ben Fisher; 16 Jason Netherton; 12 Ben Galea; 11 Clint Newton; 13 Scott Murrell. Subs (all used): 22 Scott Taylor; 18 Josh Hodgson; 8 Rhys Lovegrove; 14 Liam Watts.
Tries: Webster (28, 43), Colbon (40), Green (69), Newton (73), Dobson (79); **Goals:** Dobson 5/6.
Rugby Leaguer & League Express Men of the Match:
Harlequins: Lee Mitchell; *Rovers:* Jake Webster.
Penalty count: 8-5; **Half-time:** 0-10;
Referee: Ben Thaler; **Attendance:** 2,927.

WIGAN WARRIORS 46 HUDDERSFIELD GIANTS 12

WARRIORS: 1 Sam Tomkins; 25 Josh Charnley; 12 Joel Tomkins; 4 George Carmont; 5 Pat Richards; 6 Paul Deacon; 17 Brett Finch; 21 Lee Mossop; 7 Thomas Leuluai; 15 Jeff Lima; 11 Harrison Hansen; 16 Ryan Hoffman; 13 Sean O'Loughlin (C). Subs (all used): 9 Michael McIlorum; 10 Andy Coley; 14 Paul Prescott; 34 Gareth Hock.
Tries: S Tomkins (2, 9, 76), Leuluai (17), Carmont (25), Richards (39), Charnley (54), Mossop (68);
Goals: Richards 7/8.
GIANTS: 1 Scott Grix; 20 Jermaine McGillvary; 29 Joe Wardle; 3 Leroy Cudjoe; 5 David Hodgson; 6 Kevin Brown (C); 9 Luke Robinson; 8 Eorl Crabtree; 13 David Faiumu; 15 Keith Mason; 4 Lee Gilmour; 37 Dale Ferguson; 12 David Fa'alogo. Subs (all used): 14 Shaun Lunt; 10 Darrell Griffin; 17 Danny Kirmond; 18 Larne Patrick.
Tries: Hodgson (6), Kirmond (71); **Goals:** Grix 2/2.
Rugby Leaguer & League Express Men of the Match:
Warriors: Sam Tomkins; *Giants:* Shaun Lunt.
Penalty count: 5-6; **Half-time:** 28-6;
Referee: Phil Bentham; **Attendance:** 19,169.

CATALAN DRAGONS 54 CASTLEFORD TIGERS 20

DRAGONS: 1 Clint Greenshields; 2 Damien Blanch; 15 Jean-Philippe Baile; 18 Darryl Millard; 19 Frederic Vaccari; 4 Setaimata Sa; 7 Scott Dureau; 8 David Ferriol; 9 Ian Henderson; 22 Jamal Fakir; 11 Steve Menzies; 23 Lopini Paea; 13 Gregory Mounis (C). Subs (all used): 10 Remi Casty; 20 Michael Simon; 24 Jason Baitieri; 26 Eloi Pelissier.
Tries: Menzies (5), Paea (19, 72), Blanch (21), Dureau (24), Greenshields (34), Baitieri (43), Vaccari (47, 60), Baile (49); **Goals:** Dureau 7/10.
TIGERS: 1 Richard Mathers; 2 Kirk Dixon; 4 Joe Arundel; 22 Jordan Thompson; 5 Richard Owen; 6 Rangi Chase; 7 Danny Orr (C); 8 Paul Jackson; 9 Ryan Hudson; 11 Jake Emmitt; 13 Brett Ferres; 12 Steve Snitch; 23 Ryan McGoldrick. Subs (all used): 19 Nick Fozzard; 21 Nathan Massey; 25 Dean Widders; 27 Daryl Clark.
Tries: Owen (13, 79), Widders (37), Mathers (66); **Goals:** Dixon 2/4.
Rugby Leaguer & League Express Men of the Match:
Dragons: Scott Dureau; *Tigers:* Richard Mathers.
Penalty count: 7-8; **Half-time:** 26-10;
Referee: Thierry Alibert; **Attendance:** 8,695.

Sunday 26th June 2011

WAKEFIELD TRINITY WILDCATS 18 HULL FC 52

WILDCATS: 1 Matt Blaymire; 30 Greg Johnson; 5 Luke George; 3 Aaron Murphy; 29 Josh Griffin; 35 Gareth Moore; 16 Jeremy Smith; 17 Paul Johnson; 9 Julien Rinaldi; 31 Kyle Amor; 21 Frankie Mariano; 13 Glenn Morrison (C); 14 Tommy Lee. Subs (all used): 36 Jarrad Hickey; 26 Matthew Wildie; 10 Paul King; 11 Kevin Henderson.
Tries: Moore (7), Amor (10), George (53);
Goals: Moore 3/3.
Sin bin: Smith (65) - dissent.
HULL: 20 Cameron Phelps; 3 Richard Whiting; 19 Jordan Turner; 4 Kirk Yeaman; 5 Tom Briscoe; 6 Richard Horne; 30 Sam Obst; 8 Mark O'Meley; 9 Danny Houghton; 23 Sam Moa; 16 Willie Manu; 12 Danny Tickle; 11 Joe Westerman. Subs (all used): 14 Danny Washbrook; 15 Epalahame Lauaki; 10 Lee Radford (C); 17 Ewan Dowes.
Tries: Westerman (18), Yeaman (27), Horne (37), Tickle (42), Whiting (50, 58), Turner (61), O'Meley (66), Briscoe (73), Radford (75); **Goals:** Tickle 6/10.
Rugby Leaguer & League Express Men of the Match:
Wildcats: Julien Rinaldi; *Hull:* Richard Horne.
Penalty count: 5-12; **Half-time:** 12-16;
Referee: James Child; **Attendance:** 7,965.

Wigan's Gareth Hock, in his first game back in Rugby League, looks for a way past Huddersfield's Danny Kirmond

ROUND 20

Friday 1st July 2011

CASTLEFORD TIGERS 18 WARRINGTON WOLVES 48

TIGERS: 1 Richard Mathers; 28 Greg Eden; 4 Joe Arundel; 13 Brett Ferres; 5 Richard Owen; 6 Rangi Chase; 23 Ryan McGoldrick; 19 Nick Fozzard; 7 Danny Orr (C); 11 Jake Emmitt; 14 Stuart Jones; 12 Steve Snitch; 9 Ryan Hudson. Subs (all used): 8 Paul Jackson; 16 Adam Milner; 21 Nathan Massey; 24 Oliver Holmes.
Tries: Ferres (59), Chase (62), Hudson (64), Eden (74);
Goals: Orr 1/4.
WOLVES: 1 Brett Hodgson; 5 Joel Monaghan; 20 Matty Blythe; 23 Ryan Atkins; 3 Matt King; 4 Chris Bridge; 7 Richard Myler; 16 Paul Wood; 9 Michael Monaghan (C); 10 Garreth Carvell; 17 Simon Grix; 12 Ben Westwood; 13 Ben Harrison. Subs (all used): 14 Mick Higham; 15 Jon Clarke; 18 Michael Cooper; 26 David Solomona.
Tries: Hodgson (2, 69), Myler (28), Blythe (32), King (38, 43, 53), J Monaghan (48), Atkins (78);
Goals: Hodgson 6/8, Bridge 0/1.
Sin bin: Cooper (55) - fighting.
Rugby Leaguer & League Express Men of the Match:
Tigers: Brett Ferres; *Wolves:* Brett Hodgson.
Penalty count: 8-8; **Half-time:** 0-24;
Referee: James Child; **Attendance:** 5,947.

SALFORD CITY REDS 26 HARLEQUINS 18

CITY REDS: 1 Luke Patten; 2 Jodie Broughton; 11 Vinnie Anderson; 5 Ashley Gibson; 3 Mark Henry; 6 Stefan Ratchford; 7 Daniel Holdsworth (C); 8 Ray Cashmere; 14 Matty Smith; 19 Ryan Boyle; 18 Adam Sidlow; 4 Chris Nero; 15 Luke Adamson. Subs (all used): 23 Marc Sneyd; 10 Lee Jewitt; 17 Iafeta Palea'aesina; 22 Adam Neal.
Tries: Gibson (11, 78), Anderson (29), Broughton (58), Henry (73); **Goals:** Holdsworth 3/5.
HARLEQUINS: 2 Jamie O'Callaghan; 23 Mark Calderwood; 3 Tony Clubb; 24 Dan Sarginson; 31 Karl Pryce; 35 Kyle Briggs; 6 Luke Gale; 17 Danny Ward; 9 Andy Ellis; 8 Karl Temata; 16 Mike Burnett; 33 Lee Mitchell; 12 Chris Bailey. Subs (all used): 13 Rob Purdham (C); 18 Dave Williams; 21 Olsi Krasniqi; 15 Luke Ambler.
Tries: Sarginson (8, 53), Clubb (63); **Goals:** Gale 3/3.
Rugby Leaguer & League Express Men of the Match:
City Reds: Adam Sidlow; *Harlequins:* Dan Sarginson.
Penalty count: 6-4; **Half-time:** 8-6;
Referee: Richard Silverwood; **Attendance:** 3,065.

ST HELENS 28 HULL FC 14

SAINTS: 1 Paul Wellens (C); 28 Tom Makinson; 4 Iosia Soliola; 5 Francis Meli; 22 Jamie Foster; 25 Lee Gaskell; 20 Jonny Lomax; 10 James Graham (C); 9 James Roby; 8 Josh Perry; 13 Chris Flannery; 12 Jon Wilkin; 11 Tony Puletua. Subs (all used): 7 Kyle Eastmond; 14 Scott Moore; 18 Matty Ashurst; 21 Shaun Magennis.
Tries: Flannery (15), Meli (18, 21), Makinson (61), Lomax (68); **Goals:** Foster 4/6.
HULL: 20 Cameron Phelps; 3 Richard Whiting; 19 Jordan Turner; 4 Kirk Yeaman; 5 Tom Briscoe; 14 Danny Washbrook; 6 Richard Horne; 8 Mark O'Meley; 9 Danny Houghton; 23 Sam Moa; 16 Willie Manu; 11 Joe Westerman; 12 Danny Tickle. Subs (all used): 10 Lee Radford (C); 15 Epalahame Lauaki; 17 Ewan Dowes; 21 Reece Lyne.
Tries: Briscoe (25, 80), Turner (46);
Goals: Tickle 0/2, Westerman 1/1.
Rugby Leaguer & League Express Men of the Match:
Saints: Tony Puletua; *Hull:* Willie Manu.
Penalty count: 8-6; **Half-time:** 14-4;
Referee: Ben Thaler; **Attendance:** 7,053.

WIGAN WARRIORS 26 LEEDS RHINOS 24

WARRIORS: 1 Sam Tomkins; 25 Josh Charnley; 12 Joel Tomkins; 4 George Carmont; 5 Pat Richards; 6 Paul Deacon; 17 Brett Finch; 21 Lee Mossop; 7 Thomas Leuluai; 15 Jeff Lima; 11 Harrison Hansen; 16 Ryan Hoffman; 13 Sean O'Loughlin (C). Subs (all used): 9 Michael McIlorum; 10 Andy Coley; 14 Paul Prescott; 23 Chris Tuson.
Tries: Charnley (14), Hoffman (30), Richards (42), Carmont (45); **Goals:** Richards 5/5.
RHINOS: 1 Brent Webb; 23 Ben Jones-Bishop; 2 Lee Smith; 12 Carl Ablett; 27 Zak Hardaker; 13 Kevin Sinfield (C); 6 Danny McGuire; 8 Kylie Leuluai; 9 Danny Buderus; 10 Jamie Peacock; 3 Brett Delaney; 11 Jamie Jones-Buchanan; 21 Chris Clarkson. Subs (all used): 16 Ryan Bailey; 17 Ian Kirke; 14 Ali Lauitiiti; 7 Rob Burrow.
Tries: Jones-Bishop (18), Webb (27), Hardaker (39, 70); **Goals:** Sinfield 4/5.
Rugby Leaguer & League Express Men of the Match:
Warriors: George Carmont; *Rhinos:* Danny McGuire.
Penalty count: 7-4; **Half-time:** 12-18;
Referee: Thierry Alibert; **Attendance:** 16,426.

Saturday 2nd July 2011

BRADFORD BULLS 28 CATALAN DRAGONS 34

BULLS: 6 Brett Kearney; 24 Jason Crookes; 5 Patrick Ah Van; 1 Michael Platt; 19 Gareth Raynor; 33 Ben Jeffries;

7 Marc Herbert; 10 Andy Lynch (C); 14 Matt Diskin; 15 Bryn Hargreaves; 11 Olivier Elima; 12 Elliott Whitehead; 16 Craig Kopczak. Subs (all used): 8 Nick Scruton; 20 James Donaldson; 21 Danny Addy; 29 Tom Burgess.
Tries: Elima (8), Burgess (51), Jeffries (33), Raynor (79); **Goals:** Ah Van 6/7.
DRAGONS: 1 Clint Greenshields; 2 Damien Blanch; 15 Jean-Philippe Baile; 18 Darryl Millard; 19 Frederic Vaccari; 11 Steve Menzies; 7 Scott Dureau; 8 David Ferriol; 9 Ian Henderson; 22 Jamal Fakir; 12 Sebastien Raguin; 23 Lopini Paea; 13 Gregory Mounis (C). Subs (all used): 10 Remi Casty; 21 Sebastien Martins; 24 Jason Baitieri; 26 Eloi Pelissier.
Tries: Greenshields (14, 76), Blanch (22, 68), Raguin (42), Henderson (57), Dureau (63); **Goals:** Dureau 3/7.
Dismissal: Ferriol (46) - high tackle on Donaldson.
Rugby Leaguer & League Express Men of the Match: *Bulls:* Brett Kearney; *Dragons:* Steve Menzies.
Penalty count: 10-6; **Half-time:** 10-8;
Referee: Phil Bentham; **Attendance:** 12,670.

Sunday 3rd July 2011

HUDDERSFIELD GIANTS 40 CRUSADERS 12

GIANTS: 28 Gregg McNally (D); 20 Jermaine McGillvary; 29 Joe Wardle; 3 Leroy Cudjoe; 5 David Hodgson; 6 Kevin Brown (C); 1 Scott Grix; 12 David Fa'alogo; 9 Luke Robinson; 10 Darrell Griffin; 37 Dale Ferguson; 2 Michael Lawrence; 11 Luke O'Donnell. Subs (all used): 8 Eorl Crabtree; 18 Larne Patrick; 15 Keith Mason; 23 Kyle Wood.
Tries: Fa'alogo (3), Wardle (6), Brown (23), Hodgson (50, 61, 70), Lawrence (75); **Goals:** McNally 6/7.
CRUSADERS: 27 Jordan Tansey; 5 Stuart Reardon; 2 Gareth Thomas; 3 Tony Martin; 4 Vince Mellars; 6 Michael Witt (C); 7 Jarrod Sammut; 16 Ben Flower; 9 Lincoln Withers; 8 Ryan O'Hara; 13 Frank Winterstein; 12 Jason Chan; 11 Hep Cahill. Subs (all used): 10 Mark Bryant; 15 Jordan James; 22 Richard Moore; 18 Elliot Kear.
Tries: Martin (43, 45); **Goals:** Witt 2/2.
Sin bin: Moore (60) - late challenge on Robinson; Cahill (80) - late challenge on Brown.
Rugby Leaguer & League Express Men of the Match: *Giants:* Kevin Brown; *Crusaders:* Jordan Tansey.
Penalty count: 20-7; **Half-time:** 18-0; **Referee:** Steve Ganson; **Attendance:** 4,892 *(at The Shay, Halifax).*

HULL KINGSTON ROVERS 70
WAKEFIELD TRINITY WILDCATS 14

ROVERS: 1 Shaun Briscoe; 2 Peter Fox; 3 Kris Welham; 4 Jake Webster; 5 Liam Colbon; 6 Blake Green; 7 Michael Dobson; 20 Michael Vella (C); 9 Ben Fisher; 16 Jason Netherton; 11 Clint Newton; 12 Ben Galea; 13 Scott Murrell. Subs (all used): 15 Scott Wheeldon; 22 Scott Taylor; 18 Josh Hodgson; 8 Rhys Lovegrove.
Tries: Colbon (2, 38, 77), Fox (9, 40, 53), Welham (19, 58, 70), Webster (31, 47), Dobson (36), Newton (43, 66); **Goals:** Dobson 7/14.
WILDCATS: 1 Matt Blaymire; 30 Greg Johnson; 29 Josh Griffin; 5 Luke George; 37 Semi Tadulala (D2); 27 Kieran Hyde; 14 Tommy Lee; 8 Michael Korkidas; 9 Julien Rinaldi (C); 31 Kyle Amor; 21 Frankie Mariano; 11 Kevin Henderson; 15 Motu Tony. Subs (all used): 25 Liam Higgins; 26 Matthew Wildie; 36 Jarrad Hickey; 38 Sammy Masselot (D).
Tries: Henderson (7), Lee (15), George (73);
Goals: Griffin 1/3.
Rugby Leaguer & League Express Men of the Match: *Rovers:* Clint Newton; *Wildcats:* Tommy Lee.
Penalty count: 11-5; **Half-time:** 34-10;
Referee: Robert Hicks; **Attendance:** 8,025.

ROUND 3

Wednesday 6th July 2011

WIGAN WARRIORS 26 CASTLEFORD TIGERS 16

WARRIORS: 1 Sam Tomkins; 25 Josh Charnley; 12 Joel Tomkins; 4 George Carmont; 2 Darrell Goulding; 17 Brett Finch; 6 Paul Deacon; 15 Jeff Lima; 7 Thomas Leuluai; 21 Lee Mossop; 11 Harrison Hansen; 22 Liam Farrell; 13 Sean O'Loughlin (C). Subs (all used): 9 Michael McIlorum; 16 Ryan Hoffman; 23 Chris Tuson; 34 Gareth Hock.
Tries: Charnley (7, 29), Farrell (47), Carmont (54), Hoffman (56); **Goals:** Deacon 3/5.
TIGERS: 23 Ryan McGoldrick; 5 Richard Owen; 4 Joe Arundel; 13 Brett Ferres; 28 Greg Eden; 25 Dean Widders; 6 Rangi Chase (C); 19 Nick Fozzard; 16 Adam Milner; 11 Jake Emmitt; 14 Stuart Jones; 24 Oliver Holmes; 12 Steve Snitch. Subs (all used): 21 Nathan Massey; 26 John Davies; 27 Daryl Clark; 29 Rob Parker (D).
Tries: Jones (11), Owen (19), J Davies (37);
Goals: Arundel 2/3.
Rugby Leaguer & League Express Men of the Match: *Warriors:* Josh Charnley; *Tigers:* Ryan McGoldrick.
Penalty count: 10-6; **Half-time:** 10-16;
Referee: Steve Ganson; **Attendance:** 13,096.

ROUND 21

Friday 8th July 2011

HULL FC 52 SALFORD CITY REDS 16

HULL: 20 Cameron Phelps; 3 Richard Whiting; 19 Jordan Turner; 4 Kirk Yeaman; 5 Tom Briscoe; 14 Danny Washbrook; 6 Richard Horne; 8 Mark O'Meley; 9 Danny Houghton; 23 Sam Moa; 16 Willie Manu; 12 Danny Tickle; 11 Joe Westerman. Subs (all used): 2 Will Sharp; 10 Lee Radford (C); 17 Ewan Dowes; 15 Epalahame Lauaki.
Tries: Tickle (9, 32), Briscoe (11, 38, 62), Turner (23, 58), Westerman (50), Washbrook (65); **Goals:** Tickle 8/9.
CITY REDS: 1 Luke Patten; 2 Jodie Broughton; 5 Ashley Gibson; 6 Stefan Ratchford; 3 Mark Henry; 7 Daniel Holdsworth (C); 14 Matty Smith; 8 Ray Cashmere; 9 Wayne Godwin; 19 Ryan Boyle; 4 Chris Nero; 15 Luke Adamson; 11 Vinnie Anderson. Subs (all used): 18 Adam Sidlow; 10 Lee Jewitt; 17 Iafeta Palea'aesina; 22 Adam Neal.
Tries: Broughton (54), Anderson (71), Nero (77);
Goals: Holdsworth 2/3.
Rugby Leaguer & League Express Men of the Match: *Hull:* Joe Westerman; *City Reds:* Chris Nero.
Penalty count: 7-3; **Half-time:** 28-0;
Referee: Phil Bentham; **Attendance:** 11,699.

WARRINGTON WOLVES 28 HUDDERSFIELD GIANTS 16

WOLVES: 1 Brett Hodgson; 5 Joel Monaghan; 20 Matty Blythe; 23 Ryan Atkins; 3 Matt King; 4 Chris Bridge; 7 Richard Myler; 16 Paul Wood; 9 Michael Monaghan (C); 10 Garreth Carvell; 11 Louis Anderson; 12 Ben Westwood; 17 Simon Grix. Subs (all used): 13 Ben Harrison; 15 Jon Clarke; 18 Michael Cooper; 26 David Solomona.
Tries: Hodgson (3), J Monaghan (6, 25), Myler (17), Anderson (78); **Goals:** Hodgson 4/5.
GIANTS: 3 Leroy Cudjoe; 20 Jermaine McGillvary; 29 Joe Wardle; 2 Michael Lawrence; 5 David Hodgson; 6 Kevin Brown (C); 1 Scott Grix; 8 Eorl Crabtree; 9 Luke Robinson; 12 David Fa'alogo; 19 Graeme Horne; 4 Lee Gilmour; 11 Luke O'Donnell. Subs (all used): 18 Larne Patrick; 15 Keith Mason; 23 Kyle Wood; 37 Dale Ferguson.
Tries: McGillvary (52), Fa'alogo (54), Brown (71);
Goals: Grix 2/3.
Rugby Leaguer & League Express Men of the Match: *Wolves:* Michael Monaghan; *Giants:* Luke Robinson.
Penalty count: 11-6; **Half-time:** 22-0;
Referee: Ben Thaler; **Attendance:** 10,283.

Saturday 9th July 2011

CRUSADERS 10 HULL KINGSTON ROVERS 38

CRUSADERS: 1 Clinton Schifcofske (C); 5 Stuart Reardon; 2 Gareth Thomas; 4 Vince Mellars; 18 Elliot Kear; 3 Tony Martin; 6 Michael Witt; 8 Ryan O'Hara; 9 Lincoln Withers; 10 Mark Bryant; 29 Aled James; 13 Frank Winterstein; 16 Ben Flower. Subs (all used): 15 Jordan James; 30 Joe Burke (D); 31 Dalton Grant (D); 24 Lee Williams.
Tries: Kear (28), Winterstein (33); **Goals:** Schifcofske 1/2.
ROVERS: 1 Shaun Briscoe; 2 Peter Fox; 4 Jake Webster; 3 Kris Welham; 21 Sam Latus; 6 Blake Green; 7 Michael Dobson; 20 Michael Vella (C); 9 Ben Fisher; 16 Jason Netherton; 11 Clint Newton; 12 Ben Galea; 13 Scott Murrell. Subs (all used): 15 Scott Wheeldon; 22 Scott Taylor; 18 Josh Hodgson; 8 Rhys Lovegrove.
Tries: Latus (5), Galea (8, 46, 52), Briscoe (43), Newton (62), Dobson (74); **Goals:** Dobson 5/7.
Rugby Leaguer & League Express Men of the Match: *Crusaders:* Lincoln Withers; *Rovers:* Ben Galea.
Penalty count: 3-8; **Half-time:** 10-12;
Referee: Thierry Alibert; **Attendance:** 2,820.

HARLEQUINS 6 WIGAN WARRIORS 38

HARLEQUINS: 1 Luke Dorn; 23 Mark Calderwood; 3 Tony Clubb; 2 Jamie O'Callaghan; 31 Karl Pryce; 24 Dan Sarginson; 6 Luke Gale; 17 Danny Ward; 9 Andy Ellis; 8 Karl Temata; 13 Rob Purdham (C); 33 Lee Mitchell; 12 Chris Bailey. Subs (all used): 16 Mike Burnett; 10 Oliver Wilkes; 21 Olsi Krasniqi; 18 Dave Williams.
Try: Pryce (25); **Goals:** Gale 1/1.
WARRIORS: 1 Sam Tomkins; 25 Josh Charnley; 12 Joel Tomkins; 24 Stefan Marsh; 5 Pat Richards; 17 Brett Finch; 7 Thomas Leuluai (C); 21 Lee Mossop; 9 Michael McIlorum; 10 Andy Coley; 11 Harrison Hansen; 16 Ryan Hoffman; 23 Chris Tuson. Subs (all used): 6 Paul Deacon; 15 Jeff Lima; 22 Liam Farrell; 34 Gareth Hock.
Tries: Richards (17), Hoffman (19), Hansen (36), Deacon (46, 51), Marsh (68), Finch (78);
Goals: Richards 5/7.
Rugby Leaguer & League Express Men of the Match: *Harlequins:* Olsi Krasniqi; *Warriors:* Sam Tomkins.
Penalty count: 11-6; **Half-time:** 6-14;
Referee: Robert Hicks; **Attendance:** 4,423.

Sunday 10th July 2011

CASTLEFORD TIGERS 34 BRADFORD BULLS 30

TIGERS: 23 Ryan McGoldrick; 3 Nick Youngquest; 2 Kirk Dixon; 4 Joe Arundel; 5 Richard Owen; 6 Rangi Chase; 7 Danny Orr (C); 8 Paul Jackson; 16 Adam Milner; 29 Rob Parker; 13 Brett Ferres; 14 Stuart Jones; 9 Ryan Hudson. Subs (all used): 21 Nathan Massey; 22 Jordan Thompson; 25 Dean Widders; 26 John Davies.
Tries: Milner (7), Arundel (24, 56), Chase (26), Parker (46), Jones (66); **Goals:** Dixon 5/6.
BULLS: 6 Brett Kearney; 5 Patrick Ah Van; 3 Paul Sykes; 12 Elliott Whitehead; 19 Gareth Raynor; 33 Ben Jeffries; 7 Marc Herbert; 10 Andy Lynch (C); 14 Matt Diskin; 29 Tom Burgess; 11 Olivier Elima; 13 Jamie Langley; 15 Bryn Hargreaves. Subs (all used): 21 Danny Addy; 25 Shad Royston; 16 Craig Kopczak; 8 Nick Scruton.
Tries: Kearney (2, 4), Raynor (17), Royston (40), Sykes (41); **Goals:** Ah Van 5/5.
On report: Diskin (27) - alleged high tackle.
Rugby Leaguer & League Express Men of the Match: *Tigers:* Danny Orr; *Bulls:* Matt Diskin.
Penalty count: 11-16; **Half-time:** 18-24;
Referee: Richard Silverwood; **Attendance:** 7,004.

WAKEFIELD TRINITY WILDCATS 6 ST HELENS 46

WILDCATS: 1 Matt Blaymire; 30 Greg Johnson; 5 Luke George; 3 Aaron Murphy; 37 Semi Tadulala; 27 Kieran Hyde; 14 Tommy Lee; 8 Michael Korkidas; 9 Julien Rinaldi (C); 31 Kyle Amor; 21 Frankie Mariano; 17 Paul Johnson; 15 Motu Tony. Subs (all used): 36 Jarrad Hickey; 24 James Davey; 10 Paul King; 11 Kevin Henderson.
Try: Murphy (76); **Goals:** Hyde 1/1.
SAINTS: 7 Kyle Eastmond; 28 Tom Makinson; 3 Michael Shenton; 5 Francis Meli; 22 Jamie Foster; 25 Lee Gaskell; 20 Jonny Lomax; 10 James Graham (C); 9 James Roby; 15 Louie McCarthy-Scarsbrook; 4 Iosia Soliola; 12 Jon Wilkin; 11 Tony Puletua. Subs (all used): 14 Scott Moore; 16 Paul Clough; 13 Chris Flannery; 24 Tom Armstrong.
Tries: Eastmond (6, 29), Foster (8, 39), Wilkin (24), Lomax (40), Meli (52), Flannery (56); **Goals:** Foster 7/8.
Rugby Leaguer & League Express Men of the Match: *Wildcats:* Kyle Amor; *Saints:* James Roby.
Penalty count: 11-13; **Half-time:** 0-34;
Referee: Steve Ganson; **Attendance:** 5,985.

CATALAN DRAGONS 38 LEEDS RHINOS 18

DRAGONS: 1 Clint Greenshields; 2 Damien Blanch; 25 Vincent Duport; 18 Darryl Millard; 19 Frederic Vaccari; 11 Steve Menzies; 7 Scott Dureau; 10 Remi Casty; 9 Ian Henderson; 24 Jason Baitieri; 12 Sebastien Raguin; 23 Lopini Paea; 13 Gregory Mounis (C). Subs (all used): 17 Cyrille Gossard; 20 Michael Simon; 26 Eloi Pelissier; 30 Thibaut Ancely (D).
Tries: Raguin (14), Vaccari (35, 80), Blanch (38), Menzies (44), Greenshields (67), Duport (70);
Goals: Dureau 5/8, Mounis 0/1.
RHINOS: 1 Brent Webb; 23 Ben Jones-Bishop; 2 Lee Smith; 12 Carl Ablett; 5 Ryan Hall; 13 Kevin Sinfield (C); 6 Danny McGuire; 8 Kylie Leuluai; 9 Danny Buderus; 10 Jamie Peacock; 3 Brett Delaney; 11 Jamie Jones-Buchanan; 21 Chris Clarkson. Subs (all used): 16 Ryan Bailey; 17 Ian Kirke; 20 Weller Hauraki; 24 Paul McShane.
Tries: Hall (23), Jones-Buchanan (62), Buderus (65);
Goals: Sinfield 3/3.
Sin bin: Delaney (51) - late challenge on Dureau.
Rugby Leaguer & League Express Men of the Match: *Dragons:* Scott Dureau; *Rhinos:* Jamie Jones-Buchanan.
Penalty count: 12-4; **Half-time:** 20-6;
Referee: James Child; **Attendance:** 10,688.

ROUND 22

Friday 15th July 2011

LEEDS RHINOS 20 HULL FC 0

RHINOS: 23 Ben Jones-Bishop; 27 Zak Hardaker; 3 Brett Delaney; 12 Carl Ablett; 5 Ryan Hall; 13 Kevin Sinfield (C); 6 Danny McGuire; 16 Ryan Bailey; 9 Danny Buderus; 10 Jamie Peacock; 20 Weller Hauraki; 11 Jamie Jones-Buchanan; 21 Chris Clarkson. Subs (all used): 14 Ali Lauitiiti; 22 Jay Pitts; 17 Ian Kirke; 7 Rob Burrow.
Tries: Hall (13), Jones-Bishop (73), McGuire (79);
Goals: Sinfield 4/4.
HULL: 20 Cameron Phelps; 3 Richard Whiting; 19 Jordan Turner; 4 Kirk Yeaman; 5 Tom Briscoe; 6 Richard Horne; 30 Sam Obst; 8 Mark O'Meley; 9 Danny Houghton; 13 Craig Fitzgibbon (C); 16 Willie Manu; 12 Danny Tickle; 11 Joe Westerman. Subs (all used): 23 Sam Moa; 10 Lee Radford; 15 Epalahame Lauaki; 14 Danny Washbrook.
Rugby Leaguer & League Express Men of the Match: *Rhinos:* Jamie Peacock; *Hull:* Jordan Turner.
Penalty count: 7-9; **Half-time:** 6-0;
Referee: Richard Silverwood; **Attendance:** 14,809.

ST HELENS 40 CATALAN DRAGONS 18

SAINTS: 7 Kyle Eastmond; 28 Tom Makinson; 3 Michael Shenton; 5 Francis Meli; 22 Jamie Foster; 25 Lee Gaskell; 20 Jonny Lomax; 10 James Graham (C); 9 James Roby; 15 Louie McCarthy-Scarsbrook; 12 Jon Wilkin; 4 Iosia Soliola; 11 Tony Puletua. Subs (all used): 6 Leon Pryce; 13 Chris Flannery; 14 Scott Moore; 21 Shaun Magennis.
Tries: Foster (5, 53, 79), Meli (24, 75), Shenton (72);
Goals: Foster 8/8.
DRAGONS: 1 Clint Greenshields; 2 Damien Blanch; 15 Jean-Philippe Baile; 18 Darryl Millard; 19 Frederic Vaccari; 11 Steve Menzies; 29 Remy Marginet (D); 10 Remi Casty; 9 Ian Henderson; 24 Jason Baitieri; 23 Lopini Paea; 12 Sebastien Raguin; 13 Gregory Mounis (C). Subs (all used): 17 Cyrille Gossard; 20 Michael Simon; 22 Jamal Fakir; 26 Eloi Pelissier.
Tries: Menzies (14, 50), Vaccari (44), Greenshields (59);
Goals: Marginet 1/4.
Rugby Leaguer & League Express Men of the Match: *Saints:* James Roby; *Dragons:* Steve Menzies.
Penalty count: 9-5; **Half-time:** 14-6;
Referee: Phil Bentham; **Attendance:** 7,026.

WIGAN WARRIORS 48
WAKEFIELD TRINITY WILDCATS 6

WARRIORS: 1 Sam Tomkins; 25 Josh Charnley; 24 Stefan Marsh; 4 George Carmont; 5 Pat Richards; 6 Paul Deacon; 17 Brett Finch; 21 Lee Mossop; 9 Michael McIlorum; 15 Jeff Lima; 11 Harrison Hansen; 34 Gareth Hock; 13 Sean O'Loughlin (C). Subs (all used): 10 Andy Coley; 35 Ben Cross (D); 22 Liam Farrell; 23 Chris Tuson.

Tries: Hock (4, 68, 78), Carmont (10), Richards (32), S Tomkins (37, 65), Charnley (38); **Goals:** Richards 8/8.
WILDCATS: 23 Josh Veivers; 29 Josh Griffin; 3 Aaron Murphy; 18 Chris Dean; 37 Semi Tadulala; 16 Jeremy Smith; 14 Tommy Lee; 8 Michael Korkidas; 26 Matthew Wildie; 31 Kyle Amor; 21 Frankie Mariano; 17 Paul Johnson; 11 Kevin Henderson. Subs (all used): 9 Julien Rinaldi (C); 10 Paul King; 15 Motu Tony; 25 Liam Higgins.
Try: Griffin (16); **Goals:** Veivers 1/1.
Rugby Leaguer & League Express Men of the Match: *Warriors:* Gareth Hock; *Wildcats:* Kyle Amor.
Penalty count: 9-7; **Half-time:** 30-6;
Referee: Thierry Alibert; **Attendance:** 13,095.

Saturday 16th July 2011

HARLEQUINS 24 WARRINGTON WOLVES 54

HARLEQUINS: 1 Luke Dorn; 23 Mark Calderwood; 3 Tony Clubb; 2 Jamie O'Callaghan; 5 Chris Melling; 24 Dan Sarginson; 6 Luke Gale; 17 Danny Ward; 7 Chad Randall; 10 Oliver Wilkes; 13 Rob Purdham (C); 33 Lee Mitchell; 12 Chris Bailey. Subs (all used): 15 Luke Ambler; 21 Olsi Krasniqi; 9 Andy Ellis; 14 Jason Golden.
Tries: Gale (15), Dorn (50), Sarginson (66), Ellis (80);
Goals: Gale 4/4.
WOLVES: 1 Brett Hodgson; 5 Joel Monaghan; 3 Matt King; 23 Ryan Atkins; 22 Rhys Williams; 6 Lee Briers (C); 7 Richard Myler; 16 Paul Wood; 9 Michael Monaghan; 10 Garreth Carvell; 11 Louis Anderson; 17 Simon Grix; 4 Chris Bridge. Subs (all used): 14 Mick Higham; 15 Jon Clarke; 12 Ben Westwood; 20 Matty Blythe.
Tries: Carvell (2), Bridge (6, 9, 28, 43), J Monaghan (22), Briers (25), Myler (46), Wood (74);
Goals: Hodgson 8/8, Briers 1/1.
Rugby Leaguer & League Express Men of the Match: *Harlequins:* Dan Sarginson; *Wolves:* Chris Bridge.
Penalty count: 6-2; **Half-time:** 6-36;
Referee: Steve Ganson; **Attendance:** 3,842.

CRUSADERS 20 CASTLEFORD TIGERS 26

CRUSADERS: 1 Clinton Schifcofske (C); 5 Stuart Reardon; 3 Tony Martin; 4 Vince Mellars; 27 Jordan Tansey; 6 Michael Witt; 19 Lloyd White; 8 Ryan O'Hara; 9 Lincoln Withers; 22 Richard Moore; 13 Frank Winterstein; 12 Jason Chan; 11 Hep Cahill. Subs (all used): 7 Jarrod Sammut; 15 Jordan James; 16 Ben Flower; 24 Lee Williams.
Tries: Chan (22), White (26), Tansey (37), Sammut (45);
Goals: Schifcofske 2/4.
TIGERS: 1 Richard Mathers; 2 Kirk Dixon; 3 Nick Youngquest; 4 Joe Arundel; 5 Richard Owen; 23 Ryan McGoldrick; 7 Danny Orr (C); 8 Paul Jackson; 27 Daryl Clark; 29 Rob Parker; 13 Brett Ferres; 14 Stuart Jones; 9 Ryan Hudson. Subs (all used): 12 Steve Snitch; 22 Jordan Thompson; 25 Dean Widders; 31 Ben Davies (D).
Tries: Thompson (18), Youngquest (41), B Davies (53), Parker (77); **Goals:** Dixon 5/5.
Rugby Leaguer & League Express Men of the Match: *Crusaders:* Jason Chan; *Tigers:* Brett Ferres.
Penalty count: 6-9; **Half-time:** 14-6;
Referee: Ben Thaler; **Attendance:** 3,055.

Sunday 17th July 2011

BRADFORD BULLS 36 HUDDERSFIELD GIANTS 0

BULLS: 6 Brett Kearney; 5 Patrick Ah Van; 3 Paul Sykes; 1 Michael Platt; 19 Gareth Raynor; 33 Ben Jeffries; 7 Marc Herbert; 10 Andy Lynch (C); 14 Matt Diskin; 15 Bryn Hargreaves; 11 Olivier Elima; 12 Elliott Whitehead; 16 Craig Kopczak. Subs (all used): 8 Nick Scruton; 20 James Donaldson; 21 Danny Addy; 29 Tom Burgess.
Tries: Jeffries (10), Sykes (16, 30), Platt (39), Ah Van (64), Kearney (69); **Goals:** Ah Van 4/5, Sykes 2/3.
GIANTS: 1 Scott Grix; 20 Jermaine McGillvary; 29 Joe Wardle; 3 Leroy Cudjoe; 5 David Hodgson; 6 Kevin Brown (C); 7 Danny Brough; 8 Eorl Crabtree; 9 Luke Robinson; 10 Darrell Griffin; 4 Lee Gilmour; 2 Michael Lawrence; 11 Luke O'Donnell. Subs (all used): 18 Larne Patrick; 37 Dale Ferguson; 17 Danny Kirmond; 15 Keith Mason.
Sin bin: Crabtree (63) - interference.
Rugby Leaguer & League Express Men of the Match: *Bulls:* Ben Jeffries; *Giants:* Luke Robinson.
Penalty count: 11-9; **Half-time:** 22-0;
Referee: James Child; **Attendance:** 14,047.

HULL KINGSTON ROVERS 21 SALFORD CITY REDS 8

ROVERS: 1 Shaun Briscoe; 2 Peter Fox; 3 Kris Welham; 4 Jake Webster; 5 Liam Colbon; 13 Scott Murrell; 7 Michael Dobson; 20 Michael Vella (C); 18 Josh Hodgson; 16 Jason Netherton; 11 Clint Newton; 12 Ben Galea; 17 Matt Cook. Subs (all used): 8 Rhys Lovegrove; 22 Scott Taylor; 9 Ben Fisher; 21 Sam Latus.
Tries: Galea (55), Cook (69), Welham (80);
Goals: Dobson 4/4; **Field goal:** Dobson (75).
CITY REDS: 1 Luke Patten; 2 Jodie Broughton; 11 Vinnie Anderson; 3 Mark Henry; 30 Danny Williams (D); 14 Matty Smith; 7 Daniel Holdsworth (C); 8 Ray Cashmere; 9 Wayne Godwin; 19 Ryan Boyle; 22 Adam Neal; 4 Chris Nero; 13 Stephen Wild. Subs (all used): 23 Marc Sneyd; 15 Luke Adamson; 10 Lee Jewitt; 17 Iafeta Palea'aesina.
Try: Anderson (5); **Goals:** Holdsworth 2/2.
Rugby Leaguer & League Express Men of the Match: *Rovers:* Matt Cook; *City Reds:* Luke Patten.
Penalty count: 11-7; **Half-time:** 0-8;
Referee: Tim Roby; **Attendance:** 7,834.

ROUND 23

Friday 29th July 2011

HULL FC 16 WIGAN WARRIORS 30

HULL: 20 Cameron Phelps; 3 Richard Whiting; 19 Jordan Turner; 4 Kirk Yeaman; 5 Tom Briscoe; 6 Richard Horne; 30 Sam Obst; 8 Mark O'Meley; 9 Danny Houghton; 23 Sam Moa; 16 Willie Manu; 12 Danny Tickle; 14 Danny Washbrook. Subs (all used): 10 Lee Radford (C); 15 Epalahame Lauaki; 17 Ewan Dowes; 2 Will Sharp.
Tries: Yeaman (3), Turner (40), Manu (47);
Goals: Tickle 2/3.
WARRIORS: 1 Sam Tomkins; 25 Josh Charnley; 12 Joel Tomkins; 4 George Carmont; 5 Pat Richards; 6 Paul Deacon; 17 Brett Finch; 15 Jeff Lima; 7 Thomas Leuluai; 10 Andy Coley; 22 Liam Farrell; 16 Ryan Hoffman; 13 Sean O'Loughlin (C). Subs (all used): 9 Michael Mcllorum; 21 Lee Mossop; 34 Gareth Hock; 35 Ben Cross.
Tries: S Tomkins (13, 72), Richards (27, 33), Carmont (30); **Goals:** Richards 5/6.
Rugby Leaguer & League Express Men of the Match: *Hull:* Willie Manu; *Warriors:* Sam Tomkins.
Penalty count: 14-7; **Half-time:** 10-22;
Referee: Ben Thaler; **Attendance:** 11,729.

SALFORD CITY REDS 22 LEEDS RHINOS 30

CITY REDS: 1 Luke Patten; 2 Jodie Broughton; 3 Mark Henry; 20 Sean Gleeson; 30 Danny Williams; 6 Stefan Ratchford; 7 Daniel Holdsworth (C); 8 Ray Cashmere; 14 Matty Smith; 19 Ryan Boyle; 11 Vinnie Anderson; 4 Chris Nero; 13 Stephen Wild. Subs (all used): 10 Lee Jewitt; 22 Adam Neal; 18 Adam Sidlow; 9 Wayne Godwin.
Tries: Patten (52), Broughton (59), Anderson (66), Jewitt (78); **Goals:** Holdsworth 3/4.
RHINOS: 1 Brent Webb; 2 Lee Smith; 19 Kallum Watkins; 12 Carl Ablett; 5 Ryan Hall; 13 Kevin Sinfield (C); 7 Rob Burrow; 16 Ryan Bailey; 9 Danny Buderus; 10 Jamie Peacock; 11 Jamie Jones-Buchanan; 22 Jay Pitts; 21 Chris Clarkson. Subs (all used): 8 Kylie Leuluai; 14 Ali Lauitiiti; 6 Danny McGuire; 17 Ian Kirke.
Tries: Hall (17), Bailey (19), McGuire (37), Webb (54), Smith (74); **Goals:** Sinfield 5/6.
Rugby Leaguer & League Express Men of the Match: *City Reds:* Matty Smith; *Rhinos:* Rob Burrow.
Penalty count: 13-10; **Half-time:** 0-18;
Referee: Richard Silverwood; **Attendance:** 4,024.

Saturday 30th July 2011

CATALAN DRAGONS 48 HARLEQUINS 22

DRAGONS: 1 Clint Greenshields; 2 Damien Blanch; 15 Jean-Philippe Baile; 18 Darryl Millard; 25 Vincent Duport; 4 Setaimata Sa; 29 Remy Marginet; 10 Remi Casty; 9 Ian Henderson; 24 Jason Baitieri; 23 Lopini Paea; 12 Sebastien Raguin; 13 Gregory Mounis (C). Subs (all used): 17 Cyrille Gossard; 20 Michael Simon; 26 Eloi Pelissier; 30 Thibaut Ancely.
Tries: Greenshields (2, 60), Baile (12), Mounis (18, 50), Baitieri (23), Blanch (45), Simon (72);
Goals: Marginet 8/8.
HARLEQUINS: 2 Jamie O'Callaghan; 5 Chris Melling; 3 Tony Clubb; 4 David Howell; 31 Karl Pryce; 1 Luke Dorn; 24 Dan Sarginson; 17 Danny Ward; 7 Chad Randall; 8 Karl Temata; 33 Lee Mitchell; 13 Rob Purdham (C); 14 Jason Golden. Subs (all used): 9 Andy Ellis; 10 Oliver Wilkes; 15 Luke Ambler; 21 Olsi Krasniqi.
Tries: Wilkes (32), Pryce (40), Randall (54), Clubb (63);
Goals: Purdham 1/2, Melling 2/2.
Rugby Leaguer & League Express Men of the Match: *Dragons:* Setaimata Sa; *Harlequins:* Luke Dorn.
Penalty count: 9-6; **Half-time:** 24-10;
Referee: James Child; **Attendance:** 8,471.

HUDDERSFIELD GIANTS 46 HULL KINGSTON ROVERS 26

GIANTS: 1 Scott Grix; 20 Jermaine McGillvary; 3 Leroy Cudjoe; 19 Graeme Horne; 5 David Hodgson; 7 Danny Brough; 9 Luke Robinson (C); 8 Eorl Crabtree; 13 David Faiumu; 10 Darrell Griffin; 4 Lee Gilmour; 17 Danny Kirmond; 27 Jacob Fairbank. Subs (all used): 16 Andy Raleigh; 18 Larne Patrick; 23 Kyle Wood; 24 Adam Walker.
Tries: Cudjoe (15), Faiumu (19), Grix (35, 65), Horne (40, 45), Kirmond (50), Crabtree (71);
Goals: Grix 5/6, Cudjoe 2/2.
ROVERS: 26 Louis Sheriff; 2 Peter Fox; 3 Kris Welham; 4 Jake Webster; 21 Sam Latus; 6 Blake Green; 7 Michael Dobson; 20 Michael Vella (C); 18 Josh Hodgson; 15 Scott Wheeldon; 11 Clint Newton; 12 Ben Galea; 22 Scott Taylor. Subs (all used): 9 Ben Fisher; 13 Scott Murrell; 16 Jason Netherton; 27 Jordan Cox.
Tries: Taylor (6), Hodgson (22), Fisher (42), Webster (52); **Goals:** Dobson 5/5.
Rugby Leaguer & League Express Men of the Match: *Giants:* Leroy Cudjoe; *Rovers:* Josh Hodgson.
Penalty count: 4-8; **Half-time:** 24-14;
Referee: Thierry Alibert; **Attendance:** 6,464.

Sunday 31st July 2011

WARRINGTON WOLVES 64 BRADFORD BULLS 6

WOLVES: 1 Brett Hodgson; 5 Joel Monaghan; 4 Chris Bridge; 23 Ryan Atkins; 3 Matt King; 17 Simon Grix; 7 Richard Myler; 16 Paul Wood; 9 Michael Monaghan (C); 10 Garreth Carvell; 11 Louis Anderson; 12 Ben Westwood; 18 Michael Cooper. Subs (all used): 14 Mick Higham; 21 Tyrone McCarthy; 13 Ben Harrison; 20 Matty Blythe.
Tries: Atkins (2, 21, 67, 72), King (4, 26), J Monaghan (35, 58, 64), Hodgson (44, 51), M Monaghan (76); **Goals:** Hodgson 5/7, Bridge 3/5.
BULLS: 6 Brett Kearney; 5 Patrick Ah Van; 3 Paul Sykes; 1 Michael Platt; 19 Gareth Raynor; 33 Ben Jeffries; 7 Marc Herbert; 10 Andy Lynch (C); 14 Matt Diskin; 15 Bryn Hargreaves; 11 Olivier Elima; 12 Elliott Whitehead; 16 Craig Kopczak. Subs (all used): 8 Nick Scruton; 20 James Donaldson; 21 Danny Addy; 29 Tom Burgess.
Try: Ah Van (79); **Goals:** Ah Van 1/1.
Rugby Leaguer & League Express Men of the Match: *Wolves:* Ryan Atkins; *Bulls:* Danny Addy.
Penalty count: 5-6; **Half-time:** 26-0;
Referee: Steve Ganson; **Attendance:** 10,641.

CASTLEFORD TIGERS 26 ST HELENS 46

TIGERS: 23 Ryan McGoldrick; 2 Kirk Dixon; 3 Nick Youngquest; 4 Joe Arundel; 5 Richard Owen; 25 Dean Widders; 6 Rangi Chase; 21 Nathan Massey; 16 Adam Milner; 31 Ben Davies; 13 Brett Ferres; 24 Oliver Holmes; 22 Jordan Thompson. Subs (all used): 9 Ryan Hudson (C); 17 Willie Isa; 20 Martin Aspinwall; 26 John Davies.
Tries: Chase (25), Dixon (29), Youngquest (33), Owen (71), Widders (80); **Goals:** Dixon 3/4, Arundel 0/1.
Sin bin: Chase (13) - holding down.
SAINTS: 1 Paul Wellens (C); 28 Tom Makinson; 3 Michael Shenton; 7 Kyle Eastmond; 22 Jamie Foster; 6 Leon Pryce; 20 Jonny Lomax; 10 James Graham (C); 9 James Roby; 15 Louie McCarthy-Scarsbrook; 13 Chris Flannery; 12 Jon Wilkin; 11 Tony Puletua. Subs (all used): 14 Scott Moore; 21 Shaun Magennis; 19 Andrew Dixon; 25 Lee Gaskell.
Tries: Graham (8), Shenton (11), McCarthy-Scarsbrook (13), Wellens (37, 50), Puletua (59), Gaskell (67), Eastmond (77); **Goals:** Foster 7/8.
On report:
Roby (37) - alleged dangerous tackle on Dixon.
Rugby Leaguer & League Express Men of the Match: *Tigers:* Rangi Chase; *Saints:* Tony Puletua.
Penalty count: 10-7; **Half-time:** 16-24;
Referee: Robert Hicks; **Attendance:** 6,802.

WAKEFIELD TRINITY WILDCATS 6 CRUSADERS 40

WILDCATS: 23 Josh Veivers; 29 Josh Griffin; 3 Aaron Murphy; 18 Chris Dean; 37 Semi Tadulala; 16 Jeremy Smith; 14 Tommy Lee; 25 Liam Higgins; 26 Matthew Wildie; 31 Kyle Amor; 21 Frankie Mariano; 17 Paul Johnson; 11 Kevin Henderson. Subs (all used): 8 Michael Korkidas (C); 15 Motu Tony; 20 Ben Gledhill; 22 Stuart Howarth.
Try: Veivers (57); **Goals:** Veivers 1/1.
CRUSADERS: 1 Clinton Schifcofske (C); 5 Stuart Reardon; 3 Tony Martin; 4 Vince Mellars; 18 Elliot Kear; 6 Michael Witt; 23 Peter Lupton; 8 Ryan O'Hara; 9 Lincoln Withers; 15 Jordan James; 11 Hep Cahill; 12 Jason Chan; 24 Lee Williams. Subs (all used): 22 Richard Moore; 20 Gil Dudson; 13 Frank Winterstein; 19 Lloyd White.
Tries: Withers (33), White (42, 49), Reardon (51), Mellars (70), J James (75), Kear (77);
Goals: Schifcofske 3/4, Witt 2/2, Martin 1/1.
Rugby Leaguer & League Express Men of the Match: *Wildcats:* Kyle Amor; *Crusaders:* Lincoln Withers.
Penalty count: 11-9; **Half-time:** 0-6;
Referee: Phil Bentham; **Attendance:** 6,428.

ROUND 24

Friday 12th August 2011

CRUSADERS 31 HARLEQUINS 12

CRUSADERS: 1 Clinton Schifcofske (C); 5 Stuart Reardon; 4 Vince Mellars; 3 Tony Martin; 18 Elliot Kear; 27 Jordan Tansey; 6 Michael Witt; 15 Jordan James; 9 Lincoln Withers; 20 Gil Dudson; 12 Jason Chan; 13 Frank Winterstein; 23 Peter Lupton. Subs (all used): 10 Mark Bryant; 19 Lloyd White; 22 Richard Moore; 24 Lee Williams.
Tries: Chan (7), Reardon (10), White (45), Moore (67), Kear (76); **Goals:** Schifcofske 5/5; **Field goal:** Witt (70).
HARLEQUINS: 1 Luke Dorn; 5 Chris Melling; 3 Tony Clubb; 2 Jamie O'Callaghan; 23 Mark Calderwood; 24 Dan Sarginson; 6 Luke Gale; 8 Karl Temata; 7 Chad Randall; 17 Danny Ward; 13 Rob Purdham (C); 33 Lee Mitchell; 12 Chris Bailey. Subs (all used): 14 Jason Golden; 16 Mike Burnett; 18 Dave Williams; 21 Olsi Krasniqi.
Tries: Sarginson (24, 60); **Goals:** Gale 2/2.
Rugby Leaguer & League Express Men of the Match: *Crusaders:* Jordan Tansey; *Harlequins:* Dan Sarginson.
Penalty count: 6-6; **Half-time:** 12-6;
Referee: Richard Silverwood; **Attendance:** 2,259.

HULL FC 40 CATALAN DRAGONS 8

HULL: 20 Cameron Phelps; 3 Richard Whiting; 19 Jordan Turner; 4 Kirk Yeaman; 5 Tom Briscoe; 11 Joe Westerman; 6 Richard Horne; 8 Mark O'Meley; 9 Danny Houghton; 23 Sam Moa; 16 Willie Manu; 12 Danny Tickle; 13 Craig Fitzgibbon (C). Subs (all used): 2 Will Sharp; 10 Lee Radford; 14 Danny Washbrook; 15 Epalahame Lauaki.
Tries: Moa (2), Yeaman (16), Phelps (41), Radford (44), Westerman (52), Horne (61); **Goals:** Tickle 8/8.
Sin bin: Yeaman (74) - punching.
DRAGONS: 1 Clint Greenshields; 2 Damien Blanch; 15 Jean-Philippe Baile; 18 Daryl Millard; 25 Vincent Duport; 4 Setaimata Sa; 7 Scott Dureau; 8 David Ferriol; 9 Ian Henderson; 24 Jason Baitieri; 23 Lopini Paea; 12 Sebastien Raguin; 13 Gregory Mounis (C). Subs (all used): 17 Cyrille Gossard; 20 Michael Simon; 10 Remi Casty; 26 Eloi Pelissier.

Tries: Millard (9), Duport (65); **Goals:** Dureau 0/2.
Sin bin: Gossard (37) - interference.
Rugby Leaguer & League Express Men of the Match: *Hull:* Joe Westerman; *Dragons:* Scott Dureau.
Penalty count: 11-10; **Half-time:** 16-4;
Referee: Steve Ganson; **Attendance:** 10,739.

LEEDS RHINOS 56 CASTLEFORD TIGERS 0

RHINOS: 1 Brent Webb; 23 Ben Jones-Bishop; 19 Kallum Watkins; 12 Carl Ablett; 5 Ryan Hall; 13 Kevin Sinfield (C); 6 Danny McGuire; 8 Kylie Leuluai; 9 Danny Buderus; 10 Jamie Peacock; 20 Weller Hauraki; 11 Jamie Jones-Buchanan; 21 Chris Clarkson. Subs (all used): 16 Ryan Bailey; 7 Rob Burrow; 17 Ian Kirke; 14 Ali Lauitiiti.
Tries: Jones-Buchanan (18), Hall (24), Watkins (27), Webb (42, 76), Jones-Bishop (44), Lauitiiti (49), Burrow (63, 65), McGuire (70); **Goals:** Sinfield 6/7, Burrow 2/4.
TIGERS: 23 Ryan McGoldrick; 17 Willie Isa; 3 Nick Youngquest; 4 Joe Arundel; 5 Richard Owen; 25 Dean Widders; 7 Danny Orr (C); 29 Rob Parker; 16 Adam Milner; 31 Ben Davies; 14 Stuart Jones; 24 Oliver Holmes; 20 Martin Aspinwall. Subs (all used): 21 Nathan Massey; 26 John Davies; 22 Jordan Thompson; 27 Daryl Clark.
Rugby Leaguer & League Express Men of the Match: *Rhinos:* Jamie Jones-Buchanan; *Tigers:* Danny Orr.
Penalty count: 6-6; **Half-time:** 20-0;
Referee: Thierry Alibert; **Attendance:** 15,156.

ST HELENS 19 HUDDERSFIELD GIANTS 6

SAINTS: 1 Paul Wellens (C); 24 Tom Armstrong; 3 Michael Shenton; 5 Francis Meli; 22 Jamie Foster; 6 Leon Pryce; 25 Lee Gaskell; 10 James Graham (C); 9 James Roby; 15 Louie McCarthy-Scarsbrook; 12 Jon Wilkin; 4 Iosia Soliola; 19 Andrew Dixon. Subs: 14 Scott Moore; 16 Paul Clough; 17 Gary Wheeler (not used); 18 Matty Ashurst.
Tries: Pryce (26), Wellens (42), McCarthy-Scarsbrook (56); **Goals:** Foster 3/3; **Field goal:** Gaskell (73).
Sin bin: Clough (68) - dissent.
GIANTS: 1 Scott Grix; 20 Jermaine McGillvary; 19 Graeme Horne; 2 Michael Lawrence; 3 Leroy Cudjoe; 6 Kevin Brown (C); 7 Danny Brough; 10 Darrell Griffin; 9 Luke Robinson; 11 Luke O'Donnell; 17 Danny Kirmond; 4 Lee Gilmour; 13 David Faiumu. Subs (all used): 8 Eorl Crabtree; 12 David Fa'alogo; 16 Andy Raleigh; 18 Larne Patrick.
Try: Fa'alogo (62); **Goals:** Grix 1/1.
On report: Crabtree (45) - alleged use of the elbow on McCarthy-Scarsbrook.
Rugby Leaguer & League Express Men of the Match: *Saints:* Louie McCarthy-Scarsbrook; *Giants:* David Fa'alogo.
Penalty count: 4-9; **Half-time:** 6-0;
Referee: Phil Bentham; **Attendance:** 6,421.

Sunday 14th August 2011

WARRINGTON WOLVES 66 WAKEFIELD TRINITY WILDCATS 12

WOLVES: 1 Brett Hodgson; 5 Joel Monaghan; 4 Chris Bridge; 23 Ryan Atkins; 3 Matt King; 17 Simon Grix; 7 Richard Myler; 16 Paul Wood; 9 Michael Monaghan (C); 10 Garreth Carvell; 11 Louis Anderson; 12 Ben Westwood; 18 Michael Cooper. Subs (all used): 13 Ben Harrison; 15 Jon Clarke; 24 Rhys Evans; 26 David Solomona.
Tries: Bridge (2), Atkins (11, 52, 60), Myler (19), J Monaghan (38), King (45, 68), Anderson (50, 66), Cooper (72); **Goals:** Hodgson 1/1, Bridge 10/10.
WILDCATS: 23 Josh Veivers; 19 Dale Morton; 18 Chris Dean; 39 Ryan Tongia (D); 37 Semi Tadulala; 16 Jeremy Smith; 14 Tommy Lee; 31 Kyle Amor; 9 Julien Rinaldi; 17 Paul Johnson; 21 Frankie Mariano; 13 Glenn Morrison (C); 11 Kevin Henderson. Subs (all used): 8 Michael Korkidas; 26 Matthew Wildie; 20 Ben Gledhill; 22 Stuart Howarth.
Tries: Amor (16), Smith (78); **Goals:** Veivers 2/2.
Rugby Leaguer & League Express Men of the Match: *Wolves:* Chris Bridge; *Wildcats:* Ryan Tongia.
Penalty count: 13-3; **Half-time:** 24-6;
Referee: Ben Thaler; **Attendance:** 10,296.

WIGAN WARRIORS 52 SALFORD CITY REDS 18

WARRIORS: 1 Sam Tomkins; 25 Josh Charnley; 12 Joel Tomkins; 4 George Carmont; 5 Pat Richards; 7 Thomas Leuluai; 17 Brett Finch; 21 Lee Mossop; 9 Michael McIlorum; 10 Andy Coley; 11 Harrison Hansen; 16 Ryan Hoffman; 13 Sean O'Loughlin (C). Subs (all used): 2 Darrell Goulding; 35 Ben Cross; 34 Gareth Hock; 22 Liam Farrell.
Tries: S Tomkins (4, 34, 39, 79), Coley (14), Charnley (23), McIlorum (43), Farrell (51), J Tomkins (69);
Goals: Richards 8/9.
On report: Mossop (75) - alleged late challenge.
CITY REDS: 1 Luke Patten; 2 Jodie Broughton; 3 Mark Henry; 20 Sean Gleeson; 30 Danny Williams; 6 Stefan Ratchford; 7 Daniel Holdsworth (C); 8 Ray Cashmere; 14 Matty Smith; 19 Ryan Boyle; 11 Vinnie Anderson; 22 Adam Neal; 13 Stephen Wild. Subs (all used): 10 Lee Jewitt; 15 Luke Adamson; 17 Iafeta Palea'aesina; 9 Wayne Godwin.
Tries: Williams (10, 75), Gleeson (55);
Goals: Holdsworth 3/3.
Sin bin: Ratchford (50) - late challenge on Finch.
Rugby Leaguer & League Express Men of the Match: *Warriors:* Sam Tomkins; *City Reds:* Danny Williams.
Penalty count: 8-5; **Half-time:** 28-6;
Referee: Robert Hicks; **Attendance:** 13,607.

BRADFORD BULLS 8 HULL KINGSTON ROVERS 34

BULLS: 6 Brett Kearney; 5 Patrick Ah Van; 1 Michael Platt; 12 Elliott Whitehead; 19 Gareth Raynor; 33 Ben Jeffries; 7 Marc Herbert; 10 Andy Lynch (C); 21 Danny Addy; 15 Bryn Hargreaves; 11 Olivier Elima; 17 Ian Sibbit; 13 Jamie Langley. Subs (all used): 8 Nick Scruton; 16 Craig Kopczak; 27 Adam O'Brien; 29 Tom Burgess.
Try: Herbert (16); **Goals:** Ah Van 2/2.
ROVERS: 1 Shaun Briscoe; 2 Peter Fox; 3 Kris Welham; 4 Jake Webster; 21 Sam Latus; 6 Blake Green; 7 Michael Dobson; 20 Michael Vella (C); 18 Josh Hodgson; 22 Scott Taylor; 11 Clint Newton; 12 Ben Galea; 14 Liam Watts. Subs (all used): 13 Scott Murrell; 27 Jordan Cox; 9 Ben Fisher; 15 Scott Wheeldon.
Tries: Galea (34), Murrell (42), Fox (45), Hodgson (72), Welham (75), Green (79); **Goals:** Dobson 5/6.
Rugby Leaguer & League Express Men of the Match: *Bulls:* Elliott Whitehead; *Rovers:* Michael Dobson.
Penalty count: 6-7; **Half-time:** 8-6;
Referee: James Child; **Attendance:** 13,441.

ROUND 25

Friday 19th August 2011

SALFORD CITY REDS 24 HUDDERSFIELD GIANTS 18

CITY REDS: 1 Luke Patten; 2 Jodie Broughton; 5 Ashley Gibson; 20 Sean Gleeson; 30 Danny Williams; 6 Stefan Ratchford; 7 Daniel Holdsworth (C); 8 Ray Cashmere; 14 Matty Smith; 19 Ryan Boyle; 3 Mark Henry; 15 Luke Adamson; 13 Stephen Wild. Subs (all used): 9 Wayne Godwin; 22 Adam Neal; 17 Iafeta Palea'aesina; 10 Lee Jewitt.
Tries: Holdsworth (3), Williams (25, 50, 67);
Goals: Holdsworth 4/5.
GIANTS: 1 Scott Grix; 20 Jermaine McGillvary; 3 Leroy Cudjoe; 2 Michael Lawrence; 5 David Hodgson; 6 Kevin Brown (C); 9 Luke Robinson; 8 Eorl Crabtree; 36 Jamie Simpson; 10 Darrell Griffin; 4 Lee Gilmour; 12 David Fa'alogo; 13 David Faiumu. Subs (all used): 18 Larne Patrick; 17 Danny Kirmond; 16 Andy Raleigh; 19 Graeme Horne.
Tries: McGillvary (21), Gilmour (28), Fa'alogo (34);
Goals: Grix 3/3.
Rugby Leaguer & League Express Men of the Match: *City Reds:* Danny Williams; *Giants:* Scott Grix.
Penalty count: 6-6; **Half-time:** 12-18;
Referee: James Child; **Attendance:** 3,458.

WIGAN WARRIORS 60 BRADFORD BULLS 12

WARRIORS: 1 Sam Tomkins; 25 Josh Charnley; 12 Joel Tomkins; 4 George Carmont; 5 Pat Richards; 13 Sean O'Loughlin (C); 6 Paul Deacon; 15 Jeff Lima; 7 Thomas Leuluai; 34 Gareth Hock; 11 Harrison Hansen; 16 Ryan Hoffman; 22 Liam Farrell. Subs (all used): 2 Darrell Goulding; 9 Michael McIlorum; 14 Paul Prescott; 20 Eamon O'Carroll.
Tries: Carmont (5, 20), Hoffman (9), Richards (31, 60, 79), S Tomkins (46, 65), Charnley (50, 76), O'Loughlin (54), Hansen (70); **Goals:** Richards 6/12.
BULLS: 6 Brett Kearney; 5 Patrick Ah Van; 3 Paul Sykes; 25 Shad Royston; 19 Gareth Raynor; 33 Ben Jeffries; 7 Marc Herbert; 10 Andy Lynch (C); 21 Danny Addy; 15 Bryn Hargreaves; 11 Olivier Elima; 17 Ian Sibbit; 13 Jamie Langley. Subs (all used): 31 John Bateman; 16 Craig Kopczak; 27 Adam O'Brien; 29 Tom Burgess.
Tries: Kopczak (24), Bateman (36); **Goals:** Ah Van 2/2.
Rugby Leaguer & League Express Men of the Match: *Warriors:* Sam Tomkins; *Bulls:* John Bateman.
Penalty count: 7-4; **Half-time:** 18-12;
Referee: Ben Thaler; **Attendance:** 13,940.

Saturday 20th August 2011

HARLEQUINS 32 LEEDS RHINOS 22

HARLEQUINS: 1 Luke Dorn; 23 Mark Calderwood; 2 Jamie O'Callaghan; 3 Tony Clubb; 5 Chris Melling; 24 Dan Sarginson; 6 Luke Gale; 17 Danny Ward; 7 Chad Randall; 8 Karl Temata; 13 Rob Purdham (C); 14 Jason Golden; 12 Chris Bailey. Subs (all used): 15 Luke Ambler; 10 Oliver Wilkes; 16 Mike Burnett; 20 Ben Bolger.
Tries: Dorn (14, 16, 44), O'Callaghan (36), Calderwood (65); **Goals:** Gale 6/6.
RHINOS: 1 Brent Webb; 23 Ben Jones-Bishop; 19 Kallum Watkins; 12 Carl Ablett; 5 Ryan Hall; 13 Kevin Sinfield (C); 6 Danny McGuire; 8 Kylie Leuluai; 9 Danny Buderus; 17 Ian Kirke; 20 Weller Hauraki; 3 Brett Delaney; 21 Chris Clarkson. Subs (all used): 22 Jay Pitts; 14 Ali Lauitiiti; 2 Lee Smith; 7 Rob Burrow.
Tries: Hall (53), McGuire (72), Burrow (75), Pitts (78);
Goals: Sinfield 3/4.
Sin bin: Sinfield (34) - professional foul.
Rugby Leaguer & League Express Men of the Match: *Harlequins:* Luke Gale; *Rhinos:* Brett Delaney.
Penalty count: 7-3; **Half-time:** 20-0;
Referee: Robert Hicks; **Attendance:** 3,241.

WAKEFIELD TRINITY WILDCATS 30 CASTLEFORD TIGERS 34

WILDCATS: 39 Ryan Tongia; 19 Dale Morton; 11 Kevin Henderson; 18 Chris Dean; 37 Semi Tadulala; 16 Jeremy Smith; 14 Tommy Lee; 31 Kyle Amor; 9 Julien Rinaldi; 25 Liam Higgins; 17 Paul Johnson; 13 Glenn Morrison (C); 22 Stuart Howarth. Subs (all used): 26 Matthew Wildie; 15 Motu Tony; 20 Ben Gledhill; 36 Jarrad Hickey.
Tries: Morrison (2), P Johnson (5), Wildie (31), Tadulala (36), Dean (64); **Goals:** Morton 5/6.
TIGERS: 23 Ryan McGoldrick; 17 Willie Isa; 3 Nick Youngquest; 1 Richard Mathers; 5 Richard Owen; 6 Rangi Chase; 7 Danny Orr (C); 29 Rob Parker; 16 Adam Milner; 21 Nathan Massey; 14 Stuart Jones; 20 Martin Aspinwall; 9 Ryan Hudson. Subs (all used): 22 Jordan Thompson; 24 Chris Holmes; 25 Dean Widders; 31 Ben Davies.
Tries: Mathers (17), Isa (23, 26), B Davies (34), Youngquest (55), Widders (77); **Goals:** Orr 5/6.
Sin bin: Youngquest (63) - interference.
Rugby Leaguer & League Express Men of the Match: *Wildcats:* Matthew Wildie; *Tigers:* Rangi Chase.
Penalty count: 10-6; **Half-time:** 24-22;
Referee: Richard Silverwood; **Attendance:** 6,784.

CATALAN DRAGONS 12 WARRINGTON WOLVES 25

DRAGONS: 1 Clint Greenshields; 2 Damien Blanch; 15 Jean-Philippe Baile; 18 Darryl Millard; 19 Frederic Vaccari; 4 Setaimata Sa; 7 Scott Dureau; 8 David Ferriol; 9 Ian Henderson; 10 Remi Casty; 11 Steve Menzies; 12 Sebastien Raguin; 13 Gregory Mounis (C). Subs (all used): 22 Jamal Fakir; 23 Lopini Paea; 24 Jason Baitieri; 26 Eloi Pelissier.
Tries: Blanch (16), Menzies (33); **Goals:** Dureau 2/3.
WOLVES: 2 Chris Riley; 5 Joel Monaghan; 20 Matty Blythe; 23 Ryan Atkins; 3 Matt King; 6 Lee Briers (C); 7 Richard Myler; 16 Paul Wood; 9 Michael Monaghan; 10 Garreth Carvell; 11 Louis Anderson; 18 Michael Cooper; 4 Chris Bridge. Subs (all used): 13 Ben Harrison; 15 Jon Clarke; 19 Lee Mitchell; 26 David Solomona.
Tries: Bridge (20, 45), Atkins (69), Briers (76);
Goals: Bridge 4/4; **Field goal:** Briers (73).
Rugby Leaguer & League Express Men of the Match: *Dragons:* Scott Dureau; *Wolves:* Lee Briers.
Penalty count: 9-8; **Half-time:** 12-6;
Referee: Thierry Alibert; **Attendance:** 9,495.

Sunday 21st August 2011

CRUSADERS 18 HULL FC 58

CRUSADERS: 1 Clinton Schifcofske (C); 5 Stuart Reardon; 3 Tony Martin; 4 Vince Mellars; 18 Elliot Kear; 6 Michael Witt; 19 Lloyd White; 15 Jordan James; 9 Lincoln Withers; 8 Ryan O'Hara; 11 Hep Cahill; 13 Frank Winterstein; 23 Peter Lupton. Subs (all used): 16 Ben Flower; 24 Lee Williams; 27 Jordan Tansey; 22 Richard Moore.
Tries: Mellars (53), Martin (69), Lupton (78);
Goals: Schifcofske 3/3.
HULL: 20 Cameron Phelps; 2 Will Sharp; 19 Jordan Turner; 3 Richard Whiting; 5 Tom Briscoe; 11 Joe Westerman; 6 Richard Horne; 8 Mark O'Meley; 9 Danny Houghton; 23 Sam Moa; 12 Danny Tickle; 16 Willie Manu; 13 Craig Fitzgibbon (C). Subs (all used): 10 Lee Radford; 14 Danny Washbrook; 15 Epalahame Lauaki; 30 Sam Obst.
Tries: Fitzgibbon (4, 30), O'Meley (6), Whiting (20), Radford (34), Houghton (38), Phelps (44), Westerman (47), Turner (49), Obst (64, 72);
Goals: Westerman 5/7, Tickle 2/4.
Rugby Leaguer & League Express Men of the Match: *Crusaders:* Clinton Schifcofske; *Hull:* Sam Obst.
Penalty count: 3-8; **Half-time:** 0-32;
Referee: Phil Bentham; **Attendance:** 3,827.

HULL KINGSTON ROVERS 24 ST HELENS 22

ROVERS: 1 Shaun Briscoe; 19 Craig Hall; 4 Jake Webster; 3 Kris Welham; 21 Sam Latus; 6 Blake Green; 7 Michael Dobson; 20 Michael Vella (C); 18 Josh Hodgson; 22 Scott Taylor; 11 Clint Newton; 12 Ben Galea; 14 Liam Watts. Subs (all used): 15 Scott Wheeldon; 13 Scott Murrell; 9 Ben Fisher; 27 Jordan Cox.
Tries: Green (13, 34), Latus (16), Hall (60);
Goals: Dobson 4/6.
SAINTS: 1 Paul Wellens (C); 24 Tom Armstrong; 3 Michael Shenton; 5 Francis Meli; 22 Jamie Foster; 6 Leon Pryce; 20 Jonny Lomax; 4 Iosia Soliola; 9 James Roby; 15 Louie McCarthy-Scarsbrook; 13 Chris Flannery; 12 Jon Wilkin; 19 Andrew Dixon. Subs (all used): 16 Paul Clough; 14 Scott Moore; 18 Matty Ashurst; 25 Lee Gaskell.
Tries: Foster (5, 39), Ashurst (23), Gaskell (80);
Goals: Foster 3/4.
Rugby Leaguer & League Express Men of the Match: *Rovers:* Craig Hall; *Saints:* Louie McCarthy-Scarsbrook.
Penalty count: 7-5; **Half-time:** 16-16;
Referee: Steve Ganson; **Attendance:** 8,356.

ROUND 26

Friday 2nd September 2011

LEEDS RHINOS 64 WAKEFIELD TRINITY WILDCATS 20

RHINOS: 2 Lee Smith; 23 Ben Jones-Bishop; 27 Zak Hardaker; 12 Carl Ablett; 5 Ryan Hall; 13 Kevin Sinfield (C); 6 Danny McGuire; 8 Kylie Leuluai; 9 Danny Buderus; 10 Jamie Peacock; 11 Jamie Jones-Buchanan; 3 Brett Delaney; 20 Weller Hauraki. Subs (all used): 16 Ryan Bailey; 14 Ali Lauitiiti; 24 Paul McShane; 22 Jay Pitts.
Tries: Hall (2, 35, 63), Jones-Bishop (13), Ablett (15), McGuire (25, 69), Lauitiiti (44), Buderus (60), Peacock (73), Smith (75); **Goals:** Sinfield 10/11.
Sin bin: McShane (38) - dangerous tackle on Tongia.
WILDCATS: 15 Motu Tony; 19 Dale Morton; 23 Josh Veivers; 37 Semi Tadulala; 39 Ryan Tongia; 35 Gareth Moore; 14 Tommy Lee; 31 Kyle Amor; 9 Julien Rinaldi; 25 Liam Higgins; 17 Paul Johnson; 13 Glenn Morrison (C); 22 Stuart Howarth. Subs (all used): 20 Ben Gledhill; 26 Matthew Wildie; 36 Jarrad Hickey; 40 Lucas Walshaw (D).
Tries: Tongia (19), Veivers (48), Tony (54), Amor (78);
Goals: Moore 2/4.

Rugby Leaguer & League Express Men of the Match: *Rhinos:* Danny McGuire; *Wildcats:* Kyle Amor.
Penalty count: 9-7; **Half-time:** 28-4;
Referee: Ben Thaler; **Attendance:** 15,511.

ST HELENS 31 SALFORD CITY REDS 6

SAINTS: 1 Paul Wellens (C); 28 Tom Makinson; 3 Michael Shenton; 5 Francis Meli; 22 Jamie Foster; 6 Leon Pryce; 20 Jonny Lomax; 10 James Graham (C); 9 James Roby; 15 Louie McCarthy-Scarsbrook; 4 Iosia Soliola; 19 Andrew Dixon; 14 Scott Moore. Subs (all used): 16 Paul Clough; 18 Matty Ashurst; 25 Lee Gaskell; 29 Scott Hale.
Tries: Soliola (20), Makinson (25), Meli (50), Ashurst (55), Gaskell (74); **Goals:** Foster 5/5;
Field goal: Lomax (40).
Sin bin: Graham (16) - dissent.
CITY REDS: 1 Luke Patten; 2 Jodie Broughton; 5 Ashley Gibson; 20 Sean Gleeson; 30 Danny Williams; 6 Stefan Ratchford; 7 Daniel Holdsworth (C); 8 Ray Cashmere; 14 Matty Smith; 19 Ryan Boyle; 3 Mark Henry; 11 Vinnie Anderson; 13 Stephen Wild. Subs (all used): 9 Wayne Godwin; 10 Lee Jewitt; 15 Luke Adamson; 17 Iafeta Palea'aesina.
Try: Williams (5); **Goals:** Holdsworth 1/1.
Sin bin: Cashmere (17) - high tackle on Roby.
Rugby Leaguer & League Express Men of the Match: *Saints:* Jonny Lomax; *City Reds:* Danny Williams.
Penalty count: 15-5; **Half-time:** 13-6;
Referee: Phil Bentham; **Attendance:** 7,377.

Saturday 3rd September 2011

CATALAN DRAGONS 28 HULL KINGSTON ROVERS 30

DRAGONS: 1 Clint Greenshields; 2 Damien Blanch; 15 Jean-Philippe Baile; 18 Darryl Millard; 19 Frederic Vaccari; 11 Steve Menzies; 7 Scott Dureau; 8 David Ferriol; 9 Ian Henderson; 10 Remi Casty; 4 Setaimata Sa; 12 Sebastien Raguin; 13 Gregory Mounis (C). Subs (all used): 22 Jamal Fakir; 23 Lopini Paea; 24 Jason Baitieri; 26 Eloi Pelissier.
Tries: Sa (21), Baile (30), Millard (45, 71), Raguin (51);
Goals: Dureau 4/5.
ROVERS: 1 Shaun Briscoe; 21 Sam Latus; 4 Jake Webster; 3 Kris Welham; 19 Craig Hall; 12 Ben Galea; 7 Michael Dobson; 20 Michael Vella (C); 18 Josh Hodgson; 14 Liam Watts; 11 Clint Newton; 8 Rhys Lovegrove; 22 Scott Taylor. Subs (all used): 9 Ben Fisher; 13 Scott Murrell; 15 Scott Wheeldon; 27 Jordan Cox.
Tries: Lovegrove (4), Welham (7, 40), Latus (35), Hall (55); **Goals:** Dobson 5/6.
Rugby Leaguer & League Express Men of the Match: *Dragons:* Scott Dureau; *Rovers:* Michael Dobson.
Penalty count: 10-7; **Half-time:** 10-24;
Referee: James Child; **Attendance:** 8,252.

CASTLEFORD TIGERS 18 HULL FC 50

TIGERS: 23 Ryan McGoldrick; 5 Richard Owen; 17 Willie Isa; 4 Joe Arundel; 3 Nick Youngquest; 6 Rangi Chase; 7 Danny Orr (C); 21 Nathan Massey; 9 Ryan Hudson; 31 Ben Davies; 14 Stuart Jones; 20 Martin Aspinwall; 24 Oliver Holmes. Subs (all used): 1 Richard Mathers; 12 Steve Snitch; 19 Nick Fozzard; 25 Dean Widders.
Tries: Orr (19), Youngquest (49), Isa (78); **Goals:** Orr 3/3.
On report: McGoldrick (63) - alleged high tackle on Obst.
HULL: 20 Cameron Phelps; 3 Richard Whiting; 19 Jordan Turner; 4 Kirk Yeaman; 5 Tom Briscoe; 6 Richard Horne; 30 Sam Obst; 8 Mark O'Meley; 9 Danny Houghton; 23 Sam Moa; 16 Willie Manu; 11 Joe Westerman; 13 Craig Fitzgibbon (C). Subs (all used): 14 Danny Washbrook; 15 Epalahame Lauaki; 10 Lee Radford; 2 Will Sharp.
Tries: Yeaman (6), Turner (16, 54), Briscoe (36, 69), Manu (40, 65), Houghton (63), Sharp (73);
Goals: Westerman 7/9.
Rugby Leaguer & League Express Men of the Match: *Tigers:* Rangi Chase; *Hull:* Tom Briscoe.
Penalty count: 6-9; **Half-time:** 6-22;
Referee: Steve Ganson; **Attendance:** 7,866.

Sunday 4th September 2011

WARRINGTON WOLVES 39 WIGAN WARRIORS 12

WOLVES: 2 Chris Riley; 5 Joel Monaghan; 4 Chris Bridge; 23 Ryan Atkins; 3 Matt King; 6 Lee Briers; 7 Richard Myler; 8 Adrian Morley (C); 9 Michael Monaghan; 10 Garreth Carvell; 11 Louis Anderson; 17 Simon Grix; 18 Michael Cooper. Subs (all used): 13 Ben Harrison; 15 Jon Clarke; 19 Lee Mitchell; 20 Matty Blythe.
Tries: King (10), Briers (13), M Monaghan (18, 25), Clarke (60), J Monaghan (66); **Goals:** Bridge 7/7;
Field goal: M Monaghan (37).
WARRIORS: 1 Sam Tomkins; 25 Josh Charnley; 12 Joel Tomkins; 4 George Carmont; 5 Pat Richards; 6 Paul Deacon; 17 Brett Finch; 15 Jeff Lima; 7 Thomas Leuluai; 10 Andy Coley; 11 Harrison Hansen; 16 Ryan Hoffman; 13 Sean O'Loughlin (C). Subs (all used): 34 Gareth Hock; 9 Michael McIlorum; 14 Paul Prescott; 22 Liam Farrell.
Tries: Deacon (24), O'Loughlin (73); **Goals:** Richards 2/2.
On report: Hock (79) - alleged gouging on Harrison.
Rugby Leaguer & League Express Men of the Match: *Wolves:* Michael Monaghan; *Warriors:* Paul Deacon.
Penalty count: 12-9; **Half-time:** 25-6;
Referee: Richard Silverwood; **Attendance:** 13,024.

BRADFORD BULLS 48 CRUSADERS 24

BULLS: 6 Brett Kearney; 5 Patrick Ah Van; 3 Paul Sykes; 1 Michael Platt; 18 Shaun Ainscough; 33 Ben Jeffries; 32 Kyle Briggs; 10 Andy Lynch (C); 21 Danny Addy; 15 Bryn Hargreaves; 11 Olivier Elima; 17 Ian Sibbit; 13 Jamie Langley. Subs (all used): 4 Chev Walker; 16 Craig Kopczak; 27 Adam O'Brien; 29 Tom Burgess.
Tries: Elima (5, 20), Kearney (27, 78), Kopczak (43), Ainscough (48), Ah Van (55), Lynch (67);
Goals: Ah Van 8/8.
CRUSADERS: 1 Clinton Schifcofske (C); 5 Stuart Reardon; 3 Tony Martin; 4 Vince Mellars; 18 Elliott Kear; 27 Jordan Tansey; 19 Lloyd White; 15 Jordan James; 9 Lincoln Withers; 10 Mark Bryant; 11 Hep Cahill; 12 Jason Chan; 23 Peter Lupton. Subs (all used): 16 Ben Flower; 21 Paul Johnson; 24 Lee Williams; 28 Andy Bracek (D).
Tries: White (12), Reardon (23, 72), Lupton (58), Martin (80); **Goals:** Schifcofske 2/5.
Sin bin: Flower (38) - obstruction.
Rugby Leaguer & League Express Men of the Match: *Bulls:* Adam O'Brien; *Crusaders:* Tony Martin.
Penalty count: 5-6; **Half-time:** 18-10;
Referee: Robert Hicks; **Attendance:** 12,998.

HUDDERSFIELD GIANTS 50 HARLEQUINS 12

GIANTS: 1 Scott Grix; 2 Michael Lawrence; 3 Leroy Cudjoe; 29 Joe Wardle; 20 Jermaine McGillvary; 6 Kevin Brown (C); 7 Danny Brough; 8 Eorl Crabtree; 9 Luke Robinson; 10 Darrell Griffin; 4 Lee Gilmour; 12 David Fa'alogo; 37 Dale Ferguson. Subs (all used): 16 Andy Raleigh; 18 Larne Patrick; 13 David Faiumu; 19 Graeme Horne.
Tries: Cudjoe (7, 75), Wardle (25), Horne (29), McGillvary (38, 44, 72), Brough (52), Grix (80);
Goals: Brough 7/9.
HARLEQUINS: 24 Dan Sarginson; 5 Chris Melling; 3 Tony Clubb; 2 Jamie O'Callaghan; 23 Mark Calderwood; 1 Luke Dorn; 6 Luke Gale; 8 Karl Temata; 7 Chad Randall; 17 Danny Ward; 16 Mike Burnett; 13 Rob Purdham (C); 12 Chris Bailey. Subs (all used): 10 Oliver Wilkes; 15 Luke Ambler; 21 Olsi Krasniqi; 20 Ben Bolger.
Tries: Melling (34), Clubb (66); **Goals:** Gale 2/2.
Rugby Leaguer & League Express Men of the Match: *Giants:* Leroy Cudjoe; *Harlequins:* Rob Purdham.
Penalty count: 7-6; **Half-time:** 22-6;
Referee: Thierry Alibert; **Attendance:** 5,220.

ROUND 27

Friday 9th September 2011

HULL FC 12 WARRINGTON WOLVES 34

HULL: 20 Cameron Phelps; 3 Richard Whiting; 19 Jordan Turner; 4 Kirk Yeaman; 5 Tom Briscoe; 6 Richard Horne; 30 Sam Obst; 8 Mark O'Meley; 9 Danny Houghton; 23 Sam Moa; 16 Willie Manu; 11 Joe Westerman; 14 Danny Washbrook. Subs (all used): 10 Lee Radford (C); 15 Epalahame Lauaki; 17 Ewan Dowes; 2 Will Sharp.
Tries: Westerman (10, 62); **Goals:** Westerman 2/2.
WOLVES: 1 Brett Hodgson; 5 Joel Monaghan; 3 Matt King; 23 Ryan Atkins; 2 Chris Riley; 6 Lee Briers (C); 7 Richard Myler; 18 Michael Cooper; 9 Michael Monaghan; 10 Garreth Carvell; 11 Louis Anderson; 17 Simon Grix; 4 Chris Bridge. Subs (all used): 15 Jon Clarke; 13 Ben Harrison; 26 David Solomona; 20 Matty Blythe.
Tries: Atkins (6), Riley (19, 30), M Monaghan (25), Bridge (38), J Monaghan (69);
Goals: Bridge 4/5, Briers 1/1.
On report: Carvell (63) - alleged high tackle on Sharp.
Rugby Leaguer & League Express Men of the Match: *Hull:* Joe Westerman; *Wolves:* Ryan Atkins.
Penalty count: 5-4; **Half-time:** 6-28;
Referee: Steve Ganson; **Attendance:** 16,121.

WAKEFIELD TRINITY WILDCATS 26 BRADFORD BULLS 14

WILDCATS: 15 Motu Tony; 19 Dale Morton; 23 Josh Veivers; 29 Josh Griffin; 39 Ryan Tongia; 16 Jeremy Smith; 14 Tommy Lee; 31 Kyle Amor; 9 Julien Rinaldi; 25 Liam Higgins; 21 Frankie Mariano; 13 Glenn Morrison (C); 17 Paul Johnson. Subs (all used): 8 Michael Korkidas; 22 Stuart Howarth; 20 Ben Gledhill; 26 Matthew Wildie.
Tries: P Johnson (14), Tongia (23), Korkidas (39), Lee (60), Rinaldi (79); **Goals:** Veivers 3/4, Korkidas 0/1.
BULLS: 25 Shad Royston; 18 Shaun Ainscough; 3 Paul Sykes; 5 Patrick Ah Van; 19 Gareth Raynor; 33 Ben Jeffries; 32 Kyle Briggs; 10 Andy Lynch (C); 21 Danny Addy; 15 Bryn Hargreaves; 11 Olivier Elima; 31 John Bateman; 13 Jamie Langley. Subs (all used): 4 Chev Walker; 22 Steve Crossley; 27 Adam O'Brien; 29 Tom Burgess.
Tries: Briggs (30), Ainscough (32), Royston (67);
Goals: Ah Van 1/3.
Rugby Leaguer & League Express Men of the Match: *Wildcats:* Julien Rinaldi; *Bulls:* Shad Royston.
Penalty count: 7-9; **Half-time:** 16-8;
Referee: Phil Bentham; **Attendance:** 6,502.

WIGAN WARRIORS 42 CRUSADERS 10

WARRIORS: 1 Sam Tomkins; 25 Josh Charnley; 12 Joel Tomkins; 4 George Carmont; 5 Pat Richards; 6 Paul Deacon; 17 Brett Finch; 15 Jeff Lima; 7 Thomas Leuluai; 14 Paul Prescott; 11 Harrison Hansen; 16 Ryan Hoffman; 13 Sean O'Loughlin (C). Subs (all used): 23 Chris Tuson; 9 Michael McIlorum; 20 Eamon O'Carroll; 22 Liam Farrell.
Tries: Finch (4), Charnley (33, 53), Hoffman (35), Farrell (42), Richards (55), J Tomkins (64);
Goals: Richards 7/7.
CRUSADERS: 1 Clinton Schifcofske (C); 5 Stuart Reardon; 3 Tony Martin; 4 Vince Mellars; 18 Elliot Kear; 19 Lloyd White; 7 Jarrod Sammut; 22 Richard Moore; 9 Lincoln Withers; 10 Mark Bryant; 13 Frank Winterstein; 12 Jason Chan; 23 Peter Lupton. Subs (all used): 16 Ben Flower; 21 Paul Johnson; 24 Lee Williams; 28 Andy Bracek.
Tries: Lupton (22), Sammut (73);
Goals: Schifcofske 1/1, Chan 0/1.
Rugby Leaguer & League Express Men of the Match: *Warriors:* Sean O'Loughlin; *Crusaders:* Clinton Schifcofske.
Penalty count: 11-8; **Half-time:** 18-6;
Referee: Robert Hicks; **Attendance:** 19,104.

Saturday 10th September 2011

HARLEQUINS 16 ST HELENS 34

HARLEQUINS: 1 Luke Dorn; 5 Chris Melling; 2 Jamie O'Callaghan; 31 Karl Pryce; 23 Mark Calderwood; 24 Dan Sarginson; 6 Luke Gale; 17 Danny Ward; 7 Chad Randall; 8 Karl Temata; 12 Chris Bailey; 13 Rob Purdham (C); 3 Tony Clubb. Subs (all used): 14 Jason Golden; 18 Dave Williams; 9 Andy Ellis; 10 Oliver Wilkes.
Tries: Temata (15), Pryce (28), O'Callaghan (70);
Goals: Gale 2/2, Purdham 0/1.
SAINTS: 1 Paul Wellens (C); 28 Tom Makinson; 3 Michael Shenton; 17 Gary Wheeler; 24 Tom Armstrong; 25 Lee Gaskell; 20 Jonny Lomax; 10 James Graham (C); 14 Scott Moore; 15 Louie McCarthy-Scarsbrook; 12 Jon Wilkin; 18 Matty Ashurst; 16 Paul Clough. Subs (all used): 19 Andrew Dixon; 26 Carl Forster (D); 29 Scott Hale; 27 Nathan Ashe.
Tries: Armstrong (11, 57, 67), Gaskell (51), Hale (63), McCarthy-Scarsbrook (75); **Goals:** Makinson 5/6.
Rugby Leaguer & League Express Men of the Match: *Harlequins:* Jamie O'Callaghan; *Saints:* Tom Armstrong.
Penalty count: 9-11; **Half-time:** 12-4;
Referee: Tim Roby; **Attendance:** 3,546.

HULL KINGSTON ROVERS 26 CASTLEFORD TIGERS 24

ROVERS: 1 Shaun Briscoe; 21 Sam Latus; 3 Kris Welham; 4 Jake Webster; 19 Craig Hall; 6 Blake Green; 7 Michael Dobson; 20 Michael Vella (C); 18 Josh Hodgson; 22 Scott Taylor; 11 Clint Newton; 12 Ben Galea; 14 Liam Watts. Subs (all used): 8 Rhys Lovegrove; 9 Ben Fisher; 13 Scott Murrell; 27 Jordan Cox.
Tries: Dobson (22), Vella (26), Latus (40, 72), Webster (54); **Goals:** Dobson 3/6.
TIGERS: 5 Richard Owen; 4 Joe Arundel; 25 Dean Widders; 17 Willie Isa; 22 Jordan Thompson; 6 Rangi Chase; 7 Danny Orr (C); 19 Nick Fozzard; 16 Adam Milner; 21 Nathan Massey; 14 Stuart Jones; 24 Oliver Holmes; 9 Ryan Hudson. Subs (all used): 12 Steve Snitch; 26 John Davies; 27 Daryl Clark; 29 Rob Parker.
Tries: Orr (6), Owen (35), Snitch (47), Thompson (63);
Goals: Orr 4/4.
Rugby Leaguer & League Express Men of the Match: *Rovers:* Craig Hall; *Tigers:* Richard Owen.
Penalty count: 10-8; **Half-time:** 18-12;
Referee: Richard Silverwood; **Attendance:** 8,936.

Sunday 11th September 2011

HUDDERSFIELD GIANTS 24 LEEDS RHINOS 31

GIANTS: 1 Scott Grix; 20 Jermaine McGillvary; 19 Graeme Horne; 3 Leroy Cudjoe; 2 Michael Lawrence; 6 Kevin Brown (C); 7 Danny Brough; 8 Eorl Crabtree; 9 Luke Robinson; 10 Darrell Griffin; 4 Lee Gilmour; 12 David Fa'alogo; 37 Dale Ferguson. Subs (all used): 13 David Faiumu; 15 Keith Mason; 18 Larne Patrick; 36 Jamie Simpson.
Tries: Lawrence (24), Robinson (27), Patrick (40), McGillvary (79); **Goals:** Brough 4/5.
RHINOS: 1 Brent Webb; 23 Ben Jones-Bishop; 27 Zak Hardaker; 12 Carl Ablett; 5 Ryan Hall; 13 Kevin Sinfield (C); 6 Danny McGuire; 8 Kylie Leuluai; 9 Danny Buderus; 10 Jamie Peacock; 3 Brett Delaney; 11 Jamie Jones-Buchanan; 21 Chris Clarkson. Subs (all used): 7 Rob Burrow; 14 Ali Lauitiiti; 16 Ryan Bailey; 17 Ian Kirke.
Tries: Hardaker (17), Webb (20), Hall (41, 67), Jones-Buchanan (77); **Goals:** Sinfield 5/6;
Field goal: Sinfield (80).
Rugby Leaguer & League Express Men of the Match: *Giants:* Luke Robinson; *Rhinos:* Jamie Peacock.
Penalty count: 9-9; **Half-time:** 18-12;
Referee: James Child; **Attendance:** 10,428.

SALFORD CITY REDS 18 CATALAN DRAGONS 44

CITY REDS: 1 Luke Patten; 2 Jodie Broughton; 5 Ashley Gibson; 20 Sean Gleeson; 30 Danny Williams; 6 Stefan Ratchford; 7 Daniel Holdsworth (C); 8 Ray Cashmere; 14 Matty Smith; 19 Ryan Boyle; 3 Mark Henry; 15 Luke Adamson; 13 Stephen Wild. Subs (all used): 9 Wayne Godwin; 10 Lee Jewitt; 17 Iafeta Palea'aesina; 22 Adam Neal.
Tries: Williams (19, 57), Adamson (29);
Goals: Holdsworth 3/3.
Sin bin: Boyle (64) - interference.
DRAGONS: 1 Clint Greenshields; 2 Damien Blanch; 18 Darryl Millard; 4 Setaimata Sa; 19 Frederic Vaccari; 6 Thomas Bosc; 7 Scott Dureau; 8 David Ferriol; 9 Ian Henderson; 23 Lopini Paea; 11 Steve Menzies; 10 Remi Casty; 13 Gregory Mounis (C). Subs (all used): 12 Sebastien Raguin; 22 Jamal Fakir; 24 Jason Baitieri; 26 Eloi Pelissier.
Tries: Sa (13, 26), Menzies (17, 79), Paea (50), Bosc (71), Henderson (74); **Goals:** Dureau 6/6, Bosc 2/2.
Rugby Leaguer & League Express Men of the Match: *City Reds:* Danny Williams; *Dragons:* Setaimata Sa.
Penalty count: 8-10; **Half-time:** 12-18;
Referee: Ben Thaler; **Attendance:** 10,146.

PLAY-OFFS

QUALIFYING PLAY-OFFS

Friday 16th September 2011

WARRINGTON WOLVES 47 HUDDERSFIELD GIANTS 0

WOLVES: 1 Brett Hodgson; 5 Joel Monaghan; 3 Matt King; 23 Ryan Atkins; 2 Chris Riley; 6 Lee Briers; 7 Richard Myler; 8 Adrian Morley (C); 9 Michael Monaghan; 10 Garreth Carvell; 11 Louis Anderson; 17 Simon Grix; 4 Chris Bridge. Subs (all used): 15 Jon Clarke; 13 Ben Harrison; 18 Michael Cooper; 26 David Solomona.
Tries: Riley (8, 21), Bridge (12), J Monaghan (18, 46), King (31), Hodgson (52), Myler (60), Atkins (74);
Goals: Bridge 2/4, Briers 3/5; **Field goal:** Briers (38).
GIANTS: 1 Scott Grix; 20 Jermaine McGillvary; 19 Graeme Horne; 2 Michael Lawrence; 5 David Hodgson; 6 Kevin Brown (C); 7 Danny Brough; 15 Keith Mason; 13 David Faiumu; 10 Darrell Griffin; 4 Lee Gilmour; 12 David Fa'alogo; 18 Larne Patrick. Subs (all used): 8 Eorl Crabtree; 16 Andy Raleigh; 17 Danny Kirmond; 9 Luke Robinson.
Sin bin: Grix (43) - holding down.
Rugby Leaguer & League Express Men of the Match: *Wolves:* Lee Briers; *Giants:* David Faiumu.
Penalty count: 13-9; **Half-time:** 25-0;
Referee: Steve Ganson; **Attendance:** 10,006.

Sunday 18th September 2011

WIGAN WARRIORS 18 ST HELENS 26

WARRIORS: 1 Sam Tomkins; 25 Josh Charnley; 12 Joel Tomkins; 4 George Carmont; 5 Pat Richards; 6 Paul Deacon; 17 Brett Finch; 15 Jeff Lima; 7 Thomas Leuluai; 10 Andy Coley; 11 Harrison Hansen; 16 Ryan Hoffman; 13 Sean O'Loughlin (C). Subs (all used): 14 Paul Prescott; 9 Michael McIlorum; 22 Liam Farrell; 35 Ben Cross.
Tries: Richards (40), O'Loughlin (43), J Tomkins (67);
Goals: Richards 3/3.
On report: Coley (11) - alleged high tackle on Makinson.
SAINTS: 1 Paul Wellens (C); 28 Tom Makinson; 3 Michael Shenton; 5 Francis Meli; 22 Jamie Foster; 25 Lee Gaskell; 20 Jonny Lomax; 10 James Graham (C); 9 James Roby; 11 Tony Puletua; 12 Jon Wilkin; 4 Iosia Soliola; 16 Paul Clough. Subs: 19 Andrew Dixon; 14 Scott Moore; 15 Louie McCarthy-Scarsbrook; 24 Tom Armstrong (not used).
Tries: Wellens (13, 47), Lomax (18), McCarthy-Scarsbrook (58); **Goals:** Foster 5/5.
Rugby Leaguer & League Express Men of the Match: *Warriors:* Sean O'Loughlin; *Saints:* Jonny Lomax.
Penalty count: 10-6; **Half-time:** 6-14;
Referee: Phil Bentham; **Attendance:** 12,893.

ELIMINATION PLAY-OFFS

Saturday 17th September 2011

CATALAN DRAGONS 56 HULL KINGSTON ROVERS 6

DRAGONS: 1 Clint Greenshields; 2 Damien Blanch; 15 Jean-Philippe Baile; 18 Darryl Millard; 5 Cyril Stacul; 6 Thomas Bosc; 7 Scott Dureau; 8 David Ferriol; 9 Ian Henderson; 23 Lopini Paea; 11 Steve Menzies; 10 Remi Casty; 13 Gregory Mounis (C). Subs (all used): 12 Sebastien Raguin; 22 Jamal Fakir; 24 Jason Baitieri; 26 Eloi Pelissier.
Tries: Blanch (2, 18, 78), Menzies (12, 27), Millard (41), Pelissier (47), Raguin (56), Stacul (60), Greenshields (70); **Goals:** Dureau 8/11.
ROVERS: 1 Shaun Briscoe; 21 Sam Latus; 4 Jake Webster; 3 Kris Welham; 19 Craig Hall; 6 Blake Green; 7 Michael Dobson; 20 Michael Vella (C); 18 Josh Hodgson; 22 Scott Taylor; 11 Clint Newton; 12 Ben Galea; 14 Liam Watts. Subs (all used): 8 Rhys Lovegrove; 9 Ben Fisher; 13 Scott Murrell; 27 Jordan Cox.
Try: Hall (51); **Goals:** Dobson 1/1.
Rugby Leaguer & League Express Men of the Match: *Dragons:* Scott Dureau; *Rovers:* Kris Welham.
Penalty count: 5-8; **Half-time:** 22-0; **Referee:** James Child *(replaced by Robert Hicks, 28)*; **Attendance:** 8,413.

Sunday 18th September 2011

LEEDS RHINOS 42 HULL FC 10

RHINOS: 1 Brent Webb; 23 Ben Jones-Bishop; 27 Zak Hardaker; 4 Ryan Hall; 13 Kevin Sinfield (C); 6 Danny McGuire; 8 Kylie Leuluai; 9 Danny Buderus; 10 Jamie Peacock; 11 Jamie Jones-Buchanan; 20 Weller Hauraki; 21 Chris Clarkson. Subs (all used): 19 Ryan Bailey; 17 Ian Kirke; 14 Ali Lauitiiti; 7 Rob Burrow.
Tries: Jones-Buchanan (9), Jones-Bishop (33), Webb (38), Hauraki (45), Sinfield (55), McGuire (72), Bailey (78); **Goals:** Sinfield 7/8.
HULL: 21 Cameron Phelps; 3 Richard Whiting; 19 Jordan Turner; 4 Kirk Yeaman; 5 Tom Briscoe; 11 Joe Westerman; 6 Richard Horne; 8 Mark O'Meley; 9 Danny Houghton; 23 Sam Moa; 12 Danny Tickle (C); 16 Willie Manu; 10 Lee Radford. Subs (all used): 18 Danny Washbrook; 15 Epalahame Lauaki; 17 Ewan Dowes; 2 Will Sharp.
Tries: Whiting (42), Briscoe (76); **Goals:** Tickle 1/2.
Rugby Leaguer & League Express Men of the Match: *Rhinos:* Jamie Jones-Buchanan; *Hull:* Mark O'Meley.
Penalty count: 12-9; **Half-time:** 18-0;
Referee: Ben Thaler; **Attendance:** 9,075.

Warrington's Garreth Carvell driven back by Leeds's Jamie Peacock and Carl Ablett

PRELIMINARY SEMI-FINALS

Friday 23rd September 2011

HUDDERSFIELD GIANTS 28 LEEDS RHINOS 34

GIANTS: 1 Scott Grix; 20 Jermaine McGillvary; 29 Joe Wardle; 3 Leroy Cudjoe; 2 Michael Lawrence; 6 Kevin Brown (C); 7 Danny Brough; 15 Keith Mason; 9 Luke Robinson; 10 Darrell Griffin; 4 Lee Gilmour; 12 David Fa'alogo; 19 Graeme Horne. Subs (all used): 8 Eorl Crabtree; 13 David Faiumu; 18 Larne Patrick; 37 Dale Ferguson.
Tries: Grix (35, 73), Ferguson (44), Fa'alogo (70, 75); **Goals:** Brough 4/5.
RHINOS: 1 Brent Webb; 23 Ben Jones-Bishop; 3 Brett Delaney; 27 Zak Hardaker; 5 Ryan Hall; 13 Kevin Sinfield (C); 6 Danny McGuire; 8 Kylie Leuluai; 9 Danny Buderus; 10 Jamie Peacock; 11 Jamie Jones-Buchanan; 20 Weller Hauraki; 21 Chris Clarkson. Subs (all used): 7 Rob Burrow; 16 Ryan Bailey; 14 Ali Lauitiiti; 17 Ian Kirke.
Tries: Jones-Bishop (7), Hardaker (10, 24, 56), Webb (54, 58); **Goals:** Sinfield 5/6.
Rugby Leaguer & League Express Men of the Match: *Giants:* David Fa'alogo; *Rhinos:* Zak Hardaker.
Penalty count: 7-4; **Half-time:** 6-16;
Referee: Phil Bentham; **Attendance:** 7,872.

Sunday 25th September 2011

WIGAN WARRIORS 44 CATALAN DRAGONS 0

WARRIORS: 1 Sam Tomkins; 25 Josh Charnley; 12 Joel Tomkins; 4 George Carmont; 5 Pat Richards; 17 Brett Finch; 7 Thomas Leuluai; 15 Jeff Lima; 9 Michael McIlorum; 10 Andy Coley; 11 Harrison Hansen; 16 Ryan Hoffman; 13 Sean O'Loughlin (C). Subs (all used): 14 Paul Prescott; 20 Eamon O'Carroll; 22 Liam Farrell; 23 Chris Tuson.
Tries: Charnley (25), Hoffman (30), Farrell (40), Carmont (60), Finch (63), S Tomkins (66), Hansen (75); **Goals:** Richards 8/9.
DRAGONS: 1 Clint Greenshields; 2 Damien Blanch; 4 Setaimata Sa; 18 Darryl Millard; 5 Cyril Stacul; 6 Thomas Bosc; 7 Scott Dureau; 22 Jamal Fakir; 9 Ian Henderson; 23 Lopini Paea; 11 Steve Menzies; 10 Remi Casty; 13 Gregory Mounis (C). Subs (all used): 12 Sebastien Raguin; 20 Michael Simon; 24 Jason Baitieri; 26 Eloi Pelissier.
Rugby Leaguer & League Express Men of the Match: *Warriors:* Brett Finch; *Dragons:* Ian Henderson.
Penalty count: 8-6; **Half-time:** 18-0;
Referee: Steve Ganson; **Attendance:** 6,790.

QUALIFYING SEMI-FINALS

Friday 30th September 2011

WARRINGTON WOLVES 24 LEEDS RHINOS 26

WOLVES: 1 Brett Hodgson; 5 Joel Monaghan; 3 Matt King; 23 Ryan Atkins; 2 Chris Riley; 6 Lee Briers; 7 Richard Myler; 8 Adrian Morley (C); 9 Michael Monaghan; 10 Garreth Carvell; 11 Louis Anderson; 17 Simon Grix; 4 Chris Bridge. Subs (all used): 12 Ben Westwood; 15 Jon Clarke; 18 Michael Cooper; 26 David Solomona.
Tries: J Monaghan (14), Riley (34, 69), King (48); **Goals:** Bridge 4/4.

RHINOS: 1 Brent Webb; 23 Ben Jones-Bishop; 27 Zak Hardaker; 12 Carl Ablett; 5 Ryan Hall; 13 Kevin Sinfield (C); 6 Danny McGuire; 8 Kylie Leuluai; 9 Danny Buderus; 10 Jamie Peacock; 11 Jamie Jones-Buchanan; 3 Brett Delaney; 21 Chris Clarkson. Subs (all used): 7 Rob Burrow; 16 Ryan Bailey; 17 Ian Kirke; 20 Weller Hauraki.
Tries: Ablett (4), Hall (41, 58), Burrow (62);
Goals: Sinfield 5/6.
Rugby Leaguer & League Express Men of the Match: *Wolves:* Adrian Morley; *Rhinos:* Danny Buderus.
Penalty count: 5-5; **Half-time:** 12-6;
Referee: Steve Ganson; **Attendance:** 12,074.

Saturday 1st October 2011

ST HELENS 26 WIGAN WARRIORS 18

SAINTS: 1 Paul Wellens (C); 28 Tom Makinson; 3 Michael Shenton; 5 Francis Meli; 22 Jamie Foster; 25 Lee Gaskell; 20 Jonny Lomax; 10 James Graham (C); 9 James Roby; 11 Tony Puletua; 12 Jon Wilkin; 4 Iosia Soliola; 16 Paul Clough. Subs: 19 Andrew Dixon; 14 Scott Moore; 15 Louie McCarthy-Scarsbrook; 17 Gary Wheeler (not used).
Tries: Gaskell (24), Wellens (46), Foster (57), Roby (75); **Goals:** Foster 5/6.
WARRIORS: 1 Sam Tomkins; 25 Josh Charnley; 12 Joel Tomkins; 4 George Carmont; 5 Pat Richards; 17 Brett Finch; 7 Thomas Leuluai; 15 Jeff Lima; 9 Michael McIlorum; 10 Andy Coley; 11 Harrison Hansen; 16 Ryan Hoffman; 13 Sean O'Loughlin (C). Subs (all used): 14 Paul Prescott; 20 Eamon O'Carroll; 22 Liam Farrell; 23 Chris Tuson.
Tries: Charnley (8), O'Carroll (32), S Tomkins (76); **Goals:** Richards 3/4.
Rugby Leaguer & League Express Men of the Match: *Saints:* Lee Gaskell; *Warriors:* Thomas Leuluai.
Penalty count: 9-5; **Half-time:** 8-12;
Referee: Phil Bentham; **Attendance:** 9,421.

GRAND FINAL

Saturday 8th October 2011

LEEDS RHINOS 32 ST HELENS 16

RHINOS: 1 Brent Webb; 23 Ben Jones-Bishop; 27 Zak Hardaker; 12 Carl Ablett; 5 Ryan Hall; 13 Kevin Sinfield (C); 6 Danny McGuire; 8 Kylie Leuluai; 9 Danny Buderus; 10 Jamie Peacock; 11 Jamie Jones-Buchanan; 3 Brett Delaney; 21 Chris Clarkson. Subs (all used): 7 Rob Burrow; 16 Ryan Bailey; 17 Ian Kirke; 14 Ali Lauitiiti.
Tries: Burrow (34), Webb (65), Hall (70), Ablett (74), Hardaker (80); **Goals:** Sinfield 6/7.
SAINTS: 1 Paul Wellens (C); 28 Tom Makinson; 3 Michael Shenton; 5 Francis Meli; 22 Jamie Foster; 25 Lee Gaskell; 20 Jonny Lomax; 10 James Graham (C); 9 James Roby; 11 Tony Puletua; 12 Jon Wilkin; 4 Iosia Soliola; 16 Paul Clough. Subs (all used): 19 Andrew Dixon; 14 Scott Moore; 15 Louie McCarthy-Scarsbrook; 17 Gary Wheeler.
Tries: Makinson (50), Shenton (55); **Goals:** Foster 4/5.
Rugby Leaguer & League Express Men of the Match: *Rhinos:* Rob Burrow; *Saints:* Lee Gaskell.
Penalty count: 5-7; **Half-time:** 8-2;
Referee: Phil Bentham; **Attendance:** 69,107
(at Old Trafford, Manchester).

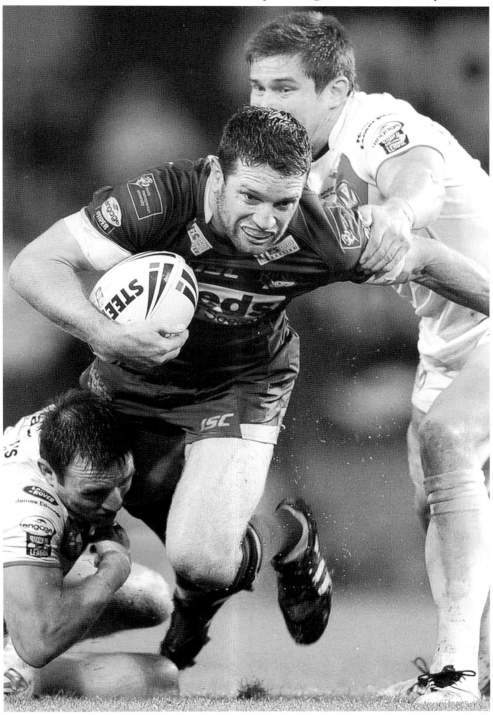

Leeds's Danny Buderus, in his final game for the Rhinos, takes on St Helens duo James Roby and Louie McCarthy-Scarsbrook during the Super League Grand Final

SUPER LEAGUE XVI
Opta Analysis

TACKLES
Danny Houghton	Hull FC	1060
James Roby	St Helens	1032
Ian Henderson	Catalan Dragons	1019
Luke Adamson	Salford	811
Craig Fitzgibbon	Hull FC	809
Andy Ellis	Harlequins	796
Sean O'Loughlin	Wigan	764
Jamie Jones-Buchanan	Leeds	757
Gregory Mounis	Catalan Dragons	740
Andy Lynch	Bradford	739

TACKLES MADE *(% success)*
Eorl Crabtree	Huddersfield	98.27
Andy Lynch	Bradford	98.27
Jordan James	Crusaders	98.14
Danny Washbrook	Hull FC	98.10
Lee Radford	Hull FC	98.01
Jamie Peacock	Leeds	97.85
Danny Houghton	Hull FC	97.79
James Graham	St Helens	97.78
Remi Casty	Catalan Dragons	97.41
Ewan Dowes	Hull FC	97.31

OFFLOADS
Chris Bailey	Harlequins	67
Clinton Schifcofske	Crusaders	59
Andy Lynch	Bradford	55
Sam Moa	Hull FC	52
David Faiumu	Huddersfield	49
Ray Cashmere	Salford	47
Steve Menzies	Catalan Dragons	46
David Ferriol	Catalan Dragons	45
Michael Monaghan	Warrington	45
Garreth Carvell	Warrington	43

CLEAN BREAKS
Sam Tomkins	Wigan	41
Pat Richards	Wigan	25
Tom Briscoe	Hull FC	24
Jamie Foster	St Helens	23
Ryan Hall	Leeds	23
Brett Hodgson	Warrington	22
Jermaine McGillvary	Huddersfield	21
Kirk Yeaman	Hull FC	21
Damien Blanch	Catalan Dragons	20
Chris Bridge	Warrington	20

TRY ASSISTS
Rangi Chase	Castleford	27
Daniel Holdsworth	Salford	26
Brett Hodgson	Warrington	24
Michael Dobson	Hull KR	22
Blake Green	Hull KR	22
Kevin Sinfield	Leeds	22
Scott Dureau	Catalan Dragons	20
Lee Briers	Warrington	19
Luke Patten	Salford	19
Sam Tomkins	Wigan	18

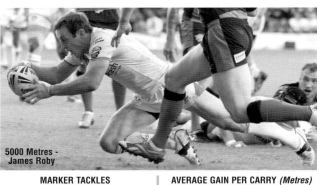

5000 Metres - James Roby

MARKER TACKLES
Danny Houghton	Hull FC	189
Ian Henderson	Catalan Dragons	160
Craig Fitzgibbon	Hull FC	154
Andy Ellis	Harlequins	145
James Roby	St Helens	138
Olivier Elima	Bradford	130
Liam Farrell	Wigan	130
Jon Wilkin	St Helens	124
Paul Wood	Warrington	122
Luke Adamson	Salford	121

METRES
James Roby	St Helens	5000
Sam Tomkins	Wigan	3996
James Graham	St Helens	3936
Andy Lynch	Bradford	3285
Jermaine McGillvary	Huddersfield	3175
Clinton Schifcofske	Crusaders	3167
Tom Briscoe	Hull FC	3154
Ryan Hall	Leeds	3062
Jodie Broughton	Salford	2948
Jamie O'Callaghan	Harlequins	2928

CARRIES
James Roby	St Helens	948
Rangi Chase	Castleford	625
James Graham	St Helens	559
Sam Tomkins	Wigan	518
Andy Lynch	Bradford	499
Daniel Holdsworth	Salford	497
Kevin Sinfield	Leeds	481
Luke Patten	Salford	463
Clinton Schifcofske	Crusaders	463
Ian Henderson	Catalan Dragons	444

*All statistics in Opta Analysis include
Super League regular season games only*

AVERAGE GAIN PER CARRY *(Metres)*
Tom Briscoe	Hull FC	9.83
Daryl Clark	Castleford	9.34
Luke George	Wakefield	9.27
Jermaine McGillvary	Huddersfield	9.20
Nick Youngquest	Castleford	8.95
Damien Blanch	Catalan Dragons	8.92
Tom Burgess	Bradford	8.88
Pat Richards	Wigan	8.87
George Carmont	Wigan	8.68
Ryan Atkins	Warrington	8.66

TACKLE BUSTS
Sam Tomkins	Wigan	169
Rangi Chase	Castleford	102
Willie Manu	Hull FC	91
Jonny Lomax	St Helens	83
Tom Briscoe	Hull FC	81
Scott Grix	Huddersfield	77
Rob Burrow	Leeds	71
James Roby	St Helens	71
Ryan Hall	Leeds	70
Luke Patten	Salford	70

40/20s
Scott Dureau	Catalan Dragons	5
Rangi Chase	Castleford	3
Michael Dobson	Hull KR	3
Blake Green	Hull KR	3
Daniel Holdsworth	Salford	3
Matty Smith	Salford	3

PENALTIES CONCEDED
Gregory Mounis	Catalan Dragons	29
Michael Witt	Crusaders	29
Jamie Jones-Buchanan	Leeds	28
Ian Henderson	Catalan Dragons	27
Richard Moore	Crusaders	27
Sean O'Loughlin	Wigan	26
Ben Westwood	Warrington	26
Chris Bailey	Harlequins	25
Jason Chan	Crusaders	24
David Ferriol	Catalan Dragons	24

Warrington's Paul Wood holds off Harlequins duo Luke Ambler and Chris Melling to score. The Wolves scored 189 tries in 2011, the most in Super League XVI

SUPER LEAGUE XVI AVERAGES PER MATCH

TACKLES		OFFLOADS		METRES		ERRORS	
Salford City Reds	328.0	Warrington Wolves	15.9	St Helens	1457.1	Catalan Dragons	15.2
Harlequins	321.9	Hull FC	15.1	Warrington Wolves	1430.5	Warrington Wolves	15.1
Wigan Warriors	321.6	Catalan Dragons	14.1	Wigan Warriors	1403.5	Leeds Rhinos	14.7
Huddersfield Giants	313.9	Crusaders	14.1	Hull FC	1355.8	Bradford Bulls	14.5
Hull Kingston Rovers	310.8	Leeds Rhinos	12.9	Leeds Rhinos	1349.3	Hull FC	14.0
Wakefield T Wildcats	309.7	Salford City Reds	12.7	Catalan Dragons	1315.4	Huddersfield Giants	13.5
Bradford Bulls	306.9	Bradford Bulls	10.8	Huddersfield Giants	1312.9	Harlequins	13.4
St Helens	303.8	St Helens	10.0	Castleford Tigers	1263.4	St Helens	13.0
Leeds Rhinos	299.7	Wigan Warriors	9.9	Hull Kingston Rovers	1247.6	Wigan Warriors	12.7
Hull FC	298.7	Harlequins	9.2	Harlequins	1234.4	Salford City Reds	12.0
Castleford Tigers	297.6	Huddersfield Giants	9.1	Bradford Bulls	1233.0	Hull Kingston Rovers	11.6
Crusaders	295.6	Wakefield T Wildcats	8.2	Crusaders	1221.0	Crusaders	11.5
Catalan Dragons	292.2	Hull Kingston Rovers	7.7	Salford City Reds	1203.4	Wakefield T Wildcats	11.3
Warrington Wolves	276.7	Castleford Tigers	7.4	Wakefield T Wildcats	1118.9	Castleford Tigers	11.1

MISSED TACKLES		CLEAN BREAKS		CARRIES		KICKS IN GENERAL PLAY	
Wakefield T Wildcats	29.1	Warrington Wolves	7.2	St Helens	227.9	Wakefield T Wildcats	20.6
Bradford Bulls	27.0	Wigan Warriors	6.6	Wigan Warriors	217.0	Huddersfield Giants	19.9
Salford City Reds	26.0	Hull FC	6.0	Hull FC	211.2	Salford City Reds	19.9
Crusaders	25.9	Catalan Dragons	5.9	Leeds Rhinos	210.3	St Helens	19.3
Castleford Tigers	24.7	St Helens	5.9	Warrington Wolves	204.6	Hull Kingston Rovers	19.2
Hull Kingston Rovers	24.3	Leeds Rhinos	5.8	Salford City Reds	204.3	Wigan Warriors	19.2
Harlequins	24.1	Huddersfield Giants	5.7	Catalan Dragons	202.0	Crusaders	18.8
Catalan Dragons	22.6	Hull Kingston Rovers	5.0	Huddersfield Giants	200.2	Castleford Tigers	18.6
St Helens	20.8	Castleford Tigers	4.4	Castleford Tigers	197.5	Hull FC	18.3
Warrington Wolves	19.9	Crusaders	4.3	Bradford Bulls	197.0	Bradford Bulls	18.0
Leeds Rhinos	19.7	Salford City Reds	3.9	Hull Kingston Rovers	194.4	Harlequins	17.7
Huddersfield Giants	17.9	Bradford Bulls	3.4	Harlequins	192.1	Leeds Rhinos	16.3
Hull FC	16.7	Wakefield T Wildcats	3.4	Crusaders	189.7	Warrington Wolves	16.2
Wigan Warriors	16.2	Harlequins	3.2	Wakefield T Wildcats	184.7	Catalan Dragons	15.9

SUPER LEAGUE XVI TRIES SCORED/CONCEDED

TOTAL TRIES SCORED		TOTAL TRIES CONCEDED		SCORED FROM KICKS		CONCEDED FROM KICKS	
Warrington Wolves	189	Wakefield T Wildcats	173	Wigan Warriors	23	Crusaders	19
Wigan Warriors	150	Harlequins	166	Bradford Bulls	21	Hull Kingston Rovers	18
St Helens	135	Bradford Bulls	151	Huddersfield Giants	20	Castleford Tigers	17
Leeds Rhinos	130	Crusaders	149	Warrington Wolves	19	Hull FC	17
Hull FC	128	Castleford Tigers	147	Leeds Rhinos	18	Leeds Rhinos	16
Hull Kingston Rovers	127	Salford City Reds	139	Hull Kingston Rovers	16	St Helens	16
Huddersfield Giants	123	Hull Kingston Rovers	124	Salford City Reds	14	Salford City Reds	15
Catalan Dragons	122	Catalan Dragons	107	Crusaders	12	Wigan Warriors	15
Castleford Tigers	116	Leeds Rhinos	103	Wakefield T Wildcats	12	Harlequins	13
Salford City Reds	100	Hull FC	100	Catalan Dragons	11	Warrington Wolves	13
Bradford Bulls	97	Huddersfield Giants	89	Castleford Tigers	10	Wakefield T Wildcats	12
Crusaders	94	St Helens	89	Hull FC	10	Bradford Bulls	11
Harlequins	91	Wigan Warriors	75	St Helens	9	Huddersfield Giants	11
Wakefield T Wildcats	80	Warrington Wolves	70	Harlequins	6	Catalan Dragons	8

Super League XVI - Opta Analysis

SUPER LEAGUE XVI TRIES SCORED/CONCEDED

TRIES SCORED FROM OWN HALF
Warrington Wolves	33
Catalan Dragons	24
Leeds Rhinos	21
St Helens	19
Wigan Warriors	18
Crusaders	17
Huddersfield Giants	17
Castleford Tigers	14
Hull Kingston Rovers	14
Wakefield T Wildcats	13
Hull FC	12
Bradford Bulls	10
Harlequins	10
Salford City Reds	10

TRIES CONCEDED FROM OVER 50M
Wakefield T Wildcats	30
Harlequins	27
Castleford Tigers	25
Bradford Bulls	24
Catalan Dragons	24
Salford City Reds	17
Crusaders	16
Hull Kingston Rovers	15
Hull FC	14
Warrington Wolves	12
Huddersfield Giants	8
Leeds Rhinos	8
Wigan Warriors	8
St Helens	4

TRIES SCORED FROM UNDER 10M
Warrington Wolves	82
St Helens	68
Wigan Warriors	68
Castleford Tigers	64
Leeds Rhinos	63
Hull FC	62
Catalan Dragons	57
Harlequins	57
Bradford Bulls	52
Huddersfield Giants	52
Salford City Reds	52
Hull Kingston Rovers	49
Crusaders	45
Wakefield T Wildcats	41

TRIES CONCEDED FROM UNDER 10M
Harlequins	84
Wakefield T Wildcats	80
Salford City Reds	79
Crusaders	72
Castleford Tigers	67
Hull Kingston Rovers	62
Bradford Bulls	61
Leeds Rhinos	60
St Helens	47
Huddersfield Giants	46
Hull FC	44
Catalan Dragons	41
Wigan Warriors	37
Warrington Wolves	32

SUPER LEAGUE XVI PENALTIES

TOTAL PENALTIES AWARDED
Bradford Bulls	236
Warrington Wolves	229
Wakefield T Wildcats	226
Catalan Dragons	217
Castleford Tigers	214
Huddersfield Giants	213
Hull FC	209
St Helens	203
Hull Kingston Rovers	202
Leeds Rhinos	199
Harlequins	198
Wigan Warriors	193
Crusaders	176
Salford City Reds	174

TOTAL PENALTIES CONCEDED
Crusaders	253
Wakefield T Wildcats	241
Catalan Dragons	235
Leeds Rhinos	229
Bradford Bulls	226
Salford City Reds	212
Castleford Tigers	206
Huddersfield Giants	204
Wigan Warriors	199
Warrington Wolves	197
Harlequins	174
Hull Kingston Rovers	174
Hull FC	172
St Helens	167

FOUL PLAY - AWARDED
Wakefield T Wildcats	57
Catalan Dragons	50
St Helens	46
Castleford Tigers	44
Harlequins	42
Hull FC	41
Hull Kingston Rovers	40
Leeds Rhinos	38
Huddersfield Giants	34
Warrington Wolves	31
Bradford Bulls	30
Wigan Warriors	30
Crusaders	29
Salford City Reds	28

FOUL PLAY - CONCEDED
Castleford Tigers	52
Crusaders	51
Salford City Reds	47
Catalan Dragons	45
Wakefield T Wildcats	42
Warrington Wolves	40
Hull FC	36
Huddersfield Giants	35
St Helens	35
Bradford Bulls	33
Harlequins	33
Leeds Rhinos	33
Hull Kingston Rovers	30
Wigan Warriors	28

OFFSIDE - AWARDED
Bradford Bulls	29
Huddersfield Giants	28
Castleford Tigers	24
Leeds Rhinos	23
Harlequins	22
Hull Kingston Rovers	22
Hull FC	21
Wigan Warriors	21
Salford City Reds	20
Wakefield T Wildcats	19
Warrington Wolves	19
Crusaders	17
St Helens	12
Catalan Dragons	8

OFFSIDE - CONCEDED
Salford City Reds	30
Catalan Dragons	27
Crusaders	26
Wakefield T Wildcats	25
Leeds Rhinos	24
Bradford Bulls	22
Huddersfield Giants	19
Castleford Tigers	18
St Helens	18
Warrington Wolves	18
Wigan Warriors	17
Harlequins	16
Hull Kingston Rovers	14
Hull FC	11

INTERFERENCE - AWARDED
Warrington Wolves	95
Bradford Bulls	85
Catalan Dragons	83
Huddersfield Giants	81
Wakefield T Wildcats	78
Harlequins	75
Leeds Rhinos	75
Wigan Warriors	71
St Helens	70
Hull FC	69
Castleford Tigers	68
Hull Kingston Rovers	65
Crusaders	61
Salford City Reds	52

INTERFERENCE - CONCEDED
Crusaders	88
Bradford Bulls	84
Leeds Rhinos	80
Catalan Dragons	79
Castleford Tigers	77
Huddersfield Giants	77
Wakefield T Wildcats	74
Wigan Warriors	74
Salford City Reds	73
Hull Kingston Rovers	70
Harlequins	68
Hull FC	64
Warrington Wolves	64
St Helens	56

OBSTRUCTION - AWARDED
Castleford Tigers	19
Hull Kingston Rovers	16
Crusaders	15
St Helens	15
Bradford Bulls	12
Salford City Reds	12
Wakefield T Wildcats	11
Warrington Wolves	11
Hull FC	10
Leeds Rhinos	10
Catalan Dragons	9
Harlequins	9
Huddersfield Giants	9
Wigan Warriors	7

OBSTRUCTION - CONCEDED
Huddersfield Giants	19
Hull FC	16
Salford City Reds	15
Catalan Dragons	14
Warrington Wolves	14
Wigan Warriors	13
Wakefield T Wildcats	11
Crusaders	10
Leeds Rhinos	10
Bradford Bulls	9
Harlequins	9
St Helens	9
Hull Kingston Rovers	8
Castleford Tigers	7

BALL STEALING - AWARDED
Bradford Bulls	26
Hull Kingston Rovers	18
Castleford Tigers	16
Wigan Warriors	16
Crusaders	15
Hull FC	15
Salford City Reds	15
Huddersfield Giants	14
Warrington Wolves	14
Catalan Dragons	13
Leeds Rhinos	12
St Helens	12
Wakefield T Wildcats	11
Harlequins	10

BALL STEALING - CONCEDED
Leeds Rhinos	25
Wakefield T Wildcats	23
Warrington Wolves	21
Catalan Dragons	19
Crusaders	18
Hull Kingston Rovers	15
Wigan Warriors	15
Bradford Bulls	13
Harlequins	12
Huddersfield Giants	10
St Helens	10
Castleford Tigers	9
Hull FC	9
Salford City Reds	8

OFFSIDE MARKERS - AWARDED
Bradford Bulls	30
Warrington Wolves	28
Wigan Warriors	27
Catalan Dragons	24
Huddersfield Giants	24
Wakefield T Wildcats	19
Crusaders	18
Hull FC	18
Leeds Rhinos	18
St Helens	18
Castleford Tigers	17
Hull Kingston Rovers	17
Harlequins	14
Salford City Reds	13

OFFSIDE MARKERS - CONCEDED
Wakefield T Wildcats	31
Bradford Bulls	25
Wigan Warriors	24
Castleford Tigers	23
Crusaders	23
Huddersfield Giants	22
Leeds Rhinos	22
Catalan Dragons	21
Warrington Wolves	18
Harlequins	17
Hull Kingston Rovers	17
St Helens	16
Hull FC	13
Salford City Reds	13

NOT PLAYING BALL CORRECTLY - AWARDED
Harlequins	4
Wakefield T Wildcats	4
Bradford Bulls	3
Catalan Dragons	3
Huddersfield Giants	2
Hull FC	2
Leeds Rhinos	2
Castleford Tigers	1
Hull Kingston Rovers	1
Salford City Reds	1
St Helens	1
Warrington Wolves	1
Crusaders	0
Wigan Warriors	0

NOT PLAYING BALL CORRECTLY - CONCEDED
Catalan Dragons	4
Crusaders	3
Leeds Rhinos	3
St Helens	3
Wakefield T Wildcats	3
Bradford Bulls	1
Castleford Tigers	1
Harlequins	1
Hull FC	1
Hull Kingston Rovers	1
Salford City Reds	1
Warrington Wolves	1
Wigan Warriors	1
Huddersfield Giants	0

DISSENT - AWARDED
(including advances)
St Helens	9
Hull FC	8
Catalan Dragons	7
Salford City Reds	7
Warrington Wolves	7
Harlequins	5
Huddersfield Giants	4
Leeds Rhinos	4
Castleford Tigers	3
Hull Kingston Rovers	3
Wakefield T Wildcats	3
Wigan Warriors	3
Bradford Bulls	2
Crusaders	1

DISSENT - CONCEDED
(including advances)
Leeds Rhinos	10
Wakefield T Wildcats	8
Harlequins	7
Crusaders	6
Catalan Dragons	5
Huddersfield Giants	5
St Helens	5
Bradford Bulls	4
Hull Kingston Rovers	4
Wigan Warriors	4
Salford City Reds	3
Castleford Tigers	2
Hull FC	2
Warrington Wolves	2

BRADFORD BULLS

Andy Lynch

Olivier Elima

MARKER TACKLES
Olivier Elima 130
Andy Lynch 102
Elliott Whitehead 99
Matt Diskin 89
Bryn Hargreaves 77

METRES
Andy Lynch 3285
Patrick Ah Van 2565
Brett Kearney 2312
Craig Kopczak 2170
Gareth Raynor 1701

CARRIES
Andy Lynch 499
Brett Kearney 379
Matt Diskin 338
Craig Kopczak 316
Patrick Ah Van 303

TACKLE BUSTS
Patrick Ah Van 47
Brett Kearney 43
Gareth Raynor 41
Andy Lynch 41
Shaun Ainscough 38

TACKLES
Andy Lynch 739
Olivier Elima 723
Elliott Whitehead 626
Matt Diskin 623
Craig Kopczak 584

CLEAN BREAKS
Elliott Whitehead 10
Ben Jeffries 9
Brett Kearney 9
Shad Royston 9
Patrick Ah Van 7

TOTAL FRONTLINE INDEX
Andy Lynch 14276
Olivier Elima 10518
Craig Kopczak 9494
Brett Kearney 8972
Marc Herbert 8511

OFFLOADS
Andy Lynch 55
Gareth Raynor 29
Olivier Elima 26
Michael Platt 24
Elliott Whitehead 24

TRY ASSISTS
Marc Herbert 18
Brett Kearney 9
Ben Jeffries 7
Heath L'Estrange 6
Danny Addy 4

CASTLEFORD TIGERS

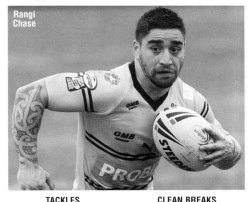

Rangi Chase

Danny Orr

MARKER TACKLES
Joe Arundel 94
Paul Jackson 87
Stuart Jones 85
Oliver Holmes 84
Adam Milner 76

METRES
Rangi Chase 2898
Richard Mathers 2331
Jake Emmitt..................2318
Richard Owen 2176
Brett Ferres 1962

CARRIES
Rangi Chase 625
Richard Mathers 373
Danny Orr 362
Jake Emmitt..................330
Kirk Dixon 281

TACKLE BUSTS
Rangi Chase 102
Richard Mathers 60
Daryl Clark......................36
Richard Owen 32
Kirk Dixon 30

TACKLES
Stuart Jones 590
Brett Ferres 532
Adam Milner 521
Joe Arundel 511
Oliver Holmes 510

CLEAN BREAKS
Nick Youngquest 15
Rangi Chase 14
Richard Owen 13
Joe Arundel 9
Danny Orr 9

TOTAL FRONTLINE INDEX
Rangi Chase 15083
Danny Orr 9465
Joe Arundel 8966
Brett Ferres 8372
Richard Mathers 8237

OFFLOADS
Rangi Chase 37
Craig Huby......................23
Ryan Hudson..................18
Brett Ferres 17
Richard Mathers 13

TRY ASSISTS
Rangi Chase 27
Richard Mathers 13
Ryan McGoldrick 8
Danny Orr 8
Martin Aspinwall 3

CATALAN DRAGONS

Jason Baitieri

Ian Henderson

TACKLES
Ian Henderson 1019
Gregory Mounis.............740
Jason Baitieri.................689
Sebastien Raguin...........620
Remi Casty 526

OFFLOADS
Steve Menzies 46
David Ferriol 45
Setaimata Sa 34
Jason Baitieri 30
Damien Blanch 23

CLEAN BREAKS
Damien Blanch 20
Steve Menzies 15
Jean-Philippe Baile 13
Darryl Millard..................12
Clint Greenshields 11

TRY ASSISTS
Scott Dureau 20
Setaimata Sa 13
Clint Greenshields 12
Darryl Millard...................9
Steve Menzies 6

METRES
Damien Blanch 2925
Jason Baitieri...............2348
Ian Henderson 2213
Clint Greenshields 2091
Jean-Philippe Baile 1866

TACKLE BUSTS
Clint Greenshields 43
Jean-Philippe Baile 38
Ian Henderson 36
Lopini Paea 34
Cyril Stacul 34

MARKER TACKLES
Ian Henderson 160
Gregory Mounis.............118
Jason Baitieri.................104
Remi Casty 74
Sebastien Raguin.............69

CARRIES
Ian Henderson 444
Jason Baitieri.................356
Damien Blanch 328
Setaimata Sa 307
Clint Greenshields 295

TOTAL FRONTLINE INDEX
Ian Henderson 13899
Jason Baitieri..............11322
Sebastien Raguin..........9312
Gregory Mounis.............9253
Steve Menzies 9194

CRUSADERS

Michael Witt

Jason Chan

TACKLES
Jason Chan 664
Lincoln Withers 647
Ryan O'Hara 614
Ben Flower.....................574
Mark Bryant...................501

OFFLOADS
Clinton Schifcofske 59
Michael Witt 38
Jason Chan 33
Richard Moore.................33
Mark Bryant....................27

CLEAN BREAKS
Tony Martin 17
Jarrod Sammut 10
Stuart Reardon 9
Jordan Tansey 9
Lloyd White 9

TRY ASSISTS
Michael Witt 17
Tony Martin 8
Jarrod Sammut 4
Jordan Tansey 4
Lincoln Withers 4

METRES
Clinton Schifcofske 3167
Ryan O'Hara 2262
Jason Chan 2195
Vince Mellars...............1906
Mark Bryant.................1827

TACKLE BUSTS
Jason Chan 70
Tony Martin 40
Clinton Schifcofske 39
Stuart Reardon 37
Vince Mellars...................36

MARKER TACKLES
Ben Flower.....................106
Jason Chan 104
Lincoln Withers 97
Ryan O'Hara 80
Mark Bryant.....................74

CARRIES
Clinton Schifcofske 463
Lincoln Withers 394
Ryan O'Hara 343
Jason Chan 314
Mark Bryant...................291

TOTAL FRONTLINE INDEX
Jason Chan 11130
Michael Witt 9783
Clinton Schifcofske 9247
Lincoln Withers 9063
Ryan O'Hara 8848

HARLEQUINS

Luke
Gale

Chris
Bailey

MARKER TACKLES
Andy Ellis	145
Chad Randall	108
Oliver Wilkes	90
Rob Purdham	88
Chris Bailey	81

METRES
Jamie O'Callaghan	2928
Tony Clubb	2433
Chris Bailey	2316
Chris Melling	2206
Luke Dorn	2103

CARRIES
Chris Bailey	401
Jamie O'Callaghan	378
Tony Clubb	361
Chad Randall	350
Luke Gale	344

TACKLES
Andy Ellis	796
Chris Bailey	693
Chad Randall	647
Oliver Wilkes	587
Danny Ward	581

CLEAN BREAKS
Luke Dorn	10
Chris Melling	9
Dan Sarginson	9
Karl Pryce	8
Jamie O'Callaghan	6

TACKLE BUSTS
Tony Clubb	55
Jamie O'Callaghan	52
Karl Pryce	46
Luke Dorn	36
Luke Gale	31

OFFLOADS
Chris Bailey	67
Tony Clubb	20
Luke Gale	15
Rob Purdham	15
Andy Ellis	13

TRY ASSISTS
Luke Gale	15
Luke Dorn	9
Chad Randall	7
Rob Purdham	4
Danny Ward	4

TOTAL FRONTLINE INDEX
Luke Gale	10724
Chris Bailey	10315
Tony Clubb	10292
Chad Randall	10242
Andy Ellis	10027

HUDDERSFIELD GIANTS

Scott
Grix

MARKER TACKLES
Eorl Crabtree	87
Lee Gilmour	87
David Faiumu	82
Luke Robinson	75
Michael Lawrence	65

METRES
Jermaine McGillvary	3175
Scott Grix	2438
Eorl Crabtree	2357
David Faiumu	1980
Leroy Cudjoe	1911

CARRIES
Luke Robinson	389
Scott Grix	378
Kevin Brown	363
Jermaine McGillvary	345
Eorl Crabtree	337

TACKLES
Lee Gilmour	649
Eorl Crabtree	624
Luke Robinson	574
Michael Lawrence	524
Leroy Cudjoe	485

CLEAN BREAKS
Jermaine McGillvary	21
Scott Grix	17
David Hodgson	13
Danny Brough	12
Kevin Brown	12

TACKLE BUSTS
Scott Grix	77
Eorl Crabtree	68
Jermaine McGillvary	63
Kevin Brown	50
Leroy Cudjoe	45

OFFLOADS
David Faiumu	49
Eorl Crabtree	20
Kevin Brown	19
Scott Grix	18
Leroy Cudjoe	17

TRY ASSISTS
Luke Robinson	15
Kevin Brown	14
Scott Grix	13
Danny Brough	11
Leroy Cudjoe	9

TOTAL FRONTLINE INDEX
Scott Grix	12122
Eorl Crabtree	11690
Danny Brough	11264
Jermaine McGillvary	10877
Leroy Cudjoe	10466

Eorl
Crabtree

HULL F.C.

Willie Manu

Danny Houghton

TACKLES
Danny Houghton	1060
Craig Fitzgibbon	809
Danny Tickle	691
Joe Westerman	649
Mark O'Meley	528

OFFLOADS
Sam Moa	52
Willie Manu	43
Tom Briscoe	40
Mark O'Meley	27
Richard Whiting	24

CLEAN BREAKS
Tom Briscoe	24
Kirk Yeaman	21
Joe Westerman	14
Richard Horne	13
Willie Manu	13

TRY ASSISTS
Richard Horne	17
Willie Manu	13
Sam Obst	9
Joe Westerman	8
Kirk Yeaman	7

MARKER TACKLES
Danny Houghton	189
Craig Fitzgibbon	154
Joe Westerman	118
Danny Tickle	93
Mark O'Meley	87

METRES
Tom Briscoe	3154
Mark O'Meley	2463
Kirk Yeaman	2391
Danny Houghton	2386
Willie Manu	2315

CARRIES
Danny Houghton	438
Mark O'Meley	374
Willie Manu	348
Danny Tickle	348
Richard Horne	334

TACKLE BUSTS
Willie Manu	91
Tom Briscoe	81
Kirk Yeaman	61
Joe Westerman	55
Richard Horne	47

TOTAL FRONTLINE INDEX
Danny Houghton	14599
Willie Manu	12043
Joe Westerman	11578
Craig Fitzgibbon	11476
Danny Tickle	10998

HULL KINGSTON ROVERS

Blake Green

Ben Galea

TACKLES
Ben Galea	718
Josh Hodgson	652
Scott Murrell	652
Ben Fisher	620
Rhys Lovegrove	519

OFFLOADS
Clint Newton	34
Blake Green	15
Craig Hall	15
Michael Vella	15
Josh Hodgson	13

CLEAN BREAKS
Kris Welham	18
Jake Webster	14
Ben Galea	13
Blake Green	12
Sam Latus	10

TRY ASSISTS
Michael Dobson	22
Blake Green	22
Jake Webster	8
Kris Welham	7
Craig Hall	6

MARKER TACKLES
Ben Fisher	117
Ben Galea	108
Josh Hodgson	108
Rhys Lovegrove	98
Scott Murrell	95

METRES
Kris Welham	2645
Ben Galea	2397
Jake Webster	2016
Michael Vella	1960
Shaun Briscoe	1801

CARRIES
Ben Galea	431
Kris Welham	341
Blake Green	334
Michael Dobson	303
Michael Vella	277

TACKLE BUSTS
Kris Welham	60
Ben Galea	46
Jake Webster	46
Blake Green	34
Ben Cockayne	30

TOTAL FRONTLINE INDEX
Ben Galea	13084
Blake Green	12651
Kris Welham	11620
Scott Murrell	9104
Josh Hodgson	8785

LEEDS RHINOS

Kevin Sinfield

Jamie Jones-Buchanan

MARKER TACKLES
Jamie Jones-Buchanan	113
Danny Buderus	85
Brett Delaney	84
Chris Clarkson	82
Weller Hauraki	78

METRES
Ryan Hall	3062
Brent Webb	2378
Jamie Jones-Buchanan	2316
Carl Ablett	2054
Rob Burrow	1989

CARRIES
Kevin Sinfield	481
Rob Burrow	377
Ryan Hall	374
Brent Webb	366
Jamie Jones-Buchanan	362

TACKLES
Jamie Jones-Buchanan	757
Danny Buderus	663
Kevin Sinfield	525
Carl Ablett	524
Chris Clarkson	499

CLEAN BREAKS
Ryan Hall	23
Carl Ablett	14
Danny McGuire	13
Jamie Jones-Buchanan	12
Brent Webb	11

TACKLE BUSTS
Rob Burrow	71
Ryan Hall	70
Brent Webb	45
Kallum Watkins	38
Danny Buderus	31

OFFLOADS
Kevin Sinfield	37
Ali Lauitiiti	35
Jamie Jones-Buchanan	30
Weller Hauraki	27
Carl Ablett	24

TRY ASSISTS
Kevin Sinfield	22
Brent Webb	18
Danny McGuire	12
Carl Ablett	10
Kallum Watkins	5

TOTAL FRONTLINE INDEX
Kevin Sinfield	13527
Jamie Jones-Buchanan	12798
Ryan Hall	11403
Carl Ablett	9611
Brent Webb	9453

SALFORD CITY REDS

Daniel Holdsworth

Luke Patten

MARKER TACKLES
Luke Adamson	121
Ray Cashmere	105
Stephen Wild	100
Daniel Holdsworth	89
Chris Nero	87

METRES
Jodie Broughton	2948
Ray Cashmere	2680
Luke Patten	2438
Mark Henry	2139
Ryan Boyle	2110

CARRIES
Daniel Holdsworth	497
Luke Patten	463
Ray Cashmere	388
Jodie Broughton	354
Mark Henry	351

TACKLES
Luke Adamson	811
Matty Smith	728
Ray Cashmere	675
Stephen Wild	666
Daniel Holdsworth	619

CLEAN BREAKS
Jodie Broughton	15
Stefan Ratchford	12
Mark Henry	11
Luke Patten	10
Danny Williams	9

TACKLE BUSTS
Luke Patten	70
Mark Henry	53
Stefan Ratchford	52
Jodie Broughton	47
Luke Adamson	32

OFFLOADS
Ray Cashmere	47
Vinnie Anderson	38
Luke Patten	33
Adam Sidlow	33
Stephen Wild	29

TRY ASSISTS
Daniel Holdsworth	26
Luke Patten	19
Stefan Ratchford	11
Sean Gleeson	6
Matty Smith	4

TOTAL FRONTLINE INDEX
Daniel Holdsworth	13621
Luke Patten	11837
Luke Adamson	11444
Matty Smith	10781
Ray Cashmere	10408

ST HELENS

James Roby

TACKLES
James Roby	1032
Jon Wilkin	685
Louie McCarthy-Scarsbrook	675
James Graham	660
Michael Shenton	618

OFFLOADS
James Roby	40
James Graham	23
Francis Meli	22
Tony Puletua	20
Jon Wilkin	19

CLEAN BREAKS
Jamie Foster	23
Jonny Lomax	15
James Roby	14
Jon Wilkin	11
Francis Meli	10

TRY ASSISTS
James Roby	18
Francis Meli	14
Jonny Lomax	11
Lee Gaskell	10
Paul Wellens	9

MARKER TACKLES
James Roby	138
Jon Wilkin	124
Louie McCarthy-Scarsbrook	105
James Graham	95
Michael Shenton	92

METRES
James Roby	5000
James Graham	3936
Louie McCarthy-Scarsbrook	2672
Tony Puletua	2376
Jonny Lomax	2230

CARRIES
James Roby	948
James Graham	559
Jonny Lomax	433
Paul Wellens	373
Louie McCarthy-Scarsbrook	348

TACKLE BUSTS
Jonny Lomax	83
James Roby	71
Jon Wilkin	59
Paul Wellens	45
Francis Meli	43

TOTAL FRONTLINE INDEX
James Roby	20239
James Graham	13954
Jon Wilkin	12600
Jonny Lomax	11766
Louie McCarthy-Scarsbrook	10808

James Graham

WAKEFIELD T WILDCATS

Paul Johnson

TACKLES
Paul Johnson	691
Julien Rinaldi	636
Frankie Mariano	635
Glenn Morrison	588
Kyle Amor	552

OFFLOADS
Kevin Henderson	24
Glenn Morrison	22
Kyle Amor	20
Paul King	14
Julien Rinaldi	13

CLEAN BREAKS
Chris Dean	9
Luke George	6
Frankie Mariano	6
Julien Rinaldi	6
Greg Johnson	5

TRY ASSISTS
Tommy Lee	9
Julien Rinaldi	6
Jeremy Smith	5
Stuart Howarth	4
Greg Johnson	2

MARKER TACKLES
Julien Rinaldi	106
Paul Johnson	93
Glenn Morrison	93
Stuart Howarth	84
Frankie Mariano	68

METRES
Paul Johnson	2568
Kyle Amor	2439
Josh Griffin	1871
Glenn Morrison	1861
Michael Korkidas	1745

CARRIES
Paul Johnson	433
Kyle Amor	353
Julien Rinaldi	313
Glenn Morrison	308
Tommy Lee	285

TACKLE BUSTS
Frankie Mariano	37
Glenn Morrison	27
Josh Griffin	26
Luke George	25
Tommy Lee	25

TOTAL FRONTLINE INDEX
Paul Johnson	11062
Tommy Lee	9748
Glenn Morrison	8769
Kyle Amor	8521
Julien Rinaldi	8052

Tommy Lee

WARRINGTON WOLVES

Brett
Hodgson

Michael
Monaghan

MARKER TACKLES
Paul Wood	122
Ben Harrison	109
Michael Monaghan	109
Garreth Carvell	103
Ben Westwood	103

METRES
Brett Hodgson	2643
Paul Wood	2631
Michael Monaghan	2459
Garreth Carvell	2378
Ben Westwood	2319

CARRIES
Michael Monaghan	436
Brett Hodgson	379
Paul Wood	372
Ben Westwood	332
Garreth Carvell	316

TACKLES
Michael Monaghan	649
Paul Wood	618
Garreth Carvell	602
Ben Westwood	581
Ben Harrison	530

CLEAN BREAKS
Brett Hodgson	22
Ryan Atkins	20
Chris Bridge	20
Matt King	19
Richard Myler	16

TACKLE BUSTS
Ryan Atkins	61
Brett Hodgson	59
Chris Bridge	57
Michael Monaghan	48
Ben Westwood	45

OFFLOADS
Michael Monaghan	45
Garreth Carvell	43
Paul Wood	43
David Solomona	36
Matty Blythe	32

TRY ASSISTS
Brett Hodgson	24
Lee Briers	19
Chris Bridge	14
Michael Monaghan	13
Ryan Atkins	12

TOTAL FRONTLINE INDEX
Brett Hodgson	12512
Michael Monaghan	11535
Ryan Atkins	10508
Chris Bridge	10239
Paul Wood	10158

WIGAN WARRIORS

Sam
Tomkins

Thomas
Leuluai

MARKER TACKLES
Liam Farrell	130
Sean O'Loughlin	115
Lee Mossop	114
Jeff Lima	92
Harrison Hansen	90

METRES
Sam Tomkins	3996
Pat Richards	2733
Josh Charnley	2722
Jeff Lima	2599
Ryan Hoffman	2415

CARRIES
Sam Tomkins	518
Thomas Leuluai	399
Michael McIlorum	359
Jeff Lima	357
Ryan Hoffman	355

TACKLES
Sean O'Loughlin	764
Michael McIlorum	699
Liam Farrell	654
Ryan Hoffman	645
Lee Mossop	620

CLEAN BREAKS
Sam Tomkins	41
Pat Richards	25
Josh Charnley	17
George Carmont	16
Ryan Hoffman	13

TACKLE BUSTS
Sam Tomkins	169
Josh Charnley	59
George Carmont	48
Thomas Leuluai	43
Joel Tomkins	41

OFFLOADS
George Carmont	32
Ryan Hoffman	30
Joel Tomkins	29
Brett Finch	28
Gareth Hock	21

TRY ASSISTS
Sam Tomkins	18
Brett Finch	15
George Carmont	11
Joel Tomkins	11
Paul Deacon	10

TOTAL FRONTLINE INDEX
Sam Tomkins	19869
Thomas Leuluai	11462
Ryan Hoffman	11201
Sean O'Loughlin	11081
George Carmont	10446

CHAMPIONSHIP 2011
Club by Club

BARROW RAIDERS

DATE	FIXTURE	RESULT	SCORERS	LGE	ATT
6/2/11	York (h) (NRC)	W24-20	t:Gleeson,Nixon(2),Catic,Ostler g:Rooney(2)	4th(P1)	1,305
13/2/11	Rochdale (a) (NRC)	W18-30	t:Harrison(3),Ballard,James,Nixon g:Rooney(3)	3rd(P1)	600
20/2/11	Featherstone (h) (NRC)	L22-28	t:Nixon,Rooney,Fletcher,Harrison g:Rooney(3)	4th(P1)	1,852
27/2/11	Dewsbury (a) (NRC)	L16-12	t:Catic,Ostler g:Rooney(2)	5th(P1)	911
5/3/11	Leigh Miners Rangers (a) (CCR3)	W26-56	t:Rooney,Mossop,Harrison,Nixon(2),Coyle,James,Fletcher(2),Ballard,Thackray g:Rooney(2),Ballard(2),Fletcher(2)	N/A	633
19/3/11	Leigh (h)	L32-36	t:Catic,Gleeson,Knowles,Nixon,Harrison,Rooney g:Rooney(4)	10th	1,799
27/3/11	York (a)	W16-42	t:Fletcher,Broadbent,Ballard(2),Harrison,Larkin,Luisi,Rooney g:Rooney(5)	6th	1,064
2/4/11	Batley (h)	L22-30	t:Rooney,Catic,Knowles,Coyle g:Rooney,Ballard(2)	7th	1,741
14/4/11	Featherstone (a)	L48-12	t:Ballard,Wardle g:Rooney(2)	8th	1,755
22/4/11	Leigh (a)	L26-24	t:Ballard(2),Harrison,Catic,Larkin g:Rooney(2)	8th	2,583
25/4/11	Widnes (h)	W30-12	t:Catic,Ballard(2),Harrison,Larkin g:Rooney(5)	7th	1,965
1/5/11	Halifax (a)	W25-43	t:Catic,Larkin(2),Knowles,Ballard,Hughes,Rooney g:Rooney(7) fg:Rooney	6th	1,757
8/5/11	Wigan (a) (CCR4)	L52-0		N/A	8,026
14/5/11	York (h)	W34-12	t:Thackray,Campbell,James,McNally,Catic,Ballard(2) g:Rooney(3)	4th	1,271
21/5/11	Dewsbury (h)	W18-14	t:Backhouse,Ballard,Larkin g:Rooney(3)	4th	1,339
26/5/11	Widnes (a)	L42-14	t:Ballard(2) g:Rooney(3)	6th	3,331
4/6/11	Toulouse (h)	W30-18	t:Ostler,Knowles(3),Larkin g:McNally(5)	5th	1,245
12/6/11	Batley (a)	L10-6	t:Blackwood g:Rooney	5th	888
23/6/11	Featherstone (h)	L28-36	t:McNally(2),Broadbent,Ballard(2) g:Rooney(4)	6th	1,832
30/6/11	Sheffield (a)	L30-26	t:Hughes,Rooney,Knowles,Broadbent g:Rooney(5)	6th	1,054
9/7/11	Halifax (h)	L16-24	t:Luisi,Harrison,Catic g:Rooney(2)	6th	1,640
23/7/11	Hunslet (h)	W26-25	t:Larkin,Knowles,Hughes,Backhouse,Thackray g:Rooney(3)	6th	1,150
31/7/11	Dewsbury (a)	L40-34	t:James(2),Larkin,Knowles,Rooney,Luisi g:Rooney(5)	7th	862
13/8/11	Sheffield (h)	W36-26	t:Blackwood,Luisi,Knowles,Ballard(2),Larkin,Finch g:Rooney(4)	7th	1,179
21/8/11	Hunslet (h)	L42-12	t:Gleeson,Broadbent g:Knowles(2)	7th	501
3/9/11	Toulouse (a)	W28-42	t:Ballard(3),Harrison(2),Larkin,Blackwood,Gleeson g:Rooney(4),Broadbent	7th	602

On 29th July, deducted six league points (a further six suspended until end of 2012) after being found guilty of breaching salary cap and operational rules during 2010
On 7th October, deducted 29 league points for breaching RFL operational rules over four-year period from 2007

		APP		TRIES		GOALS		FG		PTS	
	D.O.B.	ALL	Ch	ALL	Ch	ALL	Ch	ALL	Ch	ALL	Ch
Mike Backhouse	14/6/82	5(4)	4(4)	2	2	0	0	0	0	8	8
Andy Ballard	10/5/86	24(1)	18(1)	22	20	4	2	0	0	96	84
Anthony Blackwood	13/9/82	9	9	3	3	0	0	0	0	12	12
Gary Broadbent	31/10/76	19	17	4	4	1	1	0	0	18	18
Jamie Butler	29/8/80	13(7)	12(6)	0	0	0	0	0	0	0	0
Liam Campbell	5/6/86	11(5)	8(4)	1	1	0	0	0	0	4	4
Ned Catic	2/8/78	16	10	9	7	0	0	0	0	36	28
James Coyle	28/12/85	7	6	2	1	0	0	0	0	8	4
Ben Davies	2/11/89	2(8)	2(8)	0	0	0	0	0	0	0	0
Marc Dixon	6/3/85	5(6)	3(4)	0	0	0	0	0	0	0	0
Liam Finch	19/3/85	3(1)	3(1)	1	1	0	0	0	0	4	4
Richard Fletcher	17/5/81	3(7)	1(4)	4	1	2	0	0	0	20	4
Mark Gleeson	16/6/82	12(12)	11(8)	4	3	0	0	0	0	16	12
Liam Harrison	3/12/82	26	20	12	7	0	0	0	0	48	28
Jack Hughes	4/1/92	6(2)	6(2)	3	3	0	0	0	0	12	12
Matt James	26/3/87	16(8)	14(4)	5	3	0	0	0	0	20	12
Michael Knowles	2/5/87	20(6)	16(4)	10	10	2	2	0	0	44	44
Chris Larkin	20/6/86	20	17	11	11	0	0	0	0	44	44
Zebastian Luisi	22/12/84	22(3)	17(2)	4	4	0	0	0	0	16	16
Brett McDermott	10/9/78	1(1)	0	0	0	0	0	0	0	0	0
Gregg McNally	2/1/91	8	5	3	3	5	5	0	0	22	22
Nathan Mossop	21/2/88	16(6)	11(5)	1	0	0	0	0	0	4	0
Adam Nicholson	22/9/89	(1)	0	0	0	0	0	0	0	0	0
James Nixon	10/8/85	8(1)	4(1)	7	1	0	0	0	0	28	4
Martin Ostler	21/6/80	13(6)	8(5)	3	1	0	0	0	0	12	4
Jamie Rooney	17/3/80	24(1)	18(1)	8	6	75	63	1	1	183	151
Jamie Thackray	30/9/79	14(7)	9(6)	3	2	0	0	0	0	12	8
Adam Walker	20/2/91	9(7)	7(7)	0	0	0	0	0	0	0	0
Jonny Walker	26/3/88	3	3	0	0	0	0	0	0	0	0
Joe Wardle	22/9/91	3	1	1	1	0	0	0	0	4	4

Andy Ballard

LEAGUE RECORD
P20-W9-D0-L11-BP8
F527, A540, Diff-13
0 points. *(All points deducted for salary cap & operational rules breaches)*
(11th, Championship)

CHALLENGE CUP
Round Four

NORTHERN RAIL CUP
5th, Pool 1

ATTENDANCES
Best - v Widnes (Ch - 1,965)
Worst - v Hunslet (Ch - 1,150)
Total (excluding Challenge Cup) - 18,318
Average (excluding Challenge Cup) - 1,527
(Down by 263 on 2010)

CLUB RECORDS MATCH RECORDS	**Highest score:** 138-0 v Nottingham City, 27/11/94 **Highest score against:** 0-90 v Leeds, 11/2/90 **Record attendance:** 21,651 v Salford, 15/4/38 **Tries:** 6 Val Cumberbatch v Batley, 21/11/36; Jim Thornburrow v Maryport, 19/2/38; Steve Rowan v Nottingham City, 15/11/92 **Goals:** 17 Darren Carter v Nottingham City, 27/11/94 **Points:** 42 Darren Carter v Nottingham City, 27/11/94
SEASON RECORDS CAREER RECORDS	**Tries:** 50 Jim Lewthwaite 1956-57 **Goals:** 135 Joe Ball 1956-57 **Points:** 323 Jamie Rooney 2010 **Tries:** 352 Jim Lewthwaite 1943-57 **Goals:** 741 Willie Horne 1943-59 **Points:** 1,818 Willie Horne 1943-59 **Appearances:** 500 Jim Lewthwaite 1943-57

BATLEY BULLDOGS

DATE	FIXTURE	RESULT	SCORERS	LGE	ATT
6/2/11	Leigh (h) (NRC)	L4-24	t:Brown	10th(P2)	1,073
13/2/11	Hunslet (a) (NRC)	W8-12	t:Moore,Handforth g:Moore(2)	6th(P2)	666
20/2/11	Gateshead (h) (NRC)	W60-6	t:Daley Williams(3),Handforth(2),Moore,Lythe(2),Bretherton,Darren Williams g:Moore(7),Handforth(3)	4th(P2)	612
27/2/11	Halifax (a) (NRC)	W25-26	t:Hesketh,Reittie,Manning,Moore g:Handforth(4),Moore	2nd(P2)	1,968
6/3/11	Fryston (h) (CCR3)	W64-10	t:Maun,Brown(2),Darren Williams(2),Campbell,Moore(3),Walton(2),Manning g:Moore(8)	N/A	774
13/3/11	Dewsbury (h)	W28-0	t:Daley Williams,Lindsay,Handforth,Preece,Walton g:Moore(4)	1st	1,402
20/3/11	Featherstone (a)	L36-6	t:Moore g:Moore	6th	1,786
27/3/11	Hunslet (h)	W38-12	t:Bretherton,Potter,Campbell,Handforth(2),Mennell,Robinson g:Handforth(5)	2nd	940
2/4/11	Barrow (a)	W22-30	t:Lythe,Bretherton,Toohey,Mennell,Brown g:Handforth(5)	3rd	1,741
10/4/11	Dewsbury (a) (NRCQF)	L38-22	t:Handforth,Hesketh,Bretherton,Smith g:Handforth(3)	N/A	1,643
17/4/11	Widnes (h)	W32-12	t:Reittie(2),Preece,Flanagan,Bretherton,Lindsay g:Handforth(2),Flanagan(2)	3rd	1,101
21/4/11	Dewsbury (a)	W20-36	t:Tootill,Walton,Manning,Maun,Brown,Flanagan g:Flanagan(4),Handforth(2)	2nd	1,184
25/4/11	Sheffield (h)	L16-28	t:Daley Williams,Flanagan,Campbell g:Flanagan(2)	2nd	843
1/5/11	Leigh (a)	L36-12	t:Reittie,Daley Williams g:Handforth(2)	3rd	2,285
8/5/11	Huddersfield (h) (CCR4)	L18-28	t:Manning,Walton,Brown g:Handforth(3)	N/A	2,676
19/5/11	York (h)	W50-16	t:Bretherton,Reittie(2),Brown(3),Maun,Hesketh,Preece,Robinson g:Handforth(5)	3rd	806
28/5/11	Toulouse (a)	W18-28	t:Walton(2),Preece(2),Lythe g:Handforth(3),Mennell	3rd	1,855
5/6/11	Hunslet (a)	W12-34	t:Reittie,Robinson,Smith,Hesketh(2),Bretherton g:Handforth(5)	3rd	801
12/6/11	Barrow (h)	W10-6	t:Brown g:Handforth(3)	2nd	888
26/6/11	Halifax (a)	W28-36	t:Bretherton(2),Lindsay,Brown,Campbell,Maun g:Handforth(6)	2nd	2,483
1/7/11	York (a)	L18-10	t:Bretherton,Flanagan g:Handforth	3rd	1,098
7/7/11	Leigh (h)	L16-40	t:Toohey,Brown,Darren Williams g:Handforth(2)	3rd	1,533
21/7/11	Featherstone (h)	L18-24	t:Flanagan,Robinson,Manning g:Handforth(3)	4th	1,539
31/7/11	Widnes (a)	L24-22	t:Mennell,Daley Williams,Campbell,Hesketh g:Handforth(3)	4th	3,873
7/8/11	Halifax (h)	W18-16	t:Manning(2),Campbell g:Handforth(3)	4th	1,131
13/8/11	Toulouse (h)	W32-10	t:Handforth,Bretherton,Toohey(2),Walton,Daley Williams g:Handforth(4)	3rd	801
21/8/11	Sheffield (a)	L28-26	t:Manning,Preece,Lindsay,Buttery,Flanagan g:Handforth(3)	3rd	1,174
8/9/11	Halifax (h) (EPO)	L22-32	t:Preece(2),Daley Williams,Manning g:Handforth(2),Mennell	N/A	1,179

		APP		TRIES		GOALS		FG		PTS	
	D.O.B.	ALL	Ch	ALL	Ch	ALL	Ch	ALL	Ch	ALL	Ch
Alex Bretherton	5/12/82	27	20	11	9	0	0	0	0	44	36
Alex Brown	28/8/87	17(2)	13(1)	12	8	0	0	0	0	48	32
Chris Buttery	23/12/85	1(13)	1(12)	1	1	0	0	0	0	4	4
Johnny Campbell	17/7/87	19(1)	16	6	5	0	0	0	0	24	20
George Flanagan	8/10/86	(14)	(13)	6	6	8	8	0	0	40	40
Paul Handforth	6/10/81	27	21	8	4	72	59	0	0	176	134
Sean Hesketh	17/8/86	8(16)	5(15)	6	4	0	0	0	0	24	16
Elliot Hodgson	2/11/90	(1)	(1)	0	0	0	0	0	0	0	0
Ashley Lindsay	31/7/83	22(2)	18(1)	4	4	0	0	0	0	16	16
Kris Lythe	29/3/83	26	19	4	2	0	0	0	0	16	8
Dane Manning	15/4/89	26(1)	21	9	6	0	0	0	0	36	24
James Martin	11/11/87	2(4)	(2)	0	0	0	0	0	0	0	0
Danny Maun	5/1/81	25	19	4	3	0	0	0	0	16	12
Paul Mennell	26/10/86	18(2)	13	3	3	2	2	0	0	16	16
Gareth Moore	3/6/89	5(2)	2	7	1	23	5	0	0	74	14
Craig Potter	17/12/80	18(6)	15(2)	1	1	0	0	0	0	4	4
Ian Preece	13/6/85	25(1)	19	8	8	0	0	0	0	32	32
Wayne Reittie	21/1/88	26	20	7	6	0	0	0	0	28	24
Adam Robinson	8/4/87	(15)	(13)	4	4	0	0	0	0	16	16
Byron Smith	5/3/84	28	21	2	1	0	0	0	0	8	4
Mark Toohey	16/6/82	10(10)	6(8)	4	4	0	0	0	0	16	16
David Tootill	22/5/86	(15)	(10)	1	1	0	0	0	0	4	4
Jason Walton	13/6/90	14(7)	10(6)	8	5	0	0	0	0	32	20
Daley Williams	15/5/86	17	13	9	6	0	0	0	0	36	24
Darren Williams	28/6/89	3	1	4	1	0	0	0	0	16	4

Paul Handforth

LEAGUE RECORD
P20-W12-D0-L8-BP5
(3rd, Championship/
Elimination Play-Off)
F498, A406, Diff+92
41 points.

CHALLENGE CUP
Round Four

NORTHERN RAIL CUP
Quarter Finalists/3rd, Pool 2

ATTENDANCES
Best - v Huddersfield (CC - 2,676)
Worst - v Gateshead (NRC - 612)
Total (excluding Challenge Cup) - 13,848
Average (excluding
Challenge Cup) - 1,065
(Up by 73 on 2010)

CLUB RECORDS
MATCH RECORDS
Highest score: 100-4 v Gateshead, 17/3/2010 Highest score against: 9-78 v Wakefield, 26/8/67 Record attendance: 23,989 v Leeds, 14/3/25
Tries: 5 Joe Oakland v Bramley, 19/12/1908; Tommy Brannan v Swinton, 17/1/20; Jim Wale v Bramley, 4/12/26; Jim Wale v Cottingham, 12/2/27;
Tommy Oldroyd v Highfield, 6/3/94; Ben Feehan v Halifax, 10/8/2008; Jermaine McGillvary v Whitehaven, 24/5/2009
Goals: 16 Gareth Moore v Gateshead, 17/3/2010 Points: 40 Gareth Moore v Gateshead, 17/3/2010
SEASON RECORDS Tries: 30 Johnny Campbell 2010 Goals: 144 Barry Eaton 2004 Points: 308 Richard Price 1997
CAREER RECORDS Tries: 142 Craig Lingard 1998-2008 Goals: 463 Wharton 'Wattie' Davies 1897-1912 Points: 1,297 Wharton 'Wattie' Davies 1897-1912
Appearances: 421 Wharton 'Wattie' Davies 1897-1912

DEWSBURY RAMS

DATE	FIXTURE	RESULT	SCORERS	LGE	ATT
5/2/11	Toulouse (a) (NRC)	L40-38	t:Buchanan(2),Craven(2),Turner,Menzies,Lockwood g:P Walker,Brambani(4)	6th(P1)	1,000
13/2/11	Keighley (h) (NRC)	W14-0	t:Tonks,Hirst g:Brambani(3)	4th(P1)	758
20/2/11	Doncaster (a) (NRC)	W18-30	t:England,Turner,Brambani,Blake,Tonks g:Brambani(5)	3rd(P1)	555
27/2/11	Barrow (h) (NRC)	W16-12	t:England g:Brambani(6)	3rd(P1)	911
6/3/11	South Wales (a) (CCR3)	W6-62	t:Spicer,Buchanan(2),England,Cosgrove,Horton,Turner,Hirst,Brambani(2),Menzies g:Brambani(9)	N/A	356
13/3/11	Batley (a)	L28-0		11th	1,402
19/3/11	Toulouse (h)	W35-6	t:Buchanan,Wainwright(3),Wandless g:Brambani(7) fg:Brambani	5th	928
31/3/11	Hunslet (h)	W4-22	t:Lockwood,Buchanan(2),Faal g:Brambani(3)	6th	1,190
10/4/11	Batley (h) (NRCQF)	W38-22	t:Lockwood(2),Faal(2),Blake g:Brambani(9)	N/A	1,643
17/4/11	Sheffield (h)	L12-36	t:Buchanan,Brambani g:Brambani(2)	7th	1,010
21/4/11	Batley (h)	L20-36	t:Cosgrove,Brambani,Spicer g:Brambani(4)	7th	1,184
25/4/11	Halifax (a)	L56-24	t:Cosgrove,Turner,Tonks,Horton g:Brambani(3),P Walker	9th	1,745
1/5/11	York (a)	L30-26	t:Menzies,Buchanan,Wainwright,Spicer,Faal g:Brambani(3)	9th	1,098
8/5/11	Swinton (h) (CCR4)	L38-44	t:P Walker,Brambani(2),Buchanan(2),Spicer g:Brambani(7)	N/A	692
15/5/11	Widnes (h)	D34-34	t:Faal,Turner,Buchanan,Cosgrove,Brambani,Buchanan g:Brambani(5)	8th	1,087
21/5/11	Barrow (a)	L18-14	t:Buchanan(2),Brambani g:Brambani	8th	1,339
29/5/11	Featherstone (h)	L18-38	t:Faal,Brambani,Cosgrove g:Brambani(2),P Walker	9th	1,167
3/6/11	Sheffield (a) ●	L40-12	t:Spicer,Glynn g:Brambani(2)	9th	683
12/6/11	Leigh (h)	L34-6	t:England g:Brambani	9th	1,942
19/6/11	Leigh (a) (NRCSF)	L44-10	t:Lockwood,Brambani g:Brambani	N/A	2,234
26/6/11	York (h)	L28-30	t:Turner(3),P Walker,Smith g:Brambani(3),P Walker	10th	974
3/7/11	Halifax (a)	L16-30	t:Faal,Craven g:P Walker(4)	10th	1,102
10/7/11	Widnes (a)	L36-22	t:Buchanan,Chapman(2),Brambani g:Brambani(3)	11th	4,030
31/7/11	Barrow (h)	W40-34	t:Wainwright(2),Blake,Nicholson,Lockwood,Spicer,Faal g:P Walker(6)	9th	862
6/8/11	Toulouse (a)	L16-8	t:Blake g:P Walker(2)	9th	800
14/8/11	Hunslet (h)	W30-18	t:Wainwright,P Walker,Faal,Welham g:P Walker(7)	8th	1,066
21/8/11	Featherstone (a)	L54-24	t:Craven,P Walker,Blake,Wainwright g:P Walker(4)	10th	1,782
1/9/11	Leigh (h)	L22-40	t:Faal,Wainwright,Nicholson,Buchanan g:P Walker(3)	10th	933

● Played at Mount St Marys, Spinkhill

		D.O.B.	APP		TRIES		GOALS		FG		PTS	
			ALL	Ch	ALL	Ch	ALL	Ch	ALL	Ch	ALL	Ch
Mark Barlow		16/2/84	2(1)	2(1)	0	0	0	0	0	0	0	0
William Barthau		30/1/90	5(1)	5(1)	0	0	0	0	0	0	0	0
Kyle Bibb		25/1/88	4(3)	3(2)	0	0	0	0	0	0	0	0
Luke Blake		10/8/89	25	18	5	3	0	0	0	0	20	12
Ben Bolger		13/9/89	1(3)	1(2)	0	0	0	0	0	0	0	0
Dominic Brambani		10/5/85	28	20	12	6	83	39	1	1	215	103
Matty Brooks		9/10/86	(2)	0	0	0	0	0	0	0	0	0
Brooke Broughton		30/10/90	(2)	(1)	0	0	0	0	0	0	0	0
Austin Buchanan		22/5/84	27	19	16	10	0	0	0	0	64	40
Richard Chapman		5/9/75	(3)	(3)	2	2	0	0	0	0	8	8
Elliott Cosgrove		31/3/91	18(4)	13(2)	5	4	0	0	0	0	20	16
James Craven		14/10/88	15	10	4	2	0	0	0	0	16	8
Steve Crossley		28/11/89	5	5	0	0	0	0	0	0	0	0
Shaun Emblem		18/3/83	(10)	(5)	0	0	0	0	0	0	0	0
Anthony England		19/10/86	19(6)	14(5)	4	1	0	0	0	0	16	4
Ayden Faal		12/12/86	22(2)	16(2)	10	8	0	0	0	0	40	32
Richard Fletcher		17/5/81	8(2)	7(2)	0	0	0	0	0	0	0	0
Scott Glassell		14/8/88	2(1)	2(1)	0	0	0	0	0	0	0	0
Ryan Glynn		3/9/87	4	3	1	1	0	0	0	0	4	4
Adam Hayes		30/11/81	(2)	0	0	0	0	0	0	0	0	0
Keegan Hirst		13/12/88	21(1)	13(1)	2	0	0	0	0	0	8	0
Elliot Hodgson		2/11/90	5(1)	5(1)	1	1	0	0	0	0	4	4
Jonny Horton		7/11/87	1(9)	(6)	2	1	0	0	0	0	8	4
James Lockwood		21/3/86	24(3)	16(3)	6	2	0	0	0	0	24	8
Luke Menzies		29/6/88	2(23)	1(16)	3	1	0	0	0	0	12	4
Matt Nicholson		11/9/91	(4)	(4)	2	2	0	0	0	0	8	8
Rob Roberts		21/6/78	1	0	0	0	0	0	0	0	0	0
Matthew Sarsfield		10/9/91	3(1)	2(1)	0	0	0	0	0	0	0	0
Andy Smith		6/7/84	6(8)	5(8)	1	1	0	0	0	0	4	4
Rob Spicer		22/9/84	23	16	6	4	0	0	0	0	24	16
Jordan Tansey		9/9/86	3(1)	1	0	0	0	0	0	0	0	0
Matthew Tebb		4/9/90	(3)	(2)	0	0	0	0	0	0	0	0
Josh Tonks		14/8/91	18(3)	12(2)	3	1	0	0	0	0	12	4
Scott Turner		15/4/88	21	14	8	5	0	0	0	0	32	20
Michael Wainwright		4/11/80	26	18	9	9	0	0	0	0	36	36
James Walker		15/4/77	(5)	(3)	0	0	0	0	0	0	0	0
Pat Walker		24/3/86	15(1)	12(1)	4	3	30	29	0	0	76	70
Tom Wall		3/12/88	(1)	0	0	0	0	0	0	0	0	0
Tom Wandless		27/12/86	7	4	1	1	0	0	0	0	4	4
Liam Welham		11/11/88	2(1)	2(1)	1	1	0	0	0	0	4	4
Aston Wilson		23/10/90	1(1)	1(1)	0	0	0	0	0	0	0	0
Jake Wilson		25/3/89	(4)	(3)	0	0	0	0	0	0	0	0

Dominic Brambani

LEAGUE RECORD
P20-W4-D1-L15-BP4
(9th, Championship)
F413, A618, Diff-205
18 points.

CHALLENGE CUP
Round Four

NORTHERN RAIL CUP
Semi-Finalists/3rd, Pool 1

ATTENDANCES
Best - v Batley (NRCQF - 1,643)
Worst - v Swinton (CC - 692)
Total (excluding Challenge Cup) - 13,625
Average (excluding Challenge Cup) - 1,048
(Down by 97 on 2010)

CLUB RECORDS
MATCH RECORDS
Highest score: 90-5 v Blackpool, 4/4/93 Highest score against: 0-82 v Widnes, 30/11/86 Record attendance: 26,584 v Halifax, 30/10/20
Tries: 8 Dai Thomas v Liverpool, 13/4/1907
Goals: 13 Greg Pearce v Blackpool Borough, 4/4/93; Francis Maloney v Hunslet, 25/3/2007 Points: 32 Les Holliday v Barrow, 11/9/94
SEASON RECORDS Tries: 40 Dai Thomas 1906-07 Goals: 169 Barry Eaton 2000 Points: 394 Barry Eaton 2000
CAREER RECORDS Tries: 144 Joe Lyman 1913-31 Goals: 863 Nigel Stephenson 1967-78; 1984-86 Points: 2,082 Nigel Stephenson 1967-78; 1984-86
Appearances: 454 Joe Lyman 1913-31

FEATHERSTONE ROVERS

DATE	FIXTURE	RESULT	SCORERS	LGE	ATT
4/2/11	Doncaster (h) (NRC)	W54-10	t:Kain(2),Tonks,Smeaton(3),Finn,Hardman,Saxton,Bostock,Hardaker g:Finn(5)	2nd(P1)	1,223
13/2/11	York (a) (NRC)	W22-32	t:Morrison,Dale,Saxton,Hardaker,Bostock,Finn g:Finn(4)	2nd(P1)	1,387
20/2/11	Barrow (a) (NRC)	W22-28	t:Tonks,Welham,Hardaker(2),Saxton g:Finn(4)	2nd(P1)	1,852
26/2/11	Widnes (h) (NRC)	L16-22	t:Dickens,Hardaker,Smeaton g:Finn(2)	2nd(P1)	1,719
5/3/11	The Army (h) (CCR3)	W86-0	t:Hardman(3),Worthington,Welham(4),Carr(2),Finn,Powell,Johnson(2),Bostock, Mvududu g:Finn(11)	N/A	723
10/3/11	Leigh (a)	L36-10	t:Hardaker,Powell g:Finn	9th	1,940
20/3/11	Batley (h)	W36-6	t:Finn(2),Dickens,Powell,Bostock,Saxton g:Finn(6)	4th	1,786
24/3/11	Halifax (h)	W20-32	t:Tonks,Dickens,Powell,Bostock(2),Kain g:Finn(4)	3rd	2,638
2/4/11	Toulouse (a)	W18-56	t:Finn(2),Bostock,Saxton(2),Smeaton,Hardman,Grayshon,Kain(2) g:Finn(8)	2nd	1,500
8/4/11	Hunslet (a) (NRCQF)	W12-50	t:Tonks(2),Powell,Kain,Grayshon(3),Dickens,Smeaton g:Finn(7)	N/A	877
14/4/11	Barrow (h)	W48-12	t:Bostock(3),Smeaton(2),Powell(2),Kain,Dickens,Grayshon g:Finn(4)	1st	1,755
25/4/11	Leigh (h)	D28-28	t:Powell(2),Hardman,Grayshon,Bostock g:Finn(4)	4th	2,375
1/5/11	Hunslet (a)	W12-48	t:Saxton,Dale,Hepworth(2),Divorty,Hemingway,Chappell,Finn,Kain g:Finn(6)	2nd	905
7/5/11	Lezignan (h) (CCR4)	W42-16	t:Hepworth,Chappell,Powell,Smeaton(2),Kain,Divorty,Saxton g:Finn(5)	N/A	827
15/5/11	Halifax (h)	W30-18	t:Bostock,Hepworth(2),Worthington,Dale,Powell g:Finn(3)	2nd	1,377
22/5/11	St Helens (a) (CCR5)	L70-0		N/A	2,905
29/5/11	Dewsbury (a)	W18-38	t:Bostock,Dickens,Spears,Haley,Netherton,Dale,Divorty g:Finn(5)	2nd	1,167
5/6/11	York (h)	W44-24	t:Grayshon,Powell(2),Finn(2),Kain,Bostock,Smeaton,Hepworth g:Finn(4)	2nd	1,287
16/6/11	Halifax (h) (NRCSF)	L30-31		N/A	1,987
		(aet)			
23/6/11	Barrow (a)	W28-36	t:Worthington(3),Smeaton,Hepworth,Powell,Finn g:Finn(4)	3rd	1,832
3/7/11	Toulouse (h)	W90-10	t:Dickens,Kain(3),Smeaton,Saxton(3),Kaye(2),Finn,Hepworth,Powell(2), Grayshon,Hardman(2) g:Finn(11)	1st	1,307
10/7/11	Hunslet (h)	W54-22	t:Grayshon,Hepworth(3),Dale(2),Netherton,Powell,Kain g:Finn(9)	1st	1,271
21/7/11	Batley (a)	W18-24	t:Grayshon,Netherton,Kain,Saxton g:Finn(4)	1st	1,539
28/7/11	Sheffield (h)	W34-6	t:Powell(3),Hepworth,Netherton,Cockayne,Dale,Finn g:Finn	1st	1,527
5/8/11	York (a)	W16-44	t:Cockayne,Hepworth,Saxton,Hardman(2),Bostock,Worthington(2) g:Finn(6)	1st	1,193
17/8/11	Widnes (h)	W56-16	t:Smeaton(2),Saxton(2),Cockayne(2),Powell(3),Dickens,Hepworth g:Finn(6)	1st	2,021
21/8/11	Dewsbury (h)	W54-24	t:Cockayne(2),Dale(2),Grayshon,Divorty,Hepworth,Tonks(2),Hardman g:Finn(7)	1st	1,782
28/8/11	Sheffield (a)	W12-34	t:Saxton,Cockayne,Worthington,Kain(2),Hardman g:Finn(5)	1st	1,336
4/9/11	Widnes (a)	W4-44	t:Cockayne(2),Saxton(2),Hardman(2),Tonks,Finn g:Finn(6)	1st	5,021
15/9/11	Leigh (h) (QSF)	W35-20	t:Cockayne,Finn,Saxton(3),Bostock g:Finn(5) fg:Finn	N/A	2,031
2/10/11	Sheffield (GF) ●	W40-4	t:Spears,Finn(2),Hardman,Cockayne,Hepworth,Saxton g:Finn(6)	N/A	7,263

● Played at Halliwell Jones Stadium, Warrington

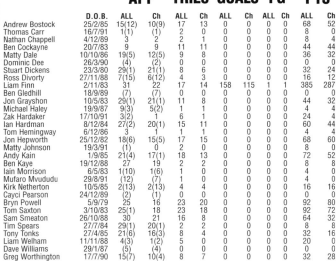

	D.O.B.	APP		TRIES		GOALS		FG		PTS	
		ALL	Ch	ALL	Ch	ALL	Ch	ALL	Ch	ALL	Ch
Andrew Bostock	25/2/85	15(12)	10(9)	17	13	0	0	0	0	68	52
Thomas Carr	16/7/91	1(1)	(1)	2	0	0	0	0	0	8	0
Nathan Chappell	4/12/89	3	2	2	1	0	0	0	0	8	4
Ben Cockayne	20/7/83	9	9	11	11	0	0	0	0	44	44
Matty Dale	10/10/86	19(5)	12(5)	9	8	0	0	0	0	36	32
Dominic Dee	26/3/90	(4)	(2)	0	0	0	0	0	0	0	0
Stuart Dickens	23/3/80	29(1)	21(1)	8	6	0	0	0	0	32	24
Ross Divorty	27/11/88	7(15)	6(12)	4	3	0	0	0	0	16	12
Liam Finn	2/11/83	31	22	17	14	158	115	1	1	385	287
Ben Gledhill	18/9/89	(7)	(7)	0	0	0	0	0	0	0	0
Jon Grayshon	10/5/83	29(1)	21(1)	11	8	0	0	0	0	44	32
Michael Haley	19/9/87	9(3)	5(2)	1	1	0	0	0	0	4	4
Zak Hardaker	17/10/91	3(2)	1	6	1	0	0	0	0	24	4
Ian Hardman	8/12/84	27(2)	20(1)	15	11	0	0	0	0	60	44
Tom Hemingway	6/12/86	3	1	1	1	0	0	0	0	4	4
Jon Hepworth	25/12/82	18(6)	15(5)	17	15	0	0	0	0	68	60
Matty Johnson	19/3/91	(1)	0	2	0	0	0	0	0	8	0
Andy Kain	1/9/85	21(4)	17(1)	18	13	0	0	0	0	72	52
Ben Kaye	19/12/88	27	19	2	2	0	0	0	0	8	8
Iain Morrison	6/5/83	1(10)	1(6)	1	0	0	0	0	0	4	0
Mufaro Mvududu	29/8/91	(12)	(7)	1	0	0	0	0	0	4	0
Kirk Netherton	10/5/85	2(13)	2(13)	4	4	0	0	0	0	16	16
Cayci Pearson	24/12/89	(2)	(1)	0	0	0	0	0	0	0	0
Bryn Powell	5/9/79	25	16	23	20	0	0	0	0	92	80
Tom Saxton	3/10/83	25(1)	18	23	18	0	0	0	0	92	72
Sam Smeaton	26/10/88	30	21	16	8	0	0	0	0	64	32
Tim Spears	27/7/84	29(1)	20(1)	2	2	0	0	0	0	8	8
Tony Tonks	27/4/85	21(6)	16(3)	8	4	0	0	0	0	32	16
Liam Welham	11/11/88	4(3)	1(2)	5	0	0	0	0	0	20	0
Dave Williams	29/1/87	(5)	(4)	0	0	0	0	0	0	0	0
Greg Worthington	17/7/90	15(7)	10(4)	8	7	0	0	0	0	32	28

Liam Finn

LEAGUE RECORD
P20-W18-D1-L1-BP0
(1st, Championship)
Grand Final Winners, Champions)
F840, A348, Diff+492
56 points.

CHALLENGE CUP
Round Five

NORTHERN RAIL CUP
Semi-Finalists/2nd, Pool 1

ATTENDANCES
Best - v Leigh (Ch - 2,375)
Worst - v The Army (CC - 723)
Total (excluding Challenge Cup) - 23,448
Average (excluding Challenge Cup) - 1,675
(Down by 147 on 2010)

CLUB RECORDS
MATCH RECORDS Highest score: 96-0 v Castleford Lock Lane, 8/2/2004 Highest score against: 14-80 v Bradford, 3/4/2005 Record attendance: 17,531 v St Helens, 21/3/59
Tries: 6 Mike Smith v Doncaster, 13/4/68; Chris Bibb v Keighley, 17/9/89
Goals: 13 Mark Knapper v Keighley, 17/9/89 Points: 40 Martin Pearson v Whitehaven, 26/11/95
SEASON RECORDS Tries: 48 Paul Newlove 1992-93 Goals: 165 (inc 9 fg) Jamie Rooney 2002 Points: 429 Jamie Rooney 2002
CAREER RECORDS Tries: 162 Don Fox 1953-66 Goals: 1,210 Steve Quinn 1975-88 Points: 2,654 Steve Quinn 1975-88 Appearances: 440 Jim Denton 1921-34

HALIFAX

DATE	FIXTURE	RESULT	SCORERS	LGE	ATT
4/2/11	Swinton (a) (NRC)	W22-28	t:Haley,White,Worrincy,Paterson(2),S Barlow g:Paterson(2)	3rd(P2)	916
13/2/11	Oldham (h) (NRC)	W50-10	t:Ostick,Black(2),Worrincy,Aizue,S Barlow(2),Jones,Gannon g:Paterson(5),Jones(2)	2nd(P2)	2,027
27/2/11	Batley (h) (NRC)	L25-26	t:White,Chandler,Worrincy(2) g:Jones(4) fg:Black	5th(P2)	1,968
6/3/11	Castleford Lock Lane (h) (CCR3)	W76-6	t:Worrincy(2),Nash,Greenwood,Bannister(2),Penkywicz,Holroyd,Jones, White(2),Fieldhouse,Beswick g:Jones(10)	N/A	1,684
12/3/11	Toulouse (a)	L26-12	t:Worrincy,Penkywicz g:Jones,Holroyd	8th	1,021
16/3/11	Whitehaven (a) (NRC)	W6-60	t:White(2),Worrincy(2),Fieldhouse,Chandler(2),Black,Penkywicz(2) g:Jones(10)	2nd(P2)	771
24/3/11	Featherstone (h)	L20-32	t:Penkywicz,Worrincy,White(2) g:Jones(2)	11th	2,638
3/4/11	Sheffield (a)	L41-22	t:Chandler(2),White,Worrincy g:Holroyd(3)	11th	1,282
9/4/11	Toulouse (a) (NRCQF)	W26-36	t:Worrincy,Penkywicz,Cherryholme,Jones(2),White g:Holroyd(6)	N/A	851
17/4/11	Leigh (h)	L22-32	t:Chandler,Greenwood,Worrincy,Paterson g:Holroyd(3)	10th	2,479
21/4/11	Widnes (a)	L47-36	t:Ostick,Paterson,Nash(2),White,S Barlow g:Holroyd(6)	9th	3,669
25/4/11	Dewsbury (h)	W56-24	t:Penkywicz(2),Worrincy,S Barlow(3),Nash(2),Smith,Greenwood g:Holroyd(8)	8th	1,745
1/5/11	Barrow (h)	L25-43	t:Worrincy,White,Jones,S Barlow g:Holroyd(4) fg:Holroyd	10th	1,757
8/5/11	Bradford (h) (CCR4)	L34-46	t:Gannon,Penkywicz,Watene,Jones,S Barlow,Beswick g:Jones(4),Holroyd	N/A	5,045
15/5/11	Featherstone (a)	L30-18	t:Jones,White,Bannister g:Paterson(3)	10th	1,377
22/5/11	Sheffield (h)	W14-12	t:Bannister,Penkywicz g:Jones(3)	9th	1,788
2/6/11	Leigh (a)	W16-36	t:Worrincy(2),Beswick,Bannister,Greenwood,Jones,S Barlow g:Jones(4)	7th	2,525
9/6/11	Hunslet (h)	W24-18	t:Fairbank,Black,Worrincy,White g:Jones(4)	7th	1,963
16/6/11	Featherstone (a) (NRCSF)	W30-31 (aet)	t:Paterson,White(2),Worrincy,Black,Nash g:Paterson(3) fg:Jones	N/A	1,987
26/6/11	Batley (h)	L28-36	t:Beswick,Nash,Penkywicz,Jones,Worrincy g:Jones(3),Paterson	7th	2,483
3/7/11	Dewsbury (a)	W16-30	t:Penkywicz,White(2),Beswick,S Barlow g:Jones(5)	7th	1,102
9/7/11	Barrow (a)	W16-24	t:Haley,Nash,Penkywicz,White g:Jones(4)	7th	1,640
17/7/11	Leigh (NRCF) ●	L16-20	t:Greenwood,Bannister,Worrincy g:Jones(2)	N/A	8,820
24/7/11	York (h)	W76-38	t:Bannister,Smith,Fairbank,Aizue,Penkywicz(2),Worrincy,White(3),Clayton,Nash(2) g:Jones(12)	7th	1,920
30/7/11	Toulouse (h)	W44-28	t:Bowman,Jones,Goddard,Greenwood,Chandler,White(2),Smith g:Jones(6)	6th	1,876
7/8/11	Batley (a)	L18-16	t:Smith,Jones,Chandler g:Jones(2)	6th	1,131
11/8/11	Widnes (h)	W26-24	t:Beswick,Greenwood,Smith,Bowman g:Jones(5)	6th	2,090
18/8/11	York (a)	L22-8	t:White(2)	6th	1,056
4/9/11	Hunslet (a)	W24-32	t:Haley,Worrincy(2),S Barlow(2) g:Jones(6)	6th	1,053
8/9/11	Batley (a) (EPO)	W22-32	t:Haley,Bannister,Worrincy,Penkywicz,Beswick g:Jones(6)	N/A	1,179
18/9/11	Sheffield (a) (ESF)	L50-12	t:Goddard,Penkywicz g:Jones(2)	N/A	1,233

● Played at Bloomfield Road, Blackpool

	D.O.B.	APP ALL	APP Ch	TRIES ALL	TRIES Ch	GOALS ALL	GOALS Ch	FG ALL	FG Ch	PTS ALL	PTS Ch
Makali Aizue	30/12/77	5(20)	3(15)	2	1	0	0	0	0	8	4
Steve Bannister	10/10/87	24(2)	17(1)	8	5	0	0	0	0	32	20
Josh Barlow	15/5/91	(4)	(1)	0	0	0	0	0	0	0	0
Sam Barlow	7/3/88	18(7)	13(5)	13	9	0	0	0	0	52	36
Bob Beswick	8/12/84	26(4)	19(2)	7	5	0	0	0	0	28	20
Ben Black	29/4/81	18(4)	11(4)	5	1	0	0	1	0	21	4
Anthony Bowman	18/3/92	5(1)	5(1)	2	2	0	0	0	0	8	8
Joe Chandler	2/11/88	7(12)	5(10)	8	5	0	0	0	0	32	20
Neil Cherryholme	20/12/86	21(5)	16(4)	1	0	0	0	0	0	4	0
Ryan Clayton	22/11/82	14(4)	10(4)	1	1	0	0	0	0	4	4
Gil Dudson	16/6/90	(2)	(2)	0	0	0	0	0	0	0	0
Jacob Fairbank	4/3/90	13(6)	10(4)	2	2	0	0	0	0	8	8
Ryan Fieldhouse	10/4/88	7(3)	6(1)	2	0	0	0	0	0	8	0
Jim Gannon	16/6/77	24(3)	17(2)	2	0	0	0	0	0	8	0
Jon Goddard	21/6/82	10	7	2	2	0	0	0	0	8	8
Miles Greenwood	30/7/87	27(1)	19(1)	8	5	0	0	0	0	32	20
James Haley	2/7/85	20	15	4	3	0	0	0	0	16	12
Graham Holroyd	25/10/75	9	6	1	0	32	25	1	1	69	51
Danny Jones	6/3/86	27(3)	19(2)	11	6	97	65	1	0	239	154
David Larder	5/6/76	4(1)	1(1)	0	0	0	0	0	0	0	0
Dylan Nash	28/12/86	15(5)	11(4)	10	8	0	0	0	0	40	32
Michael Ostick	23/1/88	7(2)	4(2)	2	1	0	0	0	0	8	4
Lee Paterson	20/7/82	13	8	5	2	14	4	0	0	48	16
Sean Penkywicz	18/5/82	9(18)	7(11)	17	12	0	0	0	0	68	48
Mike Ratu	16/10/87	1	0	0	0	0	0	0	0	0	0
Paul Smith	17/5/77	18(4)	14(2)	5	5	0	0	0	0	20	20
Frank Watene	15/2/77	(13)	(9)	1	0	0	0	0	0	4	0
Paul White	7/12/82	31	22	26	17	0	0	0	0	104	68
Rob Worrincy	9/7/85	30	21	25	14	0	0	0	0	100	56

Paul White

LEAGUE RECORD
P20-W10-D0-L10-BP6
(6th, Championship/
Elimination Semi-Final)
F569, A543, Diff+26
36 points.

CHALLENGE CUP
Round Four

NORTHERN RAIL CUP
Runners-Up/2nd, Pool 2

ATTENDANCES
Best - v Bradford (CC - 5,045)
Worst - v Castleford Lock Lane
(CC - 1,684)
Total (excluding Challenge Cup) - 24,734
Average (excluding
Challenge Cup) - 2,061
(Down by 284 on 2010)

CLUB RECORDS Highest score: 88-6 v Workington, 2/3/2008; 88-10 v Ovenden, 7/3/2010 Highest score against: 6-88 v Hull KR, 23/4/2006
Record attendance: 29,153 v Wigan, 21/3/59 *(Thrum Hall)*; 9,827 v Bradford, 12/3/2000 *(The Shay)*
MATCH RECORDS Tries: 8 Keith Williams v Dewsbury, 9/11/57 Goals: 14 Bruce Burton v Hunslet, 27/8/72 Points: 32 John Schuster v Doncaster, 9/10/94
SEASON RECORDS Tries: 48 Johnny Freeman 1956-57 Goals: 156 Graham Holroyd 2008 Points: 362 John Schuster 1994-95
CAREER RECORDS Tries: 290 Johnny Freeman 1954-67 Goals: 1,028 Ronnie James 1961-71 Points: 2,191 Ronnie James 1961-71 Appearances: 482 Stan Kielty 1946-58

HUNSLET HAWKS

DATE	FIXTURE	RESULT	SCORERS	LGE	ATT
6/2/11	Oldham (a) (NRC)	L28-22	t:Kain,Haughey,Clayton,Yates g:D March(3)	5th(P2)	685
13/2/11	Batley (h) (NRC)	L8-12	t:Houston g:Ratcliffe(2)	8th(P2)	666
20/2/11	Workington (h) (NRC)	W30-0	t:D March,McLocklan,P March,Haughey,Kain g:D March(5)	5th(P2)	379
27/2/11	Sheffield (a) (NRC) ●	W12-16	t:Haughey,Grimshaw g:Ratcliffe(4)	3rd(P2)	854
6/3/11	Warrington Wizards (h) (CCR3)	W48-10	t:Clayton,Pryce,Haigh,Grimshaw(2),Ratcliffe,Harding(2),Chapman,Oakes g:Ratcliffe(4)	N/A	316
13/3/11	York (h)	D28-28	t:Kain,Kear,Ratcliffe,Barnett,Grimshaw g:Ratcliffe(4)	5th	606
20/3/11	Widnes (a)	W10-18	t:D March,Grimshaw,Pryce g:Ratcliffe(3)	3rd	3,023
27/3/11	Batley (a)	L38-12	t:Barnett,D March g:Ratcliffe(2)	5th	940
31/3/11	Dewsbury (h)	L4-22	t:Haughey	8th	1,190
8/4/11	Featherstone (h) (NRCQF)	L12-50	t:Pryce,Kear g:Kear(2)	N/A	877
17/4/11	Toulouse (h)	W28-6	t:Lowe,Barnett,Kain,Ratcliffe,Kear g:Kear(4)	5th	518
22/4/11	York (a)	W12-50	t:Barnett(2),Haughey,Grimshaw,Pryce(2),Kear(2),Yates g:Kear(7)	5th	1,036
1/5/11	Featherstone (h)	L12-48	t:Kain,Ratcliffe g:Kear(2)	7th	905
8/5/11	Salford (h) (CCR4)	L2-68	g:Ratcliffe	N/A	649
14/5/11	Toulouse (a)	L28-6	t:Pryce g:D March	7th	645
22/5/11	Leigh (a)	L56-18	t:Chapman,Oakes,Tuffour g:Ratcliffe(3)	7th	2,071
29/5/11	Sheffield (a)	L70-12	t:Tuffour,Grimshaw g:Ratcliffe(2)	7th	907
5/6/11	Batley (h)	L12-34	t:Haigh,Grimshaw g:Ratcliffe,D March	8th	801
9/6/11	Halifax (a)	L24-18	t:Grimshaw,P March,Tuffour,Ratcliffe g:Ratcliffe	8th	1,963
3/7/11	Widnes (h)	L22-24	t:Grimshaw,Kain,Haughey,Haigh g:Ratcliffe(2),D March	9th	1,101
10/7/11	Featherstone (a)	L54-22	t:Grimshaw(2),Haughey,Pryce g:Latus(2),D March	9th	1,271
23/7/11	Barrow (a)	L26-25	t:Clayton(2),Grimshaw,Kelly g:Latus(4) fg:McLocklan	9th	1,150
31/7/11	Leigh (a)	L0-44		10th	713
7/8/11	Sheffield (h)	L24-32	t:Ratcliffe(2),P March,Barnett g:Latus(4)	11th	424
14/8/11	Dewsbury (a)	L30-18	t:P March,Ratcliffe(2) g:Latus(3)	9th	1,066
21/8/11	Barrow (h)	W42-12	t:Pryce(4),Grimshaw,Ratcliffe(2) g:Latus(7)	8th	501
4/9/11	Halifax (h)	L24-32	t:Ratcliffe(2),P March,D March g:Latus(4)	8th	1,053

● Played at Don Valley Stadium

		APP		TRIES		GOALS		FG		PTS	
	D.O.B.	ALL	Ch	ALL	Ch	ALL	Ch	ALL	Ch	ALL	Ch
Richie Barnett	26/4/81	21	16	6	6	0	0	0	0	24	24
Richard Blakeway	22/7/83	14(5)	10(4)	0	0	0	0	0	0	0	0
Tabua Cakacaka	8/3/77	4(1)	2	0	0	0	0	0	0	0	0
Richard Chapman	5/9/75	3(5)	1(2)	2	1	0	0	0	0	8	4
David Clayton	23/9/88	21(3)	14(3)	4	2	0	0	0	0	16	8
Steve Dooler	31/12/77	6(5)	5(2)	0	0	0	0	0	0	0	0
Danny Grimshaw	25/2/86	27	20	14	11	0	0	0	0	56	44
Luke Haigh	24/7/87	23	19	3	2	0	0	0	0	12	8
Chris Hall	12/12/82	(1)	(1)	0	0	0	0	0	0	0	0
Matthew Harding	2/10/90	2	1	2	0	0	0	0	0	8	0
Tom Haughey	30/1/82	24	18	7	4	0	0	0	0	28	16
Joe Helme	1/4/84	7(8)	6(4)	0	0	0	0	0	0	0	0
James Houston	28/12/82	13(7)	9(7)	1	0	0	0	0	0	4	0
Stuart Kain	18/9/85	22(1)	16(1)	6	4	0	0	0	0	24	16
Elliot Kear	29/11/88	10	6	5	4	15	13	0	0	50	42
Rob Kelly	1/3/86	17(7)	12(6)	1	1	0	0	0	0	4	4
Jack Latus	14/9/88	8	8	0	0	24	24	0	0	48	48
Neil Lowe	20/12/78	(20)	(16)	1	1	0	0	0	0	4	4
David March	25/7/79	23(1)	16(1)	4	3	12	4	0	0	40	20
Paul March	25/7/79	14(3)	8(3)	5	4	0	0	0	0	20	16
Joe McLocklan	2/10/86	2(18)	1(14)	1	0	0	0	1	1	5	1
John Oakes	12/2/88	17(4)	15(1)	2	1	0	0	0	0	8	4
Waine Pryce	3/10/81	23	17	11	9	0	0	0	0	44	36
Danny Ratcliffe	14/3/87	20(1)	16	13	12	29	18	0	0	110	84
Adam Sullivan	14/11/82	23	18	0	0	0	0	0	0	0	0
Dennis Tuffour	17/2/89	4	4	3	3	0	0	0	0	12	12
Scott Woodcock	15/11/83	(1)	0	0	0	0	0	0	0	0	0
Andrew Yates	23/2/90	3(17)	2(15)	2	1	0	0	0	0	8	4

Danny Grimshaw

LEAGUE RECORD
P20-W4-D1-L15-BP6
(7th, Championship)
F395, A630, Diff-235
20 points.

CHALLENGE CUP
Round Four

NORTHERN RAIL CUP
Quarter Finalists/4th, Pool 2

ATTENDANCES
Best - v Dewsbury (Ch - 1,190)
Worst - v Warrington Wizards
(CC - 316)
Total (excluding Challenge Cup) - 9,734
Average (excluding
Challenge Cup) - 749
(Up by 199 on 2010, Ch1)

CLUB RECORDS	**Highest score:** 82-0 v Highfield, 21/1/96 **Highest score against:** 0-82 v Bradford, 2/3/2003 **Record attendance:** 24,700 v Wigan, 15/3/24
MATCH RECORDS	**Tries:** 7 George Dennis v Bradford, 20/1/34 **Goals:** 12 Billy Langton v Keighley, 18/8/59 **Points:** 30 Simon Wilson v Highfield, 21/1/96
SEASON RECORDS	**Tries:** 34 Alan Snowden 1956-57 **Goals:** 181 Billy Langton 1958-59 **Points:** 380 Billy Langton 1958-59
CAREER RECORDS	**Tries:** 154 Fred Williamson 1943-55 **Goals:** 1,044 Billy Langton 1955-66 **Points:** 2,202 Billy Langton 1955-66 **Appearances:** 579 Geoff Gunney 1951-73

LEIGH CENTURIONS

DATE	FIXTURE	RESULT	SCORERS	LGE	ATT
6/2/11	Batley (a) (NRC)	W4-24	t:Goulden,Armstrong(2),Donlan,Hunter-Paul g:Nanyn(2)	1st(P2)	1,073
13/2/11	Swinton (h) (NRC)	W42-22	t:Ellis,Duffy,Hill(2),Nanyn(2),Goulden g:Nanyn(7)	3rd(P2)	1,623
20/2/11	Sheffield (h) (NRC)	W68-6	t:Ellis,Maden(2),Ridyard(3),Mills,Donlan,Duffy,McGilvray(2) g:Nanyn(10)	1st(P2)	1,520
27/2/11	Workington (a) (NRC)	W12-42	t:Goulden,Maden(2),Ridyard,Donlan,Ellis,Littler,Gorski g:Nanyn(5)	1st(P2)	592
6/3/11	Hull Dockers (h) (CCR3)	W68-24	t:Ellis(4),Gorski,Hopkins(2),Pownall,Nicholson,Briscoe,Thornley,Murphy g:Ellis(7),Ridyard(2),Govin	N/A	1,083
10/3/11	Featherstone (h)	W36-10	t:Armstrong,Nanyn(2),Ellis,McGilvray,Donlan g:Nanyn(6)	3rd	1,940
19/3/11	Barrow (h)	W32-36	t:McCarthy,Thornley,Maden,Armstrong,Donlan(2),Nanyn g:Nanyn(4)	1st	1,799
27/3/11	Widnes (h)	W54-16	t:Nanyn,Ridyard(3),Goulden,McCarthy(2),McGilvray,Hill,Hopkins g:Nanyn(7)	1st	3,198
7/4/11	Widnes (h) (NRCQF)	W50-18	t:Ellis(2),Maden,Armstrong,Mills(2),Goulden,Duffy g:Nanyn(9)	N/A	2,737
17/4/11	Halifax (a)	W22-32	t:Ellis,Littler(2),Hill,Maden(2) g:Nanyn(4)	2nd	2,479
22/4/11	Barrow (h)	W26-24	t:Donlan(2),Evans,Nanyn,Ellis g:Nanyn(3)	1st	2,583
25/4/11	Featherstone (a)	D28-28	t:Ellis(2),Evans,Goulden,Nanyn g:Nanyn(4)	1st	2,375
1/5/11	Batley (h)	W36-12	t:Blythe,Donlan(2),Ellis,Nanyn,Nash g:Nanyn(4),Ridyard(2)	1st	2,285
6/5/11	Catalan Dragons (h) (CCR4)	L16-22	t:Higson,Goulden,Donlan g:Ridyard(2)	N/A	2,237
15/5/11	Sheffield (a)	W8-44	t:Nanyn,McGilvray,Ridyard(2),Blythe,Littler,Goulden,Ellis g:Nanyn(6)	1st	1,778
22/5/11	Hunslet (h)	W56-18	t:Maden(2),Goulden,Ellis(2),Nash,Nanyn,Higson,Littler g:Nanyn(8)	1st	2,071
29/5/11	York (a)	W38-48	t:Ridyard(2),Govin,Ellis(2),Goulden,Nash,Mills g:Nanyn(8)	1st	1,010
2/6/11	Halifax (h)	L16-36	t:Ridyard(2),Maden g:Nanyn(2)	1st	2,525
12/6/11	Dewsbury (h)	W34-6	t:Nanyn(3),Goulden,Littler,Donlan,Maden g:Nanyn(2),Ellis	1st	1,942
19/6/11	Dewsbury (h) (NRCSF)	W44-10	t:Mills,Goulden,Duffy(2),McGilvray,Ellis,Nanyn(2) g:Nanyn(6)	N/A	2,234
25/6/11	Toulouse (a)	W14-36	t:Ridyard,McGilvray,Hunter-Paul,Ellis,Nanyn,Taylor g:Nanyn(6)	1st	2,300
7/7/11	Batley (a)	W16-40	t:Donlan,Ridyard,Ellis,Maden,McGilvray,Nash,Armstrong g:Nanyn(6)	2nd	1,533
17/7/11	Halifax (NRCF) ●	W16-20	t:Ellis(2),Hill,Armstrong g:Nanyn(2)	N/A	8,820
24/7/11	Sheffield (h)	W34-22	t:Evans,Goulden(2),Littler,Nanyn(2) g:Nanyn(5)	2nd	2,633
31/7/11	Hunslet (h)	W0-44	t:Ellis(2),Goulden,Taylor,Maden,Evans,Nash,Thornley g:Ellis(6)	2nd	713
7/8/11	Widnes (a)	W18-24	t:Ridyard,Ellis(2),Nanyn g:Nanyn(4)	2nd	4,732
14/8/11	York (h)	W66-10	t:Ridyard,Ellis(3),Hill,Nanyn(2),Hopkins,Thornley,Higson,Goulden,McGilvray g:Nanyn(9)	1st	2,207
20/8/11	Toulouse (h)	W46-16	t:Higson,Nanyn,Ridyard(2),Hunter-Paul,Littler,Ellis,Taylor g:Nanyn(7)	2nd	2,407
1/9/11	Dewsbury (a)	W22-40	t:Taylor,Donlan,Nanyn(2),Hill,Ridyard,Ellis g:Nanyn(6)	2nd	933
15/9/11	Featherstone (a) (QSF)	L35-20	t:Maden,Mills,Ridyard,Nanyn g:Nanyn(2)	N/A	2,031
22/9/11	Sheffield (h) (FE)	L10-20	t:Donlan,Nanyn g:Nanyn	N/A	1,818

● Played at Bloomfield Road, Blackpool

	D.O.B.	APP ALL	APP Ch	TRIES ALL	TRIES Ch	GOALS ALL	GOALS Ch	FG ALL	FG Ch	PTS ALL	PTS Ch
Tom Armstrong	12/9/89	9(6)	6(4)	7	3	0	0	0	0	28	12
Ricky Bibey	22/9/81	4	0	0	0	0	0	0	0	0	0
Matty Blythe	20/11/88	2	2	2	2	0	0	0	0	8	8
Craig Briscoe	8/12/92	(4)	(3)	1	0	0	0	0	0	4	0
Stuart Donlan	29/8/78	30	21	18	13	0	0	0	0	72	52
John Duffy	2/7/80	23(3)	16(2)	5	0	0	0	0	0	20	0
Jamie Ellis	4/10/89	31	22	34	22	14	7	0	0	164	102
Rhys Evans	30/10/92	8	8	4	4	0	0	0	0	16	16
Andy Gorski	31/3/81	1(3)	(2)	2	0	0	0	0	0	8	0
Tommy Goulden	30/6/81	29(1)	20(1)	15	9	0	0	0	0	60	36
Mick Govin	5/11/84	5(10)	2(7)	1	1	1	0	0	0	6	4
Adam Higson	19/5/87	12(9)	8(7)	4	3	0	0	0	0	16	12
Chris Hill	3/11/87	27(2)	19(2)	7	4	0	0	0	0	28	16
Sam Hopkins	17/2/90	3(10)	2(8)	4	2	0	0	0	0	16	8
Robbie Hunter-Paul	3/2/76	5(8)	4(6)	3	2	0	0	0	0	12	8
Stuart Littler	19/2/79	30(1)	21(1)	8	7	0	0	0	0	32	28
Steve Maden	13/9/82	28(1)	20(1)	15	10	0	0	0	0	60	40
Tyrone McCarthy	21/4/88	2(2)	2(2)	3	3	0	0	0	0	12	12
Dean McGilvray	24/4/88	28(1)	19(1)	9	6	0	0	0	0	36	24
David Mills	1/6/81	15(15)	11(11)	6	2	0	0	0	0	24	8
Lee Mitchell	8/9/88	2	1	0	0	0	0	0	0	0	0
Chris Murphy	15/12/93	(1)	0	1	0	0	0	0	0	4	0
Mick Nanyn	3/6/82	28	21	26	22	145	104	0	0	394	296
Stephen Nash	14/1/86	9(6)	8(9)	5	5	0	0	0	0	20	20
Anthony Nicholson	28/11/90	3(8)	3(6)	2	1	0	0	0	0	8	4
Jonathan Pownall	22/8/91	1(1)	(1)	1	0	0	0	0	0	4	0
Martyn Ridyard	25/7/86	28(2)	21	21	17	6	2	0	0	96	72
James Taylor	11/9/84	29	21	4	4	0	0	0	0	16	16
Andy Thornley	1/3/89	11(19)	8(14)	4	3	0	0	0	0	16	12

Jamie Ellis

LEAGUE RECORD
P20-W18-D1-L1-BP0
(2nd, Championship/Final Eliminator)
F776, A368, Diff+408
53 points. *(3 points deducted for 2010 salary cap breach)*

CHALLENGE CUP
Round Four

NORTHERN RAIL CUP
Winners/1st, Pool 2

ATTENDANCES
Best - v Widnes (Ch - 3,198)
Worst - v Hull Dockers (CC - 1,083)
Total (excluding Challenge Cup) - 33,723
Average (excluding Challenge Cup) - 2,248
(Up by 222 on 2010)

CLUB RECORDS MATCH RECORDS	**Highest score:** 92-2 v Keighley, 30/4/86 **Highest score against:** 4-94 v Workington, 26/2/95 **Record attendance:** 31,326 v St Helens, 14/3/53
	Tries: 6 Jack Wood v York, 4/10/47; Neil Turley v Workington, 31/1/2001
	Goals: 15 Mick Stacey v Doncaster, 28/3/76 **Points:** 42 Neil Turley v Chorley, 4/4/2004
SEASON RECORDS	**Tries:** 55 Neil Turley 2001 **Goals:** 187 Neil Turley 2004 **Points:** 468 Neil Turley 2004
CAREER RECORDS	**Tries:** 189 Mick Martyn 1954-67 **Goals:** 1,043 Jimmy Ledgard 1948-58 **Points:** 2,492 John Woods 1976-85; 1990-92
	Appearances: 503 Albert Worrall 1920-38

SHEFFIELD EAGLES

DATE	FIXTURE	RESULT	SCORERS	LGE	ATT
6/2/11	Gateshead (a) (NRC)	W20-32	t:Bergin,Yere(3),Mills,Hanson g:Brown(2),Bergin(2)	2nd(P2)	444
13/2/11	Whitehaven (h) (NRC) ●	D16-16	t:Bergin,Hepworth,Stringer g:Bergin(2)	4th(P2)	727
20/2/11	Leigh (a) (NRC)	L68-6	t:Cottle g:Bergin	6th(P2)	1,520
27/2/11	Hunslet (h) (NRC) ●	L12-16	t:Yere,Hanson g:Brown(2)	8th(P2)	854
6/3/11	Leeds Met University (h) (CCR3) ●	W82-0	t:Hanson,Howieson,Green,Yere(2),Szostak(2),Rowe,Cottle,Bergin,Hirst,McDonald(2),Mills,Henderson g:Brown(11)	N/A	350
13/3/11	Widnes (h)	L16-44	t:McDonald,Rowe,Hanson g:Brown(2)	10th	1,831
17/3/11	York (a)	W10-28	t:Laulu-Togagae,Mills(2),Crookes,Rowe g:Brown(4)	7th	2,022
26/3/11	Toulouse (h)	W34-16	t:Yere(2),Hirst(2),Finigan,Crookes g:Brown(5)	4th	1,076
3/4/11	Halifax (h)	W41-22	t:Yere,Finigan,Rowe,Bergin,Henderson,Wood,Hepworth g:Brown(6) fg:Brown	4th	1,282
17/4/11	Dewsbury (a)	W12-36	t:Crookes(2),Yere,Laulu-Togagae,McDonald,Rowe g:Brown(6)	4th	1,010
25/4/11	Batley (a)	W16-28	t:Laulu-Togagae,Henderson,Yere,Hirst,Finigan g:Brown(4)	3rd	843
7/5/11	St Helens (a) (CCR4)	L52-26	t:Szostak(2),Laulu-Togagae(3) g:Brown(3)	N/A	3,563
15/5/11	Leigh (h)	L8-44	t:Laulu-Togagae g:Brown,Stringer	6th	1,778
22/5/11	Halifax (a)	L14-12	t:Laulu-Togagae,Szostak,Finigan	5th	1,788
29/5/11	Hunslet (h)	W70-12	t:Finigan,Hirst,Taulapapa,Yere(2),Laulu-Togagae(2),Stringer(2),Howieson,Hanson,Rowe,Cording g:Brown(7),Stringer(2)	4th	907
3/6/11	Dewsbury (h) ●●	W40-12	t:Mills,Laulu-Togagae,Rowe(2),Yere,Bergin,Hanson g:Brown(6)	4th	683
11/6/11	Toulouse (a)	W16-32	t:Bergin,Henderson,Laulu-Togagae,Taulapapa,Yere,Green g:Brown(4)	4th	1,200
26/6/11	Widnes (a)	L38-24	t:Cording,Wood,Yere,Brown g:Brown(4)	4th	4,027
30/6/11	Barrow (h)	W30-26	t:Szostak(2),Yere,Brown,Laulu-Togagae g:Brown(5)	4th	1,054
24/7/11	Leigh (a)	L34-22	t:Taulapapa,Yere,Bergin,McDonald g:Brown(2),Bergin	5th	2,633
28/7/11	Featherstone (a)	L34-6	t:Taulapapa g:Brown	5th	1,527
7/8/11	Hunslet (a)	W24-32	t:Taulapapa(2),Hanson(2),Stringer g:Brown(6)	5th	424
13/8/11	Barrow (a)	L36-26	t:Henderson,Laulu-Togagae(2),Yere,Hanson g:Brown(3)	5th	1,179
21/8/11	Batley (h)	W28-26	t:McDonald(2),Hanson,Hirst,Bergin g:Brown(4)	5th	1,174
28/8/11	Featherstone (h)	L12-34	t:Hirst,Finigan g:Brown(2)	5th	1,336
4/9/11	York (h)	W52-18	t:Laulu-Togagae,Hirst,Szostak,Hanson(2),Taulapapa,Yere(3),Stringer g:Brown(2),Bergin(4)	4th	1,147
9/9/11	Widnes (h) (EPO)	W36-20	t:Laulu-Togagae(2),McDonald(2),Taulapapa g:Brown(8)	N/A	564
18/9/11	Halifax (h) (ESF)	W50-12	t:Laulu-Togagae,Hirst,Henderson(2),McDonald(2),Taulapapa,Woodcock g:Brown(9)	N/A	1,233
22/9/11	Leigh (a) (FE)	W10-20	t:S Scott,Finigan,Laulu-Togagae g:Brown(4)	N/A	1,818
2/10/11	Featherstone (GF) ●●●	L40-4	t:McDonald	N/A	7,263

● Played at Don Valley Stadium ●● Played at Mount St Marys, Spinkhill ●●● Played at Halliwell Jones Stadium, Warrington

		APP		TRIES		GOALS		FG		PTS	
	D.O.B.	ALL	Ch	ALL	Ch	ALL	Ch	ALL	Ch	ALL	Ch
Eddie Battye	24/7/91	(6)	(3)	0	0	0	0	0	0	0	0
Tim Bergin	29/7/85	26(1)	20(1)	8	5	10	5	0	0	52	30
Simon Brown	23/6/89	28	24	2	2	113	95	1	1	235	199
Jamie Cording	30/12/89	4(5)	1(5)	2	2	0	0	0	0	8	8
Jamie Cottle	20/5/90	6	1	2	0	0	0	0	0	8	0
Jason Crookes	21/4/90	9	9	4	4	0	0	0	0	16	16
Vinny Finigan	4/8/89	19(2)	19(2)	7	7	0	0	0	0	28	28
Peter Green	2/12/81	29(1)	23(1)	2	1	0	0	0	0	8	4
Corey Hanson	11/8/92	17(3)	12(3)	12	9	0	0	0	0	48	36
Andrew Henderson	17/6/79	30	24	7	6	0	0	0	0	28	24
Ryan Hepworth	16/1/81	3(26)	3(21)	2	1	0	0	0	0	8	4
Liam Higgins	19/7/83	4(4)	3	0	0	0	0	0	0	0	0
Joe Hirst	21/4/87	28	22	9	8	0	0	0	0	36	32
Jack Howieson	28/7/81	27	21	2	1	0	0	0	0	8	4
Quentin Laulu-Togagae	1/12/84	19(3)	18(3)	20	17	0	0	0	0	80	68
Dane McDonald	14/7/87	20(2)	14(2)	12	10	0	0	0	0	48	40
Danny Mills	10/8/82	15(3)	9(3)	5	3	0	0	0	0	20	12
Alex Rowe	11/3/85	1(21)	(16)	8	7	0	0	0	0	32	28
Connor Scott	27/5/93	(2)	(2)	0	0	0	0	0	0	0	0
Sam Scott	5/6/90	(12)	(11)	1	1	0	0	0	0	4	4
Pat Smith	4/3/90	1(12)	(11)	0	0	0	0	0	0	0	0
Mitchell Stringer	1/11/83	28(2)	23(1)	5	4	3	3	0	0	26	22
Alex Szostak	4/3/86	26(1)	23(1)	8	4	0	0	0	0	32	16
Misi Taulapapa	25/1/82	16(2)	16(2)	9	9	0	0	0	0	36	36
Nick Turnbull	22/11/82	(2)	(1)	0	0	0	0	0	0	0	0
Scott Watson	16/3/88	3	0	0	0	0	0	0	0	0	0
Kyle Wood	18/6/89	8(1)	7(1)	2	2	0	0	0	0	8	8
Jonny Woodcock	8/12/81	1(4)	1(4)	1	1	0	0	0	0	4	4
Menzie Yere	24/10/83	25(1)	19(1)	22	16	0	0	0	0	88	64

Simon Brown

LEAGUE RECORD
P20-W12-D0-L8-BP3
(4th, Championship/
Grand Final Runners-Up)
F577, A488, Diff+89
39 points.

CHALLENGE CUP
Round Four

NORTHERN RAIL CUP
7th, Pool 2

ATTENDANCES
Best - v Widnes (Ch - 1,831)
Worst - v Leeds Met University
(CC - 350)
Total (excluding Challenge Cup) - 15,646
Average (excluding
Challenge Cup) - 1,118
(Down by 110 on 2010)

CLUB RECORDS Highest score: 98-4 v London Skolars, 3/8/2003 Highest score against: 0-88 v Hull, 2/3/2003 Record attendance: 10,603 v Bradford, 16/8/97
MATCH RECORDS Tries: 5 Daryl Powell v Mansfield, 2/1/89 Goals: 13 Gavin Brown v London Skolars, 3/8/2003 Points: 32 Roy Rafferty v Fulham, 21/9/86
SEASON RECORDS Tries: 30 Iva Ropati 1991-92 Goals: 148 Mark Aston 1988-89 Points: 307 Mark Aston 1988-89
CAREER RECORDS Tries: 114 Daryl Powell 1984-95 Goals: 986 Mark Aston 1986-2004 Points: 2,142 Mark Aston 1986-2004 Appearances: 389 Mark Aston 1986-2004

TOULOUSE OLYMPIQUE

DATE	FIXTURE	RESULT	SCORERS	LGE	ATT
5/2/11	Dewsbury (h) (NRC)	W40-38	t:Ormeno(2),Lewis,Anselme(2),Pelo,Cook g:Lewis(6)	5th(P1)	1,000
12/2/11	Widnes (a) (NRC)	L44-28	t:Lewis,Planas,White,Nicholls,Ormeno g:Lewis(4)	6th(P1)	2,376
19/2/11	Keighley (a) (NRC)	W22-36	t:White,Olari,Nicholls(3),Lewis g:Lewis(6)	5th(P1)	513
26/2/11	London Skolars (h) (NRC)	W34-22	t:Nicholls,Cook,Tisseyre,Olari,Lewis,Worth g:Lewis(5)	4th(P1)	800
5/3/11	Keighley (a) (CCR3)	L16-10	t:White,Lewis g:Lewis	N/A	479
12/3/11	Halifax (h)	W26-12	t:Olari,Corcoran,Cook,Worth g:Nicholls(5)	4th	1,021
19/3/11	Dewsbury (a)	L35-6	t:Nicholls g:Nicholls	8th	928
26/3/11	Sheffield (a)	L34-16	t:Nicholls,White,Payan g:Nicholls(2)	9th	1,076
2/4/11	Featherstone (h)	L18-56	t:Nicholls(2),Lewis g:Lewis(3)	9th	1,500
9/4/11	Halifax (h) (NRCQF)	L26-36	t:White,Wynn,Faure,Villegas,Nicholls g:Couturier(3)	N/A	851
17/4/11	Hunslet (a)	L28-6	t:Nicholls g:Lewis	9th	518
25/4/11	York (h)	L10-16	t:Planas,Nicholls g:Couturier	11th	650
28/4/11	Widnes (a)	L26-12	t:White,Tisseyre g:Nicholls(2)	11th	3,601
14/5/11	Hunslet (h)	W28-6	t:Houles,Tisseyre(2),Ormeno,Nicholls g:Nicholls(4)	11th	645
28/5/11	Batley (h)	L18-28	t:Corcoran,Nicholls(2) g:Nicholls(3)	11th	1,855
4/6/11	Barrow (a)	L30-18	t:Ormeno,Wynn,Nicholls g:Nicholls(3)	10th	1,245
11/6/11	Sheffield (h)	L16-32	t:Wynn,White(2) g:Nicholls(2)	11th	1,200
25/6/11	Leigh (h)	L14-36	t:Houles,Tisseyre,White g:Nicholls	11th	2,300
3/7/11	Featherstone (a)	L90-10	t:Nicholls,Tisseyre g:Nicholls	11th	1,307
9/7/11	York (a)	W32-46	t:White(2),Anselme,Ormeno(2),Pelo,Cook,Wynn g:Nicholls(7)	10th	902
23/7/11	Widnes (h)	L16-30	t:White,Gigot,Cook g:Nicholls(2)	10th	1,157
30/7/11	Halifax (a)	L44-28	t:Ormeno,Nicholls(2),White,Gigot g:Nicholls(4)	11th	1,876
6/8/11	Dewsbury (h)	W16-8	t:Mercier,White,Maria g:Nicholls(2)	10th	800
13/8/11	Batley (a)	L32-10	t:Gout,Mercier g:Nicholls	11th	801
20/8/11	Leigh (a)	L46-16	t:Gigot,Bromley,Couturier g:Couturier(2)	11th	2,407
3/9/11	Barrow (h)	L28-42	t:Mercier(3),Gigot(2) g:Couturier(4)	11th	602

		APP		TRIES		GOALS		FG		PTS	
	D.O.B.	ALL	Ch	ALL	Ch	ALL	Ch	ALL	Ch	ALL	Ch
Lilian Albert	25/6/91	2	2	0	0	0	0	0	0	0	0
Thibaut Ancely	18/5/88	5(1)	5(1)	0	0	0	0	0	0	0	0
Eric Anselme	20/5/79	8(10)	7(6)	3	1	0	0	0	0	12	4
Clement Bienes	21/1/90	4(1)	3	0	0	0	0	0	0	0	0
Rory Bromley	1/5/84	10	10	1	1	0	0	0	0	4	4
Craig Cook	26/5/83	15(5)	10(5)	5	3	0	0	0	0	20	12
Ged Corcoran	28/3/83	9(4)	8(3)	2	2	0	0	0	0	8	8
Damien Couturier	9/7/81	17	12	1	1	10	7	0	0	24	18
Nicolas Faure	30/5/84	4(14)	3(10)	1	0	0	0	0	0	4	0
Yohann Gigord	4/1/89	6(5)	6(5)	0	0	0	0	0	0	0	0
Tony Gigot	27/12/90	10(2)	10(2)	5	5	0	0	0	0	20	20
Theo Gonzalez-Trique	11/1/91	(3)	(3)	0	0	0	0	0	0	0	0
Jerome Gout	13/5/86	7(13)	5(11)	1	1	0	0	0	0	4	4
Sylvain Houles	3/8/81	22(1)	16(1)	2	2	0	0	0	0	8	8
Kevin Larroyer	19/6/89	12(10)	9(7)	0	0	0	0	0	0	0	0
Josh Lewis	5/10/85	7	2	6	1	26	4	0	0	76	12
Antoni Maria	21/3/87	21(3)	17(1)	1	1	0	0	0	0	4	4
Sebastien Martins	18/11/84	(4)	(4)	0	0	0	0	0	0	0	0
Mathieu Mercier	8/10/82	7	7	5	5	0	0	0	0	20	20
Cyril Moliner	8/1/90	2(3)	2(2)	0	0	0	0	0	0	0	0
Darren Nicholls	14/4/89	24	18	19	13	40	40	0	0	156	132
Andrei Olari	4/11/88	8	3	3	1	0	0	0	0	12	4
Bruno Ormeno	3/12/82	16(2)	11(2)	8	5	0	0	0	0	32	20
Sebastien Payan	12/7/86	10	7	1	1	0	0	0	0	4	4
Teli Pelo	22/7/84	5(9)	3(5)	2	1	0	0	0	0	8	4
Sebastien Planas	5/5/84	21	15	2	1	0	0	0	0	8	4
Antoine Reveillon	15/11/89	4	4	0	0	0	0	0	0	0	0
Yoan Tisseyre	8/5/89	14(10)	10(9)	6	5	0	0	0	0	24	20
Remi Vignau	13/11/91	1	1	0	0	0	0	0	0	0	0
Constant Villegas	21/10/86	15	14	1	0	0	0	0	0	4	0
Gregory White	28/8/81	23(1)	18	14	10	0	0	0	0	56	40
Brendan Worth	18/7/84	14	8	2	1	0	0	0	0	8	4
Tim Wynn	19/7/85	15(2)	14(2)	4	3	0	0	0	0	16	12

Darren Nicholls

LEAGUE RECORD
P20-W4-D0-L16-BP3
(10th, Championship)
F358, A663, Diff-305
15 points.

CHALLENGE CUP
Round Three

NORTHERN RAIL CUP
Quarter Finalists/4th, Pool 1

ATTENDANCES
Best - v Leigh (Ch - 2,300)
Worst - v Barrow (Ch - 602)
Total (excluding Challenge Cup) - 14,381
Average (excluding
Challenge Cup) - 1,106
(Down by 217 on 2010)

CLUB RECORDS MATCH RECORDS	**Highest score:** 60-22 v Batley, 13/4/2009 **Highest score against:** 10-90 v Featherstone, 3/7/2011 **Record attendance:** 3,507 v Leigh, 20/4/2009 **Tries:** 3 Nathan Wynn v Batley, 13/4/2009; Vincent Duport v Widnes, 10/4/2009; Martin Mitchell v Dewsbury, 3/7/2010; Darren Nicholls v Keighley, 19/2/2011; Mathieu Mercier v Barrow, 3/9/2011 **Goals:** 8 Nathan Wynn v Doncaster, 26/4/2009; Nathan Wynn v Batley, 13/4/2010 **Points:** 22 Nathan Wynn v Batley, 13/4/2009; Nathan Wynn v Widnes, 10/4/2010
SEASON RECORDS CAREER RECORDS	**Tries:** 19 Darren Nicholls 2011 **Goals:** 81 *(inc 1 fg)* Nathan Wynn 2010 **Points:** 189 Nathan Wynn 2010 **Tries:** 28 Rory Bromley 2009-11 **Goals:** 158 (inc 1 fg) Nathan Wynn 2009-10 **Points:** 363 Nathan Wynn 2009-10 **Appearances:** 66 Antoni Maria 2009-11

WIDNES VIKINGS

DATE	FIXTURE	RESULT	SCORERS	LGE	ATT
6/2/11	London Skolars (a) (NRC)	W18-62	t:Flynn(2),Allen,Craven(2),Kavanagh,Gardner,T Coyle,Thackeray,Haggerty,Ropati g:Craven(9)	1st(P1)	643
12/2/11	Toulouse (h) (NRC)	W44-28	t:Allen,Thackeray(2),Ropati,Tyrer,Netherton,Gerrard,Kavanagh g:Tyrer(6)	1st(P1)	2,376
20/2/11	Rochdale (h) (NRC)	W50-10	t:Netherton,T Coyle,Craven,Grady,Tyrer(2),Finnigan,Ropati,Thackeray g:Tyrer(6),Ropati	1st(P1)	3,155
26/2/11	Featherstone (a) (NRC)	W16-22	t:Grady,Tyrer,Thackeray g:Tyrer(5)	1st(P1)	1,719
6/3/11	Siddal (a) (CCR3)	W6-54	t:Tyrer(3),Craven(2),Finnigan,Gaskell(2),I'Anson,Gardner g:Tyrer(7)	N/A	951
13/3/11	Sheffield (a)	W16-44	t:Tyrer(2),Finnigan(2),Netherton,Allen(3) g:Tyrer(6)	2nd	1,831
20/3/11	Hunslet (h)	L10-18	t:Varkulis,Thackeray g:Tyrer	2nd	3,023
27/3/11	Leigh (a)	L54-16	t:Finnigan,Thackeray,Flynn g:Tyrer(2)	7th	3,198
3/4/11	York (h)	W76-12	t:Flynn,Tyrer(3),Craven,Leuluai,Varkulis,Lunt,Thackeray(2),Pickersgill(2),Finnigan g:Tyrer(12)	5th	4,087
7/4/11	Leigh (a) (NRCQF)	L50-18	t:Kavanagh(2),Leuluai g:Tyrer(3)	N/A	2,737
17/4/11	Batley (a)	L32-12	t:Hulme,Varkulis g:Grady(2)	6th	1,101
21/4/11	Halifax (h)	W47-36	t:Hulme(3),Finnigan(2),Tomkins(2),T Coyle g:Tyrer(7) fg:I'Anson	6th	3,669
25/4/11	Barrow (a)	L30-12	t:Mellor(2) g:Tyrer(2)	6th	1,965
28/4/11	Toulouse (h)	W26-12	t:Crosby,Gaskell,Mellor,Tomkins,Ropati g:Tyrer(3)	5th	3,601
8/5/11	London Skolars (a) (CCR4)	W18-62	t:Leuluai(2),T Coyle,Flynn(4),Ropati,Varkulis,Gore,Tyrer,Allen g:Tyrer(7)	N/A	415
15/5/11	Dewsbury (a)	D34-34	t:I'Anson(2),Leuluai,Allen,Flynn,Tyrer g:Tyrer(5)	5th	1,087
21/5/11	Hull FC (h) (CCR5)	L26-50	t:Leuluai,Tyrer(2),Varkulis,Ropati g:Tyrer(3)	N/A	3,387
26/5/11	Barrow (h)	W42-14	t:I'Anson,Flynn,Owens,Penny,Tomkins,Tyrer,Mellor,T Coyle g:Tyrer(5)	5th	3,331
12/6/11	York (a)	W18-22	t:Haggerty,Leuluai,Crosby,Ropati g:Haggerty,Tyrer(2)	6th	1,172
26/6/11	Sheffield (h)	W38-24	t:Hulme,Leuluai,Varkulis,Penny(2),Haggerty,Allen g:Haggerty(4),Ropati	5th	4,027
3/7/11	Hunslet (a)	W22-24	t:Kavanagh,Tyrer,Grady,Flynn,Haggerty g:Tyrer(2)	5th	1,101
10/7/11	Dewsbury (h)	W36-22	t:Gore,Tomkins,Kavanagh(2),Tyrer,Penny g:Tyrer(6)	4th	4,030
23/7/11	Toulouse (a)	W16-30	t:Tyrer(2),Gardner,Allen,Finnigan g:Tyrer(5)	3rd	1,157
31/7/11	Batley (h)	W24-22	t:Kavanagh,Flynn,Mellor,Penny g:Tyrer(4)	3rd	3,873
7/8/11	Leigh (h)	L18-24	t:Tyrer,Crosby,Tomkins g:Tyrer(3)	3rd	4,732
11/8/11	Halifax (a)	L26-24	t:Hulme,Mellor(2),Varkulis g:Tyrer(4)	4th	2,090
17/8/11	Featherstone (a)	L56-16	t:Hulme(2),Grady g:Haggerty(2)	4th	2,021
4/9/11	Featherstone (h)	L4-44	t:Craven	5th	5,021
9/9/11	Sheffield (a) (EPO)	L36-20	t:Flynn(2),Ropati,Craven g:Craven(2)	N/A	564

		APP		TRIES		GOALS		FG		PTS	
	D.O.B.	ALL	Ch	ALL	Ch	ALL	Ch	ALL	Ch	ALL	Ch
Dave Allen	15/9/85	18(7)	13(6)	9	6	0	0	0	0	36	24
James Coyle	28/12/85	5(1)	5(1)	0	0	0	0	0	0	0	0
Thomas Coyle	10/5/88	28(1)	20(1)	5	2	0	0	0	0	20	8
Danny Craven	21/11/91	9	5	8	3	12	2	0	0	56	16
Dominic Crosby	11/12/90	2(11)	2(11)	3	3	0	0	0	0	12	12
Simon Finnigan	8/12/81	21(1)	17	9	7	0	0	0	0	36	28
Paddy Flynn	11/12/87	26	20	14	8	0	0	0	0	56	32
James Ford	29/9/82	4	3	0	0	0	0	0	0	0	0
Gareth Frodsham	18/12/89	(1)	(0)	0	0	0	0	0	0	0	0
Matt Gardner	24/8/84	22(3)	15(2)	3	1	0	0	0	0	12	4
Dean Gaskell	12/4/83	11(1)	6(1)	3	1	0	0	0	0	12	4
Chris Gerrard	1/10/89	2(6)	1(2)	1	0	0	0	0	0	4	0
Grant Gore	21/11/91	1(3)	1	2	1	0	0	0	0	8	4
Shane Grady	13/12/89	13(8)	9(6)	4	2	2	2	0	0	20	12
Kurt Haggerty	8/1/89	15(3)	10(2)	4	3	7	7	0	0	30	26
Daniel Heckenberg	27/10/79	8(1)	3(1)	0	0	0	0	0	0	0	0
David Houghton	2/11/89	(3)	(2)	0	0	0	0	0	0	0	0
Danny Hulme	15/2/91	11	11	8	8	0	0	0	0	32	32
Chaz I'Anson	30/11/86	17(4)	14(3)	4	3	0	0	1	1	17	13
Ben Kavanagh	4/3/88	26(1)	19(1)	8	4	0	0	0	0	32	16
Macgraff Leuluai	9/2/90	19(5)	14(4)	8	4	0	0	0	0	32	16
Chris Lunt	18/12/90	2(3)	(2)	1	1	0	0	0	0	4	4
Joe Mellor	28/11/90	14	14	7	7	0	0	0	0	28	28
Kirk Netherton	10/5/85	8(1)	3	3	1	0	0	0	0	12	4
Jack Owens	3/6/94	2	1	1	1	0	0	0	0	4	4
Kevin Penny	3/10/87	11	10	5	5	0	0	0	0	20	20
Steve Pickersgill	28/11/85	21(3)	18(1)	2	2	0	0	0	0	8	8
Tangi Ropati	15/11/84	22	14	8	3	1	1	0	0	34	14
Danny Sculthorpe	8/9/79	1(10)	(7)	0	0	0	0	0	0	0	0
Anthony Thackeray	19/2/86	9(1)	4(1)	9	4	0	0	0	0	36	16
Logan Tomkins	1/8/91	1(13)	1(13)	6	6	0	0	0	0	24	24
Steve Tyrer	16/3/89	25	18	22	12	106	69	0	0	300	186
Richard Varkulis	21/5/82	3(24)	2(17)	7	5	0	0	0	0	28	20

Steve Tyrer

LEAGUE RECORD
P20-W11-D1-L8-BP3
(5th, Championship/
Elimination Play-Off)
F555, A532, Diff+23
38 points.

CHALLENGE CUP
Round Five

NORTHERN RAIL CUP
Quarter Finalists/1st, Pool 1

ATTENDANCES
Best - v Featherstone (Ch - 5,021)
Worst - v Toulouse (NRC - 2,376)
Total (excluding Challenge Cup) - 44,925
Average (excluding
Challenge Cup) - 3,744
(Up by 886 on 2010)

CLUB RECORDS
MATCH RECORDS
Highest score: 90-4 v Doncaster, 10/6/2007 Highest score against: 24-74 v Bradford, 7/8/2005 Record attendance: 24,205 v St Helens, 16/2/61
Tries: 7 Phil Cantillon v York, 18/2/2001
Goals: 14 Mark Hewitt v Oldham, 25/7/99; Tim Hartley v Saddleworth, 7/3/2009 Points: 38 Gavin Dodd v Doncaster, 10/6/2007
SEASON RECORDS
CAREER RECORDS
Tries: 58 Martin Offiah 1988-89 Goals: 161 Mick Nanyn 2007 Points: 434 Mick Nanyn 2007
Tries: 234 Mal Aspey 1964-80 Goals: 1,083 Ray Dutton 1966-78 Points: 2,195 Ray Dutton 1966-78 Appearances: 591 Keith Elwell 1970-86

YORK CITY KNIGHTS

DATE	FIXTURE	RESULT	SCORERS	LGE	ATT
6/2/11	Barrow (a) (NRC)	L24-20	t:Wilson,Esders,Sutton,Presley g:Thorman(2)	7th(P1)	1,305
13/2/11	Featherstone (h) (NRC)	L22-32	t:Esders(2),Davies,Presley g:Thorman(3)	8th(P1)	1,387
20/2/11	London Skolars (a) (NRC)	D16-16	t:Davies,Barlow,Wilson g:Thorman(2)	6th(P1)	264
27/2/11	Keighley (h) (NRC)	W28-22	t:Straugheir(2),Presley(2),Davies g:Thorman(4)	6th(P1)	748
6/3/11	Northumbria University (a) (CCR3) ●	W0-132	t:Wilson(2),Thorman(4),Presley(6),Sutton,Lee,Lewis,Tuffour(2),Straugheir, Barlow(2),Clarke,Smith,Stearman g:Thorman(20)	N/A	434
13/3/11	Hunslet (a)	D28-28	t:Lee,Lewis,Sutton,Garside(2) g:Thorman(4)	5th	606
17/3/11	Sheffield (h)	L10-28	t:Davies,Presley g:Thorman	9th	2,022
27/3/11	Barrow (h)	L16-42	t:Presley,Sutton,Davies g:Thorman(2)	10th	1,064
3/4/11	Widnes (a)	L76-12	t:Barron,Davies g:Waterman,Barlow	10th	4,087
22/4/11	Hunslet (h)	L12-50	t:Hardcastle,Thorman g:Thorman(2)	11th	1,036
25/4/11	Toulouse (a)	W10-16	t:Waterman,Lee,Clarke g:Hardcastle(2)	10th	650
1/5/11	Dewsbury (h)	W30-26	t:Thorman,Waller,Garside,Clarke,Esders g:Waterman(5)	8th	1,098
8/5/11	Hull KR (h) (CCR4)	L22-64	t:Barlow(2),Stearman,Waterman g:Waterman(3)	N/A	2,463
14/5/11	Barrow (a)	L34-12	t:Stearman,Barlow g:Waterman(2)	9th	1,271
19/5/11	Batley (a)	L50-16	t:Ford,Straugheir,Stearman g:Bush,Barlow	10th	806
29/5/11	Leigh (h)	L38-48	t:Thorman,Presley(2),Stearman,Garside,Clarke,Straugheir g:Bush(3),Thorman(2)	10th	1,010
5/6/11	Featherstone (a)	L44-24	t:Lee,Garside,Bush,Thackeray g:Bush(4)	11th	1,287
12/6/11	Widnes (h)	L18-22	t:Smith,Jones,Esders g:Bush(3)	10th	1,172
26/6/11	Dewsbury (a)	W28-30	t:Thackeray(2),Garside,Esders,Sutton g:Bush(4),Thorman	8th	974
1/7/11	Batley (h)	W18-10	t:Esders,Freer,Straugheir g:Bush(3)	8th	1,098
9/7/11	Toulouse (h)	L32-46	t:Esders,Lee,Sutton,Freer,Garside(2),Haynes g:Bush,Haynes	8th	902
24/7/11	Halifax (a)	L76-38	t:Tuffour,Straugheir,Garside,Lewis(2),Thackeray,Ford g:Bush(5)	8th	1,920
5/8/11	Featherstone (h)	L16-44	t:Freer,Garside,Haynes g:Bush(2)	8th	1,193
14/8/11	Leigh (a)	L66-10	t:Thackeray,Freer g:Bush	10th	2,207
18/8/11	Halifax (h)	W22-8	t:Benson,Waller,Esders g:Thorman(5)	9th	1,056
4/9/11	Sheffield (a)	L52-18	t:Bush(2),Garside g:Thorman(3)	9th	1,147

● Played at Huntington Stadium

	D.O.B.	APP		TRIES		GOALS		FG		PTS	
		ALL	Ch	ALL	Ch	ALL	Ch	ALL	Ch	ALL	Ch
Jack Aldous	3/4/91	(3)	(3)	0	0	0	0	0	0	0	0
Mark Barlow	16/2/84	6(6)	3(3)	6	1	2	2	0	0	28	8
Matt Barron	17/11/86	(5)	(4)	1	1	0	0	0	0	4	4
Ian Bell	28/1/83	2(1)	0	0	0	0	0	0	0	0	0
Alex Benson	22/5/85	24	20	1	1	0	0	0	0	4	4
Kris Brinning	16/11/93	(1)	(1)	0	0	0	0	0	0	0	0
Davey Burns	22/6/86	(2)	(1)	0	0	0	0	0	0	0	0
Tom Bush	25/1/90	20(1)	18(1)	3	3	27	27	0	0	66	66
Mark Castle	19/2/86	(1)	(1)	0	0	0	0	0	0	0	0
Rhys Clarke	12/3/91	20(2)	19(1)	4	3	0	0	0	0	16	12
John Davies	8/1/91	8	4	6	3	0	0	0	0	24	12
Ryan Esders	20/10/86	18(1)	13(1)	9	6	0	0	0	0	36	24
James Ford	29/9/82	12	11	2	2	0	0	0	0	8	8
Nathan Freer	21/5/89	17(3)	16(3)	4	4	0	0	0	0	16	16
Matt Garside	1/10/90	18(5)	15(5)	11	11	0	0	0	0	44	44
Ben Hardcastle	4/1/90	3	2	1	1	2	2	0	0	8	8
James Haynes	22/3/89	10(3)	8(3)	2	2	1	1	0	0	10	10
Joe Hemmings	10/1/89	(2)	(2)	0	0	0	0	0	0	0	0
Adam Howard	22/7/87	(1)	0	0	0	0	0	0	0	0	0
Ben Jones	8/10/88	6(9)	2(9)	1	1	0	0	0	0	4	4
Jack Lee	1/11/88	23	18	5	4	0	0	0	0	20	16
Steve Lewis	22/10/86	8(12)	6(9)	4	3	0	0	0	0	16	12
Sam Lynch	21/6/90	2	0	0	0	0	0	0	0	0	0
Nathan Massey	11/7/89	8	4	0	0	0	0	0	0	0	0
Jon Presley	8/7/84	16(9)	12(8)	14	4	0	0	0	0	56	16
Jordan Rice	9/5/90	(1)	(1)	0	0	0	0	0	0	0	0
Ed Smith	12/11/92	2(9)	2(5)	2	1	0	0	0	0	8	4
Paul Stamp	25/1/89	2(1)	1	0	0	0	0	0	0	0	0
Jack Stearman	30/1/88	1(13)	(8)	5	3	0	0	0	0	20	12
Duane Straugheir	29/9/89	19	16	7	4	0	0	0	0	28	16
Dave Sutton	21/9/89	23	19	6	4	0	0	0	0	24	16
Anthony Thackeray	19/2/86	14	13	5	5	0	0	0	0	20	20
Jordan Thompson	4/9/91	5	4	0	0	0	0	0	0	0	0
Chris Thorman	26/9/80	20	15	7	3	51	20	0	0	130	52
Dennis Tuffour	17/2/89	10(1)	7(1)	3	1	0	0	0	0	12	4
Brett Waller	3/7/87	(11)	(10)	2	2	0	0	0	0	8	8
Lee Waterman	13/4/87	8(1)	5	2	1	11	8	0	0	30	20
Danny Wilson	3/6/82	10	5	4	0	0	0	0	0	16	0
Scott Woods	10/12/90	3	2	0	0	0	0	0	0	0	0

Jon Presley

LEAGUE RECORD
P20-W5-D1-L14-BP2
(8th, Championship)
F416, A788, Diff-372
19 points.

CHALLENGE CUP
Round Four

NORTHERN RAIL CUP
6th, Pool 1

ATTENDANCES
Best - v Hull KR (CC - 2,463)
Worst - v Keighley (NRC - 748)
Total (excluding Challenge Cup) - 13,786
Average (excluding
Challenge Cup) - 1,149
(Up by 419 on 2010, Ch1)

CLUB RECORDS MATCH RECORDS	**Highest score:** 132-0 v Northumbria University, 6/3/2011 **Highest score against:** 0-98 v Rochdale, 8/4/2001 **Record attendance:** 14,689 v Swinton, 10/2/34 **Tries:** 7 Brad Davis v Highfield, 17/9/95 **Goals:** 20 Chris Thorman v Northumbria University, 6/3/2011 **Points:** 56 Chris Thorman v Northumbria University, 6/3/2011
SEASON RECORDS CAREER RECORDS	**Tries:** 35 John Crossley 1980-81 **Goals:** 178 *(inc 4 fg)* Danny Brough 2004 **Points:** 412 Danny Brough 2004 **Tries:** 167 Peter Foster 1955-67 **Goals:** 1,060 Vic Yorke 1954-67 **Points:** 2,159 Vic Yorke 1954-67 **Appearances:** 449 Willie Hargreaves 1952-65

CHAMPIONSHIP 2011
Round by Round

ROUND 1

Thursday 10th March 2011

LEIGH CENTURIONS 36 FEATHERSTONE ROVERS 10

CENTURIONS: 1 Stuart Donlan; 2 Steve Maden; 22 Tom Armstrong; 4 Mick Nanyn; 5 Dean McGilvray; 6 Martyn Ridyard; 25 Jamie Ellis; 8 Chris Hill; 9 John Duffy; 26 David Mills; 3 Stuart Littler; 12 Tommy Goulden; 11 James Taylor. Subs (all used): 13 Stephen Nash; 15 Andy Thornley; 23 Mick Govin; 24 Andy Gorski.
Tries: Armstrong (10), Nanyn (13, 72), Ellis (34), McGilvray (49), Donlan (76); **Goals:** Nanyn 6/7.
ROVERS: 19 Zak Hardaker; 2 Bryn Powell; 3 Sam Smeaton; 14 Liam Welham; 5 Tom Saxton; 6 Andy Kain; 7 Liam Finn; 10 Stuart Dickens; 9 Ben Kaye; 11 Jon Grayshon; 13 Matty Dale; 12 Tim Spears; 17 Greg Worthington. Subs (all used): 27 Dave Williams; 1 Ian Hardman; 24 Mufaro Mvududu; 31 Cayci Pearson.
Tries: Hardaker (32), Powell (58); **Goals:** Finn 1/2.
Rugby Leaguer & League Express Men of the Match:
Centurions: Tommy Goulden; *Rovers:* Liam Finn.
Penalty count: 5-4; **Half-time:** 16-6;
Referee: Matthew Thomason; **Attendance:** 1,940.

Saturday 12th March 2011

TOULOUSE OLYMPIQUE 26 HALIFAX 12

OLYMPIQUE: 5 Clement Bienes; 18 Andrei Olari; 20 Bruno Ormeno; 3 Sebastien Planas; 24 Gregory White; 6 Darren Nicholls; 16 Sylvain Houles; 8 Brendan Worth; 9 Craig Cook; 15 Jerome Gout; 14 Antoni Maria; 12 Yoan Tisseyre; 13 Eric Anselme. Subs (all used): 10 Ged Corcoran; 11 Tim Wynn; 17 Kevin Larroyer; 21 Nicolas Faure.
Tries: Olari (6), Corcoran (26), Cook (55), Worth (78);
Goals: Nicholls 5/5.
HALIFAX: 1 Miles Greenwood; 23 Rob Worrincy; 4 Dylan Nash; 5 James Haley; 20 Paul White; 28 Graham Holroyd; 6 Danny Jones; 10 Neil Cherryholme; 13 Bob Beswick; 15 Jim Gannon; 11 David Larder; 24 Steve Bannister; 19 Jacob Fairbank. Subs (all used): 9 Sean Penkywicz; 7 Ben Black; 12 Sam Barlow; 25 Michael Ostick.
Tries: Worrincy (50), Penkywicz (71);
Goals: Jones 1/1, Holroyd 1/1.
Rugby Leaguer & League Express Men of the Match:
Olympique: Craig Cook; *Halifax:* Graham Holroyd.
Penalty count: 6-6; **Half-time:** 14-0;
Referee: Tim Roby; **Attendance:** 1,021.

Sunday 13th March 2011

BATLEY BULLDOGS 28 DEWSBURY RAMS 0

BULLDOGS: 30 Johnny Campbell; 5 Wayne Reittie; 3 Daley Williams; 4 Danny Maun; 2 Alex Brown; 6 Paul Handforth; 7 Gareth Moore; 8 Byron Smith; 1 Ian Preece; 10 Sean Hesketh; 18 Dane Manning; 11 Alex Bretherton; 13 Ashley Lindsay. Subs (all used): 19 Mark Toohey; 12 Jason Walton; 21 James Martin; 20 David Tootill.
Tries: Daley Williams (24), Lindsay (27), Handforth (42), Preece (60), Walton (79); **Goals:** Moore 4/5.
RAMS: 1 James Craven; 2 Michael Wainwright; 32 Elliott Cosgrove; 4 Scott Turner; 5 Austin Buchanan; 26 Jordan Tansey; 7 Dominic Brambani; 8 Anthony England; 9 Luke Blake; 10 Keegan Hirst; 11 Rob Spicer; 12 James Lockwood; 15 Josh Tonks. Subs (all used): 23 Luke Menzies; 22 Jonny Horton; 13 Ayden Faal; 31 Ben Bolger.
Rugby Leaguer & League Express Men of the Match:
Bulldogs: Byron Smith; *Rams:* Jonny Horton.
Penalty count: 10-6; **Half-time:** 10-0;
Referee: Clint Sharrad; **Attendance:** 1,402.

HUNSLET HAWKS 28 YORK CITY KNIGHTS 28

HAWKS: 22 Danny Ratcliffe; 5 Waine Pryce; 27 Elliot Kear; 2 Richie Barnett; 1 Stuart Kain; 6 Danny Grimshaw; 7 Paul March; 8 Adam Sullivan; 14 Luke Haigh; 21 Tabua Cakacaka; 17 Rob Kelly; 12 Tom Haughey; 13 David March. Subs (all used): 10 James Houston; 11 Richard Blakeway; 19 Neil Lowe; 23 Joe McLocklan.
Tries: Kain (8), Kear (28), Ratcliffe (30), Barnett (34), Grimshaw (53); **Goals:** Ratcliffe 4/6.
CITY KNIGHTS: 20 Tom Bush; 2 Dave Sutton; 3 Duane Straugheir; 30 Jordan Thompson; 5 Danny Wilson; 6 Chris Thorman; 7 Jon Presley; 33 Nathan Massey; 9 Jack Lee; 10 Alex Benson; 11 Rhys Clarke; 37 Ben Jones; 31 John Davies. Subs (all used): 8 Nathan Freer; 12 Matt Barron; 19 Matt Garside; 25 Steve Lewis.
Tries: Lee (13), Lewis (57), Sutton (62), Garside (69, 78); **Goals:** Thorman 4/5.
Rugby Leaguer & League Express Men of the Match:
Hawks: Danny Ratcliffe; *City Knights:* Chris Thorman.
Penalty count: 9-9; **Half-time:** 20-4;
Referee: George Stokes; **Attendance:** 606.

SHEFFIELD EAGLES 16 WIDNES VIKINGS 44

EAGLES: 28 Jamie Cottle; 2 Danny Mills; 26 Corey Hanson; 19 Joe Hirst; 5 Tim Bergin; 13 Dane McDonald; 7 Simon Brown; 8 Jack Howieson; 9 Andrew Henderson; 15 Liam Higgins; 11 Alex Szostak; 10 Mitchell Stringer; 12 Peter Green. Subs (all used): 22 Ryan Hepworth; 23 Nick Turnbull; 17 Alex Rowe; 6 Quentin Laulu-Togagae.
Tries: McDonald (14), Rowe (32), Hanson (62);
Goals: Brown 2/3.
VIKINGS: 1 Danny Craven; 2 Dean Gaskell; 18 James Ford; 4 Scott Tyrer; 19 Matt Gardner; 6 Anthony Thackeray; 14 Thomas Coyle; 17 Ben Kavanagh; 9 Kirk Netherton; 10 Daniel Heckenberg; 20 Shane Grady; 12 Kurt Haggerty; 13 Simon Finnigan. Subs (all used): 7 Chaz I'Anson; 8 Steve Pickersgill; 11 Dave Allen; 42 Danny Sculthorpe.
Tries: Tyrer (7, 25), Finnigan (20, 59), Netherton (28), Allen (41, 64, 73); **Goals:** Tyrer 6/8.
Rugby Leaguer & League Express Men of the Match:
Eagles: Mitchell Stringer; *Vikings:* Simon Finnigan.
Penalty count: 10-10; **Half-time:** 12-22;
Referee: Jamie Leahy; **Attendance:** 1,831.

ROUND 2

Thursday 17th March 2011

YORK CITY KNIGHTS 10 SHEFFIELD EAGLES 28

CITY KNIGHTS: 20 Tom Bush; 2 Dave Sutton; 30 Jordan Thompson; 3 Duane Straugheir; 5 Danny Wilson; 6 Chris Thorman; 7 Jon Presley; 33 Nathan Massey; 9 Jack Lee; 10 Alex Benson; 11 Rhys Clarke; 31 John Davies; 37 Ben Jones. Subs (all used): 8 Nathan Freer; 19 Matt Garside; 12 Matt Barron; 25 Steve Lewis.
Tries: Davies (16), Presley (23); **Goals:** Thorman 1/2.
EAGLES: 6 Quentin Laulu-Togagae; 2 Danny Mills; 3 Menzie Yere; 4 Jason Crookes; 5 Tim Bergin; 24 Kyle Wood; 7 Simon Brown; 8 Jack Howieson; 9 Andrew Henderson; 15 Liam Higgins; 11 Alex Szostak; 12 Peter Green; 19 Joe Hirst. Subs (all used): 22 Ryan Hepworth; 17 Alex Rowe; 20 Pat Smith; 10 Mitchell Stringer.
Tries: Laulu-Togagae (12), Mills (30, 53), Crookes (56), Rowe (75); **Goals:** Brown 4/5.
Rugby Leaguer & League Express Men of the Match:
City Knights: John Davies; *Eagles:* Andrew Henderson.
Penalty count: 3-5; **Half-time:** 10-12;
Referee: Tim Roby; **Attendance:** 2,022.

Saturday 19th March 2011

DEWSBURY RAMS 35 TOULOUSE OLYMPIQUE 6

RAMS: 17 Ryan Glynn; 2 Michael Wainwright; 32 Elliott Cosgrove; 4 Scott Turner; 5 Austin Buchanan; 7 Dominic Brambani; 25 Tom Wandless; 8 Anthony England; 9 Luke Blake; 21 Kyle Bibb; 11 Rob Spicer; 12 James Lockwood; 15 Josh Tonks. Subs (all used): 23 Luke Menzies; 19 James Walker; 22 Jonny Horton; 31 Ben Bolger.
Tries: Buchanan (20), Wainwright (44, 72, 74), Wandless (56); **Goals:** Brambani 7/9;
Field goal: Brambani (79).
OLYMPIQUE: 32 Lilian Albert; 2 Sebastien Payan; 3 Sebastien Planas; 22 Damien Couturier; 18 Andrei Olari; 6 Darren Nicholls; 4 Constant Villegas; 8 Brendan Worth; 9 Craig Cook; 21 Nicolas Faure; 11 Tim Wynn; 17 Kevin Larroyer; 16 Sylvain Houles. Subs (all used): 10 Ged Corcoran; 23 Teli Pelo; 12 Yoan Tisseyre; 13 Eric Anselme.
Try: Nicholls (67); **Goals:** Nicholls 1/1.
Rugby Leaguer & League Express Men of the Match:
Rams: Michael Wainwright; *Olympique:* Brendan Worth.
Penalty count: 7-6; **Half-time:** 12-0;
Referee: Ronnie Laughton; **Attendance:** 928.

BARROW RAIDERS 32 LEIGH CENTURIONS 36

RAIDERS: 1 Gary Broadbent; 5 James Nixon; 12 Ned Catic; 4 Liam Harrison; 2 Andy Ballard; 6 Jamie Rooney; 7 James Coyle; 10 Matt James; 9 Mark Gleeson; 8 Jamie Thackray; 11 Michael Knowles; 15 Martin Ostler; 16 Zebastian Luisi. Subs (all used): 13 Richard Fletcher; 14 Liam Campbell; 24 Adam Walker; 18 Nathan Mossop.
Tries: Catic (1), Gleeson (6), Knowles (8), Nixon (18), Harrison (35), Rooney (80); **Goals:** Rooney 4/6.
CENTURIONS: 1 Stuart Donlan; 2 Steve Maden; 22 Tom Armstrong; 4 Mick Nanyn; 5 Dean McGilvray; 23 Mick Govin; 25 Jamie Ellis; 8 Chris Hill; 9 John Duffy; 32 Tyrone McCarthy; 3 Stuart Littler; 12 Tommy Goulden; 11 James Taylor. Subs (all used): 16 Anthony Nicholson; 15 Andy Thornley; 24 Andy Gorski; 26 David Mills.
Tries: McCarthy (13), Thornley (24), Maden (38), Armstrong (54), Donlan (58, 67), Nanyn (77);
Goals: Nanyn 4/7.
Rugby Leaguer & League Express Men of the Match:
Raiders: Jamie Rooney; *Centurions:* David Mills.
Penalty count: 6-8; **Half-time:** 26-16;
Referee: Matthew Thomason; **Attendance:** 1,799.

Sunday 20th March 2011

FEATHERSTONE ROVERS 36 BATLEY BULLDOGS 6

ROVERS: 1 Ian Hardman; 2 Bryn Powell; 3 Sam Smeaton; 4 Andrew Bostock; 5 Tom Saxton; 6 Andy Kain; 7 Liam Finn; 8 Tony Tonks; 9 Ben Kaye; 10 Stuart Dickens; 11 Jon Grayshon; 12 Tim Spears; 17 Greg Worthington. Subs (all used): 24 Mufaro Mvududu; 27 Dave Williams; 23 Thomas Carr; 20 Dominic Dee.
Tries: Finn (21, 27), Dickens (24), Powell (58), Bostock (70), Saxton (72); **Goals:** Finn 6/6.
BULLDOGS: 1 Ian Preece; 30 Johnny Campbell; 3 Daley Williams; 4 Danny Maun; 5 Wayne Reittie; 6 Paul Handforth; 7 Gareth Moore; 8 Byron Smith; 13 Ashley Lindsay; 10 Sean Hesketh; 2 Alex Brown; 11 Alex Bretherton; 18 Dane Manning. Subs (all used): 19 Mark Toohey; 12 Jason Walton; 20 David Tootill; 21 James Martin.
Try: Moore (75); **Goals:** Moore 1/1, Handforth 0/1.
Rugby Leaguer & League Express Men of the Match:
Rovers: Liam Finn; *Bulldogs:* Byron Smith.
Penalty count: 6-10; **Half-time:** 18-0;
Referee: Craig Halloran; **Attendance:** 1,786.

WIDNES VIKINGS 10 HUNSLET HAWKS 18

VIKINGS: 5 Paddy Flynn; 2 Dean Gaskell; 18 James Ford; 4 Steve Tyrer; 19 Matt Gardner; 6 Anthony Thackeray; 14 Thomas Coyle; 17 Ben Kavanagh; 9 Kirk Netherton; 8 Steve Pickersgill; 11 Dave Allen; 12 Kurt Haggerty; 13 Simon Finnigan. Subs (all used): 3 Richard Varkulis; 7 Chaz I'Anson; 10 Daniel Heckenberg; 20 Shane Grady.
Tries: Varkulis (47), Thackeray (52); **Goals:** Tyrer 1/2.
Sin bin: Pickersgill (62) - late challenge on Ratcliffe.
HAWKS: 1 Stuart Kain; 5 Waine Pryce; 12 Tom Haughey; 16 John Oakes; 2 Richie Barnett; 6 Danny Grimshaw; 22 Danny Ratcliffe; 8 Adam Sullivan; 14 Luke Haigh; 20 Andrew Yates; 17 Rob Kelly; 25 Steve Dooler; 13 David March. Subs (all used): 10 James Houston; 11 Richard Blakeway; 19 Neil Lowe; 23 Joe McLocklan.
Tries: D March (7), Grimshaw (26), Pryce (76);
Goals: Ratcliffe 3/4.
Rugby Leaguer & League Express Men of the Match:
Vikings: Paddy Flynn; *Hawks:* David March.
Penalty count: 12-12; **Half-time:** 0-12;
Referee: Warren Turley; **Attendance:** 3,023.

ROUND 3

Thursday 24th March 2011

HALIFAX 20 FEATHERSTONE ROVERS 32

HALIFAX: 33 Ryan Fieldhouse; 20 Paul White; 3 Jon Goddard; 2 Lee Paterson; 23 Rob Worrincy; 6 Danny Jones; 7 Ben Black; 8 Makali Aizue; 9 Sean Penkywicz; 15 Jim Gannon; 24 Steve Bannister; 18 Joe Chandler; 12 Sam Barlow. Subs (all used): 1 Miles Greenwood; 19 Jacob Fairbank; 13 Bob Beswick; 17 Frank Watene.
Tries: Penkywicz (8), Worrincy (17), White (29, 32);
Goals: Jones 2/4.
ROVERS: 1 Ian Hardman; 2 Bryn Powell; 3 Sam Smeaton; 4 Andrew Bostock; 5 Tom Saxton; 6 Andy Kain; 7 Liam Finn; 8 Tony Tonks; 9 Ben Kaye; 10 Stuart Dickens; 11 Jon Grayshon; 12 Tim Spears; 17 Greg Worthington. Subs (all used): 20 Dominic Dee; 28 Jon Hepworth; 16 Iain Morrison; 27 Dave Williams.
Tries: Tonks (11), Dickens (25), Powell (45), Bostock (52, 60), Kain (56); **Goals:** Finn 4/6.
Rugby Leaguer & League Express Men of the Match:
Halifax: Bob Beswick; *Rovers:* Liam Finn.
Penalty count: 8-9; **Half-time:** 20-12;
Referee: Ronnie Laughton; **Attendance:** 2,638.

Saturday 26th March 2011

SHEFFIELD EAGLES 34 TOULOUSE OLYMPIQUE 16

EAGLES: 6 Quentin Laulu-Togagae; 16 Vinny Finigan; 3 Menzie Yere; 4 Jason Crookes; 5 Tim Bergin; 7 Simon Brown; 24 Kyle Wood; 15 Liam Higgins; 9 Andrew Henderson; 10 Mitchell Stringer; 11 Alex Szostak; 12 Peter Green; 19 Joe Hirst. Subs (all used): 22 Ryan Hepworth; 25 Jamie Cording; 17 Alex Rowe; 27 Eddie Battye.
Tries: Yere (9, 40), Hirst (17, 34), Finigan (21), Crookes (58); **Goals:** Brown 5/6.
OLYMPIQUE: 5 Clement Bienes; 2 Sebastien Payan; 3 Sebastien Planas; 33 Remi Vignau; 24 Gregory White; 6 Darren Nicholls; 4 Constant Villegas; 8 Brendan Worth; 13 Eric Anselme; 10 Ged Corcoran; 14 Antoni Maria; 17 Kevin Larroyer; 16 Sylvain Houles. Subs (all used): 11 Tim Wynn; 15 Jerome Gout; 12 Yoan Tisseyre; 19 Yohann Gigord.
Tries: Nicholls (13), White (31), Payan (80);
Goals: Nicholls 2/3.
Rugby Leaguer & League Express Men of the Match:
Eagles: Joe Hirst; *Olympique:* Darren Nicholls.
Penalty count: 12-10; **Half-time:** 28-10;
Referee: Jamie Leahy; **Attendance:** 1,076.

Sunday 27th March 2011

BATLEY BULLDOGS 38 HUNSLET HAWKS 12

BULLDOGS: 1 Ian Preece; 5 Wayne Reittie; 3 Daley Williams; 12 Jason Walton; 30 Johnny Campbell; 6 Paul Handforth; 16 Paul Mennell; 8 Byron Smith; 9 Kris Lythe; 10 Sean Hesketh; 11 Alex Bretherton; 18 Dane Manning; 13 Ashley Lindsay. Subs (all used): 22 Elliot Hodgson; 19 Mark Toohey; 15 Adam Robinson; 17 Craig Potter.
Tries: Bretherton (25), Potter (34), Campbell (56), Handforth (58, 61), Mennell (66), Robinson (79);
Goals: Handforth 5/7.
HAWKS: 1 Stuart Kain; 27 Elliot Kear; 16 John Oakes; 4 David Clayton; 2 Richie Barnett; 6 Danny Grimshaw; 22 Danny Ratcliffe; 20 Andrew Yates; 14 Luke Haigh; 21 Tabua Cakacaka; 17 Rob Kelly; 25 Steve Dooler; 13 David March. Subs (all used): 23 Joe McLocklan; 11 Richard Blakeway; 19 Neil Lowe; 10 James Houston.
Tries: Barnett (46), D March (76); **Goals:** Ratcliffe 2/2.
Rugby Leaguer & League Express Men of the Match:
Bulldogs: Paul Handforth; *Hawks:* David March.
Penalty count: 8-15; **Half-time:** 10-0;
Referee: Gareth Hewer; **Attendance:** 940.

LEIGH CENTURIONS 54 WIDNES VIKINGS 16

CENTURIONS: 1 Stuart Donlan; 2 Steve Maden; 22 Tom Armstrong; 4 Mick Nanyn; 5 Dean McGilvray; 6 Martyn Ridyard; 25 Jamie Ellis; 8 Chris Hill; 9 John Duffy; 32 Tyrone McCarthy; 3 Stuart Littler; 12 Tommy Goulden; 11 James Taylor. Subs (all used): 23 Mick Govin; 15 Andy Thornley; 20 Sam Hopkins; 26 David Mills.
Tries: Nanyn (15), Ridyard (24, 47, 64), Goulden (41), McCarthy (50, 56), McGilvray (61), Hill (70), Hopkins (77); **Goals:** Nanyn 7/10.
VIKINGS: 1 Danny Craven; 5 Paddy Flynn; 23 Tangi Ropati; 4 Steve Tyrer; 19 Matt Gardner; 6 Anthony Thackeray; 7 Chaz I'Anson; 8 Steve Pickersgill; 9 Kirk Netherton; 10 Daniel Heckenberg; 11 Dave Allen; 13 Simon Finnigan; 17 Ben Kavanagh. Subs (all used): 3 Richard Varkulis; 14 Thomas Coyle; 15 Chris Gerrard; 16 Macgraff Leuluai.

No way through the Dewsbury defence for Hunslet's Rob Kelly

Tries: Finnigan (19), Thackeray (29), Flynn (32);
Goals: Tyrer 2/3.
Rugby Leaguer & League Express Men of the Match:
Centurions: Tommy Goulden; *Vikings:* Richard Varkulis.
Penalty count: 8-4; **Half-time:** 8-16;
Referee: Tim Roby; **Attendance:** 3,198.

YORK CITY KNIGHTS 16 BARROW RAIDERS 42

CITY KNIGHTS: 20 Tom Bush; 2 Dave Sutton; 30 Jordan
Thompson; 3 Duane Straugheir; 5 Danny Wilson; 6 Chris
Thorman; 7 Jon Presley; 33 Nathan Massey; 23 Paul
Stamp; 10 Alex Benson; 11 Rhys Clarke; 31 John
Davies; 8 Nathan Freer. Subs (all used): 25 Steve Lewis;
19 Matt Garside; 12 Matt Barron; 14 Jack Stearman.
Tries: Presley (4), Sutton (36), Davies (76);
Goals: Thorman 2/3.
RAIDERS: 1 Gary Broadbent; 2 Andy Ballard; 3 Chris
Larkin; 4 Liam Harrison; 5 James Nixon; 6 Jamie
Rooney; 7 James Coyle; 24 Adam Walker; 9 Mark
Gleeson; 10 Matt James; 11 Michael Knowles; 15 Martin
Ostler; 12 Ned Catic. Subs (all used): 14 Liam Campbell;
16 Zebastian Luisi; 13 Richard Fletcher; 21 Jamie Butler.
Tries: Fletcher (17), Broadbent (23), Ballard (27, 43),
Harrison (46), Larkin (49), Luisi (52), Rooney (68);
Goals: Rooney 5/8.
Rugby Leaguer & League Express Men of the Match:
City Knights: Alex Benson; *Raiders:* Liam Harrison.
Penalty count: 9-4; **Half-time:** 10-16;
Referee: Clint Sharrad; **Attendance:** 1,064.

ROUND 4

Thursday 31st March 2011

HUNSLET HAWKS 4 DEWSBURY RAMS 22

HAWKS: 1 Stuart Kain; 22 Danny Ratcliffe; 27 Elliot
Kear; 4 David Clayton; 2 Richie Barnett; 6 Danny
Grimshaw; 7 Paul March; 10 James Houston; 14 Luke
Haigh; 17 Rob Kelly; 25 Steve Dooler; 12 Tom Haughey;
13 David March. Subs (all used): 9 Richard Chapman;
18 Joe Helme; 16 John Oakes; 20 Andrew Yates.
Try: Haughey (39); **Goals:** Ratcliffe 0/1.
RAMS: 17 Ryan Glynn; 2 Michael Wainwright; 32 Elliott
Cosgrove; 31 Ben Bolger; 5 Austin Buchanan; 7 Dominic
Brambani; 25 Tom Wandless; 8 Anthony England; 9 Luke
Blake; 21 Kyle Bibb; 11 Rob Spicer; 12 James Lockwood;
15 Josh Tonks. Subs (all used): 23 Luke Menzies; 22
Jonny Horton; 19 James Walker; 13 Ayden Faal.
Tries: Lockwood (12), Buchanan (57, 62), Faal (66);
Goals: Brambani 3/6.
Rugby Leaguer & League Express Men of the Match:
Hawks: Stuart Kain; *Rams:* Dominic Brambani.
Penalty count: 6-9; **Half-time:** 4-8;
Referee: Tim Roby; **Attendance:** 1,190.

Saturday 2nd April 2011

BARROW RAIDERS 22 BATLEY BULLDOGS 30

RAIDERS: 1 Gary Broadbent; 2 Andy Ballard; 12 Ned
Catic; 4 Liam Harrison; 3 Chris Larkin; 6 Jamie Rooney;
7 James Coyle; 24 Adam Walker; 9 Mark Gleeson; 10
Matt James; 11 Michael Knowles; 26 Jack Hughes; 16
Zebastian Luisi. Subs (all used): 13 Richard Fletcher; 14
Liam Campbell; 21 Jamie Butler; 25 Ben Davies.
Tries: Rooney (20), Catic (44), Knowles (58), Coyle (64);
Goals: Rooney 1/1, Ballard 2/3.
BULLDOGS: 1 Ian Preece; 30 Johnny Campbell; 3 Daley
Williams; 4 Danny Maun; 5 Wayne Reittie; 6 Paul
Handforth; 16 Paul Mennell; 8 Byron Smith; 9 Kris Lythe;
10 Sean Hesketh; 11 Alex Bretherton; 12 Jason Walton;
18 Dane Manning. Subs (all used): 2 Alex Brown; 19
Mark Toohey; 17 Craig Potter; 15 Adam Robinson.
Tries: Lythe (13), Bretherton (17), Toohey (30),
Mennell (68), Brown (76); **Goals:** Handforth 5/7.
Rugby Leaguer & League Express Men of the Match:
Raiders: Gary Broadbent; *Bulldogs:* Paul Handforth.
Penalty count: 8-7; **Half-time:** 6-18;
Referee: Ronnie Laughton; **Attendance:** 1,741.

TOULOUSE OLYMPIQUE 18 FEATHERSTONE ROVERS 56

OLYMPIQUE: 22 Damien Couturier; 24 Gregory White; 3
Sebastien Planas; 12 Yoan Tisseyre; 5 Clement Bienes; 6
Darren Nicholls; 7 Josh Lewis; 8 Brendan Worth; 13 Eric
Anselme; 10 Ged Corcoran; 11 Tim Wynn; 14 Antoni
Maria; 16 Sylvain Houles. Subs (all used): 17 Kevin
Larroyer; 15 Jerome Gout; 23 Teli Pelo; 19 Yohann
Gigord.
Tries: Nicholls (35, 61), Lewis (58); **Goals:** Lewis 3/3.
ROVERS: 1 Ian Hardman; 2 Bryn Powell; 3 Sam
Smeaton; 4 Andrew Bostock; 5 Tom Saxton; 6 Andy
Kain; 7 Liam Finn; 8 Tony Tonks; 9 Ben Kaye; 10 Stuart
Dickens; 11 Jon Grayshon; 12 Tim Spears; 17 Greg
Worthington. Subs (all used): 13 Matty Dale; 16 Iain
Morrison; 27 Dave Williams; 28 Jon Hepworth.
Tries: Finn (5, 26), Bostock (9), Saxton (13, 19),
Smeaton (29), Hardman (47), Grayshon (64),
Kain (72, 79); **Goals:** Finn 8/10.
Rugby Leaguer & League Express Men of the Match:
Olympique: Brendan Worth; *Rovers:* Liam Finn.
Penalty count: 4-4; **Half-time:** 6-32;
Referee: Gareth Hewer; **Attendance:** 1,500.

Sunday 3rd April 2011

SHEFFIELD EAGLES 41 HALIFAX 22

EAGLES: 6 Quentin Laulu-Togagae; 16 Vinny Finigan; 3
Menzie Yere; 4 Jason Crookes; 15 Tim Bergin; 2 Simon
Brown; 24 Kyle Wood; 22 Ryan Hepworth; 9 Andrew
Henderson; 10 Mitchell Stringer; 11 Alex Szostak; 12

Peter Green; 19 Joe Hirst. Subs (all used): 25 Jamie
Cording; 17 Alex Rowe; 27 Eddie Battye; 13 Dane
McDonald.
Tries: Yere (12), Finigan (16), Rowe (23), Bergin (28),
Henderson (51), Wood (55), Hepworth (80);
Goals: Brown 6/7; **Field goal:** Brown (74).
HALIFAX: 1 Miles Greenwood; 20 Paul White; 5 James
Haley; 3 Jon Goddard; 23 Rob Worrincy; 28 Graham
Holroyd; 7 Ben Black; 15 Jim Gannon; 13 Bob Beswick;
25 Michael Ostick; 18 Joe Chandler; 16 Paul Smith; 12
Sam Barlow. Subs (all used): 6 Danny Jones; 9 Sean
Penkywicz; 8 Makali Aizue; 10 Neil Cherryholme.
Tries: Chandler (6, 44), White (60), Worrincy (68);
Goals: Holroyd 3/4.
Rugby Leaguer & League Express Men of the Match:
Eagles: Mitchell Stringer; *Halifax:* Joe Chandler.
Penalty count: 7-9; **Half-time:** 22-6;
Referee: Matthew Thomason; **Attendance:** 1,282.

WIDNES VIKINGS 76 YORK CITY KNIGHTS 12

VIKINGS: 1 Danny Craven; 5 Paddy Flynn; 23 Tangi
Ropati; 4 Steve Tyrer; 2 Dean Gaskell; 15 Chris Gerrard; 7
Chaz I'Anson; 8 Steve Pickersgill; 14 Thomas Coyle; 17
Ben Kavanagh; 11 Dave Allen; 16 Macgraff Leuluai; 13
Simon Finnigan. Subs (all used): 3 Richard Varkulis; 6
Anthony Thackeray; 25 Chris Lunt; 42 Danny Sculthorpe.
Tries: Flynn (15), Tyrer (18, 22, 40), Craven (26), Leuluai
(45), Varkulis (50), Lunt (54), Thackeray (57, 77),
Pickersgill (65, 69), Finnigan (75); **Goals:** Tyrer 12/13.
Sin bin: Finnigan (44) - fighting.
CITY KNIGHTS: 30 Jordan Thompson; 4 Lee Waterman;
3 Duane Straugheir; 19 Matt Garside; 20 Tom Bush; 6
Chris Thorman; 7 Jon Presley; 33 Nathan Massey; 24
Mark Barlow; 10 Alex Benson; 31 John Davies; 25 Steve
Lewis; 11 Rhys Clarke. Subs (all used): 12 Matt Barron;
14 Jack Stearman; 28 Kris Brinning; 8 Nathan Freer.
Tries: Barron (38), Davies (59);
Goals: Waterman 1/1, Barlow 1/1.
Sin bin: Benson (44) - fighting.
Rugby Leaguer & League Express Men of the Match:
Vikings: Steve Tyrer; *City Knights:* John Davies.
Penalty count: 6-7; **Half-time:** 28-6;
Referee: Craig Halloran; **Attendance:** 4,087.

ROUND 5

Thursday 14th April 2011

FEATHERSTONE ROVERS 48 BARROW RAIDERS 12

ROVERS: 1 Ian Hardman; 2 Bryn Powell; 3 Sam
Smeaton; 4 Andrew Bostock; 5 Tom Saxton; 6 Andy
Kain; 7 Liam Finn; 8 Tony Tonks; 9 Ben Kaye; 10 Stuart
Dickens; 11 Jon Grayshon; 12 Tim Spears; 13 Matty
Dale. Subs (all used): 15 Michael Haley; 16 Iain
Morrison; 18 Ross Divorty; 28 Jon Hepworth.

Tries: Bostock (6, 40, 47), Smeaton (10, 49), Powell (18, 78), Kain (23), Dickens (26), Grayshon (55); **Goals:** Finn 4/10.
RAIDERS: 1 Gary Broadbent; 2 Andy Ballard; 39 Joe Wardle; 4 Liam Harrison; 5 James Nixon; 6 Jamie Rooney; 7 James Coyle; 25 Ben Davies; 9 Mark Gleeson; 10 Matt James; 13 Richard Fletcher; 26 Jack Hughes; 12 Ned Catic. Subs (all used): 11 Michael Knowles; 16 Zebastian Luisi; 24 Adam Walker; 8 Jamie Thackray.
Tries: Ballard (1), Wardle (68); **Goals:** Rooney 2/2.
Rugby Leaguer & League Express Men of the Match: *Rovers:* Liam Finn; *Raiders:* Zebastian Luisi.
Penalty count: 3-4; **Half-time:** 28-6;
Referee: Gareth Hewer; **Attendance:** 1,755.

Sunday 17th April 2011

HUNSLET HAWKS 28 TOULOUSE OLYMPIQUE 6

HAWKS: 1 Stuart Kain; 5 Waine Pryce; 12 Tom Haughey; 27 Elliot Kear; 2 Richie Barnett; 6 Danny Grimshaw; 22 Danny Ratcliffe; 8 Adam Sullivan; 14 Luke Haigh; 10 James Houston; 17 Rob Kelly; 11 Richard Blakeway; 13 David March. Subs (all used): 4 David Clayton; 19 Neil Lowe; 20 Andrew Yates; 23 Joe McLocklan.
Tries: Lowe (33), Barnett (35), Kain (61), Ratcliffe (69), Kear (78); **Goals:** Kear 4/5.
OLYMPIQUE: 24 Gregory White; 2 Sebastien Payan; 3 Sebastien Planas; 4 Constant Villegas; 18 Andrei Olari; 6 Darren Nicholls; 7 Josh Lewis; 8 Brendan Worth; 25 Tony Gigot; 21 Nicolas Faure; 11 Tim Wynn; 17 Kevin Larroyer; 13 Eric Anselme. Subs (all used): 10 Ged Corcoran; 14 Antoni Maria; 15 Jerome Gout; 20 Bruno Ormeno.
Try: Nicholls (26); **Goals:** Lewis 1/1.
Rugby Leaguer & League Express Men of the Match: *Hawks:* Stuart Kain; *Olympique:* Darren Nicholls.
Penalty count: 9-9; **Half-time:** 12-6;
Referee: George Stokes; **Attendance:** 518.

BATLEY BULLDOGS 32 WIDNES VIKINGS 12

BULLDOGS: 30 Johnny Campbell; 5 Wayne Reittie; 12 Jason Walton; 4 Danny Maun; 2 Alex Brown; 6 Paul Handforth; 1 Ian Preece; 8 Byron Smith; 9 Kris Lythe; 17 Craig Potter; 11 Alex Bretherton; 18 Dane Manning; 13 Ashley Lindsay. Subs (all used): 25 George Flanagan; 10 Sean Hesketh; 23 Chris Buttery; 20 David Tootill.
Tries: Reittie (33, 65), Preece (36), Flanagan (46), Bretherton (59), Lindsay (70);
Goals: Handforth 2/4, Flanagan 2/2.
VIKINGS: 24 Danny Hulme; 19 Matt Gardner; 23 Tangi Ropati; 18 James Ford; 5 Paddy Flynn; 6 Anthony Thackeray; 7 Chaz I'Anson; 8 Steve Pickersgill; 14 Thomas Coyle; 10 Daniel Heckenberg; 20 Shane Grady; 16 Macgraff Leuluai; 11 Dave Allen. Subs (all used): 3 Richard Varkulis; 15 Chris Gerrard; 38 Logan Tomkins; 39 Dominic Crosby.
Tries: Hulme (22), Varkulis (30); **Goals:** Grady 2/2.
Sin bin: Varkulis (77) - dissent.
Rugby Leaguer & League Express Men of the Match: *Bulldogs:* Ian Preece; *Vikings:* Anthony Thackeray.
Penalty count: 14-5; **Half-time:** 10-12;
Referee: Jamie Leahy; **Attendance:** 1,101.

DEWSBURY RAMS 12 SHEFFIELD EAGLES 36

RAMS: 4 Scott Turner; 2 Michael Wainwright; 32 Elliott Cosgrove; 35 Andy Smith; 5 Austin Buchanan; 25 Tom Wandless; 7 Dominic Brambani; 10 Keegan Hirst; 9 Luke Blake; 21 Kyle Bibb; 11 Rob Spicer; 12 James Lockwood; 13 Ayden Faal. Subs (all used): 23 Luke Menzies; 22 Jonny Horton; 24 Jake Wilson; 33 Shaun Emblem.
Tries: Buchanan (35), Brambani (74);
Goals: Brambani 2/3.
EAGLES: 6 Quentin Laulu-Togagae; 16 Vinny Finigan; 3 Menzie Yere; 4 Jason Crookes; 5 Tim Bergin; 24 Kyle Wood; 7 Simon Brown; 8 Jack Howieson; 9 Andrew Henderson; 10 Mitchell Stringer; 11 Alex Szostak; 12 Peter Green; 19 Joe Hirst. Subs (all used): 17 Alex Rowe; 13 Dane McDonald; 22 Ryan Hepworth; 25 Jamie Cording.
Tries: Crookes (20, 55), Yere (38), Laulu-Togagae (50), McDonald (76), Rowe (78); **Goals:** Brown 6/6.
Rugby Leaguer & League Express Men of the Match: *Rams:* Scott Turner; *Eagles:* Kyle Wood.
Penalty count: 10-8; **Half-time:** 4-12;
Referee: Ronnie Laughton; **Attendance:** 1,010.

HALIFAX 22 LEIGH CENTURIONS 32

HALIFAX: 1 Miles Greenwood; 20 Paul White; 2 Lee Paterson; 5 James Haley; 23 Rob Worrincy; 6 Danny Jones; 28 Graham Holroyd; 25 Michael Ostick; 13 Bob Beswick; 10 Neil Cherryholme; 16 Paul Smith; 24 Steve Bannister; 19 Jacob Fairbank. Subs (all used): 8 Makali Aizue; 9 Sean Penkywicz; 15 Jim Gannon; 18 Joe Chandler.
Tries: Chandler (32), Greenwood (38), Worrincy (76), Paterson (80); **Goals:** Holroyd 3/4.
CENTURIONS: 1 Stuart Donlan; 2 Steve Maden; 22 Tom Armstrong; 4 Mick Nanyn; 5 Dean McGilvray; 6 Martyn Ridyard; 25 Jamie Ellis; 8 Chris Hill; 9 John Duffy; 32 Lee Mitchell; 3 Stuart Littler; 12 Tommy Goulden; 11 James Taylor. Subs (all used): 15 Andy Thornley; 20 Sam Hopkins; 23 Mick Govin; 26 David Mills.
Tries: Ellis (5), Littler (20, 67), Hill (51), Maden (58, 63);
Goals: Nanyn 4/6.
Rugby Leaguer & League Express Men of the Match: *Halifax:* Miles Greenwood; *Centurions:* Chris Hill.
Penalty count: 5-8; **Half-time:** 10-10;
Referee: Clint Sharrad; **Attendance:** 2,479.

ROUND 6

Thursday 21st April 2011

DEWSBURY RAMS 20 BATLEY BULLDOGS 36

RAMS: 4 Scott Turner; 2 Michael Wainwright; 32 Elliott Cosgrove; 35 Andy Smith; 5 Austin Buchanan; 6 Pat Walker; 7 Dominic Brambani; 8 Anthony England; 9 Luke Blake; 10 Keegan Hirst; 11 Rob Spicer; 12 James Lockwood; 15 Josh Tonks. Subs (all used): 23 Luke Menzies; 21 Kyle Bibb; 36 Brooke Broughton; 22 Jonny Horton.
Tries: Cosgrove (10), Brambani (46), Spicer (75);
Goals: Brambani 4/5.
Dismissal: England (20) - punching.
BULLDOGS: 30 Johnny Campbell; 5 Wayne Reittie; 3 Daley Williams; 4 Danny Maun; 2 Alex Brown; 6 Paul Handforth; 1 Ian Preece; 8 Byron Smith; 9 Kris Lythe; 17 Craig Potter; 11 Alex Bretherton; 18 Dane Manning; 13 Ashley Lindsay. Subs (all used): 25 George Flanagan; 12 Jason Walton; 10 Sean Hesketh; 20 David Tootill.
Tries: Tootill (32), Walton (38), Manning (54), Maun (63), Brown (70), Flanagan (79);
Goals: Flanagan 4/4, Handforth 2/3.
Rugby Leaguer & League Express Men of the Match: *Rams:* Keegan Hirst; *Bulldogs:* Paul Handforth.
Penalty count: 6-10; **Half-time:** 8-12;
Referee: Tim Roby; **Attendance:** 1,184.

WIDNES VIKINGS 47 HALIFAX 36

VIKINGS: 24 Danny Hulme; 5 Paddy Flynn; 23 Tangi Ropati; 4 Steve Tyrer; 19 Matt Gardner; 7 Chaz I'Anson; 41 Joe Mellor; 3 Richard Varkulis; 14 Thomas Coyle; 17 Ben Kavanagh; 13 Simon Finnigan; 16 Macgraff Leuluai; 11 Dave Allen. Subs (all used): 20 Shane Grady; 22 David Houghton; 38 Logan Tomkins; 42 Danny Sculthorpe.
Tries: Hulme (2, 7, 10), Finnigan (19, 55), Tomkins (24, 34), T Coyle (29); **Goals:** Tyrer 7/10;
Field goal: I'Anson (71).
HALIFAX: 1 Miles Greenwood; 20 Paul White; 2 Lee Paterson; 5 James Haley; 23 Rob Worrincy; 7 Ben Black; 28 Graham Holroyd; 25 Michael Ostick; 13 Bob Beswick; 15 Jim Gannon; 18 Joe Chandler; 24 Steve Bannister; 19 Jacob Fairbank. Subs (all used): 4 Dylan Nash; 8 Makali Aizue; 9 Sean Penkywicz; 12 Sam Barlow.
Tries: Ostick (15), Paterson (21), Nash (37, 75), White (43), S Barlow (61); **Goals:** Holroyd 6/6.
On report:
Penkywicz (75) - alleged late challenge on I'Anson.
Rugby Leaguer & League Express Men of the Match: *Vikings:* Chaz I'Anson; *Halifax:* Graham Holroyd.
Penalty count: 6-6; **Half-time:** 38-18;
Referee: Ronnie Laughton; **Attendance:** 3,669.

Friday 22nd April 2011

LEIGH CENTURIONS 26 BARROW RAIDERS 24

CENTURIONS: 1 Stuart Donlan; 2 Steve Maden; 32 Rhys Evans; 4 Mick Nanyn; 5 Dean McGilvray; 6 Martyn Ridyard; 25 Jamie Ellis; 8 Chris Hill; 9 John Duffy; 20 Sam Hopkins; 3 Stuart Littler; 12 Tommy Goulden; 11 James Taylor. Subs (all used): 14 Adam Higson; 15 Andy Thornley; 16 Anthony Nicholson; 26 David Mills.
Tries: Donlan (30, 75), Evans (50), Nanyn (53), Ellis (68); **Goals:** Nanyn 3/5.
RAIDERS: 1 Gary Broadbent; 2 Andy Ballard; 3 Chris Larkin; 4 Liam Harrison; 19 Marc Dixon; 14 Liam Campbell; 7 James Coyle; 10 Matt James; 18 Nathan Mossop; 21 Jamie Butler; 12 Ned Catic; 26 Jack Hughes; 16 Zebastian Luisi. Subs: 6 Jamie Rooney; 9 Mark Gleeson; 11 Michael Knowles; 5 James Nixon (not used).
Tries: Ballard (24, 63), Harrison (34), Catic (71), Larkin (79); **Goals:** Ballard 0/1, Rooney 2/4.
Rugby Leaguer & League Express Men of the Match: *Centurions:* James Taylor; *Raiders:* Jack Hughes.
Penalty count: 6-3; **Half-time:** 6-8;
Referee: Gareth Hewer; **Attendance:** 2,583.

YORK CITY KNIGHTS 12 HUNSLET HAWKS 50

CITY KNIGHTS: 6 Chris Thorman; 2 Dave Sutton; 13 Ryan Esders; 3 Duane Straugheir; 4 Lee Waterman; 28 Ben Hardcastle; 7 Jon Presley; 8 Nathan Freer; 9 Jack Lee; 10 Alex Benson; 25 Steve Lewis; 19 Matt Garside; 11 Rhys Clarke. Subs (all used): 24 Mark Barlow; 15 Brett Waller; 35 Mark Castle; 14 Jack Stearman.
Tries: Hardcastle (8), Thorman (67); **Goals:** Thorman 2/2.
Sin bin: Esders (52) - dangerous tackle.
HAWKS: 1 Stuart Kain; 5 Waine Pryce; 12 Tom Haughey; 27 Elliot Kear; 2 Richie Barnett; 6 Danny Grimshaw; 22 Danny Ratcliffe; 8 Adam Sullivan; 14 Luke Haigh; 10 James Houston; 17 Rob Kelly; 11 Richard Blakeway; 13 David March. Subs (all used): 23 Joe McLocklan; 19 Neil Lowe; 20 Andrew Yates; 4 David Clayton.
Tries: Barnett (18, 49), Haughey (24), Grimshaw (38), Pryce (46, 58), Kear (70, 79), Yates (76); **Goals:** Kear 7/9.
Rugby Leaguer & League Express Men of the Match: *City Knights:* Steve Lewis; *Hawks:* Elliot Kear.
Penalty count: 7-12; **Half-time:** 6-18;
Referee: Jamie Leahy; **Attendance:** 1,036.

ROUND 7

Monday 25th April 2011

BARROW RAIDERS 30 WIDNES VIKINGS 12

RAIDERS: 1 Gary Broadbent; 2 Andy Ballard; 3 Chris Larkin; 4 Liam Harrison; 19 Marc Dixon; 6 Jamie Rooney; 7 James Coyle; 10 Matt James; 18 Nathan Mossop; 21 Jamie Butler; 12 Ned Catic; 26 Jack Hughes; 16 Zebastian Luisi. Subs (all used): 5 James Nixon; 9 Mark Gleeson; 11 Michael Knowles; 25 Ben Davies.
Tries: Catic (3), Ballard (10, 34), Harrison (29), Larkin (69); **Goals:** Rooney 5/5.
Sin bin: Davies (39) - interference.
VIKINGS: 24 Danny Hulme; 5 Paddy Flynn; 23 Tangi Ropati; 4 Steve Tyrer; 19 Matt Gardner; 7 Chaz I'Anson; 41 Joe Mellor; 8 Steve Pickersgill; 14 Thomas Coyle; 17 Ben Kavanagh; 13 Simon Finnigan; 16 Macgraff Leuluai; 11 Dave Allen. Subs (all used): 2 Dean Gaskell; 3 Richard Varkulis; 22 David Houghton; 38 Logan Tomkins.
Tries: Mellor (21, 79); **Goals:** Tyrer 2/2.
Rugby Leaguer & League Express Men of the Match: *Raiders:* Andy Ballard; *Vikings:* Joe Mellor.
Half-time: 24-6; **Referee:** Jamie Leahy;
Attendance: 1,965.

BATLEY BULLDOGS 16 SHEFFIELD EAGLES 28

BULLDOGS: 30 Johnny Campbell; 5 Wayne Reittie; 3 Daley Williams; 4 Danny Maun; 2 Alex Brown; 6 Paul Handforth; 19 Mark Toohey; 8 Byron Smith; 9 Kris Lythe; 17 Craig Potter; 11 Alex Bretherton; 18 Dane Manning; 13 Ashley Lindsay. Subs (all used): 25 George Flanagan; 23 Chris Buttery; 10 Sean Hesketh; 20 David Tootill.
Tries: Daley Williams (15), Flanagan (61), Campbell (78); **Goals:** Flanagan 2/2, Handforth 0/1.
EAGLES: 6 Quentin Laulu-Togagae; 16 Vinny Finigan; 3 Menzie Yere; 4 Jason Crookes; 5 Tim Bergin; 13 Dane McDonald; 7 Simon Brown; 8 Jack Howieson; 9 Andrew Henderson; 10 Mitchell Stringer; 11 Alex Szostak; 12 Peter Green; 19 Joe Hirst. Subs (all used): 17 Alex Rowe; 26 Corey Hanson; 22 Ryan Hepworth; 2 Danny Mills.
Tries: Laulu-Togagae (2), Henderson (6), Yere (20), Hirst (31), Finigan (35); **Goals:** Brown 4/5.
Rugby Leaguer & League Express Men of the Match: *Bulldogs:* George Flanagan;
Eagles: Quentin Laulu-Togagae.
Half-time: 4-28; **Referee:** Gareth Hewer;
Attendance: 843.

HALIFAX 56 DEWSBURY RAMS 24

HALIFAX: 1 Miles Greenwood; 20 Paul White; 3 Jon Goddard; 4 Dylan Nash; 23 Rob Worrincy; 7 Ben Black; 28 Graham Holroyd; 10 Neil Cherryholme; 9 Sean Penkywicz; 15 Jim Gannon; 16 Paul Smith; 12 Sam Barlow; 14 Ryan Clayton. Subs (all used): 6 Danny Jones; 19 Jacob Fairbank; 17 Frank Watene; 8 Makali Aizue.
Tries: Penkywicz (1, 45), Worrincy (22), S Barlow (25, 66, 75), Nash (38, 62), Smith (51), Greenwood (70); **Goals:** Holroyd 8/10.
RAMS: 1 James Craven; 2 Michael Wainwright; 4 Scott Turner; 13 Ayden Faal; 35 Andy Smith; 6 Pat Walker; 7 Dominic Brambani; 8 Anthony England; 9 Luke Blake; 10 Keegan Hirst; 11 Rob Spicer; 32 Elliott Cosgrove; 15 Josh Tonks. Subs (all used): 12 James Lockwood; 23 Luke Menzies; 33 Shaun Emblem; 22 Jonny Horton.
Tries: Cosgrove (32), Turner (77), Tonks (79), Horton (80); **Goals:** Brambani 3/3, P Walker 1/1.
Rugby Leaguer & League Express Men of the Match: *Halifax:* Sean Penkywicz; *Rams:* Rob Spicer.
Half-time: 22-6; **Referee:** Chris Leatherbarrow;
Attendance: 1,745.

FEATHERSTONE ROVERS 28 LEIGH CENTURIONS 28

ROVERS: 1 Ian Hardman; 2 Bryn Powell; 3 Sam Smeaton; 4 Andrew Bostock; 5 Tom Saxton; 6 Andy Kain; 7 Liam Finn; 8 Tony Tonks; 9 Ben Kaye; 10 Stuart Dickens; 11 Jon Grayshon; 12 Tim Spears; 13 Matty Dale. Subs (all used): 15 Michael Haley; 16 Iain Morrison; 18 Ross Divorty; 28 Jon Hepworth.
Tries: Powell (2, 18), Hardman (31), Grayshon (49), Bostock (52); **Goals:** Finn 4/5.
CENTURIONS: 1 Stuart Donlan; 2 Steve Maden; 32 Rhys Evans; 4 Mick Nanyn; 5 Dean McGilvray; 6 Martyn Ridyard; 25 Jamie Ellis; 8 Chris Hill; 16 Anthony Nicholson; 20 Sam Hopkins; 3 Stuart Littler; 12 Tommy Goulden; 11 James Taylor. Subs (all used): 15 Andy Thornley; 23 Mick Govin; 26 David Mills; 14 Adam Higson.
Tries: Ellis (11, 27), Evans (36), Goulden (62), Nanyn (78); **Goals:** Nanyn 4/5.
Rugby Leaguer & League Express Men of the Match: *Rovers:* Stuart Dickens; *Centurions:* Rhys Evans.
Half-time: 18-16; **Referee:** Tim Roby; **Attendance:** 2,375.

TOULOUSE OLYMPIQUE 10 YORK CITY KNIGHTS 16

OLYMPIQUE: 24 Gregory White; 2 Sebastien Payan; 3 Sebastien Planas; 20 Bruno Ormeno; 22 Damien Couturier; 6 Darren Nicholls; 4 Constant Villegas; 8 Brendan Worth; 25 Tony Gigot; 10 Ged Corcoran; 11 Tim Wynn; 14 Antoni Maria; 13 Eric Anselme. Subs (all used): 12 Yoan Tisseyre; 15 Jerome Gout; 21 Nicolas Faure; 16 Sylvain Houles.
Tries: Planas (32), Nicholls (64);
Goals: Nicholls 0/1, Couturier 1/1.
Dismissal: Worth (75) - fighting.
CITY KNIGHTS: 6 Chris Thorman; 2 Dave Sutton; 19 Matt Garside; 4 Lee Waterman; 5 Danny Wilson; 28 Ben Hardcastle; 7 Jon Presley; 8 Nathan Freer; 9 Jack Lee; 10 Alex Benson; 11 Rhys Clarke; 3 Duane Straugheir; 24 Mark Barlow. Subs (all used): 15 Brett Waller; 20 Tom Bush; 14 Jack Stearman; 25 Steve Lewis.
Tries: Waterman (3), Lee (9), Clarke (54);
Goals: Thorman 0/2, Hardcastle 2/2.
Dismissal: Waller (75) - fighting.
Rugby Leaguer & League Express Men of the Match: *Olympique:* Darren Nicholls; *City Knights:* Nathan Freer.
Half-time: 4-8; **Referee:** Warren Turley; **Attendance:** 650.

ROUND 8

Thursday 28th April 2011

WIDNES VIKINGS 26 TOULOUSE OLYMPIQUE 12

VIKINGS: 5 Paddy Flynn; 2 Dean Gaskell; 23 Tangi Ropati; 4 Steve Tyrer; 19 Matt Gardner; 7 Chaz I'Anson; 41 Joe Mellor; 8 Steve Pickersgill; 14 Thomas Coyle; 17 Ben Kavanagh; 13 Simon Finnigan; 16 Macgraff Leuluai; 11 Dave Allen. Subs (all used): 20 Shane Grady; 38 Logan Tomkins; 42 Danny Sculthorpe; 39 Dominic Crosby.
Tries: Crosby (23), Gaskell (40), Mellor (42), Tomkins (48), Ropati (53); **Goals:** Tyrer 3/5.
OLYMPIQUE: 22 Damien Couturier; 2 Sebastien Payan; 3 Sebastien Planas; 4 Constant Villegas; 24 Gregory White; 6 Darren Nicholls; 25 Tony Gigot; 8 Brendan Worth; 19 Yohann Gigord; 10 Ged Corcoran; 11 Tim Wynn; 14 Antoni Maria; 13 Eric Anselme. Subs (all used): 12 Yoan Tisseyre; 23 Teli Pelo; 32 Theo Gonzalez-Trique; 34 Cyril Moliner.
Tries: White (32), Tisseyre (65); **Goals:** Nicholls 2/3.
Rugby Leaguer & League Express Men of the Match:
Vikings: Tangi Ropati; *Olympique:* Darren Nicholls.
Penalty count: 6-4; **Half-time:** 10-6;
Referee: Matthew Thomason; **Attendance:** 3,601.

Sunday 1st May 2011

HALIFAX 25 BARROW RAIDERS 43

HALIFAX: 1 Miles Greenwood; 23 Rob Worrincy; 4 Dylan Nash; 5 James Haley; 20 Paul White; 28 Graham Holroyd; 6 Danny Jones; 15 Jim Gannon; 9 Sean Penkywicz; 10 Neil Cherryholme; 16 Paul Smith; 14 Ryan Clayton; 12 Sam Barlow. Subs (all used): 13 Bob Beswick; 17 Frank Watene; 18 Joe Chandler; 19 Jacob Fairbank.
Tries: Worrincy (10), White (25), Jones (31), S Barlow (65); **Goals:** Holroyd 4/4; **Field goal:** Holroyd (70).
RAIDERS: 1 Gary Broadbent; 5 James Nixon; 3 Chris Larkin; 4 Liam Harrison; 2 Andy Ballard; 6 Jamie Rooney; 9 Mark Gleeson; 24 Adam Walker; 18 Nathan Mossop; 21 Jamie Butler; 11 Michael Knowles; 12 Ned Catic; 16 Zebastian Luisi. Subs: 10 Matt James; 25 Ben Davies; 26 Jack Hughes; 7 James Coyle (not used).
Tries: Catic (16), Larkin (37, 76), Knowles (43), Ballard (56), Hughes (70), Rooney (80);
Goals: Rooney 7/7; **Field goal:** Rooney (79).
Rugby Leaguer & League Express Men of the Match:
Halifax: Sam Barlow; *Raiders:* Zebastian Luisi.
Penalty count: 8-6; **Half-time:** 18-12;
Referee: Gareth Hewer; **Attendance:** 1,757.

HUNSLET HAWKS 12 FEATHERSTONE ROVERS 48

HAWKS: 1 Stuart Kain; 5 Waine Pryce; 12 Tom Haughey; 27 Elliot Kear; 2 Richie Barnett; 6 Danny Grimshaw; 22 Danny Ratcliffe; 8 Adam Sullivan; 14 Luke Haigh; 10 James Houston; 11 Richard Blakeway; 17 Rob Kelly; 13 David March. Subs (all used): 4 David Clayton; 19 Neil Lowe; 20 Andrew Yates; 23 Joe McLocklan.
Tries: Kain (45), Ratcliffe (65); **Goals:** Kear 2/2.
ROVERS: 28 Jon Hepworth; 2 Bryn Powell; 3 Sam Smeaton; 31 Nathan Chappell; 5 Tom Saxton; 6 Andy Kain; 7 Liam Finn; 16 Iain Morrison; 29 Tom Hemingway; 15 Michael Haley; 11 Jon Grayshon; 18 Ross Divorty; 13 Matty Dale. Subs (all used): 8 Tony Tonks; 10 Stuart Dickens; 12 Tim Spears; 14 Liam Welham.
Tries: Saxton (8), Dale (11), Hepworth (14, 48), Divorty (33), Hemingway (36), Chappell (38), Finn (41), Kain (75); **Goals:** Finn 6/9.
Rugby Leaguer & League Express Men of the Match:
Hawks: Danny Grimshaw; *Rovers:* Liam Finn.
Penalty count: 5-6; **Half-time:** 0-32;
Referee: Ronnie Laughton; **Attendance:** 905.

LEIGH CENTURIONS 36 BATLEY BULLDOGS 12

CENTURIONS: 1 Stuart Donlan; 32 Rhys Evans; 21 Matty Blythe; 4 Mick Nanyn; 5 Dean McGilvray; 6 Martyn Ridyard; 25 Jamie Ellis; 8 Chris Hill; 16 Anthony Nicholson; 13 Stephen Nash; 3 Stuart Littler; 12 Tommy Goulden; 11 James Taylor. Subs (all used): 14 Adam Higson; 15 Andy Thornley; 23 Mick Govin; 26 David Mills.
Tries: Blythe (4), Donlan (18, 45), Ellis (29), Nicholson (70), Nash (80); **Goals:** Nanyn 4/4, Ridyard 2/2.
BULLDOGS: 30 Johnny Campbell; 5 Wayne Reittie; 3 Daley Williams; 4 Danny Maun; 2 Alex Brown; 6 Paul Handforth; 1 Ian Preece; 8 Byron Smith; 9 Kris Lythe; 17 Craig Potter; 11 Alex Bretherton; 18 Dane Manning; 23 Chris Buttery. Subs (all used): 10 Sean Hesketh; 13 Ashley Lindsay; 20 David Tootill; 25 George Flanagan.
Tries: Reittie (53), Daley Williams (57);
Goals: Handforth 2/2.
Rugby Leaguer & League Express Men of the Match:
Centurions: Jamie Ellis; *Bulldogs:* Paul Handforth.
Penalty count: 10-5; **Half-time:** 18-0;
Referee: Tim Roby; **Attendance:** 2,285.

YORK CITY KNIGHTS 30 DEWSBURY RAMS 26

CITY KNIGHTS: 20 Tom Bush; 2 Dave Sutton; 29 James Ford; 13 Ryan Esders; 4 Lee Waterman; 27 Anthony Thackeray; 7 Jon Presley; 8 Nathan Freer; 9 Jack Lee; 10 Alex Benson; 3 Duane Straugheir; 11 Rhys Clarke; 6 Chris Thorman. Subs (all used): 24 Mark Barlow; 15 Brett Waller; 19 Matt Garside; 25 Steve Lewis.
Tries: Thorman (30), Waller (34), Garside (45), Clarke (62), Esders (64); **Goals:** Waterman 5/6.
RAMS: 4 Scott Turner; 2 Michael Wainwright; 32 Elliott Cosgrove; 13 Ayden Faal; 5 Austin Buchanan; 25 Tom Wandless; 7 Dominic Brambani; 10 Keegan Hirst; 9 Luke Blake; 23 Luke Menzies; 11 Rob Spicer; 12 James Lockwood; 6 Pat Walker. Subs (all used): 33 Shaun Emblem; 8 Anthony England; 21 Kyle Bibb; 15 Josh Tonks.
Tries: Menzies (7), Buchanan (19), Wainwright (40), Spicer (55), Faal (72); **Goals:** Brambani 3/5.
Rugby Leaguer & League Express Men of the Match:
City Knights: Anthony Thackeray;
Rams: Dominic Brambani.
Penalty count: 2-7; **Half-time:** 12-18;
Referee: George Stokes; **Attendance:** 1,098.

ROUND 9

Saturday 14th May 2011

TOULOUSE OLYMPIQUE 28 HUNSLET HAWKS 6

OLYMPIQUE: 24 Gregory White; 2 Sebastien Payan; 3 Sebastien Planas; 20 Bruno Ormeno; 33 Antoine Reveillon; 6 Darren Nicholls; 4 Constant Villegas; 8 Brendan Worth; 9 Craig Cook; 10 Ged Corcoran; 11 Tim Wynn; 14 Antoni Maria; 16 Sylvain Houles. Subs (all used): 12 Yoan Tisseyre; 15 Jerome Gout; 21 Nicolas Faure; 19 Yohann Gigord.
Tries: Houles (10), Tisseyre (30, 34), Ormeno (58), Nicholls (71); **Goals:** Nicholls 4/5.
HAWKS: 1 Stuart Kain; 4 David Clayton; 16 John Oakes; 12 Tom Haughey; 5 Waine Pryce; 6 Danny Grimshaw; 7 Paul March; 8 Adam Sullivan; 14 Luke Haigh; 10 James Houston; 11 Richard Blakeway; 25 Steve Dooler; 13 David March. Subs (all used): 17 Rob Kelly; 9 Richard Chapman; 18 Joe Helme; 20 Andrew Yates.
Try: Pryce (17); **Goals:** D March 1/2.
Sin bin: D March (68) - interference;
P March (72) - punching.
Rugby Leaguer & League Express Men of the Match:
Olympique: Sylvain Houles; *Hawks:* Luke Haigh.
Penalty count: 9-9; **Half-time:** 16-6;
Referee: Craig Halloran; **Attendance:** 645.

BARROW RAIDERS 34 YORK CITY KNIGHTS 12

RAIDERS: 23 Gregg McNally; 2 Andy Ballard; 3 Chris Larkin; 4 Liam Harrison; 27 Mike Backhouse; 6 Jamie Rooney; 14 Liam Campbell; 21 Jamie Butler; 18 Nathan Mossop; 24 Adam Walker; 15 Martin Ostler; 12 Ned Catic; 16 Zebastian Luisi. Subs (all used): 8 Jamie Thackray; 10 Matt James; 11 Michael Knowles; 25 Ben Davies.
Tries: Thackray (15), Campbell (25), James (40), McNally (47), Catic (62), Ballard (69, 77);
Goals: Rooney 3/7.
CITY KNIGHTS: 20 Tom Bush; 2 Dave Sutton; 19 Matt Garside; 29 James Ford; 4 Lee Waterman; 27 Anthony Thackeray; 7 Jon Presley; 8 Nathan Freer; 9 Jack Lee; 10 Alex Benson; 13 Ryan Esders; 3 Duane Straugheir; 6 Chris Thorman. Subs (all used): 14 Jack Stearman; 15 Brett Waller; 24 Mark Barlow; 11 Rhys Clarke.
Tries: Stearman (35), Barlow (75); **Goals:** Waterman 2/2.
Rugby Leaguer & League Express Men of the Match:
Raiders: Matt James; *City Knights:* Lee Waterman.
Penalty count: 9-8; **Half-time:** 16-6;
Referee: Jamie Leahy; **Attendance:** 1,271.

Sunday 15th May 2011

DEWSBURY RAMS 34 WIDNES VIKINGS 34

RAMS: 38 Elliot Hodgson; 2 Michael Wainwright; 4 Scott Turner; 13 Ayden Faal; 5 Austin Buchanan; 6 Pat Walker; 7 Dominic Brambani; 8 Anthony England; 9 Luke Blake; 10 Keegan Hirst; 15 Josh Tonks; 11 Rob Spicer; 32 Elliott Cosgrove. Subs (all used): 19 James Walker; 20 Scott Glassell; 23 Luke Menzies; 35 Andy Smith.
Tries: Faal (6), Turner (13), Hodgson (16), Cosgrove (48), Brambani (53), Buchanan (79); **Goals:** Brambani 5/6.
VIKINGS: 5 Paddy Flynn; 2 Dean Gaskell; 23 Tangi Ropati; 4 Steve Tyrer; 41 Kevin Penny; 7 Chaz I'Anson; 40 Joe Mellor; 8 Steve Pickersgill; 14 Thomas Coyle; 17 Ben Kavanagh; 16 Macgraff Leuluai; 20 Shane Grady; 11 Dave Allen. Subs (all used): 3 Richard Varkulis; 38 Logan Tomkins; 39 Dominic Crosby; 42 Danny Sculthorpe.
Tries: I'Anson (20, 30), Leuluai (25), Allen (39), Flynn (63), Tyrer (70); **Goals:** Tyrer 5/6.
Rugby Leaguer & League Express Men of the Match:
Rams: Dominic Brambani; *Vikings:* Thomas Coyle.
Penalty count: 8-4; **Half-time:** 16-24;
Referee: Tim Roby; **Attendance:** 1,087.

FEATHERSTONE ROVERS 30 HALIFAX 18

ROVERS: 1 Ian Hardman; 2 Bryn Powell; 3 Sam Smeaton; 4 Andrew Bostock; 28 Jon Hepworth; 6 Andy Kain; 7 Liam Finn; 15 Michael Haley; 30 Kirk Netherton; 10 Stuart Dickens; 11 Jon Grayshon; 12 Tim Spears; 13 Matty Dale. Subs (all used): 8 Tony Tonks; 18 Ross Divorty; 16 Iain Morrison; 17 Greg Worthington.
Tries: Bostock (6), Hepworth (15, 80), Worthington (23), Dale (26), Powell (68); **Goals:** Finn 3/8.
HALIFAX: 6 Danny Jones; 20 Paul White; 2 Lee Paterson; 4 Dylan Nash; 23 Rob Worrincy; 13 Bob Beswick; 7 Ben Black; 15 Jim Gannon; 9 Sean Penkywicz; 10 Neil Cherryholme; 12 Sam Barlow; 24 Steve Bannister; 19 Jacob Fairbank. Subs (all used): 8 Makali Aizue; 14 Ryan Clayton; 17 Frank Watene; 18 Joe Chandler.
Tries: Jones (26), White (42), Bannister (48);
Goals: Paterson 3/3.
Sin bin: Penkywicz (39) - dissent.
Rugby Leaguer & League Express Men of the Match:
Rovers: Michael Haley; *Halifax:* Makali Aizue.
Penalty count: 5-6; **Half-time:** 20-6;
Referee: Gareth Hewer; **Attendance:** 1,377.

SHEFFIELD EAGLES 8 LEIGH CENTURIONS 44

EAGLES: 6 Quentin Laulu-Togagae; 2 Danny Mills; 3 Menzie Yere; 4 Jason Crookes; 16 Vinny Finigan; 24 Kyle Wood; 7 Simon Brown; 8 Jack Howieson; 9 Andrew Henderson; 10 Mitchell Stringer; 11 Alex Szostak; 19 Joe Hirst; 13 Dane McDonald. Subs (all used): 1 Misi Taulapapa; 12 Peter Green; 17 Alex Rowe; 22 Ryan Hepworth.
Try: Laulu-Togagae (70); **Goals:** Brown 1/1, Stringer 1/1.
CENTURIONS: 1 Stuart Donlan; 32 Rhys Evans; 21 Matty Blythe; 4 Mick Nanyn; 5 Dean McGilvray; 6 Martyn Ridyard; 25 Jamie Ellis; 8 Chris Hill; 9 John Duffy; 26 David Mills; 3 Stuart Littler; 12 Tommy Goulden; 11 James Taylor. Subs (all used): 2 Steve Maden; 13 Stephen Nash; 15 Andy Thornley; 23 Mick Govin.
Tries: Nanyn (11), McGilvray (23), Ridyard (32, 76), Blythe (34), Littler (37), Goulden (66), Ellis (77);
Goals: Nanyn 6/8.
Rugby Leaguer & League Express Men of the Match:
Eagles: Quentin Laulu-Togagae;
Centurions: Martyn Ridyard.
Penalty count: 4-5; **Half-time:** 2-26;
Referee: Matthew Thomason; **Attendance:** 1,778.

ROUND 10

Thursday 19th May 2011

BATLEY BULLDOGS 50 YORK CITY KNIGHTS 16

BULLDOGS: 1 Ian Preece; 5 Wayne Reittie; 3 Daley Williams; 4 Danny Maun; 2 Alex Brown; 6 Paul Handforth; 16 Paul Mennell; 8 Byron Smith; 9 Kris Lythe; 17 Craig Potter; 18 Dane Manning; 11 Alex Bretherton; 13 Ashley Lindsay. Subs (all used): 23 Chris Buttery; 12 Jason Walton; 10 Sean Hesketh; 15 Adam Robinson.
Tries: Bretherton (4), Reittie (9, 40), Brown (14, 45, 57), Maun (21), Hesketh (48), Preece (72), Robinson (75);
Goals: Handforth 5/10.
CITY KNIGHTS: 20 Tom Bush; 2 Dave Sutton; 3 Duane Straugheir; 29 James Ford; 5 Danny Wilson; 27 Anthony Thackeray; 7 Jon Presley; 13 Ryan Esders; 9 Jack Lee; 10 Alex Benson; 11 Rhys Clarke; 24 Mark Barlow; 6 Chris Thorman. Subs (all used): 14 Jack Stearman; 34 Davey Burns; 19 Matt Garside; 1 James Haynes.
Tries: Ford (25), Straugheir (36), Stearman (80);
Goals: Bush 1/2, Barlow 1/1.
Rugby Leaguer & League Express Men of the Match:
Bulldogs: Paul Handforth;
City Knights: Anthony Thackeray.
Penalty count: 9-8; **Half-time:** 24-10;
Referee: Ronnie Laughton; **Attendance:** 806.

Saturday 21st May 2011

BARROW RAIDERS 18 DEWSBURY RAMS 14

RAIDERS: 23 Gregg McNally; 2 Andy Ballard; 3 Chris Larkin; 4 Liam Harrison; 27 Mike Backhouse; 6 Jamie Rooney; 14 Liam Campbell; 21 Jamie Butler; 18 Nathan Mossop; 10 Matt James; 11 Michael Knowles; 15 Martin Ostler; 16 Zebastian Luisi. Subs (all used): 25 Ben Davies; 9 Mark Gleeson; 8 Jamie Thackray; 24 Adam Walker.
Tries: Backhouse (2), Ballard (7), Larkin (33);
Goals: Rooney 3/3.
RAMS: 38 Elliot Hodgson; 2 Michael Wainwright; 4 Scott Turner; 13 Ayden Faal; 5 Austin Buchanan; 6 Pat Walker; 7 Dominic Brambani; 8 Anthony England; 20 Scott Glassell; 10 Keegan Hirst; 32 Elliott Cosgrove; 11 Rob Spicer; 15 Josh Tonks. Subs (all used): 23 Luke Menzies; 12 James Lockwood; 35 Andy Smith; 33 Shaun Emblem.
Tries: Buchanan (17, 36), Brambani (57);
Goals: Brambani 1/3.
On report:
Cosgrove (10) - alleged dangerous tackle on Knowles.
Rugby Leaguer & League Express Men of the Match:
Raiders: Andy Ballard; *Rams:* Dominic Brambani.
Penalty count: 7-6; **Half-time:** 18-8;
Referee: George Stokes; **Attendance:** 1,339.

Sunday 22nd May 2011

HALIFAX 14 SHEFFIELD EAGLES 12

HALIFAX: 1 Miles Greenwood; 20 Paul White; 2 Lee Paterson; 3 Jon Goddard; 23 Rob Worrincy; 6 Danny Jones; 13 Bob Beswick; 15 Jim Gannon; 9 Sean Penkywicz; 10 Neil Cherryholme; 16 Paul Smith; 24 Steve Bannister; 19 Jacob Fairbank. Subs (all used): 4 Dylan Nash; 8 Makali Aizue; 14 Ryan Clayton; 17 Frank Watene.
Tries: Bannister (13), Penkywicz (52); **Goals:** Jones 3/4.
Sin bin: Nash (77) - fighting.
EAGLES: 6 Quentin Laulu-Togagae; 2 Danny Mills; 3 Menzie Yere; 4 Jason Crookes; 16 Vinny Finigan; 24 Kyle Wood; 7 Simon Brown; 8 Jack Howieson; 9 Andrew Henderson; 10 Mitchell Stringer; 11 Alex Szostak; 12 Peter Green; 19 Joe Hirst. Subs: 1 Misi Taulapapa; 26 Corey Hanson (not used); 17 Alex Rowe; 22 Ryan Hepworth.
Tries: Laulu-Togagae (21), Szostak (31), Finigan (72);
Goals: Stringer 0/2, Wood 0/1.
Sin bin: Rowe (77) - fighting.
Rugby Leaguer & League Express Men of the Match:
Halifax: Sean Penkywicz; *Eagles:* Andrew Henderson.
Penalty count: 16-8; **Half-time:** 6-8;
Referee: Warren Turley; **Attendance:** 1,788.

LEIGH CENTURIONS 56 HUNSLET HAWKS 18

CENTURIONS: 1 Stuart Donlan; 2 Steve Maden; 14 Adam Higson; 4 Mick Nanyn; 5 Dean McGilvray; 6 Martyn Ridyard; 25 Jamie Ellis; 8 Chris Hill; 9 John Duffy; 26 David Mills; 3 Stuart Littler; 12 Tommy Goulden; 11 James Taylor. Subs (all used): 13 Stephen Nash; 15 Andy Thornley; 19 Jonathan Pownall; 23 Mick Govin.

Halifax's Rob Worrincy leaps for a high ball against Leigh

Tries: Maden (9, 79), Donlan (12, 49), Ellis (15, 31), Nash (37), Nanyn (42), Higson (57), Littler (66);
Goals: Nanyn 8/10.
HAWKS: 1 Stuart Kain; 28 Dennis Tuffour; 16 John Oakes; 4 David Clayton; 24 Matthew Harding; 6 Danny Grimshaw; 22 Danny Ratcliffe; 8 Adam Sullivan; 9 Richard Chapman; 10 James Houston; 11 Richard Blakeway; 17 Rob Kelly; 13 David March. Subs (all used): 19 Neil Lowe; 20 Andrew Yates; 23 Joe McLocklan; 25 Steve Dooler.
Tries: Chapman (2), Oakes (20), Tuffour (74);
Goals: Ratcliffe 3/4.
Rugby Leaguer & League Express Men of the Match: *Centurions:* Jamie Ellis; *Hawks:* Andrew Yates.
Penalty count: 8-9; **Half-time:** 28-12;
Referee: Clint Sharrad; **Attendance:** 2,071.

ROUND 11

Thursday 26th May 2011

WIDNES VIKINGS 42 BARROW RAIDERS 14

VIKINGS: 34 Jack Owens; 5 Paddy Flynn; 23 Tangi Ropati; 4 Steve Tyrer; 41 Kevin Penny; 7 Chaz I'Anson; 40 Joe Mellor; 8 Steve Pickersgill; 14 Thomas Coyle; 17 Ben Kavanagh; 13 Simon Finnigan; 16 Macgraff Leuluai; 11 Dave Allen. Subs (all used): 3 Richard Varkulis; 19 Matt Gardner; 38 Logan Tomkins; 39 Dominic Crosby.
Tries: I'Anson (8), Flynn (20), Owens (24), Penny (35), Tomkins (55), Tyrer (55), Mellor (70), T Coyle (80);
Goals: Tyrer 5/8.
RAIDERS: 23 Gregg McNally; 2 Andy Ballard; 3 Chris Larkin; 4 Liam Harrison; 19 Marc Dixon; 16 Zebastian Luisi; 6 Jamie Rooney; 24 Adam Walker; 9 Mark Gleeson; 21 Jamie Butler; 26 Jack Hughes; 10 Matt James; 11 Michael Knowles. Subs (all used): 8 Jamie Thackray; 18 Nathan Mossop; 25 Ben Davies; 15 Martin Ostler.
Tries: Ballard (17, 60); **Goals:** Rooney 3/3.
Sin bin: Davies (44) - late challenge on I'Anson.
Rugby Leaguer & League Express Men of the Match: *Vikings:* Paddy Flynn; *Raiders:* Andy Ballard.
Penalty count: 7-4; **Half-time:** 22-8;
Referee: Clint Sharrad; **Attendance:** 3,331.

Saturday 28th May 2011

TOULOUSE OLYMPIQUE 18 BATLEY BULLDOGS 28

OLYMPIQUE: 25 Tony Gigot; 24 Gregory White; 3 Sebastien Planas; 20 Bruno Ormeno; 33 Antoine Reveillon; 6 Darren Nicholls; 4 Constant Villegas; 11 Tim Wynn; 9 Craig Cook; 10 Ged Corcoran; 14 Antoni Maria; 12 Yoan Tisseyre; 16 Sylvain Houles. Subs (all used): 13 Eric Anselme; 15 Jerome Gout; 21 Nicolas Faure; 17 Kevin Larroyer.

Tries: Corcoran (21), Nicholls (44, 57);
Goals: Nicholls 3/3.
BULLDOGS: 1 Ian Preece; 2 Alex Brown; 4 Danny Maun; 12 Jason Walton; 5 Wayne Reittie; 6 Paul Handforth; 16 Paul Mennell; 8 Byron Smith; 9 Kris Lythe; 17 Craig Potter; 18 Dane Manning; 11 Alex Bretherton; 13 Ashley Lindsay. Subs (all used): 23 Chris Buttery; 19 Mark Toohey; 10 Sean Hesketh; 15 Adam Robinson.
Tries: Walton (8, 55), Preece (26, 73), Lythe (68);
Goals: Handforth 3/4, Mennell 1/1.
Rugby Leaguer & League Express Men of the Match: *Olympique:* Tim Wynn; *Bulldogs:* Paul Handforth.
Penalty count: 3-7; **Half-time:** 6-12;
Referee: George Stokes; **Attendance:** 1,855.

Sunday 29th May 2011

DEWSBURY RAMS 18 FEATHERSTONE ROVERS 38

RAMS: 38 Elliot Hodgson; 2 Michael Wainwright; 4 Scott Turner; 13 Ayden Faal; 5 Austin Buchanan; 34 William Barthau; 7 Dominic Brambani; 8 Anthony England; 20 Scott Glassell; 10 Keegan Hirst; 11 Rob Spicer; 32 Elliott Cosgrove; 15 Josh Tonks. Subs (all used): 33 Shaun Emblem; 35 Andy Smith; 6 Pat Walker; 12 James Lockwood.
Tries: Faal (45), Brambani (52), Cosgrove (79);
Goals: Brambani 2/2, P Walker 1/1.
ROVERS: 1 Ian Hardman; 2 Bryn Powell; 17 Greg Worthington; 4 Andrew Bostock; 28 Jon Hepworth; 6 Andy Kain; 7 Liam Finn; 15 Michael Haley; 9 Ben Kaye; 10 Stuart Dickens; 11 Jon Grayshon; 12 Tim Spears; 13 Matty Dale. Subs (all used): 24 Mufaro Mvududu; 18 Ross Divorty; 30 Kirk Netherton; 14 Liam Welham.
Tries: Bostock (7), Dickens (10), Spears (12), Haley (16), Netherton (33), Dale (39), Divorty (65);
Goals: Finn 5/7.
Rugby Leaguer & League Express Men of the Match: *Rams:* William Barthau; *Rovers:* Liam Finn.
Penalty count: 7-5; **Half-time:** 0-32;
Referee: Matthew Thomason; **Attendance:** 1,167.

SHEFFIELD EAGLES 70 HUNSLET HAWKS 12

EAGLES: 1 Misi Taulapapa; 2 Danny Mills; 3 Menzie Yere; 26 Corey Hanson; 16 Vinny Finigan; 7 Simon Brown; 24 Kyle Wood; 8 Jack Howieson; 9 Andrew Henderson; 10 Mitchell Stringer; 11 Alex Szostak; 12 Peter Green; 19 Joe Hirst. Subs (all used): 6 Quentin Laulu-Togagae; 22 Ryan Hepworth; 17 Alex Rowe; 25 Jamie Cording.
Tries: Finigan (23), Hirst (29), Taulapapa (35), Yere (39, 45), Laulu-Togagae (42, 74), Stringer (48, 53), Howieson (57), Hanson (62), Rowe (77), Cording (79);
Goals: Brown 7/10, Stringer 2/3.
HAWKS: 1 Stuart Kain; 28 Dennis Tuffour; 16 John Oakes; 12 Tom Haughey; 5 Waine Pryce; 6 Danny Grimshaw; 22

Danny Ratcliffe; 8 Adam Sullivan; 14 Luke Haigh; 10 James Houston; 17 Rob Kelly; 25 Steve Dooler; 13 David March. Subs (all used): 23 Joe McLocklan; 19 Neil Lowe; 18 Joe Helme; 20 Andrew Yates.
Tries: Tuffour (4), Grimshaw (65); **Goals:** Ratcliffe 2/2.
Rugby Leaguer & League Express Men of the Match: *Eagles:* Mitchell Stringer; *Hawks:* Tom Haughey.
Penalty count: 8-7; **Half-time:** 18-6;
Referee: Gareth Hewer; **Attendance:** 907.

YORK CITY KNIGHTS 38 LEIGH CENTURIONS 48

CITY KNIGHTS: 20 Tom Bush; 22 Ed Smith; 29 James Ford; 2 Dave Sutton; 1 James Haynes; 27 Anthony Thackeray; 6 Chris Thorman; 8 Nathan Freer; 9 Jack Lee; 10 Alex Benson; 3 Duane Straugheir; 19 Matt Garside; 11 Rhys Clarke. Subs (all used): 14 Jack Stearman; 33 Jordan Rice; 7 Jon Presley; 25 Steve Lewis.
Tries: Thorman (21), Presley (35, 78), Stearman (40), Garside (59), Clarke (62), Straugheir (80);
Goals: Bush 3/4, Thorman 2/3.
CENTURIONS: 1 Stuart Donlan; 2 Steve Maden; 32 Rhys Evans; 4 Mick Nanyn; 5 Dean McGilvray; 6 Martyn Ridyard; 25 Jamie Ellis; 15 Andy Thornley; 9 John Duffy; 13 Stephen Nash; 14 Adam Higson; 3 Stuart Littler; 23 Mick Govin. Subs (all used): 16 Anthony Nicholson; 8 Chris Hill; 12 Tommy Goulden; 26 David Mills.
Tries: Ridyard (6, 19), Govin (12), Ellis (25, 38), Goulden (54), Nash (66), Mills (72); **Goals:** Nanyn 8/8.
Rugby Leaguer & League Express Men of the Match: *City Knights:* Duane Straugheir; *Centurions:* Jamie Ellis.
Penalty count: 8-5; **Half-time:** 16-30;
Referee: Ronnie Laughton; **Attendance:** 1,010.

ROUND 12

Thursday 2nd June 2011

LEIGH CENTURIONS 16 HALIFAX 36

CENTURIONS: 1 Stuart Donlan; 2 Steve Maden; 22 Tom Armstrong; 4 Mick Nanyn; 5 Dean McGilvray; 6 Martyn Ridyard; 25 Jamie Ellis; 26 David Mills; 16 Anthony Nicholson; 13 Stephen Nash; 3 Stuart Littler; 12 Tommy Goulden; 11 James Taylor. Subs (all used): 8 Chris Hill; 9 John Duffy; 14 Adam Higson; 15 Andy Thornley.
Tries: Ridyard (15, 79), Maden (74); **Goals:** Nanyn 2/3.
HALIFAX: 22 Danny White; 20 Paul White; 2 Lee Paterson; 4 Dylan Nash; 23 Rob Worrincy; 6 Danny Jones; 7 Ben Black; 15 Jim Gannon; 13 Bob Beswick; 8 Makali Aizue; 16 Paul Smith; 24 Steve Bannister; 12 Sam Barlow. Subs (all used): 10 Neil Cherryholme; 17 Frank Watene; 19 Jacob Fairbank; 9 Andy Thornley.
Tries: Worrincy (6, 25), Beswick (10), Bannister (18), Greenwood (31), Jones (39), S Barlow (53);
Goals: Jones 4/7.

Barrow's Ben Davies looks to get an offload away under pressure from the Toulouse defence

Rugby Leaguer & League Express Men of the Match:
Centurions: Andy Thornley; *Halifax:* Bob Beswick.
Penalty count: 8-8; **Half-time:** 6-32;
Referee: Tim Roby; **Attendance:** 2,525.

Friday 3rd June 2011

SHEFFIELD EAGLES 40 DEWSBURY RAMS 12

EAGLES: 1 Misi Taulapapa; 2 Danny Mills; 3 Menzie Yere;
26 Corey Hanson; 16 Vinny Finigan; 6 Quentin Laulu-
Togagae; 7 Simon Brown; 8 Jack Howieson; 9 Andrew
Henderson; 10 Mitchell Stringer; 11 Alex Szostak; 12
Peter Green; 19 Joe Hirst. Subs (all used): 5 Tim Bergin;
22 Ryan Hepworth; 17 Alex Rowe; 25 Jamie Cording.
Tries: Mills (15), Laulu-Togagae (27), Rowe (40, 70),
Yere (51), Bergin (74), Hanson (78); **Goals:** Brown 6/7.
Sin bin: Taulapapa (35) - holding down.
RAMS: 4 Scott Turner; 38 Elliot Hodgson; 37 Aston
Wilson; 13 Ayden Faal; 5 Austin Buchanan; 34 William
Barthau; 7 Dominic Brambani; 10 Keegan Hirst; 9 Luke
Blake; 8 Anthony England; 11 Rob Spicer; 12 James
Lockwood; 17 Ryan Glynn. Subs (all used): 23 Luke
Menzies; 39 Matthew Sarsfield; 24 Jake Wilson; 33
Matthew Tebb.
Tries: Spicer (44), Glynn (67); **Goals:** Brambani 2/2.
Rugby Leaguer & League Express Men of the Match:
Eagles: Andrew Henderson; *Rams:* Dominic Brambani.
Penalty count: 3-11; **Half-time:** 18-0;
Referee: Ronnie Laughton; **Attendance:** 683
(at Mount St Marys, Spinkhill).

Saturday 4th June 2011

BARROW RAIDERS 30 TOULOUSE OLYMPIQUE 18

RAIDERS: 1 Gary Broadbent; 2 Andy Ballard; 4 Liam
Harrison; 11 Michael Knowles; 3 Chris Larkin; 14 Liam
Campbell; 23 Gregg McNally; 24 Adam Walker; 9 Mark
Gleeson; 21 Jamie Butler; 10 Matt James; 15 Martin
Ostler; 16 Zebastian Luisi. Subs (all used): 8 Jamie
Thackray; 25 Ben Davies; 18 Nathan Mossop; 13
Richard Fletcher.
Tries: Ostler (4), Knowles (28, 61, 65), Larkin (69);
Goals: McNally 5/5.
OLYMPIQUE: 1 Rory Bromley; 32 Antoine Reveillon; 12
Yoan Tisseyre; 20 Bruno Ormeno; 24 Gregory White; 6
Darren Nicholls; 4 Constant Villegas; 15 Jerome Gout; 9
Craig Cook; 10 Ged Corcoran; 11 Tim Wynn; 14 Antoni
Maria; 19 Eric Anselme. Subs (all used): 21 Nicolas Faure;
25 Tony Gigot; 33 Thibaut Ancely; 17 Kevin Larroyer.
Tries: Ormeno (7), Wynn (26), Nicholls (78);
Goals: Nicholls 3/3.
Rugby Leaguer & League Express Men of the Match:
Raiders: Michael Knowles; *Olympique:* Darren Nicholls.
Penalty count: 10-4; **Half-time:** 12-12;
Referee: Jamie Leahy; **Attendance:** 1,245.

Sunday 5th June 2011

FEATHERSTONE ROVERS 44 YORK CITY KNIGHTS 24

ROVERS: 1 Ian Hardman; 2 Bryn Powell; 31 Nathan
Chappell; 4 Andrew Bostock; 3 Sam Smeaton; 6 Andy
Kain; 7 Liam Finn; 15 Michael Haley; 9 Ben Kaye; 10
Stuart Dickens; 11 Jon Grayshon; 12 Tim Spears; 18
Ross Divorty. Subs (all used): 32 Ben Gledhill; 30 Kirk
Netherton; 16 Iain Morrison; 28 Jon Hepworth.
Tries: Grayshon (17), Powell (22, 34), Finn (26, 70),
Kain (48), Bostock (66), Smeaton (76), Hepworth (79);
Goals: Finn 4/9.
CITY KNIGHTS: 20 Tom Bush; 22 Ed Smith; 29 James
Ford; 2 Dave Sutton; 1 James Haynes; 6 Chris Thorman;
27 Anthony Thackeray; 8 Nathan Freer; 9 Jack Lee; 10
Alex Benson; 3 Duane Straugheir; 19 Matt Garside; 11
Rhys Clarke. Subs (all used): 14 Jack Stearman; 13
Ryan Esders; 7 Jon Presley; 37 Ben Jones.
Tries: Lee (9), Garside (12), Bush (37), Thackeray (42);
Goals: Bush 4/4.
Rugby Leaguer & League Express Men of the Match:
Rovers: Andy Kain; *City Knights:* Chris Thorman.
Penalty count: 6-5; **Half-time:** 20-18;
Referee: Clint Sharrad; **Attendance:** 1,287.

HUNSLET HAWKS 12 BATLEY BULLDOGS 34

HAWKS: 1 Stuart Kain; 5 Waine Pryce; 16 John Oakes; 4
David Clayton; 28 Dennis Tuffour; 6 Danny Grimshaw;
22 Danny Ratcliffe; 8 Adam Sullivan; 14 Luke Haigh; 10
James Houston; 17 Rob Kelly; 12 Tom Haughey; 13
David March. Subs (all used): 7 Paul March; 25 Steve
Dooler; 19 Neil Lowe; 20 Andrew Yates.
Tries: Haigh (19), Grimshaw (70);
Goals: Ratcliffe 1/2, D March 1/1.
BULLDOGS: 1 Ian Preece; 2 Alex Brown; 4 Danny Maun;
12 Jason Walton; 5 Wayne Reittie; 6 Paul Handforth; 16
Paul Mennell; 8 Byron Smith; 9 Kris Lythe; 17 Craig
Potter; 11 Alex Bretherton; 18 Dane Manning; 13 Ashley
Lindsay. Subs (all used): 23 Chris Buttery; 10 Sean
Hesketh; 15 Adam Robinson; 19 Mark Toohey.
Tries: Reittie (12), Robinson (48), Smith (61),
Hesketh (73, 76), Bretherton (80); **Goals:** Handforth 5/6.
Rugby Leaguer & League Express Men of the Match:
Hawks: Danny Grimshaw; *Bulldogs:* Byron Smith.
Penalty count: 4-8; **Half-time:** 6-4;
Referee: Matthew Thomason; **Attendance:** 801.

ROUND 13

Thursday 9th June 2011

HALIFAX 24 HUNSLET HAWKS 18

HALIFAX: 1 Miles Greenwood; 20 Paul White; 2 Lee
Paterson; 4 Dylan Nash; 23 Rob Worrincy; 6 Danny

Jones; 7 Ben Black; 15 Jim Gannon; 13 Bob Beswick; 10
Neil Cherryholme; 12 Sam Barlow; 24 Steve Bannister;
19 Jacob Fairbank. Subs (all used): 8 Makali Aizue; 16
Paul Smith; 26 Anthony Bowman; 34 Gil Dudson.
Tries: Fairbank (9), Black (35), Worrincy (61),
White (79); **Goals:** Jones 4/6.
HAWKS: 1 Stuart Kain; 5 Waine Pryce; 4 David Clayton;
2 Richie Barnett; 28 Dennis Tuffour; 6 Danny Grimshaw;
22 Danny Ratcliffe; 8 Adam Sullivan; 14 Luke Haigh; 18
Joe Helme; 16 John Oakes; 12 Tom Haughey; 13 David
March. Subs (all used): 7 Paul March; 19 Neil Lowe; 20
Andrew Yates; 30 Chris Hall.
Tries: Grimshaw (31), P March (44), Tuffour (48),
Ratcliffe (75); **Goals:** Ratcliffe 1/3, D March 0/1.
Rugby Leaguer & League Express Men of the Match:
Halifax: Bob Beswick; *Hawks:* Neil Lowe.
Penalty count: 4-6; **Half-time:** 10-6;
Referee: Clint Sharrad; **Attendance:** 1,963.

Saturday 11th June 2011

TOULOUSE OLYMPIQUE 16 SHEFFIELD EAGLES 32

OLYMPIQUE: 1 Rory Bromley; 32 Lilian Albert; 20 Bruno
Ormeno; 12 Yoan Tisseyre; 24 Gregory White; 6 Darren
Nicholls; 4 Constant Villegas; 33 Thibaut Ancely; 9 Craig
Cook; 10 Ged Corcoran; 11 Tim Wynn; 14 Antoni Maria;
16 Sylvain Houles. Subs (all used): 15 Jerome Gout; 17
Kevin Larroyer; 21 Nicolas Faure; 19 Yohann Gigord.
Tries: Wynn (8), White (33, 45); **Goals:** Nicholls 2/3.
EAGLES: 1 Misi Taulapapa; 2 Danny Mills; 3 Menzie
Yere; 26 Corey Hanson; 5 Tim Bergin; 6 Quentin Laulu-
Togagae; 7 Simon Brown; 8 Jack Howieson; 9 Andrew
Henderson; 10 Mitchell Stringer; 11 Alex Szostak; 12
Peter Green; 19 Joe Hirst. Subs (all used): 22 Ryan
Hepworth; 17 Alex Rowe; 20 Pat Smith; 30 Sam Scott.
Tries: Bergin (17), Brown (28), Howieson (48),
Taulapapa (57), Yere (59), Green (77); **Goals:** Brown 4/6.
Rugby Leaguer & League Express Men of the Match:
Olympique: Rory Bromley; *Eagles:* Andrew Henderson.
Penalty count: 4-6; **Half-time:** 10-16;
Referee: Jamie Leahy; **Attendance:** 1,200.

Sunday 12th June 2011

BATLEY BULLDOGS 10 BARROW RAIDERS 6

BULLDOGS: 1 Ian Preece; 30 Johnny Campbell; 19 Mark
Toohey; 4 Danny Maun; 2 Alex Brown; 6 Paul Handforth;
16 Paul Mennell; 8 Byron Smith; 9 Kris Lythe; 17 Craig
Potter; 18 Dane Manning; 11 Alex Bretherton; 13 Ashley
Lindsay. Subs (all used): 23 Chris Buttery; 25 George
Flanagan; 10 Sean Hesketh; 15 Adam Robinson.
Try: Brown (12); **Goals:** Handforth 3/3.
RAIDERS: 1 Gary Broadbent; 3 Chris Larkin; 28 Anthony
Blackwood; 4 Liam Harrison; 2 Andy Ballard; 6 Jamie
Rooney; 14 Liam Campbell; 21 Jamie Butler; 18 Nathan

Mossop; 10 Matt James; 11 Michael Knowles; 15 Martin Ostler; 16 Zebastian Luisi. Subs (all used): 8 Jamie Thackray; 9 Mark Gleeson; 24 Adam Walker; 27 Mike Backhouse.
Try: Blackwood (69); **Goals:** Rooney 1/2.
Rugby Leaguer & League Express Men of the Match: *Bulldogs:* Paul Handforth; *Raiders:* Zebastian Luisi.
Penalty count: 12-6; **Half-time:** 6-2;
Referee: Ronnie Laughton; **Attendance:** 888.

LEIGH CENTURIONS 34 DEWSBURY RAMS 6

CENTURIONS: 1 Stuart Donlan; 2 Steve Maden; 3 Stuart Littler; 4 Mick Nanyn; 14 Adam Higson; 6 Martyn Ridyard; 25 Jamie Ellis; 8 Chris Hill; 9 John Duffy; 13 Stephen Nash; 15 Andy Thornley; 12 Tommy Goulden; 11 James Taylor. Subs (all used): 5 Dean McGilvray; 17 Craig Briscoe; 16 Anthony Nicholson; 26 David Mills.
Tries: Nanyn (4, 61, 67), Goulden (7), Littler (18), Donlan (54), Maden (74); **Goals:** Nanyn 2/6, Ellis 1/1.
RAMS: 1 James Craven; 2 Michael Wainwright; 4 Scott Turner; 13 Ayden Faal; 5 Austin Buchanan; 34 William Barthau; 7 Dominic Brambani; 8 Anthony England; 9 Luke Blake; 10 Keegan Hirst; 40 Richard Fletcher; 12 James Lockwood; 39 Matthew Sarsfield. Subs (all used): 23 Luke Menzies; 24 Jake Wilson; 38 Elliot Hodgson; 37 Aston Wilson.
Try: England (77); **Goals:** Brambani 1/1.
Rugby Leaguer & League Express Men of the Match: *Centurions:* James Taylor; *Rams:* Anthony England.
Penalty count: 4-2; **Half-time:** 16-0;
Referee: George Stokes; **Attendance:** 1,942.

YORK CITY KNIGHTS 18 WIDNES VIKINGS 22

CITY KNIGHTS: 20 Tom Bush; 2 Dave Sutton; 29 James Ford; 13 Ryan Esders; 1 James Haynes; 27 Anthony Thackeray; 6 Chris Thorman; 8 Nathan Freer; 9 Jack Lee; 10 Alex Benson; 3 Duane Straugheir; 19 Matt Garside; 11 Rhys Clarke. Subs (all used): 22 Ed Smith; 25 Steve Lewis; 7 Jon Presley; 37 Ben Jones.
Tries: Smith (13), Jones (29), Esders (75);
Goals: Bush 3/3.
Sin bin: Garside (1) - late challenge on I'Anson.
VIKINGS: 5 Paddy Flynn; 2 Dean Gaskell; 23 Tangi Ropati; 4 Steve Tyrer; 41 Kevin Penny; 44 James Coyle; 7 Chaz I'Anson; 8 Steve Pickersgill; 14 Thomas Coyle; 17 Ben Kavanagh; 13 Simon Finnigan; 16 Macgraff Leuluai; 12 Kurt Haggerty. Subs (all used): 19 Matt Gardner; 3 Richard Varkulis; 25 Chris Lunt; 39 Dominic Crosby.
Tries: Haggerty (19), Leuluai (37), Crosby (43), Ropati (59); **Goals:** Haggerty 1/1, Tyrer 2/3.
Rugby Leaguer & League Express Men of the Match: *City Knights:* Duane Straugheir; *Vikings:* Steve Pickersgill.
Penalty count: 11-7; **Half-time:** 12-12;
Referee: Craig Halloran; **Attendance:** 1,172.

ROUND 14

Thursday 23rd June 2011

BARROW RAIDERS 28 FEATHERSTONE ROVERS 36

RAIDERS: 1 Gary Broadbent; 3 Chris Larkin; 28 Anthony Blackwood; 4 Liam Harrison; 2 Andy Ballard; 14 Liam Campbell; 23 Gregg McNally; 8 Jamie Thackray; 9 Mark Gleeson; 24 Adam Walker; 11 Michael Knowles; 10 Matt James; 6 Jamie Rooney. Subs (all used): 18 Nathan Mossop; 15 Martin Ostler; 21 Jamie Butler; 25 Ben Davies.
Tries: McNally (5, 30), Broadbent (21), Ballard (63, 66);
Goals: Rooney 4/5.
ROVERS: 1 Ian Hardman; 2 Bryn Powell; 3 Sam Smeaton; 17 Greg Worthington; 28 Jon Hepworth; 6 Andy Kain; 7 Liam Finn; 15 Michael Haley; 30 Kirk Netherton; 10 Stuart Dickens; 11 Jon Grayshon; 12 Tim Spears; 18 Ross Divorty. Subs (all used): 8 Tony Tonks; 32 Ben Gledhill; 24 Mufaro Mvududu; 4 Andrew Bostock.
Tries: Worthington (10, 38, 60), Smeaton (16), Hepworth (35), Powell (48), Finn (71); **Goals:** Finn 4/7.
Rugby Leaguer & League Express Men of the Match: *Raiders:* Liam Harrison; *Rovers:* Liam Finn.
Penalty count: 3-7; **Half-time:** 18-22;
Referee: Matthew Thomason; **Attendance:** 1,832.

Saturday 25th June 2011

TOULOUSE OLYMPIQUE 14 LEIGH CENTURIONS 36

OLYMPIQUE: 1 Rory Bromley; 32 Antoine Reveillon; 20 Bruno Ormeno; 22 Damien Couturier; 24 Gregory White; 6 Darren Nicholls; 4 Constant Villegas; 33 Thibaut Ancely; 9 Craig Cook; 11 Tim Wynn; 12 Yoan Tisseyre; 14 Antoni Maria; 16 Sylvain Houles. Subs (all used): 13 Eric Anselme; 15 Jerome Gout; 17 Kevin Larroyer; 25 Tony Gigot.
Tries: Houles (23), Tisseyre (61), White (66);
Goals: Nicholls 1/3.
CENTURIONS: 1 Stuart Donlan; 2 Steve Maden; 14 Adam Higson; 4 Mick Nanyn; 5 Dean McGilvray; 6 Martyn Ridyard; 25 Jamie Ellis; 8 Chris Hill; 9 John Duffy; 26 David Mills; 3 Stuart Littler; 12 Tommy Goulden; 11 James Taylor. Subs (all used): 7 Robbie Hunter-Paul; 13 Stephen Nash; 15 Andy Thornley; 17 Craig Briscoe.
Tries: Ridyard (9), McGilvray (29), Hunter-Paul (34), Ellis (49), Nanyn (69), Taylor (80); **Goals:** Nanyn 6/6.
Rugby Leaguer & League Express Men of the Match: *Olympique:* Yoan Tisseyre; *Centurions:* Tommy Goulden.
Penalty count: 8-5; **Half-time:** 6-18;
Referee: Ronnie Laughton; **Attendance:** 2,300.

Sunday 26th June 2011

DEWSBURY RAMS 28 YORK CITY KNIGHTS 30

RAMS: 38 Elliot Hodgson; 35 Andy Smith; 13 Ayden Faal; 4 Scott Turner; 5 Austin Buchanan; 7 Dominic Brambani; 6 Pat Walker; 10 Keegan Hirst; 9 Luke Blake; 12 James Lockwood; 39 Matthew Sarsfield; 32 Elliott Cosgrove; 15 Josh Tonks. Subs (all used): 40 Richard Fletcher; 34 William Barthau; 8 Anthony England; 33 Matthew Tebb.
Tries: Turner (11, 39, 56), P Walker (36), Smith (50);
Goals: Brambani 3/5, P Walker 1/1.
CITY KNIGHTS: 20 Tom Bush; 2 Dave Sutton; 13 Ryan Esders; 29 James Ford; 1 James Haynes; 6 Chris Thorman; 27 Anthony Thackeray; 8 Nathan Freer; 9 Jack Lee; 10 Alex Benson; 3 Duane Straugheir; 19 Matt Garside; 11 Rhys Clarke. Subs (all used): 7 Jon Presley; 32 Jack Aldous; 21 Dennis Tuffour; 37 Ben Jones.
Tries: Thackeray (4, 57), Garside (26), Esders (33), Sutton (79); **Goals:** Bush 4/4, Thorman 1/1.
Rugby Leaguer & League Express Men of the Match: *Rams:* James Lockwood; *City Knights:* James Ford.
Penalty count: 6-5; **Half-time:** 16-18;
Referee: Chris Leatherbarrow; **Attendance:** 974.

HALIFAX 28 BATLEY BULLDOGS 36

HALIFAX: 1 Miles Greenwood; 20 Paul White; 2 Lee Paterson; 4 Dylan Nash; 23 Rob Worrincy; 6 Danny Jones; 7 Ben Black; 15 Jim Gannon; 13 Bob Beswick; 10 Neil Cherryholme; 14 Ryan Clayton; 24 Steve Bannister; 19 Jacob Fairbank. Subs (all used): 9 Sean Penkywicz; 11 David Larder; 12 Sam Barlow; 16 Paul Smith.
Tries: Beswick (14), Nash (40), Penkywicz (44), Jones (56), Worrincy (64); **Goals:** Jones 3/5, Paterson 1/1.
BULLDOGS: 30 Johnny Campbell; 5 Wayne Reittie; 12 Jason Walton; 4 Danny Maun; 2 Alex Brown; 6 Paul Handforth; 16 Paul Mennell; 8 Byron Smith; 9 Kris Lythe; 17 Craig Potter; 18 Dane Manning; 11 Alex Bretherton; 13 Ashley Lindsay. Subs (all used): 10 Sean Hesketh; 15 Adam Robinson; 23 Chris Buttery; 25 George Flanagan.
Tries: Bretherton (9, 23), Lindsay (27), Brown (38), Campbell (76), Maun (79); **Goals:** Handforth 6/7.
Rugby Leaguer & League Express Men of the Match: *Halifax:* Sean Penkywicz; *Bulldogs:* Dane Manning.
Penalty count: 11-7; **Half-time:** 10-22;
Referee: Tim Roby; **Attendance:** 2,483.

WIDNES VIKINGS 38 SHEFFIELD EAGLES 24

VIKINGS: 24 Danny Hulme; 5 Paddy Flynn; 23 Tangi Ropati; 19 Matt Gardner; 41 Kevin Penny; 7 Chaz I'Anson; 40 Joe Mellor; 8 Steve Pickersgill; 14 Thomas Coyle; 17 Ben Kavanagh; 13 Simon Finnigan; 16 Macgraff Leuluai; 12 Kurt Haggerty. Subs (all used): 3 Richard Varkulis; 11 Dave Allen; 39 Dominic Crosby; 44 James Coyle.
Tries: Hulme (10), Leuluai (13), Varkulis (25), Penny (38, 58), Haggerty (50), Allen (70);
Goals: Haggerty 4/6, Ropati 1/1.
EAGLES: 1 Misi Taulapapa; 16 Vinny Finigan; 3 Menzie Yere; 25 Jamie Cording; 5 Tim Bergin; 6 Quentin Laulu-Togagae; 7 Simon Brown; 8 Jack Howieson; 9 Andrew Henderson; 10 Mitchell Stringer; 11 Alex Szostak; 12 Peter Green; 19 Joe Hirst. Subs (all used): 17 Alex Rowe; 22 Ryan Hepworth; 24 Kyle Wood; 26 Corey Hanson.
Tries: Cording (39), Wood (43), Yere (65), Brown (79);
Goals: Brown 4/4.
Rugby Leaguer & League Express Men of the Match: *Vikings:* Kurt Haggerty; *Eagles:* Simon Brown.
Penalty count: 10-6; **Half-time:** 22-6;
Referee: Jamie Leahy; **Attendance:** 4,027.

ROUND 15

Thursday 30th June 2011

SHEFFIELD EAGLES 30 BARROW RAIDERS 26

EAGLES: 1 Misi Taulapapa; 16 Vinny Finigan; 3 Menzie Yere; 26 Corey Hanson; 5 Tim Bergin; 6 Quentin Laulu-Togagae; 7 Simon Brown; 8 Jack Howieson; 9 Andrew Henderson; 10 Mitchell Stringer; 11 Alex Szostak; 12 Peter Green; 19 Joe Hirst. Subs (all used): 2 Danny Mills; 22 Ryan Hepworth; 32 Connor Scott; 17 Alex Rowe.
Tries: Szostak (17, 62), Yere (41), Brown (68), Laulu-Togagae (75); **Goals:** Brown 5/6.
RAIDERS: 1 Gary Broadbent; 2 Andy Ballard; 28 Anthony Blackwood; 12 Ned Catic; 4 Liam Harrison; 16 Zebastian Luisi; 6 Jamie Rooney; 25 Ben Davies; 9 Mark Gleeson; 8 Jamie Thackray; 10 Matt James; 26 Jack Hughes; 11 Michael Knowles. Subs (all used): 21 Jamie Butler; 15 Martin Ostler; 24 Adam Walker; 14 Liam Campbell.
Tries: Hughes (20), Rooney (45), Knowles (48), Broadbent (58); **Goals:** Rooney 5/5.
Rugby Leaguer & League Express Men of the Match: *Eagles:* Andrew Henderson; *Raiders:* Zebastian Luisi.
Penalty count: 10-6; **Half-time:** 8-8;
Referee: Tim Roby; **Attendance:** 1,054.

Friday 1st July 2011

YORK CITY KNIGHTS 18 BATLEY BULLDOGS 10

CITY KNIGHTS: 20 Tom Bush; 2 Dave Sutton; 29 James Ford; 13 Ryan Esders; 21 Dennis Tuffour; 27 Anthony Thackeray; 7 Jon Presley; 8 Nathan Freer; 9 Jack Lee; 10 Alex Benson; 3 Duane Straugheir; 19 Matt Garside; 11 Rhys Clarke. Subs (all used): 22 Ed Smith; 25 Steve Lewis; 15 Brett Waller; 32 Jack Aldous.
Tries: Esders (4), Freer (55), Straugheir (71);
Goals: Bush 3/3.
BULLDOGS: 1 Ian Preece; 5 Wayne Reittie; 12 Jason Walton; 4 Danny Maun; 2 Alex Brown; 6 Paul Handforth; 16 Paul Mennell; 8 Byron Smith; 9 Kris Lythe; 10 Sean Hesketh; 18 Dane Manning; 11 Alex Bretherton; 19 Mark Toohey. Subs (all used): 23 Chris Buttery; 25 George Flanagan; 15 Adam Robinson; 20 David Tootill.
Tries: Bretherton (13), Flanagan (77);
Goals: Handforth 1/2.
Rugby Leaguer & League Express Men of the Match: *City Knights:* Tom Bush; *Bulldogs:* Byron Smith.
Penalty count: 6-8; **Half-time:** 6-4;
Referee: George Stokes; **Attendance:** 1,098.

Sunday 3rd July 2011

FEATHERSTONE ROVERS 90 TOULOUSE OLYMPIQUE 10

ROVERS: 1 Ian Hardman; 2 Bryn Powell; 3 Sam Smeaton; 28 Jon Hepworth; 5 Tom Saxton; 6 Andy Kain; 7 Liam Finn; 8 Tony Tonks; 9 Ben Kaye; 10 Stuart Dickens; 11 Jon Grayshon; 12 Tim Spears; 18 Ross Divorty. Subs (all used): 32 Ben Gledhill; 30 Kirk Netherton; 24 Mufaro Mvududu; 13 Matty Dale.
Tries: Dickens (2), Kain (5, 16, 62), Smeaton (7), Saxton (12, 58, 77), Kaye (18, 79), Finn (23), Hepworth (25), Powell (33, 48), Grayshon (40), Hardman (45, 64); **Goals:** Finn 11/17.
OLYMPIQUE: 1 Rory Bromley; 20 Bruno Ormeno; 3 Sebastien Planas; 22 Damien Couturier; 24 Gregory White; 6 Darren Nicholls; 4 Constant Villegas; 11 Tim Wynn; 9 Craig Cook; 17 Kevin Larroyer; 14 Antoni Maria; 12 Yoan Tisseyre; 16 Sylvain Houles. Subs (all used): 21 Nicolas Faure; 15 Jerome Gout; 26 Cyril Moliner; 19 Yohann Gigord.
Tries: Nicholls (51), Tisseyre (71); **Goals:** Nicholls 1/2.
Rugby Leaguer & League Express Men of the Match: *Rovers:* Andy Kain; *Olympique:* Darren Nicholls.
Penalty count: 3-4; **Half-time:** 52-0;
Referee: Gareth Hewer; **Attendance:** 1,307.

DEWSBURY RAMS 16 HALIFAX 30

RAMS: 1 James Craven; 2 Michael Wainwright; 13 Ayden Faal; 4 Scott Turner; 5 Austin Buchanan; 34 William Barthau; 7 Dominic Brambani; 10 Keegan Hirst; 9 Luke Blake; 12 James Lockwood; 40 Richard Fletcher; 32 Elliott Cosgrove; 6 Pat Walker. Subs (all used): 8 Anthony England; 15 Josh Tonks; 35 Andy Smith; 23 Luke Menzies.
Tries: Faal (7), Craven (20); **Goals:** P Walker 4/5.
HALIFAX: 1 Miles Greenwood; 20 Paul White; 5 James Haley; 33 Ryan Fieldhouse; 23 Rob Worrincy; 6 Danny Jones; 7 Ben Black; 15 Jim Gannon; 13 Bob Beswick; 10 Neil Cherryholme; 18 Joe Chandler; 24 Steve Bannister; 12 Sam Barlow. Subs (all used): 4 Dylan Nash; 9 Sean Penkywicz; 8 Makali Aizue; 25 Michael Ostick.
Tries: Penkywicz (34), White (39, 61), Beswick (54), S Barlow (75); **Goals:** Jones 5/6.
Rugby Leaguer & League Express Men of the Match: *Rams:* Dominic Brambani; *Halifax:* Sean Penkywicz.
Penalty count: 8-9; **Half-time:** 14-10;
Referee: Matthew Thomason; **Attendance:** 1,102.

HUNSLET HAWKS 22 WIDNES VIKINGS 24

HAWKS: 1 Stuart Kain; 5 Waine Pryce; 4 David Clayton; 31 Jack Latus; 2 Richie Barnett; 6 Danny Grimshaw; 22 Danny Ratcliffe; 8 Adam Sullivan; 14 Luke Haigh; 18 Joe Helme; 16 John Oakes; 12 Tom Haughey; 13 David March. Subs (all used): 7 Paul March; 10 James Houston; 17 Rob Kelly; 19 Neil Lowe.
Tries: Grimshaw (6), Kain (28), Haughey (37), Haigh (67); **Goals:** Ratcliffe 2/5, D March 1/1.
VIKINGS: 24 Danny Hulme; 5 Paddy Flynn; 23 Tangi Ropati; 4 Steve Tyrer; 19 Matt Gardner; 40 Joe Mellor; 7 Chaz I'Anson; 8 Steve Pickersgill; 14 Thomas Coyle; 3 Richard Varkulis; 16 Macgraff Leuluai; 12 Kurt Haggerty; 17 Ben Kavanagh. Subs (all used): 20 Shane Grady; 37 Danny Sculthorpe; 38 Logan Tomkins; 39 Dominic Crosby.
Tries: Kavanagh (16), Tyrer (51), Grady (57), Flynn (63), Haggerty (80); **Goals:** Tyrer 2/5.
Rugby Leaguer & League Express Men of the Match: *Hawks:* Danny Grimshaw; *Vikings:* Kurt Haggerty.
Penalty count: 6-7; **Half-time:** 16-6;
Referee: Ronnie Laughton; **Attendance:** 1,101.

ROUND 16

Thursday 7th July 2011

BATLEY BULLDOGS 16 LEIGH CENTURIONS 40

BULLDOGS: 29 Darren Williams; 5 Wayne Reittie; 12 Jason Walton; 4 Danny Maun; 2 Alex Brown; 6 Paul Handforth; 1 Ian Preece; 8 Byron Smith; 9 Kris Lythe; 19 Mark Toohey; 11 Alex Bretherton; 18 Dane Manning; 13 Ashley Lindsay. Subs (all used): 25 George Flanagan; 23 Chris Buttery; 10 Sean Hesketh; 15 Adam Robinson.
Tries: Toohey (9), Brown (40), Darren Williams (74);
Goals: Handforth 2/3.
CENTURIONS: 1 Stuart Donlan; 2 Steve Maden; 22 Tom Armstrong; 4 Mick Nanyn; 5 Dean McGilvray; 6 Martyn Ridyard; 25 Jamie Ellis; 8 Chris Hill; 9 John Duffy; 13 Stephen Nash; 3 Stuart Littler; 12 Tommy Goulden; 11 James Taylor. Subs (all used): 7 Robbie Hunter-Paul; 14 Adam Higson; 15 Andy Thornley; 26 David Mills.
Tries: Donlan (5), Ridyard (24), Ellis (33), Maden (47), McGilvray (57), Nash (69), Armstrong (76);
Goals: Nanyn 6/7.
Rugby Leaguer & League Express Men of the Match: *Bulldogs:* Paul Handforth; *Centurions:* Mick Nanyn.
Penalty count: 4-6; **Half-time:** 10-18;
Referee: George Stokes; **Attendance:** 1,533.

Championship 2011 - Round by Round

Saturday 9th July 2011

YORK CITY KNIGHTS 32 TOULOUSE OLYMPIQUE 46

CITY KNIGHTS: 20 Tom Bush; 2 Dave Sutton; 29 James Ford; 13 Ryan Esders; 21 Dennis Tuffour; 27 Anthony Thackeray; 7 Jon Presley; 8 Nathan Freer; 9 Jack Lee; 10 Alex Benson; 3 Duane Straugheir; 19 Matt Garside; 11 Rhys Clarke. Subs (all used): 22 Ed Smith; 1 James Haynes; 37 Ben Jones; 32 Jack Aldous.
Tries: Esders (15), Lee (18), Sutton (22), Freer (27), Garside (30, 80), Haynes (56);
Goals: Bush 1/4, Haynes 1/2, Esders 0/1.
OLYMPIQUE: 1 Rory Bromley; 24 Gregory White; 12 Yoan Tisseyre; 20 Bruno Ormeno; 28 Mathieu Mercier; 6 Darren Nicholls; 25 Tony Gigot; 11 Tim Wynn; 19 Yohann Gigord; 15 Jerome Gout; 26 Cyril Moliner; 14 Antoni Maria; 16 Sylvain Houles. Subs (all used): 17 Kevin Larroyer; 23 Teli Pelo; 13 Eric Anselme; 9 Craig Cook.
Tries: White (4, 71), Anselme (36), Ormeno (41, 60), Pelo (48), Cook (52), Wynn (66); **Goals:** Nicholls 7/8.
Rugby Leaguer & League Express Men of the Match: *City Knights:* Duane Straugheir; *Olympique:* Craig Cook.
Penalty count: 7-8; **Half-time:** 24-12;
Referee: Ronnie Laughton; **Attendance:** 902.

BARROW RAIDERS 16 HALIFAX 24

RAIDERS: 1 Gary Broadbent; 3 Chris Larkin; 28 Anthony Blackwood; 4 Liam Harrison; 2 Andy Ballard; 6 Jamie Rooney; 14 Liam Campbell; 8 Jamie Thackray; 9 Mark Gleeson; 21 Jamie Butler; 12 Ned Catic; 11 Michael Knowles; 16 Zebastian Luisi. Subs (all used): 18 Nathan Mossop; 15 Martin Ostler; 19 Marc Dixon; 24 Adam Walker.
Tries: Luisi (22), Harrison (30), Catic (71);
Goals: Rooney 2/3.
On report: Broadbent & Knowles (32) - alleged dangerous tackle on Greenwood.
HALIFAX: 1 Miles Greenwood; 20 Paul White; 4 Dylan Nash; 33 Ryan Fieldhouse; 5 James Haley; 6 Danny Jones; 7 Ben Black; 15 Jim Gannon; 13 Bob Beswick; 8 Makali Aizue; 16 Paul Smith; 14 Ryan Clayton; 12 Sam Barlow. Subs (all used): 9 Sean Penkywicz; 10 Neil Cherryholme; 17 Frank Watene; 18 Joe Chandler.
Tries: Haley (10), Nash (39), Penkywicz (65), White (79); **Goals:** Jones 4/5.
Dismissal: Watene (39) - late challenge on Broadbent.
Rugby Leaguer & League Express Men of the Match: *Raiders:* Gary Broadbent; *Halifax:* Sean Penkywicz.
Penalty count: 9-8; **Half-time:** 12-10;
Referee: Jamie Leahy; **Attendance:** 1,640.

Sunday 10th July 2011

FEATHERSTONE ROVERS 54 HUNSLET HAWKS 22

ROVERS: 1 Ian Hardman; 2 Bryn Powell; 3 Sam Smeaton; 28 Jon Hepworth; 5 Tom Saxton; 6 Andy Kain; 7 Liam Finn; 8 Tony Tonks; 9 Ben Kaye; 10 Stuart Dickens; 11 Jon Grayshon; 12 Tim Spears; 18 Ross Divorty. Subs (all used): 32 Ben Gledhill; 30 Kirk Netherton; 4 Andrew Bostock; 13 Matty Dale.
Tries: Grayshon (5), Hepworth (10, 24, 75), Dale (38, 79), Netherton (56), Powell (62), Kain (65);
Goals: Finn 9/9.
Dismissal: Kaye (69) - use of the elbow on Haigh.
HAWKS: 1 Stuart Kain; 2 Richie Barnett; 4 David Clayton; 31 Jack Latus; 5 Waine Pryce; 6 Danny Grimshaw; 7 Paul March; 8 Adam Sullivan; 14 Luke Haigh; 18 Joe Helme; 16 John Oakes; 12 Tom Haughey; 13 David March. Subs (all used): 10 James Houston; 23 Joe McLocklan; 17 Rob Kelly; 19 Neil Lowe.
Tries: Grimshaw (30, 71), Haughey (60), Pryce (77);
Goals: Latus 2/3, D March 1/1.
Sin bin: P March (15) - dissent.
Rugby Leaguer & League Express Men of the Match: *Rovers:* Tony Tonks; *Hawks:* Danny Grimshaw.
Penalty count: 13-9; **Half-time:** 24-6;
Referee: Matthew Thomason; **Attendance:** 1,271.

WIDNES VIKINGS 36 DEWSBURY RAMS 22

VIKINGS: 24 Danny Hulme; 5 Paddy Flynn; 19 Matt Gardner; 4 Steve Tyrer; 41 Kevin Penny; 29 Grant Gore; 14 Thomas Coyle; 17 Ben Kavanagh; 38 Logan Tomkins; 39 Dominic Crosby; 16 Macgraff Leuluai; 13 Simon Finnigan; 12 Kurt Haggerty. Subs (all used): 3 Richard Varkulis; 11 Dave Allen; 20 Shane Grady; 37 Danny Sculthorpe.
Tries: Gore (3), Tomkins (6), Kavanagh (13, 50), Tyrer (34), Penny (46); **Goals:** Tyrer 6/6.
RAMS: 1 James Craven; 2 Michael Wainwright; 13 Ayden Faal; 4 Scott Turner; 5 Austin Buchanan; 34 William Barthau; 7 Dominic Brambani; 8 Anthony England; 9 Luke Blake; 10 Keegan Hirst; 40 Richard Fletcher; 12 James Lockwood; 32 Elliott Cosgrove. Subs (all used): 23 Luke Menzies; 35 Andy Smith; 39 Richard Chapman; 42 Matt Nicholson.
Tries: Buchanan (32), Chapman (39, 57), Brambani (61);
Goals: Brambani 3/4.
Sin bin: England (49) - late challenge on Gore.
Rugby Leaguer & League Express Men of the Match: *Vikings:* Ben Kavanagh; *Rams:* Richard Chapman.
Penalty count: 6-7; **Half-time:** 24-10;
Referee: Tim Roby; **Attendance:** 4,030.

ROUND 17

Thursday 21st July 2011

BATLEY BULLDOGS 18 FEATHERSTONE ROVERS 24

BULLDOGS: 1 Ian Preece; 5 Wayne Reittie; 12 Jason Walton; 4 Danny Maun; 30 Johnny Campbell; 19 Mark Toohey; 6 Paul Handforth; 8 Byron Smith; 9 Kris Lythe; 17 Craig Potter; 18 Dane Manning; 11 Alex Bretherton; 13 Ashley Lindsay. Subs (all used): 25 George Flanagan; 15 Adam Robinson; 10 Sean Hesketh; 20 David Tootill.
Tries: Flanagan (40), Robinson (46), Manning (63);
Goals: Handforth 3/3.
ROVERS: 1 Ian Hardman; 33 Ben Cockayne; 3 Sam Smeaton; 28 Jon Hepworth; 5 Tom Saxton; 6 Andy Kain; 7 Liam Finn; 8 Tony Tonks; 9 Ben Kaye; 10 Stuart Dickens; 18 Ross Divorty; 12 Tim Spears; 13 Matty Dale. Subs (all used): 4 Andrew Bostock; 30 Kirk Netherton; 32 Ben Gledhill; 11 Jon Grayshon.
Tries: Grayshon (32), Netherton (51), Kain (58), Saxton (76); **Goals:** Finn 4/6.
Rugby Leaguer & League Express Men of the Match: *Bulldogs:* Ian Preece; *Rovers:* Liam Finn.
Penalty count: 9-7; **Half-time:** 6-6;
Referee: Tim Roby; **Attendance:** 1,539.

Saturday 23rd July 2011

TOULOUSE OLYMPIQUE 16 WIDNES VIKINGS 30

OLYMPIQUE: 1 Rory Bromley; 28 Mathieu Mercier; 20 Bruno Ormeno; 22 Damien Couturier; 24 Gregory White; 6 Darren Nicholls; 25 Tony Gigot; 15 Jerome Gout; 19 Yohann Gigord; 11 Tim Wynn; 26 Cyril Moliner; 12 Yoan Tisseyre; 16 Sylvain Houles. Subs (all used): 9 Craig Cook; 13 Eric Anselme; 23 Teli Pelo; 29 Sebastien Martins.
Tries: White (21), Gigot (30), Cook (36);
Goals: Nicholls 2/3.
VIKINGS: 24 Danny Hulme; 34 Kevin Penny; 19 Matt Gardner; 4 Steve Tyrer; 5 Paddy Flynn; 40 Joe Mellor; 7 Chaz l'Anson; 8 Steve Pickersgill; 14 Thomas Coyle; 17 Ben Kavanagh; 20 Shane Grady; 13 Simon Finnigan; 12 Kurt Haggerty. Subs (all used): 3 Richard Varkulis; 11 Dave Allen; 16 Macgraff Leuluai; 38 Logan Tomkins.
Tries: Tyrer (4, 15), Gardner (48), Allen (55), Finnigan (73); **Goals:** Tyrer 5/5.
Rugby Leaguer & League Express Men of the Match: *Olympique:* Rory Bromley; *Vikings:* Steve Tyrer.
Penalty count: 6-6; **Half-time:** 16-12;
Referee: Matthew Thomason; **Attendance:** 1,157.

BARROW RAIDERS 26 HUNSLET HAWKS 25

RAIDERS: 1 Gary Broadbent; 3 Chris Larkin; 28 Anthony Blackwood; 4 Liam Harrison; 27 Mike Backhouse; 6 Jamie Rooney; 14 Liam Campbell; 8 Jamie Thackray; 18 Nathan Mossop; 10 Matt James; 11 Michael Knowles; 30 Jonny Walker; 16 Zebastian Luisi. Subs (all used): 9 Mark Gleeson; 21 Jamie Butler; 26 Jack Hughes; 29 Liam Finch.
Tries: Larkin (9), Knowles (18), Hughes (42), Backhouse (58), Thackray (80); **Goals:** Rooney 3/5.
HAWKS: 1 Stuart Kain; 2 Richie Barnett; 31 Jack Latus; 4 David Clayton; 5 Waine Pryce; 6 Danny Grimshaw; 13 David March; 8 Adam Sullivan; 14 Luke Haigh; 18 Joe Helme; 16 John Oakes; 12 Tom Haughey; 11 Richard Blakeway. Subs (all used): 23 Joe McLocklan; 19 Neil Lowe; 20 Andrew Yates; 17 Rob Kelly.
Tries: Clayton (34, 46), Grimshaw (52), Kelly (65);
Goals: Latus 4/4; **Field goal:** McLocklan (69).
Rugby Leaguer & League Express Men of the Match: *Raiders:* Michael Knowles; *Hawks:* Danny Grimshaw.
Penalty count: 8-12; **Half-time:** 10-6;
Referee: Warren Turley; **Attendance:** 1,150.

Sunday 24th July 2011

HALIFAX 76 YORK CITY KNIGHTS 38

HALIFAX: 1 Miles Greenwood; 20 Paul White; 5 James Haley; 4 Dylan Nash; 23 Rob Worrincy; 6 Danny Jones; 26 Anthony Bowman; 15 Jim Gannon; 13 Bob Beswick; 10 Neil Cherryholme; 16 Paul Smith; 24 Steve Bannister; 19 Jacob Fairbank. Subs (all used): 8 Makali Aizue; 9 Sean Penkywicz; 12 Sam Barlow; 14 Ryan Clayton.
Tries: Bannister (14), Smith (17), Fairbank (27), Aizue (32), Penkywicz (34, 77), Worrincy (39), White (44, 61, 75), Clayton (55), Nash (68, 72); **Goals:** Jones 12/13.
CITY KNIGHTS: 20 Tom Bush; 21 Dennis Tuffour; 13 Ryan Esders; 29 James Ford; 2 Dave Sutton; 7 Jon Presley; 27 Anthony Thackeray; 8 Nathan Freer; 9 Jack Lee; 10 Alex Benson; 3 Duane Straugheir; 19 Matt Garside; 11 Rhys Clarke. Subs (all used): 1 James Haynes; 15 Brett Waller; 37 Ben Jones; 25 Steve Lewis.
Tries: Tuffour (5), Straugheir (9), Garside (22), Lewis (49, 51), Thackeray (59), Ford (79); **Goals:** Bush 5/7.
Rugby Leaguer & League Express Men of the Match: *Halifax:* Sean Penkywicz; *City Knights:* Anthony Thackeray.
Penalty count: 6-3; **Half-time:** 36-14;
Referee: Chris Leatherbarrow; **Attendance:** 1,920.

LEIGH CENTURIONS 34 SHEFFIELD EAGLES 22

CENTURIONS: 1 Stuart Donlan; 2 Steve Maden; 3 Stuart Littler; 4 Mick Nanyn; 32 Rhys Evans; 6 Martyn Ridyard; 25 Jamie Ellis; 8 Chris Hill; 7 Robbie Hunter-Paul; 13 Stephen Nash; 12 Tommy Goulden; 15 Andy Thornley; 11 James Taylor. Subs (all used): 14 Adam Higson; 22 Tom Armstrong; 26 David Mills; 33 Tyrone McCarthy.
Tries: Evans (11), Goulden (16, 48), Littler (21), Nanyn (35, 50); **Goals:** Nanyn 5/6.
EAGLES: 1 Misi Taulapapa; 5 Tim Bergin; 3 Menzie Yere; 4 Jason Crookes; 16 Vinny Finigan; 13 Dane McDonald; 7 Simon Brown; 8 Jack Howieson; 9 Andrew Henderson; 10 Mitchell Stringer; 11 Alex Szostak; 12 Peter Green; 19 Joe Hirst. Subs (all used): 2 Danny Mills; 17 Alex Rowe; 22 Ryan Hepworth; 30 Sam Scott.
Tries: Taulapapa (13), Yere (40), Bergin (67), McDonald (77); **Goals:** Brown 2/3, Bergin 1/1.
Rugby Leaguer & League Express Men of the Match: *Centurions:* Tommy Goulden; *Eagles:* Dane McDonald.
Penalty count: 10-8; **Half-time:** 24-10;
Referee: Jamie Leahy; **Attendance:** 2,633.

ROUND 18

Thursday 28th July 2011

FEATHERSTONE ROVERS 34 SHEFFIELD EAGLES 6

ROVERS: 1 Ian Hardman; 2 Bryn Powell; 3 Sam Smeaton; 33 Ben Cockayne; 5 Tom Saxton; 28 Jon Hepworth; 7 Liam Finn; 8 Tony Tonks; 9 Ben Kaye; 10 Stuart Dickens; 11 Jon Grayshon; 12 Tim Spears; 13 Matty Dale. Subs (all used): 32 Ben Gledhill; 30 Kirk Netherton; 4 Andrew Bostock; 18 Ross Divorty.
Tries: Powell (3, 20, 39), Hepworth (27), Netherton (44), Cockayne (54), Dale (60), Finn (73);
Goals: Finn 1/6, Dickens 0/2.
EAGLES: 1 Misi Taulapapa; 2 Danny Mills; 3 Menzie Yere; 4 Jason Crookes; 5 Tim Bergin; 13 Dane McDonald; 7 Simon Brown; 8 Jack Howieson; 9 Andrew Henderson; 22 Ryan Hepworth; 11 Alex Szostak; 12 Peter Green; 10 Mitchell Stringer. Subs (all used): 16 Vinny Finigan; 17 Alex Rowe; 30 Sam Scott; 32 Connor Scott.
Try: Taulapapa (18); **Goals:** Brown 1/1.
Rugby Leaguer & League Express Men of the Match: *Rovers:* Jon Hepworth; *Eagles:* Misi Taulapapa.
Penalty count: 6-6; **Half-time:** 16-6;
Referee: Jamie Leahy; **Attendance:** 1,527.

Saturday 30th July 2011

HALIFAX 44 TOULOUSE OLYMPIQUE 28

HALIFAX: 1 Miles Greenwood; 20 Paul White; 5 James Haley; 3 Jon Goddard; 23 Rob Worrincy; 6 Danny Jones; 26 Anthony Bowman; 15 Jim Gannon; 13 Bob Beswick; 10 Neil Cherryholme; 16 Paul Smith; 24 Steve Bannister; 12 Sam Barlow. Subs (all used): 8 Makali Aizue; 9 Sean Penkywicz; 14 Ryan Clayton; 18 Joe Chandler.
Tries: Bowman (5), Jones (24), Goddard (31), Greenwood (36), Chandler (48), White (64, 78), Smith (67); **Goals:** Jones 6/8.
OLYMPIQUE: 22 Damien Couturier; 24 Gregory White; 3 Sebastien Planas; 20 Bruno Ormeno; 28 Mathieu Mercier; 6 Darren Nicholls; 25 Tony Gigot; 11 Tim Wynn; 9 Craig Cook; 23 Teli Pelo; 17 Kevin Larroyer; 14 Antoni Maria; 16 Sylvain Houles. Subs (all used): 12 Yoan Tisseyre; 13 Eric Anselme; 21 Nicolas Faure; 29 Sebastien Martins.
Tries: Ormeno (12), Nicholls (21, 44), White (51), Gigot (56); **Goals:** Nicholls 4/5.
Rugby Leaguer & League Express Men of the Match: *Halifax:* Sean Penkywicz; *Olympique:* Tony Gigot.
Penalty count: 7-3; **Half-time:** 22-12;
Referee: George Stokes; **Attendance:** 1,876.

Sunday 31st July 2011

DEWSBURY RAMS 40 BARROW RAIDERS 34

RAMS: 1 James Craven; 2 Michael Wainwright; 11 Rob Spicer; 13 Ayden Faal; 5 Austin Buchanan; 46 Mark Barlow; 7 Dominic Brambani; 43 Steve Crossley; 9 Luke Blake; 8 Anthony England; 12 James Lockwood; 40 Richard Fletcher; 6 Pat Walker. Subs (all used): 23 Luke Menzies; 39 Richard Chapman; 42 Matt Nicholson; 35 Andy Smith.
Tries: Wainwright (6, 12), Blake (27), Nicholson (29), Lockwood (49), Spicer (53), Faal (62);
Goals: P Walker 6/8.
Sin bin: Chapman (73) - dissent.
RAIDERS: 1 Gary Broadbent; 27 Mike Backhouse; 28 Anthony Blackwood; 4 Liam Harrison; 3 Chris Larkin; 6 Jamie Rooney; 29 Liam Finch; 8 Jamie Thackray; 18 Nathan Mossop; 10 Matt James; 11 Michael Knowles; 30 Jonny Walker; 16 Zebastian Luisi. Subs (all used): 9 Mark Gleeson; 2 Andy Ballard; 21 Jamie Butler; 19 Marc Dixon.
Tries: James (32, 80), Larkin (42), Knowles (68), Rooney (71), Luisi (73); **Goals:** Rooney 5/6.
Sin bin: Rooney (17) - professional foul.
Rugby Leaguer & League Express Men of the Match: *Rams:* Rob Spicer; *Raiders:* Zebastian Luisi.
Penalty count: 3-6; **Half-time:** 22-6;
Referee: Ronnie Laughton; **Attendance:** 862.

HUNSLET HAWKS 0 LEIGH CENTURIONS 44

HAWKS: 1 Stuart Kain; 2 Richie Barnett; 4 David Clayton; 31 Jack Latus; 5 Waine Pryce; 6 Danny Grimshaw; 13 David March; 8 Adam Sullivan; 14 Luke Haigh; 18 Joe Helme; 16 John Oakes; 12 Tom Haughey; 11 Richard Blakeway. Subs (all used): 10 James Houston; 17 Rob Kelly; 20 Andrew Yates; 23 Joe McLocklan.
CENTURIONS: 1 Stuart Donlan; 2 Steve Maden; 32 Rhys Evans; 14 Adam Higson; 5 Dean McGilvray; 6 Martyn Ridyard; 25 Jamie Ellis; 13 Stephen Nash; 7 Robbie Hunter-Paul; 26 David Mills; 3 Stuart Littler; 12 Tommy Goulden; 11 James Taylor. Subs (all used): 15 Andy Thornley; 16 Anthony Nicholson; 20 Sam Hopkins; 22 Tom Armstrong.
Tries: Ellis (8, 56), Goulden (25), Taylor (30), Maden (33), Evans (40), Nash (69), Thornley (79);
Goals: Ellis 6/8.
Rugby Leaguer & League Express Men of the Match: *Hawks:* Adam Sullivan; *Centurions:* Jamie Ellis.
Penalty count: 10-4; **Half-time:** 0-26;
Referee: Clint Sharrad; **Attendance:** 713.

Leigh's Stuart Littler finds his path blocked by Widnes's Joe Mellor and Logan Tomkins

WIDNES VIKINGS 24 BATLEY BULLDOGS 22

VIKINGS: 24 Danny Hulme; 5 Paddy Flynn; 19 Matt Gardner; 4 Steve Tyrer; 34 Kevin Penny; 7 Chaz I'Anson; 40 Joe Mellor; 8 Steve Pickersgill; 14 Thomas Coyle; 17 Ben Kavanagh; 20 Shane Grady; 13 Simon Finnigan; 12 Kurt Haggerty. Subs (all used): 3 Richard Varkulis; 11 Dave Allen; 16 Macgraff Leuluai; 39 Dominic Crosby.
Tries: Kavanagh (2), Flynn (24), Mellor (37), Penny (61);
Goals: Tyrer 4/5.
BULLDOGS: 1 Ian Preece; 5 Wayne Reittie; 4 Danny Maun; 3 Daley Williams; 30 Johnny Campbell; 6 Paul Handforth; 16 Paul Mennell; 8 Byron Smith; 9 Kris Lythe; 17 Craig Potter; 18 Dane Manning; 11 Alex Bretherton; 13 Ashley Lindsay. Subs (all used): 10 Sean Hesketh; 15 Adam Robinson; 19 Mark Toohey; 25 George Flanagan.
Tries: Mennell (6), Daley Williams (12), Campbell (16), Hesketh (31); **Goals:** Handforth 3/5.
Rugby Leaguer & League Express Men of the Match:
Vikings: Steve Pickersgill; *Bulldogs:* Paul Handforth.
Penalty count: 6-7; **Half-time:** 16-20;
Referee: Matthew Thomason; **Attendance:** 3,873.

ROUND 19

Friday 5th August 2011

YORK CITY KNIGHTS 16 FEATHERSTONE ROVERS 44

CITY KNIGHTS: 20 Tom Bush; 2 Dave Sutton; 1 James Haynes; 19 Matt Garside; 21 Dennis Tuffour; 27 Anthony Thackeray; 28 Scott Woods; 8 Nathan Freer; 9 Jack Lee; 10 Alex Benson; 25 Steve Lewis; 13 Ryan Esders; 11 Rhys Clarke. Subs (all used): 32 Joe Hemmings; 7 Jon Presley; 37 Ben Jones; 15 Brett Waller.
Tries: Freer (24), Garside (28), Haynes (79);
Goals: Bush 2/3.
ROVERS: 1 Ian Hardman; 33 Ben Cockayne; 3 Sam Smeaton; 4 Andrew Bostock; 5 Tom Saxton; 28 Jon Hepworth; 7 Liam Finn; 8 Tony Tonks; 9 Ben Kaye; 10 Stuart Dickens; 11 Jon Grayshon; 12 Tim Spears; 13 Matty Dale. Subs (all used): 30 Kirk Netherton; 17 Greg Worthington; 18 Ross Divorty; 32 Ben Gledhill.
Tries: Cockayne (7), Hepworth (18), Saxton (32), Hardman (56, 69), Bostock (59), Worthington (66, 74);
Goals: Finn 6/8.
Rugby Leaguer & League Express Men of the Match:
City Knights: Nathan Freer; *Rovers:* Stuart Dickens.
Penalty count: 7-10; **Half-time:** 12-16;
Referee: Matthew Thomason; **Attendance:** 1,193.

Saturday 6th August 2011

TOULOUSE OLYMPIQUE 16 DEWSBURY RAMS 8

OLYMPIQUE: 1 Rory Bromley; 28 Mathieu Mercier; 3 Sebastien Planas; 22 Damien Couturier; 24 Gregory White; 6 Darren Nicholls; 4 Constant Villegas; 34 Thibaut Ancely; 9 Craig Cook; 23 Teli Pelo; 17 Kevin Larroyer; 14 Antoni Maria; 16 Sylvain Houles. Subs (all used): 21 Nicolas Faure; 29 Sebastien Martins; 12 Yoan Tisseyre; 20 Bruno Ormeno.
Tries: Mercier (41), White (56), Maria (66);
Goals: Nicholls 2/4.
Sin bin: Faure (35) - late challenge on Brambani.
RAMS: 1 James Craven; 2 Michael Wainwright; 11 Rob Spicer; 13 Ayden Faal; 5 Austin Buchanan; 6 Pat Walker; 7 Dominic Brambani; 8 Anthony England; 9 Luke Blake; 43 Steve Crossley; 12 James Lockwood; 40 Richard Fletcher; 15 Josh Tonks. Subs (all used): 23 Luke Menzies; 10 Keegan Hirst; 44 Liam Welham; 35 Andy Smith.
Try: Blake (71); **Goals:** P Walker 2/2.
On report: Fletcher (12) - alleged dangerous tackle.
Rugby Leaguer & League Express Men of the Match:
Olympique: Craig Cook; *Rams:* James Lockwood.
Penalty count: 5-8; **Half-time:** 0-0;
Referee: Chris Leatherbarrow; **Attendance:** 800.

Sunday 7th August 2011

BATLEY BULLDOGS 18 HALIFAX 16

BULLDOGS: 1 Ian Preece; 5 Wayne Reittie; 3 Daley Williams; 4 Danny Maun; 30 Johnny Campbell; 6 Paul Handforth; 16 Paul Mennell; 8 Byron Smith; 9 Kris Lythe; 17 Craig Potter; 11 Alex Bretherton; 18 Dane Manning; 13 Ashley Lindsay. Subs (all used): 25 George Flanagan; 19 Mark Toohey; 10 Sean Hesketh; 20 David Tootill.
Tries: Manning (3, 51), Campbell (40);
Goals: Handforth 3/3.
Sin bin: Flanagan (56) - dissent.
HALIFAX: 1 Miles Greenwood; 20 Paul White; 5 James Haley; 4 Dylan Nash; 23 Rob Worrincy; 6 Danny Jones; 26 Anthony Bowman; 15 Jim Gannon; 13 Bob Beswick; 10 Neil Cherryholme; 14 Ryan Clayton; 24 Steve Bannister; 16 Paul Smith. Subs (all used): 8 Makali Aizue; 9 Sean Penkywicz; 12 Sam Barlow; 18 Joe Chandler.
Tries: Smith (14), Jones (56), Chandler (61);
Goals: Jones 2/3.
Sin bin: Smith (50) - dissent.
Rugby Leaguer & League Express Men of the Match:
Bulldogs: Paul Mennell; *Halifax:* Danny Jones.
Penalty count: 10-9; **Half-time:** 12-6;
Referee: Jamie Leahy; **Attendance:** 1,131.

HUNSLET HAWKS 24 SHEFFIELD EAGLES 32

HAWKS: 22 Danny Ratcliffe; 2 Richie Barnett; 31 Jack Latus; 4 David Clayton; 5 Waine Pryce; 6 Danny Grimshaw; 7 Paul March; 8 Adam Sullivan; 14 Luke Haigh; 18 Joe Helme; 11 Richard Blakeway; 16 John Oakes; 12 Tom Haughey. Subs (all used): 10 James Houston; 17 Rob Kelly; 20 Andrew Yates; 23 Joe McLocklan.
Tries: Ratcliffe (35, 47), P March (59), Barnett (66);
Goals: Latus 4/4.

EAGLES: 1 Misi Taulapapa; 2 Danny Mills; 26 Corey Hanson; 3 Menzie Yere; 5 Tim Bergin; 6 Quentin Laulu-Togagae; 7 Simon Brown; 8 Jack Howieson; 9 Andrew Henderson; 10 Mitchell Stringer; 19 Joe Hirst; 12 Peter Green; 13 Dane McDonald. Subs (all used): 11 Alex Szostak; 17 Alex Rowe; 20 Pat Smith; 22 Ryan Hepworth.
Tries: Taulapapa (4, 77), Hanson (22, 69), Stringer (52);
Goals: Brown 6/6.
Rugby Leaguer & League Express Men of the Match:
Hawks: Danny Ratcliffe; *Eagles:* Corey Hanson.
Penalty count: 4-6; **Half-time:** 6-12;
Referee: Craig Halloran; **Attendance:** 424.

WIDNES VIKINGS 18 LEIGH CENTURIONS 24

VIKINGS: 24 Danny Hulme; 34 Kevin Penny; 4 Steve Tyrer; 19 Matt Gardner; 5 Paddy Flynn; 40 Joe Mellor; 7 Chaz I'Anson; 17 Ben Kavanagh; 14 Thomas Coyle; 8 Steve Pickersgill; 16 Macgraff Leuluai; 13 Simon Finnigan; 11 Dave Allen. Subs (all used): 20 Shane Grady; 3 Richard Varkulis; 39 Dominic Crosby; 38 Logan Tomkins.
Tries: Tyrer (5), Crosby (30), Tomkins (37);
Goals: Tyrer 3/3.
CENTURIONS: 1 Stuart Donlan; 2 Steve Maden; 32 Rhys Evans; 4 Mick Nanyn; 5 Dean McGilvray; 6 Martyn Ridyard; 25 Jamie Ellis; 8 Chris Hill; 7 Robbie Hunter-Paul; 26 David Mills; 3 Stuart Littler; 12 Tommy Goulden; 11 James Taylor. Subs (all used): 15 Andy Thornley; 13 Stephen Nash; 9 John Duffy; 33 Tyrone McCarthy.
Tries: Ridyard (15), Ellis (23, 67), Nanyn (51);
Goals: Nanyn 4/5.
Rugby Leaguer & League Express Men of the Match:
Vikings: Simon Finnigan; *Centurions:* Jamie Ellis.
Penalty count: 9-12; **Half-time:** 18-12;
Referee: Tim Roby; **Attendance:** 4,732.

ROUND 20

Thursday 11th August 2011

HALIFAX 26 WIDNES VIKINGS 24

HALIFAX: 1 Miles Greenwood; 20 Paul White; 5 James Haley; 4 Dylan Nash; 23 Rob Worrincy; 6 Danny Jones; 26 Anthony Bowman; 25 Michael Ostick; 13 Bob Beswick; 10 Neil Cherryholme; 14 Ryan Clayton; 24 Steve Bannister; 16 Paul Smith. Subs (all used): 8 Makali Aizue; 17 Frank Watene; 18 Joe Chandler; 33 Ryan Fieldhouse.
Tries: Beswick (3), Greenwood (30), Smith (63), Bowman (69); **Goals:** Jones 5/5.
VIKINGS: 24 Danny Hulme; 34 Kevin Penny; 4 Steve Tyrer; 23 Rangi Ropati; 5 Paddy Flynn; 40 Joe Mellor; 44 James Coyle; 39 Dominic Crosby; 14 Thomas Coyle; 8 Steve Pickersgill; 13 Simon Finnigan; 20 Shane Grady; 12 Kurt Haggerty. Subs (all used): 3 Richard Varkulis; 11 Dave Allen; 38 Logan Tomkins; 17 Ben Kavanagh.

Tries: Hulme (14), Mellor (25, 39), Varkulis (50);
Goals: Tyrer 4/4.
Rugby Leaguer & League Express Men of the Match:
Halifax: Bob Beswick; *Vikings:* Joe Mellor.
Penalty count: 14-6; **Half-time:** 12-18;
Referee: Matthew Thomason; **Attendance:** 2,090.

Saturday 13th August 2011

BATLEY BULLDOGS 32 TOULOUSE OLYMPIQUE 10

BULLDOGS: 1 Ian Preece; 30 Johnny Campbell; 19 Mark Toohey; 3 Daley Williams; 5 Wayne Reittie; 6 Paul Handforth; 16 Paul Mennell; 8 Byron Smith; 9 Kris Lythe; 17 Craig Potter; 11 Alex Bretherton; 18 Dane Manning; 13 Ashley Lindsay. Subs (all used): 23 Chris Buttery; 12 Jason Walton; 10 Sean Hesketh; 20 David Tootill.
Tries: Handforth (3), Bretherton (15), Toohey (45, 59), Walton (59), Daley Williams (78); **Goals:** Handforth 4/6.
On report: Hesketh (79) - alleged late challenge.
OLYMPIQUE: 1 Rory Bromley; 24 Gregory White; 3 Sebastien Planas; 22 Damien Couturier; 28 Mathieu Mercier; 6 Darren Nicholls; 25 Tony Gigot; 34 Thibault Ancely; 19 Yohann Gigord; 23 Teli Pelo; 14 Antoni Maria; 17 Kevin Larroyer; 16 Sylvain Houles. Subs (all used): 29 Sebastien Martins; 15 Jerome Gout; 12 Yoan Tisseyre; 9 Craig Cook.
Tries: Gout (38), Mercier (64); **Goals:** Nicholls 1/2.
Rugby Leaguer & League Express Men of the Match:
Bulldogs: Byron Smith; *Olympique:* Craig Cook.
Penalty count: 6-5; **Half-time:** 12-6;
Referee: Clint Sharrad; **Attendance:** 801.

BARROW RAIDERS 36 SHEFFIELD EAGLES 26

RAIDERS: 1 Gary Broadbent; 2 Andy Ballard; 28 Anthony Blackwood; 4 Liam Harrison; 3 Chris Larkin; 6 Jamie Rooney; 29 Liam Finch; 8 Jamie Thackray; 18 Nathan Mossop; 21 Jamie Butler; 11 Michael Knowles; 30 Jonny Walker; 16 Zebastian Luisi. Subs: 9 Mark Gleeson; 15 Martin Ostler; 19 Marc Dixon (not used); 27 Mike Backhouse.
Tries: Blackwood (5), Luisi (7), Knowles (10), Ballard (14, 20), Larkin (63), Finch (76); **Goals:** Rooney 4/7.
EAGLES: 1 Misi Taulapapa; 2 Danny Mills; 3 Menzie Yere; 26 Corey Hanson; 5 Tim Bergin; 6 Quentin Laulu-Togagae; 7 Simon Brown; 8 Jack Howieson; 9 Andrew Henderson; 10 Mitchell Stringer; 11 Alex Szostak; 13 Dane McDonald. Subs (all used): 20 Pat Smith; 22 Ryan Hepworth; 16 Vinny Finigan; 30 Sam Scott.
Tries: Henderson (26), Laulu-Togagae (33, 48), Yere (56), Hanson (68); **Goals:** Brown 3/4, Bergin 0/1.
Rugby Leaguer & League Express Men of the Match:
Raiders: Michael Knowles; *Eagles:* Quentin Laulu-Togagae.
Penalty count: 4-10; **Half-time:** 26-10;
Referee: Chris Leatherbarrow; **Attendance:** 1,179.

Sunday 14th August 2011

DEWSBURY RAMS 30 HUNSLET HAWKS 18

RAMS: 1 James Craven; 2 Michael Wainwright; 44 Liam Welham; 13 Ayden Faal; 5 Austin Buchanan; 6 Pat Walker; 7 Dominic Brambani; 12 James Lockwood; 9 Luke Blake; 43 Steve Crossley; 11 Rob Spicer; 40 Richard Fletcher; 15 Josh Tonks. Subs (all used): 8 Anthony England; 23 Luke Menzies; 32 Elliott Cosgrove; 46 Mark Barlow.
Tries: Wainwright (31), P Walker (45), Faal (53), Welham (70); **Goals:** P Walker 7/8.
HAWKS: 22 Danny Ratcliffe; 2 Richie Barnett; 4 David Clayton; 31 Jack Latus; 5 Waine Pryce; 6 Danny Grimshaw; 7 Paul March; 8 Adam Sullivan; 14 Luke Haigh; 10 James Houston; 11 Richard Blakeway; 16 John Oakes; 12 Tom Haughey. Subs (all used): 18 Joe Helme; 19 Neil Lowe; 20 Andrew Yates; 23 Joe McLocklan.
Tries: P March (7), Ratcliffe (58, 60); **Goals:** Latus 3/4.
Sin bin: Clayton (17) - interference.
Rugby Leaguer & League Express Men of the Match:
Rams: Dominic Brambani; *Hawks:* Danny Ratcliffe.
Penalty count: 10-5; **Half-time:** 6-6;
Referee: George Stokes; **Attendance:** 1,066.

LEIGH CENTURIONS 66 YORK CITY KNIGHTS 10

CENTURIONS: 7 Robbie Hunter-Paul; 2 Steve Maden; 14 Adam Higson; 4 Mick Nanyn; 5 Dean McGilvray; 6 Martyn Ridyard; 25 Jamie Ellis; 8 Chris Hill; 9 John Duffy; 26 David Mills; 15 Andy Thornley; 12 Tommy Goulden; 11 James Taylor. Subs (all used): 16 Anthony Nicholson; 13 Stephen Nash; 20 Sam Hopkins; 3 Stuart Littler.
Tries: Ridyard (4), Ellis (12, 26, 59), Hill (17), Nanyn (22, 49), Hopkins (38), Thornley (42), Higson (65), Goulden (69), McGilvray (70); **Goals:** Nanyn 9/11, Ridyard 0/1.
CITY KNIGHTS: 20 Tom Bush; 2 Dave Sutton; 1 James Haynes; 18 Matt Garside; 21 Dennis Tuffour; 27 Anthony Thackeray; 26 Scott Woods; 8 Nathan Freer; 9 Jack Lee; 10 Alex Benson; 25 Steve Lewis; 13 Ryan Esders; 11 Rhys Clarke. Subs (all used): 7 Jon Presley; 15 Brett Waller; 32 Joe Hemmings; 37 Ben Jones.
Tries: Thackeray (7), Freer (77); **Goals:** Bush 1/2.
Rugby Leaguer & League Express Men of the Match:
Centurions: Jamie Ellis; *City Knights:* Nathan Freer.
Penalty count: 5-2; **Half-time:** 36-4;
Referee: Tim Roby; **Attendance:** 2,207.

ROUND 10

Wednesday 17th August 2011

FEATHERSTONE ROVERS 56 WIDNES VIKINGS 16

ROVERS: 1 Ian Hardman; 2 Bryn Powell; 3 Sam Smeaton; 33 Ben Cockayne; 5 Tom Saxton; 28 Jon

Sheffield's Sam Scott takes on Batley's Paul Handforth

Hepworth; 7 Liam Finn; 8 Tony Tonks; 9 Ben Kaye; 10 Stuart Dickens; 11 Jon Grayshon; 12 Tim Spears; 13 Matty Dale. Subs (all used): 17 Greg Worthington; 30 Kirk Netherton; 4 Andrew Bostock; 18 Ross Divorty.
Tries: Smeaton (7, 36), Saxton (16, 55), Cockayne (21, 64), Powell (29, 58, 79), Dickens (44), Hepworth (50); **Goals:** Finn 6/11.
VIKINGS: 24 Danny Hulme; 5 Paddy Flynn; 23 Tangi Ropati; 4 Steve Tyrer; 19 Matt Gardner; 40 Joe Mellor; 44 James Coyle; 8 Steve Pickersgill; 14 Thomas Coyle; 17 Ben Kavanagh; 20 Shane Grady; 13 Simon Finnigan; 11 Dave Allen. Subs (all used): 3 Richard Varkulis; 12 Kurt Haggerty; 16 Macgraff Leuluai; 38 Logan Tomkins.
Tries: Hulme (47, 76), Grady (74); **Goals:** Haggerty 2/3.
Rugby Leaguer & League Express Men of the Match:
Rovers: Stuart Dickens; *Vikings:* Danny Hulme.
Penalty count: 7-7; **Half-time:** 26-0;
Referee: Ronnie Laughton; **Attendance:** 2,021.

ROUND 21

Thursday 18th August 2011

YORK CITY KNIGHTS 22 HALIFAX 8

CITY KNIGHTS: 1 James Haynes; 2 Dave Sutton; 20 Tom Bush; 13 Ryan Esders; 21 Dennis Tuffour; 27 Anthony Thackeray; 6 Chris Thorman; 8 Nathan Freer; 9 Jack Lee; 10 Alex Benson; 25 Steve Lewis; 19 Matt Garside; 11 Rhys Clarke. Subs (all used): 22 Ed Smith; 7 Jon Presley; 37 Ben Jones; 15 Brett Waller.
Tries: Benson (13), Waller (34), Esders (59);
Goals: Thorman 5/6.
HALIFAX: 1 Miles Greenwood; 20 Paul White; 5 James Haley; 33 Ryan Fieldhouse; 23 Rob Worrincy; 6 Danny Jones; 26 Anthony Bowman; 18 Joe Chandler; 13 Bob Beswick; 10 Neil Cherryholme; 14 Ryan Clayton; 24 Steve Bannister; 16 Paul Smith. Subs (all used): 4 Dylan Nash; 7 Ben Black; 8 Makali Aizue; 17 Frank Watene.
Tries: White (17, 78); **Goals:** Jones 0/2.
Rugby Leaguer & League Express Men of the Match:
City Knights: Chris Thorman; *Halifax:* Miles Greenwood.
Penalty count: 9-7; **Half-time:** 14-4;
Referee: Tim Roby; **Attendance:** 1,056.

Saturday 20th August 2011

LEIGH CENTURIONS 46 TOULOUSE OLYMPIQUE 16

CENTURIONS: 1 Stuart Donlan; 2 Steve Maden; 3 Stuart Littler; 4 Mick Nanyn; 14 Adam Higson; 6 Martyn Ridyard; 25 Jamie Ellis; 8 Chris Hill; 9 John Duffy; 26 David Mills; 15 Andy Thornley; 12 Tommy Goulden; 11 James Taylor. Subs (all used): 7 Robbie Hunter-Paul; 13 Stephen Nash; 17 Craig Briscoe; 20 Sam Hopkins.
Tries: Higson (18), Nanyn (25), Ridyard (29, 66), Hunter-Paul (33), Littler (41), Ellis (64), Taylor (78);
Goals: Nanyn 7/8.
OLYMPIQUE: 1 Rory Bromley; 2 Sebastien Payan; 22 Damien Couturier; 3 Sebastien Planas; 28 Mathieu Mercier; 4 Constant Villegas; 25 Tony Gigot; 15 Jerome Gout; 19 Yohann Gigord; 17 Kevin Larroyer; 14 Antoni Maria; 12 Yoan Tisseyre; 16 Sylvain Houles. Subs: 9 Craig Cook; 21 Nicolas Faure; 24 Gregory White (not used); 32 Theo Gonzalez-Trique.
Tries: Gigot (7), Bromley (36), Couturier (75);

Goals: Couturier 2/3.
Rugby Leaguer & League Express Men of the Match:
Centurions: David Mills; *Olympique:* Rory Bromley.
Penalty count: 6-3; **Half-time:** 22-10;
Referee: Dave Merrick; **Attendance:** 2,407.

Sunday 21st August 2011

FEATHERSTONE ROVERS 54 DEWSBURY RAMS 24

ROVERS: 1 Ian Hardman; 2 Bryn Powell; 3 Sam Smeaton; 33 Ben Cockayne; 5 Tom Saxton; 28 Jon Hepworth; 7 Liam Finn; 8 Tony Tonks; 9 Ben Kaye; 10 Stuart Dickens; 11 Jon Grayshon; 4 Andrew Bostock; 13 Matty Dale. Subs (all used): 30 Kirk Netherton; 24 Mufaro Mvududu; 18 Ross Divorty; 17 Greg Worthington.
Tries: Cockayne (9, 57), Dale (14, 47), Grayshon (18), Divorty (26), Hepworth (38), Tonks (67, 75), Hardman (79); **Goals:** Finn 7/10.
RAMS: 1 James Craven; 2 Michael Wainwright; 44 Liam Welham; 13 Ayden Faal; 5 Austin Buchanan; 6 Pat Walker; 7 Dominic Brambani; 12 James Lockwood; 9 Luke Blake; 43 Steve Crossley; 11 Rob Spicer; 40 Richard Fletcher; 15 Josh Tonks. Subs (all used): 8 Anthony England; 39 Richard Chapman; 35 Andy Smith; 42 Matt Nicholson.
Tries: Craven (4), P Walker (43), Blake (51), Wainwright (53); **Goals:** P Walker 4/4.
Rugby Leaguer & League Express Men of the Match:
Rovers: Tony Tonks; *Rams:* Pat Walker.
Penalty count: 6-6; **Half-time:** 28-6;
Referee: Chris Leatherbarrow; **Attendance:** 1,782.

HUNSLET HAWKS 42 BARROW RAIDERS 12

HAWKS: 22 Danny Ratcliffe; 2 Richie Barnett; 31 Jack Latus; 4 David Clayton; 5 Waine Pryce; 6 Danny Grimshaw; 7 Paul March; 8 Adam Sullivan; 14 Luke Haigh; 17 Rob Kelly; 16 John Oakes; 12 Tom Haughey; 23 Joe McLocklan. Subs (all used): 1 Stuart Kain; 11 Richard Blakeway; 19 Neil Lowe; 20 Andrew Yates.
Tries: Pryce (11, 25, 48, 79), Grimshaw (29), Ratcliffe (34, 51); **Goals:** Latus 7/8.
Dismissal: Blakeway (70) - grapple tackle on Blackwood.
RAIDERS: 1 Gary Broadbent; 2 Andy Ballard; 28 Anthony Blackwood; 4 Liam Harrison; 3 Chris Larkin; 16 Zebastian Luisi; 6 Jamie Rooney; 8 Jamie Thackray; 18 Nathan Mossop; 21 Jamie Butler; 11 Michael Knowles; 15 Martin Ostler; 9 Mark Gleeson. Subs (all used): 10 Matt James; 19 Marc Dixon; 24 Adam Walker; 27 Mike Backhouse.
Tries: Gleeson (44), Broadbent (62); **Goals:** Knowles 2/2.
Rugby Leaguer & League Express Men of the Match:
Hawks: Waine Pryce; *Raiders:* Zebastian Luisi.
Penalty count: 7-4; **Half-time:** 26-0;
Referee: Matthew Thomason; **Attendance:** 501.

SHEFFIELD EAGLES 28 BATLEY BULLDOGS 26

EAGLES: 1 Misi Taulapapa; 16 Vinny Finigan; 3 Menzie Yere; 26 Corey Hanson; 5 Tim Bergin; 13 Dane McDonald; 7 Simon Brown; 8 Jack Howieson; 9 Andrew Henderson; 10 Mitchell Stringer; 11 Alex Szostak; 12 Peter Green; 19 Joe Hirst. Subs (all used): 21 Jonny Woodcock; 30 Sam Scott; 20 Pat Smith; 22 Ryan Hepworth.
Tries: McDonald (34, 66), Hanson (41), Hirst (46), Bergin (57); **Goals:** Brown 4/5.
On report: Smith (30) - alleged dangerous tackle.

Leigh's Tommy Goulden and Mick Nanyn combine to halt Dewsbury's James Craven

BULLDOGS: 1 Ian Preece; 5 Wayne Reittie; 4 Danny Maun; 3 Daley Williams; 30 Johnny Campbell; 6 Paul Handforth; 16 Paul Mennell; 8 Byron Smith; 9 Kris Lythe; 17 Craig Potter; 12 Jason Walton; 18 Dane Manning; 13 Ashley Lindsay. Subs (all used): 23 Chris Buttery; 25 George Flanagan; 10 Sean Hesketh; 15 Adam Robinson. **Tries:** Manning (6), Preece (10), Lindsay (21), Buttery (37), Flanagan (78); **Goals:** Handforth 3/5.
Rugby Leaguer & League Express Men of the Match: *Eagles:* Dane McDonald; *Bulldogs:* Paul Handforth.
Penalty count: 7-6; **Half-time:** 6-22;
Referee: Ronnie Laughton; **Attendance:** 1,174.

ROUND 6

Sunday 28th August 2011

SHEFFIELD EAGLES 12 FEATHERSTONE ROVERS 34

EAGLES: 14 Jonny Woodcock; 16 Vinny Finigan; 3 Menzie Yere; 1 Misi Taulapapa; 5 Tim Bergin; 13 Dane McDonald; 7 Simon Brown; 22 Ryan Hepworth; 9 Andrew Henderson; 10 Mitchell Stringer; 11 Alex Szostak; 12 Peter Green; 19 Joe Hirst. Subs (all used): 6 Quentin Laulu-Togagae; 30 Sam Scott; 20 Pat Smith; 27 Eddie Battye.
Tries: Hirst (19), Finigan (36); **Goals:** Brown 2/4.
ROVERS: 1 Ian Hardman; 33 Ben Cockayne; 3 Sam Smeaton; 17 Greg Worthington; 5 Tom Saxton; 28 Jon Hepworth; 7 Liam Finn; 8 Tony Tonks; 9 Ben Kaye; 10 Stuart Dickens; 11 Jon Grayshon; 12 Tim Spears; 13 Matty Dale. Subs (all used): 6 Andy Kain; 30 Kirk Netherton; 4 Andrew Bostock; 18 Ross Divorty.
Tries: Saxton (31), Cockayne (46), Worthington (53), Kain (64, 70), Hardman (73); **Goals:** Finn 5/6.
Rugby Leaguer & League Express Men of the Match: *Eagles:* Vinny Finigan; *Rovers:* Tom Saxton.
Penalty count: 12-10; **Half-time:** 12-6;
Referee: Matthew Thomason; **Attendance:** 1,336.

ROUND 22

Thursday 1st September 2011

DEWSBURY RAMS 22 LEIGH CENTURIONS 40

RAMS: 1 James Craven; 2 Michael Wainwright; 35 Andy Smith; 13 Ayden Faal; 5 Austin Buchanan; 6 Pat Walker; 7 Dominic Brambani; 8 Anthony England; 9 Luke Blake; 43 Steve Crossley; 11 Rob Spicer; 12 James Lockwood; 46 Mark Barlow. Subs (all used): 23 Luke Menzies; 42 Matt Nicholson; 32 Elliott Cosgrove; 40 Richard Fletcher.
Tries: Faal (10), Wainwright (25), Nicholson (27, pen), Buchanan (39); **Goals:** P Walker 3/5.

CENTURIONS: 1 Stuart Donlan; 2 Steve Maden; 3 Stuart Littler; 4 Mick Nanyn; 5 Dean McGilvray; 6 Martyn Ridyard; 25 Jamie Ellis; 8 Chris Hill; 9 John Duffy; 13 Stephen Nash; 15 Andy Thornley; 12 Tommy Goulden; 11 James Taylor. Subs (all used): 7 Robbie Hunter-Paul; 20 Sam Hopkins; 22 Tom Armstrong; 26 David Mills.
Tries: Taylor (8), Donlan (15), Nanyn (22, 30), Hill (46), Ridyard (66), Ellis (74); **Goals:** Nanyn 6/7.
Rugby Leaguer & League Express Men of the Match: *Rams:* James Craven; *Centurions:* Mick Nanyn.
Penalty count: 8-9; **Half-time:** 22-22;
Referee: George Stokes; **Attendance:** 933.

Saturday 3rd September 2011

TOULOUSE OLYMPIQUE 28 BARROW RAIDERS 42

OLYMPIQUE: 1 Rory Bromley; 28 Mathieu Mercier; 3 Sebastien Planas; 22 Damien Couturier; 24 Gregory White; 25 Tony Gigot; 4 Constant Villegas; 34 Thibaut Ancely; 19 Yohann Gigord; 21 Nicolas Faure; 17 Kevin Larroyer; 14 Antoni Maria; 16 Sylvain Houles. Subs (all used): 15 Jerome Gout; 32 Theo Gonzalez-Trique; 12 Yoan Tisseyre; 9 Craig Cook.
Tries: Mercier (3, 9, 76), Gigot (9, 32);
Goals: Couturier 4/5.
RAIDERS: 1 Gary Broadbent; 2 Andy Ballard; 28 Anthony Blackwood; 4 Liam Harrison; 3 Chris Larkin; 6 Jamie Rooney; 29 Liam Finch; 8 Jamie Thackray; 18 Nathan Mossop; 21 Jamie Butler; 11 Michael Knowles; 15 Martin Ostler; 16 Zebastian Luisi. Subs (all used): 9 Mark Gleeson; 10 Matt James; 19 Marc Dixon; 27 Mike Backhouse.
Tries: Ballard (7, 21, 62), Harrison (18, 54), Larkin (38), Blackwood (59), Gleeson (80);
Goals: Rooney 4/7, Broadbent 1/1.
Rugby Leaguer & League Express Men of the Match: *Olympique:* Rory Bromley; *Raiders:* Liam Harrison.
Penalty count: 5-15; **Half-time:** 22-20;
Referee: Warren Turley; **Attendance:** 602.

Sunday 4th September 2011

HUNSLET HAWKS 24 HALIFAX 32

HAWKS: 22 Danny Ratcliffe; 2 Richie Barnett; 31 Jack Latus; 4 David Clayton; 5 Waine Pryce; 6 Danny Grimshaw; 7 Paul March; 8 Adam Sullivan; 14 Luke Haigh; 17 Rob Kelly; 16 John Oakes; 12 Tom Haughey; 11 Richard Blakeway. Subs (all used): 13 David March; 19 Neil Lowe; 20 Andrew Yates; 23 Joe McLocklan.
Tries: Ratcliffe (4, 24), P March (37), D March (60);
Goals: Latus 4/7.
HALIFAX: 1 Miles Greenwood; 20 Paul White; 5 James Haley; 33 Ryan Fieldhouse; 23 Rob Worrincy; 6 Danny

Jones; 7 Ben Black; 12 Sam Barlow; 13 Bob Beswick; 10 Neil Cherryholme; 14 Ryan Clayton; 24 Steve Bannister; 19 Jacob Fairbank. Subs (all used): 8 Makali Aizue; 9 Sean Penkywicz; 15 Jim Gannon; 18 Joe Chandler.
Tries: Haley (31), Worrincy (53, 80), S Barlow (67, 75);
Goals: Jones 6/6.
Rugby Leaguer & League Express Men of the Match: *Hawks:* Danny Ratcliffe; *Halifax:* Rob Worrincy.
Penalty count: 10-8; **Half-time:** 20-6;
Referee: Ronnie Laughton; **Attendance:** 1,053.

SHEFFIELD EAGLES 52 YORK CITY KNIGHTS 18

EAGLES: 6 Quentin Laulu-Togagae; 16 Vinny Finigan; 1 Misi Taulapapa; 26 Corey Hanson; 5 Tim Bergin; 13 Dane McDonald; 7 Simon Brown; 8 Jack Howieson; 9 Andrew Henderson; 10 Mitchell Stringer; 11 Alex Szostak; 12 Peter Green; 19 Joe Hirst. Subs (all used): 3 Menzie Yere; 30 Sam Scott; 20 Pat Smith; 22 Ryan Hepworth.
Tries: Laulu-Togagae (8), Hirst (20), Szostak (26), Hanson (39, 55), Taulapapa (45), Yere (51, 55, 63), Stringer (69); **Goals:** Brown 2/3, Bergin 4/7.
CITY KNIGHTS: 1 James Haynes; 21 Dennis Tuffour; 13 Ryan Esders; 29 James Ford; 2 Dave Sutton; 20 Tom Bush; 6 Chris Thorman; 10 Alex Benson; 9 Jack Lee; 8 Nathan Freer; 11 Rhys Clarke; 19 Matt Garside; 25 Steve Lewis. Subs (all used): 22 Ed Smith; 7 Jon Presley; 37 Ben Jones; 15 Brett Waller.
Tries: Bush (17, 73), Garside (80); **Goals:** Thorman 3/3.
Rugby Leaguer & League Express Men of the Match: *Eagles:* Corey Hanson; *City Knights:* Tom Bush.
Penalty count: 7-7; **Half-time:** 20-6;
Referee: Chris Leatherbarrow; **Attendance:** 1,147.

WIDNES VIKINGS 4 FEATHERSTONE ROVERS 44

VIKINGS: 1 Danny Craven; 5 Paddy Flynn; 4 Steve Tyrer; 20 Shane Grady; 34 Kevin Penny; 44 James Coyle; 40 Joe Mellor; 8 Steve Pickersgill; 14 Thomas Coyle; 17 Ben Kavanagh; 16 Macgraff Leuluai; 11 Dave Allen; 12 Kurt Haggerty. Subs (all used): 3 Richard Varkulis; 7 Chaz I'Anson; 39 Dominic Crosby; 38 Logan Tomkins.
Try: Craven (55); **Goals:** Haggerty 0/1.
Sin bin: Pickersgill (62) - punching.
ROVERS: 1 Ian Hardman; 33 Ben Cockayne; 3 Sam Smeaton; 17 Greg Worthington; 5 Tom Saxton; 6 Andy Kain; 7 Liam Finn; 8 Tony Tonks; 9 Ben Kaye; 10 Stuart Dickens; 11 Jon Grayshon; 12 Tim Spears; 28 Jon Hepworth. Subs (all used): 4 Andrew Bostock; 18 Ross Divorty; 24 Mufaro Mvududu; 30 Kirk Netherton.
Tries: Cockayne (17, 23), Saxton (38, 49), Hardman (41, 59), Tonks (63), Finn (65); **Goals:** Finn 6/8.
Rugby Leaguer & League Express Men of the Match: *Vikings:* Shane Grady; *Rovers:* Jon Hepworth.
Penalty count: 7-10; **Half-time:** 0-16;
Referee: Tim Roby; **Attendance:** 5,021.

Halifax's Makali Aizue swamped by the Batley defence

PLAY-OFFS

ELIMINATION PLAY-OFFS

Thursday 8th September 2011

BATLEY BULLDOGS 22 HALIFAX 32

BULLDOGS: 1 Ian Preece; 5 Wayne Reittie; 3 Daley Williams; 4 Danny Maun; 30 Johnny Campbell; 6 Paul Handforth; 16 Paul Mennell; 8 Byron Smith; 9 Kris Lythe; 17 Craig Potter; 11 Alex Bretherton; 18 Dane Manning; 13 Ashley Lindsay. Subs (all used): 25 George Flanagan; 23 Chris Buttery; 12 Jason Walton; 15 Adam Robinson.
Tries: Preece (22, 63), Daley Williams (24), Manning (60); **Goals:** Handforth 2/3, Mennell 1/3.
HALIFAX: 1 Miles Greenwood; 23 Rob Worrincy; 5 James Haley; 3 Jon Goddard; 20 Paul White; 13 Bob Beswick; 6 Danny Jones; 10 Neil Cherryholme; 9 Sean Penkywicz; 12 Sam Barlow; 14 Ryan Clayton; 16 Paul Smith; 19 Jacob Fairbank. Subs (all used): 7 Ben Black; 8 Makali Aizue; 18 Joe Chandler; 24 Steve Bannister.
Tries: Haley (30), Bannister (48), Worrincy (54), Penkywicz (58), Beswick (74); **Goals:** Jones 6/6.
Rugby Leaguer & League Express Men of the Match: *Bulldogs:* Ian Preece; *Halifax:* Ben Black.
Penalty count: 5-9; **Half-time:** 12-6;
Referee: Clint Sharrad; **Attendance:** 1,179.

Friday 9th September 2011

SHEFFIELD EAGLES 36 WIDNES VIKINGS 20

EAGLES: 6 Quentin Laulu-Togagae; 16 Vinny Finigan; 1 Misi Taulapapa; 26 Corey Hanson; 5 Tim Bergin; 13 Dane McDonald; 7 Simon Brown; 8 Jack Howieson; 9 Andrew Henderson; 10 Mitchell Stringer; 11 Alex Szostak; 12 Peter Green; 19 Joe Hirst. Subs (all used): 14 Jonny Woodcock; 30 Sam Scott; 20 Pat Smith; 22 Ryan Hepworth.
Tries: Laulu-Togagae (5, 78), McDonald (18, 52), Taulapapa (59); **Goals:** Brown 8/9.
VIKINGS: 1 Danny Craven; 5 Paddy Flynn; 23 Tangi Ropati; 20 Shane Grady; 19 Matt Gardner; 40 Joe Mellor; 44 James Coyle; 8 Steve Pickersgill; 14 Thomas Coyle; 17 Ben Kavanagh; 16 Macgraff Leuluai; 13 Simon Finnigan; 11 Dave Allen. Subs (all used): 3 Richard Varkulis; 12 Kurt Haggerty; 38 Logan Tomkins; 39 Dominic Crosby.
Tries: Flynn (14, 50), Ropati (66), Craven (74); **Goals:** Craven 2/4.
Rugby Leaguer & League Express Men of the Match: *Eagles:* Peter Green; *Vikings:* Danny Craven.
Penalty count: 12-7; **Half-time:** 14-4;
Referee: Matthew Thomason; **Attendance:** 564.

QUALIFYING SEMI-FINAL

Thursday 15th September 2011

FEATHERSTONE ROVERS 35 LEIGH CENTURIONS 20

ROVERS: 1 Ian Hardman; 33 Ben Cockayne; 3 Sam Smeaton; 17 Greg Worthington; 5 Tom Saxton; 6 Andy Kain; 7 Liam Finn; 8 Tony Tonks; 9 Ben Kaye; 10 Stuart Dickens; 11 Jon Grayshon; 12 Tim Spears; 28 Jon Hepworth. Subs (all used): 18 Ross Divorty; 13 Matty Dale; 4 Andrew Bostock; 30 Kirk Netherton.
Tries: Cockayne (3), Finn (8), Saxton (38, 47, 55), Bostock (66); **Goals:** Finn 5/7; **Field goal:** Finn (60).
Sin bin: Saxton (70) - holding down.
CENTURIONS: 1 Stuart Donlan; 2 Steve Maden; 3 Stuart Littler; 4 Mick Nanyn; 5 Dean McGilvray; 6 Martyn Ridyard; 25 Jamie Ellis; 8 Chris Hill; 9 John Duffy; 26 David Mills; 15 Andy Thornley; 12 Tommy Goulden; 11 James Taylor. Subs (all used): 14 Adam Higson; 7 Robbie Hunter-Paul; 20 Sam Hopkins; 13 Stephen Nash.
Tries: Maden (22), Mills (58), Ridyard (74), Nanyn (78); **Goals:** Nanyn 2/4.
Rugby Leaguer & League Express Men of the Match: *Rovers:* Tony Tonks; *Centurions:* Martyn Ridyard.
Penalty count: 9-9; **Half-time:** 18-4;
Referee: Tim Roby; **Attendance:** 2,031.

ELIMINATION SEMI-FINAL

Sunday 18th September 2011

SHEFFIELD EAGLES 50 HALIFAX 12

EAGLES: 6 Quentin Laulu-Togagae; 16 Vinny Finigan; 1 Misi Taulapapa; 26 Corey Hanson; 5 Tim Bergin; 13 Dane McDonald; 7 Simon Brown; 8 Jack Howieson; 9 Andrew Henderson; 10 Mitchell Stringer; 11 Alex Szostak; 12 Peter Green; 19 Joe Hirst. Subs (all used): 14 Jonny Woodcock; 30 Sam Scott; 20 Pat Smith; 22 Ryan Hepworth.
Tries: Laulu-Togagae (11), Hirst (13), Henderson (20, 62), McDonald (27, 54), Taulapapa (66), Woodcock (78); **Goals:** Brown 9/11.
HALIFAX: 33 Ryan Fieldhouse; 20 Paul White; 3 Jon Goddard; 5 James Haley; 23 Rob Worrincy; 6 Danny Jones; 13 Bob Beswick; 15 Jim Gannon; 9 Sean Penkywicz; 12 Sam Barlow; 14 Ryan Clayton; 24 Steve Bannister; 16 Paul Smith. Subs (all used): 7 Ben Black; 21 Josh Barlow; 10 Neil Cherryholme; 18 Joe Chandler.
Tries: Goddard (6), Penkywicz (50); **Goals:** Jones 2/2.
Sin bin: S Barlow (55) - dissent.
Rugby Leaguer & League Express Men of the Match: *Eagles:* Hanson; *Halifax:* Sean Penkywicz.
Penalty count: 11-12; **Half-time:** 26-6;
Referee: Matthew Thomason; **Attendance:** 1,233.

FINAL ELIMINATOR

Thursday 22nd September 2011

LEIGH CENTURIONS 10 SHEFFIELD EAGLES 20

CENTURIONS: 1 Stuart Donlan; 2 Steve Maden; 14 Adam Higson; 4 Mick Nanyn; 5 Dean McGilvray; 6 Martyn Ridyard; 25 Jamie Ellis; 8 Chris Hill; 9 John Duffy; 26 David Mills; 15 Andy Thornley; 3 Stuart Littler; 11 James Taylor. Subs (all used): 7 Robbie Hunter-Paul; 13 Stephen Nash; 20 Sam Hopkins; 22 Tom Armstrong.
Tries: Donlan (44), Nanyn (72); **Goals:** Nanyn 1/2.
EAGLES: 6 Quentin Laulu-Togagae; 16 Vinny Finigan; 1 Misi Taulapapa; 3 Menzie Yere; 5 Tim Bergin; 13 Dane McDonald; 7 Simon Brown; 8 Jack Howieson; 9 Andrew Henderson; 10 Mitchell Stringer; 11 Alex Szostak; 12 Peter Green; 19 Joe Hirst. Subs (all used): 20 Pat Smith; 22 Ryan Hepworth; 26 Corey Hanson; 30 Sam Scott.
Tries: S Scott (32), Finigan (54), Laulu-Togagae (56); **Goals:** Brown 4/4.
Rugby Leaguer & League Express Men of the Match: *Centurions:* Dean McGilvray; *Eagles:* Joe Hirst.
Penalty count: 9-8; **Half-time:** 0-8;
Referee: Ben Thaler; **Attendance:** 1,818.

GRAND FINAL

Sunday 2nd October 2011

FEATHERSTONE ROVERS 40 SHEFFIELD EAGLES 4

ROVERS: 1 Ian Hardman; 33 Ben Cockayne; 3 Sam Smeaton; 17 Greg Worthington; 5 Tom Saxton; 6 Andy Kain; 7 Liam Finn; 8 Tony Tonks; 9 Ben Kaye; 10 Stuart Dickens; 11 Jon Grayshon; 12 Tim Spears; 28 Jon Hepworth. Subs (all used): 18 Ross Divorty; 13 Matty Dale; 4 Andrew Bostock; 30 Kirk Netherton.
Tries: Spears (4), Finn (7, 39), Hardman (42), Cockayne (56), Hepworth (59), Saxton (79); **Goals:** Finn 6/7.
Sin bin: Netherton (54) - fighting.
EAGLES: 6 Quentin Laulu-Togagae; 5 Tim Bergin; 26 Corey Hanson; 1 Misi Taulapapa; 16 Vinny Finigan; 13 Dane McDonald; 7 Simon Brown; 8 Jack Howieson; 9 Andrew Henderson; 10 Mitchell Stringer; 11 Alex Szostak; 12 Peter Green; 19 Joe Hirst. Subs (all used): 22 Ryan Hepworth; 30 Sam Scott; 20 Pat Smith; 14 Jonny Woodcock.
Try: McDonald (12); **Goals:** Brown 0/1.
Sin bin: Hirst (54) - fighting.
Rugby Leaguer & League Express Men of the Match: *Rovers:* Liam Finn; *Eagles:* Joe Hirst.
Penalty count: 7-11; **Half-time:** 18-4;
Referee: Matthew Thomason; **Attendance:** 7,263 *(at Halliwell Jones Stadium, Warrington).*

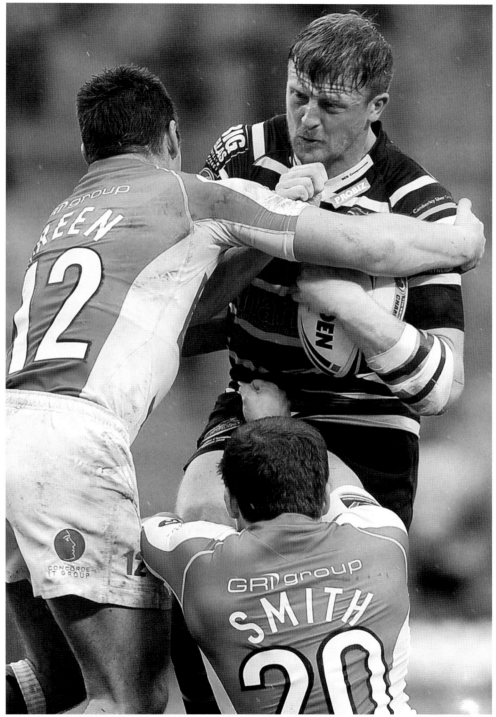

Featherstone's Jon Grayshon meets Sheffield's Peter Green and Pat Smith
head on during the Championship Grand Final

CHAMPIONSHIP ONE 2011
Club by Club

DONCASTER
RUGBY LEAGUE CLUB

DONCASTER

DATE	FIXTURE	RESULT	SCORERS	LGE	ATT
4/2/11	Featherstone (a) (NRC)	L54-10	t:Butterfield,Emmett g:Spaven	10th(P1)	1,223
13/2/11	London Skolars (h) (NRC)	W32-4	t:Spurr,Crawley,Spaven,Ely(2),Kesik g:Spaven,Sanderson(3)	7th(P1)	420
20/2/11	Dewsbury (h) (NRC)	L18-30	t:P Hughes,Robinson,Scott g:Spaven(3)	7th(P1)	555
27/2/11	Rochdale (a) (NRC)	W36-40	t:Williams,P Hughes,Kesik,Spaven,Carbutt,Wilson,Spurr,Butterfield g:Spaven(4)	7th(P1)	442
5/3/11	Thatto Heath (h) (CCR3)	W34-22	t:Ely,Sanderson,Kesik,Colton,Butterfield,Bovill g:Spaven(5)	N/A	352
13/3/11	South Wales (h)	W40-10	t:Colton(2),Spaven(2),Steen,Butterfield,Green g:Spaven(6)	3rd	895
20/3/11	London Skolars (a)	W22-42	t:Spaven(2),Butterfield,Steen,Green(2),Sanderson g:Spaven(7)	2nd	326
27/3/11	Workington (h)	W26-16	t:Leaf(2),Kesik,Fawcett,Steen g:Spaven(2),Sanderson	2nd	493
3/4/11	Rochdale (h)	L8-24	t:Green(2)	3rd	589
17/4/11	Whitehaven (a)	L26-16	t:Kesik,Colton,Robinson g:Spaven(2)	5th	727
25/4/11	Swinton (h)	L32-36	t:Sanderson(2),Emmett,Fawcett,Spurr,C Hughes g:Spaven(4)	6th	649
1/5/11	Oldham (a)	L46-24	t:Sanderson,Kesik,Colton,C Hughes,Spaven g:Spaven(2)	7th	672
8/5/11	Wakefield (h) (CCR4)	L10-50	t:Spaven,Sanderson g:Dobek	N/A	1,823
15/5/11	Keighley (h)	L20-24	t:Sanderson,Kesik,Colton,Ely g:Spaven(2)	7th	549
29/5/11	Workington (a)	W32-34	t:Potts(2),Sanderson(2),Ely,Green(2) g:Dobek(3)	6th	544
5/6/11	Oldham (h)	W30-0	t:Spaven,Spurr(3),Colton g:Spaven(5)	6th	617
19/6/11	Gateshead (a)	W6-22	t:Spaven,Spurr,Coady,Morrison g:Spaven(3)	6th	256
26/6/11	London Skolars (h)	W40-22	t:Morrison(2),Ely,Robinson,Dee,Spurr,C Hughes g:Spaven(6)	6th	456
3/7/11	Rochdale (a)	W16-26	t:Spurr(3),C Hughes,Morrison g:Spaven(3)	4th	423
10/7/11	Gateshead (h)	W32-0	t:Edwards,Spurr(2),Kesik(2),C Hughes g:Spaven(4)	3rd	681
15/7/11	Swinton (a)	L30-28	t:Potts(2),Morrison(3) g:Spaven(4)	3rd	425
24/7/11	South Wales (a)	W20-41	t:Edwards,C Hughes,Butterfield,Kesik,Coady,Spurr,Emmett g:Spaven(6) fg:Spaven	2nd	304
31/7/11	Keighley (a)	L34-6	t:Dee g:Spaven	4th	937
14/8/11	Whitehaven (h)	W20-18	t:Coady,Kesik,Morrison,Fawcett g:Spaven(2)	4th	501
21/8/11	Workington (h)	L6-37	t:Dee g:Spaven	5th	659
4/9/11	Gateshead (a)	W14-38	t:Potts,Sanderson,Butterfield,C Hughes(2),Fawcett,Morrison g:Spaven(2),Sanderson(3)	5th	527
11/9/11	Whitehaven (h) (EPO)	W34-16	t:Potts(2),Sanderson(2),Butterfield,Edwards g:Spaven(5)	N/A	418
18/9/11	Rochdale (a) (ESF)	L26-18	t:Robinson,Scott,Spurr g:Spaven(3)	N/A	552

		APP		TRIES		GOALS		FG		PTS	
	D.O.B.	ALL	Ch1	ALL	Ch1	ALL	Ch1	ALL	Ch1	ALL	Ch1
Jamie Bovill	21/3/83	11(1)	6(1)	1	0	0	0	0	0	4	0
Mick Butterfield	5/12/84	24(1)	19	8	5	0	0	0	0	32	20
Matt Carbutt	3/10/85	12(15)	8(13)	1	0	0	0	0	0	4	0
Michael Coady	14/4/87	11(2)	11(2)	3	3	0	0	0	0	12	12
Dean Colton	18/2/83	15	10	7	6	0	0	0	0	28	24
Liam Crawley	18/4/87	10(8)	9(3)	1	0	0	0	0	0	4	0
Dominic Dee	26/3/90	2(11)	2(11)	3	3	0	0	0	0	12	12
Aaron Dobek	10/9/87	4(1)	3(1)	0	0	4	3	0	0	8	6
Grant Edwards	22/3/87	11(2)	11(1)	3	3	0	0	0	0	12	12
Jack Ely	3/12/89	18(3)	14(2)	6	3	0	0	0	0	24	12
Mike Emmett	13/5/87	20(5)	15(5)	3	2	0	0	0	0	12	8
Craig Fawcett	8/11/85	18	16	4	4	0	0	0	0	16	16
Lee Gomersall	14/11/86	(1)	0	0	0	0	0	0	0	0	0
Chris Green	3/1/90	4(1)	4(1)	7	7	0	0	0	0	28	28
Carl Hughes	30/11/82	8(13)	6(12)	8	8	0	0	0	0	32	32
Paul Hughes	28/12/84	9	5	2	0	0	0	0	0	8	0
Kyle Kesik	3/6/89	4(23)	4(17)	11	8	0	0	0	0	44	32
Craig Lawton	17/2/81	4(3)	3(3)	0	0	0	0	0	0	0	0
Shaun Leaf	10/2/84	7	4	2	2	0	0	0	0	8	8
Nev Morrison	27/5/90	19	18	9	9	0	0	0	0	36	36
Gareth Potts	25/7/90	10	10	7	7	0	0	0	0	28	28
Craig Robinson	30/7/85	22(2)	16(2)	4	3	0	0	0	0	16	12
Kyle Sampson	13/9/89	6(13)	5(10)	0	0	0	0	0	0	0	0
Stewart Sanderson	10/4/85	22(2)	17(1)	12	10	7	4	0	0	62	48
Adam Scott	1/1/85	27(1)	21(1)	2	1	0	0	0	0	8	4
Scott Spaven	6/3/90	27	21	10	7	84	70	1	1	209	169
Chris Spurr	7/7/80	25	19	15	13	0	0	0	0	60	52
Ryan Steen	26/6/89	8	7	3	3	0	0	0	0	12	12
Richard Tafa	10/10/79	1	1	0	0	0	0	0	0	0	0
Ashley Williams	1/8/88	1(1)	0	1	0	0	0	0	0	4	0
Scott Wilson	21/9/88	4(2)	1(1)	1	0	0	0	0	0	4	0

Kyle Kesik

LEAGUE RECORD
P20-W12-D0-L8-BP4
(5th, Championship 1/
Elimination Semi-Final)
F531, A433, Diff+98
40 points.

CHALLENGE CUP
Round Four

NORTHERN RAIL CUP
7th, Pool 1

ATTENDANCES
Best - v Wakefield (CC - 1,823)
Worst - v Thatto Heath (CC - 352)
Total (excluding Challenge Cup) - 7,482
Average (excluding
Challenge Cup) - 575
(Up by 66 on 2010)

CLUB RECORDS
MATCH RECORDS
Highest score: 96-0 v Highfield, 20/3/94 Highest score against: 4-90 v Widnes, 10/6/2007 Record attendance: 10,000 v Bradford, 16/2/52
Tries: 6 Kane Epati v Oldham, 30/7/2006 Goals: 12 Tony Zelei v Nottingham City, 1/9/91; Robert Turner v Highfield, 20/3/94
Points: 32 Tony Zelei v Nottingham City, 1/9/91

SEASON RECORDS
CAREER RECORDS
Tries: 30 Luke Gale 2008 Goals: 129 Jonny Woodcock 2002 Points: 306 Jonny Woodcock 2002
Tries: 112 Mark Roache 1985-97 Goals: 850 David Noble 1976-77; 1980-89; 1992 Points: 1,751 David Noble 1976-77; 1980-89; 1992
Appearances: 327 Audley Pennant 1980-83; 1985-97

GATESHEAD THUNDER

DATE	FIXTURE	RESULT	SCORERS	LGE	ATT
6/2/11	Sheffield (h) (NRC)	L20-32	t:Norman,Green,Ward,Peers g:Clarke(2)	7th(P2)	444
13/2/11	Workington (a) (NRC)	L82-0		10th(P2)	381
20/2/11	Batley (a) (NRC)	L60-6	t:Morris g:Clarke	10th(P2)	612
27/2/11	Swinton (h) (NRC)	L4-76	t:Massey	10th(P2)	285
5/3/11	Milford (a) (CCR3)	W16-38	t:Massey,Barron,Green,Staveley,Morris,Jason Payne,Welton g:Clarke(5)	N/A	400
13/3/11	Oldham (a)	L66-12	t:Peers,Clarke g:Clarke(2)	8th	562
20/3/11	Keighley (h)	L10-44	t:Ward,Brown g:Clarke	9th	327
27/3/11	South Wales (a)	L60-20	t:Morris,Green,O'Sullivan,Hodgson g:Clarke(2)	10th	302
3/4/11	Swinton (a)	L48-24	t:Bate,Love,Condron,Jason Payne g:Clarke(4)	10th	493
17/4/11	Workington (h)	L0-64		10th	273
25/4/11	London Skolars (a)	D32-32	t:Jason Payne,Love,Clarke(2),Condron g:Clarke(6)	10th	263
1/5/11	Whitehaven (h)	L10-54	t:Jason Payne,Harding g:Clarke	10th	237
6/5/11	Harlequins (h) (CCR4)	L0-70		N/A	402
15/5/11	Rochdale (h)	L68-0		10th	504
22/5/11	South Wales (h)	L32-66	t:Welton(2),Cash(2),Hodgson,Williams g:Clarke(4)	10th	162
5/6/11	Swinton (h)	L16-62	t:Shields,Kelly,Causer g:Clarke(2)	10th	252
12/6/11	Workington (a)	L84-12	t:Bate,Welton g:Clarke(2)	10th	384
19/6/11	Doncaster (h)	L6-22	t:Wilson g:Clarke	10th	256
26/6/11	Oldham (h)	L16-52	t:Brown,Shields,Clarke g:Clarke(2)	10th	436
3/7/11	Keighley (a)	L92-6	t:Clarke g:Clarke	10th	899
10/7/11	Doncaster (a)	L32-0		10th	681
31/7/11	Whitehaven (a)	L64-10	t:Wilson,Jason Payne g:Stamp	10th	651
7/8/11	Rochdale (h)	L14-48	t:Mitchell,Clarke,Brown g:Clarke	10th	242
14/8/11	London Skolars (h)	L16-36	t:Welton,O'Sullivan,O'Mara g:Stamp,Clarke	10th	292
21/8/11	Rochdale (a)	L62-18	t:Peers,Jason Payne,Welton g:Stamp(3)	10th	401
4/9/11	Doncaster (h)	L14-38	t:O'Sullivan(2) g:Clarke,Stamp(2)	10th	527

		APP		TRIES		GOALS		FG		PTS	
	D.O.B.	ALL	Ch1	ALL	Ch1	ALL	Ch1	ALL	Ch1	ALL	Ch1
Ade Aderiye	26/2/85	(8)	(8)	0	0	0	0	0	0	0	0
Gareth Barron	31/5/82	(2)	(1)	1	0	0	0	0	0	4	0
Will Bate	6/12/89	22(1)	19(1)	2	2	0	0	0	0	8	8
Karl Brandt	9/2/86	(2)	(1)	0	0	0	0	0	0	0	0
Joe Brown	24/4/87	21	20	3	3	0	0	0	0	12	12
Chris Burnett	22/6/85	(1)	(1)	0	0	0	0	0	0	0	0
Tabua Cakacaka	8/3/77	5(2)	5(2)	0	0	0	0	0	0	0	0
David Cash	20/12/89	8(2)	8(2)	2	2	0	0	0	0	8	8
Joe Causer	20/5/88	(2)	(2)	1	1	0	0	0	0	4	4
Ryan Clarke	8/9/85	23(3)	17(3)	6	6	39	31	0	0	102	86
James Clarkson	24/4/89	2	0	0	0	0	0	0	0	0	0
Connor Condron	29/11/91	17	15	2	2	0	0	0	0	8	8
Steve Coutts	19/3/84	4(1)	3(1)	0	0	0	0	0	0	0	0
Sam Crowther	21/10/86	1(3)	0	0	0	0	0	0	0	0	0
Michael Ellis	6/6/83	2(1)	1(1)	0	0	0	0	0	0	0	0
Wayne Green	1/1/88	5(2)	(2)	3	1	0	0	0	0	12	4
Matthew Harding	2/10/90	6(2)	6(2)	1	1	0	0	0	0	4	4
Tom Hodgson	12/5/88	15(3)	11(3)	2	2	0	0	0	0	8	8
Craig Jones	15/7/89	1	0	0	0	0	0	0	0	0	0
Michael Kelly	23/5/89	21(3)	16(2)	1	1	0	0	0	0	4	4
Jamie Love	7/3/93	5(1)	3(1)	2	2	0	0	0	0	8	8
Matthew Massey	6/10/90	4(1)	2	2	0	0	0	0	0	8	0
Mike Mitchell	7/4/85	8	8	1	1	0	0	0	0	4	4
Andy Morris	16/6/84	10(4)	6(3)	3	1	0	0	0	0	12	4
David Norman	26/12/79	3(3)	1(1)	1	0	0	0	0	0	4	0
Craig Olugbode	30/4/85	3(1)	2	0	0	0	0	0	0	0	0
Oliver O'Mara	14/7/86	4(4)	4(4)	1	1	0	0	0	0	4	4
Dan O'Sullivan	30/7/89	7(6)	6(5)	4	4	0	0	0	0	16	16
Chris Parker	9/9/78	15(10)	11(8)	0	0	0	0	0	0	0	0
Jason Payne	20/1/88	18(4)	14(2)	6	5	0	0	0	0	24	20
Jonny Payne	26/1/88	2	2	0	0	0	0	0	0	0	0
Robin Peers	18/1/82	15(2)	9(2)	3	2	0	0	0	0	12	8
Gary Sargeant	21/2/91	2(3)	2(3)	0	0	0	0	0	0	0	0
Jonny Shields	30/12/92	3	3	2	2	0	0	0	0	8	8
Ben Smith	11/10/93	(2)	(2)	0	0	0	0	0	0	0	0
Paul Stamp	25/1/89	5	5	0	0	7	7	0	0	14	14
Nick Staveley	24/6/82	5(2)	2	1	0	0	0	0	0	4	0
Mitchell Stevens	9/4/89	11	10	0	0	0	0	0	0	0	0
Josh Stoker	26/7/92	16(4)	12(4)	0	0	0	0	0	0	0	0
Ashley Thackeray	6/11/87	4	4	0	0	0	0	0	0	0	0
Clarke Thompson	6/10/91	(2)	(2)	0	0	0	0	0	0	0	0
Michael Ward	13/1/89	9(1)	3(1)	2	1	0	0	0	0	8	4
Stephen Welton	15/3/91	11(9)	9(6)	6	5	0	0	0	0	24	20
Ashley Williams	1/8/88	12	11	1	1	0	0	0	0	4	4
Danny Wilson	3/6/82	7	7	2	2	0	0	0	0	8	8
Scott Woods	10/12/90	2	1	0	0	0	0	0	0	0	0
Reece Young	29/1/91	2(7)	2(4)	0	0	0	0	0	0	0	0

Jason Payne

LEAGUE RECORD
P20-W0-D1-L19-BP0
(10th, Championship 1)
F268, A1094, Diff-826
2 points.

CHALLENGE CUP
Round Four

NORTHERN RAIL CUP
10th, Pool 2

ATTENDANCES
Best - v Doncaster (Ch1 - 527)
Worst - v South Wales (Ch1 - 162)
Total (excluding Challenge Cup) - 3,733
Average (excluding
Challenge Cup) - 311
(Down by 62 on 2010)

CLUB RECORDS	**Highest score:** 66-6 v Wakefield, 5/9/99 **Highest score against:** 0-132 v Blackpool Panthers, 16/5/2010 **Record attendance:** 6,631 v Bradford, 16/5/99
MATCH RECORDS	**Tries:** 5 Andy Walker v London Skolars, 22/6/03 **Goals:** 11 Ian Herron v Wakefield, 5/9/99 **Points:** 26 Ian Herron v Wakefield, 5/9/99
SEASON RECORDS	**Tries:** 25 Matt Daylight 1999 **Goals:** 129 (inc 1 fg) Dan Russell 2008 **Points:** 293 Dan Russell 2008
CAREER RECORDS	**Tries:** 74 Kevin Neighbour 2001-06; 2008-10 **Goals:** 151 Paul Thorman 2001-04 **Points:** 387 Paul Thorman 2001-04
	Appearances: 211 Robin Peers 2002-11

KEIGHLEY COUGARS

DATE	FIXTURE	RESULT	SCORERS	LGE	ATT
6/2/11	Rochdale (h) (NRC)	W24-6	t:Hutchinson,Duffy(2),Cartledge,Rawlins g:Lawton(2)	3rd(P1)	627
13/2/11	Dewsbury (a) (NRC)	L14-0		5th(P1)	758
19/2/11	Toulouse (h) (NRC)	L22-36	t:Sagar,Cartledge,Wray,Demetriou g:Belcher(3)	8th(P1)	513
27/2/11	York (a) (NRC)	L28-22	t:Benjafield,Rawlins,Drake,Belcher g:Lawton(3)	8th(P1)	748
5/3/11	Toulouse (h) (CCR3)	W16-10	t:Burton,Lawton,Baines g:Lawton(2)	N/A	479
13/3/11	London Skolars (h)	W66-6	t:Law,Helliwell,Cartledge(2),Lawton(3),Duffy,Baines,Sagar,Wray,Haythornthwaite g:Lawton(9)	1st	640
20/3/11	Gateshead (a)	W10-44	t:Pursglove(2),Jones,Hutchinson,Belcher,Baines,Cartledge,Feather g:Belcher(6)	1st	327
27/3/11	Whitehaven (a)	L24-10	t:Belcher,Duffy g:Lawton	3rd	754
3/4/11	Oldham (h)	W40-14	t:Helliwell(2),Haythornthwaite,Jones,Feather,Lawton,Pursglove g:Lawton(6)	2nd	995
17/4/11	Rochdale (a)	W32-40	t:Hutchinson,Haythornthwaite(3),Demetriou,Shickell,Pursglove g:Lawton(6)	2nd	515
25/4/11	Workington (h)	W38-18	t:Moss(2),Feather,Lawton(2),Shickell g:Lawton(7)	2nd	892
1/5/11	South Wales (h)	W46-26	t:Jones,Hutchinson,Demetriou(2),Duffy,Sagar,Feather,Smith g:Lawton(7)	2nd	558
8/5/11	Warrington (a) (CCR4)	L80-0		N/A	6,583
15/5/11	Doncaster (a)	W20-24	t:Sagar,Smith,Hutchinson,Demetriou g:Baines(4)	2nd	549
29/5/11	Whitehaven (h)	L14-18	t:Benjafield,Lawton,Shickell g:Lawton	2nd	754
5/6/11	Rochdale (h)	L30-31	t:Helliwell,Haythornthwaite,Cartledge,Hutchinson,Jones g:Lawton(5)	2nd	690
12/6/11	London Skolars (a)	L18-16	t:Demetriou,Wray,Benjafield g:Lawton(2)	3rd	327
26/6/11	South Wales (a) ●	L32-24	t:Elliott,Hutchinson,Sagar,Demetriou,Benjafield g:Lawton(2)	3rd	505
3/7/11	Gateshead (h)	W92-6	t:Baines(2),Moss,Shickell,Feather,Nicholson(3),Sagar,Smith(2),Coleman, Demetriou,Law,Normington,Elliott(2) g:Baines(9),Coleman(3)	2nd	899
10/7/11	Swinton (h)	W35-30	t:Sagar,Smith,Benjafield,Coleman,Shickell,Normington g:Baines(4),Coleman fg:Coleman	2nd	1,099
24/7/11	Oldham (a)	L36-14	t:Cartledge,Wray,Hutchinson g:Baines	3rd	637
31/7/11	Doncaster (h)	W34-6	t:Sagar(2),Cartledge,Feather,Duffy,Halley,Normington g:Baines(3)	2nd	937
4/8/11	Swinton (a)	W18-20	t:Feather,Moss(2),Pursglove g:Baines(2)	2nd	1,346
14/8/11	Workington (a)	L35-18	t:Shickell,Cartledge,Demetriou g:Moss,Baines(2)	2nd	544
26/8/11	London Skolars (a)	W12-30	t:Demetriou,Benjafield,Rawlins,Duffy,Normington(2) g:Lawton(3)	2nd	1,083
4/9/11	Whitehaven (h)	W28-20	t:Cartledge,Baines g:Baines(8)	2nd	964
18/9/11	Workington (h) (QSF)	L10-19	t:Moss(2) g:Moss	N/A	1,072
25/9/11	Rochdale (h) (FE)	W38-23	t:Sagar(2),Lawton,Duffy,Haythornthwaite(2),Normington g:Lawton(5)	N/A	982
2/10/11	Workington (GF) ●●	W32-12	t:Lawton,Feather,Rawlins,Pursglove,Normington(2) g:Lawton(4)	N/A	N/A

● Played at Virginia Park, Caerphilly
●● Played at Halliwell Jones Stadium, Warrington

		APP		TRIES		GOALS		FG		PTS	
	D.O.B.	ALL	Ch1	ALL	Ch1	ALL	Ch1	ALL	Ch1	ALL	Ch1
Chris Baines	25/9/84	13(10)	11(7)	6	5	33	33	0	0	90	86
Rick Barr	17/9/90	(10)	(6)	0	0	0	0	0	0	0	0
Dan Belcher	30/12/88	4	2	3	2	9	6	0	0	30	20
Ryan Benjafield	3/8/82	9(12)	8(10)	6	5	0	0	0	0	24	20
Tom Burton	5/11/87	3	0	1	0	0	0	0	0	4	0
Will Cartledge	11/9/79	23(2)	18(2)	11	9	0	0	0	0	44	36
Jy-Mel Coleman	13/10/88	6(1)	6(1)	2	2	4	4	1	1	17	17
Jason Demetriou	13/1/76	26	21	10	9	0	0	0	0	40	36
Paul Drake	18/8/82	5	2	1	0	0	0	0	0	4	0
Gavin Duffy	9/4/87	23	20	8	6	0	0	0	0	32	24
George Elliott	21/9/91	3	3	3	3	0	0	0	0	12	12
James Feather	15/4/84	28(1)	22(1)	8	8	0	0	0	0	32	32
Dave Halley	12/10/86	8	8	1	1	0	0	0	0	4	4
James Haythornthwaite	19/10/90	15	12	8	8	0	0	0	0	32	32
Luke Helliwell	1/3/88	13	10	4	4	0	0	0	0	16	16
James Hutchinson	27/11/85	19	13	8	7	0	0	0	0	32	28
Richard Jones	7/7/89	10(10)	8(10)	4	4	0	0	0	0	16	16
Scott Law	19/2/85	17(8)	14(6)	2	2	0	0	0	0	8	8
Danny Lawton	10/3/90	20	15	10	9	65	58	0	0	170	152
Richard Lopag	13/9/89	1	0	0	0	0	0	0	0	0	0
Craig Moss	4/8/84	14	10	7	7	2	2	0	0	32	32
Greg Nicholson	24/9/85	6(5)	6(2)	3	3	0	0	0	0	12	12
Jake Normington	11/10/91	12	12	8	8	0	0	0	0	32	32
Oliver Pursglove	18/1/86	25	20	6	6	0	0	0	0	24	24
Brendan Rawlins	28/1/86	3(25)	2(17)	4	2	0	0	0	0	16	8
Ben Sagar	19/12/89	26	22	11	10	0	0	0	0	44	40
Jamie Shepherd	14/8/90	4(5)	2(4)	0	0	0	0	0	0	0	0
Andy Shickell	9/5/81	25(2)	20(2)	6	6	0	0	0	0	24	24
Ryan Smith	25/10/88	15(6)	11(6)	5	5	0	0	0	0	20	20
Jamaine Wray	15/3/84	1(24)	1(18)	4	3	0	0	0	0	16	12

Jason Demetriou

LEAGUE RECORD
P20-W13-D0-L7-BP4
(2nd, Championship 1/
Grand Final Winners)
F663, A412, Diff+251
43 points.

CHALLENGE CUP
Round Four

NORTHERN RAIL CUP
8th, Pool 1

ATTENDANCES
Best - v Swinton (Ch1 - 1,099)
Worst - v Toulouse (CC - 479)
Total (excluding Challenge Cup) - 11,622
Average (excluding
Challenge Cup) - 830
(Down by 215 on 2010, Ch)

CLUB RECORDS
MATCH RECORDS
Highest score: 104-4 v Highfield, 23/4/95 **Highest score against:** 2-92 v Leigh, 30/4/86 **Record attendance:** 14,500 v Halifax, 3/3/51
Tries: 6 Jason Critchley v Widnes, 18/8/96
Goals: 15 John Wasyliw v Nottingham City, 1/11/92; Martyn Wood v Lancashire Lynx, 1/5/2000 **Points:** 36 John Wasyliw v Nottingham City, 1/11/92
SEASON RECORDS **Tries:** 45 Nick Pinkney 1994-95 **Goals:** 187 John Wasyliw 1992-93 **Points:** 490 John Wasyliw 1992-93
CAREER RECORDS **Tries:** 155 Sam Stacey 1904-1920 **Goals:** 967 Brian Jefferson 1965-77 **Points:** 2,116 Brian Jefferson 1965-77
Appearances: 372 Hartley Tempest 1902-1915; David McGoun 1925-38

LONDON SKOLARS

DATE	FIXTURE	RESULT	SCORERS	LGE	ATT
6/2/11	Widnes (h) (NRC)	L18-62	t:M Thomas,May,Thorman,Adebisi g:Prescott	9th(P1)	643
13/2/11	Doncaster (a) (NRC)	L32-4	t:Arnot	10th(P1)	420
20/2/11	York (h) (NRC)	D16-16	t:Adebisi(2),May g:Thorman(2)	9th(P1)	264
26/2/11	Toulouse (a) (NRC)	L34-22	t:Adebisi(2),M Thomas,Arnot g:Thorman(3)	9th(P1)	800
5/3/11	Egremont (h) (CCR3)	W60-24	t:T Williams,Honor(2),Bloom(2),Jy-Mel Coleman,Cook,Adebisi,McMeeken, Iwenofu,Ball g:Thorman(4),Prescott(4)	N/A	342
13/3/11	Keighley (a)	L66-6	t:Jy-Mel Coleman g:Thorman	9th	640
20/3/11	Doncaster (h)	L22-42	t:May,Hart,Honor,Aggrey g:Thorman(3)	8th	326
27/3/11	Rochdale (a)	L40-20	t:Arnot,Gee,Adebisi,Thorman g:Thorman(2)	9th	434
3/4/11	Whitehaven (h)	L16-48	t:Jy-Mel Coleman,Adebisi,Aggrey g:Thorman(2)	9th	542
9/4/11	Swinton (a)	L38-30	t:Arnot,Bryan,Adebisi(2),Latus g:Thorman(5)	9th	395
17/4/11	Oldham (a)	L52-26	t:Arnot,Adebisi,Clement-Pascall(2),Skee g:Latus(3)	9th	566
22/4/11	South Wales (a)	L20-18	t:McMeeken,Aggrey,Clement-Pascall g:Latus(3)	9th	280
25/4/11	Gateshead (h)	D32-32	t:Aggrey,Purslow,Latus,Arnot,Thorman,Honor g:Latus(4)	9th	263
8/5/11	Widnes (h) (CCR4)	L18-62	t:Obuchowski,Anthony,Arnot g:Skee(3)	N/A	415
15/5/11	Workington (h)	L12-33	t:Anthony,Adebisi g:Skee(2)	9th	397
29/5/11	Rochdale (h)	W44-22	t:Adebisi,Bryan(2),Aggrey,Skee(2),Honor g:Skee(8)	9th	290
5/6/11	Whitehaven (a)	L14-12	t:Aggrey,Anthony g:Jy-Mel Coleman,Skee	9th	716
12/6/11	Keighley (h)	W18-16	t:Obuchowski,Bolger,Adebisi g:Skee(3)	9th	327
26/6/11	Doncaster (a)	L40-22	t:Anthony,Aggrey,D Williams,Bolger g:Skee(3)	9th	456
2/7/11	South Wales (h)	W27-26	t:Obuchowski(2),Colleran,Adebisi(2) g:Skee(3) fg:Skee	9th	437
9/7/11	Oldham (h) ●	W36-34	t:Skee,Adebisi,Anthony,Gee,Obuchowski,Honor g:Skee(6)	9th	1,105
24/7/11	Workington (a)	L41-14	t:Aggrey,Skee,Anthony g:Skee	9th	454
30/7/11	Swinton (a)	L14-42	t:Bryan,Jermaine Coleman,Aggrey g:Skee	9th	429
6/8/11	South Wales (a)	L26-16	t:Murtza,Junor,Gee g:Skee(2)	9th	232
14/8/11	Gateshead (a)	W16-36	t:Junor,M Thomas,Small,Anthony(2),Skee,Colleran g:Skee(4)	9th	292
26/8/11	Keighley (h)	L12-30	t:Paxton,Aggrey g:Skee(2)	9th	1,083

● Played at Twickenham Stoop

		APP		TRIES		GOALS		FG		PTS	
	D.O.B.	ALL	Ch1	ALL	Ch1	ALL	Ch1	ALL	Ch1	ALL	Ch1
Ade Adebisi	7/1/86	21(1)	16	17	11	0	0	0	0	68	44
Austen Aggrey	12/5/79	17(6)	15(4)	9	9	0	0	0	0	36	36
Guy Aldam	3/9/89	(2)	(1)	0	0	0	0	0	0	0	0
James Anthony	18/2/86	17	12	8	7	0	0	0	0	32	28
Dave Arnot	27/6/88	19	13	7	4	0	0	0	0	28	16
Stephen Ball	15/3/89	9(4)	6(2)	1	0	0	0	0	0	4	0
Oliver Bloom	16/4/86	5(3)	3(3)	2	0	0	0	0	0	8	0
Ben Bolger	13/9/89	6	4	2	2	0	0	0	0	8	8
Jamie Boston	5/1/88	2	1	0	0	0	0	0	0	0	0
Michael Brown	9/9/86	4	4	0	0	0	0	0	0	0	0
Lamont Bryan	12/4/88	8	8	4	4	0	0	0	0	16	16
Danny Burke	26/7/86	1(7)	(7)	0	0	0	0	0	0	0	0
Cariern Clement-Pascall	28/9/90	3(9)	3(9)	3	3	0	0	0	0	12	12
Jermaine Coleman	17/6/82	3(3)	3(3)	1	1	0	0	0	0	4	4
Jy-Mel Coleman	13/10/88	12(2)	11	3	2	1	1	0	0	14	10
Will Colleran	24/5/91	7(1)	7(1)	2	2	0	0	0	0	8	8
Jason Cook	10/6/89	6	5	1	0	0	0	0	0	4	0
Sam Gee	28/2/87	4(15)	4(13)	3	3	0	0	0	0	12	12
Jason Hart	19/10/86	9(2)	6(2)	1	1	0	0	0	0	4	4
Gareth Honor	1/10/81	24	18	6	4	0	0	0	0	24	16
Olu Iwenofu	28/9/81	4	3	1	0	0	0	0	0	4	0
Smokie Junor	15/4/90	9	5	2	2	0	0	0	0	8	8
Mourad Kriouache	10/5/91	7	7	1	1	0	0	0	0	4	4
Jack Latus	14/9/88	5	5	2	2	10	10	0	0	28	28
Luke May	23/8/89	8	4	3	1	0	0	0	0	12	4
Joe Mbu	6/11/83	1(1)	1(1)	0	0	0	0	0	0	0	0
Dave McMeeken	25/9/86	1(6)	1(2)	2	1	0	0	0	0	8	4
Chris McNamara	13/7/88	1	1	0	0	0	0	0	0	0	0
Saqib Murtza	18/11/85	8(8)	5(6)	1	1	0	0	0	0	4	4
Jaroslaw Obuchowski	20/9/90	13	12	5	4	0	0	0	0	20	16
John Paxton	20/4/85	6(1)	5(1)	1	1	0	0	0	0	4	4
Liam Prescott	31/8/88	(6)	(3)	0	0	5	0	0	0	10	0
Oliver Purslow	17/9/87	23(1)	20	1	1	0	0	0	0	4	4
Dave Samson	1/6/91	1(1)	0	0	0	0	0	0	0	0	0
James Simon	20/1/87	3(6)	2(5)	0	0	0	0	0	0	0	0
Dylan Skee	13/1/86	26	20	6	6	39	36	1	1	103	97
Aaron Small	28/10/91	14	13	1	1	0	0	0	0	4	4
Michael Sykes	10/12/86	1(7)	1(6)	0	0	0	0	0	0	0	0
Matt Thomas	8/1/80	5(1)	1(1)	3	1	0	0	0	0	12	4
Rob Thomas	9/10/90	1(1)	1(1)	0	0	0	0	0	0	0	0
Neil Thorman	4/6/84	12	7	3	2	22	13	0	0	56	34
Dave Williams	29/1/87	5(3)	5(2)	1	1	0	0	0	0	4	4
Tony Williams	4/5/84	7(7)	2(7)	1	0	0	0	0	0	4	0

Ade Adebisi

LEAGUE RECORD
P20-W5-D1-L14-BP4
(9th, Championship 1)
F433, A678, Diff-245
21 points.

CHALLENGE CUP
Round Four

NORTHERN RAIL CUP
9th, Pool 1

ATTENDANCES
Best - v Oldham (Ch1 - 1,105)
Worst - v Gateshead (Ch1 - 263)
Total (excluding Challenge Cup) - 6,106
Average (excluding
Challenge Cup) - 509
(Up by 8 on 2010)

CLUB RECORDS **Highest score:** 70-28 v St Albans, 19/3/2006 **Highest score against:** 4-98 v Sheffield, 3/8/2003 **Record attendance:** 1,427 v Keighley, 29/8/2008
MATCH RECORDS **Tries:** 5 Mark Cantoni v Gateshead, 27/6/2004 **Goals:** 10 Jake Johnstone v Gateshead, 24/8/2003 **Points:** 24 Dylan Skee v Rochdale, 29/5/2011
SEASON RECORDS **Tries:** 20 Mark Cantoni 2004 **Goals:** 79 Paul Thorman 2008 **Points:** 170 Paul Thorman 2008
CAREER RECORDS **Tries:** 56 Austen Aggrey 2004-11 **Goals:** 223 (inc 2 fg) Paul Thorman 2007-10 **Points:** 488 Paul Thorman 2007-10 **Appearances:** 198 Gareth Honor 2003-11

OLDHAM

DATE	FIXTURE	RESULT	SCORERS	LGE	ATT
6/2/11	Hunslet (h) (NRC)	W28-22	t:Bradbury(2),Clough,Diveney,Gillam g:Diveney(4)	4th(P2)	685
13/2/11	Halifax (a) (NRC)	L50-10	t:Onyango(2) g:Diveney	7th(P2)	2,027
20/2/11	Swinton (a) (NRC)	L29-20	t:Brocklehurst(2),Gillam(2) g:Diveney(2)	8th(P2)	774
27/2/11	Whitehaven (h) (NRC)	L4-14	t:Brocklehurst	9th(P2)	544
6/3/11	Hunslet Warriors (h) (CCR3)	W28-16	t:Clarke,Fogarty,Brocklehurst,N Roden,Wood g:Diveney(4)	N/A	538
13/3/11	Gateshead (h)	W66-12	t:Brocklehurst(4),Isherwood(3),Bentley(2),Fogarty,Bradbury g:Diveney(9)	2nd	562
20/3/11	Workington (a)	L31-12	t:Wood,Clough g:Diveney(2)	5th	473
27/3/11	Swinton (h)	L24-68	t:Wood,Diveney,Boults(2) g:Diveney(4)	7th	744
3/4/11	Keighley (a)	L40-14	t:Heaton,Robinson,Onyango g:Diveney	8th	995
17/4/11	London Skolars (h)	W52-26	t:Diveney(2),Robinson(2),Boults,Noone,Onyango(2),N Roden,Brocklehurst g:Diveney(6)	7th	566
22/4/11	Rochdale (h)	W38-6	t:M Roden,Clough,Clarke,Fogarty,Forber,Isherwood,Onyango g:Forber(5)	6th	876
25/4/11	Whitehaven (a)	L40-24	t:Ellison(2),N Roden,Onyango g:Forber(4)	7th	946
1/5/11	Doncaster (h)	W46-24	t:Wood(2),Clough,Noone,Forber,Brocklehurst,Heaton,Boults g:Forber(7)	6th	672
7/5/11	Hull FC (a) (CCR4)	L82-0		N/A	6,235
15/5/11	South Wales (a) ●	L40-20	t:Clough,Fogerty,Robinson,Heaton g:Forber(2)	6th	420
27/5/11	Swinton (a)	L18-16	t:Noone,Stenchion,Clarke g:Noone(2)	7th	674
5/6/11	Doncaster (a)	L30-0		7th	617
12/6/11	South Wales (h)	W35-18	t:Dallimore(2),Heaton(2),Wood,St Hilaire g:Forber(5) fg:Dallimore	7th	514
26/6/11	Gateshead (a)	W16-52	t:Fogarty(2),Isherwood,Sutton,Clough(2),Brocklehurst(2),Forber(2) g:Forber(6)	7th	436
3/7/11	Whitehaven (h)	W40-20	t:Brocklehurst,Robinson,Heaton(2),Fogarty,Clough,Stenchion g:Forber(6)	7th	537
9/7/11	London Skolars (a) ●●	L36-34	t:Sutton(2),Bentley,Gillam,Brocklehurst,Forber g:Forber(5)	7th	1,105
24/7/11	Keighley (h)	W36-14	t:N Roden,McCully,Heaton(2),Noone,Brocklehurst g:Forber(6)	7th	637
31/7/11	Workington (h)	L22-24	t:McCully,Casey,Robinson,Isherwood g:Forber(3)	7th	684
14/8/11	Rochdale (a)	W16-38	t:Heaton(2),N Roden,Whitmore,Casey,Robinson,St Hilaire g:Forber(5)	7th	928
21/8/11	South Wales (h)	W48-34	t:Noone,Heaton(2),Bravo(3),N Roden,Whitmore g:Forber(8)	7th	501
4/9/11	Workington (a)	W20-24	t:Brocklehurst,Fogarty,N Roden,Dallimore,Casey g:Dallimore(2)	7th	716
11/9/11	Rochdale (a) (EPO)	L39-18	t:Robinson,N Roden,Brocklehurst,McCully g:Forber	N/A	1,053

● Played at Virginia Park, Caerphilly
●● Played at Twickenham Stoop

APP   TRIES   GOALS   FG   PTS

	D.O.B.	ALL	Ch1	ALL	Ch1	ALL	Ch1	ALL	Ch1	ALL	Ch1
Matt Ashe	4/9/85	1	0	0	0	0	0	0	0	0	0
Valu Bentley	9/10/82	9(16)	7(13)	3	3	0	0	0	0	12	12
Jason Boults	7/9/83	23(2)	20	4	4	0	0	0	0	16	16
Jack Bradbury	4/11/90	9	5	3	1	0	0	0	0	12	4
Danny Bravo	25/10/90	9	9	3	3	0	0	0	0	12	12
Mark Brocklehurst	27/9/86	23	20	17	13	0	0	0	0	68	52
Callum Casey	6/6/90	1(8)	1(8)	3	3	0	0	0	0	12	12
Chris Clarke	29/3/89	14(1)	9	3	2	0	0	0	0	12	8
John Clough	13/9/84	11(14)	8(11)	8	7	0	0	0	0	32	28
Jamie Dallimore	20/8/88	3	2	3	3	2	2	1	1	17	17
Mick Diveney	12/3/87	10	5	4	3	33	22	0	0	82	56
Dave Ellison	2/4/82	9(8)	6(7)	2	2	0	0	0	0	8	8
Matthew Fogarty	16/3/92	11(1)	9(1)	8	7	0	0	0	0	32	28
Mick Fogerty	19/2/81	1	1	1	1	0	0	0	0	4	4
Carl Forber	17/3/85	14	14	5	5	63	63	0	0	146	146
Liam Gilchrist	28/3/89	5(6)	3(6)	0	0	0	0	0	0	0	0
John Gillam	15/10/84	9	4	4	1	0	0	0	0	16	4
Ben Heaton	12/3/90	19	15	13	13	0	0	0	0	52	52
Andrew Isherwood	23/11/79	14(3)	11(2)	6	6	0	0	0	0	24	24
Scott Mansfield	16/12/90	(1)	0	0	0	0	0	0	0	0	0
Mark McCully	24/10/79	9	9	3	3	0	0	0	0	12	12
Steven Nield	20/11/90	1	0	0	0	0	0	0	0	0	0
Paul Noone	22/4/81	27	21	5	5	2	2	0	0	24	24
Lucas Onyango	12/4/81	10	6	7	5	0	0	0	0	28	20
Shaun Robinson	13/7/89	19	18	8	8	0	0	0	0	32	32
Martin Roden	26/12/79	22(1)	19	1	1	0	0	0	0	4	4
Neil Roden	9/4/80	23	18	8	7	0	0	0	0	32	28
Marcus St Hilaire	26/1/77	13	10	2	2	0	0	0	0	8	8
Luke Stenchion	15/2/86	8(8)	8(7)	2	2	0	0	0	0	8	8
Luke Sutton	25/2/86	4(16)	(14)	3	3	0	0	0	0	12	12
Michael Ward	10/2/91	(6)	(5)	0	0	0	0	0	0	0	0
Danny Whitmore	22/12/88	4(11)	4(9)	2	2	0	0	0	0	8	8
Alistair Williams	17/9/87	1	1	0	0	0	0	0	0	0	0
Ben Wood	6/10/89	15(1)	10	6	5	0	0	0	0	24	20
Tom Wood-Hulme	27/6/90	(5)	(1)	0	0	0	0	0	0	0	0

Ben Heaton

LEAGUE RECORD
P20-W11-D0-L9-BP3
(7th, Championship 1/
Elimination Play-Off)
F641, A533, Diff+108
36 points.

CHALLENGE CUP
Round Four

NORTHERN RAIL CUP
9th, Pool 2

ATTENDANCES
Best - v Rochdale (Ch1 - 876)
Worst - v South Wales (Ch1 - 501)
Total (excluding Challenge Cup) - 7,522
Average (excluding
Challenge Cup) - 627
(Down by 181 on 2010)

CLUB RECORDS
MATCH RECORDS
Highest score: 80-6 v Blackwood, 7/3/2010 Highest score against: 0-84 v Widnes, 25/7/99 Record attendance: 28,000 v Huddersfield, 24/2/12
Tries: 7 James Miller v Barry, 31/10/1908
Goals: 14 Bernard Ganley v Liverpool City, 4/4/59 Points: 34 Andy Ballard v London Skolars, 2/5/2009; Chris Baines v Hunslet, 20/9/2009

SEASON RECORDS
CAREER RECORDS
Tries: 49 Reg Farrar 1921-22 Goals: 200 Bernard Ganley 1957-58 Points: 412 Bernard Ganley 1957-58
Tries: 174 Alan Davies 1950-61 Goals: 1,358 Bernard Ganley 1951-61 Points: 2,761 Bernard Ganley 1951-61 Appearances: 627 Joe Ferguson 1899-1923

ROCHDALE HORNETS

DATE	FIXTURE	RESULT	SCORERS	LGE	ATT
6/2/11	Keighley (a) (NRC)	L24-6	t:English g:Crook	8th(P1)	627
13/2/11	Barrow (h) (NRC)	L18-30	t:Bloomfield,Crook,Roper g:Crook(2),McGovern	9th(P1)	600
20/2/11	Widnes (a) (NRC)	L50-10	t:Ashall,Johnson g:Crook	10th(P1)	3,155
27/2/11	Doncaster (h) (NRC)	L36-40	t:McGovern(2),Crook,Johnson(2),Hobson,Hough g:Crook(4)	10th(P1)	442
6/3/11	Workington (h) (CCR3)	W22-20	t:Ashall,McDermott,Roper,McGovern g:Crook,McGovern(2)	N/A	358
13/3/11	Whitehaven (a)	L30-22	t:Saywell(3),Ashall g:Crook(3)	5th	704
20/3/11	Swinton (h)	L26-46	t:Bloomfield(2),Yates,Samuel,Saywell g:Crook(3)	6th	743
27/3/11	London Skolars (h)	W40-20	t:Ashall,Cookson,Bloomfield,Saywell(2),Crook,Ekis g:McGovern,Crook(5)	6th	434
3/4/11	Doncaster (a)	W8-24	t:Saywell(2),McHugh,Ekis g:McGovern(3) fg:McGovern(2)	5th	589
10/4/11	Whitehaven (h)	W49-18	t:Saywell(2),Mervill(2),McHugh(2),Ekis,English g:Crook(5),McGovern(3) fg:McGovern	2nd	457
17/4/11	Keighley (h)	L32-40	t:Bloomfield(2),Keavney,Newton,Crook(2) g:Crook(3),McGovern	4th	515
22/4/11	Oldham (a)	L38-6	t:English g:Crook	4th	876
25/4/11	South Wales (h)	W40-18	t:Cookson,Crook,Ashall,Newton,Bloomfield,Donoghue,McDermott g:Crook(6)	3rd	402
1/5/11	Workington (a)	W34-38	t:Crook,Yates,McDermott,Cookson,English g:Crook(9)	3rd	443
8/5/11	Castleford (h) (CCR4)	L10-72	t:Yates,Saywell g:Crook	N/A	1,675
15/5/11	Gateshead (h)	W68-0	t:Roper,Gorton(3),Bloomfield,Crook,Hough,Johnson,Ashall,Hobson,Saywell, McGovern g:Crook(10)	3rd	504
29/5/11	London Skolars (a)	L44-22	t:Saywell,Mervill,Ashall,Yates g:Crook(3)	3rd	290
5/6/11	Keighley (a)	W30-31	t:Roper,Johnson,Ashall,Hough,Yates g:Crook(5) fg:Crook	3rd	690
24/6/11	Swinton (a)	L22-20	t:Ashall,Saywell(2),McGovern g:Crook(2)	5th	586
3/7/11	Doncaster (h)	L16-26	t:Cookson,Bloomfield,Ashall g:Crook(2)	6th	423
10/7/11	Workington (h)	W45-20	t:Johnson,Cookson,McGovern,Bloomfield,McDermott,Ashall,Reid g:Crook(8) fg:Crook	6th	1,021
31/7/11	South Wales (a)	W6-13	t:McDermott,English g:McGovern(2) fg:Crook	6th	252
7/8/11	Gateshead (a)	W14-48	t:Bloomfield(3),Gorton(2),Ekis,Ashall,Samuel,McGovern g:Crook(6)	4th	242
14/8/11	Oldham (h)	L16-38	t:Bloomfield,Newton,Hobson g:Crook(2)	5th	928
21/8/11	Gateshead (h)	W62-18	t:Ashall(2),Crook,Bloomfield(2),Gorton,McDermott,Saywell,Pyke,English(2) g:Crook(8),Hough	4th	401
2/9/11	Swinton (a)	W28-34	t:Crook,Pyke,McDermott(2),Cookson,Donoghue g:Crook(5)	4th	1,063
11/9/11	Oldham (h) (EPO)	W39-18	t:Crook(2),Mervill,Gorton,Saywell,Bloomfield g:Crook(6) fg:Ashall,Crook,Roper	N/A	1,053
18/9/11	Doncaster (h) (ESF)	W26-18	t:Bloomfield(3),Saywell,Hough g:Crook(3)	N/A	552
25/9/11	Keighley (a) (FE)	L38-23	t:Saywell,English,McDermott g:Crook(5) fg:Crook	N/A	982

		APP		TRIES		GOALS		FG		PTS	
	D.O.B.	ALL	Ch1	ALL	Ch1	ALL	Ch1	ALL	Ch1	ALL	Ch1
Craig Ashall	26/9/85	28	22	14	12	0	0	1	1	57	49
Mark Biggins	19/3/83	(1)	(1)	0	0	0	0	0	0	0	0
Dale Bloomfield	24/10/87	28	23	20	19	0	0	0	0	80	76
Adam Bowman	12/11/87	13(6)	12(5)	0	0	0	0	0	0	0	0
Chris Clough	20/1/87	3(5)	1(4)	0	0	0	0	0	0	0	0
John Cookson	12/12/84	27	22	6	6	0	0	0	0	24	24
Paul Crook	28/8/86	29	23	12	10	110	100	5	5	273	245
Dayne Donoghue	22/9/88	23(1)	18(1)	2	2	0	0	0	0	8	8
Danny Ekis	17/1/82	1(18)	1(17)	4	4	0	0	0	0	16	16
Wayne English	8/3/80	21(3)	17(2)	8	7	0	0	0	0	32	28
Dean Gorton	16/1/84	21	16	7	7	0	0	0	0	28	28
Gareth Hayes	15/6/85	(3)	0	0	0	0	0	0	0	0	0
Mark Hobson	14/1/87	17(9)	15(6)	3	2	0	0	0	0	12	8
Chris Hough	30/8/81	7(6)	6(4)	4	3	1	1	0	0	18	14
Craig Johnson	17/4/87	15	11	6	3	0	0	0	0	24	12
Martin Keavney	5/12/87	1(4)	1(4)	1	1	0	0	0	0	4	4
Scott Mansfield	16/12/90	(2)	0	0	0	0	0	0	0	0	0
Steve McDermott	27/12/85	2(12)	2(9)	9	8	0	0	0	0	36	32
Liam McGovern	6/10/84	20(2)	15(2)	7	4	13	10	3	3	57	39
Wayne McHugh	1/2/80	4	4	3	3	0	0	0	0	12	12
Danny Meekin	16/3/89	(2)	0	0	0	0	0	0	0	0	0
Richard Mervill	24/6/81	9(6)	8(6)	4	4	0	0	0	0	16	16
Gary Middlehurst	24/10/83	6	6	0	0	0	0	0	0	0	0
Dave Newton	22/12/81	9(14)	7(12)	3	3	0	0	0	0	12	12
Jamie Peasnall	4/7/88	2(1)	(1)	0	0	0	0	0	0	0	0
Ryan Powell	3/2/88	(1)	0	0	0	0	0	0	0	0	0
Danny Pyke	1/10/86	6(2)	5(2)	2	2	0	0	0	0	8	8
Damien Reid	14/3/84	10	5	1	1	0	0	0	0	4	4
Steve Roper	10/11/86	23(3)	18(3)	4	2	0	0	1	1	17	9
Danny Samuel	8/8/85	9(7)	7(5)	2	2	0	0	0	0	8	8
Andy Saywell	1/1/79	20	18	19	18	0	0	0	0	76	72
Mike Stewart	3/1/91	(3)	(3)	0	0	0	0	0	0	0	0
Matthew Strong	17/2/87	12(2)	8(2)	0	0	0	0	0	0	0	0
Phil Wood	25/10/83	1(1)	1(1)	0	0	0	0	0	0	0	0
Scott Yates	8/9/88	10(2)	7(2)	5	4	0	0	0	0	20	16

Paul Crook

LEAGUE RECORD
P20-W12-D0-L8-BP4
(4th, Championship 1/
Final Eliminator)
F652, A498, Diff+154
40 points.

CHALLENGE CUP
Round Four

NORTHERN RAIL CUP
10th, Pool 1

ATTENDANCES
Best - v Castleford (CC - 1,675)
Worst - v Workington (CC - 358)
Total (excluding Challenge Cup) - 8,475
Average (excluding
Challenge Cup) - 605
(Up by 38 on 2010)

CLUB RECORDS **MATCH RECORDS**	**Highest score:** 120-4 v Illingworth, 13/3/2005 **Highest score against:** 0-106 v Castleford, 9/9/2007 **Record attendance:** 26,664 v Oldham, 25/3/22 **Tries:** 5 Jack Corsi v Barrow, 31/12/21; Jack Corsi v Broughton Moor, 25/2/22; Jack Williams v St Helens, 4/4/33; Norman Brelsford v Whitehaven, 3/9/73; Marlon Billy v York, 8/4/2001 **Goals:** 18 Lee Birdseye v Illingworth, 13/3/2005 **Points:** 44 Lee Birdseye v Illingworth, 13/3/2005
SEASON RECORDS	**Tries:** 31 Marlon Billy 2001 **Goals:** 150 Martin Strett 1994-95 **Points:** 350 Mick Nanyn 2003
CAREER RECORDS	**Tries:** 103 Jack Williams 1931-37 **Goals:** 741 Walter Gowers 1922-36 **Points:** 1,497 Walter Gowers 1922-36 **Appearances:** 456 Walter Gowers 1922-36

SOUTH WALES SCORPIONS

DATE	FIXTURE	RESULT	SCORERS	LGE	ATT
6/3/11	Dewsbury (h) (CCR3)	L6-62	t:Gay g:Reece	N/A	356
13/3/11	Doncaster (a)	L40-10	t:Parry,Lock g:Reece	7th	895
20/3/11	Whitehaven (h)	L18-22	t:Dallimore,Burke(2) g:Reece(3)	7th	271
27/3/11	Gateshead (h)	W60-20	t:Roets(2),Gay(2),Reece(2),Bromilow(2),Cunningham(2),Greville g:Reece(8)	5th	302
3/4/11	Workington (a)	L38-24	t:Gay(2),Greville,Bateman g:Reece(4)	6th	357
17/4/11	Swinton (h)	L22-74	t:Murphy,Parry,Bromilow,Reece g:Reece(3)	8th	370
22/4/11	London Skolars (h)	W20-18	t:Gay,Bateman,Grant(2) g:Murphy(2)	8th	280
25/4/11	Rochdale (a)	L40-18	t:Gay,Murphy,Bateman,Dallimore g:Murphy	8th	402
1/5/11	Keighley (a)	L46-26	t:James,Gay(2),Williams,Grant g:Reece(3)	8th	558
15/5/11	Oldham (h) ●	W40-20	t:Parry,Dallimore,Murphy,Bromilow,Cunningham,Gay,Wildbore g:Murphy(3),Bromilow(3)	8th	420
22/5/11	Gateshead (a)	W32-66	t:Grant(4),Cunningham(2),Bromilow,Reece,Roets,Parry,Wildbore,Burnell g:Reece(9)	6th	162
5/6/11	Workington (h) ●	L28-46	t:Roets,Parry(2),Reece,Grant g:Reece(4)	8th	403
12/6/11	Oldham (a)	L35-18	t:Parry,Dallimore,Murphy g:Reece(3)	8th	514
26/6/11	Keighley (h) ●	W32-24	t:Parry,Roets,Grant,Gay,Bromilow,Murphy g:Murphy,Wildbore,Reece(2)	8th	505
2/7/11	London Skolars (a)	L27-26	t:Gay(2),Parry,Grant,Cunningham g:Reece(3)	8th	437
10/7/11	Whitehaven (h)	L34-14	t:Gay,Cocka g:Reece(3)	8th	815
24/7/11	Doncaster (h)	L20-41	t:James(2),Parry(2) g:Reece(2)	8th	304
31/7/11	Rochdale (h)	L6-13	t:Lloyd g:Reece	8th	252
6/8/11	London Skolars (h)	W26-16	t:Gay(2),C Davies,Roets g:Reece(5)	8th	232
14/8/11	Swinton (a)	L40-28	t:James,Lloyd,Murphy,Bromilow,Roets g:Murphy(4)	8th	509
21/8/11	Oldham (a)	L48-34	t:Parry(2),James,Gay,Bromilow,Cunningham g:Murphy(5)	8th	501

● Played at Virginia Park, Caerphilly

	D.O.B.	APP		TRIES		GOALS		FG		PTS	
		ALL	Ch1	ALL	Ch1	ALL	Ch1	ALL	Ch1	ALL	Ch1
Ashley Bateman	11/2/90	19(1)	18(1)	3	3	0	0	0	0	12	12
Casey Bromilow	12/2/84	19	18	8	8	3	3	0	0	38	38
Joe Burke	18/5/90	16(1)	16(1)	2	2	0	0	0	0	8	8
Tom Burnell	7/3/81	1(10)	(10)	1	1	0	0	0	0	4	4
Phil Carleton	2/5/83	(3)	(3)	0	0	0	0	0	0	0	0
Dafydd Carter	12/2/92	(2)	(1)	0	0	0	0	0	0	0	0
Chris Clough	20/1/87	3(5)	3(5)	0	0	0	0	0	0	0	0
Semisi Cocka	14/3/79	(10)	(10)	1	1	0	0	0	0	4	4
Curtis Cunningham	16/12/86	16(1)	15(1)	7	7	0	0	0	0	28	28
Neil Dallimore	24/2/81	6(12)	5(12)	4	4	0	0	0	0	16	16
Chris Davies	24/12/91	(14)	(13)	1	1	0	0	0	0	4	4
Hywel Davies	19/12/81	7(7)	6(7)	0	0	0	0	0	0	0	0
Gil Dudson	16/6/90	2	2	0	0	0	0	0	0	0	0
Andrew Gay	5/10/89	21	20	17	16	0	0	0	0	68	64
Dalton Grant	21/4/90	12	12	10	10	0	0	0	0	40	40
Harri Greville	28/11/90	10(5)	9(5)	2	2	0	0	0	0	8	8
Bradley Hill	14/11/92	(2)	(2)	0	0	0	0	0	0	0	0
Aled James	17/2/82	9(1)	8(1)	5	5	0	0	0	0	20	20
Rhodri Lloyd	22/7/93	12	12	2	2	0	0	0	0	8	8
Robin Lock	23/6/89	2	1	1	1	0	0	0	0	4	4
Tylon Mafi	5/1/82	(1)	(1)	0	0	0	0	0	0	0	0
Lewis Mills	30/3/89	2(4)	2(4)	0	0	0	0	0	0	0	0
Jamie Murphy	29/12/89	15	15	6	6	16	16	0	0	56	56
Steve Parry	19/10/88	20(1)	20	13	13	0	0	0	0	52	52
Tom Philip	25/6/83	1	1	0	0	0	0	0	0	0	0
Barrie Phillips	27/5/86	(1)	(1)	0	0	0	0	0	0	0	0
Jack Pring	25/1/93	3	3	0	0	0	0	0	0	0	0
Paul Raftrey	26/1/78	15(1)	15(1)	0	0	0	0	0	0	0	0
Lewis Reece	17/6/91	15(1)	14(1)	5	5	55	54	0	0	130	128
Christiaan Roets	5/9/80	21	20	7	7	0	0	0	0	28	28
Loz Wildbore	23/9/84	14	13	2	2	1	1	0	0	10	10
Lee Williams	19/2/88	12	12	1	1	0	0	0	0	4	4

Andrew Gay

LEAGUE RECORD
P20-W6-D0-L14-BP4
(8th, Championship 1)
F536, A674, Diff-138
22 points.

CHALLENGE CUP
Round Three

NORTHERN RAIL CUP
Not entered

ATTENDANCES
Best - v Keighley (Ch1 - 505)
Worst - v London Skolars (Ch1 - 232)
Total (excluding Challenge Cup) - 3,339
Average (excluding Challenge Cup) - 334
(Down by 297 on 2010)

CLUB RECORDS	
	Highest score: 70-22 v London Skolars, 23/5/2010; 70-16 v Gateshead, 11/7/2010 **Highest score against:** 22-74 v Swinton, 17/4/2011
	Record attendance: 890 v Swinton, 13/6/2010
MATCH RECORDS	**Tries:** 4 Dalton Grant v Gateshead, 22/5/2011 **Goals:** 11 Lewis Reece v Gateshead, 11/7/2010 **Points:** 30 Lewis Reece v Gateshead, 11/7/2010
SEASON RECORDS	**Tries:** 19 Steve Parry 2010 **Goals:** 55 Lewis Reece 2011 **Points:** 130 Lewis Reece 2011
CAREER RECORDS	**Tries:** 32 Steve Parry 2010-11 **Goals:** 66 Lewis Reece 2010-11 **Points:** 160 Lewis Reece 2010-11 **Appearances:** 42 Andrew Gay 2010-11

SWINTON LIONS

DATE	FIXTURE	RESULT	SCORERS	LGE	ATT
4/2/11	Halifax (h) (NRC)	L22-28	t:Foxen,Smith,D Thompson,Holland g:Dodd(3)	6th(P2)	916
13/2/11	Leigh (a) (NRC)	L42-22	t:Mort(2),Rigby,R Hawkyard,Cunniffe g:Mort	9th(P2)	1,623
20/2/11	Oldham (h) (NRC)	W29-20	t:Foxen,Ainscough,R Hawkyard,Dodd(2),D Hawkyard g:Dodd(2) fg:Dodd	7th(P2)	774
27/2/11	Gateshead (a) (NRC)	W4-76	t:D Hawkyard(2),D Thompson(3),Gallagher,Hamilton,Rigby,Ainscough,Wingfield(2),Ashall,Stewart,Smith,Foxen g:Dodd(8)	4th(P2)	285
5/3/11	East Hull (h) (CCR3)	W44-4	t:D Thompson(2),Ainscough,Gallagher,Fitzpatrick(2),Mort,Ashall g:Mort(6)	N/A	305
13/3/11	Workington (h)	W22-10	t:Ainscough,Gallagher,Dodd,Wingfield g:Mort(3)	4th	651
20/3/11	Rochdale (a)	W26-46	t:D Thompson(2),Wilson,Ainscough,Mort,Dodd(2),Cunniffe g:Mort(7)	3rd	743
27/3/11	Oldham (a)	W24-68	t:Gallagher,Wilson,Dodd(2),Ashall(2),Mort(2),Wingfield,Flooks,Ainscough,Cunniffe g:Mort(10)	1st	744
3/4/11	Gateshead (h)	W48-24	t:Cunniffe(2),Mort,Dodd,Foxen(3),Ainscough,Smith g:Mort(6)	1st	493
9/4/11	London Skolars (h)	W38-30	t:Dodd(2),Mort,Foxen,D Hawkyard,Ashall,Cunniffe g:Mort(5)	1st	395
17/4/11	South Wales (a)	W22-74	t:Flooks(2),Foxen,Dodd(3),Ashall,Ainscough(2),D Hawkyard,Watson,Mort(2) g:Mort(11)	1st	370
25/4/11	Doncaster (a)	W32-36	t:Mort,Ainscough,Cunniffe,Watson,Foxen,D Hawkyard g:Mort(6)	1st	649
8/5/11	Dewsbury (a) (CCR4)	W38-44	t:Mort,Flooks,Dodd,Gallagher,Joseph(2),Wingfield g:Mort(8)	N/A	692
15/5/11	Whitehaven (a)	D22-22	t:Foxen,Ainscough,Mort(2) g:Mort(3)	1st	917
20/5/11	Warrington (a) (CCR5)	L112-0		N/A	4,440
27/5/11	Oldham (h)	W18-16	t:Foxen,Ainscough,Joseph g:Mort(3)	1st	674
5/6/11	Gateshead (a)	W16-62	t:Mort(2),Flooks(3),D Hawkyard,W Thompson,Wilson,Dodd,Hurst,Ashall g:Mort(9)	1st	252
24/6/11	Rochdale (h)	W22-20	t:Dodd,Cunniffe,Foxen,Joseph g:Mort(3)	1st	586
3/7/11	Workington (a)	L36-16	t:Foxen,Morrison,Cunniffe g:Mort(2)	1st	512
10/7/11	Keighley (a)	L35-30	t:Flooks,Joseph,Cunniffe,Mort(3) g:Mort(3)	1st	1,099
15/7/11	Doncaster (h)	W30-28	t:Gorski,Ainscough,Mort(2),R Hawkyard g:Mort(5)	1st	425
24/7/11	Whitehaven (h)	W44-0	t:Mort(3),Wilson(2),Foxen,Ainscough,Joseph g:Mort(6)	1st	679
30/7/11	London Skolars (a)	W14-42	t:Wingfield,Ainscough,Gorski,Dodd,Cunniffe,Meekin,Mort g:Mort(7)	1st	429
4/8/11	Keighley (h)	L18-20	t:Joseph,Hurst,Gorski g:Mort(3)	1st	1,346
14/8/11	South Wales (h)	W40-28	t:W Thompson,Cunniffe,Hurst,R Hawkyard,Wingfield,Dodd,Gorski g:Mort(6)	1st	509
21/8/11	Whitehaven (a)	L42-16	t:Fitzpatrick,R Hawkyard,Foxen g:Mort(2)	1st	863
2/9/11	Rochdale (h)	L28-34	t:Flooks,Wingfield(2),Dodd(2) g:Mort(4)	1st	1,063

Ian Mort

		APP		TRIES		GOALS		FG		PTS	
	D.O.B.	ALL	Ch1	ALL	Ch1	ALL	Ch1	ALL	Ch1	ALL	Ch1
Martin Ainscough	23/10/85	26(1)	19(1)	15	12	0	0	0	0	60	48
Karl Ashall	3/11/89	7(19)	6(14)	7	5	0	0	0	0	28	20
Dale Cunniffe	25/3/87	24	18	12	11	0	0	0	0	48	44
Gavin Dodd	28/2/81	26	20	20	17	13	0	1	0	107	68
Joe Fitzpatrick	22/10/85	(4)	(2)	3	1	0	0	0	0	12	4
Richard Flooks	8/8/86	17	14	9	8	0	0	0	0	36	32
Carl Forber	17/3/85	2(1)	1	0	0	0	0	0	0	0	0
Rob Foxen	12/12/87	23(1)	17(1)	15	12	0	0	0	0	60	48
Tommy Gallagher	10/9/83	7(6)	5(3)	5	2	0	0	0	0	20	8
Andy Gorski	31/3/81	7	7	4	4	0	0	0	0	16	16
Barry Hamilton	25/2/86	2	0	1	0	0	0	0	0	4	0
Darren Hawkyard	14/10/84	15(10)	11(9)	7	4	0	0	0	0	28	16
Richie Hawkyard	21/1/86	7(3)	4(2)	5	3	0	0	0	0	20	12
Neil Holland	24/2/89	8(7)	4(5)	1	0	0	0	0	0	4	0
Alex Hurst	17/3/90	12	10	3	3	0	0	0	0	12	12
Bruce Johnson	26/1/84	(4)	(2)	0	0	0	0	0	0	0	0
Phil Joseph	10/1/85	18(3)	15(2)	7	5	0	0	0	0	28	20
Danny Meekin	16/3/89	(5)	(4)	1	1	0	0	0	0	4	4
Richard Mervill	24/6/81	(2)	(1)	0	0	0	0	0	0	0	0
Mike Morrison	9/9/87	20(3)	14(3)	1	1	0	0	0	0	4	4
Ian Mort	21/6/88	25(1)	20	25	21	119	104	0	0	338	292
Lee Paterson	5/7/81	(1)	(1)	0	0	0	0	0	0	0	0
Sam Reay	23/5/84	10	8	0	0	0	0	0	0	0	0
Neil Rigby	5/2/86	7(3)	4(2)	2	0	0	0	0	0	8	0
Mark Smith	18/8/81	24(1)	18	3	1	0	0	0	0	12	4
Anthony Stewart	5/3/79	(1)	0	1	0	0	0	0	0	4	0
Dean Thompson	22/11/88	11	6	8	2	0	0	0	0	32	8
Warren Thompson	24/2/90	10(5)	10(5)	2	2	0	0	0	0	8	8
Chris Tyrer	10/10/85	2(3)	1(2)	0	0	0	0	0	0	0	0
Ian Watson	27/10/76	22	15	2	2	0	0	0	0	8	8
Dana Wilson	22/5/83	1(20)	1(17)	5	5	0	0	0	0	20	20
Lee Wingfield	9/6/81	18(3)	12(3)	9	6	0	0	0	0	36	24

LEAGUE RECORD
P20-W14-D1-L5-BP3
(Champions/1st, Championship 1)
F720, A479, Diff+241
47 points.

CHALLENGE CUP
Round Five

NORTHERN RAIL CUP
5th, Pool 2

ATTENDANCES
Best - v Keighley (Ch1 - 1,346)
Worst - v East Hull (CC - 305)
Total (excluding Challenge Cup) - 8,511
Average (excluding Challenge Cup) - 709
(Up by 290 on 2010)

CLUB RECORDS **MATCH RECORDS**	**Highest score:** 94-0 v Gateshead, 22/8/2010 **Highest score against:** 0-112 v Warrington, 20/5/2011 **Record attendance:** 26,891 v Wigan, 12/2/64 **Tries:** 6 Mark Riley v Prescot, 11/8/96 **Goals:** 12 Ken Gowers v Liverpool City, 3/10/59 **Points:** 30 Greg Pearce v Prescot, 11/8/96; Mick Nanyn v York, 25/3/2001; Gavin Dodd v Gateshead, 22/8/2010; Ian Mort v South Wales, 17/4/2011
SEASON RECORDS **CAREER RECORDS**	**Tries:** 42 John Stopford 1963-64 **Goals:** 128 Albert Blan 1960-61 **Points:** 338 Ian Mort 2011 **Tries:** 197 Frank Evans 1921-31 **Goals:** 970 Ken Gowers 1954-73 **Points:** 2,105 Ken Gowers 1954-73 **Appearances:** 601 Ken Gowers 1954-73

WHITEHAVEN

DATE	FIXTURE	RESULT	SCORERS	LGE	ATT
8/2/11	Workington (h) (NRC)	L18-28	t:Palfrey,McAvoy,Culnean,Eilbeck g:Palfrey	7th(P2)	1,005
13/2/11	Sheffield (a) (NRC) ●	D16-16	t:Sice,D Miller g:Palfrey(4)	5th(P2)	727
27/2/11	Oldham (a) (NRC)	W4-14	t:Barker,Beattie g:Palfrey(3)	7th(P2)	544
5/3/11	Lezignan (h) (CCR3)	L14-27	t:Barker,D Miller g:Palfrey(3)	N/A	651
13/3/11	Rochdale (h)	W30-22	t:McAvoy,Smith,Calvert(2),Palfrey,Hill g:Palfrey(3)	10th	704
16/3/11	Halifax (h) (NRC)	L6-60	t:McAvoy g:Palfrey	8th(P2)	771
20/3/11	South Wales (a)	W18-22	t:Rudd,Calvert,Sice,Ford g:Palfrey(3)	10th	271
27/3/11	Keighley (h)	W24-10	t:Calvert,Hamzat,Eilbeck,Ford g:Palfrey(4)	8th	754
3/4/11	London Skolars (a)	W16-48	t:Doran,McAvoy(2),Calvert,Isakka,Smith,Benson,Wiper,Palfrey g:Palfrey(6)	7th	542
10/4/11	Rochdale (a)	L49-18	t:Calvert,Smith,McAvoy g:Palfrey(3)	7th	457
17/4/11	Doncaster (h)	W26-16	t:Smith,Culnean,Palfrey,Dalton g:Palfrey(5)	6th	727
22/4/11	Workington (a)	D30-30	t:Benson,Dalton,Fleming,Doran,Wiper,Smith g:Palfrey(3)	7th	1,592
25/4/11	Oldham (h)	W40-24	t:Calvert(2),McAvoy,Smith(3),Culnean g:Palfrey(6)	5th	946
1/5/11	Gateshead (a)	W10-54	t:McAvoy,S Miller,Doran(2),Rudd,Calvert,Sice,Smith,Eilbeck,Palfrey g:Palfrey(7)	4th	237
15/5/11	Swinton (h)	D22-22	t:Palfrey,Beattie,Hamzat,Calvert g:Palfrey(3)	5th	917
29/5/11	Keighley (a)	W14-18	t:Wiper,Culnean,Sice g:Palfrey(3)	4th	754
5/6/11	London Skolars (h)	W14-12	t:Smith,McAvoy,Hamzat g:Palfrey	4th	716
26/6/11	Workington (h)	W22-10	t:Wiper,Calvert,Hamzat,Doran g:Palfrey(3)	4th	1,523
3/7/11	Oldham (a)	L40-20	t:Beattie,McAvoy,Wiper(2) g:Palfrey(2)	5th	537
10/7/11	South Wales (h)	W34-14	t:Rudd,S Miller,Sice,D Miller,Smith,Hamzat g:Rudd(5)	5th	815
24/7/11	Swinton (a)	L44-0		6th	679
31/7/11	Gateshead (h)	W64-10	t:Sice(3),Culnean(2),Calvert(2),Eilbeck,Haggerty,Hamzat,Wilson g:Rudd(10)	5th	651
14/8/11	Doncaster (a)	L20-18	t:Hamzat(2),Isakka g:Palfrey(3)	6th	501
21/8/11	Swinton (h)	W42-16	t:Sice(2),Calvert,Benson,McAvoy,S Miller,Smith g:Rudd(7)	6th	863
4/9/11	Keighley (a)	L28-20	t:Calvert,McAvoy,Wilton g:Rudd(4)	6th	964
11/9/11	Doncaster (a) (EPO)	L34-16	t:Sice,Doran,Crellin g:Palfrey,Rudd	N/A	418

● Played at Don Valley Stadium

	APP		TRIES		GOALS		FG		PTS	
	ALL	Ch1	ALL	Ch1	ALL	Ch1	ALL	Ch1	ALL	Ch1
	D.O.B.									
Shane Ackerley	19/11/91	1	0	0	0	0	0	0	0	0	0
Daniel Barker	1/12/88	3(2)	0	2	0	0	0	0	0	8	0
Andreas Bauer	26/9/82	8	7	0	0	0	0	0	0	0	0
Andrew Beattie	12/1/81	25	21	3	2	0	0	0	0	12	8
Craig Benson	19/8/85	21	17	3	3	0	0	0	0	12	12
Craig Calvert	10/2/84	26	21	15	15	0	0	0	0	60	60
Brad Crellin	2/7/89	(5)	(4)	1	1	0	0	0	0	4	4
Paul Culnean	8/1/77	11(13)	8(11)	6	5	0	0	0	0	24	20
Tyrone Dalton	7/1/89	4(2)	4(2)	2	2	0	0	0	0	8	8
Lee Doran	23/3/81	22	21	6	6	0	0	0	0	24	24
Derry Eilbeck	1/6/84	14	9	4	3	0	0	0	0	16	12
Richard Farrer	25/11/85	2(8)	2(8)	0	0	0	0	0	0	0	0
Chris Fleming	11/1/91	3	3	1	1	0	0	0	0	4	4
David Ford	29/5/87	5(6)	3(6)	2	2	0	0	0	0	8	8
David Fox	3/2/90	(1)	0	0	0	0	0	0	0	0	0
Reece Fox	1/5/89	(3)	(1)	0	0	0	0	0	0	0	0
Chris Gerrard	1/10/89	3	3	0	0	0	0	0	0	0	0
Matthew Haggerty	8/1/91	6(2)	6(2)	1	1	0	0	0	0	4	4
Loz Hamzat	26/10/90	14	13	8	8	0	0	0	0	32	32
Howard Hill	16/1/75	11(14)	10(10)	1	1	0	0	0	0	4	4
Luke Isakka	1/11/80	16(6)	12(5)	2	2	0	0	0	0	8	8
Paul King	28/6/79	2(2)	2(2)	0	0	0	0	0	0	0	0
Tane Manihera	6/8/74	6	2	0	0	0	0	0	0	0	0
Scott McAvoy	9/4/86	25	20	12	10	0	0	0	0	48	40
Dexter Miller	3/6/82	2(9)	(7)	3	1	0	0	0	0	12	4
Spencer Miller	27/2/80	23(2)	18(2)	3	3	0	0	0	0	12	12
Lewis Palfrey	25/2/90	23	18	6	5	68	56	0	0	160	132
Jay Rossi	26/6/93	4	2	0	0	0	0	0	0	0	0
Carl Rudd	10/10/82	15(1)	14(1)	3	3	27	27	0	0	66	66
Carl Sice	13/4/80	6(20)	6(15)	11	10	0	0	0	0	44	40
Chris Smith	21/1/90	23(2)	18(2)	12	12	0	0	0	0	48	48
Martyn Wilson	22/10/82	1	1	1	1	0	0	0	0	4	4
Kurt Wilton	26/6/89	2(6)	1(6)	1	1	0	0	0	0	4	4
Max Wiper	18/9/90	11	11	6	6	0	0	0	0	24	24

Lewis Palfrey

LEAGUE RECORD
P20-W13-D2-L5-BP2
(6th, Championship 1/
Elimination Play-Off)
F566, A425, Diff+141
36 points. *(9 points deducted for
entering administration)*

CHALLENGE CUP
Round Three

NORTHERN RAIL CUP
8th, Pool 2

ATTENDANCES
Best - v Workington (Ch1 - 1,523)
Worst - v Lezignan (CC - 651)
v Gateshead (Ch1 - 651)
Total (excluding Challenge Cup) - 10,392
Average (excluding
Challenge Cup) - 866
(Down by 118 on 2010, Ch)

CLUB RECORDS — **Highest score:** 86-6 v Highfield, 25/1/95 **Highest score against:** 8-106 v Wigan, 12/5/2008 **Record attendance:** 18,500 v Wakefield, 19/3/60
MATCH RECORDS — **Tries:** 6 Vince Gribbin v Doncaster, 18/11/84 **Goals:** 13 Lee Anderson v Highfield, 25/1/95 **Points:** 32 Mick Nanyn v Batley, 22/8/2004
SEASON RECORDS — **Tries:** 34 Mike Pechey 1994-95 **Goals:** 141 John McKeown 1956-57 **Points:** 398 Mick Nanyn 2004
CAREER RECORDS — **Tries:** 248 David Seeds 1993-2007 **Goals:** 1,050 John McKeown 1948-61 **Points:** 2,133 John McKeown 1948-61
Appearances: 417 John McKeown 1948-61

WORKINGTON TOWN

DATE	FIXTURE	RESULT	SCORERS	LGE	ATT
8/2/11	Whitehaven (a) (NRC)	W18-28	t:Stack(2),McGoff g:Kaighan(8)	3rd(P2)	1,005
13/2/11	Gateshead (h) (NRC)	W82-0	t:Kaighan,Coward(2),Patrick(2),Bainbridge(2),McKenna,McDonald,Stack(2),Olstrum,Miller,Mossop,Carter g:Kaighan(11)	1st(P2)	381
20/2/11	Hunslet (a) (NRC)	L30-0		2nd(P2)	379
27/2/11	Leigh (h) (NRC)	L12-42	t:Kaighan(2) g:Kaighan(2)	6th(P2)	592
6/3/11	Rochdale (a) (CCR3)	L22-20	t:Kaighan,Mattinson,Low,Miller g:Kaighan(2)	N/A	358
13/3/11	Swinton (a)	L22-10	t:Shackley,Mossop g:Kaighan	6th	651
20/3/11	Oldham (h)	W31-12	t:Mossop,Low,Frazer(2),Kaighan,Bainbridge g:Kaighan(3) fg:Kaighan	4th	473
27/3/11	Doncaster (a)	L26-16	t:Patrick,Frazer,Pedley g:Kaighan(2)	4th	493
3/4/11	South Wales (h)	W38-24	t:Mattinson,Low,Frazer,Stack(2),Pedley,Bainbridge g:Kaighan(5)	4th	357
17/4/11	Gateshead (a)	W0-64	t:Patrick(2),Mossop(3),Kaighan(2),Stack(2),Finch,Carter,Jackson,Frazer g:Kaighan(5),Carter	3rd	273
22/4/11	Whitehaven (h)	D30-30	t:Patrick(2),Frazer,Kaighan,Pedley g:Holt(5)	2nd	1,592
25/4/11	Keighley (a)	L38-18	t:Finch(2),Frazer g:Holt(3)	4th	892
1/5/11	Rochdale (h)	L34-38	t:Low(2),King,Patrick(2),Kaighan,Frazer g:Holt(3)	5th	443
15/5/11	London Skolars (a)	W12-33	t:Kaighan,Whitehead,King,Miller,Stack g:Holt(6) fg:Holt	4th	397
29/5/11	Doncaster (h)	L32-34	t:Kaighan(2),Pedley,Stack(2) g:Holt(6)	5th	544
5/6/11	South Wales (a) ●	W28-46	t:Low,Stack,Armitstead,Frazer,Pedley,Coward(2),Carter,Mossop g:Holt(5)	5th	403
12/6/11	Gateshead (h)	W84-12	t:Kaighan(2),Dawes(3),Low(2),Miller(4),McDonald,Bainbridge,McKenna g:Holt(14)	2nd	384
26/6/11	Whitehaven (h)	L22-10	t:Pedley,Frazer g:Holt	2nd	1,523
3/7/11	Swinton (h)	W36-16	t:Patrick,Armitstead,Kaighan(2),Pedley(2) g:Holt(2),Bainbridge(3) fg:Bainbridge,Holt	3rd	512
10/7/11	Rochdale (a)	L45-20	t:Holt,Miller,Low,Kaighan g:Holt,Bainbridge	4th	1,021
24/7/11	London Skolars (h)	W41-14	t:Miller,Whitehead,Stack,Low,Kaighan(2),Patrick g:Holt(5),Bainbridge fg:Armitstead	4th	454
31/7/11	Oldham (a)	W22-24	t:Miller,Stack,Carter,Kaighan g:Holt(4)	3rd	684
14/8/11	Keighley (h)	W35-18	t:Miller,McGoff,Kaighan(2),Carter(2) g:Holt(5) fg:Holt	3rd	544
21/8/11	Doncaster (a)	W6-37	t:Pedley(2),Carter,Miller,Kaighan,Coward g:Holt(6) fg:Holt	2nd	659
4/9/11	Oldham (h)	L20-24	t:Pedley,Coward,Carter,Kaighan g:Holt(2)	3rd	716
18/9/11	Keighley (a) (QSF)	W10-19	t:Frazer(2),Miller g:Holt(3) fg:Holt	N/A	1,072
2/10/11	Keighley (GF) ●●	L32-12	t:Kaighan,Frazer g:Holt(2)	N/A	N/A

● Played at Virginia Park, Caerphilly
●● Played at Halliwell Jones Stadium, Warrington

	APP		TRIES		GOALS		FG		PTS	
	D.O.B.	ALL	Ch1	ALL	Ch1	ALL	Ch1	ALL	Ch1	ALL	Ch1
Dave Armitstead	15/1/84	11(1)	11(1)	2	2	0	0	1	1	9	9
Marc Bainbridge	22/12/87	10(11)	6(11)	5	3	5	5	1	1	31	23
Brett Carter	9/7/88	26	22	8	7	1	1	0	0	34	30
Chris Clough	20/1/87	(5)	(5)	0	0	0	0	0	0	0	0
Kris Coward	1/10/81	24	19	6	4	0	0	0	0	24	16
Stephen Dawes	14/1/85	6(2)	4(2)	3	3	0	0	0	0	12	12
Liam Finch	19/3/85	2(2)	1(2)	3	3	0	0	0	0	12	12
Neil Frazer	7/3/76	24	20	13	13	0	0	0	0	52	52
Darren Holt	21/9/76	17	17	1	1	73	73	5	5	155	155
Marc Jackson	21/8/79	6(5)	4(2)	1	1	0	0	0	0	4	4
Scott Kaighan	11/11/88	25	20	25	21	39	16	1	1	179	117
Darren King	9/3/82	4	4	2	2	0	0	0	0	8	8
Aaron Low	5/5/88	24(1)	20(1)	10	9	0	0	0	0	40	36
Jamie Marshall	17/7/78	(2)	(1)	0	0	0	0	0	0	0	0
Graeme Mattinson	24/4/85	13(1)	8(1)	2	1	0	0	0	0	8	4
Keiron McAvoy	4/9/92	(1)	(1)	0	0	0	0	0	0	0	0
Ryan McDonald	24/2/78	10(8)	10(3)	2	1	0	0	0	0	8	4
Ruairi McGoff	5/1/85	6(17)	3(16)	2	1	0	0	0	0	8	4
Joe McKenna	21/8/87	7(11)	6(10)	2	1	0	0	0	0	8	4
Elliott Miller	14/9/90	17	12	13	11	0	0	0	0	52	44
Jason Mossop	12/9/85	21	17	7	6	0	0	0	0	28	24
Karl Olstrum	21/9/91	16(1)	12(1)	1	0	0	0	0	0	4	0
John Patrick	29/11/82	17(1)	15(1)	11	9	0	0	0	0	44	36
Jack Pedley	9/11/89	12(11)	12(7)	11	11	0	0	0	0	44	44
James Robinson	4/3/79	(13)	(11)	0	0	0	0	0	0	0	0
Marc Shackley	14/1/89	3(9)	2(6)	1	1	0	0	0	0	4	4
Jarrad Stack	13/2/88	26	21	14	10	0	0	0	0	56	40
Matthew Tunstall	7/9/77	(5)	(5)	0	0	0	0	0	0	0	0
Mike Whitehead	25/8/78	24(1)	20(1)	2	2	0	0	0	0	8	8

Scott Kaighan

LEAGUE RECORD
P20-W11-D1-L8-BP6
(3rd, Championship 1/
Grand Final Runners-Up)
F659, A443, Diff+216
41 points.

CHALLENGE CUP
Round Three

NORTHERN RAIL CUP
6th, Pool 2

ATTENDANCES
Best - v Whitehaven (Ch1 - 1,592)
Worst - v South Wales (Ch1 - 357)
Total (excluding Challenge Cup) - 6,992
Average (excluding
Challenge Cup) - 583
(Up by 113 on 2010)

CLUB RECORDS MATCH RECORDS	**Highest score:** 94-4 v Leigh, 26/2/95 **Highest score against:** 0-92 v Bradford, 14/2/99 **Record attendance:** 17,741 v Wigan, 3/3/65 **Tries:** 7 Ike Southward v Blackpool, 17/9/55 **Goals:** 14 Darren Holt v Gateshead, 12/6/2011 **Points:** 42 Dean Marwood v Highfield, 1/11/92; Dean Marwood v Leigh, 26/2/95
SEASON RECORDS CAREER RECORDS	**Tries:** 49 Johnny Lawrenson 1951-52 **Goals:** 186 Lyn Hopkins 1981-82 **Points:** 438 Lyn Hopkins 1981-82 **Tries:** 274 Ike Southward 1952-59; 1960-68 **Goals:** 809 Iain MacCorquodale 1972-80 **Points:** 1,800 Iain MacCorquodale 1972-80 **Appearances:** 419 Paul Charlton 1961-69; 1975-80

CHAMPIONSHIP ONE 2011
Round by Round

ROUND 1

Sunday 13th March 2011

DONCASTER 40 SOUTH WALES SCORPIONS 10

DONCASTER: 1 Mick Butterfield; 5 Dean Colton; 4 Shaun Leaf; 30 Nev Morrison; 2 Stewart Sanderson; 7 Craig Fawcett; 19 Scott Spaven; 8 Matt Carbutt; 13 Jack Ely; 17 Adam Scott; 15 Craig Robinson; 12 Ryan Steen; 16 Mike Emmett. Subs (all used): 9 Kyle Kesik; 22 Carl Hughes; 11 Kyle Sampson; 29 Chris Green.
Tries: Colton (13, 71), Spaven (17, 19), Steen (25), Butterfield (50), Green (66); **Goals:** Spaven 6/7.
SCORPIONS: 2 Lewis Reece; 29 Robin Lock; 3 Christiaan Roets; 4 Ashley Bateman; 5 Curtis Cunningham; 1 Andrew Gay; 7 Casey Bromilow; 20 Hywel Davies; 9 Steve Parry; 15 Neil Dallimore; 12 Loz Wildbore; 21 Rhodri Lloyd; 13 Aled James. Subs (all used): 31 Dafydd Carter; 16 Joe Burke; 8 Semisi Cocka; 18 Chris Davies.
Tries: Parry (36), Lock (59); **Goals:** Reece 1/2.
Rugby Leaguer & League Express Men of the Match: *Doncaster:* Scott Spaven; *Scorpions:* Robin Lock.
Penalty count: 6-10; **Half-time:** 24-6;
Referee: Matthew Kidd; **Attendance:** 895.

KEIGHLEY COUGARS 66 LONDON SKOLARS 6

COUGARS: 2 Craig Moss; 5 Gavin Duffy; 22 Ben Sagar; 4 Danny Lawton; 26 James Hutchinson; 29 Jason Demetriou; 6 Luke Helliwell; 8 Andy Shickell; 9 James Feather; 10 Scott Law; 11 Will Cartledge; 12 Oliver Pursglove; 18 James Haythornthwaite. Subs (all used): 14 Jamaine Wray; 20 Rick Barr; 16 Brendan Rawlins; 23 Chris Baines.
Tries: Law (2), Helliwell (5), Cartledge (17, 68), Lawton (20, 24, 39), Duffy (28), Baines (42), Sagar (48), Wray (53), Haythornthwaite (70); **Goals:** Lawton 9/12.
SKOLARS: 18 Aaron Small; 2 Smokie Junor; 6 Jy-Mel Coleman; 4 Luke May; 5 Ade Adebisi; 7 Dylan Skee; 1 Neil Thorman; 8 Tony Williams; 9 Gareth Honor; 24 Dave McMeeken; 33 Jamie Boston; 15 Oliver Purslow; 13 Stephen Ball. Subs (all used): 23 Liam Prescott; 10 Jason Hart; 25 Austen Aggrey; 16 James Simon.
Try: Jy-Mel Coleman (36); **Goals:** Thorman 1/1.
Rugby Leaguer & League Express Men of the Match: *Cougars:* Danny Lawton; *Skolars:* Oliver Purslow.
Penalty count: 7-5; **Half-time:** 38-6;
Referee: Warren Turley; **Attendance:** 640.

OLDHAM 66 GATESHEAD THUNDER 12

OLDHAM: 1 Ben Heaton; 26 Matthew Fogarty; 12 Ben Wood; 4 Jack Bradbury; 21 Mark Brocklehurst; 6 Neil Roden; 7 Mick Diveney; 8 Jason Boults; 25 Martin Roden; 16 Liam Gilchrist; 11 Andrew Isherwood; 24 Paul Noone; 14 Chris Clarke. Subs (all used): 9 Danny Whitmore; 13 Valu Bentley; 15 Luke Sutton; 22 Tom Wood-Hulme.
Tries: Brocklehurst (5, 38, 68, 76), Isherwood (12, 60, 78), Bentley (24, 44), Fogarty (33, 53), Bradbury (49); **Goals:** Diveney 9/12.
THUNDER: 26 Connor Condron; 17 Joe Brown; 15 Andy Morris; 21 Matthew Harding; 16 Robin Peers; 34 Scott Woods; 6 Steve Coutts; 22 Chris Parker; 7 Ryan Clarke; 8 Jason Payne; 4 Josh Stoker; 38 David Norman; 12 Michael Ward. Subs (all used): 9 Tom Hodgson; 10 Stephen Welton; 28 Gareth Barron; 31 Will Bate.
Tries: Peers (63), Clarke (73); **Goals:** Clarke 2/2.
Rugby Leaguer & League Express Men of the Match: *Oldham:* Danny Whitmore; *Thunder:* Matthew Harding.
Penalty count: 9-3; **Half-time:** 30-0;
Referee: Craig Halloran; **Attendance:** 562.

SWINTON LIONS 22 WORKINGTON TOWN 10

LIONS: 21 Ian Mort; 2 Rob Foxen; 3 Gavin Dodd; 4 Dean Thompson; 23 Alex Hurst; 6 Martin Ainscough; 7 Ian Watson; 12 Lee Wingfield; 9 Mark Smith; 8 Mike Morrison; 11 Dale Cunniffe; 19 Neil Rigby; 14 Tommy Gallagher. Subs (all used): 25 Karl Ashall; 15 Darren Hawkyard; 10 Dana Wilson; 16 Neil Holland.
Tries: Ainscough (16), Gallagher (25), Dodd (67), Wingfield (69); **Goals:** Mort 3/4.
TOWN: 1 Brett Carter; 3 Jason Mossop; 21 John Patrick; 4 Aaron Low; 5 Neil Frazer; 23 Marc Bainbridge; 7 Scott Kaighan; 15 Ruairi McGoff; 9 Graeme Mattinson; 10 Kris Coward; 11 Mike Whitehead; 12 Jarrad Stack; 13 Karl Olstrum. Subs (all used): 14 Jack Pedley; 28 Matthew Tunstall; 19 Marc Shackley; 18 Joe McKenna.
Tries: Shackley (54), Mossop (75); **Goals:** Kaighan 1/2.
Rugby Leaguer & League Express Men of the Match: *Lions:* Ian Watson; *Town:* Scott Kaighan.
Penalty count: 8-5; **Half-time:** 12-0;
Referee: Chris Leatherbarrow; **Attendance:** 651.

WHITEHAVEN 30 ROCHDALE HORNETS 22

WHITEHAVEN: 1 Craig Benson; 31 Jay Rossi; 4 Scott McAvoy; 3 Derry Eilbeck; 2 Craig Calvert; 6 Lewis Palfrey; 32 Carl Rudd; 23 Paul Culnean; 14 Chris Smith; 26 Luke Isakka; 11 Spencer Miller; 35 Lee Doran; 17 Andrew Beattie. Subs (all used): 9 Carl Sice; 8 David Ford; 10 Howard Hill; 12 Dexter Miller.
Tries: McAvoy (5), Smith (7), Calvert (16, 36), Palfrey (52), Hill (73); **Goals:** Palfrey 3/6.
HORNETS: 1 Wayne English; 2 Craig Johnson; 17 Dale Bloomfield; 3 Dean Gorton; 25 Andy Saywell; 6 Liam McGovern; 7 Steve Roper; 18 John Cookson; 15 Paul Crook; 20 Chris Clough; 4 Matthew Strong; 11 Craig Ashall; 13 Dayne Donoghue. Subs (all used): 28 Chris Hough; 21 Mark Hobson; 30 Danny Pyke; 9 Steve McDermott.
Tries: Saywell (44, 64, 79), Ashall (69); **Goals:** Crook 3/4.
Rugby Leaguer & League Express Men of the Match: *Whitehaven:* Andrew Beattie; *Hornets:* Andy Saywell.
Penalty count: 5-6; **Half-time:** 18-0;
Referee: Dave Merrick; **Attendance:** 704.

ROUND 2

Sunday 20th March 2011

SOUTH WALES SCORPIONS 18 WHITEHAVEN 22

SCORPIONS: 27 Jamie Murphy; 26 Lee Williams; 2 Lewis Reece; 4 Ashley Bateman; 5 Curtis Cunningham; 1 Andrew Gay; 7 Casey Bromilow; 20 Hywel Davies; 9 Steve Parry; 16 Joe Burke; 12 Loz Wildbore; 3 Christiaan Roets; 21 Rhodri Lloyd. Subs (all used): 14 Tom Burnell; 15 Neil Dallimore; 8 Semisi Cocka; 29 Tylon Mafi.
Tries: Dallimore (25), Burke (75, 78); **Goals:** Reece 3/3.
WHITEHAVEN: 1 Craig Benson; 31 Jay Rossi; 3 Derry Eilbeck; 4 Scott McAvoy; 2 Craig Calvert; 6 Lewis Palfrey; 32 Carl Rudd; 8 David Ford; 14 Chris Smith; 26 Luke Isakka; 11 Spencer Miller; 35 Lee Doran; 17 Andrew Beattie. Subs (all used): 23 Paul Culnean; 9 Carl Sice; 18 Kurt Wilton; 10 Howard Hill.
Tries: Rudd (17), Calvert (40), Sice (55), Ford (68); **Goals:** Palfrey 3/4.
Rugby Leaguer & League Express Men of the Match: *Scorpions:* Lewis Reece; *Whitehaven:* Andrew Beattie.
Penalty count: 6-8; **Half-time:** 6-10;
Referee: Clint Sharrad; **Attendance:** 271.

GATESHEAD THUNDER 10 KEIGHLEY COUGARS 44

THUNDER: 26 Connor Condron; 2 Craig Olugbode; 15 Andy Morris; 21 Matthew Harding; 17 Joe Brown; 7 Ryan Clarke; 6 Steve Coutts; 8 Jason Payne; 9 Tom Hodgson; 22 Chris Parker; 4 Josh Stoker; 12 Michael Ward; 31 Will Bate. Subs (all used): 37 Karl Brandt; 14 Reece Young; 11 Gary Sargeant; 38 David Norman.
Tries: Ward (59), Brown (65); **Goals:** Clarke 1/2.
COUGARS: 1 Dan Belcher; 5 Gavin Duffy; 22 Ben Sagar; 23 Chris Baines; 26 James Hutchinson; 24 Paul Drake; 7 Ryan Smith; 8 Andy Shickell; 9 James Feather; 21 Richard Jones; 12 Oliver Pursglove; 25 Jamie Shepherd; 18 James Haythornthwaite. Subs (all used): 14 Jamaine Wray; 20 Rick Barr; 17 Ryan Benjafield; 11 Will Cartledge.
Tries: Pursglove (2, 31), Jones (9), Hutchinson (14), Belcher (17), Baines (24), Cartledge (38), Feather (71); **Goals:** Belcher 6/8.
Rugby Leaguer & League Express Men of the Match: *Thunder:* Jason Payne; *Cougars:* Chris Baines.
Penalty count: 4-4; **Half-time:** 0-38;
Referee: Chris Leatherbarrow; **Attendance:** 327.

LONDON SKOLARS 22 DONCASTER 42

SKOLARS: 1 Neil Thorman; 30 Olu Iwenofu; 17 Dave Arnot; 4 Luke May; 5 Ade Adebisi; 6 Jy-Mel Coleman; 7 Dylan Skee; 25 Austen Aggrey; 9 Gareth Honor; 10 Jason Hart; 14 Jason Cook; 15 Oliver Purslow; 13 Stephen Ball. Subs (all used): 23 Liam Prescott; 8 Tony Williams; 16 James Simon; 27 Cariern Clement-Pascall.
Tries: May (2), Hart (12), Honor (14), Aggrey (73); **Goals:** Thorman 3/4.
DONCASTER: 1 Mick Butterfield; 5 Dean Colton; 4 Shaun Leaf; 30 Nev Morrison; 2 Stewart Sanderson; 7 Craig Fawcett; 19 Scott Spaven; 20 Jamie Bovill; 13 Jack Ely; 17 Adam Scott; 29 Chris Green; 12 Ryan Steen; 16 Mike Emmett. Subs (all used): 9 Kyle Kesik; 15 Craig Robinson; 22 Carl Hughes; 8 Matt Carbutt.
Tries: Spaven (7, 36), Butterfield (19), Steen (26), Green (43, 56), Sanderson (63); **Goals:** Spaven 7/7.
Rugby Leaguer & League Express Men of the Match: *Skolars:* Austen Aggrey; *Doncaster:* Scott Spaven.
Penalty count: 4-5; **Half-time:** 16-24;
Referee: Peter Brooke; **Attendance:** 326.

ROCHDALE HORNETS 26 SWINTON LIONS 46

HORNETS: 1 Wayne English; 17 Dale Bloomfield; 3 Dean Gorton; 22 Damien Reid; 25 Andy Saywell; 6 Liam McGovern; 7 Steve Roper; 18 John Cookson; 15 Paul Crook; 8 Dave Newton; 16 Danny Samuel; 11 Craig Ashall; 13 Dayne Donoghue. Subs (all used): 21 Mark Hobson; 9 Steve McDermott; 20 Chris Clough; 5 Scott Yates.
Tries: Bloomfield (8, 23), Yates (50), Samuel (53), Saywell (60); **Goals:** Crook 3/5.
LIONS: 21 Ian Mort; 2 Rob Foxen; 3 Gavin Dodd; 4 Dean Thompson; 23 Alex Hurst; 6 Martin Ainscough; 7 Ian Watson; 8 Mike Morrison; 13 Phil Joseph; 12 Lee Wingfield; 19 Neil Rigby; 11 Dale Cunniffe; 14 Tommy Gallagher. Subs (all used): 25 Karl Ashall; 15 Darren Hawkyard; 10 Dana Wilson; 37 Richard Mervill.
Tries: D Thompson (11, 39), Wilson (31), Ainscough (35), Mort (41), Dodd (45, 79), Cunniffe (70); **Goals:** Mort 7/8.
Rugby Leaguer & League Express Men of the Match: *Hornets:* Damien Reid; *Lions:* Martin Ainscough.
Penalty count: 4-2; **Half-time:** 10-24;
Referee: George Stokes; **Attendance:** 743.

WORKINGTON TOWN 31 OLDHAM 12

TOWN: 1 Brett Carter; 4 Aaron Low; 3 Jason Mossop; 21 John Patrick; 5 Neil Frazer; 23 Marc Bainbridge; 7 Scott Kaighan; 16 Ryan McDonald; 9 Graeme Mattinson; 10 Kris Coward; 11 Mike Whitehead; 12 Jarrad Stack; 13 Karl Olstrum. Subs (all used): 14 Jack Pedley; 15 Ruairi McGoff; 8 Marc Jackson; 19 Marc Shackley.
Tries: Mossop (1), Low (4), Frazer (18, 43), Kaighan (41), Bainbridge (80); **Goals:** Kaighan 3/7;
Field goal: Kaighan (70).
Dismissal: McDonald (64) - use of the forearm.
OLDHAM: 21 Mark Brocklehurst; 2 Lucas Onyango; 4 Jack Bradbury; 12 Ben Wood; 26 Matthew Fogarty; 6 Neil Roden; 7 Mick Diveney; 8 Jason Boults; 17 John Clough; 16 Liam Gilchrist; 11 Andrew Isherwood; 24 Paul Noone; 14 Chris Clarke. Subs (all used): 13 Valu Bentley; 9 Danny Whitmore; 15 Luke Sutton; 10 Dave Ellison.
Tries: Wood (57), Clough (78); **Goals:** Diveney 2/2.
Rugby Leaguer & League Express Men of the Match: *Town:* Scott Kaighan; *Oldham:* Ben Wood.
Penalty count: 12-10; **Half-time:** 12-0;
Referee: Jamie Leahy; **Attendance:** 473.

ROUND 3

Sunday 27th March 2011

SOUTH WALES SCORPIONS 60 GATESHEAD THUNDER 20

SCORPIONS: 1 Andrew Gay; 26 Lee Williams; 2 Lewis Reece; 4 Ashley Bateman; 5 Curtis Cunningham; 12 Loz Wildbore; 7 Casey Bromilow; 20 Hywel Davies; 9 Steve Parry; 16 Joe Burke; 17 Harri Greville; 3 Christiaan Roets; 13 Aled James. Subs (all used): 14 Tom Burnell; 11 Lewis Mills; 8 Semisi Cocka; 18 Chris Davies.
Tries: Roets (5, 28), Gay (10, 74), Reece (17, 25), Bromilow (34, 79), Cunningham (37, 41), Greville (77); **Goals:** Reece 8/11.
THUNDER: 26 Connor Condron; 2 Craig Olugbode; 15 Andy Morris; 21 Matthew Harding; 17 Joe Brown; 7 Ryan Clarke; 6 Steve Coutts; 8 Jason Payne; 9 Tom Hodgson; 22 Chris Parker; 4 Josh Stoker; 12 Michael Ward; 31 Will Bate. Subs (all used): 1 Wayne Green; 29 David Cash; 13 Michael Kelly; 5 Dan O'Sullivan.
Tries: Morris (32), Green (40), O'Sullivan (46), Hodgson (64); **Goals:** Clarke 2/4.
Rugby Leaguer & League Express Men of the Match: *Scorpions:* Casey Bromilow; *Thunder:* Tom Hodgson.
Penalty count: 2-2; **Half-time:** 36-10;
Referee: George Stokes; **Attendance:** 302.

DONCASTER 26 WORKINGTON TOWN 16

DONCASTER: 1 Mick Butterfield; 5 Dean Colton; 4 Shaun Leaf; 30 Nev Morrison; 2 Stewart Sanderson; 7 Craig Fawcett; 19 Scott Spaven; 17 Adam Scott; 13 Jack Ely; 11 Kyle Sampson; 29 Chris Green; 12 Ryan Steen; 16 Mike Emmett. Subs (all used): 9 Kyle Kesik; 6 Aaron Dobek; 32 Craig Lawton; 8 Matt Carbutt.
Tries: Leaf (13, 48), Kesik (27), Fawcett (32), Steen (64); **Goals:** Spaven 2/3, Sanderson 1/2.
TOWN: 1 Brett Carter; 4 Aaron Low; 3 Jason Mossop; 21 John Patrick; 5 Neil Frazer; 23 Marc Bainbridge; 7 Scott Kaighan; 16 Ryan McDonald; 9 Graeme Mattinson; 10 Kris Coward; 11 Mike Whitehead; 19 Marc Shackley; 13 Karl Olstrum. Subs (all used): 14 Jack Pedley; 15 Ruairi McGoff; 8 Marc Jackson; 18 Joe McKenna.
Tries: Patrick (45), Frazer (61), Pedley (79); **Goals:** Kaighan 2/3.
Rugby Leaguer & League Express Men of the Match: *Doncaster:* Shaun Leaf; *Town:* John Patrick.
Penalty count: 7-10; **Half-time:** 16-0;
Referee: Dave Merrick; **Attendance:** 493.

OLDHAM 24 SWINTON LIONS 68

OLDHAM: 21 Mark Brocklehurst; 2 Lucas Onyango; 18 Alistair Williams; 4 Jack Bradbury; 27 Shaun Robinson; 9 Danny Whitmore; 7 Mick Diveney; 8 Jason Boults; 25 Martin Roden; 14 Chris Clarke; 11 Andrew Isherwood; 12 Ben Wood; 24 Paul Noone. Subs (all used): 16 Liam Gilchrist; 13 Valu Bentley; 17 John Clough; 10 Dave Ellison.
Tries: Wood (2), Diveney (10), Boults (65, 77); **Goals:** Diveney 4/4.
LIONS: 21 Ian Mort; 2 Rob Foxen; 3 Gavin Dodd; 5 Sam Reay; 20 Richard Flooks; 6 Martin Ainscough; 7 Ian Watson; 12 Lee Wingfield; 9 Mark Smith; 8 Mike Morrison; 11 Dale Cunniffe; 14 Tommy Gallagher; 13 Phil Joseph. Subs (all used): 25 Karl Ashall; 15 Darren Hawkyard; 10 Dana Wilson; 29 Chris Tyrer.
Tries: Gallagher (23), Wilson (26), Dodd (31, 47), Ashall (37, 58), Mort (45, 80), Wingfield (53), Flooks (55), Ainscough (69), Cunniffe (73); **Goals:** Mort 10/12.
Rugby Leaguer & League Express Men of the Match: *Oldham:* Shaun Robinson; *Lions:* Ian Mort.
Penalty count: 10-8; **Half-time:** 12-22;
Referee: Matthew Thomason; **Attendance:** 744.

ROCHDALE HORNETS 40 LONDON SKOLARS 20

HORNETS: 1 Wayne English; 25 Andy Saywell; 22 Damien Reid; 23 Wayne McHugh; 17 Dale Bloomfield; 6 Liam McGovern; 7 Steve Roper; 8 Dave Newton; 15 Paul Crook; 18 John Cookson; 21 Mark Hobson; 11 Craig Ashall; 13 Dayne Donoghue. Subs (all used): 5 Scott Yates; 32 Danny Ekis; 29 Mark Biggins; 31 Martin Keavney.
Tries: Ashall (17), Cookson (38), Bloomfield (49), Saywell (54, 63), Crook (68), Ekis (77);
Goals: McGovern 1/1, Crook 5/6.
SKOLARS: 1 Neil Thorman; 30 Olu Iwenofu; 17 Dave Arnot; 4 Luke May; 5 Ade Adebisi; 7 Dylan Skee; 6 Jy-Mel Coleman; 10 Jason Hart; 9 Gareth Honor; 25 Austen Aggrey; 15 Oliver Purslow; 27 Cariern Clement-Pascall; 13 Stephen Ball. Subs (all used): 22 Saqib Murtza; 8 Tony Williams; 32 Sam Gee; 23 Liam Prescott.
Tries: Arnot (6), Gee (36), Adebisi (44), Thorman (71); **Goals:** Thorman 2/4.
Sin bin: Aggrey (76) - holding down.
Rugby Leaguer & League Express Men of the Match: *Hornets:* Andy Saywell; *Skolars:* Gareth Honor.
Penalty count: 12-7; **Half-time:** 12-10;
Referee: Craig Halloran; **Attendance:** 434.

WHITEHAVEN 24 KEIGHLEY COUGARS 10

WHITEHAVEN: 1 Craig Benson; 5 Loz Hamzat; 4 Scott McAvoy; 3 Derry Eilbeck; 2 Craig Calvert; 6 Lewis Palfrey; 7 Tane Manihera; 23 Paul Culnean; 14 Chris Smith; 26 Luke Isakka; 11 Spencer Miller; 35 Lee Doran; 17 Andrew Beattie. Subs (all used): 9 Carl Sice; 8 David Ford; 10 Howard Hill; 18 Kurt Wilton.
Tries: Calvert (11), Hamzat (23), Eilbeck (27), Ford (38);
Goals: Palfrey 4/6.
Sin bin: McAvoy (67) - interference.
COUGARS: 1 Dan Belcher; 5 Gavin Duffy; 22 Ben Sagar; 4 Danny Lawton; 26 James Hutchinson; 24 Paul Drake; 6 Luke Helliwell; 8 Andy Shickell; 9 James Feather; 10 Scott Law; 12 Oliver Pursglove; 11 Will Cartledge; 18 James Haythornthwaite. Subs (all used): 14 Jamaine Wray; 16 Brendan Rawlins; 21 Richard Jones; 23 Chris Baines.
Tries: Belcher (45), Duffy (69); **Goals:** Lawton 1/2.
Rugby Leaguer & League Express Men of the Match:
Whitehaven: Spencer Miller; *Cougars:* Luke Helliwell.
Penalty count: 12-6; **Half-time:** 22-0;
Referee: Warren Turley; **Attendance:** 754.

ROUND 4

Sunday 3rd April 2011

WORKINGTON TOWN 38 SOUTH WALES SCORPIONS 24

TOWN: 1 Brett Carter; 4 Aaron Low; 3 Jason Mossop; 21 John Patrick; 5 Neil Frazer; 23 Marc Bainbridge; 7 Scott Kaighan; 8 Marc Jackson; 9 Graeme Mattinson; 10 Kris Coward; 11 Mike Whitehead; 12 Jarrad Stack; 13 Karl Olstrum. Subs (all used): 14 Jack Pedley; 15 Ruairi McGoff; 28 Matthew Tunstall; 17 James Robinson.
Tries: Mattinson (13), Low (32), Frazer (40), Stack (48, 75), Pedley (57), Bainbridge (63); **Goals:** Kaighan 5/7.
On report: Bainbridge (44) - alleged use of the forearm.
SCORPIONS: 1 Andrew Gay; 27 Jamie Murphy; 4 Ashley Bateman; 2 Lewis Reece; 26 Lee Williams; 12 Loz Wildbore; 7 Casey Bromilow; 20 Hywel Davies; 9 Steve Parry; 29 Gil Dudson; 16 Joe Burke; 17 Harri Greville; 3 Christiaan Roets. Subs (all used): 14 Tom Burnell; 8 Semisi Cocka; 11 Lewis Mills; 18 Chris Davies.
Tries: Gay (1, 11), Greville (24), Bateman (37);
Goals: Reece 4/4, Murphy 0/1.
Rugby Leaguer & League Express Men of the Match:
Town: Graeme Mattinson; *Scorpions:* Harri Greville.
Penalty count: 12-5; **Half-time:** 16-24;
Referee: Peter Brooke; **Attendance:** 357.

LONDON SKOLARS 16 WHITEHAVEN 48

SKOLARS: 1 Neil Thorman; 30 Olu Iwenofu; 17 Dave Arnot; 4 Luke May; 5 Ade Adebisi; 7 Dylan Skee; 6 Jy-Mel Coleman; 10 Jason Hart; 9 Gareth Honor; 22 Saqib Murtza; 15 Oliver Purslow; 14 Jason Cook; 27 Cariern Clement-Pascall. Subs (all used): 32 Sam Gee; 25 Austen Aggrey; 8 Tony Williams; 16 James Simon.
Tries: Jy-Mel Coleman (13), Adebisi (31), Aggrey (77);
Goals: Thorman 2/3.
WHITEHAVEN: 1 Craig Benson; 5 Loz Hamzat; 33 Max Wiper; 4 Scott McAvoy; 2 Craig Calvert; 6 Lewis Palfrey; 7 Tane Manihera; 23 Paul Culnean; 14 Chris Smith; 26 Luke Isakka; 11 Spencer Miller; 35 Lee Doran; 17 Andrew Beattie. Subs (all used): 9 Carl Sice; 10 Howard Hill; 15 Richard Farrer; 18 Kurt Wilton.
Tries: Doran (19), McAvoy (21, 49), Calvert (26), Isakka (57), Smith (60), Benson (66), Wiper (69), Palfrey (74); **Goals:** Palfrey 6/9.
Rugby Leaguer & League Express Men of the Match:
Skolars: Jy-Mel Coleman; *Whitehaven:* Scott McAvoy.
Penalty count: 10-12; **Half-time:** 10-14;
Referee: Warren Turley; **Attendance:** 542.

DONCASTER 8 ROCHDALE HORNETS 24

DONCASTER: 2 Stewart Sanderson; 14 Scott Wilson; 4 Shaun Leaf; 30 Nev Morrison; 31 Michael Coady; 7 Craig Fawcett; 19 Scott Spaven; 20 Jamie Bovill; 13 Jack Ely; 17 Adam Scott; 25 Chris Spurr; 29 Chris Green; 12 Ryan Steen. Subs (all used): 16 Mike Emmett; 8 Matt Carbutt; 11 Kyle Sampson; 32 Craig Lawton.
Tries: Green (5, 73); **Goals:** Spaven 0/2.
Dismissal: Bovill (65) - use of the elbow.
HORNETS: 1 Wayne English; 17 Dale Bloomfield; 23 Wayne McHugh; 4 Matthew Strong; 25 Andy Saywell; 6 Liam McGovern; 7 Steve Roper; 8 Dave Newton; 15 Paul Crook; 18 John Cookson; 16 Danny Samuel; 13 Dayne Donoghue; 11 Craig Ashall. Subs (all used): 20 Chris Clough; 32 Danny Ekis; 21 Mark Hobson; 31 Martin Keavney.
Tries: Saywell (19, 29), McHugh (23), Ekis (63);
Goals: Crook 0/1, McGovern 3/3;
Field goals: McGovern (57, 80).
Rugby Leaguer & League Express Men of the Match:
Doncaster: Chris Green; *Hornets:* Danny Ekis.
Penalty count: 3-6; **Half-time:** 4-16;
Referee: Chris Leatherbarrow; **Attendance:** 589.

KEIGHLEY COUGARS 40 OLDHAM 14

COUGARS: 18 James Haythornthwaite; 5 Gavin Duffy; 22 Ben Sagar; 4 Danny Lawton; 26 James Hutchinson; 29 Jason Demetriou; 6 Luke Helliwell; 8 Andy Shickell; 9 James Feather; 16 Brendan Rawlins; 11 Will Cartledge; 12 Oliver Pursglove; 23 Chris Baines. Subs (all used): 14 Jamaine Wray; 10 Scott Law; 17 Ryan Benjafield; 21 Richard Jones.
Tries: Helliwell (3, 26), Haythornthwaite (16), Jones (47), Feather (49), Lawton (68), Pursglove (71);
Goals: Lawton 6/7.
OLDHAM: 1 Ben Heaton; 2 Lucas Onyango; 21 Mark Brocklehurst; 4 Jack Bradbury; 27 Shaun Robinson; 9 Danny Whitmore; 7 Mick Diveney; 8 Jason Boults; 25 Martin Roden; 14 Chris Clarke; 11 Andrew Isherwood; 12 Ben Wood; 24 Paul Noone. Subs (all used): 10 Dave Ellison; 13 Valu Bentley; 17 John Clough; 16 Liam Gilchrist.
Tries: Heaton (43), Robinson (54), Onyango (76);
Goals: Diveney 1/3.
Rugby Leaguer & League Express Men of the Match:
Cougars: Danny Lawton; *Oldham:* Shaun Robinson.
Penalty count: 6-5; **Half-time:** 18-0;
Referee: Dave Merrick; **Attendance:** 995.

SWINTON LIONS 48 GATESHEAD THUNDER 24

LIONS: 21 Ian Mort; 2 Rob Foxen; 3 Gavin Dodd; 5 Sam Reay; 20 Richard Flooks; 17 Carl Forber; 7 Ian Watson; 8 Mike Morrison; 9 Mark Smith; 29 Chris Tyrer; 11 Dale Cunniffe; 15 Darren Hawkyard; 14 Tommy Gallagher. Subs (all used): 6 Martin Ainscough; 25 Karl Ashall; 27 Bruce Johnson; 26 Joe Fitzpatrick.
Tries: Cunniffe (4, 76), Mort (29), Dodd (31), Foxen (33, 38, 70), Ainscough (48), Smith (62); **Goals:** Mort 6/9.
THUNDER: 26 Connor Condron; 17 Joe Brown; 23 Jamie Love; 4 Josh Stoker; 16 Robin Peers; 6 Mitchell Stevens; 7 Ryan Clarke; 8 Jason Payne; 9 Tom Hodgson; 11 Gary Sargeant; 13 Michael Kelly; 5 Dan O'Sullivan; 31 Will Bate. Subs (all used): 37 Chris Burnett; 1 Wayne Green; 41 Joe Causer; 29 David Cash.
Tries: Bate (12), Love (17), Condron (21), Jason Payne (56); **Goals:** Clarke 4/4.
Rugby Leaguer & League Express Men of the Match:
Lions: Dale Cunniffe; *Thunder:* Jason Payne.
Penalty count: 8-6; **Half-time:** 28-18;
Referee: Matthew Kidd; **Attendance:** 493.

ROUND 8

Saturday 9th April 2011

SWINTON LIONS 38 LONDON SKOLARS 30

LIONS: 21 Ian Mort; 2 Rob Foxen; 3 Gavin Dodd; 5 Sam Reay; 20 Richard Flooks; 6 Martin Ainscough; 7 Ian Watson; 8 Mike Morrison; 9 Mark Smith; 10 Dana Wilson; 11 Dale Cunniffe; 15 Darren Hawkyard; 13 Phil Joseph. Subs (all used): 25 Karl Ashall; 38 Lee Paterson; 29 Chris Tyrer; 27 Bruce Johnson.
Tries: Dodd (1, 20), Mort (17), Foxen (22), D Hawkyard (29), Ashall (40), Cunniffe (45); **Goals:** Mort 5/7.
SKOLARS: 1 Neil Thorman; 31 Jack Latus; 17 Dave Arnot; 14 Jason Cook; 5 Ade Adebisi; 7 Dylan Skee; 6 Jy-Mel Coleman; 22 Saqib Murtza; 9 Gareth Honor; 10 Jason Hart; 33 Lamont Bryan; 15 Oliver Purslow; 25 Austen Aggrey. Subs (all used): 32 Sam Gee; 16 James Simon; 8 Tony Williams; 27 Cariern Clement-Pascall.
Tries: Arnot (14), Bryan (35), Adebisi (37, 69), Latus (57); **Goals:** Thorman 5/5.
Rugby Leaguer & League Express Men of the Match:
Lions: Ian Mort; *Skolars:* Neil Thorman.
Penalty count: 4-9; **Half-time:** 34-18;
Referee: Clint Sharrad; **Attendance:** 395.

ROUND 12

Sunday 10th April 2011

ROCHDALE HORNETS 49 WHITEHAVEN 18

HORNETS: 1 Wayne English; 17 Dale Bloomfield; 4 Matthew Strong; 23 Wayne McHugh; 25 Andy Saywell; 6 Liam McGovern; 7 Steve Roper; 8 Dave Newton; 15 Paul Crook; 18 John Cookson; 21 Mark Hobson; 13 Dayne Donoghue; 11 Craig Ashall. Subs (all used): 32 Danny Ekis; 31 Martin Keavney; 20 Chris Clough; 35 Richard Mervill.
Tries: Saywell (15, 73), Mervill (27, 80), McHugh (54, 78), Ekis (64), English (66); **Goals:** Crook 5/7, McGovern 3/3; **Field goal:** McGovern (40).
WHITEHAVEN: 1 Craig Benson; 5 Loz Hamzat; 3 Derry Eilbeck; 4 Scott McAvoy; 2 Craig Calvert; 6 Lewis Palfrey; 21 Tyrone Dalton; 23 Paul Culnean; 14 Chris Smith; 26 Luke Isakka; 11 Spencer Miller; 35 Lee Doran; 17 Andrew Beattie. Subs (all used): 9 Carl Sice; 10 Howard Hill; 15 Richard Farrer; 12 Dexter Miller.
Tries: Calvert (49), Smith (57), McAvoy (70);
Goals: Palfrey 3/3.
Rugby Leaguer & League Express Men of the Match:
Hornets: Wayne McHugh; *Whitehaven:* Lewis Palfrey.
Penalty count: 13-6; **Half-time:** 15-0;
Referee: George Stokes; **Attendance:** 457.

ROUND 5

Sunday 17th April 2011

GATESHEAD THUNDER 0 WORKINGTON TOWN 64

THUNDER: 1 Mitchell Stevens; 43 Ashley Williams; 23 Jamie Love; 21 Matthew Harding; 17 Joe Brown; 26 Connor Condron; 40 Matthew Massey; 8 Jason Payne; 7 Ryan Clarke; 22 Chris Parker; 4 Josh Stoker; 13 Michael Kelly; 31 Will Bate. Subs (all used): 5 Dan O'Sullivan; 15 Andy Morris; 6 Steve Coutts; 11 Gary Sargeant.
TOWN: 1 Brett Carter; 4 Aaron Low; 3 Jason Mossop; 21 John Patrick; 5 Neil Frazer; 23 Marc Bainbridge; 7 Scott Kaighan; 10 Kris Coward; 9 Graeme Mattinson; 8 Marc Jackson; 11 Mike Whitehead; 12 Jarrad Stack; 26 Darren King. Subs (all used): 6 Liam Finch; 18 Joe McKenna; 19 Marc Shackley; 28 Matthew Tunstall.
Tries: Patrick (6, 37), Mossop (8, 32, 73), Kaighan (42, 58), Stack (49, 76), Finch (63), Carter (66), Jackson (70), Frazer (80); **Goals:** Kaighan 5/11, Carter 1/2.
Rugby Leaguer & League Express Men of the Match:
Thunder: Mitchell Stevens; *Town:* Scott Kaighan.
Penalty count: 3-4; **Half-time:** 0-18;
Referee: Dave Merrick; **Attendance:** 273.

OLDHAM 52 LONDON SKOLARS 26

OLDHAM: 21 Mark Brocklehurst; 2 Lucas Onyango; 26 Matthew Fogarty; 3 Marcus St Hilaire; 27 Shaun Robinson; 6 Neil Roden; 7 Mick Diveney; 8 Jason Boults; 17 John Clough; 14 Chris Clarke; 11 Andrew Isherwood; 24 Paul Noone; 25 Martin Roden. Subs (all used): 9 Danny Whitmore; 10 Dave Ellison; 13 Valu Bentley; 28 Luke Stenchion.
Tries: Diveney (6, 42), Robinson (10, 34), Boults (22), Noone (25), Onyango (28, 61), N Roden (32), Brocklehurst (37); **Goals:** Diveney 6/10.
SKOLARS: 1 Neil Thorman; 31 Jack Latus; 17 Dave Arnot; 14 Jason Cook; 5 Ade Adebisi; 7 Dylan Skee; 6 Jy-Mel Coleman; 22 Saqib Murtza; 9 Gareth Honor; 10 Jason Hart; 15 Oliver Purslow; 27 Cariern Clement-Pascall; 25 Austen Aggrey. Subs (all used): 32 Sam Gee; 16 James Simon; 8 Tony Williams; 21 Danny Burke.
Tries: Arnot (1), Adebisi (16), Clement-Pascall (54, 72), Skee (77); **Goals:** Thorman 0/2, Latus 3/3.
On report: Adebisi (78) - alleged high tackle.
Rugby Leaguer & League Express Men of the Match:
Oldham: Mick Diveney; *Skolars:* Jy-Mel Coleman.
Penalty count: 3-3; **Half-time:** 42-8;
Referee: Chris Leatherbarrow; **Attendance:** 566.

ROCHDALE HORNETS 32 KEIGHLEY COUGARS 40

HORNETS: 1 Wayne English; 17 Dale Bloomfield; 4 Matthew Strong; 23 Wayne McHugh; 25 Andy Saywell; 6 Liam McGovern; 7 Steve Roper; 8 Dave Newton; 15 Paul Crook; 35 Richard Mervill; 21 Mark Hobson; 13 Dayne Donoghue; 11 Craig Ashall. Subs (all used): 32 Danny Ekis; 31 Martin Keavney; 20 Chris Clough; 36 Mike Stewart.
Tries: Bloomfield (24, 75), Keavney (30), Newton (51), Crook (67, 80); **Goals:** Crook 3/5, McGovern 1/1.
COUGARS: 18 James Haythornthwaite; 5 Gavin Duffy; 4 Danny Lawton; 22 Ben Sagar; 26 James Hutchinson; 29 Jason Demetriou; 6 Luke Helliwell; 8 Andy Shickell; 9 James Feather; 17 Ryan Benjafield; 11 Will Cartledge; 12 Oliver Pursglove; 21 Richard Jones. Subs (all used): 20 Rick Barr; 10 Scott Law; 7 Ryan Smith; 23 Chris Baines.
Tries: Hutchinson (3), Haythornthwaite (10, 44, 47), Demetriou (40), Shickell (63), Pursglove (70);
Goals: Lawton 6/8.
Rugby Leaguer & League Express Men of the Match:
Hornets: Paul Crook; *Cougars:* Jason Demetriou.
Penalty count: 3-4; **Half-time:** 10-16;
Referee: Craig Halloran; **Attendance:** 515.

SOUTH WALES SCORPIONS 22 SWINTON LIONS 74

SCORPIONS: 27 Jamie Murphy; 26 Lee Williams; 4 Ashley Bateman; 3 Christiaan Roets; 2 Lewis Reece; 1 Andrew Gay; 7 Casey Bromilow; 16 Joe Burke; 9 Steve Parry; 10 Paul Raftrey; 11 Lewis Mills; 17 Harri Greville; 13 Aled James. Subs (all used): 14 Tom Burnell; 15 Neil Dallimore; 8 Semisi Cocka; 20 Hywel Davies.
Tries: Murphy (1), Parry (7), Bromilow (11), Reece (63);
Goals: Reece 3/4.
Sin bin: Dallimore (78) - fighting.
LIONS: 21 Ian Mort; 2 Rob Foxen; 3 Gavin Dodd; 5 Sam Reay; 20 Richard Flooks; 6 Martin Ainscough; 7 Ian Watson; 12 Lee Wingfield; 9 Mark Smith; 8 Mike Morrison; 11 Dale Cunniffe; 15 Darren Hawkyard; 13 Phil Joseph. Subs (all used): 25 Karl Ashall; 19 Neil Rigby; 10 Dana Wilson; 39 Warren Thompson.
Tries: Flooks (14, 41), Foxen (20), Dodd (26, 35, 67), Ashall (28), Ainscough (39, 47), D Hawkyard (53), Watson (56), Mort (72, 76); **Goals:** Mort 11/13.
Sin bin: Morrison (78) - fighting.
Rugby Leaguer & League Express Men of the Match:
Scorpions: Steve Parry; *Lions:* Gavin Dodd.
Penalty count: 4-9; **Half-time:** 18-32;
Referee: Warren Turley; **Attendance:** 370.

WHITEHAVEN 26 DONCASTER 16

WHITEHAVEN: 1 Craig Benson; 31 Chris Fleming; 33 Max Wiper; 3 Derry Eilbeck; 2 Craig Calvert; 6 Lewis Palfrey; 21 Tyrone Dalton; 23 Paul Culnean; 14 Chris Smith; 8 David Ford; 11 Spencer Miller; 35 Lee Doran; 17 Andrew Beattie. Subs (all used): 9 Carl Sice; 15 Richard Farrer; 10 Howard Hill; 12 Dexter Miller.
Tries: Smith (2), Culnean (18), Palfrey (36), Dalton (66);
Goals: Palfrey 5/5.
DONCASTER: 1 Mick Butterfield; 5 Dean Colton; 30 Nev Morrison; 31 Michael Coady; 2 Stewart Sanderson; 21 Paul Hughes; 19 Scott Spaven; 17 Adam Scott; 16 Mike Emmett; 8 Matt Carbutt; 15 Craig Robinson; 12 Ryan Steen; 25 Chris Spurr. Subs (all used): 9 Kyle Kesik; 10 Liam Crawley; 22 Carl Hughes; 11 Kyle Sampson.
Tries: Kesik (24), Colton (62), Robinson (78);
Goals: Spaven 2/3.
Rugby Leaguer & League Express Men of the Match:
Whitehaven: Craig Benson; *Doncaster:* Dean Colton.
Penalty count: 9-11; **Half-time:** 18-6;
Referee: Matthew Kidd; **Attendance:** 727.

ROUND 6

Friday 22nd April 2011

OLDHAM 38 ROCHDALE HORNETS 6

OLDHAM: 21 Mark Brocklehurst; 2 Lucas Onyango; 26

Workington's Marc Shackley meets Whitehaven's Howard Hill head on

Matthew Fogarty; 3 Marcus St Hilaire; 27 Shaun Robinson; 6 Neil Roden; 7 Carl Forber; 8 Jason Boults; 25 Martin Roden, 10 Dave Ellison; 11 Andrew Isherwood; 14 Chris Clarke; 24 Paul Noone. Subs (all used): 13 Valu Bentley; 15 Luke Sutton; 17 John Clough; 28 Luke Stenchion.
Tries: M Roden (17), Clough (24), Clarke (30), Fogarty (47), Forber (56), Isherwood (62), Onyango (78); **Goals:** Forber 5/7.
Sin bin: Clough (67) - holding down.
HORNETS: 1 Wayne English; 17 Dale Bloomfield; 4 Matthew Strong; 13 Dayne Donoghue; 25 Andy Saywell; 15 Paul Crook; 7 Steve Roper; 18 John Cookson; 31 Mark Hobson; 11 Craig Ashall. Subs (all used): 6 Liam McGovern; 8 Dave Newton; 36 Mike Stewart; 30 Danny Pyke.
Try: English (66); **Goals:** Crook 1/1.
Rugby Leaguer & League Express Men of the Match: *Oldham:* John Clough; *Hornets:* Wayne English.
Penalty count: 9-12; **Half-time:** 16-0;
Referee: Craig Halloran; **Attendance:** 876.

WORKINGTON TOWN 30 WHITEHAVEN 30

TOWN: 1 Brett Carter; 4 Aaron Low; 3 Jason Mossop; 21 John Patrick; 5 Neil Frazer; 24 Darren Holt; 7 Scott Kaighan; 8 Marc Jackson; 9 Graeme Mattinson; 10 Kris Coward; 11 Mike Whitehead; 12 Jarrad Stack; 13 Karl Olstrum. Subs (all used): 14 Jack Pedley; 19 Marc Shackley; 16 Ryan McDonald; 28 Matthew Tunstall.
Tries: Stack (25, 27), Frazer (64), Kaighan (67), Pedley (70); **Goals:** Holt 5/5.
On report: Jackson (59) - alleged punching.
WHITEHAVEN: 1 Craig Benson; 31 Chris Fleming; 33 Max Wiper; 4 Scott McAvoy; 2 Craig Calvert; 6 Lewis Palfrey; 21 Tyrone Dalton; 23 Paul Culnean; 14 Chris Smith; 26 Luke Isakka; 11 Spencer Miller; 35 Lee Doran; 17 Andrew Beattie. Subs (all used): 9 Carl Sice; 10 Howard Hill; 8 David Ford; 12 Dexter Miller.
Tries: Benson (4), Dalton (10), Fleming (17), Doran (43), Wiper (52), Smith (75); **Goals:** Palfrey 3/6.
Sin bin: Dalton (24) - late challenge on Kaighan.
Rugby Leaguer & League Express Men of the Match: *Town:* Darren Holt; *Whitehaven:* Craig Benson.
Penalty count: 8-8; **Half-time:** 12-16.
Referee: Chris Leatherbarrow; **Attendance:** 1,592.

SOUTH WALES SCORPIONS 20 LONDON SKOLARS 18

SCORPIONS: 27 Jamie Murphy; 26 Lee Williams; 4 Ashley Bateman; 3 Christiaan Roets; 24 Dalton Grant; 1 Andrew Gay; 12 Loz Wildbore; 16 Joe Burke; 9 Steve Parry; 20 Hywel Davies; 10 Paul Raftrey; 17 Harri Greville; 11 Lewis Mills. Subs (all used): 14 Tom Burnell; 15 Neil Dallimore; 8 Semisi Cocka; 18 Chris Davies.
Tries: Gay (32), Bateman (36), Grant (47, 65);
Goals: Murphy 2/4.

SKOLARS: 36 John Paxton; 31 Jack Latus; 17 Dave Arnot; 14 Jason Cook; 5 Ade Adebisi; 6 Jy-Mel Coleman; 7 Dylan Skee; 25 Austen Aggrey; 9 Gareth Honor; 8 James Simon; 37 Jaroslaw Obuchowski; 15 Oliver Purslow; 32 Sam Gee. Subs (all used): 27 Cariern Clement-Pascall; 24 Dave McMeeken; 29 Michael Sykes; 21 Danny Burke.
Tries: McMeeken (52), Aggrey (68), Clement-Pascall (76); **Goals:** Latus 3/3.
Rugby Leaguer & League Express Men of the Match: *Scorpions:* Dalton Grant; *Skolars:* Austen Aggrey.
Penalty count: 10-10; **Half-time:** 10-0;
Referee: Matthew Kidd; **Attendance:** 280.

ROUND 7

Monday 25th April 2011

LONDON SKOLARS 32 GATESHEAD THUNDER 32

SKOLARS: 36 John Paxton; 1 Neil Thorman; 31 Jack Latus; 17 Dave Arnot; 5 Ade Adebisi; 7 Dylan Skee; 6 Jy-Mel Coleman; 16 James Simon; 9 Gareth Honor; 25 Austen Aggrey; 37 Jaroslaw Obuchowski; 15 Oliver Purslow; 32 Sam Gee. Subs (all used): 27 Cariern Clement-Pascall; 29 Michael Sykes; 21 Danny Burke; 24 Dave McMeeken.
Tries: Aggrey (18), Purslow (21), Latus (31), Arnot (38), Thorman (40), Honor (76); **Goals:** Latus 4/6.
THUNDER: 17 Joe Brown; 43 Ashley Williams; 6 Mitchell Stevens; 4 Josh Stoker; 16 Robin Peers; 26 Connor Condron; 7 Ryan Clarke; 10 Stephen Welton; 40 Matthew Massey; 22 Chris Parker; 13 Michael Kelly; 8 Jason Payne; 31 Will Bate. Subs (all used): 23 Jamie Love; 15 Andy Morris; 5 Dan O'Sullivan; 21 Matthew Harding.
Tries: Jason Payne (12), Love (48), Clarke (51, 63), Condron (71); **Goals:** Clarke 6/6.
Sin bin: Massey (54) - delaying restart.
Rugby Leaguer & League Express Men of the Match: *Skolars:* Austen Aggrey; *Thunder:* Ryan Clarke.
Half-time: 26-6; **Referee:** Peter Brooke; **Attendance:** 263.

DONCASTER 32 SWINTON LIONS 36

DONCASTER: 1 Mick Butterfield; 5 Dean Colton; 7 Ryan Steen; 25 Chris Spurr; 2 Stewart Sanderson; 19 Scott Spaven; 7 Craig Fawcett; 17 Adam Scott; 21 Paul Hughes; 8 Matt Carbutt; 15 Craig Robinson; 10 Liam Crawley; 16 Mike Emmett. Subs (all used): 9 Kyle Kesik; 13 Jack Ely; 22 Carl Hughes; 14 Scott Wilson.
Tries: Sanderson (19, 36), Emmett (40), Fawcett (73), Spurr (76), C Hughes (80); **Goals:** Spaven 4/6.
Sin bin: Scott (47) - use of the elbow.
LIONS: 21 Ian Mort; 2 Rob Foxen; 3 Gavin Dodd; 5 Sam Reay; 20 Richard Flooks; 6 Martin Ainscough; 7 Ian

Watson; 12 Lee Wingfield; 9 Mark Smith; 8 Mike Morrison; 11 Dale Cunniffe; 15 Darren Hawkyard; 13 Phil Joseph. Subs (all used): 25 Karl Ashall; 19 Neil Rigby; 10 Dana Wilson; 39 Warren Thompson.
Tries: Mort (5), Ainscough (9), Cunniffe (13), Watson (30), Foxen (56), D Hawkyard (59); **Goals:** Mort 6/6.
Sin bin: Watson (76) - dissent.
Rugby Leaguer & League Express Men of the Match: *Doncaster:* Carl Hughes; *Lions:* Ian Watson.
Half-time: 16-24; **Referee:** Ronnie Laughton; **Attendance:** 649.

KEIGHLEY COUGARS 38 WORKINGTON TOWN 18

COUGARS: 2 Craig Moss; 5 Gavin Duffy; 4 Danny Lawton; 22 Ben Sagar; 26 James Hutchinson; 29 Jason Demetriou; 6 Luke Helliwell; 8 Andy Shickell; 9 James Feather; 1 Ryan Benjafield; 11 Will Cartledge; 12 Oliver Pursglove; 21 Richard Jones. Subs (all used): 20 Rick Barr; 10 Scott Law; 7 Ryan Smith; 13 Greg Nicholson.
Tries: Moss (10, 63), Feather (26), Lawton (46, 52), Shickell (57); **Goals:** Lawton 7/8.
TOWN: 1 Brett Carter; 4 Aaron Low; 3 Jason Mossop; 21 John Patrick; 5 Neil Frazer; 24 Darren Holt; 6 Liam Finch; 16 Ryan McDonald; 14 Jack Pedley; 10 Kris Coward; 11 Mike Whitehead; 12 Jarrad Stack; 26 Darren King. Subs (all used): 9 Graeme Mattinson; 18 Joe McKenna; 19 Marc Shackley; 17 James Robinson.
Tries: Finch (5, 37), Frazer (78); **Goals:** Holt 3/3.
Sin bin: Carter (24) - high tackle.
Rugby Leaguer & League Express Men of the Match: *Cougars:* Jason Demetriou; *Town:* Darren Holt.
Half-time: 14-12; **Referee:** Craig Halloran; **Attendance:** 892.

ROCHDALE HORNETS 40 SOUTH WALES SCORPIONS 18

HORNETS: 5 Scott Yates; 17 Dale Bloomfield; 4 Matthew Strong; 3 Dean Gorton; 2 Craig Johnson; 15 Paul Crook; 28 Chris Hough; 18 John Cookson; 11 Craig Ashall; 35 Richard Mervill; 21 Mark Hobson; 10 Adam Bowman; 13 Dayne Donoghue. Subs (all used): 8 Dave Newton; 9 Steve McDermott; 32 Danny Ekis; 1 Wayne English.
Tries: Cookson (5), Crook (20), Ashall (31), Newton (42), Bloomfield (50), Donoghue (58), McDermott (79); **Goals:** Crook 6/7.
SCORPIONS: 27 Jamie Murphy; 26 Lee Williams; 4 Ashley Bateman; 3 Christiaan Roets; 24 Dalton Grant; 12 Loz Wildbore; 1 Andrew Gay; 20 Hywel Davies; 9 Steve Parry; 10 Paul Raftrey; 16 Joe Burke; 17 Harri Greville; 13 Aled James. Subs (all used): 14 Tom Burnell; 15 Neil Dallimore; 8 Semisi Cocka; 11 Lewis Mills.
Tries: Gay (16), Murphy (65), Bateman (71), Dallimore (74); **Goals:** Murphy 1/4.

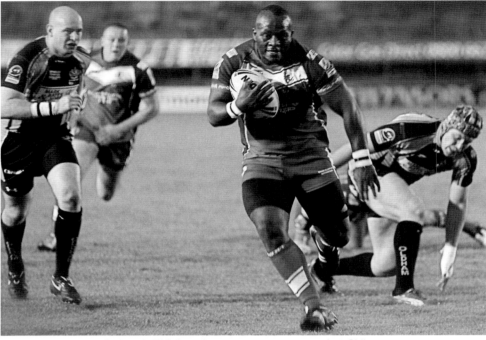

Swinton's Phil Joseph races away to score against Oldham

Rugby Leaguer & League Express Men of the Match:
Hornets: Paul Crook; *Scorpions:* Andrew Gay.
Half-time: 18-6; **Referee:** Dave Merrick; **Attendance:** 402.

WHITEHAVEN 40 OLDHAM 24

WHITEHAVEN: 1 Craig Benson; 31 Chris Fleming; 33 Max Wiper; 4 Scott McAvoy; 2 Craig Calvert; 32 Carl Rudd; 6 Lewis Palfrey; 8 David Ford; 14 Chris Smith; 15 Richard Farrer; 11 Spencer Miller; 35 Lee Doran; 17 Andrew Beattie. Subs (all used): 9 Carl Sice; 23 Paul Culnean; 10 Howard Hill; 26 Luke Isakka.
Tries: Calvert (5, 30), McAvoy (20), Smith (24, 32, 62), Culnean (68); **Goals:** Palfrey 6/9.
Sin bin: S Miller (50) - fighting.
OLDHAM: 1 Ben Heaton; 2 Lucas Onyango; 21 Mark Brocklehurst; 4 Jack Bradbury; 27 Shaun Robinson; 6 Neil Roden; 7 Carl Forber; 8 Jason Boults; 17 John Clough; 10 Dave Ellison; 12 Ben Wood; 24 Paul Noone; 25 Martin Roden. Subs (all used): 9 Danny Whitmore; 13 Valu Bentley; 28 Luke Stenchion; 15 Luke Sutton.
Tries: Ellison (9, 78), N Roden (27), Onyango (43);
Goals: Forber 4/4.
Dismissal: Boults (78) - dissent.
Sin bin: Clough (50) - fighting.
On report: Brocklehurst (49) - alleged dangerous tackle.
Rugby Leaguer & League Express Men of the Match:
Whitehaven: Chris Smith; *Oldham:* Dave Ellison.
Half-time: 24-12; **Referee:** Matthew Kidd;
Attendance: 946.

ROUND 8

Sunday 1st May 2011

GATESHEAD THUNDER 10 WHITEHAVEN 54

THUNDER: 17 Joe Brown; 43 Ashley Williams; 6 Mitchell Stevens; 4 Josh Stoker; 21 Matthew Harding; 26 Connor Condron; 7 Ryan Clarke; 20 Nick Staveley; 9 Tom Hodgson; 22 Chris Parker; 23 Jamie Love; 13 Michael Kelly; 31 Will Bate. Subs (all used): 12 Michael Ward; 15 Andy Morris; 8 Jason Payne; 32 Tabua Cakacaka.
Tries: Jason Payne (62), Harding (71); **Goals:** Clarke 1/2.
WHITEHAVEN: 1 Craig Benson; 5 Loz Hamzat; 3 Derry Eilbeck; 4 Scott McAvoy; 2 Craig Calvert; 6 Lewis Palfrey; 32 Carl Rudd; 15 Richard Farrer; 9 Carl Sice; 10 Howard Hill; 11 Spencer Miller; 35 Lee Doran; 17 Andrew Beattie. Subs (all used): 14 Chris Smith; 8 David Ford; 23 Paul Culnean; 19 Brad Crellin.
Tries: McAvoy (5), S Miller (8), Doran (16, 43), Rudd (20), Calvert (52), Sice (58), Smith (66), Eilbeck (74), Palfrey (79); **Goals:** Palfrey 7/10.
Rugby Leaguer & League Express Men of the Match:
Thunder: Joe Brown; *Whitehaven:* Lee Doran.
Penalty count: 8-4; **Half-time:** 0-20;
Referee: Matthew Kidd; **Attendance:** 237.

**KEIGHLEY COUGARS 46
SOUTH WALES SCORPIONS 26**

COUGARS: 7 Ryan Smith; 5 Gavin Duffy; 4 Danny Lawton; 22 Ben Sagar; 26 James Hutchinson; 29 Jason Demetriou; 6 Luke Helliwell; 8 Andy Shickell; 14 Jamaine Wray; 17 Ryan Benjafield; 23 Chris Baines; 21 Richard Jones; 13 Greg Nicholson. Subs (all used): 9 James Feather; 10 Scott Law; 20 Rick Barr; 25 Jamie Shepherd.
Tries: Jones (7), Hutchinson (18), Demetriou (21, 45), Duffy (23), Sagar (48), Feather (54), Smith (57);
Goals: Lawton 7/8.
SCORPIONS: 2 Lewis Reece; 5 Curtis Cunningham; 4 Ashley Bateman; 26 Lee Williams; 24 Dalton Grant; 1 Andrew Gay; 7 Casey Bromilow; 16 Joe Burke; 9 Steve Parry; 10 Paul Raftrey; 12 Loz Wildbore; 3 Christiaan Roets; 13 Aled James. Subs (all used): 14 Tom Burnell; 15 Neil Dallimore; 18 Chris Davies; 11 Lewis Mills.
Tries: James (12), Gay (15, 73), Williams (39), Grant (78); **Goals:** Reece 3/5.
Rugby Leaguer & League Express Men of the Match:
Cougars: Jason Demetriou; *Scorpions:* Andrew Gay.
Penalty count: 6-4; **Half-time:** 24-16;
Referee: Peter Brooke; **Attendance:** 558.

OLDHAM 46 DONCASTER 24

OLDHAM: 1 Ben Heaton; 21 Mark Brocklehurst; 24 Paul Noone; 12 Ben Wood; 5 John Gillam; 6 Neil Roden; 7 Carl Forber; 8 Jason Boults; 17 John Clough; 10 Dave Ellison; 14 Chris Clarke; 13 Valu Bentley; 25 Martin Roden. Subs (all used): 15 Luke Sutton; 9 Danny Whitmore; 28 Luke Stenchion; 20 Michael Ward.
Tries: Wood (4, 26), Clough (7), Noone (41), Forber (48), Brocklehurst (53), Heaton (60), Boults (68);
Goals: Forber 7/8.
DONCASTER: 7 Craig Fawcett; 5 Dean Colton; 25 Chris Spurr; 30 Nev Morrison; 2 Stewart Sanderson; 6 Aaron Dobek; 19 Scott Spaven; 17 Adam Scott; 21 Paul Hughes; 10 Liam Crawley; 15 Craig Robinson; 12 Ryan Steen; 16 Mike Emmett. Subs (all used): 9 Kyle Kesik; 13 Jack Ely; 22 Carl Hughes; 32 Craig Lawton.
Tries: Sanderson (11), Kesik (38), Colton (50), C Hughes (65), Spaven (80); **Goals:** Spaven 2/5.
Dismissal: Kesik (72) - fighting.
Rugby Leaguer & League Express Men of the Match:
Oldham: Ben Wood; *Doncaster:* Carl Hughes.
Penalty count: 5-4; **Half-time:** 16-10;
Referee: Clint Sharrad; **Attendance:** 580.

WORKINGTON TOWN 34 ROCHDALE HORNETS 38

TOWN: 1 Brett Carter; 4 Aaron Low; 3 Jason Mossop; 21 John Patrick; 5 Neil Frazer; 24 Darren Holt; 7 Scott Kaighan; 8 Marc Jackson; 9 Graeme Mattinson; 10 Kris Coward; 11 Mike Whitehead; 12 Jarrad Stack; 26 Darren King. Subs (all used): 14 Jack Pedley; 15 Ruairi McGoff; 28 Matthew Tunstall; 18 Joe McKenna.

Tries: Low (6, 72), King (10), Patrick (20, 41), Kaighan (63), Frazer (75); **Goals:** Holt 3/7.
HORNETS: 5 Scott Yates; 17 Dale Bloomfield; 4 Matthew Strong; 3 Dean Gorton; 25 Andy Saywell; 15 Paul Crook; 7 Steve Roper; 18 John Cookson; 11 Craig Ashall; 35 Richard Mervill; 8 Dave Newton; 10 Adam Bowman; 13 Dayne Donoghue. Subs (all used): 32 Danny Ekis; 9 Steve McDermott; 6 Liam McGovern; 1 Wayne English.
Tries: Crook (8), Yates (14), McDermott (23), Cookson (35), English (79); **Goals:** Crook 9/9.
Rugby Leaguer & League Express Men of the Match:
Town: John Patrick; *Hornets:* Paul Crook.
Penalty count: 7-5; **Half-time:** 16-26;
Referee: Warren Turley; **Attendance:** 443.

ROUND 9

Sunday 15th May 2011

LONDON SKOLARS 12 WORKINGTON TOWN 33

SKOLARS: 31 Jack Latus; 18 Aaron Small; 36 John Paxton; 17 Dave Arnot; 5 Ade Adebisi; 7 Dylan Skee; 3 James Anthony; 29 Michael Sykes; 9 Gareth Honor; 10 Jason Hart; 35 Ben Bolger; 15 Oliver Purslow; 34 Lamont Bryan. Subs (all used): 32 Sam Gee; 22 Saqib Murtza; 25 Austen Aggrey; 33 Dave Williams.
Tries: Anthony (25), Adebisi (30); **Goals:** Skee 2/2.
TOWN: 1 Brett Carter; 2 Elliott Miller; 3 Jason Mossop; 21 John Patrick; 5 Neil Frazer; 24 Darren Holt; 7 Scott Kaighan; 16 Ryan McDonald; 14 Jack Pedley; 10 Kris Coward; 11 Mike Whitehead; 12 Jarrad Stack; 26 Darren King. Subs (all used): 4 Aaron Low; 15 Ruairi McGoff; 19 Marc Shackley; 17 James Robinson.
Tries: Kaighan (11), Whitehead (34), King (41), Miller (47), Stack (80); **Goals:** Holt 6/7; **Field goal:** Holt (73).
Rugby Leaguer & League Express Men of the Match:
Skolars: Lamont Bryan; *Town:* Darren Holt.
Penalty count: 7-7; **Half-time:** 12-12;
Referee: Chris Leatherbarrow; **Attendance:** 397.

DONCASTER 20 KEIGHLEY COUGARS 24

DONCASTER: 1 Mick Butterfield; 2 Stewart Sanderson; 25 Chris Spurr; 32 Craig Lawton; 5 Dean Colton; 6 Aaron Dobek; 19 Scott Spaven; 17 Adam Scott; 13 Jack Ely; 10 Liam Crawley; 31 Richard Tafa; 8 Matt Carbutt; 16 Mike Emmett. Subs (all used): 9 Kyle Kesik; 22 Carl Hughes; 26 Dominic Dee; 11 Kyle Sampson.
Tries: Sanderson (3), Kesik (31), Colton (36), Ely (64);
Goals: Spaven 2/4.
COUGARS: 5 Gavin Duffy; 22 Ben Sagar; 18 James Haythornthwaite; 23 Chris Baines; 26 James Hutchinson; 29 Jason Demetriou; 7 Ryan Smith; 8 Andy Shickell; 9 James Feather; 17 Ryan Benjafield; 11 Will Cartledge; 12 Oliver Pursglove; 25 Jamie Shepherd. Subs (all used): 10 Scott Law; 13 Greg Nicholson; 14 Jamaine Wray; 16 Brendan Rawlins.

Tries: Sagar (10), Smith (43), Hutchinson (47), Demetriou (78); **Goals:** Baines 4/5.
Rugby Leaguer & League Express Men of the Match: *Doncaster:* Matt Carbutt; *Cougars:* Jason Demetriou.
Penalty count: 8-8; **Half-time:** 14-4;
Referee: Warren Turley; **Attendance:** 549.

ROCHDALE HORNETS 68 GATESHEAD THUNDER 0

HORNETS: 5 Scott Yates; 2 Craig Johnson; 3 Dean Gorton; 17 Dale Bloomfield; 25 Andy Saywell; 15 Paul Crook; 7 Steve Roper; 18 John Cookson; 6 Liam McGovern; 10 Adam Bowman; 16 Danny Samuel; 13 Dayne Donoghue; 11 Craig Ashall. Subs (all used): 35 Richard Mervill; 36 Mike Stewart; 21 Mark Hobson; 28 Chris Hough.
Tries: Roper (2), Gorton (7, 17, 79), Bloomfield (11), Crook (22), Hough (31), Johnson (62), Ashall (68), Hobson (75), Saywell (77), McGovern (80);
Goals: Crook 10/12.
THUNDER: 34 Mitchell Stevens; 6 Ashley Williams; 15 Andy Morris; 4 Josh Stoker; 17 Joe Brown; 26 Connor Condron; 7 Ryan Clarke; 20 Nick Staveley; 9 Tom Hodgson; 22 Chris Parker; 33 Jonny Payne; 13 Michael Kelly; 31 Will Bate. Subs (all used): 5 Dan O'Sullivan; 8 Jason Payne; 10 Stephen Welton; 32 Tabua Cakacaka.
Dismissal: Staveley (62) – head-butt.
Rugby Leaguer & League Express Men of the Match: *Hornets:* Steve Roper; *Thunder:* Will Bate.
Penalty count: 8-3; **Half-time:** 34-0;
Referee: Peter Brooke; **Attendance:** 504.

SOUTH WALES SCORPIONS 40 OLDHAM 20

SCORPIONS: 27 Jamie Murphy; 5 Curtis Cunningham; 4 Ashley Bateman; 26 Lee Williams; 24 Dalton Grant; 1 Andrew Gay; 7 Casey Bromilow; 10 Paul Raftrey; 9 Steve Parry; 16 Joe Burke; 12 Loz Wildbore; 11 Craig Ashall; 3 Christiaan Roets. Subs (all used): 14 Tom Burnell; 15 Neil Dallimore; 28 Chris Clough; 18 Chris Davies.
Tries: Parry (7), Dallimore (23), Murphy (35), Bromilow (39), Cunningham (54), Gay (71), Wildbore (74); **Goals:** Murphy 3/4, Bromilow 3/3.
OLDHAM: 1 Ben Heaton; 26 Matthew Fogerty; 12 Ben Wood; 29 Mick Fogerty; 27 Shaun Robinson; 6 Neil Roden; 7 Carl Forber; 8 Jason Boults; 17 John Clough; 10 Dave Ellison; 24 Paul Noone; 14 Chris Clarke; 25 Martin Roden. Subs (all used): 28 Luke Stenchion; 16 Liam Gilchrist; 13 Valu Bentley; 11 Andrew Isherwood.
Tries: Clough (12), Fogerty (31), Robinson (76), Heaton (79); **Goals:** Forber 2/4.
Rugby Leaguer & League Express Men of the Match: *Scorpions:* Curtis Cunningham; *Oldham:* Neil Roden.
Penalty count: 4-7; **Half-time:** 22-10; **Referee:** Clint Sharrad; **Attendance:** 420 *(at Virginia Park, Caerphilly)*.

WHITEHAVEN 22 SWINTON LIONS 22

WHITEHAVEN: 3 Derry Eilbeck; 5 Loz Hamzat; 33 Max Wiper; 4 Scott McAvoy; 2 Craig Calvert; 6 Lewis Palfrey; 32 Carl Rudd; 10 Howard Hill; 9 Carl Sice; 26 Luke Isakka; 11 Spencer Miller; 35 Lee Doran; 17 Andrew Beattie. Subs (all used): 21 Tyrone Dalton; 23 Paul Culnean; 8 David Ford; 18 Kurt Wilton.
Tries: Palfrey (19), Beattie (45), Hamzat (69), Calvert (74); **Goals:** Palfrey 3/5.
LIONS: 21 Ian Mort; 2 Rob Foxen; 3 Gavin Dodd; 4 Dean Thompson; 20 Richard Flooks; 7 Ian Watson; 6 Martin Ainscough; 8 Mike Morrison; 9 Mark Smith; 12 Lee Wingfield; 15 Darren Hawkyard; 11 Dale Cunniffe; 13 Phil Joseph. Subs (all used): 39 Warren Thompson; 25 Karl Ashall; 10 Dana Wilson; 16 Neil Holland.
Tries: Foxen (26), Ainscough (31), Mort (33, 60);
Goals: Mort 3/4.
Rugby Leaguer & League Express Men of the Match: *Whitehaven:* Lee Doran; *Lions:* Karl Ashall.
Penalty count: 5-7; **Half-time:** 8-18;
Referee: George Stokes; **Attendance:** 917.

ROUND 10

Sunday 22nd May 2011

GATESHEAD THUNDER 32 SOUTH WALES SCORPIONS 66

THUNDER: 17 Joe Brown; 5 Dan O'Sullivan; 4 Josh Stoker; 15 Andy Morris; 6 Ashley Williams; 26 Connor Condron; 7 Ryan Clarke; 22 Chris Parker; 9 Tom Hodgson; 32 Tabua Cakacaka; 29 David Cash; 39 Jonny Payne; 31 Will Bate. Subs (all used): 10 Stephen Welton; 14 Reece Young; 13 Michael Kelly; 11 Gary Sargeant.
Tries: Welton (25, 50), Cash (62, 79), Hodgson (64), Williams (75); **Goals:** Clarke 4/6.
SCORPIONS: 2 Lewis Reece; 5 Curtis Cunningham; 4 Ashley Bateman; 26 Lee Williams; 24 Dalton Grant; 1 Andrew Gay; 7 Casey Bromilow; 16 Joe Burke; 9 Steve Parry; 10 Paul Raftrey; 12 Loz Wildbore; 21 Rhodri Lloyd; 3 Christiaan Roets. Subs (all used): 14 Tom Burnell; 20 Hywel Davies; 22 Bradley Hill; 15 Neil Dallimore.
Tries: Grant (2, 6, 16, 68), Cunningham (13, 45), Bromilow (29), Reece (38), Roets (42), Parry (56), Wildbore (70), Burnell (80); **Goals:** Reece 9/12.
Rugby Leaguer & League Express Men of the Match: *Thunder:* Tom Hodgson; *Scorpions:* Dalton Grant.
Penalty count: 8-5; **Half-time:** 4-32;
Referee: Matthew Kidd; **Attendance:** 162.

Friday 27th May 2011

SWINTON LIONS 18 OLDHAM 16

LIONS: 21 Ian Mort; 2 Rob Foxen; 3 Gavin Dodd; 4 Dean Thompson; 23 Alex Hurst; 7 Ian Watson; 6 Martin Ainscough; 8 Mike Morrison; 9 Mark Smith; 12 Lee Wingfield; 15 Darren Hawkyard; 11 Dale Cunniffe; 13 Phil Joseph. Subs (all used): 25 Karl Ashall; 16 Neil Holland; 39 Warren Thompson; 10 Dana Wilson.
Tries: Foxen (20), Ainscough (26), Joseph (69);
Goals: Mort 3/3.
OLDHAM: 1 Ben Heaton; 21 Mark Brocklehurst; 26 Matthew Fogerty; 12 Ben Wood; 27 Shaun Robinson; 6 Neil Roden; 9 Danny Whitmore; 10 Dave Ellison; 25 Martin Roden; 16 Liam Gilchrist; 11 Andrew Isherwood; 14 Chris Clarke; 24 Paul Noone. Subs (all used): 28 Luke Stenchion; 15 Luke Sutton; 13 Valu Bentley; 17 John Clough.
Tries: Noone (31), Stenchion (35), Clarke (46);
Goals: Noone 2/3.
Rugby Leaguer & League Express Men of the Match: *Lions:* Phil Joseph; *Oldham:* Neil Roden.
Penalty count: 8-7; **Half-time:** 12-10;
Referee: Warren Turley; **Attendance:** 674.

Sunday 29th May 2011

KEIGHLEY COUGARS 14 WHITEHAVEN 18

COUGARS: 18 James Haythornthwaite; 5 Gavin Duffy; 4 Danny Lawton; 22 Ben Sagar; 26 James Hutchinson; 29 Jason Demetriou; 6 Luke Helliwell; 8 Andy Shickell; 9 James Feather; 17 Ryan Benjafield; 11 Will Cartledge; 12 Oliver Pursglove; 21 Richard Jones. Subs (all used): 10 Scott Law; 14 Jamaine Wray; 16 Brendan Rawlins; 23 Chris Baines.
Tries: Benjafield (12), Lawton (55), Shickell (66);
Goals: Lawton 1/3.
WHITEHAVEN: 38 Andreas Bauer; 5 Loz Hamzat; 33 Max Wiper; 4 Scott McAvoy; 2 Craig Calvert; 6 Lewis Palfrey; 32 Carl Rudd; 10 Howard Hill; 14 Chris Smith; 26 Luke Isakka; 35 Lee Doran; 11 Spencer Miller; 17 Andrew Beattie. Subs (all used): 9 Carl Sice; 23 Paul Culnean; 8 David Ford; 18 Kurt Wilton.
Tries: Wiper (5), Culnean (34), Sice (80);
Goals: Palfrey 3/3.
On report: Doran (32) - alleged grapple tackle.
Rugby Leaguer & League Express Men of the Match: *Cougars:* Andy Shickell; *Whitehaven:* Lee Doran.
Penalty count: 9-7; **Half-time:** 4-12;
Referee: Chris Leatherbarrow; **Attendance:** 754.

LONDON SKOLARS 44 ROCHDALE HORNETS 22

SKOLARS: 3 James Anthony; 18 Aaron Small; 30 Michael Brown; 17 Dave Arnot; 5 Ade Adebisi; 6 Jy-Mel Coleman; 7 Dylan Skee; 25 Austen Aggrey; 9 Gareth Honor; 22 Saqib Murtza; 37 Jaroslaw Obuchowski; 15 Oliver Purslow; 35 Lamont Bryan. Subs (all used): 32 Sam Gee; 36 John Paxton; 29 Michael Sykes; 31 Dave Williams.
Tries: Adebisi (16), Bryan (31, 34), Aggrey (59), Skee (67, 80), Honor (77); **Goals:** Skee 8/8.
HORNETS: 5 Scott Yates; 2 Craig Johnson; 3 Dean Gorton; 17 Dale Bloomfield; 25 Andy Saywell; 15 Paul Crook; 7 Steve Roper; 18 John Cookson; 6 Liam McGovern; 8 Dave Newton; 10 Adam Bowman; 13 Dayne Donoghue; 11 Craig Ashall. Subs (all used): 32 Danny Ekis; 35 Richard Mervill; 21 Mark Hobson; 4 Matthew Strong.
Tries: Saywell (10), Mervill (28), Ashall (54), Yates (57);
Goals: Crook 3/4.
Dismissal: Mervill (79) - high tackle.
Rugby Leaguer & League Express Men of the Match: *Skolars:* Dylan Skee; *Hornets:* Craig Ashall.
Penalty count: 6-7; **Half-time:** 18-10;
Referee: Craig Halloran; **Attendance:** 290.

WORKINGTON TOWN 32 DONCASTER 34

TOWN: 1 Brett Carter; 2 Elliott Miller; 3 Jason Mossop; 4 Aaron Low; 5 Neil Frazer; 24 Darren Holt; 7 Scott Kaighan; 16 Ryan McDonald; 9 Graeme Mattinson; 10 Kris Coward; 11 Mike Whitehead; 19 Marc Shackley; 12 Jarrad Stack. Subs (all used): 14 Jack Pedley; 15 Ruairi McGoff; 6 Liam Finch; 29 Dave Armitstead.
Tries: Kaighan (13, 42), Pedley (34), Stack (39, 42);
Goals: Holt 6/6.
DONCASTER: 5 Dean Colton; 30 Gareth Potts; 29 Chris Green; 25 Chris Spurr; 2 Stewart Sanderson; 6 Aaron Dobek; 7 Craig Fawcett; 17 Adam Scott; 13 Jack Ely; 10 Liam Crawley; 8 Matt Carbutt; 15 Craig Robinson; 16 Mike Emmett. Subs: 9 Kyle Kesik; 11 Kyle Sampson; 26 Dominic Dee; 23 Grant Edwards (not used).
Tries: Potts (16, 26), Sanderson (20, 66), Ely (61), Green (73, 80); **Goals:** Dobek 3/6, Sanderson 0/2.
Rugby Leaguer & League Express Men of the Match: *Town:* Jarrad Stack; *Doncaster:* Chris Green.
Penalty count: 8-6; **Half-time:** 18-16;
Referee: Dave Merrick; **Attendance:** 544.

ROUND 11

Sunday 5th June 2011

SOUTH WALES SCORPIONS 28 WORKINGTON TOWN 46

SCORPIONS: 27 Jamie Murphy; 5 Curtis Cunningham; 4 Ashley Bateman; 2 Lewis Reece; 24 Dalton Grant; 1 Andrew Gay; 7 Casey Bromilow; 16 Joe Burke; 9 Steve Parry; 10 Paul Raftrey; 12 Loz Wildbore; 21 Rhodri Lloyd; 3 Christiaan Roets. Subs (all used): 14 Tom Burnell; 15 Neil Dallimore; 28 Chris Clough; 17 Harri Greville.
Tries: Roets (15), Parry (32, 55), Reece (39), Grant (50); **Goals:** Reece 4/5.
TOWN: 1 Brett Carter; 2 Elliott Miller; 3 Jason Mossop; 4 Aaron Low; 5 Neil Frazer; 23 Marc Bainbridge; 24 Darren Holt; 16 Ryan McDonald; 14 Jack Pedley; 10 Kris Coward; 11 Mike Whitehead; 29 Dave Armitstead; 12 Jarrad Stack. Subs (all used): 15 Ruairi McGoff; 20 Stephen Dawes; 17 James Robinson; 18 Joe McKenna.
Tries: Low (11), Stack (21), Armitstead (27), Frazer (42), Pedley (62), Coward (65, 79), Carter (68), Mossop (71); **Goals:** Holt 5/9.
Rugby Leaguer & League Express Men of the Match: *Scorpions:* Steve Parry; *Town:* Kris Coward.
Penalty count: 2-6; **Half-time:** 16-16;
Referee: Chris Leatherbarrow; **Attendance:** 403 *(at Virginia Park, Caerphilly)*.

WHITEHAVEN 14 LONDON SKOLARS 12

WHITEHAVEN: 38 Andreas Bauer; 5 Loz Hamzat; 33 Max Wiper; 3 Derry Eilbeck; 2 Craig Calvert; 6 Lewis Palfrey; 32 Carl Rudd; 10 Howard Hill; 14 Chris Smith; 34 Matthew Haggerty; 4 Scott McAvoy; 35 Lee Doran; 17 Andrew Beattie. Subs (all used): 9 Carl Sice; 23 Paul Culnean; 26 Luke Isakka; 22 Reece Fox.
Tries: Smith (3), McAvoy (42), Hamzat (72);
Goals: Palfrey 1/3.
SKOLARS: 3 James Anthony; 18 Aaron Small; 35 Michael Brown; 17 Dave Arnot; 5 Ade Adebisi; 6 Jy-Mel Coleman; 7 Dylan Skee; 25 Austen Aggrey; 9 Gareth Honor; 22 Saqib Murtza; 37 Jaroslaw Obuchowski; 15 Oliver Purslow; 19 Jermaine Coleman. Subs (all used): 32 Sam Gee; 27 Cariern Clement-Pascall; 8 Tony Williams; 13 Stephen Ball.
Tries: Aggrey (18), Anthony (63);
Goals: Jy-Mel Coleman 1/1, Skee 1/1.
Rugby Leaguer & League Express Men of the Match: *Whitehaven:* Andreas Bauer; *Skolars:* Austen Aggrey.
Penalty count: 10-5; **Half-time:** 6-6;
Referee: George Stokes; **Attendance:** 716.

DONCASTER 30 OLDHAM 0

DONCASTER: 1 Mick Butterfield; 30 Gareth Potts; 24 Craig Lawton; 25 Chris Spurr; 5 Dean Colton; 19 Scott Spaven; 7 Craig Fawcett; 17 Adam Scott; 13 Jack Ely; 10 Liam Crawley; 15 Craig Robinson; 8 Matt Carbutt; 16 Mike Emmett. Subs (all used): 9 Kyle Kesik; 20 Jamie Bovill; 23 Grant Edwards; 26 Dominic Dee.
Tries: Spaven (15), Spurr (22, 76, 79), Colton (56);
Goals: Spaven 5/5.
OLDHAM: 1 Ben Heaton; 21 Mark Brocklehurst; 3 Marcus St Hilaire; 12 Ben Wood; 27 Shaun Robinson; 6 Neil Roden; 7 Carl Forber; 8 Jason Boults; 17 John Clough; 10 Dave Ellison; 11 Andrew Isherwood; 24 Paul Noone; 25 Martin Roden. Subs (all used): 15 Luke Sutton; 28 Luke Stenchion; 13 Valu Bentley; 9 Danny Whitmore.
Rugby Leaguer & League Express Men of the Match: *Doncaster:* Chris Spurr; *Oldham:* John Clough.
Penalty count: 9-3; **Half-time:** 12-0;
Referee: Craig Halloran; **Attendance:** 617.

GATESHEAD THUNDER 16 SWINTON LIONS 62

THUNDER: 43 Michael Ellis; 23 Jonny Shields; 13 Michael Kelly; 17 Joe Brown; 6 Ashley Williams; 7 Ryan Clarke; 31 Will Bate; 39 Tabua Cakacaka; 9 Tom Hodgson; 22 Chris Parker; 4 Josh Stoker; 29 David Cash; 11 Gary Sargeant. Subs (all used): 14 Reece Young; 10 Stephen Welton; 42 Oliver O'Mara; 41 Joe Causer.
Tries: Shields (25), Kelly (46), Causer (72);
Goals: Clarke 2/3.
LIONS: 21 Ian Mort; 2 Rob Foxen; 3 Gavin Dodd; 23 Alex Hurst; 20 Richard Flooks; 6 Martin Ainscough; 7 Ian Watson; 8 Mike Morrison; 9 Mark Smith; 12 Lee Wingfield; 19 Neil Rigby; 15 Darren Hawkyard; 13 Phil Joseph. Subs (all used): 25 Karl Ashall; 10 Dana Wilson; 38 Warren Thompson; 39 Danny Meekin.
Tries: Mort (9, 14), Flooks (29, 56, 63), D Hawkyard (40), W Thompson (41), Wilson (50), Dodd (53), Hurst (67), Ashall (79); **Goals:** Mort 9/11.
Rugby Leaguer & League Express Men of the Match: *Thunder:* Josh Stoker; *Lions:* Phil Joseph.
Penalty count: 11-8; **Half-time:** 4-22;
Referee: Dave Merrick; **Attendance:** 252.

KEIGHLEY COUGARS 30 ROCHDALE HORNETS 31

COUGARS: 18 James Haythornthwaite; 5 Gavin Duffy; 4 Danny Lawton; 22 Ben Sagar; 26 James Hutchinson; 29 Jason Demetriou; 6 Luke Helliwell; 8 Andy Shickell; 9 James Feather; 16 Brendan Rawlins; 23 Chris Baines; 12 Oliver Pursglove; 21 Richard Jones. Subs (all used): 17 Ryan Benjafield; 20 Rick Barr; 7 Ryan Smith; 11 Will Cartledge.
Tries: Helliwell (13), Haythornthwaite (23), Cartledge (29), Hutchinson (62), Jones (65); **Goals:** Lawton 5/5.
Sin bin: Demetriou (78) - fighting.
HORNETS: 5 Scott Yates; 2 Craig Johnson; 3 Dean Gorton; 17 Dale Bloomfield; 25 Andy Saywell; 15 Paul Crook; 7 Steve Roper; 18 John Cookson; 6 Liam McGovern; 16 Danny Samuel; 21 Mark Hobson; 13 Dayne Donoghue; 11 Craig Ashall. Subs (all used): 8 Dave Newton; 10 Adam Bowman; 28 Chris Hough; 4 Matthew Strong.
Tries: Roper (10), Johnson (20), Ashall (51), Hough (70), Yates (72);
Goals: Crook 5/5; **Field goal:** Crook (75).
Sin bin: Bowman (78) - fighting.
On report: Ashall (28) - alleged high tackle.
Rugby Leaguer & League Express Men of the Match: *Cougars:* Luke Helliwell; *Hornets:* John Cookson.
Penalty count: 6-8; **Half-time:** 18-12;
Referee: Gareth Hewer; **Attendance:** 690.

ROUND 12

Sunday 12th June 2011

LONDON SKOLARS 18 KEIGHLEY COUGARS 16

SKOLARS: 3 James Anthony; 18 Aaron Small; 30 Michael Brown; 17 Dave Arnot; 5 Ade Adebisi; 7 Dylan

Skee; 6 Jy-Mel Coleman; 25 Austen Aggrey; 9 Gareth Honor; 13 Stephen Ball; 37 Jaroslaw Obuchowski; 31 Ben Bolger; 15 Oliver Purslow. Subs (all used): 27 Cariern Clement-Pascall; 8 Tony Williams; 32 Sam Gee; 35 Will Colleran.
Tries: Obuchowski (20), Bolger (43), Adebisi (68); **Goals:** Skee 3/5.
COUGARS: 18 James Haythornthwaite; 5 Gavin Duffy; 4 Danny Lawton; 23 Chris Baines; 26 James Hutchinson; 29 Jason Demetriou; 6 Luke Helliwell; 17 Ryan Benjafield; 9 James Feather; 10 Scott Law; 11 Will Cartledge; 12 Oliver Pursglove; 22 Ben Sagar. Subs (all used): 7 Ryan Smith; 14 Jamaine Wray; 16 Brendan Rawlins; 21 Richard Jones.
Tries: Demetriou (50), Wray (58), Benjafield (64); **Goals:** Lawton 2/3.
Rugby Leaguer & League Express Men of the Match: *Skolars:* James Anthony; *Cougars:* Scott Law.
Penalty count: 8-9; **Half-time:** 8-0; **Referee:** Matthew Kidd; **Attendance:** 327.

OLDHAM 35 SOUTH WALES SCORPIONS 18

OLDHAM: 1 Ben Heaton; 21 Mark Brocklehurst; 3 Marcus St Hilaire; 29 Mark McCully; 27 Shaun Robinson; 7 Carl Forber; 30 Jamie Dallimore; 8 Jason Boults; 25 Martin Roden; 28 Luke Stenchion; 11 Andrew Isherwood; 12 Ben Wood; 24 Paul Noone. Subs (all used): 15 Luke Sutton; 17 John Clough; 10 Dave Ellison; 13 Valu Bentley.
Tries: Dallimore (21, 24), Heaton (30, 68), Wood (58), St Hilaire (65); **Goals:** Forber 5/6; **Field goal:** Dallimore (80).
SCORPIONS: 27 Jamie Murphy; 26 Lee Williams; 4 Ashley Bateman; 2 Lewis Reece; 24 Dalton Grant; 1 Andrew Gay; 7 Casey Bromilow; 16 Joe Burke; 9 Steve Parry; 10 Paul Raftrey; 21 Rhodri Lloyd; 3 Christiaan Roets; 12 Loz Wildbore. Subs (all used): 5 Curtis Cunningham; 15 Neil Dallimore; 28 Chris Clough; 17 Harri Greville.
Tries: Parry (2), Dallimore (26), Murphy (55); **Goals:** Reece 3/3.
Rugby Leaguer & League Express Men of the Match: *Oldham:* Jamie Dallimore; *Scorpions:* Steve Parry.
Penalty count: 6-6; **Half-time:** 18-12; **Referee:** Dave Merrick; **Attendance:** 514.

WORKINGTON TOWN 84 GATESHEAD THUNDER 12

TOWN: 1 Brett Carter; 2 Elliott Miller; 3 Jason Mossop; 4 Aaron Low; 20 Stephen Dawes; 7 Scott Kaighan; 24 Darren Holt; 16 Ryan McDonald; 14 Jack Pedley; 10 Kris Coward; 29 Dave Armitstead; 12 Jarrad Stack; 13 Karl Olstrum. Subs (all used): 23 Marc Bainbridge; 15 Ruairi McGoff; 18 Joe McKenna; 25 Keiron McAvoy.
Tries: Kaighan (3, 26), Dawes (6, 59, 77), Low (11, 56), Miller (19, 29, 53, 67), McDonald (71), Bainbridge (75), McKenna (80); **Goals:** Holt 14/14.
Sin bin: Kaighan (50) - fighting.
On report: Brawl (50).
THUNDER: 34 Mitchell Stevens; 15 Andy Morris; 17 Joe Brown; 13 Michael Kelly; 6 Ashley Williams; 7 Ryan Clarke; 31 Will Bate; 10 Stephen Welton; 14 Reece Young; 39 Tabua Cakacaka; 42 Oliver O'Mara; 29 David Cash; 5 Dan O'Sullivan. Subs (all used): 32 Ade Aderiye; 4 Josh Stoker; 43 Michael Ellis; 22 Chris Parker.
Tries: Bate (36), Welton (39); **Goals:** Clarke 2/2.
Dismissal: Stevens (50) - dissent.
Sin bin: Stevens (50) - fighting.
On report: Brawl (50).
Rugby Leaguer & League Express Men of the Match: *Town:* Darren Holt; *Thunder:* Ryan Clarke.
Penalty count: 9-9; **Half-time:** 36-12; **Referee:** Peter Brooke; **Attendance:** 384.

ROUND 6

Sunday 19th June 2011

GATESHEAD THUNDER 6 DONCASTER 22

THUNDER: 34 Mitchell Stevens; 6 Ashley Williams; 17 Joe Brown; 40 Mike Mitchell; 3 Danny Wilson; 31 Will Bate; 7 Ryan Clarke; 39 Tabua Cakacaka; 14 Reece Young; 8 Jason Payne; 13 Michael Kelly; 29 David Cash; 42 Oliver O'Mara. Subs (all used): 10 Stephen Welton; 22 Chris Parker; 4 Josh Stoker; 16 Robin Peers.
Try: Wilson (12); **Goals:** Clarke 1/2.
DONCASTER: 1 Mick Butterfield; 2 Stewart Sanderson; 30 Michael Coady; 31 Nev Morrison; 33 Gareth Potts; 19 Scott Spaven; 7 Craig Fawcett; 10 Liam Crawley; 16 Mike Emmett; 11 Kyle Sampson; 15 Craig Robinson; 25 Chris Spurr; 23 Grant Edwards. Subs (all used): 9 Kyle Kesik; 22 Carl Hughes; 17 Adam Scott; 8 Matt Carbutt.
Tries: Spaven (6), Spurr (49), Coady (69), Morrison (80); **Goals:** Spaven 3/4.
Rugby Leaguer & League Express Men of the Match: *Thunder:* Will Bate; *Doncaster:* Scott Spaven.
Penalty count: 9-13; **Half-time:** 6-6; **Referee:** Matthew Kidd; **Attendance:** 256.

ROUND 13

Friday 24th June 2011

SWINTON LIONS 22 ROCHDALE HORNETS 20

LIONS: 21 Ian Mort; 20 Richard Flooks; 4 Dean Thompson; 3 Gavin Dodd; 2 Rob Foxen; 6 Martin Ainscough; 7 Ian Watson; 38 Warren Thompson; 9 Mark Smith; 12 Lee Wingfield; 11 Dale Cunniffe; 15 Darren Hawkyard; 13 Phil Joseph. Subs (all used): 25 Karl Ashall; 10 Dana Wilson; 16 Neil Holland; 14 Tommy Gallagher.
Tries: Dodd (38), Cunniffe (50), Foxen (63), Joseph (72); **Goals:** Mort 3/4.
HORNETS: 5 Scott Yates; 2 Craig Johnson; 17 Dale Bloomfield; 4 Matthew Strong; 25 Andy Saywell; 15 Paul Crook; 6 Liam McGovern; 18 John Cookson; 11 Craig Ashall; 10 Adam Bowman; 16 Danny Samuel; 21 Mark Hobson; 13 Dayne Donoghue. Subs (all used): 28 Chris Hough; 35 Richard Mervill; 8 Dave Newton; 7 Steve Roper.
Tries: Ashall (4), Saywell (7, 67), McGovern (28); **Goals:** Crook 2/4.
Rugby Leaguer & League Express Men of the Match: *Lions:* Phil Joseph; *Hornets:* Liam McGovern.
Penalty count: 9-7; **Half-time:** 6-14; **Referee:** Warren Turley; **Attendance:** 586.

Sunday 26th June 2011

DONCASTER 40 LONDON SKOLARS 22

DONCASTER: 1 Mick Butterfield; 5 Dean Colton; 30 Michael Coady; 31 Nev Morrison; 2 Stewart Sanderson; 7 Craig Fawcett; 19 Scott Spaven; 17 Adam Scott; 13 Jack Ely; 26 Dominic Dee; 25 Chris Spurr; 24 Craig Lawton; 23 Grant Edwards. Subs (all used): 9 Kyle Kesik; 15 Craig Robinson; 22 Carl Hughes; 8 Matt Carbutt.
Tries: Morrison (11, 64), Ely (17), Robinson (35), Dee (55), Spurr (66), C Hughes (71); **Goals:** Spaven 6/7.
SKOLARS: 3 James Anthony; 18 Aaron Small; 33 Michael Brown; 35 Will Colleran; 5 Ade Adebisi; 30 Mourad Kriouache; 7 Dylan Skee; 25 Austen Aggrey; 9 Gareth Honor; 40 Dave Williams; 37 Jaroslaw Obuchowski; 31 Ben Bolger; 15 Oliver Purslow. Subs (all used): 27 Cariern Clement-Pascall; 34 Rob Thomas; 32 Sam Gee; 20 Guy Aldam.
Tries: Anthony (5), Kriouache (22), D Williams (45), Bolger (75); **Goals:** Skee 3/4.
Rugby Leaguer & League Express Men of the Match: *Doncaster:* Nev Morrison; *Skolars:* James Anthony.
Penalty count: 11-6; **Half-time:** 18-10; **Referee:** Craig Halloran; **Attendance:** 456.

GATESHEAD THUNDER 16 OLDHAM 52

THUNDER: 3 Danny Wilson; 16 Robin Peers; 40 Mike Mitchell; 17 Joe Brown; 23 Jonny Shields; 31 Will Bate; 7 Ryan Clarke; 39 Tabua Cakacaka; 9 Tom Hodgson; 22 Chris Parker; 13 Michael Kelly; 42 Oliver O'Mara; 8 Jason Payne. Subs (all used): 14 Reece Young; 10 Stephen Welton; 36 Clarke Thompson; 32 Ade Aderiye.
Tries: Brown (8), Shields (73), Clarke (77); **Goals:** Clarke 2/3.
OLDHAM: 1 Ben Heaton; 21 Mark Brocklehurst; 26 Matthew Fogarty; 29 Mark McCully; 27 Shaun Robinson; 6 Neil Roden; 7 Carl Forber; 8 Jason Boults; 25 Martin Roden; 28 Luke Stenchion; 30 Danny Bravo; 11 Andrew Isherwood; 24 Paul Noone. Subs (all used): 10 Dave Ellison; 23 Callum Casey; 17 John Clough; 15 Luke Sutton.
Tries: Fogarty (13, 36), Isherwood (23), Sutton (26), Clough (29, 45), Brocklehurst (55, 57), Forber (49, 80); **Goals:** Forber 6/10.
Rugby Leaguer & League Express Men of the Match: *Thunder:* Jonny Shields; *Oldham:* Dave Ellison.
Penalty count: 3-2; **Half-time:** 6-28; **Referee:** George Stokes; **Attendance:** 436.

SOUTH WALES SCORPIONS 32 KEIGHLEY COUGARS 24

SCORPIONS: 27 Jamie Murphy; 24 Dalton Grant; 19 Tom Philip; 4 Ashley Bateman; 5 Curtis Cunningham; 1 Andrew Gay; 7 Casey Bromilow; 16 Joe Burke; 9 Steve Parry; 10 Paul Raftrey; 3 Christiaan Roets; 21 Rhodri Lloyd; 12 Loz Wildbore. Subs (all used): 2 Lewis Reece; 15 Neil Dallimore; 28 Chris Clough; 18 Chris Davies.
Tries: Parry (8), Roets (13), Grant (16), Gay (32), Bromilow (50), Murphy (62); **Goals:** Murphy 1/3, Wildbore 1/1, Reece 2/3.
COUGARS: 18 James Haythornthwaite; 26 James Hutchinson; 4 Danny Lawton; 33 Jake Normington; 32 George Elliott; 29 Jason Demetriou; 6 Luke Helliwell; 8 Andy Shickell; 9 James Feather; 10 Scott Law; 11 Will Cartledge; 12 Oliver Pursglove; 22 Ben Sagar. Subs (all used): 36 Jy-Mel Coleman; 21 Richard Jones; 16 Brendan Rawlins; 17 Ryan Benjafield.
Tries: Elliott (5), Hutchinson (47), Sagar (51), Demetriou (54), Benjafield (70); **Goals:** Lawton 2/5.
Rugby Leaguer & League Express Men of the Match: *Scorpions:* Jamie Murphy; *Cougars:* Jason Demetriou.
Penalty count: 7-7; **Half-time:** 22-4; **Referee:** Peter Brooke; **Attendance:** 505 *(at Virginia Park, Caerphilly).*

WHITEHAVEN 22 WORKINGTON TOWN 10

WHITEHAVEN: 1 Craig Benson; 5 Loz Hamzat; 33 Max Wiper; 4 Scott McAvoy; 2 Craig Calvert; 6 Lewis Palfrey; 32 Carl Rudd; 10 Howard Hill; 14 Chris Smith; 34 Matthew Haggerty; 11 Spencer Miller; 35 Lee Doran; 17 Andrew Beattie. Subs (all used): 9 Carl Sice; 23 Paul Culnean; 26 Luke Isakka; 19 Brad Crellin.
Tries: Wiper (10), Calvert (36), Hamzat (48), Doran (79); **Goals:** Palfrey 3/4.
On report: Haggerty (13) - alleged dangerous tackle.
TOWN: 1 Brett Carter; 20 Stephen Dawes; 4 Aaron Low; 21 John Patrick; 5 Neil Frazer; 24 Darren Holt; 7 Scott Kaighan; 10 Kris Coward; 14 Jack Pedley; 16 Ryan McDonald; 29 Dave Armitstead; 12 Jarrad Stack; 13 Karl Olstrum. Subs (all used): 23 Marc Bainbridge; 15 Ruairi McGoff; 18 Joe McKenna; 11 Mike Whitehead.
Tries: Pedley (60), Frazer (74); **Goals:** Holt 1/2.
Rugby Leaguer & League Express Men of the Match: *Whitehaven:* Lee Doran; *Town:* Scott Kaighan.
Penalty count: 4-7; **Half-time:** 12-0; **Referee:** Clint Sharrad; **Attendance:** 1,523.

ROUND 14

Saturday 2nd July 2011

LONDON SKOLARS 27 SOUTH WALES SCORPIONS 26

SKOLARS: 3 James Anthony; 18 Aaron Small; 35 Will Colleran; 17 Dave Arnot; 5 Ade Adebisi; 7 Dylan Skee; 30 Mourad Kriouache; 13 Stephen Ball; 9 Gareth Honor; 34 Rob Thomas; 37 Jaroslaw Obuchowski; 31 Ben Bolger; 15 Oliver Purslow. Subs (all used): 12 Oliver Bloom; 27 Cariern Clement-Pascall; 32 Sam Gee; 19 Jermaine Coleman.
Tries: Obuchowski (1, 17), Colleran (7), Adebisi (42, 67); **Goals:** Skee 3/6; **Field goal:** Skee (77).
SCORPIONS: 27 Jamie Murphy; 5 Curtis Cunningham; 4 Ashley Bateman; 2 Lewis Reece; 24 Dalton Grant; 1 Andrew Gay; 7 Casey Bromilow; 10 Paul Raftrey; 9 Steve Parry; 16 Joe Burke; 17 Harri Greville; 3 Christiaan Roets; 12 Loz Wildbore. Subs (all used): 18 Chris Davies; 20 Hywel Davies; 15 Neil Dallimore; 28 Chris Clough.
Tries: Gay (13, 23), Parry (33), Grant (36), Cunningham (64); **Goals:** Reece 3/5.
Rugby Leaguer & League Express Men of the Match: *Skolars:* Rob Thomas; *Scorpions:* Steve Parry.
Penalty count: 14-7; **Half-time:** 16-22; **Referee:** Matthew Kidd; **Attendance:** 437.

Sunday 3rd July 2011

KEIGHLEY COUGARS 92 GATESHEAD THUNDER 6

COUGARS: 2 Craig Moss; 5 Gavin Duffy; 22 Ben Sagar; 33 Jake Normington; 32 George Elliott; 36 Jy-Mel Coleman; 7 Ryan Smith; 8 Andy Shickell; 9 James Feather; 10 Scott Law; 23 Chris Baines; 13 Greg Nicholson; 29 Jason Demetriou. Subs (all used): 14 Jamaine Wray; 16 Brendan Rawlins; 17 Ryan Benjafield; 25 Jamie Shepherd.
Tries: Baines (3, 30), Moss (8), Shickell (13), Feather (18), Nicholson (21, 23, 62), Sagar (34), Smith (38, 74), Coleman (43), Demetriou (47), Law (58), Normington (66), Elliott (78, 79); **Goals:** Baines 9/13, Coleman 3/4.
THUNDER: 16 Robin Peers; 6 Ashley Williams; 17 Joe Brown; 40 Mike Mitchell; 3 Danny Wilson; 26 Connor Condron; 7 Ryan Clarke; 22 Chris Parker; 9 Tom Hodgson; 10 Stephen Welton; 13 Michael Kelly; 42 Oliver O'Mara; 31 Will Bate. Subs (all used): 4 Josh Stoker; 5 Dan O'Sullivan; 32 Ade Aderiye; 36 Clarke Thompson.
Try: Clarke (40); **Goals:** Clarke 1/1.
Rugby Leaguer & League Express Men of the Match: *Cougars:* Jy-Mel Coleman; *Thunder:* Ryan Clarke.
Penalty count: 6-5; **Half-time:** 52-6; **Referee:** Greg Dolan; **Attendance:** 899.

OLDHAM 40 WHITEHAVEN 20

OLDHAM: 1 Ben Heaton; 21 Mark Brocklehurst; 26 Matthew Fogarty; 29 Mark McCully; 27 Shaun Robinson; 6 Neil Roden; 7 Carl Forber; 8 Jason Boults; 25 Martin Roden; 28 Luke Stenchion; 30 Danny Bravo; 24 Paul Noone; 13 Valu Bentley. Subs (all used): 15 Luke Sutton; 17 John Clough; 10 Dave Ellison; 23 Callum Casey.
Tries: Brocklehurst (10), Robinson (36), Heaton (39, 75), Fogarty (46), Clough (52), Stenchion (62); **Goals:** Forber 6/8.
WHITEHAVEN: 1 Craig Benson; 5 Loz Hamzat; 33 Max Wiper; 4 Scott McAvoy; 2 Craig Calvert; 6 Lewis Palfrey; 32 Carl Rudd; 10 Howard Hill; 14 Chris Smith; 34 Matthew Haggerty; 11 Spencer Miller; 35 Lee Doran; 17 Andrew Beattie. Subs (all used): 9 Carl Sice; 23 Paul Culnean; 26 Luke Isakka; 12 Dexter Miller.
Tries: Beattie (15), McAvoy (25), Wiper (70, 78); **Goals:** Palfrey 2/4.
Rugby Leaguer & League Express Men of the Match: *Oldham:* Ben Heaton; *Whitehaven:* Carl Rudd.
Penalty count: 6-4; **Half-time:** 14-8; **Referee:** George Stokes; **Attendance:** 537.

ROCHDALE HORNETS 16 DONCASTER 26

HORNETS: 1 Wayne English; 2 Craig Johnson; 17 Dale Bloomfield; 5 Scott Yates; 25 Andy Saywell; 15 Paul Crook; 7 Steve Roper; 18 John Cookson; 6 Liam McGovern; 35 Richard Mervill; 16 Danny Samuel; 21 Mark Hobson; 11 Craig Ashall. Subs (all used): 32 Danny Ekis; 8 Dave Newton; 10 Adam Bowman; 27 Jamie Peasnall.
Tries: Cookson (12), Bloomfield (17), Ashall (39); **Goals:** Crook 2/3.
DONCASTER: 1 Mick Butterfield; 30 Gareth Potts; 31 Nev Morrison; 25 Chris Spurr; 32 Michael Coady; 19 Scott Spaven; 7 Craig Fawcett; 17 Adam Scott; 13 Jack Ely; 26 Dominic Dee; 15 Craig Robinson; 23 Grant Edwards; 16 Mike Emmett. Subs (all used): 9 Kyle Kesik; 8 Matt Carbutt; 10 Liam Crawley; 22 Carl Hughes.
Tries: Spurr (21, 27, 79), C Hughes (33), Morrison (74); **Goals:** Spaven 3/5.
Rugby Leaguer & League Express Men of the Match: *Hornets:* John Cookson; *Doncaster:* Chris Spurr.
Penalty count: 10-11; **Half-time:** 16-18; **Referee:** Mohammed Drizza; **Attendance:** 423.

WORKINGTON TOWN 36 SWINTON LIONS 16

TOWN: 1 Brett Carter; 20 Stephen Dawes; 21 John Patrick; 4 Aaron Low; 5 Neil Frazer; 24 Darren Holt; 7 Scott Kaighan; 29 Dave Armitstead; 14 Jack Pedley; 15 Ruairi McGoff; 11 Mike Whitehead; 12 Jarrad Stack; 13 Karl Olstrum. Subs (all used): 23 Marc Bainbridge; 16 Ryan McDonald; 18 Joe McKenna; 17 James Robinson.
Tries: Patrick (17), Armitstead (33), Kaighan (46, 58), Pedley (74, 77); **Goals:** Holt 2/3, Kaighan 0/2, Bainbridge 3/3; **Field goals:** Bainbridge (39), Holt (73).

Keighley's Greg Nicholson and James Feather get to grips with Swinton's Darren Hawkyard

LIONS: 21 Ian Mort; 20 Richard Flooks; 4 Dean Thompson; 3 Gavin Dodd; 2 Rob Foxen; 6 Martin Ainscough; 7 Ian Watson; 38 Warren Thompson; 9 Mark Smith; 8 Mike Morrison; 11 Dale Cunniffe; 14 Tommy Gallagher; 13 Phil Joseph. Subs (all used): 25 Karl Ashall; 10 Dana Wilson; 15 Darren Hawkyard; 12 Lee Wingfield.
Tries: Foxen (24), Morrison (50), Cunniffe (61); **Goals:** Mort 2/3.
Rugby Leaguer & League Express Men of the Match:
Town: Jarrad Stack; *Lions:* Warren Thompson.
Penalty count: 10-5; **Half-time:** 13-4;
Referee: Jamie Leahy *(replaced by Sarah Bennison, half-time)*; **Attendance:** 512.

ROUND 15

Saturday 9th July 2011

LONDON SKOLARS 36 OLDHAM 34

SKOLARS: 3 James Anthony; 18 Aaron Small; 35 Will Colleran; 17 Dave Arnot; 5 Ade Adebisi; 30 Mourad Kriouache; 7 Dylan Skee; 15 Oliver Purslow; 9 Gareth Honor; 13 Stephen Ball; 37 Jaroslaw Obuchowski; 31 Lamont Bryan; 19 Jermaine Coleman. Subs (all used): 25 Austen Aggrey; 32 Sam Gee; 33 Joe Mbu; 12 Oliver Bloom.
Tries: Skee (4), Adebisi (16), Anthony (29), Gee (35), Obuchowski (44), Honor (73); **Goals:** Skee 6/6.
OLDHAM: 1 Ben Heaton; 5 John Gillam; 21 Mark Brocklehurst; 29 Mark McCully; 27 Shaun Robinson; 6 Neil Roden; 7 Carl Forber; 8 Jason Boults; 25 Martin Roden; 28 Luke Stenchion; 30 Danny Bravo; 24 Paul Noone; 13 Valu Bentley. Subs (all used): 11 Andrew Isherwood; 15 Luke Sutton; 17 John Clough; 23 Callum Casey.
Tries: Sutton (22, 57), Bentley (26), Gillam (50), Brocklehurst (53), Forber (65); **Goals:** Forber 5/6.
Rugby Leaguer & League Express Men of the Match:
Skolars: Ade Adebisi; *Oldham:* Carl Forber.
Penalty count: 5-8; **Half-time:** 24-12;
Referee: Warren Turley; **Attendance:** 1,105
(at Twickenham Stoop).

Sunday 10th July 2011

WHITEHAVEN 34 SOUTH WALES SCORPIONS 14

WHITEHAVEN: 1 Craig Benson; 5 Loz Hamzat; 38 Andreas Bauer; 4 Scott McAvoy; 2 Craig Calvert; 32 Carl Rudd; 21 Tyrone Dalton; 34 Matthew Haggerty; 14 Chris Smith; 10 Howard Hill; 11 Spencer Miller; 35 Lee Doran; 17 Andrew Beattie. Subs (all used): 9 Carl Sice; 23 Paul Culnean; 26 Luke Isakka; 12 Dexter Miller.
Tries: Rudd (16), S Miller (33), Sice (47), D Miller (62), Smith (67), Hamzat (71); **Goals:** Rudd 5/7.

SCORPIONS: 27 Jamie Murphy; 2 Lewis Reece; 3 Christiaan Roets; 4 Ashley Bateman; 5 Curtis Cunningham; 1 Andrew Gay; 7 Casey Bromilow; 28 Chris Clough; 9 Steve Parry; 10 Paul Raftrey; 15 Neil Dallimore; 21 Rhodri Lloyd; 17 Harri Greville. Subs (all used): 20 Hywel Davies; 18 Chris Davies; 29 Phil Carleton; 8 Semisi Cocka.
Tries: Gay (19), Cocka (50); **Goals:** Reece 3/3.
Rugby Leaguer & League Express Men of the Match:
Whitehaven: Andrew Beattie; *Scorpions:* Semisi Cocka.
Penalty count: 8-9; **Half-time:** 12-6;
Referee: Greg Dolan; **Attendance:** 815.

DONCASTER 32 GATESHEAD THUNDER 0

DONCASTER: 1 Mick Butterfield; 30 Michael Coady; 31 Nev Morrison; 25 Chris Spurr; 2 Stewart Sanderson; 19 Scott Spaven; 9 Kyle Kesik; 20 Jamie Bovill; 13 Jack Ely; 10 Liam Crawley; 17 Adam Scott; 8 Matt Carbutt; 23 Grant Edwards. Subs (all used): 16 Mike Emmett; 22 Carl Hughes; 26 Dominic Dee; 11 Kyle Sampson.
Tries: Edwards (19), Spurr (29, 70), Kesik (33, 56), C Hughes (49); **Goals:** Spaven 4/6.
THUNDER: 16 Robin Peers; 3 Danny Wilson; 40 Mike Mitchell; 17 Joe Brown; 23 Jonny Shields; 31 Will Bate; 26 Connor Condron; 8 Jason Payne; 9 Tom Hodgson; 10 Stephen Welton; 13 Michael Kelly; 29 David Cash; 4 Josh Stoker. Subs (all used): 7 Ryan Clarke; 24 Ben Smith; 22 Chris Parker; 21 Matthew Harding.
Rugby Leaguer & League Express Men of the Match:
Doncaster: Kyle Kesik; *Thunder:* Jonny Shields.
Penalty count: 9-6; **Half-time:** 18-0;
Referee: Matthew Kidd; **Attendance:** 681.

KEIGHLEY COUGARS 35 SWINTON LIONS 30

COUGARS: 31 Dave Halley; 2 Craig Moss; 22 Ben Sagar; 33 Jake Normington; 32 George Elliott; 36 Jy-Mel Coleman; 7 Ryan Smith; 8 Andy Shickell; 9 James Feather; 10 Scott Law; 23 Chris Baines; 13 Greg Nicholson; 29 Jason Demetriou. Subs (all used): 14 Jamaine Wray; 17 Ryan Benjafield; 16 Brendan Rawlins; 25 Jamie Shepherd.
Tries: Sagar (2), Smith (38), Benjafield (42), Coleman (44), Shickell (66), Normington (75); **Goals:** Baines 4/5, Coleman 1/1; **Field goal:** Coleman (80).
Sin bin: Feather (25) - late challenge on Watson.
LIONS: 1 Richie Hawkyard; 20 Richard Flooks; 23 Alex Hurst; 3 Gavin Dodd; 21 Ian Mort; 6 Martin Ainscough; 7 Ian Watson; 8 Mike Morrison; 25 Karl Ashall; 38 Warren Thompson; 13 Dale Cunniffe; 13 Phil Joseph. Subs: 10 Dana Wilson; 16 Neil Holland; 39 Anthony Stewart (on used); 12 Lee Wingfield.
Tries: Flooks (6), Joseph (12), Cunniffe (21), Mort (49, 53, 62); **Goals:** Mort 3/6.
Rugby Leaguer & League Express Men of the Match:
Cougars: Dave Halley; *Lions:* Dale Cunniffe.

Penalty count: 8-5; **Half-time:** 10-18;
Referee: Peter Brooke *(replaced by Adam Gill, half-time)*; **Attendance:** 1,099.

ROCHDALE HORNETS 45 WORKINGTON TOWN 20

HORNETS: 1 Wayne English; 2 Craig Johnson; 3 Dean Gorton; 22 Damien Reid; 17 Dale Bloomfield; 15 Paul Crook; 7 Steve Roper; 18 John Cookson; 6 Liam McGovern; 10 Adam Bowman; 29 Gary Middlehurst; 21 Mark Hobson; 11 Craig Ashall. Subs (all used): 8 Dave Newton; 32 Danny Ekis; 16 Danny Samuel; 9 Steve McDermott.
Tries: Johnson (17), Cookson (22), McGovern (26), Bloomfield (35), McDermott (39), Ashall (41), Reid (76); **Goals:** Crook 8/9; **Field goal:** Crook (75).
TOWN: 1 Brett Carter; 2 Elliott Miller; 21 John Patrick; 4 Aaron Low; 5 Neil Frazer; 24 Darren Holt; 7 Scott Kaighan; 15 Ruairi McGoff; 14 Jack Pedley; 29 Dave Armitstead; 11 Mike Whitehead; 12 Jarrad Stack; 13 Karl Olstrum. Subs (all used): 23 Marc Bainbridge; 18 Joe McKenna; 16 Ryan McDonald; 17 James Robinson.
Tries: Holt (12), Miller (54), Low (60), Kaighan (73); **Goals:** Holt 1/3, Bainbridge 1/1.
Rugby Leaguer & League Express Men of the Match:
Hornets: John Cookson; *Town:* Scott Kaighan.
Penalty count: 7-6; **Half-time:** 28-4;
Referee: Craig Halloran; **Attendance:** 1,021.

ROUND 12

Friday 15th July 2011

SWINTON LIONS 30 DONCASTER 28

LIONS: 1 Richie Hawkyard; 20 Richard Flooks; 23 Alex Hurst; 3 Gavin Dodd; 21 Ian Mort; 6 Martin Ainscough; 7 Ian Watson; 38 Warren Thompson; 9 Mark Smith; 16 Neil Holland; 37 Andy Gorski; 11 Dale Cunniffe; 13 Phil Joseph. Subs (all used): 25 Karl Ashall; 10 Dana Wilson; 2 Rob Foxen; 15 Darren Hawkyard.
Tries: Gorski (7), Ainscough (13), Mort (26, 37), R Hawkyard (51); **Goals:** Mort 5/6.
DONCASTER: 1 Mick Butterfield; 30 Michael Coady; 25 Chris Spurr; 31 Nev Morrison; 32 Gareth Potts; 19 Scott Spaven; 9 Kyle Kesik; 17 Adam Scott; 13 Jack Ely; 20 Jamie Bovill; 8 Matt Carbutt; 22 Carl Hughes. Subs (all used): 18 Dale Cunniffe; 11 Kyle Sampson; 26 Dominic Dee; 10 Liam Crawley.
Tries: Potts (1, 71), Morrison (22, 57, 78); **Goals:** Spaven 4/6.
Rugby Leaguer & League Express Men of the Match:
Lions: Ian Watson; *Doncaster:* Nev Morrison.
Penalty count: 8-14; **Half-time:** 22-12;
Referee: Ronnie Laughton; **Attendance:** 425.

ROUND 16

Sunday 24th July 2011

WORKINGTON TOWN 41 LONDON SKOLARS 14

TOWN: 1 Brett Carter; 2 Elliott Miller; 21 John Patrick; 4 Aaron Low; 5 Neil Frazer; 24 Darren Holt; 7 Scott Kaighan; 29 Dave Armitstead; 14 Jack Pedley; 16 Ryan McDonald; 11 Mike Whitehead; 18 Joe McKenna; 12 Jarrad Stack. Subs (all used): 23 Marc Bainbridge; 15 Ruairi McGoff; 27 Jamie Marshall; 17 James Robinson.
Tries: Miller (6), Whitehead (12), Stack (20), Low (37), Kaighan (45, 73), Patrick (48); **Goals:** Holt 5/6, Bainbridge 1/1; **Field goal:** Armitstead (40).
SKOLARS: 3 James Anthony; 18 Aaron Small; 33 Joe Mbu; 35 Will Colleran; 5 Ade Adebisi; 7 Dylan Skee; 30 Mourad Kriouache; 34 Dave Williams; 9 Gareth Honor; 25 Austen Aggrey; 37 Jaroslaw Obuchowski; 31 Lamont Bryan; 15 Oliver Purslow. Subs (all used): 21 Danny Burke; 19 Jermaine Coleman; 12 Oliver Bloom; 13 Stephen Ball.
Tries: Aggrey (58), Skee (61), Anthony (77);
Goals: Skee 1/3.
Rugby Leaguer & League Express Men of the Match: *Town:* Jarrad Stack; *Skolars:* Lamont Bryan.
Penalty count: 3-6; **Half-time:** 25-0;
Referee: Matthew Kidd; **Attendance:** 454.

OLDHAM 36 KEIGHLEY COUGARS 14

OLDHAM: 1 Ben Heaton; 21 Mark Brocklehurst; 3 Marcus St Hilaire; 29 Mark McCully; 27 Shaun Robinson; 6 Neil Roden; 7 Carl Forber; 8 Jason Boults; 25 Martin Roden; 28 Luke Stenchion; 30 Danny Bravo; 24 Paul Noone; 13 Valu Bentley. Subs (all used): 15 Luke Sutton; 17 John Clough; 20 Michael Ward; 23 Callum Casey.
Tries: N Roden (8), McCully (32), Heaton (45, 72), Noone (60), Brocklehurst (64); **Goals:** Forber 6/7.
COUGARS: 31 Dave Halley; 26 James Hutchinson; 4 Danny Lawton; 33 Jake Normington; 5 Gavin Duffy; 36 Jy-Mel Coleman; 7 Ryan Smith; 8 Andy Shickell; 9 James Feather; 12 Oliver Pursglove; 11 Will Cartledge; 23 Chris Baines; 29 Jason Demetriou. Subs (all used): 14 Jamaine Wray; 17 Ryan Benjafield; 16 Brendan Rawlins; 25 Jamie Shepherd.
Tries: Cartledge (19), Wray (30), Hutchinson (79);
Goals: Baines 1/3.
Dismissal: Feather (71) - high tackle.
Sin bin: Shickell (54) - professional foul.
Rugby Leaguer & League Express Men of the Match: *Oldham:* Neil Roden; *Cougars:* Jy-Mel Coleman.
Penalty count: 15-10; **Half-time:** 14-10;
Referee: Ronnie Laughton; **Attendance:** 637.

SOUTH WALES SCORPIONS 20 DONCASTER 41

SCORPIONS: 2 Lewis Reece; 24 Dalton Grant; 26 Lee Williams; 4 Ashley Bateman; 5 Curtis Cunningham; 1 Andrew Gay; 7 Casey Bromilow; 29 Gil Dudson; 9 Steve Parry; 16 Joe Burke; 3 Christiaan Roets; 21 Rhodri Lloyd; 13 Aled James. Subs (all used): 10 Paul Raftrey; 15 Neil Dallimore; 17 Harri Greville; 18 Chris Davies.
Tries: James (3, 31), Parry (41, 62);
Goals: Reece 2/3, Williams 0/1.
DONCASTER: 1 Mick Butterfield; 30 Gareth Potts; 31 Nev Morrison; 25 Chris Spurr; 29 Michael Coady; 9 Kyle Kesik; 19 Scott Spaven; 20 Jamie Bovill; 13 Jack Ely; 17 Adam Scott; 15 Craig Robinson; 23 Grant Edwards; 22 Carl Hughes. Subs (all used): 8 Matt Carbutt; 16 Mike Emmett; 11 Kyle Sampson; 2 Stewart Sanderson.
Tries: Edwards (13), C Hughes (17), Butterfield (28), Kesik (35), Coady (57), Spurr (68), Emmett (77);
Goals: Spaven 6/8; **Field goal:** Spaven (73).
Rugby Leaguer & League Express Men of the Match: *Scorpions:* Steve Parry; *Doncaster:* Scott Spaven.
Penalty count: 3-9; **Half-time:** 10-24;
Referee: Greg Dolan; **Attendance:** 304.

SWINTON LIONS 44 WHITEHAVEN 0

LIONS: 21 Ian Mort; 20 Richard Flooks; 3 Gavin Dodd; 23 Alex Hurst; 2 Rob Foxen; 6 Martin Ainscough; 7 Ian Watson; 38 Warren Thompson; 9 Mark Smith; 16 Neil Holland; 11 Dale Cunniffe; 37 Andy Gorski; 13 Phil Joseph. Subs (all used): 25 Karl Ashall; 10 Dana Wilson; 15 Darren Hawkyard; 39 Danny Meekin.
Tries: Mort (1, 19, 33), Wilson (25, 69), Foxen (47), Ainscough (53), Joseph (57); **Goals:** Mort 6/9.
WHITEHAVEN: 1 Craig Benson; 5 Loz Hamzat; 4 Scott McAvoy; 38 Andreas Bauer; 2 Craig Calvert; 6 Lewis Palfrey; 32 Carl Rudd; 26 Luke Isakka; 14 Chris Smith; 23 Paul Culnean; 11 Spencer Miller; 35 Lee Doran; 17 Andrew Beattie. Subs (all used): 9 Carl Sice; 10 Howard Hill; 12 Dexter Miller; 34 Matthew Haggerty.
On report: Sice (29) - alleged dangerous contact.
Rugby Leaguer & League Express Men of the Match: *Lions:* Dana Wilson; *Whitehaven:* Scott McAvoy.
Penalty count: 8-7; **Half-time:** 24-0;
Referee: Dave Merrick; **Attendance:** 679.

ROUND 17

Saturday 30th July 2011

LONDON SKOLARS 14 SWINTON LIONS 42

SKOLARS: 3 James Anthony; 18 Aaron Small; 31 Lamont Bryan; 35 Will Colleran; 2 Smokie Junor; 30 Mourad Kriouache; 7 Dylan Skee; 34 Dave Williams; 9 Gareth Honor; 25 Austen Aggrey; 37 Jaroslaw Obuchowski; 12 Oliver Bloom; 15 Oliver Purslow. Subs (all used): 32 Sam Gee; 19 Jermaine Coleman; 10 Jason Hart; 22 Saqib Murtza.
Tries: Bryan (20), Jermaine Coleman (42), Aggrey (67);
Goals: Skee 1/3.
LIONS: 21 Ian Mort; 5 Sam Reay; 3 Gavin Dodd; 15 Darren Hawkyard; 20 Richard Flooks; 6 Martin Ainscough; 25 Karl Ashall; 38 Warren Thompson; 9 Mark Smith; 16 Neil Holland; 11 Dale Cunniffe; 37 Andy Gorski; 12 Lee Wingfield. Subs (all used): 10 Dana Wilson; 8 Mike Morrison; 39 Danny Meekin; 13 Phil Joseph.
Tries: Wingfield (2), Ainscough (26), Gorski (39), Dodd (45), Cunniffe (50), Meekin (55), Mort (60);
Goals: Mort 7/7.
Rugby Leaguer & League Express Men of the Match: *Skolars:* Jermaine Coleman; *Lions:* Karl Ashall.
Penalty count: 3-9; **Half-time:** 4-18;
Referee: Craig Halloran; **Attendance:** 429.

Sunday 31st July 2011

KEIGHLEY COUGARS 34 DONCASTER 6

COUGARS: 31 Dave Halley; 2 Craig Moss; 22 Ben Sagar; 33 Jake Normington; 5 Gavin Duffy; 29 Jason Demetriou; 7 Ryan Smith; 8 Andy Shickell; 9 James Feather; 10 Scott Law; 12 Oliver Pursglove; 11 Will Cartledge; 13 Greg Nicholson. Subs (all used): 14 Jamaine Wray; 16 Brendan Rawlins; 21 Richard Jones; 23 Chris Baines.
Tries: Sagar (25, 34), Cartledge (51), Feather (69), Duffy (73), Halley (75), Normington (80);
Goals: Baines 3/6, Halley 0/1.
DONCASTER: 1 Mick Butterfield; 29 Michael Coady; 25 Chris Spurr; 31 Nev Morrison; 30 Gareth Potts; 9 Kyle Kesik; 19 Scott Spaven; 20 Jamie Bovill; 13 Jack Ely; 17 Adam Scott; 15 Craig Robinson; 23 Grant Edwards; 22 Carl Hughes. Subs (all used): 8 Matt Carbutt; 11 Kyle Sampson; 16 Mike Emmett; 26 Dominic Dee.
Try: Dee (40); **Goals:** Spaven 1/1.
Rugby Leaguer & League Express Men of the Match: *Cougars:* Jason Demetriou; *Doncaster:* Adam Scott.
Penalty count: 6-11; **Half-time:** 8-6;
Referee: Dave Merrick; **Attendance:** 937.

OLDHAM 22 WORKINGTON TOWN 24

OLDHAM: 1 Ben Heaton; 21 Mark Brocklehurst; 3 Marcus St Hilaire; 29 Mark McCully; 27 Shaun Robinson; 6 Neil Roden; 7 Carl Forber; 8 Jason Boults; 25 Martin Roden; 11 Andrew Isherwood; 30 Danny Bravo; 24 Paul Noone; 13 Valu Bentley. Subs (all used): 15 Luke Sutton; 17 John Clough; 20 Michael Ward; 23 Callum Casey.
Tries: McCully (19), Casey (53), Robinson (57), Isherwood (75); **Goals:** Forber 3/4.
TOWN: 1 Brett Carter; 2 Elliott Miller; 21 John Patrick; 4 Aaron Low; 5 Neil Frazer; 24 Darren Holt; 7 Scott Kaighan; 29 Dave Armitstead; 14 Jack Pedley; 10 Kris Coward; 11 Mike Whitehead; 18 Joe McKenna; 12 Jarrad Stack. Subs (all used): 15 Ruairi McGoff; 20 Stephen Dawes; 23 Marc Bainbridge; 17 James Robinson.
Tries: Miller (16), Stack (30), Carter (38), Kaighan (63);
Goals: Holt 4/6.
Rugby Leaguer & League Express Men of the Match: *Oldham:* Ben Heaton; *Town:* Darren Holt.
Penalty count: 9-7; **Half-time:** 6-14;
Referee: Chris Leatherbarrow; **Attendance:** 684.

SOUTH WALES SCORPIONS 6 ROCHDALE HORNETS 13

SCORPIONS: 27 Jamie Murphy; 2 Lewis Reece; 3 Christiaan Roets; 6 Jack Pring; 5 Curtis Cunningham; 1 Andrew Gay; 7 Casey Bromilow; 10 Paul Raftrey; 9 Steve Parry; 15 Neil Dallimore; 17 Harri Greville; 28 Chris Clough; 21 Rhodri Lloyd. Subs (all used): 20 Hywel Davies; 22 Bradley Hill; 29 Phil Carleton; 18 Chris Davies.
Try: Lloyd (36); **Goals:** Reece 1/1.
HORNETS: 1 Wayne English; 2 Craig Johnson; 3 Dean Gorton; 22 Damien Reid; 17 Dale Bloomfield; 6 Liam McGovern; 7 Steve Roper; 18 John Cookson; 15 Paul Crook; 10 Adam Bowman; 29 Gary Middlehurst; 21 Mark Hobson; 11 Craig Ashall. Subs (all used): 32 Danny Ekis; 8 Dave Newton; 16 Danny Samuel; 9 Steve McDermott.
Tries: McDermott (23), English (29);
Goals: McGovern 2/2; **Field goal:** Crook (80).
Rugby Leaguer & League Express Men of the Match: *Scorpions:* Christiaan Roets; *Hornets:* Wayne English.
Penalty count: 11-6; **Half-time:** 6-12;
Referee: Matthew Kidd; **Attendance:** 252.

WHITEHAVEN 64 GATESHEAD THUNDER 10

WHITEHAVEN: 1 Craig Benson; 5 Loz Hamzat; 3 Derry Eilbeck; 4 Scott McAvoy; 2 Craig Calvert; 6 Lewis Palfrey; 14 Chris Smith; 34 Matthew Haggerty; 9 Carl Sice; 35 Lee Doran; 11 Spencer Miller; 36 Martyn Wilson; 17 Andrew Beattie. Subs (all used): 32 Carl Rudd; 23 Paul Culnean; 15 Richard Farrer; 19 Brad Crellin.
Tries: Sice (15, 53, 67), Culnean (28, 34), Calvert (36, 51), Eilbeck (65), Haggerty (69), Hamzat (75), Wilson (78); **Goals:** Rudd 10/11.
THUNDER: 16 Robin Peers; 3 Danny Wilson; 44 Mitchell Stevens; 17 Joe Brown; 4 Josh Stoker; 26 Connor Condron; 40 Paul Stamp; 8 Jason Payne; 31 Will Bate; 10 Stephen Welton; 13 Michael Kelly; 29 David Cash; 21 Matthew Harding. Subs (all used): 7 Ryan Clarke; 22 Chris Parker; 32 Ade Aderiye; 23 Ben Smith.
Tries: Wilson (9), Jason Payne (60); **Goals:** Stamp 1/2.
Rugby Leaguer & League Express Men of the Match: *Whitehaven:* Carl Sice; *Thunder:* Jason Payne.
Penalty count: 9-9; **Half-time:** 24-4;
Referee: Warren Turley; **Attendance:** 651.

ROUND 6

Thursday 4th August 2011

SWINTON LIONS 18 KEIGHLEY COUGARS 20

LIONS: 21 Ian Mort; 5 Sam Reay; 3 Gavin Dodd; 23 Alex Hurst; 2 Rob Foxen; 6 Martin Ainscough; 25 Karl Ashall; 38 Warren Thompson; 9 Mark Smith; 12 Lee Wingfield; 11 Dale Cunniffe; 37 Andy Gorski; 13 Phil Joseph. Subs (all used): 1 Richie Hawkyard; 15 Darren Hawkyard; 39 Danny Meekin; 8 Mike Morrison.
Tries: Joseph (9), Hurst (36), Gorski (67);
Goals: Mort 3/3.
COUGARS: 31 Dave Halley; 2 Craig Moss; 22 Ben Sagar; 33 Jake Normington; 5 Gavin Duffy; 29 Jason Demetriou; 7 Ryan Smith; 8 Andy Shickell; 9 James Feather; 10 Scott Law; 11 Will Cartledge; 12 Oliver Pursglove; 13 Greg Nicholson. Subs (all used): 14 Jamaine Wray; 16 Brendan Rawlins; 23 Chris Baines; 21 Richard Jones.
Tries: Feather (19), Moss (24, 61), Pursglove (55);
Goals: Halley 0/1, Moss 0/1, Baines 2/3.
Rugby Leaguer & League Express Men of the Match: *Lions:* Phil Joseph; *Cougars:* Jason Demetriou.
Penalty count: 4-9; **Half-time:** 12-8;
Referee: George Stokes; **Attendance:** 1,346.

ROUND 20

Saturday 6th August 2011

SOUTH WALES SCORPIONS 26 LONDON SKOLARS 16

SCORPIONS: 27 Jamie Murphy; 5 Curtis Cunningham; 6 Jack Pring; 3 Christiaan Roets; 2 Lewis Reece; 1 Andrew Gay; 7 Casey Bromilow; 10 Paul Raftrey; 9 Steve Parry; 15 Neil Dallimore; 28 Chris Clough; 21 Rhodri Lloyd; 26 Lee Williams. Subs (all used): 17 Harri Greville; 18 Chris Davies; 13 Aled James; 4 Ashley Bateman.
Tries: Gay (9, 65), C Davies (45), Roets (50);
Goals: Reece 5/5.
SKOLARS: 3 James Anthony; 18 Aaron Small; 35 Chris McNamara; 31 Will Colleran; 2 Smokie Junor; 30 Mourad Kriouache; 7 Dylan Skee; 25 Austen Aggrey; 32 Sam Gee; 34 Dave Williams; 12 Oliver Bloom; 37 Jaroslaw Obuchowski; 15 Oliver Purslow. Subs (all used): 29 Michael Sykes; 21 Danny Burke; 27 Carlern Clement-Pascall; 22 Saqib Murtza.
Tries: Murtza (24), Junor (58), Gee (68); **Goals:** Skee 2/3.
Rugby Leaguer & League Express Men of the Match: *Scorpions:* Christiaan Roets; *Skolars:* Austen Aggrey.
Penalty count: 8-10; **Half-time:** 6-6;
Referee: Matthew Kidd; **Attendance:** 232.

ROUND 16

Sunday 7th August 2011

GATESHEAD THUNDER 14 ROCHDALE HORNETS 48

THUNDER: 44 Mitchell Stevens; 34 Ashley Thackeray; 30 Mike Mitchell; 17 Joe Brown; 16 Robin Peers; 40 Paul Stamp; 26 Connor Condron; 8 Jason Payne; 9 Tom Hodgson; 10 Stephen Welton; 13 Michael Kelly; 29 David Cash; 31 Will Bate. Subs (all used): 7 Ryan Clarke; 22 Chris Parker; 4 Josh Stoker; 32 Ade Aderiye.
Tries: Mitchell (17), Clarke (20), Brown (79);
Goals: Clarke 1/3.
HORNETS: 1 Wayne English; 2 Craig Johnson; 3 Dean Gorton; 22 Damien Reid; 17 Dale Bloomfield; 15 Paul Crook; 7 Steve Roper; 18 John Cookson; 6 Liam McGovern; 10 Adam Bowman; 16 Danny Samuel; 29 Gary Middlehurst; 11 Craig Ashall. Subs (all used): 8 Dave Newton; 34 Phil Wood; 32 Danny Ekis; 21 Mark Hobson.
Tries: Bloomfield (6, 10, 42), Gorton (13, 67), Ekis (28), Ashall (38), Samuel (55), McGovern (66);
Goals: Crook 6/9.
Rugby Leaguer & League Express Men of the Match: *Thunder:* Will Bate; *Hornets:* Dave Newton.
Penalty count: 3-4; **Half-time:** 10-28;
Referee: Ronnie Laughton; **Attendance:** 242.

ROUND 18

Sunday 14th August 2011

GATESHEAD THUNDER 16 LONDON SKOLARS 36

THUNDER: 44 Mitchell Stevens; 34 Ashley Thackeray; 30 Mike Mitchell; 17 Joe Brown; 16 Robin Peers; 40 Paul Stamp; 26 Connor Condron; 8 Jason Payne; 7 Ryan Clarke; 10 Stephen Welton; 13 Michael Kelly; 5 Dan O'Sullivan; 31 Will Bate. Subs (all used): 22 Chris Parker; 9 Tom Hodgson; 32 Ade Aderiye; 42 Oliver O'Mara.
Tries: Welton (35), O'Sullivan (51), O'Mara (79);
Goals: Stamp 1/2, Clarke 1/1.
SKOLARS: 3 James Anthony; 2 Smokie Junor; 36 John Paxton; 35 Will Colleran; 18 Aaron Small; 19 Jermaine Coleman; 7 Dylan Skee; 25 Austen Aggrey; 32 Sam Gee; 15 Oliver Purslow; 34 Lamont Bryan; 37 Jaroslaw Obuchowski; 12 Oliver Bloom. Subs (all used): 21 Danny Burke; 11 Matt Thomas; 22 Saqib Murtza; 29 Michael Sykes.
Tries: Junor (20), M Thomas (39), Small (42), Anthony (47, 74), Skee (55), Colleran (72); **Goals:** Skee 4/7.
Rugby Leaguer & League Express Men of the Match: *Thunder:* Stephen Welton; *Skolars:* Dylan Skee.
Penalty count: 13-3; **Half-time:** 6-10;
Referee: Jon Downham; **Attendance:** 292.

DONCASTER 20 WHITEHAVEN 18

DONCASTER: 1 Mick Butterfield; 2 Stewart Sanderson; 31 Nev Morrison; 25 Chris Spurr; 30 Michael Coady; 19 Scott Spaven; 7 Craig Fawcett; 17 Adam Scott; 21 Paul Hughes; 10 Liam Crawley; 15 Craig Robinson; 23 Grant Edwards; 22 Carl Hughes. Subs (all used): 9 Kyle Kesik; 26 Dominic Dee; 8 Matt Carbutt; 11 Kyle Sampson.
Tries: Coady (9), Kesik (43), Morrison (77), Fawcett (79); **Goals:** Spaven 2/4.
WHITEHAVEN: 1 Craig Benson; 5 Loz Hamzat; 33 Max Wiper; 4 Scott McAvoy; 2 Craig Calvert; 6 Lewis Palfrey; 36 Chris Gerrard; 23 Paul Culnean; 14 Chris Smith; 26 Luke Isakka; 11 Spencer Miller; 35 Lee Doran; 17 Andrew Beattie. Subs (all used): 9 Carl Sice; 10 Howard Hill; 15 Richard Farrer; 37 Paul King.
Tries: Hamzat (20, 35), Isakka (63); **Goals:** Palfrey 3/3.
Rugby Leaguer & League Express Men of the Match: *Doncaster:* Grant Edwards; *Whitehaven:* Loz Hamzat.
Penalty count: 5-8; **Half-time:** 4-12;
Referee: Ronnie Laughton; **Attendance:** 501.

ROCHDALE HORNETS 16 OLDHAM 38

HORNETS: 1 Wayne English; 2 Craig Johnson; 3 Dean Gorton; 13 Dayne Donoghue; 17 Dale Bloomfield; 15 Paul Crook; 6 Liam McGovern; 18 John Cookson; 34 Phil Wood; 35 Richard Mervill; 21 Mark Hobson; 10 Adam Bowman; 11 Craig Ashall. Subs (all used): 32 Danny Ekis; 8 Dave Newton; 9 Steve McDermott; 16 Danny Samuel.
Tries: Bloomfield (17), Newton (29), Hobson (76);
Goals: Crook 2/3.
OLDHAM: 1 Ben Heaton; 21 Mark Brocklehurst; 3 Marcus St Hilaire; 29 Mark McCully; 27 Shaun Robinson; 6 Neil Roden; 7 Carl Forber; 8 Jason Boults; 25 Martin Roden; 28 Luke Stenchion; 30 Danny Bravo; 24 Paul Noone; 13 Valu Bentley. Subs (all used): 9 Danny Whitmore; 15 Luke Sutton; 23 Callum Casey; 20 Michael Ward.
Tries: Heaton (25, 54), N Roden (37), Whitmore (42), Casey (47), Robinson (58), St Hilaire (74);
Goals: Forber 5/7.
Rugby Leaguer & League Express Men of the Match: *Hornets:* John Cookson; *Oldham:* Danny Whitmore.
Penalty count: 7-9; **Half-time:** 10-12;
Referee: Dave Merrick; **Attendance:** 928.

SWINTON LIONS 40 SOUTH WALES SCORPIONS 28

LIONS: 1 Richie Hawkyard; 2 Rob Foxen; 3 Gavin Dodd; 23 Alex Hurst; 21 Ian Mort; 6 Martin Ainscough; 25 Karl Ashall; 16 Neil Holland; 9 Mark Smith; 38 Warren Thompson; 11 Dale Cunniffe; 37 Andy Gorski; 13 Phil Joseph. Subs (all used): 15 Darren Hawkyard; 10 Dana Wilson; 12 Lee Wingfield; 8 Mike Morrison.
Tries: W Thompson (10), Cunniffe (13), Hurst (29), R Hawkyard (44), Wingfield (53), Dodd (65), Gorski (72); **Goals:** Mort 6/7.
SCORPIONS: 27 Jamie Murphy; 5 Curtis Cunningham; 4 Ashley Bateman; 3 Christiaan Roets; 24 Dalton Grant; 1 Andrew Gay; 7 Casey Bromilow; 10 Paul Raftrey; 9 Steve Parry; 16 Joe Burke; 15 Neil Dallimore; 21 Rhodri Lloyd; 13 Aled James. Subs: 17 Harri Greville; 8 Semisi Cocka; 20 Hywel Davies; 2 Lewis Reece (not used).
Tries: James (3), Lloyd (8), Murphy (39), Bromilow (57), Roets (76); **Goals:** Murphy 4/5.
Rugby Leaguer & League Express Men of the Match: *Lions:* Mark Smith; *Scorpions:* Jamie Murphy.
Penalty count: 6-11; **Half-time:** 16-18;
Referee: Matthew Kidd; **Attendance:** 509.

WORKINGTON TOWN 35 KEIGHLEY COUGARS 18

TOWN: 1 Brett Carter; 2 Elliott Miller; 3 Jason Mossop; 4 Aaron Low; 5 Neil Frazer; 24 Darren Holt; 7 Scott Kaighan; 29 Dave Armitstead; 14 Jack Pedley; 10 Kris Coward; 11 Mike Whitehead; 18 Joe McKenna; 12 Jarrad Stack. Subs (all used): 23 Marc Bainbridge; 15 Ruairi McGoff; 13 Karl Olstrum; 32 Chris Clough.
Tries: Miller (5), McGoff (26), Kaighan (35, 65), Carter (51, 56); **Goals:** Holt 5/6; **Field goal:** Holt (53).
COUGARS: 31 Dave Halley; 2 Craig Moss; 22 Ben Sagar; 33 Jake Normington; 5 Gavin Duffy; 29 Jason Demetriou; 7 Ryan Smith; 8 Andy Shickell; 9 James Feather; 10 Scott Law; 11 Will Cartledge; 12 Oliver Pursglove; 13 Greg Nicholson. Subs (all used): 14 Jamaine Wray; 16 Brendan Rawlins; 23 Chris Baines; 21 Richard Jones.
Tries: Shickell (17), Cartledge (33), Demetriou (60);
Goals: Moss 1/1, Baines 2/2.
Rugby Leaguer & League Express Men of the Match: *Town:* Darren Holt; *Cougars:* Will Cartledge.
Penalty count: 6-5; **Half-time:** 18-12;
Referee: Craig Halloran; **Attendance:** 544.

ROUND 19

Sunday 21st August 2011

DONCASTER 6 WORKINGTON TOWN 37

DONCASTER: 1 Mick Butterfield; 30 Michael Coady; 25 Chris Spurr; 31 Nev Morrison; 2 Stewart Sanderson; 7 Craig Fawcett; 19 Scott Spaven; 17 Adam Scott; 21 Paul Hughes; 10 Liam Crawley; 15 Craig Robinson; 23 Grant Edwards; 16 Mike Emmett. Subs (all used): 9 Kyle Kesik; 22 Carl Hughes; 8 Matt Carbutt; 26 Dominic Dee.
Try: Dee (80); **Goals:** Spaven 1/1.
TOWN: 1 Brett Carter; 2 Elliott Miller; 3 Jason Mossop; 21 John Patrick; 20 Stephen Dawes; 24 Darren Holt; 7 Scott Kaighan; 29 Dave Armitstead; 14 Jack Pedley; 10 Kris Coward; 11 Mike Whitehead; 18 Joe McKenna; 12 Jarrad Stack. Subs (all used): 23 Marc Bainbridge; 15 Ruairi McGoff; 32 Chris Clough; 17 James Robinson.
Tries: Pedley (3, 72), Carter (17), Miller (26), Kaighan (45), Coward (63);
Goals: Holt 6/7; **Field goal:** Holt (52).
Rugby Leaguer & League Express Men of the Match: *Doncaster:* Dominic Dee; *Town:* Darren Holt.
Penalty count: 9-7; **Half-time:** 0-18;
Referee: Warren Turley; **Attendance:** 659.

OLDHAM 48 SOUTH WALES SCORPIONS 34

OLDHAM: 1 Ben Heaton; 21 Mark Brocklehurst; 3 Marcus St Hilaire; 29 Mark McCully; 27 Shaun Robinson; 6 Neil Roden; 7 Carl Forber; 8 Jason Boults; 9 Danny Whitmore; 28 Luke Stenchion; 30 Danny Bravo; 24 Paul Noone; 23 Callum Casey. Subs (all used): 13 Valu Bentley; 17 John Clough; 16 Liam Gilchrist; 20 Michael Ward.
Tries: Noone (17), Heaton (20, 48), Bravo (27, 45, 53), N Roden (59), Whitmore (80); **Goals:** Forber 8/8.
Sin bin: St Hilaire (68) - holding down.
SCORPIONS: 27 Jamie Murphy; 5 Curtis Cunningham; 6 Jack Pring; 3 Christiaan Roets; 24 Dalton Grant; 1 Andrew Gay; 7 Casey Bromilow; 10 Paul Raftrey; 9 Steve Parry; 16 Joe Burke; 21 Rhodri Lloyd; 4 Ashley Bateman; 13 Aled James. Subs (all used): 29 Phil Carleton; 18 Chris Davies; 20 Hywel Davies; 8 Semisi Cocka.
Tries: Parry (9, 72), James (38), Gay (57), Bromilow (65), Cunningham (75); **Goals:** Murphy 5/6.
Rugby Leaguer & League Express Men of the Match: *Oldham:* Danny Bravo; *Scorpions:* Steve Parry.
Penalty count: 4-7; **Half-time:** 18-12; **Referee:** Craig Halloran *(replaced by Adam Gill, 42)*; **Attendance:** 501.

ROCHDALE HORNETS 62 GATESHEAD THUNDER 18

HORNETS: 1 Wayne English; 17 Dale Bloomfield; 3 Dean Gorton; 30 Danny Pyke; 25 Andy Saywell; 28 Chris Hough; 15 Paul Crook; 18 John Cookson; 9 Steve McDermott; 10 Adam Bowman; 13 Dayne Donoghue; 21 Mark Hobson; 11 Craig Ashall. Subs (all used): 35 Richard Mervill; 7 Steve Roper; 32 Danny Ekis; 16 Danny Samuel.
Tries: Ashall (1, 29), Crook (5), Bloomfield (21, 54), Gorton (26), McDermott (34), Saywell (38), Pyke (68), English (70, 72); **Goals:** Crook 8/10, Hough 1/1.
THUNDER: 3 Danny Wilson; 34 Ashley Thackeray; 30 Mike Mitchell; 17 Joe Brown; 23 Ashley Williams; 40 Paul Stamp; 26 Connor Condron; 8 Jason Payne; 7 Ryan Clarke; 10 Stephen Welton; 13 Michael Kelly; 5 Dan O'Sullivan; 31 Will Bate. Subs (all used): 22 Chris Parker; 16 Robin Peers; 32 Ade Aderiye; 42 Oliver O'Mara.
Tries: Peers (45), Jason Payne (60), Welton (62);
Goals: Stamp 3/3.
Rugby Leaguer & League Express Men of the Match: *Hornets:* Craig Ashall; *Thunder:* Will Bate.
Penalty count: 7-5; **Half-time:** 38-0;
Referee: Tom Crashley; **Attendance:** 401.

WHITEHAVEN 42 SWINTON LIONS 16

WHITEHAVEN: 1 Craig Benson; 38 Andreas Bauer; 33 Max Wiper; 4 Scott McAvoy; 2 Craig Calvert; 14 Chris Smith; 32 Carl Rudd; 10 Howard Hill; 9 Carl Sice; 37 Paul King; 35 Lee Doran; 26 Luke Isakka; 17 Andrew Beattie. Subs (all used): 21 Tyrone Dalton; 15 Richard Farrer; 23 Paul Culnean; 11 Spencer Miller.
Tries: Sice (10, 30), Calvert (15), Benson (34), McAvoy (58), S Miller (61), Smith (77); **Goals:** Rudd 7/8.
On report: McAvoy (26) - alleged punching.
Sin bin: Doran (45) - holding down.
LIONS: 1 Richie Hawkyard; 2 Rob Foxen; 3 Gavin Dodd; 5 Sam Reay; 21 Ian Mort; 6 Martin Ainscough; 25 Karl Ashall; 8 Mike Morrison; 9 Mark Smith; 38 Warren Thompson; 15 Darren Hawkyard; 19 Neil Rigby; 37 Andy Gorski. Subs (all used): 13 Phil Joseph; 10 Dana Wilson; 26 Joe Fitzpatrick; 14 Tommy Gallagher.
Tries: Fitzpatrick (41), R Hawkyard (68), Foxen (73);
Goals: Mort 2/3.
On report: Dodd (26) - alleged punching.
Rugby Leaguer & League Express Men of the Match: *Whitehaven:* Carl Sice; *Lions:* Phil Joseph.
Penalty count: 9-11; **Half-time:** 24-0;
Referee: Greg Dolan; **Attendance:** 863.

Friday 26th August 2011

LONDON SKOLARS 12 KEIGHLEY COUGARS 30

SKOLARS: 3 James Anthony; 18 Aaron Small; 11 Matt Thomas; 36 John Paxton; 2 Smokie Junor; 7 Dylan Skee; 30 Mourad Kriouache; 8 Tony Williams; 9 Gareth Honor; 34 Dave Williams; 33 Lamont Bryan; 15 Oliver Purslow; 25 Austen Aggrey. Subs (all used): 32 Sam Gee; 21 Danny Burke; 22 Saqib Murtza; 29 Michael Sykes.
Tries: Paxton (18), Aggrey (22); **Goals:** Skee 2/2.
Sin bin: Purslow (52) - fighting.
COUGARS: 2 Craig Moss; 31 Dave Halley; 4 Danny Lawton; 33 Jake Normington; 5 Gavin Duffy; 29 Jason Demetriou; 7 Ryan Smith; 8 Andy Shickell; 9 James Feather; 10 Scott Law; 11 Will Cartledge; 12 Oliver Pursglove; 26 Ben Sagar. Subs (all used): 14 Jamaine Wray; 16 Brendan Rawlins; 17 Ryan Benjafield; 21 Richard Jones.
Tries: Demetriou (4), Benjafield (21), Rawlins (31), Duffy (52), Normington (61, 75); **Goals:** Lawton 3/7.
Sin bin: Halley (52) - fighting.
Rugby Leaguer & League Express Men of the Match: *Skolars:* Austen Aggrey; *Cougars:* Jamaine Wray.
Penalty count: 7-18; **Half-time:** 12-16;
Referee: Tim Roby; **Attendance:** 1,083.

ROUND 20

Friday 2nd September 2011

SWINTON LIONS 28 ROCHDALE HORNETS 34

LIONS: 21 Ian Mort; 20 Richard Flooks; 2 Rob Foxen; 3 Gavin Dodd; 23 Alex Hurst; 6 Martin Ainscough; 25 Karl Ashall; 8 Mike Morrison; 9 Mark Smith; 38 Warren Thompson; 37 Andy Gorski; 11 Dale Cunniffe; 12 Lee Wingfield. Subs (all used): 1 Richie Hawkyard; 15 Darren Hawkyard; 14 Tommy Gallagher; 10 Dana Wilson.
Tries: Flooks (7), Wingfield (10, 33), Dodd (50, 61);
Goals: Mort 4/5.
Sin bin: Cunniffe (4) - fighting.
HORNETS: 1 Wayne English; 17 Dale Bloomfield; 3 Dean Gorton; 30 Danny Pyke; 25 Andy Saywell; 28 Chris Hough; 15 Paul Crook; 18 John Cookson; 9 Steve McDermott; 10 Adam Bowman; 13 Dayne Donoghue; 29 Gary Middlehurst; 11 Craig Ashall. Subs (all used): 8 Dave Newton; 35 Richard Mervill; 32 Danny Ekis; 7 Steve Roper.
Tries: Crook (28), Pyke (37), McDermott (42, 80), Cookson (70), Donoghue (75); **Goals:** Crook 5/6.
Sin bin: Middlehurst (4) - fighting.
Rugby Leaguer & League Express Men of the Match: *Lions:* Lee Wingfield; *Hornets:* Wayne English.
Penalty count: 4-5; **Half-time:** 18-12;
Referee: Clint Sharrad; **Attendance:** 1,063.

Sunday 4th September 2011

GATESHEAD THUNDER 14 DONCASTER 38

THUNDER: 3 Danny Wilson; 34 Ashley Thackeray; 30 Mike Mitchell; 17 Joe Brown; 23 Ashley Williams; 40 Paul Stamp; 31 Will Bate; 8 Jason Payne; 7 Ryan Clarke; 10 Stephen Welton; 13 Michael Kelly; 29 David Cash; 5 Dan O'Sullivan. Subs (all used): 22 Chris Parker; 9 Tom Hodgson; 32 Ade Aderiye; 42 Oliver O'Mara.
Tries: O'Sullivan (9, 33); **Goals:** Clarke 1/1, Stamp 2/2.
DONCASTER: 1 Mick Butterfield; 2 Stewart Sanderson; 31 Nev Morrison; 25 Chris Spurr; 32 Gareth Potts; 19 Scott Spaven; 7 Craig Fawcett; 17 Adam Scott; 13 Jack Ely; 11 Kyle Sampson; 15 Craig Robinson; 23 Grant Edwards; 16 Mike Emmett. Subs (all used): 9 Kyle Kesik; 22 Carl Hughes; 8 Matt Carbutt; 26 Dominic Dee.
Tries: Potts (18), Sanderson (24), Butterfield (42), C Hughes (44, 72), Fawcett (55), Morrison (61);
Goals: Spaven 2/4, Sanderson 3/3.
Rugby Leaguer & League Express Men of the Match: *Thunder:* Dan O'Sullivan; *Doncaster:* Gareth Potts.
Penalty count: 11-5; **Half-time:** 14-10;
Referee: Craig Halloran; **Attendance:** 527.

KEIGHLEY COUGARS 28 WHITEHAVEN 20

COUGARS: 2 Craig Moss; 4 Danny Lawton; 22 Ben Sagar; 33 Jake Normington; 31 Dave Halley; 29 Jason Demetriou; 36 Jy-Mel Coleman; 8 Andy Shickell; 9 James Feather; 10 Scott Law; 11 Will Cartledge; 12 Oliver Pursglove; 23 Chris Baines. Subs (all used): 14 Jamaine Wray; 16 Brendan Rawlins; 17 Ryan Benjafield; 21 Richard Jones.
Tries: Cartledge (40, 52), Baines (64); **Goals:** Baines 8/8.
WHITEHAVEN: 1 Craig Benson; 38 Andreas Bauer; 17 Andrew Beattie; 4 Scott McAvoy; 2 Craig Calvert; 36 Chris Gerrard; 32 Carl Rudd; 10 Howard Hill; 9 Carl Sice; 37 Paul King; 35 Lee Doran; 26 Luke Isakka; 18 Kurt Wilton. Subs (all used): 11 Spencer Miller; 14 Chris Smith; 15 Richard Farrer; 34 Matthew Haggerty.
Tries: Calvert (46), McAvoy (61), Wilton (71);
Goals: Rudd 4/5.
Rugby Leaguer & League Express Men of the Match: *Cougars:* Jason Demetriou; *Whitehaven:* Carl Rudd.
Penalty count: 11-8; **Half-time:** 12-4;
Referee: Jamie Leahy; **Attendance:** 964.

WORKINGTON TOWN 20 OLDHAM 24

TOWN: 1 Brett Carter; 2 Elliott Miller; 3 Jason Mossop; 4 Aaron Low; 5 Neil Frazer; 24 Darren Holt; 7 Scott Kaighan; 16 Ryan McDonald; 14 Jack Pedley; 10 Kris Coward; 11 Mike Whitehead; 12 Jarrad Stack; 13 Karl Olstrum. Subs (all used): 21 John Patrick; 15 Ruairi McGoff; 23 Marc Bainbridge; 32 Chris Clough.
Tries: Pedley (1), Coward (13), Carter (66), Kaighan (72); **Goals:** Holt 2/4.
OLDHAM: 27 Shaun Robinson; 5 John Gillam; 3 Marcus St Hilaire; 26 Matthew Fogarty; 21 Mark Brocklehurst; 6 Neil Roden; 7 Jamie Dallimore; 8 Jason Boults; 17 John Clough; 28 Luke Stenchion; 30 Danny Bravo; 24 Paul Noone; 25 Martin Roden. Subs (all used): 9 Danny Whitmore; 16 Liam Gilchrist; 23 Callum Casey; 13 Valu Bentley.
Tries: Brocklehurst (31), Fogarty (36), N Roden (41), Dallimore (52), Casey (58); **Goals:** Dallimore 2/5.
Rugby Leaguer & League Express Men of the Match: *Town:* Brett Carter; *Oldham:* Neil Roden.
Penalty count: 10-7; **Half-time:** 10-8;
Referee: Dave Merrick; **Attendance:** 716.

Doncaster's Dominic Dee stretches past Whitehaven's Paul King, Andrew Beattie and Carl Sice, but the 'try' was subsequently disallowed

PLAY-OFFS

ELIMINATION PLAY-OFFS

Sunday 11th September 2011

ROCHDALE HORNETS 39 OLDHAM 18

HORNETS: 1 Wayne English; 17 Dale Bloomfield; 3 Dean Gorton; 30 Danny Pyke; 25 Andy Saywell; 15 Paul Crook; 7 Steve Roper; 18 John Cookson; 11 Craig Ashall; 35 Richard Mervill; 13 Dayne Donoghue; 21 Mark Hobson; 28 Chris Hough. Subs (all used): 32 Danny Ekis; 8 Dave Newton; 10 Adam Bowman; 16 Danny Samuel.
Tries: Crook (2, 36), Mervill (5), Gorton (16), Saywell (65), Bloomfield (79); **Goals:** Crook 6/8;
Field goals: Ashall (39), Crook (60), Roper (75).
OLDHAM: 27 Shaun Robinson; 21 Mark Brocklehurst; 3 Marcus St Hilaire; 29 Mark McCully; 5 John Gillam; 6 Neil Roden; 7 Carl Forber; 8 Jason Boults; 17 John Clough; 13 Valu Bentley; 30 Danny Bravo; 24 Paul Noone; 25 Martin Roden. Subs (all used): 26 Matthew Fogarty; 9 Danny Whitmore; 16 Liam Gilchrist; 23 Callum Casey.
Tries: Robinson (12), N Roden (21), Brocklehurst (70), McCully (80); **Goals:** Forber 1/4.
Rugby Leaguer & League Express Men of the Match:
Hornets: Paul Crook; *Oldham:* Jason Boults.
Penalty count: 8-14; **Half-time:** 23-10;
Referee: George Stokes; **Attendance:** 1,053.

DONCASTER 34 WHITEHAVEN 16

DONCASTER: 1 Mick Butterfield; 29 Gareth Potts; 25 Chris Spurr; 31 Nev Morrison; 2 Stewart Sanderson; 7 Craig Fawcett; 19 Scott Spaven; 17 Adam Scott; 16 Mike Emmett; 11 Kyle Sampson; 15 Craig Robinson; 23 Grant Edwards; 22 Carl Hughes. Subs (all used): 9 Kyle Kesik; 26 Dominic Dee; 8 Matt Carbutt; 30 Michael Coady.
Tries: Potts (6, 50), Sanderson (16, 31), Butterfield (21), Edwards (64); **Goals:** Spaven 5/6.
WHITEHAVEN: 9 Carl Sice; 38 Andreas Bauer; 17 Andrew Beattie; 4 Scott McAvoy; 2 Craig Calvert; 6 Lewis Palfrey; 32 Carl Rudd; 34 Matthew Haggerty; 14 Chris Smith; 10 Howard Hill; 11 Spencer Miller; 35 Lee Doran; 36 Chris Gerrard. Subs (all used): 18 Kurt Wilton; 37 Paul King; 15 Richard Farrer; 19 Brad Crellin.
Tries: Sice (26), Doran (70), Crellin (75);
Goals: Palfrey 1/1, Rudd 1/2.
Rugby Leaguer & League Express Men of the Match:
Doncaster: Grant Edwards; *Whitehaven:* Howard Hill.
Penalty count: 7-8; **Half-time:** 24-6;
Referee: Ronnie Laughton; **Attendance:** 418.

QUALIFYING SEMI-FINAL

Sunday 18th September 2011

KEIGHLEY COUGARS 10 WORKINGTON TOWN 19

COUGARS: 2 Craig Moss; 5 Gavin Duffy; 22 Ben Sagar; 33 Jake Normington; 31 Dave Halley; 29 Jason Demetriou; 7 Ryan Smith; 8 Andy Shickell; 9 James Feather; 10 Scott Law; 11 Will Cartledge; 12 Oliver Pursglove; 23 Chris Baines. Subs (all used): 14 Jamaine Wray; 16 Brendan Rawlins; 17 Ryan Benjafield; 21 Richard Jones.
Tries: Moss (52, 61); **Goals:** Moss 1/1, Baines 0/1.
TOWN: 1 Brett Carter; 5 Neil Frazer; 3 Jason Mossop; 4 Aaron Low; 2 Elliott Miller; 24 Darren Holt; 7 Scott Kaighan; 10 Kris Coward; 13 Karl Olstrum; 29 Dave Armitstead; 18 Joe McKenna; 11 Mike Whitehead; 12 Jarrad Stack. Subs (all used): 15 Ruairi McGoff; 17 James Robinson; 23 Marc Bainbridge; 32 Chris Clough.
Tries: Frazer (3, 47), Miller (18); **Goals:** Holt 3/5;
Field goal: Holt (36).
Rugby Leaguer & League Express Men of the Match:
Cougars: Craig Moss; *Town:* Darren Holt.
Penalty count: 11-9; **Half-time:** 0-13;
Referee: Ronnie Laughton; **Attendance:** 1,072.

ELIMINATION SEMI-FINAL

Sunday 18th September 2011

ROCHDALE HORNETS 26 DONCASTER 18

HORNETS: 1 Wayne English; 17 Dale Bloomfield; 3 Dean Gorton; 30 Danny Pyke; 25 Andy Saywell; 15 Paul Crook; 7 Steve Roper; 18 John Cookson; 28 Chris Hough; 35 Richard Mervill; 11 Craig Ashall; 21 Mark Hobson; 29 Gary Middlehurst. Subs (all used): 13 Dayne Donoghue; 32 Danny Ekis; 9 Steve McDermott; 10 Adam Bowman.
Tries: Bloomfield (3, 39, 65), Saywell (55), Hough (75);
Goals: Crook 3/6.
DONCASTER: 1 Mick Butterfield; 2 Stewart Sanderson; 31 Nev Morrison; 25 Chris Spurr; 32 Gareth Potts; 19 Scott Spaven; 7 Craig Fawcett; 17 Adam Scott; 16 Mike Emmett; 11 Kyle Sampson; 15 Craig Robinson; 23 Grant Edwards; 22 Carl Hughes. Subs (all used): 9 Kyle Kesik; 8 Matt Carbutt; 26 Dominic Dee; 30 Michael Coady.
Tries: Robinson (7), Scott (10), Spurr (20);
Goals: Spaven 3/3.
Rugby Leaguer & League Express Men of the Match:
Hornets: Wayne English; *Doncaster:* Scott Spaven.
Penalty count: 4-7; **Half-time:** 8-18;
Referee: Clint Sharrad; **Attendance:** 552.

FINAL ELIMINATOR

Sunday 25th September 2011

KEIGHLEY COUGARS 38 ROCHDALE HORNETS 23

COUGARS: 18 James Haythornthwaite; 4 Danny Lawton; 22 Ben Sagar; 33 Jake Normington; 5 Gavin Duffy; 29 Jason Demetriou; 36 Jy-Mel Coleman; 17 Ryan Benjafield; 9 James Feather; 10 Scott Law; 11 Will Cartledge; 12 Oliver Pursglove; 21 Richard Jones. Subs (all used): 14 Jamaine Wray; 7 Ryan Smith; 16 Brendan Rawlins; 8 Andy Shickell.
Tries: Sagar (38, 47), Lawton (51), Duffy (58), Haythornthwaite (70, 80), Normington (74);
Goals: Lawton 5/8.
HORNETS: 1 Wayne English; 17 Dale Bloomfield; 3 Dean Gorton; 30 Danny Pyke; 25 Andy Saywell; 15 Paul Crook; 7 Steve Roper; 18 John Cookson; 28 Chris Hough; 35 Richard Mervill; 13 Dayne Donoghue. Subs (all used): 32 Danny Ekis; 9 Steve McDermott; 10 Adam Bowman; 8 Dave Newton.
Tries: Saywell (15), English (34), McDermott (54);
Goals: Crook 5/5; **Field goal:** Crook (63).
Rugby Leaguer & League Express Men of the Match:
Cougars: James Feather; *Hornets:* Paul Crook.
Penalty count: 7-4; **Half-time:** 8-16;
Referee: Robert Hicks; **Attendance:** 982.

GRAND FINAL

Sunday 2nd October 2011

KEIGHLEY COUGARS 32 WORKINGTON TOWN 12

COUGARS: 18 James Haythornthwaite; 4 Danny Lawton; 22 Ben Sagar; 33 Jake Normington; 5 Gavin Duffy; 6 Jason Demetriou; 36 Jy-Mel Coleman; 17 Ryan Benjafield; 9 James Feather; 10 Scott Law; 11 Will Cartledge; 12 Oliver Pursglove; 21 Richard Jones. Subs (all used): 14 Jamaine Wray; 8 Andy Shickell; 16 Brendan Rawlins; 7 Ryan Smith.
Tries: Lawton (5), Feather (20), Rawlins (25), Pursglove (32), Normington (69, 77); **Goals:** Lawton 4/6.
TOWN: 1 Brett Carter; 2 Elliott Miller; 3 Jason Mossop; 4 Aaron Low; 5 Neil Frazer; 24 Darren Holt; 7 Scott Kaighan; 10 Kris Coward; 29 Dave Armitstead; 11 Mike Whitehead; 18 Joe McKenna; 12 Jarrad Stack. Subs (all used): 23 Marc Bainbridge; 15 Ruairi McGoff; 32 Chris Clough; 17 James Robinson.
Tries: Kaighan (65), Frazer (74); **Goals:** Holt 2/2.
Rugby Leaguer & League Express Men of the Match:
Cougars: Jason Demetriou; *Town:* Jarrad Stack.
Penalty count: 7-5; **Half-time:** 22-0; **Referee:** Tim Roby.
(at Halliwell Jones Stadium, Warrington).

Keighley's Jamaine Wray takes on Workington's Dave Armitstead during the
Championship One Grand Final

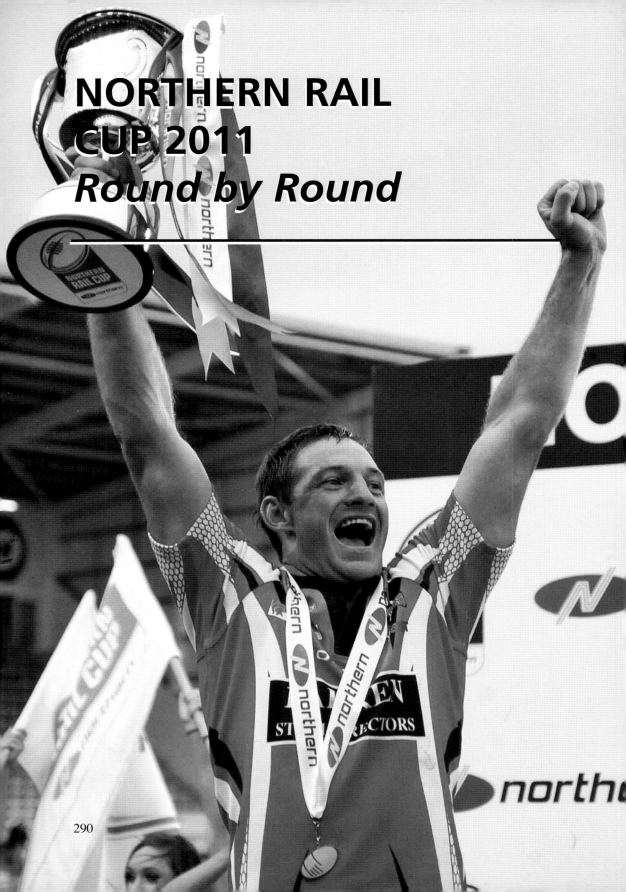

NORTHERN RAIL CUP 2011
Round by Round

ROUND 1

Friday 4th February 2011

POOL 1

FEATHERSTONE ROVERS 54 DONCASTER 10

ROVERS: 1 Ian Hardman; 2 Bryn Powell; 3 Sam Smeaton; 17 Greg Worthington; 5 Tom Saxton; 6 Andy Kain; 7 Liam Finn; 8 Tony Tonks; 9 Ben Kaye; 10 Stuart Dickens; 11 Jon Grayshon; 12 Tim Spears; 13 Matty Dale. Subs (all used): 16 Iain Morrison; 15 Michael Haley; 4 Andrew Bostock; 19 Zak Hardaker.
Tries: Kain (12, 50), Tonks (14), Smeaton (16, 41, 78), Finn (36), Hardman (44), Saxton (61), Bostock (64), Hardaker (71); **Goals:** Finn 5/11.
Sin bin: Spears (39) - fighting.
DONCASTER: 1 Mick Butterfield; 5 Dean Colton; 4 Shaun Leaf; 25 Chris Spurr; 2 Stewart Sanderson; 7 Craig Fawcett; 19 Scott Spaven; 20 Jamie Bovill; 21 Paul Hughes; 17 Adam Scott; 11 Kyle Sampson; 15 Craig Robinson; 16 Mike Emmett. Subs (all used): 8 Matt Carbutt; 10 Liam Crawley; 3 Lee Gomersall; 9 Kyle Kesik.
Tries: Butterfield (2), Emmett (68); **Goals:** Spaven 1/2.
Dismissal: Kesik (39) - fighting.
Sin bin: Spurr (39) - fighting.
Rugby Leaguer & League Express Men of the Match:
Rovers: Tony Tonks; *Doncaster:* Michael Butterfield.
Penalty count: 9-10; **Half-time:** 22-4;
Referee: Ben Thaler; **Attendance:** 1,223.

POOL 2

SWINTON LIONS 22 HALIFAX 28

LIONS: 1 Richie Hawkyard; 2 Rob Foxen; 3 Gavin Dodd; 4 Dean Thompson; 20 Richard Flooks; 6 Martin Ainscough; 7 Ian Watson; 8 Mike Morrison; 25 Karl Ashall; 16 Neil Holland; 15 Darren Hawkyard; 11 Dale Cunniffe; 12 Lee Wingfield. Subs (all used): 9 Mark Smith; 21 Ian Mort; 19 Neil Rigby; 27 Bruce Johnson.
Tries: Foxen (27), Smith (37), D Thompson (40), Holland (62); **Goals:** Dodd 3/4.
Sin bin: D Thompson (21) - holding down.
HALIFAX: 1 Miles Greenwood; 20 Paul White; 2 Lee Paterson; 5 James Haley; 23 Rob Worrincy; 6 Danny Jones; 7 Ben Black; 12 Sam Barlow; 13 Bob Beswick; 15 Jim Gannon; 24 Steve Bannister; 14 Ryan Clayton; 16 Paul Smith. Subs (all used): 9 Sean Penkywicz; 18 Joe Chandler; 19 Jacob Fairbank; 21 Josh Barlow.
Tries: Haley (6), White (9), Worrincy (33), Paterson (56, 66), S Barlow (79); **Goals:** Paterson 2/5, Jones 0/1.
Sin bin: Paterson (25) - holding down.
Rugby Leaguer & League Express Men of the Match:
Lions: Ian Watson; *Halifax:* Ben Black.
Penalty count: 11-13; **Half-time:** 16-14;
Referee: Robert Hicks; **Attendance:** 916.

Saturday 5th February 2011

POOL 1

TOULOUSE OLYMPIQUE 40 DEWSBURY RAMS 38

OLYMPIQUE: 5 Clement Bienes; 2 Sebastien Payan; 3 Sebastien Planas; 20 Bruno Ormeno; 18 Andrei Olari; 6 Darren Nicholls; 7 Josh Lewis; 8 Brendan Worth; 9 Craig Cook; 23 Teli Pelo; 17 Kevin Larroyer; 12 Yoan Tisseyre; 16 Sylvain Houles. Subs (all used): 10 Ged Corcoran; 14 Antoni Maria; 13 Eric Anselme; 24 Gregory White.
Tries: Ormeno (4, 16), Lewis (7), Anselme (34, 47), Pelo (69), Cook (77); **Goals:** Lewis 6/7.
Sin bin: Pelo (58) - fighting.
RAMS: 1 James Craven; 2 Michael Wainwright; 13 Ayden Faal; 4 Scott Turner; 5 Austin Buchanan; 6 Pat Walker; 7 Dominic Brambani; 10 Keegan Hirst; 22 Jonny Horton; 8 Anthony England; 12 James Lockwood; 11 Rob Spicer; 14 Rob Roberts. Subs (all used): 32 Elliott Cosgrove; 21 Kyle Bibb; 23 Luke Menzies; 15 Josh Tonks.
Tries: Buchanan (21, 50), Craven (27, 65), Turner (33), Menzies (44), Lockwood (54);
Goals: P Walker 1/2, Brambani 4/5.
Sin bin: Cosgrove (58) - fighting.
Rugby Leaguer & League Express Men of the Match:
Olympique: Brendan Worth; *Rams:* Keegan Hirst.
Penalty count: 5-5; **Half-time:** 22-16;
Referee: Gareth Hewer; **Attendance:** 1,000.

Sunday 6th February 2011

POOL 1

BARROW RAIDERS 24 YORK CITY KNIGHTS 20

RAIDERS: 2 Andy Ballard; 19 Marc Dixon; 12 Ned Catic; 4 Liam Harrison; 5 James Nixon; 6 Jamie Rooney; 14 Liam Campbell; 8 Jamie Thackray; 9 Mark Gleeson; 10 Matt James; 15 Martin Ostler; 13 Richard Fletcher; 16 Zebastian Luisi. Subs (all used): 18 Nathan Mossop; 17 Brett McDermott; 11 Michael Knowles; 38 Adam Nicholson.
Tries: Gleeson (9), Nixon (19, 43), Catic (28), Ostler (55); **Goals:** Rooney 2/5.
CITY KNIGHTS: 1 James Haynes; 5 Danny Wilson; 3 Duane Straugheir; 19 Matt Garside; 2 Dave Sutton; 6 Chris Thorman; 7 Jon Presley; 37 Ben Jones; 9 Jack Lee; 32 Nathan Massey; 31 John Davies; 13 Ryan Esders; 10 Alex Benson. Subs (all used): 14 Jack Stearman; 22 Ed Smith; 24 Mark Barlow; 4 Lee Waterman.
Tries: Wilson (34), Esders (38), Sutton (70), Presley (79); **Goals:** Thorman 2/4.
Rugby Leaguer & League Express Men of the Match:
Raiders: Richard Fletcher; *City Knights:* Chris Thorman.
Penalty count: 6-9; **Half-time:** 12-10;
Referee: Richard Silverwood; **Attendance:** 1,305.

KEIGHLEY COUGARS 24 ROCHDALE HORNETS 6

COUGARS: 2 Craig Moss; 5 Gavin Duffy; 18 James Haythornthwaite; 4 Danny Lawton; 26 James Hutchinson; 24 Paul Drake; 7 Ryan Smith; 10 Scott Law; 9 James Feather; 8 Andy Shickell; 11 Will Cartledge; 12 Oliver Pursglove; 29 Jason Demetriou. Subs (all used): 14 Jamaine Wray; 20 Rick Barr; 23 Chris Baines; 16 Brendan Rawlins.
Tries: Hutchinson (5), Duffy (17, 77), Cartledge (25), Rawlins (72); **Goals:** Lawton 2/7.
HORNETS: 5 Scott Yates; 17 Dale Bloomfield; 3 Dean Gorton; 22 Damien Reid; 1 Wayne English; 6 Liam McGovern; 15 Paul Crook; 8 Dave Newton; 28 Chris Hough; 18 John Cookson; 11 Craig Ashall; 4 Matthew Strong; 13 Dayne Donoghue. Subs (all used): 14 Ryan Powell; 20 Chris Clough; 16 Danny Samuel; 10 Adam Bowman.
Try: English (35); **Goals:** Crook 1/1.
Rugby Leaguer & League Express Men of the Match:
Cougars: Jason Demetriou; *Hornets:* Dayne Donoghue.
Penalty count: 14-11; **Half-time:** 12-6;
Referee: Phil Bentham; **Attendance:** 627.

LONDON SKOLARS 18 WIDNES VIKINGS 62

SKOLARS: 1 Neil Thorman; 2 Smokie Junor; 17 Dave Arnot; 4 Luke May; 5 Ade Adebisi; 7 Dylan Skee; 6 Jy-Mel Coleman; 8 Tony Williams; 9 Gareth Honor; 13 Stephen Ball; 11 Matt Thomas; 10 Jason Hart; 15 Oliver Purslow. Subs (all used): 24 Dave McMeeken; 25 Austen Aggrey; 23 Liam Prescott; 22 Saqib Murtza.
Tries: M Thomas (7), May (14), Thorman (61), Adebisi (80); **Goals:** Jy-Mel Coleman 0/3, Prescott 1/1.
VIKINGS: 1 Danny Craven; 19 Matt Gardner; 18 James Ford; 23 Tangi Ropati; 5 Paddy Flynn; 6 Anthony Thackeray; 14 Thomas Coyle; 3 Richard Varkulis; 9 Kirk Netherton; 10 Daniel Heckenberg; 11 Dave Allen; 16 Macgraff Leuluai; 17 Ben Kavanagh. Subs (all used): 8 Steve Pickersgill; 12 Kurt Haggerty; 13 Simon Finnigan; 29 Grant Gore.
Tries: Flynn (11, 77), Allen (19), Craven (26, 39), Kavanagh (34), Gardner (40), T Coyle (48), Thackeray (51), Haggerty (70), Ropati (74); **Goals:** Craven 9/11.
Rugby Leaguer & League Express Men of the Match:
Skolars: Luke May; *Vikings:* Danny Craven.
Penalty count: 8-19; **Half-time:** 8-34;
Referee: Chris Leatherbarrow; **Attendance:** 643.

POOL 2

BATLEY BULLDOGS 4 LEIGH CENTURIONS 24

BULLDOGS: 1 Ian Preece; 5 Wayne Reittie; 3 Daley Williams; 4 Danny Maun; 2 Alex Brown; 6 Paul Handforth; 7 Gareth Moore; 8 Byron Smith; 9 Kris Lythe; 21 James Martin; 11 Alex Bretherton; 12 Jason Walton; 19 Mark Toohey. Subs (all used): 13 Ashley Lindsay; 17 Craig Potter; 10 Sean Hesketh; 16 Paul Mennell.
Try: Brown (47); **Goals:** Moore 0/1.
Dismissal: Mennell (60) - high tackle.
On report: Martin (20) - alleged high tackle.
CENTURIONS: 1 Stuart Donlan; 2 Steve Maden; 22 Tom Armstrong; 4 Mick Nanyn; 5 Dean McGilvray; 23 Mick Govin; 25 Jamie Ellis; 8 Chris Hill; 7 Robbie Hunter-Paul; 10 Ricky Bibey; 3 Stuart Littler; 12 Tommy Goulden; 11 James Taylor. Subs (all used): 9 John Duffy; 6 Martyn Ridyard; 13 Stephen Nash; 26 David Mills.
Tries: Goulden (9), Armstrong (11, 16), Donlan (61), Hunter-Paul (78); **Goals:** Nanyn 2/5.
Rugby Leaguer & League Express Men of the Match:
Bulldogs: Gareth Moore; *Centurions:* Robbie Hunter-Paul.
Penalty count: 18-11; **Half-time:** 0-14;
Referee: Steve Ganson; **Attendance:** 1,073.

GATESHEAD THUNDER 20 SHEFFIELD EAGLES 32

THUNDER: 17 Joe Brown; 2 Craig Olugbode; 15 Andy Morris; 1 Wayne Green; 16 Robin Peers; 6 James Clarkson; 7 Ryan Clarke; 10 Stephen Welton; 9 Tom Hodgson; 19 Sam Crowther; 13 Michael Kelly; 12 Michael Ward; 8 Jason Payne. Subs (all used): 14 Reece Young; 38 David Norman; 20 Nick Staveley; 22 Chris Parker.
Tries: Norman (44), Green (52), Ward (60), Peers (72);
Goals: Clarke 2/4.
EAGLES: 28 Jamie Cottle; 2 Danny Mills; 3 Menzie Yere; 26 Corey Hanson; 5 Tim Bergin; 13 Dane McDonald; 7 Simon Brown; 8 Jack Howieson; 9 Andrew Henderson; 17 Alex Rowe; 11 Alex Szostak; 12 Peter Green; 19 Joe Hirst. Subs (all used): 20 Pat Smith; 15 Liam Higgins; 10 Mitchell Stringer; 18 Scott Watson.
Tries: Bergin (4), Yere (9, 55, 76), Mills (16), Hanson (65); **Goals:** Brown 2/3, Bergin 2/3.
Rugby Leaguer & League Express Men of the Match:
Thunder: Wayne Green; *Eagles:* Menzie Yere.
Penalty count: 10-8; **Half-time:** 0-16;
Referee: Ronnie Laughton; **Attendance:** 444.

OLDHAM 28 HUNSLET HAWKS 22

OLDHAM: 1 Ben Heaton; 2 Lucas Onyango; 12 Ben Wood; 4 Jack Bradbury; 5 John Gillam; 6 Neil Roden; 7 Mick Diveney; 15 Luke Sutton; 25 Martin Roden; 10 Dave Ellison; 11 Andrew Isherwood; 24 Paul Noone; 14 Chris Clarke. Subs (all used): 8 Jason Boults; 13 Valu Bentley; 17 John Clough; 22 Tom Wood-Hulme.
Tries: Bradbury (21, 72), Clough (32), Diveney (35), Gillam (45); **Goals:** Diveney 4/5.
Sin bin: N Roden (76) - high tackle.
HAWKS: 1 Stuart Kain; 5 Waine Pryce; 4 David Clayton; 12 Tom Haughey; 2 Richie Barnett; 6 Danny Grimshaw; 7 Paul March; 8 Adam Sullivan; 14 Luke Haigh; 10 James Houston; 17 Rob Kelly; 11 Richard Blakeway; 13 David March. Subs (all used): 15 Scott Woodcock; 16 John Oakes; 20 Andrew Yates; 23 Joe McLocklan.
Tries: Kain (3), Haughey (14), Clayton (52), Yates (78);
Goals: D March 3/4.
Sin bin: D March (31) - use of the knee.
Rugby Leaguer & League Express Men of the Match:
Oldham: Ben Heaton; *Hawks:* Tom Haughey.
Penalty count: 12-14; **Half-time:** 16-12;
Referee: Thierry Alibert; **Attendance:** 685.

Tuesday 8th February 2011

POOL 2

WHITEHAVEN 18 WORKINGTON TOWN 28

WHITEHAVEN: 1 Craig Benson; 31 Jay Rossi; 3 Derry Eilbeck; 4 Scott McAvoy; 2 Craig Calvert; 6 Lewis Palfrey; 7 Tane Manihera; 23 Paul Culnean; 14 Chris Smith; 10 Howard Hill; 11 Spencer Miller; 12 Dexter Miller; 17 Andrew Beattie. Subs (all used): 9 Carl Sice; 26 Luke Isakka; 22 Reece Fox; 13 Daniel Barker.
Tries: Palfrey (20), McAvoy (28), Culnean (51), Eilbeck (78); **Goals:** Palfrey 1/4.
Sin bin: Hill (15) - use of the knee;
Sice (70) - delaying restart.
TOWN: 1 Brett Carter; 2 Elliott Miller; 3 Jason Mossop; 4 Aaron Low; 5 Neil Frazer; 23 Marc Bainbridge; 7 Scott Kaighan; 15 Ruairi McGoff; 9 Graeme Mattinson; 10 Kris Coward; 11 Mike Whitehead; 12 Jarrad Stack; 13 Karl Olstrum. Subs (all used): 14 Jack Pedley; 8 Marc Jackson; 16 Ryan McDonald; 19 Marc Shackley.
Tries: Stack (3, 12), McGoff (7); **Goals:** Kaighan 8/9.
Rugby Leaguer & League Express Men of the Match:
Whitehaven: Paul Culnean; *Town:* Jarrad Stack.
Penalty count: 9-22; **Half-time:** 8-18;
Referee: James Child; **Attendance:** 1,005.

ROUND 2

Saturday 12th February 2011

POOL 1

WIDNES VIKINGS 44 TOULOUSE OLYMPIQUE 28

VIKINGS: 1 Danny Craven; 5 Paddy Flynn; 23 Tangi Ropati; 4 Steve Tyrer; 19 Matt Gardner; 6 Anthony Thackeray; 14 Thomas Coyle; 17 Ben Kavanagh; 9 Kirk Netherton; 10 Daniel Heckenberg; 11 Dave Allen; 16 Macgraff Leuluai; 12 Kurt Haggerty. Subs (all used): 3 Richard Varkulis; 15 Chris Gerrard; 20 Shane Grady; 35 Gareth Frodsham.
Tries: Allen (9), Thackeray (16, 54), Ropati (51), Tyrer (67), Netherton (73), Gerrard (75), Kavanagh (78);
Goals: Tyrer 6/8.
OLYMPIQUE: 22 Damien Couturier; 24 Gregory White; 3 Sebastian Planas; 20 Bruno Ormeno; 2 Sebastien Payan; 6 Darren Nicholls; 7 Josh Lewis; 8 Brendan Worth; 9 Craig Cook; 23 Teli Pelo; 12 Yoan Tisseyre; 17 Kevin Larroyer; 16 Sylvain Houles. Subs (all used): 13 Eric Anselme; 14 Antoni Maria; 15 Jerome Gout; 21 Nicolas Faure.
Tries: Lewis (4), Planas (29), White (33), Nicholls (47), Ormeno (64); **Goals:** Lewis 4/5.
Rugby Leaguer & League Express Men of the Match:
Vikings: Anthony Thackeray; *Olympique:* Josh Lewis.
Penalty count: 4-1; **Half-time:** 12-16;
Referee: Ronnie Laughton; **Attendance:** 2,376.

Sunday 13th February 2011

POOL 1

DEWSBURY RAMS 14 KEIGHLEY COUGARS 0

RAMS: 1 James Craven; 5 Austin Buchanan; 13 Ayden Faal; 17 Ryan Glynn; 2 Michael Wainwright; 7 Dominic Brambani; 25 Tom Wandless; 8 Anthony England; 9 Luke Blake; 10 Keegan Hirst; 11 Rob Spicer; 12 James Lockwood; 15 Josh Tonks. Subs (all used): 23 Luke Menzies; 19 James Walker; 32 Elliott Cosgrove; 29 Matty Brooks.
Tries: Tonks (16), Hirst (70); **Goals:** Brambani 3/3.
COUGARS: 2 Craig Moss; 5 Gavin Duffy; 3 Tom Burton; 4 Danny Lawton; 26 James Hutchinson; 24 Paul Drake; 7 Ryan Smith; 8 Andy Shickell; 9 James Feather; 10 Scott Law; 11 Will Cartledge; 12 Oliver Pursglove; 29 Jason Demetriou. Subs (all used): 14 Jamaine Wray; 16 Brendan Rawlins; 23 Chris Baines; 13 Greg Nicholson.
Sin bin: Drake (36) - punching.
Rugby Leaguer & League Express Men of the Match:
Rams: James Craven; *Cougars:* Jamaine Wray.
Penalty count: 10-14; **Half-time:** 8-0;
Referee: Dave Merrick; **Attendance:** 758.

DONCASTER 32 LONDON SKOLARS 4

DONCASTER: 1 Mick Butterfield; 2 Stewart Sanderson; 25 Chris Spurr; 4 Shaun Leaf; 5 Dean Colton; 7 Craig Fawcett; 19 Scott Spaven; 17 Adam Scott; 13 Jack Ely; 20 Jamie Bovill; 15 Craig Robinson; 8 Matt Carbutt; 16 Mike Emmett. Subs (all used): 14 Scott Wilson; 9 Kyle Kesik; 10 Liam Crawley; 11 Kyle Sampson.
Tries: Spurr (7), Crawley (29), Spaven (37), Ely (52, 56), Kesik (63); **Goals:** Spaven 1/2, Sanderson 3/4.
SKOLARS: 3 James Anthony; 2 Smokie Junor; 17 Dave Arnot; 4 Luke May; 5 Ade Adebisi; 7 Dylan Skee; 1 Neil Thorman; 8 Tony Williams; 9 Gareth Honor; 10 Jason Hart; 11 Matt Thomas; 33 Dave Samson; 31 Ben Bolger. Subs (all used): 25 Austen Aggrey; 22 Saqib Murtza; 32 Sam Gee; 13 Stephen Ball.
Try: Arnot (15); **Goals:** Thorman 0/1.
Sin bin: Arnot (49) - interference.

Rugby Leaguer & League Express Men of the Match: *Doncaster:* Craig Fawcett; *Skolars:* Neil Thorman.
Penalty count: 12-8; **Half-time:** 16-4;
Referee: Mohammed Drizza; **Attendance:** 420.

ROCHDALE HORNETS 18 BARROW RAIDERS 30

HORNETS: 1 Wayne English; 2 Craig Johnson; 3 Dean Gorton; 22 Damien Reid; 17 Dale Bloomfield; 6 Liam McGovern; 7 Steve Roper; 18 John Cookson; 15 Paul Crook; 27 Jamie Peasnall; 11 Craig Ashall; 16 Danny Samuel; 13 Dayne Donoghue. Subs (all used): 29 Danny Meekin; 19 Gareth Hayes; 21 Mark Hobson; 36 Scott Mansfield.
Tries: Bloomfield (28), Crook (42), Roper (75);
Goals: Crook 2/2, McGovern 1/1.
RAIDERS: 1 Gary Broadbent; 2 Andy Ballard; 12 Ned Catic; 4 Liam Harrison; 5 James Nixon; 6 Jamie Rooney; 14 Liam Campbell; 8 Jamie Thackray; 18 Nathan Mossop; 17 Brett McDermott; 11 Michael Knowles; 15 Martin Ostler; 16 Zebastian Luisi. Subs (all used): 10 Matt James; 19 Marc Dixon; 13 Richard Fletcher; 9 Mark Gleeson.
Tries: Harrison (6, 52, 69), Ballard (30), James (67), Nixon (79); **Goals:** Rooney 3/6.
Rugby Leaguer & League Express Men of the Match: *Hornets:* Paul Crook; *Raiders:* Liam Harrison.
Penalty count: 7-7; **Half-time:** 6-12;
Referee: Craig Halloran; **Attendance:** 600.

YORK CITY KNIGHTS 22 FEATHERSTONE ROVERS 32

CITY KNIGHTS: 21 Dennis Tuffour; 2 Dave Sutton; 19 Matt Garside; 4 Lee Waterman; 5 Danny Wilson; 6 Chris Thorman; 7 Jon Presley; 32 Nathan Massey; 9 Jack Lee; 37 Ben Jones; 31 John Davies; 13 Ryan Esders; 23 Paul Stamp. Subs (all used): 14 Jack Stearman; 24 Mark Barlow; 25 Steve Lewis; 17 Ian Bell.
Tries: Esders (33, 79), Davies (37), Presley (70);
Goals: Thorman 3/4.
Sin bin: Bell (42) - late challenge on Morrison.
ROVERS: 1 Ian Hardman; 2 Bryn Powell; 3 Sam Smeaton; 17 Greg Worthington; 5 Tom Saxton; 6 Andy Kain; 7 Liam Finn; 8 Tony Tonks; 9 Ben Kaye; 10 Stuart Dickens; 11 Jon Grayshon; 12 Tim Spears; 13 Matty Dale. Subs (all used): 16 Iain Morrison; 20 Dominic Dee; 4 Andrew Bostock; 19 Zak Hardaker.
Tries: Morrison (17), Dale (21), Saxton (30), Hardaker (43), Bostock (50), Finn (67); **Goals:** Finn 4/6.
Rugby Leaguer & League Express Men of the Match: *City Knights:* John Davies; *Rovers:* Liam Finn.
Penalty count: 10-13; **Half-time:** 12-16;
Referee: Gareth Hewer; **Attendance:** 1,387.

POOL 2

HALIFAX 50 OLDHAM 10

HALIFAX: 1 Miles Greenwood; 20 Paul White; 2 Lee Paterson; 27 Mike Ratu; 23 Rob Worrincy; 6 Danny Jones; 7 Ben Black; 25 Michael Ostick; 13 Bob Beswick; 15 Jim Gannon; 24 Steve Bannister; 4 Dylan Nash; 12 Sam Barlow. Subs (all used): 8 Makali Aizue; 9 Sean Penkywicz; 17 Frank Watene; 33 Ryan Fieldhouse.
Tries: Ostick (5), Black (11, 43), Worrincy (29), Aizue (41), S Barlow (46, 63), Jones (53), Gannon (79);
Goals: Paterson 5/7, Jones 2/2.
OLDHAM: 1 Ben Heaton; 2 Lucas Onyango; 12 Ben Wood; 4 Jack Bradbury; 5 John Gillam; 6 Neil Roden; 7 Mick Diveney; 10 Dave Ellison; 17 John Clough; 16 Liam Gilchrist; 11 Andrew Isherwood; 24 Paul Noone; 13 Valu Bentley. Subs (all used): 8 Jason Boults; 9 Danny Whitmore; 14 Chris Clarke; 15 Luke Sutton.
Tries: Onyango (26, 59); **Goals:** Diveney 1/2.
Rugby Leaguer & League Express Men of the Match: *Halifax:* Ryan Fieldhouse; *Oldham:* Lucas Onyango.
Penalty count: 14-6; **Half-time:** 14-6;
Referee: Jamie Leahy; **Attendance:** 2,027.

HUNSLET HAWKS 8 BATLEY BULLDOGS 12

HAWKS: 22 Danny Ratcliffe; 2 Richie Barnett; 27 Elliot Kear; 4 David Clayton; 1 Stuart Kain; 6 Danny Grimshaw; 7 Paul March; 8 Adam Sullivan; 14 Luke Haigh; 10 James Houston; 17 Rob Kelly; 12 Tom Haughey; 13 David March. Subs (all used): 9 Richard Chapman; 18 Joe Helme; 19 Neil Lowe; 25 Steve Dooler.
Try: Houston (23); **Goals:** Ratcliffe 2/2.
BULLDOGS: 1 Ian Preece; 5 Wayne Reittie; 3 Daley Williams; 4 Danny Maun; 30 Johnny Campbell; 6 Paul Handforth; 16 Paul Mennell; 17 Craig Potter; 9 Kris Lythe; 8 Byron Smith; 19 Mark Toohey; 11 Alex Bretherton; 13 Ashley Lindsay. Subs (all used): 7 Gareth Moore; 18 Dane Manning; 12 Jason Walton; 20 David Tootill.
Tries: Moore (57), Handforth (78); **Goals:** Moore 2/2.
Rugby Leaguer & League Express Men of the Match: *Hawks:* Neil Lowe; *Bulldogs:* Paul Handforth.
Penalty count: 12-8; **Half-time:** 8-0;
Referee: Matthew Thomason; **Attendance:** 666.

LEIGH CENTURIONS 42 SWINTON LIONS 22

CENTURIONS: 1 Stuart Donlan; 14 Adam Higson; 22 Tom Armstrong; 4 Mick Nanyn; 5 Dean McGilvray; 23 Mick Govin; 25 Jamie Ellis; 8 Chris Hill; 9 John Duffy; 10 Ricky Bibey; 12 Tommy Goulden; 3 Stuart Littler; 11 James Taylor. Subs (all used): 13 Stephen Nash; 26 David Mills; 6 Martyn Ridyard; 15 Andy Thornley.
Tries: Ellis (5), Duffy (12), Hill (16, 28), Nanyn (52, 60), Goulden (74); **Goals:** Nanyn 7/7.
LIONS: 21 Ian Mort; 23 Alex Hurst; 3 Gavin Dodd; 6 Martin Ainscough; 5 Sam Reay; 17 Carl Forber; 7 Ian Watson; 8 Mike Morrison; 9 Mark Smith; 16 Neil Holland; 19 Neil Rigby; 11 Dale Cunniffe; 12 Lee Wingfield. Subs (all used): 1 Richie Hawkyard; 13 Phil Joseph; 29 Chris Tyrer; 14 Tommy Gallagher.
Tries: Mort (9, 39), Rigby (48), R Hawkyard (57), Cunniffe (69); **Goals:** Mort 1/5.
On report: Wingfield (63) - alleged high tackle.
Rugby Leaguer & League Express Men of the Match: *Centurions:* Chris Hill; *Lions:* Ian Watson.
Penalty count: 5-12; **Half-time:** 24-10;
Referee: Chris Leatherbarrow; **Attendance:** 1,623.

SHEFFIELD EAGLES 16 WHITEHAVEN 16

EAGLES: 28 Jamie Cottle; 2 Danny Mills; 3 Menzie Yere; 25 Jamie Cording; 5 Tim Bergin; 13 Dane McDonald; 24 Kyle Wood; 8 Jack Howieson; 9 Andrew Henderson; 15 Liam Higgins; 10 Mitchell Stringer; 12 Peter Green; 19 Joe Hirst. Subs (all used): 22 Ryan Hepworth; 18 Scott Watson; 17 Alex Rowe; 27 Eddie Battye.
Tries: Bergin (14), Hepworth (21), Stringer (80);
Goals: Bergin 2/3.
WHITEHAVEN: 1 Craig Benson; 38 Andreas Bauer; 3 Derry Eilbeck; 4 Scott McAvoy; 2 Craig Calvert; 6 Lewis Palfrey; 7 Tane Manihera; 26 Luke Isakka; 14 Chris Smith; 23 Paul Culnean; 11 Spencer Miller; 13 Daniel Barker; 17 Andrew Beattie. Subs (all used): 9 Carl Sice; 10 Howard Hill; 36 David Fox; 12 Dexter Miller.
Tries: Sice (31), D Miller (58); **Goals:** Palfrey 4/4.
Rugby Leaguer & League Express Men of the Match: *Eagles:* Andrew Henderson; *Whitehaven:* Carl Sice.
Penalty count: 5-6; **Half-time:** 10-8; **Referee:** Peter Brooke; **Attendance:** 727 *(at Don Valley Stadium).*

WORKINGTON TOWN 82 GATESHEAD THUNDER 0

TOWN: 1 Brett Carter; 2 Elliott Miller; 3 Jason Mossop; 21 John Patrick; 20 Stephen Dawes; 23 Marc Bainbridge; 7 Scott Kaighan; 8 Marc Jackson; 9 Graeme Mattinson; 10 Kris Coward; 18 Joe McKenna; 12 Jarrad Stack; 13 Karl Olstrum. Subs (all used): 14 Jack Pedley; 19 Marc Shackley; 16 Ryan McDonald; 17 James Robinson.
Tries: Kaighan (5), Coward (9, 26), Patrick (14, 64), Bainbridge (17, 70), McKenna (32), McDonald (35), Stack (42, 73), Olstrum (51), Miller (61), Mossop (67), Carter (76); **Goals:** Kaighan 11/15.
THUNDER: 17 Joe Brown; 5 Dan O'Sullivan; 15 Andy Morris; 1 Wayne Green; 16 Robin Peers; 6 James Clarkson; 7 Ryan Clarke; 10 Stephen Welton; 9 Tom Hodgson; 22 Chris Parker; 12 Michael Ward; 13 Michael Kelly; 8 Jason Payne. Subs (all used): 14 Reece Young; 38 David Norman; 20 Nick Staveley; 19 Sam Crowther.
Rugby Leaguer & League Express Men of the Match: *Town:* Scott Kaighan; *Thunder:* Michael Kelly.
Penalty count: 10-6; **Half-time:** 36-0;
Referee: Matthew Kidd; **Attendance:** 381.

ROUND 3

Saturday 19th February 2011

POOL 1

KEIGHLEY COUGARS 22 TOULOUSE OLYMPIQUE 36

COUGARS: 1 Dan Belcher; 2 Craig Moss; 3 Tom Burton; 22 Ben Sagar; 26 James Hutchinson; 6 Luke Helliwell; 7 Ryan Smith; 8 Andy Shickell; 9 James Feather; 21 Richard Jones; 11 Will Cartledge; 12 Oliver Pursglove; 29 Jason Demetriou. Subs (all used): 14 Jamaine Wray; 25 Jamie Shepherd; 10 Scott Law; 17 Ryan Benjafield.
Tries: Sagar (16), Cartledge (38), Wray (49), Demetriou (73); **Goals:** Belcher 3/4.
OLYMPIQUE: 22 Damien Couturier; 24 Gregory White; 3 Sebastian Planas; 20 Bruno Ormeno; 18 Andrei Olari; 6 Darren Nicholls; 7 Josh Lewis; 8 Brendan Worth; 9 Craig Cook; 15 Jerome Gout; 17 Kevin Larroyer; 14 Antoni Maria; 16 Sylvain Houles. Subs (all used): 21 Nicolas Faure; 23 Teli Pelo; 12 Yoan Tisseyre; 13 Eric Anselme.
Tries: White (5), Olari (7), Nicholls (22, 59, 69), Lewis (75); **Goals:** Lewis 6/6.
Rugby Leaguer & League Express Men of the Match: *Cougars:* Jason Demetriou; *Olympique:* Darren Nicholls.
Penalty count: 8-5; **Half-time:** 10-18;
Referee: Jamie Leahy; **Attendance:** 513.

Sunday 20th February 2011

POOL 1

BARROW RAIDERS 22 FEATHERSTONE ROVERS 28

RAIDERS: 1 Gary Broadbent; 2 Andy Ballard; 39 Joe Wardle; 4 Liam Harrison; 5 James Nixon; 6 Jamie Rooney; 23 Gregg McNally; 8 Jamie Thackray; 18 Nathan Mossop; 24 Adam Walker; 15 Martin Ostler; 11 Michael Knowles; 12 Ned Catic. Subs (all used): 16 Zebastian Luisi; 10 Matt James; 9 Mark Gleeson; 13 Richard Fletcher.
Tries: Nixon (8), Rooney (43), Fletcher (58), Harrison (66); **Goals:** Rooney 3/4.
ROVERS: 1 Ian Hardman; 2 Bryn Powell; 3 Sam Smeaton; 14 Liam Welham; 19 Zak Hardaker; 17 Greg Worthington; 7 Liam Finn; 15 Michael Haley; 9 Ben Kaye; 10 Stuart Dickens; 4 Andrew Bostock; 12 Tim Spears; 13 Matty Dale. Subs (all used): 8 Tony Tonks; 6 Andy Kain; 24 Mufaro Mvududu; 5 Tom Saxton.
Tries: Tonks (22), Welham (27), Hardaker (39, 70), Saxton (63); **Goals:** Finn 4/5.
On report:
Dickens (58) - alleged dangerous contact on Fletcher.
Rugby Leaguer & League Express Men of the Match: *Raiders:* Jamie Thackray; *Rovers:* Liam Finn.
Penalty count: 8-5; **Half-time:** 6-18;
Referee: Ronnie Laughton; **Attendance:** 1,852.

DONCASTER 18 DEWSBURY RAMS 30

DONCASTER: 1 Mick Butterfield; 5 Dean Colton; 4 Shaun Leaf; 25 Chris Spurr; 2 Stewart Sanderson; 14 Scott Wilson; 19 Scott Spaven; 20 Jamie Bovill; 21 Paul Hughes; 17 Adam Scott; 8 Matt Carbutt; 15 Craig Robinson; 16 Mike Emmett. Subs (all used): 9 Kyle Kesik; 13 Jack Ely; 18 Ashley Williams; 10 Liam Crawley.
Tries: P Hughes (6), Robinson (12), Scott (60);
Goals: Spaven 3/3.
On report: Bovill (40) - alleged tripping.
RAMS: 1 James Craven; 2 Michael Wainwright; 13 Ayden Faal; 4 Scott Turner; 5 Austin Buchanan; 7 Dominic Brambani; 25 Tom Wandless; 8 Anthony England; 9 Luke Blake; 10 Keegan Hirst; 11 Rob Spicer; 12 James Lockwood; 15 Josh Tonks. Subs (all used): 23 Luke Menzies; 26 Jordan Tansey; 16 Adam Hayes; 31 Shaun Emblem.
Tries: England (20), Turner (23), Brambani (25), Blake (44), Tonks (65); **Goals:** Brambani 5/5.
Rugby Leaguer & League Express Men of the Match: *Doncaster:* Adam Scott; *Rams:* Dominic Brambani.
Penalty count: 6-11; **Half-time:** 12-18;
Referee: Chris Leatherbarrow; **Attendance:** 555.

LONDON SKOLARS 16 YORK CITY KNIGHTS 16

SKOLARS: 3 James Anthony; 2 Smokie Junor; 17 Dave Arnot; 4 Luke May; 5 Ade Adebisi; 7 Dylan Skee; 1 Neil Thorman; 8 Tony Williams; 9 Gareth Honor; 22 Saqib Murtza; 11 Matt Thomas; 31 Ben Bolger; 25 Austen Aggrey. Subs (all used): 34 Dave Williams; 33 Dave Samson; 13 Stephen Ball; 23 Liam Prescott.
Tries: Adebisi (9, 65), May (40); **Goals:** Thorman 2/3.
CITY KNIGHTS: 20 Tom Bush; 2 Dave Sutton; 17 Ian Bell; 4 Lee Waterman; 5 Danny Wilson; 6 Chris Thorman; 27 Scott Woods; 32 Nathan Massey; 9 Jack Lee; 37 Ben Jones; 13 Ryan Esders; 31 John Davies; 24 Mark Barlow. Subs (all used): 14 Jack Stearman; 22 Ed Smith; 25 Steve Lewis; 34 Adam Howard.
Tries: Davies (24), Barlow (28), Wilson (67);
Goals: Thorman 2/3.
Sin bin: Thorman (38) - dissent.
Rugby Leaguer & League Express Men of the Match: *Skolars:* Neil Thorman; *City Knights:* John Davies.
Penalty count: 11-11; **Half-time:** 10-12;
Referee: Matthew Kidd; **Attendance:** 264.

WIDNES VIKINGS 50 ROCHDALE HORNETS 10

VIKINGS: 6 Anthony Thackeray; 2 Dean Gaskell; 23 Tangi Ropati; 4 Steve Tyrer; 19 Matt Gardner; 1 Danny Craven; 14 Thomas Coyle; 17 Ben Kavanagh; 9 Kirk Netherton; 10 Daniel Heckenberg; 20 Shane Grady; 12 Kurt Haggerty; 13 Simon Finnigan. Subs (all used): 3 Richard Varkulis; 15 Chris Gerrard; 16 Macgraff Leuluai; 25 Chris Lunt.
Tries: Netherton (4), T Coyle (13), Craven (19), Grady (38), Tyrer (44, 79), Finnigan (49), Ropati (54), Thackeray (73); **Goals:** Tyrer 6/7, Craven 1/2.
HORNETS: 1 Wayne English; 2 Craig Johnson; 3 Dean Gorton; 22 Damien Reid; 17 Dale Bloomfield; 6 Liam McGovern; 7 Steve Roper; 18 John Cookson; 15 Paul Crook; 27 Jamie Peasnall; 11 Craig Ashall; 16 Danny Samuel; 13 Dayne Donoghue. Subs (all used): 29 Danny Meekin; 19 Gareth Hayes; 21 Mark Hobson; 36 Scott Mansfield.
Tries: Ashall (8), Johnson (33); **Goals:** Crook 1/2.
Rugby Leaguer & League Express Men of the Match: *Vikings:* Steve Tyrer; *Hornets:* Craig Ashall.
Penalty count: 10-10; **Half-time:** 22-10;
Referee: Tim Roby; **Attendance:** 3,155.

POOL 2

BATLEY BULLDOGS 60 GATESHEAD THUNDER 6

BULLDOGS: 1 Ian Preece; 5 Wayne Reittie; 3 Daley Williams; 19 Mark Toohey; 29 Darren Williams; 6 Paul Handforth; 7 Gareth Moore; 8 Byron Smith; 9 Kris Lythe; 10 Sean Hesketh; 18 Dane Manning; 11 Alex Bretherton; 13 Ashley Lindsay. Subs (all used): 16 Paul Mennell; 20 David Tootill; 17 Craig Potter; 30 Johnny Campbell.
Tries: Daley Williams (3, 39, 45), Handforth (6, 78), Moore (33), Lythe (54, 77), Bretherton (68), Darren Williams (80); **Goals:** Moore 7/7, Handforth 3/3.
THUNDER: 43 Michael Ellis; 23 Jamie Love; 15 Andy Morris; 12 Michael Ward; 16 Robin Peers; 1 Wayne Green; 31 Will Bate; 20 Nick Staveley; 7 Ryan Clarke; 8 Jason Payne; 4 Josh Stoker; 38 David Norman; 13 Michael Kelly. Subs (all used): 14 Reece Young; 19 Sam Crowther; 10 Stephen Welton; 22 Chris Parker.
Try: Morris (20); **Goals:** Clarke 1/1.
Sin bin: Green (52) - dangerous tackle;
Bate (76) - holding down.
Rugby Leaguer & League Express Men of the Match: *Bulldogs:* Paul Handforth; *Thunder:* Jason Payne.
Penalty count: 10-8; **Half-time:** 24-6;
Referee: Dave Merrick; **Attendance:** 612.

HUNSLET HAWKS 30 WORKINGTON TOWN 0

HAWKS: 1 Stuart Kain; 2 Richie Barnett; 27 Elliot Kear; 4 David Clayton; 5 Waine Pryce; 6 Danny Grimshaw; 7 Paul March; 8 Adam Sullivan; 14 Luke Haigh; 20 Andrew Yates; 11 Richard Blakeway; 12 Tom Haughey; 13 David March. Subs (all used): 23 Joe McLocklan; 21 Tabua Cakacaka; 22 Danny Ratcliffe; 25 Steve Dooler.
Tries: D March (10), McLocklan (37), P March (52), Haughey (62), Kain (80); **Goals:** D March 5/6.
TOWN: 2 Elliott Miller; 20 Stephen Dawes; 3 Jason Mossop; 4 Aaron Low; 5 Neil Frazer; 6 Liam Finch; 7 Scott Kaighan; 8 Marc Jackson; 9 Graeme Mattinson; 10 Kris Coward; 19 Marc Shackley; 11 Mike Whitehead; 12 Jarrad Stack. Subs (all used): 27 Jamie Marshall; 15 Ruairi McGoff; 16 Ryan McDonald; 17 James Robinson.
Dismissal: Robinson (78) - punching.

Rugby Leaguer & League Express Men of the Match: *Hawks:* Stuart Kain; *Town:* Ryan McDonald.
Penalty count: 9-7; **Half-time:** 14-0;
Referee: George Stokes; **Attendance:** 379.

LEIGH CENTURIONS 68 SHEFFIELD EAGLES 6

CENTURIONS: 1 Stuart Donlan; 2 Steve Maden; 14 Adam Higson; 4 Mick Nanyn; 5 Dean McGilvray; 6 Martyn Ridyard; 25 Jamie Ellis; 8 Chris Hill; 9 John Duffy; 10 Ricky Bibey; 12 Tommy Goulden; 3 Stuart Littler; 11 James Taylor. Subs (all used): 13 Stephen Nash; 26 David Mills; 15 Andy Thornley; 7 Robbie Hunter-Paul.
Tries: Ellis (8), Maden (15, 56), Ridyard (23, 36, 53), Mills (29), Donlan (32, 44), Duffy (60), McGilvray (72, 79); **Goals:** Nanyn 10/12.
Sin bin: Hill (68) - late challenge on Smith.
EAGLES: 28 Jamie Cottle; 2 Danny Mills; 3 Menzie Yere; 26 Corey Hanson; 5 Tim Bergin; 13 Dane McDonald; 20 Pat Smith; 8 Jack Howieson; 9 Andrew Henderson; 10 Mitchell Stringer; 25 Jamie Cording; 12 Peter Green; 19 Joe Hirst. Subs (all used): 18 Scott Watson; 22 Ryan Hepworth; 17 Alex Rowe; 15 Liam Higgins.
Try: Cottle (76); **Goals:** Bergin 1/1.
Rugby Leaguer & League Express Men of the Match: *Centurions:* Martyn Ridyard; *Eagles:* Jamie Cottle.
Penalty count: 6-2; **Half-time:** 34-0;
Referee: Matthew Thomason; **Attendance:** 1,520.

SWINTON LIONS 29 OLDHAM 20

LIONS: 1 Richie Hawkyard; 2 Rob Foxen; 3 Gavin Dodd; 4 Dean Thompson; 21 Ian Mort; 6 Martin Ainscough; 7 Ian Watson; 8 Mike Morrison; 9 Mark Smith; 12 Lee Wingfield; 11 Dale Cunniffe; 19 Neil Rigby; 13 Phil Joseph. Subs (all used): 25 Karl Ashall; 15 Darren Hawkyard; 16 Neil Holland; 26 Joe Fitzpatrick.
Tries: Foxen (15), Ainscough (18), R Hawkyard (20), Dodd (26, 76), D Hawkyard (66); **Goals:** Dodd 2/6;
Field goal: Dodd (75).
On report: Smith (42) - alleged dangerous contact.
OLDHAM: 3 Marcus St Hilaire; 2 Lucas Onyango; 21 Mark Brocklehurst; 4 Jack Bradbury; 5 John Gillam; 6 Neil Roden; 7 Mick Diveney; 8 Jason Boults; 17 John Clough; 15 Luke Sutton; 11 Andrew Isherwood; 24 Paul Noone; 14 Chris Clarke. Subs (all used): 9 Danny Whitmore; 25 Martin Roden; 12 Ben Wood; 22 Tom Wood-Hulme.
Tries: Brocklehurst (11, 69), Gillam (51, 54);
Goals: Diveney 2/4.
Rugby Leaguer & League Express Men of the Match: *Lions:* Ian Watson; *Oldham:* Neil Roden.
Penalty count: 9-17; **Half-time:** 20-6;
Referee: Clint Sharrad; **Attendance:** 774.

ROUND 4

Saturday 26th February 2011

POOL 1

TOULOUSE OLYMPIQUE 34 LONDON SKOLARS 22

OLYMPIQUE: 22 Damien Couturier; 18 Andrei Olari; 3 Sebastien Planas; 20 Bruno Ormeno; 24 Gregory White; 6 Darren Nicholls; 7 Josh Lewis; 8 Brendan Worth; 9 Craig Cook; 15 Jerome Gout; 12 Yoan Tisseyre; 14 Antoni Maria; 16 Sylvain Houles. Subs (all used): 17 Kevin Larroyer; 21 Nicolas Faure; 23 Teli Pelo; 29 Cyril Moliner.
Tries: Nicholls (9), Cook (24), Tisseyre (29), Olari (57), Lewis (62), Worth (75); **Goals:** Lewis 5/6.
SKOLARS: 3 James Anthony; 2 Smokie Junor; 17 Dave Arnot; 4 Luke May; 5 Ade Adebisi; 1 Neil Thorman; 7 Dylan Skee; 22 Saqib Murtza; 9 Gareth Honor; 8 Tony Williams; 11 Matt Thomas; 12 Oliver Bloom; 13 Stephen Ball. Subs (all used): 6 Jy-Mel Coleman; 15 Oliver Purslow; 16 James Simon; 24 Dave McMeeken.
Tries: Adebisi (17, 21), M Thomas (66), Arnot (73);
Goals: Thorman 3/4.
Rugby Leaguer & League Express Men of the Match: *Olympique:* Brendan Worth; *Skolars:* Saqib Murtza.
Penalty count: 4-5; **Half-time:** 18-10;
Referee: Chris Leatherbarrow; **Attendance:** 800.

FEATHERSTONE ROVERS 16 WIDNES VIKINGS 22

ROVERS: 19 Zak Hardaker; 2 Bryn Powell; 3 Sam Smeaton; 14 Liam Welham; 5 Tom Saxton; 17 Greg Worthington; 7 Liam Finn; 8 Tony Tonks; 9 Ben Kaye; 10 Stuart Dickens; 11 Jon Grayshon; 12 Tim Spears; 13 Matty Dale. Subs (all used): 27 Dave Williams; 6 Andy Kain; 4 Andrew Bostock; 1 Ian Hardman.
Tries: Dickens (67), Hardaker (71), Smeaton (75);
Goals: Finn 2/3.
VIKINGS: 5 Paddy Flynn; 2 Dean Gaskell; 23 Tangi Ropati; 4 Steve Tyrer; 19 Matt Gardner; 6 Anthony Thackeray; 14 Thomas Coyle; 17 Ben Kavanagh; 9 Kirk Netherton; 10 Daniel Heckenberg; 20 Shane Grady; 12 Kurt Haggerty; 13 Simon Finnigan. Subs (all used): 3 Richard Varkulis; 8 Steve Pickersgill; 11 Dave Allen; 15 Chris Gerrard.
Tries: Grady (3), Tyrer (8), Thackeray (32);
Goals: Tyrer 5/5.
Rugby Leaguer & League Express Men of the Match: *Rovers:* Tony Tonks; *Vikings:* Anthony Thackeray.
Penalty count: 13-9; **Half-time:** 0-18;
Referee: Matthew Thomason; **Attendance:** 1,719.

Sunday 27th February 2011

POOL 1

DEWSBURY RAMS 16 BARROW RAIDERS 12

RAMS: 1 James Craven; 2 Michael Wainwright; 32 Elliott Cosgrove; 4 Scott Turner; 5 Austin Buchanan; 26 Jordan Tansey; 7 Dominic Brambani; 8 Anthony England; 9 Luke Blake; 10 Keegan Hirst; 11 Rob Spicer; 12 James Lockwood; 15 Josh Tonks. Subs (all used): 23 Luke Menzies; 31 Shaun Emblem; 29 Matty Brooks; 33 Ben Bolger.
Try: England (59); **Goals:** Brambani 6/6.
Sin bin: Tansey (49) - dissent.
RAIDERS: 16 Zebastian Luisi; 2 Andy Ballard; 39 Joe Wardle; 4 Liam Harrison; 3 Chris Larkin; 6 Jamie Rooney; 23 Gregg McNally; 24 Adam Walker; 18 Nathan Mossop; 13 Richard Fletcher; 11 Michael Knowles; 15 Martin Ostler; 12 Ned Catic. Subs (all used): 8 Jamie Thackray; 10 Matt James; 9 Mark Gleeson; 21 Jamie Butler.
Tries: Catic (12), Ostler (63); **Goals:** Rooney 2/2.
Sin bin: James (25) - late challenge on Tansey.
Rugby Leaguer & League Express Men of the Match: *Rams:* Dominic Brambani; *Raiders:* Jamie Rooney.
Penalty count: 7-5; **Half-time:** 6-6;
Referee: Craig Halloran; **Attendance:** 911.

ROCHDALE HORNETS 36 DONCASTER 40

HORNETS: 5 Scott Yates; 25 Andy Saywell; 30 Danny Pyke; 22 Damien Reid; 2 Craig Johnson; 6 Liam McGovern; 7 Steve Roper; 8 Dave Newton; 15 Paul Crook; 20 Chris Clough; 21 Mark Hobson; 11 Craig Ashall; 4 Matthew Strong. Subs (all used): 19 Gareth Hayes; 9 Steve McDermott; 16 Danny Samuel; 28 Chris Hough.
Tries: McGovern (4, 70), Crook (9), Johnson (13, 53), Hobson (21), Hough (44);
Goals: Crook 4/5, McGovern 0/2.
DONCASTER: 2 Stewart Sanderson; 18 Ashley Williams; 12 Ryan Steen; 25 Chris Spurr; 14 Scott Wilson; 21 Paul Hughes; 19 Scott Spaven; 20 Jamie Bovill; 13 Jack Ely; 17 Adam Scott; 8 Matt Carbutt; 15 Craig Robinson; 22 Carl Hughes. Subs (all used): 9 Kyle Kesik; 11 Kyle Sampson; 10 Liam Crawley; 1 Mick Butterfield.
Tries: Williams (25), P Hughes (29), Kesik (31), Spaven (34), Carbutt (38), Wilson (48), Spurr (50), Butterfield (59); **Goals:** Spaven 4/8.
Rugby Leaguer & League Express Men of the Match: *Hornets:* Chris Clough; *Doncaster:* Paul Hughes.
Penalty count: 10-9; **Half-time:** 22-26;
Referee: Peter Brooke; **Attendance:** 442.

YORK CITY KNIGHTS 28 KEIGHLEY COUGARS 22

CITY KNIGHTS: 18 Sam Lynch; 17 Ian Bell; 30 Jordan Thompson; 3 Duane Straugheir; 21 Dennis Tuffour; 6 Chris Thorman; 7 Jon Presley; 33 Nathan Massey; 9 Jack Lee; 37 Ben Jones; 31 John Davies; 13 Ryan Esders; 10 Alex Benson. Subs (all used): 14 Jack Stearman; 24 Mark Barlow; 11 Rhys Clarke; 25 Steve Lewis.
Tries: Straugheir (6, 58), Presley (34, 51), Davies (77);
Goals: Thorman 4/5.
Sin bin: Esders (64) - punching.
COUGARS: 1 Dan Belcher; 28 Richard Lopag; 4 Danny Lawton; 22 Ben Sagar; 26 James Hutchinson; 24 Paul Drake; 6 Luke Helliwell; 16 Brendan Rawlins; 9 James Feather; 21 Richard Jones; 23 Chris Baines; 25 Jamie Shepherd; 18 James Haythornthwaite. Subs (all used): 14 Jamaine Wray; 20 Rick Barr; 13 Greg Nicholson; 17 Ryan Benjafield.
Tries: Benjafield (28), Rawlins (55), Drake (66), Belcher (72); **Goals:** Lawton 3/4.
Rugby Leaguer & League Express Men of the Match: *City Knights:* Jon Presley; *Cougars:* Chris Baines.
Penalty count: 7-8; **Half-time:** 12-6;
Referee: Warren Turley; **Attendance:** 748.

POOL 2

GATESHEAD THUNDER 4 SWINTON LIONS 76

THUNDER: 31 Will Bate; 23 Jamie Love; 28 Craig Jones; 40 Matthew Massey; 16 Robin Peers; 1 Wayne Green; 34 Scott Woods; 8 Jason Payne; 7 Ryan Clarke; 22 Chris Parker; 4 Josh Stoker; 38 David Norman; 12 Michael Ward. Subs (all used): 37 Karl Brandt; 10 Stephen Welton; 19 Sam Crowther; 13 Michael Kelly.
Try: Massey (24); **Goals:** Clarke 0/1.
LIONS: 1 Richie Hawkyard; 24 Barry Hamilton; 3 Gavin Dodd; 4 Dean Thompson; 2 Rob Foxen; 6 Martin Ainscough; 7 Ian Watson; 12 Lee Wingfield; 9 Mark Smith; 29 Chris Tyrer; 15 Darren Hawkyard; 19 Neil Rigby; 14 Tommy Gallagher. Subs (all used): 25 Karl Ashall; 37 Richard Mervill; 39 Anthony Stewart; 27 Bruce Johnson.
Tries: D Hawkyard (7, 37), D Thompson (12, 39, 42), Gallagher (14), Hamilton (17), Rigby (35), Ainscough (48), Wingfield (51, 70), Ashall (54), Stewart (60), Smith (68), Foxen (74); **Goals:** Dodd 8/15.
Rugby Leaguer & League Express Men of the Match: *Thunder:* Ryan Clarke; *Lions:* Ian Watson.
Penalty count: 11-7; **Half-time:** 4-38;
Referee: Gareth Hewer; **Attendance:** 285.

HALIFAX 25 BATLEY BULLDOGS 26

HALIFAX: 1 Miles Greenwood; 20 Paul White; 5 James Haley; 24 Steve Bannister; 23 Rob Worrincy; 6 Danny Jones; 7 Ben Black; 8 Makali Aizue; 13 Bob Beswick; 15 Jim Gannon; 11 David Larder; 14 Ryan Clayton; 12 Sam Barlow. Subs (all used): 9 Sean Penkywicz; 18 Joe Chandler; 19 Jacob Fairbank; 21 Josh Barlow.
Tries: White (9), Chandler (42), Worrincy (58, 60);
Goals: Jones 4/4; **Field goal:** Black (77).
Sin bin: Penkywicz (70) - punching.
BULLDOGS: 1 Ian Preece; 5 Wayne Reittie; 3 Daley Williams; 4 Danny Maun; 2 Alex Brown; 6 Paul Handforth; 16 Paul Mennell; 8 Byron Smith; 9 Kris Lythe; 10 Sean Hesketh; 11 Alex Bretherton; 18 Dane Manning; 13 Ashley Lindsay. Subs (all used): 7 Gareth Moore; 19 Mark Toohey; 17 Craig Potter; 21 James Martin.
Tries: Hesketh (4), Reittie (16), Manning (20), Moore (30); **Goals:** Handforth 4/5, Moore 1/1.
Dismissal: Lythe (70) - head-butt.
Sin bin: Preece (62) - interference.
Rugby Leaguer & League Express Men of the Match: *Halifax:* Danny Jones; *Bulldogs:* Paul Handforth.
Penalty count: 9-8; **Half-time:** 6-22;
Referee: Jamie Leahy; **Attendance:** 1,968.

OLDHAM 4 WHITEHAVEN 14

OLDHAM: 1 Ben Heaton; 2 Lucas Onyango; 3 Marcus St Hilaire; 21 Mark Brocklehurst; 5 John Gillam; 6 Neil Roden; 23 Matt Ashe; 8 Jason Boults; 25 Martin Roden; 15 Luke Sutton; 12 Ben Wood; 24 Paul Noone; 14 Chris Clarke. Subs (all used): 17 John Clough; 13 Valu Bentley; 11 Andrew Isherwood; 22 Tom Wood-Hulme.
Try: Brocklehurst (16); **Goals:** Ashe 0/1.
WHITEHAVEN: 1 Craig Benson; 31 Jay Rossi; 3 Derry Eilbeck; 4 Scott McAvoy; 2 Craig Calvert; 6 Lewis Palfrey; 7 Tane Manihera; 8 David Ford; 14 Chris Smith; 26 Luke Isakka; 11 Spencer Miller; 13 Daniel Barker; 17 Andrew Beattie. Subs (all used): 9 Carl Sice; 23 Paul Culnean; 10 Howard Hill; 12 Dexter Miller.
Tries: Barker (26), Beattie (43); **Goals:** Palfrey 3/4.
Rugby Leaguer & League Express Men of the Match: *Oldham:* Mark Brocklehurst; *Whitehaven:* Carl Sice.
Penalty count: 9-4; **Half-time:** 4-6;
Referee: George Stokes; **Attendance:** 544.

SHEFFIELD EAGLES 12 HUNSLET HAWKS 16

EAGLES: 28 Jamie Cottle; 2 Danny Mills; 3 Menzie Yere; 26 Corey Hanson; 5 Tim Bergin; 13 Dane McDonald; 7 Simon Brown; 8 Jack Howieson; 9 Andrew Henderson; 10 Mitchell Stringer; 25 Jamie Cording; 12 Peter Green; 19 Joe Hirst. Subs (all used): 22 Ryan Hepworth; 27 Eddie Battye; 17 Alex Rowe; 15 Liam Higgins.
Tries: Yere (42), Hanson (62); **Goals:** Brown 2/2.
HAWKS: 22 Danny Ratcliffe; 5 Waine Pryce; 4 David Clayton; 27 Elliot Kear; 2 Richie Barnett; 6 Danny Grimshaw; 7 Paul March; 21 Tabua Cakacaka; 9 Richard Chapman; 17 Rob Kelly; 11 Richard Blakeway; 12 Tom Haughey; 13 David March. Subs (all used): 23 Joe McLocklan; 18 Joe Helme; 16 John Oakes; 19 Neil Lowe.
Tries: Haughey (13), Grimshaw (72); **Goals:** Ratcliffe 4/5.
Rugby Leaguer & League Express Men of the Match: *Eagles:* Andrew Henderson; *Hawks:* Tom Haughey.
Penalty count: 7-8; **Half-time:** 0-6; **Referee:** Dave Merrick; **Attendance:** 854 *(at Don Valley Stadium)*.

WORKINGTON TOWN 12 LEIGH CENTURIONS 42

TOWN: 1 Brett Carter; 2 Elliott Miller; 3 Jason Mossop; 4 Aaron Low; 5 Neil Frazer; 23 Marc Bainbridge; 7 Scott Kaighan; 15 Ruairi McGoff; 9 Graeme Mattinson; 10 Kris Coward; 11 Mike Whitehead; 12 Jarrad Stack; 13 Karl Olstrum. Subs (all used): 14 Jack Pedley; 8 Marc Jackson; 16 Ryan McDonald; 18 Joe McKenna.
Tries: Kaighan (24, 43); **Goals:** Kaighan 2/3.
CENTURIONS: 1 Stuart Donlan; 2 Steve Maden; 14 Adam Higson; 4 Mick Nanyn; 5 Dean McGilvray; 6 Martyn Ridyard; 25 Jamie Ellis; 8 Chris Hill; 9 John Duffy; 10 Ricky Bibey; 3 Stuart Littler; 12 Tommy Goulden; 11 James Taylor. Subs (all used): 13 Stephen Nash; 15 Andy Thornley; 23 Mick Govin; 24 Andy Gorski.
Tries: Goulden (2), Maden (20, 32), Ridyard (30), Donlan (60), Ellis (70), Littler (78), Gorski (80);
Goals: Nanyn 5/8.
Sin bin: Bibey (39) - holding down.
Rugby Leaguer & League Express Men of the Match: *Town:* Scott Kaighan; *Centurions:* Chris Hill.
Penalty count: 10-3; **Half-time:** 6-18;
Referee: Clint Sharrad; **Attendance:** 592.

ROUND 3

Wednesday 16th March 2011

POOL 2

WHITEHAVEN 6 HALIFAX 60

WHITEHAVEN: 20 Shane Ackerley; 5 Loz Hamzat; 4 Scott McAvoy; 3 Derry Eilbeck; 2 Craig Calvert; 6 Lewis Palfrey; 32 Carl Rudd; 23 Paul Culnean; 14 Chris Smith; 26 Luke Isakka; 11 Spencer Miller; 18 Kurt Wilton; 13 Daniel Barker. Subs (all used): 9 Carl Sice; 22 Reece Fox; 10 Howard Hill; 19 Brad Crellin.
Try: McAvoy (15); **Goals:** Palfrey 1/1.
HALIFAX: 33 Ryan Fieldhouse; 20 Paul White; 3 Jon Goddard; 2 Lee Paterson; 23 Rob Worrincy; 6 Danny Jones; 7 Ben Black; 15 Jim Gannon; 9 Sean Penkywicz; 8 Makali Aizue; 14 Ryan Clayton; 18 Joe Chandler; 16 Paul Smith. Subs (all used): 13 Bob Beswick; 17 Frank Watene; 10 Neil Cherryholme; 24 Steve Bannister.
Tries: White (17, 33), Worrincy (23, 58), Fieldhouse (29), Chandler (38, 68), Black (51), Penkywicz (62, 73); **Goals:** Jones 10/10.
Rugby Leaguer & League Express Men of the Match: *Whitehaven:* Luke Isakka; *Halifax:* Frank Watene.
Penalty count: 8-14; **Half-time:** 6-30;
Referee: Warren Turley; **Attendance:** 771.

Northern Rail Cup 2011 - Round by Round

FINAL TABLES

POOL 1

	P	W	D	L	BP	F	A	Diff	Pts
Widnes Vikings	4	4	0	0	0	178	72	106	12
Featherstone Rovers	4	3	0	1	1	130	76	54	10
Dewsbury Rams	4	3	0	1	1	98	70	28	10
Toulouse Olympique	4	3	0	1	0	138	126	12	9
Barrow Raiders	4	2	0	2	2	88	82	6	8
York City Knights	4	1	1	2	2	86	94	-8	7
Doncaster	4	2	0	2	1	100	124	-24	7
Keighley Cougars	4	1	0	3	1	68	84	-16	4
London Skolars	4	0	1	3	1	60	144	-84	3
Rochdale Hornets	4	0	0	4	2	70	144	-74	2

POOL 2

	P	W	D	L	BP	F	A	Diff	Pts
Leigh Centurions	4	4	0	0	0	176	44	132	12
Halifax	4	3	0	1	1	163	64	99	10
Batley Bulldogs	4	3	0	1	0	102	63	39	9
Hunslet Hawks	4	2	0	2	2	76	52	24	8
Swinton Lions	4	2	0	2	1	149	94	55	7
Workington Town	4	2	0	2	0	122	90	32	6
Sheffield Eagles	4	1	1	2	1	66	120	-54	6
Whitehaven	4	1	1	2	1	54	108	-54	6
Oldham	4	1	0	3	2	62	115	-53	5
Gateshead Thunder	4	0	0	4	1	30	250	-220	1

Top four teams from each Pool progressed to Quarter Finals.

QUARTER FINALS

Thursday 7th April 2011

LEIGH CENTURIONS 50 WIDNES VIKINGS 18

CENTURIONS: 1 Stuart Donlan; 2 Steve Maden; 22 Tom Armstrong; 4 Mick Nanyn; 5 Dean McGilvray; 6 Martyn Ridyard; 25 Jamie Ellis; 8 Chris Hill; 9 John Duffy; 32 Lee Mitchell; 3 Stuart Littler; 12 Tommy Goulden; 11 James Taylor. Subs (all used): 23 Mick Govin; 15 Andy Thornley; 20 Sam Hopkins; 26 David Mills.
Tries: Ellis (5, 55), Maden (31), Armstrong (33), Mills (36, 78), Goulden (58), Duffy (73); **Goals:** Nanyn 9/10.
VIKINGS: 6 Anthony Thackeray; 2 Dean Gaskell; 23 Tangi Ropati; 4 Steve Tyrer; 5 Paddy Flynn; 15 Chris Gerrard; 7 Chaz l'Anson; 8 Steve Pickersgill; 14 Thomas Coyle; 17 Ben Kavanagh; 11 Dave Allen; 16 Macgraff Leuluai; 13 Simon Finnigan. Subs (all used): 3 Richard Varkulis; 9 Kirk Netherton; 19 Matt Gardner; 42 Danny Sculthorpe.
Tries: Kavanagh (12, 16), Leuluai (19); **Goals:** Tyrer 3/4.
Rugby Leaguer & League Express Men of the Match: *Centurions:* Jamie Ellis; *Vikings:* Ben Kavanagh.
Penalty count: 10-7; **Half-time:** 22-18;
Referee: Gareth Hewer; **Attendance:** 2,737.

Friday 8th April 2011

HUNSLET HAWKS 12 FEATHERSTONE ROVERS 50

HAWKS: 1 Stuart Kain; 2 Richie Barnett; 4 David Clayton; 27 Elliot Kear; 5 Waine Pryce; 6 Danny Grimshaw; 7 Paul March; 8 Adam Sullivan; 23 Joe McLocklan; 10 James Houston; 11 Richard Blakeway; 17 Rob Kelly; 13 David March. Subs (all used): 9 Richard Chapman; 16 John Oakes; 18 Joe Helme; 19 Neil Lowe.
Tries: Pryce (43), Kear (59); **Goals:** Kear 2/2.
Sin bin: Helme (53) - persistent offending; Kelly (54) - dissent.
ROVERS: 1 Ian Hardman; 2 Bryn Powell; 3 Sam Smeaton; 4 Andrew Bostock; 5 Tom Saxton; 6 Andy Kain; 7 Liam Finn; 8 Tony Tonks; 9 Sam Barlow; 10 Stuart Dickens; 11 Jon Grayshon; 12 Tim Spears; 13 Matty Dale. Subs (all used): 16 Iain Morrison; 17 Greg Worthington; 19 Ross Divorty; 28 Jon Hepworth.
Tries: Tonks (5, 57), Powell (12), Kain (15), Grayshon (20, 31, 74), Dickens (55), Smeaton (77); **Goals:** Finn 7/9.
On report:
Finn (68) - alleged dangerous tackle on S Kain.
Rugby Leaguer & League Express Men of the Match: *Hawks:* Elliot Kear; *Rovers:* Liam Finn.
Penalty count: 8-11; **Half-time:** 0-28;
Referee: Jamie Leahy; **Attendance:** 877.

Saturday 9th April 2011

TOULOUSE OLYMPIQUE 26 HALIFAX 36

OLYMPIQUE: 24 Gregory White; 18 Andrei Olari; 3 Sebastien Planas; 22 Damien Couturier; 2 Sebastien Payan; 4 Constant Villegas; 6 Darren Nicholls; 8 Brendan Worth; 13 Eric Anselme; 10 Ged Corcoran; 11 Tim Wynn; 14 Antoni Maria; 16 Sylvain Houles. Subs (all used): 23 Teli Pelo; 21 Nicolas Faure; 17 Kevin Larroyer; 5 Clement Bienes.
Tries: White (32), Wynn (41), Faure (46), Villegas (60), Nicholls (69); **Goals:** Couturier 3/5.
On report: Nicholls (72) - alleged high tackle.
HALIFAX: 1 Miles Greenwood; 20 Paul White; 3 Jon Goddard; 5 James Haley; 23 Rob Worrincy; 6 Danny Jones; 28 Graham Holroyd; 25 Michael Ostick; 9 Sean Penkywicz; 10 Neil Cherryholme; 11 David Larder; 18 Joe Chandler; 19 Jacob Fairbank. Subs (all used): 13 Bob Beswick; 15 Jim Gannon; 16 Paul Smith; 17 Frank Watene.
Tries: Worrincy (4), Penkywicz (16), Cherryholme (19), Jones (23, 35), White (60); **Goals:** Holroyd 6/6.
Rugby Leaguer & League Express Men of the Match: *Olympique:* Gregory White; *Halifax:* Graham Holroyd.
Penalty count: 7-11; **Half-time:** 4-30;
Referee: Matthew Thomason; **Attendance:** 851.

Halifax's Rob Worrincy halted by Featherstone's Ben Kaye and Ross Divorty during a golden point semi-final thriller

Sunday 10th April 2011

DEWSBURY RAMS 38 BATLEY BULLDOGS 22

RAMS: 2 Michael Wainwright; 35 Andy Smith; 4 Scott Turner; 32 Elliott Cosgrove; 5 Austin Buchanan; 13 Ayden Faal; 7 Dominic Brambani; 10 Keegan Hirst; 25 Tom Wandless; 12 James Lockwood; 21 Kyle Bibb; 11 Rob Spicer; 9 Luke Blake. Subs (all used): 23 Luke Menzies; 22 Jonny Horton; 24 Jake Wilson; 33 Shaun Emblem.
Tries: Lockwood (22, 66), Faal (42, 76), Blake (69); **Goals:** Brambani 9/9.
BULLDOGS: 1 Ian Preece; 5 Wayne Reittie; 12 Jason Walton; 4 Danny Maun; 30 Johnny Campbell; 6 Paul Handforth; 16 Paul Mennell; 8 Byron Smith; 9 Kris Lythe; 10 Sean Hesketh; 11 Alex Bretherton; 18 Dane Manning; 17 Craig Potter. Subs (all used): 2 Alex Brown; 19 Mark Toohey; 21 James Martin; 20 David Tootill.
Tries: Handforth (30), Hesketh (33), Bretherton (38), Smith (58); **Goals:** Handforth 3/4.
Rugby Leaguer & League Express Men of the Match: *Rams:* Dominic Brambani; *Bulldogs:* Paul Handforth.
Penalty count: 5-5; **Half-time:** 8-16;
Referee: Ronnie Laughton; **Attendance:** 1,643.

SEMI-FINALS

Thursday 16th June 2011

FEATHERSTONE ROVERS 30 HALIFAX 31

(after golden point extra time)

ROVERS: 1 Ian Hardman; 2 Bryn Powell; 3 Sam Smeaton; 4 Andrew Bostock; 5 Tom Saxton; 28 Jon Hepworth; 7 Liam Finn; 15 Michael Haley; 9 Ben Kaye; 10 Stuart Dickens; 11 Jon Grayshon; 12 Tim Spears; 18 Ross Divorty. Subs (all used): 8 Tony Tonks; 16 Iain Morrison; 6 Andy Kain; 24 Mufaro Mvududu.
Tries: Saxton (14), Smeaton (19), Kain (30), Hepworth (40), Bostock (71); **Goals:** Finn 5/7.
HALIFAX: 1 Miles Greenwood; 20 Paul White; 2 Lee Paterson; 4 Dylan Nash; 23 Rob Worrincy; 6 Danny Jones; 7 Ben Black; 15 Jim Gannon; 13 Bob Beswick; 10 Neil Cherryholme; 14 Ryan Clayton; 24 Steve Bannister; 19 Jacob Fairbank. Subs (all used): 8 Makali Aizue; 12 Sam Barlow; 16 Paul Smith; 9 Sean Penkywicz.
Tries: Paterson (22), White (33, 37), Worrincy (45), Black (53), Nash (76); **Goals:** Jones 0/1, Paterson 3/5.
Field goal: Jones (83).
Rugby Leaguer & League Express Men of the Match: *Rovers:* Michael Haley; *Halifax:* Danny Jones.
Penalty count: 3-4; **Half-time:** 22-14;
Referee: Gareth Hewer; **Attendance:** 1,987.

Sunday 19th June 2011

LEIGH CENTURIONS 44 DEWSBURY RAMS 10

CENTURIONS: 1 Stuart Donlan; 2 Steve Maden; 3 Stuart Littler; 4 Mick Nanyn; 5 Dean McGilvray; 6 Martyn Ridyard; 25 Jamie Ellis; 8 Chris Hill; 9 John Duffy; 26 David Mills; 15 Andy Thornley; 12 Tommy Goulden; 11 James Taylor. Subs (all used): 13 Stephen Nash; 14 Adam Higson; 16 Anthony Nicholson; 22 Tom Armstrong.
Tries: Mills (3), Goulden (9), Duffy (24, 36), McGilvray (30), Ellis (39), Nanyn (47, 78); **Goals:** Nanyn 6/8.
RAMS: 4 Scott Turner; 2 Michael Wainwright; 32 Elliott Cosgrove; 13 Ayden Faal; 5 Austin Buchanan; 6 Pat Walker; 7 Dominic Brambani; 10 Keegan Hirst; 9 Luke Blake; 12 James Lockwood; 40 Richard Fletcher; 39 Matthew Sarsfield; 15 Josh Tonks. Subs (all used): 8 Anthony England; 23 Luke Menzies; 33 Matthew Tebb; 36 Tom Wall.
Tries: Lockwood (18), Brambani (64);
Goals: Brambani 1/2.
Rugby Leaguer & League Express Men of the Match: *Centurions:* John Duffy; *Rams:* Matthew Tebb.
Penalty count: 6-7; **Half-time:** 34-6;
Referee: Matthew Thomason; **Attendance:** 2,234.

FINAL

Sunday 17th July 2011

HALIFAX 16 LEIGH CENTURIONS 20

HALIFAX: 1 Miles Greenwood; 20 Paul White; 5 James Haley; 3 Jon Goddard; 23 Rob Worrincy; 6 Danny Jones; 7 Ben Black; 15 Jim Gannon; 13 Bob Beswick; 10 Neil Cherryholme; 16 Paul Smith; 24 Steve Bannister; 19 Jacob Fairbank. Subs (all used): 4 Dylan Nash; 8 Makali Aizue; 9 Sean Penkywicz; 12 Sam Barlow.
Tries: Greenwood (18), Bannister (28), Worrincy (67);
Goals: Jones 2/4.
CENTURIONS: 1 Stuart Donlan; 2 Steve Maden; 3 Stuart Littler; 4 Mick Nanyn; 5 Dean McGilvray; 6 Martyn Ridyard; 25 Jamie Ellis; 8 Chris Hill; 9 John Duffy; 26 David Mills; 15 Andy Thornley; 12 Tommy Goulden; 11 James Taylor. Subs (all used): 7 Robbie Hunter-Paul; 13 Stephen Nash; 22 Tom Armstrong; 14 Adam Higson.
Tries: Ellis (47, 75), Hill (55), Armstrong (80);
Goals: Nanyn 2/4.
Rugby Leaguer & League Express Men of the Match: *Halifax:* Bob Beswick; *Centurions:* Chris Hill.
Penalty count: 9-7; **Half-time:** 10-0;
Referee: Matthew Thomason;
Attendance: 8,820. *(at Bloomfield Road, Blackpool).*

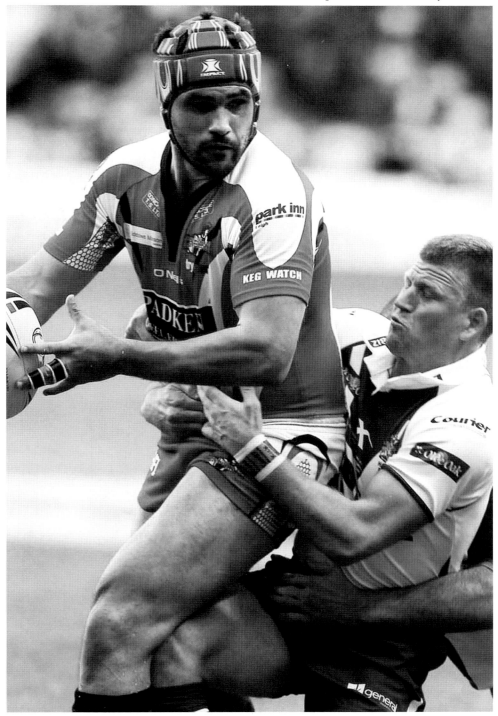

Leigh's Mick Nanyn looks for support under pressure from Halifax's Ben Black
during the Northern Rail Cup Final

ROUND 3

Saturday 5th March 2011

SWINTON LIONS 44 EAST HULL 4

LIONS: 21 Ian Mort; 2 Rob Foxen; 5 Sam Reay; 4 Dean Thompson; 24 Barry Hamilton; 6 Martin Ainscough; 7 Ian Watson; 8 Mike Morrison; 9 Mark Smith; 16 Neil Holland; 11 Dale Cunniffe; 14 Tommy Gallagher; 12 Lee Wingfield. Subs (all used): 25 Karl Ashall; 17 Carl Forber; 26 Joe Fitzpatrick; 10 Dana Wilson.
Tries: D Thompson (2, 46), Ainscough (10), Gallagher (15), Fitzpatrick (21, 59), Mort (27), Ashall (39); **Goals:** Mort 6/8.
EAST HULL: 1 Jason Abdul; 2 Ashley Thackeray; 3 Jamie Edwards; 4 Jordan Precious; 5 Gary King; 6 Gary Blanchard; 7 Carl Puckering; 8 Lee Brown; 9 Shaun Painter; 10 Michael Docherty; 11 Danny Bell; 12 Craig Poucher; 13 Dale Blakeley. Subs (all used): 14 Lee Roberts; 15 Lee Cator; 16 Scott Partis; 17 Chris Lyth.
Try: Poucher (36); **Goals:** Edwards 0/1.
Rugby Leaguer & League Express Men of the Match: *Lions:* Martin Ainscough; *East Hull:* Ashley Thackeray.
Penalty count: 9-9; **Half-time:** 34-4;
Referee: Peter Brooke; **Attendance:** 305.

FEATHERSTONE ROVERS 86 THE ARMY 0

ROVERS: 5 Tom Saxton; 2 Bryn Powell; 1 Ian Hardman; 14 Liam Welham; 23 Thomas Carr; 17 Greg Worthington; 7 Liam Finn; 8 Tony Tonks; 9 Ben Kaye; 11 Jon Grayshon; 4 Andrew Bostock; 12 Tim Spears; 3 Sam Smeaton. Subs (all used): 24 Mufaro Mvududu; 20 Dominic Dee; 31 Cayci Pearson; 22 Matty Johnson.
Tries: Hardman (3, 46, 60), Worthington (6), Welham (11, 14, 25, 55), Carr (18, 64), Finn (27), Powell (42), Johnson (50, 79), Bostock (73), Mvududu (76); **Goals:** Finn 11/16.
THE ARMY: 1 Stuart Butters; 2 Ben Seru; 3 Tony Gregory; 4 Josh Lyons; 5 David Kearns; 6 Andy Gray; 7 Michael Brown; 8 Marc Donnolly; 9 Andy Kay; 10 Sanivalati Ligani; 11 Jamie Laing; 12 Andre Zuhnen; 13 Colin Marangon. Subs (all used): 14 Rob Smart; 15 Darrell Wynn; 16 Vuniani Cuvuilati; 17 Casey Shaw.
Rugby Leaguer & League Express Men of the Match: *Rovers:* Dominic Dee; *The Army:* Michael Brown.
Penalty count: 4-5; **Half-time:** 36-0;
Referee: Dave Merrick; **Attendance:** 723.

LEIGH MINERS RANGERS 26 BARROW RAIDERS 56

MINERS RANGERS: 1 James Muir; 2 Alistair Peters; 3 John Woods; 4 Tom Bradbury; 5 Haydn Bud-Skinkis; 6 Scott O'Brien; 7 Ryan Smith; 8 Craig Connor; 9 Danny Jones; 10 Darryl Kay; 11 Dave Patterson; 12 Ross Bradley; 13 Adam Thomason. Subs (all used): 14 Joe Harrison; 15 Daryl Flannery; 16 Dean Balmer; 17 Tom Eckersley.
Tries: Bradley (20), O'Brien (28), Bradbury (36, 64), Smith (45); **Goals:** Bradbury 3/5.
RAIDERS: 2 Andy Ballard; 19 Marc Dixon; 3 Chris Larkin; 4 Liam Harrison; 5 James Nixon; 6 Jamie Rooney; 7 James Coyle; 8 Jamie Thackray; 18 Nathan Mossop; 10 Matt James; 11 Michael Knowles; 12 Ned Catic; 16 Zebastian Luisi. Subs (all used): 13 Richard Fletcher; 15 Martin Ostler; 9 Mark Gleeson; 14 Liam Campbell.
Tries: Rooney (5), Mossop (8), Harrison (22), Nixon (33, 71), Coyle (39), James (48), Fletcher (51, 75), Ballard (59), Thackray (68); **Goals:** Rooney 2/4, Ballard 2/3, Fletcher 2/3, Knowles 0/1.
Rugby Leaguer & League Express Men of the Match: *Miners Rangers:* Scott O'Brien; *Raiders:* Matt James.
Penalty count: 6-5; **Half-time:** 16-26; **Referee:** Richard Cowling; **Attendance:** 633 *(at Leigh Sports Village).*

MILFORD MARLINS 16 GATESHEAD THUNDER 38

MARLINS: 1 Andy McGann; 2 Sam Hood; 3 John Richardson; 4 Arron Jones-Bishop; 5 Ben Hood; 6 Ryan Oxtoby; 7 Josh Parle; 8 Anthony Ward; 9 James Coates; 10 John Elkington; 11 Simon Speight; 12 Andy Barker; 13 James Barker. Subs (all used): 14 Craig Green; 15 Luke Greaves; 16 John Elliker; 17 Dave Watmough.
Tries: Parle (21), S Hood (45), Oxtoby (79);
Goals: Oxtoby 2/3.
Dismissals: Coates (74) - use of the elbow; Jones-Bishop (77) - punching; Watmough (79) - punching.
Sin bin: J Barker (65) - dissent; McGann (72) - holding down.
THUNDER: 26 Connor Condron; 1 Wayne Green; 15 Andy Morris; 40 Matthew Massey; 16 Robin Peers; 6 Steve Coutts; 7 Ryan Clarke; 20 Nick Staveley; 9 Tom Hodgson; 22 Chris Parker; 4 Josh Stoker; 13 Michael Kelly; 12 Michael Ward. Subs (all used): 2 Craig Olugbode; 10 Stephen Welton; 8 Jason Payne; 28 Gareth Barron.
Tries: Massey (6), Barron (31), Green (39), Staveley (43), Morris (55), Jason Payne (65), Welton (70); **Goals:** Clarke 5/7.
Rugby Leaguer & League Express Men of the Match: *Marlins:* James Barker; *Thunder:* Michael Ward.
Penalty count: 8-22; **Half-time:** 6-16; **Referee:** Craig Halloran; **Attendance:** 400 *(at West Park Bramhope).*

DONCASTER 34 THATTO HEATH CRUSADERS 22

DONCASTER: 1 Mick Butterfield; 5 Dean Colton; 30 Nev Morrison; 25 Chris Spurr; 17 Scott Wilson; 21 Paul Hughes; 19 Scott Spaven; 20 Jamie Bovill; 13 Jack Ely; 17 Adam Scott; 22 Carl Hughes; 15 Craig Robinson; 16 Mike Emmett. Subs (all used): 8 Matt Carbutt; 10 Liam Crawley; 9 Kyle Kesik; 2 Stewart Sanderson.
Tries: Ely (18), Sanderson (26), Kesik (36), Colton (55), Butterfield (59), Bovill (64); **Goals:** Spaven 5/6.
CRUSADERS: 1 Shaun Quinn; 2 Adam Walsh; 3 Dave Hull; 4 Dave Pike; 5 Darren Woods; 6 Andy Stott; 7 Chris Frodsham; 8 Mick Ledger; 9 Kieron Maddocks; 10 Martin Shea; 11 Alex Trumper; 12 Mark Beech; 13 Barry McGilvray. Subs (all used): 14 James Hitchmough; 15 Stephen Lucas; 16 Dave Johnson; 17 Steve Woods.
Tries: D Woods (2, 39, 49), Frodsham (66);
Goals: Quinn 3/4.
Rugby Leaguer & League Express Men of the Match: *Doncaster:* Jamie Bovill; *Crusaders:* Darren Woods.
Penalty count: 6-5; **Half-time:** 18-12;
Referee: Brandon Robinson; **Attendance:** 352.

LONDON SKOLARS 60 EGREMONT RANGERS 24

SKOLARS: 3 James Anthony; 30 Olu Iwenofu; 14 Jason Cook; 33 Jamie Boston; 17 Dave Arnot; 7 Dylan Skee; 1 Neil Thorman; 8 Tony Williams; 9 Gareth Honor; 16 James Simon; 12 Oliver Bloom; 15 Oliver Purslow; 13 Stephen Ball. Subs (all used): 6 Jy-Mel Coleman; 23 Liam Prescott; 24 Dave McMeeken; 5 Ade Adebisi.
Tries: T Williams (5), Honor (15, 27), Bloom (36, 55), Jy-Mel Coleman (40), Cook (45), Adebisi (58), McMeeken (61), Iwenofu (63), Ball (76);
Goals: Thorman 4/6, Prescott 4/5.
Sin bin: Simon (70) - fighting.
RANGERS: 1 Rhys Davies; 2 Ryan Barnes; 3 Ben Walker; 4 Blake Mahovic; 5 Leon Crellin; 6 James McDonald; 7 Paul Corkhill; 8 David Butler; 9 Dan Telford; 10 John Young; 11 Peter Bewsher; 12 David Hartley; 13 John-Paul Brocklebank. Subs (all used): 14 Alastair Leak; 15 Keiron Glenn; 16 Tom Whalley; 17 Kevin Brown.
Tries: Corkhill (12, 70), Brocklebank (32, 80);
Goals: Brocklebank 4/4.
Sin bin: Bewsher (54) - persistent offending; Hartley (70) - fighting.
Rugby Leaguer & League Express Men of the Match: *Skolars:* Neil Thorman; *Rangers:* John-Paul Brocklebank.
Penalty count: 15-7; **Half-time:** 28-12;
Referee: George Stokes; **Attendance:** 342.

KEIGHLEY COUGARS 16 TOULOUSE OLYMPIQUE 10

COUGARS: 2 Craig Moss; 3 Tom Burton; 22 Ben Sagar; 4 Danny Lawton; 26 James Hutchinson; 29 Jason Demetriou; 6 Luke Helliwell; 8 Andy Shickell; 9 James Feather; 10 Scott Law; 11 Will Cartledge; 12 Oliver Pursglove; 18 James Haythornthwaite. Subs (all used): 14 Jamaine Wray; 20 Rick Barr; 16 Brendan Rawlins; 23 Chris Baines.
Tries: Burton (9), Lawton (20), Baines (67);
Goals: Lawton 2/7.
OLYMPIQUE: 22 Damien Couturier; 24 Gregory White; 3 Sebastien Planas; 20 Bruno Ormeno; 18 Andrei Olari; 6 Darren Nicholls; 7 Josh Lewis; 8 Brendan Worth; 9 Craig Cook; 21 Nicolas Faure; 14 Antoni Maria; 12 Yoan Tisseyre; 16 Sylvain Houles. Subs (all used): 15 Jerome Gout; 23 Teli Pelo; 17 Kevin Larroyer; 13 Eric Anselme.
Tries: White (6), Lewis (33); **Goals:** Lewis 1/2.
Rugby Leaguer & League Express Men of the Match: *Cougars:* Scott Law; *Olympique:* Josh Lewis.
Penalty count: 9-5; **Half-time:** 10-10;
Referee: Ronnie Laughton; **Attendance:** 479.

WHITEHAVEN 14 LEZIGNAN 27

WHITEHAVEN: 1 Craig Benson; 3 Derry Eilbeck; 12 Dexter Miller; 4 Scott McAvoy; 2 Craig Calvert; 6 Lewis Palfrey; 7 Tane Manihera; 8 David Ford; 14 Chris Smith; 26 Luke Isakka; 11 Spencer Miller; 35 Lee Doran; 17 Andrew Beattie. Subs (all used): 9 Carl Sice; 23 Paul Culnean; 10 Howard Hill; 13 Daniel Barker.
Tries: Barker (77), D Miller (79); **Goals:** Palfrey 3/3.
LEZIGNAN: 1 Jye Mullane; 2 Nicolas Piquemal; 3 Cedric Bringuier; 4 Mickeal Triballic; 5 Fabien Poggi; 6 Mathieu Alberola; 7 Nathan Wynn; 8 Phil Leuluai; 9 Nicolas Munoz; 10 Frank Rovira; 11 Florian Quintilla; 12 Pierre Negre; 13 Jordi Ligneres. Subs (all used): 14 Julien Bousquet; 15 Mathieu Griffi; 16 Mustafa Mahfoudi; 17 Aurelien Cologni.
Tries: Poggi (5), Bringuier (15, 35), Mullane (48), Quintilla (56); **Goals:** Wynn 3/5; **Field goal:** Wynn (69).
Rugby Leaguer & League Express Men of the Match: *Whitehaven:* Lee Doran; *Lezignan:* Nathan Wynn.
Penalty count: 6-7; **Half-time:** 2-16;
Referee: Matthew Thomason; **Attendance:** 651.

Sunday 6th March 2011

SIDDAL 6 WIDNES VIKINGS 54

SIDDAL: 1 Scott Caley; 2 Craig Sanderson; 3 Luke Simeunovich; 4 Steven Illingworth; 5 Jack Holmes; 6 Steven Hope; 7 Mark Boothroyd; 8 Nick Smith; 9 Gareth English; 10 Gareth Blackburn; 11 Chris Marsh; 12 Chris Brooke; 13 James Simeunovich. Subs (all used): 14 Josh Bentley; 15 Richard Casonove; 16 Simeon Hoyle; 17 Luke Garnett.
Try: Hoyle (34); **Goals:** Blackburn 1/1.
VIKINGS: 34 Jack Owens; 2 Dean Gaskell; 23 Tangi Ropati; 4 Steve Tyrer; 19 Matt Gardner; 1 Danny Craven; 14 Thomas Coyle; 17 Ben Kavanagh; 9 Kirk Netherton; 8 Steve Pickersgill; 12 Kurt Haggerty; 20 Shane Grady; 13 Simon Finnigan. Subs (all used): 42 Danny Sculthorpe; 3 Richard Varkulis; 7 Chaz I'Anson; 15 Chris Gerrard.
Tries: Tyrer (4, 43, 45), Craven (22, 49), Finnigan (25), Gaskell (60, 74), I'Anson (64), Gardner (70);
Goals: Tyrer 7/10.
Rugby Leaguer & League Express Men of the Match: *Siddal:* Scott Caley; *Vikings:* Steve Tyrer.
Penalty count: 3-8; **Half-time:** 6-16; **Referee:** David Sharpe; **Attendance:** 951 *(at The Shay, Halifax).*

BATLEY BULLDOGS 64 FRYSTON WARRIORS 10

BULLDOGS: 30 Johnny Campbell; 29 Darren Williams; 12 Jason Walton; 4 Danny Maun; 2 Alex Brown; 16 Paul Mennell; 7 Gareth Moore; 8 Byron Smith; 9 Kris Lythe; 21 James Martin; 18 Dane Manning; 11 Alex Bretherton; 19 Mark Toohey. Subs (all used): 15 Adam Robinson; 20 David Tootill; 17 Craig Potter; 1 Ian Preece.
Tries: Maun (16), Brown (19, 37), Darren Williams (23, 42), Campbell (25), Moore (35, 40, 68), Walton (40, 73), Manning (75); **Goals:** Moore 8/13.
WARRIORS: 1 Chris Ainley; 2 James Cryer; 3 Dale Cogan; 4 Lee Land; 5 Andy Matthews; 6 Andy Speake; 7 Dave Probert; 8 Gareth Handford; 9 Andy Dickenson; 10 Jonny Jones; 11 Mark Castle; 12 Gareth Lumb; 13 Scott Horner. Subs (all used): 14 Steve Hayes; 15 Steve Scott; 16 Stuart Flowers; 17 Gareth Swinson.
Tries: Land (5), Scott (59); **Goals:** Speake 1/2.
Rugby Leaguer & League Express Men of the Match: *Bulldogs:* Gareth Moore; *Warriors:* Gareth Handford.
Penalty count: 16-8; **Half-time:** 38-6;
Referee: Warren Turley; **Attendance:** 774.

HUNSLET HAWKS 48 WARRINGTON WIZARDS 10

HAWKS: 1 Stuart Kain; 24 Matthew Harding; 16 John Oakes; 4 David Clayton; 5 Waine Pryce; 6 Danny Grimshaw; 22 Danny Ratcliffe; 8 Adam Sullivan; 14 Luke Haigh; 21 Tabua Cakacaka; 17 Rob Kelly; 12 Tom Haughey; 13 David March. Subs (all used): 9 Richard Chapman; 18 Joe Helme; 20 Andrew Yates; 25 Steve Dooler.
Tries: Clayton (1), Pryce (9), Haigh (12), Grimshaw (14, 74), Ratcliffe (22), Harding (44, 54), Chapman (51), Oakes (62); **Goals:** Ratcliffe 4/8, D March 0/2.
Sin bin: Grimshaw (48) - foul play.
WIZARDS: 1 Dave Yii; 2 Darren Forshaw; 3 Matt Taylor; 4 Mike Stout; 5 Craig Middlemore; 6 Alan Reddecliff; 7 Chris Campbell; 8 Dan Stubbs; 9 Warren Ayres; 10 Matt Clarke; 11 Paul Alcock; 12 Wesley Lawton; 13 Nick Owen. Subs (all used): 14 Graham Healey; 15 Mike Grady; 16 Dan Faulkner; 17 Ian Harris.
Tries: Forshaw (29), Taylor (78); **Goals:** Ayres 1/2.
Rugby Leaguer & League Express Men of the Match: *Hawks:* Danny Grimshaw; *Wizards:* Darren Forshaw.
Penalty count: 8-9; **Half-time:** 24-4;
Referee: Tony Mahar; **Attendance:** 316.

LEIGH CENTURIONS 68 HULL DOCKERS 24

CENTURIONS: 1 Stuart Donlan; 19 Jonathan Pownall; 3 Stuart Littler; 2 Steve Maden; 5 Dean McGilvray; 6 Martyn Ridyard; 25 Jamie Ellis; 13 Stephen Nash; 23 Mick Govin; 26 David Mills; 24 Andy Gorski; 12 Tommy Goulden; 20 Sam Hopkins. Subs (all used): 17 Craig Briscoe; 15 Andy Thornley; 16 Anthony Nicholson; 32 Chris Murphy.
Tries: Ellis (3, 22, 28, 38), Gorski (5), Hopkins (14, 67), Pownall (43), Nicholson (53), Briscoe (57), Thornley (69), Murphy (79);
Goals: Ellis 7/7, Ridyard 2/2, Govin 1/3.
DOCKERS: 1 Danny Ulyatt; 2 Jack Snowden; 3 Martin Johnson; 4 Jason Bowsley; 5 Paul Taylor; 6 Chris Stephenson; 7 Carl Smirk; 8 Aaron Bradley; 9 Steven Sellars; 10 Matthew Emmerson; 11 Nick Powley; 12 John Eccles; 13 Andrew Kay. Subs (all used): 14 Gareth Moore; 15 Craig Render; 16 Callum Birch; 17 Lee Forth.
Tries: Snowden (11, 40), Johnson (16), Birch (47);
Goals: Stephenson 4/4.
Rugby Leaguer & League Express Men of the Match: *Centurions:* Jamie Ellis; *Dockers:* Steven Sellars.
Penalty count: 12-4; **Half-time:** 36-18;
Referee: Tom Crashley; **Attendance:** 1,083.

NORTHUMBRIA UNIVERSITY 0 YORK CITY KNIGHTS 132

NORTHUMBRIA UNIVERSITY: 1 Luke Bradley; 2 Connor Sheridan; 3 Jack Wilshire; 4 Marcus Broad; 5 Danny Chetwynd; 6 Scott Whiteley; 7 Richard Whiteley; 8 Karl Brandt; 9 Gary Sargent; 10 Ian Sherwood; 11 Josh Taylor; 12 David Cash; 13 Neil Eyes. Subs (all used): 14 Mike Ellis; 15 Austin Phillips; 16 Gareth Schofield; 17 Andy Forbes.
CITY KNIGHTS: 18 Sam Lynch; 5 Danny Wilson; 2 Dave Sutton; 3 Duane Straugheir; 21 Dennis Tuffour; 6 Chris Thorman; 7 Jon Presley; 14 Jack Stearman; 9 Jack Lee; 10 Alex Benson; 11 Rhys Clarke; 25 Steve Lewis; 24 Mark Barlow. Subs (all used): 23 Paul Stamp; 22 Ed Smith; 12 Matt Barron; 34 Davey Burns.
Tries: Wilson (3, 47), Thorman (8, 34, 53, 65), Presley (11, 13, 40, 41, 49, 71), Sutton (16), Lee (27), Lewis (30), Tuffour (45, 55), Straugheir (57), Barlow (59, 69), Clarke (63), Smith (73), Stearman (79);
Goals: Thorman 20/23.
Rugby Leaguer & League Express Men of the Match: *Northumbria University:* Gary Sargent; *City Knights:* Chris Thorman.
Penalty count: 8-4; **Half-time:** 0-52; **Referee:** Joe Cobb; **Attendance:** 434 *(at Huntington Stadium).*

OLDHAM 28 HUNSLET WARRIORS 16

OLDHAM: 1 Ben Heaton; 26 Matthew Fogarty; 3 Marcus St Hilaire; 4 Jack Bradbury; 21 Mark Brocklehurst; 6 Neil Roden; 7 Mick Diveney; 8 Jason Boults; 25 Martin Roden; 15 Luke Sutton; 12 Ben Wood; 24 Paul Noone; 14 Chris Clarke. Subs (all used): 10 Dave Ellison; 13 Valu Bentley; 17 John Clough; 22 Tom Wood-Hulme.
Tries: Clarke (3), Fogarty (26), Brocklehurst (32), N Roden (70), Wood (73); **Goals:** Diveney 4/6.
WARRIORS: 1 Gary McClelland; 2 Aaron Niles; 3 Mark Cunningham; 4 Tony Swift; 5 Chris Hartley; 6 Mick Lyons; 7 Jim Baker; 8 Paul Sebine; 9 Aaron Pratt; 10 Jonny Dawson; 11 Ryan Angus; 12 Omar Medhi; 13 Caldon Bravo. Subs (all used): 14 Mark Holmes; 15 Jason Milner; 16 Liam Gale; 17 Karl Featherstone.

Tries: Niles (8), Cunningham (39, 58);
Goals: McClelland 2/3.
Rugby Leaguer & League Express Men of the Match: *Oldham:* Neil Roden; *Warriors:* Caldon Bravo.
Penalty count: 15-6; **Half-time:** 16-10;
Referee: Chris Leatherbarrow; **Attendance:** 538.

ROCHDALE HORNETS 22 WORKINGTON TOWN 20

HORNETS: 1 Wayne English; 2 Craig Johnson; 3 Dean Gorton; 22 Damien Reid; 17 Dale Bloomfield; 6 Liam McGovern; 7 Steve Roper; 18 John Cookson; 15 Paul Crook; 20 Chris Clough; 4 Matthew Strong; 11 Craig Ashall; 13 Dayne Donoghue. Subs (all used): 8 Dave Newton; 21 Mark Hobson; 28 Chris Hough; 9 Steve McDermott.
Tries: Ashall (16), McDermott (44), Roper (47), McGovern (64); **Goals:** Crook 1/2, McGovern 2/2.
TOWN: 1 Brett Carter; 2 Elliott Miller; 21 John Patrick; 4 Aaron Low; 5 Neil Frazer; 23 Marc Bainbridge; 7 Scott Kaighan; 15 Ruairi McGoff; 9 Graeme Mattinson; 10 Kris Coward; 11 Mike Whitehead; 12 Jarrad Stack; 13 Karl Olstrum. Subs (all used): 14 Jack Pedley; 8 Marc Jackson; 16 Ryan McDonald; 19 Marc Shackley.
Tries: Kaighan (7), Mattinson (20), Low (26), Miller (31); **Goals:** Kaighan 2/4.
Rugby Leaguer & League Express Men of the Match: *Hornets:* Craig Ashall; *Town:* Jarrad Stack.
Penalty count: 8-8; **Half-time:** 4-20;
Referee: Tim Roby; **Attendance:** 358.

SHEFFIELD EAGLES 82 LEEDS MET UNIVERSITY 0

EAGLES: 28 Jamie Cottle; 2 Danny Mills; 3 Menzie Yere; 26 Corey Hanson; 5 Tim Bergin; 13 Dane McDonald; 7 Simon Brown; 8 Jack Howieson; 9 Andrew Henderson; 10 Mitchell Stringer; 11 Alex Szostak; 12 Peter Green; 19 Joe Hirst. Subs (all used): 23 Nick Turnbull; 22 Ryan Hepworth; 17 Alex Rowe; 15 Liam Higgins.
Tries: Hanson (5), Howieson (11), Green (19), Yere (26, 79), Szostak (29, 33), Rowe (37), Cottle (39), Bergin (47), Hirst (58), McDonald (64, 80), Mills (67), Henderson (76); **Goals:** Brown 11/15.
LEEDS MET UNIVERSITY: 1 John Paxton; 2 Matt Holding; 3 Reece Griffiths; 4 Ethan Longhorn; 5 Zac Cotton; 6 Mark Wool; 7 Pat Toft; 8 Mike Sykes; 9 Owain Griffiths; 10 Danny Jackson; 11 Tom Dransfield; 12 Sean Richards; 13 Chris Clark. Subs (all used): 14 Gareth Hynes; 15 Danny Ventner; 16 Ben Tyers; 17 Ben Parkinson.
Rugby Leaguer & League Express Men of the Match: *Eagles:* Simon Brown; *Leeds Met University:* Mark Wool.
Penalty count: 9-7; **Half-time:** 44-0; **Referee:** Matthew Kidd; **Attendance:** 350 *(at Don Valley Stadium).*

SOUTH WALES SCORPIONS 6 DEWSBURY RAMS 62

SCORPIONS: 2 Lewis Reece; 29 Robin Lock; 4 Ashley Bateman; 3 Christiaan Roets; 5 Curtis Cunningham; 1 Andrew Gay; 7 Casey Bromilow; 20 Hywel Davies; 14 Tom Burnell; 15 Neil Dallimore; 12 Loz Wildbore; 17 Harri Greville; 13 Aled James. Subs (all used): 9 Steve Parry; 30 Barrie Phillips; 18 Chris Davies; 31 Dafydd Carter.
Try: Gay (49); **Goals:** Reece 1/1.
Sin bin: Roets (53) - late challenge.
RAMS: 1 James Craven; 2 Michael Wainwright; 32 Elliott Cosgrove; 4 Scott Turner; 5 Austin Buchanan; 26 Jordan Tansey; 7 Dominic Brambani; 8 Anthony England; 9 Luke Blake; 10 Keegan Hirst; 11 Rob Spicer; 12 James Lockwood; 15 Josh Tonks. Subs (all used): 22 Jonny Horton; 23 Luke Menzies; 16 Adam Hayes; 31 Shaun Emblem.
Tries: Spicer (3), Buchanan (7, 38), England (15), Cosgrove (20), Horton (40), Turner (60), Hirst (63), Brambani (69, 79), Menzies (75); **Goals:** Brambani 9/11.
Rugby Leaguer & League Express Men of the Match: *Scorpions:* Andrew Gay; *Rams:* Dominic Brambani.
Penalty count: 9-13; **Half-time:** 0-32;
Referee: Jamie Leahy; **Attendance:** 356.

HALIFAX 76 CASTLEFORD LOCK LANE 6

HALIFAX: 1 Miles Greenwood; 20 Paul White; 5 James Haley; 4 Dylan Nash; 23 Rob Worrincy; 28 Graham Holroyd; 6 Danny Jones; 10 Neil Cherryholme; 13 Bob Beswick; 25 Michael Ostick; 11 David Larder; 24 Steve Bannister; 12 Sam Barlow. Subs (all used): 8 Makali Aizue; 9 Sean Penkywicz; 21 Josh Barlow; 33 Ryan Fieldhouse.
Tries: Worrincy (2, 25), Nash (7), Greenwood (21, 40), Bannister (28, 48), Penkywicz (31), Holroyd (42), Jones (45), White (55, 75), Fieldhouse (60), Beswick (62); **Goals:** Jones 10/14.
LOCK LANE: 1 Craig Duncan; 2 Darren Holmes; 3 John Walton; 4 Chris Tudor; 5 Adam Garlick; 6 Mark Spears; 7 Lee Cartwright; 8 Craig Jones; 9 Steve Bolderson; 10 Mark Kear; 11 Robert Firth; 12 Wayne Hardy; 13 Craig Jeffels. Subs (all used): 14 Joe Groves; 15 James Gilpin; 16 James Rayner; 17 Tom Wood.
Try: Garlick (13); **Goals:** Hardy 1/1.
Sin bin: Jeffels (78) - dissent.
Rugby Leaguer & League Express Men of the Match: *Halifax:* Graham Holroyd; *Lock Lane:* Wayne Hardy.
Penalty count: 13-7; **Half-time:** 38-6;
Referee: Clint Sharrad; **Attendance:** 1,684.

ROUND 4

Friday 6th May 2011

GATESHEAD THUNDER 0 HARLEQUINS 70

THUNDER: 17 Joe Brown; 43 Ashley Williams; 6 Mitchell Stevens; 12 Michael Ward; 16 Robin Peers; 26 Connor Condron; 7 Ryan Clarke; 20 Nick Staveley; 9 Tom Hodgson; 22 Chris Parker; 4 Josh Stoker; 13 Michael Kelly; 31 Will Bate. Subs (all used): 5 Dan O'Sullivan; 8 Jason Payne; 40 Matthew Massey; 15 Andy Morris.
HARLEQUINS: 2 Jamie O'Callaghan; 23 Mark Calderwood; 3 Tony Clubb; 4 David Howell; 5 Chris Melling; 6 Luke Gale; 7 Chad Randall (C); 17 Danny Ward; 9 Andy Ellis; 8 Karl Temata; 10 Oliver Wilkes; 11 Nick Kouparitsas; 15 Luke Ambler. Subs (all used): 20 Ben Bolger; 18 Dave Williams; 21 Olsi Krasniqi; 24 Dan Sarginson (D).
Tries: Wilkes (14), Gale (23), Bolger (29, 62), O'Callaghan (31), Howell (34), Clubb (37, 51, 71), Sarginson (43), Melling (53), Kouparitsas (64), Randall (78); **Goals:** Gale 7/9, Melling 2/4.
Rugby Leaguer & League Express Men of the Match: *Thunder:* Nick Staveley; *Harlequins:* Tony Clubb.
Penalty count: 2-7; **Half-time:** 0-32;
Referee: Craig Halloran; **Attendance:** 402.

LEIGH CENTURIONS 16 CATALAN DRAGONS 22

CENTURIONS: 1 Stuart Donlan; 2 Steve Maden; 3 Stuart Littler; 14 Adam Higson; 5 Dean McGilvray; 6 Martyn Ridyard; 25 Jamie Ellis; 8 Chris Hill; 9 John Duffy; 26 David Mills; 15 Andy Thornley; 12 Tommy Goulden; 11 James Taylor. Subs: 13 Stephen Nash; 19 Jonathan Pownall (not used); 20 Sam Hopkins; 23 Mick Govin.
Tries: Higson (5), Goulden (12), Donlan (76);
Goals: Ridyard 2/4.
DRAGONS: 5 Cyril Stacul; 2 Damien Blanch; 3 Ben Farrar; 15 Jean-Philippe Baile; 19 Frederic Vaccari; 6 Thomas Bosc (C); 7 Scott Dureau; 8 David Ferriol; 26 Eloi Pelissier; 20 Michael Simon; 10 Remi Casty; 12 Sebastien Raguin; 13 Gregory Mounis. Subs (all used): 9 Ian Henderson; 22 Jamal Fakir; 24 Jason Baitieri; 28 Julien Touxagas.
Tries: Blanch (25), Baile (38), Stacul (44), Henderson (70); **Goals:** Dureau 1/3, Bosc 2/2.
Rugby Leaguer & League Express Men of the Match: *Centurions:* Stuart Donlan; *Dragons:* Ian Henderson.
Penalty count: 10-11; **Half-time:** 12-10;
Referee: James Child; **Attendance:** 2,237.

Saturday 7th May 2011

HULL FC 82 OLDHAM 0

HULL: 3 Richard Whiting; 2 Will Sharp; 33 Martin Gleeson; 19 Jordan Turner; 5 Tom Briscoe; 6 Richard Horne; 30 Sam Obst; 23 Sam Moa; 9 Danny Houghton; 17 Ewan Dowes; 16 Willie Manu; 15 Epalahame Lauaki; 14 Danny Washbrook. Subs (all used): 21 Reece Lyne; 32 Jack Aldous (D); 24 Liam Kent (D); 10 Lee Radford (C).
Tries: Obst (7, 15), Turner (9, 29, 80), Houghton (17), Sharp (21), Whiting (40, 73), Gleeson (45), Lyne (50, 67), Horne (56), Moa (60), Radford (75);
Goals: Whiting 11/15.
OLDHAM: 30 Steven Nield; 27 Shaun Robinson; 26 Matthew Fogarty; 12 Ben Wood; 5 John Gillam; 29 Jamie Dallimore; 7 Mick Diveney; 10 Dave Ellison; 17 John Clough; 16 Liam Gilchrist; 24 Paul Noone; 14 Chris Clarke; 13 Valu Bentley. Subs (all used): 20 Michael Ward; 19 Scott Mansfield; 28 Luke Stenchion; 15 Luke Sutton.
Rugby Leaguer & League Express Men of the Match: *Hull:* Richard Whiting; *Oldham:* Shaun Robinson.
Penalty count: 2-2; **Half-time:** 42-0;
Referee: Chris Leatherbarrow; **Attendance:** 6,235.

ST HELENS 52 SHEFFIELD EAGLES 26

SAINTS: 27 Nathan Ashe; 2 Ade Gardner; 3 Michael Shenton; 5 Francis Meli; 22 Jamie Foster; 12 Jon Wilkin; 7 Kyle Eastmond; 10 James Graham (C); 9 James Roby; 8 Josh Perry; 4 Iosia Soliola; 13 Chris Flannery; 21 Shaun Magennis. Subs (all used): 15 Louie McCarthy-Scarsbrook; 18 Matty Ashurst; 19 Andrew Dixon; 24 Tom Armstrong.
Tries: Foster (3, 50), Soliola (13), Meli (16, 42), Shenton (32), Wilkin (48), Eastmond (56), Flannery (80); **Goals:** Foster 8/9.
EAGLES: 6 Quentin Laulu-Togagae; 2 Danny Mills; 3 Menzie Yere; 26 Corey Hanson; 5 Tim Bergin; 13 Dane McDonald; 7 Simon Brown; 8 Jack Howieson; 9 Andrew Henderson; 10 Mitchell Stringer; 11 Alex Szostak; 12 Peter Green; 19 Joe Hirst. Subs (all used): 17 Alex Rowe; 22 Ryan Hepworth; 27 Eddie Battye; 30 Sam Scott.
Tries: Szostak (28, 54), Laulu-Togagae (71, 75, 77);
Goals: Brown 3/5.
Rugby Leaguer & League Express Men of the Match: *Saints:* Jon Wilkin; *Eagles:* Quentin Laulu-Togagae.
Penalty count: 6-1; **Half-time:** 22-6;
Referee: Ben Thaler; **Attendance:** 3,563.

LEEDS RHINOS 30 CRUSADERS 20

RHINOS: 1 Brent Webb; 2 Lee Smith; 3 Brett Delaney; 4 Keith Senior; 5 Ryan Hall; 13 Kevin Sinfield (C); 7 Rob Burrow; 8 Kylie Leuluai; 9 Danny Buderus; 10 Jamie Peacock; 22 Jay Pitts; 21 Chris Clarkson; 12 Carl Ablett. Subs (all used): 6 Danny McGuire; 24 Paul McShane; 17 Ian Kirke; 18 Luke Burgess.
Tries: McShane (23), Pitts (25), Burrow (32), Hall (42), Buderus (72); **Goals:** Sinfield 5/5.
CRUSADERS: 1 Clinton Schifcofske (C); 5 Stuart Reardon; 4 Vince Mellars; 2 Gareth Thomas; 18 Elliot Kear; 6 Michael Witt; 17 Rhys Hanbury; 8 Ryan O'Hara; 19 Lloyd White; 22 Richard Moore; 11 Hep Cahill; 13 Frank Winterstein; 23 Peter Lupton. Subs (all used): 16 Ben Flower; 7 Jarrod Sammut; 10 Mark Bryant; 20 Gil Dudson.
Tries: Cahill (6), Hanbury (14), Kear (52), Lupton (69);
Goals: Schifcofske 2/4.
Dismissal: Cahill (58) - kick on Burrow.
On report:
Bryant (35) - alleged use of the elbow on Smith.
Rugby Leaguer & League Express Men of the Match: *Rhinos:* Danny Buderus; *Crusaders:* Clinton Schifcofske.
Penalty count: 7-6; **Half time:** 18-10;
Referee: Steve Ganson; **Attendance:** 10,954.

FEATHERSTONE ROVERS 42 LEZIGNAN 16

ROVERS: 28 Jon Hepworth; 2 Bryn Powell; 3 Sam Smeaton; 31 Nathan Chappell; 5 Tom Saxton; 6 Andy Kain; 7 Liam Finn; 15 Michael Haley; 29 Tom Hemingway; 10 Stuart Dickens; 11 Jon Grayshon; 12 Tim Spears; 13 Matty Dale. Subs (all used): 8 Tony Tonks; 18 Ross Divorty; 17 Greg Worthington; 24 Mufaro Mvududu.
Tries: Hepworth (8), Chappell (13), Powell (17), Smeaton (21, 30), Kain (34), Divorty (39), Saxton (48);
Goals: Finn 5/8.
LEZIGNAN: 1 Vincent Michalu; 2 Nicolas Piquemal; 3 Cedric Bringuier; 4 Damien Cardace; 5 Fabien Poggi; 6 Jye Mullane; 7 Nathan Wynn; 8 Mathieu Griffi; 9 Aurelien Cologni; 10 Frank Rovira; 11 Charly Clottes; 12 Pierre Negre; 13 Andrew Bentley. Subs (all used): 14 Fabien Croux; 15 Phil Leuluai; 16 Julien Bousquet; 17 Aurelien Bourrell.
Tries: Mullane (25, 78), Cologni (63); **Goals:** Wynn 2/3.
Rugby Leaguer & League Express Men of the Match: *Rovers:* Andy Kain; *Lezignan:* Mathieu Griffi.
Penalty count: 7-6; **Half-time:** 38-4;
Referee: Ronnie Laughton; **Attendance:** 827.

Sunday 8th May 2011

BATLEY BULLDOGS 18 HUDDERSFIELD GIANTS 28

BULLDOGS: 1 Ian Preece; 5 Wayne Reittie; 12 Jason Walton; 4 Danny Maun; 2 Alex Brown; 6 Paul Handforth; 16 Paul Mennell; 8 Byron Smith; 9 Kris Lythe; 17 Craig Potter; 18 Dane Manning; 11 Alex Bretherton; 13 Ashley Lindsay. Subs (all used): 25 George Flanagan; 23 Chris Buttery; 15 Adam Robinson; 20 David Tootill.
Tries: Manning (24), Walton (26), Brown (50);
Goals: Handforth 3/4.
Dismissal: Manning (65) - high tackle.
GIANTS: 3 Leroy Cudjoe; 2 Michael Lawrence; 29 Joe Wardle; 4 Lee Gilmour; 5 David Hodgson; 6 Kevin Brown (C); 7 Danny Brough; 18 Larne Patrick; 14 Shaun Lunt; 10 Darrell Griffin; 26 Jamie Cording; 17 Danny Kirmond; 11 Luke O'Donnell. Subs (all used): 23 Kyle Wood; 8 Eorl Crabtree; 32 Jon Molloy; 27 Jacob Fairbank (D).
Tries: Brown (8), Gilmour (33), Brough (67), Wardle (70), Hodgson (74), Cudjoe (79); **Goals:** Brough 2/6.
Rugby Leaguer & League Express Men of the Match: *Bulldogs:* Paul Handforth; *Giants:* Kevin Brown.
Penalty count: 4-4; **Half-time:** 10-10;
Referee: Robert Hicks; **Attendance:** 2,676.

DEWSBURY RAMS 38 SWINTON LIONS 44

RAMS: 4 Scott Turner; 2 Michael Wainwright; 32 Elliott Cosgrove; 13 Ayden Faal; 5 Austin Buchanan; 6 Pat Walker; 7 Dominic Brambani; 23 Luke Menzies; 9 Luke Blake; 10 Keegan Hirst; 11 Rob Spicer; 12 James Lockwood; 15 Josh Tonks. Subs (all used): 22 Jonny Horton; 33 Shaun Emblem; 19 James Walker; 36 Brooke Broughton.
Tries: P Walker (22), Brambani (25, 77), Buchanan (30, 75), Spicer (38); **Goals:** Brambani 7/8.
Sin bin: P Walker (73) - fighting.
LIONS: 21 Ian Mort; 2 Rob Foxen; 3 Gavin Dodd; 4 Dean Thompson; 20 Richard Flooks; 7 Ian Watson; 6 Martin Ainscough; 8 Mike Morrison; 9 Mark Smith; 12 Lee Wingfield; 15 Darren Hawkyard; 11 Dale Cunniffe; 13 Phil Joseph. Subs (all used): 25 Karl Ashall; 16 Neil Holland; 10 Dana Wilson; 14 Tommy Gallagher.
Tries: Mort (3), Flooks (6), Dodd (16), Gallagher (35), Joseph (50, 61), Wingfield (63); **Goals:** Mort 8/8.
Sin bin: Watson (73) - fighting; Cunniffe (73) - fighting.
Rugby Leaguer & League Express Men of the Match: *Rams:* Dominic Brambani; *Lions:* Ian Mort.
Penalty count: 14-6; **Half-time:** 24-24;
Referee: Jamie Leahy; **Attendance:** 692.

DONCASTER 10 WAKEFIELD TRINITY WILDCATS 50

DONCASTER: 1 Mick Butterfield; 2 Stewart Sanderson; 25 Chris Spurr; 32 Craig Lawton; 5 Dean Colton; 6 Aaron Dobek; 19 Scott Spaven; 17 Adam Scott; 13 Jack Ely; 10 Liam Crawley; 15 Craig Robinson; 8 Matt Carbutt; 16 Mike Emmett. Subs (all used): 9 Kyle Kesik; 22 Carl Hughes; 23 Grant Edwards; 11 Kyle Sampson.
Tries: Spaven (25), Sanderson (44);
Goals: Spaven 0/1, Dobek 1/1.
WILDCATS: 23 Josh Veivers; 29 Josh Griffin; 5 Luke George; 3 Aaron Murphy; 19 Dale Morton; 27 Kieran Hyde; 14 Tommy Lee; 10 Paul King; 26 Matthew Wildie; 31 Kyle Amor; 13 Glenn Morrison (C); 21 Frankie Mariano; 22 Stuart Howarth. Subs (all used): 8 Michael Korkidas; 11 Kevin Henderson; 18 Chris Dean; 24 James Davey.
Tries: Amor (8), Griffin (12, 57), Murphy (31), Henderson (52), Morton (68), Dean (71), Veivers (75), Hyde (79); **Goals:** Veivers 7/10.
Rugby Leaguer & League Express Men of the Match: *Doncaster:* Adam Scott; *Wildcats:* Kieran Hyde.
Penalty count: 4-9; **Half-time:** 4-18;
Referee: Matthew Thomason; **Attendance:** 1,823.

HUNSLET HAWKS 2 SALFORD CITY REDS 68

HAWKS: 22 Danny Ratcliffe; 1 Stuart Kain; 16 John Oakes; 4 David Clayton; 5 Waine Pryce; 6 Danny Grimshaw; 7 Paul March; 18 Joe Helme; 9 Richard Chapman; 10 James Houston; 12 Tom Haughey; 25 Steve Dooler; 13 David March. Subs (all used): 11 Richard Blakeway; 17 Rob Kelly; 19 Neil Lowe; 23 Joe McLocklan.
Goals: Ratcliffe 1/1.
CITY REDS: 1 Luke Patten; 2 Jodie Broughton; 6 Stefan Ratchford; 5 Ashley Gibson; 27 Adam Clay; 14 Matty Smith; 7 Daniel Holdsworth (C); 19 Ryan Boyle; 9 Wayne Godwin; 17 Iafeta Palea'aesina; 18 Adam Sidlow; 4 Chris Nero; 15 Luke Adamson. Subs (all used): 8 Ray Cashmere; 10 Lee Jewitt; 22 Adam Neal; 23 Marc Sneyd.
Tries: Adamson (13, 41), Palea'aesina (16, 68), Neal (28), Jewitt (33), Broughton (46, 58), Ratchford (50), Nero (61), Clay (66, 78);
Goals: Holdsworth 6/7, Ratchford 3/4, Smith 1/1.
Rugby Leaguer & League Express Men of the Match: *Hawks:* John Oakes; *City Reds:* Matty Smith.
Penalty count: 6-5; **Half-time:** 2-22;
Referee: Warren Turley; **Attendance:** 649.

LONDON SKOLARS 18 WIDNES VIKINGS 62

SKOLARS: 3 James Anthony; 18 Aaron Small; 17 Dave Arnot; 36 John Paxton; 5 Ade Adebisi; 21 Danny Burke; 7 Dylan Skee; 22 Saqib Murtza; 9 Gareth Honor; 10 Jason Hart; 37 Jaroslaw Obuchowski; 15 Oliver Purslow; 25 Austen Aggrey. Subs (all used): 24 Dave McMeeken; 20 Guy Aldam; 32 Sam Gee; 29 Michael Sykes.
Tries: Obuchowski (42), Anthony (57), Arnot (62);
Goals: Skee 3/3.
VIKINGS: 5 Paddy Flynn; 2 Dean Gaskell; 23 Tangi Ropati; 4 Steve Tyrer; 19 Matt Gardner; 7 Chaz I'Anson; 14 Thomas Coyle; 42 Danny Sculthorpe; 25 Chris Lunt; 10 Daniel Heckenberg; 20 Shane Grady; 16 Macgraff Leuluai; 11 Dave Allen. Subs: 3 Richard Varkulis; 17 Ben Kavanagh (not used); 22 David Houghton; 29 Grant Gore.
Tries: Leuluai (5, 10), T Coyle (18), Flynn (34, 39, 51, 75), Ropati (37), Varkulis (46), Gore (48), Tyrer (66), Allen (80); **Goals:** Tyrer 7/12.
Rugby Leaguer & League Express Men of the Match: *Skolars:* James Anthony; *Vikings:* Paddy Flynn.
Penalty count: 5-6; **Half-time:** 0-32;
Referee: Clint Sharrad; **Attendance:** 415.

ROCHDALE HORNETS 10 CASTLEFORD TIGERS 72

HORNETS: 5 Scott Yates; 17 Dale Bloomfield; 4 Matthew Strong; 3 Dean Gorton; 25 Andy Saywell; 15 Paul Crook; 7 Steve Roper; 35 Richard Mervill; 11 Craig Ashall; 18 John Cookson; 21 Mark Hobson; 10 Adam Bowman; 13 Dayne Donoghue. Subs (all used): 32 Danny Ekis; 8 Dave Newton; 9 Steve McDermott; 1 Wayne English.
Tries: Yates (12), Saywell (73); **Goals:** Crook 1/2.
TIGERS: 5 Richard Owen; 22 Jordan Thompson; 4 Joe Arundel; 2 Kirk Dixon; 28 Greg Eden (D); 23 Ryan McGoldrick; 6 Rangi Chase; 19 Nick Fozzard; 16 Adam Milner; 11 Jake Emmitt; 24 Oliver Holmes; 25 Dean Widders; 9 Ryan Hudson. Subs (all used): 7 Danny Orr (C); 12 Steve Snitch; 21 Nathan Massey; 27 Daryl Clark.
Tries: Dixon (17, 69), Arundel (20, 31), Chase (24), Snitch (42, 55), Clark (47, 66), Massey (51, 57), Milner (64), Owen (77); **Goals:** Dixon 9/12, Orr 1/1.
Rugby Leaguer & League Express Men of the Match: *Hornets:* Craig Ashall; *Tigers:* Richard Owen.
Penalty count: 7-4; **Half-time:** 6-22;
Referee: Thierry Alibert; **Attendance:** 1,675.

WARRINGTON WOLVES 80 KEIGHLEY COUGARS 0

WOLVES: 2 Chris Riley; 22 Rhys Williams; 20 Matty Blythe; 23 Ryan Atkins; 3 Matt King; 6 Lee Briers (C); 27 Gareth O'Brien (D); 10 Garreth Carvell; 14 Mick Higham; 18 Michael Cooper; 26 David Solomona; 17 Simon Grix; 13 Ben Harrison. Subs (all used): 8 Adrian Morley (C); 9 Michael Monaghan; 16 Paul Wood; 24 Rhys Evans.
Tries: Atkins (1, 34, 42), Grix (21), Wood (24), Cooper (31), Briers (40, 74), O'Brien (41), Williams (50, 78), King (54), M Monaghan (56), Evans (66); **Goals:** Briers 12/14.
COUGARS: 5 Gavin Duffy; 22 Ben Sagar; 4 Danny Lawton; 23 Chris Baines; 26 James Hutchinson; 29 Jason Demetriou; 7 Ryan Smith; 8 Andy Shickell; 9 James Feather; 17 Ryan Benjafield; 11 Will Cartledge; 12 Oliver Pursglove; 25 Jamie Shepherd. Subs (all used): 10 Scott Law; 13 Greg Nicholson; 14 Jamaine Wray; 20 Rick Barr.
Rugby Leaguer & League Express Men of the Match: *Wolves:* Ryan Atkins; *Cougars:* Jason Demetriou.
Penalty count: 3-2; **Half-time:** 34-0;
Referee: George Stokes; **Attendance:** 6,583.

WIGAN WARRIORS 52 BARROW RAIDERS 0

WARRIORS: 1 Sam Tomkins; 25 Josh Charnley; 12 Joel Tomkins; 4 George Carmont; 5 Pat Richards; 17 Brett Finch; 7 Thomas Leuluai; 10 Andy Coley; 9 Michael McIlorum; 15 Jeff Lima; 22 Liam Farrell; 16 Ryan Hoffman; 13 Sean O'Loughlin (C). Subs (all used): 14 Paul Prescott; 6 Paul Deacon; 23 Chris Tuson; 33 Jack Hughes (D).
Tries: Leuluai (12, 53), Coley (15), Carmont (19), Deacon (34), S Tomkins (41, 71), O'Loughlin (44), Richards (64); **Goals:** Richards 8/9.
Sin bin: Lima (46) - professional foul.
RAIDERS: 23 Gregg McNally; 2 Andy Ballard; 3 Chris Larkin; 4 Liam Harrison; 27 Mike Backhouse; 6 Jamie Rooney; 14 Liam Campbell; 8 Jamie Thackray; 18 Nathan Mossop; 21 Jamie Butler; 15 Martin Ostler; 12 Ned Catic; 16 Zebastian Luisi. Subs: 9 Mark Gleeson (not used); 10 Matt James; 11 Michael Knowles; 19 Marc Dixon.
Rugby Leaguer & League Express Men of the Match: *Warriors:* Sam Tomkins; *Raiders:* Andy Ballard.
Penalty count: 7-2; **Half-time:** 24-0;
Referee: Tim Roby; **Attendance:** 8,026.

YORK CITY KNIGHTS 22 HULL KINGSTON ROVERS 64

CITY KNIGHTS: 20 Tom Bush; 5 Danny Wilson; 29 James Ford; 4 Lee Waterman; 1 James Haynes; 27 Anthony Thackeray; 28 Ben Hardcastle; 8 Nathan Freer; 24 Mark Barlow; 10 Alex Benson; 13 Ryan Esders; 19 Matt Garside; 25 Steve Lewis. Subs (all used): 14 Jack Stearman; 15 Brett Waller; 7 Jon Presley; 22 Ed Smith.
Tries: Barlow (12, 50), Stearman (46), Waterman (79);
Goals: Waterman 3/4.
ROVERS: 26 Louis Sheriff; 2 Peter Fox; 3 Kris Welham; 4 Jake Webster; 28 Ben Cockayne; 6 Blake Green; 7 Michael Dobson; 15 Scott Wheeldon; 18 Josh Hodgson; 10 Joel Clinton; 17 Matt Cook; 12 Ben Galea (C); 16 Jason Netherton. Subs (all used): 8 Rhys Lovegrove; 9 Ben Fisher; 14 Liam Watts; 27 Jordan Cox (D).
Tries: Fox (5, 71), Green (9), Galea (18), Sheriff (23), Dobson (24), Cook (27), Cox (35, 68), Welham (54), Webster (64); **Goals:** Dobson 10/11.
Rugby Leaguer & League Express Men of the Match: *City Knights:* Mark Barlow; *Rovers:* Blake Green.
Penalty count: 4-6; **Half-time:** 6-42;
Referee: Gareth Hewer; **Attendance:** 2,463.

HALIFAX 34 BRADFORD BULLS 46

HALIFAX: 1 Miles Greenwood; 20 Paul White; 2 Lee Paterson; 4 Dylan Nash; 23 Rob Worrincy; 28 Graham Holroyd; 7 Ben Black; 15 Jim Gannon; 13 Bob Beswick; 10 Neil Cherryholme; 16 Paul Smith; 24 Steve Bannister; 12 Sam Barlow. Subs (all used): 6 Danny Jones; 8 Makali Aizue; 9 Sean Penkywicz; 17 Frank Watene.
Tries: Gannon (16), Penkywicz (24), Watene (33), Jones (40), S Barlow (44), Beswick (80);
Goals: Jones 4/5, Holroyd 1/1.
BULLS: 25 Shad Royston; 5 Patrick Ah Van; 1 Michael Platt; 4 Chev Walker; 19 Gareth Raynor; 32 Kyle Briggs; 7 Marc Herbert; 10 Andy Lynch (C); 9 Heath L'Estrange; 16 Craig Kopczak; 12 Elliott Whitehead; 17 Ian Sibbit; 20 James Donaldson. Subs (all used): 15 Bryn Hargreaves; 27 Adam O'Brien; 29 Tom Burgess; 31 John Bateman.
Tries: Royston (5), Raynor (11, 62), Platt (21), Whitehead (30), Ah Van (35), Burgess (38), Sibbit (53);
Goals: Ah Van 7/9.
Rugby Leaguer & League Express Men of the Match: *Halifax:* Sean Penkywicz; *Bulls:* Elliott Whitehead.
Penalty count: 5-11; **Half-time:** 24-32;
Referee: Phil Bentham; **Attendance:** 5,045.

ROUND 5

Friday 20th May 2011

LEEDS RHINOS 40 HARLEQUINS 20

RHINOS: 2 Lee Smith; 27 Zak Hardaker; 3 Brett Delaney; 4 Keith Senior; 5 Ryan Hall; 13 Kevin Sinfield (C); 7 Rob Burrow; 8 Kylie Leuluai; 9 Danny Buderus; 10 Jamie Peacock; 11 Jamie Jones-Buchanan; 21 Chris Clarkson; 12 Carl Ablett. Subs (all used): 17 Ian Kirke; 16 Ryan Bailey; 14 Ali Lauitiiti; 24 Paul McShane.
Tries: Hardaker (4), Jones-Buchanan (30), Delaney (36), Lauitiiti (38), Leuluai (52), Hall (66), Clarkson (76);
Goals: Sinfield 6/8.
HARLEQUINS: 1 Luke Dorn; 5 Chris Melling; 4 David Howell; 3 Tony Clubb; 23 Mark Calderwood; 6 Luke Gale; 12 Chris Bailey; 8 Karl Temata; 7 Chad Randall (C); 17 Danny Ward; 16 Mike Burnett; 10 Oliver Wilkes; 21 Olsi Krasniqi. Subs (all used): 15 Luke Ambler; 18 Dave Williams; 9 Andy Ellis; 20 Ben Bolger.
Tries: Melling (8), Dorn (21), Calderwood (26), Bolger (72); **Goals:** Gale 2/4.
Rugby Leaguer & League Express Men of the Match: *Rhinos:* Jamie Jones-Buchanan; *Harlequins:* Tony Clubb.
Penalty count: 9-3; **Half-time:** 22-14;
Referee: Ben Thaler; **Attendance:** 7,147.

SALFORD CITY REDS 0 HULL KINGSTON ROVERS 25

CITY REDS: 1 Luke Patten; 2 Jodie Broughton; 6 Stefan Ratchford; 20 Sean Gleeson; 27 Adam Clay; 14 Matty Smith; 7 Daniel Holdsworth (C); 8 Ray Cashmere; 23 Marc Sneyd; 19 Ryan Boyle; 4 Chris Nero; 15 Luke Adamson; 13 Stephen Wild. Subs (all used): 10 Lee Jewitt; 22 Adam Neal; 17 Iafeta Palea'aesina; 11 Vinnie Anderson.
ROVERS: 1 Shaun Briscoe; 2 Peter Fox; 3 Kris Welham; 4 Jake Webster; 28 Ben Cockayne; 6 Blake Green; 7 Michael Dobson; 20 Michael Vella (C); 18 Josh Hodgson; 15 Scott Wheeldon; 8 Rhys Lovegrove; 12 Ben Galea; 13 Scott Murrell. Subs (all used): 9 Ben Fisher; 17 Matt Cook; 10 Joel Clinton; 16 Jason Netherton.
Tries: Green (38), Cockayne (43), Welham (51), Webster (79); **Goals:** Dobson 4/4; **Field goal:** Dobson (77).
Rugby Leaguer & League Express Men of the Match: *City Reds:* Stefan Ratchford; *Rovers:* Michael Dobson.
Penalty count: 12-3; **Half-time:** 0-6;
Referee: Thierry Alibert; **Attendance:** 2,087.

WARRINGTON WOLVES 112 SWINTON LIONS 0

WOLVES: 2 Chris Riley; 5 Joel Monaghan; 4 Chris Bridge; 23 Ryan Atkins; 22 Rhys Williams; 27 Gareth O'Brien; 6 Lee Briers; 8 Adrian Morley (C); 9 Michael Monaghan; 10 Garreth Carvell; 3 Matt King; 12 Ben Westwood; 17 Simon Grix. Subs (all used): 15 Jon Clarke; 18 Michael Cooper; 20 Matty Blythe; 26 David Solomona.
Tries: J Monaghan (2, 18, 32, 62), Briers (6, 44, 46), Atkins (12), Carvell (23, 25, 78), Grix (28), M Monaghan (40), Riley (48, 71, 80), Westwood (50, 58), Williams (54), Bridge (75); **Goals:** Briers 16/20.
LIONS: 21 Ian Mort; 20 Richard Flooks; 23 Alex Hurst; 3 Gavin Dodd; 2 Rob Foxen; 7 Ian Watson; 6 Martin Ainscough; 8 Mike Morrison; 9 Mark Smith; 16 Neil Holland; 11 Dale Cunniffe; 15 Darren Hawkyard; 13 Phil Joseph. Subs (all used): 25 Karl Ashall; 10 Dana Wilson; 39 Danny Meekin; 14 Tommy Gallagher.
Rugby Leaguer & League Express Men of the Match: *Wolves:* Lee Briers; *Lions:* Alex Hurst.
Penalty count: 3-2; **Half-time:** 48-0;
Referee: Tim Roby; **Attendance:** 4,440.

Saturday 21st May 2011

WAKEFIELD TRINITY WILDCATS 18 CASTLEFORD TIGERS 20
(after golden point extra time)

WILDCATS: 23 Josh Veivers; 30 Greg Johnson; 3 Aaron Murphy; 29 Josh Griffin; 19 Dale Morton; 27 Kieran Hyde; 14 Tommy Lee; 8 Michael Korkidas; 9 Julien Rinaldi; 17 Paul Johnson; 13 Glenn Morrison (C); 11 Kevin Henderson; 22 Stuart Howarth. Subs (all used): 21 Frankie Mariano; 10 Paul King; 31 Kyle Amor; 26 Matthew Wildie.
Tries: Morrison (15), Lee (47); **Goals:** Veivers 5/5.
TIGERS: 1 Richard Mathers; 2 Kirk Dixon; 17 Willie Isa; 4 Joe Arundel; 5 Richard Owen; 6 Rangi Chase; 7 Danny Orr (C); 19 Nick Fozzard; 9 Ryan Hudson; 11 Jake Emmitt; 24 Oliver Holmes; 13 Brett Ferres; 12 Steve Snitch. Subs (all used): 21 Nathan Massey; 22 Jordan Thompson; 25 Dean Widders; 27 Daryl Clark.
Tries: Ferres (6), Chase (52), Orr (62); **Goals:** Dixon 4/5.
Rugby Leaguer & League Express Men of the Match: *Wildcats:* Tommy Lee; *Tigers:* Kirk Dixon.
Penalty count: 5-4; **Half-time:** 8-6;
Referee: Richard Silverwood; **Attendance:** 6,604.

WIDNES VIKINGS 26 HULL FC 50

VIKINGS: 5 Paddy Flynn; 41 Kevin Penny; 23 Tangi Ropati; 4 Steve Tyrer; 19 Matt Gardner; 7 Chaz I'Anson; 14 Thomas Coyle; 8 Steve Pickersgill; 25 Chris Lunt; 17 Ben Kavanagh; 12 Kurt Haggerty; 16 Macgraff Leuluai; 11 Dave Allen. Subs (all used): 3 Richard Varkulis; 20 Shane Grady; 29 Grant Gore; 37 Danny Sculthorpe.
Tries: Leuluai (16), Tyrer (28, 78), Varkulis (43), Ropati (61); **Goals:** Tyrer 3/5.
HULL: 20 Cameron Phelps; 2 Will Sharp; 3 Richard Whiting; 4 Kirk Yeaman; 5 Tom Briscoe; 19 Jordan Turner; 6 Richard Horne; 8 Mark O'Meley; 9 Danny Houghton; 23 Sam Moa; 16 Willie Manu; 11 Joe Westerman; 12 Danny Tickle. Subs (all used): 10 Lee Radford (C); 14 Danny Washbrook; 15 Epalahame Lauaki; 17 Ewan Dowes.
Tries: Whiting (9), Sharp (12), Horne (32, 75), Westerman (37), Lauaki (45), Briscoe (54, 68), Phelps (80); **Goals:** Tickle 4/5, Westerman 3/4.
Rugby Leaguer & League Express Men of the Match: *Vikings:* Macgraff Leuluai; *Hull:* Tom Briscoe.
Penalty count: 5-8; **Half-time:** 8-22;
Referee: Robert Hicks; **Attendance:** 3,387.

Sunday 22nd May 2011

HUDDERSFIELD GIANTS 30 CATALAN DRAGONS 16

GIANTS: 1 Scott Grix; 20 Jermaine McGillvary; 3 Leroy Cudjoe; 2 Michael Lawrence; 5 David Hodgson; 6 Kevin Brown (C); 7 Danny Brough; 8 Eorl Crabtree; 9 Luke Robinson; 10 Darrell Griffin; 4 Lee Gilmour; 37 Dale Ferguson; 17 Danny Kirmond. Subs (all used): 13 David Faiumu; 14 Shaun Lunt; 15 Keith Mason; 18 Larne Patrick.
Tries: McGillvary (5), Cudjoe (29), Hodgson (37), Brown (43, 75), Griffin (72); **Goals:** Brough 3/6.
DRAGONS: 5 Cyril Stacul; 2 Damien Blanch; 15 Jean-Philippe Baile; 18 Darryl Millard; 19 Frederic Vaccari; 6 Thomas Bosc (C); 7 Scott Dureau; 8 David Ferriol; 9 Ian Henderson; 22 Jamal Fakir; 4 Setaimata Sa; 12 Sebastien Raguin; 23 Lopini Paea. Subs (all used): 13 Gregory Mounis; 14 Tony Gigot; 20 Michael Simon; 24 Jason Baitieri.
Tries: Henderson (18), Baile (26), Stacul (55);
Goals: Dureau 2/3.
Rugby Leaguer & League Express Men of the Match: *Giants:* Darrell Griffin; *Dragons:* Scott Dureau.
Penalty count: 6-4; **Half-time:** 12-10;
Referee: Phil Bentham; **Attendance:** 3,198.

ST HELENS 70 FEATHERSTONE ROVERS 0

SAINTS: 1 Paul Wellens (C); 2 Ade Gardner; 3 Michael Shenton; 5 Francis Meli; 22 Jamie Foster; 12 Jon Wilkin; 27 Nathan Ashe; 10 James Graham (C); 9 James Roby; 15 Louie McCarthy-Scarsbrook; 18 Matty Ashurst; 4 Iosia Soliola; 21 Shaun Magennis. Subs (all used): 24 Tom Armstrong; 28 Tom Makinson; 29 Scott Hale; 33 Warren Thompson (D).
Tries: Meli (11), Thompson (26), Wellens (35), Graham (44), Ashe (52), Shenton (57, 75), Ashurst (59), Makinson (64, 67), Soliola (73), Armstrong (77);
Goals: Foster 11/12.
ROVERS: 1 Ian Hardman; 2 Bryn Powell; 4 Andrew Bostock; 3 Sam Smeaton; 28 Jon Hepworth; 29 Tom Hemingway; 7 Liam Finn; 15 Michael Haley; 9 Ben Kaye; 10 Stuart Dickens; 11 Jon Grayshon; 12 Tim Spears; 13 Matty Dale. Subs (all used): 14 Liam Welham; 17 Greg Worthington; 18 Ross Divorty; 24 Mufaro Mvududu.
Rugby Leaguer & League Express Men of the Match: *Saints:* Jamie Foster; *Rovers:* Liam Finn.
Penalty count: 5-4; **Half-time:** 18-0;
Referee: James Child; **Attendance:** 2,905.

Castleford's Danny Orr gets a pass away as Huddersfield's Lee Gilmour and Danny Brough move in

BRADFORD BULLS 22 WIGAN WARRIORS 26

BULLS: 25 Shad Royston; 19 Gareth Raynor; 1 Michael Platt; 12 Elliott Whitehead; 5 Patrick Ah Van; 33 Ben Jeffries; 32 Kyle Briggs; 10 Andy Lynch (C); 9 Heath L'Estrange; 15 Bryn Hargreaves; 17 Ian Sibbit; 11 Olivier Elima; 13 Jamie Langley. Subs (all used): 16 Craig Kopczak; 29 Tom Burgess; 14 Matt Diskin; 23 Tom Olbison.
Tries: Whitehead (11), Ah Van (48, 80), Royston (64); **Goals:** Ah Van 3/4.
Dismissal: Raynor (30) - high tackle on S Tomkins.
WARRIORS: 1 Sam Tomkins; 25 Josh Charnley; 12 Joel Tomkins; 2 Darrell Goulding; 5 Pat Richards; 17 Brett Finch; 7 Thomas Leuluai; 10 Andy Coley; 9 Michael McIlorum; 21 Lee Mossop; 22 Liam Farrell; 16 Ryan Hoffman; 13 Sean O'Loughlin (C). Subs (all used): 15 Jeff Lima; 6 Paul Deacon; 14 Paul Prescott; 23 Chris Tuson.
Tries: Richards (18, 45), S Tomkins (30), Finch (43), Farrell (75); **Goals:** Richards 3/5.
Sin bin: Lima (36) - use of the forearm.
Rugby Leaguer & League Express Men of the Match: *Bulls:* Elliott Whitehead; *Warriors:* Sean O'Loughlin.
Penalty count: 9-2; **Half-time:** 6-10;
Referee: Steve Ganson; **Attendance:** 5,828.

QUARTER FINALS

Saturday 23rd July 2011

WARRINGTON WOLVES 24 WIGAN WARRIORS 44

WOLVES: 1 Brett Hodgson; 5 Joel Monaghan; 20 Matty Blythe; 23 Ryan Atkins; 3 Matt King; 4 Chris Bridge; 7 Richard Myler; 16 Paul Wood; 9 Michael Monaghan (C); 10 Garreth Carvell; 11 Louis Anderson; 12 Ben Westwood; 17 Simon Grix. Subs (all used): 14 Mick Higham; 15 Jon Clarke; 18 Michael Cooper; 26 David Solomona.
Tries: King (27, 59), Myler (32, 37), Solomona (42); **Goals:** Hodgson 2/5.
WARRIORS: 1 Sam Tomkins; 25 Josh Charnley; 12 Joel Tomkins; 4 George Carmont; 5 Pat Richards; 17 Brett Finch; 6 Paul Deacon; 10 Andy Coley; 7 Thomas Leuluai; 15 Jeff Lima; 11 Harrison Hansen; 16 Ryan Hoffman; 13 Sean O'Loughlin (C). Subs (all used): 9 Michael McIlorum; 14 Paul Prescott; 21 Lee Mossop; 34 Gareth Hock.
Tries: Hansen (10), S Tomkins (12), Coley (17), Richards (24, 49), Charnley (62, 65), O'Loughlin (77); **Goals:** Richards 6/8.
Rugby Leaguer & League Express Men of the Match: *Wolves:* Matt King; *Warriors:* George Carmont.
Penalty count: 7-8; **Half-time:** 16-22;
Referee: Richard Silverwood; **Attendance:** 13,105.

Sunday 24th July 2011

ST HELENS 54 HULL KINGSTON ROVERS 6

SAINTS: 1 Paul Wellens (C); 28 Tom Makinson; 3 Michael Shenton; 5 Francis Meli; 22 Jamie Foster; 6 Leon Pryce; 20 Jonny Lomax; 10 James Graham (C); 9 James Roby; 11 Tony Puletua; 13 Chris Flannery; 4 Iosia Soliola; 12 Jon Wilkin. Subs (all used): 7 Kyle Eastmond; 15 Louie McCarthy-Scarsbrook; 14 Scott Moore; 21 Shaun Magennis.
Tries: Pryce (8), Soliola (11), Wilkin (19, 64), Makinson (31, 56), Moore (42), Lomax (52), Roby (54), Shenton (68); **Goals:** Foster 7/10.

ROVERS: 1 Shaun Briscoe; 2 Peter Fox; 3 Kris Welham; 4 Jake Webster; 5 Liam Colbon; 6 Blake Green; 7 Michael Dobson; 20 Michael Vella (C); 18 Josh Hodgson; 16 Jason Netherton; 11 Clint Newton; 12 Ben Galea; 13 Scott Murrell. Subs (all used): 8 Rhys Lovegrove; 22 Scott Taylor; 9 Ben Fisher; 15 Scott Wheeldon.
Try: Galea (25); **Goals:** Dobson 1/1.
Rugby Leaguer & League Express Men of the Match: *Saints:* Leon Pryce; *Rovers:* Kris Welham.
Penalty count: 11-6; **Half-time:** 20-6;
Referee: Ben Thaler; **Attendance:** 6,449.

CASTLEFORD TIGERS 22 HUDDERSFIELD GIANTS 18

TIGERS: 23 Ryan McGoldrick; 2 Kirk Dixon; 3 Nick Youngquest; 4 Joe Arundel; 5 Richard Owen; 6 Rangi Chase; 7 Danny Orr (C); 8 Paul Jackson; 16 Adam Milner; 29 Rob Parker; 13 Brett Ferres; 14 Stuart Jones; 9 Ryan Hudson. Subs (all used): 21 Nathan Massey; 22 Jordan Thompson; 27 Daryl Clark; 31 Ben Davies.
Tries: Dixon (16), Thompson (22), Orr (46), Hudson (62); **Goals:** Dixon 3/4.
GIANTS: 1 Scott Grix; 20 Jermaine McGillvary; 29 Joe Wardle; 4 Lee Gilmour; 5 David Hodgson; 3 Leroy Cudjoe; 7 Danny Brough; 8 Eorl Crabtree; 9 Luke Robinson (C); 15 Keith Mason; 2 Michael Lawrence; 18 Larne Patrick; 37 Dale Ferguson. Subs (all used): 10 Darrell Griffin; 13 David Faiumu; 17 Danny Kirmond; 23 Kyle Wood.
Tries: Grix (38), McGillvary (42), Cudjoe (55), Lawrence (71); **Goals:** Brough 1/4.
Rugby Leaguer & League Express Men of the Match: *Tigers:* Kirk Dixon; *Giants:* Luke Robinson.
Penalty count: 6-6; **Half-time:** 12-6;
Referee: Phil Bentham; **Attendance:** 6,336.

HULL FC 22 LEEDS RHINOS 38

HULL: 20 Cameron Phelps; 3 Richard Whiting; 19 Jordan Turner; 4 Kirk Yeaman; 5 Tom Briscoe; 6 Richard Horne; 30 Sam Obst; 8 Mark O'Meley; 9 Danny Houghton; 23 Sam Moa; 16 Willie Manu; 12 Danny Tickle; 11 Joe Westerman. Subs (all used): 15 Epalahame Lauaki; 17 Ewan Dowes; 2 Will Sharp; 10 Lee Radford (C).
Tries: Obst (16), Turner (20, 39), Westerman (63); **Goals:** Tickle 3/4.
RHINOS: 1 Brent Webb; 23 Ben Jones-Bishop; 3 Brett Delaney; 5 Ryan Hall; 13 Kevin Sinfield (C); 6 Danny McGuire; 16 Ryan Bailey; 9 Danny Buderus; 20 Weller Hauraki; 21 Chris Clarkson. Subs (all used): 7 Rob Burrow; 8 Kylie Leuluai; 14 Ali Lauitiiti; 17 Ian Kirke.
Tries: Jones-Bishop (22, 80), Lauitiiti (46), Delaney (49), Ablett (54, 70); **Goals:** Sinfield 7/8.
Rugby Leaguer & League Express Men of the Match: *Hull:* Jordan Turner; *Rhinos:* Ben Jones-Bishop.
Penalty count: 7-8; **Half-time:** 6-16;
Referee: Steve Ganson; **Attendance:** 9,496.

SEMI-FINALS

Saturday 6th August 2011

ST HELENS 12 WIGAN WARRIORS 18

SAINTS: 1 Paul Wellens (C); 28 Tom Makinson; 3 Michael Shenton; 5 Francis Meli; 22 Jamie Foster; 6 Leon Pryce; 20 Jonny Lomax; 10 James Graham (C); 9 James Roby; 11 Tony Puletua; 13 Chris Flannery; 4 Iosia Soliola; 12 Jon Wilkin. Subs (all used): 15 Louie

McCarthy-Scarsbrook; 14 Scott Moore; 16 Paul Clough; 25 Lee Gaskell.
Tries: Foster (65, 70); **Goals:** Foster 2/3.
WARRIORS: 1 Sam Tomkins; 25 Josh Charnley; 12 Joel Tomkins; 4 George Carmont; 5 Pat Richards; 17 Brett Finch; 6 Paul Deacon; 15 Jeff Lima; 7 Thomas Leuluai; 10 Andy Coley; 11 Harrison Hansen; 16 Ryan Hoffman; 13 Sean O'Loughlin (C). Subs (all used): 9 Michael McIlorum; 21 Lee Mossop; 22 Liam Farrell; 35 Ben Cross.
Tries: Carmont (34), Charnley (56), S Tomkins (59); **Goals:** Richards 3/5.
Rugby Leaguer & League Express Men of the Match: *Saints:* James Roby; *Warriors:* Sam Tomkins.
Penalty count: 9-9; **Half-time:** 2-6;
Referee: Richard Silverwood; **Attendance:** 12,713 *(at Halliwell Jones Stadium, Warrington).*

Sunday 7th August 2011

CASTLEFORD TIGERS 8 LEEDS RHINOS 10
(after golden point extra time)

TIGERS: 23 Ryan McGoldrick; 2 Kirk Dixon; 3 Nick Youngquest; 4 Joe Arundel; 5 Richard Owen; 6 Rangi Chase; 7 Danny Orr (C); 8 Paul Jackson; 16 Adam Milner; 29 Rob Parker; 13 Brett Ferres; 14 Stuart Jones; 20 Martin Aspinwall. Subs (all used): 9 Ryan Hudson; 17 Willie Isa; 22 Jordan Thompson; 31 Ben Davies.
Try: Chase (43); **Goals:** Dixon 2/3.
RHINOS: 1 Brent Webb; 23 Ben Jones-Bishop; 19 Kallum Watkins; 12 Carl Ablett; 5 Ryan Hall; 13 Kevin Sinfield (C); 7 Rob Burrow; 8 Kylie Leuluai; 9 Danny Buderus; 10 Jamie Peacock; 11 Jamie Jones-Buchanan; 3 Brett Delaney; 21 Chris Clarkson. Subs (all used): 6 Danny McGuire; 16 Ryan Bailey; 17 Ian Kirke; 20 Weller Hauraki.
Try: Watkins (74); **Goals:** Sinfield 3/3.
Rugby Leaguer & League Express Men of the Match: *Tigers:* Danny Orr; *Rhinos:* Danny Buderus.
Penalty count: 7-10; **Half-time:** 0-2;
Referee: Phil Bentham; **Attendance:** 13,158 *(at Keepmoat Stadium, Doncaster).*

FINAL

Saturday 27th August 2011

LEEDS RHINOS 18 WIGAN WARRIORS 28

RHINOS: 1 Brent Webb; 23 Ben Jones-Bishop; 19 Kallum Watkins; 12 Carl Ablett; 5 Ryan Hall; 13 Kevin Sinfield (C); 6 Danny McGuire; 8 Kylie Leuluai; 9 Danny Buderus; 10 Jamie Peacock; 11 Jamie Jones-Buchanan; 3 Brett Delaney; 20 Weller Hauraki. Subs (all used): 7 Rob Burrow; 16 Ryan Bailey; 17 Ian Kirke; 21 Chris Clarkson.
Tries: Hall (34, 71), Jones-Bishop (37), Ablett (59); **Goals:** Sinfield 1/4.
WARRIORS: 1 Sam Tomkins; 25 Josh Charnley; 12 Joel Tomkins; 4 George Carmont; 5 Pat Richards; 6 Paul Deacon; 17 Brett Finch; 15 Jeff Lima; 7 Thomas Leuluai; 10 Andy Coley; 11 Harrison Hansen; 16 Ryan Hoffman; 13 Sean O'Loughlin (C). Subs (all used): 22 Liam Farrell; 21 Lee Mossop; 9 Michael McIlorum; 14 Paul Prescott.
Tries: Charnley (9), Lima (24, 61), J Tomkins (29), Carmont (78); **Goals:** Richards 4/5.
Rugby Leaguer & League Express Men of the Match: *Rhinos:* Rob Burrow; *Warriors:* Jeff Lima.
Penalty count: 5-2; **Half-time:** 10-16; **Referee:** Phil Bentham; **Attendance:** 78,482 *(at Wembley Stadium).*

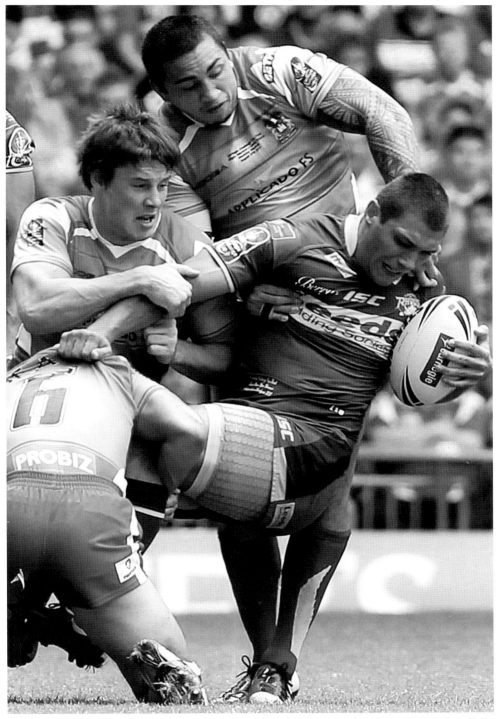

Wigan's Harrison Hansen, Joel Tomkins and Paul Deacon combine to bring down Leeds's Ryan Hall during the Challenge Cup Final

AMATEUR, RESERVES & ACADEMY 2011

THE CO-OPERATIVE RUGBY LEAGUE CONFERENCE NATIONAL

FINAL TABLE

	P	W	L	F	A	D	BP	Pts
Hudds-Underbank	18	17	1	716	358	358	1	52
Kippax Knights	18	13	5	700	352	348	4	43
Featherstone Lions	18	12	6	625	388	237	3	39
Hemel Stags	18	10	8	509	402	107	6	36
Valley Cougars	18	9	9	560	586	-26	5	32
Dewsbury Celtic	18	9	9	521	417	104	3	30
Coventry Bears	18	8	10	520	572	-52	4	28
Warrington Wizards	18	6	12	505	667	-162	4	22
Nottingham Outlaws	18	4	14	330	714	-384	0	12
Bramley Buffaloes	18	2	16	264	794	-530	0	3

ELIMINATION PLAY-OFFS

Sunday 11th September 2011
Featherstone Lions 8 ....Dewsbury Celtic 32
Hemel Stags 40 ....Valley Cougars 18

QUALIFYING SEMI-FINAL

Saturday 17th September 2011
Huddersfield Underbank Rangers 8 ....Kippax Knights 17

ELIMINATION SEMI-FINAL

Sunday 18th September 2011
Hemel Stags 25 ....Dewsbury Celtic 4

FINAL ELIMINATOR

Saturday 24th September 2011
Huddersfield Underbank Rangers 40 ......Hemel Stags 14

GRAND FINAL

Sunday 2nd October 2011

Huddersfield Underbank Rangers **40**
Kippax Knights **18**
Rangers: T - Ryder (5), Allette (11), Briggs (24),
Midgley (27), Carroll (43), Geoghegan (47, 79);
G - Barrett 6/9
Knights: T - Brown (7), Dobek (32), Eastham (77);
G - Speake 2/2, Brown 1/1
(at Halliwell Jones Stadium, Warrington)

HATTONS SOLICITORS NATIONAL CONFERENCE

PREMIER DIVISION

	P	W	D	L	F	A	D	Pts
Siddal	26	19	0	7	708	481	227	38
Thatto Heath	26	19	0	7	746	527	219	38
Leigh East	26	16	0	10	766	487	279	32
Wath Brow Hornets	26	15	2	9	671	554	117	32
Hull Dockers	26	16	0	10	610	562	48	32
West Hull	26	15	1	10	660	548	112	31
Leigh Miners	26	15	0	11	719	584	135	30
Skirlaugh	26	12	2	12	572	536	36	26
Saddleworth	26	11	1	14	570	710	-140	23
East Hull	26	9	2	15	533	602	-69	20
Wigan St Patricks	26	9	1	16	505	620	-115	19
Bradford Dudley Hill	26	9	0	17	592	702	-110	18
Wigan St Judes	26	7	0	19	470	875	-405	14
York Acorn	26	5	1	20	471	805	-334	11

ELIMINATION PLAY-OFFS

Saturday 7th May 2011
Leigh East 40 ....West Hull 28
Wath Brow Hornets 30 ....Hull Dockers 6

QUALIFYING SEMI-FINAL

Saturday 14th May 2011
Siddal 40 ....Thatto Heath Crusaders 8

Sharlston Rovers - BARLA National Cup Winners

ELIMINATION SEMI-FINAL

Saturday 14th May 2011
Leigh East 16 ....Wath Brow Hornets 0

FINAL ELIMINATOR

Saturday 21st May 2011
Thatto Heath Crusaders 24 ....Leigh East 19

GRAND FINAL

Sunday 29th May 2011

Siddal 18 ....**Thatto Heath Crusaders 30**
Siddal: T - Caley (26), English (39), Hoyle (68);
G - Blackburn 2/2, Brooke 1/1
Crusaders: T - Maddocks (17, 65), Walsh (26),
Quinn (41), Johnson (55); G - Quinn 5/5
(at Stobart Stadium, Widnes)

DIVISION ONE

	P	W	D	L	F	A	D	Pts
Oulton Raiders	22	19	2	1	805	334	471	40
Myton Warriors	22	16	1	5	651	442	209	33
Ince Rose Bridge	22	14	1	7	624	367	257	29
Rochdale Mayfield	22	14	0	8	589	480	109	28
Stanley Rangers	22	12	0	10	480	460	20	24
Milford Marlins	22	10	0	12	458	496	-38	20
Oldham St Annes	22	9	0	13	547	611	-64	18
Millom	22	9	0	13	390	713	-323	18
Castleton Panthers	22	8	0	14	426	532	-106	16
Stanningley	22	8	0	14	383	489	-106	16
Eccles	22	8	0	14	497	605	-108	16
Normanton Knights	22	3	0	19	384	705	-321	6

DIVISION TWO

	P	W	D	L	F	A	D	Pts
Hunslet Warriors	22	20	1	1	856	256	600	41
Egremont Rangers	22	18	0	4	810	406	404	36
Castleford Lock Lane	22	15	0	7	580	336	244	30
Eastmoor Dragons	22	14	1	7	524	396	128	29
Ovenden	22	10	2	10	510	432	78	22
Elland	22	9	1	12	406	449	-43	19
East Leeds	22	9	1	12	446	548	-102	19
West Bowling	22	9	0	13	425	473	-48	18
Shaw Cross Sharks	22	7	1	14	362	547	-185	15
Crosfields	22	7	0	15	408	711	-303	14
Waterhead	22	7	0	15	377	702	-325	14
Heworth	22	3	1	18	270	718	-448	7

ACE INSURANCE BARLA NATIONAL CUP

QUARTER FINALS

Saturday 26th March 2011
Drighlington 4................................Sharlston Rovers 35
Queens 48 ....Bradford Dudley Hill 18
West Hull 20......................................Fryston Warriors 22
Saturday 2nd April 2011
Wigan St Patricks 34 ....Leigh East 22

SEMI-FINALS

Saturday 9th April 2011
Fryston Warriors 29.......................Wigan St Patricks 10
Sharlston Rovers 22 ....Queens 21

FINAL

Saturday 28th May 2011

Fryston Warriors 18 ....**Sharlston Rovers 20**
Warriors: T - Cryer (5, 69), G Handford (20, 60);
G - Speake 1/4
Rovers: T - Hick (27), Miles (34), Lingard (52),
Davies (80); G - Malyan 2/4
(at Woodlands Memorial Ground, Fylde)

THE CO-OPERATIVE RUGBY LEAGUE CONFERENCE PREMIER

MIDLANDS

	P	W	L	D	F	A	D	Pts
Bristol Sonics	3	3	0	0	142	40	102	6
Leicester Storm	3	2	1	0	64	96	-32	4
Birmingham Bulldogs	3	1	2	0	74	80	-6	2
Northampton Demons	3	0	3	0	56	120	-64	0

NORTH EAST

	P	W	L	D	F	A	D	Pts
Jarrow Vikings	15	12	3	0	564	324	240	24
Peterlee Pumas	15	9	5	1	535	402	133	19
Gateshead Spartans	15	8	7	0	452	442	10	16
Gateshead Storm	15	7	8	0	371	472	-101	14
Sunderland	15	5	9	1	454	511	-57	11
Wallsend Eagles	15	2	11	2	330	555	-225	6

NORTH WEST

	P	W	L	D	F	A	D	Pts
Accrington & Leyland	10	9	1	0	321	130	191	18
Liverpool Buccaneers	10	7	3	0	256	126	130	14
Widnes West Bank	10	7	3	0	280	200	80	14
Wigan Riversiders	10	5	5	0	226	171	55	10
East Lancashire V	10	2	8	0	64	280	-216	4
Mancunians	10	0	10	0	0	240	-240	0

SCOTLAND

	P	W	L	D	F	A	D	Pts
Edinburgh Eagles	8	7	0	1	282	78	204	15
Fife Lions	8	5	3	0	254	264	-10	10
Ayrshire Storm	8	4	4	0	214	230	-16	8
Carluke Tigers	8	3	4	1	192	186	6	7
Easterhouse Panthers	8	0	8	0	136	320	-184	0

SOUTH

	P	W	L	D	F	A	D	Pts
Hammersmith Hill	13	13	0	0	482	176	306	26
St Albans Centurions	13	8	5	0	352	297	55	16
Eastern Rhinos	13	7	5	1	338	328	10	15
West London Sharks	13	4	9	0	258	346	-88	8
London Skolars	13	3	9	1	209	314	-105	7
South London Storm	13	3	10	0	240	418	-178	6

WALES

	P	W	L	D	F	A	D	Pts
Bridgend Blue Bulls	10	10	0	0	412	178	234	20
Valley Cougars A	10	7	2	1	332	244	88	15
Titans	10	6	4	0	404	222	182	12
Cardiff Demons	10	3	7	0	176	358	-182	6
Torfaen Tigers	10	2	7	1	298	384	-86	5
CPC Bears	10	1	9	0	82	318	-236	2

YORKSHIRE (East)

	P	W	L	D	F	A	D	Pts
Cutsyke Raiders	14	11	2	1	475	280	195	23
Knottingley Rockware	14	10	3	1	444	278	166	21
Scarborough Pirates	14	9	5	0	366	248	118	18
Moorend Thorne M	14	7	4	3	318	240	78	17
York Lokomotive	14	7	6	1	357	319	38	15
Walton Warriors	14	4	9	1	281	367	-86	9
Rotherham Giants	14	3	10	1	262	389	-127	7
Barnsley Broncos	14	1	13	0	116	498	-382	2

YORKSHIRE (West)

	P	W	L	D	F	A	D	Pts
Parkside Hawks	10	7	0	3	284	172	112	17
Prospect Pirates	10	7	3	0	340	143	197	14
Shaw Cross Sharks	10	6	2	2	280	262	18	14
Lindley Swifts	10	5	4	1	236	203	33	11
Leeds Akkies	10	2	8	0	196	316	-120	4
Doncaster Toll Bar	10	0	10	0	0	240	-240	0

HARRY JEPSON TROPHY - GRAND FINAL

Sunday 11th September 2011

Accrington & Leyland Warriors..........................16
Parkside Hawks..24
Warriors: T - Lever (43, 76), O'Rourke (63);
G - Quinn 2/3
Hawks: T - Dean (15), O'Malley (36), Boyce (57),
Bradley (73); G - Fields 3/4, Austin 1/1
(at Butts Arena, Coventry)

THE CO-OPERATIVE RUGBY LEAGUE CONFERENCE REGIONAL

EAST

	P	W	L	D	F	A	D	Pts
Bedford Tigers	10	8	2	0	358	190	168	16
Sudbury Gladiators	10	8	2	0	334	176	158	16
St Ives Roosters	10	7	3	0	302	268	34	14
Bury Titans	10	5	5	0	270	260	10	10
Northampton D 'A'	10	2	8	0	150	280	-130	4
Norwich City Saxons	10	0	10	0	0	240	-240	0

MIDLANDS

	P	W	L	D	F	A	D	Pts
Telford Raiders	4	4	0	0	154	56	98	8
Coventry Dragons	4	2	2	0	122	110	12	4
Leamington Royals	4	1	3	0	114	142	-28	2
Nottingham O 'A'	4	1	3	0	76	158	-82	2

NORTH EAST

	P	W	L	D	F	A	D	Pts
East Cumbria C	14	13	1	0	757	181	576	26
North Yorkshire S	14	12	2	0	784	316	468	24
Cramlington Rockets	14	11	3	0	710	289	421	22
Durham Demons	14	6	8	0	570	424	146	12
Warriors	14	4	10	0	351	654	-303	8
Peterlee Pumas 2nd	14	4	10	0	330	676	-346	8
Whitley Bay B	14	4	10	0	348	730	-382	8
Hartlepool	14	2	12	0	262	842	-580	4

NORTH WEST

	P	W	L	D	F	A	D	Pts
Cadishead Rhinos	10	8	2	0	298	238	60	16
Rochdale Cobras	10	7	2	1	426	140	286	15
Chorley Panthers	10	5	4	1	210	244	-34	11
Blackpool Sea Eagles	10	5	5	0	220	278	-58	10
Chester Gladiators	10	4	6	0	254	268	-14	8
Crewe & Nantwich	10	0	10	0	0	240	-240	0

SCOTLAND

	P	W	L	D	F	A	D	Pts
Aberdeen Warriors	7	6	0	1	294	82	212	13
Moray Titans	7	3	3	1	186	174	12	7
Cumbernauld	7	3	4	0	152	202	-50	6
Ayr Knights	7	1	6	0	52	226	-174	2

SOUTH EAST

	P	W	L	D	F	A	D	Pts
Elmbridge Eagles	12	11	1	0	578	166	412	22
Portsmouth Navy	12	10	2	0	560	258	302	20
Greenwich Admirals	12	7	5	0	458	262	196	14
Southampton Spitfires	12	6	6	0	308	418	-110	12
Guildford Giants	12	3	9	0	280	422	-142	6
Medway Dragons	12	3	9	0	254	546	-292	6
Sussex Merlins	12	2	10	0	170	536	-366	4

SOUTH WEST

	P	W	L	D	F	A	D	Pts
Somerset Vikings	10	10	0	0	390	171	219	20
East Devon Eagles	10	9	1	0	532	168	364	18
Devon Sharks	10	6	4	0	342	250	92	12
South Dorset Giants	10	4	6	0	234	288	-54	8
North Devon Raiders	10	4	6	0	310	416	-106	8
Exeter Centurions	10	3	6	1	282	403	-121	7
Plymouth Titans	10	3	6	1	304	458	-154	7
South Somerset W	10	0	10	0	0	240	-240	0

WALES

	P	W	L	D	F	A	D	Pts
Bonymaen Broncos	9	9	0	0	414	96	318	18
Neath Port Talbot	9	5	4	0	284	338	-54	10
Tydfil Wildcats	9	2	6	1	212	336	-124	5
Dyffryn Devils	9	1	7	1	212	352	-140	3

WEST

	P	W	L	D	F	A	D	Pts
Gloucestershire W	10	9	0	1	487	136	351	19
Wiltshire Wyverns	10	5	5	0	300	319	-19	10
Bristol Sonics "A"	10	4	5	1	242	330	-88	9
Oxford Cavaliers	10	3	7	0	194	272	-78	6
Swindon St George	10	3	7	0	216	382	-166	6

REGIONAL GRAND FINAL

Sunday 11th September 2011

Elmbridge Eagles 76 ....North Yorkshire Stallions 6
Eagles: T – Mee (5), Cripps (9, 26, 61), Coates (12, 51), Kyle (16, 53), Reynolds (30), Pugsley (33), Naldrett (41, 70), Rodman (56), Gosbell (68); G - Mee 10/14
Stallions: T - Park (78); G - Worsnop 1/1
(at Butts Arena, Coventry)

Elmbridge Eagles - Conference Regional Champions

VALVOLINE CUP *(Under 20s)*

FINAL TABLE

	P	W	D	L	F	A	D	Pts
Wigan Warriors	20	17	0	3	755	427	328	34
Warrington Wolves	20	16	0	4	781	436	345	32
Hull FC	20	12	1	7	556	426	130	25
Wakefield T Wildcats	20	12	1	7	615	539	76	25
Leeds Rhinos	20	12	0	8	678	500	178	24
St Helens	20	11	0	9	698	522	176	22
Castleford Tigers	20	10	1	9	709	663	46	21
Hull KR	20	10	0	10	640	634	6	20
Harlequins	20	6	1	13	556	642	-86	13
Bradford Bulls	20	5	0	15	520	800	-280	10
Salford City Reds	20	4	0	16	512	905	-393	8
Huddersfield Giants	20	3	0	17	327	853	-526	6

QUALIFYING PLAY-OFFS

Saturday 10th September 2011
Warrington Wolves 30 ....Hull FC 14
Wigan Warriors 30 ....Wakefield Trinity Wildcats 20

ELIMINATION PLAY-OFFS

Saturday 10th September 2011
Leeds Rhinos 42 ....Hull Kingston Rovers 18
Sunday 11th September 2011
St Helens 28 ....Castleford Tigers 30

PRELIMINARY SEMI-FINALS

Saturday 17th September 2011
Hull FC 24 ....Castleford Tigers 38
Wakefield Trinity Wildcats 26 ....Leeds Rhinos 20

QUALIFYING SEMI-FINALS

Saturday 24th September 2011
Warrington Wolves 38 ....Castleford Tigers 18
Wigan Warriors 56 ....Wakefield Trinity Wildcats 6

GRAND FINAL

Saturday 1st October 2011

Warrington Wolves 16 ....Wigan Warriors 24
Wolves: T - Goulding (14), Saltonstall (39, 80);
G - Shaw 2/3
Warriors: T - Marsh (34), King (37), Sandford (54),
Hughes (73); G - Murphy 4/6
(at Leigh Sports Village)

RESERVES CHAMPIONSHIP

FINAL TABLE

	P	W	D	L	F	A	D	Pts
Widnes Vikings	18	15	2	1	728	356	372	32
Oldham	18	13	1	4	664	456	208	27
Leigh Centurions	18	13	0	5	569	450	119	26
Whitehaven	18	12	0	6	585	479	106	24
Featherstone Rovers	18	9	2	7	515	390	125	20
Halifax	18	7	0	11	450	510	-60	14
York City Knights	18	6	1	11	496	570	-74	13
Keighley Cougars	18	6	0	12	394	509	-115	12
Dewsbury Rams	18	4	0	14	414	713	-299	8
Sheffield Eagles	18	2	0	16	332	714	-382	4

ELIMINATION PLAY-OFFS

Wednesday 31st August 2011
Leigh Centurions 26 ....Halifax 20
Saturday 3rd September 2011
Whitehaven 0.............................Featherstone Rovers 38

QUALIFYING SEMI-FINAL

Saturday 10th September 2011
Widnes Vikings 22..Oldham 46

ELIMINATION SEMI-FINAL

Thursday 8th September 2011
Leigh Centurions 19 ....Featherstone Rovers 18
(after golden point extra time)

FINAL ELIMINATOR

Saturday 17th September 2011
Widnes Vikings 44 ....Leigh Centurions 18

GRAND FINAL

Sunday 25th September 2011

Oldham 29 ....Widnes Vikings 24
Oldham: T - Bridge (18, 25, 71), Dallimore (40),
Thompson (54); G - Dallimore 4/5; FG - Dallimore (39)
Vikings: T - Houghton (3), Smith (34, 62, 74);
G - Youds 4/4
(at Whitebank Stadium)

GRAND FINALS
1998-2011

1998

DIVISION ONE GRAND FINAL

Saturday 26th September 1998

FEATHERSTONE ROVERS 22 WAKEFIELD TRINITY 24

ROVERS: 1 Steve Collins; 2 Carl Hall; 3 Shaun Irwin; 4 Danny Baker; 5 Karl Pratt; 6 Jamie Coventry; 7 Ty Fallins; 8 Chico Jackson; 9 Richard Chapman; 10 Stuart Dickens; 11 Gary Price; 12 Neil Lowe; 13 Richard Slater. Subs: 14 Paddy Handley for Coventry (70); 15 Asa Amone for Lowe (50); 16 Micky Clarkson for Jackson (50); 17 Steve Dooler (not used).
Tries: Baker (15), Jackson (45), Collins (49), Hall (69).
Goals: Chapman 3.
TRINITY: 1 Martyn Holland; 2 Josh Bostock; 3 Adam Hughes; 4 Martin Law; 5 Kevin Gray; 6 Garen Casey; 7 Roger Kenworthy; 8 Francis Stephenson; 9 Roy Southernwood; 10 Gary Lord; 11 Ian Hughes; 12 Sonny Whakarau; 13 Matt Fuller. Subs: 14 Sean Richardson for I Hughes (32); 15 Andy Fisher for Lord (26); 16 David Mycoe (not used); 17 Wayne McDonald for Whakarau (70); Lord for Stephenson (40); Stephenson for Lord (70).
Tries: Southernwood (2), Bostock (7, 25), Casey (58), Stephenson (76). **Goals:** Casey 2.
League Express Men of the Match:
Rovers: Richard Chapman; *Trinity:* Garen Casey.
Penalty count: 8-3; **Half time:** 6-12; **Referee:** Nick Oddy (Halifax); **Attendance:** 8,224 *(at McAlpine Stadium, Huddersfield).*

SUPER LEAGUE GRAND FINAL

Saturday 24th October 1998

LEEDS RHINOS 4 WIGAN WARRIORS 10

RHINOS: 1 Iestyn Harris (C); 22 Leroy Rivett; 3 Richie Blackmore; 4 Brad Godden; 5 Francis Cummins; 13 Daryl Powell; 7 Ryan Sheridan; 8 Martin Masella; 21 Terry Newton; 25 Darren Fleary; 11 Adrian Morley; 17 Anthony Farrell; 12 Marc Glanville. Subs: 20 Jamie Mathiou for Masella (25); 24 Marcus St Hilaire for Powell (40); 14 Graham Holroyd for Newton (49); 27 Andy Hay for Fleary (54); Powell for Godden (58); Masella for Mathiou (71).
Try: Blackmore (20).
WARRIORS: 1 Kris Radlinski; 2 Jason Robinson; 3 Danny Moore; 4 Gary Connolly; 5 Mark Bell; 6 Henry Paul; 7 Tony Smith; 16 Terry O'Connor; 9 Robbie McCormack; 10 Tony Mestrov; 20 Lee Gilmour; 17 Stephen Holgate; 13 Andy Farrell (C). Subs: 8 Neil Cowie for O'Connor (18BB, rev 48); 14 Mick Cassidy for McCormack (19BB, rev 27); 25 Paul Johnson for Moore (37); 12 Simon Haughton for Gilmour (27BB, rev 33); Haughton for Holgate (33); Cowie for Mestrov (54); Cassidy for Haughton (64); Holgate for Cowie (68); Haughton for Gilmour (71BB, rev 75); Mestrov for O'Connor (75BB).
Try: Robinson (37); **Goals:** Farrell 3.
League Express Men of the Match:
Rhinos: Iestyn Harris; *Warriors:* Jason Robinson.
Penalty count: 7-13; **Half-time:** 4-6; **Referee:** Russell Smith (Castleford); **Attendance:** 43,553 *(at Old Trafford, Manchester).*

1999

NORTHERN FORD PREMIERSHIP GRAND FINAL

Saturday 25th September 1999

DEWSBURY RAMS 11 HUNSLET HAWKS 12

RAMS: 1 Nathan Graham; 2 Alex Godfrey; 3 Paul Evans; 4 Brendan O'Meara; 5 Adrian Flynn; 6 Richard Agar; 7 Barry Eaton; 8 Alan Boothroyd; 9 Paul Delaney; 10 Matthew Long; 11 Andy Spink; 12 Mark Haigh; 13 Damian Ball. Subs: 14 Brendan Williams for Eaton (5BB, rev 15); 15 Sean Richardson for Haigh (50); 16 Simon Hicks for Long (25); 17 Paul Medley for Spink (50); Williams for Evans (61); Long for Boothroyd (71); Spink for Long (78).
Tries: Flynn (27), Ball (54); **Goal:** Eaton; **Field goal:** Agar.
HAWKS: 1 Abraham Fatnowna; 2 Chris Ross; 3 Shaun Irwin; 4 Paul Cook; 5 Iain Higgins; 6 Marcus Vassilakopoulos; 7 Latham Tawhai; 8 Richard Hayes; 9 Richard Pachniuk; 10 Steve Pryce; 11 Rob Wilson; 12 Jamie Leighton; 13 Lee St Hilaire. Subs: 14 Mick Coyle for Wilson (57); 15 Phil Kennedy for Pryce (35); 16 Jamie Thackray for St Hilaire (25); 17 Richard Baker for Higgins (55); Higgins for Fatnowna (62); Pryce for Kennedy (65).
Tries: Cook (31), Higgins (46);
Goal: Ross; **Field goals:** Tawhai, Leighton.
League Express Men of the Match:
Rams: Barry Eaton; *Hawks:* Latham Tawhai.
Penalty count: 8-5; **Half-time:** 7-7; **Referee:** Steve Ganson (St Helens); **Attendance:** 5,783 *(at Headingley Stadium, Leeds).*

SUPER LEAGUE GRAND FINAL

Saturday 9th October 1999

BRADFORD BULLS 6 ST HELENS 8

BULLS: 28 Stuart Spruce; 2 Tevita Vaikona; 20 Scott Naylor; 5 Michael Withers; 17 Leon Pryce; 6 Henry Paul; 1 Robbie Paul (C); 10 Paul Anderson; 9 James Lowes; 29 Stuart Fielden; 15 David Boyle; 23 Bernard Dwyer; 13 Steve McNamara. Subs: 14 Paul Deacon for R Paul (53); 4 Nathan McAvoy (not used); 12 Mike Forshaw for McNamara (18); 22 Brian McDermott for Anderson (18); Anderson for Fielden (61); Fielden for Dwyer (65); R Paul for Deacon (72).
Try: H Paul (18); **Goal:** H Paul.
SAINTS: 1 Paul Atcheson; 14 Chris Smith; 3 Kevin Iro; 4 Paul Newlove; 5 Anthony Sullivan; 13 Paul Sculthorpe; 20 Tommy Martyn; 8 Apollo Perelini; 9 Keiron Cunningham; 10 Julian O'Neill; 2 Fereti Tuilagi; 21 Sonny Nickle; 11 Chris Joynt (C). Subs: 26 Paul Wellens for Martyn (52); 6 Sean Hoppe for Newlove (43); 16 Vila Matautia for O'Neill (20); 7 Sean Long for Perelini (24); Perelini for Matautia (46); O'Neill for Perelini (69).
Tries: Iro (65); **Goals:** Long 2.
League Express Men of the Match:
Bulls: Henry Paul; *Saints:* Kevin Iro.
Penalty count: 4-7; **Half-time:** 6-2; **Referee:** Stuart Cummings (Widnes); **Attendance:** 50,717 *(at Old Trafford, Manchester).*

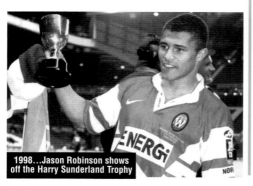

1998...Jason Robinson shows off the Harry Sunderland Trophy

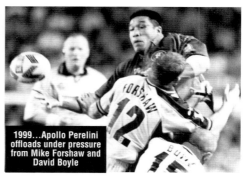

1999...Apollo Perelini offloads under pressure from Mike Forshaw and David Boyle

2000

NORTHERN FORD PREMIERSHIP GRAND FINAL

Saturday 29th July 2000

DEWSBURY RAMS 13 LEIGH CENTURIONS 12

RAMS: 1 Nathan Graham; 2 Richard Baker; 4 Dan Potter; 3 Brendan O'Meara; 5 Adrian Flynn; 6 Richard Agar; 7 Barry Eaton; 8 Shayne Williams; 9 David Mycoe; 10 Mark Haigh; 11 Sean Richardson; 12 Daniel Frame; 13 Damian Ball. Subs: 14 Gavin Wood (not used); 15 Paul Delaney for Mycoe (53); 16 Ryan McDonald for Haigh (30); 17 Matthew Long for Williams (23); Haigh for McDonald (64).
Tries: Eaton (2), Long (23); **Goals:** Eaton 2; **Field goal:** Agar.
Sin bin: Williams (66) - use of the elbow.
On report: Richardson (20) - high tackle on Donlan.
CENTURIONS: 1 Stuart Donlan; 5 David Ingram; 3 Paul Anderson; 4 Andy Fairclough; 2 Alan Cross; 6 Liam Bretherton; 7 Kieron Purtill; 8 Tim Street; 9 Mick Higham; 10 Andy Leathem; 11 Simon Baldwin; 12 Heath Cruckshank; 13 Adam Bristow. Subs: 14 James Arkwright for Cross (68); 15 Paul Norman for Street (36); 16 Radney Bowker (not used); 17 David Whittle for Leathem (24); Street for Norman (62).
Tries: Higham (29, 69); **Goals:** Bretherton 2.
Sin bin: Whittle (66) - retaliation.
League Express Men of the Match:
Rams: Richard Agar; *Centurions:* Mick Higham.
Penalty count: 4-4; **Half-time:** 10-6; **Referee:** Robert Connolly (Wigan); **Attendance:** 8,487 *(at Gigg Lane, Bury).*

SUPER LEAGUE GRAND FINAL

Saturday 14th October 2000

ST HELENS 29 WIGAN WARRIORS 16

SAINTS: 17 Paul Wellens; 24 Steve Hall; 3 Kevin Iro; 15 Sean Hoppe; 5 Anthony Sullivan; 20 Tommy Martyn; 7 Sean Long; 8 Apollo Perelini; 9 Keiron Cunningham; 10 Julian O'Neill; 11 Chris Joynt (C); 22 Tim Jonkers; 13 Paul Sculthorpe. Subs: 14 Fereti Tuilagi for O'Neill (20); 12 Sonny Nickle for Perelini (28); 26 John Stankevitch for Jonkers (50); 23 Scott Barrow (not used); Perelini for Nickle (52); Jonkers for Stankevitch (66); Stankevitch for Perelini (67BB); O'Neill for Hall (74).
Tries: Hoppe (7), Joynt (28, 50), Tuilagi (69), Jonkers (80); **Goals:** Long 4; **Field goal:** Sculthorpe.
WARRIORS: 9 Jason Robinson; 2 Brett Dallas; 1 Kris Radlinski; 3 Steve Renouf; 26 David Hodgson; 6 Tony Smith; 7 Willie Peters; 8 Terry O'Connor; 9 Terry Newton; 10 Neil Cowie; 11 Mick Cassidy; 12 Denis Betts; 13 Andy Farrell (C). Subs: 23 Brady Malam for Cowie (30); 17 Tony Mestrov for O'Connor (43); 19 Chris Chester for Cassidy (47BB, rev 69); 14 Lee Gilmour for Betts (51); O'Connor for Mestrov (61); Cowie for Malam (67); Chester for Newton (75).
Tries: Farrell (13), Hodgson (58), Smith (61); **Goals:** Farrell 2.
League Express Men of the Match:
Saints: Chris Joynt; *Warriors:* Andy Farrell.
Penalty count: 10-6; **Half-time:** 11-4; **Referee:** Russell Smith (Castleford); **Attendance:** 58,132 *(at Old Trafford, Manchester).*

2000...Dewsbury Rams get the party started

2001

NORTHERN FORD PREMIERSHIP GRAND FINAL

Saturday 28th July 2001

OLDHAM 14 WIDNES VIKINGS 24

OLDHAM: 1 Mark Sibson; 2 Joey Hayes; 3 Anthony Gibbons; 4 Pat Rich; 5 Joe McNicholas; 6 David Gibbons; 7 Neil Roden; 8 Leo Casey; 9 Keith Brennan; 10 Paul Norton; 11 Phil Farrell; 12 Bryan Henare; 13 Kevin Mannion. Subs: 14 Mike Ford for Mannion (27); 15 Jason Clegg for Casey (18); 16 John Hough for Brennan (44); 17 Danny Guest for Norton (40BB, rev 54); Mannion for Henare (66); Guest for Clegg (73).
Tries: Brennan (9), Ford (74), Mannion (80); **Goal:** Rich.
VIKINGS: 1 Paul Atcheson; 2 Damian Munro; 3 Craig Weston; 4 Jason Demetriou; 5 Chris Percival; 6 Richard Agar; 7 Martin Crompton; 8 Simon Knox; 9 Phil Cantillon; 10 Stephen Holgate; 11 Steve Gee; 12 Sean Richardson; 13 Tommy Hodgkinson. Subs: 14 Andy Craig for Percival (65); 15 Chris McKinney for Gee (41); 16 Joe Faimalo for Knox (32); 17 Matthew Long for Holgate (23); Knox for Long (49BB, rev 61); Holgate for Long (74).
Tries: Gee (17), Demetriou (38, 60), Cantillon (50), Munro (69); **Goals:** Weston 2.
League Express Men of the Match:
Oldham: Jason Clegg; *Vikings:* Phil Cantillon.
Penalty count: 8-5; **Half-time:** 4-10; **Referee:** Steve Ganson (St Helens); **Attendance:** 8,974 *(at Spotland, Rochdale).*

SUPER LEAGUE GRAND FINAL

Saturday 13th October 2001

BRADFORD BULLS 37 WIGAN WARRIORS 6

BULLS: 5 Michael Withers; 2 Tevita Vaikona; 20 Scott Naylor; 23 Graham Mackay; 3 Leon Pryce; 6 Henry Paul; 1 Robbie Paul (C); 8 Joe Vagana; 9 James Lowes; 22 Brian McDermott; 11 Daniel Gartner; 19 Jamie Peacock; 12 Mike Forshaw. Subs: 29 Stuart Fielden for McDermott (21BB, rev 65); 10 Paul Anderson for Vagana (22); 15 Shane Rigon for Pryce (40); 7 Paul Deacon for R Paul (69); Vagana for Anderson (53); Fielden for Gartner (72); Anderson for Vagana (74).
Tries: Lowes (9), Withers (11, 27, 31), Fielden (65), Mackay (72); **Goals:** H Paul 5, Mackay; **Field goal:** H Paul.
WARRIORS: 1 Kris Radlinski; 2 Brett Dallas; 4 Gary Connolly; 3 Steve Renouf; 5 Brian Carney; 6 Matthew Johns; 7 Adrian Lam; 8 Terry O'Connor; 9 Terry Newton; 20 Harvey Howard; 11 Mick Cassidy; 14 David Furner; 13 Andy Farrell (C). Subs: 15 Paul Johnson for Carney (12BB); 10 Neil Cowie for Howard (17); 12 Denis Betts for O'Connor (32); 19 Chris Chester for Farrell (59); O'Connor for Cowie (55); Howard for Newton (64); Cowie for Cassidy (72).
Try: Lam (63); **Goal:** Furner.
League Express Men of the Match:
Bulls: Michael Withers; *Warriors:* Adrian Lam.
Penalty count: 6-7; **Half-time:** 26-0; **Referee:** Stuart Cummings (Widnes); **Attendance:** 60,164 *(at Old Trafford, Manchester).*

2001...Henry Paul races away from Adrian Lam and Kris Radlinski

2002

NORTHERN FORD PREMIERSHIP GRAND FINAL

Saturday 12th October 2002

HUDDERSFIELD GIANTS 38 LEIGH CENTURIONS 16

GIANTS: 1 Ben Cooper; 2 Hefin O'Hare; 3 Eorl Crabtree; 4 Graeme Hallas; 5 Marcus St Hilaire; 6 Stanley Gene; 7 Chris Thorman; 8 Michael Slicker; 9 Paul March; 10 Jeff Wittenberg; 11 David Atkins; 12 Robert Roberts; 13 Steve McNamara. Subs: 14 Heath Cruckshank for Roberts (24BB); 15 Chris Molyneux for Slicker (53); 16 Darren Turner for March (21); 17 Andy Rice for Cruckshank (57); Roberts for Wittenberg (34); Wittenberg for Roberts (74).
Tries: O'Hare (12, 78), St Hilaire (34, 53), Thorman (46), Gene (57); **Goals:** McNamara 7.
Sin bin: Roberts (47) - fighting.
CENTURIONS: 1 Neil Turley; 2 Leon Felton; 4 Jon Roper; 3 Dale Cardoza; 5 Oliver Marns; 6 Willie Swann; 7 Bobbie Goulding; 8 Vila Matautia; 9 Paul Rowley; 10 David Bradbury; 11 Simon Baldwin; 12 Andrew Isherwood; 13 Adam Bristow. Subs: 14 Gareth Price for Bradbury (24BB, rev 35); 15 John Duffy for Swann (32); 16 John Hamilton for Bristow (46BB, rev 57); 17 David Whittle for Matautia (22); Matautia for Bradbury (53BB); Swann for Goulding (58); Hamilton for Whittle (67); Bradbury for Turley (72); Goulding for Swann (75).
Tries: Cardoza (9), Marns (18), Hamilton (70); **Goals:** Turley 2.
Sin bin: Whittle (47) - fighting; Bristow (74) - interference.
On report: Isherwood (66) - high tackle on Roberts.
Rugby Leaguer & League Express Men of the Match:
Giants: Chris Thorman; *Centurions:* Adam Bristow.
Penalty count: 11-11; **Half-time:** 14-10;
Referee: Karl Kirkpatrick (Warrington).
Attendance: 9,051 *(at Halton Stadium, Widnes).*

SUPER LEAGUE GRAND FINAL

Saturday 19th October 2002

BRADFORD BULLS 18 ST HELENS 19

BULLS: 6 Michael Withers; 2 Tevita Vaikona; 20 Scott Naylor; 15 Brandon Costin; 5 Lesley Vainikolo; 1 Robbie Paul (C); 7 Paul Deacon; 8 Joe Vagana; 9 James Lowes; 29 Stuart Fielden; 11 Daniel Gartner; 12 Jamie Peacock; 13 Mike Forshaw. Subs: 14 Lee Gilmour for Gartner (21); 10 Paul Anderson for Vagana (25); 22 Brian McDermott for Fielden (34); 3 Leon Pryce for Vainikolo (53); Fielden for Anderson (55); Vainikolo for Paul (77).
Tries: Naylor (3), Paul (44), Withers (47); **Goals:** Deacon 3.
SAINTS: 1 Paul Wellens; 5 Darren Albert; 3 Martin Gleeson; 4 Paul Newlove; 19 Anthony Stewart; 13 Paul Sculthorpe; 7 Sean Long; 8 Darren Britt; 9 Keiron Cunningham; 10 Barry Ward; 23 Mike Bennett; 15 Tim Jonkers; 11 Chris Joynt (C). Subs: 2 Sean Hoppe for Wellens (3); 12 Peter Shiels for Ward (27); 14 John Stankevitch for Britt (31BB, rev 58); 17 Mick Higham for Joynt (54); Stankevitch for Shiels (58); Joynt for Britt (75); Shiels for Jonkers (77).
Tries: Bennett (24), Long (32), Gleeson (56);
Goals: Long 3; **Field goal:** Long.
Rugby Leaguer & League Express Men of the Match:
Bulls: Paul Deacon; *Saints:* Mike Bennett.
Penalty count: 5-4; **Half-time:** 12-8; **Referee:** Russell Smith (Castleford); **Attendance:** 61,138 *(at Old Trafford, Manchester).*

2002...Huddersfield celebrate promotion

2003

NATIONAL LEAGUE TWO GRAND FINAL

Sunday 5th October 2003

KEIGHLEY COUGARS 13 SHEFFIELD EAGLES 11

COUGARS: 1 Matt Foster; 2 Max Tomlinson; 3 David Foster; 4 James Rushforth; 5 Andy Robinson; 6 Paul Ashton; 7 Matt Firth; 8 Phil Stephenson; 9 Simeon Hoyle; 10 Danny Ekis; 11 Oliver Wilkes; 12 Ian Sinfield; 13 Lee Patterson. Subs (all used): 14 Chris Wainwright; 15 Richard Mervill; 16 Mick Durham; 17 Jason Ramshaw.
Tries: M Foster (7), Robinson (74); **Goals:** Ashton 2;
Field goal: Firth.
EAGLES: 1 Andy Poynter; 2 Tony Weller; 3 Richard Goddard; 4 Tom O'Reilly; 5 Greg Hurst; 6 Gavin Brown; 7 Mark Aston; 8 Jack Howieson; 9 Gareth Stanley; 10 Dale Laughton; 11 Andy Raleigh; 12 Craig Brown; 13 Wayne Flynn. Subs (all used): 14 Peter Reilly; 15 Simon Tillyer; 16 Nick Turnbull; 17 Mitchell Stringer.
Try: O'Reilly (51); **Goals:** G Brown 3; **Field goal:** Reilly.
Rugby Leaguer & League Express Men of the Match:
Cougars: Simeon Hoyle; *Eagles:* Andy Raleigh.
Penalty count: 6-8; **Half-time:** 9-4; **Referee:** Peter Taberner (Wigan). *(at Halton Stadium, Widnes).*

NATIONAL LEAGUE ONE GRAND FINAL

Sunday 5th October 2003

LEIGH CENTURIONS 14 SALFORD CITY REDS 31

CENTURIONS: 1 Neil Turley; 2 Damian Munro; 3 Alan Hadcroft; 4 Danny Halliwell; 5 Leroy Rivett; 6 John Duffy; 7 Tommy Martyn; 8 Sonny Nickle; 9 Patrick Weisner; 10 Paul Norman; 11 Sean Richardson; 12 Willie Swann; 13 Adam Bristow. Subs (all used): 14 David Bradbury; 15 Lee Sanderson; 16 Bryan Henare; 17 Ricky Bibey.
Tries: Richardson (33), Halliwell (38), Swann (65);
Goal: Turley.
On report: Nickle (60) - late tackle on Clinch.
CITY REDS: 1 Jason Flowers; 2 Danny Arnold; 3 Stuart Littler; 4 Alan Hunte; 5 Andy Kirk; 6 Cliff Beverley; 7 Gavin Clinch; 8 Neil Baynes; 9 Malcolm Alker; 10 Andy Coley; 11 Simon Baldwin; 12 Paul Highton; 13 Chris Charles. Subs (all used): 14 Steve Blakeley; 15 David Highton; 16 Martin Moana; 17 Gareth Haggerty.
Tries: Hunte (3, 52), Beverley (23), Littler (73);
Goals: Charles 6, Blakeley; **Field goal:** Blakeley.
Rugby Leaguer & League Express Men of the Match:
Centurions: Willie Swann; *City Reds:* Gavin Clinch.
Penalty count: 10-10; **Half-time:** 10-16;
Referee: Richard Silverwood (Dewsbury);
Attendance: 9,186 *(at Halton Stadium, Widnes).*

SUPER LEAGUE GRAND FINAL

Saturday 18th October 2003

BRADFORD BULLS 25 WIGAN WARRIORS 12

BULLS: 17 Stuart Reardon; 2 Tevita Vaikona; 6 Michael Withers; 4 Shontayne Hape; 5 Lesley Vainikolo; 15 Karl Pratt; 7 Paul Deacon; 8 Joe Vagana; 9 James Lowes; 29 Stuart Fielden; 11 Daniel Gartner; 12 Jamie Peacock; 13 Mike Forshaw. Subs (all used): 10 Paul Anderson; 18 Lee Radford; 3 Leon Pryce; 1 Robbie Paul (C).
Tries: Reardon (51), Hape (59), Lowes (75);
Goals: Deacon 6/6; **Field goal:** Deacon.
WARRIORS: 1 Kris Radlinski; 5 Brian Carney; 18 Martin Aspinwall; 14 David Hodgson; 2 Brett Dallas; 15 Sean O'Loughlin; 20 Luke Robinson; 30 Quentin Pongia; 9 Terry Newton; 10 Craig Smith; 11 Mick Cassidy; 12 Danny Tickle; 13 Andy Farrell (C). Subs (all used): 4 Paul Johnson; 8 Terry O'Connor; 23 Gareth Hock; 17 Mark Smith.
Tries: Tickle (17), Radlinski (72); **Goals:** Farrell 2/3.
Rugby Leaguer & League Express Men of the Match:
Bulls: Stuart Reardon; *Warriors:* Kris Radlinski.
Penalty count: 7-6; **Half-time:** 4-6; **Referee:** Karl Kirkpatrick (Warrington); **Attendance:** 65,537 *(at Old Trafford, Manchester).*

2004

NATIONAL LEAGUE ONE GRAND FINAL

Sunday 10th October 2004

LEIGH CENTURIONS 32 WHITEHAVEN 16
(after extra time)

CENTURIONS: 1 Neil Turley; 2 Rob Smyth; 3 Danny Halliwell; 4 Ben Cooper; 5 David Alstead; 6 John Duffy; 7 Tommy Martyn; 8 Simon Knox; 9 Paul Rowley; 10 Matt Sturm; 11 David Larder; 12 Oliver Wilkes; 13 Ian Knott. Subs (all used): 14 Dave McConnell; 15 Heath Cruckshank; 16 Richard Marshall; 17 Willie Swann.
Tries: Cooper (27, 83), Martyn (61), Turley (87);
Goals: Turley 6/8; **Field goals:** Turley 2, Rowley, Martyn.
WHITEHAVEN: 1 Gary Broadbent; 2 Craig Calvert; 3 David Seeds; 4 Mick Nanyn; 5 Wesley Wilson; 6 Leroy Joe; 7 Sam Obst; 8 Marc Jackson; 9 Aaron Lester; 10 David Fatialofa; 11 Paul Davidson; 12 Howard Hill; 13 Craig Walsh. Subs (all used): 14 Spencer Miller; 15 Carl Sice; 16 Chris McKinney; 17 Ryan Tandy.
Tries: Wilson (2, 71), Calvert (45); **Goals:** Nanyn 2/6.
Rugby Leaguer & League Express Men of the Match:
Centurions: Neil Turley; *Whitehaven:* Aaron Lester.
Penalty count: 5-9; **Half-time:** 7-6; **Full-time:** 16-16;
Referee: Ronnie Laughton (Barnsley);
Attendance: 11,005 *(at Halton Stadium, Widnes).*

SUPER LEAGUE GRAND FINAL

Saturday 16th October 2004

BRADFORD BULLS 8 LEEDS RHINOS 16

BULLS: 6 Michael Withers; 17 Stuart Reardon; 16 Paul Johnson; 4 Shontayne Hape; 5 Lesley Vainikolo; 18 Iestyn Harris; 7 Paul Deacon; 8 Joe Vagana; 1 Robbie Paul (C); 29 Stuart Fielden; 12 Jamie Peacock; 13 Logan Swann; 11 Lee Radford. Subs: 10 Paul Anderson for Vagana (14); 15 Karl Pratt for Paul (23); 27 Rob Parker for Anderson (24); 19 Jamie Langley for Peacock (32); Paul for Withers (ht); Peacock for Radford (48); Radford for Swann (54); Vagana for Parker (56); Parker for Fielden (63); Fielden for Vagana (67); Swann for Langley (68).
Tries: Vainikolo (7), Hape (43); **Goals:** Deacon 0/2.
RHINOS: 21 Richard Mathers; 18 Mark Calderwood; 5 Chev Walker; 4 Keith Senior; 22 Marcus Bai; 13 Kevin Sinfield (C); 6 Danny McGuire; 19 Danny Ward; 9 Matt Diskin; 8 Ryan Bailey; 3 Chris McKenna; 29 Ali Lauitiiti; 11 David Furner. Subs: 16 Willie Poching for Furner (19); 10 Barrie McDermott for Ward (22); Ward for Bailey (29); 7 Rob Burrow for Lauitiiti (30); Bailey for McDermott (41); 20 Jamie Jones-Buchanan for McKenna (48); Lauitiiti for Ward (50); Furner for Sinfield (60); McKenna for Poching (63); Sinfield for Diskin (67); Poching for McKenna (72); Ward for Bailey (73).
Tries: Diskin (15), McGuire (75); **Goals:** Sinfield 4/4.
Rugby Leaguer & League Express Men of the Match:
Bulls: Lesley Vainikolo; *Rhinos:* Richard Mathers.
Penalty count: 5-5; **Half-time:** 4-10; **Referee:** Steve Ganson (St Helens); **Attendance:** 65,547 *(at Old Trafford, Manchester).*

2005

NATIONAL LEAGUE ONE GRAND FINAL

Sunday 9th October 2005

CASTLEFORD TIGERS 36 WHITEHAVEN 8

TIGERS: 1 Michael Platt; 2 Waine Pryce; 3 Michael Shenton; 4 Jon Hepworth; 5 Damien Blanch; 6 Brad Davis; 7 Andrew Henderson; 8 Adam Watene; 9 Aaron Smith; 10 Richard Fletcher; 11 Tom Haughey; 12 Steve Crouch; 13 Deon Bird. Subs (all used): 14 Paul Handforth; 15 Craig Huby; 16 Adrian Vowles; 17 Frank Watene.
Tries: Huby (22), Crouch (24), Blanch (26), Davis (33, 45), Haughey (52); **Goals:** Fletcher 2/3, Huby 3/4, Hepworth 1/1.
WHITEHAVEN: 1 Gary Broadbent; 2 Craig Calvert; 3 David Seeds; 4 Mick Nanyn; 5 Wesley Wilson; 6 Leroy Joe; 7 Joel Penny; 8 Ryan Tandy; 9 Carl Sice; 10 David Fatialofa; 11 Spencer Miller; 12 Howard Hill; 13 Aaron Lester. Subs (all used): 14 Carl Rudd; 15 Aaron Summers; 16 Craig Chambers; 17 Marc Jackson.
Tries: Seeds (56), Calvert (78); **Goals:** Nanyn 0/2.
Sin bin: Joe (16) - late tackle on Davis.
On report: Joe (16) - late tackle on Davis;
Sice (40) - alleged biting.
Rugby Leaguer & League Express Men of the Match:
Tigers: Brad Davis; *Whitehaven:* Wesley Wilson.
Penalty count: 4-9; **Half-time:** 26-0;
Referee: Steve Ganson (St Helens);
Attendance: 13,300 *(at Halton Stadium, Widnes).*

SUPER LEAGUE GRAND FINAL

Saturday 15th October 2005

BRADFORD BULLS 15 LEEDS RHINOS 6

BULLS: 6 Michael Withers; 3 Leon Pryce; 13 Ben Harris; 4 Shontayne Hape; 5 Lesley Vainikolo; 18 Iestyn Harris; 7 Paul Deacon; 9 Ian Henderson; 29 Stuart Fielden; 16 Paul Johnson; 10 Brad Meyers; 11 Lee Radford. Subs (all used): 24 Adrian Morley for Johnson (5); 19 Jamie Langley for Peacock (24); 8 Joe Vagana for Fielden (24); Johnson for Radford (24); 1 Robbie Paul for Henderson (31); Peacock for Vagana (45); Fielden for Morley (49); Henderson for Paul (54); Radford for Meyers (60); Morley for Peacock (62); Meyers for Langley (73); Peacock for Johnson (74).
Tries: L Pryce (29), Vainikolo (53); **Goals:** Deacon 3/5;
Field goal: I Harris.
RHINOS: 1 Richard Mathers; 2 Mark Calderwood; 3 Chev Walker; 4 Chris McKenna; 5 Marcus Bai; 6 Danny McGuire; 7 Rob Burrow; 8 Ryan Bailey; 14 Andrew Dunemann; 15 Danny Ward; 20 Gareth Ellis; 16 Willie Poching; 13 Kevin Sinfield (C). Subs (all used): 10 Barrie McDermott for Ward (17); 11 Ali Lauitiiti for Poching (21); 18 Jamie Jones-Buchanan for Bailey (31); Ward for McDermott (34); 9 Matt Diskin for Ellis (48); Poching for Lauitiiti (48); McDermott for Ward (54); Ellis for Poching (54); Lauitiiti for McDermott (61); Poching for Dunemann (65); Ward for Jones-Buchanan (68); Dunemann for Ellis (71).
Try: McGuire (22); **Goals:** Sinfield 1/2.
Rugby Leaguer & League Express Men of the Match:
Bulls: Leon Pryce; *Rhinos:* Danny McGuire.
Penalty count: 6-8; **Half-time:** 8-6; **Referee:** Ashley Klein (Keighley); **Attendance:** 65,537 *(at Old Trafford, Manchester).*

2004...Kevin Sinfield leads the Rhinos' celebrations

2005...Craig Huby shows his delight at scoring

2006

NATIONAL LEAGUE TWO GRAND FINAL

Sunday 8th October 2006

SHEFFIELD EAGLES 35 SWINTON LIONS 10

EAGLES: 1 Johnny Woodcock; 5 Greg Hurst; 4 Jimmy Walker; 3 James Ford; 2 Rob Worrincy; 6 Brendon Lindsay; 7 Gavin Brown; 8 Jack Howieson; 9 Paul Pickering; 10 Mitchell Stringer; 11 Andy Hay; 12 Dale Holdstock; 13 Andy Smith. Subs (all used): 14 Craig Poucher; 15 Martin Ostler; 16 Sean Dickinson; 17 Waisale Sovatabua.
Tries: Worrincy (21, 43), Lindsay (38), Woodcock (39), Walker (51), Hay (60); **Goals:** Woodcock 5/6;
Field goal: G Brown.
LIONS: 1 Wayne English; 2 Andy Saywell; 3 Darren Woods; 4 David Alstead; 5 Marlon Billy; 6 Martin Moana; 7 Chris Hough; 8 Bruce Johnson; 9 Phil Wood; 10 Dave Newton; 11 Kris Smith; 12 Ian Sinfield; 13 Lee Marsh. Subs (all used): 14 Liam McGovern; 15 Chris Morley; 16 Danny Aboushakra; 17 Ian Parry.
Tries: Saywell (35), Alstead (74); **Goals:** McGovern 1/2.
Rugby Leaguer & League Express Men of the Match:
Eagles: Johnny Woodcock; *Lions:* Wayne English.
Penalty count: 3-4; **Half-time:** 16-4;
Referee: Peter Taberner (Wigan).
(at Halliwell Jones Stadium, Warrington).

Dewsbury Rams were National League Two Champions in 2006. This game was to determine who took the second promotion place.

NATIONAL LEAGUE ONE GRAND FINAL

Sunday 8th October 2006

HULL KINGSTON ROVERS 29 WIDNES VIKINGS 16

ROVERS: 1 Ben Cockayne; 2 Leroy Rivett; 3 Gareth Morton; 4 Jon Goddard; 5 Byron Ford; 6 Scott Murrell; 7 James Webster; 8 Makali Aizue; 9 Ben Fisher; 10 David Tangata-Toa; 11 Iain Morrison; 12 Michael Smith; 13 Tommy Gallagher. Subs (all used): 14 Pat Weisner; 15 Dwayne Barker; 16 Jason Netherton; 17 Dave Wilson.
Tries: Ford (6), Goddard (18, 36), Murrell (24), Weisner (43); **Goals:** Morton 4/6; **Field goal:** Murrell.
VIKINGS: 1 Gavin Dodd; 2 Damien Blanch; 3 Sean Gleeson; 4 Daryl Cardiss; 5 John Kirkpatrick; 6 Dennis Moran; 7 Ian Watson; 8 Terry O'Connor; 9 Mark Smith; 10 Barrie McDermott; 11 Mick Cassidy; 12 David Allen; 13 Bob Beswick. Subs (all used): 14 Aaron Summers; 15 Oliver Wilkes; 16 Jordan James; 17 Ryan Tandy.
Tries: Dodd (32), Tandy (57), Blanch (70); **Goals:** Dodd 2/3.
Rugby Leaguer & League Express Men of the Match:
Rovers: James Webster; *Vikings:* Mark Smith.
Penalty count: 8-5; **Half-time:** 22-4;
Referee: Phil Bentham (Warrington);
Attendance: 13,024 *(at Halliwell Jones Stadium, Warrington).*

2006...The departing Jamie Lyon carried from the Old Trafford pitch by his teammates

SUPER LEAGUE GRAND FINAL

Saturday 14th October 2006

HULL FC 4 ST HELENS 26

HULL: 1 Shaun Briscoe; 14 Motu Tony; 4 Sid Domic; 3 Kirk Yeaman; 5 Gareth Raynor; 13 Paul Cooke; 7 Richard Horne; 8 Ewan Dowes; 9 Richard Swain (C); 10 Garreth Carvell; 11 Lee Radford; 12 Shayne McMenemy; 24 Danny Washbrook. Subs: 15 Paul King for Carvell (17); 19 Graeme Horne for Radford (23); 26 Scott Wheeldon for Dowes (27); 6 Richard Whiting for McMenemy (29); Dowes for Wheeldon (49); Carvell for King (49); Radford for G Horne (51); McMenemy for Whiting (54); King for Carvell (68); Wheeldon for Dowes (73); Whiting for Tony (76); G Horne for Radford (77).
Try: Domic (24); **Goals:** Cooke 0/1.
SAINTS: 1 Paul Wellens; 2 Ade Gardner; 3 Jamie Lyon; 4 Willie Talau; 5 Francis Meli; 6 Leon Pryce; 7 Sean Long (C); 17 Paul Anderson; 9 Keiron Cunningham; 10 Jason Cayless; 11 Lee Gilmour; 12 Jon Wilkin; 16 Jason Hooper. Subs: 23 Maurie Fa'asavalu for P Anderson (12); 19 James Graham for Cayless (25); 15 Mike Bennett for Fa'asavalu (28); 14 James Roby for Cunningham (31); P Anderson for Wilkin (33); Cunningham for Gilmour (49); Cayless for P Anderson (52); Wilkin for Hooper (56); Fa'asavalu for Cayless (58); Gilmour for Graham (66); Cayless for Fa'asavalu (72); P Anderson for Wilkin (75).
Tries: Meli (17), Pryce (29), Talau (49), Gardner (52), Cunningham (62); **Goals:** Lyon 3/5.
Rugby Leaguer & League Express Men of the Match:
Hull: Shaun Briscoe; *Saints:* Paul Wellens.
Penalty count: 4-2; **Half-time:** 4-10;
Referee: Karl Kirkpatrick (Warrington);
Attendance: 72,582 *(at Old Trafford, Manchester).*

2007

NATIONAL LEAGUE TWO GRAND FINAL

Sunday 7th October 2007

FEATHERSTONE ROVERS 24 OLDHAM 6

ROVERS: 1 Loz Wildbore; 2 Danny Kirmond; 3 Jon Whittle; 4 Wayne McHugh; 5 Ade Adebisi; 6 Andy Kain; 7 Paul Handforth; 8 Gareth Handford; 9 Joe McLocklan; 10 Stuart Dickens; 11 Jamie Field; 12 Richard Blakeway; 13 Tom Haughey. Subs (all used): 14 Jamie Benn; 15 Ian Tonks; 16 James Houston; 17 Gavin Swinson.
Tries: McHugh (39, 49), Handforth (46); **Goals:** Dickens 5/6;
Field goals: Wildbore (66, 70).
Dismissal: Blakeway (64) – head butt on Roberts.
OLDHAM: 1 Gareth Langley; 2 Byron Ford; 3 Craig Littler; 4 Adam Hughes; 5 Lucas Onyango; 6 Neil Roden; 7 James Coyle; 8 Anthony Tonks; 9 Simeon Hoyle; 10 Richard Mervill; 11 Ian Sinfield; 12 Robert Roberts; 13 Geno Costin. Subs (all used): 14 Ian Hodson; 15 Alex Wilkinson; 16 Said Tamghart; 17 Matty Brooks.
Try: Hughes (31); **Goals:** Langley 1/2.
Rugby Leaguer & League Express Men of the Match:
Rovers: Paul Handforth; *Oldham:* Robert Roberts.
Penalty count: 9-5; **Half-time:** 10-6; **Referee:** Gareth Hewer.
(at Headingley Carnegie, Leeds).

Celtic Crusaders were National League Two Champions in 2007. This game was to determine who took the second promotion place.

NATIONAL LEAGUE ONE GRAND FINAL

Sunday 7th October 2007

CASTLEFORD TIGERS 42 WIDNES VIKINGS 10

TIGERS: 1 Stuart Donlan; 2 Danny Williams; 3 Michael Shenton; 4 Ryan McGoldrick; 5 Kirk Dixon; 6 Anthony Thackeray; 7 Danny Brough; 8 Liam Higgins; 9 Andrew Henderson; 10 Awen Guttenbeil; 11 Joe Westerman; 12 Ryan Clayton; 13 Peter Lupton. Subs (all used): 14 Mark Leafa; 15 Chris Charles; 16 Michael Wainwright; 17 Ryan Boyle.
Tries: Wainwright (20), McGoldrick (29), Guttenbeil (44, 76), M Shenton (52), Westerman (62), Clayton (66);
Goals: Brough 6/9; **Field goals:** Brough (25, 55).
VIKINGS: 1 Scott Grix; 2 Damien Blanch; 3 Toa Kohe-Love; 4 Mick Nanyn; 5 Gavin Dodd; 6 Dennis Moran; 7 Joel Penny; 8 Mick Cassidy; 9 Mark Smith; 10 Oliver Wilkes; 11 Joel Tomkins; 12 Paul Noone; 13 Bob Beswick. Subs (all used): 14 Aaron Summers; 15 Jordan James; 16 Ian Webster; 17 Lee Doran.
Tries: Nanyn (35), Wilkes (69); **Goals:** Nanyn 1/2.
Rugby Leaguer & League Express Men of the Match:
Tigers: Danny Brough; *Vikings:* Scott Grix.
Penalty count: 7-2; **Half-time:** 13-4; **Referee:** Phil Bentham; **Attendance:** 20,814 *(at Headingley Carnegie, Leeds).*

SUPER LEAGUE GRAND FINAL

Saturday 13th October 2007

LEEDS RHINOS 33 ST HELENS 6

RHINOS: 1 Brent Webb; 5 Lee Smith; 3 Clinton Toopi; 4 Keith Senior; 2 Scott Donald; 6 Danny McGuire; 7 Rob Burrow; 8 Kylie Leuluai; 9 Matt Diskin; 10 Jamie Peacock; 11 Jamie Jones-Buchanan; 12 Gareth Ellis; 13 Kevin Sinfield. Subs (all used): 14 Ali Lauitiiti for Diskin (23); 16 Ryan Bailey for Leuluai (18); 18 Ian Kirke for Jones-Buchanan (33); 22 Carl Ablett for Kirke (57); Leuluai for Bailey (55); Jones-Buchanan for Lauitiiti (60); Diskin for Ablett (63); Kirke for Leuluai (65); Bailey for Kirke (76).
Tries: Webb (19), Lauitiiti (50), Donald (52), Smith (69), Jones-Buchanan (80); **Goals:** Sinfield 6/7;
Field goal: Burrow (55).
SAINTS: 1 Paul Wellens; 2 Ade Gardner; 3 Matt Gidley; 4 Willie Talau; 5 Francis Meli; 6 Leon Pryce; 7 Sean Long; 8 Nick Fozzard; 9 Keiron Cunningham (C); 10 Jason Cayless; 11 Lee Gilmour; 30 Chris Flannery; 12 Jon Wilkin. Subs (all used): 17 James Graham for Cayless (15); 14 James Roby for Cunningham (23); 23 Maurie Fa'asavalu for Fozzard (23); 15 Mike Bennett for Wilkin (31); Cayless for Fa'asavalu (34); Cunningham for Flannery (51); Wilkin for Bennett (55); Fa'asavalu for Cayless (55); Fozzard for Graham (57); Cayless for Fozzard (68); Graham for Fa'asavalu (68); Bennett for Gilmour (72).
Try: Roby (27); **Goals:** Long 1/2.
Rugby Leaguer & League Express Men of the Match:
Rhinos: Rob Burrow; *Saints:* Sean Long.
Penalty count: 4-5; **Half-time:** 8-6; **Referee:** Ashley Klein; **Attendance:** 71,352 *(at Old Trafford, Manchester).*

2007...Jon Whittle brought down by Ian Sinfield

2008

NATIONAL LEAGUE TWO GRAND FINAL

Sunday 28th September 2008

DONCASTER 18 OLDHAM 10

DONCASTER: 1 Zebastian Luisi; 2 Dean Colton; 3 Andreas Bauer; 4 Shaun Leaf; 5 Wayne Reittie; 6 Kyle Wood; 7 Luke Gale; 8 Nathan Freer; 9 Corey Lawrie; 10 Alex Benson; 11 Peter Green; 12 Craig Lawton; 13 Josh Weeden. Subs (all used): 14 Kyle Briggs; 15 Chris Buttery; 16 Michael Haley; 17 Mark Castle.
Tries: Buttery (44), Gale (49), Briggs (73); **Goals:** Gale 3/4.
OLDHAM: 1 Paul O'Connor; 2 Gareth Langley; 3 Marcus St Hilaire; 4 Mick Nanyn; 5 Daryl Cardiss; 6 Phil Joseph; 7 James Coyle; 8 Adam Robinson; 9 Matty Brooks; 10 Richard Mervill; 11 Tommy Goulden; 12 Danny Halliwell; 13 Robert Roberts. Subs (all used): 14 Ian Hodson; 15 Luke Menzies; 16 Chris Baines; 17 Said Tamghart.
Tries: Hodson (34), Nanyn (62); **Goals:** Nanyn 1/4.
Rugby Leaguer & League Express Men of the Match:
Doncaster: Luke Gale; *Oldham:* Adam Robinson.
Penalty count: 7-8; **Half-time:** 2-6; **Referee:** Ronnie Laughton. *(at Halliwell Jones Stadium, Warrington).*

Gateshead Thunder were National League Two Champions in 2008. This game was to determine who took the second promotion place.

NATIONAL LEAGUE ONE GRAND FINAL

Sunday 28th September 2008

CELTIC CRUSADERS 18 SALFORD CITY REDS 36
(after extra time)

CRUSADERS: 1 Tony Duggan; 2 Luke Dyer; 3 Josh Hannay; 4 Mark Dalle Cort; 5 Anthony Blackwood; 6 Damien Quinn; 7 Jace Van Dijk; 8 Jordan James; 9 Neil Budworth; 10 David Tangata-Toa; 11 Chris Beasley; 12 Darren Mapp; 13 Terry Martin. Subs (all used): 14 Aaron Summers; 15 Ian Webster; 16 Mark Lennon; 17 Neale Wyatt.
Tries: Blackwood (38), Dyer (50), J James (54), Tangata-Toa (66); **Goals:** Hannay 0/1, Lennon 1/3.
CITY REDS: 1 Karl Fitzpatrick; 2 Matt Gardner; 3 Stuart Littler; 4 John Wilshere; 5 Paul White; 6 Robbie Paul; 7 Richard Myler; 8 Paul Highton; 9 Malcolm Alker; 10 Craig Stapleton; 11 Ian Sibbit; 12 Luke Adamson; 13 Jordan Turner. Subs (all used): 14 Stefan Ratchford; 15 Steve Bannister; 16 Lee Jewitt; 17 Phil Leuluai.
Tries: White (5, 86), Gardner (26), Fitzpatrick (63), Sibbit (83), Myler (99); **Goals:** Wilshere 6/7.
Rugby Leaguer & League Express Men of the Match:
Crusaders: Tony Duggan; *City Reds:* John Wilshere.
Penalty count: 5-5; **Half-time:** 4-10; **Full-time:** 18-18;
Referee: Ben Thaler; **Attendance:** 7,104
(at Halliwell Jones Stadium, Warrington).

SUPER LEAGUE GRAND FINAL

Saturday 4th October 2008

LEEDS RHINOS 24 ST HELENS 16

RHINOS: 5 Lee Smith; 22 Ryan Hall; 19 Carl Ablett; 4 Keith Senior; 2 Scott Donald; 6 Danny McGuire; 7 Rob Burrow; 8 Kylie Leuluai; 9 Matt Diskin; 10 Jamie Peacock; 11 Jamie Jones-Buchanan; 12 Gareth Ellis; 13 Kevin Sinfield (C). Subs (all used): 17 Nick Scruton; 14 Ali Lauitiiti; 18 Ian Kirke; 16 Ryan Bailey.
Tries: Smith (23), Hall (37), McGuire (49, 63);
Goals: Sinfield 4/4.
SAINTS: 1 Paul Wellens; 2 Ade Gardner; 3 Matt Gidley; 4 Willie Talau; 5 Francis Meli; 6 Leon Pryce; 7 Sean Long; 18 Bryn Hargreaves; 9 Keiron Cunningham (C); 17 James Graham; 11 Lee Gilmour; 12 Jon Wilkin; 16 Chris Flannery. Subs (all used): 8 Nick Fozzard; 21 Paul Clough; 14 James Roby; 23 Maurie Fa'asavalu.
Tries: Graham (6), Gidley (43), Gardner (59); **Goals:** Long 2/3.
Rugby Leaguer & League Express Men of the Match:
Rhinos: Jamie Peacock; *Saints:* Sean Long.
Penalty count: 6-8; **Half-time:** 12-6; **Referee:** Ashley Klein; **Attendance:** 68,810 *(at Old Trafford, Manchester).*

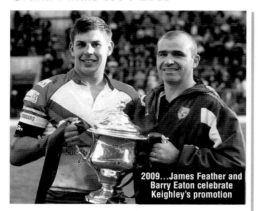

2009...James Feather and Barry Eaton celebrate Keighley's promotion

2009...Zebastian Luisi gets a pass away under pressure from Shad Royston

2009

CHAMPIONSHIP ONE GRAND FINAL

Sunday 4th October 2009

KEIGHLEY COUGARS 28 OLDHAM 26

COUGARS: 1 George Rayner; 2 Sam Gardner; 3 Dan Potter; 4 Oliver Pursglove; 5 Gavin Duffy; 6 Jon Presley; 7 Danny Jones; 17 Scott Law; 14 Jamaine Wray; 8 Andy Shickell; 11 Will Cartledge; 18 Greg Nicholson; 13 Carl Hughes. Subs (all used): 21 Ryan Smith; 28 Ryan Benjafield; 9 James Feather; 16 Brendan Rawlins.
Tries: Gardner (24), Jones (42, 50), Presley (63), Pursglove (67); **Goals:** Jones 4/5.
OLDHAM: 4 Paul Reilly; 21 Lucas Onyango; 24 Marcus St Hilaire; 22 Phil Joseph; 1 Paul O'Connor; 18 Neil Roden; 7 Thomas Coyle; 15 Jason Boults; 30 Martin Roden; 16 Wayne Kerr; 23 Chris Baines; 12 Tommy Goulden; 28 Craig Lawton. Subs (all used): 10 Jamie I'Anson; 25 Luke Menzies; 27 Matt Ashe; 29 Ben Heaton.
Tries: Menzies (35, 76), N Roden (54), St Hilaire (70), Kerr (78); **Goals:** Baines 3/4, Ashe 0/1.
Rugby Leaguer & League Express Men of the Match:
Cougars: Danny Jones; *Oldham:* Luke Menzies.
Penalty count: 9-2; **Half-time:** 4-6; **Referee:** Ronnie Laughton. *(at Halliwell Jones Stadium, Warrington).*

Dewsbury Rams were Championship One Champions in 2009. This game was to determine who took the second promotion place.

CHAMPIONSHIP GRAND FINAL

Sunday 4th October 2009

BARROW RAIDERS 26 HALIFAX 18

RAIDERS: 1 Gary Broadbent; 36 Andy Ballard; 32 Andreas Bauer; 4 Liam Harrison; 5 James Nixon; 24 Jamie Rooney; 31 James Coyle; 34 Rob Roberts; 9 Andy Ellis; 8 Brett McDermott; 33 Dave Allen; 22 Ned Catic; 26 Zebastian Luisi. Subs (all used): 15 Chris Young; 13 Andy Bracek; 35 Danny Halliwell; 14 Paul Noone.
Tries: Harrison (33), Ballard (37), Allen (61), Bauer (66, 78); **Goals:** Rooney 3/5.
HALIFAX: 4 Shad Royston; 5 James Haley; 15 Mark Roberts; 2 Lee Paterson; 23 Rob Worrincy; 19 Mick Govin; 7 Ben Black; 21 Neil Cherryholme; 9 Sean Penkywicz; 22 David Wrench; 11 David Larder; 27 Steve Bannister; 12 Paul Smith. Subs (all used): 13 Bob Beswick; 14 Mark Gleeson; 16 Said Tamghart; 26 Dominic Maloney.
Tries: Haley (12), Royston (31), Black (45), Govin (70); **Goals:** Paterson 1/5.
Rugby Leaguer & League Express Men of the Match:
Raiders: Gary Broadbent; *Halifax:* Mick Govin.
Penalty count: 8-5; **Half-time:** 10-10; **Referee:** Phil Bentham; **Attendance:** 11,398 *(at Halliwell Jones Stadium, Warrington).*

SUPER LEAGUE GRAND FINAL

Saturday 10th October 2009

LEEDS RHINOS 18 ST HELENS 10

RHINOS: 1 Brent Webb; 2 Scott Donald; 3 Lee Smith; 4 Keith Senior; 5 Ryan Hall; 6 Danny McGuire; 7 Rob Burrow; 8 Kylie Leuluai; 14 Matt Diskin; 10 Jamie Peacock; 11 Jamie Jones-Buchanan; 18 Carl Ablett; 13 Kevin Sinfield (C). Subs (all used): 16 Ryan Bailey for Leuluai (19); 19 Luke Burgess for Peacock (29); 17 Ian Kirke for Jones-Buchanan (29); 12 Ali Lauitiiti for Ablett (29); Jones-Buchanan for Lauitiiti (36); Peacock for Burgess (46); Leuluai for Bailey (53); Ablett for Kirke (57); Burgess for Diskin (62); Bailey for Leuluai (67); Diskin for Burgess (69); Kirke for Jones-Buchanan (76).
Tries: Diskin (30), Smith (37, 72); **Goals:** Sinfield 2/4;
Field goals: Sinfield (42), Burrow (78).
SAINTS: 1 Paul Wellens; 2 Ade Gardner; 3 Matt Gidley; 18 Kyle Eastmond; 5 Francis Meli; 6 Leon Pryce; 7 Sean Long; 10 James Graham; 9 Keiron Cunningham (C); 16 Tony Puletua; 12 Jon Wilkin; 11 Lee Gilmour; 13 Chris Flannery. Subs (all used): 14 James Roby for Cunningham (25); 15 Bryn Hargreaves for Puletua (24); 17 Paul Clough for Gilmour (31); 23 Maurie Fa'asavalu for Graham (31); Graham for Fa'asavalu (48); Puletua for Hargreaves (50); Gilmour for Wilkin (55); Cunningham for Clough (64); Wilkin for Roby (65); Roby for Flannery (73).
Try: Eastmond (13); **Goals:** Eastmond 3/3.
Rugby Leaguer & League Express Men of the Match:
Rhinos: Kevin Sinfield; *Saints:* James Graham.
Penalty count: 8-7; **Half-time:** 8-8; **Referee:** Steve Ganson; **Attendance:** 63,259 *(at Old Trafford, Manchester).*

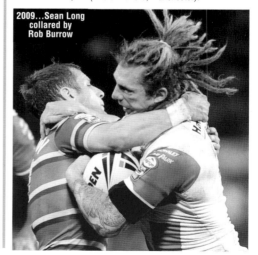

2009...Sean Long collared by Rob Burrow

2010...York celebrate defeating Oldham

2010...Ben Black lands Halifax's golden point field goal

2010

CHAMPIONSHIP ONE GRAND FINAL

Sunday 26th September 2010

OLDHAM 4 YORK CITY KNIGHTS 25

OLDHAM: 1 Paul O'Connor; 2 Lucas Onyango; 24 Marcus St Hilaire; 4 Mick Fogerty; 5 John Gillam; 6 Neil Roden; 28 Gregg McNally; 8 Jason Boults; 9 Martin Roden; 16 Wayne Kerr; 18 Chris Clarke; 13 Joe Chandler; 21 Valu Bentley. Subs (all used): 10 Dave Ellison; 19 Ben Heaton; 17 Danny Whitmore; 7 Matt Ashe.
Try: Fogerty (20); **Goals:** McNally 0/1.
CITY KNIGHTS: 31 James Haynes; 2 Wayne Reittie; 3 Mike Mitchell; 4 Lee Waterman; 28 Danny Wilson; 6 Chris Thorman; 1 Danny Ratcliffe; 17 Nathan Freer; 33 Jack Lee; 10 Alex Benson; 11 Jordan Ross; 29 Ryan Esders; 15 Luke Hardbottle. Subs (all used): 32 Paul Stamp; 36 Callum Dinsdale; 26 Steve Lewis; 30 Jack Stearman.
Tries: Reittie (7), Haynes (26), Thorman (64), Lewis (74);
Goals: Waterman 2/3, Thorman 2/2; **Field goal:** Thorman (69).
Rugby Leaguer & League Express Men of the Match:
Oldham: Neil Roden; *City Knights:* Chris Thorman.
Penalty count: 2-7; **Half-time:** 4-10; **Referee:** Gareth Hewer.
(at Halliwell Jones Stadium, Warrington).

Hunslet Hawks were Championship One Champions in 2010. This game was to determine who took the second promotion place.

CHAMPIONSHIP GRAND FINAL

Sunday 26th September 2010

FEATHERSTONE ROVERS 22 HALIFAX 23
(after golden point extra time)

ROVERS: 1 Ian Hardman; 26 Zak Hardaker; 3 Sam Smeaton; 4 Liam Welham; 2 Tom Saxton; 6 Kyle Briggs; 9 Liam Finn; 17 Tony Tonks; 31 Ben Kaye; 10 Stuart Dickens; 18 Tim Spears; 13 Jamie Field; 11 Matty Dale. Subs (all used): 19 Ross Divorty; 16 Dane Manning; 12 Jon Grayshon; 7 Andy Kain.
Tries: Briggs (28), Hardaker (30, 52), Dale (45);
Goals: Briggs 3/4.
HALIFAX: 4 Shad Royston; 2 Lee Paterson; 6 Luke Branighan; 18 Dylan Nash; 23 Rob Worrincy; 26 Graham Holroyd; 7 Ben Black; 10 Neil Cherryholme; 13 Bob Beswick; 8 Makali Aizue; 11 David Larder; 22 David Wrench; 27 Sam Barlow. Subs (all used): 9 Sean Penkywicz; 17 Frank Watene; 19 Dominic Maloney; 24 Steve Bannister.
Tries: Worrincy (20), Black (58), Branighan (60), Bannister (75); **Goals:** Paterson 3/4; **Field goal:** Black (82).
On report: Barlow (35) - alleged high tackle on Divorty.
Rugby Leaguer & League Express Men of the Match:
Rovers: Tom Saxton; *Halifax:* Ben Black.
Penalty count: 6-3; **Half-time:** 12-4; **Full-time:** 22-22;
Referee: Robert Hicks; **Attendance:** 9,443
(at Halliwell Jones Stadium, Warrington).

SUPER LEAGUE GRAND FINAL

Saturday 2nd October 2010

ST HELENS 10 WIGAN WARRIORS 22

SAINTS: 1 Paul Wellens; 30 Jamie Foster; 3 Matt Gidley; 5 Francis Meli; 24 Jonny Lomax; 12 Jon Wilkin; 34 Matty Smith; 10 James Graham; 9 Keiron Cunningham (C); 15 Bryn Hargreaves; 4 Iosia Soliola; 13 Chris Flannery; 11 Tony Puletua. Subs (all used): 17 Paul Clough; 14 James Roby; 22 Andrew Dixon; 25 Jacob Emmitt.
Tries: Dixon (28), Meli (74); **Goals:** Foster 1/2.
WARRIORS: 6 Sam Tomkins; 24 Darrell Goulding; 3 Martin Gleeson; 4 George Carmont; 5 Pat Richards; 19 Paul Deacon; 7 Thomas Leuluai; 8 Stuart Fielden; 15 Michael McIlorum; 10 Andy Coley; 11 Harrison Hansen; 12 Joel Tomkins; 13 Sean O'Loughlin (C). Subs (all used): 9 Mark Riddell; 17 Iafeta Palea'aesina; 25 Liam Farrell; 14 Paul Prescott.
Tries: Gleeson (4, 16), Goulding (20), S Tomkins (53);
Goals: Richards 2/3, Riddell 1/3, S Tomkins 0/1.
Rugby Leaguer & League Express Men of the Match:
Saints: Tony Puletua; *Warriors:* Thomas Leuluai.
Penalty count: 6-11; **Half time:** 6-16;
Referee: Richard Silverwood;
Attendance: 71,526 *(at Old Trafford, Manchester).*

2010...Sam and Joel Tomkins show off the Super League Trophy

313

SUPER LEAGUE
2012 FIXTURES

ROUND 1

February 3, 2012
Widnes Vikings v Wakefield Trinity Wildcats
Leeds Rhinos v Hull Kingston Rovers
February 4, 2012
London Broncos v St Helens
Salford City Reds v Castleford Tigers
February 5, 2012
Hull FC v Warrington Wolves
Wigan Warriors v Huddersfield Giants
Bradford Bulls v Catalan Dragons

ROUND 2

February 10, 2012
St Helens v Salford City Reds
February 11, 2012
Wigan Warriors v Leeds Rhinos
Catalan Dragons v Hull FC
February 12, 2012
Castleford Tigers v Bradford Bulls
Huddersfield Giants v Widnes Vikings
Wakefield Trinity Wildcats v Hull Kingston Rovers
Warrington Wolves v London Broncos

WORLD CLUB CHALLENGE

February 17, 2012
Leeds Rhinos v Manly Sea Eagles
(at Headingley Carnegie)

ROUND 3

February 18, 2012
Catalan Dragons v Castleford Tigers
Huddersfield Giants v Warrington Wolves
February 19, 2012
Bradford Bulls v Wigan Warriors
Hull FC v London Broncos
Hull Kingston Rovers v St Helens
Widnes Vikings v Salford City Reds
TBC - Leeds Rhinos v Wakefield Trinity Wildcats

ROUND 4

February 24, 2012
Salford City Reds v Hull FC
St Helens v Catalan Dragons
February 25, 2012
Wakefield Trinity Wildcats v Bradford Bulls
February 26, 2012
Castleford Tigers v Wigan Warriors
London Broncos v Huddersfield Giants
Warrington Wolves v Hull Kingston Rovers
Widnes Vikings v Leeds Rhinos

ROUND 5

March 2, 2012
Salford City Reds v London Broncos
Castleford Tigers v Leeds Rhinos
March 3, 2012
Bradford Bulls v Warrington Wolves
March 4, 2012
Huddersfield Giants v St Helens
Hull FC v Wakefield Trinity Wildcats
Hull Kingston Rovers v Widnes Vikings
Wigan Warriors v Catalan Dragons

ROUND 6

March 9, 2012
Leeds Rhinos v Warrington Wolves
St Helens v Hull FC
March 10, 2012
Catalan Dragons v Salford City Reds
Hull Kingston Rovers v Bradford Bulls
London Broncos v Castleford Tigers
March 11, 2012
Wakefield Trinity Wildcats v Huddersfield Giants
Widnes Vikings v Wigan Warriors

ROUND 7

March 16, 2012
Salford City Reds v Leeds Rhinos
Huddersfield Giants v Castleford Tigers
March 17, 2012
Catalan Dragons v Hull Kingston Rovers
Bradford Bulls v St Helens
March 18, 2012
Hull FC v Widnes Vikings
Warrington Wolves v Wakefield Trinity Wildcats
Wigan Warriors v London Broncos

ROUND 8

March 23, 2012
Wigan Warriors v Warrington Wolves
March 24, 2012
St Helens v Leeds Rhinos
March 25, 2012
Bradford Bulls v Salford City Reds
Castleford Tigers v Hull FC
Hull Kingston Rovers v Huddersfield Giants
Wakefield Trinity Wildcats v Catalan Dragons
Widnes Vikings v London Broncos

ROUND 9

March 30, 2012
Castleford Tigers v Hull Kingston Rovers
Hull FC v Bradford Bulls
Leeds Rhinos v Huddersfield Giants
Salford City Reds v Wigan Warriors
Warrington Wolves v St Helens
March 31, 2012
London Broncos v Wakefield Trinity Wildcats
Catalan Dragons v Widnes Vikings

ROUND 10

April 5, 2012
Warrington Wolves v Widnes Vikings
London Broncos v Catalan Dragons
April 6, 2012
Bradford Bulls v Leeds Rhinos
Huddersfield Giants v Salford City Reds
Hull Kingston Rovers v Hull FC
St Helens v Wigan Warriors
Wakefield Trinity Wildcats v Castleford Tigers

ROUND 11

April 9, 2012
Castleford Tigers v St Helens
Salford City Reds v Hull Kingston Rovers
Huddersfield Giants v Hull FC
Catalan Dragons v Warrington Wolves
Leeds Rhinos v London Broncos
Widnes Vikings v Bradford Bulls
April 10, 2012
Wigan Warriors v Wakefield Trinity Wildcats

CHALLENGE CUP ROUND 4

Weekend of April 13/14/15, 2012

ROUND 12

April 20, 2012
Leeds Rhinos v Catalan Dragons
St Helens v Widnes Vikings
April 21, 2012
Wakefield Trinity Wildcats v Salford City Reds
April 22, 2012
Bradford Bulls v Huddersfield Giants
Hull FC v Wigan Warriors
Hull Kingston Rovers v London Broncos
Warrington Wolves v Castleford Tigers

CHALLENGE CUP ROUND 5

Weekend of April 27/28/29, 2012

ROUND 13

May 4, 2012
St Helens v Wakefield Trinity Wildcats
Wigan Warriors v Hull Kingston Rovers
May 5, 2012
Catalan Dragons v Huddersfield Giants
Hull FC v Leeds Rhinos
May 6, 2012
London Broncos v Bradford Bulls
Warrington Wolves v Salford City Reds
May 7, 2012
Castleford Tigers v Widnes Vikings

CHALLENGE CUP QUARTER FINALS

Weekend of May 11/12/13, 2012

ROUND 14

May 18, 2012
Leeds Rhinos v St Helens
Salford City Reds v Bradford Bulls
Huddersfield Giants v Wigan Warriors
May 20, 2012
Hull Kingston Rovers v Castleford Tigers
Wakefield Trinity Wildcats v Warrington Wolves
Widnes Vikings v Catalan Dragons
London Broncos v Hull FC

ROUND 15 - MAGIC WEEKEND

Weekend of May 26/27, 2012
Bradford Bulls v Leeds Rhinos
Castleford Tigers v Wakefield Trinity Wildcats
Catalan Dragons v London Broncos
Huddersfield Giants v Salford City Reds
Hull FC v Hull Kingston Rovers
St Helens v Wigan Warriors
Warrington Wolves v Widnes Vikings

ROUND 16

June 1, 2012
Leeds Rhinos v Wigan Warriors
Salford City Reds v Catalan Dragons
June 3, 2012
Hull FC v St Helens
Hull Kingston Rovers v Warrington Wolves
Wakefield Trinity Wildcats v London Broncos
Widnes Vikings v Huddersfield Giants
June 4, 2012
Bradford Bulls v Castleford Tigers

ROUND 17

June 8, 2012
St Helens v Bradford Bulls
June 9, 2012
Catalan Dragons v Wigan Warriors
June 10, 2012
Castleford Tigers v Salford City Reds
Huddersfield Giants v Hull Kingston Rovers
Wakefield Trinity Wildcats v Hull FC
Warrington Wolves v Leeds Rhinos
London Broncos v Widnes Vikings

INTERNATIONAL ORIGIN MATCH

Weekend of June 15/16/17, 2012

ROUND 18

June 22, 2012
Salford City Reds v St Helens
Wigan Warriors v Widnes Vikings
June 24, 2012
Leeds Rhinos v Castleford Tigers
Bradford Bulls v Wakefield Trinity Wildcats
Huddersfield Giants v London Broncos
Hull Kingston Rovers v Catalan Dragons
Warrington Wolves v Hull FC

ROUND 19

June 29, 2012
St Helens v Hull Kingston Rovers
Salford City Reds v Warrington Wolves
Wigan Warriors v Bradford Bulls
June 30, 2012
Catalan Dragons v Wakefield Trinity Wildcats
July 1, 2012
Hull FC v Huddersfield Giants
Widnes Vikings v Castleford Tigers
London Broncos v Leeds Rhinos

ROUND 20

July 6, 2012
Leeds Rhinos v Hull FC
July 8, 2012
Bradford Bulls v London Broncos
Castleford Tigers v Huddersfield Giants
Hull Kingston Rovers v Salford City Reds
Wakefield Trinity Wildcats v Wigan Warriors
Warrington Wolves v Catalan Dragons
Widnes Vikings v St Helens

CHALLENGE CUP SEMI-FINALS

Weekend of July 13/14/15, 2012

ROUND 21

July 20, 2012
Leeds Rhinos v Bradford Bulls
Salford City Reds v Widnes Vikings
Catalan Dragons v St Helens
Hull FC v Hull Kingston Rovers
July 21, 2012
London Broncos v Wigan Warriors
July 22, 2012
Castleford Tigers v Warrington Wolves
Huddersfield Giants v Wakefield Trinity Wildcats

ROUND 22

July 27, 2012
St Helens v Huddersfield Giants
Wigan Warriors v Castleford Tigers
July 28, 2012
Catalan Dragons v London Broncos
July 29, 2012
Hull FC v Salford City Reds
Wakefield Trinity Wildcats v Leeds Rhinos
Warrington Wolves v Bradford Bulls
Widnes Vikings v Hull Kingston Rovers

ROUND 23

August 3, 2012
St Helens v Warrington Wolves
Wigan Warriors v Hull FC
August 5, 2012
Bradford Bulls v Widnes Vikings
Castleford Tigers v Wakefield Trinity Wildcats
Huddersfield Giants v Catalan Dragons
Hull Kingston Rovers v Leeds Rhinos
London Broncos v Salford City Reds

ROUND 24

August 10, 2012
Leeds Rhinos v Widnes Vikings
Salford City Reds v Huddersfield Giants
August 12, 2012
Bradford Bulls v Hull Kingston Rovers
Castleford Tigers v London Broncos
Hull FC v Catalan Dragons
Wakefield Trinity Wildcats v St Helens
Warrington Wolves v Wigan Warriors

ROUND 25

August 17, 2012
St Helens v Castleford Tigers
Wigan Warriors v Salford City Reds
London Broncos v Warrington Wolves
August 18, 2012
Catalan Dragons v Leeds Rhinos
August 19, 2012
Huddersfield Giants v Bradford Bulls
Hull Kingston Rovers v Wakefield Trinity Wildcats
Widnes Vikings v Hull FC

CHALLENGE CUP FINAL

Saturday August 25, 2012
(at Wembley Stadium)

ROUND 26

August 31, 2012
Leeds Rhinos v Salford City Reds
St Helens v London Broncos
September 2, 2012
Bradford Bulls v Hull FC
Castleford Tigers v Catalan Dragons
Hull Kingston Rovers v Wigan Warriors
Wakefield Trinity Wildcats v Widnes Vikings
Warrington Wolves v Huddersfield Giants

ROUND 27

September 7, 2012
Salford City Reds v Wakefield Trinity Wildcats
Wigan Warriors v St Helens
September 8, 2012
Catalan Dragons v Bradford Bulls
September 9, 2012
Huddersfield Giants v Leeds Rhinos
Hull FC v Castleford Tigers
Widnes Vikings v Warrington Wolves
London Broncos v Hull Kingston Rovers

PLAY-OFFS

Weekend of September 14/15/16, 2012
Play-offs Week 1

Weekend of September 21/22/23, 2012
Play-offs Week 2

Weekend of September 28/29/30, 2012
Play-offs Week 3

GRAND FINAL

Saturday, 6 October
(at Old Trafford, Manchester)

2011 SEASON
Stats round-up

Sam Tomkins

Kevin Sinfield

TRIES *(play-offs in brackets, included in total)*

1	Ryan Hall	Leeds Rhinos	28 (3)
	Sam Tomkins	Wigan Warriors	28 (2)
3	Joel Monaghan	Warrington Wolves	26 (3)
4	Kris Welham	Hull Kingston Rovers	24 (0)
5	Josh Charnley	Wigan Warriors	23 (2)
6	Ryan Atkins	Warrington Wolves	22 (1)
7	Kirk Yeaman	Hull FC	21 (0)
	Jamie Foster	St Helens	21 (1)
	Pat Richards	Wigan Warriors	21 (1)
10	Damien Blanch	Catalan Dragons	20 (3)

GOALS *(play-offs in brackets, included in total)*

1	Kevin Sinfield	Leeds Rhinos	138 (23)
2	Jamie Foster	St Helens	123 (14)
3	Brett Hodgson	Warrington Wolves	121 (0)
4	Pat Richards	Wigan Warriors	115 (14)
5	Scott Dureau	Catalan Dragons	92 (8)
6	Patrick Ah Van	Bradford Bulls	87 (-)
7	Kirk Dixon	Castleford Tigers	84 (-)
8	Danny Tickle	Hull FC	83 (1)
9	Danny Brough	Huddersfield Giants	82 (4)
10	Michael Dobson	Hull Kingston Rovers	76 (1)

GOALS PERCENTAGE *(play-offs included)*

			G	Att	%
1	Michael Witt	Crusaders	12	13	92.3
2	Luke Gale	Harlequins	75	88	85.2
3	Chris Bridge	Warrington Wolves	34	40	85.0
4	Jamie Foster	St Helens	123	145	84.8
5	Pat Richards	Wigan Warriors	115	136	84.6
6	Gareth Moore	Wakefield Trinity Wildcats	14	17	82.4
7	Scott Grix	Huddersfield Giants	18	22	81.8
8	Kevin Sinfield	Leeds Rhinos	138	169	81.7
9	Danny Brough	Huddersfield Giants	82	102	80.4
10	Brett Hodgson	Warrington Wolves	121	151	80.1

(10 minimum attempts to qualify)

POINTS *(play-offs in brackets, included in total)*

			T	G	FG	Pts
1	Jamie Foster	St Helens	21	123	0	330 (32)
2	Brett Hodgson	Warrington Wolves	18	121	0	314 (4)
3	Pat Richards	Wigan Warriors	21	115	0	314 (32)
4	Kevin Sinfield	Leeds Rhinos	2	138	2	286 (50)
5	Scott Dureau	Catalan Dragons	11	92	5	233 (16)
6	Patrick Ah Van	Bradford Bulls	9	87	0	210 (-)
7	Danny Tickle	Hull FC	9	83	0	202 (2)
8	Danny Brough	Huddersfield Giants	8	82	1	197 (8)
9	Kirk Dixon	Castleford Tigers	7	84	0	196 (-)
10	Luke Gale	Harlequins	8	75	2	184 (-)

CONSECUTIVE APPEARANCES
(Super League, including play-offs, Challenge Cup and World Club Challenge)

1	Tony Clubb	Harlequins	60
2	Danny Houghton	Hull FC	55
	Matty Smith	Salford City Reds/St Helens	55
4	Jodie Broughton	Salford City Reds	43
5	Tom Briscoe	Hull FC	42
6	Kevin Sinfield	Leeds Rhinos	41
7	Michael McIlorum	Wigan Warriors	40
8	Andy Lynch	Bradford Bulls	38
9	Josh Hodgson	Hull Kingston Rovers	37
10	Ben Galea	Hull Kingston Rovers	34
	Kris Welham	Hull Kingston Rovers	34

FINAL TABLE

	P	W	D	L	F	A	D	Pts
Warrington Wolves	27	22	0	5	1072	401	671	44
Wigan Warriors	27	20	3	4	852	432	420	43
St Helens	27	17	3	7	782	515	267	37
Huddersfield Giants	27	16	0	11	707	524	183	32
Leeds Rhinos	27	15	1	11	757	603	154	31
Catalan Dragons	27	15	1	11	689	626	63	31
Hull Kingston Rovers	27	14	0	13	713	692	21	28
Hull FC	27	13	1	13	718	569	149	27
Castleford Tigers	27	12	2	13	664	808	-144	26
Bradford Bulls	27	9	2	16	570	826	-256	20
Salford City Reds	27	10	0	17	542	809	-267	20
Harlequins	27	6	1	20	524	951	-427	13
Wakefield Trinity Wildcats *	27	7	0	20	453	957	-504	10
Crusaders *	27	6	0	21	527	857	-330	8

* 4 points deducted for entering administration

AVERAGE ATTENDANCES

	2011 Avg	2010 Avg	Diff
Wigan Warriors	15,287	15,177	+110
Leeds Rhinos	14,669	15,237	-568
Bradford Bulls	13,967	8,436	+5,531
Hull FC	12,431	14,014	-1,583
Warrington Wolves	11,149	10,738	+411
Catalan Dragons	8,387	6,814	+1,573
Hull Kingston Rovers	8,320	8,234	+86
St Helens	7,975	11,569	-3,594
Castleford Tigers	7,156	6,616	+540
Huddersfield Giants	7,147	7,233	-86
Wakefield Trinity Wildcats	6,552	5,984	+568
Salford City Reds	4,754	4,166	+588
Crusaders	3,377	4,621	-1,244
Harlequins	3,132	3,380	-248

2011 Average	8,879
2010 Average	8,730
Difference	+149

BEST ATTENDANCES

		Round	Date
69,107	Leeds v St Helens	GF	8/10/11
	(at Old Trafford, Manchester)		
24,057	Wigan v St Helens	11	22/4/11
21,056	Wigan v Warrington	7	25/3/11
19,795	Hull FC v Hull KR	11	22/4/11
19,275	Bradford v Leeds	11	21/4/11
19,169	Wigan v Huddersfield	19	25/6/11
19,104	Wigan v Crusaders	27	9/9/11
18,095	Leeds v Bradford	19	24/6/11
17,276	Leeds v Warrington	15	27/5/11
16,426	Wigan v Leeds	20	1/7/11

WORST ATTENDANCES

		Round	Date
1,776	Harlequins v Crusaders	2	20/2/11
1,957	Harlequins v Salford	13	30/4/11
2,069	Harlequins v Catalan Dragons	11	22/4/11
2,259	Crusaders v Harlequins	24	12/8/11
2,576	Crusaders v Salford	19	24/6/11
2,615	Crusaders v Bradford	3	26/2/11
2,624	Harlequins v Huddersfield	4	4/3/11
2,809	Salford v Bradford	10	16/4/11
2,820	Crusaders v Hull KR	21	9/7/11
2,875	Harlequins v Wakefield	18	18/6/11

* Super League attendance figures include play-offs.

CHALLENGE CUP

TRIES

1	Steve Tyrer	Widnes Vikings	6
	Jon Presley	York City Knights	6
3	Jordan Turner	Hull FC	5
	Lee Briers	Warrington Wolves	5
	Pat Richards	Wigan Warriors	5
	Sam Tomkins	Wigan Warriors	5

GOALS

1	Lee Briers	Warrington Wolves	28
	Jamie Foster	St Helens	28
3	Pat Richards	Wigan Warriors	24
4	Kevin Sinfield	Leeds Rhinos	22
5	Chris Thorman	York City Knights	20

POINTS

			T	G	FG	Pts
1	Lee Briers	Warrington Wolves	5	28	0	76
2	Jamie Foster	St Helens	4	28	0	72
3	Pat Richards	Wigan Warriors	5	24	0	68
4	Steve Tyrer	Widnes Vikings	6	17	0	58
5	Chris Thorman	York City Knights	4	20	0	56

BEST ATTENDANCES

		Round	Date
78,482	Leeds v Wigan	F	27/8/11
	(at Wembley Stadium)		
13,158	Castleford v Leeds	SF	7/8/11
	(at Keepmoat Stadium, Doncaster)		
13,105	Warrington v Wigan	QF	23/7/11
12,713	St Helens v Wigan	SF	6/8/11
	(at Halliwell Jones Stadium, Warrington)		
10,954	Leeds v Crusaders	4	7/5/11

WORST ATTENDANCES

		Round	Date
305	Swinton v East Hull	3	5/3/11
316	Hunslet v Warrington Wizards	3	6/3/11
342	London Skolars v Egremont	3	5/3/11
350	Sheffield v Leeds Met University	3	6/3/11
	(at Don Valley Stadium)		
352	Doncaster v Thatto Heath	3	5/3/11

NORTHERN RAIL CUP

TRIES

1	Rob Worrincy	Halifax	9
2	Jamie Ellis	Leigh Centurions	8
3	Paul White	Halifax	7
4	Sam Smeaton	Featherstone Rovers	6
	Darren Nicholls	Toulouse Olympique	6

GOALS

1	Mick Nanyn	Leigh Centurions	41
2	Dominic Brambani	Dewsbury Rams	28
3	Liam Finn	Featherstone Rovers	27
4	Scott Kaighan	Workington Town	21
	Josh Lewis	Toulouse Olympique	21

POINTS

			T	G	FG	Pts
1	Mick Nanyn	Leigh Centurions	4	41	0	98
2	Dominic Brambani	Dewsbury Rams	2	28	0	64
3	Liam Finn	Featherstone Rovers	2	27	0	62
4	Josh Lewis	Toulouse Olympique	4	21	0	58
5	Steve Tyrer	Widnes Vikings	4	20	0	56

BEST ATTENDANCES

		Round	Date
8,820	Halifax v Leigh	F	17/7/11
	(at Bloomfield Road, Blackpool)		
3,155	Widnes v Rochdale	3	20/2/11
2,737	Leigh v Widnes	QF	7/4/11
2,376	Widnes v Toulouse	2	12/2/11
2,234	Leigh v Dewsbury	SF	19/6/11

WORST ATTENDANCES

		Round	Date
264	London Skolars v York	3	20/2/11
285	Gateshead v Swinton	4	27/2/11
379	Hunslet v Workington	3	20/2/11
381	Workington v Gateshead	2	13/2/11
420	Doncaster v London Skolars	2	13/2/11

2011 Season - Stats round-up

CHAMPIONSHIP

Jamie Ellis

TRIES *(play-offs in brackets, included in total)*

1	Jamie Ellis	Leigh Centurions	22 (0)
	Mick Nanyn	Leigh Centurions	22 (2)
3	Andy Ballard	Barrow Raiders	20 (-)
	Bryn Powell	Featherstone Rovers	20 (0)
5	Tom Saxton	Featherstone Rovers	18 (4)
6	Paul White	Halifax	17 (0)
	Martyn Ridyard	Leigh Centurions	17 (1)
	Quentin Laulu-Togagae		
		Sheffield Eagles	17 (4)
9	Menzie Yere	Sheffield Eagles	16 (0)
10	Jon Hepworth	Featherstone Rovers	15 (1)

GOALS *(play-offs in brackets, included in total)*

1	Liam Finn	Featherstone Rovers	115 (11)
2	Mick Nanyn	Leigh Centurions	104 (3)
3	Simon Brown	Sheffield Eagles	95 (21)
4	Steve Tyrer	Widnes Vikings	69 (0)
5	Danny Jones	Halifax	65 (8)
6	Jamie Rooney	Barrow Raiders	63 (-)
7	Paul Handforth	Batley Bulldogs	59 (2)
8	Darren Nicholls	Toulouse Olympique	40 (-)
9	Dominic Brambani		
		Dewsbury Rams	39 (-)
10	Pat Walker	Dewsbury Rams	29 (-)

POINTS *(play-offs in brackets, included in total)*

			T	G	FG	Pts
1	Mick Nanyn	Leigh Centurions	22	104	0	296 (14)
2	Liam Finn	Featherstone Rovers	14	115	1	287 (35)
3	Simon Brown	Sheffield Eagles	2	95	1	199 (42)
4	Steve Tyrer	Widnes Vikings	12	69	0	186 (0)
5	Danny Jones	Halifax	6	65	0	154 (16)
6	Jamie Rooney	Barrow Raiders	6	63	1	151 (-)
7	Paul Handforth	Batley Bulldogs	4	59	0	134 (4)
8	Darren Nicholls	Toulouse Olympique	13	40	0	132 (-)
9	Dominic Brambani					
		Dewsbury Rams	6	39	1	103 (-)
10	Jamie Ellis	Leigh Centurions	22	7	0	102 (0)

FINAL TABLE

	P	W	D	L	BP	F	A	D	Pts
Featherstone Rovers	20	18	1	1	0	840	348	492	56
Leigh Centurions *	20	18	1	1	0	776	368	408	53
Batley Bulldogs	20	12	0	8	5	498	406	92	41
Sheffield Eagles	20	12	0	8	3	577	488	89	39
Widnes Vikings	20	11	1	8	3	555	532	23	38
Halifax	20	10	0	10	6	569	543	26	36
Hunslet Hawks	20	4	1	15	6	395	630	-235	20
York City Knights	20	5	1	14	2	416	788	-372	19
Dewsbury Rams	20	4	1	15	4	413	618	-205	18
Toulouse Olympique	20	4	0	16	3	358	663	-305	15
Barrow Raiders **	20	9	0	11	8	527	540	-13	0

* 3 points deducted for 2010 salary cap breach
** All points deducted for salary cap & operational rules breaches

AVERAGE ATTENDANCES

	2011 Avg	2010 Avg	Diff
Widnes Vikings	3,744	2,858	+886
Leigh Centurions	2,248	2,026	+222
Halifax	2,061	2,345	-284
Featherstone Rovers	1,675	1,822	-147
Barrow Raiders	1,527	1,790	-263
York City Knights	1,149	730	+419 (Ch1)
Sheffield Eagles	1,118	1,228	-110
Toulouse Olympique	1,106	1,323	-217
Batley Bulldogs	1,065	992	+73
Dewsbury Rams	1,048	1,145	-97
Hunslet Hawks	749	550	+199 (Ch1)

2011 Average	1,590
2010 Average	1,596
Difference	-6

BEST ATTENDANCES

		Round	Date
7,263	Featherstone v Sheffield	GF	2/10/11
	(at Halliwell Jones Stadium, Warrington)		
5,021	Widnes v Featherstone	22	4/9/11
4,732	Widnes v Leigh	19	7/8/11
4,087	Widnes v York	4	3/4/11
4,030	Widnes v Dewsbury	16	10/7/11
4,027	Widnes v Sheffield	14	26/6/11
3,873	Widnes v Batley	18	31/7/11
3,669	Widnes v Halifax	6	21/4/11
3,601	Widnes v Toulouse	8	28/4/11
3,331	Widnes v Barrow	11	26/5/11

WORST ATTENDANCES

		Round	Date
424	Hunslet v Sheffield	19	7/8/11
501	Hunslet v Barrow	21	21/8/11
518	Hunslet v Toulouse	5	17/4/11
564	Sheffield v Widnes	EPO	9/9/11
602	Toulouse v Barrow	22	3/9/11
606	Hunslet v York	1	13/3/11
645	Toulouse v Hunslet	9	14/5/11
650	Toulouse v York	7	25/4/11
683	Sheffield v Dewsbury	12	3/6/11
	(at Mount St Marys, Spinkhill)		
713	Hunslet v Leigh	18	31/7/11

* Championship attendance figures include play-offs and Northern Rail Cup. Challenge Cup not included.

CHAMPIONSHIP ONE

TRIES *(play-offs in brackets, included in total)*

1	Ian Mort	Swinton Lions	21 (-)
	Scott Kaighan	Workington Town	21 (1)
3	Dale Bloomfield	Rochdale Hornets	19 (4)
4	Andy Saywell	Rochdale Hornets	18 (3)
5	Gavin Dodd	Swinton Lions	17 (-)
6	Andrew Gay	South Wales Scorpions	16 (-)
7	Craig Calvert	Whitehaven	15 (0)
8	Chris Spurr	Doncaster	13 (1)
	Mark Brocklehurst		
		Oldham	13 (1)
	Ben Heaton	Oldham	13 (0)
	Steve Parry	South Wales Scorpions	13 (-)
	Neil Frazer	Workington Town	13 (3)

GOALS *(play-offs in brackets, included in total)*

1	Ian Mort	Swinton Lions	104 (-)
2	Paul Crook	Rochdale Hornets	100 (14)
3	Darren Holt	Workington Town	73 (5)
4	Scott Spaven	Doncaster	70 (8)
5	Carl Forber	Oldham	63 (1)
6	Danny Lawton	Keighley Cougars	58 (9)
7	Lewis Palfrey	Whitehaven	56 (1)
8	Lewis Reece	South Wales Scorpions	54 (-)
9	Dylan Skee	London Skolars	36 (-)
10	Chris Baines	Keighley Cougars	33 (0)

POINTS *(play-offs in brackets, included in total)*

			T	G	FG	Pts
1	Ian Mort	Swinton Lions	21	104	0	292 (-)
2	Paul Crook	Rochdale Hornets	10	100	5	245 (38)
3	Scott Spaven	Doncaster	7	70	1	169 (16)
4	Darren Holt	Workington Town	1	73	5	155 (11)
5	Danny Lawton	Keighley Cougars	9	58	0	152 (26)
6	Carl Forber	Oldham	5	63	0	146 (2)
7	Lewis Palfrey	Whitehaven	5	56	0	132 (2)
8	Lewis Reece	South Wales Scorpions	5	54	0	128 (-)
9	Scott Kaighan	Workington Town	21	16	1	117 (4)
10	Dylan Skee	London Skolars	6	36	1	97 (-)

FINAL TABLE

	P	W	D	L	BP	F	A	D	Pts
Swinton Lions	20	14	1	5	3	720	479	241	47
Keighley Cougars	20	13	0	7	4	663	412	251	43
Workington Town	20	11	1	8	6	659	443	216	41
Rochdale Hornets	20	12	0	8	4	652	498	154	40
Doncaster	20	12	0	8	4	531	433	98	40
Whitehaven *	20	13	2	5	2	566	425	141	36
Oldham	20	11	0	9	3	641	533	108	36
South Wales Scorpions	20	6	0	14	4	536	674	-138	22
London Skolars	20	5	1	14	4	433	678	-245	21
Gateshead Thunder	20	0	1	19	0	268	1094	-826	2

* 9 points deducted for entering administration

AVERAGE ATTENDANCES

	2011 Avg	2010 Avg	Diff
Whitehaven	866	984	-118 (Ch)
Keighley Cougars	830	1,045	-215 (Ch)
Swinton Lions	709	419	+290
Oldham	627	808	-181
Rochdale Hornets	605	567	+38
Workington Town	583	470	+113
Doncaster	575	509	+66
London Skolars	509	501	+8
South Wales Scorpions	334	631	-297
Gateshead Thunder	311	373	-62
2011 Average	595		
2010 Average	539		
Difference	+56		

BEST ATTENDANCES *(figure unavailable for Grand Final)*

		Round	Date
1,592	Workington v Whitehaven	6	22/4/11
1,523	Whitehaven v Workington	13	26/6/11
1,346	Swinton v Keighley	6	4/8/11
1,105	London Skolars v Oldham	15	9/7/11
		(at Twickenham Stoop)	
1,099	Keighley v Swinton	15	10/7/11
1,083	London Skolars v Keighley	19	26/8/11
1,072	Keighley v Workington	QSF	18/9/11
1,063	Swinton v Rochdale	20	2/9/11
1,053	Rochdale v Oldham	EPO	11/9/11
1,021	Rochdale v Workington	15	10/7/11

WORST ATTENDANCES

		Round	Date
162	Gateshead v South Wales	10	22/5/11
232	South Wales v London Skolars	20	6/8/11
237	Gateshead v Whitehaven	8	1/5/11
242	Gateshead v Rochdale	16	7/8/11
252	Gateshead v Swinton	11	5/6/11
252	South Wales v Rochdale	17	31/7/11
256	Gateshead v Doncaster	6	19/6/11
263	London Skolars v Gateshead	7	25/4/11
271	South Wales v Whitehaven	2	20/3/11
273	Gateshead v Workington	5	17/4/11

* Championship One attendance figures include play-offs and Northern Rail Cup. Challenge Cup not included.

2011 TOP SCORERS - ALL COMPETITIONS

Jamie Foster

TRIES

1	Jamie Ellis	Leigh Centurions	34
2	Sam Tomkins	Wigan Warriors	33
3	Ryan Hall	Leeds Rhinos	32
4	Joel Monaghan	Warrington Wolves	30
5	Josh Charnley	Wigan Warriors	27
6	Paul White	Halifax	26
	Kris Welham	Hull Kingston Rovers	26
	Mick Nanyn	Leigh Centurions	26
	Ryan Atkins	Warrington Wolves	26
	Pat Richards	Wigan Warriors	26

GOALS

1	Kevin Sinfield	Leeds Rhinos	160
2	Liam Finn	Featherstone Rovers	158
3	Jamie Foster	St Helens	151
4	Mick Nanyn	Leigh Centurions	145
5	Pat Richards	Wigan Warriors	139
6	Brett Hodgson	Warrington Wolves	123
7	Ian Mort	Swinton Lions	119
8	Simon Brown	Sheffield Eagles	113
9	Paul Crook	Rochdale Hornets	110
10	Steve Tyrer	Widnes Vikings	106

POINTS

			T	G	FG	Pts
1	Jamie Foster	St Helens	25	151	0	402
2	Mick Nanyn	Leigh Centurions	26	145	0	394
3	Liam Finn	Featherstone Rovers	17	158	1	385
4	Pat Richards	Wigan Warriors	26	139	0	382
5	Ian Mort	Swinton Lions	25	119	0	338
6	Kevin Sinfield	Leeds Rhinos	2	160	2	330
7	Brett Hodgson	Warrington Wolves	18	123	0	318
8	Steve Tyrer	Widnes Vikings	22	106	0	300
9	Paul Crook	Rochdale Hornets	12	110	5	273
10	Kirk Dixon	Castleford Tigers	10	102	0	244

FIELD GOALS

1	Paul Crook	Rochdale Hornets	5
	Scott Dureau	Catalan Dragons	5
	Darren Holt	Workington Town	5
4	Lee Briers	Warrington Wolves	4
	Michael Dobson	Hull Kingston Rovers	4